The Longman Anthology of British Literature

VOLUME 2C

THE TWENTIETH CENTURY AND BEYOND

David Damrosch
HARVARD UNIVERSITY

Kevin J. H. Dettmar
POMONA COLLEGE

Christopher Baswell
BARNARD COLLEGE AND COLUMBIA UNIVERSITY

Clare Carroll
QUEENS COLLEGE, CITY UNIVERSITY OF NEW YORK

Andrew Hadfield
UNIVERSITY OF SUSSEX

Heather Henderson

Peter J. Manning
STATE UNIVERSITY OF NEW YORK, STONY BROOK

Anne Howland Schotter
WAGNER COLLEGE

William Chapman Sharpe
BARNARD COLLEGE

Stuart Sherman
FORDHAM UNIVERSITY

Susan J. Wolfson
PRINCETON UNIVERSITY

The Longman Anthology of British Literature
Fourth Edition

David Damrosch and Kevin J. H. Dettmar
General Editors

VOLUME 2C

THE TWENTIETH CENTURY AND BEYOND
Kevin J. H. Dettmar

Longman

Boston Columbus Indianapolis New York San Francisco Upper Saddle River
Amsterdam Cape Town Dubai London Madrid Milan Munich Paris Montreal Toronto
Delhi Mexico City Sao Paulo Sydney Hong Kong Seoul Singapore Taipei Tokyo

Editor-in-Chief: *Joseph Terry*
Associate Development Editor: *Erin Reilly*
Executive Marketing Manager: *Joyce Nilsen*
Senior Supplements Editor: *Donna Campion*
Production Manager: *Ellen MacElree*
Project Coordination, Text Design, and Page Makeup: GGS *Higher Education Resources, a Division of PreMedia Global, Inc.*
Cover Design Manager: *Nancy Danahy*
On the Cover: *The Sensation of Crossing the Street—The West End, Edinburgh, 1913, oils, by Stanley Cursiter, Private Collection, Scotland / Courtesy of William Hardie, Ltd., Glasglow.*
Photo Researcher: *Pearson Image Resource Center/Julie Tesser*
Image Permission Coordinator: *Debbie Latronica*
Senior Manufacturing Buyer: *Dennis J. Para*
Printer and Binder: *RRD-Crawfordsville, In.*
Cover Printer: *Lehigh-Phoenix Color/Hagerstown*

For permission to use copyrighted material, grateful acknowledgment is made to the copyright holders on pages 2873–2876, which are hereby made part of this copyright page.

Library of Congress Cataloging-in-Publication Data
The Longman anthology of British literature / David Damrosch and Kevin J. H. Dettmar, general editors.—4th ed.
p. cm.
Includes bibliographical references and index.
ISBN–13: 978–0–205–65524–3 (v. 1 : alk. paper)
ISBN–10: 0–205–65524–6 (v. 1 : alk. paper)
ISBN–13: 978–0–205–65519–9 (v. 2 : alk. paper)
ISBN–10: 0–205–65519–X (v. 2 : alk. paper) 1. English literature. 2. Great Britain—Literary collections. I. Damrosch, David. II. Dettmar, Kevin J. H., 1958–
PR1109.L69 2010
820.8—dc22

2009020241

ISBN-10 Single Volume Edition, Volume 2: 0-205-65519-X
ISBN-13 Single Volume Edition, Volume 2: 978-0-205-65519-9

ISBN-10 Volume 2A, The Romantics and Their Contemporaries: 0-205-65528-9
ISBN-13 Volume 2A, The Romantics and Their Contemporaries: 978-0-205-65528-1

ISBN-10 Volume 2B, The Victorian Age: 0-205-65526-2
ISBN-13 Volume 2B, The Victorian Age: 978-0-205-65526-7

ISBN-10 Volume 2C, The Twentieth Century and Beyond: 0-205-65531-9
ISBN-13 Volume 2C, The Twentieth Century and Beyond: 978-0-205-65531-1

Longman
is an imprint of

PEARSON

6 7 8 9 0—DOC—17 16 15

www.pearsonhighered.com

CONTENTS

PERSPECTIVES
The Great War: Confronting the Modern 2112

ADDITIONAL RESOURCES

Cultural Editions

Longman Cultural Editions present major texts along with a generous selection of contextual material that reveal the conversations and controversies of its historical moment. Taken together, our new edition and the Longman Cultural Editions offer an unparalleled set of materials for the enjoyment and study of British literary culture from its earliest beginnings to the present. One Longman Cultural Edition is available at no additional cost when packaged with the anthology. Contact your local Pearson Publisher's Representative for packaging details. Some titles of interest for Volume Two include the following works:

The Castle of Otranto and *The Man of Feeling*, Walpole and MacKenzie. ed. Mandell
ISBN-10: 0-321-39892-0 | ISBN-13: 978-0-321-39892-5

A Vindication of the Rights of Woman and The Wrongs of Woman; or Maria, Wollstonecraft. ed. Mellor and Chao
ISBN-10: 0-321-18273-1 | ISBN-13: 978-0-321-18273-9

Northanger Abbey, Austen. ed. Gaull
ISBN-10: 0-321-20208-2 | ISBN-13: 978-0-321-20208-6

Pride and Prejudice, Austen. ed. Wolfson and Johnson
ISBN-10: 0-321-10507-9 | ISBN-13: 978-0-321-10507-3

Emma, Austen. ed. Ferguson
ISBN-10: 0-321-22504-X | ISBN-13: 978-0-321-22504-7

Persuasion, Austen. ed. Galperin
ISBN-10: 0-321-19822-0 | ISBN-13: 978-0-321-19822-8

Dorothy Wordsworth, Wordsworth. ed. Levin
ISBN-10: 0-321-27775-9 | ISBN-13: 978-0-321-27775-6

Frankenstein, Shelley. ed. Wolfson
ISBN-10: 0-321-39953-6 | ISBN-13: 978-0-321-39953-3

John Keats, Keats. ed. Wolfson
ISBN-10: 0-321-23616-5 | ISBN-13: 978-0-321-23616-6

Percy Bysshe Shelley, Shelley. ed. Behrendt
ISBN-10: 0-321-20210-4 | ISBN-13: 978-0-321-20210-9

Wuthering Heights, Brontë. ed. Booth
ISBN-10: 0-321-21298-3 | ISBN-13: 978-0-321-21298-6

Dr Jekyll and Mr. Hyde, *The Secret Sharer*, and *Transformation: Three Tales of Doubles*, Stevenson, Conrad, and Shelley. ed. Wolfson and Qualls
ISBN-10: 0-321-41561-2 | ISBN-13: 978-0-321-41561-5

Hard Times, Dickens. ed. Nunokawa and McWeeney
ISBN-10: 0-321-10721-7 | ISBN-13: 978-0-321-10721-3

The Heart of Darkness, *The Man Who Would Be King and Other Works on Empire*, Conrad and Kipling. ed. Damrosch
ISBN-10: 0-321-36467-8 | ISBN-13: 978-0-321-36467-8

The Picture of Dorian Gray, Wilde. ed. Elfenbein
ISBN-10: 0-321-42713-0 | ISBN-13: 978-0-321-42713-7

Howards End, Forster. ed. Mao
ISBN-10: 0-205-53737-5 | ISBN-13: 978-0-205-53737-2

For a complete listing of Longman Cultural Edition titles, please visit www.pearsonhighered.com/literature.

WEB SITE FOR *THE LONGMAN ANTHOLOGY OF BRITISH LITERATURE*

www.myliteraturekit.com

The fourth edition makes connections beyond its covers as well as within them. The Web site we have developed for the course provides a wealth of resources:

Student Resources

- **Discussion Questions for Major Selections and Perspectives Sections.** Designed to prepare students for the kind of deeper-level analysis expected in class discussions, these compelling prompts are available for each period introduction and for major selections and Perspectives groupings.
- **Self-Grading Multiple Choice Practice Questions.** Available for each period introduction and for all major authors and Perspectives groupings, these objective practice quizzes are designed to help students review their basic understanding of the reading.
- **An Interactive Timeline.** Our interactive timeline helps students visualize the key literary, political, and cultural events of an era. Each event is accompanied by a detailed explanation, usually including references to relevant texts that can be found in the anthology, and colorful pictures and illustrations.
- **Links to Valuable British Literature Resources.** Our Online Research Guide provides a wealth of annotated links to excellent Web resources on major authors, texts, and related historical and cultural movements and events.
- **An Archive of Additional Texts.** Our new online archive contains a wealth of selections that could not fit within the bounds of the print anthology. A listing of many of these works can be found in context in our table of contents.

- **Additional Reference Materials.** The Web site also features an extensive glossary of literary and cultural terms, useful summaries of British political and religious organizations, and of money, weights, and measures. For further reading, we provide carefully selected, up-to-date bibliographies for each period and author.

Instructor's Section

- **An Online Instructor's Manual.** The online version of our print manual uses a hyperlink format to allow instructors to jump directly to the author or selection they want to access.
- **PowerPoint Presentations.** A visually rich presentation is available for each period.
- **Sample Syllabi.** Our collection of syllabi include samples of a wide variety of approaches to both the survey-level and period-specific courses.

PREFACE

Literature has a double life. Born in one time and place and read in another, literary works are at once products of their age and independent creations, able to live on long after their original world has disappeared. The goal of *The Longman Anthology of British Literature* is to present a wealth of poetry, prose, and drama from the full sweep of the literary history of Great Britain and its empire, and to do so in ways that will bring out both the works' original cultural contexts and their lasting aesthetic power. These aspects are in fact closely related: form and content, verbal music and social meanings, go hand in hand. This double life makes literature, as Aristotle said, "the most philosophical" of all the arts, intimately connected to ideas and to realities that the writer transforms into moving patterns of words. The challenge is to show these works in the contexts in which, and for which, they were written, while at the same time not trapping them within those contexts. The warm response this anthology has received from the hundreds of teachers who have adopted it in its first three editions reflects the growing consensus that we are not forced to choose between the literature's aesthetic and cultural dimensions. Our users' responses have now guided us in seeing how we can improve our anthology further, so as to be most pleasurable and stimulating to students, most useful to teachers, and most responsive to ongoing developments in literary studies. This preface can serve as a road map to this book's goals and structure.

New to This Edition

- **Period at a Glance features.** These informative illustrated features open each volume, providing thumbnail sketches of daily life during each period.
- **Enhanced Web site.** A new fourth edition site includes an archive of valuable texts from previous editions, detailed bibliographies, an interactive timeline, discussion questions, and Web resources for major selections and authors.
- **New major, classic texts.** In response to instructors' requests, major additions of important works frequently taught in the British Literature course have been added, including the following selections:
  - A new unit on the poetry of Emily Brontë
  - A new unit on British Poet Laureate Carol Ann Duffy
  - Expanded coverage of Postwar English Voices includes enriched coverage of W. H. Auden, Philip Larkin, Seamus Heaney, and Derek Walcott.
  - A selection from Alan Moore and David Lloyd's highly regarded graphic novel *V for Vendetta*
  - Tom Stoppard's *The Invention of Love*
  - A new unit on contemporary British short fiction featuring stories by well known authors including Hanif Kureishi, Nick Hornby, and Zadie Smith.

- **New selections across the anthology.** We have continued to refine our contents, adding new selections to established units across the anthology, including authors such as Anna Letitia Barbauld, James Macpherson, Sir Walter Scott, Elizabeth Barrett Browning, John Ruskin, Sarah Grand, Mona Caird, Dante Gabriel Rossetti, William Ewart Gladstone, Benjamin Disraeli, Thomas Hardy, and T. S. Eliot.
- **New Response pairings.** Newly added Dante Gabriel Rossetti's "Jenny" is paired with a selection from Augusta Webster's "A Castaway" and Thomas Hardy's "The Ruined Maid;" Samuel Taylor Coleridge's "Christabel" is paired with Mary Elizabeth Coleridge's "The Witch."

LITERATURE IN ITS TIME—AND IN OURS

When we engage with a rich literary history that extends back over a thousand years, we often encounter writers who assume their readers know all sorts of things that are little known today: historical facts, social issues, literary and cultural references. Beyond specific information, these works will have come out of a very different literary culture than our own. Even the contemporary British Isles present a cultural situation—or a mix of cultures—very different from what North American readers encounter at home, and these differences only increase as we go farther back in time. A major emphasis of this anthology is to bring the works' original cultural moment to life: not because the works simply or naively reflect that moment of origin, but because they do refract it in fascinating ways. British literature is both a major heritage for modern North America and, in many ways, a very distinct culture; reading British literature will regularly give an experience both of connection and of difference. Great writers create imaginative worlds that have their own compelling internal logic, and a prime purpose of this anthology is to help readers to understand the formal means—whether of genre, rhetoric, or style—with which these writers have created works of haunting beauty. At the same time, as Virginia Woolf says in *A Room of One's Own*, the gossamer threads of the artist's web are joined to reality "with bands of steel."

The Longman Anthology pursues a range of strategies to bring out both the beauty of these webs of words and their points of contact with reality and to bring related authors and works together in several ways:

☞ **PERSPECTIVES: Broad groupings that illuminate underlying issues in a variety of the major works of a period.**

☞ **AND ITS TIME: A focused cluster that illuminates a specific cultural moment or a debate to which an author is responding.**

☞ **RESPONSES: One or more texts in which later authors in the tradition respond creatively to the challenging texts of their forebears.**

These groupings provide a range of means of access to the literary culture of each period. The Perspectives sections do much more than record what major writers thought about an issue: they give a variety of views in a range of voices, to illustrate the wider culture within which the literature was being written. Passionate voices on both sides of the debate over slavery; fiction and essays on the competing claims of science and religion; poetic voices from the trenches of WWI: these and many other vivid readings featured in Volume Two give rhetorical as well as social contexts for the poems, plays, and stories around them. Perspectives sections typically relate to several major authors of the period, as with a section on the industrial landscape that brings the writing of Charles Dickens and Friedrich Engels into conversation with less widely read figures like Thomas Babington Macaulay and Benjamin Disraeli. Most of the writers included in Perspectives sections are important figures of the period who might be neglected if they were listed on their own with just a few pages each; grouping them together has proved to be useful pedagogically as well as intellectually. Perspectives sections may also include work by a major author whose primary listing appears elsewhere in the period; thus, a Perspective section on Victorian Ladies and Gentlemen features selections from Charlotte and Anne Brontë, George Eliot, and Queen Victoria, so as to give a rounded presentation of the issue in ways that can inform the reading of those authors in their individual sections.

When we present a major work "And Its Time," we give a cluster of related materials to suggest the context within which the work was written. Thus Joseph Conrad's *Heart of Darkness* is accompanied by a speech given by the "real-life Kurtz," Sir Henry Morton Stanley, suggesting the nexus of racism and profiteering driving the Congo exploration. Some of the writers in these groupings and in our Perspectives sections have not traditionally been seen as literary figures, but all have produced lively and intriguing works, from the aesthetic philosophy of Immanuel Kant's *Critique of Judgement* to the salacious double-entendres of the ballad "The Steam Loom Weaver," to speeches inspiring support in the Irish fight for independence.

We also include "Responses" to significant texts in the British literary tradition, demonstrating the sometimes far-reaching influence these works have had over the decades and centuries, and sometimes across oceans and continents. Judge John M. Woolsey, in the legal decision allowing the sale of James Joyce's *Ulysses* in the United States, succinctly makes the case for dangerous and unsettling art in the contemporary world.

What Is British Literature?

Stepping back from the structure of the book, let us define our basic terms: What is "British" literature? What is literature itself? And just what should an anthology of this material look like at the present time? The term "British" can mean many things, some of them contradictory, some of them even offensive to people on whom the name has been imposed. If the term "British" has no ultimate essence, it does have a history. The first British were Celtic people who inhabited the British Isles and the northern coast of France (still called Brittany) before various Germanic tribes of Angles and Saxons moved onto the islands in the fifth and sixth centuries. Gradually the Angles and Saxons amalgamated into the Anglo-Saxon culture that became dominant in the southern and eastern regions of Britain and then spread outward; the old British people were pushed west, toward what became known as Cornwall, Wales, and Ireland, which remained independent kingdoms for centuries, as did Celtic Scotland to the north. By an ironic twist of linguistic fate, the Anglo-Saxons began to appropriate the term "British" from the Britons they had displaced, and they took as a national hero the early, semimythic Welsh King Arthur. By the seventeenth century, English monarchs had extended their sway over Wales, Ireland, and

Scotland, and they began to refer to their holdings as "Great Britain." Today, Great Britain includes England, Wales, Scotland, and Northern Ireland, but does not include the Republic of Ireland, which has been independent since 1922.

This anthology uses "British" in a broad sense, as a geographical term encompassing the whole of the British Isles. For all its fraught history, it seems a more satisfactory term than to speak simply of "English" literature, for two reasons. First, most speakers of English live in countries that are not the focus of this anthology (for instance, the United States and Canada); second, while the English language and its literature have long been dominant in the British Isles, other cultures in the region have always used other languages and have produced great literature in these languages. Important works by Irish, Welsh, and Scots writers appear regularly in the body of this anthology, some of them written directly in their languages and presented here in translation, and others written in an English inflected by the rhythms, habits of thought, and modes of expression characteristic of these other languages and the people who use them.

We use the term "literature" in a similarly capacious sense, to refer to a range of artistically shaped works written in a charged language, appealing to the imagination at least as much as to discursive reasoning. It is only relatively recently that creative writers have been able to make a living composing poems, plays, and novels, and only in the past hundred years or so has creating "belles lettres" or high literary art been thought of as a sharply separate sphere of activity from other sorts of writing that the same authors would regularly produce. The past two decades have seen the lowly "comic book" re-emerge as the respectable "graphic novel" and, in the process, bring the immediacy and dynamism of visual form to contemporary British fiction in a new and powerful fashion.

Varieties of Literary Experience

Above all, we have strived to give as full a presentation as possible to the varieties of great literature produced from the Romantic period to the present in the British Isles, by women as well as by men, in outlying regions as well as in the metropolitan center of London, and in prose, drama, and verse alike. We have taken particular care to do justice to prose fiction: we include entire novels or novellas by Charles Dickens, Robert Louis Stevenson, Joseph Conrad, and Virginia Woolf, as well as a wealth of short fiction from the eighteenth century to the present. New in this fourth edition is a selection of contemporary short fiction, including stories by Zadie Smith, Nick Hornby, and Hanif Kureishi, as well as the opening of Alan Moore's landmark graphic novel, *V for Vendetta*. Drama appears throughout, with Tom Stoppard's *The Invention of Love* a notable addition to this newest edition. Finally, lyric poetry appears in profusion throughout the anthology, ranging from the acknowledged masters of Romantic poetry to the powerful contemporary voices of Philip Larkin, Seamus Heaney, Eavan Boland, Gwyneth Lewis, Carol Ann Duffy, and Derek Walcott—himself a product of colonial British education, heir of Shakespeare, Joseph Conrad, and James Joyce. We hope that this anthology will show that the great works of earlier centuries can speak to us compellingly today, their value only increased by the resistance they offer to our views of ourselves and our world. To read and reread the full sweep of this literature is to be struck anew by the degree to which the most radically new works are rooted in centuries of prior innovation.

Illustrating Visual Culture

Another important context for literary production has been a different kind of culture: the visual. This edition includes a suite of color plates in each volume, along with hundreds of black-and-white illustrations throughout the anthology, chosen to show artistic and cultural images that figured importantly for literary creation. Sometimes, a poem refers to a specific painting, or more generally emulates qualities of a school of visual art. At other times, more popular materials like advertisements may illuminate scenes in modern writing. In some cases, visual and literary creation have merged, as in William Morris's, John Waterhouse's, and Dante Gabriel Rossetti's illustrations of scenes from pre-Raphaelite poetry. Thumbnail portraits of many major authors mark the beginning of author introductions.

Aids to Understanding

We have attempted to contextualize our selections in suggestive rather than exhaustive ways, trying to enhance rather than overwhelm the experience of reading the texts themselves. Thus, when difficult or archaic words need defining in poems, we use glosses in the margins, so as to disrupt the reader's eye as little as possible; footnotes are intended to be concise and informative, rather than massive or interpretive. Important literary and social terms are defined when they are used. For convenience of reference, new Period at a Glance features appear at the beginning of each period, providing a thumbnail sketch of daily life during the period. With these informative, illustrated features readers can begin to connect with the world that the anthology is illuminating. Sums of money, for instance, can be understood better when one knows what a loaf of bread cost at the time; the symbolic values attached to various articles of clothing are sometimes difficult for today's readers to decipher, without some information about contemporary apparel and its class associations. And the gradual shift of the Empire's population from rural regions to urban centers is graphically presented in charts for each period.

Looking—and Listening—Further

Beyond the boundaries of the anthology itself, we have expanded our Web site, available to all readers at www.myliteraturekit.com; this site gives a wealth of information, annotated links to related sites, and an archive of texts for further reading. For reference, there is also an extensive glossary of literary and cultural terms available there, together with useful summaries of British political and religious organization, and of money, weights, and measures. For further reading, carefully selected, up-to-date bibliographies for each period and for each author can be found in on the Web site. A guide to our media resources can be found at the end of the table of contents.

For instructors, we have revised and expanded our popular companion volume, *Teaching British Literature*, written directly by the anthology editors, 600 pages in length, available free to everyone who adopts the anthology.

David Damrosch & Kevin J. H. Dettmar

ACKNOWLEDGMENTS

In planning and preparing the fourth edition of our anthology, the editors have been fortunate to have the support, advice, and assistance of many committed and gifted people. Our editor, Joe Terry, has been unwavering in his enthusiasm for the book and his commitment to it; he and his associates Roth Wilkofsky, Mary Ellen Curley, and Joyce Nilsen have supported us in every possible way throughout the process, ably assisted by Rosie Ellis and Annie England. Our developmental editor Erin Reilly guided us and our manuscript from start to finish with unfailing acuity and seemingly unwavering patience. Our copyeditor Stephanie Magean seamlessly integrated the work of a dozen editors. Erin Reilly, Elizabeth Bravo and Stefanie Liebman have devoted enormous energy and creativity to revising our Web site. Karyn Morrison cleared our many permissions, and Julie Tesser tracked down and cleared our many new illustrations. Finally, Nancy Wolitzer and Ellen MacElree oversaw the production with sunny good humor and kept the book successfully on track on a very challenging schedule, working closely with Doug Bell at GGS Higher Education Resources.

Our plans for the new edition have been shaped by comments and suggestions from many faculty who have used the book over the years. We are specifically grateful for the thoughtful advice of our reviewers for this edition, Jesse T. Airaudi (Baylor University), Thomas Crofts (East Tennessee State University), Lois Feuer (California State University, Dominguez Hills), Daniel P. Galvin (Clemson University), S. E. Gontarski (Florida State University), Stephen Harris (University of Massachusetts), Roxanne Kent-Drury (Northern Kentucky University), Carol A. Lowe (McLennan Community College), Darin A Merrill (Brigham Young University—Idaho), David G. Miller (Mississippi College), Crystal L. Mueller (University of Wisconsin Oshkosh), and Gary Schneider (University of Texas—Pan American).

We remain grateful as well for the guidance of the many reviewers who advised us on the creation of the first three editions, the base on which this new edition has been built. In addition to the people named above, we would like to thank Lucien Agosta (California State University, Sacramento), Anne W. Astell (Purdue University), Derek Attridge (Rutgers University), Linda Austin (Oklahoma State University), Arthur D. Barnes (Louisiana State University), Robert Barrett (University of Pennsylvania), Candice Barrington (Central Connecticut State University), Joseph Bartolomeo (University of Massachusetts, Amherst), Mary Been (Clovis Community College), Stephen Behrendt (University of Nebraska), Todd Bender (University of Wisconsin, Madison), Bruce Boehrer (Florida State University), Bruce Brandt (South Dakota State University), Joel J. Brattin (Worcester Polytechnic Institute), James Campbell (University of Central Florida), J. Douglas Canfield (University of Arizona), Paul A. Cantor (University of Virginia), George Allan Cate (University of Maryland, College Park), Philip Collington (Niagra University), Linda McFerrin

Cook (McLellan Community College), Eugene R. Cunnar (New Mexico State University), Earl Dachslager (University of Houston), Elizabeth Davis (University of California, Davis), Andrew Elfenbein (University of Minnesota), Hilary Englert (New Jersey City University), Margaret Ferguson (University of California, Davis), Sandra K. Fisher (State University of New York, Albany), Sandra C. Fowler (The University of Alabama), Allen J. Frantzen (Loyola University, Chicago), Kevin Gardner (Baylor University), Kate Gartner Frost (University of Texas), Leon Gottfried (Purdue University), Leslie Graff (University at Buffalo), Mark L. Greenberg (Drexel University), Peter Greenfield (University of Puget Sound), Natalie Grinnell (Wofford College), James Hala (Drew University), Wayne Hall (University of Cincinnati), Donna Hamilton (University of Maryland), Wendell Harris (Pennsylvania State University), Richard H. Haswell (Washington State University), Susan Sage Heinzelman (University of Texas, Austin), Standish Henning (University of Wisconsin, Madison), Noah Heringman (University of Missouri—Columbia), Jack W. Herring (Baylor University), Carrie Hintz (Queens College), Romana Huk (University of Notre Dame), Maurice Hunt (Baylor University), Mary Anne Hutchison (Utica College), Patricia Clare Ingham (Indiana University), Kim Jacobs (University of Cincinnati Clermont College), Carol Jamison (Armstrong Atlantic State University), Eric Johnson (Dakota State College), Mary Susan Johnston (Minnesota State University), Eileen A. Joy (Southern Illinois University—Edwardsville), Colleen Juarretche (University of California, Los Angeles), George Justice (University of Missouri), Roxanne Kent-Drury (Northern Kentucky University), R. B. Kershner (University of Florida), Lisa Klein (Ohio State University), Adam Komisaruk (West Virginia University), Rita S. Kranidis (Radford University), Leslie M. LaChance (University of Tennessee at Martin), John Laflin (Dakota State University), Lisa Lampert (University of California, San Diego), Dallas Liddle (Augsburg College), Paulino Lim (California State University, Long Beach), Elizabeth B. Loizeaux (University of Maryland), Ed Malone (Missouri Western State College), John J. Manning (University of Connecticut), William W. Matter (Richland College), Evan Matthews (Navarro College), Michael Mays (University of Southern Mississippi), Lawrence McCauley (College of New Jersey), Michael B. McDonald (Iowa State University), James J. McKeown Jr. (McLennan Community College), Kathryn McKinley (Florida International University), Peter E. Medine (University of Arizona), Barry Milligan (Wright State University), Celia Millward (Boston University), Charlotte Morse (Virginia Commonwealth University), Mary Morse (Rider University), Thomas C. Moser, Jr. (University of Maryland), James Najarian (Boston College), Deborah Craig Wester (Worcester State College), Jude V. Nixon (Baylor University), Richard Nordquist (Armstrong Atlantic State University), Daniel Novak (Tulane University), John Ottenhoff (Alma College), Violet O'Valle (Tarrant County Junior College, Texas), Joyce Cornette Palmer (Texas Women's University), Leslie Palmer (University of North Texas), Richard Pearce (Wheaton College), Rebecca Phillips (West Virginia University), Renée Pigeon (California State University, San Bernardino), Tadeusz Pioro (Southern Methodist University), Deborah Preston (Dekalb College), William Rankin (Abilene Christian University), Sherry Rankin (Abilene Christian University), Luke Reinsma (Seattle Pacific University), Elizabeth Robertson (University of Colorado), Deborah Rogers (University of Maine), David Rollison (College of Marin), Brian Rosenberg (Allegheny College), Charles Ross (Purdue University), Kathryn Rummel (California Polytechnic), Harry Rusche (Emory University), Laura E. Rutland (Berry College), Kenneth D. Shields

(Southern Methodist University), R. G. Siemens (Malaspina University-College), Clare A. Simmons (Ohio State University), Sally Slocum (University of Akron), Phillip Snyder (Brigham Young University), Isabel Bonnyman Stanley (East Tennessee University), Brad Sullivan (Florida Gulf Coast University), Margaret Sullivan (University of California, Los Angeles), Herbert Sussmann (Northeastern University), Mary L. Tanter (Tarleton State University), Ronald R. Thomas (Trinity College), Theresa Tinkle (University of Michigan), William A. Ulmer (University of Alabama), Jennifer A. Wagner (University of Memphis), Anne D. Wallace (University of Southern Mississippi), Brett Wallen (Cleveland Community College), Jackie Walsh (McNeese State University, Louisiana), Daniel Watkins (Duquesne University), John Watkins (University of Minnesota), Martin Wechselblatt (University of Cincinnati), Arthur Weitzman (Northeastern University), Bonnie Wheeler (Southern Methodist University), Jan Widmayer (Boise State University), Dennis L. Williams (Central Texas College), William A. Wilson (San Jose State University), Paula Woods (Baylor University), and Julia Wright (University of Waterloo).

Other colleagues brought our developing book into the classroom, teaching from portions of the work-in-progress. Our thanks go to Lisa Abney (Northwestern State University), Charles Lynn Batten (University of California, Los Angeles), Brenda Riffe Brown (College of the Mainland, Texas), John Brugaletta (California State University, Fullerton), Dan Butcher (Southeastern Louisiana University), Lynn Byrd (Southern University at New Orleans), David Cowles (Brigham Young University), Sheila Drain (John Carroll University), Lawrence Frank (University of Oklahoma), Leigh Garrison (Virginia Polytechnic Institute), David Griffin (New York University), Rita Harkness (Virginia Commonwealth University), Linda Kissler (Westmoreland County Community College, Pennsylvania), Brenda Lewis (Motlow State Community College, Tennessee), Paul Lizotte (River College), Wayne Luckman (Green River Community College, Washington), Arnold Markely (Pennsylvania State University, Delaware County), James McKusick (University of Maryland, Baltimore), Eva McManus (Ohio Northern University), Manuel Moyrao (Old Dominion University), Kate Palguta (Shawnee State University, Ohio), Paul Puccio (University of Central Florida), Sarah Polito (Cape Cod Community College), Meredith Poole (Virginia Western Community College), Tracy Seeley (University of San Francisco), Clare Simmons (Ohio State University), and Paul Yoder (University of Arkansas, Little Rock).

As if all this help weren't enough, the editors also drew directly on friends and colleagues in many ways, for advice, for information, sometimes for outright contributions to headnotes and footnotes, even (in a pinch) for aid in proofreading. In particular, we wish to thank David Ackiss, Marshall Brown, James Cain, Cathy Corder, Jeffrey Cox, Michael Coyle, Pat Denison, Tom Farrell, Andrew Fleck, Jane Freilich, Laurie Glover, Lisa Gordis, Joy Hayton, Ryan Hibbet, V. Lauryl Hicks, Nelson Hilton, Jean Howard, David Kastan, Stanislas Kemper, Andrew Krull, Ron Levao, Carol Levin, David Lipscomb, Denise MacNeil, Jackie Maslowski, Richard Matlak, Anne Mellor, James McKusick, Melanie Micir, Michael North, David Paroissien, Stephen M. Parrish, Peter Platt, Cary Plotkin, Desma Polydorou, Gina Renee, Alan Richardson, Esther Schor, Catherine Siemann, Glenn Simshaw, David Tresilian, Shasta Turner, Nicholas Watson, Michael Winckleman, Gillen Wood, and Sarah Zimmerman for all their guidance and assistance.

The pages on the Restoration and the eighteenth century are the work of many collaborators, diligent and generous. Michael F. Suarez, S. J. (Campion Hall,

Oxford) edited the Swift and Pope sections; Mary Bly (Fordham University) edited Sheridan's *School for Scandal*; Michael Caldwell (University of Chicago) edited the portions of "Reading Papers" on *The Craftsman* and the South Sea Bubble. Steven N. Zwicker (Washington University) co-wrote the period introduction, and the headnotes for the Dryden section. Bruce Redford (Boston University) crafted the footnotes for Dryden, Gay, Johnson, and Boswell. Susan Brown, Janice Cable, Christine Coch, Marnie Cox, Tara Czechowski, Susan Greenfield, Mary Nassef, Paige Reynolds, and Andrew Tumminia helped with texts, footnotes, and other matters throughout; William Pritchard gathered texts, wrote notes, and prepared the bibliography. Doug Thomson (Georgia Southern University) prepared The Romantics: At a Glance. To all, abiding thanks.

It has been a pleasure to work with all of these colleagues in the ongoing collaborative process that has produced this book and brought it to this new stage of its life and use. This book exists for its readers, whose reactions and suggestions we warmly welcome, as these will in turn reshape this book for later users in the years to come.

David Damrosch
HARVARD UNIVERSITY

Kevin J. H. Dettmar
POMONA COLLEGE

Christopher Baswell
BARNARD COLLEGE AND COLUMBIA UNIVERSITY

Clare Carroll
QUEENS COLLEGE, CITY UNIVERSITY OF NEW YORK

Andrew Hadfield
UNIVERSITY OF SUSSEX

Heather Henderson

Peter J. Manning
STATE UNIVERSITY OF NEW YORK, STONY BROOK

Anne Howland Schotter
WAGNER COLLEGE

William Chapman Sharpe
BARNARD COLLEGE

Stuart Sherman
FORDHAM UNIVERSITY

Susan J. Wolfson
PRINCETON UNIVERSITY

ABOUT THE EDITORS

David Damrosch is Professor of Comparative Literature at Harvard University. He is past President of the American Comparative Literature Association, and has written widely on world literature from antiquity to the present. His books include *What is World Literature?* (2003), *The Buried Book: The Loss and Rediscovery of the Great Epic of Gilgamesh* (2007), and *How to Read World Literature* (2009). He is the founding general editor of the six-volume *Longman Anthology of World Literature*, 2/e (2009) and the editor of *Teaching World Literature* (2009).

Kevin J. H. Dettmar is W. M. Keck Professor and Chair of the Department of English at Pomona College, and Past President of the Modernist Studies Association. He is the author of *The Illicit Joyce of Postmodernism* and *Is Rock Dead?*, and the editor of *Rereading the New: A Backward Glance at Modernism; Marketing Modernisms: Self-Promotion, Canonization, and Rereading; Reading Rock & Roll: Authenticity, Appropriation, Aesthetics*; the Barnes & Noble Classics edition of James Joyce's *A Portrait of the Artist as a Young Man* and *Dubliners*; *The Blackwell Companion to Modernist Literature and Culture*; and *The Cambridge Companion to Bob Dylan*.

Christopher Baswell is A.W. Olin Chair of English at Barnard College, and Professor of English and Comparative Literature at Columbia University. His interests include classical and medieval literature and culture, and contemporary poetry. He is author of *Virgil in Medieval England: Figuring the "Aeneid" from the Twelfth Century to Chaucer*, which won the 1998 Beatrice White Prize of the English Association. He has held fellowships from the NEH, the National Humanities Center, and the Institute for Advanced Study, Princeton.

Clare Carroll is Director of Renaissance Studies at The Graduate Center, City University of New York and Professor of Comparative Literature at Queens College, CUNY. Her research is in Renaissance Studies, with particular interests in early modern colonialism, epic poetry, historiography, and translation. She is the author of *The Orlando Furioso: A Stoic Comedy*, and editor of Richard Beacon's humanist dialogue on the colonization of Ireland, *Solon His Follie*. Her most recent book is *Circe's Cup: Cultural Transformations in Early Modern Ireland*. She has received Fulbright Fellowships for her research and the Queens College President's Award for Excellence in Teaching.

Andrew Hadfield is Professor of English at The University of Sussex. He is the author of a number of books, including *Shakespeare and Republicanism* (2005), which was awarded the 2006 Sixteenth-Century Society Conference Roland H. Bainton Prize for Literature; *Literature, Travel and Colonialism in the English Renaissance, 1540–1625* (1998); and *Spenser's Irish Experience: Wild Fruyt and Salvage Soyl* (1997).

He has also edited a number of texts, most recently, with Matthew Dimmock, *Religions of the Book: Co-existence and Conflict, 1400–1660* (2008), and with Raymond Gillespie, *The Oxford History of the Irish Book, Vol. III: The Irish Book in English, 1550–1800* (2006). He is a regular reviewer for the TLS.

Heather Henderson is a freelance writer and former Associate Professor of English Literature at Mount Holyoke College. A specialist in Victorian literature, she is the recipient of a fellowship from the National Endowment for the Humanities. She is the author of *The Victorian Self: Autobiography and Biblical Narrative*. Her current interests include homeschooling, travel literature, and autobiography.

Peter J. Manning is Professor at Stony Brook University. He is the author of *Byron and His Fictions* and *Reading Romantics*, and of numerous essays on the British Romantic poets and prose writers. With Susan J. Wolfson, he has co-edited *Selected Poems of Byron*, and *Selected Poems of Beddoes, Hood, and Praed*. He has received fellowships from the National Endowment for the Humanities and the John Simon Guggenheim Memorial Foundation, and the Distinguished Scholar Award of the Keats-Shelley Association.

Anne Howland Schotter is Professor of English at Wagner College. She is the co-editor of *Ineffability: Naming the Unnamable from Dante to Beckett* and author of articles on Middle English poetry, Dante, and medieval Latin poetry. Her current interests include the medieval reception of classical literature, particularly the work of Ovid. She has held fellowships from the Woodrow Wilson and Andrew W. Mellon foundations.

William Chapman Sharpe is Professor of English Literature at Barnard College. A specialist in Victorian poetry and the literature of the city, he is the author of *Unreal Cities: Urban Figuration in Wordsworth, Baudelaire, Whitman, Eliot, and Williams*. He is also co-editor of *The Passing of Arthur* and *Visions of the Modern City*. He is the recipient of Guggenheim, National Endowment of the Humanities, Fulbright, and Mellon fellowships, and recently published *New York Nocturne: The City After Dark in Literature, Painting, and Photography*.

Stuart Sherman is Associate Professor of English at Fordham University. He received the Gottschalk Prize from the American Society for Eighteenth-Century Studies for his book *Telling Time: Clocks, Diaries, and English Diurnal Form, 1660–1775*, and is currently at work on a study called "News and Plays: Evanescences of Page and Stage, 1620–1779." He has received the Quantrell Award for Undergraduate Teaching, as well as fellowships from the American Council of Learned Societies and the Chicago Humanities Institute.

Susan J. Wolfson is Professor of English at Princeton University and is general editor of Longman Cultural Editions. She has also produced editions of Felicia Hemans, Lord Byron, Thomas L. Beddoes, William M. Praed, and Thomas Hood. She is the editor of the innovative Longman Cultural Editions of John Keats, and of Mary Shelley's *Frankenstein*, and coeditor (with Barry V. Qualls) of *Three Tales of Doubles*, and (with Claudia Johnson) of Jane Austen's *Pride and Prejudice*. She is author of *The Questioning Presence* (1986), *Formal Charges: The Shaping of Poetry in British Romanticism* (1997), and *Borderlines: The Shiftings of Gender* (2007).

The Longman Anthology of British Literature

VOLUME 2C

THE TWENTIETH CENTURY AND BEYOND

Richard Nevinson, *The Arrival*, 1913–1914.

THE TWENTIETH CENTURY AND BEYOND

POPULATION

NATIONAL POPULATIONS (IN MILLIONS)

Year	England and Wales	Scotland	Ireland
1901	32.5	4.5	4.5
2001	52.1	5.1	3.8[1]

URBAN POPULATIONS

Year	London	Manchester	Edinburgh	Dublin
1901	6,507,000	649,246	413,000	448,000
2001	7,172,000	395,806	449,000	491,000

LIFE EXPECTANCY

Life expectancy for a child born in 1901 in Great Britain is 41 years; by 2001 it has soared to 75 for males and almost 81 for females.

DAILY LIFE

CURRENCY[2]

4 farthings	1d. (1 penny)	One penny (a 240th of a pound) in 1910 would be worth 25 U.S. cents today.
12d.	1s. (1shilling)	One shilling (a 20th of a pound) in 1910 would be worth $2.98 today.
5s.	1 crown	One crown (a 4th of a pound) in 1910 would be worth $14.90 today.
20s.	1£ (1 pound)	One pound in 1910 would be worth $59.57 today.
21s.	1 guinea	One guinea (1 pound, 1 shilling) in 1910 would be worth $62.55 today.

In 1971, the British changed to decimalization, with £1 denominated into 100 pence. On independence in 1922, Ireland established its own currency, the Irish pound (IR£, "punt Éireannach"); in 2002, Ireland adopted the Euro (€).

SOCIAL STRUCTURE[3]

Grade	Status	Occupation	Estimated Population, in 2006	Percentage of the Population, in 2006
A	Upper middle class	Higher managerial, administrative, or professional	1,594,000	3.4
B	Middle class	Intermediate managerial, administrative, or professional	10,189,000	21.6

1. Republic of Ireland only (after 1922); the population of Northern Ireland in 2001 is 1.7 million.
2. Historical equivalences for the purchasing power of a given sum are very approximate. Different types of calculations provide quite different results. A calculation based on wages, for instance, yields a different figure from a calculation based on the prices of basic consumer goods; and those consumer goods thought essential to daily life change drastically over time. These conversions, then, are meant to be only approximations.
3. These classifications were created by the National Readership Survey (http://www.nrs.co.uk/about_nrs/data_available/definitions_of_social_grade).

Social Structure

Grade	Status	Occupation	Estimated Population, in 2006	Percentage of the Population, in 2006
C1	Lower middle class	Supervisory or clerical and junior managerial, administrative, or professional	13,757,000	29.1
C2	Skilled Working class	Skilled manual workers	9,924,000	21
D	Working class	Semiskilled and unskilled manual workers	7,636,000	16.2
E	Those at lowest level of subsistence	Casual or lowest grade workers, pensioners, and others who depend on the state for their income	4,166,000	8.8

Wages in London in 1922

£30 Starting annual salary for hospital nurse, London Hospital
£40 Average annual salary, housemaid
£90 Average annual salary, farm laborer
£150 Annual salary, coal miner
£150 Annual salary, dockworker
£350 Annual salary offered for a "clever young advertising man"
£600 Annual salary, county medical inspector

Cost of Goods, 1922

1d. 1 pint milk
2d. 2 lbs. sugar
4d. 1 lb. cheddar cheese
5d. Daily edition, *The Times* (London)
6d. 1 dozen eggs
6d. 10 cigarettes
6d. Average fare on London Underground
7d. Average price of a pint of beer
15s. Umbrella
£1 Woman's summer hat
£2 Moderate London hotel room for two
£5 5s. Woman's winter coat
£12 Round-trip air fare, London-Paris
£40 Monthly rent on a furnished, 3-bedroom flat on Marylebone Road, London
£125 "His Master's Voice" Model 15 electric gramophone, in mahogany
£625 Aston Martin 20 h.p. 4-seater coupe

Food and Drink

Like so much else in the twentieth century, the traditions associated with British foodways were greatly affected by technological advances. In T. S. Eliot's *The Waste Land,* the young woman typist in the third section "home at teatime . . . lights / Her stove, and lays out food in tins" (page 2304); for Eliot, this is incontrovertible proof of the soulless character of contemporary urban life. But it also points to the collapsing class distinctions surrounding food in the period; mass-manufactured food products made a wide variety of foods that could be prepared quickly (after a long day at work) available at affordable prices.

Convenience foods then constitute one pole of the twentieth-century British dining continuum, at the opposite end from dining out; household servants (including cooks), a staple of even lower-middle-class households at the turn of the century, became increasingly scarce as the century progressed, and elaborately prepared home meals thus became more and more unusual, especially as, in the second half of the century, two-income households became increasingly common. In 1930, fewer than 15% of households included a working wife; by 1968, that figure had increased to 45%, and a majority (51%) of households had two incomes a decade later. In the process, "dining out" had paradoxically been transformed from a luxury enjoyed by the wealthy to a practical fact of urban working life, in the form of "fast food" (witness, for instance, the recent popularity of the British take-away sandwich chain, Pret a Manger ["Ready to Eat"], with nearly 200 restaurants opened since 1986).

Apparel

Here, too, the pace of technological change had a profound impact on the quality of day-to-day life. Skirts for women became shorter, in order to accommodate a greater range of motion, including the mounting of trams and trains; dresses became lighter in their construction and materials. In the 1930s nylon was invented, and was used to manufacture women's stockings by 1940; a wave of other synthetic materials followed, making clothing less expensive, more durable, and easier to care for.

The British Empire's incursion into India provided it with cheap rubber and latex, both of which found their way into clothing manufacture, especially for waterproofing garments and manufacturing waterproof footwear. This technology

dates back to the Macintosh coat of the 1820s, but the increasing integration of new synthetic materials with traditional, organic materials such as cotton, wool, and silk, made clothing more convenient, durable, and affordable; Keds had the first big marketing success with their canvas-topped rubber-soled "sneakers," so named by an advertising executive because one could walk silently on them.

In broad strokes, the evolution of clothing from 1900 to the present moves in the direction of comfort, convenience, affordability, and casualness: looking back at photographs from 1962 of the Beatles on their first trip to the United States (page 1944), for instance, one is struck that for all their reputation as rebels, they are all wearing coats and ties. Women only stopped wearing gloves and started wearing trousers in polite society in the mid-1960s, when men stopped wearing hats.

RULERS

MONARCHS	PRIME MINISTERS
Victoria, Queen of the United Kingdom of Great Britain and Ireland and Empress of India of the British Raj (1837–1901)	Arthur Balfour (1902–1905), Conservative
Edward VII, King of the United Kingdom and the British Dominions and Emperor of India (1901–1910)	Herbert Henry Asquith (1908–1916), Liberal; after 1908, coalition government
George V, King of the United Kingdom and the British Dominions and Emperor of India (1910–1936)	David Lloyd George (1916–1922), coalition government
Edward VIII, King of the United Kingdom and the British Dominions and Emperor of India (1936; abdicates to marry a twice-divorced American commoner, Wallis Simpson)	Neville Chamberlain (1937–1940), national government
George VI, King of the United Kingdom and the British Dominions (1936—1952); Emperor of India (until 1947); King of Ireland (until 1949); Head of the Commonwealth (1936–1952)	Winston Churchill (1940–1945), national government
	Clement Attlee (1945–1951), Labour
Elizabeth II, Queen of the United Kingdom, Canada, Australia and the other Commonwealth realms (1952-)	Sir Winston Churchill (1951–1955), Conservative
	Harold Wilson (1964–1970, 1974–1976), Labour
	Margaret Thatcher (1979–1990), Conservative
	John Major (1990–1997), Conservative
	Tony Blair (1997–2007), Labour
	Gordon Brown (2007–) Labour

Margaret Thatcher

Gordon Brown and Queen Elizabeth II

TIMELINE

1901 Queen Victoria dies.

1902 The Treaty of Vereeniging ends the Boer War.

1902 Based on personal experience, Joseph Conrad's *Heart of Darkness* (page 1954) is published in *Blackwood's Magazine* in 1898. It explores the atrocities of colonialism in Africa.

1903 The Wright Brothers launch the first manned flight.

1905 Albert Einstein publishes his *Special Theory of Relativity* and Sigmund Freud publishes his *Three Essays in the Theory of Sexuality*. In addition to revolutionizing their fields and establishing the groundwork for later advances, these widely influential works ignite popular interest in physics and psychology.

1906–1914 A Liberal-run government passes a series of measures aimed at improving life for the working class and the poor. This includes making education and medical visits compulsory for children, instituting an eight-hour workday, and establishing a minimum wage in trades without any standard.

1912 The RMS *Titanic* hits an iceberg and sinks during its maiden voyage.

1914 James Joyce's *Dubliners* (page 2218)

1914 Bernard Shaw's *Pygmalion* (page 2032)

1914 Released only weeks before the onset of World War I, Wyndham Lewis' *Blast* exemplifies modernist experimentation with typography and radical content (page 2114).

1914–1918 As a result of a complex series of alliances, the assassination of Archduke Francis Ferdinand of Austria draws the nations of Europe into the Great War. The atrocities of mechanized total warfare foster a sense of alienation and senselessness captured by the war poets (page 2112).

1916 Seeking liberation from British rule, Irish Republicans occupy the Dublin Post Office in an attempt to institute an independent government. The British government executes the leaders of the Easter Rising, an event memorialized in William Butler Yeats' *Easter 1916* (page 2181).

1918 Women over age 30 are given right to vote; women's voting age lowers to 21 in 1928.
1922 The British Broadcasting Company (BBC) begins daily transmissions, providing entertainment and news programs on a mass scale.
1922 T. S. Eliot's *The Waste Land* (page 2297) and James Joyce's *Ulysses* (page 2472) break with traditional literary techniques while at the same time asserting the importance of mythology and history. Both works challenge the reader's sense of authority and mark a conscious departure from traditional literary form and content.
1922 The Irish Free State is established, granting dominion status to the 26 southern counties of Ireland but leaving the remaining six northern counties still under British rule.
1925 Virginia Woolf's *Mrs Dalloway* (page 2338)
1930 W. H. Auden's *Poems* (page 2614)
1932–1948 The decline of the British empire begins in earnest with independence for Iraq in 1932, Egypt in 1936, India in 1947, and Palestine in 1948.
1933 Adolf Hitler comes to power in Germany.
1936 Edward VIII abdicates his throne after creating political turmoil by proposing marriage to American Wallis Simpson.
1936–1939 The Spanish Civil War, a bloody and complex conflict, signals the rise of fascism in Europe. The war evokes strong reactions in the literary and artistic worlds, including Auden's *Spain 1937* (page 2617) and much of George Orwell's writing (page 2566).
1939–1945 After a period of aggressive German expansionism is met with little interference by the major European powers, Hitler invades Poland on 11 September 1939. Britain and France declare war on Germany in response, but offer little military support for Poland. World War II quickly launches the world into a state of total warfare between the Axis (led by Germany, Italy, and Japan) and Allies (led by Great Britain, France, and later the Soviet Union and United States).
1940 Winston Churchill's inspiring speeches encourage Britons under attack by Luftwaffe (German air force) during the Battle of Britain (page 2528).
1941 Britain declares war on Japan in response to the Japanese bombing of Pearl Harbor, which officially draws the United States into the war as a British ally.
1944 On 26 June, Allied troops land on the coast of Normandy. The assault, known as D-Day, is considered the turning point of World War II.

1946 In the wake of World War II, the government assumes control of many private industries involved with national interests, including the Bank of England and the railway system.
1946 Dylan Thomas publishes *Fern Hill* (page 2574), a pastoral elegy based on summers spent at his aunt's dairy farm.
1949 George Orwell's novel *1984* explores a dystopia ruled by "Big Brother" characterized by totalitarian rule, loss of freedom, and violence.
1952 George VI dies; Elizabeth II ascends the throne.
1956 During the Suez Canal Crisis, Britain, France, and Israel attack Egypt in response to their attempts to nationalize the canal.
1957 Samuel Beckett's *Endgame* (page 2579) continues the Theater of the Absurd tradition established by his masterpiece *Waiting for Godot* (1953).
1962 The Beatles release their first single, "Love Me Do / P.S. I Love You."
1963 In a political scandal known as the Profumo Affair, Secretary of State for War John Profumo is forced to resign after his brief affair with Christine Keeler (rumored to be the mistress of a Russian official) becomes public knowledge.
1968 The Booker Prize is established to annually reward the author of the best original novel written in the English language by a citizen of the United Kingdom.
1969 The Open University, a government-sponsored, open-admissions distance-learning institution, is established.
1969 Anti-British violence ferments in Ulster.
1972 On 30 January, better known as "Bloody Sunday" British paratroopers open fire on unarmed civil rights marchers in Derry, killing 13.

1973 Britain joins the European Community (EC), later the European Union (EU), though without adopting its common currency (the Euro).
1979–1990 Under Margaret Thatcher's leadership, the government dismantles many of the social programs established during the postwar period.
1980–1981 Hunger strikes by IRA prisoners in Northern Ireland result in ten deaths by starvation and the election of one striker to Parliament, drawing international media attention.
1981 Salman Rushdie (page 2748) wins the Booker Prize for his novel *Midnight's Children.*
1982 Argentina invades disputed British possessions the Falkland Islands as well as South Georgia and South Sandwich Islands, prompting the Falkland War. After a few months, Argentina surrenders and the British retain control of the islands; nevertheless, Argentina claims possession to this day.
1985 The Anglo-Irish Agreement grants the Irish government an advisory voice in North Ireland's government in an effort to quell the violence in Northern Ireland.
1995 Irish poet Seamus Heaney (page 2739) wins the Nobel Prize in Literature.
1997 A revitalized Labour Party, under Tony Blair, returns to power in a landslide election. Among its first measures, it establishes a national minimum wage and grants additional autonomy to Wales, Scotland, and Northern Ireland.
1997 Britain returns control of Hong Kong to China.
1997 Diana Spencer, Princess of Wales, dies in an automobile accident.

1997 Tom Stoppard's *The Invention of Love* (page 2684).
1998 A major step in the peace process for Northern Ireland, the Belfast Agreement, or "Good Friday" Agreement, addresses a number of political, economic, and social issues.
2001 Al-Qaeda terrorists attack the Twin Towers in New York and the Pentagon in Washington, D.C., as well as United Airlines Flight 93 over Shanksville, Pennsylvania, killing 2,974 victims.
2003 Britain becomes a member of the "coalition of the willing" in George W. Bush's invasion of Iraq in response to the September 11, 2001, terrorist attacks in the United States.
2008 Irish voters reject EU membership.

The Twentieth Century and Beyond

Beyond the Pale

Modern British literature has consistently been distinguished by its movement "beyond the pale." The Pale was originally the fenced-in territory established around Dublin by the invading English in the medieval period, a border between English civilization and Celtic foreignness. In later usage, the phrase "beyond the pale" came to have a purely metaphoric meaning: to stand outside the conventional boundaries of law, behavior, or social class. To snobbish members of the British elite, a poor flower-seller like Eliza Doolittle in Shaw's *Pygmalion* would be beyond the pale in a social sense; at its most serious, the phrase can designate actions violating universal standards of human decency, such as the colonists' appalling treatment of Africans that Conrad chillingly describes in *Heart of Darkness*. Throughout the twentieth century, writers active in the British Isles increasingly probed actions and locations beyond the pale of proper middle-class Englishness. Many of the century's greatest writers, such as the Pole Joseph Conrad, the Irishmen William Butler Yeats and James Joyce, and the Americans Ezra Pound and T. S. Eliot, themselves came from beyond the boundaries of England; others came from social strata within England less often visible before: provincial working-class writers like D. H. Lawrence and the Scots writer James Kelman; women like Rebecca West and Katherine Mansfield; men and women whose sexuality transcended conventional boundaries, such as E. M. Forster, Virginia Woolf, and W. H. Auden.

As the century went on, more and more writers active in the British Isles and its former colonies have been "beyond the pale" in a very literal sense, as people of color: Salman Rushdie, who grew up in India and Pakistan before establishing himself as a writer in England; V. S. Naipaul, a Caribbean of Indian ancestry; Ngugi wa-Thiongo, educated by British missionaries in Kenya; Derek Walcott, whose poetry moves between the Caribbean, England, North America, and Africa. With the ending of England's role as a colonial power, a new and dynamic relation of former colonies and colonizers has arisen, a pervasive interfusion of people and of roles, aptly symbolized by dizzying role changes in Caryl Churchill's comic masterpiece *Cloud 9*. British literature has become a world literature, overflowing what were once its borders.

> *British literature has become a world literature, overflowing what were once its borders.*

Earlier centuries had periodically seen the eruption of writers, and of issues, from beyond the pale of accepted norms and educated social groups, but these writers had often faced severe struggles against dominant values of upper-middle-class propriety and the strictures of established literary conventions. The fate of Oscar Wilde was a case in point: his arrest on sodomy charges in 1895 at the peak of his career as a playwright, his sentencing to hard labor and then his exile and death in France in 1900, all pointed up the ways in which late Victorian society could retaliate against the challenges posed by a brilliant, flamboyant, homosexual Irishman. A new generation of writers at the turn of the century set themselves to change this situation, seeking variously to infiltrate the Pale of established British literary expression, to expand its dimensions, or to abolish it altogether. For many of these young writers, a prime strategy for achieving these goals was to attack their predecessors, and they set about this task with gusto.

Burying Victoria

Writing in 1928, Virginia Woolf described the cultural atmosphere of the Victorian era in the following way:

> Damp now began to make its way into every house. . . . The damp struck within. Men felt the chill in their hearts; the damp in their minds. . . . The life of the average woman was a succession of childbirths. She married at nineteen and had fifteen or eighteen children by the time she was thirty; for twins abounded. Thus the British Empire came into existence; and thus—for there is no stopping damp; it gets into inkpots as it gets into the woodwork—sentences swelled, adjectives multiplied, lyrics became epics, and little trifles that had been essays a column long were now encyclopedias in ten or twenty volumes.

Woolf of course exaggerates here for her own effect; yet this passage does capture nicely the stereotypical view of the Victorians that flourished during the modern period—and helped make it possible. Ezra Pound, for instance, called the later nineteenth century "a rather blurry, messy sort of period, a rather sentimentalistic, mannerish sort of period." Polemical descriptions like these served the rhetorical purposes of writers at the start of the new century as they attempted to stake out their terrain and to forge a literature and a perspective of their own.

The opening decade of the new century was a time of transition. Woolf later suggested, her tongue perhaps in her cheek, that as a result of a Post-Impressionist exhibition of paintings in London, "on or about December, 1910, human character changed." Almost no one, however, seems to have maintained that anything changed very decisively on the morning of 1 January 1900. Queen Victoria, at that time on the throne for nearly sixty-five years and in mourning for her husband Prince Albert for almost forty, lived and ruled on into the following year; the subsequent reign of Edward VII (1901–1910) differed only slightly from that of his mother in many respects, the entire nation mourning the loss of their queen as she had the loss of her husband. But Woolf, in a 1924 essay, saw a gulf between herself and the Edwardians: Edwardian novelists, she writes, "established conventions which do their business; and that business is not our business." Edward VII himself, in fact, was clearly not a Victorian. He had a reputation as a playboy and implicitly rebelled against the conventions that his mother had upheld. During his reign, the mannered decadence of the 1890s modulated into a revived social realism seen in ambitious novels like Joseph Conrad's *Nostromo* and H. G. Wells's darkly comic masterpiece *Tono-Bungay*, while poets like Yeats and Hardy produced major poems probing the relations of self, society, and history. Writers in general considered themselves to be voices of a nation taking stock of its place in the world in a new century. They saw their times as marked by accelerating social and technological change and by the burden of a worldwide empire, which achieved its greatest extent in the years between 1900 and 1914—encompassing as much as a quarter of the world's population and dominating world trade through a global network of ports.

Writers in general considered themselves to be voices of a nation taking stock of its place in the world in a new century.

This period of consolidation and reflection abruptly came to an end four years into the reign of George V, with the start of World War I in August 1914; the relatively tranquil prewar years of George's early reign were quickly memorialized, and nostalgized, in the wake of the war's disruption to the traditionally English way of life. This first Georgian period was abruptly elevated into a cultural "golden age" by the British public and British publishers, a process that was typified by the pastoral poetry gathered by Edward Marsh in his hugely popular series of five anthologies called *Georgian Poetry*, the first of which was published in 1912. As a consequence of Marsh's skill as a tastemaker, this brief period before the war is frequently known as the Georgian period in British literature, though George V himself remained on the throne until 1936, when the distant rumble of World War II was to be heard by those with ears to hear.

The quarter century from 1914 until the start of the war in 1939 is now conventionally known as the modernist period. To be modern was, in one respect, to rebel openly and loudly against one's philosophical and artistic inheritance, in much the same way that the Romantic writers of the late eighteenth and early nineteenth centuries had sought to distinguish themselves from their Augustan forebears. This gesture—the way in which a new artistic movement seeks to define itself through caricature of the movement(s) that gave it birth—is a recurrent feature in literary history, but it took on a particular urgency and energy among the modernists, who advanced the view summarized in Pound's bold slogan, "Make It New." A great modernist monument to this anti-Victorian sentiment was Lytton Strachey's elegantly ironic *Eminent Victorians* (1918), whose probing biographical portraits punctured a series of Victorian pieties. Much of Bernard Shaw's writing (including *Pygmalion*) is animated by anti-Victorian animus as well, taking the theatrical wit of Oscar Wilde and turning it against specific targets. Exaggerated though it was, the ritualized slaughter performed by modernists like Woolf, Strachey, and Shaw seems to have achieved a clearing of the literary and artistic terrain that formed a necessary prelude to further innovation. The modernists' "Victorians" were oversimplified, sometimes straw figures, but the battle that was waged against them was real indeed, and the principles of modernism were forged and refined in the process.

To be modern was, in one respect, to rebel openly and loudly against one's philosophical and artistic inheritance . . .

The Foundations of Modern Skepticism

The best Victorian writers had not been afraid to ask difficult, unsettling questions. Tennyson's restless skepticism in *In Memoriam*, for example, exemplifies the spirit of Victorian inquiry. But the conclusion of that poem foresees an ongoing progress toward future perfection, guided by "One God, one law, one element, / And one far-off divine event, / To which the whole creation moves." Tennyson himself doubted that such unities could be embodied in the present; twentieth-century writers found increasing fragmentation around them and became more and more suspicious of narratives of historical progress and of social unity.

Modern explorations are undertaken with absolutely no confidence as to the results that will be discovered, still less that a public exists who could understand the writers' discoveries. For that reason Thomas Hardy's ruthless skepticism now seems quintessentially modern. This new attitude is quite clear in Ford Madox Ford's *The Good Soldier* (1915), the first installment of which was published in the inaugural issue of Wyndham Lewis's violently modern magazine *Blast*. John Dowell, the narrator/protagonist of Ford's novel, worries for 250 pages about his sense that the "givens" of civil society seem to have been knocked out from under him, and that he has been left to create values and meaning on his own. Struggling to extract the moral of the story he tells us—the story of his wife's long-standing affair with his best friend, and their consequent deaths—Dowell can only conclude:

> I don't know. And there is nothing to guide us. And if everything is so nebulous about a matter so elementary as the morals of sex, what is there to guide us in the more subtle morality of all other personal contacts, associations, and activities? Or are we meant to act on impulse alone? It is all a darkness.

In Conrad's *Heart of Darkness*, the narrator Charlie Marlow suffers from a similar moral vertigo. When, at the novella's close, he resolves to perform an action he finds deeply repugnant—to tell a lie—he worries that his willful violation of the moral order will provoke an immediate act of divine retribution. None, however, is forthcoming: "It seemed to me that the house would collapse before I could escape, that the heavens would fall upon my head. But nothing happened. The heavens do not fall for such a trifle." In works like these, a voyage is undertaken into a vast, unknown, dark expanse. Those few who come out alive have seen too much ever to be the same.

Similar perceptions underlie modern humor. The Theater of the Absurd that flourished in the 1950s and 1960s, in the work of playwrights like Samuel Beckett and Harold Pinter, had roots in Wilde and Shaw and their comic explorations of the arbitrary conventionality of long-held social values. Throughout the twentieth century, writers devoted themselves to unfolding many varieties of irony—from the severe ironies of Conrad and Yeats to the more tender ironies of Woolf and Auden, to the farcical absurdities of Tom Stoppard and Joe Orton. Joyce described his mixture of high and low comedy as "jocoserious"; asked the meaning of his dense book *Finnegans Wake*, he replied, "It's meant to make you laugh."

Whether seen in comic or tragic light, the sense of a loss of moorings was pervasive.

Whether seen in comic or tragic light, the sense of a loss of moorings was pervasive. Following the rapid social and intellectual changes of the previous century, the early twentieth century suffered its share of further concussions tending to heighten modern uncertainty. It was even becoming harder to understand the grounds of uncertainty itself. The critiques of Marx and Darwin had derived new messages from bodies of evidence available in principle to all literate citizens; the most important paradigm shifts of the early twentieth century, on the other hand, occurred in the fields of philosophy, psychology, and physics, and often rested on evidence invisible to the average citizen. The German philosopher Friedrich Nietzsche (1844–1900) was, as his dates suggest, wholly a nineteenth-century man, yet his ideas had their most profound impact in the twentieth century. Nietzsche described his lifelong philosophical project as "the revaluation of all values"; in his 1882 treatise *The Joyful Science*, he went so far as to assert that "God is dead." This deliberately provocative statement came as the culmination of a long and complicated argument, and did not mean simply that Nietzsche was an atheist (though he was). Nietzsche was suggesting that traditional religion had been discredited by advances in the natural and physical sciences, and as transcendent standards of truth disappeared, so logically must all moral and ethical systems depending on some faith for their force. It was from this base that Nietzsche created the idea of the *Übermensch*, the "superman" who because of his intellectual and moral superiority to others must not be bound by social conventions. Conrad's tragic figure Kurtz and Shaw's comic Professor Henry Higgins represent two very different takes on this idea, building on Nietzsche's interest in showing how all values are "constructed" rather than given—at some level arbitrary, all truths being merely opinions, all social identities merely roles.

The new psychology, whose earliest stirrings are to be found in the last decades of the nineteenth century, came of age at the turn of the twentieth. Sigmund Freud's *The Interpretation of Dreams* (1900) and *Psychopathology of Everyday Life* (1901) together illustrate in an especially vivid way his evolving theories about the influence of the unconscious mind, and past (especially childhood) experience, on our daily lives. The whole of Freud's work was translated into English by James Strachey (Lytton's brother), and was published in conjunction with the Hogarth Press, owned and run by Leonard and Virginia Woolf; for this reason, among others, the Freudian revolution was felt early, and strongly, among the London intelligentsia. The new psychology was frequently distorted and misunderstood by the larger public; among the artistic community Freud provoked a wide range of response, from the enthusiastic adoption of his theories by some to nervous rejection by writers like Joyce. This response is complicated, in part, by the fact that Freud himself took an interest in artistic and creative processes, and presumed to explain to writers the psychopathology at the heart of their own genius; as the Freudian literary critic Lionel Trilling succinctly put it, "the poet is a poet by reason of his sickness as well as by reason of his power." As Freud's supporter W. H. Auden wrote in his elegy, *In Memory of Sigmund Freud* (1939):

> If often he was wrong and at times absurd,
> To us he is no more a person
> Now but a whole climate of opinion
> Under whom we conduct our different lives.

A further intellectual shock wave was the revolution in physics that was spearheaded by Albert Einstein's *Special Theory of Relativity* (1905). In both this theory (dealing with motion) and later in the general theory of relativity (dealing with gravity), Einstein shook the traditional understanding of the universe and our relationship to it; the certainty and predictability of the Newtonian description of the universe had been undone. The "uncertainty" of Einstein's universe was seemingly reinforced by developments in quantum physics, such as the work of Niels Bohr (who won the Nobel Prize in physics in 1922) and Werner Heisenberg, author of the famous "Uncertainty Principle" and the principle of complementarity, which together assert that the movement of subatomic particles can only be predicted by probability and not measured, as the very act of measurement alters their behavior. Ironically enough, the true import of these ideas is not, as the truism has it, that "everything is

. . . the certainty and predictability of the Newtonian description of the universe had been undone.

relative"—in fact, Einstein says almost the exact opposite. In Einstein's vision of the world, *nothing* is relative: everything is absolute, and absolutely fixed—except for us, fallible and limited observers, who have no secure standpoint from which "to see the thing as in itself it really is," to quote Matthew Arnold's 1867 formulation of the critic's goal. The only way to experience the truth, it would seem, would be to find what T. S. Eliot called "the still point of the turning world," an "unmoved mover" outside the flux and change of our day-to-day world. Einstein himself never really rejected the idea of transcendent truth; he once said to an interviewer that to him, the idea of our universe without a Creator was inconceivable. In this case, however, the popular fiction has been more influential than the facts, and the work of Einstein, Heisenberg, and Bohr has been used to support the widespread sense that, as Irish playwright Sean O'Casey's character Captain Jack Boyle puts it in *Juno and the Paycock* (1924), "the whole worl's in a state o' chassis!"

Notions of British invincibility, of honor, even of the viability of civilization all weakened over the years of vicious trench warfare in France.

The philosophical and moral upheavals of these years were given added force by the profound shock of World War I—"The Great War," as it came to be known. The British entered the conflict against Germany partly in order to preserve their influence in Europe and their dominance around the globe, and partly out of altruistic notions of gallantry and fair play—to aid their weaker allies against German aggression. The conflict was supposed to take a few weeks; it lasted four grueling years and cost hundreds of thousands of British lives. Notions of British invincibility, of honor, even of the viability of civilization all weakened over the years of vicious trench warfare in France. The progress of technology, which had raised Victorian standards of living, now led to a mechanization of warfare that produced horrific numbers of deaths—as many as a million soldiers died in the single protracted battle of the Somme in 1916. As poets discovered as they served in the trenches, and as the people back home came to learn, modernity had arrived with a vengeance.

Revolutions of Style

The end of the war was accompanied by a sense of physical and moral exhaustion. To be modern has been defined as a persistent sense of having arrived on the stage of history after history has finished. The critic Perry Meisel, for instance, describes modernism as "a structure of compensation, a way of adjusting to the paradox of belatedness." Behind Ezra Pound's struggle to reinvent poetry lay a nagging suspicion that there was nothing new left to make or say, and Pound claimed that the very slogan "Make It New" was taken off the bathtub of an ancient Chinese emperor. As T. S. Eliot explains in his essay *Tradition and the Practice of Poetry*, "The perpetual task of poetry is to *make all things new*. Not necessarily to make new things. . . . It is always partly a revolution, or a reaction, from the work of the previous generation."

That revolution was carried out both on the level of subject matter and often on the level of style. Some important early twentieth-century fiction writers, like John Galsworthy and H. G. Wells, felt no real need to depart from inherited narrative

Soldiers of the 9th Cameronians division prepare to go "over the top" during a daylight raid near Arras, France, 24 March 1917. During such an offensive, troops would make their way quickly across the contested territory between the opposing armies' trenches—the area known as No Man's Land—and attempt to take control of an enemy trench in order to conduct bombing raids and gain whatever intelligence might be found in the abandoned foxholes. The pace of this warfare—where a week's progress might be measured in yards, rather than miles—was, according to troops on both sides, the most salient feature of trench warfare. The human costs included diseases caused by standing water (like infamous "trench foot") and emotional disorders caused by the stress of waiting and constant shelling ("shell shock").

models, and hewed more or less to a realist or naturalist line, carrying on from the French naturalists like Emile Zola and the Norwegian dramatist Henrik Ibsen. But for those writers we now call modernist, these conventions came to seem too limiting and lifeless. The modern writer was faced with an enormous, Nietzschean task: to create new and appropriate values for modern culture, and a style appropriate to those values. As a consequence, there is often a probing, nervous quality in the modernist explorations of ultimate questions. This quality can be seen at the very start of the century in Conrad's *Heart of Darkness*, a novel about psychological depth and social disintegration that simultaneously implicates its readers in the moral ambiguities of its events. These ambiguities, moreover, are reflected in the very presentation of the narrative itself. In the modern novel, we are no longer allowed to watch from a safe distance while our protagonists mature and change through their trials; instead, we are made to undergo those trials ourselves, through the machinations of the narrative. This technique had already been employed in the nineteenth century, as for instance in the dramatic monologues of Robert Browning; but this narrative of process becomes pervasive in modernist texts, where the uncertainties of the form, the waverings and unpredictability of the narrative, mirror similar qualities in the mind of the narrator or protagonist. Often the reader is drawn into the story's crisis by a heightened use of the technique of plunging the narrative suddenly *in medias res:* "There was no hope for him this time: it was the third stroke" (Joyce, *The Sisters*); "A sudden blow:" (Yeats, *Leda and the Swan*); "'Yes, of course, if it's fine tomorrow,' said Mrs. Ramsay" (Woolf, *To the Lighthouse*). The customary preliminary information—the sort of dossier about the characters that we expect—isn't given; the reader is put in the position of a detective who has to sort all this information out unaided. This narrative decontextualization reaches its culmination in the theater of Beckett and Pinter, who typically withhold any and all background information about characters. "Confusion," Samuel Beckett told an interviewer in 1956, "is all around us and our only chance now is to let it in. The only chance of renovation is to open our eyes and see the mess. It is not a mess you can make sense of."

Early in the century, a number of poets began to dispense with the frames of reference provided by conventional poetic forms. The first important Anglo-American poetic movement of the century was Imagism, a reaction against the expansive wordiness of Victorian poetry like Tennyson's *Idylls of the King* or Browning's *The Ring and the Book*. Imagists like Pound and H. D. wrote short, spare poems embodying a revelatory image or moment. The most memorable Imagist poems have the concentrated impact of a haiku. But the form leaves little scope for narrative development; that path seems to have been opened by a rediscovery of the seventeenth-century metaphysical poets, notably by T. S. Eliot. The techniques of metaphysical poets like John Donne suggested to Eliot a means for expanding the repertory of Imagist poetry, which he used to good effect in poems like *The Love Song of J. Alfred Prufrock*, which opens with a thoroughly modernized metaphysical conceit:

> Let us go then, you and I,
> when the evening is spread out against the sky
> Like a patient etherized upon a table.

One strategy for making literature new was to make it difficult; this notion was, in part, a response to the proliferation of popular entertainments during the early twentieth century, a development that both disturbed and intrigued many artists, writers, and cultural critics. In such a context, "difficult" literature (such as the densely allusive poetry of Eliot, or the multilayered prose of Joyce) was seen to be of greater artistic merit than the products of an easily consumable mass culture—even as both Eliot and Joyce drew on popular culture and diction as they reshaped the norms of their literary art. Thus, while one of the primary targets of modernist renovation was Victorian literary manners, another was the complacent taste and sensibility of a large, and growing, middle class. Artists had been declaring the need to shock the bourgeoisie since time immemorial; Matthew Arnold worried publicly, and at length, about the dilution of a natural aristocracy of taste by the pseudoculture of newly educated British philistines, at the same time that he campaigned for greatly expanded public education. The Education Act of 1870 resulted in the explosive growth of elementary education, which meant that the reading class grew exponentially. Within the art world, the most obvious result of this anxiety was the "art for art's sake" movement associated with Walter Pater that began in the 1870s. Art was becoming its own material—as, for instance, in French artist Marcel Duchamp's mustache on the Mona Lisa.

In some ways modernist art and literature turned inward, becoming cannibalistic and self-referential. This is demonstrated well in Joyce's novel *A Portrait of the Artist as a Young Man*, whose protagonist is autobiographical in genesis yet critical in intent; the way Joyce accomplishes this is by moving Stephen Dedalus, his artist-protagonist, through various prose poses—writing now like Gustave Flaubert, now like Cardinal Newman, now like Pater. Stephen can only mimic—not create—a style; such is the situation of the modern writer, Joyce suggests, and his novel *Ulysses* dramatizes this by adopting a kaleidoscopic array of styles in its eighteen chapters. It thus becomes increasingly difficult to think of "style" as the achievement of an individual, and more and more it becomes the culmination of a cultural, national, or ethnic project or history. As the French critic Roland Barthes has written, the text in the modern period becomes a "multidimensional space in which a variety of writings, none of them original, blend and clash," "a tissue of quotations drawn from innumerable centres of culture"—an apt and dramatic description of modernist texts like Eliot's *The Waste Land*, Joyce's *Ulysses*, and Pound's *Cantos*. To be textual is, during this period, to be intertextual and interdisciplinary as well.

> *Stephen Dedalus, [Joyce's] artist-protagonist . . . can only mimic—not create—a style; such is the situation of the modern writer . . .*

The stylistic experimentation of modernist writers was fueled by the era's technological advances. From the mid-nineteenth century on, Britain had prided itself on its industrial strength and leadership; with the electrification of Britain at the turn of the century, however, the Industrial Revolution was gradually overtaken by a technological revolution. If the sinking of the *Titanic* on her maiden voyage in 1912 stands as a symbol of the vulnerability of progress—a sort of watery funeral for traditional British industry—the first transatlantic flight in 1919 pointed toward the future. Advances in photographic technology made documentary photographs a part of daily life and brought a heightened visual dimension to political campaigns and to advertising; the advent of quick and inexpensive newspaper photographs put vivid images of the carnage of World War I on Britain's breakfast tables. The texture and pace of daily life changed in the early years of the century to such a degree that average men and women were comfortable referring to themselves by that hopelessly awkward designation, "modern" (from the Latin *modo*, "just now"). And clearly, the London inhabited by the denizens of Eliot's *Waste Land* is a profoundly different place from the London of Dickens. Eliot portrays a woman who works in an office, composes letters on a typewriter, talks to clients on the telephone, plays records on the phonograph at her flat after having casual sex with a co-worker, and eats her evening meal from tins.

The advent of technology had far-reaching effects on the writing of the period. Beckett, famously, imagined a tape recorder before he had ever seen one in order to make possible the memory play of his *Krapp's Last Tape* (1959); more generally, the technology of the transistor radio, and government sponsorship of radio and television by the British Broadcasting Corporation, made possible wholly new literary genres. Beckett and Dylan Thomas were among the first to take advantage of the new media, writing plays for radio and then for television. A generation earlier, Joyce

The advent of technology had far-reaching effects on the writing of the period.

made use of early art film strategies in his "Circe" episode of *Ulysses*. In the most advanced writing of the modernist period we find an increasing sense that the technologies of print affect the text itself. Pound's *Cantos* were composed, not just transcribed, on a typewriter, and cannot be imagined in their current form composed with pen and ink; Joyce plays with the typographic conventions of newspaper headlines in the "Aeolus" chapter of *Ulysses* to create an ironic running commentary on the action. A crucial scene in Joyce's *Finnegans Wake* features a television broadcast (which was not available commercially when the novel was published), blending with a nuclear explosion (also several years before the fact). The scene culminates in "the abnihilisation of the etym"—both a destruction of atom/Adam/etym and its recovery *from* ("ab") nothingness.

Modernism and the Modern City

Paralleling the new social and artistic opportunities of the twentieth century was a kind of anomie or alienation created by the rush toward industrialization. Vast numbers of human figures remained undifferentiated and the mass-manufactured hats and clothing worn by British industrial workers served only to heighten the monotony of their daily routines. Newspapers eagerly published photographs of thousands of sooty-faced miners. The members of the workforce, which Marx had called "alienated labor," were seen to be estranged not just from their work but from one another as well, as they themselves became mass products. This situation is dramatized especially vividly in the silent films of the period—from the dystopian vision of Fritz Lang's *Metropolis* (1926) to the more comic vision presented by the British-American Charlie Chaplin in *Modern Times* (1936). The sense of major cities being overrun by crowds of nameless human locusts recurs in the poetry of the period:

A crowd flowed over London Bridge, so many,
I had not thought death had undone so many.
Sighs, short and infrequent, were exhaled,
And each man fixed his eyes before his feet.

(Eliot, *The Waste Land*)

I have met them at close of day
Coming with vivid faces
From counter or desk among grey
Eighteenth-century houses.

(Yeats, *Easter 1916*)

The Victorian concern over huge numbers of urban poor was seconded by a fear of large numbers of restive urban lower-middle-class workers and their families.

The city also appeared in far more positive guises, as the modernists were urban sophisticates above all else. Joyce famously remarked that if Dublin were one day destroyed, it could be recreated whole from the pages of his *Ulysses*. Virginia Woolf's great novel *Mrs Dalloway* is among other things a glowing tribute to London as the center of incongruous juxtapositions and unexpected connections,

Archibald Hatrick, *A Lift Girl,* 1916. The Scottish artist A. S. Hatrick (1864–1950) was part of the vibrant art movement in Glasgow, which he joined after studying art in France, where he had met the painters Van Gogh and Gauguin; as a wartime artist, he became especially interested in recording women's efforts. *A Lift Girl* is a multidimensional portrait of these efforts, as it depicts a young woman whose service to her country in the war comes about as an elevator operator carrying civilians and military personnel down to the underground refuges meant to protect families and soldiers alike from the constant aerial bombardment of German airplanes.

the quintessence of life itself: "Heaven only knows why one loves it so," Clarissa Dalloway thinks,

> how one sees it so, making it up, building it round one, tumbling it, creating it every moment afresh. . . . In people's eyes, in the swing, tramp, and trudge; in the bellow and the uproar; the carriages, motor cars, omnibuses, vans, sandwich men shuffling and swinging; brass bands; barrel organs; in the triumph and the jingle and the strange high singing of some aeroplane overhead was what she loved; life; London; this moment of June.

London had a magnetic attraction for many American writers as well, as a transatlantic literary culture blossomed. Henry James based novels like *The American* and *Portrait of a Lady* on the adventures of Americans living abroad; James himself was an American who lived most of the last thirty-five years of his life in London, and was naturalized as a British citizen three months before his death. T. S. Eliot moved to London in 1915 and lived there until his death in 1965, becoming a British subject, a communicant of the Church of England, and being knighted along the way. The great comic writer P. G. Wodehouse commuted back and forth across the Atlantic in the 1920s and 1930s as his plays and musical comedies were staged in New York and London. In many ways, New York and London had never been so close. This artistic diaspora resulted in a richer, more complex and urbane literature.

Plotting the Self

The Freudian revolution grew from and reinforced an intense interest in the workings of the individual psyche, and modernists like Woolf and Joyce devoted themselves to capturing the mind's modulations. Both Woolf and Joyce employed versions of what came to be known as the "stream-of-consciousness" technique, in which fragmentary thoughts gradually build up a portrayal of characters' perceptions and of their unstated concerns. Consider this passage from the "interior monologue" of Joyce's protagonist Leopold Bloom, as he prepares a saucer of milk for his cat:

> They call them stupid. They understand what we say better than we understand them. She understands all she wants to. Vindictive too. Wonder what I look like to her. Height of a tower? No, she can jump me. . . . Cruel. Her nature. Curious mice never squeal. Seem to like it.

On the surface, Bloom's staccato thoughts reflect on the cat; at the same time, he identifies the cat with his unfaithful wife Molly, and—without admitting it to himself—he reflects on the cat's foreign psyche as a way of coming to terms with Molly's needs and desires. The development of stream-of-consciousness narrative grows out of a sense that the self is not "natural" or "given" but a construction—specifically a social construction—and that, consequently, traditional methods for depicting character no longer suffice. We are all the products of our own past and we are also, powerfully, products of larger social forces that shape the stories we tell about ourselves, and which others tell about us.

In the Victorian novel, plot crises were typically resolved in some definitive way, such as by a marriage or a change in the financial status of the protagonist. In the modern novel, lasting resolutions growing out of a common vision are few and far between. Walter Pater had counseled his readers, at the conclusion of *The Renaissance*, that "to burn always with a hard, gemlike flame, to maintain this ecstasy" was "success in life"; in the modern period, everyone wants that ecstasy, but no one is sure quite what it looks like amid the ruthless individualism of modern life. "We live as we dream, alone," Conrad's narrator Marlow mutters despondently; "Only connect," the epigraph to E. M. Forster's *Howards End* (1910) implores. On the eve of the London Blitz, however, the characters in Woolf's *Between the Acts* (still the most powerful British novel of World War II) are united only as they sing the refrain, "Dispersed are we." The texts of the modern period, bookended as they are by two world wars, represent a real, agonized meditation on how modern individuals can become united as community again. Woolf herself was skeptical of the possibility and her last novel remains unfinished—or finished only by her husband Leonard—because she took her own life before she could complete it. In the novels of Woolf and Joyce, and in the poetry of Yeats and Auden, community is the glimpsed prospect, the promised land: seen as a possibility but never realized, or embodied precariously in a gesture, a moment, a metaphor, and above all in art itself.

The texts of the modern period . . . represent a real, agonized meditation on how modern individuals can become united as community again.

After the modernist high-water mark of the 1920s, the atmosphere darkened amid the international financial depression of the 1930s triggered by the U.S. stock market crash of 1929. The decade saw the growth of British Marxism and widespread labor agitation. The decade also witnessed the international growth of fascism and totalitarianism; writers like Shaw, Wyndham Lewis, Eliot, Yeats, Pound, and Lawrence for a time saw the order and stability promised by authoritarian governments as the only antidote to the "mere anarchy" Yeats decries in his poem *The Second Coming*. In the late thirties, however, intellectual sentiment turned increasingly against the fascist movements being led in Germany by Hitler, in Italy by Mussolini and in Spain by Franco. During Spain's brutal civil war (1936–1939), many writers supported the democratic Republicans against the ultimately victorious fascist General Franco. Meanwhile a series of weak British governments did little to oppose Hitler's increasing belligerence and extremism; the failure to stand up for democratic principles, coupled with worldwide economic depression, led many young intellectuals and artists to become Leftists.

Compared to the stylistic experiments of the previous two decades, British writing of the 1930s sometimes looks rather flat, neutral. This can be attributed in part to the disillusionment that followed World War I, and the very real sense throughout the thirties that things were building up to another war, that art had become something of an irrelevancy. The German cultural critic Theodor Adorno was to write after the war, "no poetry after Auschwitz"; writers of the thirties seem to have had this sense well in advance of Auschwitz. Yeats admired the character in Auguste de Villiers de L'Isle-Adam's drama *Axël* who said, "As for living, we let the servants do that for us"; the young writers of the thirties, however, were concerned that (in Auden's phrase) "poetry makes nothing happen," and were committed to the idea that it must. "Late modernism," as the critic Tyrus Miller has described this writing, was newly engaged with popular culture and political events alike.

The Return of the Repressed

Modern British literature is characterized by the increasing presence of women's voices, working-class voices, and voices expressing varied ethnic, religious, and sexual perspectives which, whether methodically or inadvertently, had often been excluded from the British literary tradition. The writings of an author like Woolf made England think hard about who she really was, as did, in another sense, the writings of the former colonial administrator George Orwell. In the modern period, Britain begins to deal in a fully conscious way with its human rights problems—most significantly, its treatment of women and the diverse ethnic groups of its colonial possessions.

The gradual enfranchisement and political and economic liberation of British women in the early years of the twentieth century comprised a fundamental social change; the novelist D. H. Lawrence, a rather equivocal friend of the women's movement, called it "perhaps the greatest revolution of modern times." The Women's Property Act—passed in 1882, the year of Woolf's birth—for the first time allowed married women to own property. Decades of sometimes violent suffragist agitation led finally to full voting rights for women in 1928 and to the gradual opening up of opportunities in higher education and the professions.

The quick pace of these changes naturally made many men uneasy. In their monumental three-volume study *No Man's Land: The Place of the Woman Writer in the Twentieth Century*, critics Sandra Gilbert and Susan Gubar suggest that this "war between the sexes" was one of the primary driving forces behind the modernist literary movement. Having emphasized the revolutionary force of the women's movement, Lawrence goes on to warn that the movement, "is even going beyond, and becoming a tyranny of woman, of the individual woman in the house, and of the feminine ideas and ideals in the world." In a half-serious essay titled *Cocksure Women and Hensure Men*, Lawrence complained of women

> more cocky, in their assurance, than the cock himself. . . . It is really out of scheme, it is not in relation to the rest of things. . . . They find, so often, that instead of having laid an egg, they have laid a vote, or an empty ink-bottle, or some other absolutely unhatchable object, which means nothing to them.

On the level of literary principles, a masculinist emphasis can be seen in Ezra Pound's insistence that modern poetry should "move against poppy-cock," "be harder and saner . . . 'nearer the bone' . . . as much like granite as it can be."

Other writers, male and female, supported women's rights; almost all writers sought to rebel against Victorian sexual norms and gender roles. Joyce battled with censors beginning in 1906, and his *Ulysses* was put on trial in New York on obscenity charges in 1933 (and cleared of those charges in the same week that the United States repealed Prohibition). Defending his sexual and scatological scenes, Joyce put the modernists' case for frankness this way:

> The modern writer has other problems facing him, problems which are more intimate and unusual. We prefer to search in the corners for what has been hidden, and moods, atmospheres and intimate relationships are the modern writers' theme. . . . The modern theme is the subterranean forces, those hidden tides which govern everything and run humanity counter to the apparent flood: those poisonous subtleties which envelop the soul, the ascending fumes of sex.

In defense of his "dirty" book *Lady Chatterley's Lover* (1928), whose full text was banned as obscene until 1960, Lawrence wrote: "In spite of all antagonism, I put forth this novel as an honest, healthy book, necessary for us today. . . . We are today, as human beings, evolved and cultured far beyond the taboos which are inherent in our culture. . . . The mind has an old groveling fear of the body and the body's potencies. It is the mind we have to liberate, to civilize on these points." In a rich irony, Joyce and Lawrence hated one another's writing: Joyce insisted on calling Lawrence's best-known novel "Lady Chatterbox's Lover." He dismissed the novel as "a piece of propaganda in favour of something which, outside of D. H. L.'s country at any rate, makes all the propaganda for itself." Lawrence, for his part, thought the last chapter of *Ulysses* (Molly Bloom's famous soliloquy) "the dirtiest, most indecent, obscene thing ever written."

Sexuality of all stripes was on trial.

Sexuality of all stripes was on trial. The lesbian writer Radclyffe Hall was tried for obscenity in 1928 for her novel *The Well of Loneliness*—whose most obscene sentence is, "That night they were not divided." The trial became a public spectacle, and was a rallying point for writers like Woolf and E. M. Forster, who spoke valiantly in favor of Hall's right to explore her subject, which was primarily the loneliness, rather than the fleshly joys, of same-sex love. Forster's overtly homosexual writings, including his novel *Maurice*, were not

Christopher Richard Wynne Nevinson, *Poster for the Wembley Exhibition*, 1925. Advertising the Wembley Empire Exhibition, this bus poster conveys its quite effective attempt to turn empire into spectacular entertainment, and imperial colonies into a multicultural festival for the British masses. Labor strikes and unemployment within England had made the working public aware of the huge costs of maintaining empire at their expense; the ruling class responded by trying to force the working class and the poor to emigrate to the colonies. The latter coercive approach appears in *Mrs Dalloway*, where Lady Bruton, whose last name conveys the brutality of this attempt to get rid of what she calls a "superfluous" population, is joined by Clarissa Dalloway's husband, a prominent member of the government, at a posh luncheon meeting to launch what was called in real life, although not in Woolf's novel, the "Get Out!" movement.

published until after his death in 1970. Woolf was somewhat more open in her novel *Orlando* (1928), whose protagonist changes sex from male to female. In Joyce's *Ulysses*, Leopold Bloom fantasizes about becoming a "new womanly man" and dreams of being chastised by a dominatrix who appears first as Bella and then as Bello Cohen. It was not only sexual taboos that were challenged in the writing of the period; in practice there began to be a loosening of the strict gender and sexual roles, which had been reinforced by the homophobia resulting from Oscar Wilde's trial. Gay, lesbian, and bisexual writers like Forster, Woolf, Hall, Stein, Natalie Barney, Djuna Barnes, H. D., Ronald Firbank, and Carl Van Vechten pushed the comfort level of the British reading public; even the "healthy" version of sexuality celebrated by D. H. Lawrence in his greatest novel *Women in Love* begins to suggest that heterosexuality and homosexuality are shifting boundaries, not immutable categories.

The growing independence of the individual subject began to be matched by drives for independence among imperial subjects as well. In "John Bull's other island," as Bernard Shaw called Ireland in his play of that title, agitations for independence grew widespread from the late nineteenth century onward, culminating in the Easter Rising of 1916 and the 1922 partitioning of Ireland, when the Irish Republic became an independent nation while Northern Ireland remained part of Great Britain. No match for England militarily, the Irish used words as their chief weapon in the struggle for independence.

The liberation of Britain's overseas colonial holdings began in the early decades of the century and gathered momentum thereafter. The history of Great Britain in the twentieth century is, in some ways, the story of the centrifugal forces that have largely stripped Britain of its colonial possessions. Britain suffered humiliating losses in the Boer War (1899–1902), fought by the British to take possession of the Boer Republic of South Africa. Half a million British troops were unable to win outright victory over eighty thousand Boers; finally the British adopted a scorched-earth policy that entailed massive arrests and the deaths of thousands of captives in unsanitary camps. This debilitating and unsavory conquest marked the low point of British imperialism, and public disgust led to a reaction against empire itself. Independence movements sprang up in colonies around the world, most notably in India, Britain's largest colony, "the jewel in the crown" of Queen Victoria, where Mohandas Gandhi's Congress Party struggled through nonviolent resistance to force Britain to grant its independence.

Independence movements sprang up in colonies around the world . . .

World War II and Its Aftermath

The year 1939 and the start of World War II closed the modernist era. It was the year that saw the publication of Joyce's *Finnegans Wake*, which the critic Ihab Hassan calls a "monstrous prophecy" of postmodernity. The seminal modernist careers of Joyce, Woolf, Yeats, Ford, and Freud all came to an end—as did the social and political order of the previous decades. Throughout the late thirties, the government had engaged in futile efforts at diplomacy as Hitler expanded German control in central Europe. Prime Minister Neville Chamberlain finally denounced Hitler when the Germans invaded Czechoslovakia early in 1939; on September 1, Germany invaded Poland, and within days Britain declared war. In contrast to the "Great War," this conflict began with few illusions—but with the knowledge that Britain was facing an implacable and better-armed enemy. Unlike the Great War, fought on foreign soil, the new war hit home directly; during "the Blitz" from July 1940 through 1941, the German Luftwaffe carried out massive bombing raids on London and many other targets around Britain.

During these years, Winston Churchill emerged as a pivotal figure both strategically and morally. First as commander in chief of the navy, and starting in May 1940 as prime minister, he directed British military operations while rallying popular support through stirring speeches and radio addresses. The war had profound effects throughout British society, as almost every man—and many women—between the ages of 14 and 64 came to be involved in the war effort, in conditions that weakened old divisions of region and class and that provided the impetus for new levels of government involvement in social planning. At the war's end in September of 1945, Britain emerged victorious, in concert with its allies. In contrast with the United States, though, Britain had suffered enormous civilian casualties and crushing economic losses, both within Great Britain and throughout its far-flung colonies. As much as a quarter of Britain's national wealth had been consumed by the war. The great city of London had undergone horrific bombing during the the Blitz, whose attacks left the face of this world capital as scarred as had the Great Fire three centuries

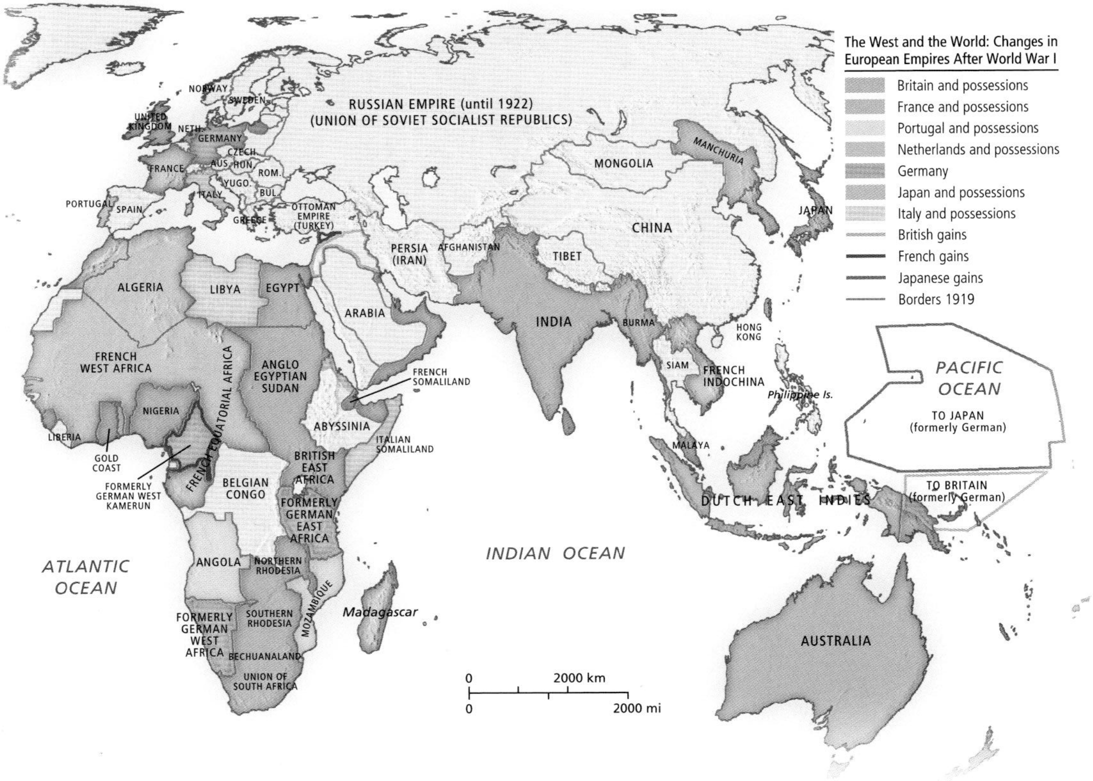

Color Plate 21 The British Empire Stretched Thin. At its greatest extent, the British Empire covered 14.1 million square miles, nearly 25 percent of the earth's surface, and ruled over 400–500 million people. Shortly after the close of World War I, however, the British Empire had stopped growing and had begun to contract; the first territories to win their independence, Ireland and far-flung Ascension Island (off the east coast of South America), broke ties with Great Britain in 1922. The great tide of decolonization, however, was to follow in the wake of World War II. *(Courtesy of David Damrosch.)*

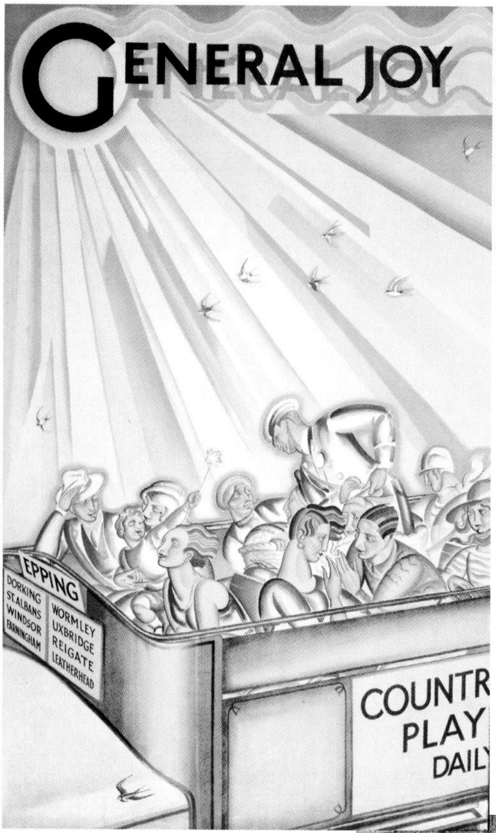

Color Plate 22 The Glories of Commercial Art. Vera Willoughby, *General Joy*, 1928. In an era when color printing first became practical for large-scale commercial purposes, British artists rose to the occasion, creating memorable images that opened both imaginations and pocketbooks. Willoughby's work reflects the exuberance of London in the 1920s; just as often though the posters for London public transportation offered public art, political messages, and cultural rallying points. In Virginia Woolf's *Mrs Dalloway*, Clarissa Dalloway's daughter Elizabeth rides just such an open-air bus through a sparkling London day in June. *(London Transport Museum.)*

Color Plate 23 Urban Energies. Charles Ginner, *Piccadilly Circus*, 1912. Like Eliza Doolittle in Bernard Shaw's *Pygmalion*, the quaint flower seller in this scene is surrounded by evidence of the energies and transformations of the modern city: automobiles, advertising, and even an unescorted woman boldly strolling down the sidewalk. The word "new" on the bus poster sums up the social scene. *(Copyright © Tate Gallery, London/Art Resource, New York.)*

Color Plates 24 and 25 A Nation Goes to War. Anna Airy, *Shop for Machining 15-inch Shells* (above), 1915, *(Tate Gallery, London, Great Britain/Art Resource, New York)* and Sir William Orpen, *Ready to Start* (left), 1917 *(Imperial War Museum, London, Great Britain/Art Resource, New York)*. Airy's painting might serve as an illustration for Siegfried Sassoon's line in *Glory of Women*, "You make us shells," though with none of Sassoon's bitterness. This fascinating oil painting of an all-female staffed weapons factory transmutes the arduous and exacting labor of designing and manufacturing enormous artillery shells for battleship guns into a symphony of gold "to airy thinness beat," as John Donne's sonnet puts it. Orpen's self-portrait depicts the artist in a rather aesthetic pose as he gazes into a mirror at a French café. The aristocratic Orpen was a leading London-based society painter before the war, considered superior to John Singer Sargent. Through royal connections and friendship with the literary Sassoon family, he was sent to battlefronts and wartime events to record them for the public. He made numerous striking and controversial paintings that depicted his gradual judgment that the British generals had betrayed their rank and file.

Color Plate 26 Bloomsbury Arts. Vanessa Bell, *The Tub*, 1917. Bell, along with her sister Virginia Woolf, was a member of the Bloomsbury Group—an informal association of friends, family, and lovers at the forefront of Britain's literary, artistic, and cultural scene for three decades. In addition to her painting, Bell was known for decorative and crafts work such as the furniture, painting, and china with which she adorned Charleston, the legendary Bloomsbury country house, today on England's register of cultural landmarks. *(Copyright © Tate Gallery, London/Art Resource, New York.)*

Color Plate 27 Kathleen Ni Houlihan. Sir John Lavery, *Lady Lavery as Kathleen Ni Houlihan*, 1928. In this portrait the artist's wife stands in for Kathleen Ni Houlihan, a Celtic heroine from the distant past of Irish glory celebrated in the work of W. B. Yeats; many of Yeats's poems celebrate the dynamic role that women played in Ireland's revolutionary movement, almost as if they were latter-day incarnations of the spirit of this great female cultural ancestor. Lavery (1857–1941) not only depicts his striking wife in the modern face and fashions of the time but also gives her an iconic status: the harp, the symbol of Ireland, is placed prominently in the foreground, as if to show that the woman sitting for the portrait knows full well that she conveys the symbolic hopes of a liberated Ireland, not the image of a real person. *(National Gallery of Ireland.)*

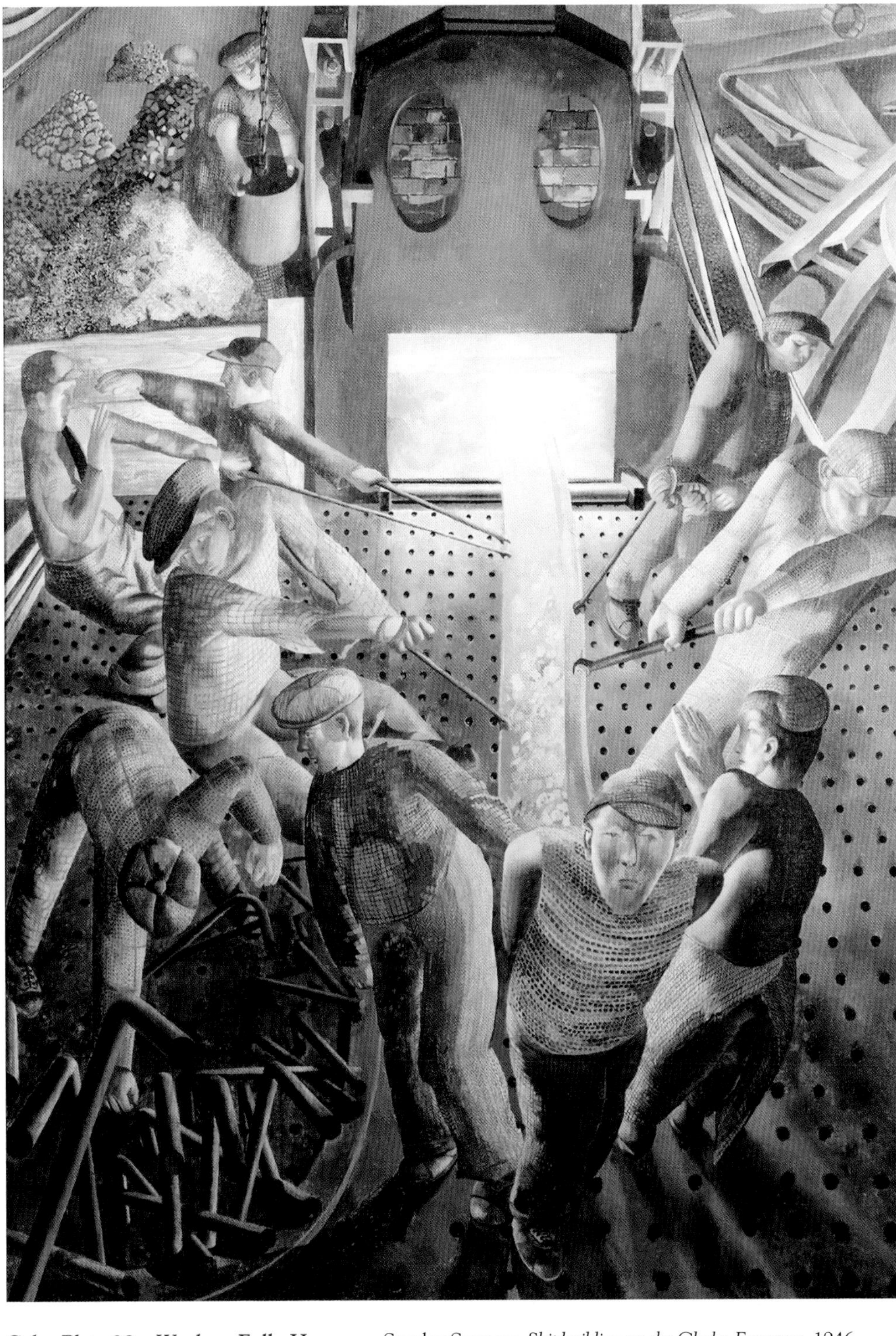

Color Plate 28 Workers Fully Human. Stanley Spencer, *Shipbuilding on the Clyde: Furnaces*, 1946. Twentieth-century British painting is unusual in modern art, for the best of it is based not on abstraction but on the human figure. Spencer's work was resolutely figural, yet it manages to be modern nonetheless because of the almost transcendent, mystical effects his images create. Spencer spent most of his eccentric life in a small English village, whose citizens he depicted swept up in great religious mysteries, such as the Annunciation or the Resurrection. Even his portraits of everyday activities—from shipbuilding to baking—are gilded with radiant transfiguration. *(Copyright © Imperial War Museum, London, UK/The Bridgeman Art Library.)*

Color Plate 29 Beyond Swinging London. Gilbert and George, *Death Hope Life Fear*, 1984. As performance artists and photographers, the gay couple Gilbert and George have offered provocative art for decades. Since the 1980s, they have produced huge photographic canvases incorporating religious, political, and homoerotic imagery. Cultural agents-provocateurs, Gilbert and George try to create witty yet highly charged confrontations between spectators and their own cultural beliefs, wishes, and secrets. *(Tate Gallery, London, Great Britain/Art Resource, New York.)*

Color Plate 30 After Such Knowledge, What Forgiveness? Francis Bacon, *Study After Velasquez*, 1950. Irish painter Francis Bacon (1909–1992) lived for most of his life in London, where his squalid studio was famous as a hub of creativity. Bacon's innovations in portraiture are unforgettable icons of modernity; perhaps his most familiar works depict a series of screaming popes. Based on classical portraits by Velasquez, Bacon's unnamed pope has a face haunted with knowledge of the holocausts of the twentieth century; he seems to scream at us from behind an arrangement of bars symbolizing totalitarianism. *(Copyright © 2003 Estate of Francis Bacon/Artists Rights Society [ARS], New York.)*

Color Plate 31 Consumerism as Modern Art. Richard Hamilton, *Just What Is It That Makes Today's Homes So Different, So Appealing?*, 1956. With its title taken directly from an advertising slogan, this whimsical collage puts together a fantasy domicile that features the motifs and icons of contemporary consumerism: the TV permanently tuned into its advertising spokeswoman, a vacuum cleaner close by, a canned ham ready for the next meal, and a Tootsie Roll lollipop held like a tennis racket by the muscularly endowed man of the house. Intruding upon this patchwork is the old-fashioned portrait hanging on a lurid yellow wall, positioned next to a Romance comic book page and a "picture" window that frames a marquee featuring an Al Jolson film. Hamilton's juxtapositions imply that we all now live in homes that are cultural tissues made up of ads, celebrities' wishes, dreams, and empty consumer desires. *(Copyright © 2007 Artists Rights Society [ARS], New York/ DACS, London. Photo by Kunsthalle Tubingen.)*

Color Plate 32 Multicultural Britain at the End of Empire. Chris Ofili, *No Woman, No Cry*, 1998. As one of the most exciting artists to emerge from the 1990s London art scene, Nigerian-born Chris Ofili represents the multicultural Britain that is remaking British art, literature, and popular culture. In *No Woman, No Cry*, titled after a Bob Marley song, he makes a vivid, almost religious, icon out of a black British woman, her clothes and the landscape of hot color studded with dried elephant dung, a sacred substance in some African rites. *(Copyright © Victoria Miro Gallery. Tate Gallery, London/Art Resource, New York.)*

London during the Blitz, seen from the north transept of Saint Paul's Cathedral.

before. Although morally and socially triumphant in its defeat of Nazism and fascism, Britain was left shattered economically and exhausted spiritually. Its people had come through the war gallantly, only to face grim conditions at home and political unrest throughout the empire.

Although morally and socially triumphant in its defeat of Nazism and fascism, Britain was left shattered economically and exhausted spiritually.

The global effort of that war, whose battles were fought not only in Europe but in Africa, Asia, Latin America, the Middle East, and the Pacific, had forced Britain to draw massively on its colonies for raw materials, money, and soldiers. Since the resistance to the British empire had begun long before World War II, the drafting of millions of already restive colonial subjects into the armed forces intensified the tensions and the conflicts running beneath the surface of the empire. One of the most important political phenomena of the twentieth century was about to hit a depleted Britain with a vengeance: the decolonization of most of the conquered globe in the great wave of independence movements that swept the world after 1945. One by one, with greater and lesser degrees of violence and agony, colonies slipped out of Britain's imperial net. From the independence of India (1947) to the independence struggles of Kenya, Nigeria, Zaire, Palestine, Egypt, and many others, Britain experienced the accelerated loss of the largest empire in Western history. Retaining only a handful of Caribbean, Latin American, and Pacific Rim possessions, the empire had radically shrunk. India, Pakistan, Canada, Australia, and a few other countries adopted

The empire on which the sun never set was fast becoming largely confined to England, Scotland, Wales, and Northern Ireland . . .

commonwealth status, remaining commercially linked but becoming essentially independent politically. The empire on which the sun never set was fast becoming largely confined to England, Scotland, Wales, and Northern Ireland—the latter, especially, an ongoing area of tension and conflict to the present day.

The dizzying pace of decolonization after the war put Britain in a paradoxically modern position ahead of many other Western countries: the unquestioned ability, and the rarely questioned right, of Western societies to dominate the globe had finally encountered decisive opposition. Within fifty years Britain found itself transformed from the dominant global power into a relatively small and, for a time, impoverished island nation, no longer a dictator of the world's history, but merely part of it. This dislocation was profoundly registered in British culture, and British writers strove to assess these losses—and to define the new possibilities for a freer and more open society that might emerge from the wreckage of empire.

One of the exciting aspects of British literature after World War II, then, is its very incoherence. New players not only joined the game, but in some instances began to call the shots, as the struggles for independence from British colonial control provided vivid and critical literary subjects—"subjects" in the sense of topics as well as those newly empowered writers whose subjectivity emerged on the page. At the same time, the shrinking of empire was turning Great Britain back into a small nation. Vita Sackville-West's story *Seducers in Ecuador* serves as a beautiful pre-war parable of Britain's precarious global significance; its main character travels around the Mediterranean by yacht with a group of fellow English citizens, with many if not most of their exotic ports of call under British imperial control. When the man buys a pair of blue spectacles in Egypt, he finds that he cannot bear to take them off: the story subtly suggests that they are imperial sunglasses, affording him a way of looking at the world—a gaze of control and domination—that ironically destroys his life when he tries to wear them back in England. The British literature that comes after the loss of Suez, of Egypt and Palestine and Arabia, reverses Sackville-West's prescient parable. The inhabitants of colonized zones don spectacles themselves, and use them to look unsparingly at their colonizers.

A new generation of writers also took on the task of evaluating English culture from inside. John of Gaunt's beautiful paean to "this sceptered isle, this England," in Shakespeare's *Richard II* had to be rewritten now: what was "this England" to be? In the absence of its colonial possessions, and in the general misery of shortages and rationing after the war, there was suddenly a sharp new scrutiny of British society. Its class-bound hierarchies appeared in an even harsher light, and its failures at home became the source of profound self-examination. Rage and anger accompanied this process of self-awareness, and a generation of literary artists dubbed the "angry young men" arose to meet the failures head-on, often in realist drama so faithful to its shabby subjects it was called "kitchen sink" drama, after the cold-water flat settings where the characters played out their rage. Playwrights such as John Osborne (as in the aptly titled *Look Back in Anger*) and novelists such as Anthony Burgess (*A Clockwork Orange*) angrily or satirically probed the discrepancy between England's glorious past and its seemingly squalid present.

A sense of diminishment in the world's eyes led to a passionate critique of British institutions . . .

A sense of diminishment in the world's eyes led to a passionate critique of British institutions, particularly its class structure, even where the literature produced was conservative in its looking backward. The extraordinary poet Philip Larkin might be seen as a key figure in this generation of writers. Larkin was a librarian in a rural town for most of his adult life. His poetry takes on the sardonic voice of the disenfranchised and the dispossessed—speaking not for the poor or the downtrodden but instead articulating the sense of loss and fury of middle and upper-class England, bereft of its historical prestige, impoverished by modern culture. He sings of nature, home, and country in a voice that is lacerating and self-mocking, using jazzy and colloquial poetic diction and Anglo-Saxon expletives. As one of his poems memorably declares:

> They fuck you up, your mum and dad.
> They may not mean to, but they do.
> They fill you with the faults they had
> And add some extra, just for you.

Larkin also wrote several notable novels at this time, among them *A Girl in Winter*, which explores from a surprisingly feminine and even feminist point of view the struggles of an emigré to Britain who must conceal the traumas her family experienced during the war, in order to "fit in" with a blithe and cavalier aristocratic British family. Larkin's artistry joins that of a host of other postwar writers, mostly male, who write from the center of an England now put off-kilter by the wrenching changes after the war.

Profound historical changes were to continue after the war with the commencement of the Cold War, in which the new world superpowers, the United States and the former Soviet Union, became locked in an intense battle for ideological, political, and economic dominance. Human beings now possessed the technological means to destroy the planet and its inhabitants, and these weapons of destruction were amassed by two societies with sharply conflicting goals. Britain along with Western Europe unequivocally aligned itself on the side of the United States, joining in the long fight against communism and Soviet socialism. While not itself a superpower, Britain had to shape its own social goals in light of the Cold War raging around it. A supremely eloquent voice in the articulation of what was at stake was that of the British writer George Orwell, known for his lucid essays on politics and language, including *Politics and the English Language*, to cite one of his classic works. Immediately after the war Orwell crafted *1984*, an enduring parable of Cold War culture. This book envisions a future society in the year 1984 when the infamous "Big Brother" is watching everyone. That tale of a society of totalitarian surveillance was a thinly veiled allegory of the possibilities inherent not only in a Soviet takeover but even in Western societies and their implicit tendencies toward control and bureaucracy. It may be that Orwell was able to be prophetic about the cultural touchstones of the next several decades because as a British writer he wrote from an oblique angle: the colonial relationship of Britain to the United States had become reversed, with Britain almost becoming an outpost of the United States in terms of its Cold War dominance, reminiscent of Britain's dominance of the fate of the American colonies in the centuries leading up to the American Revolution. It is sometimes possible to see more clearly from a position outside the exact center—and Britain was, in this sense, no longer the center of English-speaking Western civilization. Strangely enough, that ex-centricity granted its literary writers a certain kind of insight.

The British novel after World War II made a retreat from modernist experimentalism. One explanation for a return to the realism that Woolf had so passionately argued against comes, paradoxically, from feminism of the very sort Woolf espouses in *A Room of One's Own* and *Three Guineas*. For as women began to write in large numbers, the novel with characters and a plot became a kind of room these writers needed to make their own. A host of important women writers emerged who revived the novel—which had been declared dead by the French, at least, around 1950—by using its traditions to incorporate their experiences as women, "making it new" not by formal experiments, but by opening that familiar, even a little shabby, room to new voices and new stories. Among the practitioners of this "feminist realism"—although some of them would vehemently deny the label "feminist"—are Jean Rhys, Doris Lessing, Margaret Drabble, A. S. Byatt, Muriel Spark, Iris Murdoch, Nadine Gordimer, and Buchi Emecheta. In every case these are writers who ring changes on ostensibly traditional forms.

A particularly vibrant arena of British literary innovation after the postwar period was British drama; the dramatic form seemed to lend itself to the staging of new social and aesthetic experiments which, with the exception of women's writing as noted above, largely bypassed the British novel of this period. The most innovative of all British dramatists of the twentieth century after World War I was indubitably the Irishman Samuel Beckett. Living in a form of self-imposed exile in France, and a further self-imposed exile within the French language, Beckett moved from being the writer of mordant novels (*Molloy; Malone Dies*) to becoming an extraordinary dramatist. He often wrote his plays first in French, later translating them into English, so that English was their "secondary" language, leading to multiple puns in both English and French. Beckett's contribution to dramatic form, for which he received the Nobel Prize, is nonetheless a creation within British literature. Beckett sculpted his plays out of silence, paring down lines of dialogue until their short sentences and sometimes single words reverberate with the unspoken. More than any other dramatist in English, Samuel Beckett found the pockets of silence in English speech, and made those silences speak. His characters do not inhabit a real place, like England, but instead occupy an abstract space of human existence, where the human predicaments of longing and desire for redemption, the failures of understanding, and the bafflement of death are experienced in their purest form.

. . . the dramatic form seemed to lend itself to the staging of new social and aesthetic experiments . . .

Within England a host of dramatic luminaries gave vital energy to the British stage after 1945. While John Osborne created realist dramas of rage and dispossession, Harold Pinter emphasized the careful chiseling of language, bringing out the full ambiguity hidden in seemingly innocuous social conversation. Tom Stoppard joins Harold Pinter in his postwar longevity as a master of the British drama, despite or perhaps because of being an immigrant—"a bounced Czech," as he has called himself. Stoppard employs a brilliant rhetorical surface in his plays, which are often modernist puzzle boxes in their annihilation of the rules of time and space. In his meteoric but short dramatic career the playwright Joe Orton took a reverse tack to that of Beckettian silence and economy, or Pinterian ordinary language, and returned to the example of Oscar Wilde. Using a wildly baroque vocabulary and an epigrammatic wit, Orton brought an explicit gay drama and gay sensibility to the postwar theater, in works like *Loot*, which revolves around a seductive lower-class character who wreaks sexual havoc with all the inhabitants of a country estate, male and female, young and old. In *What the Butler Saw*, Orton imagines a monumental statue, bearing the national "phallus," which is hilariously blown to bits.

The impoverishment of the fifties abated in the sixties, at least for the middle class, as British banking and finance reinvigorated the economy. "Swinging London" became a household phrase, as British urban culture set the pace in music, fashion, and style. The Carnaby Street mode of dress and fashion mavens like Mary Quant, Jean Muir, and Zandra Rhodes were copied all over the world, worn by Jean Shrimpton and Twiggy, who were among the first supermodels. British film came out of a postwar slump and movies like *Morgan* and *Georgy Girl* had huge audiences at home and in the United States. A delirious excitement invested British popular culture, and London became a hub of the new once more. The critique of British society mounted by Joe Orton's work found its double in the youth culture of "Mods" and "Rockers." Asked which he was, the Beatles' drummer Ringo Starr claimed to synthesize both: "I'm a mocker."

A delirious excitement invested British popular culture, and London became a hub of the new once more.

Amid the cultural ferment of the sixties and seventies, successive British governments struggled with intractable problems of inflation and unemployment, punctuated by frequent strikes by Britain's powerful unions, and rising violence in Northern Ireland. The generally pro-union government of Harold Wilson (1964–1970) was followed by the Conservative government of Edward Heath, who put new stress on private enterprise. A major shift away from the "welfare state," however, came only at the end of the decade, when Heath was succeeded by the formidable Margaret Thatcher, the prime minister of Britain for a record twelve years. The daughter of a lower middle-class family, Thatcher vaulted into politics when that was an exceptionally rare opportunity not only for a woman, but for a person whose father was a shopkeeper. Trained as a chemist, Thatcher worked long and hard for the Conservative (Tory) Party, even as Britain was ruled by a succession of Labour and Socialist governments. When her chance came to lead England as its Tory prime minister, Thatcher and her political and ideological colleagues began a governmental revolution by adopting free-market policies similar to those identified with the Ronald Reagan school of U.S. Republicanism. Thatcher set about dismantling as much of the welfare state of postwar modern Britain as she could—and that was a considerable amount.

Margaret Thatcher had an enormous impact on British identity, as well as on British society. Among the very small number of women worldwide who have ever wielded such substantial political power—Golda Meir and Indira Gandhi come to mind as others—Thatcher's polished good looks, her extreme toughness, and her uncompromising political dictates combined to produce a caricature of her as the domineering English governness, laying down the rules of what would be good for Britain's unruly citizens. Thatcher's economic policies emphasized productivity as never before; under her rule, an entrepreneurial culture began to flourish at the expense of once-sacred British social entitlements in education, health care, and

The Beatles preparing for a television broadcast, c. 1963.

civic subsidy of the arts and culture. Margaret Thatcher's most breathtaking quotation, and the one summing up her philosophy of government, was uttered in response to complaints about what was happening to the fabric of British society and, especially, to its poor, elderly, immigrants, and the mass numbers of the unemployed. "There is no such thing as society," she declared. What she meant was that government had no role to play in creating a unitary, egalitarian society. The forces of the unleashed free market, and the will of private individuals, would replace any notion of a social contract or social compact between and among British citizens. There was irony, of course, in Thatcher's seeming to turn her back on members of her own class and those below it, and despite the power and immense reputation she acquired worldwide, there was always scathing and vocal opposition to her within Britain, as she privatized the universities and abolished tenure, made inroads on the National Health Service, dissolved city councils and established poll taxes. Prime Minister Thatcher declared and fought Britain's last imperial war of modern times, against Argentina over the control of the Falkland Islands, and she was a fierce opponent of nationalist sentiment among the Scottish and the Welsh, a firm upholder of Britain's right to control Northern Ireland in perpetuity, and strongly against the move toward joining the European Community. Thatcher became an icon in Britain, as well as its longest-governing prime minister: an icon for her certainty, confidence, and her personification of the huge changes she brought about. Though she provoked sharp opposition, her brilliance and energy were never in question, nor was her international influence.

By and large, the literary response to Thatcher's vision of Britain was electrifying in its opposition to everything she stood for. The jolt of anti-Thatcherism galvanized fiction, poetry, drama, visual art, and film. Among the many superb artists honed in the crucible of anti-Thatcherism is the playwright Caryl Churchill. While Churchill was plying her craft well before Maggie's reign began, she is an apt symbol of the passionate creativity unleashed from the later 1970s into the mid–1990s, especially given the gender she shares with Thatcher. Without question Caryl Churchill is among the foremost playwrights in the world today; such singularity means for her that gender—in addition to class, race, age, sexuality, nationality, ethnicity and the like—is foregrounded in her plays. Churchill's provocative theater is designed in part to open that Pandora's box which Thatcher herself ignored. Her play *Top Girls*, for example, sets Thatcher's political rise into collision with a contemporary feminism that questions whether female power is simply identical to masculine power—i.e., just a matter of who's on top, and who's at the top. By those lights, Thatcher's success made her a top girl par excellence, yet the play sets up a dinner party to debate this, a conversation between and among powerful women throughout the centuries from around the world, some of them historical figures, others images and icons, legends or myths, all eager to investigate whether or not women's liberation inheres in a simple exchange of dominance.

The jolt of anti-Thatcherism galvanized fiction, poetry, drama, visual art, and film.

Major changes occurred in the last several years of the twentieth century, changes sweeping enough to have diminished Margaret Thatcher's iconic stature, and to have partially reversed the social revolution she began. At the turn of the century, the Labour Party reclaimed control of the country, changing course economically and emphasizing the very social contract Thatcher had set aside. Despite its refusal to adopt the European common currency, the Euro, Britain is an increasingly pivotal member of the European Community alliance, and its own internal divisions have come productively to the fore. Surprisingly, the twentieth century ended in much the same way as did the nineteenth century for Britain, with a nationwide debate on home rule. In 1886 and again in 1893 the eminent British prime minister William Gladstone fought for the establishment of a separate Irish parliament—thus the term "home rule"—to allow the Irish colony, with its differing religion of Roman Catholicism and its unique Gaelic culture, to have control over its own internal affairs. Gladstone and his Liberal Party formed an alliance with the Irish National Party's members of Parliament, who were led by the great Charles Stewart Parnell, a Protestant Irishman known as "the uncrowned king of Ireland." Parnell's political fall due to an extramarital scandal removed a key player in Gladstone's strategy, and his final attempt in 1893 at voting in home rule failed. This failure led to the Irish revolution, the Irish Civil War, and the continuing violence within Northern Ireland, the six counties still belonging to Britain and occupied by their army.

Surprisingly, the twentieth century ended in much the same way as did the nineteenth century for Britain . . .

Britain's new prime minister, Tony Blair, was elected in 1997 from the Labour Party, breaking the Conservative Party's eighteen-year hold on the position under

Thatcher and her chosen successor, the rather low-key John Major. One of Blair's main campaign promises was bringing home rule to both Scotland and Wales, regions of Britain with their own language and dialect, their own cultural mores, and a long history of armed conflict with England. The referendum on the Scottish parliament, with the power to raise and lower income taxes within Scotland, and a considerable budget to operate as Scotland chooses, for its schools, health, housing and transport, overwhelmingly passed the popular vote; Wales has voted as well for the creation of a Welsh assembly with many of the same powers and responsibilities. While the Republic of Ireland is now a nation in its own right, Tony Blair's commitment to the peace talks in Northern Ireland, and to the inclusion of Sinn Fein in those talks, has also provided the first stirrings of political momentum in resolving the century-old conflict between Northern Irish Protestants who largely wish to remain attached to Britain, and the Northern Irish Catholics who have fought for the autonomy of this part of Ireland.

Language and Identity

Complicated questions of language and identity have increasingly come to dominate the most recent phase of British literature. A great paradox of the British postwar period, in its time of imperial shrinkage, involves the fate of the English language. Britain may have been "kicked out" of many of its former colonies as a governing presence, but English was rarely shown the door at the same time. For economic and cultural reasons English as a global language became even more widely dispersed and dominant after World War II. Of course, the spread of U.S. interests has played a role in the hegemony of English. However, the old contours of the British empire continue to shape much of the production of English literature today. In this way, the former British empire has become part of the fabric of British literature. V. S. Naipaul, for example, has long resided in England, but he was born to Indian parents in Trinidad, where the British had deployed Indian labor. His writing is as much in dialogue with the British literary tradition, and an extension of it, as that of any native-born British author. Naipaul's winning of the 2001 Nobel Prize for literature both confirms his international standing and highlights the altered literary geography of England itself.

For economic and cultural reasons English as a global language became even more widely dispersed and dominant after World War II.

Salman Rushdie, who is of Pakistani parentage, is another intriguing example of this process of crossing the increasingly porous boundaries of Britishness, as well as a cautionary tale of how powerful literature can be. Rushdie's novels are part of British literature at its modernist best, drawing on the entire English literary tradition, yet informed by a cosmopolitan and a non-Western literary tradition as well. Eight years after he achieved great acclaim for his novel *Midnight's Children* (1980), a book that adapted the "magic realism" of Latin American fiction to the history of Indian independence, Rushdie published *The Satanic Verses*. This novel recounts a magical mystery tour of sorts, the arrival of two South Asian refugees to modern London: one a film star from Bombay, the other a kind of trickster figure. Embedded in this complex tale of migration and identity is a brief dream sequence satirizing the prophet Mohammed. In response to this dream-within-a-dream passage, the Iranian theocratic government delivered a *fatwa*—an edict sentencing Rushdie to death for treachery to the religion of Islam. Rushdie did not write the book in Arabic, nor did he write it for a Muslim audience, but that was irrelevant to the clerics who pronounced sentence on him before millions of devout adherents. From that time until the late 1990s, Rushdie was forced to live in a form of self-imposed house arrest, guarded by the British government. In an ironic twist, British literature itself had become his prison house of language, his internal exile. It is this tradition that "protects" him as a great writer, and, because of its porous literary borders, is responsible for his predicament.

In recent years British literature has been infused with new life both from foreign-born writers and from new voices bubbling up from within the British Isles, in the shape of Welsh, Scottish, and Irish literary prose and poetry. The Nobel Prize–winning Irish poet Seamus Heaney is a kind of internal outsider, since, as he has written, he does not consider himself to be part of "British" literature as ordinarily defined, while he nonetheless writes English poetry deeply influenced by English poets from Milton to Wordsworth to Eliot. Some writers have deliberately taken themselves out of British literature for political and literary reasons, using the strongest means possible: they have decided to write in a language other than English. For example, the Kenyan writer Ngugi wa Thiong'o, educated by British missionaries and then at a British university, whose first memorized poem was Wordsworth's *Daffodils*, now writes in the Kikuyu language, and translates his work into English. The Irish poet Nuala Ní Dhomhnaill has made a similar decision: she writes and publishes her poetry first in Irish, and only later translates it into English as a "second" language.

In recent years British writing has been invigorated from "below," as well as from "outside" . . .

In recent years British writing has been invigorated from "below," as well as from "outside": there has been a profusion of working-class or lower-middle-class novelists, poets, and screenwriters, many of whom adopt the dialect or argot of lower-class Welsh, Scots, and Irish English. The Scots writer Irvine Welsh is one example of this cross-fertilization today; his novel *Trainspotting* received ample literary accolades and was made into a widely seen film that, like the book, circulated throughout Europe, the Americas, and much of the globe. Its picaresque tale of down-and-out yet lively and smart urban twenty-somethings trying to find fulfillment in drugs, travel, and petty crime made Glaswegian knockabouts and their dialect emblematic of the modern condition. When James Kelman won the Booker Prize for the best novel published in England in 1994, there was widespread outrage: the working-class, expletive-laced speech of his Scottish protagonist was deemed unliterary by many, or at least unreadable and not in conformity with what was revered as the Queen's English. Poetry too has become a vehicle for a range of literary experiments, linking music and film to rhymed and unrhymed, and often performed, verse, connecting the popular and the literary. This upsurge of vivacious and often provocative writing is primarily the work of younger writers, and in many instances the novels are almost immediately being turned into films with international audiences.

In the past hundred years British literature has seen upheavals of aesthetic form, of geographic location, and of linguistic content. What is no longer in question, oddly enough, despite the current age of cyberspace and interactive media, is whether literature itself will survive. As Mark Twain once commented dryly after reading his own obituary in the newspaper: "The reports of my death are greatly exaggerated." The reports of literature's inevitable eclipse at the hands of media and mass culture have, it seems, been greatly exaggerated too. At this moment, British literary creativity is fed from many streams, welling up unpredictably, located in unexpected places. British literature has not merely survived; it remains a vital index of contemporary social and cultural life, and a crucial indication of the shape of things to come.

For additional resources on the twentieth century, including an interactive timeline of the period, go to *The Longman Anthology of British Literature* Web site at www.myliteraturekit.com.

Joseph Conrad

1857–1924

Joseph Conrad, London, 11 March 1916.

One of the ironies of twentieth-century British literature is that many of its greatest writers were not conventionally "British." In the case of Joseph Conrad, arguably the first modern British writer, the irony is even more extreme, because Conrad was born a Pole, and learned English only when he was in his twenties. The transformation of Josef Konrad Nalecz Korzeniowski into "Joseph Conrad" is as fascinating and mysterious a story as the transforming journeys at the heart of his fiction.

Joseph Conrad was a lifelong exile from a country that no longer existed on the map of Europe as a separate country. At the time of Conrad's birth in 1857, Poland was divided between Russia and the Austro-Hungarian empire. His parents, Apollo and Eva, were Polish patriots, and after an uprising against Russia in 1863, the family was exiled to a village in the far north of Russia. Eva died when Josef was seven years old; Apollo when he was twelve. Apollo had been both a political activist and a man of letters, a poet and a translator of French and English literature into Polish. In a sense, by becoming a British novelist writing in English, Conrad was carrying on a project of translation begun by his father, a translation across cultures and literatures as well as languages. Hidden within Conrad's poetic and impressionistic literary language is a secret language—Polish—and a secret history of exile from his homeland.

After Conrad's parents died, he was raised by a cosmopolitan uncle, Tadeusz Bobrowski, who was also imbued with patriotic political leanings and a deep love of literature. Josef was sent to school in Cracow, Poland, where he was bored and restless. His uncle then sent him to Switzerland with a private tutor; they argued constantly for a year, and the tutor resigned. Not quite seventeen years old, Conrad proceeded to Marseilles and joined the French merchant navy. He spent twenty years as a sailor and as a ship's captain, spending four years sailing under the French flag, and then sixteen years with British trading ships. In 1894 Josef Korzeniowski completed his transformation into the writer Joseph Conrad by changing his name and settling in England to become a full-time writer.

By the end of the nineteenth century, the nationalistic wars that had led to a divided Poland had been followed by another historical phenomenon: the dividing-up of the globe by the nations of Europe as these powers consolidated empires. The oceans were crucial pathways in these struggles, not simply vast, watery landscapes outside of history. The seafaring Conrad, who had wanted to leave the frustrations of school behind him and see the world, became intimately involved in the everyday business of the making of empires, playing a minor role behind the scenes of the major political forces of the age. Merchant ships of the kind he served on traced the routes of trade and commerce, which now had become the routes of colonization and political conquest as well. As he came to realize he was an eyewitness to modern history in the making, Joseph Conrad discovered his abiding subject as a writer.

Conrad's voyages during this twenty-year odyssey took him East and West, to Indonesia and the Philippines, to Venezuela, the West Indies, and Africa. Working all the while, he watched as bit by bit the patchwork quilt of empire was put together. Wishing to avoid conscription in the French navy when he came of age, in 1878 Conrad joined the British merchant navy. The British empire had become the most extensive and mighty of any imperial power, and in his capacity as seaman Conrad worked in the main ports of call of the empire upon which the sun supposedly never set. He adopted British citizenship in 1886; after his uncle Tadeusz's death in 1894, Conrad made the final decision to become a writer, and to write in English rather than in French. At the age of thirty-seven, Joseph Conrad was newly born.

As a British writer, Conrad was a sort of ventriloquist. On the surface, he was as English as any other writer in his circle: he married an Englishwoman, Jessie George, and became a recognized part of British literary life, forming friendships with other major writers like Henry James and Ford Madox Ford, and achieving great popularity with the British reading public. A stranger from an exotically foreign place, by British standards, a newcomer to the English language, he nonetheless spoke through an English "voice" he created. From his distanced perspective, he was able to make English do things it had not done in the past for native writers of English. Language in Conrad's writing is always a bit off kilter, reading as if it had been translated instead of being, as it was, originally written in English. His prose has a hallucinatory effect, and a poetic intensity linked to his approaching the words of the English language afresh. The most famous of Conrad's narrators is the character Marlow, who appears in several of his major works as an elusive commentator on the action. His Englishness is as real as it can be, for an imitation. Marlow is perhaps even more British than the British, lapsing often into British slang like "By Jove!" as if to authenticate the reality of Conrad's vision of the British world. Through narrative voices like that of Marlow, Conrad can tell stories that may appear to be familiar and ordinary but are in fact anything but that. If modernist writers succeed in making us doubt that we can truly be at home in the world, Conrad can be said to have been the first writer to convey this homelessness in English.

There is another paradox at the heart of Joseph Conrad's work. His writing straddles the nineteenth and the twentieth centuries, with the five major works he wrote in the years before 1900—*Almayer's Folly*, *The Nigger of the "Narcissus," Heart of Darkness*, *Lord Jim*, and *Typhoon*—thought of by many critics as more modernist and experimental than later novels he wrote in the twentieth century—*Nostromo*, *The Secret Agent*, *Under Western Eyes*, *Chance*, and *Victory*. The critic Ian Watt claims that the "intense experimentation which began in 1896 and ended in 1900" resulted from Conrad's concentration in those five earlier works on his own personal experience, a personal experience of travel, exile, and solitude that was a radical premonition of the conditions of modernity. Works like *Heart of Darkness*, written during Queen Victoria's reign, for Watt present "the obdurate incompatibility of the self and the world in which it exists." In book after book, he sets a lone individual into confrontation with the complexities of the modern world, whether the world be that of European imperialism, or political anarchism, or the secret world of spies, or the world of political revolution. His heroes and (much less often) heroines have to find their bearings as society crumbles around them, and Conrad usually depicts them at a moment of choice, when they have to act on their lonely knowledge without any guarantee that they have chosen rightly.

A reliance on personal experience might seem to be a recipe for a straightforward, realist style, but Conrad's prose throughout his work is complex and symbolic, relying on images that are spun into complicated and ambiguous webs of symbolism. What stands out prominently in Conrad's style is its visual nature, the emphasis on making the reader "see." Critics of Conrad's writing early on seized on the strikingly visual aspect of his effects, and his friend and fellow modernist writer Ford Madox Ford wrote an essay in 1913, *On Impressionism*, which put Conrad in a newly invented camp of impressionist writers. Conrad never fully agreed with this description of his style, nor did he have any special fondness for impressionist painting or the works of its greatest practitioners, Monet and Cézanne. Nonetheless, his own preface to *The Nigger of the "Narcissus"* describes all successful art as based on "an impression conveyed through the senses," and in each of his first five books narrators recount what they have *seen*. The narrator goes back over an experience in retelling it to an audience, an experience whose significance is not necessarily clear even to the narrator but whose meaning is revealed through the accumulation of imagistic details. The powers of sight are directly related to the powers of insight, or self-knowledge. A famous passage from *Heart of Darkness* explains the storytelling technique of the narrator Marlow, but also explains a philosophical conviction at the core of Conrad's writing: "The yarns of seamen have a direct simplicity, the whole meaning of which lies within the shell of a cracked nut. But Marlow was not typical (if his propensity to spin yarns be excepted), and to him the meaning of an episode was not inside like a kernel but outside, enveloping the tale which brought it out only as a glow brings out a haze, in the likeness of one of these misty halos that are sometimes made visible by the spectral illumination of moonshine." Events cast a visual glow and haze where meaning can be found only in the most subtle shades and ambiguous highlights of language. The reader must participate in the gradual, and partial, process of accumulating meaning.

Heart of Darkness is a work at the heart of modern British literature. First published serially in *Blackwood's Magazine* in 1899, it was reprinted as a complete work along with a companion novella, *Youth,* in 1902, and writers have returned to it again and again, in the form of quotations and allusions and imitations of its style; its story has been rewritten by each successive generation, in novels, films like *Apocalypse Now,* and even rock lyrics. Almost mythic in resonance, *Heart of Darkness* itself is structured around a mythical core—that is, the hero's quest. The journey or quest motif pervades world literature and English literature alike, from the *Odyssey* and the *Epic of Gilgamesh* to Dante's *Divine Comedy*, Bunyan's *Pilgrim's Progress*, and Byron's *Childe Harold. Heart of Darkness* condenses in its pages an epic range of theme and experience, both the social themes of empire and cultural clash, and the personal theme of the hero's quest for self-discovery.

As with all his early work, Conrad based *Heart of Darkness* on his own experience, in this case a trip he took up the Congo River in 1890 in order to become captain of a small steamship. The trip was an unusual one even by Conrad's standards, as he had been sailing the major oceans of the world on large ships. Conrad had reasons for choosing the assignment, however; he had been fascinated by maps since boyhood, and the blank space on the continent of Africa represented by the then-unexplored interior impelled him on. He was curious to see for himself the scandalous imperial practices of the Belgian King Leopold II in the Congo, who possessed what he called the Congo Free State (now Zaire) as his own private property, draining it of raw materials like ivory, while claiming to be suppressing savagery and spreading European civilization. After traveling two hundred miles upriver to Kinshasa to join his ship, however, he found it was undergoing repairs. He traveled as a passenger on a trip to Stanley Falls, to bring back an ailing company agent, Georges Klein, who died on the return trip to Kinshasa. These events provided the germ of Conrad's novella, which transformed Klein ("Little," in German) into the uncanny figure of Kurtz.

A diary Conrad kept during his journey (excerpted beginning on p. 2010) records his dawning awareness that King Leopold's policy in the Congo was nothing other than slave labor, ultimately causing the deaths of more than a million Africans. Initially an observer, Conrad became a passionately informed partisan, and made known his findings in the form of journalism and essays in the attempt to halt the King's genocidal policies. *Heart of Darkness* records these evils, and the ravages of Belgian colonialism on the African tribal societies it encountered and uprooted. Scholars of African history have shown how accurate his descriptions are, from the bit of white thread worn around the neck of a certain tribal group, to the construction of the railroad to Kinshasa and its devastating human impact. Conrad never names the Congo, nor the places and landmarks his character Marlow visits, yet he himself later called the book a "Kodak," or a snapshot, of the Congo.

The location is left unnamed in part because Conrad wishes to show that the heart of this darkness can shift on its axis. Marlow is telling the tale to several anonymous Englishmen as they sail the Thames on their yacht. Under the Roman empire, Britain had itself been thought of as a savage wilderness, a dark continent. The journey upriver, as Marlow points out, has been a reverse journey as well, a journey back from Africa to the darkness that lies at the heart of an England that claims to be civilizing those whom it is merely conquering. The seemingly clear-cut boundaries of light and dark, black and white, have blurred and even reversed themselves, and the nested narrative of the story itself challenges our understanding and even our sense of self. In this narrative, as in Conrad's other works, we are confronted with the tragic irony that human knowledge always comes too late.

For additional resources on Conrad, go to *The Longman Anthology of British Literature* Web site at www.myliteraturekit.com.

Preface to *The Nigger of the "Narcissus"*[1]

A work that aspires, however humbly, to the condition of art should carry its justification in every line. And art itself may be defined as a single-minded attempt to render the highest kind of justice to the visible universe, by bringing to light the truth, manifold and one, underlying its every aspect. It is an attempt to find in its forms, in its colours, in its light, in its shadows, in the aspects of matter, and in the facts of life what of each is fundamental, what is enduring and essential—their one illuminating and convincing quality—the very truth of their existence. The artist, then, like the thinker or the scientist, seeks the truth and makes his appeal. Impressed by the aspect of the world the thinker plunges into ideas, the scientist into facts—whence, presently, emerging they make their appeal to those qualities of our being that fit us best for the hazardous enterprise of living. They speak authoritatively to our common sense, to our intelligence, to our desire of peace, or to our desire of unrest; not seldom to our prejudices, sometimes to our fears, often to our egoism—but always to our credulity. And their words are heard with reverence, for their concern is with weighty matters: with the cultivation of our minds and the proper care of our bodies, with the attainment of our ambitions, with the perfection of the means and the glorification of our precious aims.

It is otherwise with the artist.

Confronted by the same enigmatical spectacle the artist descends within himself, and in that lonely region of stress and strife, if he be deserving and fortunate, he finds the terms of his appeal. His appeal is made to our less obvious capacities: to that part of our nature which, because of the warlike conditions of existence, is necessarily kept out of sight within the more resisting and hard qualities—like the vulnerable body within a steel armour. His appeal is less loud, more profound, less distinct, more stirring—and sooner forgotten. Yet its effect endures for ever. The changing wisdom of successive generations discards ideas, questions facts, demolishes theories. But the artist appeals to that part of our being which is not dependent on wisdom; to that in us which is a gift and not an acquisition—and, therefore, more permanently enduring. He speaks to our capacity for delight and wonder, to the sense of mystery surrounding our lives; to our sense of pity, and beauty, and pain; to the latent feeling of fellowship with all creation—and to the subtle but invincible conviction of solidarity that knits together the loneliness of innumerable hearts, to the solidarity in dreams, in joy, in sorrow, in aspirations, in illusions, in hope, in fear, which binds men to each other, which binds together all humanity—the dead to the living and the living to the unborn.

1. Conrad's novella *The Nigger of the "Narcissus"* deals with the tragic death of a black seaman aboard a merchant ship named the *Narcissus;* Conrad had served as first mate on a ship of that name in the Indian Ocean in 1883. He published the novella in *The New Review* in 1897, then added this preface when it came out in book form in 1898.

It is only some such train of thought, or rather of feeling, that can in a measure explain the aim of the attempt, made in the tale which follows, to present an unrestful episode in the obscure lives of a few individuals out of all the disregarded multitude of the bewildered, the simple, and the voiceless. For, if any part of truth dwells in the belief confessed above, it becomes evident that there is not a place of splendour or a dark corner of the earth that does not deserve, if only a passing glance of wonder and pity. The motive, then, may be held to justify the matter of the work; but this preface, which is simply an avowal of endeavour, cannot end here—for the avowal is not yet complete.

Fiction—if it at all aspires to be art—appeals to temperament. And in truth it must be, like painting, like music, like all art, the appeal of one temperament to all the other innumerable temperaments whose subtle and resistless power endows passing events with their true meaning, and creates the moral, the emotional atmosphere of the place and time. Such an appeal to be effective must be an impression conveyed through the senses; and, in fact, it cannot be made in any other way, because temperament, whether individual or collective, is not amenable to persuasion. All art, therefore, appeals primarily to the senses, and the artistic aim when expressing itself in written words must also make its appeal through the senses, if its high desire is to reach the secret spring of responsive emotions. It must strenuously aspire to the plasticity of sculpture, to the colour of painting, and to the magic suggestiveness of music—which is the art of arts. And it is only through complete, unswerving devotion to the perfect blending of form and substance; it is only through an unremitting never-discouraged care for the shape and ring of sentences that an approach can be made to plasticity, to colour, and that the light of magic suggestiveness may be brought to play for an evanescent instant over the commonplace surface of words: of the old, old words, worn thin, defaced by ages of careless usage.

The sincere endeavour to accomplish that creative task, to go as far on that road as his strength will carry him, to go undeterred by faltering, weariness, or reproach, is the only valid justification for the worker in prose. And if his conscience is clear, his answer to those who, in the fullness of a wisdom which looks for immediate profit, demand specifically to be edified, consoled, amused; who demand to be promptly improved, or encouraged, or frightened, or shocked, or charmed, must run thus: My task which I am trying to achieve is, by the power of the written word to make you hear, to make you feel—it is, before all, to make you see. That—and no more, and it is everything. If I succeed, you shall find there according to your deserts: encouragement, consolation, fear, charm—all you demand—and, perhaps, also that glimpse of truth for which you have forgotten to ask.

To snatch in a moment of courage, from the remorseless rush of time, a passing phase of life, is only the beginning of the task. The task approached in tenderness and faith is to hold up unquestioningly, without choice and without fear, the rescued fragment before all eyes in the light of a sincere mood. It is to show its vibration, its colour, its form; and through its movement, its form, and its colour, reveal the substance of its truth—disclose its inspiring secret: the stress and passion within the core of each convincing moment. In a single-minded attempt of that kind, if one be deserving and fortunate, one may perchance attain to such clearness of sincerity that at last the presented vision of regret or pity, of terror or mirth, shall awaken in the hearts of the beholders that feeling of unavoidable solidarity; of the solidarity in mysterious origin, in toil, in joy, in hope, in uncertain fate, which binds men to each other and all mankind to the visible world.

It is evident that he who, rightly or wrongly, holds by the convictions expressed above cannot be faithful to any one of the temporary formulas of his craft. The enduring part of them—the truth which each only imperfectly veils—should abide with him as the most precious of his possessions, but they all: Realism, Romanticism, Naturalism, even the unofficial sentimentalism (which, like the poor, is exceedingly difficult to get rid of), all these gods must, after a short period of fellowship, abandon him—even on the very threshold of the temple—to the stammerings of his conscience and to the outspoken consciousness of the difficulties of his work. In that uneasy solitude the supreme cry of Art for Art itself, loses the exciting ring of its apparent immorality. It sounds far off. It has ceased to be a cry, and is heard only as a whisper, often incomprehensible, but at times and faintly encouraging.

Sometimes, stretched at ease in the shade of a roadside tree, we watch the motions of a labourer in a distant field, and after a time, begin to wonder languidly as to what the fellow may be at. We watch the movements of his body, the waving of his arms, we see him bend down, stand up, hesitate, begin again. It may add to the charm of an idle hour to be told the purpose of his exertions. If we know he is trying to lift a stone, to dig a ditch, to uproot a stump, we look with a more real interest at his efforts; we are disposed to condone the jar of his agitation upon the restfulness of the landscape; and even, if in a brotherly frame of mind, we may bring ourselves to forgive his failure. We understood his object, and, after all, the fellow has tried, and perhaps he had not the strength—and perhaps he had not the knowledge. We forgive, go on our way—and forget.

And so it is with the workman of art. Art is long and life is short, and success is very far off. And thus, doubtful of strength to travel so far, we talk a little about the aim—the aim of art, which, like life itself, is inspiring, difficult—obscured by mists. It is not in the clear logic of a triumphant conclusion; it is not in the unveiling of one of those heartless secrets which are called the Laws of Nature. It is not less great, but only more difficult.

To arrest, for the space of a breath, the hands busy about the work of the earth, and compel men entranced by the sight of distant goals to glance for a moment at the surrounding vision of form and colour, of sunshine and shadows; to make them pause for a look, for a sigh, for a smile—such is the aim, difficult and evanescent, and reserved only for a very few to achieve. But sometimes, by the deserving and the fortunate, even that task is accomplished. And when it is accomplished—behold!—all the truth of life is there: a moment of vision, a sigh, a smile—and the return to an eternal rest.

Heart of Darkness

1

The *Nellie*, a cruising yawl,[1] swung to her anchor without a flutter of the sails, and was at rest. The flood had made, the wind was nearly calm, and being bound down the river, the only thing for it was to come to and wait for the turn of the tide.

The sea-reach of the Thames stretched before us like the beginning of an interminable waterway. In the offing the sea and the sky were welded together without a joint, and in the luminous space the tanned sails of the barges drifting up with the tide seemed to stand still in red clusters of canvas sharply peaked, with gleams of var-

1. A two-masted ship.

nished sprits. A haze rested on the low shores that ran out to sea in vanishing flatness. The air was dark above Gravesend, and farther back still seemed condensed into a mournful gloom, brooding motionless over the biggest, and the greatest, town on earth.[2]

The Director of Companies was our captain and our host. We four affectionately watched his back as he stood in the bows looking to seaward. On the whole river there was nothing that looked half so nautical. He resembled a pilot, which to a seaman is trustworthiness personified. It was difficult to realise his work was not out there in the luminous estuary, but behind him, within the brooding gloom.

Between us there was, as I have already said somewhere, the bond of the sea. Besides holding our hearts together through long periods of separation, it had the effect of making us tolerant of each other's yarns—and even convictions. The Lawyer—the best of old fellows—had, because of his many years and many virtues, the only cushion on deck, and was lying on the only rug. The Accountant had brought out already a box of dominoes, and was toying architecturally with the bones. Marlow sat cross-legged right aft, leaning against the mizzen-mast.[3] He had sunken cheeks, a yellow complexion, a straight back, an ascetic aspect, and, with his arms dropped, the palms of hands outwards, resembled an idol. The Director, satisfied the anchor had good hold, made his way aft and sat down amongst us. We exchanged a few words lazily. Afterwards there was silence on board the yacht. For some reason or other we did not begin that game of dominoes. We felt meditative, and fit for nothing but placid staring. The day was ending in a serenity of still and exquisite brilliance. The water shone pacifically; the sky, without a speck, was a benign immensity of unstained light; the very mist on the Essex marshes was like a gauzy and radiant fabric, hung from the wooded rises inland, and draping the low shores in diaphanous folds. Only the gloom to the west, brooding over the upper reaches, became more sombre every minute, as if angered by the approach of the sun.

And at last, in its curved and imperceptible fall, the sun sank low, and from glowing white changed to a dull red without rays and without heat, as if about to go out suddenly, stricken to death by the touch of that gloom brooding over a crowd of men.

Forthwith a change came over the waters, and the serenity became less brilliant but more profound. The old river in its broad reach rested unruffled at the decline of day, after ages of good service done to the race that peopled its banks, spread out in the tranquil dignity of a waterway leading to the uttermost ends of the earth. We looked at the venerable stream not in the vivid flush of a short day that comes and departs for ever, but in the august light of abiding memories. And indeed nothing is easier for a man who has, as the phrase goes, "followed the sea" with reverence and affection, than to evoke the great spirit of the past upon the lower reaches of the Thames. The tidal current runs to and fro in its unceasing service, crowded with memories of men and ships it has borne to the rest of home or to the battles of the sea. It had known and served all the men of whom the nation is proud, from Sir Francis Drake to Sir John Franklin, knights all, titled and untitled—the great knights-errant of the sea.[4] It had borne all the ships whose

2. London. Gravesend is the last major town on the Thames estuary, from which the river joins the North Sea.

3. A secondary mast at the stern of the ship.

4. Sir Francis Drake (1540–1596) was captain of *The Golden Hind* in the service of Queen Elizabeth I; his reputation came from the successful raids he mounted against Spanish ships returning laden with gold from the New World (South America). In 1845 Sir John Franklin led an expedition in the *Erebus* and *Terror* in search of the Northwest Passage (to the Pacific); all perished.

names are like jewels flashing in the night of time, from the *Golden Hind* returning with her round flanks full of treasure, to be visited by the Queen's Highness and thus pass out of the gigantic tale, to the *Erebus* and *Terror*, bound on other conquests—and that never returned. It had known the ships and the men. They had sailed from Deptford, from Greenwich, from Erith—the adventurers and the settlers; kings' ships and the ships of men on 'Change; captains, admirals, the dark "interlopers" of the Eastern trade, and the commissioned "generals" of East India fleets.[5] Hunters for gold or pursuers of fame, they all had gone out on that stream, bearing the sword, and often the torch, messengers of the might within the land, bearers of a spark from the sacred fire. What greatness had not floated on the ebb of that river into the mystery of an unknown earth! . . . The dreams of men, the seed of commonwealths, the germs of empires.

The sun set; the dusk fell on the stream, and lights began to appear along the shore. The Chapman lighthouse, a three-legged thing erect on a mudflat, shone strongly. Lights of ships moved in the fairway—a great stir of lights going up and going down. And farther west on the upper reaches the place of the monstrous town was still marked ominously on the sky, a brooding gloom in sunshine, a lurid glare under the stars.

"And this also," said Marlow suddenly, "has been one of the dark places of the earth."

He was the only man of us who still "followed the sea." The worst that could be said of him was that he did not represent his class. He was a seaman, but he was a wanderer too, while most seamen lead, if one may so express it, a sedentary life. Their minds are of the stay-at-home order, and their home is always with them—the ship; and so is their country—the sea. One ship is very much like another, and the sea is always the same. In the immutability of their surroundings the foreign shores, the foreign faces, the changing immensity of life, glide past, veiled not by a sense of mystery but by a slightly disdainful ignorance; for there is nothing mysterious to a seaman unless it be the sea itself, which is the mistress of his existence and as inscrutable as Destiny. For the rest, after his hours of work, a casual stroll or a casual spree on shore suffices to unfold for him the secret of a whole continent, and generally he finds the secret not worth knowing. The yarns of seamen have a direct simplicity, the whole meaning of which lies within the shell of a cracked nut. But Marlow was not typical (if his propensity to spin yarns be excepted), and to him the meaning of an episode was not inside like a kernel but outside, enveloping the tale which brought it out only as a glow brings out a haze, in the likeness of one of these misty halos that sometimes are made visible by the spectral illumination of moonshine.

His remark did not seem at all surprising. It was just like Marlow. It was accepted in silence. No one took the trouble to grunt even; and presently he said, very slow,—

"I was thinking of very old times, when the Romans first came here, nineteen hundred years ago[6]—the other day. . . . Light came out of this river since—you say Knights? Yes; but it is like a running blaze on a plain, like a flash of lightning in the clouds. We live in the flicker—may it last as long as the old earth keeps rolling! But

5. Deptford, Greenwich, and Erith lie on the Thames between London and Gravesend; "men on 'Change" are brokers on the Stock Exchange; the East India Company, a commercial and trading concern, became *de facto* ruler of large tracts of India in the 18th and 19th centuries.

6. A Roman force under Julius Caesar landed in Britain in 55 B.C.E., but it was not until 43 C.E. that the Emperor Claudius decided to conquer the island.

darkness was here yesterday. Imagine the feelings of a commander of a fine—what d'ye call 'em?—trireme in the Mediterranean, ordered suddenly to the north; run overland across the Gauls in a hurry;[7] put in charge of one of these craft the legionaries,—a wonderful lot of handy men they must have been too—used to build, apparently by the hundred, in a month or two, if we may believe what we read. Imagine him here—the very end of the world, a sea the colour of lead, a sky the colour of smoke, a kind of ship about as rigid as a concertina—and going up this river with stores, or orders, or what you like. Sandbanks, marshes, forests, savages,—precious little to eat fit for a civilised man, nothing but Thames water to drink. No Falernian wine here, no going ashore. Here and there a military camp lost in a wilderness, like a needle in a bundle of hay—cold, fog, tempests, disease, exile, and death,—death skulking in the air, in the water, in the bush. They must have been dying like flies here. Oh yes—he did it. Did it very well, too, no doubt, and without thinking much about it either, except afterwards to brag of what he had gone through in his time, perhaps. They were men enough to face the darkness. And perhaps he was cheered by keeping his eye on a chance of promotion to the fleet at Ravenna by-and-by, if he had good friends in Rome and survived the awful climate. Or think of a decent young citizen in a toga—perhaps too much dice, you know—coming out here in the train of some prefect, or tax-gatherer, or trader even, to mend his fortunes. Land in a swamp, march through the woods, and in some inland post feel the savagery, the utter savagery, had closed round him,—all that mysterious life of the wilderness that stirs in the forest, in the jungles, in the hearts of wild men. There's no initiation either into such mysteries. He has to live in the midst of the incomprehensible, which is also detestable. And it has a fascination, too, that goes to work upon him. The fascination of the abomination—you know. Imagine the growing regrets, the longing to escape, the powerless disgust, the surrender, the hate."

He paused.

"Mind," he began again, lifting one arm from the elbow, the palm of the hand outwards, so that, with his legs folded before him, he had the pose of a Buddha preaching in European clothes and without a lotus-flower—"Mind, none of us would feel exactly like this. What saves us is efficiency—the devotion to efficiency. But these chaps were not much account, really. They were no colonists; their administration was merely a squeeze, and nothing more, I suspect. They were conquerors, and for that you want only brute force—nothing to boast of, when you have it, since your strength is just an accident arising from the weakness of others. They grabbed what they could get for the sake of what was to be got. It was just robbery with violence, aggravated murder on a great scale, and men going at it blind—as is very proper for those who tackle a darkness. The conquest of the earth, which mostly means the taking it away from those who have a different complexion or slightly flatter noses than ourselves, is not a pretty thing when you look into it too much. What redeems it is the idea only. An idea at the back of it; not a sentimental pretence but an idea; and an unselfish belief in the idea—something you can set up, and bow down before, and offer a sacrifice to. . . ."

He broke off. Flames glided in the river, small green flames, red flames, white flames, pursuing, overtaking, joining, crossing each other—then separating slowly or hastily. The traffic of the great city went on in the deepening night upon the sleep-

7. A *trireme* is an ancient warship, propelled by oarsmen; the Gauls were the pre-Roman tribes who occupied present-day France; they were subdued by Julius Caesar between 58–50 B.C.E.

less river. We looked on, waiting patiently—there was nothing else to do till the end of the flood; but it was only after a long silence, when he said, in a hesitating voice, "I suppose you fellows remember I did once turn fresh-water sailor for a bit," that we knew we were fated, before the ebb began to run, to hear about one of Marlow's inconclusive experiences.

"I don't want to bother you much with what happened to me personally," he began, showing in this remark the weakness of many tellers of tales who seem so often unaware of what their audience would best like to hear; "yet to understand the effect of it on me you ought to know how I got out there, what I saw, how I went up that river to the place where I first met the poor chap. It was the farthest point of navigation and the culminating point of my experience. It seemed somehow to throw a kind of light on everything about me—and into my thoughts. It was sombre enough too—and pitiful—not extraordinary in any way—not very clear either. No, not very clear. And yet it seemed to throw a kind of light.

"I had then, as you remember, just returned to London after a lot of Indian Ocean, Pacific, China Seas—a regular dose of the East—six years or so, and I was loafing about, hindering you fellows in your work and invading your homes, just as though I had got a heavenly mission to civilise you. It was very fine for a time, but after a bit I did get tired of resting. Then I began to look for a ship—I should think the hardest work on earth. But the ships wouldn't even look at me. And I got tired of that game too.

"Now when I was a little chap I had a passion for maps. I would look for hours at South America, or Africa, or Australia, and lose myself in all the glories of exploration. At that time there were many blank spaces on the earth, and when I saw one that looked particularly inviting on a map (but they all look that) I would put my finger on it and say, When I grow up I will go there. The North Pole was one of these places, I remember. Well, I haven't been there yet, and shall not try now. The glamour's off. Other places were scattered about the Equator, and in every sort of latitude all over the two hemispheres. I have been in some of them, and. . . well, we won't talk about that. But there was one yet—the biggest, the most blank, so to speak—that I had a hankering after.

"True, by this time it was not a blank space any more. It had got filled since my boyhood with rivers and lakes and names. It had ceased to be a blank space of delightful mystery—a white patch for a boy to dream gloriously over. It had become a place of darkness. But there was in it one river especially, a mighty big river, that you could see on the map, resembling an immense snake uncoiled, with its head in the sea, its body at rest curving afar over a vast country, and its tail lost in the depths of the land. And as I looked at the map of it in a shop-window, it fascinated me as a snake would a bird—a silly little bird. Then I remembered there was a big concern, a Company for trade on that river. Dash it all! I thought to myself, they can't trade without using some kind of craft on that lot of fresh water—steamboats! Why shouldn't I try to get charge of one. I went on along Fleet Street, but could not shake off the idea. The snake had charmed me.

"You understand it was a Continental concern, that Trading Society; but I have a lot of relations living on the Continent, because it's cheap and not so nasty as it looks, they say.

"I am sorry to own I began to worry them. This was already a fresh departure for me. I was not used to get things that way, you know. I always went my own road and on my own legs where I had a mind to go. I wouldn't have believed it of myself; but, then—you see—I felt somehow I must get there by hook or by crook. So I worried them. The men said 'My dear fellow,' and did nothing. Then—would you believe it?—I tried the women. I, Charlie Marlow, set the women to work—to get a job. Heavens! Well, you see, the notion drove me. I had an aunt, a dear enthusiastic soul. She wrote: 'It will be delightful. I am ready to do anything, anything for you. It is a glorious idea. I know the wife of a very high personage in the Administration, and also a man who has lots of influence with,' &c., &c. She was determined to make no end of fuss to get me appointed skipper of a river steamboat, if such was my fancy.

"I got my appointment—of course; and I got it very quick. It appears the Company had received news that one of their captains had been killed in a scuffle with the natives. This was my chance, and it made me the more anxious to go. It was only months and months afterwards, when I made the attempt to recover what was left of the body, that I heard the original quarrel arose from a misunderstanding about some hens. Yes, two black hens. Fresleven—that was the fellow's name, a Dane—thought himself wronged somehow in the bargain, so he went ashore and started to hammer the chief of the village with a stick. Oh, it didn't surprise me in the least to hear this, and at the same time to be told that Fresleven was the gentlest, quietest creature that ever walked on two legs. No doubt he was; but he had been a couple of years already out there engaged in the noble cause, you know, and he probably felt the need at last of asserting his self-respect in some way. Therefore he whacked the old nigger mercilessly, while a big crowd of his people watched him, thunderstruck, till some man,—I was told the chief's son,—in desperation at hearing the old chap yell, made a tentative jab with a spear at the white man—and of course it went quite easy between the shoulder-blades. Then the whole population cleared into the forest, expecting all kinds of calamities to happen, while, on the other hand, the steamer Fresleven commanded left also in a bad panic, in charge of the engineer, I believe. Afterwards nobody seemed to trouble much about Fresleven's remains, till I got out and stepped into his shoes. I couldn't let it rest, though; but when an opportunity offered at last to meet my predecessor, the grass growing through his ribs was tall enough to hide his bones. They were all there. The supernatural being had not been touched after he fell. And the village was deserted, the huts gaped black, rotting, all askew within the fallen enclosures. A calamity had come to it, sure enough. The people had vanished. Mad terror had scattered them, men, women, and children, through the bush, and they had never returned. What became of the hens I don't know either. I should think the cause of progress got them, anyhow. However, through this glorious affair I got my appointment, before I had fairly begun to hope for it.

"I flew around like mad to get ready, and before forty-eight hours I was crossing the Channel to show myself to my employers, and sign the contract. In a very few hours I arrived in a city that always makes me think of a whited sepulchre.[8] Prejudice no doubt. I had no difficulty in finding the Company's offices. It was the biggest thing in the town, and everybody I met was full of it. They were going to run an oversea empire, and make no end of coin by trade.

8. Brussels was the headquarters of the Société Anonyme Belge pour le Commerce du Haut-Congo (Belgian Corporation for Trade in the Upper Congo), with which Conrad obtained his post through the influence of his aunt, Marguerite Poradowska.

"A narrow and deserted street in deep shadow, high houses, innumerable windows with venetian blinds, a dead silence, grass sprouting between the stones, imposing carriage archways right and left, immense double doors standing ponderously ajar. I slipped through one of these cracks, went up a swept and ungarnished staircase, as arid as a desert, and opened the first door I came to. Two women, one fat and the other slim, sat on straw-bottomed chairs, knitting black wool. The slim one got up and walked straight at me—still knitting with downcast eyes—and only just as I began to think of getting out of her way, as you would for a somnambulist, stood still, and looked up. Her dress was as plain as an umbrella-cover, and she turned round without a word and preceded me into a waiting-room. I gave my name, and looked about. Deal table in the middle, plain chairs all round the walls, on one end a large shining map, marked with all the colours of a rainbow. There was a vast amount of red—good to see at any time, because one knows that some real work is done in there, a deuce of a lot of blue, a little green, smears of orange, and, on the East Coast, a purple patch, to show where the jolly pioneers of progress drink the jolly lager-beer.[9] However, I wasn't going into any of these. I was going into the yellow. Dead in the centre. And the river was there—fascinating—deadly—like a snake. Ough! A door opened, a white-haired secretarial head, but wearing a compassionate expression, appeared, and a skinny forefinger beckoned me into the sanctuary. Its light was dim, and a heavy writing-desk squatted in the middle. From behind that structure came out an impression of pale plumpness in a frock-coat. The great man himself. He was five feet six, I should judge, and had his grip on the handle-end of ever so many millions. He shook hands, I fancy, murmured vaguely, was satisfied with my French. *Bon voyage*.

"In about forty-five seconds I found myself again in the waiting-room with the compassionate secretary, who, full of desolation and sympathy, made me sign some document. I believe I undertook amongst other things not to disclose any trade secrets. Well, I am not going to.

"I began to feel slightly uneasy. You know I am not used to such ceremonies, and there was something ominous in the atmosphere. It was just as though I had been let into some conspiracy—I don't know—something not quite right; and I was glad to get out. In the outer room the two women knitted black wool feverishly. People were arriving, and the younger one was walking back and forth introducing them. The old one sat on her chair. Her flat cloth slippers were propped up on a foot-warmer, and a cat reposed on her lap. She wore a starched white affair on her head, had a wart on one cheek, and silver-rimmed spectacles hung on the tip of her nose. She glanced at me above the glasses. The swift and indifferent placidity of that look troubled me. Two youths with foolish and cheery countenances were being piloted over, and she threw at them the same quick glance of unconcerned wisdom. She seemed to know all about them and about me too. An eerie feeling came over me. She seemed uncanny and fateful. Often far away there I thought of these two, guarding the door of Darkness, knitting black wool as for a warm pall, one introducing, introducing continuously to the unknown, the other scrutinising the cheery and foolish faces with unconcerned old eyes. *Ave!* Old knitter of black wool. *Morituri te salutant*.[1] Not many of those she looked at ever saw her again—not half, by a long way.

9. British territories were traditionally marked in red on colonial maps; lager was originally a continental beer, not much drunk in England.

1. Hail!. . . Those who are about to die salute you!—traditional cry of Roman gladiators.

"There was yet a visit to the doctor. 'A simple formality,' assured me the secretary, with an air of taking an immense part in all my sorrows. Accordingly a young chap wearing his hat over the left eyebrow, some clerk I suppose,—there must have been clerks in the business, though the house was as still as a house in a city of the dead,—came from somewhere upstairs, and led me forth. He was shabby and careless, with ink-stains on the sleeves of his jacket, and his cravat was large and billowy, under a chin shaped like the toe of an old boot. It was a little too early for the doctor, so I proposed a drink, and thereupon he developed a vein of joviality. As we sat over our vermouths he glorified the Company's business, and by-and-by I expressed casually my surprise at him not going out there. He became very cool and collected all at once. 'I am not such a fool as I look, quoth Plato to his disciples,' he said sententiously, emptied his glass with great resolution, and we rose.

"The old doctor felt my pulse, evidently thinking of something else the while. 'Good, good for there,' he mumbled, and then with a certain eagerness asked me whether I would let him measure my head. Rather surprised, I said Yes, when he produced a thing like calipers and got the dimensions back and front and every way, taking notes carefully. He was an unshaven little man in a threadbare coat like a gaberdine, with his feet in slippers, and I thought him a harmless fool. 'I always ask leave, in the interests of science, to measure the crania of those going out there,' he said. 'And when they come back too?' I asked. 'Oh, I never see them,' he remarked; 'and moreover, the changes take place inside, you know.' He smiled, as if at some quiet joke. 'So you are going out there. Famous. Interesting too.' He gave me a searching glance, and made another note. 'Ever any madness in your family?' he asked, in a matter-of-fact tone. I felt very annoyed. 'Is that question in the interests of science too?' 'It would be,' he said, without taking notice of my irritation, 'interesting for science to watch the mental changes of individuals, on the spot, but. . . ' 'Are you an alienist?'[2] I interrupted. 'Every doctor should be—a little,' answered that original, imperturbably. 'I have a little theory which you Messieurs who go out there must help me to prove. This is my share in the advantages my country shall reap from the possession of such a magnificent dependency. The mere wealth I leave to others. Pardon my questions, but you are the first Englishman coming under my observation . . .' I hastened to assure him I was not in the least typical. 'If I were,' said I, 'I wouldn't be talking like this with you.' 'What you say is rather profound, and probably erroneous,' he said, with a laugh. 'Avoid irritation more than exposure to the sun. Adieu. How do you English say, eh? Good-bye. Ah! Good-bye. Adieu. In the tropics one must before everything keep calm.' . . . He lifted a warning forefinger. . . . *'Du calme, du calme. Adieu.'*

"One thing more remained to do—say good-bye to my excellent aunt. I found her triumphant. I had a cup of tea—the last decent cup of tea for many days—and in a room that most soothingly looked just as you would expect a lady's drawing-room to look, we had a long quiet chat by the fireside. In the course of these confidences it became quite plain to me I had been represented to the wife of the high dignitary, and goodness knows to how many more people besides, as an exceptional and gifted creature—a piece of good fortune for the Company—a man you don't get hold of every day. Good heavens! and I was going to take charge of a twopenny-half-penny river-steamboat with a penny whistle attached! It appeared, however, I was also one of the Workers, with a capital—you know. Something like an emissary of light,

2. A psychologist.

something like a lower sort of apostle. There had been a lot of such rot let loose in print and talk just about that time, and the excellent woman, living right in the rush of all that humbug, got carried off her feet. She talked about 'weaning those ignorant millions from their horrid ways,' till, upon my word, she made me quite uncomfortable. I ventured to hint that the Company was run for profit.

"'You forget, dear Charlie, that the labourer is worthy of his hire,' she said, brightly.[3] It's queer how out of touch with truth women are. They live in a world of their own, and there had never been anything like it, and never can be. It is too beautiful altogether, and if they were to set it up it would go to pieces before the first sunset. Some confounded fact we men have been living contentedly with ever since the day of creation would start up and knock the whole thing over.

"After this I got embraced, told to wear flannel, be sure to write often, and so on—and I left. In the street—I don't know why—a queer feeling came to me that I was an impostor. Odd thing that I, who used to clear out for any part of the world at twenty-four hours' notice, with less thought than most men give to the crossing of a street, had a moment—I won't say of hesitation, but of startled pause, before this commonplace affair. The best way I can explain it to you is by saying that, for a second or two, I felt as though, instead of going to the centre of a continent, I were about to set off for the centre of the earth.

"I left in a French steamer, and she called in every blamed port they have out there, for, as far as I could see, the sole purpose of landing soldiers and custom-house officers. I watched the coast. Watching a coast as it slips by the ship is like thinking about an enigma. There it is before you—smiling, frowning, inviting, grand, mean, insipid, or savage, and always mute with an air of whispering, Come and find out. This one was almost featureless, as if still in the making, with an aspect of monotonous grimness. The edge of a colossal jungle, so dark-green as to be almost black, fringed with white surf, ran straight, like a ruled line, far, far away along a blue sea whose glitter was blurred by a creeping mist. The sun was fierce, the land seemed to glisten and drip with steam. Here and there greyish-whitish specks showed up, clustered inside the white surf, with a flag flying above them perhaps—settlements some centuries old, and still no bigger than pin-heads on the untouched expanse of their background. We pounded along, stopped, landed soldiers; went on, landed custom-house clerks to levy toll in what looked like a Godforsaken wilderness, with a tin shed and a flag-pole lost in it; landed more soldiers—to take care of the custom-house clerks, presumably. Some, I heard, got drowned in the surf; but whether they did or not, nobody seemed particularly to care. They were just flung out there, and on we went. Every day the coast looked the same, as though we had not moved; but we passed various places—trading places—with names like Gran' Bassam, Little Popo,[4] names that seemed to belong to some sordid farce acted in front of a sinister backcloth. The idleness of a passenger, my isolation amongst all these men with whom I had no point of contact, the oily and languid sea, the uniform sombreness of the coast, seemed to keep me away from the truth of things, within the toil of a mournful and senseless delusion. The voice of the surf heard now and then was a positive pleasure, like the speech of a brother. It was something natural, that had its reason, that had a meaning.

3. 1 Timothy 5.18.

4. Grand Bassam and Grand Popo are the names of ports where Conrad's ship called on its way to the Congo.

Now and then a boat from the shore gave one a momentary contact with reality. It was paddled by black fellows. You could see from afar the white of their eyeballs glistening. They shouted, sang; their bodies streamed with perspiration; they had faces like grotesque masks—these chaps; but they had bone, muscle, a wild vitality, an intense energy of movement, that was as natural and true as the surf along their coast. They wanted no excuse for being there. They were a great comfort to look at. For a time I would feel I belonged still to a world of straightforward facts; but the feeling would not last long. Something would turn up to scare it away. Once, I remember, we came upon a man-of-war anchored off the coast. There wasn't even a shed there, and she was shelling the bush. It appears the French had one of their wars going on thereabouts. Her ensign dropped limp like a rag; the muzzles of the long eight-inch guns stuck out all over the low hull; the greasy, slimy swell swung her up lazily and let her down, swaying her thin masts. In the empty immensity of earth, sky, and water, there she was, incomprehensible, firing into a continent. Pop, would go one of the eight-inch guns; a small flame would dart and vanish, a little white smoke would disappear, a tiny projectile would give a feeble screech—and nothing happened. Nothing could happen. There was a touch of insanity in the proceeding, a sense of lugubrious drollery in the sight; and it was not dissipated by somebody on board assuring me earnestly there was a camp of natives—he called them enemies!—hidden out of sight somewhere.

"We gave her letters (I heard the men in that lonely ship were dying of fever at the rate of three a day) and went on. We called at some more places with farcical names, where the merry dance of death and trade goes on in a still and earthy atmosphere as of an overheated catacomb;[5] all along the formless coast bordered by dangerous surf, as if Nature herself had tried to ward off intruders; in and out of rivers, streams of death in life, whose banks were rotting into mud, whose waters, thickened into slime, invaded the contorted mangroves, that seemed to writhe at us in the extremity of an impotent despair. Nowhere did we stop long enough to get a particularised impression, but the general sense of vague and oppressive wonder grew upon me. It was like a weary pilgrimage amongst hints for nightmares.

"It was upward of thirty days before I saw the mouth of the big river. We anchored off the seat of the government. But my work would not begin till some two hundred miles farther on. So as soon as I could I made a start for a place thirty miles higher up.

"I had my passage on a little sea-going steamer. Her captain was a Swede, and knowing me for a seaman, invited me on the bridge. He was a young man, lean, fair, and morose, with lanky hair and a shuffling gait. As we left the miserable little wharf, he tossed his head contemptuously at the shore. 'Been living there?' he asked. I said, 'Yes.' 'Fine lot these government chaps—are they not?' he went on, speaking English with great precision and considerable bitterness. 'It is funny what some people will do for a few francs a month. I wonder what becomes of that kind when it goes up country?' I said to him I expected to see that soon. 'So-o-o!' he exclaimed. He shuffled athwart, keeping one eye ahead vigilantly. 'Don't be too sure,'

5. In a letter in May 1890 Conrad wrote: "What makes me rather uneasy is the information that 60 per cent. of our Company's employés return to Europe before they have completed even six months' service. Fever and dysentery! There are others who are sent home in a hurry at the end of a year, so that they shouldn't die in the Congo." According to a 1907 report, 150 out of every 2,000 native Congolese laborers died each month while in company employ; "All along the [railroad] track one would see corpses."

he continued. 'The other day I took up a man who hanged himself on the road. He was a Swede, too.' 'Hanged himself! Why, in God's name?' I cried. He kept on looking out watchfully. 'Who knows? The sun too much for him, or the country perhaps.'

"At last we opened a reach. A rocky cliff appeared, mounds of turned-up earth by the shore, houses on a hill, others, with iron roofs, amongst a waste of excavations, or hanging to the declivity. A continuous noise of the rapids above hovered over this scene of inhabited devastation. A lot of people, mostly black and naked, moved about like ants. A jetty projected into the river. A blinding sunlight drowned all this at times in a sudden recrudescence of glare. 'There's your Company's station,' said the Swede, pointing to three wooden barrack-like structures on the rocky slope. 'I will send your things up. Four boxes did you say? So. Farewell.'

"I came upon a boiler wallowing in the grass, then found a path leading up the hill. It turned aside for the boulders, and also for an undersized railway-truck lying there on its back with its wheels in the air. One was off. The thing looked as dead as the carcass of some animal. I came upon more pieces of decaying machinery, a stack of rusty rails. To the left a clump of trees made a shady spot, where dark things seemed to stir feebly. I blinked, the path was steep. A horn tooted to the right, and I saw the black people run. A heavy and dull detonation shook the ground, a puff of smoke came out of the cliff, and that was all. No change appeared on the face of the rock. They were building a railway. The cliff was not in the way or anything; but this objectless blasting was all the work going on.

"A slight clinking behind me made me turn my head. Six black men advanced in a file, toiling up the path. They walked erect and slow, balancing small baskets full of earth on their heads, and the clink kept time with their footsteps. Black rags were wound round their loins, and the short ends behind wagged to and fro like tails. I could see every rib, the joints of their limbs were like knots in a rope; each had an iron collar on his neck, and all were connected together with a chain whose bights swung between them, rhythmically clinking. Another report from the cliff made me think suddenly of that ship of war I had seen firing into a continent. It was the same kind of ominous voice; but these men could by no stretch of imagination be called enemies. They were called criminals, and the outraged law, like the bursting shells, had come to them, an insoluble mystery from over the sea. All their meagre breasts panted together, the violently dilated nostrils quivered, the eyes stared stonily uphill. They passed me within six inches, without a glance, with that complete, deathlike indifference of unhappy savages. Behind this raw matter one of the reclaimed, the product of the new forces at work, strolled despondently, carrying a rifle by its middle. He had a uniform jacket with one button off, and seeing a white man on the path, hoisted his weapon to his shoulder with alacrity. This was simple prudence, white men being so much alike at a distance that he could not tell who I might be. He was speedily reassured, and with a large, white, rascally grin, and a glance at his charge, seemed to take me into partnership in his exalted trust. After all, I also was a part of the great cause of these high and just proceedings.

"Instead of going up, I turned and descended to the left. My idea was to let that chain-gang get out of sight before I climbed the hill. You know I am not particularly tender; I've had to strike and to fend off. I've had to resist and to attack sometimes—that's only one way of resisting—without counting the exact cost, according to the demands of such sort of life as I had blundered into. I've seen the devil of violence, and the devil of greed, and the devil of hot desire; but, by all the stars! these were strong, lusty, red-eyed devils, that swayed and drove men—men, I tell you. But as I stood on this hillside, I foresaw that in the blinding sunshine of that land I would become acquainted with a flabby, pretending, weak-eyed devil of a rapacious and pitiless folly. How insidious he could be, too, I was only to find out several months later and a thousand miles farther. For a moment I stood appalled, as though by a warning. Finally I descended the hill, obliquely, towards the trees I had seen.

"I avoided a vast artificial hole somebody had been digging on the slope, the purpose of which I found it impossible to divine. It wasn't a quarry or a sandpit, anyhow. It was just a hole. It might have been connected with the philanthropic desire of giving the criminals something to do. I don't know. Then I nearly fell into a very narrow ravine, almost no more than a scar in the hillside. I discovered that a lot of imported drainage-pipes for the settlement had been tumbled in there. There wasn't one that was not broken. It was a wanton smash-up. At last I got under the trees. My purpose was to stroll into the shade for a moment; but no sooner within than it seemed to me I had stepped into the gloomy circle of some Inferno. The rapids were near, and an uninterrupted, uniform, headlong, rushing noise filled the mournful stillness of the grove, where not a breath stirred, not a leaf moved, with a mysterious sound—as though the tearing pace of the launched earth had suddenly become audible.

"Black shapes crouched, lay, sat between the trees, leaning against the trunks, clinging to the earth, half coming out, half effaced within the dim light, in all the attitudes of pain, abandonment, and despair. Another mine on the cliff went off, followed by a slight shudder of the soil under my feet. The work was going on. The work! And this was the place where some of the helpers had withdrawn to die.

"They were dying slowly—it was very clear. They were not enemies, they were not criminals, they were nothing earthly now,—nothing but black shadows of disease and starvation, lying confusedly in the greenish gloom. Brought from all the recesses of the coast in all the legality of time contracts, lost in uncongenial surroundings, fed on unfamiliar food, they sickened, became inefficient, and were then allowed to crawl away and rest. These moribund shapes were free as air—and nearly as thin. I began to distinguish the gleam of eyes under the trees. Then, glancing down, I saw a face near my hand. The black bones reclined at full length with one shoulder against the tree, and slowly the eyelids rose and the sunken eyes looked up at me, enormous and vacant, a kind of blind, white flicker in the depths of the orbs, which died out slowly. The man seemed young—almost a boy—but you know with them it's hard to tell. I found nothing else to do but to offer him one of my good Swede's ship's biscuits I had in my pocket. The fingers closed slowly on it and held—there was no other movement and no other glance. He had tied a bit of white worsted round his neck—Why? Where did he get it? Was it a badge—an ornament—a charm—a propitiatory act? Was there any idea at all connected with it? It looked startling round his black neck, this bit of white thread from beyond the seas.

"Near the same tree two more bundles of acute angles sat with their legs drawn up. One, with his chin propped on his knees, stared at nothing, in an intolerable and appalling manner: his brother phantom rested its forehead, as if overcome with a great weariness; and all about others were scattered in every pose of contorted collapse, as in some picture of a massacre or a pestilence. While I stood horror-struck, one of these creatures rose to his hands and knees, and went off on all-fours towards the river to drink. He lapped out of his hand, then sat up in the sunlight, crossing his shins in front of him, and after a time let his woolly head fall on his breastbone.

"I didn't want any more loitering in the shade, and I made haste towards the station. When near the buildings I met a white man, in such an unexpected elegance of get-up that in the first moment I took him for a sort of vision. I saw a high starched collar, white cuffs, a light alpaca jacket, snowy trousers, a clear silk necktie, and varnished boots. No hat. Hair parted, brushed, oiled, under a green-lined parasol held in a big white hand. He was amazing, and had a penholder behind his ear.

"I shook hands with this miracle, and I learned he was the Company's chief accountant, and that all the book-keeping was done at this station. He had come out for a moment, he said, 'to get a breath of fresh air.' The expression sounded wonderfully odd, with its suggestion of sedentary desk-life. I wouldn't have mentioned the fellow to you at all, only it was from his lips that I first heard the name of the man who is so indissolubly connected with the memories of that time. Moreover, I respected the fellow. Yes; I respected his collars, his vast cuffs, his brushed hair. His appearance was certainly that of a hairdresser's dummy; but in the great demoralisation of the land he kept up his appearance. That's backbone. His starched collars and got-up shirt-fronts were achievements of character. He had been out nearly three years; and, later on, I could not help asking him how he managed to sport such linen. He had just the faintest blush, and said modestly, 'I've been teaching one of the native women about the station. It was difficult. She had a distaste for the work.' Thus this man had verily accomplished something. And he was devoted to his books, which were in apple-pie order.

"Everything else in the station was in a muddle,—heads, things, buildings. Strings of dusty niggers with splay feet arrived and departed; a stream of manufactured goods, rubbishy cottons, beads, and brass-wire set into the depths of darkness, and in return came a precious trickle of ivory.

"I had to wait in the station for ten days—an eternity. I lived in a hut in the yard, but to be out of the chaos I would sometimes get into the accountant's office. It was built of horizontal planks, and so badly put together that, as he bent over his high desk, he was barred from neck to heels with narrow strips of sunlight. There was no need to open the big shutter to see. It was hot there too; big flies buzzed fiendishly, and did not sting, but stabbed. I sat generally on the floor, while, of faultless appearance (and even slightly scented), perching on a high stool, he wrote, he wrote. Sometimes he stood up for exercise. When a truckle-bed with a sick man (some invalided agent from up-country) was put in there, he exhibited a gentle annoyance. 'The groans of this sick person,' he said, 'distract my attention. And without that it is extremely difficult to guard against clerical errors in this climate.'

"One day he remarked, without lifting his head, 'In the interior you will no doubt meet Mr Kurtz.' On my asking who Mr Kurtz was, he said he was a first-class agent; and seeing my disappointment at this information, he added slowly, laying down his pen, 'He is a very remarkable person.' Further questions elicited from him that Mr Kurtz was at present in charge of a trading-post, a very important one, in the true ivory-country, at 'the very bottom of there. Sends in as much ivory as all the others put together . . . ' He began to write again. The sick man was too ill to groan. The flies buzzed in a great peace.

"Suddenly there was a growing murmur of voices and a great tramping of feet. A caravan had come in. A violent babble of uncouth sounds burst out on the other side of the planks. All the carriers were speaking together, and in the midst of the uproar the lamentable voice of the chief agent was heard 'giving it up' tearfully for the twentieth time that day. . . . He rose slowly. 'What a frightful row,' he said. He crossed the room gently to look at the sick man, and returning, said to me, 'He does not hear.' 'What! Dead?' I asked, startled. 'No, not yet,' he answered, with great composure. Then, alluding with a toss of the head to the tumult in the station-yard, 'When one has got to make correct entries, one comes to hate those savages—hate them to the death.' He remained thoughtful for a moment. 'When you see Mr Kurtz,' he went on, 'tell him from me that everything here'—he glanced at the desk—'is very satisfactory. I don't like to write to him—with those messengers of ours you never know who may get hold of your letter—at that Central Station.' He stared at me for a moment with his mild, bulging eyes. 'Oh, he will go far, very far,' he began again. 'He will be a somebody in the Administration before long. They, above—the Council in Europe, you know—mean him to be.'

"He turned to his work. The noise outside had ceased, and presently in going out I stopped at the door. In the steady buzz of flies the homeward-bound agent was lying flushed and insensible; the other, bent over his books, was making correct entries of perfectly correct transactions; and fifty feet below the doorstep I could see the still tree-tops of the grove of death.

"Next day I left that station at last, with a caravan of sixty men, for a two-hundred-mile tramp.

"No use telling you much about that. Paths, paths, everywhere; a stamped-in network of paths spreading over the empty land, through long grass, through burnt grass, through thickets, down and up chilly ravines, up and down stony hills ablaze with heat; and a solitude, a solitude, nobody, not a hut. The population had cleared out a long time ago. Well, if a lot of mysterious niggers armed with all kinds of fearful weapons suddenly took to travelling on the road between Deal[6] and Gravesend, catching the yokels right and left to carry heavy loads for them, I fancy every farm and cottage thereabouts would get empty very soon. Only here the dwellings were gone too. Still, I passed through several abandoned villages. There's something pathetically childish in the ruins of grass walls. Day after day, with the stamp and shuffle of sixty pair of bare feet behind me, each pair under a 60-lb. load. Camp, cook, sleep, strike camp, march. Now and then a carrier dead in harness, at rest in the long grass near the path, with an empty water-gourd and his long staff lying by his side. A great silence around and above. Perhaps on some quiet night the tremor of far-off drums, sinking, swelling, a tremor vast, faint; a sound weird, appealing, suggestive, and wild—and perhaps with as profound a meaning as the sound of bells in a Christian country. Once a white man in an unbuttoned uniform, camping on the path with an armed escort of lank Zanzibaris,[7] very hospitable and festive—not to say drunk. Was looking after the upkeep of the road, he declared. Can't say I saw any road or any upkeep, unless the body of a middle-aged negro, with a bullet-hole in the forehead, upon which I absolutely stumbled three miles farther on, may be considered as a permanent improvement. I had a white companion too, not a bad chap, but rather too fleshy and with the exasperating habit of fainting on the hot hillsides, miles away from the least bit of shade and water. Annoying, you know, to hold your own coat like a parasol over a

6. An English port.

7. Africans from Zanzibar, in East Africa; they were widely used as mercenaries.

man's head while he is coming-to. I couldn't help asking him once what he meant by coming there at all. 'To make money, of course. What do you think?' he said, scornfully. Then he got fever, and had to be carried in a hammock slung under a pole. As he weighed sixteen stone I had no end of rows with the carriers. They jibbed, ran away, sneaked off with their loads in the night—quite a mutiny. So, one evening, I made a speech in English with gestures, not one of which was lost to the sixty pairs of eyes before me, and the next morning I started the hammock off in front all right. An hour afterwards I came upon the whole concern wrecked in a bush—man, hammock, groans, blankets, horrors. The heavy pole had skinned his poor nose. He was very anxious for me to kill somebody, but there wasn't the shadow of a carrier near. I remembered the old doctor,—'It would be interesting for science to watch the mental changes of individuals, on the spot.' I felt I was becoming scientifically interesting. However, all that is to no purpose. On the fifteenth day I came in sight of the big river again, and hobbled into the Central Station. It was on a back water surrounded by scrub and forest, with a pretty border of smelly mud on one side, and on the three others enclosed by a crazy fence of rushes. A neglected gap was all the gate it had, and the first glance at the place was enough to let you see the flabby devil was running that show. White men with long staves in their hands appeared languidly from amongst the buildings, strolling up to take a look at me, and then retired out of sight somewhere. One of them, a stout, excitable chap with black moustaches, informed me with great volubility and many digressions, as soon as I told him who I was, that my steamer was at the bottom of the river. I was thunderstruck. What, how, why? Oh, it was 'all right.' The 'manager himself' was there. All quite correct. 'Everybody had behaved splendidly! splendidly!'—'You must,' he said in agitation, 'go and see the general manager at once. He is waiting!'

"I did not see the real significance of that wreck at once. I fancy I see it now, but I am not sure—not at all. Certainly the affair was too stupid—when I think of it—to be altogether natural. Still. . . . But at the moment it presented itself simply as a confounded nuisance. The steamer was sunk. They had started two days before in a sudden hurry up the river with the manager on board, in charge of some volunteer skipper, and before they had been out three hours they tore the bottom out of her on stones, and she sank near the south bank. I asked myself what I was to do there, now my boat was lost. As a matter of fact, I had plenty to do in fishing my command out of the river. I had to set about it the very next day. That, and the repairs when I brought the pieces to the station, took some months.

"My first interview with the manager was curious. He did not ask me to sit down after my twenty-mile walk that morning. He was commonplace in complexion, in feature, in manners, and in voice. He was of middle size and of ordinary build. His eyes, of the usual blue, were perhaps remarkably cold, and he certainly could make his glance fall on one as trenchant and heavy as an axe. But even at these times the rest of his person seemed to disclaim the intention. Otherwise there was only an indefinable, faint expression of his lips, something stealthy—a smile—not a smile—I remember it, but I can't explain. It was unconscious, this smile was, though just after he had said something it got intensified for an instant. It came at the end of his speeches like a seal applied on the words to make the meaning of the commonest phrase appear absolutely inscrutable. He was a common trader, from his youth up employed in these parts—nothing more. He was obeyed, yet he inspired neither love nor fear, nor even respect. He inspired uneasiness. That was it! Uneasiness. Not a definite mistrust—just uneasiness—nothing more. You have no idea how effective such a . . . a . . . faculty can be. He had no genius for organising, for initiative, or for order even. That was evident in such things as the deplorable state of the station. He had no learning, and no intelligence. His position had come to him—why? Perhaps because he was never ill . . . He had served three terms of three years out there . . . Because triumphant health in the general rout of constitutions is a kind of power in itself. When he went home on leave he rioted on a large scale—pompously. Jack ashore—with a difference—in externals only. This one could gather from his casual talk. He originated nothing, he could keep the routine going—that's all. But he was great. He was great by this little thing that it was impossible to tell what could control such a man. He never gave that secret away. Perhaps there was nothing within him. Such a suspicion made one pause—for out there there were no external checks. Once when various tropical diseases had laid low almost every 'agent' in the station, he was heard to say, 'Men who come out here should have no entrails.' He sealed the utterance with that smile of his, as though it had been a door opening into a darkness he had in his keeping. You fancied you had seen things—but the seal was on. When annoyed at meal-times by the constant quarrels of the white men about precedence, he ordered an immense round table to be made, for which a special house had to be built. This was the station's mess-room. Where he sat was the first place—the rest were nowhere. One felt this to be his unalterable conviction. He was neither civil nor uncivil. He was quiet. He allowed his 'boy'—an overfed young negro from the coast—to treat the white men, under his very eyes, with provoking insolence.

"He began to speak as soon as he saw me. I had been very long on the road. He could not wait. Had to start without me. The up-river stations had to be relieved. There had been so many delays already that he did not know who was dead and who was alive, and how they got on—and so on, and so on. He paid no attention to my explanations, and, playing with a stick of sealing-wax, repeated several times that the situation was 'very grave, very grave.' There were rumours that a very important station was in jeopardy, and its chief, Mr Kurtz, was ill. Hoped it was not true. Mr Kurtz was . . . I felt weary and irritable. Hang Kurtz, I thought. I interrupted him by saying I had heard of Mr Kurtz on the coast. 'Ah! So they talk of him down there,' he murmured to himself. Then he began again, assuring me Mr Kurtz was the best agent he had, an exceptional man, of the greatest importance to the Company; therefore I could understand his anxiety. He was, he said, 'very, very uneasy.' Certainly he fidgeted on his chair a good deal, exclaimed, 'Ah, Mr Kurtz!' broke the stick of sealing-wax and seemed dumbfounded by the accident. Next thing he wanted to know 'how long it would take to' . . . I interrupted him again. Being hungry, you know, and kept on my feet too, I was getting savage. 'How can I tell?' I said. 'I haven't even seen the wreck yet—some months, no doubt.' All this talk seemed to me so futile. 'Some months,' he said. 'Well, let us say three months before we can make a start. Yes. That ought to do the affair.' I flung out of his hut (he lived all alone in a clay hut with a sort of verandah) muttering to myself my opinion of him. He was a chattering idiot. Afterwards I took it back when it was borne in upon me startlingly with what extreme nicety he had estimated the time requisite for the 'affair.'

"I went to work the next day, turning, so to speak, my back on that station. In that way only it seemed to me I could keep my hold on the redeeming facts of life.

Still, one must look about sometimes; and then I saw this station, these men strolling aimlessly about in the sunshine of the yard. I asked myself sometimes what it all meant. They wandered here and there with their absurd long staves in their hands, like a lot of faithless pilgrims bewitched inside a rotten fence. The word 'ivory' rang in the air, was whispered, was sighed. You would think they were praying to it. A taint of imbecile rapacity blew through it all, like a whiff from some corpse. By Jove! I've never seen anything so unreal in my life. And outside, the silent wilderness surrounding this cleared speck on the earth struck me as something great and invincible, like evil or truth, waiting patiently for the passing away of this fantastic invasion.

"Oh, those months! Well, never mind. Various things happened. One evening a grass shed full of calico, cotton prints, beads, and I don't know what else, burst into a blaze so suddenly that you would have thought the earth had opened to let an avenging fire consume all that trash. I was smoking my pipe quietly by my dismantled steamer, and saw them all cutting capers in the light, with their arms lifted high, when the stout man with moustaches came tearing down to the river, a tin pail in his hand, assured me that everybody was 'behaving splendidly, splendidly,' dipped about a quart of water and tore back again. I noticed there was a hole in the bottom of his pail.

"I strolled up. There was no hurry. You see the thing had gone off like a box of matches. It had been hopeless from the very first. The flame had leaped high, driven everybody back, lighted up everything—and collapsed. The shed was already a heap of embers glowing fiercely. A nigger was being beaten near by. They said he had caused the fire in some way; be that as it may, he was screeching most horribly. I saw him, later on, for several days, sitting in a bit of shade looking very sick and trying to recover himself: afterwards he arose and went out—and the wilderness without a sound took him into its bosom again. As I approached the glow from the dark I found myself at the back of two men, talking. I heard the name of Kurtz pronounced, then the words, 'take advantage of this unfortunate accident.' One of the men was the manager. I wished him a good evening. 'Did you ever see anything like it—eh? it is incredible,' he said, and walked off. The other man remained. He was a first-class agent, young, gentlemanly, a bit reserved, with a forked little beard and a hooked nose. He was stand-offish with the other agents, and they on their side said he was the manager's spy upon them. As to me, I had hardly ever spoken to him before. We got into talk, and by-and-by we strolled away from the hissing ruins. Then he asked me to his room, which was in the main building of the station. He struck a match, and I perceived that this young aristocrat had not only a silver-mounted dressing-case but also a whole candle all to himself. Just at that time the manager was the only man supposed to have any right to candles. Native mats covered the clay walls; a collection of spears, assegais,[8] shields, knives was hung up in trophies. The business intrusted to this fellow was the making of bricks—so I had been informed; but there wasn't a fragment of a brick anywhere in the station, and he had been there more than a year—waiting. It seems he could not make bricks without something, I don't know what—straw maybe. Anyway, it could not be found there, and as it was not likely to be sent from Europe, it did not appear clear to me what he was waiting

8. Slender African spears.

for. An act of special creation perhaps. However, they were all waiting—all the sixteen or twenty pilgrims of them—for something; and upon my word it did not seem an uncongenial occupation, from the way they took it, though the only thing that ever came to them was disease—as far as I could see. They beguiled the time by backbiting and intriguing against each other in a foolish kind of way. There was an air of plotting about that station, but nothing came of it, of course. It was as unreal as everything else—as the philanthropic pretence of the whole concern, as their talk, as their government, as their show of work. The only real feeling was a desire to get appointed to a trading-post where ivory was to be had, so that they could earn percentages. They intrigued and slandered and hated each other only on that account,—but as to effectually lifting a little finger—oh, no. By heavens! there is something after all in the world allowing one man to steal a horse while another must not look at a halter. Steal a horse straight out. Very well. He has done it. Perhaps he can ride. But there is a way of looking at a halter that would provoke the most charitable of saints into a kick.

"I had no idea why he wanted to be sociable, but as we chatted in there it suddenly occurred to me the fellow was trying to get at something—in fact, pumping me. He alluded constantly to Europe, to the people I was supposed to know there—putting leading questions as to my acquaintances in the sepulchral city, and so on. His little eyes glittered like mica discs—with curiosity,—though he tried to keep up a bit of superciliousness. At first I was astonished, but very soon I became awfully curious to see what he would find out from me. I couldn't possibly imagine what I had in me to make it worth his while. It was very pretty to see how he baffled himself, for in truth my body was full of chills, and my head had nothing in it but that wretched steamboat business. It was evident he took me for a perfectly shameless prevaricator. At last he got angry, and, to conceal a movement of furious annoyance, he yawned. I rose. Then I noticed a small sketch in oils, on a panel, representing a woman, draped and blind-folded, carrying a lighted torch. The background was sombre—almost black. The movement of the woman was stately, and the effect of the torchlight on the face was sinister.

"It arrested me, and he stood by civilly, holding a half-pint champagne bottle (medical comforts) with the candle stuck in it. To my question he said Mr Kurtz had painted this—in this very station more than a year ago—while waiting for means to go to his trading-post. 'Tell me, pray,' said I, 'who is this Mr Kurtz?'

"'The chief of the Inner Station,' he answered in a short tone, looking away. 'Much obliged,' I said, laughing. 'And you are the brickmaker of the Central Station. Every one knows that.' He was silent for a while. 'He is a prodigy,' he said at last. 'He is an emissary of pity, and science, and progress, and devil knows what else. We want,' he began to declaim suddenly, 'for the guidance of the cause intrusted to us by Europe, so to speak, higher intelligence, wide sympathies, a singleness of purpose.' 'Who says that?' I asked. 'Lots of them,' he replied. 'Some even write that; and so *he* comes here, a special being, as you ought to know.' 'Why ought I to know?' I interrupted, really surprised. He paid no attention. 'Yes. Today he is chief of the best station, next year he will be assistant-manager, two years more and . . . but I daresay you know what he will be in two years' time. You are of the new gang—the gang of virtue. The same people who sent him specially also recommended you. Oh, don't say no. I've my own eyes to trust.' Light dawned upon me. My dear aunt's influential acquaintances were producing an unexpected effect upon that young man. I nearly burst into a laugh. 'Do you read the

Company's confidential correspondence?' I asked. He hadn't a word to say. It was great fun. 'When Mr Kurtz,' I continued severely, 'is General Manager, you won't have the opportunity.'

"He blew the candle out suddenly, and we went outside. The moon had risen. Black figures strolled about listlessly, pouring water on the glow, whence proceeded a sound of hissing; steam ascended in the moonlight; the beaten nigger groaned somewhere. 'What a row the brute makes!' said the indefatigable man with the moustaches, appearing near us. 'Serve him right. Transgression—punishment—bang! Pitiless, pitiless. That's the only way. This will prevent all conflagrations for the future. I was just telling the manager . . . ' He noticed my companion, and became crestfallen all at once. 'Not in bed yet,' he said, with a kind of servile heartiness; 'it's so natural. Ha! Danger—agitation.' He vanished. I went on to the river-side, and the other followed me. I heard a scathing murmur at my ear, 'Heap of muffs—go to.' The pilgrims could be seen in knots gesticulating, discussing. Several had still their staves in their hands. I verily believe they took these sticks to bed with them. Beyond the fence the forest stood up spectrally in the moonlight, and through the dim stir, through the faint sounds of that lamentable courtyard, the silence of the land went home to one's very heart,—its mystery, its greatness, the amazing reality of its concealed life. The hurt nigger moaned feebly somewhere near by, and then fetched a deep sigh that made me mend my pace away from there. I felt a hand introducing itself under my arm. 'My dear sir,' said the fellow, 'I don't want to be misunderstood, and especially by you, who will see Mr Kurtz long before I can have that pleasure. I wouldn't like him to get a false idea of my disposition . . . .'

"I let him run on, this papier-mâché Mephistopheles,[9] and it seemed to me that if I tried I could poke my forefinger through him, and would find nothing inside but a little loose dirt, maybe. He, don't you see, had been planning to be assistant-manager by-and-by under the present man, and I could see that the coming of that Kurtz had upset them both not a little. He talked precipitately, and I did not try to stop him. I had my shoulders against the wreck of my steamer, hauled up on the slope like a carcass of some big river animal. The smell of mud, of primeval mud, by Jove! was in my nostrils, the high stillness of primeval forest was before my eyes; there were shiny patches on the black creek. The moon had spread over everything a thin layer of silver—over the rank grass, over the mud, upon the wall of matted vegetation standing higher than the wall of a temple, over the great river I could see through a sombre gap glittering, glittering, as it flowed broadly by without a murmur. All this was great, expectant, mute, while the man jabbered about himself. I wondered whether the stillness on the face of the immensity looking at us two were meant as an appeal or as a menace. What were we who had strayed in here? Could we handle that dumb thing, or would it handle us? I felt how big, how confoundedly big, was that thing that couldn't talk, and perhaps was deaf as well. What was in there? I could see a little ivory coming out from there, and I had heard Mr Kurtz was in there. I had heard enough about it too—God knows! Yet somehow it didn't bring any image with it—no more than if I had been told an angel or a fiend was in there. I believed it in the same way one of you might believe there are inhabitants in the planet Mars. I knew once a Scotch sailmaker who was certain, dead sure, there were people in Mars. If you asked him for

9. One of the devils who tempts Faust.

some idea how they looked and behaved, he would get shy and mutter something about 'walking on all-fours.' If you as much as smiled, he would—though a man of sixty—offer to fight you. I would not have gone so far as to fight for Kurtz, but I went for him near enough to a lie. You know I hate, detest, and can't bear a lie, not because I am straighter than the rest of us, but simply because it appals me. There is a taint of death, a flavour of mortality in lies,—which is exactly what I hate and detest in the world—what I want to forget. It makes me miserable and sick, like biting something rotten would do. Temperament, I suppose. Well, I went near enough to it by letting the young fool there believe anything he liked to imagine as to my influence in Europe. I became in an instant as much of a pretence as the rest of the bewitched pilgrims. This simply because I had a notion it somehow would be of help to that Kurtz whom at the time I did not see—you understand. He was just a word for me. I did not see the man in the name any more than you do. Do you see him? Do you see the story? Do you see anything? It seems to me I am trying to tell you a dream—making a vain attempt, because no relation of a dream can convey the dream-sensation, that commingling of absurdity, surprise, and bewilderment in a tremor of struggling revolt, that notion of being captured by the incredible which is of the very essence of dreams . . . ."

He was silent for a while.

". . . No, it is impossible; it is impossible to convey the life-sensation of any given epoch of one's existence,—that which makes its truth, its meaning—its subtle and penetrating essence. It is impossible. We live, as we dream—alone . . . ."

He paused again as if reflecting, then added—

"Of course in this you fellows see more than I could then. You see me, whom you know . . . ."

It had become so pitch dark that we listeners could hardly see one another. For a long time already he, sitting apart, had been no more to us than a voice. There was not a word from anybody. The others might have been asleep, but I was awake. I listened, I listened on the watch for the sentence, for the word, that would give me the clue to the faint uneasiness inspired by this narrative that seemed to shape itself without human lips in the heavy night-air of the river.

". . . Yes—I let him run on," Marlow began again, "and think what he pleased about the powers that were behind me. I did! And there was nothing behind me! There was nothing but that wretched, old, mangled steamboat I was leaning against, while he talked fluently about 'the necessity for every man to get on.' 'And when one comes out here, you conceive, it is not to gaze at the moon.' Mr Kurtz was a 'universal genius,' but even a genius would find it easier to work with 'adequate tools—intelligent men.' He did not make bricks—why, there was a physical impossibility in the way—as I was well aware; and if he did secretarial work for the manager, it was because 'no sensible man rejects wantonly the confidence of his superiors.' Did I see it? I saw it. What more did I want? What I really wanted was rivets, by heaven! Rivets. To get on with the work—to stop the hole. Rivets I wanted. There were cases of them down at the coast—cases—piled up—burst—split! You kicked a loose rivet at every second step in that station yard on the hillside. Rivets had rolled into the grove of death. You could fill your pockets with rivets for the trouble of stooping down—and there wasn't one rivet to be found where it was wanted. We had plates that would do, but nothing to fasten them with. And every week the messenger, a lone negro, letter-bag on shoulder and staff in hand, left our station for the coast. And several times a week a coast caravan came in with trade goods,—ghastly glazed calico that made you shudder only to look at it, glass beads value about a penny a quart, confounded spotted cotton handkerchiefs. And no rivets. Three carriers could have brought all that was wanted to set that steamboat afloat.

"He was becoming confidential now, but I fancy my unresponsive attitude must have exasperated him at last, for he judged it necessary to inform me he feared neither God nor devil, let alone any mere man. I said I could see that very well, but what I wanted was a certain quantity of rivets—and rivets were what really Mr Kurtz wanted, if he had only known it. Now letters went to the coast every week. . . . 'My dear sir,' he cried, 'I write from dictation.' I demanded rivets. There was a way—for an intelligent man. He changed his manner; became very cold, and suddenly began to talk about a hippopotamus; wondered whether sleeping on board the steamer (I stuck to my salvage night and day) I wasn't disturbed. There was an old hippo that had the bad habit of getting out on the bank and roaming at night over the station grounds. The pilgrims used to turn out in a body and empty every rifle they could lay hands on at him. Some even had sat up o' nights for him. All this energy was wasted, though. 'That animal has a charmed life,' he said; 'but you can say this only of brutes in this country. No man—you apprehend me?—no man here bears a charmed life.' He stood there for a moment in the moonlight with his delicate hooked nose set a little askew, and his mica eyes glittering without a wink, then, with a curt Good night, he strode off. I could see he was disturbed and considerably puzzled, which made me feel more hopeful than I had been for days. It was a great comfort to turn from that chap to my influential friend, the battered, twisted, ruined, tin-pot steamboat. I clambered on board. She rang under my feet like an empty Huntley & Palmer[1] biscuit-tin kicked along a gutter; she was nothing so solid in make, and rather less pretty in shape, but I had expended enough hard work on her to make me love her. No influential friend would have served me better. She had given me a chance to come out a bit—to find out what I could do. No, I don't like work. I had rather laze about and think of all the fine things that can be done. I don't like work—no man does—but I like what is in the work,—the chance to find yourself. Your own reality—for yourself, not for others—what no other man can ever know. They can only see the mere show, and never can tell what it really means.

"I was not surprised to see somebody sitting aft, on the deck, with his legs dangling over the mud. You see I rather chummed with the few mechanics there were in that station, whom the other pilgrims naturally despised—on account of their imperfect manners, I suppose. This was the foreman—a boiler-maker by trade—a good worker. He was a lank, bony, yellow-faced man, with big intense eyes. His aspect was worried, and his head was as bald as the palm of my hand; but his hair in falling seemed to have stuck to his chin, and had prospered in the new locality, for his beard hung down to his waist. He was a widower with six young children (he had left them in charge of a sister of his to come out there), and the passion of his life was pigeon-flying. He was an enthusiast and a connoisseur. He would rave about pigeons. After work hours he used sometimes to come over from his hut for a talk about his children and his pigeons; at work, when he had to crawl in the mud under the bottom of the steamboat, he would tie up that beard of his in a kind of white serviette[2]

1. A brand of English cookies.

2. Napkin.

he brought for the purpose. It had loops to go over his ears. In the evening he could be seen squatted on the bank rinsing that wrapper in the creek with great care, then spreading it solemnly on a bush to dry.

"I slapped him on the back and shouted 'We shall have rivets!' He scrambled to his feet exclaiming 'No! Rivets!' as though he couldn't believe his ears. Then in a low voice, 'You . . . eh?' I don't know why we behaved like lunatics. I put my finger to the side of my nose and nodded mysteriously. 'Good for you!' he cried, snapped his fingers above his head, lifting one foot. I tried a jig. We capered on the iron deck. A frightful clatter came out of that hulk, and the virgin forest on the other bank of the creek sent it back in a thundering roll upon the sleeping station. It must have made some of the pilgrims sit up in their hovels. A dark figure obscured the lighted doorway of the manager's hut, vanished, then, a second or so after, the doorway itself vanished too. We stopped, and the silence driven away by the stamping of our feet flowed back again from the recesses of the land. The great wall of vegetation, an exuberant and entangled mass of trunks, branches, leaves, boughs, festoons, motionless in the moonlight, was like a rioting invasion of soundless life, a rolling wave of plants, piled up, crested, ready to topple over the creek, to sweep every little man of us out of his little existence. And it moved not. A deadened burst of mighty splashes and snorts reached us from afar, as though an ichthyosaurus had been taking a bath of glitter in the great river. 'After all,' said the boiler-maker in a reasonable tone, 'why shouldn't we get the rivets?' Why not, indeed! I did not know of any reason why we shouldn't. 'They'll come in three weeks,' I said, confidently.

"But they didn't. Instead of rivets there came an invasion, an infliction, a visitation. It came in sections during the next three weeks, each section headed by a donkey carrying a white man in new clothes and tan shoes, bowing from that elevation right and left to the impressed pilgrims. A quarrelsome band of footsore sulky niggers trod on the heels of the donkey; a lot of tents, camp-stools, tin boxes, white cases, brown bales would be shot down in the courtyard, and the air of mystery would deepen a little over the muddle of the station. Five such instalments came, with their absurd air of disorderly flight with the loot of innumerable outfit shops and provision stores, that, one would think, they were lugging, after a raid, into the wilderness for equitable division. It was an inextricable mess of things decent in themselves but that human folly made look like the spoils of thieving.

"This devoted band called itself the Eldorado Exploring Expedition,[3] and I believe they were sworn to secrecy. Their talk, however, was the talk of sordid buccaneers: it was reckless without hardihood, greedy without audacity, and cruel without courage; there was not an atom of foresight or of serious intention in the whole batch of them, and they did not seem aware these things are wanted for the work of the world. To tear treasure out of the bowels of the land was their desire, with no more moral purpose at the back of it than there is in burglars breaking into a safe. Who paid the expenses of the noble enterprise I don't know; but the uncle of our manager was leader of that lot.

3. Eldorado, legendary land of gold in South America and the object of many fruitless 16th-century Spanish expeditions.

"In exterior he resembled a butcher in a poor neighbourhood, and his eyes had a look of sleepy cunning. He carried his fat paunch with ostentation on his short legs, and during the time his gang infested the station spoke to no one but his nephew. You could see these two roaming about all day long with their heads close together in an everlasting confab.

"I had given up worrying myself about the rivets. One's capacity for that kind of folly is more limited than you would suppose. I said Hang!—and let things slide. I had plenty of time for meditation, and now and then I would give some thought to Kurtz. I wasn't very interested in him. No. Still, I was curious to see whether this man, who had come out equipped with moral ideas of some sort, would climb to the top after all, and how he would set about his work when there."

2

"One evening as I was lying flat on the deck of my steamboat, I heard voices approaching—and there were the nephew and the uncle strolling along the bank. I laid my head on my arm again, and had nearly lost myself in a doze, when somebody said in my ear, as it were: 'I am as harmless as a little child, but I don't like to be dictated to. Am I the manager—or am I not? I was ordered to send him there. It's incredible.'. . . I became aware that the two were standing on the shore alongside the forepart of the steamboat, just below my head. I did not move; it did not occur to me to move: I was sleepy. 'It is unpleasant,' grunted the uncle. 'He has asked the Administration to be sent there,' said the other, 'with the idea of showing what he could do; and I was instructed accordingly. Look at the influence that man must have. Is it not frightful?' They both agreed it was frightful, then made several bizarre remarks: 'Make rain and fine weather—one man—the Council—by the nose'—bits of absurd sentences that got the better of my drowsiness, so that I had pretty near the whole of my wits about me when the uncle said, 'The climate may do away with this difficulty for you. Is he alone there?' 'Yes,' answered the manager; 'he sent his assistant down the river with a note to me in these terms: "Clear this poor devil out of the country, and don't bother sending more of that sort. I had rather be alone than have the kind of men you can dispose of with me." It was more than a year ago. Can you imagine such impudence?' 'Anything since then?' asked the other, hoarsely. 'Ivory,' jerked the nephew; 'lots of it—prime sort—lots—most annoying, from him.' 'And with that?' questioned the heavy rumble. 'Invoice,' was the reply fired out, so to speak. Then silence. They had been talking about Kurtz.

"I was broad awake by this time, but, lying perfectly at ease, remained still, having no inducement to change my position. 'How did that ivory come all this way?' growled the elder man, who seemed very vexed. The other explained that it had come with a fleet of canoes in charge of an English half-caste clerk Kurtz had with him; that Kurtz had apparently intended to return himself, the station being by that time bare of goods and stores, but after coming three hundred miles, had suddenly decided to go back, which he started to do alone in a small dug-out with four paddlers, leaving the half-caste to continue down the river with the ivory. The two fellows there seemed astounded at anybody attempting such a thing. They were at a loss for an adequate motive. As to me, I seemed to see Kurtz for the first time. It was a distinct glimpse: the dug-out, four paddling savages, and the lone white man turning his back suddenly on the headquarters, on relief, on thoughts of home—perhaps; setting his face towards the depths of the wilderness, towards his empty and desolate station. I did not know the motive. Perhaps he was just simply a fine fellow who stuck to his work for its own sake. His name, you understand, had not been pronounced once. He was 'that man.' The half-caste, who, as far as I could see, had conducted a difficult trip with great prudence and pluck, was invariably alluded to as 'that scoundrel.' The 'scoundrel' had reported that the 'man' had been very ill—had recovered imperfectly. . . . The two below me moved away then a few paces, and strolled back and forth at some little distance. I heard: 'Military post—doctor—two hundred miles—quite alone now—unavoidable delays—nine months—no news—strange rumours.' They approached again, just as the manager was saying, 'No one, as far as I know, unless a species of wandering trader—a pestilential fellow, snapping ivory from the natives.' Who was it they were talking about now? I gathered in snatches that this was some man supposed to be in Kurtz's district, and of whom the manager did not approve. 'We will not be free from unfair competition till one of these fellows is hanged for an example,' he said. 'Certainly,' grunted the other; 'get him hanged! Why not? Anything—anything can be done in this country. That's what I say; nobody here, you understand, *here*, can endanger your position. And why? You stand the climate—you outlast them all. The danger is in Europe; but there before I left I took care to—' They moved off and whispered, then their voices rose again. 'The extraordinary series of delays is not my fault. I did my possible.' The fat man sighed, 'Very sad.' 'And the pestiferous absurdity of his talk,' continued the other; 'he bothered me enough when he was here. "Each station should be like a beacon on the road towards better things, a centre for trade of course, but also for humanising, improving, instructing." Conceive you—that ass! And he wants to be manager! No, it's—' Here he got choked by excessive indignation, and I lifted my head the least bit. I was surprised to see how near they were—right under me. I could have spat upon their hats. They were looking on the ground, absorbed in thought. The manager was switching his leg with a slender twig: his sagacious relative lifted his head. 'You have been well since you came out this time?' he asked. The other gave a start. 'Who? I? Oh! Like a charm—like a charm. But the rest—oh, my goodness! All sick. They die so quick, too, that I haven't the time to send them out of the country—it's incredible!' 'H'm. Just so,' grunted the uncle. 'Ah! my boy, trust to this—I say, trust to this.' I saw him extend his short flipper of an arm for a gesture that took in the forest, the creek, the mud, the river,—seemed to beckon with a dishonouring flourish before the sunlit face of the land a treacherous appeal to the lurking death, to the hidden evil, to the profound darkness of its heart. It was so startling that I leaped to my feet and looked back at the edge of the forest, as though I had expected an answer of some sort to that black display of confidence. You know the foolish notions that come to one sometimes. The high stillness confronted these two figures with its ominous patience, waiting for the passing away of a fantastic invasion.

"They swore aloud together—out of sheer fright, I believe—then, pretending not to know anything of my existence, turned back to the station. The sun was low; and leaning forward side by side, they seemed to be tugging painfully uphill their two ridiculous shadows of unequal length, that trailed behind them slowly over the tall grass without bending a single blade.

"In a few days the Eldorado Expedition went into the patient wilderness, that closed upon it as the sea closes over a diver. Long afterwards the news came that all the donkeys were dead. I know nothing as to the fate of the less valuable animals.

They, no doubt, like the rest of us, found what they deserved. I did not inquire. I was then rather excited at the prospect of meeting Kurtz very soon. When I say very soon I mean it comparatively. It was just two months from the day we left the creek when we came to the bank below Kurtz's station.

"Going up that river was like travelling back to the earliest beginnings of the world, when vegetation rioted on the earth and the big trees were kings. An empty stream, a great silence, an impenetrable forest. The air was warm, thick, heavy, sluggish. There was no joy in the brilliance of sunshine. The long stretches of the waterway ran on, deserted, into the gloom of overshadowed distances. On silvery sandbanks hippos and alligators sunned themselves side by side. The broadening waters flowed through a mob of wooded islands; you lost your way on that river as you would in a desert, and butted all day long against shoals, trying to find the channel, till you thought yourself bewitched and cut off for ever from everything you had known once—somewhere—far away—in another existence perhaps. There were moments when one's past came back to one, as it will sometimes when you have not a moment to spare to yourself; but it came in the shape of an unrestful and noisy dream, remembered with wonder amongst the overwhelming realities of this strange world of plants, and water, and silence. And this stillness of life did not in the least resemble a peace. It was the stillness of an implacable force brooding over an inscrutable intention. It looked at you with a vengeful aspect. I got used to it afterwards; I did not see it any more; I had no time. I had to keep guessing at the channel; I had to discern, mostly by inspiration, the signs of hidden banks; I watched for sunken stones; I was learning to clap my teeth smartly before my heart flew out, when I shaved by a fluke some infernal sly old snag that would have ripped the life out of the tin-pot steamboat and drowned all the pilgrims; I had to keep a look-out for the signs of dead wood we could cut up in the night for next day's steaming. When you have to attend to things of that sort, to the mere incidents of the surface, the reality—the reality, I tell you—fades. The inner truth is hidden—luckily, luckily. But I felt it all the same; I felt often its mysterious stillness watching me at my monkey tricks, just as it watches you fellows performing on your respective tight-ropes for—what is it? half-a-crown a tumble—"

"Try to be civil, Marlow," growled a voice, and I knew there was at least one listener awake besides myself.

"I beg your pardon. I forgot the heartache which makes up the rest of the price. And indeed what does the price matter, if the trick be well done? You do your tricks very well. And I didn't do badly either, since I managed not to sink that steamboat on my first trip. It's a wonder to me yet. Imagine a blindfolded man set to drive a van over a bad road. I sweated and shivered over that business considerably, I can tell you. After all, for a seaman, to scrape the bottom of the thing that's supposed to float all the time under his care is the unpardonable sin. No one may know of it, but you never forget the thump—eh? A blow on the very heart. You remember it, you dream of it, you wake up at night and think of it—years after—and go hot and cold all over. I don't pretend to say that steamboat floated all the time. More than once she had to wade for a bit, with twenty cannibals splashing around and pushing. We had enlisted some of these chaps on the way for a crew. Fine fellows—cannibals—in their place. They were men one could work with, and I am grateful to them. And, after all, they did not eat each other before my face: they had brought along a provision of hippo-meat which went rotten, and made the mystery of the wilderness stink in my nostrils. Phoo! I can sniff it now. I had the manager on board and three or four pilgrims with their staves—all complete. Sometimes we came upon a station close by the bank, clinging to the skirts of the unknown, and the white men rushing out of a tumble-down hovel, with great gestures of joy and surprise and welcome, seemed very strange,—had the appearance of being held there captive by a spell. The word 'ivory' would ring in the air for a while—and on we went again into the silence, along empty reaches, round the still bends, between the high walls of our winding way, reverberating in hollow claps the ponderous beat of the stern-wheel. Trees, trees, millions of trees, massive, immense, running up high; and at their foot, hugging the bank against the stream, crept the little begrimed steamboat, like a sluggish beetle crawling on the floor of a lofty portico. It made you feel very small, very lost, and yet it was not altogether depressing that feeling. After all, if you were small, the grimy beetle crawled on—which was just what you wanted it to do. Where the pilgrims imagined it crawled to I don't know. To some place where they expected to get something, I bet! For me it crawled towards Kurtz—exclusively; but when the steam-pipes started leaking we crawled very slow. The reaches opened before us and closed behind, as if the forest had stepped leisurely across the water to bar the way for our return. We penetrated deeper and deeper into the heart of darkness. It was very quiet there. At night sometimes the roll of drums behind the curtain of trees would run up the river and remain sustained faintly, as if hovering in the air high over our heads, till the first break of day. Whether it meant war, peace, or prayer we could not tell. The dawns were heralded by the descent of a chill stillness; the woodcutters slept, their fires burned low; the snapping of a twig would make you start. We were wanderers on a prehistoric earth, on an earth that wore the aspect of an unknown planet. We could have fancied ourselves the first of men taking possession of an accursed inheritance, to be subdued at the cost of profound anguish and of excessive toil. But suddenly, as we struggled round a bend, there would be a glimpse of rush walls, of peaked grass-roofs, a burst of yells, a whirl of black limbs, a mass of hands clapping, of feet stamping, of bodies swaying, of eyes rolling, under the droop of heavy and motionless foliage. The steamer toiled along slowly on the edge of a black and incomprehensible frenzy. The prehistoric man was cursing us, praying to us, welcoming us—who could tell? We were cut off from the comprehension of our surroundings; we glided past like phantoms, wondering and secretly appalled, as sane men would be before an enthusiastic outbreak in a madhouse. We could not understand, because we were too far and could not remember, because we were travelling in the night of first ages, of those ages that are gone, leaving hardly a sign—and no memories.

"The earth seemed unearthly. We are accustomed to look upon the shackled form of a conquered monster, but there—there you could look at a thing monstrous and free. It was unearthly, and the men were—No, they were not inhuman. Well, you know, that was the worst of it—this suspicion of their not being inhuman. It would come slowly to one. They howled, and leaped, and spun, and made horrid faces; but what thrilled you was just the thought of their humanity—like yours—the thought of your remote kinship with this wild and passionate uproar. Ugly. Yes, it was ugly enough; but if you were man enough you would admit to yourself that there was in you just the faintest trace of a response to the terrible frankness of that noise, a dim suspicion of there being a meaning in it which you—you so remote from the night of first ages—could comprehend. And why not? The mind of man is capable of anything—because everything is in it, all the past as well as all the future. What was there after all? Joy, fear, sorrow, devotion, valour, rage—who can tell?—but truth—truth stripped of its cloak of time. Let the fool gape and shudder—the man knows, and can look on without a wink. But he must at least be as much of a man as these on the shore. He must meet that truth with his own true stuff—with his own inborn strength. Principles? Principles won't do. Acquisitions, clothes, pretty rags—rags that would fly off at the first good shake. No; you want a deliberate belief. An appeal to me in this fiendish row—is there? Very well; I hear; I admit, but I have a voice too, and for good or evil mine is the speech that cannot be silenced. Of course, a fool, what with sheer fright and fine sentiments, is always safe. Who's that grunting? You wonder I didn't go ashore for a howl and a dance? Well, no—I didn't. Fine sentiments, you say? Fine sentiments be hanged! I had no time. I had to mess about with white-lead and strips of woollen blanket helping to put bandages on those leaky steam-pipes—I tell you. I had to watch the steering, and circumvent those snags, and get the tin-pot along by hook or by crook. There was surface-truth enough in these things to save a wiser man. And between whiles I had to look after the savage who was fireman. He was an improved specimen; he could fire up a vertical boiler. He was there below me, and, upon my word, to look at him was as edifying as seeing a dog in a parody of breeches and a feather hat, walking on his hind-legs. A few months of training had done for that really fine chap. He squinted at the steam-gauge and at the water-gauge with an evident effort of intrepidity—and he had filed teeth too, the poor devil, and the wool of his pate shaved into queer patterns, and three ornamental scars on each of his cheeks. He ought to have been clapping his hands and stamping his feet on the bank, instead of which he was hard at work, a thrall to strange witchcraft, full of improving knowledge. He was useful because he had been instructed; and what he knew was this—that should the water in that transparent thing disappear, the evil spirit inside the boiler would get angry through the greatness of his thirst, and take a terrible vengeance. So he sweated and fired up and watched the glass fearfully (with an impromptu charm, made of rags, tied to his arm, and a piece of polished bone, as big as a watch, stuck flatways through his lower lip), while the wooded banks slipped past us slowly, the short noise was left behind, the interminable miles of silence—and we crept on, towards Kurtz. But the snags were thick, the water was treacherous and shallow, the boiler seemed indeed to have a sulky devil in it, and thus neither that fireman nor I had any time to peer into our creepy thoughts.

"Some fifty miles below the Inner Station we came upon a hut of reeds, an inclined and melancholy pole, with the unrecognisable tatters of what had been a flag of some sort flying from it, and a neatly stacked wood-pile. This was unexpected. We came to the bank, and on the stack of firewood found a flat piece of board with some faded pencil-writing on it. When deciphered it said: 'Wood for you. Hurry up. Approach cautiously.' There was a signature, but it was illegible—not Kurtz—a much longer word. Hurry up. Where? Up the river? 'Approach cautiously.' We had not done so. But the warning could not have been meant for the place where it could be only found after approach. Something was wrong above. But what—and how much? That was the question. We commented adversely upon the imbecility of that telegraphic style. The bush around said nothing, and would not let us look very far, either. A torn curtain of red twill hung in the doorway of the hut, and flapped sadly in our faces. The dwelling was dismantled; but we could see a white man had lived there not very long ago. There remained a rude table—a plank on two posts; a heap of rubbish reposed in a dark corner, and

by the door I picked up a book. It had lost its covers, and the pages had been thumbed into a state of extremely dirty softness; but the back had been lovingly stitched afresh with white cotton thread, which looked clean yet. It was an extraordinary find. Its title was, 'An Inquiry into some Points of Seamanship,' by a man Tower, Towson—some such name—Master in his Majesty's Navy. The matter looked dreary reading enough, with illustrative diagrams and repulsive tables of figures, and the copy was sixty years old. I handled this amazing antiquity with the greatest possible tenderness, lest it should dissolve in my hands. Within, Towson or Towser was inquiring earnestly into the breaking strain of ships' chains and tackle, and other such matters. Not a very enthralling book; but at the first glance you could see there a singleness of intention, an honest concern for the right way of going to work, which made these humble pages, thought out so many years ago, luminous with another than a professional light. The simple old sailor, with his talk of chains and purchases, made me forget the jungle and the pilgrims in a delicious sensation of having come upon something unmistakably real. Such a book being there was wonderful enough; but still more astounding were the notes pencilled in the margin, and plainly referring to the text. I couldn't believe my eyes! They were in cipher! Yes, it looked like cipher. Fancy a man lugging with him a book of that description into this nowhere and studying it—and making notes—in cipher at that! It was an extravagant mystery.

"I had been dimly aware for some time of a worrying noise, and when I lifted my eyes I saw the wood-pile was gone, and the manager, aided by all the pilgrims, was shouting at me from the river-side. I slipped the book into my pocket. I assure you to leave off reading was like tearing myself away from the shelter of an old and solid friendship.

"I started the lame engine ahead. 'It must be this miserable trader—this intruder,' exclaimed the manager, looking back malevolently at the place we had left. 'He must be English,' I said. 'It will not save him from getting into trouble if he is not careful,' muttered the manager darkly. I observed with assumed innocence that no man was safe from trouble in this world.

"The current was more rapid now, the steamer seemed at her last gasp, the stern-wheel flopped languidly, and I caught myself listening on tiptoe for the next beat of the float, for in sober truth I expected the wretched thing to give up every moment. It was like watching the last flickers of a life. But still we crawled. Sometimes I would pick out a tree a little way ahead to measure our progress towards Kurtz by, but I lost it invariably before we got abreast. To keep the eyes so long on one thing was too much for human patience. The manager displayed a beautiful resignation. I fretted and fumed and took to arguing with myself whether or no I would talk openly with Kurtz; but before I could come to any conclusion it occurred to me that my speech or my silence, indeed any action of mine, would be a mere futility. What did it matter what any one knew or ignored? What did it matter who was manager? One gets sometimes such a flash of insight. The essentials of this affair lay deep under the surface, beyond my reach, and beyond my power of meddling.

"Towards the evening of the second day we judged ourselves about eight miles from Kurtz's station. I wanted to push on; but the manager looked grave, and told me the navigation up there was so dangerous that it would be advisable, the sun being very low already, to wait where we were till next morning. Moreover, he pointed out that if the warning to approach cautiously were to be followed, we must approach in daylight—not at dusk, or in the dark. This was sensible enough. Eight miles meant nearly three hours' steaming for us, and I could also see suspi-

cious ripples at the upper end of the reach. Nevertheless, I was annoyed beyond expression at the delay, and most unreasonably too, since one night more could not matter much after so many months. As we had plenty of wood, and caution was the word, I brought up in the middle of the stream. The reach was narrow, straight, with high sides like a railway cutting. The dusk came gliding into it long before the sun had set. The current ran smooth and swift, but a dumb immobility sat on the banks. The living trees, lashed together by the creepers and every living bush of the undergrowth, might have been changed into stone, even to the slenderest twig, to the lightest leaf. It was not sleep—it seemed unnatural, like a state of trance. Not the faintest sound of any kind could be heard. You looked on amazed, and began to suspect yourself of being deaf—then the night came suddenly, and struck you blind as well. About three in the morning some large fish leaped, and the loud splash made me jump as though a gun had been fired. When the sun rose there was a white fog, very warm and clammy, and more blinding than the night. It did not shift or drive; it was just there, standing all round you like something solid. At eight or nine, perhaps, it lifted as a shutter lifts. We had a glimpse of the towering multitude of trees, of the immense matted jungle, with the blazing little ball of the sun hanging over it—all perfectly still—and then the white shutter came down again, smoothly, as if sliding in greased grooves. I ordered the chain, which we had begun to heave in, to be paid out again. Before it stopped running with a muffled rattle, a cry, a very loud cry, as of infinite desolation, soared slowly in the opaque air. It ceased. A complaining clamour, modulated in savage discords, filled our ears. The sheer unexpectedness of it made my hair stir under my cap. I don't know how it struck the others: to me it seemed as though the mist itself had screamed, so suddenly, and apparently from all sides at once, did this tumultuous and mournful uproar arise. It culminated in a hurried outbreak of almost intolerably excessive shrieking, which stopped short, leaving us stiffened in a variety of silly attitudes, and obstinately listening to the nearly as appalling and excessive silence. 'Good God! What is the meaning—?' stammered at my elbow one of the pilgrims,—a little fat man, with sandy hair and red whiskers, who wore side-spring boots, and pink pyjamas tucked into his socks. Two others remained open-mouthed a whole minute, then dashed into the little cabin, to rush out incontinently and stand darting scared glances, with Winchesters at 'ready' in their hands. What we could see was just the steamer we were on, her outlines blurred as though she had been on the point of dissolving, and a misty strip of water, perhaps two feet broad, around her—and that was all. The rest of the world was nowhere, as far as our eyes and ears were concerned. Just nowhere. Gone, disappeared; swept off without leaving a whisper or a shadow behind.

"I went forward, and ordered the chain to be hauled in short, so as to be ready to trip the anchor and move the steamboat at once if necessary. 'Will they attack?' whispered an awed voice. 'We will all be butchered in this fog,' murmured another. The faces twitched with the strain, the hands trembled slightly, the eyes forgot to wink. It was very curious to see the contrast of expressions of the white men and of the black fellows of our crew, who were as much strangers to that part of the river as we, though their homes were only eight hundred miles away. The whites, of course greatly discomposed, had besides a curious look of being painfully shocked by such an outrageous row. The others had an alert, naturally interested expression; but their faces were essentially quiet, even those of the one or two who grinned as they hauled at the chain. Several exchanged short, grunt-

ing phrases, which seemed to settle the matter to their satisfaction. Their headman, a young, broad-chested black, severely draped in dark-blue fringed cloths, with fierce nostrils and his hair all done up artfully in oily ringlets, stood near me. 'Aha!' I said, just for good fellowship's sake. 'Catch 'im,' he snapped, with a bloodshot widening of his eyes and a flash of sharp teeth—'catch 'im. Give 'im to us.' 'To you, eh?' I asked; 'what would you do with them?' 'Eat 'im!' he said, curtly, and, leaning his elbow on the rail, looked out into the fog in a dignified and profoundly pensive attitude. I would no doubt have been properly horrified, had it not occurred to me that he and his chaps must be very hungry: that they must have been growing increasingly hungry for at least this month past. They had been engaged for six months (I don't think a single one of them had any clear idea of time, as we at the end of countless ages have. They still belonged to the beginnings of time—had no inherited experience to teach them, as it were), and of course, as long as there was a piece of paper written over in accordance with some farcical law or other made down the river, it didn't enter anybody's head to trouble how they would live. Certainly they had brought with them some rotten hippo-meat, which couldn't have lasted very long, anyway, even if the pilgrims hadn't, in the midst of a shocking hullabaloo, thrown a considerable quantity of it overboard. It looked like a high-handed proceeding; but it was really a case of legitimate self-defence. You can't breathe dead hippo waking, sleeping, and eating, and at the same time keep your precarious grip on existence. Besides that, they had given them every week three pieces of brass wire, each about nine inches long; and the theory was they were to buy their provisions with that currency in river-side villages. You can see how *that* worked. There were either no villages, or the people were hostile, or the director, who like the rest of us fed out of tins, with an occasional old he-goat thrown in, didn't want to stop the steamer for some more or less recondite reason. So, unless they swallowed the wire itself, or made loops of it to snare the fishes with, I don't see what good their extravagant salary could be to them. I must say it was paid with a regularity worthy of a large and honourable trading company. For the rest, the only thing to eat—though it didn't look eatable in the least—I saw in their possession was a few lumps of some stuff like half-cooked dough, of a dirty lavender colour, they kept wrapped in leaves, and now and then swallowed a piece of, but so small that it seemed done more for the looks of the thing than for any serious purpose of sustenance. Why in the name of all the gnawing devils of hunger they didn't go for us—they were thirty to five—and have a good tuck-in for once, amazes me now when I think of it. They were big powerful men, with not much capacity to weigh the consequences, with courage, with strength, even yet, though their skins were no longer glossy and their muscles no longer hard. And I saw that something restraining, one of those human secrets that baffle probability, had come into play there. I looked at them with a swift quickening of interest—not because it occurred to me I might be eaten by them before very long, though I own to you that just then I perceived—in a new light, as it were—how unwholesome the pilgrims looked, and I hoped, yes, I positively hoped, that my aspect was not so—what shall I say?—so—unappetising: a touch of fantastic vanity which fitted well with the dream-sensation that pervaded all my days at that time. Perhaps I had a little fever too. One can't live with one's finger everlastingly on one's pulse. I had often 'a little fever,' or a little touch of other things—the playful paw-strokes of the wilderness, the preliminary trifling before the more serious onslaught which came in due course. Yes; I looked at them as you would on any human being, with a curiosity of their impulses, motives, capacities, weaknesses, when brought to the test of an inexorable physical necessity. Restraint! What possible restraint? Was it superstition, disgust, patience, fear—or some kind of primitive honour? No fear can stand up to hunger, no patience can wear it out, disgust simply does not exist where hunger is; and as to superstition, beliefs, and what you may call principles, they are less than chaff in a breeze. Don't you know the devilry of lingering starvation, its exasperating torment, its black thoughts, its sombre and brooding ferocity? Well, I do. It takes a man all his inborn strength to fight hunger properly. It's really easier to face bereavement, dishonour, and the perdition of one's soul—than this kind of prolonged hunger. Sad, but true. And these chaps too had no earthly reason for any kind of scruple. Restraint! I would just as soon have expected restraint from a hyena prowling amongst the corpses of a battlefield. But there was the fact facing me—the fact dazzling, to be seen, like the foam on the depths of the sea, like a ripple on an unfathomable enigma, a mystery greater—when I thought of it—than the curious, inexplicable note of desperate grief in this savage clamour that had swept by us on the river-bank, behind the blind whiteness of the fog.

"Two pilgrims were quarrelling in hurried whispers as to which bank. 'Left.' 'No, no; how can you? Right, right, of course.' 'It is very serious,' said the manager's voice behind me; 'I would be desolated if anything should happen to Mr Kurtz before we came up.' I looked at him, and had not the slightest doubt he was sincere. He was just the kind of man who would wish to preserve appearances. That was his restraint. But when he muttered something about going on at once, I did not even take the trouble to answer him. I knew, and he knew, that it was impossible. Were we to let go our hold of the bottom, we would be absolutely in the air—in space. We wouldn't be able to tell where we were going to—whether up or down stream, or across—till we fetched against one bank or the other,—and then we wouldn't know at first which it was. Of course I made no move. I had no mind for a smash-up. You couldn't imagine a more deadly place for a shipwreck. Whether drowned at once or not, we were sure to perish speedily in one way or another. 'I authorise you to take all the risks,' he said, after a short silence. 'I refuse to take any,' I said shortly; which was just the answer he expected, though its tone might have surprised him. 'Well, I must defer to your judgment. You are captain,' he said, with marked civility. I turned my shoulder to him in sign of my appreciation, and looked into the fog. How long would it last? It was the most hopeless look-out. The approach to this Kurtz grubbing for ivory in the wretched bush was beset by as many dangers as though he had been an enchanted princess sleeping in a fabulous castle. 'Will they attack, do you think?' asked the manager, in a confidential tone.

"I did not think they would attack, for several obvious reasons. The thick fog was one. If they left the bank in their canoes they would get lost in it, as we would be if we attempted to move. Still, I had also judged the jungle of both banks quite impenetrable—and yet eyes were in it, eyes that had seen us. The river-side bushes were certainly very thick; but the undergrowth behind was evidently penetrable. However, during the short lift I had seen no canoes anywhere in the reach—certainly not abreast of the steamer. But what made the idea of attack inconceivable to me was the nature of the noise—of the cries we had heard. They had not the fierce character boding of immediate hostile intention. Unexpected, wild, and violent as they had been, they had given me an irresistible impression of sorrow. The glimpse of the steamboat had for some reason filled those savages with unrestrained grief. The danger, if any, I expounded, was from our proximity to a great human passion let loose. Even extreme grief may ultimately vent itself in violence—but more generally takes the form of apathy. . . .

"You should have seen the pilgrims stare! They had no heart to grin, or even to revile me; but I believe they thought me gone mad—with fright, maybe. I delivered a regular lecture. My dear boys, it was no good bothering. Keep a look-out? Well, you may guess I watched the fog for the signs of lifting as a cat watches a mouse; but for anything else our eyes were of no more use to us than if we had been buried miles deep in a heap of cotton-wool. It felt like it too—choking, warm, stifling. Besides, all I said, though it sounded extravagant, was absolutely true to fact. What we afterwards alluded to as an attack was really an attempt at repulse. The action was very far from being aggressive—it was not even defensive, in the usual sense: it was undertaken under the stress of desperation, and in its essence was purely protective.

"It developed itself, I should say, two hours after the fog lifted, and its commencement was at a spot, roughly speaking, about a mile and a half below Kurtz's station. We had just floundered and flopped round a bend, when I saw an islet, a mere grassy hummock of bright green, in the middle of the stream. It was the only thing of the kind; but as we opened the reach more, I perceived it was the head of a long sandbank, or rather of a chain of shallow patches stretching down the middle of the river. They were discoloured, just awash, and the whole lot was seen just under the water, exactly as a man's backbone is seen running down the middle of his back under the skin. Now, as far as I did see, I could go to the right or to the left of this. I didn't know either channel, of course. The banks looked pretty well alike, the depth appeared the same; but as I had been informed the station was on the west side, I naturally headed for the western passage.

"No sooner had we fairly entered it than I became aware it was much narrower than I had supposed. To the left of us there was the long uninterrupted shoal, and to the right a high, steep bank heavily overgrown with bushes. Above the bush the trees stood in serried ranks. The twigs overhung the current thickly, and from distance to distance a large limb of some tree projected rigidly over the stream. It was then well on in the afternoon, the face of the forest was gloomy, and a broad strip of shadow had already fallen on the water. In this shadow we steamed up—very slowly, as you may imagine. I sheered her well inshore—the water being deepest near the bank, as the sounding-pole informed me.

"One of my hungry and forbearing friends was sounding in the bows just below me. This steamboat was exactly like a decked scow.[4] On the deck there were two little teak-wood houses, with doors and windows. The boiler was in the fore-end, and the machinery right astern. Over the whole there was a light roof, supported on stanchions. The funnel projected through that roof, and in front of the funnel a small cabin built of light planks served for a pilot-house. It contained a couch, two camp-stools, a loaded Martini-Henry[5] leaning in one corner, a tiny table, and the steering-wheel. It had a wide door in front and a broad shutter at

4. A flat-bottomed boat.

5. A rifle.

each side. All these were always thrown open, of course. I spent my days perched up there on the extreme fore-end of that roof, before the door. At night I slept, or tried to, on the couch. An athletic black belonging to some coast tribe, and educated by my poor predecessor, was the helmsman. He sported a pair of brass earrings, wore a blue cloth wrapper from the waist to the ankles, and thought all the world of himself. He was the most unstable kind of fool I had ever seen. He steered with no end of a swagger while you were by; but if he lost sight of you, he became instantly the prey of an abject funk, and would let that cripple of a steamboat get the upper hand of him in a minute.

"I was looking down at the sounding-pole, and feeling much annoyed to see at each try a little more of it stick out of that river, when I saw my poleman give up the business suddenly, and stretch himself flat on the deck, without even taking the trouble to haul his pole in. He kept hold on it though, and it trailed in the water. At the same time the fireman, whom I could also see below me, sat down abruptly before his furnace and ducked his head. I was amazed. Then I had to look at the river mighty quick, because there was a snag in the fairway. Sticks, little sticks, were flying about—thick: they were whizzing before my nose, dropping below me, striking behind me against my pilot-house. All this time the river, the shore, the woods, were very quiet—perfectly quiet. I could only hear the heavy splashing thump of the stern-wheel and the patter of these things. We cleared the snag clumsily. Arrows, by Jove! We were being shot at! I stepped in quickly to close the shutter on the landside. That fool-helmsman, his hands on the spokes, was lifting his knees high, stamping his feet, champing his mouth, like a reined-in horse. Confound him! And we were staggering within ten feet of the bank. I had to lean right out to swing the heavy shutter, and I saw a face amongst the leaves on the level with my own, looking at me very fierce and steady; and then suddenly, as though a veil had been removed from my eyes, I made out, deep in the tangled gloom, naked breasts, arms, legs, glaring eyes,—the bush was swarming with human limbs in movement, glistening, of bronze colour. The twigs shook, swayed, and rustled, the arrows flew out of them, and then the shutter came to. 'Steer her straight,' I said to the helmsman. He held his head rigid, face forward; but his eyes rolled, he kept on lifting and setting down his feet gently, his mouth foamed a little. 'Keep quiet!' I said in a fury. I might just as well have ordered a tree not to sway in the wind. I darted out. Below me there was a great scuffle of feet on the iron deck; confused exclamations; a voice screamed, 'Can you turn back?' I caught sight of a V-shaped ripple on the water ahead. What? Another snag! A fusillade burst out under my feet. The pilgrims had opened with their Winchesters, and were simply squirting lead into that bush. A deuce of a lot of smoke came up and drove slowly forward. I swore at it. Now I couldn't see the ripple or the snag either. I stood in the doorway, peering, and the arrows came in swarms. They might have been poisoned, but they looked as though they wouldn't kill a cat. The bush began to howl. Our wood-cutters raised a warlike whoop; the report of a rifle just at my back deafened me. I glanced over my shoulder, and the pilot-house was yet full of noise and smoke when I made a dash at the wheel. The fool-nigger had dropped everything, to throw the shutter open and let off that Martini-Henry. He stood before the wide opening, glaring, and I yelled at him to come back, while I straightened the sudden twist out of that steamboat. There was no room to turn even if I had wanted to, the snag was somewhere very near ahead in that confounded smoke, there was no time to lose, so I just crowded her into the bank—right into the bank, where I knew the water was deep.

"We tore slowly along the overhanging bushes in a whirl of broken twigs and flying leaves. The fusillade below stopped short, as I had foreseen it would when the squirts got empty. I threw my head back to a glinting whizz that traversed the pilot-house, in at one shutter-hole and out at the other. Looking past that mad helmsman, who was shaking the empty rifle and yelling at the shore, I saw vague forms of men running bent double, leaping, gliding, distinct, incomplete, evanescent. Something big appeared in the air before the shutter, the rifle went overboard, and the man stepped back swiftly, looked at me over his shoulder in an extraordinary, profound, familiar manner, and fell upon my feet. The side of his head hit the wheel twice, and the end of what appeared a long cane clattered round and knocked over a little camp-stool. It looked as though after wrenching that thing from somebody ashore he had lost his balance in the effort. The thin smoke had blown away, we were clear of the snag, and looking ahead I could see that in another hundred yards or so I would be free to sheer off, away from the bank; but my feet felt so very warm and wet that I had to look down. The man had rolled on his back and stared straight up at me; both his hands clutched that cane. It was the shaft of a spear that, either thrown or lunged through the opening, had caught him in the side just below the ribs; the blade had gone in out of sight, after making a frightful gash; my shoes were full; a pool of blood lay very still, gleaming dark-red under the wheel; his eyes shone with an amazing lustre. The fusillade burst out again. He looked at me anxiously, gripping the spear like something precious, with an air of being afraid I would try to take it away from him. I had to make an effort to free my eyes from his gaze and attend to the steering. With one hand I felt above my head for the line of the steam-whistle, and jerked out screech after screech hurriedly. The tumult of angry and warlike yells was checked instantly, and then from the depths of the woods went out such a tremulous and prolonged wail of mournful fear and utter despair as may be imagined to follow the flight of the last hope from the earth. There was a great commotion in the bush; the shower of arrows stopped, a few dropping shots rang out sharply—then silence, in which the languid beat of the stern-wheel came plainly to my ears. I put the helm hard astarboard at the moment when the pilgrim in pink pyjamas, very hot and agitated, appeared in the doorway. 'The manager sends me—' he began in an official tone, and stopped short. 'Good God!' he said, glaring at the wounded man.

"We two whites stood over him, and his lustrous and inquiring glance enveloped us both. I declare it looked as though he would presently put to us some question in an understandable language; but he died without uttering a sound, without moving a limb, without twitching a muscle. Only in the very last moment, as though in response to some sign we could not see, to some whisper we could not hear, he frowned heavily, and that frown gave to his black death-mask an inconceivably sombre, brooding, and menacing expression. The lustre of inquiring glance faded swiftly into vacant glassiness. 'Can you steer?" I asked the agent eagerly. He looked very dubious; but I made a grab at his arm, and he understood at once I meant him to steer whether or no. To tell you the truth, I was morbidly anxious to change my shoes and socks. 'He is dead,' murmured the fellow, immensely impressed. 'No doubt about it,' said I, tugging like mad at the shoelaces. 'And, by the way, I suppose Mr Kurtz is dead as well by this time.'

"For the moment that was the dominant thought. There was a sense of extreme disappointment, as though I had found out I had been striving after something altogether without a substance. I couldn't have been more disgusted if I had travelled all this way for the sole purpose of talking with Mr Kurtz. Talking with . . . I flung one shoe overboard, and became aware that that was exactly what I had been looking forward to—a talk with Kurtz. I made the strange discovery that I had never imagined him as doing, you know, but as discoursing. I didn't say to myself, 'Now I will never see him,' or 'Now I will never shake him by the hand,' but, 'Now I will never hear him.' The man presented himself as a voice. Not of course that I did not connect him with some sort of action. Hadn't I been told in all the tones of jealousy and admiration that he had collected, bartered, swindled, or stolen more ivory than all the other agents together. That was not the point. The point was in his being a gifted creature, and that of all his gifts the one that stood out pre-eminently, that carried with it a sense of real presence, was his ability to talk, his words—the gift of expression, the bewildering, the illuminating, the most exalted and the most contemptible, the pulsating stream of light, or the deceitful flow from the heart of an impenetrable darkness.

"The other shoe went flying unto the devil-god of that river. I thought, By Jove! it's all over. We are too late; he has vanished—the gift has vanished, by means of some spear, arrow, or club. I will never hear that chap speak after all,—and my sorrow had a startling extravagance of emotion, even such as I had noticed in the howling sorrow of these savages in the bush. I couldn't have felt more of lonely desolation somehow, had I been robbed of a belief or had missed my destiny in life. . . . Why do you sigh in this beastly way, somebody? Absurd? Well, absurd. Good Lord! mustn't a man ever—Here, give me some tobacco.". . .

There was a pause of profound stillness, then a match flared, and Marlow's lean face appeared, worn, hollow, with downward folds and dropped eyelids, with an aspect of concentrated attention; and as he took vigorous draws at his pipe, it seemed to retreat and advance out of the night in the regular flicker of the tiny flame. The match went out.

"Absurd!" he cried. "This is the worst of trying to tell . . . Here you all are, each moored with two good addresses, like a hulk with two anchors, a butcher round one corner, a policeman round another, excellent appetites, and temperature normal—you hear—normal from year's end to year's end. And you say, Absurd! Absurd be—exploded! Absurd! My dear boys, what can you expect from a man who out of sheer nervousness had just flung overboard a pair of new shoes? Now I think of it, it is amazing I did not shed tears. I am, upon the whole, proud of my fortitude. I was cut to the quick at the idea of having lost the inestimable privilege of listening to the gifted Kurtz. Of course I was wrong. The privilege was waiting for me. Oh yes, I heard more than enough. And I was right, too. A voice. He was very little more than a voice. And I heard—him—it—this voice—other voices—all of them were so little more than voices—and the memory of that time itself lingers around me, impalpable, like a dying vibration of one immense jabber, silly, atrocious, sordid, savage, or simply mean, without any kind of sense. Voices, voices—even the girl herself—now—"

He was silent for a long time.

"I laid the ghost of his gifts at last with a lie," he began suddenly. "Girl! What? Did I mention a girl? Oh, she is out of it—completely. They—the women I mean—are out of it—should be out of it. We must help them to stay in that beautiful world of their own, lest ours gets worse. Oh, she had to be out of it. You should have heard the disinterred body of Mr Kurtz saying, "My Intended." You would have perceived directly then how completely she was out of it. And the lofty frontal bone of Mr

Kurtz! They say the hair goes on growing sometimes, but this—ah—specimen was impressively bald. The wilderness had patted him on the head, and, behold, it was like a ball—an ivory ball; it had caressed him, and—lo!—he had withered; it had taken him, loved him, embraced him, got into his veins, consumed his flesh, and sealed his soul to its own by the inconceivable ceremonies of some devilish initiation. He was its spoiled and pampered favourite. Ivory? I should think so. Heaps of it, stacks of it. The old mud shanty was bursting with it. You would think there was not a single tusk left either above or below the ground in the whole country. 'Mostly fossil,' the manager had remarked disparagingly. It was no more fossil than I am; but they call it fossil when it is dug up. It appears these niggers do bury the tusks sometimes—but evidently they couldn't bury this parcel deep enough to save the gifted Mr Kurtz from his fate. We filled the steamboat with it, and had to pile a lot on the deck. Thus he could see and enjoy as long as he could see, because the appreciation of this favour had remained with him to the last. You should have heard him say, 'My ivory.' Oh yes, I heard him. 'My Intended, my ivory, my station, my river, my—' everything belonged to him. It made me hold my breath in expectation of hearing the wilderness burst into a prodigious peal of laughter that would shake the fixed stars in their places. Everything belonged to him—but that was a trifle. The thing was to know what he belonged to, how many powers of darkness claimed him for their own. That was the reflection that made you creepy all over. It was impossible—it was not good for one either—trying to imagine. He had taken a high seat amongst the devils of the land—I mean literally. You can't understand. How could you?—with solid pavement under your feet, surrounded by kind neighbours ready to cheer you or to fall on you, stepping delicately between the butcher and the policeman, in the holy terror of scandal and gallows and lunatic asylums—how can you imagine what particular region of the first ages a man's untrammelled feet may take him into by the way of solitude—utter solitude without a policeman—by the way of silence—utter silence, where no warning voice of a kind neighbour can be heard whispering of public opinion? These little things make all the great difference. When they are gone you must fall back upon your own innate strength, upon your own capacity for faithfulness. Of course you may be too much of a fool to go wrong—too dull even to know you are being assaulted by the powers of darkness. I take it, no fool ever made a bargain for his soul with the devil: the fool is too much of a fool, or the devil too much of a devil—I don't know which. Or you may be such a thunderingly exalted creature as to be altogether deaf and blind to anything but heavenly sights and sounds. Then the earth for you is only a standing place—and whether to be like this is your loss or your gain I won't pretend to say. But most of us are neither one nor the other. The earth for us is a place to live in, where we must put up with sights, with sounds, with smells too, by Jove!—breathe dead hippo, so to speak, and not be contaminated. And there, don't you see? your strength comes in, the faith in your ability for the digging of unostentatious holes to bury the stuff in—your power of devotion, not to yourself, but to an obscure, back-breaking business. And that's difficult enough. Mind, I am not trying to excuse or even explain—I am trying to account to myself for—for—Mr Kurtz—for the shade of Mr Kurtz. This initiated wraith from the back of Nowhere honoured me with its amazing confidence before it vanished altogether. This was because it could speak English to me. The original Kurtz had been educated partly in England, and—as he was good enough to say himself—his sympathies were in the right place. His mother was half-English, his father was half-French. All Europe contributed to the making of Kurtz; and by-and-by I learned that, most appropriately, the

International Society for the Suppression of Savage Customs had intrusted him with the making of a report, for its future guidance. And he had written it too. I've seen it. I've read it. It was eloquent, vibrating with eloquence, but too high-strung, I think. Seventeen pages of close writing he had found time for! But this must have been before his—let us say—nerves went wrong, and caused him to preside at certain midnight dances ending with unspeakable rites, which—as far as I reluctantly gathered from what I heard at various times—were offered up to him—do you understand?—to Mr Kurtz himself. But it was a beautiful piece of writing. The opening paragraph, however, in the light of later information, strikes me now as ominous. He began with the argument that we whites, from the point of development we had arrived at, 'must necessarily appear to them [savages] in the nature of supernatural beings—we approach them with the might as of a deity,' and so on, and so on. 'By the simple exercise of our will we can exert a power for good practically unbounded,' &c., &c. From that point he soared and took me with him. The peroration was magnificent, though difficult to remember, you know. It gave me the notion of an exotic Immensity ruled by an august Benevolence. It made me tingle with enthusiasm. This was the unbounded power of eloquence—of words—of burning noble words. There were no practical hints to interrupt the magic current of phrases, unless a kind of note at the foot of the last page, scrawled evidently much later, in an unsteady hand, may be regarded as the exposition of a method. It was very simple, and at the end of that moving appeal to every altruistic sentiment it blazed at you, luminous and terrifying, like a flash of lightning in a serene sky: 'Exterminate all the brutes!' The curious part was that he had apparently forgotten all about that valuable postscriptum, because, later on, when he in a sense came to himself, he repeatedly entreated me to take good care of 'my pamphlet' (he called it), as it was sure to have in the future a good influence upon his career. I had full information about all these things, and, besides, as it turned out, I was to have the care of his memory. I've done enough for it to give me the indisputable right to lay it, if I choose, for an everlasting rest in the dust-bin of progress, amongst all the sweepings and, figuratively speaking, all the dead cats of civilisation. But then, you see, I can't choose. He won't be forgotten. Whatever he was, he was not common. He had the power to charm or frighten rudimentary souls into an aggravated witch-dance in his honour; he could also fill the small souls of the pilgrims with bitter misgivings: he had one devoted friend at least, and he had conquered one soul in the world that was neither rudimentary nor tainted with self-seeking. No; I can't forget him, though I am not prepared to affirm the fellow was exactly worth the life we lost in getting to him. I missed my late helmsman awfully,—I missed him even while his body was still lying in the pilot-house. Perhaps you will think it passing strange this regret for a savage who was no more account than a grain of sand in a black Sahara. Well, don't you see, he had done something, he had steered; for months I had him at my back—a help—an instrument. It was a kind of partnership. He steered for me—I had to look after him, I worried about his deficiencies, and thus a subtle bond had been created, of which I only became aware when it was suddenly broken. And the intimate profundity of that look he gave me when he received his hurt remains to this day in my memory—like a claim of distant kinship affirmed in a supreme moment.

"Poor fool! If he had only left that shutter alone. He had no restraint, no restraint—just like Kurtz—a tree swayed by the wind. As soon as I had put on a dry pair of slippers, I dragged him out, after first jerking the spear out of his side, which operation I confess I performed with my eyes shut tight. His heels leaped together over the little doorstep; his shoulders were pressed to my breast; I hugged him from behind desperately. Oh! he was heavy, heavy; heavier than any man on earth, I should imagine. Then without more ado I tipped him overboard. The current snatched him as though he had been a wisp of grass, and I saw the body roll over twice before I lost sight of it for ever. All the pilgrims and the manager were then congregated on the awning-deck about the pilot-house, chattering at each other like a flock of excited magpies, and there was a scandalised murmur at my heartless promptitude. What they wanted to keep that body hanging about for I can't guess. Embalm it, maybe. But I had also heard another, and a very ominous, murmur on the deck below. My friends the woodcutters were likewise scandalised, and with a better show of reason—though I admit that the reason itself was quite inadmissible. Oh, quite! I had made up my mind that if my late helmsman was to be eaten, the fishes alone should have him. He had been a very second-rate helmsman while alive, but now he was dead he might have become a first-class temptation, and possibly cause some startling trouble. Besides, I was anxious to take the wheel, the man in pink pyjamas showing himself a hopeless duffer at the business.

"This I did directly the simple funeral was over. We were going half-speed, keeping right in the middle of the stream, and I listened to the talk about me. They had given up Kurtz, they had given up the station; Kurtz was dead, and the station had been burnt—and so on—and so on. The red-haired pilgrim was beside himself with the thought that at least this poor Kurtz had been properly revenged. 'Say! We must have made a glorious slaughter of them in the bush. Eh? What do you think? Say?' He positively danced, the bloodthirsty little gingery beggar. And he had nearly fainted when he saw the wounded man! I could not help saying, 'You made a glorious lot of smoke, anyhow.' I had seen, from the way the tops of the bushes rustled and flew, that almost all the shots had gone too high. You can't hit anything unless you take aim and fire from the shoulder; but these chaps fired from the hip with their eyes shut. The retreat, I maintained—and I was right—was caused by the screeching of the steam-whistle. Upon this they forgot Kurtz, and began to howl at me with indignant protests.

"The manager stood by the wheel murmuring confidentially about the necessity of getting well away down the river before dark at all events, when I saw in the distance a clearing on the river-side and the outlines of some sort of building. 'What's this?' I asked. He clapped his hands in wonder. 'The station!' he cried. I edged in at once, still going half-speed.

"Through my glasses I saw the slope of a hill interspersed with rare trees and perfectly free from undergrowth. A long decaying building on the summit was half buried in the high grass; the large holes in the peaked roof gaped black from afar; the jungle and the woods made a background. There was no enclosure or fence of any kind; but there had been one apparently, for near the house half-a-dozen slim posts remained in a row, roughly trimmed, and with their upper ends ornamented with round carved balls. The rails, or whatever there had been between, had disappeared. Of course the forest surrounded all that. The river-bank was clear, and on the waterside I saw a white man under a hat like a cart-wheel beckoning persistently with his whole arm. Examining the edge of the forest above and below, I was almost certain I could see movements—human forms gliding here and there. I steamed past prudently, then stopped the engines and let her drift down. The man on the shore began to shout, urging us to land. 'We have been attacked,' screamed the manager. 'I know—I know. It's all right,' yelled back the other, as cheerful as you please. 'Come along. It's all right. I am glad.'

"His aspect reminded me of something I had seen—something funny I had seen somewhere. As I manoeuvred to get alongside, I was asking myself, 'What does this fellow look like?' Suddenly I got it. He looked like a harlequin. His clothes had been made of some stuff that was brown holland[6] probably, but it was covered with patches all over, with bright patches, blue, red, and yellow,—patches on the back, patches on front, patches on elbows, on knees; coloured binding round his jacket, scarlet edging at the bottom of his trousers; and the sunshine made him look extremely gay and wonderfully neat withal, because you could see how beautifully all this patching had been done. A beardless, boyish face, very fair, no features to speak of, nose peeling, little blue eyes, smiles and frowns chasing each other over that open countenance like sunshine and shadow on a wind-swept plain. 'Look out, captain!' he cried; 'there's a snag lodged in here last night.' What! Another snag? I confess I swore shamefully. I had nearly holed my cripple, to finish off that charming trip. The harlequin on the bank turned his little pug nose up to me. 'You English?' he asked, all smiles. 'Are you?' I shouted from the wheel. The smiles vanished, and he shook his head as if sorry for my disappointment. Then he brightened up. 'Never mind!' he cried encouragingly. 'Are we in time?' I asked. 'He is up there,' he replied, with a toss of the head up the hill, and becoming gloomy all of a sudden. His face was like the autumn sky, overcast one moment and bright the next.

"When the manager, escorted by the pilgrims, all of them armed to the teeth, had gone to the house, this chap came on board. 'I say, I don't like this. These natives are in the bush,' I said. He assured me earnestly it was all right. 'They are simple people,' he added; 'well, I am glad you came. It took me all my time to keep them off.' 'But you said it was all right,' I cried. 'Oh, they meant no harm,' he said; and as I stared he corrected himself, 'Not exactly.' Then vivaciously, 'My faith, your pilot-house wants a clean-up!' In the next breath he advised me to keep enough steam on the boiler to blow the whistle in case of any trouble. 'One good screech will do more for you than all your rifles. They are simple people,' he repeated. He rattled away at such a rate he quite overwhelmed me. He seemed to be trying to make up for lots of silence, and actually hinted, laughing, that such was the case. 'Don't you talk with Mr Kurtz?' I said. 'You don't talk with that man—you listen to him,' he exclaimed with severe exaltation. 'But now—' He waved his arm, and in the twinkling of an eye was in the uttermost depths of despondency. In a moment he came up again with a jump, possessed himself of both my hands, shook them continuously, while he gabbled: 'Brother sailor . . . honour . . . pleasure . . . delight . . . introduce myself . . . Russian . . . son of an arch-priest . . . Government of Tambov[7] . . . What? Tobacco! English tobacco; the excellent English tobacco! Now, that's brotherly. Smoke? Where's a sailor that does not smoke?'

"The pipe soothed him, and gradually I made out he had run away from school, had gone to sea in a Russian ship; ran away again; served some time in English ships; was now reconciled with the arch-priest. He made a point of that. 'But when one is young one must see things, gather experience, ideas; enlarge the mind.' 'Here!' I interrupted. 'You can never tell! Here I have met Mr Kurtz,' he said, youthfully solemn and reproachful. I held my tongue after that. It appears he had persuaded a Dutch trading-house on the coast to fit him out with stores and goods, and had started for

6. A smooth linen fabric.

7. A province of Western Russia.

the interior with a light heart, and no more idea of what would happen to him than a baby. He had been wandering about that river for nearly two years alone, cut off from everybody and everything. 'I am not so young as I look. I am twenty-five,' he said. 'At first old Van Shuyten would tell me to go to the devil,' he narrated with keen enjoyment; 'but I stuck to him, and talked and talked, till at last he got afraid I would talk the hind-leg off his favorite dog, so he gave me some cheap things and a few guns, and told me he hoped he would never see my face again. Good old Dutchman, Van Shuyten. I sent him one small lot of ivory a year ago, so that he can't call me a little thief when I get back. I hope he got it. And for the rest, I don't care. I had some wood stacked for you. That was my old house. Did you see?'

"I gave him Towson's book. He made as though he would kiss me, but restrained himself. 'The only book I had left, and I thought I had lost it,' he said, looking at it ecstatically. 'So many accidents happen to a man going about alone, you know. Canoes get upset sometimes—and sometimes you've got to clear out so quick when the people get angry.' He thumbed the pages. 'You made notes in Russian?' I asked. He nodded. 'I thought they were written in cipher,' I said. He laughed, then became serious. 'I had lots of trouble to keep these people off,' he said. 'Did they want to kill you?' I asked. 'Oh no!' he cried, and checked himself. 'Why did they attack us?' I pursued. He hesitated, then said shamefacedly, 'They don't want him to go.' 'Don't they?' I said, curiously. He nodded a nod full of mystery and wisdom. 'I tell you,' he cried, 'this man has enlarged my mind.' He opened his arms wide, staring at me with his little blue eyes that were perfectly round."

3

"I looked at him, lost in astonishment. There he was before me, in motley, as though he had absconded from a troupe of mimes, enthusiastic, fabulous. His very existence was improbable, inexplicable, and altogether bewildering. He was an insoluble problem. It was inconceivable how he had existed, how he had succeeded in getting so far, how he had managed to remain—why he did not instantly disappear. 'I went a little farther,' he said, 'then still a little farther—till I had gone so far that I don't know how I'll ever get back. Never mind. Plenty time. I can manage. You take Kurtz away quick—quick—I tell you.' The glamour of youth enveloped his particoloured rags, his destitution, his loneliness, the essential desolation of his futile wanderings. For months—for years—his life hadn't been worth a day's purchase; and there he was gallantly, thoughtlessly alive, to all appearance indestructible solely by the virtue of his few years and of his unreflecting audacity. I was seduced into something like admiration—like envy. Glamour urged him on, glamour kept him unscathed. He surely wanted nothing from the wilderness but space to breathe in and to push on through. His need was to exist, and to move onwards at the greatest possible risk, and with a maximum of privation. If the absolutely pure, uncalculating, unpractical spirit of adventure had ever ruled a human being, it ruled this be-patched youth. I almost envied him the possession of this modest and clear flame. It seemed to have consumed all thought of self so completely, that, even while he was talking to you, you forgot that it was he—the man before your eyes—who had gone through these things. I did not envy him his devotion to Kurtz, though. He had not meditated over it. It came to him, and he accepted it with a sort of eager fatalism. I must say that to me it appeared about the most dangerous thing in every way he had come upon so far.

"They had come together unavoidably, like two ships becalmed near each other, and lay rubbing sides at last. I suppose Kurtz wanted an audience, because on a certain occasion, when encamped in the forest, they had talked all night, or more probably Kurtz had talked. 'We talked of everything,' he said, quite transported at the recollection. 'I forgot there was such a thing as sleep. The night did not seem to last an hour. Everything! Everything! . . . Of love too.' 'Ah, he talked to you of love!' I said, much amused. 'It isn't what you think,' he cried, almost passionately. 'It was in general. He made me see things—things.'

"He threw his arms up. We were on deck at the time, and the headman of my wood-cutters, lounging near by, turned upon him his heavy and glittering eyes. I looked around, and I don't know why, but I assure you that never, never before, did this land, this river, this jungle, the very arch of this blazing sky, appear to me so hopeless and so dark, so impenetrable to human thought, so pitiless to human weakness. 'And, ever since, you have been with him, of course?' I said.

"On the contrary. It appears their intercourse had been very much broken by various causes. He had, as he informed me proudly, managed to nurse Kurtz through two illnesses (he alluded to it as you would to some risky feat), but as a rule Kurtz wandered alone, far in the depths of the forest. 'Very often coming to this station, I had to wait days and days before he would turn up,' he said. 'Ah, it was worth waiting for!—sometimes.' 'What was he doing? exploring or what?' I asked. 'Oh yes, of course'; he had discovered lots of villages, a lake too—he did not know exactly in what direction; it was dangerous to inquire too much—but mostly his expeditions had been for ivory. 'But he had no goods to trade with by that time,' I objected. 'There's a good lot of cartridges left even yet,' he answered, looking away. 'To speak plainly, he raided the country,' I said. He nodded. 'Not alone, surely!' He muttered something about the villages round that lake. 'Kurtz got the tribe to follow him, did he?' I suggested. He fidgeted a little. 'They adored him,' he said. The tone of these words was so extraordinary that I looked at him searchingly. It was curious to see his mingled eagerness and reluctance to speak of Kurtz. The man filled his life, occupied his thoughts, swayed his emotions. 'What can you expect?' he burst out; 'he came to them with thunder and lightning, you know—and they had never seen anything like it—and very terrible. He could be very terrible. You can't judge Mr Kurtz as you would an ordinary man. No, no, no! Now—just to give you an idea—I don't mind telling you, he wanted to shoot me too one day—but I don't judge him.' 'Shoot you!' I cried. 'What for?' 'Well, I had a small lot of ivory the chief of that village near my house gave me. You see I used to shoot game for them. Well, he wanted it, and wouldn't hear reason. He declared he would shoot me unless I gave him the ivory and then cleared out of the country, because he could do so, and had a fancy for it, and there was nothing on earth to prevent him killing whom he jolly well pleased. And it was true too. I gave him the ivory. What did I care! But I didn't clear out. No, no. I couldn't leave him. I had to be careful, of course, till we got friendly again for a time. He had his second illness then. Afterwards I had to keep out of the way; but I didn't mind. He was living for the most part in those villages on the lake. When he came down to the river, sometimes he would take to me, and sometimes it was better for me to be careful. This man suffered too much. He hated all this, and somehow he couldn't get away. When I had a chance I begged him to try and leave while there was time; I offered to go back with him. And he would say yes, and then he would remain; go off on another ivory hunt; disappear for weeks; forget himself amongst these people—forget himself—you know.' 'Why! he's mad,' I said. He protested indignantly. Mr Kurtz couldn't be mad. If I had heard him talk, only two days ago, I wouldn't dare hint at such a thing. . . . I had taken up my binoculars while we talked, and was looking at the shore, sweeping the limit of the forest at each side and at the back of the house. The consciousness of there being people in that bush, so silent, so quiet—as silent and quiet as the ruined house on the hill—made me uneasy. There was no sign on the face of nature of this amazing tale that was not so much told as suggested to me in desolate exclamations, completed by shrugs, in interrupted phrases, in hints ending in deep sighs. The woods were unmoved, like a mask—heavy, like the closed door of a prison—they looked with their air of hidden knowledge, of patient expectation, of unapproachable silence. The Russian was explaining to me that it was only lately that Mr Kurtz had come down to the river, bringing along with him all the fighting men of that lake tribe. He had been absent for several months—getting himself adored, I suppose—and had come down unexpectedly, with the intention to all appearance of making a raid either across the river or down stream. Evidently the appetite for more ivory had got the better of the—what shall I say?—less material aspirations. However, he had got much worse suddenly. 'I heard he was lying helpless, and so I came up—took my chance,' said the Russian. 'Oh, he is bad, very bad.' I directed my glass to the house. There were no signs of life, but there was the ruined roof, the long mud wall peeping above the grass, with three little square window-holes, no two of the same size; all this brought within reach of my hand, as it were. And then I made a brusque movement, and one of the remaining posts of that vanished fence leaped up in the field of my glass. You remember I told you I had been struck at the distance by certain attempts at ornamentation, rather remarkable in the ruinous aspect of the place. Now I had suddenly a nearer view, and its first result was to make me throw my head back as if before a blow. Then I went carefully from post to post with my glass, and I saw my mistake. These round knobs were not ornamental but symbolic; they were expressive and puzzling, striking and disturbing—food for thought and also for the vultures if there had been any looking down from the sky; but at all events for such ants as were industrious enough to ascend the pole. They would have been even more impressive, those heads on the stakes, if their faces had not been turned to the house. Only one, the first I had made out, was facing my way. I was not so shocked as you may think. The start back I had given was really nothing but a movement of surprise. I had expected to see a knob of wood there, you know. I returned deliberately to the first I had seen—and there it was, black, dried, sunken, with closed eyelids,—a head that seemed to sleep at the top of that pole, and, with the shrunken dry lips showing a narrow white line of the teeth, was smiling too, smiling continuously at some endless and jocose dream of that eternal slumber.

"I am not disclosing any trade secrets. In fact the manager said afterwards that Mr Kurtz's methods had ruined the district. I have no opinion on that point, but I want you clearly to understand that there was nothing exactly profitable in these heads being there. They only showed that Mr Kurtz lacked restraint in the gratification of his various lusts, that there was something wanting in him—some small matter which, when the pressing need arose, could not be found under his magnificent eloquence. Whether he knew of this deficiency himself I can't say. I think the knowledge came to him at last—only at the very last. But the wilderness had found him out early, and had taken on him a terrible vengeance for the fantastic invasion. I think it had whispered to him things about himself which he did not know, things of which he had no conception till he took counsel with this great solitude—and the whisper had proved irresistibly fascinating. It echoed loudly within him because he was hollow at the core. . . . I put down the glass, and the head that had appeared near enough to be spoken to seemed at once to have leaped away from me into inaccessible distance.

"The admirer of Mr Kurtz was a bit crestfallen. In a hurried, indistinct voice he began to assure me he had not dared to take these—say, symbols—down. He was not afraid of the natives; they would not stir till Mr Kurtz gave the word. His ascendancy was extraordinary. The camps of these people surrounded the place, and the chiefs came every day to see him. They would crawl . . . 'I don't want to know anything of the ceremonies used when approaching Mr Kurtz,' I shouted. Curious, this feeling that came over me that such details would be more intolerable than those heads drying on the stakes under Mr Kurtz's windows. After all, that was only a savage sight, while I seemed at one bound to have been transported into some lightless region of subtle horrors, where pure, uncomplicated savagery was a positive relief, being something that had a right to exist—obviously—in the sunshine. The young man looked at me with surprise. I suppose it did not occur to him Mr Kurtz was no idol of mine. He forgot I hadn't heard any of these splendid monologues on, what was it? on love, justice, conduct of life—or what not. If it had come to crawling before Mr Kurtz, he crawled as much as the veriest savage of them all. I had no idea of the conditions, he said: these heads were the heads of rebels. I shocked him excessively by laughing. Rebels! What would be the next definition I was to hear? There had been enemies, criminals, workers—and these were rebels. Those rebellious heads looked very subdued to me on their sticks. 'You don't know how such a life tries a man like Kurtz,' cried Kurtz's last disciple. 'Well, and you?' I said. 'I! I! I am a simple man. I have no great thoughts. I want nothing from anybody. How can you compare me to . . . ?' His feelings were too much for speech, and suddenly he broke down. 'I don't understand,' he groaned. 'I've been doing my best to keep him alive, and that's enough. I had no hand in all this. I have no abilities. There hasn't been a drop of medicine or a mouthful of invalid food for months here. He was shamefully abandoned. A man like this, with such ideas. Shamefully! Shamefully! I—I—haven't slept for the last ten nights. . . .'

"His voice lost itself in the calm of the evening. The long shadows of the forest had slipped down-hill while we talked, had gone far beyond the ruined hovel, beyond the symbolic row of stakes. All this was in the gloom, while we down there were yet in the sunshine, and the stretch of the river abreast of the clearing glittered in a still and dazzling splendour, with a murky and overshadowed bend above and below. Not a living soul was seen on the shore. The bushes did not rustle.

"Suddenly round the corner of the house a group of men appeared, as though they had come up from the ground. They waded waist-deep in the grass, in a compact body, bearing an improvised stretcher in their midst. Instantly, in the emptiness of the landscape, a cry arose whose shrillness pierced the still air like a sharp arrow flying straight to the very heart of the land; and, as if by enchantment, streams of human beings—of naked human beings—with spears in their hands, with bows, with shields, with wild glances and savage movements, were poured into the clearing by the dark-faced and pensive forest. The bushes shook, the grass swayed for a time, and then everything stood still in attentive immobility.

"'Now, if he does not say the right thing to them we are all done for,' said the Russian at my elbow. The knot of men with the stretcher had stopped too, half-way to the steamer, as if petrified. I saw the man on the stretcher sit up, lank and with an uplifted arm, above the shoulders of the bearers. 'Let us hope that the man who can talk so well of love in general will find some particular reason to spare us this time,' I said. I resented bitterly the absurd danger of our situation, as if to be at the mercy of that atrocious phantom had been a dishonouring necessity. I could not hear a sound, but through my glasses I saw the thin arm extended commandingly, the lower jaw moving, the eyes of that apparition shining darkly far in its bony head that nodded with grotesque jerks. Kurtz—Kurtz—that means 'short' in German—don't it? Well, the name was as true as everything else in his life—and death. He looked at least seven feet long. His covering had fallen off, and his body emerged from it pitiful and appalling as from a winding-sheet. I could see the cage of his ribs all astir, the bones of his arm waving. It was as though an animated image of death carved out of old ivory had been shaking its hand with menaces at a motionless crowd of men made of dark and glittering bronze. I saw him open his mouth wide—it gave him a weirdly voracious aspect, as though he had wanted to swallow all the air, all the earth, all the men before him. A deep voice reached me faintly. He must have been shouting. He fell back suddenly. The stretcher shook as the bearers staggered forward again, and almost at the same time I noticed that the crowd of savages was vanishing without any perceptible movement of retreat, as if the forest that had ejected these beings so suddenly had drawn them in again as the breath is drawn in a long aspiration.

"Some of the pilgrims behind the stretcher carried his arms—two shot-guns, a heavy rifle, and a light revolver-carbine—the thunderbolts of that pitiful Jupiter. The manager bent over him murmuring as he walked beside his head. They laid him down in one of the little cabins—just a room for a bed-place and a camp-stool or two, you know. We had brought his belated correspondence, and a lot of torn envelopes and open letters littered his bed. His hand roamed feebly amongst these papers. I was struck by the fire of his eyes and the composed languor of his expression. It was not so much the exhaustion of disease. He did not seem in pain. This shadow looked satiated and calm, as though for the moment it had had its fill of all the emotions.

"He rustled one of the letters, and looking straight in my face said, 'I am glad.' Somebody had been writing to him about me. These special recommendations were turning up again. The volume of tone he emitted without effort, almost without the trouble of moving his lips, amazed me. A voice! a voice! It was grave, profound, vibrating, while the man did not seem capable of a whisper. However, he had enough strength in him—factitious no doubt—to very nearly make an end of us, as you shall hear directly.

"The manager appeared silently in the doorway; I stepped out at once and he drew the curtain after me. The Russian, eyed curiously by the pilgrims, was staring at the shore. I followed the direction of his glance.

"Dark human shapes could be made out in the distance, flitting indistinctly against the gloomy border of the forest, and near the river two bronze figures, leaning on tall spears, stood in the sunlight under fantastic head-dresses of spotted skins, warlike and still in statuesque repose. And from right to left along the lighted shore moved a wild and gorgeous apparition of a woman.

"She walked with measured steps, draped in striped and fringed cloths, treading the earth proudly, with a slight jingle and flash of barbarous ornaments. She carried her head high; her hair was done in the shape of a helmet; she had brass leggings to the knee, brass wire gauntlets to the elbow, a crimson spot on her tawny cheek, innumerable necklaces of glass beads on her neck; bizarre things, charms, gifts of witch-men, that hung about her, glittered and trembled at every step. She must have had the value of several elephant tusks upon her. She was savage and superb, wild-eyed and magnificent; there was something ominous and stately in her deliberate progress. And in the hush that had fallen suddenly upon the whole sorrowful land, the immense wilderness, the colossal body of the fecund and mysterious life seemed to look at her, pensive, as though it had been looking at the image of its own tenebrous and passionate soul.

"She came abreast of the steamer, stood still, and faced us. Her long shadow fell to the water's edge. Her face had a tragic and fierce aspect of wild sorrow and of dumb pain mingled with the fear of some struggling, half-shaped resolve. She stood looking at us without a stir, and like the wilderness itself, with an air of brooding over an inscrutable purpose. A whole minute passed, and then she made a step forward. There was a low jingle, a glint of yellow metal, a sway of fringed draperies, and she stopped as if her heart had failed her. The young fellow by my side growled. The pilgrims murmured at my back. She looked at us all as if her life had depended upon the unswerving steadiness of her glance. Suddenly she opened her bared arms and threw them up rigid above her head, as though in an uncontrollable desire to touch the sky, and at the same time the swift shadows darted out on the earth, swept around on the river, gathering the steamer in a shadowy embrace. A formidable silence hung over the scene.

"She turned away slowly, walked on, following the bank, and passed into the bushes to the left. Once only her eyes gleamed back at us in the dusk of the thickets before she disappeared.

"'If she had offered to come aboard I really think I would have tried to shoot her,' said the man of patches, nervously. 'I had been risking my life every day for the last fortnight to keep her out of the house. She got in one day and kicked up a row about those miserable rags I picked up in the storeroom to mend my clothes with. I wasn't decent. At least it must have been that, for she talked like a fury to Kurtz for an hour, pointing at me now and then. I don't understand the dialect of this tribe. Luckily for me, I fancy Kurtz felt too ill that day to care, or there would have been mischief. I don't understand. . . . No—it's too much for me. Ah, well, it's all over now.'

"At this moment I heard Kurtz's deep voice behind the curtain, 'Save me!—save the ivory, you mean. Don't tell me. Save *me!* Why, I've had to save you. You are interrupting my plans now. Sick! Sick! Not so sick as you would like to believe. Never mind. I'll carry my ideas out yet—I will return. I'll show you what can be done. You with your little peddling notions—you are interfering with me. I will return. I. . . '

"The manager came out. He did me the honour to take me under the arm and lead me aside. 'He is very low, very low,' he said. He considered it necessary to sigh, but neglected to be consistently sorrowful. 'We have done all we could for him—haven't we? But there is no disguising the fact, Mr Kurtz has done more harm than good to the Company. He did not see the time was not ripe for vigorous action. Cautiously, cautiously—that's my principle. We must be cautious yet. The district is closed to us for a time. Deplorable! Upon the whole, the trade will suffer. I don't deny there is a remarkable quantity of ivory—mostly fossil. We must save it, at all events—but look how precarious the position is—and why? Because the method is unsound.' 'Do you,' said I, looking at the shore, 'call it "unsound method"?' 'Without doubt,' he exclaimed, hotly. 'Don't you?'. . . 'No method at all,' I murmured after a while. 'Exactly,' he exulted. 'I anticipated this. Shows a complete want of judgment. It is my duty to point it out in the proper quarter.' 'Oh,' said I, 'that fellow—what's his name?—the brickmaker, will make a readable report for you.' He appeared confounded for a moment. It seemed to me I had never breathed an atmosphere so vile, and I turned mentally to Kurtz for relief—positively for relief. 'Nevertheless, I think Mr Kurtz is a remarkable man,' I said with emphasis. He started, dropped on me a cold heavy glance, said very quietly, 'He was,' and turned his back on me. My hour of favour was over; I found myself lumped along with Kurtz as a partisan of methods for which the time was not ripe: I was unsound! Ah! but it was something to have at least a choice of nightmares.

"I had turned to the wilderness really, not to Mr Kurtz, who, I was ready to admit, was as good as buried. And for a moment it seemed to me as if I also were buried in a vast grave full of unspeakable secrets. I felt an intolerable weight oppressing my breast, the smell of the damp earth, the unseen presence of victorious corruption, the darkness of an impenetrable night. . . . The Russian tapped me on the shoulder. I heard him mumbling and stammering something about 'brother seaman—couldn't conceal—knowledge of matters that would affect Mr Kurtz's reputation.' I waited. For him evidently Mr Kurtz was not in his grave; I suspect that for him Mr Kurtz was one of the immortals. 'Well!' said I at last, 'speak out. As it happens, I am Mr Kurtz's friend—in a way.'

"He stated with a good deal of formality that had we not been 'of the same profession,' he would have kept the matter to himself without regard to consequences. He suspected 'there was an active ill-will towards him on the part of these white men that—' 'You are right,' I said, remembering a certain conversation I had overheard. 'The manager thinks you ought to be hanged.' He showed a concern at this intelligence which amused me at first. 'I had better get out of the way quietly,' he said, earnestly. 'I can do no more for Kurtz now, and they would soon find some excuse. What's to stop them? There's a military post three hundred miles from here.' 'Well, upon my word,' said I, 'perhaps you had better go if you have any friends amongst the savages near by.' 'Plenty,' he said. 'They are simple people—and I want nothing, you know.' He stood biting his lip, then: 'I don't want any harm to happen to these whites here, but of course I was thinking of Mr Kurtz's reputation—but you are a brother seaman and—' 'All right,' said I, after a time. 'Mr Kurtz's reputation is safe with me.' I did not know how truly I spoke.

"He informed me, lowering his voice, that it was Kurtz who had ordered the attack to be made on the steamer. 'He hated sometimes the idea of being taken away—and then again . . . But I don't understand these matters. I am a simple man. He thought it would scare you away—that you would give it up, thinking him dead. I could not stop him. Oh, I had an awful time of it this last month.' 'Very well,' I said. 'He is all right now.' 'Ye-e-es,' he muttered, not very convinced apparently. 'Thanks,' said I; 'I shall keep my eyes open.' 'But quiet—eh?' he urged, anxiously. 'It would be awful for his reputation if anybody here—' I promised a complete discretion with great gravity. 'I have a canoe and three black fellows waiting not very far. I am off. Could you give me a few Martini-Henry cartridges?' I could, and did, with proper secrecy. He helped himself, with a wink at me, to a handful of my tobacco. 'Between sailors—you know—good English tobacco.' At the door of the pilot-house he turned round—'I say, haven't you a pair of shoes you could spare?' He raised one leg. 'Look.' The soles were tied with knotted strings sandal-wise under his bare feet. I rooted out an old pair, at which he looked with admiration before tucking it under his left arm. One of his pockets (bright red) was bulging with cartridges, from the other (dark blue) peeped 'Towson's Inquiry,' &c., &c. He seemed to think himself excellently well equipped for a renewed encounter with the wilderness. 'Ah! I'll never, never meet such a man again. You ought to have heard him recite poetry—his own too it was, he told me. Poetry!' He rolled his eyes at the recollection of these delights. 'Oh, he enlarged my mind!' 'Good-bye,' said I. He shook hands and vanished in the night. Sometimes I ask myself whether I had ever really seen him—whether it was possible to meet such a phenomenon!. . .

"When I woke up shortly after midnight his warning came to my mind with its hint of danger that seemed, in the starred darkness, real enough to make me get up for the purpose of having a look round. On the hill a big fire burned, illuminating fitfully a crooked corner of the station-house. One of the agents with a picket of a few of our blacks, armed for the purpose, was keeping guard over the ivory; but deep within the forest, red gleams that wavered, that seemed to sink and rise from the ground amongst confused columnar shapes of intense blackness, showed the exact position of the camp where Mr Kurtz's adorers were keeping their uneasy vigil. The monotonous beating of a big drum filled the air with muffled shocks and a lingering vibration. A steady droning sound of many men chanting each to himself some weird incantation came out from the black, flat wall of the woods as the humming of bees comes out of a hive, and had a strange narcotic effect upon my half-awake senses. I believe I dozed off leaning over the rail, till an abrupt burst of yells, an overwhelming outbreak of a pent-up and mysterious frenzy, woke me up in a bewildered wonder. It was cut short all at once, and the low droning went on with an effect of audible and soothing silence. I glanced casually into the little cabin. A light was burning within, but Mr Kurtz was not there.

"I think I would have raised an outcry if I had believed my eyes. But I didn't believe them at first—the thing seemed so impossible. The fact is, I was completely unnerved by a sheer blank fright, pure abstract terror, unconnected with any distinct shape of physical danger. What made this emotion so overpowering was—how shall I define it?—the moral shock I received, as if something altogether monstrous, intolerable to thought and odious to the soul, had been thrust upon me unexpectedly. This lasted of course the merest fraction of a second, and then the usual sense of commonplace, deadly danger, the possibility of a sudden onslaught and massacre, or something of the kind, which I saw impending, was positively welcome and composing. It pacified me, in fact, so much, that I did not raise an alarm.

"There was an agent buttoned up inside an ulster[8] and sleeping on a chair on deck within three feet of me. The yells had not awakened him; he snored very slightly; I left him to his slumbers and leaped ashore. I did not betray Mr Kurtz—it was ordered I should never betray him—it was written I should be loyal to the nightmare of my choice. I was anxious to deal with this shadow by myself alone,—and to this day I don't know why I was so jealous of sharing with any one the peculiar blackness of that experience.

"As soon as I got on the bank I saw a trail—a broad trail through the grass. I remember the exultation with which I said to myself, 'He can't walk—he is crawling on all-fours—I've got him.' The grass was wet with dew. I strode rapidly with clenched fists. I fancy I had some vague notion of falling upon him and giving him a drubbing. I don't know. I had some imbecile thoughts. The knitting old woman with the cat obtruded herself upon my memory as a most improper person to be sitting at the other end of such an affair. I saw a row of pilgrims squirting lead in the air out of

8. Long overcoat.

Winchesters held to the hip. I thought I would never get back to the steamer, and imagined myself living alone and unarmed in the woods to an advanced age. Such silly things—you know. And I remember I confounded the beat of the drum with the beating of my heart, and was pleased at its calm regularity.

"I kept to the track though—then stopped to listen. The night was very clear: a dark blue space, sparkling with dew and starlight, in which black things stood very still. I thought I could see a kind of motion ahead of me. I was strangely cocksure of everything that night. I actually left the track and ran in a wide semicircle (I verily believe chuckling to myself) so as to get in front of that stir, of that motion I had seen—if indeed I had seen anything. I was circumventing Kurtz as though it had been a boyish game.

"I came upon him, and, if he had not heard me coming, I would have fallen over him too, but he got up in time. He rose, unsteady, long, pale, indistinct, like a vapour exhaled by the earth, and swayed slightly, misty and silent before me; while at my back the fires loomed between the trees, and the murmur of many voices issued from the forest. I had cut him off cleverly; but when actually confronting him I seemed to come to my senses, I saw the danger in its right proportion. It was by no means over yet. Suppose he began to shout? Though he could hardly stand, there was still plenty of vigour in his voice. 'Go away—hide yourself,' he said, in that profound tone. It was very awful. I glanced back. We were within thirty yards from the nearest fire. A black figure stood up, strode on long black legs, waving long black arms, across the glow. It had horns—antelope horns, I think—on its head. Some sorcerer, some witch-man, no doubt: it looked fiend-like enough. 'Do you know what you are doing?' I whispered. 'Perfectly,' he answered, raising his voice for that single word: it sounded to me far off and yet loud, like a hail through a speaking-trumpet. If he makes a row we are lost, I thought to myself. This clearly was not a case for fisticuffs, even apart from the very natural aversion I had to beat that Shadow—this wandering and tormented thing. 'You will be lost,' I said—'utterly lost.' One gets sometimes such a flash of inspiration, you know. I did say the right thing, though indeed he could not have been more irretrievably lost than he was at this very moment, when the foundations of our intimacy were being laid—to endure—to endure—even to the end—even beyond.

" 'I had immense plans,' he muttered irresolutely. 'Yes,' said I; 'but if you try to shout I'll smash your head with—' there was not a stick or a stone near. 'I will throttle you for good,' I corrected myself. 'I was on the threshold of great things,' he pleaded, in a voice of longing, with a wistfulness of tone that made my blood run cold. 'And now for this stupid scoundrel—' 'Your success in Europe is assured in any case,' I affirmed, steadily. I did not want to have the throttling of him, you understand—and indeed it would have been very little use for any practical purpose. I tried to break the spell—the heavy, mute spell of the wilderness—that seemed to draw him to its pitiless breast by the awakening of forgotten and brutal instincts, by the memory of gratified and monstrous passions. This alone, I was convinced, had driven him out to the edge of the forest, to the bush, towards the gleam of fires, the throb of drums, the drone of weird incantations; this alone had beguiled his unlawful soul beyond the bounds of permitted aspirations. And, don't you see, the terror of the position was not in being knocked on the head—though I had a very lively sense of that danger too—but in this, that I had to deal with a being to whom I could not appeal in the name of anything high or low. I had, even like the niggers, to invoke him—himself—his own exalted and incredible degradation. There was nothing either above or below him, and I knew it. He had kicked himself loose of the earth. Confound the man! he had kicked the very earth to pieces. He was alone, and I before

him did not know whether I stood on the ground or floated in the air. I've been telling you what we said—repeating the phrases we pronounced,—but what's the good? They were common everyday words,—the familiar, vague sounds exchanged on every waking day of life. But what of that? They had behind them, to my mind, the terrific suggestiveness of words heard in dreams, of phrases spoken in nightmares. Soul! If anybody had ever struggled with a soul, I am the man. And I wasn't arguing with a lunatic either. Believe me or not, his intelligence was perfectly clear—concentrated, it is true, upon himself with horrible intensity, yet clear; and therein was my only chance—barring, of course, the killing him there and then, which wasn't so good, on account of unavoidable noise. But his soul was mad. Being alone in the wilderness, it had looked within itself, and, by heavens! I tell you, it had gone mad. I had—for my sins, I suppose—to go through the ordeal of looking into it myself. No eloquence could have been so withering to one's belief in mankind as his final burst of sincerity. He struggled with himself, too. I saw it,—I heard it. I saw the inconceivable mystery of a soul that knew no restraint, no faith, and no fear, yet struggling blindly with itself. I kept my head pretty well; but when I had him at last stretched on the couch, I wiped my forehead, while my legs shook under me as though I had carried half a ton on my back down that hill. And yet I had only supported him, his bony arm clasped round my neck—and he was not much heavier than a child.

"When next day we left at noon, the crowd, of whose presence behind the curtain of trees I had been acutely conscious all the time, flowed out of the woods again, filled the clearing, covered the slope with a mass of naked, breathing, quivering, bronze bodies. I steamed up a bit, then swung down-stream, and two thousand eyes followed the evolutions of the splashing, thumping, fierce river-demon beating the water with its terrible tail and breathing black smoke into the air. In front of the first rank, along the river, three men, plastered with bright red earth from head to foot, strutted to and fro restlessly. When we came abreast again, they faced the river, stamped their feet, nodded their horned heads, swayed their scarlet bodies; they shook towards the fierce river-demon a bunch of black feathers, a mangy skin with a pendent tail—something that looked like a dried gourd; they shouted periodically together strings of amazing words that resembled no sounds of human language; and the deep murmurs of the crowd, interrupted suddenly, were like the responses of some satanic litany.

"We had carried Kurtz into the pilot-house: there was more air there. Lying on the couch, he stared through the open shutter. There was an eddy in the mass of human bodies, and the woman with helmeted head and tawny cheeks rushed out to the very brink of the stream. She put out her hands, shouted something, and all that wild mob took up the shout in a roaring chorus of articulated, rapid, breathless utterance.

" 'Do you understand this?' I asked.

"He kept on looking out past me with fiery, longing eyes, with a mingled expression of wistfulness and hate. He made no answer, but I saw a smile, a smile of indefinable meaning, appear on his colourless lips that a moment after twitched convulsively. 'Do I not?' he said slowly, gasping, as if the words had been torn out of him by a supernatural power.

"I pulled the string of the whistle, and I did this because I saw the pilgrims on deck getting out their rifles with an air of anticipating a jolly lark. At the sudden screech there was a movement of abject terror through that wedged mass of bodies. 'Don't! don't! you frighten them away,' cried some one on deck disconsolately. I pulled the string time after time. They broke and ran, they leaped, they crouched,

they swerved, they dodged the flying terror of the sound. The three red chaps had fallen flat, face down on the shore, as though they had been shot dead. Only the barbarous and superb woman did not so much as flinch, and stretched tragically her bare arms after us over the sombre and glittering river.

"And then that imbecile crowd down on the deck started their little fun, and I could see nothing more for smoke.

"The brown current ran swiftly out of the heart of darkness, bearing us down towards the sea with twice the speed of our upward progress; and Kurtz's life was running swiftly too, ebbing, ebbing out of his heart into the sea of inexorable time. The manager was very placid, he had no vital anxieties now, he took us both in with a comprehensive and satisfied glance: the 'affair' had come off as well as could be wished. I saw the time approaching when I would be left alone of the party of 'unsound method.' The pilgrims looked upon me with disfavour. I was, so to speak, numbered with the dead. It is strange how I accepted this unforeseen partnership, this choice of nightmares forced upon me in the tenebrous land invaded by these mean and greedy phantoms.

"Kurtz discoursed. A voice! a voice! It rang deep to the very last. It survived his strength to hide in the magnificent folds of eloquence the barren darkness of his heart. Oh, he struggled! he struggled! The wastes of his weary brain were haunted by shadowy images now—images of wealth and fame revolving obsequiously round his unextinguishable gift of noble and lofty expression. My Intended, my station, my career, my ideas—these were the subjects for the occasional utterances of elevated sentiments. The shade of the original Kurtz frequented the bedside of the hollow sham, whose fate it was to be buried presently in the mould of primeval earth. But both the diabolic love and the unearthly hate of the mysteries it had penetrated fought for the possession of that soul satiated with primitive emotions, avid of lying fame, of sham distinction, of all the appearances of success and power.

"Sometimes he was contemptibly childish. He desired to have kings meet him at railway-stations on his return from some ghastly Nowhere, where he intended to accomplish great things. 'You show them you have in you something that is really profitable, and then there will be no limits to the recognition of your ability,' he would say. 'Of course you must take care of the motives—right motives—always.' The long reaches that were like one and the same reach, monotonous bends that were exactly alike, slipped past the steamer with their multitude of secular[9] trees looking patiently after this grimy fragment of another world, the forerunner of change, of conquest, of trade, of massacres, of blessings. I looked ahead—piloting. 'Close the shutter,' said Kurtz suddenly one day; 'I can't bear to look at this.' I did so. There was a silence. 'Oh, but I will wring your heart yet!' he cried at the invisible wilderness.

"We broke down—as I had expected—and had to lie up for repairs at the head of an island. This delay was the first thing that shook Kurtz's confidence. One morning he gave me a packet of papers and a photograph,—the lot tied together with a shoestring. 'Keep this for me,' he said. 'This noxious fool' (meaning the manager) 'is capable of prying into my boxes when I am not looking.' In the afternoon I saw him. He was lying on his back with closed eyes, and I withdrew quietly, but I heard him mutter, 'Live rightly, die, die . . .' I listened. There was nothing more. Was he rehearsing

9. Ancient.

some speech in his sleep, or was it a fragment of a phrase from some newspaper article? He had been writing for the papers and meant to do so again, 'for the furthering of my ideas. It's a duty.'

"His was an impenetrable darkness. I looked at him as you peer down at a man who is lying at the bottom of a precipice where the sun never shines. But I had not much time to give him, because I was helping the engine-driver to take to pieces the leaky cylinders, to straighten a bent connecting-rod, and in other such matters. I lived in an infernal mess of rust, filings, nuts, bolts, spanners, hammers, ratchet-drills—things I abominate, because I don't get on with them. I tended the little forge we fortunately had aboard; I toiled wearily in a wretched scrap-heap—unless I had the shakes too bad to stand.

"One evening coming in with a candle I was startled to hear him say a little tremulously, 'I am lying here in the dark waiting for death.' The light was within a foot of his eyes. I forced myself to murmur, 'Oh, nonsense!' and stood over him as if transfixed.

"Anything approaching the change that came over his features I have never seen before, and hope never to see again. Oh, I wasn't touched. I was fascinated. It was as though a veil had been rent. I saw on that ivory face the expression of sombre pride, of ruthless power, of craven terror—of an intense and hopeless despair. Did he live his life again in every detail of desire, temptation, and surrender during that supreme moment of complete knowledge? He cried in a whisper at some image, at some vision,—he cried out twice, a cry that was no more than a breath—

" 'The horror! The horror!'

"I blew the candle out and left the cabin. The pilgrims were dining in the mess-room, and I took my place opposite the manager, who lifted his eyes to give me a questioning glance, which I successfully ignored. He leaned back, serene, with that peculiar smile of his sealing the unexpressed depths of his meanness. A continuous shower of small flies streamed upon the lamp, upon the cloth, upon our hands and faces. Suddenly the manager's boy put his insolent black head in the doorway, and said in a tone of scathing contempt—

" 'Mistah Kurtz—he dead.'

"All the pilgrims rushed out to see. I remained, and went on with my dinner. I believe I was considered brutally callous. However, I did not eat much. There was a lamp in there—light, don't you know—and outside it was so beastly, beastly dark. I went no more near the remarkable man who had pronounced a judgment upon the adventures of his soul on this earth. The voice was gone. What else had been there? But I am of course aware that next day the pilgrims buried something in a muddy hole.

"And then they very nearly buried me.

"However, as you see, I did not go to join Kurtz there and then. I did not. I remained to dream the nightmare out to the end, and to show my loyalty to Kurtz once more. Destiny. My destiny! Droll thing life is—that mysterious arrangement of merciless logic for a futile purpose. The most you can hope from it is some knowledge of yourself—that comes too late—a crop of unextinguishable regrets. I have wrestled with death. It is the most unexciting contest you can imagine. It takes place in an impalpable greyness, with nothing underfoot, with nothing around, without spectators, without clamour, without glory, without the great desire of victory, without the great fear of defeat, in a sickly atmosphere of tepid scepticism, without much belief in your own right, and still less in that of your adversary. If such is the form of ultimate wisdom, then life is a greater riddle than some of us think it to be. I was within a hair's-breadth of the last opportunity for pronouncement, and I found with humiliation that probably I would have nothing to say. This is the reason why I affirm that Kurtz was a remarkable man. He had something to say. He said it. Since I had peeped over the edge myself, I understand better the meaning of his stare, that could not see the flame of the candle, but was wide enough to embrace the whole universe, piercing enough to penetrate all the hearts that beat in the darkness. He had summed up—he had judged. 'The horror!' He was a remarkable man. After all, this was the expression of some sort of belief; it had candour, it had conviction, it had a vibrating note of revolt in its whisper, it had the appalling face of a glimpsed truth—the strange commingling of desire and hate. And it is not my own extremity I remember best—a vision of greyness without form filled with physical pain, and a careless contempt for the evanescence of all things—even of this pain itself. No! It is his extremity that I seem to have lived through. True, he had made that last stride, he had stepped over the edge, while I had been permitted to draw back my hesitating foot. And perhaps in this is the whole difference; perhaps all the wisdom, and all truth, and all sincerity, are just compressed into that inappreciable moment of time in which we step over the threshold of the invisible. Perhaps! I like to think my summing-up would not have been a word of careless contempt. Better his cry—much better. It was an affirmation, a moral victory paid for by innumerable defeats, by abominable terrors, by abominable satisfactions. But it was a victory! That is why I have remained loyal to Kurtz to the last, and even beyond, when a long time after I heard once more, not his own voice, but the echo of his magnificent eloquence thrown to me from a soul as translucently pure as a cliff of crystal.

"No, they did not bury me, though there is a period of time which I remember mistily, with a shuddering wonder, like a passage through some inconceivable world that had no hope in it and no desire. I found myself back in the sepulchral city resenting the sight of people hurrying through the streets to filch a little money from each other, to devour their infamous cookery, to gulp their unwholesome beer, to dream their insignificant and silly dreams. They trespassed upon my thoughts. They were intruders whose knowledge of life was to me an irritating pretence, because I felt so sure they could not possibly know the things I knew. Their bearing, which was simply the bearing of commonplace individuals going about their business in the assurance of perfect safety, was offensive to me like the outrageous flauntings of folly in the face of a danger it is unable to comprehend. I had no particular desire to enlighten them, but I had some difficulty in restraining myself from laughing in their faces, so full of stupid importance. I daresay I was not very well at that time. I tottered about the streets—there were various affairs to settle—grinning bitterly at perfectly respectable persons. I admit my behaviour was inexcusable, but then my temperature was seldom normal in these days. My dear aunt's endeavours to 'nurse up my strength' seemed altogether beside the mark. It was not my strength that wanted nursing, it was my imagination that wanted soothing. I kept the bundle of papers given me by Kurtz, not knowing exactly what to do with it. His mother had died lately, watched over, as I was told, by his Intended. A clean-shaved man, with an official manner and wearing gold-rimmed spectacles, called on me one day and made inquiries, at first circuitous, afterwards suavely pressing, about what he was pleased to denominate certain 'documents.' I was not surprised, because I had had two rows with the manager on the subject out there. I had refused to give up the smallest scrap out of that package, and I took the same attitude with the spectacled man. He became darkly menacing at last, and with much heat argued that the Company had the right to every bit of information about its 'territories.' And, said he, 'Mr Kurtz's knowledge of unexplored regions must have been necessarily extensive and peculiar—owing to his great abilities and to the deplorable circumstances in which he had been placed: therefore—' I assured him Mr Kurtz's knowledge, however extensive, did not bear upon the problems of commerce or administration. He invoked then the name of science. 'It would be an incalculable loss if,' &c., &c. I offered him the report on the 'Suppression of Savage Customs,' with the postscriptum torn off. He took it up eagerly, but ended by sniffing at it with an air of contempt. 'This is not what we had a right to expect,' he remarked. 'Expect nothing else,' I said. 'There are only private letters.' He withdrew upon some threat of legal proceedings, and I saw him no more; but another fellow, calling himself Kurtz's cousin, appeared two days later, and was anxious to hear all the details about his dear relative's last moments. Incidentally he gave me to understand that Kurtz had been essentially a great musician. 'There was the making of an immense success,' said the man, who was an organist, I believe, with lank grey hair flowing over a greasy coat-collar. I had no reason to doubt his statement; and to this day I am unable to say what was Kurtz's profession, whether he ever had any—which was the greatest of his talents. I had taken him for a painter who wrote for the papers, or else for a journalist who could paint—but even the cousin (who took snuff during the interview) could not tell me what he had been—exactly. He was a universal genius—on that point I agreed with the old chap, who thereupon blew his nose noisily into a large cotton handkerchief and withdrew in senile agitation, bearing off some family letters and memoranda without importance. Ultimately a journalist anxious to know something of the fate of his 'dear colleague' turned up. This visitor informed me Kurtz's proper sphere ought to have been politics 'on the popular side.' He had furry straight eyebrows, bristly hair cropped short, an eye-glass on a broad ribbon, and, becoming expansive, confessed his opinion that Kurtz really couldn't write a bit—'but heavens! how that man could talk! He electrified large meetings. He had faith—don't you see?—he had the faith. He could get himself to believe anything—anything. He would have been a splendid leader of an extreme party.' 'What party?' I asked. 'Any party,' answered the other. 'He was an—an—extremist.' Did I not think so? I assented. Did I know, he asked, with a sudden flash of curiosity, 'what it was that had induced him to go out there?' 'Yes,' said I, and forthwith handed him the famous Report for publication, if he thought fit. He glanced through it hurriedly, mumbling all the time, judged 'it would do,' and took himself off with this plunder.

"Thus I was left at last with a slim packet of letters and the girl's portrait. She struck me as beautiful—I mean she had a beautiful expression. I know that the sunlight can be made to lie too, yet one felt that no manipulation of light and pose could have conveyed the delicate shade of truthfulness upon those features. She seemed ready to listen without mental reservation, without suspicion, without a thought for herself. I concluded I would go and give her back her portrait and those letters myself. Curiosity? Yes; and also some other feeling perhaps. All that had been Kurtz's had passed out of my hands: his soul, his body, his station, his plans, his ivory, his career. There remained only his memory and his Intended—and I wanted to give that up too to the past, in a way,—to surrender personally all that remained of him with me to that oblivion which is the last word of our common fate. I don't defend myself. I had no clear perception of what it was I really wanted. Perhaps it was an impulse of unconscious loyalty, or the fulfilment of one of those ironic necessities that lurk in the facts of human existence. I don't know. I can't tell. But I went.

"I thought his memory was like the other memories of the dead that accumulate in every man's life,—a vague impress on the brain of shadows that had fallen on it in their swift and final passage; but before the high and ponderous door, between the tall houses of a street as still and decorous as a well-kept alley in a cemetery, I had a vision of him on the stretcher, opening his mouth voraciously, as if to devour all the earth with all its mankind. He lived then before me; he lived as much as he had ever lived—a shadow insatiable of splendid appearances, of frightful realities; a shadow darker than the shadow of the night, and draped nobly in the folds of a gorgeous eloquence. The vision seemed to enter the house with me—the stretcher, the phantom-bearers, the wild crowd of obedient worshippers, the gloom of the forests, the glitter of the reach between the murky bends, the beat of the drum, regular and muffled like the beating of a heart—the heart of a conquering darkness. It was a moment of triumph for the wilderness, an invading and vengeful rush which, it seemed to me, I would have to keep back alone for the salvation of another soul. And the memory of what I had heard him say afar there, with the horned shapes stirring at my back, in the glow of fires, within the patient woods, those broken phrases came back to me, were heard again in their ominous and terrifying simplicity. I remembered his abject pleading, his abject threats, the colossal scale of his vile desires, the meanness, the torment, the tempestuous anguish of his soul. And later on I seemed to see his collected languid manner, when he said one day, 'This lot of ivory now is really mine. The Company did not pay for it. I collected it myself at a very great personal risk. I am afraid they will try to claim it as theirs though. H'm. It is a difficult case. What do you think I ought to do—resist? Eh? I want no more than justice.' . . . He wanted no more than justice—no more than justice. I rang the bell before a mahogany door on the first floor, and while I waited he seemed to stare at me out of the glassy panel—stare with that wide and immense stare embracing, condemning, loathing all the universe. I seemed to hear the whispered cry, 'The horror! The horror!'

"The dusk was falling. I had to wait in a lofty drawing-room with three long windows from floor to ceiling that were like three luminous and bedraped columns. The bent gilt legs and backs of the furniture shone in indistinct curves. The tall marble fireplace had a cold and monumental whiteness. A grand piano stood massively in a corner, with dark gleams on the flat surfaces like a sombre and polished sarcophagus. A high door opened—closed. I rose.

"She came forward, all in black, with a pale head, floating towards me in the dusk. She was in mourning. It was more than a year since his death, more than a year since the news came; she seemed as though she would remember and mourn for ever. She took both my hands in hers and murmured, 'I had heard you were coming.' I noticed she was not very young—I mean not girlish. She had a mature capacity for fidelity, for belief, for suffering. The room seemed to have grown darker, as if all the sad light of the cloudy evening had taken refuge on her forehead. This fair hair, this pale visage, this pure brow, seemed surrounded by an ashy halo from which the dark eyes looked out at me. Their glance was guileless, profound, confident, and trustful. She carried her sorrowful head as though she were proud of that sorrow, as though she would say, I—I alone know how to mourn for him as he deserves. But while we were still shaking hands, such a look of awful desolation came upon her face that I perceived she was one of those creatures that are not the playthings of Time. For her he had died only yesterday. And, by Jove! the impression was so powerful that for me too he seemed to have died only yesterday—nay, this very minute. I saw her and him in the same instant of time—his death and her sorrow—I saw her sorrow in the very moment of his death. Do you understand? I saw them together—I heard them together. She had said, with a deep catch of the breath, 'I have survived'; while my strained ears seemed to hear distinctly, mingled with her tone of despairing regret, the summing-up whisper of his eternal condemnation. I asked myself what I was doing there, with a sensation of panic in my heart as though I had blundered into a place of cruel and absurd mysteries not fit for a human being to behold. She motioned me to a chair. We sat down. I laid the packet gently on the little table, and she put her hand over it. . . . 'You knew him well,' she murmured, after a moment of mourning silence.

" 'Intimacy grows quickly out there,' I said. 'I knew him as well as it is possible for one man to know another.'

" 'And you admired him,' she said. 'It was impossible to know him and not to admire him. Was it?'

" 'He was a remarkable man,' I said, unsteadily. Then before the appealing fixity of her gaze, that seemed to watch for more words on my lips, I went on, 'It was impossible not to—'

" 'Love him,' she finished eagerly, silencing me into an appalled dumbness. 'How true! how true! But when you think that no one knew him so well as I! I had all his noble confidence. I knew him best.'

" 'You knew him best,' I repeated. And perhaps she did. But with every word spoken the room was growing darker, and only her forehead, smooth and white, remained illumined by the unextinguishable light of belief and love.

" 'You were his friend,' she went on. 'His friend,' she repeated, a little louder. 'You must have been, if he had given you this, and sent you to me. I feel I can speak to you—and oh! I must speak. I want you—you who have heard his last words—to know I have been worthy of him. . . . It is not pride. . . . Yes! I am proud to know I understood him better than any one on earth—he told me so himself. And since his mother died I have had no one—no one—to—to—'

"I listened. The darkness deepened. I was not even sure whether he had given me the right bundle. I rather suspect he wanted me to take care of another batch of his papers which, after his death, I saw the manager examining under the lamp. And the girl talked, easing her pain in the certitude of my sympathy; she talked as thirsty men drink. I had heard that her engagement with Kurtz had been disapproved by her people. He wasn't rich enough or something. And indeed I don't know whether he had not been a pauper all his life. He had given me some reason to infer that it was his impatience of comparative poverty that drove him out there.

" '. . . Who was not his friend who had heard him speak once?' she was saying. 'He drew men towards him by what was best in them.' She looked at me with intensity. 'It is the gift of the great,' she went on, and the sound of her low voice seemed to have the accompaniment of all the other sounds, full of mystery, desolation, and sorrow, I had ever heard—the ripple of the river, the soughing of the trees swayed by the wind, the murmurs of wild crowds, the faint ring of incomprehensible words cried from afar, the whisper of a voice speaking from beyond the threshold of an eternal darkness. 'But you have heard him! You know!' she cried.

" 'Yes, I know,' I said with something like despair in my heart, but bowing my head before the faith that was in her, before that great and saving illusion that shone with an unearthly glow in the darkness, in the triumphant darkness from which I could not have defended her—from which I could not even defend myself.

" 'What a loss to me—to us!'—she corrected herself with beautiful generosity; then added in a murmur, 'To the world.' By the last gleams of twilight I could see the glitter of her eyes, full of tears—of tears that would not fall.

" 'I have been very happy—very fortunate—very proud,' she went on. 'Too fortunate. Too happy for a little while. And now I am unhappy for—for life.'

"She stood up; her fair hair seemed to catch all the remaining light in a glimmer of gold. I rose too.

" 'And of all this,' she went on, mournfully, 'of all his promise, and of all his greatness, of his generous mind, of his noble heart, nothing remains—nothing but a memory. You and I—'

" 'We shall always remember him,' I said, hastily.

" 'No!' she cried. 'It is impossible that all this should be lost—that such a life should be sacrificed to leave nothing—but sorrow. You know what vast plans he had. I knew of them too—I could not perhaps understand,—but others knew of them. Something must remain. His words, at least, have not died.'

" 'His words will remain,' I said.

" 'And his example,' she whispered to herself. 'Men looked up to him,—his goodness shone in every act. His example—'

" 'True,' I said; 'his example too. Yes, his example. I forgot that.'

" 'But I do not. I cannot—I cannot believe—not yet. I cannot believe that I shall never see him again, that nobody will see him again, never, never, never.'

"She put out her arms as if after a retreating figure, stretching them black and with clasped pale hands across the fading and narrow sheen of the window. Never see him! I saw him clearly enough then. I shall see this eloquent phantom as long as I live, and I shall see her too, a tragic and familiar Shade, resembling in this gesture another one, tragic also, and bedecked with powerless charms, stretching bare brown arms over the glitter of the infernal stream, the stream of darkness. She said suddenly very low, 'He died as he lived.'

" 'His end,' said I, with dull anger stirring in me, 'was in every way worthy of his life.'

" 'And I was not with him,' she murmured. My anger subsided before a feeling of infinite pity.

" 'Everything that could be done—' I mumbled.

" 'Ah, but I believed in him more than any one on earth—more than his own mother, more than—himself. He needed me! Me! I would have treasured every sigh, every word, every sign, every glance.'

"I felt like a chill grip on my chest. 'Don't,' I said, in a muffled voice.

" 'Forgive me. I—I—have mourned so long in silence—in silence. . . . You were with him—to the last? I think of his loneliness. Nobody near to understand him as I would have understood. Perhaps no one to hear . . . .'

" 'To the very end,' I said, shakily. 'I heard his very last words . . . .' I stopped in a fright.

" 'Repeat them,' she said in a heart-broken tone. 'I want—I want—something—something—to—to live with.'

"I was on the point of crying at her, 'Don't you hear them?' The dusk was repeating them in a persistent whisper all around us, in a whisper that seemed to swell menacingly like the first whisper of a rising wind. 'The horror! the horror!'

" 'His last word—to live with,' she murmured. 'Don't you understand I loved him—I loved him—I loved him!'

"I pulled myself together and spoke slowly.

" 'The last word he pronounced was—your name.'

"I heard a light sigh, and then my heart stood still, stopped dead short by an exulting and terrible cry, by the cry of inconceivable triumph and of unspeakable pain. 'I knew it—I was sure!' . . . She knew. She was sure. I heard her weeping; she had hidden her face in her hands. It seemed to me that the house would collapse before I could escape, that the heavens would fall upon my head. But nothing happened. The heavens do not fall for such a trifle. Would they have fallen, I wonder, if I had rendered Kurtz that justice which was his due? Hadn't he said he wanted only justice? But I couldn't. I could not tell her. It would have been too dark—too dark altogether . . . ."

Marlow ceased, and sat apart, indistinct and silent, in the pose of a meditating Buddha. Nobody moved for a time. "We have lost the first of the ebb," said the Director, suddenly. I raised my head. The offing was barred by a black bank of clouds, and the tranquil waterway leading to the uttermost ends of the earth flowed sombre under an overcast sky—seemed to lead into the heart of an immense darkness.

HEART OF DARKNESS AND ITS TIME

Joseph Conrad

from *Congo Diary*[1]

Arrived at Matadi[2] on the 13th of June, 1890.

Mr Gosse, chief of the station (O.K.) retaining us for some reason of his own.

Made the acquaintance of Mr Roger Casement,[3] which I should consider as a great pleasure under any circumstances and now it becomes a positive piece of luck.

Thinks, speaks well, most intelligent and very sympathetic.

Feel considerably in doubt about the future. Think just now that my life amongst the people (white) around here cannot be very comfortable. Intend avoid acquaintances as much as possible. * * *

24th. Gosse and R.C. gone with a large lot of ivory down to Boma. On G.['s] return to start to up the river. Have been myself busy packing ivory in casks. Idiotic employment. Health good up to now. * * *

Prominent characteristic of the social life here: people speaking ill of each other.

* * *

Friday, 4th July.

Left camp at 6h a.m. after a very unpleasant night. Marching across a chain of hills and then in a maze of hills. At 8:15 opened out into an undulating plain. Took bearings of a break in the chain of mountains on the other side. * * *

Saw another dead body lying by the path in an attitude of meditative repose.

In the evening three women of whom one albino passed our camp. Horrid chalky white with pink blotches. Red eyes. Red hair. Features very Negroid and ugly. Mosquitos. At night when the moon rose heard shouts and drumming in distant villages. Passed a bad night.

* * *

1. The following excerpts are taken from the diary Conrad kept when he was employed to go to the Congo in 1889; he kept the diary only from his landing at Matadi on 13 June, 1890, until his arrival at Kinchassa on 1 August.

2. Colonial station near the mouth of the Congo River. Conrad arrived there on his way to take up his command of a steamship upriver at Kinshasa.

3. Casement (1864–1916) and Conrad were employed at the time by the same company. Casement later served as British consul in various parts of Africa, and was the author of a report on the Congo (1904) that did much to make public the terrible conditions there. He was knighted in 1912. In 1916 he was executed by the British for his part in the Easter Rising in Ireland.

Saturday, 5th July. 90.

Left at 6:15. Morning cool, even cold and very damp. Sky densely overcast. Gentle breeze from NE. Road through a narrow plain up to R. Kwilu. Swift-flowing and deep, 50 yds. wide. Passed in canoes. After[war]ds up and down very steep hills intersected by deep ravines. Main chain of heights running mostly NW-SE or W and E at times. Stopped at Manyamba. Camp[in]g place bad—in hollow—water very indifferent. Tent set at 10:15.

Section of today's road. NNE Distance 12 m. [a drawing]

Today fell into a muddy puddle. Beastly. The fault of the man that carried me. After camp[in]g went to a small stream, bathed and washed clothes. Getting jolly well sick of this fun.

Tomorrow expect a long march to get to Nsona, 2 days from Manyanga. No sunshine today.

* * *

Saturday, 26th.

Left very early. Road ascending all the time. Passed villages. Country seems thickly inhabited. At 11h arrived at large market place. Left at noon and camped at 1h p.m.

[section of the day's march with notes]

a camp—a white man died here—market—govt. post—mount—crocodile pond—Mafiesa. * * *

Sunday, 27th.

Left at 8h am. Sent luggage carriers straight on to Luasi and went ourselves round by the Mission of Sutili.

Hospitable reception by Mrs Comber. All the missio[naries] absent.

The looks of the whole establishment eminently civilized and very refreshing to see after the lots of tumble-down hovels in which the State and Company agents are content to live—fine buildings. Position on a hill. Rather breezy.

Left at 3h pm. At the first heavy ascent met Mr Davis, miss[ionary] returning from a preaching trip. Rev. Bentley away in the South with his wife. * * *

Tuesday, 29th.

Left camp at 7h after a good night's rest. Continuous ascent; rather easy at first. Crossed wooded ravines and the river Lunzadi by a very decent bridge.

At 9h met Mr Louette escorting a sick agent of the Comp[an]y back to Matadi. Looking very well. Bad news from up the river. All the steamers disabled. One wrecked. Country wooded. At 10:30 camped at Inkissi. * * *

Today did not set the tent but put up in Gov[ernmen]t shimbek.[4] Zanzibari in charge—very obliging. Met ripe pineapple for the first time. On the road today passed a skeleton tied up to a post. Also white man's grave—no name. Heap of stones in the form of a cross.

Health good now.

Wednesday, 30th.

Left at 6 a.m. intending to camp at Kinfumu. Two hours' sharp walk brought me to Nsona na Nsefe. Market. ½ hour after, Harou arrived very ill with billious [sic] attack and fever. Laid him down in Gov[ernmen]t shimbek. Dose of Ipeca.[5]

4. A group of huts.

5. A medicine.

Vomiting bile in enormous quantities. At 11h gave him 1 gramme of quinine and lots of hot tea. Hot fit ending in heavy perspiration. At 2 p.m. put him in hammock and started for Kinfumu. Row with carriers all the way. Harou suffering much through the jerks of the hammock. Camped at a small stream.

At 4h Harou better. Fever gone. * * *

Up till noon, sky clouded and strong NW wind very chilling. From 1h pm to 4h pm sky clear and very hot day. Expect lots of bother with carriers tomorrow. Had them all called and made a speech which they did not understand. They promise good behaviour. * * *

Friday, 1st of August 1890.

* * * Row between the carriers and a man stating himself in Gov[ernmen]t employ, about a mat. Blows with sticks raining hard. Stopped it. Chief came with a youth about 13 suffering from gunshot wound in the head. Bullet entered about an inch above the right eyebrow and came out a little inside. The roots of the hair, fairly in the middle of the brow in a line with the bridge of the nose. Bone not damaged apparently. Gave him a little glycerine to put on the wound made by the bullet on coming out. Harou not very well. Mosquitos. Frogs. Beastly. Glad to see the end of this stupid tramp. Feel rather seedy. Sun rose red. Very hot day. Wind S[ou]th.

Sir Henry Morton Stanley

from *Address to the Manchester Chamber of Commerce*[1]

There is not one manufacturer here present who could not tell me if he had the opportunity how much he personally suffered through the slackness of trade; and I dare say that you have all some vague idea that if things remain as they are the future of the cotton manufacture is not very brilliant. New inventions are continually cropping up, so that your power of producing, if stimulated, is almost incalculable; but new markets for the sale of your products are not of rapid growth, and as other nations, by prohibitive tariffs, are bent upon fostering native manufacturers to the exclusion of your own, such markets as are now open to you are likely to be taken away from you in course of time. Well, then, I come to you with at least one market where there are at present, perhaps, 6,250,000 yards of cheap cottons sold every year on the Congo banks and in the Congo markets.[2]

I was interested the other day in making a curious calculation, which was, supposing that all the inhabitants of the Congo basin were simply to have one Sunday dress each, how many yards of Manchester cloth would be required; and the amazing number was 320,000,000 yards, just for one Sunday dress! (Cheers.) Proceeding still further with these figures I found that two Sunday dresses and four everyday dresses would in one year amount to 3,840,000,000 yards, which at 2d. [two

1. The journalist and adventurer Henry Morton Stanley wrote best-selling accounts of his exploits in Africa; an excerpt from his *Through the Dark Continent* begins on page 1762. He delivered this address to the textile manufacturers of Manchester in 1886, seeking their support for the commercial exploitation of the Congo. This speech gives a striking example of the outlook—and rhetoric—of the people who created the conditions Conrad encountered when he went to the Congo in 1890.

2. The Congo Free State (later Zaire), a vast area of central Africa around the Congo River, was formally brought under the ownership of Leopold II of Belgium and other investors in the International Association of the Congo by the Berlin West Africa Conference of 1884–1885. Stanley's expeditions there (from 1876) had been financed by Leopold, and from 1879 Stanley had set up trading stations along the river to facilitate the exploitation of the area's natural resources.

pence] per yard would be of the value of £16,000,000. The more I pondered upon these things I discovered that I could not limit these stores of cotton cloth to day dresses. I would have to provide for night dresses also—(laughter)—and these would consume 160,000,000 yards. (Cheers.) Then the grave cloths came into mind, and, as a poor lunatic, who burned Bolobo Station,[3] destroyed 30,000 yards of cloth in order that he should not be cheated out of a respectable burial, I really feared for a time that the millions would get beyond measurable calculation. However, putting such accidents aside, I estimate that, if my figures of population are approximately correct, 2,000,000 die every year, and to bury these decently, and according to the custom of those who possess cloth, 16,000,000 yards will be required, while the 40,000 chiefs will require an average of 100 yards each, or 4,000,000 yards. I regarded these figures with great satisfaction, and I was about to close my remarks upon the millions of yards of cloth that Manchester would perhaps be required to produce when I discovered that I had neglected to provide for the family wardrobe or currency chest, for you must know that in the Lower Congo there is scarcely a family that has not a cloth fund of about a dozen pieces of about 24 yards each. This is a very important institution, otherwise how are the family necessities to be provided for? How are the fathers and mothers of families to go to market to buy greens, bread, oil, ground nuts, chickens, fish, and goats, and how is the petty trade to be conducted? How is ivory to be purchased, the gums, rubber, dye powders, gunpowder, copper slugs, guns, trinkets, knives, and swords to be bought without a supply of cloth? Now, 8,000,000 families at 300 yards each will require 2,400,000,000. (Cheers.) You all know how perishable such currency must be; but if you sum up these several millions of yards, and value all of them at the average price of 2d. per yard, you will find that it will be possible for Manchester to create a trade—in the course of time—in cottons in the Congo basin amounting in value to about £26,000,000 annually. (Loud cheers.) I have said nothing about Rochdale savelist, or your own superior prints, your gorgeous handkerchiefs, with their variegated patterns, your checks and striped cloths, your ticking and twills.[4] I must satisfy myself with suggesting them; your own imaginations will no doubt carry you to the limbo of immeasurable and incalculable millions. (Laughter and cheers.)

Now, if your sympathy for yourselves and the fate of Manchester has been excited sufficiently, your next natural question would be as follows: We acknowledge, sir, that you have contrived by an artful array of imposing millions to excite our attention, at least, to this field; but we beg to ask you what Manchester is to do in order that we may begin realising this sale of untold millions of yards of cotton cloth? I answer that the first thing to do is for you to ask the British Government to send a cruiser to the mouth of the Congo to keep watch and ward over that river until the European nations have agreed among themselves as to what shall be done with the river, lest one of these days you will hear that it is too late. (Hear, hear.) Secondly, to study whether, seeing that it will never do to permit Portugal to assume sovereignty over that river[5]—and England publicly disclaims any wish to possess that river for herself—it would not be as well to allow the International Association to act as

3. The London *Times* carried frequent reports of disturbances in the Congo at this time; in March 1884, for example, Congolese attacks on foreign trading establishments at Nokki in the Lower Congo had caused the Europeans to "declare war against the natives."

4. Savelist is cheap fabric; ticking is a strong cotton or linen fabric; twill is a kind of textile weave.

5. The mouth of the Congo River had been discovered by the Portuguese in 1482.

guardians of international right to free trade and free entrance and exit into and out of the river. (Hear, hear.) The main point, remember, always is a guarantee that the lower river shall be free, that, however the Upper Congo may be developed, no Power, inspired by cupidity, shall seize upon the mouth of the river and build custom houses. (Hear, hear.) The Lower Congo in the future will only be valuable because down its waters will have to be floated the produce of the rich basin above to the ocean steamships. It will always have a fair trade of its own, but it bears no proportion to the almost limitless trade that the Upper Congo could furnish. If the Association could be assured that the road from Europe to Vivi[6] was for ever free, the first steps to realise the sale of those countless millions of yards of cotton cloth would be taken. Over six millions of yards are now used annually; but we have no means of absorbing more, owing to the difficulties of transport. Every man capable and willing to carry a load is employed. When human power was discovered to be not further available we tested animal power and discovered it to be feebler and more costly than the other; and we have come to the conclusion that steam power must now assist us or we remain *in statu quo* [as things now stand]. But before having recourse to this steam power, and building the iron road along which your bales of cotton fabrics may roll on to the absorbing markets of the Upper Congo unceasingly, the Association pauses to ask you, and the peoples of other English cities, such as London, Liverpool, Glasgow, Birmingham, Leeds, Preston, Sheffield, who profess to understand the importance of the work we have been doing, and the absorbing power of those markets we have reached, what help you will render us, for your own sakes, to make those markets accessible? (Hear, hear.) The Association will not build that railway to the Upper Congo, nor invest one piece of sterling gold in it, unless they are assured they will not be robbed of it, and the Lower Congo will be placed under some flag that shall be a guarantee to all the world that its waters and banks are absolutely free. (Cheers.)

You will agree with me, I am sure, that trade ought to expand and commerce grow, and if we can coax it into mature growth in this Congo basin that it would be a praiseworthy achievement, honoured by men and gods; for out of this trade, this intercourse caused by peaceful barter, proceed all those blessings which you and I enjoy. The more trade thrives, the more benefits to mankind are multipled, and nearer to gods do men become. (Hear, hear.) The builders of railroads through wildernesses generally require large concessions of lands; but the proposed builders of this railway to connect the Lower with the Upper Congo do not ask for any landed concessions; but they ask for a concession of authority over the Lower Congo in order that the beneficent policy which directs the civilising work on the Upper Congo may be extended to the Lower River, and that the mode of government and action may be uniform throughout. The beneficent policy referred to is explained in the treaty made and concluded with the United States Government.[7] That treaty says: "That with the object of enabling civilisation and commerce to penetrate into Equatorial Africa the Free States of the Congo have resolved to levy no customs duties whatever. The Free States also guarantee to all men who establish themselves in their territories the right of purchasing, selling, or leasing any land and buildings, of creating factories and of trade on the sole condition that they conform to the law. The International Association of the Congo is prepared

6. A town on the Upper Congo river; from 1882 Stanley had been arguing that a railway should be built between the Lower and Upper Congo to facilitate the exploitation of the interior. It was completed in 1898.

7. The United States was the first country to recognize the right of the International Association to govern the Congo territories in April 1884.

to enter into engagements with other nations who desire to secure the free admission of their products on the same terms as those agreed upon with the United States."

Here you have in brief the whole policy. I might end here, satisfied with having reminded you of these facts, which probably you had forgotten. Obedience to the laws—that is, laws drawn for protection of all—is the common law of all civilised communities, without which men would soon become demoralised. Can anybody object to that condition? Probably many of you here recollect reading those interesting letters from the Congo which were written by an English clerk in charge of an English factory. They ended with the cry of "Let us alone." In few words he meant to say, "We are doing very well as we are, we do not wish to be protected, and least of all taxed—therefore, let us alone. Our customers, the natives, are satisfied with us. The native chiefs are friendly and in accord with us; the disturbances, if any occur, are local; they are not general, and they right themselves quickly enough, for the trader cannot exist here if he is not just and kind in his dealings. The obstreperous and violent white is left to himself and ruin. Therefore, let us alone." Most heartily do I echo this cry; but unfortunately the European nations will not heed this cry; they think that some mode of government is necessary to curb those inclined to be refractory, and if there is at present a necessity to exhibit judicial power and to restrict evil-minded and ill-conditioned whites, as the Congo basin becomes more and more populated this necessity will be still more apparent. At the same time, if power appears on the Congo with an arbitrary and unfeeling front—with a disposition to tax and levy burdensome tariffs just as trade begins to be established—the outlook for enterprise becomes dismal and dark indeed.[8] (Hear, hear.) * * *

No part of Africa, look where I might, appeared so promising to me as this neglected tenth part of the continent. I have often fancied myself—when I had nothing to do better than dream—gazing from some lofty height, and looking down upon this square compact patch of 800,000,000 acres, with its 80,000 native towns, its population of 40,000,000 souls, its 17,000 miles of river waters, and its 30,000 square miles of lakes, all lying torpid, lifeless, inert, soaked in brutishness and bestiality, and I have never yet descended from that airy perch in the empyrean and touched earth but I have felt a purpose glow in me to strive to do something to awaken it into life and movement, and I have sometimes half fancied that the face of aged Livingstone,[9] vague and indistinct as it were, shone through the warm, hazy atmosphere, with a benignant smile encouraging me in my purpose. * * *

Yet, though examined from every point of view, a study of the Upper Congo and its capabilities produces these exciting arrays of figures and possibilities, I would not pay a two-shilling piece for it all so long as it remains as it is. It will absorb easily the revenue of the wealthiest nation in Europe without any return. I would personally one hundred times over prefer a snug little freehold in a suburb of Manchester to being the owner of the 1,300,000 English square miles of the Congo basin if it is to remain as inaccessible as it is to-day, or if it is to be blocked by that fearful tariff-loving nation, the Portuguese. (Hear, hear.) But if I were assured that the Lower Congo would remain free, and the flag of the Association guaranteed its freedom, I would if

8. The right of the International Association to govern the Congo was eventually ended in 1908, following widespread protests against the regime's brutality.

9. David Livingstone (1813–1873), Scottish explorer and missionary. His expeditions into central Africa, in search of the source of the Nile River, were heavily publicized; when Livingstone "disappeared" in the course of what proved to be his last expedition, Stanley, then a correspondent for the *New York Herald*, was sent to find him. The two men met on the banks of Lake Tanganyika in East Africa in 1871; Stanley published an account of their meeting in *How I Found Livingstone* (1872).

I were able build that railway myself—build it solid and strong—and connect the Lower Congo with the Upper Congo, perfectly satisfied that I should be followed by the traders and colonists of all nations. * * * The Portuguese have had nearly 400 years given them to demonstrate to the world what they could do with the river whose mouth they discovered, and they have been proved to be incapable to do any good with it, and now civilisation is inclined to say to them, "Stand off from this broad highway into the regions beyond—(cheers); let others who are not paralytic strive to do what they can with it to bring it within the number of accessible markets. There are 40,000,000 of naked people beyond that gateway, and the cotton spinners of Manchester are waiting to clothe them. Rochdale and Preston women are waiting for the word to weave them warm blue and crimson savelist. Birmingham foundries are glowing with the red metal that shall presently be made into ironwork in every fashion and shape for them, and the trinkets that shall adorn those dusky bosoms; and the ministers of Christ are zealous to bring them, the poor benighted heathen, into the Christian fold." (Cheers.)

Mr JACOB BRIGHT, M.P., who was received with loud cheers, said: I have listened with extreme interest to one of the ablest, one of the most eloquent addresses which have ever been delivered in this city—(cheers); and I have heard with uncommon pleasure the views of a man whose ability, whose splendid force of character, whose remarkable heroism, have given him a world-wide reputation. (Cheers.) * * *

Mr GRAFTON, M.P., moved:—

> That the best thanks of this meeting be and are hereby given to Mr H. M. Stanley for his address to the members of the Chamber, and for the interesting information conveyed by him respecting the Congo and prospects of international trade on the West Coast and interior of Africa.

He remarked that Mr Stanley's name was already enrolled in the pages of history, and would be handed down to posterity with the names of the greatest benefactors of our species, such as Columbus, who had opened out the pathways of the world. Long might Mr Stanley be spared to witness the benefit of his arduous and beneficent labours. (Cheers.)

END OF *HEART AND DARKNESS* AND ITS TIME

RESPONSES

Chinua Achebe: An Image of Africa[1]

It was a fine autumn morning at the beginning of this academic year such as encouraged friendliness to passing strangers. Brisk youngsters were hurrying in all directions, many of them obviously freshmen in their first flush of enthusiasm. An older man, going the same way as I, turned and remarked to me how very young they came these

1. More than any other author, Chinua Achebe (b. 1930) is responsible for creating a consciousness of modern African writing in the West. In 1958, Achebe published *Things Fall Apart*, a novel that has since become the single most widely read text by an African author. Achebe's demand for Western recognition of African historicity in this work is often read as a direct response to Conrad's *Heart of Darkness*, the tale of a journey into Africa, toward savagery, away from both civilization and civilized behavior; Achebe offers a critique of Conrad's novella directly in his essay, *An Image of Africa*. In later novels such as *No Longer at Ease* (1960) and *A Man of the People* (1966), Achebe concerns himself less with Africa's colonial past than with the first years of its independence.

days. I agreed. Then he asked me if I was a student too. I said no, I was a teacher. What did I teach? African literature. Now that was funny, he said, because he never had thought of Africa as having that kind of stuff, you know. By this time I was walking much faster. "Oh well," I heard him say finally, behind me, "I guess I have to take your course to find out."

A few weeks later I received two very touching letters from high school children in Yonkers, New York, who—bless their teacher—had just read *Things Fall Apart*. One of them was particularly happy to learn about the customs and superstitions of an African tribe.

I propose to draw from these rather trivial encounters rather heavy conclusions which at first sight might seem somewhat out of proportion to them: But only at first sight.

The young fellow from Yonkers, perhaps partly on account of his age but I believe also for much deeper and more serious reasons, is obviously unaware that the life of his own tribesmen in Yonkers, New York, is full of odd customs and superstitions and, like everybody else in his culture, imagines that he needs a trip to Africa to encounter those things.

The other person being fully my own age could not be excused on the grounds of his years. Ignorance might be a more likely reason; but here again I believe that something more willful than a mere lack of information was at work. For did not that erudite British historian and Regius Professor at Oxford, Hugh Trevor Roper, pronounce a few years ago that African history did not exist?

If there is something in these utterances more than youthful experience, more than a lack of factual knowledge, what is it? Quite simply it is the desire—one might indeed say the need—in Western psychology to set Africa up as a foil in Europe, a place of negations at once remote and vaguely familiar in comparison with which Europe's own state of spiritual grace will be manifest.

This need is not new: which should relieve us of considerable responsibility and perhaps make us even willing to look at this phenomenon dispassionately. I have neither the desire nor, indeed, the competence to do so with the tools of the social and biological sciences. But, I can respond, as a novelist, to one famous book of European fiction, Joseph Conrad's *Heart of Darkness*, which better than any other work I know displays that Western desire and need which I have just spoken about. Of course, there are whole libraries of books devoted to the same purpose, but most of them are so obvious and so crude that few people worry about them today. Conrad, on the other hand, is undoubtedly one of the great stylists of modern fiction and a good storyteller into the bargain. His contribution therefore falls automatically into a different class—permanent literature—read and taught and constantly evaluated by serious academics. *Heart of Darkness* is indeed so secure today that a leading Conrad scholar has numbered it "among the half-dozen greatest short novels in the English language."[2] I will return to this critical option in due course because it may seriously modify my earlier suppositions about who may or may not be guilty in the things of which I will now speak.

Heart of Darkness projects the image of Africa as "the other world," the antithesis of Europe and therefore of civilization, a place where a man's vaunted intelligence and refinement are finally mocked by triumphant bestiality. The book opens on the River Thames, tranquil, resting peacefully "at the decline of day after ages of good service done to the race that peopled its banks." But the actual story takes place on the River

2. Albert J. Guerard, Introduction to *Heart of Darkness* (New York: New American Library, 1950), p. 9 [Achebe's note].

Congo, the very antithesis of the Thames. The River Congo is quite decidedly not a River Emeritus. It has rendered no service and enjoys no old-age pension. We are told that "going up that river was like travelling back to the earliest beginning of the world."

Is Conrad saying then that these two rivers are very different, one good, the other bad? Yes, but that is not the real point. What actually worries Conrad is the lurking hint of kinship, of common ancestry. For the Thames, too, "has been one of the dark places of the earth." It conquered its darkness, of course, and is now at peace. But if it were to visit its primordial relative, the Congo, it would run the terrible risk of hearing grotesque, suggestive echoes of its own forgotten darkness, and of falling victim to an avenging recrudescence of the mindless frenzy of the first beginnings.

I am not going to waste your time with examples of Conrad's famed evocation of the African atmosphere. In the final consideration it amounts to no more than a steady, ponderous, fake-ritualistic repetition of two sentences, one about silence and the other about frenzy. An example of the former is "It was the stillness of an implacable force brooding over an inscrutable intention" and of the latter, "The steamer toiled along slowly on the edge of a black and incomprehensible frenzy." Of course, there is a judicious change of adjective from time to time so that instead of "inscrutable," for example, you might have "unspeakable," etc., etc.

The eagle-eyed English critic, F. R. Leavis, drew attention nearly thirty years ago to Conrad's "adjectival insistence upon inexpressible and incomprehensible mystery." That insistence must not be dismissed lightly, as many Conrad critics have tended to do, as a mere stylistic flaw. For it raises serious questions of artistic good faith. When a writer, while pretending to record scenes, incidents and their impact, is in reality engaged in inducing hypnotic stupor in his readers through a bombardment of emotive words and other forms of trickery much more has to be at stake than stylistic felicity. Generally, normal readers are well armed to detect and resist such underhand activity. But Conrad chose his subject well—one which was guaranteed not to put him in conflict with the psychological predisposition of his readers or raise the need for him to contend with their resistance. He chose the role of purveyor of comforting myths.

The most interesting and revealing passages in *Heart of Darkness* are, however, about people. I must quote a long passage from the middle of the story in which representatives of Europe in a steamer going down the Congo encounter the denizens of Africa:

> We were wanderers on a prehistoric earth, on an earth that wore the aspect of an unknown planet. We could have fancied ourselves the first of men taking possession of an accursed inheritance, to be subdued at the cost of profound anguish and of excessive toil. But suddenly, as we struggled round a bend, there would be a glimpse of rush walls, of peaked grass-roofs, a burst of yells, a whirl of black limbs, a mass of hands clapping, of feet stamping, of bodies swaying, of eyes rolling, under the droop of heavy and motionless foliage. The steamer toiled along slowly on the edge of a black and incomprehensible frenzy. The prehistoric man was cursing us, praying to us, welcoming us—who could tell? We were cut off from the comprehension of our surroundings; we glided past like phantoms, wondering and secretly appalled, as sane men would be before an enthusiastic outbreak in a madhouse. We could not remember because we were travelling in the night of first ages, of those ages that are gone, leaving hardly a sign—and no memories.
>
> The earth seemed unearthly. We are accustomed to look upon the shackled form of a conquered monster, but there—there you could look at a thing monstrous and free. It was unearthly, and the men were—No, they were not inhuman. Well, you know, that was the worst of it—this suspicion of their not being inhuman. It would come slowly to one. They

> howled and leaped, and spun, and made horrid faces; but what thrilled you was just the thought of your remote kinship with this wild and passionate uproar. Ugly. Yes, it was ugly enough; but if you were man enough you would admit to yourself that there was in you just the faintest trace of a response to the terrible frankness of that noise, a dim suspicion of there being a meaning in it which you—you so remote from the night of first ages—could comprehend.

Herein lies the meaning of *Heart of Darkness* and the fascination it holds over the Western mind: "What thrilled you was just the thought of their humanity—like yours. . . . Ugly."

Having shown us Africa in the mass, Conrad then zeros in on a specific example, giving us one of his rare descriptions of an African who is not just limbs or rolling eyes:

> And between whiles I had to look after the savage who was fireman. He was an improved specimen; he could fire up a vertical boiler. He was there below me, and, upon my word, to look at him was as edifying as seeing a dog in a parody of breeches and a feather hat, walking on his hind legs. A few months of training had done for that really fine chap. He squinted at the steam gauge and at the water gauge with an evident effort of intrepidity—and he had filed his teeth, too, the poor devil, and the wool of his pate shaved into queer patterns, and three ornamental scars on each of his cheeks. He ought to have been clapping his hands and stamping his feet on the bank, instead of which he was hard at work, a thrall to strange witchcraft, full of improving knowledge.

As everybody knows, Conrad is a romantic on the side. He might not exactly admire savages clapping their hands and stamping their feet but they have at least the merit of being in their place, unlike this dog in a parody of breeches. For Conrad, things (and persons) being in their place is of the utmost importance.

Towards the end of the story, Conrad lavishes great attention quite unexpectedly on an African woman who has obviously been some kind of mistress to Mr. Kurtz and now presides (if I may be permitted a little imitation of Conrad) like a formidable mystery over the inexorable imminence of his departure:

> She was savage and superb, wild-eyed and magnificent . . . She stood looking at us without a stir and like the wilderness itself, with an air of brooding over an inscrutable purpose.

This Amazon is drawn in considerable detail, albeit of a predictable nature, for two reasons. First, she is in her place and so can win Conrad's special brand of approval; and second, she fulfills a structural requirement of the story; she is a savage counterpart to the refined, European woman with whom the story will end:

> She came forward, all in black with a pale head, floating towards me in the dusk. She was in mourning. . . . She took both my hands in hers and murmured, "I had heard you were coming" . . . She had a mature capacity for fidelity, for belief, for suffering.

The difference in the attitude of the novelist to these two women is conveyed in too many direct and subtle ways to need elaboration. But perhaps the most significant difference is the one implied in the author's bestowal of human expression to the one and the withholding of it from the other. It is clearly not part of Conrad's purpose to confer language on the "rudimentary souls" of Africa. They only "exchanged short grunting phrases" even among themselves but mostly they were too busy with their frenzy. There are two occasions in the book, however, when Conrad departs somewhat from his practice and confers speech, even English speech, on the savages. The first occurs when cannibalism gets the better of them:

> "Catch 'im," he snapped, with a bloodshot widening of his eyes and a flash of sharp white teeth—"catch 'im. Give 'im to us." "To you, eh?" I asked; "what would you do with them?" "Eat 'im!" he said curtly . . .

The other occasion is the famous announcement:

> Mistah Kurtz—he dead.

At first sight, these instances might be mistaken for unexpected acts of generosity from Conrad. In reality, they constitute some of his best assaults. In the case of the cannibals, the incomprehensible grunts that had thus far served them for speech suddenly proved inadequate for Conrad's purpose of letting the European glimpse the unspeakable craving in their hearts. Weighing the necessity for consistency in the portrayal of the dumb brutes against the sensational advantages of securing their conviction by clear, unambiguous evidence issuing out of their own mouth, Conrad chose the latter. As for the announcement of Mr. Kurtz's death by the "insolent black head of the doorway," what better or more appropriate *finis* could be written to the horror story of that wayward child of civilization who willfully had given his soul to the powers of darkness and "taken a high seat amongst the devils of the land" than the proclamation of his physical death by the forces he had joined?

It might be contended, of course, that the attitude to the African in *Heart of Darkness* is not Conrad's but that of his fictional narrator, Marlow, and that far from endorsing it Conrad might indeed be holding it up to irony and criticism. Certainly, Conrad appears to go to considerable pains to set up layers of insulation between himself and the moral universe of his story. He has, for example, a narrator behind a narrator. The primary narrator is Marlow but his account is given to us through the filter of a second, shadowy person. But if Conrad's intention is to draw a *cordon sanitaire* between himself and the moral and psychological malaise of his narrator, his care seems to me totally wasted because he neglects to hint however subtly or tentatively at an alternative frame of reference by which we may judge the actions and opinions of his characters. It would not have been beyond Conrad's power to make that provision if he had thought it necessary. Marlow seems to me to enjoy Conrad's complete confidence—a feeling reinforced by the close similarities between their careers.

Marlow comes through to us not only as a witness of truth, but one holding those advanced and humane views appropriate to the English liberal tradition which required all Englishmen of decency to be deeply shocked by atrocities in Bulgaria or the Congo of King Leopold of the Belgians or wherever. Thus Marlow is able to toss out such bleeding-heart sentiments as these:

> They were all dying slowly—it was very clear. They were not enemies, they were not criminals, they were nothing earthly now—nothing but black shadows of disease and starvation, lying confusedly in the greenish gloom. Brought from all the recesses of the coast in all the legality of time contracts, lost in uncongenial surroundings, fed on unfamiliar food, they sickened, became inefficient, and were then allowed to crawl away and rest.

The kind of liberalism espoused here by Marlow/Conrad touched all the best minds of the age in England, Europe, and America. It took different forms in the minds of different people but almost always managed to sidestep the ultimate question of equality between white people and black people. That extraordinary missionary, Albert Schweitzer, who sacrificed brilliant careers in music and theology in Europe for a life of service to Africans in much the same area as Conrad writes about, epitomizes the ambivalence. In a comment which I have often quoted but must quote one last time Schweitzer says: "The African is indeed my brother but my junior brother." And so he proceeded to build a hospital appropriate to the needs of junior brothers with standards of hygiene reminiscent of medical practice in the days before the germ theory of disease came into being. Naturally, he became a sensation in Europe and America. Pilgrims flocked, and I believe still flock even after he has passed on, to witness the prodigious miracle in Lamberene, on the edge of the primeval forest.

Conrad's liberalism would not take him quite as far as Schweitzer's, though. He would not use the word "brother" however qualified; the farthest he would go was "kinship." When Marlow's African helmsman falls down with a spear in his heart he gives his white master one final disquieting look.

> And the intimate profundity of that look he gave me when he received his hurt remains to this day in my memory—like a claim of distant kinship affirmed in a supreme moment.

It is important to note that Conrad, careful as ever with his words, is not talking so much about *distant kinship* as about someone *laying a claim* on it. The black man lays a claim on the white man which is well-nigh intolerable. It is the laying of this claim which frightens and at the same time fascinates Conrad, ". . . the thought of their humanity—like yours . . . Ugly."

The point of my observations should be quite clear by now, namely, that *Conrad was a bloody racist*. That this simple truth is glossed over in criticism of his work is due to the fact that white racism against Africa is such a normal way of thinking that its manifestations go completely undetected. Students of *Heart of Darkness* will often tell you that Conrad is concerned not so much with Africa as with the deterioration of one European mind caused by solitude and sickness. They will point out to you that Conrad is, if anything, less charitable to the Europeans in the story than he is to the natives. A Conrad student told me in Scotland last year that Africa is merely a setting for the disintegration of the mind of Mr. Kurtz.

Which is partly the point: Africa as setting and backdrop which eliminates the African as human factor. Africa as a metaphysical battlefield devoid of all recognizable humanity, into which the wandering European enters at his peril. Of course, there is a preposterous and perverse kind of arrogance in thus reducing Africa to the role of props for the breakup of one petty European mind. But that is not even the point. The real question is the dehumanization of Africa and Africans which this age-long attitude has fostered and continues to foster in the world. And the question is whether a novel which celebrates this dehumanization, which depersonalizes a portion of the human race, can be called a great work of art. My answer is: No, it cannot. I would not call that man an artist, for example, who composes an eloquent instigation to one people to fall upon another and destroy them. No matter how striking his imagery or how beautiful his cadences fall such a man is no more a great artist than another may be called a priest who reads the mass backwards or a physician who poisons his patients. All those men in Nazi Germany who lent their talent to the service of virulent racism whether in science, philosophy or the arts have generally and rightly been condemned for their perversions. The time is long overdue for taking a hard look at the work of creative artists who apply their talents, alas often considerable as in the case of Conrad, to set people against people. This, I take it, is what Yevtushenko is after when he tells us that a poet cannot be a slave trader at the same time, and gives the striking example of Arthur Rimbaud who was fortunately honest enough to give up any pretenses to poetry when he opted for slave trading. For poetry surely can only be on the side of man's deliverance and not his enslavement; for the brotherhood and unity of all mankind and against the doctrines of Hitler's master races or Conrad's "rudimentary souls."

Last year was the 50th anniversary of Conrad's death. He was born in 1857, the very year in which the first Anglican missionaries were arriving among my own people in Nigeria. It was certainly not his fault that he lived his life at a time when the reputation of the black man was at a particularly low level. But even after due allowances have been made for all the influences of contemporary prejudice on his sensibility, there remains still in Conrad's attitude a residue of antipathy to black people which his peculiar psychology alone can explain. His own account of his first encounter with a black man is very revealing:

> A certain enormous buck nigger encountered in Haiti fixed my conception of blind, furious, unreasoning rage, as manifested in the human animal to the end of my days. Of the nigger I used to dream for years afterwards.

Certainly, Conrad had a problem with niggers. His inordinate love of that word itself should be of interest to psychoanalysts. Sometimes his fixation on blackness is equally interesting as when he gives us this brief description:

> A black figure stood up, strode on long black legs, waving long black arms.[3]

as though we might expect a black figure striding along on black legs to have *white* arms! But so unrelenting is Conrad's obsession.

As a matter of interest Conrad gives us in *A Personal Record* what amounts to a companion piece to the buck nigger of Haiti. At the age of sixteen Conrad encountered his first Englishman in Europe. He calls him "my unforgettable Englishman" and describes him in the following manner:

> [his] calves exposed to the public gaze . . . dazzled the beholder by the splendor of their marble-like condition and their rich tone of young ivory . . . The light of a headlong, exalted satisfaction with the world of men . . . illumined his face . . . and triumphant eyes. In passing he cast a glance of kindly curiosity and a friendly gleam of big, sound, shiny teeth . . . his white calves twinkled sturdily.[4]

Irrational love and irrational hate jostling together in the heart of that tormented man. But whereas irrational love may at worst engender foolish acts of indiscretion, irrational hate can endanger the life of the community. Naturally, Conrad is a dream for psychoanalytic critics. Perhaps the most detailed study of him in this direction is by Bernard C. Meyer, M.D. In this lengthy book, Dr. Meyer follows every conceivable lead (and sometimes inconceivable ones) to explain Conrad. As an example, he gives us long disquisitions on the significance of hair and hair-cutting in Conrad. And yet not even one word is spared for his attitude to black people. Not even the discussion of Conrad's antisemitism was enough to spark off in Dr. Meyer's mind those other dark and explosive thoughts. Which only leads one to surmise that Western psychoanalysts must regard the kind of racism displayed by Conrad as absolutely normal despite the profoundly important work done by Frantz Fanon in the psychiatric hospitals of French Algeria.

Whatever Conrad's problems were, you might say he is now safely dead. Quite true. Unfortunately, his heart of darkness plagues us still. Which is why an offensive and totally deplorable book can be described by a serious scholar as "among the half dozen greatest short novels in the English language," and why it is today perhaps the

3. Jonah Raskin, *The Mythology of Imperialism* (New York: Random House, 1971), p. 143 [Achebe's note].
4. Bernard C. Meyer, M.D., *Joseph Conrad: A Psychoanalytic Biography* (Princeton, N.J.: Princeton University Press, 1967), p. 30 [Achebe's note].

most commonly prescribed novel in the twentieth-century literature courses in our own English Department here. Indeed the time is long overdue for a hard look at things.

There are two probable grounds on which what I have said so far may be contested. The first is that it is no concern of fiction to please people about whom it is written. I will go along with that. But I am not talking about pleasing people. I am talking about a book which parades in the most vulgar fashion prejudices and insults from which a section of mankind has suffered untold agonies and atrocities in the past and continues to do so in many ways and many places today. I am talking about a story in which the very humanity of black people is called in question. It seems to me totally inconceivable that great art or even good art could possibly reside in such unwholesome surroundings.

Secondly, I may be challenged on the grounds of actuality. Conrad, after all, sailed down the Congo in 1890 when my own father was still a babe in arms, and recorded what he saw. How could I stand up in 1975, fifty years after his death and purport to contradict him? My answer is that as a sensible man I will not accept just any traveller's tales solely on the grounds that I have not made the journey myself: I will not trust the evidence even of a man's very eyes when I suspect them to be as jaundiced as Conrad's. And we also happen to know that Conrad was, in the words of his biographer, Bernard C. Meyer, "notoriously inaccurate in the rendering of his own history."[5]

But more important by far is the abundant testimony about Conrad's savages which we could gather if we were so inclined from other sources and which might lead us to think that these people must have had other occupations besides merging into the evil forest or materializing out of it simply to plague Marlow and his dispirited band. For as it happened, soon after Conrad had written his book an event of far greater consequence was taking place in the art world of Europe. This is how Frank Willett, a British art historian, describes it:

> Gaugin had gone to Tahiti, the most extravagant individual act of turning to a non-European culture in the decades immediately before and after 1900, when European artists were avid for new artistic experiences, but it was only about 1904–5 that African art began to make its distinctive impact. One piece is still identifiable; it is a mask that had been given to Maurice Vlaminck in 1905. He records that Derain was "speechless" and "stunned" when he saw it, bought it from Vlaminck and in turn showed it to Picasso and Matisse, who were also greatly affected by it. Ambroise Vollard then borrowed it and had it cast in bronze . . . The revolution of twentieth century art was under way![6]

The mask in question was made by other savages living just north of Conrad's River Congo. They have a name, the Fang people, and are without a doubt among the world's greatest masters of the sculptured form. As you might have guessed, the event to which Frank Willett refers marked the beginning of cubism and the infusion of new life into European art that had run completely out of strength.

The point of all this is to suggest that Conrad's picture of the people of the Congo seems grossly inadequate even at the height of their subjection to the ravages of King Leopold's International Association for the Civilization of Central Africa. Travellers with closed minds can tell us little except about themselves. But even those not blinkered, like Conrad, with xenophobia, can be astonishingly blind.

5. *Ibid.*, p. 30 [Achebe's note].

6. Frank Willett, *African Art* (New York: Praeger, 1971), pp. 35–36 [Achebe's note].

Let me digress a little here. One of the greatest and most intrepid travellers of all time, Marco Polo, journeyed to the Far East from the Mediterranean in the thirteenth century and spent twenty years in the court of Kublai Khan in China. On his return to Venice he set down in his book entitled *Description of the World* his impressions of the peoples and places and customs he had seen. There are at least two extraordinary omissions in his account. He says nothing about the art of printing unknown as yet in Europe but in full flower in China. He either did not notice it at all or if he did, failed to see what use Europe could possibly have for it. Whatever reason, Europe had to wait another hundred years for Gutenberg. But even more spectacular was Marco Polo's omission of any reference to the Great Wall of China nearly 4000 miles long and already more than 1000 years old at the time of his visit. Again, he may not have seen it; but the Great Wall of China is the only structure built by man which is visible from the moon![7] Indeed, travellers can be blind.

As I said earlier, Conrad did not originate the image of Africa which we find in his book. It was and is the dominant image of Africa in the Western imagination and Conrad merely brought the peculiar gifts of his own mind to bear on it. For reasons which can certainly use close psychological inquiry, the West seems to suffer deep anxieties about the precariousness of its civilization and to have a need for constant reassurance by comparing it with Africa. If Europe, advancing in civilization, could cast a backward glance periodically at Africa trapped in primordial barbarity, it could say with faith and feeling: There go I but for the grace of God. Africa is to Europe as the picture is to Dorian Gray—a carrier onto whom the master unloads his physical and moral deformities so that he may go forward, erect and immaculate. Consequently, Africa is something to be avoided just as the picture has to be hidden away to safeguard the man's jeopardous integrity. Keep away from Africa, or else! Mr. Kurtz of *Heart of Darkness* should have heeded that warning and the prowling horror in his heart would have kept its place, chained to its lair. But he foolishly exposed himself to the wild irresistible allure of the jungle and lo! the darkness found him out.

In my original conception of this talk I had thought to conclude it nicely on an appropriately positive note in which I would suggest from my privileged position in African and Western culture some advantages the West might derive from Africa once it rid its mind of old prejudices and began to look at Africa not through a haze of distortions and cheap mystification but quite simply as a continent of people—not angels, but not rudimentary souls either—just people, often highly gifted people and often strikingly successful in their enterprise with life and society. But as I thought more about the stereotype image, about its grip and pervasiveness, about the willful tenacity with which the West holds it to its heart; when I thought of your television and the cinema and newspapers, about books read in schools and out of school, of churches preaching to empty pews about the need to send help to the heathen in Africa, I realized that no easy optimism was possible. And there is something totally wrong in offering bribes to the West in return for its good opinion of Africa. Ultimately, the abandonment of unwholesome thoughts must be its own and only reward. Although I have used the word *willful* a few times in this talk to characterize the West's view of Africa it may well be that what is happening at this stage is more akin to reflex action than calculated malice. Which does not make the situation more, but less, hopeful. Let me give you one last and really minor example of what I mean.

7. About the omission of the Great Wall of China I am indebted to *The Journey of Marco Polo* as recreated by artist Michael Foreman, published by *Pegasus* Magazine, 1974 [Achebe's note].

Last November the *Christian Science Monitor* carried an interesting article written by its Education Editor on the serious psychological and learning problems faced by little children who speak one language at home and then go to school where something else is spoken. It was a wide-ranging article taking in Spanish-speaking children in this country, the children of migrant Italian workers in Germany, the quadrilingual phenomenon in Malaysia and so on. And all this while the article speaks unequivocally about *language*. But then out of the blue sky comes this:

> In London there is an enormous immigration of children who speak Indian or Nigerian dialects, or some other native language.[8]

I believe that the introduction of *dialects*, which is technically erroneous in the context, is almost a reflex action caused by an instinctive desire of the writer to downgrade the discussion to the level of Africa and India. And this is quite comparable to Conrad's withholding of language from his rudimentary souls. Language is too grand for these chaps; let's give them dialects. In all this business a lot of violence is inevitably done to words and their meaning. Look at the phrase "native language" in the above excerpt. Surely the only native language possible in London is Cockney English. But our writer obviously means something else—something Indians and Africans speak.

Perhaps a change will come. Perhaps this is the time when it can begin, when the high optimism engendered by the breathtaking achievements of Western science and industry is giving way to doubt and even confusion. There is just the possibility that Western man may begin to look seriously at the achievements of other people. I read in the papers the other day a suggestion that what America needs at this time is somehow to bring back the extended family. And I saw in my mind's eye future African Peace Corps Volunteers coming to help you set up the system.

Seriously, although the work which needs to be done may appear too daunting, I believe that it is not one day too soon to begin. And where better than at a University?

Gang of Four: We Live As We Dream, Alone[1]

Everybody is in too many pieces
No man's land surrounds our desires
To crack the shell we mix with others
Some lie in the arms of lovers

The city is the place to be
With no money you go crazy
I need an occupation
You have to pay for satisfaction

We live as we dream, alone
To crack this shell we mix with others

8. *Christian Science Monitor*, Nov. 25, 1974, p. 11 [Achebe's note].

1. In 1976 the Sex Pistols set off the British punk revolution with their first single, *Anarchy in the U.K.* The Gang of Four is one of many bands that arose during the early years of punk, when a wide range of musical possibilities seemed open to anyone with a guitar. The Gang of Four's music combines the assaultive sound of punk bands with an infectious dance sensibility—lacing this unlikely hybrid with neo-Marxist lyrics about consumerism and labor. *We Live As We Dream, Alone*, from their 1982 album *Songs of the Free*, takes a famous line from *Heart of Darkness* and makes it the cry of alienated labor, thereby reframing Conrad's message for a nation dominated by the conservative policies of Thatcherism.

Some flirt with fascism
Some lie in the arms of lovers

We live as we dream, alone
(repeat)

Everybody is in too many pieces
No man's land surrounds me
Without money we'll all go crazy

Man and woman need to work
It helps to define ourselves
We were not born in isolation
But sometimes it seems that way

We live as we dream, alone
(repeat)

We live as we dream, alone
The space between our work and its product
Some fall into fatalism
As if it started out this way

We live as we dream, alone
(repeat)

We live as we dream, alone
We were not born in isolation
But sometimes it seems that way
The space between our work and its product
As if it must always be this way

With our money we'll. . . .

Bernard Shaw

1856–1950

Few writers so dominate their times that their names become household words, let alone, as with (George) Bernard Shaw, their initials: three letters as identifiable during his lifetime as a brand name or a logo is today. G.B.S. was the shorthand code for one of the most celebrated and controversial writers of the twentieth century—a novelist, music critic, playwright, pamphleteer, political theorist, educator, and essayist. Shaw's life arc stretched a venerable ninety-four years from the midpoint of the nineteenth century to the midpoint of the twentieth. In his very long and almost unbelievably prolific career Shaw articulated most of the new ideas associated with modernity, whether in the dramatic form of the plays he is best remembered for today, or in the philosophical and political essays for which he was equally famed during his lifetime. He was awarded the Nobel Prize in Literature in 1925, although in characteristically defiant fashion, he refused to accept the money, saying that the honor "is greater than is good for my spiritual health." By the same token, when the British government tried to award him the Order of Merit, he riposted, "I have already conferred it upon myself." So well known was he, and so influential as an iconoclast, that the adjective "Shavian" sprang from his last name, denoting a worldview of exuberant and profound contradictions, where opposing ideas are brought into comic, and ultimately serious, artistic and social synthesis.

A major force on the London stage and in British cultural life, Shaw was not conventionally British. He was Irish, born in Dublin in 1856, the third child of George Carr Shaw and Bessie Gurly. Brought up in "an awful little kennel with primitive sanitary arrangements" on Synge Street in Dublin, Shaw had a startlingly unusual childhood: his father, an alchoholic clerk on his way down the social scale, had permitted Shaw's mother Bessie to bring her vocal coach and lover, Vandeleur Lee, to live in the family house. As Shaw once remarked, Bessie "was simply not a wife or mother at all." Bessie's brother Walter Gurly, a ship's surgeon, was another part of the menage; an ebullient man who electrifyingly proclaimed his idiosyncratic views of the Bible, Gurly became Shaw's "third father." The eccentricities of his upbringing, with three fathers and an absentee mother, led to Shaw's firm belief that parents and children were inevitably mismatched, and to his strong activism for equal rights for all members of the family constellation.

Shaw's experiments with schooling were abysmal failures, largely because only vocational training was available to a family of his means, and by the age of fifteen he had seen his last of school, which he likened to a jail designed "to keep the little devils locked up where they cannot drive their mothers mad." What took the place of formal schooling was Shaw's self-education as a voracious reader of Homer, Shakespeare, Shelley, Dickens, and much popular literature—"all normal people require both classics and trash," he wrote—and his constant immersion in the rich musical life of Dublin. In 1873 his "father" Vandeleur Lee left for London to become a musical impresario, followed soon after by Bessie Shaw and young Bernard's two sisters, leaving Shaw essentially abandoned in Dublin. Thrown back on his own resources, he worked miserably as a clerk and lived in a rooming house, teaching himself to play the piano and organizing musicales with other clerks in their off hours. So acute did his misery grow that in 1876 he decided to go to London himself, and moved in with his mother, Lee, and his sister Lucy.

The move to London altered everything for Shaw. London was the cornucopia that the deprived and impoverished colonial city of Dublin was not, and Shaw was simultaneously intoxicated with its grandeur and disillusioned by its poverty and inequalities. He recognized London as "the literary center of the English language," and he quickly established himself as a budding essayist and critic, and a would-be playwright, while also writing four novels that received rejection notices labeling them "sordid" and "perverse." The hub of Shaw's endeavors was the British Museum's famous reading room and library. Sitting at his assigned carrel (unbeknownst to him, Lenin sat nearby), Shaw read large numbers of books, among them Karl Marx's *Das Kapital*, a book that ironically had been written in that very same reading room. "It was the only book that ever turned me upside down," Shaw confessed, and he began attending meetings of every radical society he could find, until the Fabian Society claimed his loyalty. He delivered a paper before the group in 1884, beginning a long career as a political theorist and polemicist, writing essays such as *The Intelligent Woman's Guide to Socialism and Capitalism*.

Shaw became a charismatic public lecturer on social and political topics, and he began to write art and music criticism. In vivid essays he argued that the innovations of such radical composers as Wagner were parallel to the radical changes in politics and social arrangements Shaw also championed. Like James Joyce, he fervently admired Henrik Ibsen, the Norwegian playwright whose plays seemed to sound the death knell for Victorian social certainties. Ibsen's *The Doll House*, for example, dramatized the growing movement for the emancipation of women, a cause Shaw adamantly supported. Ibsen's drama pointed the way for Shaw's own development into a great playwright: he realized through Ibsen's example that he need not adopt an "art for art's sake" philosophy, as the reigning vision of the *fin de siècle* described its ideal; instead, art could be fully engaged in ideas, and could have as its mission nothing less than changing the world.

Shaw struggled for seven years to break free of Victorian dramatic constraints and the rigid structures of nineteenth-century drama, until in 1895 he had created his first play, *Widower's Houses*. While the play is not particularly memorable, its subtitle does give a sense of the special goals of Shavian drama at this early stage: "An Original Didactic Realist Play in Three Acts, Designed to Induce People to Vote on the Progressive Side at the Next County Council in London." Art for art's sake, indeed. "Why would art if it was just for art's sake interest me at all?" Shaw asked.

The political play of ideas was the form Shaw crafted and perfected over the next thirty years, drawing on a rich history of political thought and philosophical inquiry. He borrowed from British thinkers like Carlyle and from the German philosopher Friedrich Nietzsche, whose controversial writings argued that human beings make their own truth and thus create their own values. In plays like *Man and Superman*, *Androcles and the Lion*, *Arms and the Man*, and *The Doctor's Dilemma*, Shaw staged debates over values that only seem to be universal or eternal, likening the contemporary values of Edwardian Britain to outmoded garments that his society should change. Shaw was a political iconoclast whose democratic ideals were meshed with an unsentimental acknowledgment of human nature. He wanted the best cultural goods—education, art, freedom from drudgery—to be distributed equally to all without regard to sex, class, or race. However, he never romanticized the working class nor any other political group, and, never a utopian, Shaw always argued that lasting change should gradually be pressed with pragmatism, common sense, and energetic wit.

The "Shavian" element of all the plays, and of Shaw's essays and reviews, resides in an unwillingness to propose a simple answer to social problems, or to establish a clear-cut "right" and "wrong." Shaw's thinking is dialectical in style: ideas bounce and ricochet off one another, and things happen in his plays by means of a quicksilver collision of ideas that yields a new and unexpected synthesis. Shaw's characters are not simply ideas dressed up to look like people; instead, the characters embody the ever-changing and often arbitrary flow of ideas as these come to life in real, quirky, individual human beings, embroiled in verbal duels. One of his characters puts it this way: "I want to be an active verb." There are no outright villains, and no pure heroes or heroines, in a Shaw play: for example, while ruthless capitalism is a social evil in Shaw's universe, his plays are full of capitalist *characters* who are wise and winning.

It is helpful—if somewhat dizzying—to remember that Bernard Shaw and Sigmund Freud were born in the same year, and that each man was a powerful voice in transforming modern ideas of sex, gender, and "the woman question." Shaw in fact commented on this unexpected affinity when he first stumbled on Freud's writings in 1911, and pronounced "I have said it all before him." For Freud, the Rosetta Stone of understanding was sex, and his great discovery was that women are also sexual beings. For Shaw, too, sex is everywhere, but it is never the problem—sex is liberating for men and women alike. Shaw was an ardent proponent of free love, and had many romances and affairs, although most of them appear to have been limited to the pages of his torrid correspondence. In 1898, at the age of forty-two, he married Charlotte Payne-Townshend, a wealthy supporter of Fabian socialist causes, but he remained attached, at least on paper, to several other women.

In his famous essay *The Quintessence of Ibsenism*, Shaw used his commentary on Ibsen's plays as a way of proclaiming his own discoveries about the New Woman: "There is no such species in creation as 'Woman, lovely Woman,' the woman being simply the female of the human species, and to have one conception of humanity for the woman and another for the man, or one law for the woman and another for the man, or one artistic convention for the woman and another for the man, or, for that matter, a skirt for the woman and a pair of breeches for the man . . . is unnatural and unworkable." Shaw was dedicated to tearing down what he saw as the oppressive veil of Victorian ideals of womanhood—that women are self-sacrificing, pure, noble, and passive. Women are usually the social visionaries in his plays, not because he thought of women as "better," or even as fundamentally different, but because their struggles with orthodoxy were basic.

The modern woman can change into "modern dress"—the radical costumes of the mind—with much more ease and enthusiasm, indeed, more lightheartedly and playfully, than can men. By allying women with the newest of the new ideas, in plays including *Major Barbara*, *Mrs. Warren's Profession*, *Pygmalion*, *Misalliance*, and *Saint Joan*, Shaw indicates the excitement, the vitality, and the innovation behind women who have burst out of the confines of domestic duty.

Shaw's plays employ classic comic situations, with elements drawn from Roman comedy and from Shakespeare. Yet for all their classical economy, Shaw's plays feel experimental, perhaps because they are constructed musically rather than dramatically. Shaw, who is still considered to be the most distinguished music critic of modern times, loves to draw on the musical style of a harmony of voices rather than singling out one or two main protagonists, often creating a kind of chamber play that is reliant on its ensemble. *Pygmalion* has this ensemble structure—we don't get a "full" portrait of any single character in the play, since the characters, like the colored glass bits of a kaleidoscope, change in relation to one another and form new patterns from scene to scene.

Pygmalion—first performed in London and New York in 1914, and published in 1916—is Shaw's most enduringly popular play, due in no small part to the big-budget 1964 Warner Brothers film adaptation *My Fair Lady*, starring Rex Harrison as Professor Henry Higgins and Audrey Hepburn as Eliza Doolittle and featuring songs by the gifted team of Lerner and Loewe. *Pygmalion* foregrounds most of Shaw's characteristic themes: his distaste for and distrust of the British class system, his impatience with the second-class status afforded women in the early decades of the twentieth century, and the hollowness of what Eliza's father refers to as "middle class morality." *Pygmalion* is also characteristic in the way that Shaw uses comic means—as well as a long brow-beating postscript—to put his ideas for social reform across. In the end, aristocratic status is made to look like something of a parlor trick—and that while elegant costume and genteel pronunciation might get one accepted into polite society there is, as W. B. Yeats wrote in his poem "A Coat," "more enterprise / In walking naked."

Bernard Shaw is at once a brilliant comic dramatist—in his essays and his letters as in his plays—and one of the great political playwrights of modern British literature, infusing all his work with the conviction that our social, economic, and sexual lives need transformation. For Shaw, it is comedy and laughter that draw an audience into a generous, collective ensemble—one rather like the ensemble of characters in his plays, none of whom could exist as a full-fledged human being without the others. Shaw disarms us with laughter, dismantling our expectations about what is natural, necessary, or inevitable. In his comedy, words are deeds and gestures speak, always pointedly.

For additional resources on Shaw, go to *The Longman Anthology of British Literature* Web site at www.myliteraturekit.com.

Preface

A Professor of Phonetics

As will be seen later on, Pygmalion needs, not a preface, but a sequel, which I have supplied in its due place.

The English have no respect for their language, and will not teach their children to speak it. They cannot spell it because they have nothing to spell it with but an old foreign alphabet of which only the consonants—and not all of them—have any agreed speech value. Consequently no man can teach himself what it should sound like from reading it; and it is impossible for an Englishman to open his mouth without making some other Englishman despise him. Most European languages are now accessible in black and white to foreigners: English and French are not thus accessible even to Englishmen and Frenchmen. The reformer we need most today is an energetic phonetic enthusiast: that is why I have made such a one the hero of a popular play.

There have been heroes of that kind crying in the wilderness for many years past. When I became interested in the subject towards the end of the eighteen-seventies, the illustrious Alexander Melville Bell, the inventor of Visible Speech, had emigrated to Canada, where his son invented the telephone; but Alexander J. Ellis was still a London patriarch, with an impressive head always covered by a velvet skull cap, for which he would apologize to public meetings in a very courtly manner. He and Tito Pagliardini, another phonetic veteran, were men whom it was impossible to dislike. Henry Sweet, then a young man, lacked their sweetness of character: he was about as conciliatory to conventional mortals as Ibsen[1] or Samuel Butler.[2] His great ability as a phonetician (he was, I think, the best of them all at his job) would have entitled him to high official recognition, and perhaps enabled him to popularize his subject, but for his Satanic contempt for all academic dignitaries and persons in general who thought more of Greek than of phonetics. Once, in the days when the Imperial Institute rose in South Kensington, and Joseph Chamberlain[3] was booming the Empire, I induced the editor of a leading monthly review to commission an article from Sweet on the imperial importance of his subject. When it arrived, it contained nothing but a savagely derisive attack on a professor of language and literature whose chair Sweet regarded as proper to a phonetic expert only. The article, being libellous, had to be returned as impossible; and I had to renounce my dream of dragging its author into the limelight. When I met him afterwards, for the first time for many years, I found to my astonishment that he, who had been a quite tolerably presentable young man, had actually managed by sheer scorn to alter his personal appearance until he had become a sort of walking repudiation of Oxford and all its traditions. It must have been largely in his own despite that he was squeezed into something called a Readership of phonetics there. The future of phonetics rests probably with his pupils, who all swore by him; but nothing could bring the man himself into any sort of compliance with the university to which he nevertheless clung by divine right in an intensely Oxonian way. I daresay his papers, if he has left any, include some satires that may be published without too destructive results fifty years hence. He was, I believe, not in the least an ill-natured man: very much the opposite, I should say; but he would not suffer fools gladly; and to him all scholars who were not rabid phoneticians were fools.

Those who knew him will recognize in my third act the allusion to the Current Shorthand in which he used to write postcards. It may be acquired from a four and sixpenny manual published by the Clarendon Press. The postcards which Mrs Higgins describes are such as I have received from Sweet. I would decipher a sound which a cockney would represent by *zerr*, and a Frenchman by *seu*, and then write demanding with some heat what on earth it meant. Sweet, with boundless contempt for my stupidity, would reply that it not only meant but obviously was the word Result, as no other word containing that sound, and capable of making sense with the context, existed in any language spoken on earth. That less expert mortals should require fuller indications was beyond Sweet's patience. Therefore, though the whole point of his Current Shorthand is that it can express every sound in the language perfectly, vowels as well as consonants, and that your hand has to make no stroke except the easy and current ones with which you write m, n, and u, l, p, and q, scribbling

1. Henrik Ibsen (1828–1906), Norwegian playwright whose realist plays dealing with contemporary social problems were a large influence on Shaw.

2. Samuel Butler (1835–1902), whose satirical novels were admired by Shaw.

3. Joseph Chamberlain (1836–1914), British statesman.

them at whatever angle comes easiest to you, his unfortunate determination to make this remarkable and quite legible script serve also as a shorthand reduced it in his own practice to the most inscrutable of cryptograms. His true objective was the provision of a full, accurate, legible script for our language; but he was led past that by his contempt for the popular Pitman system of shorthand, which he called the Pitfall system. The triumph of Pitman was a triumph of business organization: there was a weekly paper to persuade you to learn Pitman: there were cheap textbooks and exercise books and transcripts of speeches for you to copy, and schools where experienced teachers coached you up to the necessary proficiency. Sweet could not organize his market in that fashion. He might as well have been the Sybil who tore up the leaves of prophecy that nobody would attend to. The four and sixpenny manual, mostly in his lithographed hand-writing, that was never vulgarly advertized, may perhaps some day be taken up by a syndicate and pushed upon the public as The Times pushed the Encyclopaedia Britannica; but until then it will certainly not prevail against Pitman. I have bought three copies of it during my lifetime; and I am informed by the publishers that its cloistered existence is still a steady and healthy one. I actually learned the system two several[4] times; and yet the shorthand in which I am writing these lines is Pitman's. And the reason is, that my secretary cannot transcribe Sweet, having been perforce taught in the schools of Pitman. In America I could use the commercially organized Gregg shorthand, which has taken a hint from Sweet by making its letters writable (current, Sweet would have called them) instead of having to be geometrically drawn like Pitman's; but all these systems, including Sweet's, are spoilt by making them available for verbatim reporting, in which complete and exact spelling and word division are impossible. A complete and exact phonetic script is neither practicable nor necessary for ordinary use; but if we enlarge our alphabet to the Russian size, and make our spelling as phonetic as Spanish, the advance will be prodigious.

Pygmalion[5] Higgins is not a portrait of Sweet, to whom the adventure of Eliza Doolittle would have been impossible; still, as will be seen, there are touches of Sweet in the play. With Higgins's physique and temperament Sweet might have set the Thames on fire. As it was, he impressed himself professionally on Europe to an extent that made his comparative personal obscurity, and the failure of Oxford to do justice to his eminence, a puzzle to foreign specialists in his subject. I do not blame Oxford, because I think Oxford is quite right in demanding a certain social amenity from its nurslings (heaven knows it is not exorbitant in its requirements!); for although I well know how hard it is for a man of genius with a seriously underrated subject to maintain serene and kindly relations with the men who underrate it, and who keep all the best places for less important subjects which they profess without originality and sometimes without much capacity for them, still, if he overwhelms them with wrath and disdain, he cannot expect them to heap honors on him.

Of the later generations of phoneticians I know little. Among them towered Robert Bridges, to whom perhaps Higgins may owe his Miltonic sympathies, though here again I must disclaim all portraiture. But if the play makes the public aware that there are such people as phoneticians, and that they are among the most important people in England at present, it will serve its turn.

4. Different.
5. In Greek myth, Pygmalion was king of Cyprus and a sculptor; he fell in love with his own creation, and Aphrodite brought the statue, Galatea, to life.

I wish to boast that Pygmalion has been an extremely successful play, both on stage and screen, all over Europe and North America as well as at home. It is so intensely and deliberately didactic, and its subject is esteemed so dry, that I delight in throwing it at the heads of the wiseacres who repeat the parrot cry that art should never be didactic. It goes to prove my contention that great art can never be anything else.

Finally, and for the encouragement of people troubled with accents that cut them off from all high employment, I may add that the change wrought by Professor Higgins in the flower-girl is neither impossible nor uncommon. The modern concierge's daughter who fulfils her ambition by playing the Queen of Spain in Ruy Blas at the Théâtre Français is only one of many thousands of men and women who have sloughed off their native dialects and acquired a new tongue. Our West End shop assistants and domestic servants are bi-lingual. But the thing has to be done scientifically, or the last state of the aspirant may be worse than the first. An honest slum dialect is more tolerable than the attempts of phonetically untaught persons to imitate the plutocracy. Ambitious flower-girls who read this play must not imagine that they can pass themselves off as fine ladies by untutored imitation. They must learn their alphabet over again, and different, from a phonetic expert. Imitation will only make them ridiculous.

NOTE FOR TECHNICIANS. A complete representation of the play as printed for the first time in this edition is technically possible only on the cinema screen or on stages furnished with exceptionally elaborate machinery. For ordinary theatrical use the scenes separated by rows of asterisks are to be omitted.

In the dialogue an e upside down indicates the indefinite vowel, sometimes called obscure or neutral, for which, though it is one of the commonest sounds in English speech, our wretched alphabet has no letter.

Pygmalion

ACT 1

London at 11.15 p.m. Torrents of heavy summer rain. Cab whistles blowing frantically in all directions. Pedestrians running for shelter into the portico of St Paul's church (not Wren's[1] *cathedral but Inigo Jones's*[2] *church in Covent Garden vegetable market), among them a lady and her daughter in evening dress. All are peering out gloomily at the rain, except one man with his back turned to the rest, wholly preoccupied with a notebook in which he is writing.*

The church clock strikes the first quarter.

THE DAUGHTER [*in the space between the central pillars, close to the one on her left*]: I'm getting chilled to the bone. What can Freddy be doing all this time? He's been gone twenty minutes.

THE MOTHER [*on her daughter's right*]: Not so long. But he ought to have got us a cab by this.

A BYSTANDER [*on the lady's right*]: He wont get no cab not until half-past eleven, missus, when they come back after dropping their theatre fares.

THE MOTHER: But we must have a cab. We cant stand here until half-past eleven. It's too bad.

THE BYSTANDER: Well it aint my fault, missus.

THE DAUGHTER: If Freddy had a bit of gumption, he would have got one at the theatre door.

1. Sir Christopher Wren (1632–1723), English architect. 2. Inigo Jones (1573–1652), English architect.

THE MOTHER: What could he have done, poor boy?

THE DAUGHTER: Other people get cabs. Why couldnt he?

[*Freddy rushes in out of the rain from the Southampton Street side, and comes between them closing a dripping umbrella. He is a young man of twenty, in evening dress, very wet round the ankles.*]

THE DAUGHTER: Well, havnt you got a cab?

FREDDY: Theres not one to be had for love or money.

THE MOTHER: Oh, Freddy, there must be one. You cant have tried.

THE DAUGHTER: It's too tiresome. Do you expect us to go and get one ourselves?

FREDDY: I tell you theyre all engaged. The rain was so sudden: nobody was prepared; and everybody had to take a cab. Ive been to Charing Cross one way and nearly to Ludgate Circus the other; and they were all engaged.

THE MOTHER: Did you try Trafalgar Square?

FREDDY: There wasnt one at Trafalgar Square.

THE DAUGHTER: Did you try?

FREDDY: I tried as far as Charing Cross Station. Did you expect me to walk to Hammersmith?

THE DAUGHTER: You havnt tried at all.

THE MOTHER: You really are very helpless, Freddy. Go again; and dont come back until you have found a cab.

FREDDY: I shall simply get soaked for nothing.

THE DAUGHTER: And what about us? Are we to stay here all night in this draught, with next to nothing on? You selfish pig—

FREDDY: Oh, very well: I'll go. I'll go. [*He opens his umbrella and dashes off Strandwards, but comes into collision with a flower girl who is hurrying in for shelter, knocking her basket out of her hands. A blinding flash of lightning, followed instantly by a rattling peal of thunder, orchestrates the incident.*]

THE FLOWER GIRL: Nah then, Freddy: look wh'y' gowin, deah.

FREDDY: Sorry. [*He rushes off.*]

THE FLOWER GIRL [*picking up her scattered flowers and replacing them in the basket*]: Theres menners f'yer! Tə -oo banches o voylets trod into the mad.

[*She sits down on the plinth of the column, sorting her flowers, on the lady's right. She is not at all a romantic figure. She is perhaps eighteen, perhaps twenty, hardly older. She wears a little sailor hat of black straw that has long been exposed to the dust and soot of London and has seldom if ever been brushed. Her hair needs washing rather badly: its mousy color can hardly be natural. She wears a shoddy black coat that reaches nearly to her knees and is shaped to her waist. She has a brown skirt with a coarse apron. Her boots are much the worse for wear. She is no doubt as clean as she can afford to be; but compared to the ladies she is very dirty. Her features are no worse than theirs; but their condition leaves something to be desired; and she needs the services of a dentist.*]

THE MOTHER: How do you know that my son's name is Freddy, pray?

THE FLOWER GIRL: Ow, eez, yə -ooa san, is e? Wal, fewd dan y' d-ooty bawmz a mather should, eed now bettern to spawl a pore gel's flahrzn than ran awy athaht pyin. Will ye-oo py me f'them? [*Here, with apologies, this desperate attempt to represent her dialect without a phonetic alphabet must be abandoned as unintelligible outside London.*]

THE DAUGHTER: Do nothing of the sort, mother. The idea!

THE MOTHER: Please allow me, Clara. Have you any pennies?

THE DAUGHTER: No. Ive nothing smaller than sixpence.

THE FLOWER GIRL [*hopefully*]: I can give you change for a tanner, kind lady.

THE MOTHER [*to Clara*]: Give it to me. [*Clara parts reluctantly.*] Now [*to the girl*] This is for your flowers.

THE FLOWER GIRL: Thank you kindly, lady.

THE DAUGHTER: Make her give you the change. These things are only a penny a bunch.

THE MOTHER: Do hold your tongue, Clara. [*To the girl*] You can keep the change.

THE FLOWER GIRL: Oh, thank you, lady.

THE MOTHER: Now tell me how you know that young gentleman's name.

THE FLOWER GIRL: I didnt.

THE MOTHER: I heard you call him by it. Dont try to deceive me.

THE FLOWER GIRL [*protesting*]: Who's trying to deceive you? I called him Freddy or Charlie same as you might yourself if you was talking to a stranger and wished to be pleasant.

THE DAUGHTER: Sixpence thrown away! Really, mamma, you might have spared Freddy that. [*She retreats in disgust behind the pillar.*]

[*An elderly gentleman of the amiable military type rushes into the shelter, and closes a dripping umbrella. He is in the same plight as Freddy, very wet about the ankles. He is in evening dress, with a light overcoat. He takes the place left vacant by the daughter.*]

THE GENTLEMAN: Phew!

THE MOTHER [*to the gentleman*]: Oh, sir, is there any sign of its stopping?

THE GENTLEMAN: I'm afraid not. It started worse than ever about two minutes ago. [*He goes to the plinth beside the flower girl; puts up his foot on it; and stoops to turn down his trouser ends.*]

THE MOTHER: Oh dear! [*She retires sadly and joins her daughter.*]

THE FLOWER GIRL [*taking advantage of the military gentleman's proximity to establish friendly relations with him*]: If it's worse, it's a sign it's nearly over. So cheer up, Captain; and buy a flower off a poor girl.

THE GENTLEMAN: I'm sorry. I havnt any change.

THE FLOWER GIRL: I can give you change, Captain.

THE GENTLEMAN: For a sovereign? Ive nothing less.

THE FLOWER GIRL: Garn! Oh do buy a flower off me, Captain. I can change half-a-crown. Take this for tuppence.

THE GENTLEMAN: Now dont be troublesome: theres a good girl. [*Trying his pockets.*] I really havnt any change—Stop: heres three hapence, if thats any use to you [*he retreats to the other pillar*].

THE FLOWER GIRL [*disappointed, but thinking three halfpence better than nothing*]: Thank you, sir.

THE BYSTANDER [*to the girl*]: You be careful: give him a flower for it. Theres a bloke here behind taking down every blessed word youre saying. [*All turn to the man who is taking notes.*]

THE FLOWER GIRL [*springing up terrified*]: I aint done nothing wrong by speaking to the gentleman. Ive a right to sell flowers if I keep off the kerb. [*Hysterically.*] I'm a respectable girl: so help me. I never spoke to him except to ask him to buy a flower off me.

[*General hubbub, mostly sympathetic to the flower girl, but deprecating her excessive sensibility. Cries of* Dont start hollerin. Who's hurting you? Nobody's going to touch you. Whats the good of fussing? Steady on. Easy easy, etc., *come from the elderly staid spectators, who pat her comfortingly. Less patient ones bid her shut her head, or ask her roughly what is wrong with her. A remoter group, not knowing what the matter is, crowd in and increase the noise with question and answer:* Whats the row? What-she-do? Where is he? A tec[3] taking her down. What! him? Yes: him over there: Took money off the gentleman, etc.]

THE FLOWER GIRL [*breaking through them to the gentleman, crying wildly*]: Oh, sir, dont let him charge me. You dunno what it means to me. Theyll take away my character and drive me on the streets for speaking to gentlemen. They—

THE NOTE TAKER [*coming forward on her right, the rest crowding after him*]: There! there! there! there! Who's hurting you, you silly girl? What do you take me for?

THE BYSTANDER: It's aw rawt: e's a genleman: look at his bə -oots. [*Explaining to the note taker.*] She thought you was a copper's nark, sir.

THE NOTE TAKER [*with quick interest*]: Whats a copper's nark?

THE BYSTANDER [*inapt at definition*]: It's a—well, it's a copper's nark, as you might say. What else would you call it? A sort of informer.

THE FLOWER GIRL [*still hysterical*]: I take my Bible oath I never said a word—

THE NOTE TAKER [*overbearing but good-humored*]: Oh, shut up, shut up. Do I look like a policeman?

THE FLOWER GIRL [*far from reassured*]: Then what did you take down my words for? How do I know whether you took me down right? You just shew[4] me what youve wrote about me. [*The note taker opens his book and holds it steadily under her nose, though the pressure of the mob trying to read it over his shoulders would upset a weaker man.*] Whats that? That aint proper writing. I cant read that.

THE NOTE TAKER: I can. [*Reads, reproducing her pronunciation exactly.*] "Cheer ap, Keptin; n' baw ya flahr orf a pore gel."

THE FLOWER GIRL [*much distressed*]: It's because I called him Captain. I meant no harm. [*To the gentleman.*] Oh, sir, dont let him lay a charge agen me for a word like that. You—

THE GENTLEMAN: Charge! I make no charge. [*To the note taker.*] Really, sir, if you are a detective, you need not begin protecting me against molestation by young women until I ask you. Anybody could see that the girl meant no harm.

THE BYSTANDERS GENERALLY [*demonstrating against police espionage*]: Course they could. What business is it of yours? You mind your own affairs. He wants promotion, he does. Taking down people's words! Girl never said a word to him. What harm if she did? Nice thing a girl cant shelter from the rain without being insulted, etc., etc., etc. [*She is conducted by the more sympathetic demonstrators back to her plinth, where she resumes her seat and struggles with her emotion.*]

THE BYSTANDER: He aint a tec. He's a blooming busy-body: thats what he is. I tell you, look at his bə -oots.

THE NOTE TAKER [*turning on him genially*]: And how are all your people down at Selsey?

THE BYSTANDER [*suspiciously*]: Who told you my people come from Selsey?

THE NOTE TAKER: Never you mind. They did. [*To the girl.*] How do you come to be up so far east? You were born in Lisson Grove.

THE FLOWER GIRL [*appalled*]: Oh, what harm is there in my leaving Lisson Grove? It wasnt fit for a pig to live in; and I had to pay four-and-six a week. [*In tears.*] Oh, boo—hoo—oo—

THE NOTE TAKER: Live where you like; but stop that noise.

3. Detective.

4. Show.

THE GENTLEMAN [*to the girl*]: Come, come! he cant touch you: you have a right to live where you please.

A SARCASTIC BYSTANDER [*thrusting himself between the note taker and the gentleman*]: Park Lane, for instance. I'd like to go into the Housing Question with you, I would.

THE FLOWER GIRL [*subsiding into a brooding melancholy over her basket, and talking very low-spiritedly to herself*]: I'm a good girl, I am.

THE SARCASTIC BYSTANDER [*not attending to her*]: Do you know where *I* come from?

THE NOTE TAKER [*promptly*]: Hoxton.

[*Titterings. Popular interest in the note taker's performance increases.*]

THE SARCASTIC ONE [*amazed*]: Well, who said I didnt? Bly me! you know everything, you do.

THE FLOWER GIRL [*still nursing her sense of injury*]: Aint no call to meddle with me, he aint.

THE BYSTANDER [*to her*]: Of course he aint. Dont you stand it from him. [*To the note taker.*] See here: what call have you to know about people what never offered to meddle with you?

THE FLOWER GIRL: Let him say what he likes. I dont want to have no truck with him.

THE BYSTANDER: You take us for dirt under your feet, dont you? Catch you taking liberties with a gentleman!

THE SARCASTIC BYSTANDER: Yes: tell him where he come from if you want to go fortune-telling.

THE NOTE TAKER: Cheltenham, Harrow, Cambridge, and India.

THE GENTLEMAN: Quite right.

[*Great laughter. Reaction in the note taker's favor. Exclamations of* He knows all about it. Told him proper. Hear him tell the toff where he come from? etc.]

THE GENTLEMAN: May I ask, sir, do you do this for your living at a music hall?

THE NOTE TAKER: I've thought of that. Perhaps I shall some day.

[*The rain has stopped; and the persons on the outside of the crowd begin to drop off.*]

THE FLOWER GIRL [*resenting the reaction*]: He's no gentleman, he aint, to interfere with a poor girl.

THE DAUGHTER [*out of patience, pushing her way rudely to the front and displacing the gentleman, who politely retires to the other side of the pillar*]: What on earth is Freddy doing? I shall get pneumownia if I stay in this draught any longer.

THE NOTE TAKER [*to himself, hastily making a note of her pronunciation of "monia"*]: Earlscourt.

THE DAUGHTER [*violently*]: Will you please keep your impertinent remarks to yourself.

THE NOTE TAKER: Did I say that out loud? I didnt mean to. I beg your pardon. Your mother's Epsom, unmistakeably.

THE MOTHER [*advancing between the daughter and the note taker*]: How very curious! I was brought up in Largelady Park, near Epsom.

THE NOTE TAKER [*uproariously amused*]: Ha! ha! what a devil of a name! Excuse me. [*To the daughter.*] You want a cab, do you?

THE DAUGHTER: Dont dare speak to me.

THE MOTHER: Oh, please, please, Clara. [*Her daughter repudiates her with an angry shrug and retires haughtily.*] We should be so grateful to you, sir, if you found us a cab. [*The note taker produces a whistle.*] Oh, thank you. [*She joins her daughter. The note taker blows a piercing blast.*]

THE SARCASTIC BYSTANDER: There! I knowed he was a plain-clothes copper.

THE BYSTANDER: That aint a police whistle: thats a sporting whistle.

THE FLOWER GIRL [*still preoccupied with her wounded feelings*]: He's no right to take away my character. My character is the same to me as any lady's.

THE NOTE TAKER: I dont know whether youve noticed it; but the rain stopped about two minutes ago.

THE BYSTANDER: So it has. Why didnt you say so before? And us losing our time listening to your silliness! [*He walks off towards the Strand.*]

THE SARCASTIC BYSTANDER: I can tell where you come from. You come from Anwell. Go back there.

THE NOTE TAKER [*helpfully*]: Hanwell.

THE SARCASTIC BYSTANDER [*affecting great distinction of speech*]: Thenk you, teacher. Haw haw! So long. [*He touches his hat with mock respect and strolls off.*]

THE FLOWER GIRL: Frightening people like that! How would he like it himself?

THE MOTHER: It's quite fine now, Clara. We can walk to a motor bus. Come. [*She gathers her skirts above her ankles and hurries off towards the Strand.*]

THE DAUGHTER: But the cab—[*her mother is out of hearing*]. Oh, how tiresome! [*She follows angrily.*]

[*All the rest have gone except the note taker, the gentleman, and the flower girl, who sits arranging her basket, and still pitying herself in murmurs.*]

THE FLOWER GIRL: Poor girl! Hard enough for her to live without being worried and chivied.

THE GENTLEMAN [*returning to his former place on the note taker's left*]: How do you do it, if I may ask?

THE NOTE TAKER: Simply phonetics. The science of speech. Thats my profession: also my hobby. Happy is the man who can make a living by his hobby! You can spot an Irishman or a Yorkshireman by his brogue. *I* can place any man within six miles. I can place him within two miles in London. Sometimes within two streets.

THE FLOWER GIRL: Ought to be ashamed of himself, unmanly coward!

THE GENTLEMAN: But is there a living in that?

THE NOTE TAKER: Oh, yes. Quite a fat one. This is an age of upstarts. Men begin in Kentish Town with £80 a year, and end in Park Lane with a hundred thousand. They want to drop Kentish Town; but they give themselves away every time they open their mouths. Now I can teach them—

THE FLOWER GIRL: Let him mind his own business and leave a poor girl—

THE NOTE TAKER [*explosively*]: Woman: cease this detestable boohooing instantly: or else seek the shelter of some other place of worship.

THE FLOWER GIRL [*with feeble defiance*]: Ive a right to be here if I like, same as you.

THE NOTE TAKER: A woman who utters such depressing and disgusting sounds has no right to be anywhere—no right to live. Remember that you are a human being with a soul and the divine gift of articulate speech: that your native language is the language of Shakespear and Milton and The Bible; and dont sit there crooning like a bilious pigeon.

THE FLOWER GIRL [*quite overwhelmed, looking up at him in mingled wonder and deprecation without daring to raise her head*]: Ah-ah-ah-ow-ow-ow-oo!

THE NOTE TAKER [*whipping out his book*]: Heavens! what a sound! [*He writes; then holds out the book and reads, reproducing her vowels exactly*.] Ah-ah-ah-ow-ow-ow-oo!

THE FLOWER GIRL [*tickled by the performance, and laughing in spite of herself*]: Garn!

THE NOTE TAKER: You see this creature with her kerbstone English: the English that will keep her in the gutter to the end of her days. Well, sir, in three months I could pass that girl off as a duchess at an ambassador's garden party. I could even get her a place as lady's maid or shop assistant, which requires better English.

THE FLOWER GIRL: What's that you say?

THE NOTE TAKER: Yes, you squashed cabbage leaf, you disgrace to the noble architecture of these columns, you incarnate insult to the English language: I could pass you off as the Queen of Sheba. [*To the Gentleman*.] Can you believe that?

THE GENTLEMAN: Of course I can. I am myself a student of Indian dialects; and—

THE NOTE TAKER [*eagerly*]: Are you? Do you know Colonel Pickering, the author of Spoken Sanscrit?

THE GENTLEMAN: I am Colonel Pickering. Who are you?

THE NOTE TAKER: Henry Higgins, author of Higgins's Universal Alphabet.

PICKERING [*with enthusiasm*]: I came from India to meet you.

HIGGINS: I was going to India to meet you.

PICKERING: Where do you live?

HIGGINS: 27a Wimpole Street. Come and see me tomorrow.

PICKERING: I'm at the Carlton. Come with me now and lets have a jaw over some supper.

HIGGINS: Right you are.

THE FLOWER GIRL [*to Pickering, as he passes her*]: Buy a flower, kind gentleman. I'm short for my lodging.

PICKERING: I really havnt any change. I'm sorry. [*He goes away*.]

HIGGINS [*shocked at the girl's mendacity*]: Liar. You said you could change half-a-crown.

THE FLOWER GIRL [*rising in desperation*]: You ought to be stuffed with nails, you ought. [*Flinging the basket at his feet*.] Take the whole blooming basket for sixpence.

[*The church clock strikes the second quarter*.]

HIGGINS [*hearing in it the voice of God, rebuking him for his Pharisaic want of charity to the poor girl*]: A reminder. [*He raises his hat solemnly; then throws a handful of money into the basket and follows Pickering*.]

THE FLOWER GIRL [*picking up a half-crown*]: Ah-ow-ooh! [*picking up a couple of florins*] Aaah-ow-ooh! [*picking up several coins*] Aaaaaah-ow-ooh! [*picking up a half-sovereign*] Aaaaaaaaaaaah-ow-ooh!!!

FREDDY [*springing out of a taxicab*]: Got one at last. Hallo! [*To the girl*.] Where are the two ladies that were here?

THE FLOWER GIRL: They walked to the bus when the rain stopped.

FREDDY: And left me with a cab on my hands! Damnation!

THE FLOWER GIRL [*with grandeur*]: Never mind, young man. I'm going home in a taxi. [*She sails off to the cab. The driver puts his hand behind him and holds the door firmly shut against her. Quite understanding his mistrust, she shews him her handful of money*.] A taxi fare aint no object to me, Charlie. [*He grins and opens the door*.] Here. What about the basket?

THE TAXIMAN: Give it here. Tuppence extra.

LIZA: No: I dont want nobody to see it. [*She crushes it into the cab and gets in, continuing the conversation through the window.*] Goodbye, Freddy.

FREDDY [*dazedly raising his hat*]: Goodbye.

TAXIMAN: Where to?

LIZA: Bucknam Pellis [Buckingham Palace].

TAXIMAN: What d'ye mean—Bucknam Pellis?

LIZA: Dont you know where it is? In the Green Park, where the King lives. Goodbye, Freddy. Dont let me keep you standing there. Goodbye.

FREDDY: Goodbye. [*He goes.*]

TAXIMAN: Here? Whats this about Bucknam Pellis? What business have you at Bucknam Pellis?

LIZA: Of course I havnt none. But I wasnt going to let him know that. You drive me home.

TAXIMAN: And wheres home?

LIZA: Angel Court, Drury Lane, next Meiklejohn's oil shop.

TAXIMAN: That sounds more like it, Judy. [*He drives off.*]

* * *

Let us follow the taxi to the entrance to Angel Court, a narrow little archway between two shops, one of them Meiklejohn's oil shop. When it stops there, Eliza gets out, dragging her basket with her.

LIZA: How much?

TAXIMAN [*indicating the taximeter*]: Cant you read? A shilling.

LIZA: A shilling for two minutes!!

TAXIMAN: Two minutes or ten: it's all the same.

LIZA: Well. I dont call it right.

TAXIMAN: Ever been in a taxi before?

LIZA [*with dignity*]: Hundreds and thousands of times, young man.

TAXIMAN [*laughing at her*]: Good for you. Judy, Keep the shilling, darling, with best love from all at home. Good luck! [*He drives off.*]

LIZA [*humiliated*]: Impidence!

[She picks up the basket and trudges up the alley with it to her lodging: a small room with very old wall paper hanging loose in the damp places. A broken pane in the window is mended with paper. A portrait of a popular actor and a fashion plate of ladies' dresses, all wildly beyond poor Eliza's means, both torn from newspapers, are pinned up on the wall. A birdcage hangs in the window; but its tenant died long ago: it remains as a memorial only.

These are the only visible luxuries: the rest is the irreducible minimum of poverty's needs: a wretched bed heaped with all sorts of coverings that have any warmth in them, a draped packing case with a basin and jug on it and a little looking glass over it, a chair and table, the refuse of some suburban kitchen, and an American alarum clock on the shelf above the unused fireplace: the whole lighted with a gas lamp with a penny in the slot meter. Rent: four shillings a week.

Here Eliza, chronically weary, but too excited to go to bed, sits, counting her new riches and dreaming and planning what to do with them, until the gas goes out, when she enjoys for the first time the sensation of being able to put in another penny without grudging it. This prodigal mood does not extinguish her gnawing sense of the need for economy sufficiently to prevent her from calculating that she can dream and plan in bed more cheaply and warmly than sitting up without a fire. So she takes off her shawl and skirt and adds them to the miscellaneous bedclothes. Then she kicks off her shoes and gets into bed without any further change.]

ACT 2

Next day at 11 a.m. Higgins's laboratory in Wimpole Street. It is a room on the first floor, looking on the street, and was meant for the drawing room. The double doors are in the middle of the back wall; and persons entering find in the corner to their right two tall file cabinets at right angles to one another against the wall. In this corner stands a flat writing-table, on which are a phonograph, a laryngoscope, a row of tiny organ pipes with a bellows, a set of lamp chimneys for singing flames with burners attached to a gas plug in the wall by an indiarubber tube, several tuning-forks of different sizes, a life-size image of half a human head, shewing in section the vocal organs, and a box containing a supply of wax cylinders for the phonograph.

Further down the room, on the same side, is a fireplace, with a comfortable leather-covered easy-chair at the side of the hearth nearest the door, and a coal-scuttle. There is a clock on the mantel-piece. Between the fireplace and the phonograph table is a stand for newspapers.

On the other side of the central door, to the left of the visitor, is a cabinet of shallow drawers. On it is a telephone and the telephone directory. The corner beyond, and most of the side wall, is occupied by a grand piano, with the keyboard at the end furthest from the door, and a bench for the player extending the full length of the keyboard. On the piano is a dessert dish heaped with fruit and sweets, mostly chocolates.

The middle of the room is clear. Besides the easy-chair, the piano bench, and two chairs at the phonograph table, there is one stray chair. It stands near the fireplace. On the walls, engravings: mostly Piranesis[1] and mezzotint[2] portraits. No paintings.

Pickering is seated at the table, putting down some cards and a tuning-fork which he has been using. Higgins is standing up near him, closing two or three file drawers which are hanging out. He appears in the morning light as a robust, vital, appetizing sort of man of forty or thereabouts, dressed in a professional-looking black frock-coat with a white linen collar and black silk tie. He is of the energetic scientific type, heartily, even violently interested in everything that can be studied as a scientific subject, and careless about himself and other people, including their feelings. He is, in fact, but for his years and size, rather like a very impetuous baby 'taking notice' eagerly and loudly, and requiring almost as much watching to keep him out of unintended mischief. His manner varies from genial bullying when he is in a good humor to stormy petulance when anything goes wrong: but he is so entirely frank and void of malice that he remains likeable even in his least reasonable moments.

HIGGINS [*as he shuts the last drawer*]: Well, I think thats the whole show.

PICKERING: It's really amazing. I havnt taken half of it in, you know.

HIGGINS: Would you like to go over any of it again?

PICKERING [*rising and coming to the fireplace, where he plants himself with his back to the fire*]: No, thank you: not now. I'm quite done up for this morning.

HIGGINS [*following him, and standing beside him on his left*]: Tired of listening to sounds?

PICKERING: Yes. It's a fearful strain. I rather fancied myself because I can pronounce twenty-four distinct vowel sounds; but your hundred and thirty beat me. I cant hear a bit of difference between most of them.

HIGGINS [*chuckling, and going over to the piano to eat sweetS*]: Oh, that comes with practice. You hear no difference at first; but you keep on listening, and presently

1. Giovanni Piranesi (1720–1778), Italian architect and engraver.

2. Prints produced with copper or steel engraved plates.

you find theyre all as different as A from B. [*Mrs Pearce looks in: she is Higgins's housekeeper.*] Whats the matter?

MRS PEARCE [*hesitating, evidently perplexed*]: A young woman asks to see you, sir.

HIGGINS: A young woman! What does she want?

MRS PEARCE: Well, sir, she says youll be glad to see her when you know what she's come about. She's quite a common girl, sir. Very common indeed. I should have sent her away, only I thought perhaps you wanted her to talk into your machines. I hope Ive not done wrong; but really you see such queer people sometimes—youll excuse me, I'm sure, sir—

HIGGINS: Oh, thats all right, Mrs Pearce. Has she an interesting accent?

MRS PEARCE: Oh, something dreadful, sir, really. I dont know how you can take an interest in it.

HIGGINS [*to Pickering*]: Lets have her up. Shew her up, Mrs Pearce. [*He rushes across to his working table and picks out a cylinder to use on the phonograph.*]

MRS PEARCE [*only half resigned to it*]: Very well, sir. It's for you to say. [*She goes downstairs.*]

HIGGINS: This is rather a bit of luck. I'll shew you how I make records. We'll set her talking; and I'll take it down first in Bell's Visible Speech; then in broad Romic; and then we'll get her on the phonograph so that you can turn her on as often as you like with the written transcript before you.

MRS PEARCE [*returning*]: This is the young woman, sir.

[*The flower girl enters in state. She has a hat with three ostrich feathers, orange, sky-blue, and red. She has a nearly clean apron and the shoddy coat has been tidied a little. The pathos of this deplorable figure, with its innocent vanity and consequential air, touches Pickering, who has already straightened himself in the presence of Mrs Pearce. But as to Higgins, the only distinction he makes between men and women is that when he is neither bullying nor exclaiming to the heavens against some featherweight cross, he coaxes women as a child coaxes its nurse when it wants to get anything out of her.*]

HIGGINS [*brusquely, recognizing her with unconcealed disappointment, and at once, babylike, making an intolerable grievance of it*]: Why, this is the girl I jotted down last night. She's no use: Ive got all the records I want of the Lisson Grove lingo; and I'm not going to waste another cylinder on it. [*To the girl.*] Be off with you: I dont want you.

THE FLOWER GIRL: Dont you be so saucy. You aint heard what I come for yet. [*To Mrs Pearce, who is waiting at the door for further instructions.*] Did you tell him I come in a taxi?

MRS PEARCE: Nonsense, girl! what do you think a gentleman like Mr Higgins cares what you came in?

THE FLOWER GIRL: Oh, we are proud! He aint above giving lessons, not him: I heard him say so. Well, I aint come here to ask for any compliment; and if my money's not good enough I can go elsewhere.

HIGGINS: Good enough for what?

THE FLOWER GIRL: Good enough for yə-oo. Now you know, dont you? I'm coming to have lessons, I am. And to pay for em tə-oo: make no mistake.

HIGGINS [*stupent*]:[3] Well!!! [*Recovering his breath with a gasp.*] What do you expect me to say to you?

3. Astonished.

THE FLOWER GIRL: Well, if you was a gentleman, you might ask me to sit down, I think. Dont I tell you I'm bringing you business?

HIGGINS: Pickering: shall we ask this baggage to sit down, or shall we throw her out of the window?

THE FLOWER GIRL [*running away in terror to the piano, where she turns at bay*]: Ah-ah-oh-ow-ow-ow-oo! [*Wounded and whimpering.*] I wont be called a baggage when Ive offered to pay like any lady.

[*Motionless, the two men stare at her from the other side of the room, amazed.*]

PICKERING [*gently*]: But what is it you want?

THE FLOWER GIRL: I want to be a lady in a flower shop stead of sellin at the corner of Tottenham Court Road. But they wont take me unless I can talk more genteel. He said he could teach me. Well, here I am ready to pay him—not asking any favor—and he treats me zif I was dirt.

MRS PEARCE: How can you be such a foolish ignorant girl as to think you could afford to pay Mr Higgins?

THE FLOWER GIRL: Why shouldnt I? I know what lessons cost as well as you do; and I'm ready to pay.

HIGGINS: How much?

THE FLOWER GIRL [*coming back to him triumphant*]: Now youre talking! I thought youd come off it when you saw a chance of getting back a bit of what you chucked at me last night. [*Confidentially.*] Youd had a drop in, hadnt you?

HIGGINS [*peremptorily*]: Sit down.

THE FLOWER GIRL: Oh, if youre going to make a compliment of it—

HIGGINS [*thundering at her*]: Sit down.

MRS PEARCE [*severely*]: Sit down, girl. Do as youre told.

THE FLOWER GIRL: Ah-ah-ah-ow-ow-oo! [*She stands, half rebellious, half-bewildered.*]

PICKERING [*very courteous*]: Wont you sit down? [*He places the stray chair near the hearthrug between himself and Higgins.*]

LIZA [*coyly*]: Dont mind if I do. [*She sits down. Pickering returns to the hearthrug.*]

HIGGINS: Whats your name?

THE FLOWER GIRL: Liza Doolittle.

HIGGINS [*declaiming gravely*]: Eliza, Elizabeth, Betsy and Bess, They went to the woods to get a bird's nes':

PICKERING: They found a nest with four eggs in it:

HIGGINS: They took one apiece, and left three in it.

[*They laugh heartily at their own fun.*]

LIZA: Oh, dont be silly.

MRS PEARCE [*placing herself behind Eliza's chair*]: You mustnt speak to the gentleman like that.

LIZA: Well, why wont he speak sensible to me?

HIGGINS: Come back to business. How much do you propose to pay me for the lessons?

LIZA: Oh, I know whats right. A lady friend of mine gets French lessons for eighteenpence an hour from a real French gentleman. Well, you wouldnt have the face to ask me the same for teaching me my own language as you would for French; so I wont give more than a shilling. Take it or leave it.

HIGGINS [*walking up and down the room, ratting his keys and his cash in his pockets*]: You know, Pickering, if you consider a shilling, not as a simple shilling, but as a percentage of this girl's income, it works out as fully equivalent to sixty or seventy guineas from a millionaire.

PICKERING: How so?

HIGGINS: Figure it out. A millionaire has about £150 a day. She earns about half-a-crown.

LIZA [*haughtily*]: Who told you I only—

HIGGINS [*continuing*]: She offers me two-fifths of her day's income for a lesson. Two-fifths of a millionaire's income for a day would be somewhere about £60. It's handsome. By George, it's enormous! it's the biggest offer I ever had.

LIZA [*rising, terrified*]: Sixty pounds! What are you talking about? I never offered you sixty pounds. Where would I get—

HIGGINS: Hold your tongue.

LIZA [*weeping*]: But I aint got sixty pounds. Oh—

MRS PEARCE: Dont cry, you silly girl. Sit down. Nobody is going to touch your money.

HIGGINS: Somebody is going to touch you, with a broom-stick, if you dont stop snivelling. Sit down.

LIZA [*obeying slowly*]: Ah-ah-ah-ow-oo-o! One would think you was my father.

HIGGINS: If I decide to teach you, I'll be worse than two fathers to you. Here [*he offers her his silk handkerchief*]!

LIZA: Whats this for?

HIGGINS: To wipe your eyes. To wipe any part of your face that feels moist. Remember: thats your handkerchief; and thats your sleeve. Dont mistake the one for the other if you wish to become a lady in a shop.

[*Liza, utterly bewildered, stares helplessly at him.*]

MRS PEARCE: It's no use talking to her like that, Mr Higgins: she doesnt understand you. Besides, youre quite wrong: she doesnt do it that way at all. [*She takes the handkerchief.*]

LIZA [*snatching it*]: Here! You give me that handkerchief. He gev it to me, not to you.

PICKERING [*laughing*]: He did. I think it must be regarded as her property, Mrs Pearce.

MRS PEARCE [*resigning herself*]: Serve you right, Mr Higgins.

PICKERING: Higgins: I'm interested. What about the ambassador's garden party? I'll say youre the greatest teacher alive if you make that good. I'll bet you all the expenses of the experiment you cant do it. And I'll pay for the lessons.

LIZA: Oh, you are real good. Thank you, Captain.

HIGGINS [*tempted, looking at her*]: It's almost irresistible. She's so deliciously low—so horribly dirty—

LIZA [*protesting extremely*]: Ah-ah-ah-ah-ow-oo-oo!!! I aint dirty: I washed my face and hands afore I come, I did.

PICKERING: Youre certainly not going to turn her head with flattery, Higgins.

MRS PEARCE [*uneasy*]: Oh, dont say that, sir: theres more ways than one of turning a girl's head; and nobody can do it better than Mr Higgins, though he may not always mean it. I do hope, sir, you wont encourage him to do anything foolish.

HIGGINS [*becoming excited as the idea grows on him*]: What is life but a series of inspired follies? The difficulty is to find them to do. Never lose a chance: it doesnt come every day. I shall make a duchess of this draggletailed guttersnipe.

LIZA [*strongly deprecating this view of her*]: Ah-ah-ah-ow-ow-oo!

HIGGINS [*carried away*]: Yes: in six months—in three if she has a good ear and a quick tongue—I'll take her anywhere and pass her off as anything. We'll start today: now! this moment! Take her away and clean her, Mrs Pearce. Monkey Brand,[4] if it wont come off any other way. Is there a good fire in the kitchen?

MRS PEARCE [*protesting*]: Yes; but—

HIGGINS [*storming on*]: Take all her clothes off and burn them. Ring up Whiteley or somebody for new ones. Wrap her up in brown paper til they come.

LIZA: Youre no gentleman, youre not, to talk of such things. I'm a good girl, I am; and I know what the like of you are, I do.

HIGGINS: We want none of your Lisson Grove prudery here, young woman. Youve got to learn to behave like a duchess. Take her away, Mrs Pearce. If she gives you any trouble, wallop her.

LIZA [*springing up and running between Pickering and Mrs Pearce for protection*]: No! I'll call the police, I will.

MRS PEARCE: But Ive no place to put her.

HIGGINS: Put her in the dustbin.

LIZA: Ah-ah-ah-ow-ow-oo!

PICKERING: Oh come, Higgins! Be reasonable.

MRS PEARCE [*resolutely*]: You must be reasonable, Mr Higgins: really you must. You cant walk over everybody like this.

[*Higgins, thus scolded, subsides. The hurricane is succeeded by a zephyr of amiable surprise.*]

HIGGINS [*with professional exquisiteness of modulation*]: I walk over everybody! My dear Mrs Pearce, my dear Pickering, I never had the slightest intention of walking over anyone. All I propose is that we should be kind to this poor girl. We must help her to prepare and fit herself for her new station in life. If I did not express myself clearly it was because I did not wish to hurt her delicacy, or yours.

[*Liza, reassured, steals back to her chair.*]

MRS PEARCE [*to Pickering*]: Well, did you ever hear anything like that, sir?

PICKERING [*laughing heartily*]: Never, Mrs Pearce: never.

HIGGINS [*patiently*]: Whats the matter?

MRS PEARCE: Well, the matter is, sir, that you cant take a girl up like that as if you were picking up a pebble on the beach.

HIGGINS: Why not?

MRS PEARCE: Why not! But you dont know anything about her. What about her parents? She may be married.

LIZA: Garn!

HIGGINS: There! As the girl very properly says, Garn! Married indeed! Dont you know that a woman of that class looks a worn out drudge of fifty a year after she's married?

LIZA: Whood marry me?

HIGGINS [*suddenly resorting to the most thrillingly beautiful low tones in his best elocutionary style*]: By George, Eliza, the streets will be strewn with the bodies of men shooting themselves for your sake before Ive done with you.

MRS PEARCE: Nonsense, sir. You mustnt talk like that to her.

LIZA [*rising and squaring herself determinedly*]: I'm going away. He's off his chump, he is. I dont want no balmies teaching me.

4. Widely advertised brand of household cleanser—"won't wash clothes!"

HIGGINS [*wounded in his tenderest point by her insensibility to his elocution*]: Oh, indeed! I'm mad, am I? Very well, Mrs Pearce: you neednt order the new clothes for her. Throw her out.

LIZA [*whimpering*]: Nah-ow. You got no right to touch me.

MRS PEARCE: You see now what comes of being saucy. [*Indicating the door.*] This way, please.

LIZA [*almost in tears*]: I didnt want no clothes. I wouldnt have taken them. [*She throws away the handkerchief.*] I can buy my own clothes.

HIGGINS [*deftly retrieving the handkerchief and intercepting her on her reluctant way to the door*]: Youre an ungrateful wicked girl. This is my return for offering to take you out of the gutter and dress you beautifully and make a lady of you.

MRS PEARCE: Stop, Mr Higgins. I wont allow it. It's you that are wicked. Go home to your parents, girl; and tell them to take better care of you.

LIZA: I aint got no parents. They told me I was big enough to earn my own living and turned me out.

MRS PEARCE: Wheres your mother?

LIZA: I aint got no mother. Her that turned me out was my sixth stepmother. But I done without them. And I'm a good girl, I am.

HIGGINS: Very well, then, what on earth is all this fuss about? The girl doesnt belong to anybody—is no use to anybody but me. [*He goes to Mrs Pearce and begins coaxing.*] You can adopt her, Mrs Pearce: I'm sure a daughter would be a great amusement to you. Now dont make any more fuss. Take her downstairs; and—

MRS PEARCE: But whats to become of her? Is she to be paid anything? Do be sensible, sir.

HIGGINS: Oh, pay her whatever is necessary: put it down in the housekeeping book. [*Impatiently.*] What on earth will she want with money? She'll have her food and her clothes. She'll only drink if you give her money.

LIZA [*turning on him*]: Oh you are a brute. It's a lie: nobody ever saw the sign of liquor on me. [*To Pickering.*] Oh, sir: youre a gentleman: dont let him speak to me like that.

PICKERING [*in good-humored remonstrance*]: Does it occur to you, Higgins, that the girl has some feelings?

HIGGINS [*looking critically at her*]: Oh no, I dont think so. Not any feelings that we need bother about. [*Cheerily.*] Have you, Eliza?

LIZA: I got my feelings same as anyone else.

HIGGINS [*to Pickering, reflectively*]: You see the difficulty?

PICKERING: Eh? What difficulty?

HIGGINS: To get her to talk grammar. The mere pronunciation is easy enough.

LIZA: I dont want to talk grammar. I want to talk like a lady in a flower-shop.

MRS PEARCE: Will you please keep to the point, Mr Higgins. I want to know on what terms the girl is to be here. Is she to have any wages? And what is to become of her when youve finished your teaching? You must look ahead a little.

HIGGINS [*impatiently*]: Whats to become of her if I leave her in the gutter? Tell me that, Mrs Pearce.

MRS PEARCE: Thats her own business, not yours. Mr Higgins.

HIGGINS: Well, when Ive done with her, we can throw her back into the gutter; and then it will be her own business again; so thats all right.

LIZA: Oh, youve no feeling heart in you: you dont care for nothing but yourself. [*She rises and takes the floor resolutely.*] Here! Ive had enough of this. I'm going [*making for the door*]. You ought to be ashamed of yourself, you ought.

HIGGINS [*snatching a chocolate cream from the piano, his eyes suddenly beginning to twinkle with mischief*]: Have some chocolates, Eliza.

LIZA [*halting, tempted*]: How do I know what might be in them? Ive heard of girls being drugged by the like of you.

[*Higgins whips out his penknife; cuts a chocolate in two; puts one half into his mouth and bolts it; and offers her the other half.*]

HIGGINS: Pledge of good faith. Eliza. I eat one half: you eat the other. [*Liza opens her mouth to retort: he pops the half chocolate into it.*] You shall have boxes of them, barrels of them, every day. You shall live on them. Eh?

LIZA [*who has disposed of the chocolate after being nearly choked by it*]: I wouldnt have ate it, only I'm too ladylike to take it out of my mouth.

HIGGINS: Listen, Eliza. I think you said you came in a taxi.

LIZA: Well, what if I did? Ive as good a right to take a taxi as anyone else.

HIGGINS: You have, Eliza; and in future you shall have as many taxis as you want. You shall go up and down and round the town in a taxi every day. Think of that, Eliza.

MRS PEARCE: Mr Higgins: youre tempting the girl. It's not right. She should think of the future.

HIGGINS: At her age! Nonsense! Time enough to think of the future when you havnt any future to think of. No, Eliza: do as this lady does: think of other people's futures; but never think of your own. Think of chocolates, and taxis, and gold, and diamonds.

LIZA: No: I dont want no gold and no diamonds. I'm a good girl, I am. [*She sits down again, with an attempt at dignity.*]

HIGGINS: You shall remain so, Eliza, under the care of Mrs Pearce. And you shall marry an officer in the Guards, with a beautiful moustache: the son of a marquis, who will disinherit him for marrying you, but will relent when he sees your beauty and goodness—

PICKERING: Excuse me, Higgins: but I really must interfere. Mrs Pearce is quite right. If this girl is to put herself in your hands for six months for an experiment in teaching, she must understand thoroughly what she's doing.

HIGGINS: How can she? She's incapable of understanding anything. Besides, do any of us understand what we are doing? If we did, would we ever do it?

PICKERING: Very clever, Higgins; but not to the present point. [*To Eliza.*] Miss Doolittle—

LIZA [*overwhelmed*]: Ah-ah-ow-oo!

HIGGINS: There! Thats all youll get out of Eliza. Ah-ah-ow-oo! No use explaining. As a military man you ought to know that. Give her her orders: thats enough for her. Eliza: you are to live here for the next six months, learning how to speak beautifully, like a lady in a florist's shop. If youre good and do whatever youre told, you shall sleep in a proper bedroom, and have lots to eat, and money to buy chocolates and take rides in taxis. If youre naughty and idle you will sleep in the back kitchen among the black beetles, and be walloped by Mrs Pearce with a broomstick. At the end of six months you shall go to Buckingham Palace in a carriage, beautifully dressed. If the King finds out youre not a lady, you will be taken by the police to the Tower of London, where your head will be cut off as a warning to other presumptuous flower girls. If you are not found out, you shall have a present of seven-and-sixpence to start life with as a lady in a shop. If you refuse this offer you will be a most ungrateful wicked girl; and the angels will weep for you.

[*To Pickering.*] Now are you satisfied, Pickering? [*To Mrs Pearce.*] Can I put it more plainly and fairly, Mrs Pearce?

MRS PEARCE [*patiently*]: I think youd better let me speak to the girl properly in private. I dont know that I can take charge of her or consent to the arrangement at all. Of course I know you dont mean her any harm; but when you get what you call interested in people's accents, you never think or care what may happen to them or you. Come with me, Eliza.

HIGGINS: Thats all right. Thank you, Mrs Pearce. Bundle her off to the bathroom.

LIZA [*rising reluctantly and suspiciously*]: Youre a great bully, you are. I wont stay here if I dont like. I wont let nobody wallop me. I never asked to go to Bucknam Palace, I didnt. I was never in trouble with the police, not me. I'm a good girl—

MRS PEARCE: Dont answer back, girl. You dont understand the gentleman. Come with me. [*She leads the way to the door, and holds it open for Eliza.*]

LIZA [*as she goes out*]: Well, what I say is right. I wont go near the King, not if I'm going to have my head cut off. If I'd known what I was letting myself in for, I wouldnt have come here. I always been a good girl; and I never offered to say a word to him; and I dont owe him nothing; and I dont care; and I wont be put upon; and I have my feelings the same as anyone else—

[*Mrs Pearce shuts the door; and Eliza's plaints are no longer audible.*]

* * *

Eliza is taken upstairs to the third floor greatly to her surprise; for she expected to be taken down to the scullery. There Mrs Pearce opens a door and takes her into a spare bedroom.

MRS PEARCE: I will have to put you here. This will be your bedroom.

LIZA: O-h, I couldnt sleep here, missus. It's too good for the likes of me. I should be afraid to touch anything. I aint a duchess yet, you know.

MRS PEARCE: You have got to make yourself as clean as the room: then you wont be afraid of it. And you must call me Mrs Pearce, not missus. [*She throws open the door of the dressing-room, now modernized as a bathroom.*]

LIZA: Gawd! whats this? Is this where you wash clothes? Funny sort of copper[5] I call it.

MRS PEARCE: It is not a copper. This is where we wash ourselves, Eliza, and where I am going to wash you.

LIZA: You expect me to get into that and wet myself all over! Not me. I should catch my death. I knew a woman did it every Saturday night; and she died of it.

MRS PEARCE: Mr Higgins has the gentlemen's bathroom down-stairs; and he has a bath every morning, in cold water.

LIZA: Ugh! He's made of iron, that man.

MRS PEARCE: If you are to sit with him and the Colonel and be taught you will have to do the same. They wont like the smell of you if you dont. But you can have the water as hot as you like. There are two taps: hot and cold.

LIZA [*weeping*]: I couldnt. I dursnt. Its not natural: It would kill me. Ive never had a bath in my life: not what youd call a proper one.

MRS PEARCE: Well, dont you want to be clean and sweet and decent, like a lady? You know you cant be a nice girl inside if youre a dirty slut outside.

LIZA: Boohoo!!!!

5. Kettle to boil laundry.

MRS PEARCE: Now stop crying and go back into your room and take off all your clothes. Then wrap yourself in this [*taking down a gown from its peg and handing it to her*] and come back to me. I will get the bath ready.

LIZA [*all tears*]: I cant. I wont. I'm not used to it. Ive never took off all my clothes before. It's not right: it's not decent.

MRS PEARCE: Nonsense, child. Dont you take off all your clothes every night when you go to bed?

LIZA [*amazed*]: No. Why should I? I should catch my death. Of course I take off my skirt.

MRS PEARCE: Do you mean that you sleep in the underclothes you wear in the daytime?

LIZA: What else have I to sleep in?

MRS PEARCE: You will never do that again as long as you live here. I will get you a proper nightdress.

LIZA: Do you mean change into cold things and lie awake shivering half the night? You want to kill me, you do.

MRS PEARCE: I want to change you from a frowzy[6] slut to a clean respectable girl fit to sit with the gentlemen in the study. Are you going to trust me and do what I tell you or be thrown out and sent back to your flower basket?

LIZA: But you dont know what the cold is to me. You dont know how I dread it.

MRS PEARCE: Your bed wont be cold here: I will put a hot water bottle in it. [*Pushing her into the bedroom.*] Off with you and undress.

LIZA: Oh, if only I'd a known what a dreadful thing it is to be clean I'd never have come. I didnt know when I was well off. I—[*Mrs Pearce pushes her through the door, but leaves it partly open lest her prisoner should take to flight.*]

[*Mrs Pearce puts on a pair of white rubber sleeves, and fills the bath, mixing hot and cold, and testing the result with the bath thermometer. She perfumes it with a handful of bath salts and adds a palmful of mustard. She then takes a formidable looking long handled scrubbing brush and soaps it profusely with a ball of scented soap.*

Eliza comes back with nothing on but the bath gown huddled tightly round her, a piteous spectacle of abject terror.]

MRS PEARCE: Now come along. Take that thing off.

LIZA: Oh I couldnt, Mrs Pearce: I reely couldnt. I never done such a thing.

MRS PEARCE: Nonsense. Here: step in and tell me whether it's hot enough for you.

LIZA: Ah-oo! Ah-oo! It's too hot.

MRS PEARCE [*deftly snatching the gown away and throwing Eliza down on her back*]: It wont hurt you. [*She sets to work with the scrubbing brush.*]

[*Eliza's screams are heartrending.*]

* * *

Meanwhile the Colonel has been having it out with Higgins about Eliza. Pickering has come from the hearth to the chair and seated himself astride of it with his arms on the back to cross-examine him.

PICKERING: Excuse the straight question, Higgins. Are you a man of good character where women are concerned?

6. Dirty, untidy.

HIGGINS [*moodily*]: Have you ever met a man of good character where women are concerned?

PICKERING: Yes: very frequently.

HIGGINS [*dogmatically, lifting himself on his hands to the level of the piano, and sitting on it with a bounce*]: Well, I havnt. I find that the moment I let a woman make friends with me, she becomes jealous, exacting, suspicious, and a damned nuisance. I find that the moment I let myself make friends with a woman, I become selfish and tyrannical. Women upset everything. When you let them into your life, you find that the woman is driving at one thing and youre driving at another.

PICKERING: At what, for example?

HIGGINS [*coming off the piano restlessly*]: Oh, Lord knows! I suppose the woman wants to live her own life; and the man wants to live his; and each tries to drag the other on to the wrong track. One wants to go north and the other south; and the result is that both have to go east, though they both hate the east wind. [*He sits down on the bench at the keyboard.*] So here I am, a confirmed old bachelor, and likely to remain so.

PICKERING [*rising and standing over him gravely*]: Come, Higgins! You know what I mean. If I'm to be in this business I shall feel responsible for that girl. I hope it's understood that no advantage is to be taken of her position.

HIGGINS: What! That thing! Sacred. I assure you. [*Rising to explain.*] You see, she'll be a pupil; and teaching would be impossible unless pupils were sacred. Ive taught scores of American millionairesses how to speak English: the best looking women in the world. I'm seasoned. They might as well be blocks of wood. I might as well be a block of wood. It's—

[*Mrs Pearce opens the door. She has Eliza's hat in her hand. Pickering retires to the easy-chair at the hearth and sits down.*]

HIGGINS [*eagerly*]: Well, Mrs Pearce: is it all right?

MRS PEARCE [*at the door*]: I just wish to trouble you with a word, if I may, Mr Higgins.

HIGGINS: Yes, certainly. Come in. [*She comes forward.*] Dont burn that, Mrs Pearce. I'll keep it as a curiosity. [*He takes the hat.*]

MRS PEARCE: Handle it carefully, sir, please. I had to promise her not to burn it; but I had better put it in the oven for a while.

HIGGINS [*putting it down hastily on the piano*]: Oh! thank you. Well, what have you to say to me?

PICKERING: Am I in the way?

MRS PEARCE: Not at all, sir. Mr Higgins: will you please be very particular what you say before the girl?

HIGGINS [*sternly*]: Of course. I'm always particular about what I say. Why do you say this to me?

MRS PEARCE [*unmoved*]: No sir: youre not at all particular when youve mislaid anything or when you get a little impatient. Now it doesnt matter before me: I'm used to it. But you really must not swear before the girl.

HIGGINS [*indignantly*]: I swear! [*Most emphatically.*] I never swear. I detest the habit. What the devil do you mean?

MRS PEARCE [*stolidly*]: Thats what I mean, sir. You swear a great deal too much. I dont mind your damning and blasting, and what the devil and where the devil and who the devil—

HIGGINS: Mrs Pearce: this language from your lips! Really!

MRS PEARCE [*not to be put off*]: —but there is a certain word I must ask you not to use. The girl used it herself when she began to enjoy the bath. It begins with the same letter as bath.[7] She knows no better: she learnt it at her mother's knee. But she must not hear it from your lips.

HIGGINS [*loftily*]: I cannot charge myself with having ever uttered it, Mrs Pearce. [*She looks at him steadfastly. He adds, hiding an uneasy conscience with a judicial air.*] Except perhaps in a moment of extreme and justifiable excitement.

MRS PEARCE: Only this morning, sir, you applied it to your boots, to the butter, and to the brown bread.

HIGGINS: Oh, that! Mere alliteration, Mrs Pearce, natural to a poet.

MRS PEARCE: Well, sir, whatever you choose to call it. I beg you not to let the girl hear you repeat it.

HIGGINS: Oh, very well, very well. Is that all?

MRS PEARCE: No, sir. We shall have to be very particular with this girl as to personal cleanliness.

HIGGINS: Certainly. Quite right. Most important.

MRS PEARCE: I mean not to be slovenly about her dress or untidy in leaving things about.

HIGGINS [*going to her solemnly*]: Just so. I intended to call your attention to that. [*He passes on to Pickering, who is enjoying the conversation immensely.*] It is these little things that matter, Pickering. Take care of the pence and the pounds will take care of themselves is as true of personal habits as of money. [*He comes to anchor on the hearthrug, with the air of a man in an unassailable position.*]

MRS PEARCE: Yes, sir. Then might I ask you not to come down to breakfast in your dressing-gown, or at any rate not to use it as a napkin to the extent you do, sir. And if you would be so good as not to eat everything off the same plate, and to remember not to put the porridge saucepan out of your hand on the clean tablecloth, it would be a better example to the girl. You know you nearly choked yourself with a fishbone in the jam only last week.

HIGGINS [*routed from the hearthrug and drifting back to the piano*]: I may do these things sometimes in absence of mind; but surely I dont do them habitually. [*Angrily.*] By the way: my dressing-gown smells most damnably of benzine.

MRS PEARCE: No doubt it does, Mr Higgins. But if you will wipe your fingers—

HIGGINS [*yelling*]: Oh very well, very well: I'll wipe them in my hair in future.

MRS PEARCE: I hope youre not offended, Mr Higgins.

HIGGINS [*shocked at finding himself thought capable of an unamiable sentiment*]: Not at all, not at all. Youre quite right, Mrs Pearce: I shall be particularly careful before the girl. Is that all?

MRS PEARCE: No, sir. Might she use some of those Japanese dresses you brought from abroad? I really cant put her back into her old things.

HIGGINS: Certainly. Anything you like. Is that all?

MRS PEARCE: Thank you, sir. Thats all. [*She goes out.*]

HIGGINS: You know, Pickering, that woman has the most extraordinary ideas about me. Here I am, a shy, diffident sort of man. Ive never been able to feel really grown-up and tremendous, like other chaps. And yet she's firmly persuaded that I'm an arbitrary overbearing bossing kind of person. I cant account for it.

7. The word in question is "bloody" which, at the time the play was written and produced, was a vulgar term not used in polite society.

[*Mrs Pearce returns.*]

MRS PEARCE: If you please, sir, the trouble's beginning already. Theres a dustman downstairs, Alfred Doolittle, wants to see you. He says you have his daughter here.

PICKERING [*rising*]: Phew! I say!

HIGGINS [*promptly*]: Send the blackguard[8] up.

MRS PEARCE: Oh, very well, sir. [*She goes out.*]

PICKERING: He may not be a blackguard, Higgins.

HIGGINS: Nonsense. Of course he's a blackguard.

PICKERING: Whether he is or not, I'm afraid we shall have some trouble with him.

HIGGINS [*confidently*]: Oh no: I think not. If theres any trouble he shall have it with me, not I with him. And we are sure to get something interesting out of him.

PICKERING: About the girl?

HIGGINS: No, I mean his dialect.

PICKERING: Oh!

MRS PEARCE [*at the door*]: Doolittle, sir. [*She admits Doolittle and retires.*]

[*Alfred Doolittle is an elderly but vigorous dustman, clad in the costume of his profession, including a hat with a back brim covering his neck and shoulders. He has well marked and rather interesting features, and seems equally free from fear and conscience. He has a remarkably expressive voice, the result of a habit of giving vent to his feelings without reserve. His present pose is that of wounded honor and stern resolution.*]

DOOLITTLE [*at the door, uncertain which of the two gentlemen is his man*]: Professor Iggins?

HIGGINS: Here, Good morning. Sit down.

DOOLITTLE: Morning, Governor. [*He sits down magisterially.*] I come about a very serious matter, Governor.

HIGGINS [*to Pickering*]: Brought up in Hounslow. Mother Welsh, I should think. [*Doolittle opens his mouth, amazed. Higgins continues.*] What do you want, Doolittle?

DOOLITTLE [*menacingly*]: I want my daughter: thats what I want. See?

HIGGINS: Of course you do. Youre her father, arnt you? You dont suppose anyone else wants her, do you? I'm glad to see you have some spark of family feeling left. She's upstairs. Take her away at once.

DOOLITTLE [*rising, fearfully taken aback*]: What!

HIGGINS: Take her away. Do you suppose I'm going to keep your daughter for you?

DOOLITTLE [*remonstrating*]: Now, now, look here, Governor. Is this reasonable? Is it fairity[9] to take advantage of a man like this? The girl belongs to me. You got her. Where do I come in? [*He sits down again.*]

HIGGINS: Your daughter had the audacity to come to my house and ask me to teach her how to speak properly so that she could get a place in a flower-shop. This gentleman and my housekeeper have been here all the time. [*Bullying him.*] How dare you come here and attempt to blackmail me? You sent her here on purpose.

DOOLITTLE [*protesting*]: No, Governor.

HIGGINS: You must have. How else could you possibly know that she is here?

DOOLITTLE: Dont take a man up like that, Governor.

HIGGINS: The police shall take you up. This is a plant—a plot to extort money by threats. I shall telephone for the police. [*He goes resolutely to the telephone and opens the directory.*]

8. Scoundrel.

9. Fair play.

DOOLITTLE: Have I asked you for a brass farthing? I leave it to the gentleman here: have I said a word about money?

HIGGINS [*throwing the book aside and marching down on Doolittle with a poser*[1]]: What else did you come for?

DOOLITTLE [*sweetly*]: Well, what would a man come for? Be human, Governor.

HIGGINS [*disarmed*]: Alfred: did you put her up to it?

DOOLITTLE: So help me, Governor, I never did. I take my Bible oath I aint seen the girl these two months past.

HIGGINS: Then how did you know she was here?

DOOLITTLE [*"most musical, most melancholy"*]: I'll tell you, Governor, if youll only let me get a word in. I'm willing to tell you. I'm wanting to tell you. I'm waiting to tell you.

HIGGINS: Pickering: this chap has a certain natural gift of rhetoric. Observe the rhythm of his native woodnotes wild. "I'm willing to tell you: I'm wanting to tell you: I'm waiting to tell you." Sentimental rhetoric! Thats the Welsh strain in him. It also accounts for his mendacity[2] and dishonesty.

PICKERING: Oh, please, Higgins: I'm west country[3] myself. [*To Doolittle.*] How did you know the girl was here if you didnt send her?

DOOLITTLE: It was like this, Governor. The girl took a boy in the taxi to give him a jaunt. Son of her landlady, he is. He hung about on the chance of her giving him another ride home. Well, she sent him back for her luggage when she heard you was willing for her to stop here. I met the boy at the corner of Long Acre and Endell Street.

HIGGINS: Public house. Yes?

DOOLITTLE: The poor man's club, Governor: why shouldnt I?

PICKERING: Do let him tell his story, Higgins.

DOOLITTLE: He told me what was up. And I ask you, what was my feelings and my duty as a father? I says to the boy, "You bring me the luggage," I says—

PICKERING: Why didnt you go for it yourself?

DOOLITTLE: Landlady wouldnt have trusted me with it, Governor. She's that kind of woman: you know. I had to give the boy a penny afore he trusted me with it, the little swine. I brought it to her just to oblige you like, and make myself agreeable. Thats all.

HIGGINS: How much luggage?

DOOLITTLE: Musical instrument, Governor. A few pictures, a trifle of jewlery, and a bird-cage. She said she didn't want no clothes. What was I to think from that, Governor? I ask you as a parent what was I to think?

HIGGINS: So you came to rescue her from worse than death eh?

DOOLITTLE [*appreciatively: relieved at being so well understood*]: Just so, Governor. Thats right.

PICKERING: But why did you bring her luggage if you intended to take her away?

DOOLITTLE: Have I said a word about taking her away? Have I now?

HIGGINS [*determinedly*]: Youre going to take her away, double quick. [*He crosses to the hearth and rings the bell.*]

DOOLITTLE [*rising*]: No, Governor. Dont say that. I'm not the man to stand in my girl's light. Heres a career opening for her as you might say; and—

1. Puzzle.
2. Tendency to lie.
3. From the west of England—perhaps even Wales.

[*Mrs Pearce opens the door and awaits orders.*]

HIGGINS: Mrs Pearce: this is Eliza's father. He has come to take her away. Give her to him. [*He goes back to the piano, with an air of washing his hands of the whole affair.*]

DOOLITTLE: No. This is a misunderstanding. Listen here—

MRS PEARCE: He cant take her away, Mr Higgins: how can he? You told me to burn her clothes.

DOOLITTLE: Thats right. I cant carry the girl through the streets like a blooming monkey, can I? I put it to you.

HIGGINS: You have put it to me that you want your daughter. Take your daughter. If she has no clothes go out and buy her some.

DOOLITTLE [*desperate*]: Wheres the clothes she come in? Did I burn them or did your missus here?

MRS PEARCE: I am the housekeeper, if you please. I have sent for some clothes for the girl. When they come you can take her away. You can wait in the kitchen. This way, please.

[*Doolittle, much troubled, accompanies her to the door; then hesitates: finally turns confidentially to Higgins.*]

DOOLITTLE: Listen here, Governor. You and me is men of the world, aint we?

HIGGINS: Oh! Men of the world, are we? Youd better go, Mrs Pearce.

MRS PEARCE: I think so, indeed, sir. [*She goes, with dignity.*]

PICKERING: The floor is yours, Mr Doolittle.

DOOLITTLE [*to Pickering*]: I thank you, Governor. [*To Higgins, who takes refuge on the piano bench, a little overwhelmed by the proximity of his visitor; for Doolittle has a professional flavor of dust about him.*] Well, the truth is, Ive taken a sort of fancy to you, Governor; and if you want the girl, I'm not so set on having her back home again but what I might be open to an arrangement. Regarded in the light of a young woman, she's a fine handsome girl. As a daughter she's not worth her keep; and so I tell you straight. All I ask is my rights as a father; and youre the last man alive to expect me to let her go for nothing; for I can see youre one of the straight sort, Governor. Well, whats a five-pound note to you? and whats Eliza to me? [*He turns to his chair and sits down judicially.*]

PICKERING: I think you ought to know, Doolittle, that Mr Higgins's intentions are entirely honorable.

DOOLITTLE: Course they are, Governor. If I thought they wasn't, I'd ask fifty.

HIGGINS [*revolted*]: Do you mean to say that you would sell your daughter for £50?

DOOLITTLE: Not in a general way I wouldnt; but to oblige a gentleman like you I'd do a good deal, I do assure you.

PICKERING: Have you no morals, man?

DOOLITTLE [*unabashed*]: Cant afford them, Governor. Neither could you if you was as poor as me. Not that I mean any harm, you know. But if Liza is going to have a bit out of this, why not me too?

HIGGINS [*troubled*]: I dont know what to do, Pickering. There can be no question that as a matter of morals it's a positive crime to give this chap a farthing. And yet I feel a sort of rough justice in his claim.

DOOLITTLE: Thats it, Governor. Thats all I say. A father's heart, as it were.

PICKERING: Well, I know the feeling; but really it seems hardly right—

DOOLITTLE: Dont say that, Governor. Dont look at it that way. What am I, Governors both? I ask you, what am I? I'm one of the undeserving poor: thats what I am. Think of what that means to a man. It means that he's up agen middle class morality all the time. If theres anything going, and I put in for a bit of it, it's always the same story: "Youre undeserving: so you cant have it." But my needs is as great as the most deserving widow's that ever got money out of six different charities in one week for the death of the same husband. I dont need less than a deserving man: I need more. I dont eat less hearty than him; and I drink a lot more. I want a bit of amusement, cause I'm a thinking man. I want cheerfulness and a song and a band when I feel low. Well, they charge me just the same for everything as they charge the deserving. What is middle class morality? Just an excuse for never giving me anything. Therefore, I ask you, as two gentlemen, not to play that game on me. I'm playing straight with you. I aint pretending to be deserving. I'm undeserving; and I mean to go on being undeserving. I like it; and thats the truth. Will you take advantage of a man's nature to do him out of the price of his own daughter what he's brought up and fed and clothed by the sweat of his brow until she's growed big enough to be interesting to you two gentlemen? Is five pounds unreasonable? I put it to you: and I leave it to you.

HIGGINS [*rising, and going over to Pickering*]: Pickering: if we were to take this man in hand for three months, he could choose between a seat in the Cabinet and a popular pulpit in Wales.

PICKERING: What do you say to that, Doolittle?

DOOLITTLE: Not me, Governor, thank you kindly. Ive heard all the preachers and all the prime ministers—for I'm a thinking man and game for politics or religion or social reform same as all the other amusements—and I tell you it's a dog's life any way you look at it. Undeserving poverty is my line. Taking one station in society with another, it's—it's—well, it's the only one that has any ginger in it, to my taste.

HIGGINS: I suppose we must give him a fiver.

PICKERING: He'll make a bad use of it, I'm afraid.

DOOLITTLE: Not me, Governor, so help me I wont. Dont you be afraid that I'll save it and spare it and live idle on it. There wont be a penny of it left by Monday: I'll have to go to work same as if I'd never had it. It wont pauperize me, you bet. Just one good spree for myself and the missus, giving pleasure to ourselves and employment to others, and satisfaction to you to think it's not been throwed away. You couldnt spend it better.

HIGGINS: [*taking out his pocket book and coming between Doolittle and the piano*]: This is irresistible. Lets give him ten. [*He offers two notes to the dustman.*]

DOOLITTLE: No. Governor. She wouldnt have the heart to spend ten; and perhaps I shouldnt neither. Ten pounds is a lot of money: it makes a man feel prudent like; and then good-bye to happiness. You give me what I ask you, Governor: not a penny more, and not a penny less.

PICKERING: Why dont you marry that missus of yours? I rather draw the line at encouraging that sort of immorality.

DOOLITTLE: Tell her so. Governor: tell her so. *I'm* willing. It's me that suffers by it. Ive no hold on her. I got to be agreeable to her. I got to give her presents. I got to buy her clothes something sinful. I'm a slave to that woman, Governor, just because I'm not her lawful husband. And she knows it too. Catch her marrying me! Take my advice, Governor—marry Eliza while she's young and dont know no better. If you dont youll be sorry for it after. If you do, she'll be sorry for it after; but better her than you, because youre a man, and she's only a woman and dont know how to be happy anyhow.

HIGGINS: Pickering: If we listen to this man another minute, we shall have no convictions left. [*To Doolittle.*] Five pounds I think you said.

DOOLITTLE: Thank you kindly, Governor.

HIGGINS: Youre sure you wont take ten?

DOOLITTLE: Not now. Another time, Governor.

HIGGINS [*handing him a five-pound note*]: Here you are.

DOOLITTLE: Thank you, Governor. Good morning. [*He hurries to the door, anxious to get away with his booty. When he opens it he is confronted with a dainty and exquisitely clean young Japanese lady in a simple blue cotton kimono printed cunningly with small white jasmine blossoms. Mrs Pearce is with her. He gets out of her way deferentially and apologizes.*] Beg pardon, miss.

THE JAPANESE LADY: Garn! Dont you know you own daughter?

DOOLITTLE: } *exclaiming* { Bly me! It's Eliza!
HIGGINS: } *simul-* { Whats that? This!
PICKERING: } *taneously* { By Jove!

LIZA: Dont I look silly?

HIGGINS: Silly?

MRS PEARCE [*at the door*]: Now, Mr Higgins, please dont say anything to make the girl conceited about herself.

HIGGINS [*conscientiously*]: Oh! Quite right, Mrs Pearce. [*To Eliza.*] Yes: damned silly.

MRS PEARCE: Please, sir.

HIGGINS [*correcting himself*]: I mean extremely silly.

LIZA: I should look all right with my hat on. [*She takes up her hat; puts it on; and walks across the room to the fireplace with a fashionable air.*]

HIGGINS: A new fashion, by George! And it ought to look horrible!

DOOLITTLE: [*with fatherly pride*]: Well, I never thought she'd clean up as good looking as that, Governor. She's a credit to me, aint she?

LIZA: I tell you, it's easy to clean up here. Hot and cold water on tap, just as much as you like, there is. Woolly towels, there is; and a towel horse[4] so hot, it burns your fingers. Soft brushes to scrub yourself, and a wooden bowl of soap smelling like primroses. Now I know why ladies is so clean. Washing's a treat for them. Wish they could see what it is for the like of me!

HIGGINS: I'm glad the bathroom met with your approval.

LIZA: It didnt: not all of it; and I dont care who hears me say it. Mrs Pearce knows.

HIGGINS: What was wrong, Mrs Pearce?

MRS PEARCE [*blandly*]: Oh, nothing, sir. It doesnt matter.

LIZA: I had a good mind to break it. I didn't know which way to look. But I hung a towel over it, I did.

HIGGINS: Over what?

MRS PEARCE: Over the looking-glass sir.

HIGGINS: Doolittle: you have brought your daughter up too strictly.

DOOLITTLE: Me! I never brought her up at all, except to give her a lick of a strap now and again. Dont put it on me, Governor. She aint accustomed to it, you see: thats all. But she'll soon pick up your free-and-easy ways.

LIZA: I'm a good girl, I am; and I wont pick up no free-and-easy ways.

4. Towel rack.

HIGGINS: Eliza: if you say again that youre a good girl, your father shall take you home.

LIZA: Not him. You dont know my father. All he come here for was to touch you for some money to get drunk on.

DOOLITTLE: Well, what else would I want money for? To put into the plate in church, I suppose. [*She puts out her tongue at him. He is so incensed by this that Pickering presently finds it necessary to step between them.*] Dont you give me none of your lip; and dont let me hear you giving this gentleman any of it neither, or youll hear from me about it. See?

HIGGINS: Have you any further advice to give her before you go, Doolittle? Your blessing, for instance.

DOOLITTLE: No, Governor: I aint such a mug as to put up my children to all I know myself. Hard enough to hold them in without that. If you want Eliza's mind improved, Governor, you do it yourself with a strap. So long, gentlemen. [*He turns to go.*]

HIGGINS [*impressively*]: Stop. Youll come regularly to see your daughter. It's your duty, you know. My brother is a clergyman; and he could help you in your talks with her.

DOOLITTLE [*evasively*]: Certainly. I'll come, Governor. Not just this week, because I have a job at a distance. But later on you may depend on me. Afternoon, gentlemen. Afternoon, maam. [*He touches his hat to Mrs Pearce, who disdains the salutation and goes out. He winks at Higgins, thinking him probably a fellow-sufferer from Mrs Pearce's difficult disposition, and follows her.*]

LIZA: Dont you believe the old liar. He'd as soon you set a bull-dog on him as a clergyman. You wont see him again in a hurry.

HIGGINS: I dont want to, Eliza. Do you?

LIZA: Not me. I dont want never to see him again. I dont. He's a disgrace to me, he is, collecting dust, instead of working at his trade.

PICKERING: What is his trade, Eliza?

LIZA: Talking money out of other people's pockets into his own. His proper trade's a navvy;[5] and he works at it sometimes too—for exercise—and earns good money at it. Aint you going to call me Miss Doolittle any more?

PICKERING: I beg your pardon, Miss Doolittle. It was a slip of the tongue.

LIZA: Oh, I dont mind; only it sounded so genteel. I should just like to take a taxi to the corner of Tottenham Court Road and get out there and tell it to wait for me, just to put the girls in their place a bit. I wouldnt speak to them, you know.

PICKERING: Better wait til we get you something really fashionable.

HIGGINS: Besides, you shouldnt cut your old friends now that you have risen in the world. Thats what we call snobbery.

LIZA: You dont call the like of them my friends now, I should hope. Theyve took it out of me often enough with their ridicule when they had the chance; and now I mean to get a bit of my own back. But if I'm to have fashionable clothes, I'll wait. I should like to have some. Mrs Pearce says youre going to give me some to wear in bed at night different to what I wear in the daytime; but it do seem a waste of money when you could get something to shew. Besides, I never could fancy changing into cold things on a winter night.

5. Manual laborer.

MRS PEARCE [*coming back*]: Now, Eliza. The new things have come for you to try on.

LIZA: Ah-ow-oo-ooh! [*She rushes out.*]

MRS PEARCE [*following her*]: Oh, dont rush about like that, girl. [*She shuts the door behind her.*]

HIGGINS: Pickering: we have taken on a stiff job.

PICKERING [*with conviction*]: Higgins: we have.

* * *

There seems to be some curiosity as to what Higgins's lessons to Eliza were like. Well, here is a sample: the first one.

Picture Eliza, in her new clothes, and feeling her inside put out of step by a lunch, dinner, and breakfast of a kind to which it is unaccustomed, seated with Higgins and the Colonel in the study, feeling like a hospital out-patient at a first encounter with the doctors.

Higgins, constitutionally unable to sit still, discomposes her still more by striding restlessly about. But for the reassuring presence and quietude of her friend the Colonel she would run for her life, even back to Drury Lane.

HIGGINS: Say your alphabet.

LIZA: I know my alphabet. Do you think I know nothing? I dont need to be taught like a child.

HIGGINS [*thundering*]: Say your alphabet.

PICKERING: Say it, Miss Doolittle. You will understand presently. Do what he tells you; and let him teach you in his own way.

LIZA: Oh well, if you put it like that—Ahyee, bə yee, cə yee, də yee—

HIGGINS [*with the roar of a wounded lion*]: Stop. Listen to this, Pickering. This is what we pay for as elementary education. This unfortunate animal has been locked up for nine years in school at our expense to teach her to speak and read the language of Shakespear and Milton. And the result is Ahyee, Bə -yee, Cə -yee, Də -yee. [*To Eliza.*] Say A, B, C, D.

LIZA [*almost in tears*]: But I'm saying it. Ahyee, Bə yee, Cə -yee—

HIGGINS: Stop. Say a cup of tea.

LIZA: A cappə tə -ee.

HIGGINS: Put your tongue forward until it squeezes against the top of your lower teeth. Now say cup.

LIZA: C-c-c—I cant. C-Cup.

PICKERING: Good. Splendid, Miss Doolittle.

HIGGINS: By Jupiter, she's done it at the first shot. Pickering: we shall make a duchess of her. [*To Eliza.*] Now do you think you could possibly say tea? Not tə -yee, mind: if you ever say bə -yee cə -yee də -yee again you shall be dragged round the room three times by the hair of your head. [*Fortissimo.*] T, T, T, T.

LIZA [*weeping*]: I cant hear no difference cep that it sounds more genteel-like when you say it.

HIGGINS: Well, if you can hear that difference, what the devil are you crying for? Pickering: give her a chocolate.

PICKERING: No, no. Never mind crying a little, Miss Doolittle: you are doing very well; and the lessons wont hurt. I promise you I wont let him drag you round the room by your hair.

HIGGINS: Be off with you to Mrs Pearce and tell her about it. Think about it. Try to do it by yourself: and keep your tongue well forward in your mouth instead of trying to roll it up and swallow it. Another lesson at half-past four this afternoon. Away with you.

[Eliza, still sobbing, rushes from the room.]

And that is the sort of ordeal poor Eliza has to go through for months before we meet her again on her first appearance in London society of the professional class.

ACT 3

It is Mrs Higgins's at-home day.[1] *Nobody has yet arrived. Her drawing room, in a flat on Chelsea Embankment, has three windows looking on the river; and the ceiling is not so lofty as it would be in an older house of the same pretension. The windows are open, giving access to a balcony with flowers in pots. If you stand with your face to the windows, you have the fireplace on your left and the door in the right-hand wall close to the corner nearest the windows.*

Mrs Higgins was brought up on Morris[2] *and Burne Jones;*[3] *and her room, which is very unlike her son's room in Wimpole Street, is not crowded with furniture and little tables and nicknacks. In the middle of the room there is a big ottoman; and this, with the carpet, the Morris wallpapers, and the Morris chintz window curtains and brocade covers of the ottoman and its cushions, supply all the ornament, and are much too handsome to be hidden by odds and ends of useless things. A few good oil-paintings from the exhibitions in the Grosvenor Gallery thirty years ago (the Burne Jones, not the Whistler*[4] *side of them) are on the walls. The only landscape is a Cecil Lawson*[5] *on the scale of a Rubens*[6]. *There is a portrait of Mrs Higgins as she was when she defied the fashion in her youth in one of the beautiful Rossettian*[7] *costumes which, when caricatured by people who did not understand, led to the absurdities of popular estheticism in the eighteen-seventies.*

In the corner diagonally opposite the door Mrs Higgins, now over sixty and long past taking the trouble to dress out of the fashion, sits writing at an elegantly simple writing-table with a bell button within reach of her hand. There is a Chippendale chair further back in the room between her and the window nearest her side. At the other side of the room, further forward, is an Elizabethan chair roughly carved in the taste of Inigo Jones. On the same side a piano in a decorated case. The corner between the fireplace and the window is occupied by a divan cushioned in Morris chintz.

It is between four and five in the afternoon.

The door is opened violently; and Higgins enters with his hat on.

MRS HIGGINS [*dismayed*]: Henry! [*Scolding him.*] What are you doing here today? It is my at-home day: you promised not to come. [*As he bends to kiss her, she takes his hat off, and presents it to him.*]

HIGGINS: Oh bother! [*He throws the hat down on the table.*]

MRS HIGGINS: Go home at once.

HIGGINS [*kissing her*]: I know, mother. I came on purpose.

MRS HIGGINS: But you mustnt. I'm serious, Henry. You offend all my friends: they stop coming whenever they meet you.

1. Reception of visitors in one's home in genteel society.
2. William Morris (1834–1896), English graphic artist, poet, and social reformer.
3. Sir Edward Coley Burne-Jones (1833–1898), English painter and designer.
4. James Abbott McNeill Whistler (1834–1903), American avant-garde painter who did much of his work living in London.
5. Cecil Gordon Lawson (1851–1882), English landscape painter.
6. Peter Paul Rubens (1577–1640), Flemish painter.
7. Dante Gabriel Rossetti (1828–1882), painter and poet, founder of the Pre-Raphaelite Brotherhood.

HIGGINS: Nonsense! I know I have no small talk; but people dont mind. [*He sits on the settee.*]

MRS HIGGINS: Oh! dont they? Small talk indeed! What about your large talk? Really, dear, you mustnt stay.

HIGGINS: I must. Ive a job for you. A phonetic job.

MRS HIGGINS: No use, dear. I'm sorry; but I cant get round your vowels; and though I like to get pretty postcards in your patent shorthand, I always have to read the copies in ordinary writing you so thoughtfully send me.

HIGGINS: Well, this isnt a phonetic job.

MRS HIGGINS: You said it was.

HIGGINS: Not your part of it. Ive picked up a girl.

MRS HIGGINS: Does that mean that some girl has picked you up?

HIGGINS: Not at all. I dont mean a love affair.

MRS HIGGINS: What a pity!

HIGGINS: Why?

MRS HIGGINS: Well, you never fall in love with anyone under forty-five. When will you discover that there are some rather nice-looking young women about?

HIGGINS: Oh, I cant be bothered with young women. My idea of a lovable woman is somebody as like you as possible. I shall never get into the way of seriously liking young women: some habits lie too deep to be changed. [*Rising abruptly and walking about, jingling his money and his keys in his trouser pockets.*] Besides, theyre all idiots.

MRS HIGGINS: Do you know what you would do if you really loved me, Henry?

HIGGINS: Oh bother! What? Marry, I suppose.

MRS HIGGINS: No. Stop fidgeting and take your hands out of your pockets. [*With a gesture of despair, he obeys and sits down again.*] Thats a good boy. Now tell me about the girl.

HIGGINS: She's coming to see you.

MRS HIGGINS: I dont remember asking her.

HIGGINS: You didnt. *I* asked her. If youd known her you wouldnt have asked her.

MRS HIGGINS: Indeed! Why?

HIGGINS: Well, It's like this. She's a common flower-girl. I picked her off the kerbstone.

MRS HIGGINS: And invited her to my at-home!

HIGGINS [*rising and coming to her to coax her*]: Oh, thatll be all right. Ive taught her to speak properly; and she has strict orders as to her behavior. She's to keep to two subjects: the weather and everybody's health—Fine day and How do you do, you know—and not to let herself go on things in general. That will be safe.

MRS HIGGINS: Safe! To talk about our health! About our insides! Perhaps about our outsides! How could you be so silly, Henry?

HIGGINS [*impatiently*]: Well, she must talk about something. [*He controls himself and sits down again.*] Oh, she'll be all right; dont you fuss. Pickering is in it with me. Ive a sort of bet on that I'll pass her off as a duchess in six months. I started on her some months ago; and she's getting on like a house on fire. I shall win my bet. She has a quick ear; and she's been easier to teach than my middle-class pupils because she's had to learn a complete new language. She talks English almost as you talk French.

MRS HIGGINS: Thats satisfactory, at all events.

HIGGINS: Well, it is and it isnt.

MRS HIGGINS: What does that mean?

HIGGINS: You see, Ive got her pronunciation all right; but you have to consider not only how a girl pronounces, but what she pronounces; and thats where—

[*They are interrupted by the parlormaid, announcing guests.*]

THE PARLORMAID: Mrs and Miss Eynsford Hill. [*She withdraws.*]

HIGGINS: Oh Lord! [*He rises: snatches his hat from the table; and makes for the door; but before he reaches it his mother introduces him.*]

[*Mrs and Miss Eynsford Hill are the mother and daughter who sheltered from the rain in Covent Garden. The mother is well bred, quiet, and has the habitual anxiety of straitened means. The daughter has acquired a gay air of being very much at home in society; the bravado of genteel poverty.*]

MRS EYNSFORD HILL [*to Mrs Higgins*]: How do you do? [*They shake hands.*]

MISS EYNSFORD HILL: How d'you do? [*She shakes.*]

MRS HIGGINS [*introducing*]: My son Henry.

MRS EYNSFORD HILL: Your celebrated son! I have so longed to meet you, Professor Higgins.

HIGGINS [*glumly, making no movement in her direction*]: Delighted. [*He backs against the piano and bows brusquely.*]

MISS EYNSFORD HILL [*going to him with confident familiarity*]: How do you do?

HIGGINS [*staring at her*]: Ive seen you before somewhere. I havnt the ghost of a notion where; but Ive heard your voice. [*Drearily*] It doesnt matter. Youd better sit down.

MRS HIGGINS: I'm sorry to say that my celebrated son has no manners. You mustnt mind him.

MISS EYNSFORD HILL [*gaily*]: I dont. [*She sits in the Elizabethan chair.*]

MRS EYNSFORD HILL [*a little bewildered*]: Not at all. [*She sits on the ottoman between her daughter and Mrs Higgins, who has turned her chair away from the writing-table.*]

HIGGINS: Oh, have I been rude? I didnt mean to be.

[*He goes to the central window, through which, with his back to the company, he contemplates the river and the flowers in Battersea Park on the opposite bank as if they were a frozen desert.*

The parlormaid returns, ushering in Pickering.]

THE PARLORMAID: Colonel Pickering. [*She withdraws.*]

PICKERING: How do you do, Mrs Higgins?

MRS HIGGINS: So glad youve come. Do you know Mrs Eynsford Hill—Miss Eynsford Hill? [*Exchange of bows. The Colonel brings the Chippendale chair a little forward between Mrs Hill and Mrs Higgins, and sits down.*]

PICKERING: Has Henry told you what weve come for?

HIGGINS [*over his shoulder*]: We were interrupted: damn it!

MRS HIGGINS: Oh Henry, Henry, really!

MRS EYNSFORD HILL [*half rising*]: Are we in the way?

MRS HIGGINS [*rising and making her sit down again*]: No, no. You couldnt have come more fortunately; we want you to meet a friend of ours.

HIGGINS [*turning hopefully*]: Yes, by George! We want two or three people. Youll do as well as anybody else.

[*The parlormaid returns, ushering Freddy.*]

THE PARLORMAID: Mr Eynsford Hill.

HIGGINS [*almost audibly, past endurance*]: God of Heaven! Another of them.

FREDDY [*shaking hands with Mrs Higgins*]: Ahdedo?

MRS HIGGINS: Very good of you to come. [*Introducing.*] Colonel Pickering.

FREDDY [*bowing*]: Ahdedo?

MRS HIGGINS: I dont think you know my son, Professor Higgins.

FREDDY [*going to Higgins*]: Ahdedo?

HIGGINS [*looking at him much as if he were a pickpocket*]: I'll take my oath Ive met you before somewhere. Where was it?

FREDDY: I dont think so.

HIGGINS [*resignedly*]: It dont matter, anyhow. Sit down.

[*He shakes Freddy's hand and almost slings him on to the ottoman with his face to the window; then comes round to the other side of it.*]

HIGGINS: Well, here we are, anyhow! [*He sits down on the ottoman next Mrs Eynsford Hill, on her left.*] And now, what the devil are we going to talk about until Eliza comes?

MRS HIGGINS: Henry: you are the life and soul of the Royal Society's soirées; but really youre rather trying on more commonplace occasions.

HIGGINS: Am I? Very sorry. [*Beaming suddenly.*] I suppose I am, you know. [*Uproariously.*] Ha, ha!

MISS EYNSFORD HILL [*who considers Higgins quite eligible matrimonially*]: I sympathize. *I* havnt any small talk. If people would only be frank and say what they really think!

HIGGINS [*relapsing into gloom*]: Lord forbid!

MRS EYNSFORD HILL [*taking up her daughter's cue*]: But why?

HIGGINS: What they think they ought to think is bad enough, Lord knows; but what they really think would break up the whole show. Do you suppose it would be really agreeable if I were to come out now with what *I* really think?

MISS EYNSFORD HILL [*gaily*]: Is it so very cynical?

HIGGINS: Cynical! Who the dickens said it was cynical? I mean it wouldnt be decent.

MRS EYNSFORD HILL [*seriously*]: Oh! I'm sure you dont mean that, Mr Higgins.

HIGGINS: You see, we're all savages, more or less. We're supposed to be civilized and cultured—to know all about poetry and philosophy and art and science, and so on; but how many of us know even the meanings of these names? [*To Miss Hill.*] What do you know of poetry? [*To Mrs Hill.*] What do you know of science? [*Indicating Freddy.*] What does he know of art or science or anything else? What the devil do you imagine I know of philosophy?

MRS HIGGINS [*warningly*]: Or of manners, Henry?

THE PARLORMAID [*opening the door*]: Miss Doolittle. [*She withdraws.*]

HIGGINS [*rising hastily and running to Mrs Higgins*]: Here she is, mother. [*He stands on tiptoe and makes signs over his mother's head to Eliza to indicate to her which lady is her hostess.*]

[*Eliza, who is exquisitely dressed, produces an impression of such remarkable distinction and beauty as she enters that they all rise, quite fluttered. Guided by Higgins's signals, she comes to Mrs Higgins with studied grace.*]

LIZA [*speaking with pedantic correctness of pronunciation and great beauty of tone*]: How do you do, Mrs Higgins? [*She gasps slightly in making sure of the H in Higgins, but is quite successful.*] Mr Higgins told me I might come.

MRS HIGGINS [*cordially*]: Quite right: I'm very glad indeed to see you.

PICKERING: How do you do, Miss Doolittle?

LIZA [*shaking hands with him*]: Colonel Pickering, is it not?

MRS EYNSFORD HILL: I feel sure we have met before, Miss Doolittle. I remember your eyes.

LIZA: How do you do? [*She sits down on the ottoman gracefully in the place just left vacant by Higgins.*]

MRS EYNSFORD HILL [*introducing*]: My daughter Clara.

LIZA: How do you do?

CLARA [*impulsively*]: How do you do? [*She sits down on the ottoman beside Eliza, devouring her with her eyes.*]

FREDDY [*coming to their side of the ottoman*]: Ive certainly had the pleasure.

MRS EYNSFORD HILL [*introducing*]: My son Freddy.

LIZA: How do you do?

[*Freddy bows and sits down in the Elizabethan chair, infatuated.*]

HIGGINS [*suddenly*]: By George, yes: It all comes back to me! [*They stare at him.*] Covent Garden! [*Lamentably.*] What a damned thing!

MRS HIGGINS: Henry, please! [*He is about to sit on the edge of the table.*] Dont sit on my writing-table: youll break it.

HIGGINS [*sulkily*]: Sorry.

[*He goes to the divan, stumbling into the fender and over the fire-irons on his way; extricating himself with muttered imprecations; and finishing his disastrous journey by throwing himself so impatiently on the divan that he almost breaks it. Mrs Higgins looks at him, but controls herself and says nothing.*

A long and painful pause ensues.]

MRS HIGGINS [*at last, conversationally*]: Will it rain, do you think?

LIZA: The shallow depression in the west of these islands is likely to move slowly in an easterly direction. There are no indications of any great change in the barometrical situation.

FREDDY: Ha! ha! how awfully funny!

LIZA: What is wrong with that, young man? I bet I got it right.

FREDDY: Killing!

MRS EYNSFORD HILL: I'm sure I hope it wont turn cold. Theres so much influenza about. It runs right through our whole family regularly every spring.

LIZA [*darkly*]: My aunt died of influenza: so they said.

MRS EYNSFORD HILL [*clicks her tongue sympathetically*]: !!!

LIZA [*in the same tragic tone*]: But it's my belief they done the old woman in.

MRS HIGGINS [*puzzled*]: Done her in?

LIZA: Y-e-e-e-es, Lord love you! Why should she die of influenza? She come through diphtheria right enough the year before. I saw her with my own eyes. Fairly blue with it, she was. They all thought she was dead; but my father he kept ladling gin down her throat til she came to so sudden that she bit the bowl off the spoon.

MRS EYNSFORD HILL [*startled*]: Dear me!

LIZA [*piling up the indictment*]: What call would a woman with that strength in her have to die of influenza? What become of her new straw hat that should have come to me? Somebody pinched it; and what I say is, them as pinched it done her in.

MRS EYNSFORD HILL: What does doing her in mean?

HIGGINS [*hastily*]: Oh, thats the new small talk. To do a person in means to kill them.

MRS EYNSFORD HILL [*to Eliza, horrified*]: You surely dont believe that your aunt was killed?

LIZA: Do I not! Them she lived with would have killed her for a hat-pin, let alone a hat.

MRS EYNSFORD HILL: But it cant have been right for your father to pour spirits down her throat like that. It might have killed her.

LIZA: Not her. Gin was mother's milk to her. Besides, he'd poured so much down his own throat that he knew the good of it.

MRS EYNSFORD HILL: Do you mean that he drank?

LIZA: Drank! My word! Something chronic.

MRS EYNSFORD HILL: How dreadful for you!

LIZA: Not a bit. It never did him no harm what I could see. But then he did not keep it up regular. [*Cheerfully.*] On the burst, as you might say, from time to time. And always more agreeable when he had a drop in. When he was out of work, my mother used to give him fourpence and tell him to go out and not come back until he'd drunk himself cheerful and loving-like. Theres lots of women has to make their husbands drunk to make them fit to live with. [*Now quite at her ease.*] You see, it's like this. If a man has a bit of a conscience, it always takes him when he's sober; and then it makes him low-spirited. A drop of booze just takes that off and makes him happy. [*To Freddy, who is in convulsions of suppressed laughter.*] Here! What are you sniggering at?

FREDDY: The new small talk. You do it so awfully well.

LIZA: If I was doing it proper, what was you laughing at? [*To Higgins.*] Have I said anything I oughtnt?

MRS HIGGINS [*interposing*]: Not at all, Miss Doolittle.

LIZA: Well, thats a mercy, anyhow. [*Expansively.*] What I always say is—

HIGGINS [*rising and looking at his watch*]: Ahem!

LIZA [*looking round at him; taking the hint; and rising*]: Well: I must go. [*They all rise. Freddy goes to the door.*] So pleased to have met you. Goodbye. [*She shakes hands with Mrs Higgins.*]

MRS HIGGINS: Goodbye.

LIZA: Goodbye, Colonel Pickering.

PICKERING: Goodbye, Miss Doolittle. [*They shake hands*].

LIZA [*nodding to the others*]: Goodbye, all.

FREDDY [*opening the door for her*]: Are you walking across the Park, Miss Doolittle? If so—

LIZA [*perfectly elegant diction*]: Walk! Not bloody likely. [*Sensation.*] I am going in a taxi. [*She goes out.*]

[*Pickering gasps and sits down. Freddy goes out on the balcony to catch another glimpse of Eliza.*]

MRS EYNSFORD HILL [*suffering from shock*]: Well, I really cant get used to the new ways.

CLARA [*throwing herself discontentedly into the Elizabethan chair*]: Oh, it's all right, mamma, quite right. People will think we never go anywhere or see anybody if you are so old-fashioned.

MRS EYNSFORD HILL: I daresay I am very old-fashioned; but I do hope you wont begin using that expression, Clara. I have got accustomed to hear you talking about men as rotters, and calling everything filthy and beastly; though I do think it horrible and unladylike. But this last is really too much. Dont you think so, Colonel Pickering?

PICKERING: Dont ask me, Ive been away in India for several years; and manners have changed so much that I sometimes dont know whether I'm at a respectable dinner-table or in a ship's forecastle.

CLARA: It's all a matter of habit. Theres no right or wrong in it. Nobody means anything by it. And it's so quaint, and gives such a smart emphasis to things that are not in themselves very witty. I find the new small talk delightful and quite innocent.

MRS EYNSFORD HILL [*rising*]: Well, after that, I think it's time for us to go.
[*Pickering and Higgins rise.*]

CLARA [*rising*]: Oh yes: we have three at-homes to go to still. Goodbye, Mrs Higgins. Goodbye, Colonel Pickering. Goodbye, Professor Higgins.

HIGGINS [*coming grimly at her from the divan, and accompanying her to the door*]: Goodbye. Be sure you try on that small talk at the three at-homes. Dont be nervous about it. Pitch it in strong.

CLARA [*all smiles*]: I will. Goodbye. Such non-sense, all this early Victorian prudery!

HIGGINS [*tempting her*]: Such damned nonsense!

CLARA: Such bloody nonsense!

MRS EYNSFORD HILL [*convulsively*]: Clara!

CLARA: Ha! ha! [*She goes out radiant, conscious of being thoroughly up to date, and is heard descending the stairs in a stream of silvery laughter.*]

FREDDY [*to the heavens at large*]: Well, I ask you—[*He gives it up, and comes to Mrs Higgins.*] Goodbye.

MRS HIGGINS [*shaking hands*]: Goodbye. Would you like to meet Miss Doolittle again?

FREDDY [*eagerly*]: Yes, I should, most awfully.

MRS HIGGINS: Well, you know my days.

FREDDY: Yes. Thanks awfully. Goodbye. [*He goes out.*]

MRS EYNSFORD HILL: Goodbye, Mr Higgins.

HIGGINS: Goodbye. Goodbye.

MRS EYNSFORD HILL [*to Pickering*]: It's no use. I shall never be able to bring myself to use that word.

PICKERING: Dont. It's not compulsory, you know. Youll get on quite well without it.

MRS EYNSFORD HILL: Only, Clara is so down on me if I am not positively reeking with the latest slang. Goodbye.

PICKERING: Goodbye. [*They shake hands.*]

MRS EYNSFORD HILL [*to Mrs Higgins*]: You mustnt mind Clara. [*Pickering, catching from her lowered tone that this is not meant for him to hear, discreetly joins Higgins at the window.*] We're so poor! and she gets so few parties, poor child! She doesnt quite know. [*Mrs Higgins, seeing that her eyes are moist, takes her hand sympathetically and goes with her to the door.*] But the boy is nice. Dont you think so?

MRS HIGGINS: Oh, quite nice. I shall always be delighted to see him.

MRS EYNSFORD HILL: Thank you, dear. Goodbye. [*She goes out.*]

HIGGINS [*eagerly*]: Well? Is Eliza presentable? [*He swoops on his mother and drags her to the ottoman, where she sits down in Eliza's place with her son on her left.*]
[*Pickering returns to his chair on her right.*]

MRS HIGGINS: You silly boy, of course she's not presentable. She's a triumph of your art and of her dressmaker's; but if you suppose for a moment that she doesnt give herself away in every sentence she utters, you must be perfectly cracked about her.

PICKERING: But dont you think something might be done? I mean something to eliminate the sanguinary element from her conversation.

MRS HIGGINS: Not as long as she is in Henry's hands.

HIGGINS [*aggrieved*]: Do you mean that my language is improper?

MRS HIGGINS: No, dearest: it would be quite proper—say on a canal barge; but it would not be proper for her at a garden party.

HIGGINS [*deeply injured*]: Well I must say—

PICKERING [*interrupting him*]: Come, Higgins: you must learn to know yourself. I havnt heard such language as yours since we used to review the volunteers in Hyde Park twenty years ago.

HIGGINS [*sulkily*]: Oh, well, if you say so, I suppose I dont always talk like a bishop.

MRS HIGGINS [*quieting Henry with a touch*]: Colonel Pickering: will you tell me what is the exact state of things in Wimpole Street?

PICKERING [*cheerfully: as if this completely changed the subject*]: Well, I have come to live there with Henry. We work together at my Indian Dialects; and we think it more convenient—

MRS HIGGINS: Quite so. I know all about that: it's an excellent arrangement. But where does this girl live?

HIGGINS: With us, of course. Where should she live?

MRS HIGGINS: But on what terms? Is she a servant? If not, what is she?

PICKERING [*slowly*]: I think I know what you mean, Mrs Higgins.

HIGGINS: Well, dash me if *I* do! Ive had to work at the girl every day for months to get her to her present pitch. Besides, she's useful. She knows where my things are, and remembers my appointments and so forth.

MRS HIGGINS: How does your housekeeper get on with her?

HIGGINS: Mrs Pearce? Oh, she's jolly glad to get so much taken off her hands; for before Eliza came, she used to have to find things and remind me of my appointments. But she's got some silly bee in her bonnet about Eliza. She keeps saying "You dont think, sir": doesnt she, Pick?

PICKERING: Yes: thats the formula. "You dont think, sir." Thats the end of every conversation about Eliza.

HIGGINS: As if I ever stop thinking about the girl and her confounded vowels and consonants. I'm worn out, thinking about her, and watching her lips and her teeth and her tongue, not to mention her soul, which is the quaintest of the lot.

MRS HIGGINS: You certainly are a pretty pair of babies, playing with your live doll.

HIGGINS: Playing! The hardest job I ever tackled: make no mistake about that, mother. But you have no idea how fright-fully interesting it is to take a human being and change her into a quite different human being by creating a new speech for her. It's filling up the deepest gulf that separates class from class and soul from soul.

PICKERING [*drawing his chair closer to Mrs Higgins and bending over to her eagerly*]: Yes: it's enormously interesting. I assure you. Mrs Higgins, we take Eliza very seriously. Every week—every day almost—there is some new change. [*Closer again.*] We keep records of every stage—dozens of gramophone disks and photographs—

HIGGINS [*assailing her at the other ear*]: Yes, by George: it's the most absorbing experiment I ever tackled. She regularly fills our lives up: doesnt she, Pick?

PICKERING: We're always talking Eliza.

HIGGINS: Teaching Eliza.

PICKERING: Dressing Eliza.

MRS HIGGINS: What!

HIGGINS: Inventing new Elizas.

HIGGINS:		You know, she has the most extraordinary quickness of ear;
PICKERING:		I assure you, my dear Mrs Higgins, that girl
HIGGINS:		just like a parrot. Ive tried her with every
PICKERING:		is a genius. She can play the piano quite beautifully.
HIGGINS:		possible sort of sound that a human being can make—
PICKERING:		We have taken her to classical concerts and to music
HIGGINS:	[*speaking*	Continental dialects, African dialects, Hottentot
PICKERING:	*together*]	halls; and it's all the same to her: she plays everything
HIGGINS:		clicks, things it took me years to get hold of; and
PICKERING:		she hears right off when she comes home, whether it's
HIGGINS:		she picks them up like a shot, right away, as if she had
PICKERING:		Beethoven and Brahms or Lehar and Lionel Monckton;
HIGGINS:		been at it all her life.
PICKERING:		though six months ago, she'd never as much as touched a piano—

MRS HIGGINS [*putting her fingers in her ears, as they are by this time shouting one another down with an intolerable noise*]: Sh-sh-sh—sh!

[*They stop.*]

PICKERING: I beg your pardon. [*He draws his chair back apologetically.*]

HIGGINS: Sorry. When Pickering starts shouting nobody can get a word in edgeways.

MRS HIGGINS: Be quiet, Henry, Colonel Pickering: dont you realize that when Eliza walked into Wimpole Street, something walked in with her?

PICKERING: Her father did. But Henry soon got rid of him.

MRS HIGGINS: It would have been more to the point if her mother had. But as her mother didnt something else did.

PICKERING: But what?

MRS HIGGINS [*unconsciously dating herself by the word*]: A problem.

PICKERING: Oh I see. The problem of how to pass her off as a lady.

HIGGINS: I'll solve that problem. Ive half solved it already.

MRS HIGGINS: No, you two infinitely stupid male creatures: the problem of what is to be done with her afterwards.

HIGGINS: I dont see anything in that. She can go her own way, with all the advantages I have given her.

MRS HIGGINS: The advantages of that poor woman who was here just now! The manners and habits that disqualify a fine lady from earning her own living without giving her a fine lady's income! Is that what you mean?

PICKERING [*indulgently, being rather bored*]: Oh, that will be all right, Mrs Higgins. [*He rises to go.*]

HIGGINS [*rising also*]: We'll find her some light employment.

PICKERING: She's happy enough. Dont you worry about her. Goodbye. [*He shakes hands as if he were consoling a frightened child, and makes for the door.*]

HIGGINS: Anyhow, theres no good bothering now. The thing's done. Goodbye, mother. [*He kisses her, and follows Pickering.*]

PICKERING [*turning for a final consolation*]: There are plenty of openings. We'll do whats right. Goodbye.

HIGGINS [*to Pickering as they go out together*]: Lets take her to the Shakespear exhibition at Earls Court.

PICKERING: Yes: lets. Her remarks will be delicious.

HIGGINS: She'll mimic all the people for us when we get home.

PICKERING: Ripping. [*Both are heard laughing as they go down-stairs.*]

MRS HIGGINS [*rises with an impatient bounce, and returns to her work at the writing-table. She sweeps a litter of disarranged papers out of the way; snatches a sheet of paper from her stationery case; and tries resolutely to write. At the third time she gives it up; flings down her pen; grips the table angrily and exclaims*]: Oh, men! men!! men!!!

* * *

Clearly Eliza will not pass as a duchess yet; and Higgins's bet remains unwon. But the six months are not yet exhausted; and just in time Eliza does actually pass as a princess. For a glimpse of how she did it imagine an Embassy in London one summer evening after dark. The hall door has an awning and a carpet across the sidewalk to the kerb, because a grand reception is in progress. A small crowd is lined up to see the guests arrive.

A Rolls-Royce car drives up. Pickering in evening dress, with medals and orders, alights, and hands out Eliza, in opera cloak, evening dress, diamonds, fan, flowers and all accessories. Higgins follows. The car drives off; and the three go up the steps and into the house, the door opening for them as they approach.

Inside the house they find themselves in a spacious hall from which the grand staircase rises. On the left are the arrangements for the gentlemen's cloaks. The male guests are depositing their hats and wraps there.

On the right is a door leading to the ladies' cloakroom. Ladies are going in cloaked and coming out in splendor. Pickering whispers to Eliza and points out the ladies' room. She goes into it. Higgins and Pickering take off their overcoats and take tickets for them from the attendant.

One of the guests, occupied in the same way, has his back turned. Having taken his ticket, he turns round and reveals himself as an important looking young man with an astonishingly hairy face. He has an enormous moustache, flowing out into luxuriant whiskers. Waves of hair cluster on his brow. His hair is cropped closely at the back, and glows with oil. Otherwise he is very smart. He wears several worthless orders. He is evidently a foreigner, guessable as a whiskered Pandour[8] *from Hungary: but in spite of the ferocity of his moustache he is amiable and genially voluble.*

Recognizing Higgins, he flings his arms wide apart and approaches him enthusiastically.

WHISKERS: Maestro, maestro. [*He embraces Higgins and kisses him on both cheeks.*] You remember me?

HIGGINS: No I dont. Who the devil are you?

WHISKERS: I am your pupil: your first pupil, your best and greatest pupil. I am little Nepommuck, the marvellous boy. I have made your name famous throughout Europe. You teach me phonetic. You cannot forget ME.

HIGGINS: Why dont you shave?

NEPOMMUCK: I have not your imposing appearance, your chin, your brow. Nobody notices me when I shave. Now I am famous: they call me Hairy Faced Dick.

HIGGINS: And what are you doing here among all these swells?

8. Member of the legendarily cruel Croatian militia.

NEPOMMUCK: I am interpreter. I speak 32 languages. I am indispensable at these international parties. You are great cockney specialist: you place a man anywhere in London the moment he open his mouth. I place any man in Europe.

[*A footman hurries down the grand staircase and comes to Nepommuck.*]

FOOTMAN: You are wanted upstairs. Her Excellency cannot understand the Greek gentleman.

NEPOMMUCK: Thank you, yes, immediately.

[*The footman goes and is lost in the crowd.*]

NEPOMMUCK [*to Higgins*]: This Greek diplomatist pretends he cannot speak nor understand English. He cannot deceive me. He is the son of a Clerkenwell watchmaker. He speaks English so villainously that he dare not utter a word of it without betraying his origin. I help him to pretend; but I make him pay through the nose. I make them all pay. Ha ha! [*He hurries upstairs.*]

PICKERING: Is this fellow really an expert? Can he find out Eliza and blackmail her?

HIGGINS: We shall see. If he finds her out I lose my bet.

[*Eliza comes from the cloakroom and joins them.*]

PICKERING: Well, Eliza, now for it. Are you ready?

LIZA: Are you nervous, Colonel?

PICKERING: Frightfully. I feel exactly as I felt before my first battle. It's the first time that frightens.

LIZA: It is not the first time for me, Colonel. I have done this fifty times—hundreds of times—in my little piggery in Angel Court in my day-dreams. I am in a dream now. Promise me not to let Professor Higgins wake me; for if he does I shall forget everything and talk as I used to in Drury Lane.

PICKERING: Not a word, Higgins. [*To Eliza.*] Now ready?

LIZA: Ready.

PICKERING: Go.

[*They mount the stairs, Higgins last. Pickering whispers to the footman on the first landing.*]

FIRST LANDING FOOTMAN: Miss Doolittle, Colonel Pickering, Professor Higgins.

SECOND LANDING FOOTMAN: Miss Doolittle, Colonel Pickering, Professor Higgins.

[*At the top of the staircase the Ambassador and his wife, with Nepommuck at her elbow, are receiving.*]

HOSTESS [*taking Eliza's hand*]: How d'ye do?

HOST [*same play*]: How d'ye do? How d'ye do, Pickering?

LIZA [*with a beautiful gravity that awes her hostess*]: How do you do? [*She passes on to the drawing room.*]

HOSTESS: Is that your adopted daughter, Colonel Pickering? She will make a sensation.

PICKERING: Most kind of you to invite her for me. [*He passes on.*]

HOSTESS [*to Nepommuck*]: Find out all about her.

NEPOMMUCK [*bowing*]: Excellency—[*He goes into the crowd.*]

HOST: How d'ye do, Higgins? You have a rival here tonight. He introduced himself as your pupil. Is he any good?

HIGGINS: He can learn a language in a fortnight—knows dozens of them. A sure mark of a fool. As a phonetician, no good whatever.

HOSTESS: How d'ye do, Professor?

HIGGINS: How do you do? Fearful bore for you this sort of thing. Forgive my part in it. [*He passes on.*]

[*In the drawing room and its suite of salons the reception is in full swing. Eliza passes through. She is so intent on her ordeal that she walks like a somnambulist in a desert instead of a débutante in a fashionable crowd. They stop talking to look at her, admiring her dress, her jewels, and her strangely attractive self. Some of the younger ones at the back stand on their chairs to see.*

The Host and Hostess come in from the staircase and mingle with their guests. Higgins, gloomy and contemptuous of the whole business, comes into the group where they are chatting.]

HOSTESS: Ah, here is Professor Higgins: he will tell us. Tell us all about the wonderful young lady, Professor.

HIGGINS [*almost morosely*]: What wonderful young lady?

HOSTESS: You know very well. They tell me there has been nothing like her in London since people stood on their chairs to look at Mrs Langtry.[9]

[*Nepommuck joins the group, full of news.*]

HOSTESS: Ah, here you are at last, Nepommuck. Have you found out all about the Doolittle lady?

NEPOMMUCK: I have found out all about her. She is a fraud.

HOSTESS: A fraud! Oh no.

NEPOMMUCK: YES, yes. She cannot deceive me. Her name cannot be Doolittle.

HIGGINS: Why?

NEPOMMUCK: Because Doolittle is an English name. And she is not English.

HOSTESS: Oh, nonsense! She speaks English perfectly.

NEPOMMUCK: Too perfectly. Can you shew me any English woman who speaks English as it should be spoken? Only foreigners who have been taught to speak it speak it well.

HOSTESS: Certainly she terrified me by the way she said How d'ye do. I had a schoolmistress who talked like that; and I was mortally afraid of her. But if she is not English what is she?

NEPOMMUCK: Hungarian.

ALL THE REST: Hungarian!

NEPOMMUCK: Hungarian. And of royal blood. I am Hungarian. My blood is royal.

HIGGINS: Did you speak to her in Hungarian?

NEPOMMUCK: I did. She was very clever. She said "Please speak to me in English: I do not understand French." French! She pretends not to know the difference between Hungarian and French. Impossible: she knows both.

HIGGINS: And the blood royal? How did you find that out?

NEPOMMUCK: Instinct, maestro, instinct. Only the Magyar races can produce that air of the divine right, those resolute eyes. She is a princess.

HOST: What do you say, Professor?

HIGGINS: I say an ordinary London girl out of the gutter and taught to speak by an expert. I place her in Drury Lane.

NEPOMMUCK: Ha ha ha! Oh, maestro, maestro, you are mad on the subject of cockney dialects. The London gutter is the whole world for you.

9. Lillie Langtry (1852–1929), English actress and celebrity spokesperson for Pears' soap.

HIGGINS [*to the Hostess*]: What does your Excellency say?
HOSTESS: Oh, of course I agree with Nepommuck. She must be a princess at least.
HOST: Not necessarily legitimate, of course. Morganatic[1] perhaps. But that is undoubtedly her class.
HIGGINS: I stick to my opinion.
HOSTESS: Oh, you are incorrigible.

[*The group breaks up, leaving Higgins isolated. Pickering joins him.*]

PICKERING: Where is Eliza? We must keep an eye on her.

[*Eliza joins them.*]

LIZA: I dont think I can bear much more. The people all stare so at me. An old lady has just told me that I speak exactly like Queen Victoria. I am sorry if I have lost your bet. I have done my best: but nothing can make me the same as these people.
PICKERING: You have not lost it, my dear. You have won it ten times over.
HIGGINS: Let us get out of this. I have had enough of chattering to these fools.
PICKERING: Eliza is tired; and I am hungry. Let us clear out and have supper somewhere.

ACT 4

The Wimpole Street laboratory. Midnight. Nobody in the room. The clock on the mantelpiece strikes twelve. The fire is not alight: it is a summer night.

Presently Higgins and Pickering are heard on the stairs.

HIGGINS [*calling down to Pickering*]: I say, Pick: lock up, will you? I shant be going out again.
PICKERING: Right. Can Mrs Pearce go to bed? We dont want anything more, do we?
HIGGINS: Lord, no!

[*Eliza opens the door and is seen on the lighted landing in all the finery in which she has just won Higgins's bet for him. She comes to the hearth, and switches on the electric lights there. She is tired: her pallor contrasts strongly with her dark eyes and hair; and her expression is almost tragic. She takes off her cloak; puts her fan and gloves on the piano; and sits down on the bench, brooding and silent. Higgins, in evening dress, with overcoat and hat, comes in, carrying a smoking jacket which he has picked up downstairs. He takes off the hat and overcoat; throws them carelessly on the newspaper stand; disposes of his coat in the same way; puts on the smoking jacket; and throws himself wearily into the easy-chair at the hearth. Pickering, similarly attired, comes in. He also takes off his hat and overcoat, and is about to throw them on Higgins's when he hesitates.*]

PICKERING: I say: Mrs Pearce will row if we leave these things lying about in the drawing room.
HIGGINS: Oh, chuck them over the bannisters into the hall. She'll find them there in the morning and put them away all right. She'll think we were drunk.
PICKERING: We are, slightly. Are there any letters?
HIGGINS: I didnt look. [*Pickering takes the overcoats and hats and goes downstairs. Higgins begins half singing half yawning an air from La Fanciulla del Golden West. Suddenly he stops and exclaims.*] I wonder where the devil my slippers are!

1. Form of marriage in which partners of unequal social station agree that neither the lower-ranking spouse nor any children will have a claim to the higher-ranking spouse's titles or property.

[*Eliza looks at him darkly; then rises suddenly and leaves the room.*
Higgins yawns again, and resumes his song.
Pickering returns, with the contents of the letterbox in his hand.]

PICKERING: Only circulars, and this coroneted billet-doux[1] for you. [*He throws the circulars into the fender, and posts himself on the hearthrug, with his back to the grate.*]

HIGGINS [*glancing at the billet-doux*]: Money-lender. [*He throws the letter after the circulars.*]

[*Eliza returns with a pair of large down-at-heel slippers. She places them on the carpet before Higgins, and sits as before without a word.*]

HIGGINS [*yawning again*]: Oh Lord! What an evening! What a crew! What a silly tomfoolery! [*He raises his shoe to unlace it, and catches sight of the slippers. He stops unlacing and looks at them as if they had appeared there of their own accord.*] Oh! theyre there, are they?

PICKERING [*stretching himself*]: Well, I feel a bit tired. It's been a long day. The garden party, a dinner party, and the reception! Rather too much of a good thing. But youve won your bet, Higgins. Eliza did the trick, and something to spare, eh?

HIGGINS [*fervently*]: Thank God it's over!

[*Eliza flinches violently; but they take no notice of her; and she recovers herself and sits stonily as before.*]

PICKERING: Were you nervous at the garden party? *I* was. Eliza didnt seem a bit nervous.

HIGGINS: Oh, she wasnt nervous. I knew she'd be all right. No: it's the strain of putting the job through all these months that has told on me. It was interesting enough at first, while we were at the phonetics; but after that I got deadly sick of it. If I hadnt backed myself to do it I should have chucked the whole thing up two months ago. It was a silly notion: the whole thing has been a bore.

PICKERING: Oh come! the garden party was frightfully exciting. My heart began beating like anything.

HIGGINS: Yes, for the first three minutes. But when I saw we were going to win hands down, I felt like a bear in a cage, hanging about doing nothing. The dinner was worse: sitting gorging there for over an hour, with nobody but a damned fool of a fashionable woman to talk to! I tell you, Pickering, never again for me. No more artificial duchesses. The whole thing has been simple purgatory.

PICKERING: Youve never been broken in properly to the social routine. [*Strolling over to the piano.*] I rather enjoy dipping into it occasionally myself: it makes me feel young again. Anyhow, it was a great success: an immense success. I was quite frightened once or twice because Eliza was doing it so well. You see, lots of the real people cant do it at all: theyre such fools that they think style comes by nature to people in their position; and so they never learn. Theres always something professional about doing a thing superlatively well.

HIGGINS: Yes: thats what drives me mad: the silly people dont know their own silly business. [*Rising.*] However, it's over and done with; and now I can go to bed at last without dreading tomorrow.

[*Eliza's beauty becomes murderous.*]

PICKERING: I think I shall turn in too. Still, it's been a great occasion: a triumph for you. Goodnight. [*He goes.*]

1. Love letter.

HIGGINS [*following him*]: Goodnight. [*Over his shoulder, at the door.*] Put out the lights, Eliza; and tell Mrs Pearce not to make coffee for me in the morning: I'll take tea. [*He goes out.*]

[*Eliza tries to control herself and feel indifferent as she rises and walks across to the hearth to switch off the lights. By the time she gets there she is on the point of screaming. She sits down in Higgins's chair and holds on hard to the arms. Finally she gives way and flings herself furiously on the floor, raging.*]

HIGGINS [*in despairing wrath outside*]: What the devil have I done with my slippers?

[*He appears at the door.*]

LIZA [*snatching up the slippers, and hurling them at him one after the other with all her force*]: There are your slippers. And there. Take your slippers; and may you never have a day's luck with them!

HIGGINS [*astounded*]: What on earth—! [*He comes to her.*] Whats the matter? Get up. [*He pulls her up.*] Anything wrong?

LIZA [*breathless*]: Nothing wrong—with you. Ive won your bet for you, havnt I? Thats enough for you. *I* dont matter, I suppose.

HIGGINS: You won my bet! You! Presumptuous insect! *I* won it. What did you throw those slippers at me for?

LIZA: Because I wanted to smash your face. I'd like to kill you, you selfish brute. Why didnt you leave me where you picked me out of—in the gutter? You thank God it's all over, and that now you can throw me back again there, do you? [*She crisps her fingers frantically.*]

HIGGINS [*looking at her in cool wonder*]: The creature is nervous, after all.

LIZA [*gives a suffocated scream of fury, and instinctively darts her nails at his face*]: !!

HIGGINS [*catching her wrists*]: Ah! would you? Claws in, you cat. How dare you shew your temper to me? Sit down and be quiet. [*He throws her roughly into the easy-chair.*]

LIZA [*crushed by superior strength and weight*]: Whats to become of me? Whats to become of me?

HIGGINS: How the devil do I know whats to become of you? What does it matter what becomes of you?

LIZA: You dont care. I know you dont care. You wouldnt care if I was dead. I'm nothing to you—not so much as them slippers.

HIGGINS [*thundering*]: Those slippers.

LIZA [*with bitter submission*]: Those slippers. I didnt think it made any difference now.

[*A pause. Eliza hopeless and crushed. Higgins a little uneasy.*]

HIGGINS [*in his loftiest manner*]: Why have you begun going on like this? May I ask whether you complain of your treatment here?

LIZA: No.

HIGGINS: Has anybody behaved badly to you? Colonel Pickering? Mrs Pearce? Any of the servants?

LIZA: No.

HIGGINS: I presume you dont pretend that *I* have treated you badly?

LIZA: No.

HIGGINS: I am glad to hear it. [*He moderates his tone.*] Perhaps youre tired after the strain of the day. Will you have a glass of champagne? [*He moves towards the door.*]

LIZA: No. [*Recollecting her manners.*] Thank you.

HIGGINS [*good-humored again*]: This has been coming on you for some days. I suppose it was natural for you to be anxious about the garden party. But thats all over now. [*He pats her kindly on the shoulder. She writhes.*] Theres nothing more to worry about.

LIZA: No. Nothing more for you to worry about. [*She suddenly rises and gets away from him by going to the piano bench, where she sits and hides her face.*] Oh God! I wish I was dead.

HIGGINS [*staring after her in sincere surprise*]: Why? In heaven's name, why? [*Reasonably, going to her.*] Listen to me, Eliza. All this irritation is purely subjective.

LIZA: I dont understand. I'm too ignorant.

HIGGINS: It's only imagination. Low spirits and nothing else. Nobody's hurting you. Nothing's wrong. You go to bed like a good girl and sleep it off. Have a little cry and say your prayers: that will make you comfortable.

LIZA: I heard your prayers. "Thank God it's all over!"

HIGGINS [*impatiently*]: Well, dont you thank God it's all over? Now you are free and can do what you like.

LIZA [*pulling herself together in desperation*]: What am I fit for? What have you left me fit for? Where am I to go? What am I to do? Whats to become of me?

HIGGINS [*enlightened, but not at all impressed*]: Oh, thats whats worrying you, is it? [*He thrusts his hands into his pockets, and walks about in his usual manner, rattling the contents of his pockets, as if condescending to a trivial subject out of pure kindness.*] I shouldnt bother about it if I were you. I should imagine you wont have much difficulty in settling yourself somewhere or other, though I hadnt quite realized that you were going away. [*She looks quickly at him: he does not look at her, but examines the dessert stand on the piano and decides that he will eat an apple.*] You might marry, you know. [*He bites a large piece out of the apple and munches it noisily.*] You see, Eliza, all men are not confirmed old bachelors like me and the Colonel. Most men are the marrying sort (poor devils!); and youre not bad-looking: it's quite a pleasure to look at you sometimes—not now, of course, because youre crying and looking as ugly as the very devil; but when youre all right and quite yourself, youre what I should call attractive. That is, to the people in the marrying line, you understand. You go to bed and have a good nice rest; and then get up and look at yourself in the glass; and you wont feel so cheap.

[*Eliza again looks at him, speechless, and does not stir.*

The look is quite lost on him: he eats his apple with a dreamy expression of happiness, as it is quite a good one.]

HIGGINS [*a genial afterthought occurring to him*]: I daresay my mother could find some chap or other who would do very well.

LIZA: We were above that at the corner of Tottenham Court Road.

HIGGINS [*waking up*]: What do you mean?

LIZA: I sold flowers. I didnt sell myself. Now youve made a lady of me I'm not fit to sell anything else. I wish youd left me where you found me.

HIGGINS [*slinging the core of the apple decisively into the grate*]: Tosh, Eliza. Dont you insult human relations by dragging all this cant about buying and selling into it. You neednt marry the fellow if you dont like him.

LIZA: What else am I to do?

HIGGINS: Oh, lots of things. What about your old idea of a florist's shop? Pickering could set you up in one: he has lots of money. [*Chuckling.*] He'll have to pay for all those togs you have been wearing today; and that, with the hire of the jewellery, will make a big hole in two hundred pounds. Why, six months ago you would have thought it the millennium to have a flower shop of your own. Come! youll be all right. I must clear off to bed: I'm devilish sleepy. By the way, I came down for something: I forget what it was.

LIZA: Your slippers.

HIGGINS: Oh yes, of course. You shied them at me. [*He picks them up, and is going out when she rises and speaks to him.*]

LIZA: Before you go, sir—

HIGGINS [*dropping the slippers in his surprise at her calling him Sir*]: Eh?

LIZA: Do my clothes belong to me or to Colonel Pickering?

HIGGINS [*coming back into the room as if her question were the very climax of unreason*]: What the devil use would they be to Pickering?

LIZA: He might want them for the next girl you pick up to experiment on.

HIGGINS [*shocked and hurt*]: Is that the way you feel towards us?

LIZA: I dont want to hear anything more about that. All I want to know is whether anything belongs to me. My own clothes were burnt.

HIGGINS: But what does it matter? Why need you start bothering about that in the middle of the night?

LIZA: I want to know what I may take away with me. I dont want to be accused of stealing.

HIGGINS [*now deeply wounded*]: Stealing! You shouldnt have said that. Eliza. That shews a want of feeling.

LIZA: I'm sorry. I'm only a common ignorant girl; and in my station I have to be careful. There cant be any feelings between the like of you and the like of me. Please will you tell me what belongs to me and what doesnt?

HIGGINS [*very sulky*]: You may take the whole damned houseful if you like. Except the jewels. Theyre hired. Will that satisfy you? [*He turns on his heel and is about to go in extreme dudgeon.*[2]]

LIZA [*drinking in his emotion like nectar, and nagging him to provoke a further supply*]: Stop, please. [*She takes off her jewels.*] Will you take these to your room and keep them safe? I dont want to run the risk of their being missing.

HIGGINS [*furious*]: Hand them over. [*She puts them into his hands.*] If these belonged to me instead of to the jeweller, I'd ram them down your ungrateful throat. [*He perfunctorily thrusts them into his pockets, unconsciously decorating himself with the protruding ends of the chains.*]

LIZA [*taking a ring off*]: This ring isnt the jeweller's: it's the one you bought me in Brighton. I dont want it now. [*Higgins dashes the ring violently into the fireplace, and turns on her so threateningly that she crouches over the piano with her hands over her face, and exclaims.*] Dont you hit me.

HIGGINS: Hit you! You infamous creature, how dare you accuse me of such a thing? It is you who have hit me. You have wounded me to the heart.

LIZA [*thrilling with hidden joy*]: I'm glad. Ive got a little of my own back, anyhow.

HIGGINS [*with dignity, in his finest professional style*]: You have caused me to lose my temper: a thing that has hardly ever happened to me before. I prefer to say nothing more tonight. I am going to bed.

LIZA [*pertly*]: Youd better leave a note for Mrs Pearce about the coffee; for she wont be told by me.

2. Anger, irritation.

HIGGINS [*formally*]: Damn Mrs Pearce; and damn the coffee: and damn you; and [*wildly*] damn my own folly in having lavished my hard-earned knowledge and the treasure of my regard and intimacy on a heartless guttersnipe. [*He goes out with impressive decorum, and spoils it by slamming the door savagely*].

[*Eliza goes down on her knees on the hearthrug to look for the ring. When she finds it she considers for a moment what to do with it. Finally she flings it down on the dessert stand and goes upstairs in a tearing rage.*]

* * *

The furniture of Eliza's room has been increased by a big wardrobe and a sumptuous dressing-table. She comes in and switches on the electric light. She goes to the wardrobe; opens it; and pulls out a walking dress, a hat, and a pair of shoes, which she throws on the bed. She takes off her evening dress and shoes: then takes a padded hanger from the wardrobe: adjusts it carefully in the evening dress; and hangs it, in the wardrobe, which she shuts with a slam. She puts on her walking shoes, her walking dress, and hat. She takes her wrist watch from the dressing-table and fastens it on. She pulls on her gloves: takes her vanity bag; and looks into it to see that her purse is there before hanging it on her wrist. She makes for the door. Every movement expresses her furious resolution.

She takes a last look at herself in the glass.

She suddenly puts out her tongue at herself; then leaves the room, switching off the electric light at the door.

Meanwhile, in the street outside, Freddy Eynsford Hill, lovelorn, is gazing up at the second floor, in which one of the windows is still lighted.

The light goes out.

FREDDY: Goodnight, darling, darling, darling.

[*Eliza comes out, giving the door a considerable bang behind her.*]

LIZA: Whatever are you doing here?

FREDDY: Nothing. I spend most of my nights here. It's the only place where I'm happy. Dont laugh at me, Miss Doolittle.

LIZA: Dont you call me Miss Doolittle, do you hear? Liza's good enough for me. [*She breaks down and grabs him by the shoulders.*] Freddy: you dont think I'm a heartless guttersnipe, do you?

FREDDY: Oh no, no, darling: how can you imagine such a thing? You are the loveliest, dearest—

[*He loses all self-control and smothers her with kisses. She, hungry for comfort, responds. They stand there in one another's arms.*

An elderly police constable arrives.]

CONSTABLE [*scandalized*]: Now then! Now then!! Now then!!!

[*They release one another hastily.*]

FREDDY: Sorry, constable. Weve only just become engaged.

[*They run away.*

The constable shakes his head, reflecting on his own courtship and on the vanity of human hopes. He moves off in the opposite direction with slow professional steps.

The flight of the lovers takes them to Cavendish Square. There they halt to consider their next move.]

LIZA [*out of breath*]: He didnt half give me a fright, that copper. But you answered him proper.

FREDDY: I hope I havnt taken you out of your way. Where were you going?

LIZA: To the river.

FREDDY: What for?

LIZA: To make a hole in it.

FREDDY [*horrified*]: Eliza, darling. What do you mean? What's the matter?

LIZA: Never mind. It doesnt matter now. Theres nobody in the world now but you and me, is there?

FREDDY: Not a soul.

[*They indulge in another embrace, and are again surprised by a much younger constable.*]

SECOND CONSTABLE: Now then, you two! What's this? Where do you think you are? Move along here, double quick.

FREDDY: As you say, sir, double quick.

[*They run away again, and are in Hanover Square before they stop for another conference.*]

FREDDY: I had no idea the police were so devilishly prudish.

LIZA: It's their business to hunt girls off the streets.

FREDDY: We must go somewhere. We cant wander about the streets all night.

LIZA: Cant we? I think it'd be lovely to wander about for ever.

FREDDY: Oh, darling.

[*They embrace again, oblivious of the arrival of a crawling taxi. It stops.*]

TAXIMAN: Can I drive you and the lady anywhere, sir?

[*They start asunder.*]

LIZA: Oh, Freddy, a taxi. The very thing.

FREDDY: But, damn it, Ive no money.

LIZA: I have plenty. The Colonel thinks you should never go out without ten pounds in your pocket. Listen. We'll drive about all night; and in the morning I'll call on old Mrs Higgins and ask her what I ought to do. I'll tell you all about it in the cab. And the police wont touch us there.

FREDDY: Righto! Ripping. [*To the Taximan.*] Wimbledon Common. [*They drive off.*]

ACT 5

Mrs Higgins's drawing room. She is at her writing-table as before. The parlormaid comes in.

THE PARLORMAID [*at the door*]: Mr Henry, maam, is downstairs with Colonel Pickering.

MRS HIGGINS: Well, shew them up.

THE PARLORMAID: Theyre using the telephone, maam. Telephoning to the police, I think.

MRS HIGGINS: What!

THE PARLORMAID [*coming further in and lowering her voice*]: Mr Henry is in a state, maam. I thought I'd better tell you.

MRS HIGGINS: If you had told me that Mr Henry was not in a state it would have been more surprising. Tell them to come up when theyve finished with the police. I suppose he's lost something.

THE PARLORMAID: Yes, maam [*Going.*]

MRS HIGGINS: Go upstairs and tell Miss Doolittle that Mr Henry and the Colonel are here. Ask her not to come down til I send for her.

THE PARLORMAID: Yes, maam.

[*Higgins bursts in. He is, as the parlormaid has said, in a state.*]

HIGGINS: Look here, mother: heres a confounded thing!

MRS HIGGINS: Yes, dear. Good morning. [*He checks his impatience and kisses her, whilst the parlormaid goes out.*] What is it?

HIGGINS: Eliza's bolted.

MRS HIGGINS [*calmly continuing her writing*]: You must have frightened her.

HIGGINS: Frightened her! nonsense! She was left last night, as usual, to turn out the lights and all that; and instead of going to bed she changed her clothes and went right off: her bed wasnt slept in. She came in a cab for her things before seven this morning; and that fool Mrs Pearce let her have them without telling me a word about it. What am I to do?

MRS HIGGINS: Do without, I'm afraid, Henry. The girl has a perfect right to leave if she chooses.

HIGGINS [*wandering distractedly across the room*]: But I cant find anything. I dont know what appointments Ive got. I'm—[*Pickering comes in. Mrs Higgins puts down her pen and turns away from the writing-table.*]

PICKERING [*shaking hands*]: Good morning. Mrs Higgins. Has Henry told you? [*He sits down on the ottoman.*]

HIGGINS: What does that ass of an inspector say? Have you offered a reward?

MRS HIGGINS [*rising in indignant amazement*]: You dont mean to say you have set the police after Eliza?

HIGGINS: Of course. What are the police for? What else could we do? [*He sits in the Elizabethan chair.*]

PICKERING: The inspector made a lot of difficulties. I really think he suspected us of some improper purpose.

MRS HIGGINS: Well, of course he did. What right have you to go to the police and give the girl's name as if she were a thief, or a lost umbrella, or something? Really! [*She sits down again, deeply vexed.*]

HIGGINS: But we want to find her.

PICKERING: We cant let her go like this, you know, Mrs Higgins. What were we to do?

MRS HIGGINS: You have no more sense, either of you, than two children. Why— [*The parlormaid comes in and breaks off the conversation.*]

THE PARLORMAID: Mr Henry: a gentleman wants to see you very particular. He's been sent on from Wimpole Street.

HIGGINS: Oh, bother! I cant see anyone now. Who is it?

THE PARLORMAID: A Mr Doolittle, sir.

PICKERING: Doolittle! Do you mean the dustman?

THE PARLORMAID: Dustman! Oh no, sir: a gentleman.

HIGGINS [*springing up excitedly*]: By George, Pick, it's some relative of hers that she's gone to. Somebody we know nothing about. [*To the parlormaid.*] Send him up, quick.

THE PARLORMAID: Yes, sir. [*She goes.*]

HIGGINS [*eagerly, going to his mother*]: Genteel relatives! now we shall hear something. [*He sits down in the Chippendale chair.*]

MRS HIGGINS: Do you know any of her people?

PICKERING: Only her father: the fellow we told you about.

THE PARLORMAID [*announcing*]: Mr Doolittle. [*She withdraws*].

[*Doolittle enters. He is resplendently dressed as for a fashionable wedding, and might, in fact, be the bridegroom. A flower in his buttonhole, a dazzling silk hat, and patent leather shoes complete the effect. He is too concerned with the business he has come on to notice Mrs Higgins. He walks straight to Higgins, and accosts him with vehement reproach.*]

DOOLITTLE [*indicating his own person*]: See here! Do you see this? You done this.
HIGGINS: Done what, man?
DOOLITTLE: This, I tell you. Look at it. Look at this hat. Look at this coat.
PICKERING: Has Eliza been buying you clothes?
DOOLITTLE: Eliza! not she. Why would she buy me clothes?
MRS HIGGINS: Good morning, Mr Doolittle. Wont you sit down?
DOOLITTLE [*taken aback as he becomes conscious that he has forgotten his hostess*]: Asking your pardon, maam. [*He approaches her and shakes her proffered hand.*] Thank you. [*He sits down on the ottoman, on Pickering's right.*] I am that full of what has happened to me that I cant think of anything else.
HIGGINS: What the dickens has happened to you?
DOOLITTLE: I shouldnt mind if it had only happened to me: anything might happen to anybody and nobody to blame but Providence, as you might say. But this is something that you done to me: yes, you, Enry Iggins.
HIGGINS: Have you found Eliza?
DOOLITTLE: Have you lost her?
HIGGINS: Yes.
DOOLITTLE: You have all the luck, you have. I aint found her: but she'll find me quick enough now after what you done to me.
MRS HIGGINS: But what has my son done to you. Mr Doolittle?
DOOLITTLE: Done to me! Ruined me. Destroyed my happiness. Tied me up and delivered me into the hands of middle class morality.
HIGGINS [*rising intolerantly and standing over Doolittle*]: Youre raving. Youre drunk. Youre mad. I gave you five pounds. After that I had two conversations with you, at half-a-crown an hour. Ive never seen you since.
DOOLITTLE: Oh! Drunk am I? Mad am I? Tell me this. Did you or did you not write a letter to an old blighter in America that was giving five millions to found Moral Reform Societies all over the world, and that wanted you to invent a universal language for him?
HIGGINS: What! Ezra D. Wannafeller! He's dead. [*He sits down again carelessly.*]
DOOLITTLE: Yes: he's dead; and I'm done for. Now did you or did you not write a letter to him to say that the most original moralist at present in England, to the best of your knowledge, was Alfred Doolittle, a common dustman?
HIGGINS: Oh, after your first visit I remember making some silly joke of the kind.
DOOLITTLE: Ah! You may well call it a silly joke. It put the lid on me right enough. Just give him the chance he wanted to shew that Americans is not like us: that they reckonize and respect merit in every class of life, however humble. Them words is in his blooming will, in which, Henry Higgins, thanks to your silly joking, he leaves me a share in his Pre-digested Cheese Trust worth three thousand a year on condition that I lecture for his Wannafeller Moral Reform World League as often as they ask me up to six times a year.
HIGGINS: The devil he does! Whew! [*Brightening suddenly.*] What a lark!
PICKERING: A safe thing for you, Doolittle. They wont ask you twice.
DOOLITTLE: It aint the lecturing I mind. I'll lecture them blue in the face, I will, and not turn a hair. It's making a gentleman of me that I object to. Who asked him to make a gentleman of me? I was happy. I was free. I touched pretty nigh everybody for money when I wanted it, same as I touched you, Enry Iggins. Now I

am worrited:[1] tied neck and heels: and everybody touches me for money. It's a fine thing for you, says my solicitor. Is it? says I. You mean it's a good thing for you, I says. When I was a poor man and had a solicitor once when they found a pram in the dust cart, he got me off, and got shut of me and got me shut of him as quick as he could. Same with the doctors: used to shove me out of the hospital before I could hardly stand on my legs, and nothing to pay. Now they finds out that I'm not a healthy man and cant live unless they looks after me twice a day. In the house I'm not let do a hand's turn for myself: somebody else must do it and touch me for it. A year ago I hadnt a relative in the world except two or three that wouldnt speak to me. Now Ive fifty, and not a decent week's wages among the lot of them. I have to live for others and not for myself: thats middle class morality. You talk of losing Eliza. Dont you be anxious: I bet she's on my doorstep by this: she that could support herself easy by selling flowers if I wasnt respectable. And the next one to touch me will be you, Enry Iggins. I'll have to learn to speak middle class language from you, instead of speaking proper English. Thats where youll come in; and I daresay thats what you done it for.

MRS HIGGINS: But, my dear Mr Doolittle, you need not suffer all this if you are really in earnest. Nobody can force you to accept this bequest. You can repudiate it. Isnt that so, Colonel Pickering?

PICKERING: I believe so.

DOOLITTLE [*softening his manner in deference to her sex*]: Thats the tragedy of it, maam. It's easy to say chuck it; but I havnt the nerve. Which of us has? We're all intimidated. Intimidated, maam: thats what we are. What is there for me if I chuck it but the workhouse in my old age? I have to dye my hair already to keep my job as a dustman. If I was one of the deserving poor, and had put by a bit, I could chuck it; but then why should I, acause[2] the deserving poor might as well be millionaires for all the happiness they ever has. They dont know what happiness is. But I, as one of the undeserving poor, have nothing between me and the pauper's uniform but this here blasted three thousand a year that shoves me into the middle class. (Excuse the expression, maam; youd use it yourself if you had my provocation.) Theyve got you every way you turn: it's a choice between the Skilly of the workhouse and the Char Bydis[3] of the middle class; and I havnt the nerve for the workhouse. Intimidated: thats what I am. Broke. Bought up. Happier men than me will call for my dust, and touch me for their tip; and I'll look on helpless, and envy them. And thats what your son has brought me to. [*He is overcome by emotion*.]

MRS HIGGINS: Well, I'm very glad youre not going to do anything foolish, Mr Doolittle. For this solves the problem of Eliza's future. You can provide for her now.

DOOLITTLE [*with melancholy resignation*]: Yes, maam: I'm expected to provide for everyone now, out of three thousand a year.

HIGGINS [*jumping up*]: Nonsense! he cant provide for her. He shant provide for her. She doesnt belong to him. I paid him five pounds for her. Doolittle: either youre an honest man or a rogue.

1. Worried.
2. Because.
3. In his odyssey to return home to Ithaca, the Greek hero Odysseus had to sail carefully between the paired hazards of Scylla, a monster who would pluck and eat mariners who passed too close, and Charybdis, an enormous whirlpool.

DOOLITTLE [*tolerantly*]: A little of both, Henry, like the rest of us: a little of both.

HIGGINS: Well, you took that money for the girl; and you have no right to take her as well.

MRS HIGGINS: Henry: dont be absurd. If you want to know where Eliza is, she is upstairs.

HIGGINS [*amazed*]: Upstairs!!! Then I shall jolly soon fetch her downstairs. [*He makes resolutely for the door*.]

MRS HIGGINS [*rising and following him*]: Be quiet, Henry. Sit down.

HIGGINS: I—

MRS HIGGINS: Sit down, dear; and listen to me.

HIGGINS: Oh very well, very well, very well. [*He throws himself ungraciously on the ottoman, with his face towards the windows*.] But I think you might have told us this half an hour ago.

MRS HIGGINS: Eliza came to me this morning. She told me of the brutal way you two treated her.

HIGGINS [*bouncing up again*]: What!

PICKERING [*rising also*]: My dear Mrs Higgins, she's been telling you stories. We didnt treat her brutally. We hardly said a word to her; and we parted on particularly good terms. [*Turning on Higgins*.] Higgins: did you bully her after I went to bed?

HIGGINS: Just the other way about. She threw my slippers in my face. She behaved in the most outrageous way. I never gave her the slightest provocation. The slippers came bang into my face the moment I entered the room—before I had uttered a word. And used perfectly awful language.

PICKERING [*astonished*]: But why? What did we do to her?

MRS HIGGINS: I think I know pretty well what you did. The girl is naturally rather affectionate, I think. Isnt she, Mr Doolittle?

DOOLITTLE: Very tender-hearted, maam. Takes after me.

MRS HIGGINS: Just so. She had become attached to you both. She worked very hard for you, Henry. I dont think you quite realize what anything in the nature of brain work means to a girl of her class. Well, it seems that when the great day of trial came, and she did this wonderful thing for you without making a single mistake, you two sat there and never said a word to her, but talked together of how glad you were that it was all over and how you had been bored with the whole thing. And then you were surprised because she threw your slippers at you! I should have thrown the fire-irons at you.

HIGGINS: We said nothing except that we were tired and wanted to go to bed. Did we, Pick?

PICKERING [*shrugging his shoulders*]: That was all.

MRS HIGGINS [*ironically*]: Quite sure?

PICKERING: Absolutely, Really, that was all.

MRS HIGGINS: You didnt thank her, or pet her, or admire her, or tell her how splendid she'd been.

HIGGINS [*impatiently*]: But she knew all about that. We didnt make speeches to her, if thats what you mean.

PICKERING [*conscience stricken*]: Perhaps we were a little inconsiderate. Is she very angry?

MRS HIGGINS [*returning to her place at the writing-table*]: Well, I'm afraid she wont go back to Wimpole Street, especially now that Mr Doolittle is able to keep up the position you have thrust on her; but she says she is quite willing to meet you on friendly terms and to let bygones be bygones.

HIGGINS [*furious*]: Is she, by George? Ho!

MRS HIGGINS: If you promise to behave yourself, Henry, I'll ask her to come down. If not, go home: for you have taken up quite enough of my time.

HIGGINS: Oh, all right. Very well. Pick: you behave yourself. Let us put on our best Sunday manners for this creature that we picked out of the mud. [*He flings himself sulkily into the Elizabethan chair.*]

DOOLITTLE [*remonstrating*]: Now, now, Enry Iggins! Have some consideration for my feelings as a middle class man.

MRS HIGGINS: Remember your promise, Henry. [*She presses the bell-button on the writing-table.*] Mr Doolittle: will you be so good as to step out on the balcony for a moment. I dont want Eliza to have the shock of your news until she has made it up with these two gentlemen. Would you mind?

DOOLITTLE: As you wish, lady. Anything to help Henry to keep her off my hands. [*He disappears through the window.*]

[*The parlormaid answers the bell. Pickering sits down in Doolittle's place.*]

MRS HIGGINS: Ask Miss Doolittle to come down, please.

THE PARLORMAID: Yes, maam. [*She goes out.*]

MRS HIGGINS: Now, Henry: be good.

HIGGINS: I am behaving myself perfectly.

PICKERING: He is doing his best, Mrs Higgins.

[*A pause. Higgins throws back his head; stretches out his legs; and begins to whistle.*]

MRS HIGGINS: Henry, dearest, you dont look at all nice in that attitude.

HIGGINS [*pulling himself together*]: I was not trying to look nice, mother.

MRS HIGGINS: It doesnt matter, dear. I only wanted to make you speak.

HIGGINS: Why?

MRS HIGGINS: Because you cant speak and whistle at the same time.

[*Higgins groans. Another very trying pause.*]

HIGGINS [*springing up, out of patience*]: Where the devil is that girl? Are we to wait here all day?

[*Eliza enters, sunny, self-possessed, and giving a staggeringly convincing exhibition of ease of manner. She carries a little work-basket, and is very much at home. Pickering is too much taken aback to rise.*]

LIZA: How do you do, Professor Higgins? Are you quite well?

HIGGINS [*choking*]: Am I—[*He can say no more.*]

LIZA: But of course you are: you are never ill. So glad to see you again, Colonel Pickering. [*He rises hastily; and they shake hands.*] Quite chilly this morning, isnt it? [*She sits down on his left. He sits beside her.*]

HIGGINS: Dont you dare try this game on me. I taught it to you; and it doesnt take me in. Get up and come home; and dont be a fool.

[*Eliza takes a piece of needlework from her basket, and begins to stitch at it, without taking the least notice of this outburst.*]

MRS HIGGINS: Very nicely put, indeed, Henry. No woman could resist such an invitation.

HIGGINS: You let her alone, mother. Let her speak for herself. You will jolly soon see whether she has an idea that I havnt put into her head or a word that I havnt put into her mouth. I tell you I have created this thing out of the squashed cabbage leaves of Covent Garden; and now she pretends to play the fine lady with me.

MRS HIGGINS [*placidly*]: Yes, dear; but youll sit down, wont you?

[*Higgins sits down again, savagely.*]

LIZA [*to Pickering, taking no apparent notice of Higgins, and working away deftly*]: Will you drop me altogether now that the experiment is over, Colonel Pickering?

PICKERING: Oh dont. You mustnt think of it as an experiment. It shocks me, somehow.

LIZA: Oh, I'm only a squashed cabbage leaf—

PICKERING [*impulsively*]: No.

LIZA [*continuing quietly*]: —but I owe so much to you that I should be very unhappy if you forgot me.

PICKERING: It's very kind of you to say so, Miss Doolittle.

LIZA: It's not because you paid for my dresses. I know you are generous to everybody with money. But it was from you that I learnt really nice manners; and that is what makes one a lady, isnt it? You see it was so very difficult for me with the example of Professor Higgins always before me. I was brought up to be just like him, unable to control myself, and using bad language on the slightest provocation. And I should never have known that ladies and gentlemen didnt behave like that if you hadnt been there.

HIGGINS: Well!!

PICKERING: Oh, thats only his way, you know. He doesnt mean it.

LIZA: Oh, *I* didnt mean it either, when I was a flower girl. It was only my way. But you see I did it; and thats what makes the difference after all.

PICKERING: No doubt. Still, he taught you to speak; and I couldnt have done that, you know.

LIZA [*trivially*]: Of course: that is his profession.

HIGGINS: Damnation!

LIZA [*continuing*]: It was just like learning to dance in the fashionable way: there was nothing more than that in it. But do you know what began my real education?

PICKERING: What?

LIZA [*stopping her work for a moment*]: Your calling me Miss Doolittle that day when I first came to Wimpole Street. That was the beginning of self-respect for me. [*She resumes her stitching.*] And there were a hundred little things you never noticed, because they came naturally to you. Things about standing up and taking off your hat and opening doors—

PICKERING: Oh, that was nothing.

LIZA: Yes: things that shewed you thought and felt about me as if I were something better than a scullery-maid; though of course I know you would have been just the same to a scullery-maid if she had been let into the drawing room. You never took off your boots in the dining room when I was there.

PICKERING: You mustnt mind that. Higgins takes off his boots all over the place.

LIZA: I know. I am not blaming him. It is his way, isnt it? But it made such a difference to me that you didnt do it. You see, really and truly, apart from the things anyone can pick up (the dressing and the proper way of speaking, and so on), the difference between a lady and a flower girl is not how she behaves, but how she's treated. I shall always be a flower girl to Professor Higgins, because he always treats me as a flower girl, and always will; but I know I can be a lady to you, because you always treat me as a lady, and always will.

MRS HIGGINS: Please dont grind your teeth. Henry.

PICKERING: Well, this is really very nice of you, Miss Doolittle.

LIZA: I should like you to call me Eliza, now, if you would.

PICKERING: Thank you. Eliza, of course.

LIZA: And I should like Professor Higgins to call me Miss Doolittle.

HIGGINS: I'll see you damned first.

MRS HIGGINS: Henry! Henry!

PICKERING [*laughing*]: Why dont you slang back at him? Dont stand it. It would do him a lot of good.

LIZA: I cant. I could have done it once but now I cant go back to it. You told me, you know, that when a child is brought to a foreign country, it picks up the language in a few weeks, and forgets its own. Well, I am a child in your country. I have forgotten my own language, and can speak nothing but yours. Thats the real break-off with the corner of Tottenham Court Road. Leaving Wimpole Street finishes it.

PICKERING [*much alarmed*]: Oh! but youre coming back to Wimpole Street, arnt you? Youll forgive Higgins?

HIGGINS [*rising*]: Forgive! Will she, by George! Let her go. Let her find out how she can get on without us. She will relapse into the gutter in three weeks without me at her elbow.

[*Doolittle appears at the centre window. With a look of dignified reproach at Higgins, he comes slowly and silently to his daughter, who, with her back to the window, is unconscious of his approach.*]

PICKERING: He's incorrigible, Eliza. You wont relapse, will you?

LIZA: No: not now. Never again. I have learnt my lesson. I dont believe I could utter one of the old sounds if I tried. [*Doolittle touches her on her left shoulder. She drops her work, losing her self-possession utterly at the spectacle of her father's splendor.*] A-a-a-a-a-ah-ow-ooh!

HIGGINS [*with a crow of triumph*]: Aha! Just so. A-a-a-a-ahowooh! A-a-a-a-ahowooh! A-a-a-a-ahowooh! Victory! Victory! [*He throws himself on the divan, folding his arms, and spraddling arrogantly.*]

DOOLITTLE: Can you blame the girl? Dont look at me like that, Eliza. It aint my fault. Ive come into some money.

LIZA: You must have touched a millionaire this time, dad.

DOOLITTLE: I have. But I'm dressed something special today. I'm going to St George's. Hanover Square. Your stepmother is going to marry me.

LIZA [*angrily*]: Youre going to let yourself down to marry that low common woman!

PICKERING [*quietly*]: He ought to, Eliza. [*To Doolittle.*] Why has she changed her mind?

DOOLITTLE [*sadly*]: Intimidated, Governor. Intimidated. Middle class morality claims its victim. Wont you put on your hat, Liza, and come and see me turned off?

LIZA: If the Colonel says I must. I—I'll [*almost sobbing*] I'll demean myself. And get insulted for my pains, like enough.

DOOLITTLE: Dont be afraid: she never comes to words with anyone now, poor woman! respectability has broke all the spirit out of her.

PICKERING [*squeezing Eliza's elbow gently*]: Be kind to them, Eliza. Make the best of it.

LIZA [*forcing a little smile for him through her vexation*]: Oh well, just to shew theres no ill feeling. I'll be back in a moment. [*She goes out.*]

DOOLITTLE [*sitting down beside Pickering*]: I feel uncommon nervous about the ceremony, Colonel. I wish youd come and see me through it.

PICKERING: But youve been through it before, man. You were married to Eliza's mother.

DOOLITTLE: Who told you that, Colonel?

PICKERING: Well, nobody told me. But I concluded—naturally—

DOOLITTLE: No: that aint the natural way, Colonel: It's only the middle class way. My way was always the undeserving way. But dont say nothing to Eliza. She dont know: I always had a delicacy about telling her.

PICKERING: Quite right. We'll leave it so, if you dont mind.

DOOLITTLE: And youll come to the church, Colonel, and put me through straight?

PICKERING: With pleasure. As far as a bachelor can.

MRS HIGGINS: May I come, Mr Doolittle? I should be very sorry to miss your wedding.

DOOLITTLE: I should indeed be honored by your condescension, maam; and my poor old woman would take it as a tremenjous compliment. She's been very low, thinking of the happy days that are no more.

MRS HIGGINS [*rising*]: I'll order the carriage and get ready. [*The men rise, except Higgins.*] I shant be more than fifteen minutes. [*As she goes to the door Eliza comes in, hatted and buttoning her gloves.*] I'm going to the church to see your father married, Eliza. You had better come in the brougham[4] with me. Colonel Pickering can go on with the bridegroom.

[*Mrs Higgins goes out. Eliza comes to the middle of the room between the centre window and the ottoman. Pickering joins her.*]

DOOLITTLE: Bridegroom! What a word! It makes a man realize his position, somehow. [*He takes up his hat and goes towards the door.*]

PICKERING: Before I go, Eliza, do forgive Higgins and come back to us.

LIZA: I dont think dad would allow me. Would you, dad?

DOOLITTLE [*sad but magnanimous*]: They played you off very cunning, Eliza, them two sportsmen. If it had been only one of them, you could have nailed him. But you see, there was two; and one of them chaperoned the other, as you might say. [*To Pickering.*] It was artful of you, Colonel: but I bear no malice: I should have done the same myself. I been the victim of one woman after another all my life, and I dont grudge you two getting the better of Liza. I shant interfere. It's time for us to go, Colonel. So long, Henry. See you in St George's, Eliza. [*He goes out.*]

PICKERING [*coaxing*]: Do stay with us, Eliza. [*He follows Doolittle.*]

[*Eliza goes out on the balcony to avoid being alone with Higgins. He rises and joins her there. She immediately comes back into the room and makes for the door; but he goes along the balcony quickly and gets his back to the door before she reaches it.*]

HIGGINS: Well, Eliza, youve had a bit of your own back, as you call it. Have you had enough? and are you going to be reasonable? Or do you want any more?

LIZA: You want me back only to pick up your slippers and put up with your tempers and fetch and carry for you.

HIGGINS: I havnt said I wanted you back at all.

LIZA: Oh, indeed. Then what are we talking about?

4. Four-wheeled horse carriage.

HIGGINS: About you, not about me. If you come back I shall treat you just as I have always treated you. I cant change my nature; and I dont intend to change my manners. My manners are exactly the same as Colonel Pickering's.

LIZA: Thats not true. He treats a flower girl as if she was a duchess.

HIGGINS: And I treat a duchess as if she was a flower girl.

LIZA: I see. [*She turns away composedly, and sits on the ottoman, facing the window.*] The same to everybody.

HIGGINS: Just so.

LIZA: Like father.

HIGGINS [*grinning, a little taken down*]: Without accepting the comparison at all points, Eliza, it's quite true that your father is not a snob, and that he will be quite at home in any station of life to which his eccentric destiny may call him. [*Seriously.*] The great secret, Eliza, is not having bad manners or good manners or any other particular sort of manners, but having the same manner for all human souls: in short, behaving as if you were in Heaven, where there are no third-class carriages, and one soul is as good as another.

LIZA: Amen. You are a born preacher.

HIGGINS [*irritated*]: The question is not whether I treat you rudely, but whether you ever heard me treat anyone else better.

LIZA [*with sudden sincerity*]: I dont care how you treat me. I dont mind your swearing at me. I shouldnt mind a black eye: Ive had one before this. But [*standing up and facing him*] I wont be passed over.

HIGGINS: Then get out of my way; for I wont stop for you. You talk about me as if I were a motor bus.

LIZA: So you are a motor bus: all bounce and go, and no consideration for anyone. But I can do without you: dont think I cant.

HIGGINS: I know you can. I told you you could.

LIZA [*wounded, getting away from him to the other side of the ottoman with her face to the hearth*]: I know you did, you brute. You wanted to get rid of me.

HIGGINS: Liar.

LIZA: Thank you. [*She sits down with dignity.*]

HIGGINS: You never asked yourself, I suppose, whether I could do without you.

LIZA [*earnestly*]: Dont you try to get round me. Youll have to do without me.

HIGGINS [*arrogant*]: I can do without anybody. I have my own soul: my own spark of divine fire. But [*with sudden humility*] I shall miss you, Eliza. [*He sits down near her on the ottoman.*] I have learnt something from your idiotic notions: I confess that humbly and gratefully. And I have grown accustomed to your voice and appearance. I like them, rather.

LIZA: Well, you have both of them on your gramophone and in your book of photographs. When you feel lonely without me, you can turn the machine on. It's got no feelings to hurt.

HIGGINS: I cant turn your soul on. Leave me those feelings; and you can take away the voice and the face. They are not you.

LIZA: Oh, you are a devil. You can twist the heart in a girl as easy as some could twist her arms to hurt her. Mrs Pearce warned me. Time and again she has wanted to leave you; and you always got round her at the last minute. And you dont care a bit for her. And you dont care a bit for me.

HIGGINS: I care for life, for humanity; and you are a part of it that has come my way and been built into my house. What more can you or anyone ask?

LIZA: I wont care for anybody that doesnt care for me.

HIGGINS: Commercial principles, Eliza. Like [*reproducing her Covent Garden pronunciation with professional exactness*] s'yollin voylets [selling violets], isnt it?

LIZA: Dont sneer at me. It's mean to sneer at me.

HIGGINS: I have never sneered in my life. Sneering doesnt become either the human face or the human soul. I am expressing my righteous contempt for Commercialism. I dont and wont trade in affection. You call me a brute because you couldnt buy a claim on me by fetching my slippers and finding my spectacles. You were a fool: I think a woman fetching a man's slippers is a disgusting sight: did I ever fetch your slippers? I think a good deal more of you for throwing them in my face. No use slaving for me and then saying you want to be cared for: who cares for a slave? If you come back, come back for the sake of good fellowship; for youll get nothing else. Youve had a thousand times as much out of me as I have out of you; and if you dare to set up your little dog's tricks of fetching and carrying slippers against my creation of a Duchess Eliza. I'll slam the door in your silly face.

LIZA: What did you do it for if you didnt care for me?

HIGGINS [*heartily*]: Why, because it was my job.

LIZA: You never thought of the trouble it would make for me.

HIGGINS: Would the world ever have been made if its maker had been afraid of making trouble? Making life means making trouble. Theres only one way of escaping trouble; and thats killing things. Cowards, you notice, are always shrieking to have troublesome people killed.

LIZA: I'm no preacher: I dont notice things like that. I notice that you dont notice me.

HIGGINS [*jumping up and walking about intolerantly*]: Eliza: youre an idiot. I waste the treasures of my Miltonic mind by spreading them before you. Once for all, understand that I go my way and do my work without caring twopence what happens to either of us. I am not intimidated, like your father and your stepmother. So you can come back or go to the devil: which you please.

LIZA: What am I to come back for?

HIGGINS [*bouncing up on his knees on the ottoman and leaning over it to her*]: For the fun of it. Thats why I took you on.

LIZA [*with averted face*]: And you may throw me out tomorrow if I dont do everything you want me to?

HIGGINS: Yes; and you may walk out tomorrow if I dont do everything you want me to.

LIZA: And live with my stepmother?

HIGGINS: Yes, or sell flowers.

LIZA: Oh! If I only could go back to my flower basket! I should be independent of both you and father and all the world! Why did you take my independence from me? Why did I give it up? I'm a slave now, for all my fine clothes.

HIGGINS: Not a bit. I'll adopt you as my daughter and settle money on you if you like. Or would you rather marry Pickering?

LIZA [*looking fiercely round at him*]: I wouldnt marry you if you asked me; and youre nearer my age than what he is.

HIGGINS [*gently*]: Than he is: not "than what he is."

LIZA [*losing her temper and rising*]: I'll talk as I like. Youre not my teacher now.

HIGGINS [*reflectively*]: I dont suppose Pickering would, though. He's as confirmed an old bachelor as I am.

LIZA: Thats not what I want; and dont you think it. Ive always had chaps enough wanting me that way. Freddy Hill writes to me twice and three times a day, sheets and sheets.

HIGGINS [*disagreeably surprised*]: Damn his impudence! [*He recoils and finds himself sitting on his heels*.]

LIZA: He has a right to if he likes, poor lad. And he does love me.

HIGGINS [*getting off the ottoman*]: You have no right to encourage him.

LIZA: Every girl has a right to be loved.

HIGGINS: What! By fools like that?

LIZA: Freddy's not a fool. And if he's weak and poor and wants me, may be he'd make me happier than my betters that bully me and dont want me.

HIGGINS: Can he make anything of you? Thats the point.

LIZA: Perhaps I could make something of him. But I never thought of us making anything of one another; and you never think of anything else. I only want to be natural.

HIGGINS: In short, you want me to be as infatuated about you as Freddy? Is that it?

LIZA: No I dont. Thats not the sort of feeling I want from you. And dont you be too sure of yourself or of me. I could have been a bad girl if I'd liked. Ive seen more of some things than you, for all your learning. Girls like me can drag gentlemen down to make love to them easy enough. And they wish each other dead the next minute.

HIGGINS: Of course they do. Then what in thunder are we quarrelling about?

LIZA [*much troubled*]: I want a little kindness. I know I'm a common ignorant girl, and you a book-learned gentleman; but I'm not dirt under your feet. What I done [*correcting herself*] what I did was not for the dresses and the taxis: I did it because we were pleasant together and I come—came—to care for you; not to want you to make love to me, and not forgetting the difference between us, but more friendly like.

HIGGINS: Well, of course. Thats just how I feel. And how Pickering feels. Eliza: youre a fool.

LIZA: Thats not a proper answer to give me [*she sinks on the chair at the writing-table in tears*].

HIGGINS: It's all youll get until you stop being a common idiot. If youre going to be a lady, youll have to give up feeling neglected if the men you know dont spend half their time snivelling over you and the other half giving you black eyes. If you cant stand the coldness of my sort of life, and the strain of it, go back to the gutter. Work til youre more a brute than a human being: and then cuddle and squabble and drink til you fall asleep. Oh, it's a fine life, the life of the gutter. It's real: it's warm: it's violent: you can feel it through the thickest skin: you can taste it and smell it without any training or any work. Not like Science and Literature and Classical Music and Philosophy and Art. You find me cold, unfeeling, selfish, dont you? Very well: be off with you to the sort of people you like. Marry some sentimental hog or other with lots of money, and a thick pair of lips to kiss you with and a thick pair of boots to kick you with. If you cant appreciate what youve got, youd better get what you can appreciate.

LIZA [*desperate*]: Oh, you are a cruel tyrant. I cant talk to you: you turn everything against me: I'm always in the wrong. But you know very well all the time that youre nothing but a bully. You know I cant go back to the gutter, as you call it, and that I have no real friends in the world but you and the Colonel. You know well I couldnt bear to live with a low common man after you two; and it's wicked and cruel of you to insult me by pretending I could. You think I must go back to Wimpole Street because I have nowhere else to go but father's. But dont you be too sure that you have me under your feet to be trampled on and talked down. I'll marry Freddy, I will, as soon as I'm able to support him.

HIGGINS [*thunderstruck*]: Freddy!!! that young fool! That poor devil who couldnt get a job as an errand boy even if he had the guts to try for it! Woman: do you not understand that I have made you a consort for a king?

LIZA: Freddy loves me: that makes him king enough for me. I dont want him to work: he wasnt brought up to it as I was. I'll go and be a teacher.

HIGGINS: Whatll you teach, in heaven's name?

LIZA: What you taught me. I'll teach phonetics.

HIGGINS: Ha! Ha! ha!

LIZA: I'll offer myself as an assistant to that hairyfaced Hungarian.

HIGGINS [*rising in a fury*]: What! That impostor! That humbug! That toadying ignoramus! Teach him my methods! my discoveries! You take one step in his direction and I'll wring your neck. [*He lays hands on her.*] Do you hear?

LIZA [*defiantly non-resistant*]: Wring away. What do I care? I knew youd strike me some day. [*He lets her go, stamping with rage at having forgotten himself, and recoils so hastily that he stumbles back into his seat on the ottoman.*] Aha! Now I know how to deal with you. What a fool I was not to think of it before! You cant take away the knowledge you gave me. You said I had a finer ear than you. And I can be civil and kind to people, which is more than you can. Aha! [*Purposely dropping her aitches to annoy him.*] Thats done you, Enry Iggins, it az. Now I dont care that [*snapping her fingers*] for your bullying and your big talk. I'll advertize it in the papers that your duchess is only a flower girl that you taught, and that she'll teach anybody to be a duchess just the same in six months for a thousand guineas. Oh, when I think of myself crawling under your feet and being trampled on and called names, when all the time I had only to lift up my finger to be as good as you, I could just kick myself.

HIGGINS [*wondering at her*]: You damned impudent slut, you! But it's better than snivelling; better than fetching slippers and finding spectacles, isnt it? [*Rising.*] By George, Eliza, I said I'd make a woman of you; and I have. I like you like this.

LIZA: Yes: you can turn round and make up to me now that I'm not afraid of you, and can do without you.

HIGGINS: Of course I do, you little fool. Five minutes ago you were like a millstone round my neck. Now youre a tower of strength: a consort battleship. You and I and Pickering will be three old bachelors instead of only two men and a silly girl.

[*Mrs Higgins returns, dressed for the wedding. Eliza instantly becomes cool and elegant.*]

MRS HIGGINS: The carriage is waiting, Eliza. Are you ready?

LIZA: Quite. Is the Professor coming?

MRS HIGGINS: Certainly not. He cant behave himself in church. He makes remarks out loud all the time on the clergyman's pronunciation.

LIZA: Then I shall not see you again, Professor. Goodbye. [*She goes to the door.*]

MRS HIGGINS [*coming to Higgins*]: Goodbye, dear.

HIGGINS: Goodbye, mother. [*He is about to kiss her, when he recollects something.*] Oh, by the way, Eliza, order a ham and a Stilton cheese, will you? And buy me a pair of reindeer gloves, number eights, and a tie to match that new suit of mine. You can choose the color. [*His cheerful, careless, vigorous voice shews that he is incorrigible.*]

LIZA [*disdainfully*]: Number eights are too small for you if you want them lined with lamb's wool. You have three new ties that you have forgotten in the drawer of your washstand. Colonel Pickering prefers double Gloucester to Stilton; and you dont notice the difference. I telephoned Mrs Pearce this morning not to forget the ham. What you are to do without me I cannot imagine. [*She sweeps out.*]

MRS HIGGINS: I'm afraid youve spoilt that girl, Henry. I should be uneasy about you and her if she were less fond of Colonel Pickering.

HIGGINS: Pickering! Nonsense: she's going to marry Freddy. Ha ha! Freddy! Freddy!! Ha ha ha ha ha!!!!! [*He roars with laughter as the play ends.*]

Sequel

The rest of the story need not be shewn in action, and indeed, would hardly need telling if our imaginations were not so enfeebled by their lazy dependence on the ready-mades and reach-me-downs of the ragshop in which Romance keeps its stock of "happy endings" to misfit all stories. Now, the history of Eliza Doolittle, though called a romance because the transfiguration it records seems exceedingly improbable, is common enough. Such transfigurations have been achieved by hundreds of resolutely ambitious young women since Nell Gwynne[1] set them the example by playing queens and fascinating kings in the theatre in which she began by selling oranges. Nevertheless, people in all directions have assumed, for no other reason than that she became the heroine of a romance, that she must have married the hero of it. This is unbearable, not only because her little drama, if acted on such a thoughtless assumption, must be spoiled, but because the true sequel is patent to anyone with a sense of human nature in general, and of feminine instinct in particular.

Eliza, in telling Higgins she would not marry him if he asked, was not coquetting: she was announcing a well-considered decision. When a bachelor interests, and dominates, and teaches, and becomes important to a spinster, as Higgins with Eliza, she always, if she has character enough to be capable of it, considers very seriously indeed whether she will play for becoming that bachelor's wife, especially if he is so little interested in marriage that a determined and devoted woman might capture him if she set herself resolutely to do it. Her decision will depend a good deal on whether she is really free to choose; and that, again, will depend on her age and income. If she is at the end of her youth, and has no security for her livelihood, she will marry him because she must marry anybody who will provide for her. But at Eliza's age a good-looking girl does not feel that pressure: she feels free to pick and choose. She is therefore guided by her instinct in the matter. Eliza's instinct tells her not to marry Higgins. It does not tell her to give him up. It is not in the slightest doubt as to his remaining one of the strongest personal interests in her life. It would be very sorely strained if there was another woman likely to supplant her with him. But as she feels sure of him on that last point, she has no doubt at all as to her course, and would not have any, even if the difference of twenty years in age, which seems so great to youth, did not exist between them.

As our own instincts are not appealed to by her conclusion, let us see whether we cannot discover some reason in it. When Higgins excused his indifference to young women on the ground that they had an irresistible rival in his mother, he gave the clue to his inveterate old-bachelordom. The case is uncommon only to the extent that remarkable mothers are uncommon. If an imaginative boy has a sufficiently rich mother who has intelligence, personal grace, dignity of character without harshness, and a cultivated sense of the best art of her time to enable her to make her house beautiful, she sets a standard for him against which very few women can struggle, besides effecting for him a disengagement of his affections, his sense of beauty,

1. Nell Gwynne (1650–1687), London theatre vendor, actor, and later mistress of Charles II.

and his idealism from his specifically sexual impulses. This makes him a standing puzzle to the huge number of uncultivated people who have been brought up in tasteless homes by commonplace or disagreeable parents, and to whom, consequently, literature, painting, sculpture, music, and affectionate personal relations come as modes of sex if they come at all. The word passion means nothing else to them; and that Higgins could have a passion for phonetics and idealize his mother instead of Eliza, would seem to them absurd and unnatural. Nevertheless, when we look round and see that hardly anyone is too ugly or disagreeable to find a wife or a husband if he or she wants one, whilst many old maids and bachelors are above the average in quality and culture, we cannot help suspecting that the disentanglement of sex from the associations with which it is commonly confused, a disentanglement which persons of genius achieve by sheer intellectual analysis, is sometimes produced or aided by parental fascination.

Now, though Eliza was incapable of thus explaining to herself Higgins's formidable powers of resistance to the charm that prostrated Freddy at the first glance, she was instinctively aware that she could never obtain a complete grip of him, or come between him and his mother (the first necessity of the married woman). To put it shortly, she knew that for some mysterious reason he had not the makings of a married man in him, according to her conception of a husband as one to whom she would be his nearest and fondest and warmest interest. Even had there been no mother-rival, she would still have refused to accept an interest in herself that was secondary to philosophic interests. Had Mrs Higgins died, there would still have been Milton and the Universal Alphabet. Landor's remark that to those who have the greatest power of loving, love is a secondary affair, would not have recommended Landor to Eliza. Put that along with her resentment of Higgins's domineering superiority, and her mistrust of his coaxing cleverness in getting round her and evading her wrath when he had gone too far with his impetuous bullying, and you will see that Eliza's instinct had good grounds for warning her not to marry her Pygmalion.

And now, whom did Eliza marry? For if Higgins was a predestinate old bachelor, she was most certainly not a predestinate old maid. Well, that can be told very shortly to those who have not guessed it from the indications she has herself given them.

Almost immediately after Eliza is stung into proclaiming her considered determination not to marry Higgins, she mentions the fact that young Mr Frederick Eynsford Hill is pouring out his love for her daily through the post. Now Freddy is young, practically twenty years younger than Higgins: he is a gentleman (or, as Eliza would qualify him, a toff[2]), and speaks like one. He is nicely dressed, is treated by the Colonel as an equal, loves her unaffectedly, and is not her master, nor ever likely to dominate her in spite of his advantage of social standing. Eliza has no use for the foolish romantic tradition that all women love to be mastered, if not actually bullied and beaten. "When you go to women" says Nietzsche[3] "take your whip with you." Sensible despots have never confined that precaution to women: they have taken their whips with them when they have dealt with men, and been slavishly idealized by the men over whom they have flourished the whip much more than by women. No doubt there are slavish women as well as slavish men; and women, like men, admire those that are stronger than themselves. But to admire a strong person and to live under that strong person's thumb are two different things. The weak may not be admired

2. Fashionable gentleman.
3. Friedrich Nietzsche (1844–1900), German philosopher whose rejection of traditional Judeo-Christian ethics and belief in the natural moral superiority of certain individuals fascinated Shaw, finding its most direct expression in his play *Man and Superman* (1903).

and hero-worshipped; but they are by no means disliked or shunned; and they never seem to have the least difficulty in marrying people who are too good for them. They may fail in emergencies: but life is not one long emergency: it is mostly a string of situations for which no exceptional strength is needed, and with which even rather weak people can cope if they have a stronger partner to help them out. Accordingly, it is a truth everywhere in evidence that strong people, masculine or feminine, not only do not marry stronger people, but do not shew any preference for them in selecting their friends. When a lion meets another with a louder roar "the first lion thinks the last a bore." The man or woman who feels strong enough for two, seeks for every other quality in a partner than strength.

The converse is also true. Weak people want to marry strong people who do not frighten them too much: and this often leads them to make the mistake we describe metaphorically as "biting off more than they can chew." They want too much for too little; and when the bargain is unreasonable beyond all bearing, the union becomes impossible: it ends in the weaker party being either discarded or borne as a cross, which is worse. People who are not only weak, but silly or obtuse as well, are often in these difficulties.

This being the state of human affairs, what is Eliza fairly sure to do when she is placed between Freddy and Higgins? Will she look forward to a lifetime of fetching Higgins's slippers or to a lifetime of Freddy fetching hers? There can be no doubt about the answer. Unless Freddy is biologically repulsive to her, and Higgins biologically attractive to a degree that overwhelms all her other instincts, she will, if she marries either of them, marry Freddy.

And that is just what Eliza did.

Complications ensued; but they were economic, not romantic. Freddy had no money and no occupation. His mother's jointure,[4] a last relic of the opulence of Largelady Park, had enabled her to struggle along in Earlscourt with an air of gentility, but not to procure any serious secondary education for her children, much less give the boy a profession. A clerkship at thirty shillings a week was beneath Freddy's dignity, and extremely distasteful to him besides. His prospects consisted of a hope that if he kept up appearances somebody would do something for him. The something appeared vaguely to his imagination as a private secretaryship or a sinecure of some sort. To his mother it perhaps appeared as a marriage to some lady of means who could not resist her boy's niceness. Fancy her feelings when he married a flower girl who had become disclassed under extraordinary circumstances which were now notorious!

It is true that Eliza's situation did not seem wholly ineligible. Her father, though formerly a dustman, and now fantastically disclassed, had become extremely popular in the smartest society by a social talent which triumphed over every prejudice and every disadvantage. Rejected by the middle class, which he loathed, he had shot up at once into the highest circles by his wit, his dustmanship (which he carried like a banner), and his Nietzschean transcendence of good and evil. At intimate ducal dinners he sat on the righthand of the Duchess; and in country houses he smoked in the pantry and was made much of by the butler when he was not feeding in the dining room and being consulted by cabinet ministers. But he found it almost as hard to do all this on four thousand a year as Mrs Eynsford Hill to live in Earlscourt on an income so pitiably smaller that I have not the heart to disclose its exact figure. He absolutely refused to add the last straw to his burden by contributing to Eliza's support.

4. Estate settled upon a widow by her late husband.

Thus Freddy and Eliza, now Mr and Mrs Eynsford Hill, would have spent a penniless honeymoon but for a wedding present of £500 from the Colonel to Eliza. It lasted a long time because Freddy did not know how to spend money, never having had any to spend, and Eliza, socially trained by a pair of old bachelors, wore her clothes as long as they held together and looked pretty, without the least regard to their being many months out of fashion. Still, £500 will not last two young people for ever; and they both knew, and Eliza felt as well, that they must shift themselves in the end. She could quarter herself on Wimpole Street because it had come to be her home; but she was quite aware that she ought not to quarter Freddy there, and that it would not be good for his character if she did.

Not that the Wimpole Street bachelors objected. When she consulted them, Higgins declined to be bothered about her housing problem when that solution was so simple. Eliza's desire to have Freddy in the house with her seemed of no more importance than if she had wanted an extra piece of bedroom furniture. Pleas as to Freddy's character, and the moral obligation on him to earn his own living, were lost on Higgins. He denied that Freddy had any character, and declared that if he tried to do any useful work some competent person would have the trouble of undoing it: a procedure involving a net loss to the community, and great unhappiness to Freddy himself, who was obviously intended by Nature for such light work as amusing Eliza, which, Higgins declared, was a much more useful and honorable occupation than working in the city. When Eliza referred again to her project of teaching phonetics, Higgins abated not a jot of his violent opposition to it. He said she was not within ten years of being qualified to meddle with his pet subject: and as it was evident that the Colonel agreed with him, she felt she could not go against them in this grave matter, and that she had no right, without Higgins's consent, to exploit the knowledge he had given her: for his knowledge seemed to her as much his private property as his watch: Eliza was no communist. Besides, she was superstitiously devoted to them both, more entirely and frankly after her marriage than before it.

It was the Colonel who finally solved the problem, which had cost him much perplexed cogitation. He one day asked Eliza, rather shyly, whether she had quite given up her notion of keeping a flower shop. She replied that she had thought of it, but had put it out of her head, because the Colonel had said, that day at Mrs Higgins's, that it would never do. The Colonel confessed that when he said that, he had not quite recovered from the dazzling impression of the day before. They broke the matter to Higgins that evening. The sole comment vouchsafed by him very nearly led to a serious quarrel with Eliza. It was to the effect that she would have in Freddy an ideal errand boy.

Freddy himself was next sounded on the subject. He said he had been thinking of a shop himself; though it had presented itself to his pennilessness as a small place in which Eliza should sell tobacco at one counter whilst he sold newspapers at the opposite one. But he agreed that it would be extraordinarily jolly to go early every morning with Eliza to Covent Garden and buy flowers on the scene of their first meeting: a sentiment which earned him many kisses from his wife. He added that he had always been afraid to propose anything of the sort, because Clara would make an awful row about a step that must damage her matrimonial chances, and his mother could not be expected to like it after clinging for so many years to that step of the social ladder on which retail trade is impossible.

This difficulty was removed by an event highly unexpected by Freddy's mother. Clara, in the course of her incursions into those artistic circles which were the highest within her reach, discovered that her conversational qualifications were ex-

pected to include a grounding in the novels of Mr H. G. Wells.[5] She borrowed them in various directions so energetically that she swallowed them all within two months. The result was a conversion of a kind quite common today. A modern Acts of the Apostles would fill fifty whole Bibles if anyone were capable of writing it.

Poor Clara, who appeared to Higgins and his mother as a disagreeable and ridiculous person, and to her own mother as in some inexplicable way a social failure, had never seen herself in either light; for, though to some extent ridiculed and mimicked in West Kensington like everybody else there, she was accepted as a rational and normal—or shall we say inevitable?—sort of human being. At worst they called her The Pusher; but to them no more than to herself had it ever occurred that she was pushing the air, and pushing it in a wrong direction. Still, she was not happy. She was growing desperate. Her one asset, the fact that her mother was what the Epsom greengrocer called a carriage lady, had no exchange value, apparently. It had prevented her from getting educated, because the only education she could have afforded was education with the Earlscourt greengrocer's daughter. It had led her to seek the society of her mother's class; and that class simply would not have her, because she was much poorer than the greengrocer, and, far from being able to afford a maid, could not afford even a house-maid, and had to scrape along at home with an illiberally treated general servant. Under such circumstances nothing could give her an air of being a genuine product of Largelady Park. And yet its tradition made her regard a marriage with anyone within her reach as an unbearable humiliation. Commercial people and professional people in a small way were odious to her. She ran after painters and novelists; but she did not charm them; and her bold attempts to pick up and practise artistic and literary talk irritated them. She was, in short, an utter failure, an ignorant, incompetent, pretentious, unwelcome, penniless, useless little snob; and though she did not admit these disqualifications (for nobody ever faces unpleasant truths of this kind until the possibility of a way out dawns on them) she felt their effects too keenly to be satisfied with her position.

Clara had a startling eyeopener when, on being suddenly wakened to enthusiasm by a girl of her own age who dazzled her and produced in her a gushing desire to take her for a model, and gain her friendship, she discovered that this exquisite apparition had graduated from the gutter in a few months time. It shook her so violently, that when Mr H. G. Wells lifted her on the point of his puissant pen, and placed her at the angle of view from which the life she was leading and the society to which she clung appeared in its true relation to real human needs and worthy social structure, he effected a conversion and a conviction of sin comparable to the most sensational feats of General Booth[6] or Gypsy Smith.[7] Clara's snobbery went bang. Life suddenly began to move with her. Without knowing how or why, she began to make friends and enemies. Some of the acquaintances to whom she had been a tedious or indifferent or ridiculous affliction, dropped her: others became cordial. To her amazement she found that some "quite nice" people were saturated with Wells, and that this accessibility to ideas was the secret of their niceness. People she had thought deeply religious and had tried to conciliate on that tack with disastrous results, suddenly took an interest in her, and revealed a hostility to conventional religion which she had never conceived possible except among the most desperate characters. They made her read Galsworthy; and Galsworthy exposed

5. H(erbert) G(eorge) Wells (1866–1946), English novelist and writer of science fiction, who shared Shaw's zeal for social reform, while their passion meant they were often at odds.

6. ("General") William Booth (1829–1912), English religious reformer and founder of the Salvation Army.

7. Rodney ("Gypsy") Smith (1860–1947), popular British preacher and evangelist.

the vanity of Largelady Park and finished her. It exasperated her to think that the dungeon in which she had languished for so many unhappy years had been unlocked all the time, and that the impulses she had so carefully struggled with and stifled for the sake of keeping well with society, were precisely those by which alone she could have come into any sort of sincere human contact. In the radiance of these discoveries, and the tumult of their reaction, she made a fool of herself as freely and conspicuously as when she so rashly adopted Eliza's expletive in Mrs Higgins's drawing room; for the new-born Wellsian had to find her bearings almost as ridiculously as a baby; but nobody hates a baby for its ineptitudes, or thinks the worse of it for trying to eat the matches; and Clara lost no friends by her follies. They laughed at her to her face this time; and she had to defend herself and fight it out as best she could.

When Freddy paid a visit to Earlscourt (which he never did when he could possibly help it) to make the desolating announcement that he and his Eliza were thinking of blackening the Largelady scutcheon by opening a shop, he found the little household already convulsed by a prior announcement from Clara that she also was going to work in an old furniture shop in Dover Street, which had been started by a fellow Wellsian. This appointment Clara owed, after all, to her old social accomplishment of Push. She had made up her mind that, cost what it might, she would see Mr Wells in the flesh; and she had achieved her end at a garden party. She had better luck than so rash an enterprise deserved, Mr Wells came up to her expectations. Age had not withered him, nor could custom stale his infinite variety in half an hour. His pleasant neatness and compactness, his small hands and feet, his teeming ready brain, his unaffected accessibility, and a certain fine apprehensiveness which stamped him as susceptible from his topmost hair to his tipmost toe, proved irresistible. Clara talked of nothing else for weeks and weeks afterwards. And as she happened to talk to the lady of the furniture shop, and that lady also desired above all things to know Mr Wells and sell pretty things to him, she offered Clara a job on the chance of achieving that end through her.

And so it came about that Eliza's luck held, and the expected opposition to the flower shop melted away. The shop is in the arcade of a railway station not very far from the Victoria and Albert Museum; and if you live in that neighborhood you may go there any day and buy a buttonhole from Eliza.

Now here is a last opportunity for romance. Would you not like to be assured that the shop was an immense success, thanks to Eliza's charms and her early business experience in Covent Garden? Alas! the truth is the truth: the shop did not pay for a long time, simply because Eliza and her Freddy did not know how to keep it. True, Eliza had not to begin at the very beginning: she knew the names and prices of the cheaper flowers; and her elation was unbounded when she found that Freddy, like all youths educated at cheap, pretentious, and thoroughly inefficient schools, knew a little Latin. It was very little, but enough to make him appear to her a Porson or Bentley,[8] and to put him at his ease with botanical nomenclature. Unfortunately he knew nothing else; and Eliza, though she could count money up to eighteen shillings or so, and had acquired a certain familiarity with the language of Milton from her struggles to qualify herself for winning Higgins's bet, could not write out a bill without utterly disgracing the establishment. Freddy's power of stating in Latin that Balbus built a wall[9] and that Gaul was divided into three parts did not carry with it the slightest

8. Richard Porson (1759–1808), English classical scholar; Richard Bentley (1662–1742), English classical scholar satirized by Jonathan Swift in *The Battle of the Books*.

9. From Cicero's *Letters to Atticus* 12.2; a common schoolboy's Latin translation exercise.

knowledge of accounts or business: Colonel Pickering had to explain to him what a cheque book and a bank account meant. And the pair were by no means easily teachable. Freddy backed up Eliza in her obstinate refusal to believe that they could save money by engaging a bookkeeper with some knowledge of the business. How, they argued, could you possibly save money by going to extra expense when you already could not make both ends meet? But the Colonel, after making the ends meet over and over again, at last gently insisted; and Eliza, humbled to the dust by having to beg from him so often, and stung by the uproarious derision of Higgins, to whom the notion of Freddy succeeding at anything was a joke that never palled, grasped the fact that business, like phonetics, has to be learned.

On the piteous spectacle of the pair spending their evenings in shorthand schools and polytechnic classes, learning book-keeping and typewriting with incipient junior clerks, male and female, from the elementary schools, let me not dwell. There were even classes at the London School of Economics, and a humble personal appeal to the director of that institution to recommend a course bearing on the flower business. He, being a humorist, explained to them the method of the celebrated Dickensian essay on Chinese Metaphysics by the gentleman who read an article on China and an article on Metaphysics and combined the information. He suggested that they should combine the London School with Kew Gardens. Eliza, to whom the procedure of the Dickensian gentleman seemed perfectly correct (as in fact it was) and not in the least funny (which was only her ignorance), took the advice with entire gravity. But the effort that cost her the deepest humiliation was a request to Higgins, whose pet artistic fancy, next to Milton's verse, was calligraphy, and who himself wrote a most beautiful Italian hand, that he would teach her to write. He declared that she was congenitally incapable of forming a single letter worthy of the least of Milton's words; but she persisted; and again he suddenly threw himself into the task of teaching her with a combination of stormy intensity, concentrated patience, and occasional bursts of interesting disquisition on the beauty and nobility, the august mission and destiny, of human handwriting. Eliza ended by acquiring an extremely uncommercial script which was a positive extension of her personal beauty, and spending three times as much on stationery as anyone else because certain qualities and shapes of paper became indispensable to her. She could not even address an envelope in the usual way because it made the margins all wrong.

Their commercial schooldays were a period of disgrace and despair for the young couple. They seemed to be learning nothing about flower shops. At last they gave it up as hopeless, and shook the dust of the shorthand schools, and the polytechnics, and the London School of Economics from their feet for ever. Besides, the business was in some mysterious way beginning to take care of itself. They had somehow forgotten their objections to employing other people. They came to the conclusion that their own way was the best, and that they had really a remarkable talent for business. The Colonel, who had been compelled for some years to keep a sufficient sum on current account at his bankers to make up their deficits, found that the provision was unnecessary: the young people were prospering. It is true that there was not quite fair play between them and their competitors in trade. Their week-ends in the country cost them nothing, and saved them the price of their Sunday dinners; for the motor car was the Colonel's; and he and Higgins paid the hotel bills. Mr F. Hill, florist and greengrocer (they soon discovered that there was money in asparagus; and asparagus led to other vegetables), had an air which stamped the business as classy; and in private life he was still Frederick Eynsford Hill, Esquire. Not that there was any swank about him; nobody but Eliza knew that he had been christened Frederick Challoner. Eliza herself swanked like anything.

That is all. That is how it has turned out. It is astonishing how much Eliza still manages to meddle in the housekeeping at Wimpole Street in spite of the shop and her own family. And it is notable that though she never nags her husband, and frankly loves the Colonel as if she were his favorite daughter, she has never got out of the habit of nagging Higgins that was established on the fatal night when she won his bet for him. She snaps his head off on the faintest provocation, or on none. He no longer dares to tease her by assuming an abysmal inferiority of Freddy's mind to his own. He storms and bullies and derides; but she stands up to him so ruthlessly that the Colonel has to ask her from time to time to be kinder to Higgins; and it is the only request of his that brings a mulish expression into her face. Nothing but some emergency or calamity great enough to break down all likes and dislikes, and throw them both back on their common humanity—and may they be spared any such trial!—will ever alter this. She knows that Higgins does not need her, just as her father did not need her. The very scrupulousness with which he told her that day that he had become used to having her there, and dependent on her for all sorts of little services, and that he should miss her if she went away (it would never have occurred to Freddy or the Colonel to say anything of the sort) deepens her inner certainty that she is "no more to him than them slippers"; yet she has a sense, too, that his indifference is deeper than the infatuation of commoner souls. She is immensely interested in him. She has even secret mischievous moments in which she wishes she could get him alone, on a desert island, away from all ties and with nobody else in the world to consider, and just drag him off his pedestal and see him making love like any common man. We all have private imaginations of that sort. But when it comes to business, to the life that she really leads as distinguished from the life of dreams and fancies, she likes Freddy and she likes the Colonel; and she does not like Higgins and Mr Doolittle. Galatea never does quite like Pygmalion; his relation to her is too godlike to be altogether agreeable.

Thomas Hardy

1840–1928

Thomas Hardy led a double life: one of the great Victorian novelists, he abandoned fiction in 1896 and reinvented himself as a poet. In a series of volumes published from 1898 through the early decades of the twentieth century, Hardy emerged as one of the most compelling voices in modern poetry. How should this strangely bifurcated literary career be read? There are continuities as well as divergences between Hardy's fiction and his poetry, and the shifts in his work provide a telling instance of the interwoven links and discontinuities between the Victorian era and the new modernism of the twentieth century.

Hardy was born and reared in the village of Higher Bockhampton, Stinsford, in the rural county of Dorset in southern England. He left home in his early twenties and worked as a church architect in London for five years, then returned to the family home in 1867; he continued to accept architectural commissions while trying his hand at fiction and poetry. In early poems such as *Hap* and *Neutral Tones* Hardy revealed his abiding sense of a universe ruled by a blind or hostile fate, a world whose landscapes are etched with traces of the fleeting stories of their inhabitants. He was not able to find a publisher for such works, and he largely stopped writing poetry, but his first novel, *Desperate Remedies*, was published in 1871. By 1874 he was earning a steady income from his writing and was able to marry Emma Lavinia Gifford, the sister-in-law of a rector whose church he had been restoring. He produced twenty novels within a twenty-five year period, achieving fame, popularity, and no little controversy for the provocative and dark worlds he created. In *Far from the Madding Crowd*, *The Return of the Native*, *Tess of the d'Urbervilles*, and *Jude the Obscure*, Hardy transformed the realist novel of manners into tragic accounts of the industrialization of rural Britain, the bankruptcy of religious faith, and irreconcilable tensions between social classes and between men and women. Though he had become a master of characterization and plot, in his later novels Hardy grew increasingly preoccupied with fundamentally lyrical questions of interiority, subjective perception, and personal voice. After the sexual frankness of *Jude the Obscure* provoked shocked reviews—the Bishop of Wakefield went so far as to burn the book—Hardy decided to abandon his prose writing altogether and to mine his chosen territory with the tools of a poet.

He began by recreating in poetry the landscape of his fiction. Hardy's first poetry collection, published when he was fifty-eight, was *Wessex Poems* (1898), its title referring to the imaginary countryside that he had created in his novels, loosely based on regions in the south of England but named for a long-vanished medieval kingdom. Hardy's "Wessex" was a place whose towns and roads and forests and fields were breathed into life by the novelist. The Wessex novels were published with maps of the territory, and the landmarks were to remain constant throughout the disparate books. The region took such a hold on readers' imaginations that a Wessex tourist industry emerged, one which is still in place today. Hardy was as painstaking in giving the precise (although imaginary) coordinates of a village pathway as he was in tracing the path of a character's destiny.

Many of Hardy's poems take root in this same creative landscape, now viewed by an intensely self-aware speaker who retraces his personal history, himself "tracked by phantoms having weird detective ways," as he says in *Wessex Heights*. Burning logs, a photograph, a diminishing figure on a train platform, a deer at a window all provide "moments of vision" (the title of one of his collections) that foreshadow the modernist "epiphanies" of Joyce and Woolf. Like the major modernists, Hardy explored the workings of memory, of perception, and of individual vision. In other poems, he focused on contemporary events, most notably in a series of poems written during World War I, unsparing in their presentation both of the necessity of waging the conflict and of its horrifying waste.

In his poetry as in his prose, Hardy's modern themes are typically set in a rural landscape with ancient roots. A constant feature of the Wessex novels involves characters setting off on one of the myriad footpaths connecting obscure villages and solitary cottages with one another. Hardy invented his own geography for Wessex, but the footpaths really existed and were the most important trails carved into the landscape by travelers over many years. Called "ley lines" in folk culture, such footpaths are thought to gather their energy over time, as hundreds of people gradually wear down a shared path and leave traces of themselves in the form of memory and tradition. Hardy's poems move between personal, historical, and natural levels of experience, but it is the landscape above all that conveys the power of these events.

Hardy embodied his moments of vision in poems that recall old oral and religious forms of verse, especially those of ballads and hymns. Like Wordsworth, Burns, and Kipling, Hardy was fascinated by the power of popular verse forms to convey deep truths in seemingly simple meters and diction; like his predecessors, Hardy brought his traditional forms to life by subtle modulations of their elements. The lines of Hardy's poetry are measured with extreme care and precision—not in any way approaching "free verse." As W. H. Auden wrote of Hardy's poetry: "No English poet, not even Donne or Browning, employed so many and so complicated stanza forms. Anyone who imitates his style will learn at least one thing, how to make words fit into a complicated structure." With architectural care, Hardy built up his words into complicated structures, lines, and stanzas following well-used poetic paths. With its compelling mixture of tradition and modernity, stoic calm and deep emotional intensity, Hardy's poetry has become a touchstone for modern poets writing in English, from Ezra Pound, who said he "needed no other poet," to Philip

Larkin, Seamus Heaney, and Derek Walcott. "Auden worshiped his honesty, Eliot disliked his heresy," the critic Irving Howe has commented; "but Hardy prepared the ground for both."

Hardy mined his native landscape, and his own memory, until his death, composing many of his best poems in his seventies and eighties. He had built a house on the outskirts of Dorchester in 1885, and he lived there for the rest of his life, with his wife Emma until her death in 1912, and subsequently with his secretary, Florence Dugdale, whom he married in 1914. When he died, his body was buried in Westminster Abbey; but his heart, as he had directed, was buried in the grave of his wife Emma, next to his father's grave, in the Stinsford churchyard.

Hardy's short story *The Withered Arm* appears on page 1448.

Hap° *chance*

If but some vengeful god would call to me
From up the sky, and laugh: "Thou suffering thing,
Know that thy sorrow is my ecstasy,
That thy love's loss is my hate's profiting!"

Then would I bear it, clench myself, and die,
Steeled by the sense of ire unmerited;
Half-eased in that a Powerfuller than I
Had willed and meted° me the tears I shed. *given*

But not so. How arrives it joy lies slain,
And why unblooms the best hope ever sown?
—Crass Casualty obstructs the sun and rain,
And dicing° Time for gladness casts a moan. . . . *gambling*
These purblind° Doomsters had as readily strown *half-blind*
Blisses about my pilgrimage as pain.

1866 1898

Neutral Tones

We stood by a pond that winter day,
And the sun was white, as though chidden° of God, *rebuked*
And a few leaves lay on the starving sod;
—They had fallen from an ash, and were gray.

Your eyes on me were as eyes that rove
Over tedious riddles of years ago;
And some words played between us to and fro
On which lost the more by our love.

The smile on your mouth was the deadest thing
Alive enough to have strength to die;
And a grin of bitterness swept thereby
Like an ominous bird a-wing. . . .

Since then, keen lessons that love deceives,
And wrings with wrong, have shaped to me
Your face, and the God-curst sun, and a tree,
And a pond edged with grayish leaves.

1867 1898

Wessex Heights

There are some heights in Wessex,[1] shaped as if by a kindly hand
For thinking, dreaming, dying on, and at crises when I stand,
Say, on Ingpen Beacon eastward, or on Wylls-Neck westwardly,
I seem where I was before my birth, and after death may be.

In the lowlands I have no comrade, not even the lone man's friend—
Her who suffereth long and is kind;[2] accepts what he is too weak to mend:
Down there they are dubious and askance; there nobody thinks as I,
But mind-chains do not clank where one's next neighbour is the sky.

In the towns I am tracked by phantoms having weird detective ways—
Shadows of beings who fellowed with myself of earlier days:
They hang about at places, and they say harsh heavy things—
Men with a wintry sneer, and women with tart disparagings.

Down there I seem to be false to myself, my simple self that was,
And is not now, and I see him watching, wondering what crass cause
Can have merged him into such a strange continuator as this,
Who yet has something in common with himself, my chrysalis.

I cannot go to the great grey Plain; there's a figure against the moon,
Nobody sees it but I, and it makes my breast beat out of tune;
I cannot go to the tall-spired town, being barred by the forms now passed
For everybody but me, in whose long vision they stand there fast.
There's a ghost at Yell'ham Bottom chiding loud at the fall of the night,
There's a ghost in Froom-side Vale, thin-lipped and vague, in a shroud
of white,
There is one in the railway train whenever I do not want it near,
I see its profile against the pane, saying what I would not hear.

As for one rare fair woman, I am now but a thought of hers,
I enter her mind and another thought succeeds me that she prefers,
Yet my love for her in its fulness she herself even did not know;
Well, time cures hearts of tenderness, and now I can let her go.

So I am found on Ingpen Beacon, or on Wylls-Neck to the west,
Or else on homely Bulbarrow, or little Pilsdon Crest,
Where men have never cared to haunt, nor women have walked with me,
And ghosts then keep their distance; and I know some liberty.

1898

The Darkling Thrush[1]

I leant upon a coppice° gate — *wood*
When Frost was spectre-gray,
And Winter's dregs made desolate
The weakening eye of day.
The tangled bine-stems° scored the sky — *stems of bushes*

1. An imaginary county in southwest England that forms the setting for Hardy's writings; the place names that follow are in "Wessex."

2. Cf. Corinthians 13.4: "Charity suffereth long, and is kind."

1. The poem was published on 31 December 1900.

Like strings of broken lyres,
And all mankind that haunted nigh
Had sought their household fires.

The land's sharp features seemed to be
The Century's corpse outleant,[2]
His crypt the cloudy canopy,
The wind his death-lament.
The ancient pulse of germ° and birth *seed*
Was shrunken hard and dry,
And every spirit upon earth
Seemed fervourless as I.

At once a voice arose among
The bleak twigs overhead
In a full-hearted evensong
Of joy illimited;
An aged thrush, frail, gaunt, and small,
In blast-beruffled plume,
Had chosen thus to fling his soul
Upon the growing gloom.

So little cause for carolings
Of such ecstatic sound
Was written on terrestrial things
Afar or nigh around,
That I could think there trembled through
His happy good-night air
Some blessed Hope, whereof he knew
And I was unaware.

On the Departure Platform

We kissed at the barrier; and passing through
She left me, and moment by moment got
Smaller and smaller, until to my view
She was but a spot;

A wee white spot of muslin fluff
That down the diminishing platform bore
Through hustling crowds of gentle and rough
To the carriage door.

Under the lamplight's fitful glowers,
Behind dark groups from far and near,
Whose interests were apart from ours,
She would disappear,

Then show again, till I ceased to see
That flexible form, that nebulous white;

2. As if leaning out from a coffin.

And she who was more than my life to me
Had vanished quite. . . .

We have penned new plans since that fair fond day,
And in season she will appear again—
Perhaps in the same soft white array—
But never as then!

—"And why, young man, must eternally fly
A joy you'll repeat, if you love her well?"
—O friend, nought happens twice thus; why,
I cannot tell!

1909

The Dead Man Walking

They hail me as one living,
But don't they know
That I have died of late years,
Untombed although?

I am but a shape that stands here,
A pulseless mould,
A pale past picture, screening
Ashes gone cold.

Not at a minute's warning,
Not in a loud hour,
For me ceased Time's enchantments
In hall and bower.

There was no tragic transit,
No catch of breath,
When silent seasons inched me
On to this death. . . .

—A Troubadour-youth I rambled
With Life for lyre,
The beats of being raging
In me like fire.

But when I practised eyeing
The goal of men,
It iced me, and I perished
A little then.

When passed my friend, my kinsfolk,
Through the Last Door,
And left me standing bleakly,
I died yet more;

And when my Love's heart kindled
In hate of me,
Wherefore I knew not, died I
One more degree.

And if when I died fully
I cannot say,
And changed into the corpse-thing
I am to-day,

Yet is it that, though whiling
The time somehow
In walking, talking, smiling,
I live not now.

A Wife and Another

"War ends, and he's returning
Early; yea,
The evening next to-morrow's!"—
—This I say
To her, whom I suspiciously survey,

Holding my husband's letter
To her view.—
She glanced at it but lightly,
And I knew
That one from him that day had reached her too.

There was no time for scruple;
Secretly
I filched her missive, conned° it, *studied*
Learnt that he
Would lodge with her ere he came home to me.

To reach the port before her,
And, unscanned,
There wait to intercept them
Soon I planned:
That, in her stead, -I- might before him stand.

So purposed, so effected;
At the inn
Assigned, I found her hidden:—
O that sin
Should bear what she bore when I entered in!

Her heavy lids grew laden
With despairs,
Her lips made soundless movements
Unawares,
While I peered at the chamber hired as theirs.

And as beside its doorway,
Deadly hued,
One inside, one withoutside
We two stood,
He came—my husband—as she knew he would.

No pleasurable triumph
Was that sight!
The ghastly disappointment
Broke them quite.
What love was theirs, to move them with such might!

"Madam, forgive me!" said she,
Sorrow bent,
"A child—I soon shall bear him . . .
Yes—I meant
To tell you—that he won me ere he went."

Then, as it were, within me
Something snapped,
As if my soul had largened:
Conscience-capped,
I saw myself the snarer—them the trapped.

"My hate dies, and I promise,
Grace-beguiled,"
I said, "to care for you, be
Reconciled;
And cherish, and take interest in the child."

Without more words I pressed him
Through the door
Within which she stood, powerless
To say more,
And closed it on them, and downstairward bore.

"He joins his wife—my sister,"
I, below,
Remarked in going—lightly–
Even as though
All had come right, and we had arranged it so . . .

As I, my road retracing,
Left them free,
The night alone embracing
Childless me,
I held° I had not stirred God wrothfully. *believe*

1909

To Sincerity

O sweet sincerity!—
Where modern methods be
What scope for thine and thee?

Life may be sad past saying,
Its greens for ever graying,
Its faiths to dust decaying;

And youth may have foreknown it,
And riper seasons shown it,
But custom cries: "Disown it:

"Say ye rejoice, though grieving,
Believe, while unbelieving,
Behold, without perceiving!"

—Yet, would men look at true things,
And unilluded° view things, *undeceived*
And count to bear undue things,

The real might mend the seeming,
Facts better their foredeeming,
And Life its disesteeming.

February 1899

The Convergence of the Twain
(Lines on the loss of the "Titanic")[1]

1

In a solitude of the sea
Deep from human vanity,
And the Pride of Life that planned her, stilly couches she.

2

Steel chambers, late the pyres
Of her salamandrine° fires, *white-hot*
Cold currents thrid,° and turn to rhythmic tidal lyres. *thread*

3

Over the mirrors meant
To glass the opulent
The sea-worm crawls—grotesque, slimed, dumb, indifferent.

4

Jewels in joy designed
To ravish the sensuous mind
Lie lightless, all their sparkles bleared and black and blind.

5

Dim moon-eyed fishes near
Gaze at the gilded gear
And query: "What does this vaingloriousness down here?". . .

6

Well: while was fashioning
This creature of cleaving wing,
The Immanent Will that stirs and urges everything

1. The largest ocean-liner of its day, the supposedly unsinkable *Titanic* sank on 15 April 1912 on its maiden voyage after colliding with an iceberg; two-thirds of its 2,200 passengers died.

7

Prepared a sinister mate
For her—so gaily great—
A Shape of Ice, for the time far and dissociate.[2]

8

And as the smart ship grew
In stature, grace, and hue,
In shadowy silent distance grew the Iceberg too.

9

Alien they seemed to be:
No mortal eye could see
The intimate welding of their later history,

10

Or sign that they were bent
By paths coincident
On being anon twin halves of one august event,

11

Till the Spinner of the Years
Said "Now!" And each one hears,
And consummation comes, and jars two hemispheres.

1912 1912

At Castle Boterel[1]

As I drive to the junction of lane and highway,
And the drizzle bedrenches the waggonette,° *cart*
I look behind at the fading byway,
And see on its slope, now glistening wet,
Distinctly yet

Myself and a girlish form benighted
In dry March weather. We climb the road
Beside a chaise.° We had just alighted *carriage*
To ease the sturdy pony's load
When he sighed and slowed.

What we did as we climbed, and what we talked of
Matters not much, nor to what it led,—
Something that life will not be balked of
Without rude reason till hope is dead,
And feeling fled.

It filled but a minute. But was there ever
A time of such quality, since or before,
In that hill's story? To one mind never,

2. According to Hardy, the Immanent Will is that which secretly guides events.

1. Hardy's first wife Emma died in November 1912; in 1913 the poet revisited scenes of their courtship in Cornwall in southwest England.

Though it has been climbed, foot-swift, foot-sore,
By thousands more.

Primaeval rocks form the road's steep border,
And much have they faced there, first and last,
Of the transitory in Earth's long order;
But what they record in colour and cast
Is—that we two passed.

And to me, though Time's unflinching rigour,
In mindless rote, has ruled from sight
The substance now, one phantom figure
Remains on the slope, as when that night
Saw us alight.

I look and see it there, shrinking, shrinking,
I look back at it amid the rain
For the very last time; for my sand is sinking,
And I shall traverse old love's domain
Never again.

March 1913 1914

Channel Firing[1]

That night your great guns, unawares,
Shook all our coffins as we lay,
And broke the chancel window-squares,
We thought it was the Judgment-day

And sat upright. While drearisome
Arose the howl of wakened hounds:
The mouse let fall the altar-crumb,
The worms drew back into the mounds,
The glebe° cow drooled. Till God called, "No; *field*
It's gunnery practice out at sea
Just as before you went below;
The world is as it used to be:

"All nations striving strong to make
Red war yet redder. Mad as hatters
They do no more for Christés sake
Than you who are helpless in such matters.

"That this is not the judgment-hour
For some of them's a blessed thing,
For if it were they'd have to scour
Hell's floor for so much threatening. . . .

"Ha, ha. It will be warmer when
I blow the trumpet (if indeed

1. The poem refers to military exercises in the English Channel prior to World War I.

I ever do; for you are men,
And rest eternal sorely need)."

So down we lay again. "I wonder,
Will the world ever saner be,"
Said one, "than when He sent us under
In our indifferent century!"

And many a skeleton shook his head.
"Instead of preaching forty year,"
My neighbour Parson Thirdly said,
"I wish I had stuck to pipes and beer."

Again the guns disturbed the hour,
Roaring their readiness to avenge,
As far inland as Stourton Tower,
And Camelot, and starlit Stonehenge.[2]

April 1914 1914

In Time of "The Breaking of Nations"[1]

1

Only a man harrowing clods
In a slow silent walk
With an old horse that stumbles and nods
Half asleep as they stalk.

2

Only thin smoke without flame
From the heaps of couch-grass;
Yet this will go onward the same
Though Dynasties pass.

3

Yonder a maid and her wight° *man*
Come whispering by:
War's annals will cloud into night
Ere their story die.

1915 1916

I Looked Up from My Writing

I looked up from my writing,
And gave a start to see,
As if rapt in my inditing,
The moon's full gaze on me.

Her meditative misty head
Was spectral in its air,

2. The town of Stour Head, which Hardy calls Stourton, is in the county of Dorset. According to legend, Camelot was the site of King Arthur's court; Stonehenge is a prehistoric site in southwest England.

1. Cf. Jeremiah 51.20: "Thou art my battle axe and weapons of war: for with thee will I break in pieces the nations, and with thee will I destroy kingdoms."

And I involuntarily said,
"What are you doing there?"

"Oh, I've been scanning pond and hole
And waterway hereabout
For the body of one with a sunken soul
Who has put his life-light out.

"Did you hear his frenzied tattle?
It was sorrow for his son
Who is slain in brutish battle,
Though he has injured none.

"And now I am curious to look
Into the blinkered mind
Of one who wants to write a book
In a world of such a kind."

Her temper overwrought me,
And I edged to shun her view,
For I felt assured she thought me
One who should drown him too.

1917

"And There Was a Great Calm"[1]
(On the Signing of the Armistice, 11 Nov. 1918)[2]

1

There had been years of Passion—scorching, cold,
And much Despair, and Anger heaving high,
Care whitely watching, Sorrows manifold,
Among the young, among the weak and old,
And the pensive Spirit of Pity whispered, "Why?"

2

Men had not paused to answer. Foes distraught
Pierced the thinned peoples in a brute-like blindness,
Philosophies that sages long had taught,
And Selflessness, were as an unknown thought,
And "Hell!" and "Shell!" were yapped at Lovingkindness.

3

The feeble folk at home had grown full-used
To "dug-outs," "snipers," "Huns,"[3] from the war-adept
In the mornings heard, and at evetides perused;
To day-dreamt men in millions, when they mused—
To nightmare-men in millions when they slept.

4

Waking to wish existence timeless, null,
Sirius[4] they watched above where armies fell;

1. A phrase from Mark 4.39, after Jesus has calmed a storm at sea.
2. The armistice ending World War I was signed by Germany and the Allies on this date.
3. Slang for "Germans" during the war.
4. The brightest star in the night sky.

He seemed to check his flapping when, in the lull
Of night a boom came thencewise, like the dull
Plunge of a stone dropped into some deep well.

5

So, when old hopes that earth was bettering slowly
Were dead and damned, there sounded "War is done!"
One morrow. Said the bereft, and meek, and lowly,
"Will men some day be given to grace? yea, wholly,
And in good sooth,° as our dreams used to run?" *truth*

6

Breathless they paused. Out there men raised their glance
To where had stood those poplars lank and lopped,
As they had raised it through the four years' dance
Of Death in the now familiar flats of France;
And murmured, "Strange, this! How? All firing stopped?"

7

Aye; all was hushed. The about-to-fire fired not,
The aimed-at moved away in trance-lipped song.
One checkless regiment slung a clinching shot
And turned. The Spirit of Irony smirked out, "What?
Spoil peradventures° woven of Rage and Wrong?" *perhaps*

8

Thenceforth no flying fires inflamed the gray,
No hurtlings shook the dewdrop from the thorn,
No moan perplexed the mute bird on the spray;
Worn horses mused: "We are not whipped to-day;"
No weft-winged engines° blurred the moon's thin horn. *early airplanes*

9

Calm fell. From Heaven distilled a clemency;
There was peace on earth, and silence in the sky;
Some could, some could not, shake off misery:
The Sinister Spirit sneered: "It had to be!"
And again the Spirit of Pity whispered, "Why?"

1918 1919, 1922

Logs on the Hearth

A Memory of a Sister[1]

The fire advances along the log
Of the tree we felled,
Which bloomed and bore striped apples by the peck° *basketful*
Till its last hour of bearing knelled.
The fork that first my hand would reach
And then my foot
In climbings upward inch by inch, lies now
Sawn, sapless, darkening with soot.

1. Hardy's sister Mary died in November 1915.

Where the bark chars is where, one year,
It was pruned, and bled—
Then overgrew the wound. But now, at last,
Its growings all have stagnated.

My fellow-climber rises dim
From her chilly grave—
Just as she was, her foot near mine on the bending limb,
Laughing, her young brown hand awave.

1915 1917

The Photograph

The flame crept up the portrait line by line
As it lay on the coals in the silence of night's profound,
And over the arm's incline,
And along the marge° of the silkwork superfine, *margin*
And gnawed at the delicate bosom's defenceless round.

Then I vented a cry of hurt, and averted my eyes;
The spectacle was one that I could not bear,
To my deep and sad surprise;
But, compelled to heed, I again looked furtivewise
Till the flame had eaten her breasts, and mouth, and hair.

"Thank God, she is out of it now!" I said at last,
In a great relief of heart when the thing was done
That had set my soul aghast,
And nothing was left of the picture unsheathed from the past
But the ashen ghost of the card it had figured on.

She was a woman long hid amid packs of years,
She might have been living or dead; she was lost to my sight,
And the deed that had nigh drawn tears
Was done in a casual clearance of life's arrears;
But I felt as if I had put her to death that night! . . .

* * *

—Well; she knew nothing thereof did she survive,
And suffered nothing if numbered among the dead;
Yet—yet—if on earth alive
Did she feel a smart, and with vague strange anguish strive?
If in heaven, did she smile at me sadly and shake her head?

1917

The Fallow Deer at the Lonely House

One without looks in to-night
Through the curtain-chink
From the sheet of glistening white;

One without looks in to-night
As we sit and think
By the fender-brink.

We do not discern those eyes
Watching in the snow;
Lit by lamps of rosy dyes
We do not discern those eyes
Wondering, aglow,
Fourfooted, tiptoe.

1922

Afterwards

When the Present has latched its postern° behind my tremulous stay, *gate*
And the May month flaps its glad green leaves like wings,
Delicate-filmed as new-spun silk, will the neighbours say,
"He was a man who used to notice such things"?

If it be in the dusk when, like an eyelid's soundless blink,
The dewfall-hawk comes crossing the shades to alight
Upon the wind-warped upland thorn, a gazer may think,
"To him this must have been a familiar sight."

If I pass during some nocturnal blackness, mothy and warm,
When the hedgehog travels furtively over the lawn,
One may say, "He strove that such innocent creatures should come to no harm,
But he could do little for them; and now he is gone."

If, when hearing that I have been stilled at last, they stand at the door,
Watching the full-starred heavens that winter sees,
Will this thought rise on those who will meet my face no more,
"He was one who had an eye for such mysteries"?

And will any say when my bell of quittance is heard in the gloom,
And a crossing breeze cuts a pause in its outrollings,
Till they rise again, as they were a new bell's boom,
"He hears it not now, but used to notice such things"?

1917

Epitaph

I never cared for Life: Life cared for me,
And hence I owed it some fidelity.
It now says, "Cease; at length thou hast learnt to grind
Sufficient toll for an unwilling mind,
And I dismiss thee—not without regard
That thou didst ask no ill-advised reward,
Nor sought in me much more than thou couldst find."

1922

PERSPECTIVES

The Great War: Confronting the Modern

The multiplying technological, artistic, and social changes at the turn of the twentieth century impressed that generation's artists as a rupture with the past. And no event so graphically suggested that human history had "changed, changed utterly," as World War I—"the Great War."

Great Britain, like its enemy Germany, entered the war with idealistic aims. Prime Minister H. H. Asquith put the justice of the British case this way in a speech to the House of Commons on 7 August 1914: "I do not think any nation ever entered into a great conflict—and this is one of the greatest that history will ever know—with a clearer conscience or stronger conviction that it is fighting not for aggression, not for the maintenance of its own selfish ends, but in defence of principles the maintenance of which is vital to the civilization of the world." But cynicism set in quickly—first among ground troops on the Western Front, dug into trenches and watching "progress" that could be measured in yards per day. Soon the British public became disillusioned with the war effort, partly as a result of technological advances in the news media. Daily papers in England carried photographs from the front, and while editorial policy generally supported the British government and printed heroic images of the fighting, this sanitized version of the war was largely offset by the long published lists of casualties; during the four years and three months that Britain was involved in the war, more than a million British troops—an average of fifteen hundred per day—were killed in action.

The war's lasting legacy was a sense of bitterly rebuffed idealism, bringing with it a suspicion of progress, technology, government, bureaucracy, nationalism, and conventional morality—themes probed in new ways by the period's writers. Just as the war had involved radically new strategies and new technologies, writers intensified their search for new forms and modes of expression as they and their compatriots found themselves in the midst of a conflict unlike anything previously known in the annals of history.

Alys Fane Trotter[1]

The Hospital Visitor

When yesterday I went to see my friends—
    (Watching their patient faces in a row
I want to give each boy a D.S.O.)
When yesterday I went to see my friends
With cigarettes, and foolish odds and ends,
    (Knowing they understand how well I know
That nothing I can do may make amends,
    But that I must not grieve, or tell them so),
A pale-faced Iniskilling, just eighteen,

1. (1863–1961), writer, graphic artist, author of a history of South Africa.

Who'd fought two years; with eyes a little dim
Smiled up and showed me, there behind the screen
On the humped bandage that replaced a limb,
How someone left him, where the leg had been
A tiny green glass pig to comfort him.

These are the men who've learned to laugh at pain.
And if their lips have quivered when they spoke,
They've said brave words, or tried to make a joke.
Said it's not worse than trenches in the rain,
Or pools of water on a chalky plain,
Or bitter cold from which you stiffly woke,
Or deep wet mud that left you hardly sane,
Or the tense wait for "Fritz's master stroke."
You seldom hear them talk of their "bad luck,"
And suffering has not spoiled their ready wit.
And oh! you'd hardly doubt their fighting pluck
When each new operation shows their grit,
Who never brag of blows for England struck,
But only yearn to "get about a bit."

1924

Cicely Hamilton[1]

Non-Combatant

Before one drop of angry blood was shed
I was sore hurt and beaten to my knee;
Before one fighting man reeled back and died
The War-Lords struck at me.

They struck me down—an idle, useless mouth,
As cumbrous—nay, more cumbrous—than the dead,
With life and heart afire to give and give
I take a dole instead.

With life and heart afire to give and give
I take and eat the bread of charity.
In all the length of all this eager land,
No man has need of me.

That is my hurt—my burning, beating wound;
That is the spear-thrust driven through my pride!

1. (1872–1952), playwright, social activist, feminist; founder of the Women Writers' Suffrage League.

With aimless hands, and mouth that must be fed,
    I wait and stand aside.

Let me endure it, then, with stiffened lip:
    I, even I, have suffered in the strife!
Let me endure it then—I give my pride
    Where others give a life.

1916

Blast

Wyndham Lewis (1884–1957), founder of the provocative arts magazine *Blast,* was often at odds with his sometime co-conspirator Ezra Pound: indeed both men were usually at odds with most of their friends. But they did agree on one thing: that the writers of Edwardian and Georgian England had failed to throw off the deadening literary mannerisms of the previous century. "As for the nineteenth century," Pound wrote, "with all respects to its achievements, I think we shall look back upon it as a rather blurry, messy sort of a period, a rather sentimentalistic, mannerish sort of a period."

Some violent corrective was needed. The name of Lewis's magazine was intended to suggest an explosive charge that would blow away tired literary and social conventions. It was a calculated assault on good taste, both in its contents and, more immediately, in its form: an oversized, bright pink cover with the single word *BLAST* splashed diagonally across it. Lewis carefully oversaw the details of typography; visually and rhetorically, *Blast* is indebted to the polemical style of the Italian artist F. T. Marinetti (1876–1944), the founder of Italian futurism. Marinetti's vivid manifestos for futurism celebrated a modern aesthetic of speed, technology, and power. Lewis in turn founded a movement he called Vorticism, and *Blast* bore the subtitle *The Review of the Great English Vortex.*

The definition of *vorticism* was left intentionally hazy; as canny an observer as the Vorticist painter William Roberts, one of the signatories of the manifesto, claimed that Vorticism was first and foremost "a slogan." In 1915 Lewis defined it this way: "By Vorticism we mean (a) ACTIVITY as opposed to the tasteful PASSIVITY of Picasso; (b) SIGNIFICANCE as opposed to the dull or anecdotal character to which the Naturalist is condemned; (c) ESSENTIAL MOVEMENT and ACTIVITY (such as the energy of a mind) as opposed to the imitative cinematography, the fuss and hysterics of the Futurists."

In its disorienting layout of typography, the *Vorticist Manifesto* is as much a visual as a literary statement, reflecting the multiple and always skewed interest of its primary author, Lewis. Born on a yacht off the coast of Nova Scotia, he had moved to London with his mother when his parents separated in 1893. A precocious painter, he won a scholarship to the progressive Slade School of Art at age sixteen, but moved to Paris before completing his studies. He returned to London in 1909 and began a career as a painter and writer. During the War, he served both as an artillery officer and as a commissioned war artist. He also wrote an experimental novel, *Tarr* (1918), and went on to produce a range of works in the dozen years thereafter, including pro-fascist political theory in *The Art of Being Ruled* (1926) and more general cultural criticism in *Time and Western Man* (1927), in which he attacked the modern cult of subjectivity. During the thirties, he became increasingly unpopular in London, first as a result of a satirical novel, *The Apes of God,* which

Wyndham Lewis, *The Creditors* (design for *Timon of Athens*), 1912–1913.

lampooned figures in the literary and art world and their patrons; following two libel actions against him, publishers became wary of taking on his works. Lewis and his wife spent the years of World War II living in poverty in America and Canada; after the war, he returned to England, where he became an art critic for the British Broadcasting Corporation. He continued to draw, paint, and write memoirs, satirical stories, and an allegorical fantasy in several volumes.

Along with the *Vorticist Manifesto*, the first issue of *Blast* included poetry by Pound, fiction by Ford Madox Ford and Rebecca West, a play by Lewis, and illustrations by Lewis and others. The timing of the first issue couldn't have been worse: after delays caused by typesetting difficulties, *Blast* went on sale in London on 20 June 1914; World War I began just a few weeks later. While Lewis and his confederates had declared war on conventional artistic and literary taste with their "puce monster"—an advertisement for the first issue announced the "END OF THE CHRISTIAN ERA"—they were usurped by a much more pressing conflict. As Lewis later wrote, "In 1914 I produced a huge review called *Blast*, which for the most part I wrote myself. That was my first public appearance. Immediately the War broke out and put an end to all that." Lewis brought out a second issue in July 1915, attempting to fend off charges of irrelevancy with a special "War Number" that included T. S. Eliot's *Preludes* and *Rhapsody on a Windy Night* and a manifesto from the sculptor Henri Gaudier-Brzeska, "written from the trenches," which concludes poignantly with an obituary for Gaudier, "Mort pour la Patrie" (died for the fatherland). But by this time, *Blast* itself was for all intents and purposes dead; its second issue was its last. Short-lived though it was, however, *Blast* was remarkably important in clearing the way for the new art of modernism.

VORTICIST MANIFESTO
LONG LIVE THE VORTEX!

Long live the great art vortex sprung up in the centre of this town!

We stand for the Reality of the Present—not for the sentimental Future, or the sacripant[1] Past.

We want to leave Nature and Men alone.

We do not want to make people wear Futurist Patches, or fuss men to take to pink and sky-blue trousers.

We are not their wives or tailors.

The only way Humanity can help artists is to remain independent and work unconsciously.

WE NEED THE UNCONSCIOUSNESS OF HUMANITY—their stupidity, animalism and dreams.

We believe in no perfectibility except our own.

Intrinsic beauty is in the Interpreter and Seer, not in the object or content.[2]

We do not want to change the appearance of the world, because we are not Naturalists, Impressionists or Futurists (the latest form of Impressionism), and do not depend on the appearance of the world for our art.

WE ONLY WANT THE WORLD TO LIVE, and to feel its crude energy flowing through us.

It may be said that great artists in England are always revolutionary, just as in France any really fine artist had a strong traditional vein.

Blast sets out to be an avenue for all those vivid and violent ideas that could reach the Public in no other way.

Blast will be popular, essentially. It will not appeal to any particular class, but to the fundamental and popular instincts in every class and description of people, **TO THE INDIVIDUAL.** The moment a man feels or realizes himself as an artist, he ceases to belong to any milieu or time. Blast is created for this timeless, fundamental Artist that exists in everybody.

The Man in the Street and the Gentleman are equally ignored.

Popular art does not mean the art of the poor people, as it is usually supposed to. It means the art of the individuals.

Education (art education and general education) tends to destroy the creative instinct. Therefore it is in times when education has been non-existent that art chiefly flourished.

1. Boasting of valor.
2. Although the Vorticists go on to differentiate themselves from the impressionists, this statement is very close to the impressionism articulated by Walter Pater in *The Renaissance* (1873); see page 1694.

But it is nothing to do with "the People."

It is a mere accident that that is the most favourable time for the individual to appear.

To make the rich of the community shed their education skin, to destroy politeness, standardization and academic, that is civilized, vision, is the task we have set ourselves.

We want to make in England not a popular art, not a revival of lost folk art, or a romantic fostering of such unactual conditions, but to make individuals, wherever found.

We will convert the King if possible.

A VORTICIST KING! WHY NOT?
DO YOU THINK LLOYD GEORGE[3] HAS THE VORTEX IN HIM?
MAY WE HOPE FOR ART FROM LADY MOND?[4]

We are against the glorification of "the People," as we are against snobbery. It is not necessary to be an outcast bohemian, to be unkempt or poor, any more than it is necessary to be rich or handsome, to be an artist. Art is nothing to do with the coat you wear. A top-hat can well hold the Sixtine.[5] A cheap cap could hide the image of Kephren.

AUTOMOBILISM (Marinetteism) bores us. We don't want to go about making a hullo-bulloo about motor cars, anymore than about knives and forks, elephants or gas-pipes.

Elephants are **VERY BIG.** Motor cars go quickly.

Wilde gushed twenty years ago about the beauty of machinery. Gissing,[6] in his romantic delight with modern lodging houses was futurist in this sense.

The futurist is a sensational and sentimental mixture of the aesthete of 1890 and the realist of 1870.

The "Poor" are detestable animals! They are only picturesque and amusing for the sentimentalist or the romantic! The "Rich" are bores without a single exception, *en tant que riches* [so far as they are rich]!

We want those simple and great people found everywhere.

Blast presents an art of Individuals.

MANIFESTO.

1

BLAST First (from politeness) **ENGLAND**

CURSE ITS CLIMATE FOR ITS SINS AND INFECTIONS

DISMAL SYMBOL, SET round our bodies,
of effeminate lout within.

3. David Lloyd George, British statesman, and Prime Minister 1916–1922.
4. A leader of fashionable London society.
5. The Sistine Chapel in the Vatican.
6. George Gissing (1857–1903), naturalist novelist.

VICTORIAN VAMPIRE, the LONDON cloud sucks
the TOWN'S heart.

A 1000 MILE LONG, 2 KILOMETER Deep

BODY OF WATER even, is pushed against us
from the Floridas, TO MAKE US MILD.
OFFICIOUS MOUNTAINS keep back DRASTIC WINDS

SO MUCH VAST MACHINERY TO PRODUCE

THE CURATE of "Eltham"
BRITANNIC AESTHETE
WILD NATURE CRANK
DOMESTICATED POLICEMAN
LONDON COLISEUM
SOCIALIST-PLAYWRIGHT
DALY'S MUSICAL COMEDY
GAIETY CHORUS GIRL
TONKS[7]

CURSE

the flabby sky that can manufacture no snow, but can only drop the sea on us in a drizzle like a poem by Mr. Robert Bridges.[8]

CURSE

the lazy air that cannot stiffen the back of the **SERPENTINE,** or put Aquatic steel half way down the **MANCHESTER CANAL.**

But ten years ago we saw distinctly both snow and ice here.

May some vulgarly inventive, but useful person, arise, and restore to us the necessary **BLIZZARDS.**

LET US ONCE MORE WEAR THE ERMINE
OF THE NORTH.

WE BELIEVE IN THE EXISTENCE OF THIS USEFUL
LITTLE CHEMIST IN OUR MIDST!

7. Henry Tonks, a teacher at the Slade School of Art (where Lewis and other Vorticists studied) who resisted as "contamination" such modern innovations as post impressionism and cubism.

8. Poet Laureate from 1913 until his death in 1930, noted for his technical skill and high moral tone.

2
OH BLAST FRANCE

pig plagiarism
BELLY
SLIPPERS
POODLE TEMPER
BAD MUSIC

SENTIMENTAL GALLIC GUSH
SENSATIONALISM
FUSSINESS.

PARISIAN PAROCHIALISM.

Complacent young man, so much respect for Papa and his son!—Oh!—Papa <u>is</u> wonderful: but <u>all</u> papas are!

BLAST

APERITIFS (Pernots, Amers picon)
Bad change
Naively seductive Houri salon-picture Cocottes
Slouching blue porters (can carry a pantechnicon)
Stupidly rapacious people at every step
Economy maniacs
Bouillon Kub (for being a bad pun)

PARIS.

Clap-trap Heaven of amative German professor.
Ubiquitous lines of silly little trees.
Arcs de Triomphe.
Imperturbable, endless prettiness.
Large empty cliques, higher up.
Bad air for the individual.

BLAST
MECCA OF THE AMERICAN

because it is not other side of Suez Canal, instead of an afternoon's ride from London.

3
CURSE

WITH EXPLETIVE OF WHIRLWIND

THE BRITANNIC AESTHETE

CREAM OF THE SNOBBISH EARTH
ROSE OF SHARON OF GOD-PRIG
OF SIMIAN VANITY
SNEAK AND SWOT OF THE SCHOOL-ROOM
IMBERB (or Berbed when in Belsize)-PEDANT

PRACTICAL JOKER
DANDY
CURATE

BLAST all products of phlegmatic cold
Life of LOOKER-ON.
CURSE

SNOBBERY
(disease of feminity)
FEAR OF RIDICULE
(arch vice of inactive, sleepy)
PLAY
STYLISM
SINS AND PLAGUES
of this LYMPHATIC finished
(we admit in every sense
finished)
VEGETABLE HUMANITY.

4
BLAST

THE SPECIALIST
"PROFESSIONAL"
"GOOD WORKMAN"
"GROVE-MAN"
ONE ORGAN MAN

BLAST THE

AMATEUR
SCIOLAST
ART-PIMP
JOURNALIST
SELF MAN
NO-ORGAN MAN

5
BLAST HUMOUR

Quack ENGLISH drug for stupidity and sleepiness.
Arch enemy of REAL, conventionalizing like
gunshot, freezing supple
REAL in ferocious chemistry
of laughter.

BLAST SPORT

HUMOUR'S FIRST COUSIN AND ACCOMPLICE.

Impossibility for Englishman to be grave and keep his end up, psychologically.
Impossible for him to use Humour as well and be persistently grave.
Alas! necessity for big doll's show in front of mouth.
Visitation of Heaven on
English Miss
gums, canines of **FIXED GRIN**
Death's head symbol of Anti-Life.

CURSE those who will hang over this
Manifesto with SILLY CANINES exposed.

6
BLAST

years 1837 to 1900

Curse abysmal inexcusable middle-class (also Aristocracy and Proletariat).

BLAST

pasty shadow cast by gigantic BOEHM[9]
(Imagined at introduction of BOURGEOIS VICTORIAN VISTAS).
WRING THE NECK OF all sick inventions born in that progressive white wake.

9. Joseph Edgar Boehm (1834–1890), sculptor for Queen Victoria.

BLAST their weeping whiskers—hirsute
RHETORIC of EUNUCH and STYLIST—
SENTIMENTAL HYGIENICS
ROUSSEAUISMS (wild Nature cranks)
FRATERNIZING WITH MONKEYS
DIABOLICS—raptures and roses
of the erotic bookshelves
culminating in
PURGATORY OF PUTNEY.[1]

CHAOS OF ENOCH ARDENS[2]
laughing Jennys[3]
Ladies with Pains
good-for-nothing Guineveres.

SNOBBISH BORROVIAN running after
GIPSY KINGS and ESPADAS[4]
bowing the knee to
wild Mother Nature,
her feminine contours,
Unimaginative insult to
MAN.

DAMN

all those to-day who have taken on that Rotten Menagerie, and still crack their whips and tumble in Piccadilly Circus, as though London were a provincial town.

WE WHISPER IN YOUR EAR A GREAT SECRET.

LONDON IS NOT A PROVINCIAL TOWN.

We will allow Wonder Zoos. But we do not want the
GLOOMY VICTORIAN CIRCUS in
Piccadilly Circus.

IT IS PICCADILLY'S CIRCUS!

NOT MEANT FOR MENAGERIES trundling
out of Sixties DICKENSIAN CLOWNS,
CORELLI[5] LADY RIDERS, TROUPS
OF PERFORMING GIPSIES (who
complain besides that 1/6 a night
does not pay fare back to Clapham).

1. A middle-class suburb of London.
2. *Enoch Arden* (1864), a sentimental narrative poem by Tennyson.
3. From Dante Gabriel Rossetti's popular poem *Jenny* (1870), again disliked for its sentimentality.
4. Refers to the contemporary popularity of the gypsy romances of George Borrow, such as *The Zincali* (1841).
5. Marie Corelli, pseud. of Mary Mackay (1855–1924), author of best-selling religious novels and romances.

BLAST[6]

The Post Office Frank Brangwyn Robertson Nicol
Rev. Pennyfeather Galloway Kyle
(Bells) (Cluster of Grapes)
Bishop of London and all his posterity
Galsworthy Dean Inge Croce Matthews
Rev Meyer Seymour Hicks
Lionel Cust C. B. Fry Bergson Abdul Bahai
Hawtrey Edward Elgar Sardlea
Filson Young Marie Corelli Geddes
Codliver Oil St. Loe Strachey Lyceum Club
Rhabindraneth Tagore Lord Glenconner of Glen
Weiniger Norman Angel Ad. Mahon
Mr. and Mrs. Dearmer Beecham Ella
A. C. Benson (Pills, Opera, Thomas) Sydney Webb
British Academy Messrs. Chapell
Countess of Warwick George Edwards
Willie Ferraro Captain Cook R. J. Campbell
Clan Thesiger Martin Harvey William Archer
George Grossmith R. H. Benson
Annie Besant Chenil Clan Meynell
Father Vaughan Joseph Holbrooke Clan Strachey

1

BLESS ENGLAND!

BLESS ENGLAND

FOR ITS SHIPS

which switchback on Blue, Green and
Red **SEAS** all around the **PINK**
EARTH-BALL,

BIG BETS ON EACH.

BLESS ALL SEAFARERS.

THEY exchange not one LAND for another, but one ELEMENT for ANOTHER. The MORE against the LESS ABSTRACT.

---

6. The list of those blasted by the Vorticists falls, according to the critic William Wees, into seven categories: (1) members of the (literary and cultural) Establishment (e.g., William Archer, drama critic of the *Nation*); (2) people who represented popular or snobbish fads (e.g., Sir Abdul Baha Bahai, leader of the Bahai faith); (3) high-minded popular writers, (e.g., Marie Corelli); (4) mediocre but popular figures (e.g., the poet Ella Wheeler Wilcox); (5) fuzzy-minded reformers and idealists (e.g., Sidney Webb, a leader of the Fabian Socialist organization); (6) "popular figures whom the Vorticists just didn't like" (e.g., C. B. Fry, a cricket player); and (7) "blasting just for the fun of it . . . or blasting that grew from special circumstances and private reasons known only to insiders" (e.g., the Post Office and Cod Liver Oil). See William C. Wees, *Vorticism and the English Avant-Garde* (1972), pp. 217–27.

BLESS the vast planetary abstraction of the **OCEAN.**

BLESS THE ARABS OF THE **ATLANTIC.**
THIS ISLAND MUST BE CONTRASTED WITH THE BLEAK WAVES.

BLESS ALL PORTS.

PORTS, RESTLESS MACHINES of

scooped out basins
heavy insect dredgers
monotonous cranes
stations
lighthouses, blazing through the frosty starlight, cutting the storm like a cake
beaks of infant boats, side by side,
heavy chaos of wharves,
steep walls of factories
womanly town

BLESS these MACHINES that work the little boats across clean liquid space, in beelines.

BLESS the great **PORTS**

HULL
LIVERPOOL
LONDON
NEWCASTLE-ON-TYNE
BRISTOL
GLASGOW

BLESS ENGLAND,

Industrial Island machine, pyramidal workshop, its apex at Shetland, discharging itself on the sea.

BLESS

cold
magnanimous
delicate
gauche
fanciful
stupid

ENGLISHMEN.

2

BLESS the HAIRDRESSER.

He attacks Mother Nature for a small fee.
Hourly he ploughs heads for sixpence,
Scours chins and lips for threepence.
He makes systematic mercenary war on this
WILDNESS.
He trims aimless and retrograde growths into
CLEAN ARCHED SHAPES and
ANGULAR PLOTS.

BLESS this HESSIAN (or SILESIAN) **EXPERT**[7]
correcting the grotesque anachronisms
of our physique.

3

BLESS ENGLISH HUMOUR

It is the great barbarous weapon of
the genius among races.
The wild MOUNTAIN RAILWAY from IDEA
to IDEA, in the ancient Fair of LIFE.

BLESS **SWIFT** for his solemn bleak
wisdom of laughter.

SHAKESPEARE for his bitter Northern
Rhetoric of humour.

BLESS ALL ENGLISH EYES
that grow crows-feet with their
FANCY and ENERGY.

BLESS this hysterical WALL built round
the EGO.

BLESS the solitude of LAUGHTER.

BLESS the separating, ungregarious

BRITISH GRIN.

4

BLESS FRANCE

for its **BUSHELS** of **VITALITY**
to the square inch.

7. From German industrial regions.

HOME OF MANNERS (the Best, the WORST and interesting mixtures).
MASTERLY PORNOGRAPHY (great enemy of progress).
COMBATIVENESS
GREAT HUMAN SCEPTICS
DEPTHS OF ELEGANCE
FEMALE QUALITIES
FEMALES
BALLADS of its PREHISTORIC APACHE
Superb hardness and hardiesse of its
Voyou° type, rebellious adolescent. *disreputable*
Modesty and humanity of many there.
GREAT FLOOD OF LIFE pouring out
of wound of 1797.[8]
Also bitterer stream from 1870.[9]
STAYING POWER, like a cat.

BLESS[1]

Bridget Berrwolf Bearline Cranmer Byng
Frieder Graham The Pope Maria de Tomaso
Captain Kemp Munroe Gaby Jenkins
R. B. Cuningham Grahame Barker
(not his brother) (John and Granville)
Mrs. Wil Finnimore Madame Strindberg Carson
Salvation Army Lord Howard de Walden
Capt. Craig Charlotte Corday Cromwell
Mrs. Duval Mary Robertson Lillie Lenton
Frank Rutter Castor Oil James Joyce
Leveridge Lydia Yavorska Preb. Carlyle Jenny
Mon. le compte de Gabulis Smithers Dick Burge
33 Church Street Sievier Gertie Millar
Norman Wallis Miss Fowler Sir Joseph Lyons
Martin Wolff Watt Mrs. Hepburn
Alfree Tommy Captain Kendell Young Ahearn
Wilfred Walter Kate Lechmere Henry Newbolt
Lady Aberconway Frank Harris Hamel
Gilbert Canaan Sir James Mathew Barry
Mrs. Belloc Lowdnes W. L. George Rayner
George Robey George Mozart Harry Weldon

8. The rise of Napoleon Bonaparte.
9. Beginning of Franco-Prussian War and end of the Second Empire, led by Napoleon Bonaparte's nephew Napoleon III.
1. This list of the blessed falls, according to William Wees, into four categories: (1) "some of the blessings, like most of the blasts, seemed designed to affront respectable public opinion" (e.g., the Pope and the Salvation Army); (2) "working class entertainments such as boxing and music halls"; (3) "a few selected representatives of the fine arts" (e.g., James Joyce); and (4) "friends of the Vorticists or of the avant-garde in general" (e.g., Frank Rutter and P. J. Konody, two sympathetic art critics).

Chaliapine George Hirst Graham White
Hucks Salmet Shirley Kellogg Bandsman Rice
Petty Officer Curran Applegarth Konody
Colin Bell Lewis Hind LEFRANC
Hubert Commercial Process Co.

MANIFESTO.

I.

1 Beyond Action and Reaction we would establish ourselves.

2 We start from opposite statements of a chosen world. Set up violent structure of adolescent clearness between two extremes.

3 We discharge ourselves on both sides.

4 We fight first on one side, then on the other, but always for the SAME cause, which is neither side or both sides and ours.

5 Mercenaries were always the best troops.

6 We are Primitive Mercenaries in the Modern World.

7 Our Cause is NO-MAN'S.

8 We set Humour at Humour's throat.
Stir up Civil War among peaceful apes.

9 We only want Humour if it has fought like Tragedy.

10 We only want Tragedy if it can clench its side-muscles like hands on its belly, and bring to the surface a laugh like a bomb.

II.

1 We hear from America and the Continent all sorts of disagreeable things about England: "the unmusical, anti-artistic, unphilosophic country."

2 We quite agree.

3 Luxury, sport, the famous English "Humour," the thrilling ascendancy and idée fixe of Class, producing the most intense snobbery in the World; heavy stagnant pools of Saxon blood, incapable of anything but the song of a frog, in home-counties:—these phenomena give England a peculiar distinction in the wrong sense, among the nations.

4 This is why England produces such good artists from time to time.

5 This is also the reason why a movement towards art and imagination could burst up here, from this lump of compressed life, with more force than anywhere else.

6 To believe that it is necessary for or conducive to art, to "improve" life, for instance—make architecture, dress, ornament, in "better taste," is absurd.

7 The Art-instinct is permanently primitive.

8 In a chaos of imperfection, discord, etc., it finds the same stimulus as in Nature.

9 The artist of the modern movement is a savage (in no sense an "advanced," perfected, democratic, Futurist individual of Mr. Marinetti's limited imagination): this enormous, jangling, journalistic, fairy desert of modern life serves him as Nature did more technically primitive man.

10 As the steppes and the rigours of the Russian winter, when the peasant has to lie for weeks in his hut, produces that extraordinary acuity of feeling and intelligence we associate with the Slav; so England is just now the most favourable country for the appearance of a great art.

III.

1 We have made it quite clear that there is nothing Chauvinistic or picturesquely patriotic about our contentions.

2 But there is violent boredom with that feeble Europeanism, abasement of the miserable "intellectual" before anything coming from Paris, Cosmopolitan sentimentality, which prevails in so many quarters.

3 Just as we believe that an Art must be organic with its Time,
So we insist that what is actual and vital for the South, is ineffectual and unactual in the North.

4 Fairies have disappeared from Ireland (despite foolish attempts to revive them)[2] and the bull-ring languishes in Spain.

5 But mysticism on the one hand, gladiatorial instincts, blood and asceticism on the other, will be always actual, and springs of Creation for these two peoples.

6 The English Character is based on the Sea.

7 The particular qualities and characteristics that the sea always engenders in men are those that are, among the many diagnostics of our race, the most fundamentally English.

8 That unexpected universality as well, found in the completest English artists, is due to this.

IV.

1 We assert that the art for these climates, then, must be a northern flower.

2 And we have implied what we believe should be the specific nature of the art destined to grow up in this country, and models of whose flue decorate the pages of this magazine.

3 It is not a question of the characterless material climate around us.
Were that so the complication of the Jungle, dramatic Tropic growth, the vastness of American trees, would not be for us.

4 But our industries, and the Will that determined, face to face with its needs, the direction of the modern world, has reared up steel trees where the green ones were lacking; has exploded in useful growths, and found wilder intricacies than those of Nature.

V.

1 We bring clearly forward the following points, before further defining the character of this necessary native art.

2. The Celtic Revival was a nostalgic movement in Irish arts and letters.

[2] At the freest and most vigorous period of ENGLAND'S history, her literature, then chief Art, was in many ways identical with that of France.
[3] Chaucer was very much cousin of Villon[3] as an artist.
[4] Shakespeare and Montaigne[4] formed one literature.
[5] But Shakespeare reflected in his imagination a mysticism, madness and delicacy peculiar to the North, and brought equal quantities of Comic and Tragic together.
[6] Humour is a phenomenon caused by sudden pouring of culture into Barbary.[5]
[7] It is intelligence electrified by flood of Naivety.
[8] It is Chaos invading Concept and bursting it like nitrogen.
[9] It is the Individual masquerading as Humanity like a child in clothes too big for him.
[10] Tragic Humour is the birthright of the North.
[11] Any great Northern Art will partake of this insidious and volcanic chaos.
[12] No great ENGLISH Art need be ashamed to share some glory with France, to-morrow it may be with Germany, where the Elizabethans did before it.
[13] But it will never be French, any more than Shakespeare was, the most catholic and subtle Englishman.

VI.

[1] The Modern World is due almost entirely to Anglo-Saxon genius,—its appearance and its spirit.
[2] Machinery, trains, steam-ships, all that distinguishes externally our time, came far more from here than anywhere else.
[3] In dress, manners, mechanical inventions, LIFE, that is, ENGLAND, has influenced Europe in the same way that France has in Art.
[4] But busy with this LIFE-EFFORT, she has been the last to become conscious of the Art that is an organism of this new Order and Will of Man.
[5] Machinery is the greatest Earth-medium: incidentally it sweeps away the doctrines of a narrow and pedantic Realism at one stroke.
[6] By mechanical inventiveness, too, just as Englishmen have spread themselves all over the Earth, they have brought all the hemispheres about them in their original island.
[7] It cannot be said that the complication of the Jungle, dramatic tropic growths, the vastness of American trees, is not for us.
[8] For, in the forms of machinery, Factories, new and vaster buildings, bridges and works, we have all that, naturally, around us.

VII.

[1] Once this consciousness towards the new possibilities of expression in present life has come, however, it will be more the legitimate property of Englishmen than of any other people in Europe.

3. François Villon (1431–1463?), French poet.
4. Michel de Montaigne (1533–1592), French essayist.
5. An old name for the western part of North Africa; possibly used here to mean "barbarity."

2 It should also, as it is by origin theirs, inspire them more forcibly and directly.
3 They are the inventors of this bareness and hardness, and should be the great enemies of Romance.
4 The Romance peoples will always be, at bottom, its defenders.
5 The Latins are at present, for instance, in their "discovery" of sport, their Futuristic gush over machines, aeroplanes, etc., the most romantic and sentimental "moderns" to be found.
6 It is only the second-rate people in France or Italy who are thorough revolutionaries.
7 In England, on the other hand, there Is no vulgarity in revolt.
8 Or, rather, there is no revolt, it is the normal state.
9 So often rebels of the North and the South are diametrically opposed species.
10 The nearest thing in England to a great traditional French artist, is a great revolutionary English one.

Signatures for Manifesto[6]

R. Aldington
Arbuthnot
L. Atkinson
Gaudier Brzeska
J. Dismorr
C. Hamilton
E. Pound
W. Roberts
H. Sanders
E. Wadsworth
Wyndham Lewis

Siegfried Sassoon

1886–1967

It is tempting to describe a poet like Siegfried Sassoon by emphasizing his differences from the hugely popular Rupert Brooke. Sassoon was born to a wealthy Jewish family, who made their fortune in India; he lived a life of ease before the war, writing slight Georgian poetry and hunting foxes. World War I suddenly and unequivocally changed all that. Sassoon served with the Royal Welch Fusiliers, and before the end of 1915 saw action in France; he helped a wounded soldier to safety during heavy fire, for which he was awarded a Military Cross. After being wounded himself, Sassoon refused to return to battle; from his hospital bed, he wrote an open letter to the war department suggesting that the war was being unnecessarily prolonged, and as a result, he narrowly avoided a court-martial. Owing to the intervention of his fellow soldier the poet Robert Graves, he was instead committed to a hospital and treated for "shell shock." He returned to the front in 1919, and was wounded a second time.

6. The signatories to the manifesto are Richard Aldington, English writer and man of letters; Malcolm Arbuthnot, professional photographer; Lawrence Atkinson, Vorticist artist; Henri Gaudier-Brzeska, Vorticist sculptor and contributor to *Blast* who was killed in the trenches in World War I and whose obituary was included in *Blast II*; Jessica Dismoor, artist whose illustrations were included in *Blast*; Cuthbert Hamilton, avant-garde artist; Ezra Pound; William Roberts, painter; Helen Saunders, Vorticist designer; Edward Wadsworth, Vorticist painter; and Wyndham Lewis.

Where the war poetry of Brooke is patriotic to the point of sentimentality, Sassoon's verse is characterized by an unrelentingly realistic portrayal of the horrors of modern warfare. And where Brooke's poetry was eagerly welcomed by an anxious public, Sassoon's was largely rejected as either unpatriotic or unnecessarily grotesque. After the war, he lived in seclusion in the country, writing memoirs and poetry—though rarely with the shock value of his early war poems.

Glory of Women

You love us when we're heroes, home on leave,
Or wounded in a mentionable place.
You worship decorations; you believe
That chivalry redeems the war's disgrace.
You make us shells. You listen with delight,
By tales of dirt and danger fondly thrilled.
You crown our distant ardours while we fight,
And mourn our laurelled memories when we're killed.
You can't believe that British troops "retire"
When hell's last horror breaks them, and they run,
Trampling the terrible corpses—blind with blood.
O German mother dreaming by the fire,
While you are knitting socks to send your son
His face is trodden deeper in the mud.

Craiglockhart,[1] 1917

"They"

The Bishop tells us: "When the boys come back
"They will not be the same; for they'll have fought
"In a just cause: they lead the last attack
"On Anti-Christ;[1] their comrades' blood has bought
"New right to breed an honourable race,
"They have challenged Death and dared him face to face."

"We're none of us the same!" the boys reply.
"For George lost both his legs; and Bill's stone blind;
"Poor Jim's shot through the lungs and like to die;
"And Bert's gone syphilitic:[2] you'll not find
"A chap who's served that hasn't found *some* change."
And the Bishop said: "The ways of God are strange!"

The Rear-Guard

(Hindenburg Line, April 1917)

Groping along the tunnel, step by step,
He winked his prying torch° with patching glare — *lantern or flashlight*
From side to side, and sniffed the unwholesome air.

Tins, boxes, bottles, shapes too vague to know;
A mirror smashed, the mattress from a bed;

1. A hospital near Edinburgh, Scotland, where Sassoon (along with Wilfred Owen) was treated for shell shock.
1. In Christian tradition, the archenemy of Christ whose appearance will signal the beginning of the "end times."
2. Infected with syphilis.

And he, exploring fifty feet below
The rosy gloom of battle overhead.

Tripping, he grabbed the wall; saw some one lie
Humped at his feet, half-hidden by a rug,
And stooped to give the sleeper's arm a tug.
"I'm looking for headquarters." No reply.
"God blast your neck!" (For days he'd had no sleep,)
"Get up and guide me through this stinking place."
Savage, he kicked a soft, unanswering heap,
And flashed his beam across the livid face
Terribly glaring up, whose eyes yet wore
Agony dying hard ten days before;
And fists of fingers clutched a blackening wound.

Alone he staggered on until he found
Dawn's ghost that filtered down a shafted stair
To the dazed, muttering creatures underground
Who hear the boom of shells in muffled sound.
At last, with sweat of horror in his hair,
He climbed through darkness to the twilight air,
Unloading hell behind him step by step.

Everyone Sang

Everyone suddenly burst out singing;
And I was filled with such delight
As prisoned birds must find in freedom,
Winging wildly across the white
Orchards and dark-green fields; on—on—and out of sight.
Everyone's voice was suddenly lifted;
And beauty came like the setting sun:
My heart was shaken with tears; and horror
Drifted away . . . O, but Everyone
Was a bird; and the song was wordless; the singing will never be done.

April 1919

Pauline Barrington[1]

"Education"

The rain is slipping, dripping down the street;
The day is grey as ashes on the hearth.
The children play with soldiers made of tin,
While you sew
Row after row.

1. Though details of her life are sketchy, Pauline Barrington's poetry was included in the important anthology *Poems Written During the Great War 1914–1918*, edited by Bertram Lloyd.

The tears are slipping, dripping one by one;
Your son has shot and wounded his small brother.
The mimic battle's ended with a sob,
While you dream
Over your seam.

The blood is slipping, dripping drop by drop;
The men are dying in the trenches' mud.
The bullets search the quick among the dead.
While you drift,
The Gods sift.

The ink is slipping, dripping from the pens,
On papers, White and Orange, Red and Grey,—
History for the children of tomorrow,—
While you prate
About Fate.

War is slipping, dripping death on earth.
If the child is father of the man,
Is the toy gun father of the Krupps?
For Christ's sake think!
While you sew
Row after row.

1918

Helen Dircks[1]

After Bourlon Wood

In one of London's most exclusive haunts,
Amid the shining lights and table ware,
We sat, where meagre Mistress Ration flaunts
Herself in syncopated music there.

He was a Major twenty-six years old,
Back from the latest party of the Hun,
He said: "The beastly blighters had me bowled
Almost before the picnic had begun.

"By Jove! I was particularly cross,
I had looked forward to a little fling!
(These censored wine lists have me at a loss.)
But what have you been doing, dear old thing?"

1. Helen Dircks's poems were published in her lifetime in the volumes *Finding* (1918) and *Passenger* (1920), from which "After Bourlon Wood" is taken.

"I go to bed," I said, "at half-past ten,
And lead the life of any simple Waac—
Alas! a meatless, sweetless one—and then
I have a little joy when you come back.

"But mostly life is dull upon this isle,
And is inclined to be a trifle limp."
"I hate," he said, "the Hun to cramp my style,
We'll try and give it just a little crimp."

"On Saturday," I cried, "we stop at one:
To help you with the crimping would be grand!"
"Sorry," he said, "it simply can't be done,
I've got a most unpleasant job on hand."

"Unpleasant job!" I asked. "What do you mean?"
"I would," he said, "avoid it if I could,
But Georgius Rex, it seems, is awfully keen
To give me the M.C.[2] for being good."

1920

Rupert Brooke
1887–1915

Rupert Brooke was the first of Britain's "war poets," and the last poem he completed during his short lifetime—*The Soldier*—is alone enough to guarantee his lasting place in modern poetry.

Brooke rose with extraordinary speed to the center of the British literary establishment. While an undergraduate, he worked with the *Cambridge Review* and came into contact with such influential writers as Henry James, W. B. Yeats, Virginia Woolf, and Lytton Strachey, and the editor and publisher Edward Marsh. In 1912, after the publication of his first volume of poetry, Brooke suffered a nervous breakdown; after a short recovery period, he spent most of the next three years traveling. World War I began shortly after he returned to England in the spring of 1914; Brooke enlisted immediately and was commissioned on a ship that sailed to Antwerp, Belgium, where Brooke saw no action through early 1915. During this lull, Brooke wrote the war sonnets for which he is best remembered today. While his ship was sailing to Gallipoli, Brooke died of blood poisoning, before seeing combat duty.

It is nearly impossible, even at this late date, to separate Brooke the myth from Brooke the poet; he was something of a national hero even before his death, thanks to the popular reception of his volume of war sonnets, *Nineteen Fourteen*. In Brooke's writings about the war, the irony of early poems like *Heaven* ("And in that Heaven of all their wish, / There shall be no more land, say fish") falls away. These patriotic poems—and most especially *The Soldier*, in which Brooke seemed to have foreseen his own death—meshed perfectly with the temperament

2. Military cross.

of the British people as the nation entered into war. When *The Soldier* was read aloud at Saint Paul's Cathedral in London on Easter Sunday, 1915, Brooke the man—whom Yeats called "the handsomest man in England"—was permanently immortalized as the symbol of English pride.

The Great Lover

I have been so great a lover: filled my days
So proudly with the splendour of Love's praise,
The pain, the calm, and the astonishment,
Desire illimitable, and still content,
And all dear names men use, to cheat despair,
For the perplexed and viewless streams that bear
Our hearts at random down the dark of life.
Now, ere the unthinking silence on that strife
Steals down, I would cheat drowsy Death so far,
My night shall be remembered for a star
That outshone all the suns of all men's days.
Shall I not crown them with immortal praise
Whom I have loved, who have given me, dared with me
High secrets, and in darkness knelt to see
The inenarrable° godhead of delight? *indescribable*
Love is a flame;—we have beaconed the world's night.
A city:—and we have built it, these and I.
An emperor:—we have taught the world to die.
So, for their sakes I loved, ere I go hence,
And the high cause of Love's magnificence,
And to keep loyalties young, I'll write those names
Golden for ever, eagles, crying flames,
And set them as a banner, that men may know,
To dare the generations, burn, and blow
Out on the wind of Time, shining and streaming. . . .

These I have loved:
White plates and cups, clean-gleaming,
Ringed with blue lines; and feathery, faëry dust;
Wet roofs, beneath the lamp-light; the strong crust
Of friendly bread; and many-tasting food;
Rainbows; and the blue bitter smoke of wood;
And radiant raindrops couching in cool flowers;
And flowers themselves, that sway through sunny hours,
Dreaming of moths that drink them under the moon;
Then, the cool kindliness of sheets, that soon
Smooth away trouble; and the rough male kiss
Of blankets; grainy wood; live hair that is
Shining and free; blue-massing clouds; the keen
Unpassioned beauty of a great machine;
The benison° of hot water; furs to touch; *benediction*
The good smell of old clothes; and other such—

The comfortable smell of friendly fingers,
Hair's fragrance, and the musty reek that lingers
About dead leaves and last year's ferns. . . .
Dear names,
And thousand other throng to me! Royal flames;
Sweet water's dimpling laugh from tap or spring;
Holes in the ground; and voices that do sing;
Voices in laughter, too; and body's pain,
Soon turned to peace; and the deep-panting train;
Firm sands; the little dulling edge of foam
That browns and dwindles as the wave goes home;
And washen stones, gay for an hour; the cold
Graveness of iron; moist black earthen mould;
Sleep; and high places; footprints in the dew;
And oaks; and brown horse-chestnuts, glossy-new;
And new-peeled sticks; and shining pools on grass;—
All these have been my loves. And these shall pass,
Whatever passes not, in the great hour,
Nor all my passion, all my prayers, have power
To hold them with me through the gate of Death.
They'll play deserter, turn with the traitor breath,
Break the high bond we made, and sell Love's trust
And sacramented covenant to the dust.
—Oh, never a doubt but, somewhere, I shall wake,
And give what's left of love again, and make
New friends, now strangers. . . .
But the best I've known,
Stays here, and changes, breaks, grows old, is blown
About the winds of the world, and fades from brains
Of living men, and dies.
Nothing remains.

O dear my loves, O faithless, once again
This one last gift I give: that after men
Shall know, and later lovers, far-removed,
Praise you, "All these were lovely"; say, "He loved."

MATAIEA, 1914

The Soldier

If I should die, think only this of me:
That there's some corner of a foreign field
That is forever England. There shall be
In that rich earth a richer dust concealed;
A dust whom England bore, shaped, made aware,
Gave, once, her flowers to love, her ways to roam,
A body of England's, breathing English air,
Washed by the rivers, blest by suns of home.

And think, this heart, all evil shed away,
A pulse in the Eternal mind, no less
Gives somewhere back the thoughts by England given,
Her sights and sounds; dreams happy as her day;
And laughter, learnt of friends; and gentleness,
In hearts at peace, under an English heaven.

Teresa Hooley[1]

A War Film

I saw,
With a catch of the breath and the heart's uplifting,
Sorrow and pride,
The "week's great draw"—
The Mons Retreat;
The "Old Contemptibles" who fought, and died,
The horror and the anguish and the glory.

As in a dream,
Still hearing machine-guns rattle and shells scream,
I came out into the street.
When the day was done,
My little son
Wondered at bath-time why I kissed him so,
Naked upon my knee.
How could he know
The sudden terror that assaulted me? . . .
The body I had borne
Nine moons beneath my heart,
A part of me . . .
If, someday,
It should be taken away
To War. Tortured. Torn.
Slain.
Rotting in No Man's Land, out in the rain—
My little son . . .
Yet all those men had mothers, every one.

How should he know
Why I kissed and kissed and kissed him, crooning his name?
He thought that I was daft.
He thought it was a game,
And laughed, and laughed.

1927

1. (1888–1973), pseud. Mrs. F. H. Butler, Derbyshire writer.

Isaac Rosenberg

1890–1918

World War I was the spur that goaded some poets, like Wilfred Owen, into the writing of poetry; for Isaac Rosenberg the war was simply the catalyst for a more vivid and powerful verse. Rosenberg began writing poetry on Jewish themes when he was just fifteen; he had published two volumes of poems and a verse play, *Moses*, by the time he joined the army in 1916. Rosenberg's experience of the war was, in important ways, different from the other poets represented here. To begin with, he was the son of Lithuanian Jewish immigrants who had settled in the East End, London's Jewish ghetto. As a child, Rosenberg lived with severe poverty; he was forced to leave school at fourteen to help support his family. He went to war not as an officer, but as a private; as the critic Irving Howe writes, "No glamorous fatality hangs over Rosenberg's head: he was just a clumsy, stuttering Jewish doughboy." He was killed while on patrol outside the trenches—a private's dangerous assignment.

His experiences on the Western Front seem to have provided him with the perfect canvas for his essentially religious art. Siegfried Sassoon, alluding to Rosenberg's training as an artist at the Slade School, later described his poems as "scriptural and sculptural": "His experiments were a strenuous effort for impassioned expression; his imagination had a sinewy and muscular aliveness; often he saw things in terms of sculpture, but he did not carve or chisel; he *modeled* words with fierce energy and aspiration." His less-than-genteel background also made Rosenberg impatient with the patriotic sentiments of a poet like Rupert Brooke, for whose "begloried sonnets" he had nothing but contempt. In the poetry of Rosenberg, by contrast—according to Sassoon—"words and images obey him, instead of leading him into over-elaboration." Interest in Rosenberg's poetry has recently been revived by critics interested in his use of Jewish themes; the critic Harold Bloom, for instance, calls Rosenberg "an English poet with a Jewish difference," and suggests that he is "the best Jewish poet writing in English that our century has given us."

Break of Day in the Trenches

The darkness crumbles away—
It is the same old druid[1] Time as ever.
Only a live thing leaps my hand—
A queer sardonic rat—
As I pull the parapet's poppy
To stick behind my ear.
Droll rat, they would shoot you if they knew
Your cosmopolitan sympathies.
Now you have touched this English hand
You will do the same to a German—
Soon, no doubt, if it be your pleasure
To cross the sleeping green between.
It seems you inwardly grin as you pass
Strong eyes, fine limbs, haughty athletes

1. Member of an ancient Celtic religion.

Less chanced than you for life,
Bonds to the whims of murder,
Sprawled in the bowels of the earth,
The torn fields of France.
What do you see in our eyes
At the shrieking iron and flame
Hurled through still heavens?
What quaver—what heart aghast?
Poppies whose roots are in man's veins
Drop, and are ever dropping;
But mine in my ear is safe,
Just a little white with the dust.

1916 1922

Dead Man's Dump

The plunging limbers over the shattered track
Racketed with their rusty freight,
Stuck out like many crowns of thorns,
And the rusty stakes like sceptres old
To stay the flood of brutish men
Upon our brothers dear.

The wheels lurched over sprawled dead
But pained them not, though their bones crunched,
Their shut mouths made no moan.
They lie there huddled, friend and foeman,
Man born of man, and born of woman,
And shells go crying over them
From night till night and now.

Earth has waited for them,
All the time of their growth
Fretting for their decay:
Now she has them at last!
In the strength of their strength
Suspended—stopped and held.

What fierce imaginings their dark souls lit?
Earth! have they gone into you!
Somewhere they must have gone,
And flung on your hard back
Is their soul's sack
Emptied of God-ancestralled essences.
Who hurled them out? Who hurled?

None saw their spirits' shadow shake the grass,
Or stood aside for the half used life to pass
Out of those doomed nostrils and the doomed mouth,

When the swift iron burning bee
Drained the wild honey of their youth.

What of us who, flung on the shrieking pyre,° *funeral bonfire*
Walk, our usual thoughts untouched,
Our lucky limbs as on ichor[1] fed,
Immortal seeming ever?
Perhaps when the flames beat loud on us,
A fear may choke in our veins
And the startled blood may stop.

The air is loud with death,
The dark air spurts with fire,
The explosions ceaseless are.
Timelessly now, some minutes past,
These dead strode time with vigorous life,
Till the shrapnel called 'An end!'
But not to all. In bleeding pangs
Some borne on stretchers dreamed of home,
Dear things, war-blotted from their hearts.

Maniac Earth! howling and flying, your bowel
Seared by the jagged fire, the iron love,
The impetuous storm of savage love.
Dark Earth! dark Heavens! swinging in chemic smoke,
What dead are born when you kiss each soundless soul
With lightning and thunder from your mined heart,
Which man's self dug, and his blind fingers loosed?

A man's brains splattered on
A stretcher-bearer's face;
His shook shoulders slipped their load,
But when they bent to look again
The drowning soul was sunk too deep
For human tenderness.

They left this dead with the older dead,
Stretched at the cross roads.

Burnt black by strange decay
Their sinister faces lie,
The lid over each eye,
The grass and coloured clay
More motion have than they,
Joined to the great sunk silences.

Here is one not long dead;
His dark hearing caught our far wheels,
And the choked soul stretched weak hands

1. The vital fluid flowing in the veins of the Gods in classical mythology.

To reach the living word the far wheels said,
The blood-dazed intelligence beating for light,
Crying through the suspense of the far torturing wheels
Swift for the end to break
Or the wheels to break,
Cried as the tide of the world broke over his sight.

Will they come? Will they ever come?
Even as the mixed hoofs of the mules,
The quivering-bellied mules,
And the rushing wheels all mixed
With his tortured upturned sight.
So we crashed round the bend,
We heard his weak scream,
We heard his very last sound,
And our wheels grazed his dead face.

Rebecca West

1892–1983

Rebecca West is increasingly appreciated as a writer of fiction, literary criticism, political commentary, and biography, as well as one of the most important journalists of the century. Born Cicely Fairfield in Ireland, she was educated in Edinburgh after her father died when she was ten years old. She became an actress in London, taking the stage name "Rebecca West" from a heroine she had played in Ibsen's drama *Rosmersholm*. By the time she was twenty, she was becoming active in left-wing journalism and in agitation for women's rights. In 1914, when she wrote *Indissoluble Matrimony*, she was involved in a love affair with the free-thinking but married novelist H. G. Wells, with whom she had a son; at the same time, she was working on a critical biography of Henry James. She went on to write searching and sometimes critical essays on male modernists like Joyce, Eliot, and Lawrence, and perceptive essays on Virginia Woolf and Katherine Mansfield. Throughout her life, she wrote both novels and political journalism, notably a major study of Balkan politics and culture, *Black Lamb and Grey Falcon* (1942), and a series of brilliant reports on the Nuremberg trials of Nazi war criminals at the end of World War II, collected as *A Train of Powder* (1955). She was made Dame Commander of the British Empire in 1959. Like her political writing, her fiction is notable for its irreverent probing of modernity's fault lines. Though never an orthodox feminist, West demonstrated a keen insight into the psychology of women and men, and portrayed the straitened thinking that made feminism's ultimate victory anything but a foregone conclusion.

Indissoluble Matrimony

When George Silverton opened the front door he found that the house was not empty for all its darkness. The spitting noise of the striking of damp matches and mild, growling exclamations of annoyance told him that his wife was trying to light the dining-room gas. He went in and with some short, hostile sound of greeting lit a match and brought brightness into the little room. Then, irritated by his own folly in bringing private papers into his wife's presence, he stuffed the letters he had brought from the office deep into the pockets of his overcoat. He looked at her suspiciously, but she had not seen them, being busy in unwinding her orange motor-veil. His eyes remained on her face to brood a little sourly on her moving loveliness, which he had not been sure of finding: for she was one of those women who create an illusion alternately of extreme beauty and extreme ugliness. Under her curious dress, designed in some pitifully cheap and worthless stuff by a successful mood of her indiscreet taste—she had black blood in her—her long body seemed pulsing with some exaltation. The blood was coursing violently under her luminous yellow skin, and her lids, dusky with fatigue, drooped contentedly over her great humid black eyes. Perpetually she raised her hand to the mass of black hair that was coiled on her thick golden neck, and stroked it with secretive enjoyment, as a cat licks its fur. And her large mouth smiled frankly, but abstractedly, at some digested pleasure.

There was a time when George would have looked on this riot of excited loveliness with suspicion. But now he knew it was almost certainly caused by some trifle—a long walk through stinging weather, the report of a Socialist victory at a by-election, or the intoxication of a waltz refrain floating from the municipal band-stand across the flats of the local recreation ground. And even if it had been caused by some amorous interlude he would not have greatly cared. In the ten years since their marriage he had lost the quality which would have made him resentful. He now believed that quality to be purely physical. Unless one was in good condition and responsive to the messages sent out by the flesh Evadne could hardly concern one. He turned the bitter thought over in his heart and stung himself by deliberately gazing unmoved upon her beautiful joyful body.

"Let's have supper now!" she said rather greedily.

He looked at the table and saw she had set it before she went out. As usual she had been in an improvident hurry: it was carelessly done. Besides, what an absurd supper to set before a hungry solicitor's clerk! In the centre, obviously intended as the principal dish, was a bowl of plums, softly red, soaked with the sun, glowing like jewels in the downward stream of the incandescent light. Besides them was a great yellow melon, its sleek sides fluted with rich growth, and a honey-comb glistening on a willow-pattern dish. The only sensible food to be seen was a plate of tongue laid at his place.

"I can't sit down to supper without washing my hands!"

While he splashed in the bathroom upstairs he heard her pull in a chair to the table and sit down to her supper. It annoyed him. There was no ritual about it. While he was eating the tongue she would be crushing honey on new bread, or stripping a plum of its purple skin and holding the golden globe up to the gas to see the light filter through. The meal would pass in silence. She would innocently take his dumbness for a sign of abstraction and forbear to babble. He would find the words choked on his lips by the weight of dullness that always oppressed him in her presence. Then, just about the time when he was beginning to feel able to formulate his obscure grievances against her, she would rise from the table without a word and run upstairs to her work, humming in that uncanny, negro way of hers.

And so it was. She ate with an appalling catholicity of taste, with a nice child's love of sweet foods, and occasionally she broke into that hoarse beautiful croon. Every now and then she looked at him with too obvious speculations as to whether his silence was due to weariness or uncertain temper. Timidly she cut him an enormous slice of the melon, which he did not want. Then she rose abruptly and flung herself into the rocking chair on the hearth. She clasped her hands behind her head and strained backwards so that the muslin stretched over her strong breasts. She sang softly to the ceiling.

There was something about the fantastic figure that made him feel as though they were not properly married.

"Evadne?"

"'S?"

"What have you been up to this evening?"

"I was at Milly Stafordale's."

He was silent again. That name brought up the memory of his courting days. It was under the benign eyes of blonde, plebeian Milly that he had wooed the distracting creature in the rocking chair.

Ten years before, when he was twenty-five, his firm had been reduced to hysteria over the estates of an extraordinarily stupid old woman, named Mrs. Mary Ellerker. Her stupidity, grappling with the complexity of the sources of the vast income which rushed in spate from the properties of four deceased husbands, demanded oceans of explanations even over her weekly rents. Silverton alone in the office, by reason of a certain natural incapacity for excitement, could deal calmly with this marvel of imbecility. He alone could endure to sit with patience in the black-panelled drawing-room amidst the jungle of shiny mahogany furniture and talk to a mass of darkness, who rested heavily in the window-seat and now and then made an idiotic remark in a bright, hearty voice. But it shook even him. Mrs. Mary Ellerker was obscene. Yet she was perfectly sane and, although of that remarkable plainness noticeable in most oft-married women, in good enough physical condition. She merely presented the loathsome spectacle of an ignorant mind, contorted by the artificial idiocy of coquetry, lack of responsibility, and hatred of discipline, stripped naked by old age. That was the real horror of her. One feared to think how many women were really like Mrs. Ellerker under their armour of physical perfection or social grace. For this reason he turned eyes of hate on Mrs. Ellerker's pretty little companion, Milly Stafordale, who smiled at him over her embroidery with wintry northern brightness. When she was old she too would be obscene.

This horror obsessed him. Never before had he feared anything. He had never lived more than half-an-hour from a police station, and, as he had by some chance missed the melancholy clairvoyance of adolescence, he had never conceived of any horror with which the police could not deal. This disgust of women revealed to him that the world is a place of subtle perils. He began to fear marriage as he feared death. The thought of intimacy with some lovely, desirable and necessary wife turned him sick as he sat at his lunch. The secret obscenity of women! He talked darkly of it to his friends. He wondered why the Church did not provide a service for the absolution of men after marriage. Wife desertion seemed to him a beautiful return of the tainted body to cleanliness.

On his fifth visit to Mrs. Ellerker he could not begin his business at once. One of Milly Stafordale's friends had come in to sing to the old lady. She stood by the piano against the light, so that he saw her washed with darkness. Amazed, of tropical fruit. And before he had time to apprehend the sleepy wonder of her beauty, she had begun to sing. Now he knew that her voice was a purely physical attribute, built in her as she lay in her mother's womb, and no index of her spiritual values. But then, as it welled up from the thick golden throat and clung to her lips, it seemed a sublime achievement of the soul. It was smouldering contralto such as only those of black blood can possess. As she sang her great black eyes lay on him with the innocent shamelessness of a young animal, and he remembered hopefully that he was good looking. Suddenly she stood in silence, playing with her heavy black plait. Mrs. Ellerker broke into silly thanks. The girl's mother, who had been playing the accompaniment, rose and stood rolling up her music. Silverton, sick with excitement, was introduced to them. He noticed that the mother was a little darker than the conventions permit. Their name was Hannan—Mrs. Arthur Hannan and Evadne. They moved lithely and quietly out of the room, the girl's eyes still lingering on his face.

The thought of her splendour and the rolling echoes of her voice disturbed him all night. Next day, going to his office, he travelled with her on the horse-car that bound his suburb to Petrick. One of the horses fell lame, and she had time to tell him that she was studying at a commercial college. He quivered with distress. All the time he had a dizzy illusion that she was nestling up against him. They parted shyly. During the next few days they met constantly. He began to go and see them in the evening at their home—a mean flat crowded with cheap glories of bead curtains and Oriental hangings that set off the women's alien beauty. Mrs. Hannan was a widow and they lived alone, in a wonderful silence. He talked more than he had ever done in his whole life before. He took a dislike to the widow, she was consumed with fiery subterranean passions, no fit guardian for the tender girl.

Now he could imagine with what silent rapture Evadne had watched his agitation. Almost from the first she had meant to marry him. He was physically attractive, though not strong. His intellect was gently stimulating like a mild white wine. And it was time she married. She was ripe for adult things. This was the real wound in his soul. He had tasted of a divine thing created in his time for dreams out of her rich beauty, her loneliness, her romantic poverty, her immaculate youth. He had known love. And Evadne had never known anything more than a magnificent physical adventure which she had secured at the right time as she would have engaged a cab to take her to the station in time for the cheapest excursion train. It was a quick way to light-hearted living. With loathing he remembered how in the days of their engagement she used to gaze purely into his blinking eyes and with her unashamed kisses incite him to extravagant embraces. Now he cursed her for having obtained his spiritual revolution on false pretences. Only for a little time had he had his illusion, for their marriage was hastened by Mrs. Hannan's sudden death. After three months of savage mourning Evadne flung herself into marriage, and her excited candour had enlightened him very soon.

That marriage had lasted ten years. And to Evadne their relationship was just the same as ever. Her vitality needed him as it needed the fruit on the table before him. He shook with wrath and a sense of outraged decency.

"O George!" She was yawning widely.

"What's the matter?" he said without interest.

"It's so beastly dull."

"I can't help that, can I?"

"No." She smiled placidly at him. "We're a couple of dull dogs, aren't we? I wish we had children."

After a minute she suggested, apparently as an alternative amusement, "Perhaps the post hasn't passed."

As she spoke there was a rat-tat and the slither of a letter under the door. Evadne picked herself up and ran out into the lobby. After a second or two, during which she made irritating inarticulate exclamations, she came in reading the letter and stroking her bust with a gesture of satisfaction.

"They want me to speak at Longton's meeting on the nineteenth," she purred.

"Longton? What's he up to?"

Stephen Longton was the owner of the biggest iron works in Petrick, a man whose refusal to adopt the livery of busy oafishness thought proper to commercial men aroused the gravest suspicions.

"He's standing as Socialist candidate for the town council."

". . . Socialist!" he muttered.

He set his jaw. That was a side of Evadne he considered as little as possible. He had never been able to assimilate the fact that Evadne had, two years after their marriage, passed through his own orthodox Radicalism[1] to a passionate Socialism, and that after reading enormously of economics she had begun to write for the Socialist press and to speak successfully at meetings. In the jaundiced recesses of his mind he took it for granted that her work would have the lax fibre of her character: that it would be infected with her Oriental crudities. Although once or twice he had been congratulated on her brilliance, he mistrusted this phase of her activity as a caper of the sensualist. His eyes blazed on her and found the depraved, over-sexed creature, looking milder than a gazelle, holding out a hand-bill to him.

"They've taken it for granted!"

He saw her name—his name—

MRS. EVADNE SILVERTON.[2]

It was at first the blaze of stout scarlet letters on the dazzling white ground that made him blink. Then he was convulsed with rage.

"Georgie dear!"

She stepped forward and caught his weak body to her bosom. He wrenched himself away. Spiritual nausea made him determined to be a better man than her.

"A pair of you! You and Longton—!" he snarled scornfully. Then, seeing her startled face, he controlled himself.

"I thought it would please you," said Evadne, a little waspishly.

"You mustn't have anything to do with Longton," he stormed.

A change passed over her. She became ugly. Her face was heavy with intellect, her lips coarse with power. He was at arms with a Socialist lead. Much he would have preferred the bland sensualist again.

1. An extreme form of Liberalism, still comfortably within the continuum of British democratic politics; Socialism, which Evadne has embraced, advocates the abolition of the current system and is thus too extreme for George's bourgeois attitudes.

2. Evadne would have been addressed in polite society as "Mrs. George Silverton"; George reads this breach of decorum as one more sign that his wife is out of control. Leopold Bloom, the protagonist of James Joyce's *Ulysses*, makes a similar observation when his wife Molly receives a letter from her lover addressed to "Mrs. Marion Bloom."

"Why?"

"Because—his lips stuck together like blotting-paper—he's not the sort of man my wife should—should—"

With movements which terrified him by their rough energy, she folded up the bills and put them back in the envelope.

"George. I suppose you mean that he's a bad man." He nodded.

"I know quite well that the girl who used to be his typist is his mistress." She spoke it sweetly, as if reasoning with an old fool. "But she's got consumption. She'll be dead in six months. In fact, I think it's rather nice of him. To look after her and all that."

"My God!" He leapt to his feet, extending a shaking forefinger. As she turned to him, the smile dying on her lips, his excited weakness wrapped him in a paramnesic illusion:[3] it seemed to him that he had been through all this before—a long, long time ago. "My God, you talk like a woman off the streets!"

Evadne's lips lifted over her strong teeth. With clever cruelty she fixed his eyes with hers, well knowing that he longed to fall forward and bury his head on the table in a transport of hysterical sobs. After a moment of this torture she turned away, herself distressed by a desire to cry.

"How can you say such dreadful, dreadful things!" she protested, chokingly.

He sat down again. His eyes looked little and red, but they blazed on her. "I wonder if you are," he said softly.

"Are what?" she asked petulantly, a tear rolling down her nose.

"You know," he answered, nodding.

"George, George, George!" she cried.

"You've always been keen on kissing and making love, haven't you, my precious? At first you startled me, you did! I didn't know women were like that." From that morass he suddenly stepped on to a high peak of terror. Amazed to find himself sincere, he cried—"I don't believe good women are!"

"Georgie, how can you be so silly!" exclaimed Evadne shrilly. "You know quite well I've been as true to you as any woman could be." She sought his eyes with a liquid glance of reproach. He averted his gaze, sickened at having put himself in the wrong. For even while he degraded his tongue his pure soul fainted with loathing of her fleshliness.

"I—I'm sorry."

Too wily to forgive him at once, she showed him a lowering profile with downcast lids. Of course, he knew it was a fraud: an imputation against her chastity was no more poignant than a reflection on the cleanliness of her nails—rude and spiteful, but that was all. But for a time they kept up the deception, while she cleared the table in a steely silence.

"Evadne, I'm sorry. I'm tired." His throat was dry. He could not bear the discord of a row added to the horror of their companionship. "Evadne, do forgive me—I don't know what I meant by—"

"That's all right, silly!" she said suddenly and bent over the table to kiss him. Her brow was smooth. It was evident from her splendid expression that she was pre-occupied. Then she finished clearing up the dishes and took them into the kitchen. While she was out of the room he rose from his seat and sat down in the armchair by the fire, setting his bull-dog pipe alight. For a very short time he was free of her voluptuous presence. But she ran back soon, having put the kettle on and changed her blouse for a loose dressing-jacket, and sat down on the arm of his

3. A condition in which fact and fiction become confused.

chair. Once or twice she bent and kissed his brow, but for the most part she lay back with his head drawn to her bosom, rocking herself rhythmically. Silverton, a little disgusted by their contact, sat quite motionless and passed into a doze. He revolved in his mind the incidents of his day's routine and remembered a snub from a superior. So he opened his eyes and tried to think of something else. It was then that he became conscious that the rhythm of Evadne's movement was not regular. It was broken as though she rocked in time to music. Music? His sense of hearing crept up to hear if there was any sound of music in the breaths she was emitting rather heavily every now and then. At first he could hear nothing. Then it struck him that each breath was a muttered phrase. He stiffened, and hatred flamed through his veins. The words came clearly through her lips. . . . "The present system of wage-slavery. . . ."

"Evadne!" He sprang to his feet. "You're preparing your speech!"

She did not move. "I am," she said.

"Damn it, you shan't speak!"

"Damn it, I will!"

"Evadne, you shan't speak! If you do I swear to God above I'll turn you out into the streets—." She rose and came towards him. She looked black and dangerous. She trod softly like a cat with her head down. In spite of himself, his tongue licked his lips in fear and he cowered a moment before he picked up a knife from the table. For a space she looked down on him and the sharp blade.

"You idiot, can't you hear the kettle's boiling over?"

He shrank back, letting the knife fall on the floor. For three minutes he stood there controlling his breath and trying to still his heart. Then he followed her into the kitchen. She was making a noise with a basinful of dishes.

"Stop that row."

She turned round with a dripping dish-cloth in her hand and pondered whether to throw it at him. But she was tired and wanted peace: so that she could finish the rough draft of her speech. So she stood waiting.

"Did you understand what I said then? If you don't promise me here and now—"

She flung her arms upwards with a cry and dashed past him. He made to run after her upstairs, but stumbled on the threshold of the lobby and sat with his ankle twisted under him, shaking with rage. In a second she ran downstairs again, clothed in a big cloak with black bundle clutched to her breast. For the first time in their married life she was seized with a convulsion of sobs. She dashed out of the front door and banged it with such passion that a glass pane shivered to fragments behind her.

"What's this? What's this?" he cried stupidly, standing up. He perceived with an insane certainty that she was going out to meet some unknown lover. "I'll come and tell him what a slut you are!" he shouted after her and stumbled to the door. It was jammed now and he had to drag at it.

The night was flooded with the yellow moonshine of midsummer: it seemed to drip from the lacquered leaves of the shrubs in the front garden. In its soft clarity he could see her plainly, although she was now two hundred yards away. She was hastening to the north end of Sumatra Crescent, an end that curled up the hill like a silly kitten's tail and stopped abruptly in green fields. So he knew that she was going to the young man who had just bought the Georgian Manor, whose elm-trees crowned the hill. Oh, how he hated her! Yet he must follow her, or else she would cover up her adulteries so that he could not take his legal revenge. So he began to run—silently, for he wore his carpet slippers. He was only a hundred yards behind her when she slipped through a gap in the hedge to tread a field-path. She still walked with pride, for though she was town-bred, night in the open seemed not at all fearful to her. As he shuffled in pursuit his carpet slippers were engulfed in a shining pool of mud: he raised one with a squelch, the other was left. This seemed the last humiliation. He kicked the other one off his feet and padded on in his socks, snuffling in anticipation of a cold. Then physical pain sent him back to the puddle to pluck out the slippers; it was a dirty job. His heart battered his breast as he saw that Evadne had gained the furthest hedge and was crossing the stile into the lane that ran up to the Manor gates.

"Go on, you beast!" he muttered, "Go on, go on!" After a scamper he climbed the stile and thrust his lean neck beyond a mass of wilted hawthorn bloom that crumbled into vagrant petals at his touch.

The lane mounted yellow as cheese to where the moon lay on his iron tracery of the Manor gates. Evadne was not there. Hardly believing his eyes he hobbled over into the lane and looked in the other direction. There he saw her disappearing round the bend of the road. Gathering himself up to a run, he tried to think out his bearings. He had seldom passed this way, and like most people without strong primitive instincts he had no sense of orientation. With difficulty he remembered that after a mile's mazy wanderings between high hedges this lane sloped suddenly to the bowl of heather overhung by the moorlands, in which lay the Petrick reservoirs, two untamed lakes.

"Eh! she's going to meet him by the water!" he cursed to himself. He remembered the withered ash tree, seared by lightning to its root, that stood by the road at the bare frontier of the moor. "May God strike her like that," he prayed," "as she fouls the other man's lips with her kisses. O God! let me strangle her. Or bury a knife deep in her breast." Suddenly he broke into a lolloping run. "O my Lord, I'll be able to divorce her. I'll be free. Free to live alone. To do my day's work and sleep my night's sleep without her. I'll get a job somewhere else and forget her. I'll bring her to the dogs. No clean man or woman in Petrick will look at her now. They won't have her to speak at that meeting now!" His throat swelled with joy, he leapt high in the air.

"I'll lie about her. If I can prove that she's wrong with this man they'll believe me if I say she's a bad woman and drinks. I'll make her name a joke. And then—"

He flung wide his arms in ecstasy: the left struck against stone. More pain than he had thought his body could hold convulsed him, so that he sank on the ground hugging his aching arm. He looked backwards as he writhed and saw that the hedge had stopped; above him was the great stone wall of the county asylum. The question broke on him—was there any lunatic in its confines so slavered with madness as he himself? Nothing but madness could have accounted for the torrent of ugly words, the sea of uglier thoughts that was now a part of him. "O God, me to turn like this!" he cried, rolling over full-length on the grassy bank by the roadside. That the infidelity of his wife, a thing that should have brought out the stern manliness of his true nature, should have discovered him as lecherous-lipped as any pot-house[4] lounger, was the most infamous accident of his married life. The sense of sin descended on him so that his tears flowed hot and bitterly. "Have I gone to the Unitarian chapel every Sunday morning and to the Ethical Society every evening for nothing?" his spirit asked itself in its travail. "All those Browning lectures for nothing. . . ."[5] He said the Lord's Prayer several times and lay for a minute quietly crying. The relaxation of his muscles brought him a sense of rest which seemed forgiveness falling from

4. Tavern.

5. George's activities—Unitarian church, Ethical Society, Browning Society—suggest that he participated in public exercises of a high moral nature without giving himself over to traditional religious faith, which he would have seen as "irrational" and "unmanly."

God. The tears dried on his cheeks. His calmer consciousness heard the sound of rushing waters mingled with the beating of blood in his ears. He got up and scrambled round the turn of the road that brought him to the withered ash-tree.

He walked forward on the parched heatherland to the mound whose scarred sides, heaped with boulders, tufted with mountain grasses, shone before him in the moonlight. He scrambled up to it hurriedly and hoisted himself from ledge to ledge till he fell on his knees with a squeal of pain. His ankle was caught in a crevice of the rock. Gulping down his agony at this final physical humiliation he heaved himself upright and raced on to the summit, and found himself before the Devil's Cauldron, filled to the brim with yellow moonshine and the fiery play of summer lightning. The rugged crags opposite him were a low barricade against the stars to which the mound where he stood shot forward like a bridge. To the left of this the long Lisbech pond lay like a trailing serpent; its silver scales glittered as the wind swept down from the vaster moorlands to the east. To the right under a steep drop of twenty feet was the Whimsey pond, more sinister, shaped in an unnatural oval, sheltered from the wind by the high ridge so that the undisturbed moonlight lay across it like a sharp-edged sword.

He looked about for some sign of Evadne. She could not be on the land by the margin of the lakes, for the light blazed so strongly that each reed could be clearly seen like a black dagger stabbing the silver. He looked down Lisbech and saw far east a knot of red and green and orange lights. Perhaps for some devilish purpose Evadne had sought Lisbech railway station. But his volcanic mind had preserved one grain of sense that assured him that, subtle as Evadne's villainy might be, it would not lead her to walk five miles out of her way to a terminus which she could have reached in fifteen minutes by taking a train from the station down the road. She must be under cover somewhere here. He went down the gentle slope that fell from the top of the ridge to Lisbech pond in a disorder of rough heather, unhappy patches of cultivated grass, and coppices of silver birch, fringed with flaming broom that seemed faintly tarnished in the moonlight. At the bottom was a roughly hewn path which he followed in hot aimless hurry. In a little he approached a riot of falling waters. There was a slice ten feet broad carved out of the ridge, and to this narrow channel of black shining rock the floods of Lisbech leapt some feet and raced through to Whimsey. The noise beat him back. The gap was spanned by a gaunt thing of paint-blistered iron, on which he stood dizzily and noticed how the wide step that ran on each side of the channel through to the other pond was smeared with sinister green slime. Now his physical distress reminded him of Evadne, whom he had almost forgotten in contemplation of these lonely waters. The idea of her had been present but obscured, as sometimes toothache may cease active torture. His blood lust set him on and he staggered forward with covered ears. Even as he went something caught his eye in a thicket high up on the slope near the crags. Against the slender pride of some silver birches stood a gnarled hawthorn tree, its branches flattened under the stern moorland winds so that it grew squat like an opened umbrella. In its dark shadows, faintly illumined by a few boughs of withered blossom, there moved a strange bluish light. Even while he did not know what it was it made his flesh stir.

The light emerged. It was the moonlight reflected from Evadne's body. She was clad in a black bathing dress, and her arms and legs and the broad streak of flesh laid bare by a rent down the back shone brilliantly white, so that she seemed like a grotesquely patterned wild animal as she ran down to the lake. Whirling her arms above her head she trampled down into the water and struck out strongly. Her movements were full of brisk delight and she swam quickly. The moonlight made her the centre of a little feathery blur of black and silver, with a comet's tail trailing in her wake.

Nothing in all his married life had ever staggered Silverton so much as this. He had imagined his wife's adultery so strongly that it had come to be. It was now as real as their marriage; more real than their courtship. So this seemed to be the last crime of the adulteress. She had dragged him over those squelching fields and these rough moors and changed him from a man of irritations, but no passions, into a cold designer of murderous treacheries, so that he might witness a swimming exhibition! For a minute he was stunned. Then he sprang down to the rushy edge and ran along in the direction of her course, crying—"Evadne! Evadne!" She did not hear him. At last he achieved a chest note and shouted—"Evadne! come here!" The black and silver feather shivered in mid-water. She turned immediately and swam back to shore. He suspected sullenness in her slowness, but was glad of it, for after the shock of this extraordinary incident he wanted to go to sleep. Drowsiness lay on him like lead. He shook himself like a dog and wrenched off his linen collar, winking at the bright moon to keep himself awake. As she came quite near he was exasperated by the happy, snorting breaths she drew, and strolled a pace or two up the bank. To his enragement the face she lifted as she waded to dry land was placid, and she scrambled gaily up the bank to his side.

"O George, why did you come!" she exclaimed quite affectionately, laying a damp hand on his shoulder.

"O damn it, what does this mean!" he cried, committing a horrid tenor squeak. "What are you doing?"

"Why. George," she said," "I came here for a bathe."

He stared into her face and could make nothing of it. It was only sweet surfaces of flesh, soft radiances of eye and lip, a lovely lie of comeliness. He forgot this present grievance in a cold search for the source of her peculiar hatefulness. Under this sick gaze she pouted and turned away with a peevish gesture. He made no sign and stood silent, watching her saunter to that gaunt iron bridge. The roar of the little waterfall did not disturb her splendid nerves and she drooped sensuously over the hand-rail, sniffing up the sweet night smell; too evidently trying to abase him to another apology.

A mosquito whirred into his face. He killed it viciously and strode off towards his wife, who showed by a common little toss of the head that she was conscious of his coming.

"Look here, Evadne!" he panted. "What did you come here for? Tell me the truth and I promise I'll not—I'll not—"

"Not WHAT, George?"

"O please, please tell me the truth, do Evadne!" he cried pitifully.

"But, dear, what is there to carry on about so? You went on so queerly about my meeting that my head felt fit to split, and I thought the long walk and the dip would do me good." She broke off, amazed at the wave of horror that passed over his face.

His heart sank. From the loose-lipped hurry in the telling of her story, from the bigness of her eyes and the lack of subtlety in her voice, he knew that this was the truth. Here was no adulteress whom he could accuse in the law courts and condemn into the street, no resourceful sinner whose merry crimes he could discover. Here was merely his good wife, the faithful attendant of his hearth, relentless wrecker of his soul.

She came towards him as a cat approaches a displeased master, and hovered about him on the stone coping of the noisy sluice.

"Indeed!" he found himself saying sarcastically. "Indeed!"

"Yes, George Silverton, indeed!" she burst out, a little frightened. "And why shouldn't I? I used to come here often enough on summer nights with poor Mamma—"

"Yes!" he shouted. It was exactly the sort of thing that would appeal to that weird half-black woman from the back of beyond. "Mamma!" he cried tauntingly, "Mamma!"

There was a flash of silence between them before Evadne, clutching her breast and balancing herself dangerously on her heels on the stone coping, broke into gentle shrieks. "You dare talk of my Mamma, my poor Mamma, and she cold in her grave! I haven't been happy since she died and I married you, you silly little misery, you!" Then the rage was suddenly wiped off her brain by the perception of a crisis.

The trickle of silence overflowed into a lake, over which their spirits flew, looking at each other's reflection in the calm waters: in the hurry of their flight they had never before seen each other. They stood facing one another with dropped heads, quietly thinking.

The strong passion which filled them threatened to disintegrate their souls as a magnetic current decomposes the electrolyte, so they fought to organise their sensations. They tried to arrange themselves and their lives for comprehension, but beyond sudden lyric visions of old incidents of hatefulness—such as a smarting quarrel of six years ago as to whether Evadne had or had not cheated the railway company out of one and eightpence on an excursion ticket—the past was intangible. It trailed behind this intense event as the pale hair trails behind the burning comet. They were pre-occupied with the moment. Quite often George had found a mean pleasure in the thought that by never giving Evadne a child he had cheated her out of one form of experience, and now he paid the price for this unnatural pride of sterility. For now the spiritual offspring of their intercourse came to birth. A sublime loathing was between them. For a little time it was a huge perilous horror, but afterwards, like men aboard a ship whose masts seek the sky through steep waves, they found a drunken pride in the adventure. This was the very absolute of hatred. It cheapened the memory of the fantasias of irritation and ill-will they had performed in the less boring moments of their marriage, and they felt dazed, as amateurs who had found themselves creating a masterpiece. For the first time they were possessed by a supreme emotion and they felt a glad desire to strip away restraint and express it nakedly. It was ecstasy; they felt tall and full of blood.

Like people who, bewitched by Christ, see the whole earth as the breathing body of God, so they saw the universe as the substance and the symbol of their hatred. The stars trembled overhead with wrath. A wind from behind the angry crags set the moonlight on Lisbech quivering with rage, and the squat hawthorn-tree creaked slowly like the irritation of a dull little man. The dry moors, parched with harsh anger, waited thirstily and, sending out the murmur of rustling mountain grass and the cry of wakening fowl, seemed to huddle closer to the lake. But this sense of the earth's sympathy slipped away from them and they loathed all matter as the dull wrapping of their flame-like passion. At their wishing matter fell away and they saw sarcastic visions. He saw her as a toad squatting on the clean earth, obscuring the stars and pressing down its hot moist body on the cheerful fields. She felt his long boneless body coiled round the roots of the lovely tree of life. They shivered fastidiously. With an uplifting sense of responsibility they realised that they must kill each other.

A bird rose over their heads with a leaping flight that made it seem as though its black body was bouncing against the bright sky. The foolish noise and motion precipitated their thoughts. They were broken into a new conception of life. They perceived that God is war and his creatures are meant to fight. When dogs walk through the world cats must climb trees. The virgin must snare the wanton, the fine lover must put the prude to the sword. The gross man of action walks, spurred on the bloodless bodies of the men of thought, who lie quiet and cunningly do not tell him where his grossness leads him. The flesh must smother the spirit, the spirit must set the flesh on fire and watch it burn. And those who were gentle by nature and shrank from the ordained brutality were betrayers of their kind, surrendering the earth to the seed of their enemies.

In this war there is no discharge. If they succumbed to peace now, the rest of their lives would be dishonourable, like the exile of a rebel who has begged his life as the reward of cowardice. It was their first experience of religious passion, and they abandoned themselves to it so that their immediate personal qualities fell away from them. Neither his weakness nor her prudence stood in the way of the event.

They measured each other with the eye. To her he was a spidery thing against the velvet blackness and hard silver surfaces of the pond. The light soaked her bathing dress so that she seemed, against the jagged shadows of the rock cutting, as though she were clad in a garment of dark polished mail. Her knees were bent so clearly, her toes gripped the coping so strongly. He understood very clearly that if he did not kill her instantly she would drop him easily into the deep riot of waters. Yet for a space he could not move, but stood expecting a degrading death. Indeed, he gave her time to kill him. But she was without power too, and struggled weakly with a hallucination. The quarrel in Sumatra Crescent with its suggestion of vast and unmentionable antagonisms; her swift race through the moon-drenched countryside, all crepitant with night noises: the swimming in the wine-like lake: their isolation on the moor, which was expressedly hostile to them, as nature always is to lonely man: and this stark contest face to face, with their resentments heaped between them like a pile of naked swords—these things were so strange that her civilised self shrank back appalled. There entered into her the primitive woman who is the curse of all women: a creature of the most utter femaleness, useless, save for childbirth, with no strong brain to make her physical weakness a light accident, abjectly and corruptingly afraid of man. A squaw, she dared not strike her lord.

The illusion passed like a moment of faintness and left her enraged at having forgotten her superiority even for an instant. In the material world she had a thousand times been defeated into making prudent reservations and practising unnatural docilities. But in the world of thought she had maintained unfalteringly her masterfulness in spite of the strong yearning of her temperament towards voluptuous surrenders. That was her virtue. Its violation whipped her to action and she would have killed him at once, had not his moment come a second before hers. Sweating horribly, he had dropped his head forward on his chest: his eyes fell on her feet and marked the plebeian moulding of her ankle, which rose thickly over a crease of flesh from the heel to the calf. The woman was coarse in grain and pattern.

He had no instinct for honourable attack, so he found himself striking her in the stomach. She reeled from pain, not because his strength overcame hers. For the first time her eyes looked into his candidly open, unveiled by languor or lust: their hard brightness told him how she despised him for that unwarlike blow. He cried out as he realised that this was another of her despicable victories and that the whole burden of the crime now lay on him, for he had begun it. But the rage was stopped on his lips as her arms, flung wildly out as she fell backwards, caught him about the waist with abominable justness of eye and evil intention. So they fell body to body into the quarrelling waters.

The feathery confusion had looked so soft, yet it seemed the solid rock they struck. The breath shot out of him and suffocation warmly stuffed his ears and nose. Then the rock cleft and he was swallowed by a brawling blackness in which whirled a vortex that flung him again and again on a sharp thing that burned his shoulder. All about him fought the waters, and they cut his flesh like knives. His pain was past belief. Though God might be war, he desired peace in his time, and he yearned for another God—a child's God, an immense arm coming down from the hills and lifting him to a kindly bosom. Soon his body would burst for breath, his agony would smash in his breast bone. So great was his pain that his consciousness was strained to apprehend it, as a too tightly stretched canvas splits and rips.

Suddenly the air was sweet on his mouth. The starlight seemed as hearty as a cheer. The world was still there, the world in which he had lived, so he must be safe. His own weakness and loveableness induced enjoyable tears, and there was a delicious moment of abandonment to comfortable whining before he realised that the water would not kindly buoy him up for long, and that even now a hostile current clasped his waist. He braced his flaccid body against the sucking blackness and flung his head back so that the water should not bubble so hungrily against the cords of his throat. Above him the slime of the rock was sticky with moonbeams, and the leprous light brought to his mind a newspaper paragraph, read years ago, which told him that the dawn had discovered floating in some oily Mersey dock, under walls as infected with wet growth as this, a corpse whose blood-encrusted finger-tips were deeply cleft. On the instant his own finger-tips seemed hot with blood and deeply cleft from clawing at the impregnable rock. He screamed gaspingly and beat his hands through the strangling flood. Action, which he had always loathed and dreaded, had broken the hard mould of his self-possession, and the dry dust of his character was blown hither and thither by fear. But one sharp fragment of intelligence which survived this detrition of his personality perceived that a certain gleam on the rock about a foot above the water was not the cold putrescence of the slime, but certainly the hard and merry light of a moon-ray striking on solid metal. His left hand clutched upwards at it, and he swung from a rounded projection. It was, his touch told him, a leaden ring hanging obliquely from the rock, to which his memory could visualise precisely in some past drier time when Lisbech sent no flood to Whimsey, a waterman mooring a boat strewn with pale-bellied perch. And behind the stooping waterman he remembered a flight of narrow steps that led up a buttress to a stone shelf that ran through the cutting. Unquestionably he was safe. He swung in a happy rhythm from the ring, his limp body trailing like a caterpillar through the stream to the foot of the steps, while he gasped in strength. A part of him was in agony, for his arm was nearly dragged out of its socket and a part of him was embarrassed because his hysteria shook him with a deep rumbling chuckle that sounded as though he meditated on some unseemly joke; the whole was pervaded by a twilight atmosphere of unenthusiastic gratitude for his rescue, like the quietly cheerful tone of a Sunday evening sacred concert. After a minute's deep breathing he hauled himself up by the other hand and prepared to swing himself on to the steps.

But first, to shake off the wet worsted rags, once his socks, that now stuck uncomfortably between his toes, he splashed his feet outwards to midstream. A certain porpoise-like surface met his left foot. Fear dappled his face with goose flesh. Without turning his head he knew what it was. It was Evadne's fat flesh rising on each side of her deep-furrowed spine through the rent in her bathing dress.

Once more hatred marched through his soul like a king: compelling service by his godhead and, like all gods, a little hated for his harsh lieu[6] on his worshipper. He saw his wife as the curtain of flesh between him and celibacy, and solitude and all those delicate abstentions from life which his soul desired. He saw her as the invisible worm destroying the rose of the world with her dark secret love.[7] Now he knelt on the lowest stone step watching her wet seal-smooth head bobbing nearer on the waters. As her strong arms, covered with little dark points where her thick hairs were clotted with moisture, stretched out towards safety he bent forward and laid his hands on her head. He held her face under water. Scornfully he noticed the bubbles that rose to the surface from her

6. Discipline.
7. A reference to William Blake's poem *The Sick Rose*, in which a worm has entered a rose's "bed / of crimson joy; And his dark secret love / Does thy life destroy."

protesting mouth and nostrils, and the foam raised by her arms and her thick ankles. To the end the creature persisted in turmoil, in movement, in action. . . .

She dropped like a stone. His hands, with nothing to resist them, slapped the water foolishly and he nearly overbalanced forward into the stream. He rose to his feet very stiffly. "I must be a very strong man," he said, as he slowly climbed the steps. "I must be a very strong man," he repeated, a little louder, as with a hot and painful rigidity of the joints he stretched himself out at full length along the stone shelf. Weakness closed him in like a lead coffin. For a little time the wetness of his clothes persisted in being felt: then the sensation oozed out of him and his body fell out of knowledge. There was neither pain nor joy nor any other reckless ploughing of the brain by nerves. He knew unconsciousness, or rather the fullest consciousness he had ever known. For the world became nothingness, and nothingness which is free from the yeasty nuisance of matter and the ugliness of generation was the law of his being. He was absorbed into vacuity, the untamed substance of the universe, round which he conceived passion and thought to circle as straws caught up by the wind. He saw God and lived.

In Heaven a thousand years are a day. And this little corner of time in which he found happiness shrank to a nut-shell as he opened his eyes again. This peace was hardly printed on his heart, yet the brightness of the night was blurred by the dawn. With the grunting carefulness of a man drunk with fatigue, he crawled along the stone shelf to the iron bridge, where he stood with his back to the roaring sluice and rested. All things seemed different now and happier. Like most timid people he disliked the night, and the commonplace hand which the dawn laid on the scene seemed to him a sanctification. The dimmed moon sank to her setting behind the crags. The jewel lights of Lisbech railway station were weak, cheerful twinklings. A steaming bluish milk of morning mist had been spilt on the hard silver surface of the lake, and the reeds no longer stabbed it like little daggers, but seemed a feathery fringe, like the pampas grass in the front garden in Sumatra Crescent. The black crags became brownish, and the mist disguised the sternness of the moor. This weakening of effects was exactly what he had always thought the extinction of Evadne would bring the world. He smiled happily at the moon.

Yet he was moved to sudden angry speech. "If I had my time over again," he said, "I wouldn't touch her with the tongs." For the cold he had known all along he would catch had settled in his head, and his handkerchief was wet through.

He leaned over the bridge and looked along Lisbech and thought of Evadne. For the first time for many years he saw her image without spirits, and wondered without indignation why she had so often looked like the cat about to steal the cream. What was the cream? And did she ever steal it? Now he would never know. He thought of her very generously and sighed over the perversity of fate in letting so much comeliness.

"If she had married a butcher or a veterinary surgeon she might have been happy," he said, and shook his head at the glassy black water that slid under the bridge to that boiling sluice.

A gust of ague[8] reminded him that wet clothes clung to his fevered body and that he ought to change as quickly as possible, or expect to be laid up for weeks. He turned along the path that led back across the moor to the withered ash tree, and was learning the torture of bare feet on gravel when he cried out to himself: "I shall be hanged for killing my wife." It did not come as a trumpet-call, for he was one of those people who never quite hear what is said to them, and this deafishness extended in him to emotional things. It stole on him clamly, like a fog closing on a city. When he first felt hemmed in by this certainty he looked over his shoulder to the crags, remembering

8. Fever.

tales of how Jacobite fugitives had hidden on the moors for many weeks. There lay at least another day of freedom. But he was the kind of man who always goes home. He stumbled on, not very unhappy, except for his feet. Like many people of weak temperament he did not fear death. Indeed, it had a peculiar appeal to him; for while it was important, exciting, it did not, like most important and exciting things try to create action. He allowed his imagination the vanity of painting pictures. He saw himself standing in their bedroom, plotting this last event, with the white sheet and the high lights of the mahogany wardrobe shining ghostly at him through the darkness. He saw himself raising a thin hand to the gas bracket and turning on the tap. He saw himself staggering to their bed while death crept in at his nostrils. He saw his corpse lying in full daylight, and for the first time knew himself certainly, unquestionably dignified.

He threw back his chest in pride: but at that moment the path stopped and he found himself staggering down the mound of heatherland and boulders with bleeding feet. Always he had suffered from sore feet, which had not exactly disgusted but, worse still, disappointed Evadne. A certain wistfulness she had always evinced when she found herself the superior animal had enraged and humiliated him many times. He felt that sting him now, and flung himself down the mound cursing. When he stumbled up to the withered ash tree he hated her so much that it seemed as though she were alive again, and a sharp wind blowing down from the moor terrified him like her touch.

He rested there. Leaning against the stripped grey trunk, he smiled up at the sky, which was now so touched to ineffectiveness by the dawn that it looked like a tent of faded silk. There was the peace of weakness in him, which he took to be spiritual, because it had no apparent physical justification: but he lost it as his dripping clothes chilled his tired flesh. His discomfort reminded him that the phantasmic night was passing from him. Daylight threatened him: the daylight in which for so many years he had worked in the solicitor's office and been snubbed and ignored. "'The garish day,'" he murmured disgustedly, quoting the blasphemy of some hymn writer. He wanted his death to happen in this phantasmic night.

So he limped his way along the road. The birds had not yet begun to sing, but the rustling noises of the night had ceased. The silent highway was consecrated to his proud progress. He staggered happily like a tired child returning from a lovely birthday walk: his death in the little bedroom, which for the first time he would have to himself, was a culminating treat to be gloated over like the promise of a favourite pudding for supper. As he walked he brooded dozingly on large and swelling thoughts. Like all people of weak passions and enterprise he loved to think of Napoleon, and in the shadow of the great asylum wall he strutted a few steps of his advance from murder to suicide, with arms crossed on his breast and thin legs trying to strut massively. He was so happy. He wished that a military band went before him, and pretended that the high hedges were solemn lines of men, stricken in awe to silence as their king rode out to some nobly self-chosen doom. Vast he seemed to himself, and magnificent like music, and solemn like the Sphinx. He had saved the earth from corruption by killing Evadne, for whom he now felt the unremorseful pity a conqueror might bestow on a devastated empire. He might have grieved that his victory brought him death, but with immense pride he found that the occasion was exactly described by a text. "He saved others, Himself He could not save."[9] He had missed the stile in the field above Sumatra Crescent and had to go back and hunt for it in the hedge. So quickly had his satisfaction borne him home.

9. These are the words of the priests and elders mocking Jesus at his crucifixion; Matthew 27.42.

The field had the fantastic air that jerry-builders[1] give to land poised on the knife-edge of town and country, so that he walked in romance to his very door. The unmarred grass sloped to a stone-hedge of towers of loose brick, trenches and mounds of shining clay, and the fine intentful spires of the scaffolding round the last unfinished house. And he looked down on Petrick. Though to the actual eye it was but a confusion of dark distances through the twilight, a breaking of velvety perspectives, he saw more intensely than ever before its squalid walls and squalid homes where mean men and mean women enlaced their unwholesome lives. Yet he did not shrink from entering for his great experience: as Christ did not shrink from being born in a stable. He swaggered with humility over the trodden mud of the field and the new white flags of Sumatra Crescent. Down the road before him there passed a dim figure, who paused at each lamp post and raised a long wand to behead the yellow gas-flowers that were now wilting before the dawn: a ghostly herald preparing the world to be his deathbed. The Crescent curved in quiet darkness, save for one house, where blazed a gas-lit room with undrawn blinds. The brightness had the startling quality of a scream. He looked in almost anxiously as he passed, and met the blank eyes of a man in evening clothes who stood by the window shaking a medicine. His face was like a wax mask softened by heat: the features were blurred with the suffering which comes from the spectacle of suffering. His eyes lay unshiftingly on George's face as he went by and he went on shaking the bottle. It seemed as though he would never stop.

In the hour of his grandeur George was not forgetful of the griefs of the little human people, but interceded with God for the sake of this stranger. Everything was beautiful, beautiful, beautiful.

His own little house looked solemn as a temple. He leaned against the lamppost at the gate and stared at its empty windows and neat bricks. The disorder of the shattered pane of glass could be overlooked by considering a sign that this house was a holy place: like the Passover blood on the lintel. The propriety of the evenly drawn blind pleased him enormously. He had always known that this was how the great tragic things of the world had accomplished themselves: quietly. Evadne's raging activity belonged to trivial or annoying things like spring-cleaning or thunderstorms. Well, the house belonged to him now. He opened the gate and went up the asphalt path, sourly noticing that Evadne had as usual left out the lawn-mower, though it might very easily have rained, with the wind coming up as it was. A stray cat that had been sleeping in the tuft of pampas grass in the middle of the lawn was roused by his coming, and fled insolently close to his legs. He hated all wild homeless things, and bent for a stone to throw at it. But instead his fingers touched a slug, which reminded him of the feeling of Evadne's flesh through the slit in her bathing dress. And suddenly the garden was possessed by her presence: she seemed to amble there as she had so often done, sowing seeds unwisely and tormenting the last days of an ailing geranium by insane transplantation, exclaiming absurdly over such mere weeds as morning glory. He caught the very clucking of her voice. . . . The front door opened at his touch.

The little lobby with its closed doors seemed stuffed with expectant silence. He realised that he had come to the theatre of his great adventure. Then panic seized him. Because this was the home where he and she had lived together so horribly he doubted whether he could do this splendid momentous thing, for here he had always been a poor thing with the habit of failure. His heart beat in him more quickly than his raw feet could pad up the oil-clothed stairs. Behind the deal door at the end of the

1. Low-wage, slipshod workers.

passage was death. Nothingness! It would escape him, even the idea of it would escape him if he did not go to it at once. When he burst at last into its presence he felt so victorious that he sank back against the door waiting for death to come to him without turning on the gas. He was so happy. His death was coming true.

But Evadne lay on his deathbed. She slept there soundly, with her head flung back on the pillows so that her eyes and brow seemed small in shadow, and her mouth and jaw huge above her thick throat in the light. Her wet hair straggled across the pillow on to a broken cane chair covered with her tumbled clothes. Her breast, silvered with sweat, shone in the ray of the street lamp that had always disturbed their nights. The counterpane rose enormously over her hips in rolls of glazed linen. Out of mere innocent sleep her sensuality was distilling a most drunken pleasure.

Not for one moment did he think this a phantasmic appearance. Evadne was not the sort of woman to have a ghost.

Still leaning against the door, he tried to think it all out: but his thoughts came brokenly, because the dawnlight flowing in at the window confused him by its pale glare and that lax figure on the bed held his attention. It must have been that when he laid his murderous hands on her head she had simply dropped below the surface and swum a few strokes under water as any expert swimmer can. Probably he had never even put her into danger, for she was a great lusty creature and the weir was a little place. He had imagined the wonder and peril of the battle as he had imagined his victory. He sneezed exhaustingly, and from his physical distress realised how absurd it was ever to have thought that he had killed her. Bodies like his do not kill bodies like hers.

Now his soul was naked and lonely as though the walls of his body had fallen in at death, and the grossness of Evadne's sleep made him suffer more unlovely a destitution than any old beggarwoman squatting by the roadside in the rain. He had thought he had had what every man most desires: one night of power over a woman for the business of murder or love. But it had been a lie. Nothing beautiful had ever happened to him. He would have wept, but the hatred he had learnt on the moors obstructed all tears in his throat. At least this night had given him passion enough to put an end to it all.

Quietly he went to the window and drew down the sash. There was no fireplace, so that sealed the room. Then he crept over to the gas bracket and raised his thin hand, as he had imagined in his hour of vain glory by the lake.

He had forgotten Evadne's thrifty habit of turning off the gas at the main to prevent leakage when she went to bed.

He was beaten. He undressed and got into bed: as he had done every night for ten years, and as he would do every night until he died. Still sleeping, Evadne caressed him with warm arms.

Wilfred Owen
1893–1918

The poet C. Day Lewis wrote that Wilfred Owen's poems were "certainly the finest written by any English poet of the First War." In his small body of poems Owen manages to combine his friend Siegfried Sassoon's outrage at the horror of the war with a formal and technical skill reminiscent of his idols Keats and Shelley. Sassoon himself characterized their differences as poets this way: "My trench-sketches were like rockets, sent up to illuminate the darkness. . . . It was Owen who revealed how, out of realistic horror and scorn, poetry might be made."

Owen grew up on the Welsh border in Shropshire, the landscape A. E. Housman was to celebrate in his poetry. After finishing technical school, Owen spent two years in training with an evangelical Church of England vicar, trying to decide whether to pursue formal training as a clergyman. As a result of his experiences, Owen became dissatisfied with the institutional church's response to the poverty and suffering of England's least privileged citizens. In October 1915 he enlisted with the Artists' Rifles, and on 29 December 1916, he left for France as a lieutenant with the Lancashire Fusiliers.

Owen quickly became disillusioned with the war; as a result of almost unimaginable privations, which included being blown into the air while he slept in a foxhole, Owen suffered a breakdown, and was sent to the Craiglockhart War Hospital in Edinburgh. Owen composed nearly all of his poetry in the fourteen months of his rehabilitation, between August 1917 and September 1918; though hard to imagine, it is quite possible that if he had not been sent back to Great Britain to recover from his "shell shock," we might now know nothing of his poetry. While at Craiglockhart he met Sassoon and found his true voice and mode; he published his first poems on war themes anonymously in the hospital's magazine, which he edited. In September 1918 Owen returned to the battlefields of France; he was killed in action at Sambre Canal on 4 November, 1918, one week before the Armistice. Dylan Thomas called Owen "one of the four most profound influences upon the poets who came after him"—the others being Hopkins, Yeats, and Eliot.

Anthem for Doomed Youth

What passing-bells for these who die as cattle?
    Only the monstrous anger of the guns.
    Only the stuttering rifles' rapid rattle
Can patter out their hasty orisons.° *prayers*
No mockeries now for them; no prayers nor bells,
    Nor any voice of mourning save the choirs,–
The shrill, demented choirs of wailing shells;
    And bugles calling for them from sad shires.

What candles may be held to speed them all?
    Not in the hands of boys, but in their eyes
Shall shine the holy glimmers of good-byes.
    The pallor of girls' brows shall be their pall;[1]
Their flowers the tenderness of patient minds,
And each slow dusk a drawing-down of blinds.

Strange Meeting

It seemed that out of battle I escaped
Down some profound dull tunnel, long since scooped
Through granites which titanic wars had groined.° *joined together*
Yet also there encumbered sleepers groaned,
Too fast in thought or death to be bestirred.
Then, as I probed them, one sprang up, and stared
With piteous recognition in fixed eyes,
Lifting distressful hands as if to bless.
And by his smile, I knew that sullen hall,

1. The cloth draped over a coffin.

By his dead smile I knew we stood in Hell.
With a thousand pains that vision's face was grained;
Yet no blood reached there from the upper ground,
And no guns thumped, or down the flues made moan.
"Strange friend," I said, "here is no cause to mourn."
"None," said that other, "save the undone years,
The hopelessness. Whatever hope is yours,
Was my life also; I went hunting wild
After the wildest beauty in the world,
Which lies not calm in eyes, or braided hair,
But mocks the steady running of the hour,
And if it grieves, grieves richlier than here.
For of my glee might many men have laughed,
And of my weeping something had been left,
Which must die now. I mean the truth untold,
The pity of war, the pity war distilled.
Now men will go content with what we spoiled,
Or, discontent, boil bloody, and be spilled.
They will be swift with swiftness of the tigress.
None will break ranks, though nations trek from progress.
Courage was mine, and I had mystery,
Wisdom was mine, and I had mastery:
To miss the march of this retreating world
Into vain citadels that are not walled.
Then, when much blood had clogged their chariot-wheels,
I would go up and wash them from sweet wells,
Even with truths that lie too deep for taint.
I would have poured my spirit without stint
But not through wounds; not on the cess of war.
Foreheads of men have bled where no wounds were.
I am the enemy you killed, my friend.
I knew you in this dark: for so you frowned
Yesterday through me as you jabbed and killed.
I parried; but my hands were loath and cold.
Let us sleep now. . . . "

Disabled

He sat in a wheeled chair, waiting for dark,
And shivered in his ghastly suit of grey,
Legless, sewn short at elbow. Through the park
Voices of boys rang saddening like a hymn,
Voices of play and pleasure after day,
Till gathering sleep had mothered them from him.

About this time Town used to swing so gay
When glow-lamps budded in the light blue trees,
And girls glanced lovelier as the air grew dim,—
In the old times, before he threw away his knees.
Now he will never feel again how slim

Girls' waists are, or how warm their subtle hands.
All of them touch him like some queer disease.

There was an artist silly for his face,
For it was younger than his youth, last year.
Now, he is old; his back will never brace;
He's lost his colour very far from here,
Poured it down shell-holes till the veins ran dry,
And half his lifetime lapsed in the hot race
And leap of purple spurted from his thigh.

One time he liked a blood-smear down his leg,
After the matches, carried shoulder-high.
It was after football, when he'd drunk a peg,[1]
He thought he'd better join.—He wonders why.
Someone had said he'd look a god in kilts,
That's why; and maybe, too, to please his Meg,
Aye, that was it, to please the giddy jilts° *girls or women*
He asked to join. He didn't have to beg;
Smiling they wrote his lie: aged nineteen years.

Germans he scarcely thought of; all their guilt,
And Austria's, did not move him. And no fears
Of Fear came yet. He thought of jewelled hilts
For daggers in plaid socks; of smart salutes;
And care of arms; and leave; and pay arrears;
Esprit de corps;[2] and hints for young recruits.
And soon, he was drafted out with drums and cheers.
Some cheered him home, but not as crowds cheer Goal.
Only a solemn man who brought him fruits
Thanked him; and then enquired about his soul.

Now, he will spend a few sick years in institutes,
And do what things the rules consider wise,
And take whatever pity they may dole.
Tonight he noticed how the women's eyes
Passed from him to the strong men that were whole.
How cold and late it is! Why don't they come
And put him into bed? Why don't they come?

Dulce Et Decorum Est[1]

Bent double, like old beggars under sacks,
Knock-kneed, coughing like hags, we cursed through sludge,
Till on the haunting flares we turned our backs
And towards our distant rest began to trudge.
Men marched asleep. Many had lost their boots
But limped on, blood-shod. All went lame; all blind;

1. Alcoholic drink, such as brandy and soda.
2. Spirit of the group (French); camaraderie.
1. From the *Odes* of the Roman satirist Horace (65–8 B.C.E.): Dulce et decorum est pro patria mori [sweet and fitting it is to die for your fatherland].

Drunk with fatigue; deaf even to the hoots
Of tired, outstripped Five-Nines[2] that dropped behind.

Gas! Gas! Quick, boys!—An ecstasy of fumbling,
Fitting the clumsy helmets just in time;
But someone still was yelling out and stumbling
And flound'ring like a man in fire or lime[3] . . .
Dim, through the misty panes and thick green light,
As under a green sea, I saw him drowning.

In all my dreams, before my helpless sight,
He plunges at me, guttering, choking, drowning.

If in some smothering dreams you too could pace
Behind the wagon that we flung him in,
And watch the white eyes writhing in his face,
His hanging face, like a devil's sick of sin;
If you could hear, at every jolt, the blood
Come gargling from the froth-corrupted lungs,
Obscene as cancer, bitter as the cud
Of vile, incurable sores on innocent tongues,—
My friend, you would not tell with such high zest
To children ardent for some desperate glory,
The old Lie: Dulce et decorum est
Pro patria mori.

May Wedderburn Cannan[1]

Lamplight

We planned to shake the world together, you and I
Being young, and very wise;
Now in the light of the green shaded lamp
Almost I see your eyes
Light with the old gay laughter; you and I
Dreamed greatly of an Empire in those days,
Setting our feet upon laborious ways,
And all you asked of fame
Was crossed swords in the Army List,
My Dear, against your name.

We planned a great Empire together, you and I,
Bound only by the sea;
Now in the quiet of a chill Winter's night
Your voice comes hushed to me

2. Artillery shells used by the Germans.

3. Calcium oxide, a powerfully caustic alkali used, among other purposes, for cleaning the flesh off the bones of corpses.

1. (1893–1973), poet, involved in espionage for the British government during the war.

Full of forgotten memories: you and I
Dreamed great dreams of our future in those days,
Setting our feet on undiscovered ways,
And all I asked of fame
A scarlet cross on my breast, my Dear,
For the swords by your name.

We shall never shake the world together, you and I,
For you gave your life away;
And I think my heart was broken by the war,
Since on a summer day
You took the road we never spoke of: you and I
Dreamed greatly of an Empire in those days;
You set your feet upon the Western ways
And have no need of fame—
There's a scarlet cross on my breast, my Dear,
And a torn cross with your name.

December 1916

Rouen
26 April–25 May 1915

Early morning over Rouen, hopeful, high, courageous morning,
And the laughter of adventure and the steepness of the stair,
And the dawn across the river, and the wind across the bridges,
And the empty littered station and the tired people there.

Can you recall those mornings and the hurry of awakening,
And the long-forgotten wonder if we should miss the way,
And the unfamiliar faces, and the coming of provisions,
And the freshness and the glory of the labour of the day?

Hot noontide over Rouen, and the sun upon the city,
Sun and dust unceasing, and the glare of cloudless skies,
And the voices of the Indians and the endless stream of soldiers,
And the clicking of the tatties, and the buzzing of the flies.

Can you recall those noontides and the reek of steam and coffee,
Heavy-laden noontides with the evening's peace to win,
And the little piles of Woodbines, and the sticky soda bottles,
And the crushes in the "Parlour," and the letters coming in?

Quiet night-time over Rouen, and the station full of soldiers,
All the youth and pride of England from the ends of all the earth;
And the rifles piled together, and the creaking of the sword-belts,
And the faces bent above them, and the gay, heart-breaking mirth.

Can I forget the passage from the cool white-bedded Aid Post
Past the long sun-blistered coaches of the khaki Red Cross train
To the truck train full of wounded, and the weariness and laughter,
And "Good-bye, and thank you, Sister," and the empty yards again?

Can you recall the parcels that we made them for the railroad,
Crammed and bulging parcels held together by their string,
And the voices of the sergeants who called the Drafts together,
And the agony and splendour when they stood to save the King?

Can you forget their passing, the cheering and the waving,
The little group of people at the doorway of the shed,
The sudden awful silence when the last train swung to darkness,
And the lonely desolation, and the mocking stars o'erhead?

Can you recall the midnights, and the footsteps of night watchers,
Men who came from darkness and went back to dark again,
And the shadows on the rail-lines and the all-inglorious labour,
And the promise of the daylight firing blue the window-pane?

Can you recall the passing through the kitchen door to morning,
Morning very still and solemn breaking slowly on the town,
And the early coastways engines that had met the ships at daybreak,
And the Drafts just out from England, and the day shift coming down?

Can you forget returning slowly, stumbling on the cobbles,
And the white-decked Red Cross barges dropping seawards for the tide,
And the search for English papers, and the blessed cool of water,
And the peace of half-closed shutters that shut out the world outside?

Can I forget the evenings and the sunsets on the island,
And the tall black ships at anchor far below our balcony,
And the distant call of bugles, and the white wine in the glasses,
And the long line of the street lamps, stretching Eastwards to the sea?

. . . When the world slips slow to darkness, when the office fire burns lower,
My heart goes out to Rouen, Rouen all the world away;
When other men remember I remember our Adventure
And the trains that go from Rouen at the ending of the day.

1916

END OF PERSPECTIVES: THE GREAT WAR: CONFRONTING THE MODERN

Speeches on Irish Independence

Through the eight centuries of British rule in Ireland, Irish nationalist sentiment remained strong, though it was often forced underground. Ireland had gained a hundred members in the British Parliament when the United Kingdom was formed in 1801, yet on crucial issues they were regularly outvoted by the English majority. As Ireland gradually recovered from the effects of the famine of the 1840s, nationalist agitation increased, only inflamed by English attempts at repression. In 1870 the Home Rule League was formed, to press for legislative independence. In 1877 the League elected as its parliamentary leader a bold young nationalist named Charles Stewart Parnell (1846–1891), who came to dominate the movement for the ensuing dozen years; his tragic fall from power in 1889 shocked both his supporters and his detractors. For Yeats and Joyce especially, Parnell was proof of their suspicion that, as Joyce's character Stephen Dedalus was to put it, Ireland is "the old sow that eats her farrow."

And though they sleep in dungeons deep,
Or flee, outlawed and banned,
We love them yet, we can't forget
The felons of our land

Jack B. Yeats, *The Felons of Our Land*, 1910. Brother of the poet William Butler Yeats and the son of the portrait painter John Butler Yeats, Jack Yeats (1871–1957) was Ireland's major modern artist of the first half of the twentieth century, beginning in the tumultuous revolutionary period prior to and culminating in the Easter Rising of 1916 and the Civil War that followed. This engraving is unlike the later vivid, modernist style of oil painting Jack Yeats was famous for, but it expresses the urgency of the political art of the period of Padraic Pearse and other orators included in this section of the anthology. The title of the engraving is deeply ironic as well as political, since ordinary Irish people who worked for independence were described as enemies of the British empire and jailed as felons.

Parnell assembled a powerful coalition in Parliament, bringing other business to a halt until Irish issues were considered. After years of negotiation, the Liberal prime minister Gladstone agreed to introduce a Home Rule bill in 1886. The bill was defeated, but passage was believed to be just a matter of time. Parnell's fortunes were quickly to turn, however. On Christmas Eve, 1889, Captain William O'Shea, a moderate Home Rule member, brought a divorce action against his wife Katherine ("Kitty"), and named Parnell as respondent. Parnell had been conducting an affair with Kitty O'Shea since 1880; some suggest that Captain O'Shea had long known this, and brought the action at this point for political gain. As a result of the divorce, the Irish parliamentary party removed Parnell from the leadership, and the Catholic hierarchy in Ireland turned against him, declaring him unfit for public office; a large portion of the Irish people abandoned him as well. Others, especially in Dublin, remained fiercely loyal to Parnell; but he was a broken man, and died just a few months after his marriage to Kitty O'Shea in June 1891.

The ensuing years were marked by token reforms and by division in Ireland, between ardent nationalists, moderate reformers, and Protestants who opposed weakened ties to England. The Irish republic can be dated from the Easter Rising in 1916 which, though unsuccessful, started the movement toward Irish independence which resulted six years later in the founding of the Irish Free State. After the failure of a third Home Rule bill in 1914, the Irish Republican Brotherhood stepped up their activities and began planning for a large-scale revolutionary uprising. In the spring of 1916 the Irish statesman Sir Roger Casement traveled to Germany to raise support for the planned uprising, but he managed only to obtain some obsolete firearms and was arrested on his return to Ireland. Three days later, on Easter Monday, 24 April, a small force of about a thousand rebels seized the General Post Office and other city buildings, and declared a provisional Republican government, in a stirring proclamation read on the Post Office steps by Padraic Pearse, the planned president. W. B. Yeats vividly evokes that historical moment, and its transformation into nationalist mythology, in his poem *Easter 1916*. Street fighting continued for about a week, until Pearse and other leaders were forced to surrender. The execution of these leaders helped to rally support for the Republican cause among the Irish people and contributed to the founding of the Irish Republican Army (IRA) in 1919. Guided by the brilliant tactician Michael Collins, the IRA harrassed British troops and kept them from crushing the nationalist resistance.

As a result of this ongoing state of virtual civil war, the British government was ultimately forced to pass the Government of Ireland Act in 1920, dividing Ireland into two self-governing areas, Northern Ireland and Southern Ireland. Historically, the south has been primarily Catholic (currently more than 90 percent), and the north Protestant (about 65 percent); all twentieth-century political divisions of Ireland have been made with the awareness of these religious and cultural differences. At the close of 1921, the Anglo-Irish Treaty laid the groundwork for Ireland's twenty-six southern counties to establish an Irish Free State, the Republic of Ireland; the six counties of Northern Ireland would retain their status as a member of the United Kingdom. Michael Collins, who negotiated the 1921 treaty, was ambushed and killed in 1922 by opponents of Irish partition. This division of the island remains in effect today, although recurrent terrorist violence of the IRA has been directed at winning independence as well for Northern Ireland. Thus while Ireland and England are still somewhat uneasy neighbors, 1922 marks the incomplete realization of a 750-year-old dream—in the words of a popular ballad, the dream that Ireland might be "a nation once again."

For additional speeches on Irish independence, go to *The Longman Anthology of British Literature* Web site at www.myliteraturekit.com.

Charles Stewart Parnell
At Limerick

I firmly believe that, bad as are the prospects of this country, out of that we will obtain good for Ireland. * * * It is the duty of the Irish tenant farmers to combine amongst themselves and ask for a reduction of rent, and if they get no reduction where a reduction is necessary, then I say that it is the duty of the tenant to pay no rent until he gets it. And if they combined in that way, if they stood together, and if being refused a reasonable and just reduction, they kept a firm grip of their homesteads, I can tell them that no power on earth could prevail against the hundreds of thousands of the tenant farmers of this country. Do not fear. You are not to be exterminated as you were in 1847,[1] and take my word for it it will not be attempted. You should ask for concessions that are just. Ask for them in a proper manner, and good landlords will give these conditions. But for the men who had always shown themselves regardless of right and justice in their dealings with these questions, I say it is necessary for you to maintain a firm and determined attitude. If you maintain that attitude victory must be yours. If when a farm was tenantless, owing to any cause, you refuse to take it, and the present most foolish competition amongst farmers came to an end, as undoubtedly it now must, these men who are forgetful of reason and of

1. After the failure of the potato crops in 1845 and 1846, and English refusal to suspend rent payments of Irish tenant farmers, 1847 was perhaps the year of most extreme suffering and starvation. During the years of the Potato Famine, the Irish population plummeted, through starvation, disease, and emigration, from about 8.5 million in 1845 to 6.6 million in 1851. This national tragedy forms the backdrop for Parnell's remarks (31 August 1879) to the tenant farmers of Limerick, who seemed to be facing an agricultural crisis of similar magnitude.

common sense must come to reconsider their position. I believe that the land of a country ought to be owned by the people of the country. And I think we should centre our exertions upon attaining that end. * * * When we have the people of this country prosperous, self-reliant, and confident of the future, we will have an Irish nation which will be able to hold its own amongst the nations of the world. We will have a country which will be able to speak with the enemy in the gate—we will have a people who will understand their rights, and, knowing those rights, will be resolved to maintain them. We must all have this without injustice to any individual.

Before the House of Commons[1]

* * * I can assure the House that it is not my belief that anything I can say, or wish to say at this time, will have the slightest effect on the public opinion of the House, or upon the public opinion of this country. I have been accustomed during my political life to rely upon the public opinion of those whom I have desired to help, and with whose aid I have worked for the cause of prosperity and freedom in Ireland: and the utmost that I desire to do in the very few words which I shall address to this House, is to make my position clear to the Irish people at home and abroad from the unjust aspersions which have been cast upon me by a man[2] who ought to be ashamed to devote his high ability to the task of traducing[3] them. I don't wish to reply to the questions of the right hon. gentleman. I consider he has no right to question me, standing as he does in a position very little better than an informer with regard to the secrets of the men with whom he was associated, and he has not even the pretext of that remarkable informer whose proceedings we have lately heard of.[4] He had not even the pretext of that miserable man that he was attempting to save his own life. No, sir: other motives of less importance seem to have weighed with the right hon. gentleman in the extraordinary course which he has adopted on the present occasion of going out of his way to collect together a series of extracts, perhaps nine or ten in number, out of a number of speeches—many hundreds and thousands—delivered during the Land League movement[5] by other people and not by me, upon which to found an accusation against me for what has been said and done by others. * * * The right hon. gentleman has asked me to defend myself. Sir, I have nothing to defend myself for. The right hon. gentleman has confessed that he attempted to obtain a declaration or public promise from me which would have the effect of discrediting me with the Irish people. He has admitted that he failed in that attempt, and failing in that attempt, he lost his own reputation. He boasted last night that he had deposed me from some imaginary position which he was pleased to assign to me; but, at least, I have this consolation—that he also deposed himself. * * * I have taken very little part in Irish politics since my release from Kilmainham.[6] I expressed my reason for that upon the passing of the Crimes Act.[7] I said that, in my judgment, the Crimes Act would result in such a state of affairs that between the Government and secret societies it would be impossible for constitutional agitation to exist in Ireland. I believe so still.

1. Delivered 23 February 1883.
2. William Edward Forster, chief secretary for Ireland, had attacked Parnell at the beginning of the 1883 session.
3. Slandering.
4. James Carcy (1845–1883), one of the Invincibles (an Irish nationalist group who killed the Irish chief secretary and undersecretary in Dublin's Phoenix Park in May 1882). After his arrest, he turned informer but was killed by another of the Invincibles while the British government attempted to transport him to safety in South Africa.
5. A division of the Home Rule Confederation, founded in 1879 by Michael Davitt and led by Parnell, that fought for the tenant farmers' security of tenure, fair rents on property, and the freedom to sell their property.
6. A jail in Dublin where Parnell was held between October 1881 and May 1882, after a series of popular speeches to the Irish people couched in violent language.
7. A coercion act against Irish agitation passed in 1881.

* * * It would have been far better if you were going to pass an Act of this kind and to administer an Act of this kind as you are going to administer it, and as you are obliged to administer it—up to the hilt—that it should be done by the seasoned politician who is now in disgrace. Call him back to his post! Send him to help Lord Spencer[8] in his congenial work of the gallows in Ireland! Send him to look after the Secret Inquisitions of Dublin Castle! Send him to superintend the payment of blood money! Send him to distribute the taxes which an unfortunate and starving peasantry have to pay for crimes not committed by them! All this would be congenial work. We invite you to man your ranks, and send your ablest and best men. Push forward the task of misgoverning Ireland! For my part I am confident as to the future of Ireland. Although her horizon may appear at this moment clouded, I believe that our people will survive the present oppression as we have survived many and worse ones. And although our progress may be slow it will be sure, and the time will come when this House and the people of this country will admit once again that they have been mistaken; that they have been deceived by those who ought to be ashamed of deceiving them; that they have been led astray as to the method of governing a noble, a generous, and an impulsive people; that they will reject their present leaders who are conducting them into the terrible course, which, I am sorry to say, the Government appears to be determined to enter; that they will reject these guides and leaders with just as much determination as they rejected the services of the right hon. gentleman the member of Bradford.[9]

At Portsmouth, After the Defeat of Mr. Gladstone's Home Rule Bill[1]

It is, I believe, about the first time I have had the honour of addressing a mainly English audience. And I have been induced to do so now because I rely greatly upon the spirit of fair play among the English masses, and because the issues for my country are so great and so vital at the present moment—the issues which underlie this present struggle—that the Irishman who remains silent when it might be possible to do something to help his country would be more unworthy than tongue could describe. * * * I have, in my career as a member of Parliament, never wittingly injured the cause of the English working man. I have done something to show my sympathy for the masses of the people of this country. * * * Some years ago it was my privilege to strike with English members a successful blow in favour of the abolition of flogging in the army and navy. We were met then by the very same arguments as we are met with today, and from the same class of persons. It was said by the late Lord Beaconsfield[2] that the integrity of the British Empire would be endangered if flogging were abolished, and he called a great meeting at one of the Ministerial offices in London, a great meeting of his supporters both in the Lords and Commons, for the purpose of exhorting them to stand shoulder to shoulder in defence of the British Empire against the abolition of flogging in the army. * * * I have shown you that in some respects the Irish settlement proposed by Mr Gladstone does not give a Parliament, a Legislature with the powers possessed by Grattan's Parliament;[3] but I have shown you on the other hand that as regards our own exclusively domestic business it gives larger powers, more important powers, more valuable powers for Ireland itself than was possessed by Grattan's, and therefore we think that this settlement proposed by Mr

8. John Poyntz, fifth Earl of Spencer; Lord Lieutenant of Ireland for a second term (1882–1885).
9. I.e., William Edward Forster.
1. The first Home Rule bill, which would have given Ireland a "wide measure of autonomy"; Parnell gave this speech (25 June 1886), shortly after the bill's defeat.
2. Benjamin Disraeli, Prime Minister of England in 1868, and from 1874 to 1880.
3. Henry Grattan was leader of the movement that gave Ireland legislative independence in 1782.

Gladstone will prove a more durable settlement than the restitution of the Grattan Parliament or the Repeal of the Union would prove. * * * Imperial unity does not require or necessitate unity of Parliaments. Will you carry that away with you and remember it, because it is the keystone of our whole proceedings. * * * I should say that Ireland would justly deserve to lose her privilege if she passed laws oppressive of the minority. * * * So far as coercion was concerned it has not brought you any nearer to the end of the Irish question. * * * One great fault in English coercion has been that no matter what your intentions have been when you have commenced coercion, you have never discriminated between political agitators and breakers of the law. * * * Lord Carnarvon[4] will not deny that he was as strong a Home Ruler as I was last August, and that when he went over to Ireland he became stronger and stronger every day he lived in that country. There is another thing he has not denied: he has not denied that he sought an interview with me in order to speak to me and consult with me about a Constitution for Ireland.[5] * * * Untold is the guilt of that man who, for party purposes, does not take advantage of the spirit which is abroad amongst the English to put the hand of the Irish into that of the English to close the strife of centuries—a strife that has been of no advantage to the people of either country; a strife that has only been for the benefit of the money-grabbing landlords; a strife that has impeded popular progress in England as well as in Ireland, and that must continue to impede it; a strife which is fanned for the purpose of cheating you out of your rights, and to divert the energies of the newly enfranchised masses of Great Britain from the redress of their grievances to the odious task of oppressing and keeping down the small sister country.

In Committee Room No. 15[1]

The men whose ability is now so conspicuously exercised as that of Mr. Healy and Mr. Sexton, will have to bear their responsibility for this. * * * Why did you encourage me to come forward and maintain my leadership in the face of the world if you were not going to stand by me? * * * I want to ask you before you vote my deposition to be sure you are getting value for it. * * * I know what Mr. Gladstone will do for you; I know what Mr. Morley[2] will do for you; and I know there is not a single one of the lot to be trusted unless you trust yourselves. Be to your own selves true and hence it follows, as the day the night, thou can'st not be false to any man.[3] * * * If I am to leave you tonight I should like to leave you in security. I should like, and it is not an unfair thing for me to ask, that I should come within sight of the Promised Land; that I should come with you, having come so far, if not to the end of this course, that I should at least come with you as far as you will allow and permit me to come with you, at least until it is absolutely sure that Ireland and I can go no further.

4. Lord lieutenant of Ireland from 1885 to 1886 and member of the British Parliament.

5. Parnell and Carnarvon met on 1 August 1885, and discussed Irish Home Rule and an Irish Constitution.

1. Office of Parnell's party in Dublin. Parnell spoke to the party leadership on 6 December 1890 following a motion by Timothy Healy and Thomas Sexton to depose him as their leader in Parliament. Healy had been a Member of Parliament allied with Parnell's legislative agenda; Sexton had also supported Parnell in Parliament. In the wake of Parnell's involvement with the O'Shea divorce case, however, both abandoned Parnell and withdrew their support for his policies—an act of treachery which inspired James Joyce's first literary production, at age 8, a poem titled *Et Tu, Healy?* This scene, imaginatively recreated, also provides the backdrop to Joyce's story *Ivy Day in the Committee Room*.

2. John Morley (1838–1923), twice Chief Secretary for Ireland.

3. A paraphrase of lines from Polonius's speech in *Hamlet*, 1.3.78–80.

Proclamation of the Irish Republic

Poblacht na h Eireann[1]

THE PROVISIONAL GOVERNMENT OF THE IRISH REPUBLIC
TO THE
PEOPLE OF IRELAND

Irishmen and Irishwomen:

In the name of God and of the dead generations from which she receives her old tradition of nationhood, Ireland, through us, summons her children to her flag and strikes for her freedom.

Having organised and trained her manhood through her secret revolutionary organisation, the Irish Republican Brotherhood, and through her open military organisations, the Irish Volunteers and the Irish Citizen Army, having patiently perfected her discipline, having resolutely waited for the right moment to reveal itself, she now seizes that moment, and, supported by her exiled children in America and by gallant allies in Europe, but relying in the first on her own strength, she strikes in full confidence of victory.

We declare the right of the people of Ireland to the ownership of Ireland, and to the unfettered control of Irish destinies, to be sovereign and indefeasible. The long usurpation of that right by a foreign people and government has not extinguished the right, nor can it ever be extinguished except by the destruction of the Irish people. In every generation the Irish have asserted their right to National freedom and sovereignty; six times during the past three hundred years they have asserted it in arms. Standing on that fundamental right and again asserting it in arms in the face of the world, we hereby proclaim the Irish Republic as a Sovereign Independent State, and we pledge our lives and the lives of our comrades-in-arms to the cause of its freedom, of its welfare, and of its exaltation among the nations.

The Irish Republic is entitled to, and hereby claims, the allegiance of every Irishman and Irishwoman. The Republic guarantees religious and civil liberty, equal rights and equal opportunities to all its citizens, and declares its resolve to pursue the happiness and prosperity of the whole nation and of all its parts, cherishing all the children of the nation equally, and oblivious of the differences carefully fostered by an alien government, which have divided a minority from the majority in the past.

Until our arms have brought the opportune moment for the establishment of a permanent National Government, representative of the whole people of Ireland and elected by the suffrages of all her men and women,[2] the Provisional Government, hereby constituted, will administer the civil and military affairs of the Republic in trust for the people.

We place the cause of the Irish Republic under the protection of the Most High God, Whose blessing we invoke upon our arms, and we pray that no one who serves that cause will dishonor it by cowardice, inhumanity, or rapine. In this supreme hour the Irish nation must, by its valour and discipline and by the readiness of its children

1. *Irish Republic*, in the Irish language.
2. This call for women's suffrage in the Irish Republic predates full British women's suffrage by twelve years, and American women's suffrage by four years.

to sacrifice themselves for the common good, prove itself worthy of the august destiny to which it is called.

Signed on Behalf of the Provisional Government,
THOMAS J. CLARKE,
SEAN MACDIARMADA,
THOMAS MACDONAGH,
P. H. PEARSE,
EAMONN CEANNT,
JAMES CONNOLLY,
JOSEPH PLUNKETT.

Easter 1916

Padraic Pearse
Kilmainham Prison[1]

The following is the substance of what I said when asked today by the President of the Court-Martial at Richmond Barracks whether I had anything to say in my defence:

I desire, in the first place, to repeat what I have already said in letters to General Maxwell and Brigadier General Lowe.[2] My object in agreeing to an unconditional surrender was to prevent the further slaughter of the civil population of Dublin and to save the lives of our gallant fellows, who, having made for six days a stand unparalleled in military history, were now surrounded, and in the case of those under the immediate command of H.Q., without food. I fully understand now, as then, that my own life is forfeit to British law, and I shall die very cheerfully if I can think that the British Government, as it has already shown itself strong, will now show itself magnanimous enough to accept my single life in forfeiture and to give a general amnesty to the brave men and boys who have fought at my bidding.[3]

In the second place, I wish it to be understood that any admissions I make here are to be taken as involving myself alone. They do not involve and must not be used against anyone who acted with me, not even those who may have set their names to documents with me. (The Court assented to this.)

I admit that I was Commandant-General Commanding-in-Chief of the forces of the Irish Republic which have been acting against you for the past week, and that I was President of the Provisional Government. I stand over all my acts and words done or spoken, in these capacities. When I was a child of ten I went on my bare knees by my bedside one night and promised God that I should devote my life to an effort to free my country. I have kept the promise. I have helped to organize, to arm, to train, and to discipline my fellow-countrymen to the sole end that, when the time came, they might fight for Irish freedom. The time, as it seemed to me, did come, and we went into the fight. I am glad we did, we seem to have lost, but we have not lost. To refuse to fight would have been to lose, to fight is to win; we have kept faith with the past, and handed on a tradition to the future. I repudiate the assertion of the prosecutor that I sought to aid and abet England's enemy. Germany is no more to me than England is. I asked and accepted German aid in the shape of arms and an expeditionary force, we neither asked for nor accepted German gold, nor had any traffic with Germany but what I state. My object was to win Irish freedom. We struck the first blow ourselves, but I should have been glad of an ally's aid.

1. 2 May 1916. Pearse had been arrested on 29 April 1916, ending the street fighting that had begun when he read the Proclamation of the Irish Republic on 16 April. Pearse was executed at the conclusion of this military trial.

2. Leaders of the British troops during the Easter Rising.

3. This was not to be the case; in addition to Pearse, several other conspirators were executed by the British.

I assume that I am speaking to Englishmen who value their freedom and who profess to be fighting for the freedom of Belgium and Serbia;[4] believe that we too love freedom and desire it. To us it is more desirable than anything in the world. If you strike us down now we shall rise again and renew the fight, you cannot conquer Ireland, you cannot extinguish the Irish passion for freedom; if our deed has not been sufficient to win freedom then our children will win it by a better deed.

Michael Collins

The Substance of Freedom[1]

* * * We gather here today to uphold and to expound the Treaty. It was not our intention to hold any meetings until the issue was definitely before the electorate. But as a campaign has been begun in the country by Mr. de Valera and his followers we cannot afford to wait longer.

Mr de Valera's campaign is spoken of as a campaign against the Treaty. It is not really that.

The Irish people have already ratified the Treaty through their elected representatives. And the people of Ireland will stand by that ratification. The weekly paper of our opponents, which they call *The Republic of Ireland*, admits that ratification. Document No. 2[2] lapsed with the approval by the Dáil of the Treaty, they said in a leading article in the issue of February 21st; and in the issue of February 28th it is said "alternative documents are no longer in question."

No, it is not a campaign against the Treaty.

Nothing would disconcert Mr. de Valera and his followers more than the wrecking of the Treaty, than the loss of what has been secured by the Treaty.

It is a campaign, not against the Treaty, but against the Free State. And not only against the Free State, but still more against those who stand for the Free State. "Please God we will win," said Mr. de Valera last Sunday at Ennis, "and then there will be an end to the Free State." And if there were an end to the Free State, what then? What is the object of our opponents? I will tell you what it is.

In the same leading article of February 28th (in *The Republic of Ireland*) they say: "The Republican position is clear," and "We stand against the Treaty for the maintenance of the Republic."

The maintenance of the Republic [exclaimed Mr. Collins]. That is very curious. Because in the previous week's issue we were told by a member of the Dáil Cabinet that before the Truce of July last[3] it had become plain that it was physically impossible to secure Ireland's ideal of a completely isolated Republic in the immediate future, otherwise than by driving the overwhelmingly superior British forces out of the country. * * *

I will tell you what has happened since.

The Treaty has been brought back. It has brought and is bringing such freedom to Ireland in the transference to us of all governmental powers, but, above all, in the departure of the British armed forces, that it has become safe, and simple, and easy, and courageous to stand now for what was surrendered in July, because the British armed forces were still here.

4. In World War I.

1. The text is compiled from reports of audience members for Collins's speech at a public meeting on 5 March 1922. The "treaty" in question is the Anglo-Irish Treaty establishing 26 of Ireland's 32 counties as the Irish Free State and setting up a parliamentary government in Ireland. The treaty was opposed by Eamon de Valera, a surviving leader of the Easter Rising and leader of Sinn Féin, the Irish Republican organization whose Irish name means "Ourselves Alone." Though he was imprisoned by the newly formed Free State for his refusal to sign the treaty, de Valera later went on to serve as both Prime Minister and President of Ireland.

2. A document proposing an alternative arrangement, put forward by a private session of the Dáil Éireann (Irish Parliament) in December 1921.

3. A 1921 truce that led to negotiations and the Anglo-Irish Treaty.

We could not beat the British out by force, so the Republican ideal was surrendered. But when we have beaten them out by the Treaty the Republican ideal, which was surrendered in July, is restored.

The object of Mr de Valera and his party emerges. They are stealing our clothes.

We have beaten out the British by means of the Treaty. While damning the Treaty, and us with it, they are taking advantage of the evacuation which the Treaty secures.

After the surrender of the Republican ideal in July we were sent over to make a Treaty with England.

Some of us were sent very much against our wishes. That is well-known to our opponents. Everyone knew then, and it is idle and dishonest to deny now, that in the event of a settlement some postponement of the realisation of our full national sentiment would have to be agreed to.

We were not strong enough to realise the full Republican ideal. In addition, we must remember that there is a strong minority in our country up in the North-East that does not yet share our national views, but has to be reckoned with. In view of these things I claim that we brought back the fullest measure of freedom obtainable—the solid substance of independence.

We signed the Treaty believing it gave us such freedom. Our opponents make use of the advantage of the Treaty while they vilify it and us. The position gained by the Treaty provides them with a jumping off ground. After dropping the Republic while the British were still here, they shout bravely for it now from the safe foothold provided for them by means of the Treaty.

It is a mean campaign.

We were left with the Herculean labour and the heavy responsibility of taking over a Government. This would be a colossal task for the most experienced men of any nation. And we are young and not experienced. While we are thus engaged our former comrades go about the country talking. They tell the people to think of their own strength and the weakness of the enemy. Yes! and what is it that has made us strong and the enemy weak in the last few months? Yes, the enemy becomes weaker every day as his numbers grow less. And as they grow less, louder and louder do our opponents shout for the Republic which they surrendered in July last.

What has made the enemy weaker? The enemy that was then too strong for us? Is it the division in our ranks, which is Mr. de Valera's achievement, and which is already threatening a suspension of the evacuation? Or is it the Treaty which is our achievement?

Mr de Valera, in Limerick last Sunday, compared Ireland to a party that had set out to cross a desert, and they had come to a green spot, he said, and there were some who came along to tell them to lie down and stay there, and be satisfied and not go on.

Yes, we had come by means of the Treaty to a green oasis, the last in the long weary desert over which the Irish nation has been travelling. Oases are the resting-places of the desert, and unless the traveller finds them and refreshes himself he never reaches his destination.

Ireland has been brought to the last one, beyond which there is but a little and an easy stretch to go. The nation has earned the right to rest for a little while we renew our strength, and restore somewhat our earlier vigour.

But there are some amongst us who, while they take full advantage of the oasis—only a fool or a madman would fail to do that—complain of those who have led them to it. They find fault with it. They do nothing to help. They are poisoning the wells, wanting now to hurry on, seeing the road ahead short and straight, wanting the glory for themselves of leading the Irish nation over it, while unwilling to fill and shoulder the pack.

We are getting the British armed forces out of Ireland. Because of that evacuation our opponents are strong enough and brave enough now to say: "They are traitors who got you this. We are men of principle. We stand for the Republic"—that Republic which it was physically impossible to secure until the traitors had betrayed you.

Have we betrayed you? * * *

The arrangement in regard to North-East Ulster is not ideal. But then the position in North-East Ulster is not ideal.

If the Free State is established, however, union is certain. Forces of persuasion and pressure are embodied in the Treaty which will bring the North-East into a united Ireland. If they join us they can have control in their own area. If they stay outside Ireland, then they can only have their own corner, and cannot, and will not, have the counties and areas which belong to Ireland and to the Irish people, according to the wishes of the inhabitants.

Then upon the area remaining outside will fall the burdens and restrictions of the 1920 Partition Act.[4] These disabilities cannot be removed without our consent. If the North-East does not come in, then they are deciding upon bankruptcy for themselves and, remember, this is not our wish but their own.

We must not, however, take a gloomy view of this situation, for, with the British gone, the incentive to partition is gone; but the evacuation is held up by our own disunion—if the Free State is threatened, as long as there is any hope of seeing it destroyed, the North-East will remain apart. Partition will remain.

Destroy the Free State, and you perpetuate Partition. You destroy all hopes of union.

It is best to speak out plainly.

Destroy the Free State now and you destroy more even than the hope, the certainty of union. You destroy our hopes of national freedom, all realisation in our generation of the democratic right of the people of Ireland to rule themselves without interference from any outside power. * * *

But the aim of all of us can be for unity and independence. In public matters it must be realised that we cannot get all each one wants. We have to agree to get what is essential.

We have to agree to sink individual differences or only to work for them on legitimate lines which do not undermine and destroy the basis on which all rests and which alone makes it possible for us all, as Irishmen and women, to pursue our own aims freely in Ireland, namely, the union and independence of the nation as a whole.

We must be Irish first and last, and must be Republicans or Document Two-ites, or Free Staters, only within the limits which leave Ireland strong, united and free.

Would any other form of freedom which was obtainable now, which would have been acquiesced in by so large a body of our countrymen, have fulfilled the objects of Sinn Féin better, have put us in such a strong position to secure any that are yet unfulfilled?

We claim that the solid substance of freedom has been won, and that full powers are in the hands of the nation to mould its own life, quite as full for that purpose as if we had already our freedom in the Republican form.

Any difficulties will not be of our own making. There is no enemy nor any foreign Government here any longer to hinder us. Will we not take the fruits of victory, or do we mean to let them decay in our hands, while we wrangle as to whether they are ripe or whether they have exactly the bloom and shape we dreamed of before they had ripened?

No freedom when realised has quite the glory dreamed of by the captive.

[END OF SPEECHES ON IRISH INDEPENDENCE]

4. The act that divided Ireland politically into Northern Ireland (Ulster) and the Republic of Ireland.

William Butler Yeats

1865–1939

William Butler Yeats, c. 1933.

Beginning his career as a poet during the languid 1880s and 1890s, William Butler Yeats fought, as Ezra Pound said of T. S. Eliot, to modernize himself on his own. At a time when Irish poetry seemed to be in danger of ossifying into a sentimental, self-indulgent luxury, Yeats instead forged a verse that would serve as an exacting instrument of introspection and national inquiry. As a consequence, all modern Irish writing—most clearly poetry, but prose, drama, and literary nonfiction as well—is directly in his debt.

Yeats was born in the Dublin suburb of Sandymount, but his spiritual home, the land of his mother Susan Pollexfen and her people, was the countryside of County Sligo. His father, John Butler Yeats, was an amateur philosopher, an insolvent painter, and a refugee from the legal profession; his grandfather and great-grandfather were both clergymen of the Church of Ireland. Through his mother's family, Yeats traced a close connection with the countryside of Ireland, and the myths and legends of the Irish people. Both parents belonged to the Anglo-Irish Protestant ascendancy, a heritage Yeats remained fiercely proud of all his life; but the success of his poetry, in part, lay in his ability to reconcile the British literary tradition with the native materials of the Irish Catholic tradition.

As he tells it in his autobiography, Yeats's childhood was not a happy one; in 1915 he wrote: "I remember little of childhood but its pain." His father, though a talented painter, lacked the ability to turn his gifts to profit; he would linger over a single portrait for months and sometimes years, revising ceaselessly. When Yeats was three, his father moved his family to London in order to put himself to school as a painter; their existence, though intellectually and artistically rich and stimulating, was quite straitened financially. The young Yeats found London sterile and joyless; fortunately for his imagination, and his future poetry, portions of each year were spent in the Sligo countryside, where Yeats spent time gathering the local folklore and taking long, wide-ranging walks and pony rides. The family remained in London until 1875, and had four more children (though one brother died in childhood). All his surviving siblings were to remain important to Yeats in his artistic life: his brother Jack B. Yeats became an important Irish painter (see engraving, page 2164), and his sisters Lily and Lolly together founded the Dun Emer Press, later called the Cuala Press, which published limited-edition volumes of some of Yeats's poetry.

In 1880 the family returned permanently to Ireland, settling first in Howth, in Dublin Bay; the city of Dublin, with its largely unsung history and tradition, fueled Yeats's imagination in a way that London never had. When the time for college came, Yeats was judged unlikely to pass Trinity College's entrance exams, and he was sent instead to the Metropolitan School of Art, apparently in preparation to follow in his father's footsteps. His true gift, it soon appeared, was not for drawing and painting but for poetry. He steeped himself in the Romantic poets, especially Shelley and Keats, as well as the English poet of Irish residence Edmund Spenser. His first poems were published in the *Dublin University Review* in March 1885.

Yeats's early work is self-evidently apprentice work; it draws heavily on the late-Romantic, Pre-Raphaelite ambience so important in the painting of his father and his father's colleagues. He also began to take an active interest in the various mystical movements that were then finding a foothold in Dublin and London, and with friends formed a Hermetic Society in Dublin as an antidote to the humanist rationalism to which his father was so passionately attached. At the same time—almost as a self-administered antidote to the teachings of mystics like the Brahmin teacher Mohini Chatterji—Yeats began to attend the meetings of several Dublin political and debating societies, and became increasingly interested in the nationalist artistic revival that would become known as the Irish Renaissance or Celtic Revival. Unlike most of his debating society comrades, Yeats imagined this political and cultural renaissance as resulting from a marriage of Blakean opposites: "I had noticed that Irish Catholics among whom had been born so many political martyrs had not the good taste, the household courtesy and decency of the Protestant Ireland I had known, yet Protestant Ireland seemed to think of nothing but getting on in the world. I thought we might bring the halves together if we had a national literature that made Ireland beautiful in the memory, and yet had been freed from provincialism by an exacting criticism, a European pose."

The Yeats family moved back to London in 1887; finances were difficult as ever, and Yeats contributed to the family's upkeep by editing two anthologies, *Poems and Ballads of Young Ireland* (1888) and *Fairy and Folk Tales of the Irish Peasantry* (1888). His own first collection of poems, *The Wanderings of Oisin and Other Poems*, was published in the following year; the poems are resolutely romantic, Yeats himself describing his manner at the time as "in all things Pre-Raphaelite." The poems were well received, but the praise of one reader in particular caught Yeats's attention. The statuesque beauty Maud Gonne appeared at Yeats's door with an introduction from the Irish revolutionary John O'Leary, and declared that the title poem had brought her to tears. It was a fateful meeting; throughout five decades Yeats continued to write to Gonne, for Gonne—the critic M. L. Rosenthal has suggested that "virtually every poem celebrating a woman's beauty or addressing a beloved woman has to do with her." Rosenthal might have added, every poem decrying the sacrifice of life to politics, including *No Second Troy, Easter 1916, A Prayer for My Daughter*, and others, all of which lament Gonne's increasing political fanaticism. This fanaticism, which Gonne considered simply patriotism, made impossible the spiritual and emotional consummation that Yeats so fervently desired. He proposed marriage, but she declined, marrying instead an Irish soldier who would later be executed for his role in the Easter Rising of 1916. Yeats is, among his other distinctions, a great poet of unrequited love.

The 1890s in London were heady times for a young poet. Yeats became even more active in his studies of the occult, studying with the charismatic Theosophist Madame Blavatsky and attending meetings of the Order of the Golden Dawn, a Christian cabalist society. The practical upshot of these activities for his later poetry was a confirmed belief in a storehouse of all human experience and knowledge, which he called variously the *Spiritus Mundi* and *Anima Mundi*, invoked in later poems like *The Second Coming* (1920). In 1891 Yeats, together with Ernest Rhys, founded the Rhymers' Club, which brought him into almost nightly contact with such important literary figures as Lionel Johnson, Ernest Dowson, Arthur Symons, and Oscar Wilde; during this same period, he established the Irish Literary Society in London, and the National Literary Society in Dublin. Clearly, something of a program for modern Irish poetry was beginning to emerge, even if Yeats himself wasn't yet quite ready to write it. Yeats also spent the years from 1887 to 1891 studying the writings of that most mystic of English poets, William Blake; working with his father's friend Edwin Ellis, he produced an edition of and extended commentary on Blake's prophetic writings. Summing up the lesson of Blake's writings, Yeats wrote: "I had learned from Blake to hate all abstractions."

Romantic abstraction was easier to abjure in principle than in practice; Yeats's poetry of the 1890s still hankers after what one of his dramatis personae would later call "the loveliness that has long faded from the world." As one critic has written, "Early Yeats was the best poetry in English in late Victorian times; but they were bad times." Yeats began the process of throwing off the false manners of his Pre-Raphaelite upbringing with his play *The Countess Cathleen*, first performed by the Abbey Theatre, funded by subscriptions collected by his good friend Lady Augusta Gregory. Yeats's play, like Synge's *Playboy of the Western World* years later on that same stage, offended Irish sensibilities; in it, Cathleen sells her soul in order to protect Irish peasants from starvation. Yeats's volume *The Wind Among the Reeds* (1899) closes out the 1890s quite conveniently; it is ethereal, beautiful, and mannered. With this volume, Yeats's early phase comes to a close.

The early years of the twentieth century found Yeats concentrating his energies on the writing of poetic dramas, including, *The Pot of Broth* (1902) and *On Baile's Strand* (1904), for his fledgling Irish National Theatre. In 1903, the small Dun Emer Press published his volume of poems *In the Seven Woods*. These poems, including *Adam's Curse*, show Yeats working in a more spare idiom, the cadences and rhythms closer to those of actual speech—a consequence, some have argued, of his years writing for the stage. New poems published in *The Green Helmet and Other Poems* (1910) display Yeats as an increasingly mature and confident poet; his treatment of Maud Gonne in *No Second Troy*, for instance, shows a tragic acceptance of the fact that he will never have her, nor master her indomitable spirit. In *A Coat*, the poem that closes the 1914 collection *Responsibilities*, Yeats writes of the embroidered cloak he had fashioned for himself in his early poems, whose vanity is now brought home to him by the gaudiness of his imitators. He resolves, in the volume's closing lines, to set his cloak aside, "For there's more enterprise / In walking naked." This sense was strengthened by his close work, during the winter of 1912–1913, with Ezra Pound, in a cottage in rural Sussex. Both studied the stripped-down Japanese Noh drama and the Orientalist Ernest Fennollosa's work on the Chinese ideogram, and both men no doubt reinforced one another's increasing desire for a poetry that would be, in Pound's phrase, "closer to the bone."

The Easter Rising of 1916 took Yeats by surprise; he was in England at the time and complained of not having been informed in advance. A number of the rebel leaders were personal friends; he writes their names into Irish literature in *Easter 1916*, an excruciatingly honest, and ambivalent, exploration of the nature of heroism and nationalism. Yeats's mixed feelings about the revolution derived in part from a concern that some of his early writings, like the nationalist *Cathleen ní Houlihan*, might have contributed to the slaughter that followed in the wake of Easter 1916; as he wrote many years later, he couldn't help but wonder, "Did that play of mine send out / Certain men the English shot?"

The intricacies of Yeats's emotional and romantic life would require an essay of their own. His first marriage proposal to Maud Gonne in 1891, politely refused, set a pattern that was to remain in place for many years; though a number of poems try to reason through the affair, Yeats remained tragically attracted to this woman who did not return his affection, and multiple proposals were turned down as routinely as the first. He would have done as well, he was to write years later, to profess his love "to a statue in a museum." In the summer of 1917 things reached such a pass that Yeats proposed to Maud Gonne's adopted daughter Iseult; here, again, he was refused. Then, hastily, in October 1917 he married a longtime friend Georgiana ("George") Hyde-Lees. For all the tragicomedy leading up to the marriage, Yeats could not have chosen better; George was intelligent and sympathetic, and she brought the additional gift of an interest in mysticism and a facility in automatic writing that Yeats was soon to take full advantage of. Since early childhood, Yeats had heard voices speaking to him, and when he was twenty-one a voice commanded him "Hammer your thoughts into unity"; this charge had weighed on his mind for years, and his various experiments in mysticism and esoteric religions were intended to discover the system wherein his thoughts might be made to cohere.

With George, Yeats finally created that system on his own; its fullest exposition is found in *A Vision* (1928), though elements of it turn up in his poems beginning as early as *No Second Troy*. The system is complicated enough to fill out over 300 pages in the revised (1937) edition; at the heart of the system, though, is a simple diagram of two interpenetrating cones, oriented horizontally, such that the tip of each cone establishes the center of the base of the opposite cone. These two cones describe the paths of two turning gyres, or spirals, representing two alternating antithetical ages which make up human history. Yeats saw history as composed of cycles of approximately 2,000 years; his apocalyptic poem *The Second Coming*, for instance, describes the anxiety caused by the recognition that the 2,000 years of Christian (in Yeats's terms, "primary") values were about to be succeeded by an antithetical age—the "rough beast" of a time characterized by values and beliefs in every way hostile to those of the Christian era. For Yeats, however, as for William Blake, this vacillation and tension between contraries was not to be regretted; Blake taught that "without Contraries is no progression," and Yeats, that "all the gains of man come from conflict with the opposite of his true being."

Yeats's greatest phase begins with the poems of *Michael Robartes and the Dancer* (1921). His mytho-historical system informs a number of the poems written in the 1920s and after; it explains, for instance, why Yeats saw the brutal rape of Leda by Zeus in the form of a swan as a precursor of the traditional Christian iconography of the Virgin Mary "visited" by God the Father in the form of a dove. A logical corollary of Yeats's belief in historical recurrence was the philosophy, articulated best in his late poem *Lapis Lazuli*, of tragic joy: "All things fall and are built again, / And those that build them again are gay." In a letter inspired by the gift of lapis lazuli that the poem celebrates, Yeats wrote to a friend: "To me the supreme aim is an act of faith or reason to make one rejoice in the midst of tragedy." The influence of the writing of Nietzsche, whom Yeats had been reading, is apparent in these formulations.

While continuing to push at the boundaries of modern literature and modern poetry, Yeats also enjoyed the role of statesman. In the fall of 1922, Yeats was made a senator of the new Irish Free State; in 1923 he was awarded the Nobel Prize in Literature, the first Irish writer ever to receive the award. The 1930s also saw Yeats flirt briefly with fascism, as did other writers like Pound and Wyndham Lewis. Yeats's belief in the importance of an aristocracy, and his disappointment over the excesses of revolutionary zeal demonstrated in the Irish civil war, for a time during the 1930s made the fascist program of the Irish Blueshirt movement look attractive. He composed *Three Songs to the Same Tune* as rallying songs for the Blueshirts, but the poems were too recherché for any such use. He soon became disillusioned with the party.

Yeats continued to write major poetry almost until his death; his growing ill health seems only to have made his poetry stronger and more defiant, as evidenced in such sinuous and clearsighted poems as *Lapis Lazuli* and the bawdy Crazy Jane poems. In the work published as *Last Poems* (1939), Yeats most satisfactorily put into practice what he had much earlier discovered in theory: that he must, as he wrote in *The Circus Animals' Desertion*, return for his poetry to "the foul rag-and-bone shop of the heart." After a long period of heart trouble, Yeats died on 28 January 1939; he was buried in Roquebrune, France, where he and George had been spending the winter. In 1948 he was reinterred, as he had wished, in Drumcliff churchyard near Sligo, where his grandfather and great-grandfather had served as rectors. Again according to his wishes, his epitaph is that which he wrote for himself in *Under Ben Bulben*:

Cast a cold eye
On life, on death.
Horseman, pass by!

For additional resources on Yeats, go to *The Longman Anthology of British Literature* Web site at www.myliteraturekit.com.

The Lake Isle of Innisfree[1]

I will arise and go now, and go to Innisfree,
And a small cabin build there, of clay and wattles° made: *woven twigs*
Nine bean-rows will I have there, a hive for the honey-bee,
And live alone in the bee-loud glade.

And I shall have some peace there, for peace comes dropping slow,
Dropping from the veils of the morning to where the cricket sings;
There midnight's all a glimmer, and noon a purple glow,
And evening full of the linnet's° wings. *song bird*

1. A small island in Lough Gill outside the town of Sligo, near the border with Northern Ireland.

I will arise and go now, for always night and day
I hear lake water lapping with low sounds by the shore;
While I stand on the roadway, or on the pavements grey,
I hear it in the deep heart's core.

1890 1890

Who Goes with Fergus?[1]

Who will go drive with Fergus now,
And pierce the deep wood's woven shade,
And dance upon the level shore?
Young man, lift up your russet brow,
And lift your tender eyelids, maid,
And brood on hopes and fear no more.

And no more turn aside and brood
Upon love's bitter mystery;
For Fergus rules the brazen° cars, *brass*
And rules the shadows of the wood,
And the white breast of the dim sea
And all dishevelled wandering stars.

1893

No Second Troy[1]

Why should I blame her that she filled my days
With misery, or that she would of late
Have taught to ignorant men most violent ways,
Or hurled the little streets upon the great,
Had they but courage equal to desire?
What could have made her peaceful with a mind
That nobleness made simple as a fire,
With beauty like a tightened bow, a kind
That is not natural in an age like this,
Being high and solitary and most stern?
Why, what could she have done, being what she is?
Was there another Troy for her to burn?

1908 1910

The Fascination of What's Difficult

The fascination of what's difficult
Has dried the sap out of my veins, and rent
Spontaneous joy and natural content
Out of my heart. There's something ails our colt[1]
That must, as if it had not holy blood
Nor on Olympus leaped from cloud to cloud,
Shiver under the lash, strain, sweat and jolt

1. The poem is a lyric from the second scene of Yeats's play *The Countess Cathleen*. Fergus was an ancient Irish king who gave up his throne to feast, fight, and hunt.

1. Yeats here compares Maud Gonne to Helen of Troy; the Trojan War began from two kings' rivalry over Helen.

1. Pegasus, winged horse of Greek mythology.

As though it dragged road metal. My curse on plays
That have to be set up in fifty ways,
On the day's war with every knave and dolt,
Theatre business, management of men.
I swear before the dawn comes round again
I'll find the stable and pull out the bolt.

1910

1910

September 1913[1]

What need you, being come to sense,
But fumble in a greasy till
And add the halfpence to the pence
And prayer to shivering prayer, until
You have dried the marrow from the bone;
For men were born to pray and save:
Romantic Ireland's dead and gone,
It's with O'Leary[2] in the grave.

Yet they were of a different kind,
The names that stilled your childish play,
They have gone about the world like wind,
But little time had they to pray
For whom the hangman's rope was spun,
And what, God help us, could they save?
Romantic Ireland's dead and gone,
It's with O'Leary in the grave.
Was it for this the wild geese[3] spread
The grey wing upon every tide;
For this that all the blood was shed,
For this Edward Fitzgerald[4] died,
And Robert Emmet[5] and Wolfe Tone,[6]
All that delirium of the brave?
Romantic Ireland's dead and gone,
It's with O'Leary in the grave.

Yet could we turn the years again,
And call those exiles as they were
In all their loneliness and pain,
You'd cry, 'Some woman's yellow hair
Has maddened every mother's son':
They weighed so lightly what they gave.

1. Yeats wrote the poem on 7 September 1913, and it was published the following day in the *Irish Times*.

2. John O'Leary (1830–1907) was involved first in the nationalist Young Ireland movement, and later went on to cofound its successor, the Fenian movement. After serving nine years of penal servitude for his republican activities, he was exiled in Paris for 15 years, before being allowed to return to Dublin in 1885. O'Leary was a friend of Yeats's father, John Butler Yeats.

3. The "wild geese" were those Irishmen who fled Ireland in the wake of the Penal Laws of 1691; many of them fought as soldiers in the French, Spanish, and Austrian armies. About 120,000 "wild geese" are thought to have left Ireland between 1691 and 1730.

4. Lord Edward Fitzgerald (1763–1798) was a leader of the nationalist United Irishmen and died of wounds he received while being taken into custody by authorities.

5. Robert Emmet (1778–1803) led an unsuccessful revolt against the British government in 1803 and was hanged.

6. Theobald Wolfe Tone (1763–1798) led a friendly French force to Ireland to help oust the British in the ill-fated "year of the French" uprising in 1798. He was arrested and committed suicide while in prison awaiting execution.

But let them be, they're dead and gone,
They're with O'Leary in the grave.

The Wild Swans at Coole[1]

The trees are in their autumn beauty,
The woodland paths are dry,
Under the October twilight the water
Mirrors a still sky;
Upon the brimming water among the stones
Are nine-and-fifty swans.

The nineteenth autumn has come upon me
Since I first made my count;
I saw, before I had well finished,
All suddenly mount
And scatter wheeling in great broken rings
Upon their clamorous wings.

I have looked upon those brilliant creatures,
And now my heart is sore.
All's changed since I, hearing at twilight,
The first time on this shore,
The bell-beat of their wings above my head,
Trod with a lighter tread.

Unwearied still, lover by lover,
They paddle in the cold
Companionable streams or climb the air;
Their hearts have not grown old;
Passion or conquest, wander where they will,
Attend upon them still.

But now they drift on the still water,
Mysterious, beautiful;
Among what rushes will they build,
By what lake's edge or pool
Delight men's eyes when I awake some day
To find they have flown away?

1916 1917

An Irish Airman Foresees His Death[1]

I know that I shall meet my fate
Somewhere among the clouds above;
Those that I fight I do not hate,
Those that I guard I do not love;

1. Coole Park was the name of the estate of Yeats's patron Lady Gregory in Galway.

1. The particular airman Yeats had in mind was Major Robert Gregory (1881–1918), only child of his dear friend Lady Augusta Gregory, who was killed in action in Italy during World War I.

My country is Kiltartan Cross,[2]
My countrymen Kiltartan's poor,
No likely end could bring them loss
Or leave them happier than before.
Nor law, nor duty bade me fight,
Nor public men, nor cheering crowds,
A lonely impulse of delight
Drove to this tumult in the clouds;
I balanced all, brought all to mind,
The years to come seemed waste of breath,
A waste of breath the years behind
In balance with this life, this death.

Easter 1916[1]

I have met them at close of day
Coming with vivid faces
From counter or desk among grey
Eighteenth-century houses.
I have passed with a nod of the head
Or polite meaningless words,
Or have lingered awhile and said
Polite meaningless words,
And thought before I had done
Of a mocking tale or a gibe° *taunt*
To please a companion
Around the fire at the club,
Being certain that they and I
But lived where motley° is worn: *jester's outfit*
All changed, changed utterly:
A terrible beauty is born.
That woman's days were spent
In ignorant good-will,
Her nights in argument
Until her voice grew shrill.[2]
What voice more sweet than hers
When, young and beautiful,
She rode to harriers?° *hunting dogs*
This man[3] had kept a school
And rode our wingèd horse;
This other[4] his helper and friend
Was coming into his force;
He might have won fame in the end,
So sensitive his nature seemed,

2. The crossroads in Kiltartan, near the Gregory estate at Coole Park.

1. The Irish Republic was declared on Easter Monday, 24 April 1916.

2. Countess Markiewicz, née Constance Gore-Booth, played a prominent part in the Easter Rising and was sentenced to be executed; her sentence was later reduced to imprisonment.

3. Padraic Pearse.

4. Thomas MacDonagh, poet executed for his role in the rebellion.

So daring and sweet his thought.
This other man[5] I had dreamed
A drunken, vainglorious lout.
He had done most bitter wrong
To some who are near my heart,
Yet I number him in the song;
He, too, has resigned his part
In the casual comedy;
He, too, has been changed in his turn,
Transformed utterly:
A terrible beauty is born.

Hearts with one purpose alone
Through summer and winter seem
Enchanted to a stone
To trouble the living stream.
The horse that comes from the road,
The rider, the birds that range
From cloud to tumbling cloud,
Minute by minute they change;
A shadow of cloud on the stream
Changes minute by minute;
A horse-hoof slides on the brim,
And a horse plashes within it;
The long-legged moor-hens dive,
And hens to moor-cocks call;
Minute by minute they live:
The stone's in the midst of all.

Too long a sacrifice
Can make a stone of the heart.
O when may it suffice?
That is Heaven's part, our part
To murmur name upon name,
As a mother names her child
When sleep at last has come
On limbs that had run wild.
What is it but nightfall?
No, no, not night but death;
Was it needless death after all?
For England may keep faith
For all that is done and said.
We know their dream; enough
To know they dreamed and are dead;
And what if excess of love
Bewildered them till they died?
I write it out in a verse—
MacDonagh and MacBride

5. Major John MacBride, briefly married to Maud Gonne, was also executed.

And Connolly[6] and Pearse
Now and in time to be,
Wherever green is worn,
Are changed, changed utterly:
A terrible beauty is born.

1916 1916

The Second Coming[1]

Turning and turning in the widening gyre° *circle or spiral*
The falcon cannot hear the falconer;
Things fall apart; the centre cannot hold;
Mere anarchy is loosed upon the world,
The blood-dimmed tide is loosed, and everywhere
The ceremony of innocence is drowned;
The best lack all conviction, while the worst
Are full of passionate intensity.

Surely some revelation is at hand;
Surely the Second Coming is at hand.
The Second Coming! Hardly are those words out
When a vast image out of *Spiritus Mundi*[2]
Troubles my sight: somewhere in sands of the desert
A shape with lion body and the head of a man,
A gaze blank and pitiless as the sun,
Is moving its slow thighs, while all about it
Reel shadows of the indignant desert birds.
The darkness drops again; but now I know
That twenty centuries° of stony sleep *the Christian era*
Were vexed to nightmare by a rocking cradle,
And what rough beast, its hour come round at last,
Slouches towards Bethlehem to be born?

1919 1921

A Prayer for My Daughter[1]

Once more the storm is howling, and half hid
Under this cradle-hood and coverlid
My child sleeps on. There is no obstacle
But Gregory's wood and one bare hill
Whereby the haystack- and roof-levelling wind,
Bred on the Atlantic, can be stayed;
And for an hour I have walked and prayed
Because of the great gloom that is in my mind.

I have walked and prayed for this young child an hour
And heard the sea-wind scream upon the tower,
And under the arches of the bridge, and scream

6. James Connolly, Marxist commander-in-chief of the Easter rebels; also executed.
1. Traditionally, the return of Christ to earth on Judgment Day.
2. A storehouse of images and symbols common to all humankind; similar to Carl Jung's notion of the collective unconscious.
1. Anne Butler Yeats was born 26 February 1919.

In the elms above the flooded stream;
Imagining in excited reverie
That the future years had come,
Dancing to a frenzied drum,
Out of the murderous innocence of the sea.

May she be granted beauty and yet not
Beauty to make a stranger's eye distraught,
Or hers before a looking-glass, for such,
Being made beautiful overmuch,
Consider beauty a sufficient end,
Lose natural kindness and maybe
The heart-revealing intimacy
That chooses right, and never find a friend.

Helen[2] being chosen found life flat and dull
And later had much trouble from a fool,
While that great Queen,[3] that rose out of the spray,
Being fatherless could have her way
Yet chose a bandy-leggèd smith[4] for man.
It's certain that fine women eat
A crazy salad with their meat
Whereby the Horn of Plenty is undone.
In courtesy I'd have her chiefly learned;
Hearts are not had as a gift but hearts are earned
By those that are not entirely beautiful;
Yet many, that have played the fool
For beauty's very self, has charm made wise,
And many a poor man that has roved,
Loved and thought himself beloved,
From a glad kindness cannot take his eyes.

May she become a flourishing hidden tree
That all her thoughts may like the linnet° be, *song bird*
And have no business but dispensing round
Their magnanimities of sound,
Nor but in merriment begin a chase,
Nor but in merriment a quarrel.
O may she live like some green laurel
Rooted in one dear perpetual place.

My mind, because the minds that I have loved,
The sort of beauty that I have approved,
Prosper but little, has dried up of late,
Yet knows that to be choked with hate
May well be of all evil chances chief.
If there's no hatred in a mind

2. Helen of Troy, who left her husband Menelaus for Paris.
3. Aphrodite, Greek goddess of love, born from the sea.
4. Aphrodite's husband Hephaestus, the god of fire, was lame.

Assault and battery of the wind
Can never tear the linnet from the leaf.

An intellectual hatred is the worst,
So let her think opinions are accursed.
Have I not seen the loveliest woman born
Out of the mouth of Plenty's horn,
Because of her opinionated mind
Barter that horn and every good
By quiet natures understood
For an old bellows full of angry wind?

Considering that, all hatred driven hence,
The soul recovers radical innocence
And learns at last that it is self-delighting,
Self-appeasing, self-affrighting,
And that its own sweet will is Heaven's will;
She can, though every face should scowl
And every windy quarter howl
Or every bellows burst, be happy still.

And may her bridegroom bring her to a house
Where all's accustomed, ceremonious;
For arrogance and hatred are the wares
Peddled in the thoroughfares.
How but in custom and in ceremony
Are innocence and beauty born?
Ceremony's a name for the rich horn,
And custom for the spreading laurel tree.

June 1919 1919

Sailing to Byzantium[1]

1

That is no country for old men. The young
In one another's arms, birds in the trees,
—Those dying generations—at their song,
The salmon-falls, the mackerel-crowded seas,
Fish, flesh, or fowl, commend all summer long
Whatever is begotten, born, and dies.
Caught in that sensual music all neglect
Monuments of unageing intellect.

2

An aged man is but a paltry thing,
A tattered coat upon a stick, unless
Soul clap its hands and sing, and louder sing
For every tatter in its mortal dress,

1. Constantinople, now called Istanbul, capital of the Byzantine Empire and the holy city of Eastern Christianity.

Nor is there singing school but studying
Monuments of its own magnificence;
And therefore I have sailed the seas and come
To the holy city of Byzantium.

3

O sages standing in God's holy fire
As in the gold mosaic of a wall,
Come from the holy fire, perne° in a gyre, *spin*
And be the singing-masters of my soul.
Consume my heart away; sick with desire
And fastened to a dying animal
It knows not what it is; and gather me
Into the artifice of eternity.

4

Once out of nature I shall never take
My bodily form from any natural thing,
But such a form as Grecian goldsmiths make
Of hammered gold and gold enamelling
To keep a drowsy Emperor awake;—
Or set upon a golden bough to sing
To lords and ladies of Byzantium
Of what is past, or passing, or to come.

1926 1927

Meditations in Time of Civil War[1]

1. Ancestral Houses

Surely among a rich man's flowering lawns,
Amid the rustle of his planted hills,
Life overflows without ambitious pains;
And rains down life until the basin spills,
And mounts more dizzy high the more it rains
As though to choose whatever shape it wills
And never stoop to a mechanical
Or servile shape, at others' beck and call.

Mere dreams, mere dreams! Yet Homer had not sung
Had he not found it certain beyond dreams
That out of life's own self-delight had sprung
The abounding glittering jet; though now it seems
As if some marvellous empty sea-shell flung
Out of the obscure dark of the rich streams,
And not a fountain, were the symbol which
Shadows the inherited glory of the rich.

1. Written at Yeats's country home at Thor Bellylee, Sligo, in 1922, during the civil war between the Free State forces and the "irregulars."

Some violent bitter man, some powerful man
Called architect and artist in, that they,
Bitter and violent men, might rear in stone
The sweetness that all longed for night and day,
The gentleness none there had ever known;
But when the master's buried mice can play,
And maybe the great-grandson of that house,
For all its bronze and marble, 's but a mouse.

O what if gardens where the peacock strays
With delicate feet upon old terraces,
Or else all Juno[2] from an urn displays
Before the indifferent garden deities;
O what if levelled lawns and gravelled ways
Where slippered Contemplation finds his ease
And Childhood a delight for every sense,
But take our greatness with our violence?
What if the glory of escutcheoned° doors, *shield-embossed*
And buildings that a haughtier age designed,
The pacing to and fro on polished floors
Amid great chambers and long galleries, lined
With famous portraits of our ancestors;
What if those things the greatest of mankind
Consider most to magnify, or to bless,
But take our greatness with our bitterness?

2. My House

An ancient bridge, and a more ancient tower,
A farmhouse that is sheltered by its wall,
An acre of stony ground,
Where the symbolic rose can break in flower,
Old ragged elms, old thorns innumerable,
The sound of the rain or sound
Of every wind that blows;
The stilted water-hen
Crossing stream again
Scared by the splashing of a dozen cows;
A winding stair, a chamber arched with stone,
A grey stone fireplace with an open hearth,
A candle and written page.
Il Penseroso's Platonist[3] toiled on
In some like chamber, shadowing forth
How the daemonic rage
Imagined everything.
Benighted travellers

2. Roman Goddess of marriage and patroness of women; the peacock was sacred to her as a symbol of immortality.

3. Follower of the idealist philosophy of Plato, in Milton's poem *Il Penseroso* ("The Contemplative").

From markets and from fairs
Have seen his midnight candle glimmering.

Two men have founded here. A man-at-arms
Gathered a score of horse and spent his days
In this tumultuous spot,
Where through long wars and sudden night alarms
His dwindling score and he seemed castaways
Forgetting and forgot;
And I, that after me
My bodily heirs may find,
To exalt a lonely mind,
Befitting emblems of adversity.

3. My Table

Two heavy trestles, and a board
Where Sato's[4] gift, a changeless sword,
By pen and paper lies,
That it may moralise
My days out of their aimlessness.
A bit of an embroidered dress
Covers its wooden sheath.
Chaucer had not drawn breath
When it was forged. In Sato's house,
Curved like new moon, moon-luminous,
It lay five hundred years.
Yet if no change appears
No moon; only an aching heart
Conceives a changeless work of art.
Our learned men have urged
That when and where 'twas forged
A marvellous accomplishment,
In painting or in pottery, went
From father unto son
And through the centuries ran
And seemed unchanging like the sword.
Soul's beauty being most adored,
Men and their business took
The soul's unchanging look;
For the most rich inheritor,
Knowing that none could pass Heaven's door
That loved inferior art,
Had such an aching heart
That he, although a country's talk
For silken clothes and stately walk,

4. Junzo Sato, Japanese consul who presented Yeats with an ancestral ceremonial sword.

Had waking wits; it seemed
Juno's peacock screamed.

4. My Descendants

Having inherited a vigorous mind
From my old fathers, I must nourish dreams
And leave a woman and a man behind
As vigorous of mind, and yet it seems
Life scarce can cast a fragrance on the wind,
Scarce spread a glory to the morning beams,
But the torn petals strew the garden plot;
And there's but common greenness after that.

And what if my descendants lose the flower
Through natural declension of the soul,
Through too much business with the passing hour,
Through too much play, or marriage with a fool?
May this laborious stair and this stark tower
Become a roofless ruin that the owl
May build in the cracked masonry and cry
Her desolation to the desolate sky.

The Primum Mobile[5] that fashioned us
Has made the very owls in circles move;
And I, that count myself most prosperous,
Seeing that love and friendship are enough,
For an old neighbour's friendship chose the house
And decked and altered it for a girl's love,
And know whatever flourish and decline
These stones remain their monument and mine.

5. The Road at My Door

An affable Irregular,[6]
A heavily-built Falstaffian[7] man,
Comes cracking jokes of civil war
As though to die by gunshot were
The finest play under the sun.

A brown Lieutenant and his men,
Half dressed in national uniform,
Stand at my door, and I complain
Of the foul weather, hail and rain,
A pear tree broken by the storm.

5. Prime mover (Latin); part of the Ptolemaic system that described the revolution of the heavens around the earth.
6. A member of the Irish Republican Army (IRA), which opposed any cooperation with British power and started the civil war.
7. Robust, bawdy, witty; after Sir John Falstaff, comic character in Shakespeare's *The Merry Wives of Windsor* and *Henry IV*.

I count those feathered balls of soot
The moor-hen guides upon the stream,
To silence the envy in my thought;
And turn towards my chamber, caught
In the cold snows of a dream.

6. The Stare's° Nest by My Window

starling's

The bees build in the crevices
Of loosening masonry, and there
The mother birds bring grubs and flies.
My wall is loosening; honey-bees,
Come build in the empty house of the stare.

We are closed in, and the key is turned
On our uncertainty; somewhere
A man is killed, or a house burned,
Yet no clear fact to be discerned:
Come build in the empty house of the stare.

A barricade of stone or of wood;
Some fourteen days of civil war;
Last night they trundled down the road
That dead young soldier in his blood:
Come build in the empty house of the stare.

We had fed the heart on fantasies,
The heart's grown brutal from the fare;
More substance in our enmities
Than in our love; O honey-bees,
Come build in the empty house of the stare.

7. I See Phantoms of Hatred and of the Heart's Fullness and of the Coming Emptiness

I climb to the tower-top and lean upon broken stone,
A mist that is like blown snow is sweeping over all,
Valley, river, and elms, under the light of a moon
That seems unlike itself, that seems unchangeable,
A glittering sword out of the east. A puff of wind
And those white glimmering fragments of the mist sweep by.
Frenzies bewilder, reveries perturb the mind;
Monstrous familiar images swim to the mind's eye.

"Vengeance upon the murderers," the cry goes up,
"Vengeance for Jacques Molay."[8] In cloud-pale rags, or in lace,
The rage-driven, rage-tormented, and rage-hungry troop,
Trooper belabouring trooper, biting at arm or at face,

8. Jacques de Molay, Grand Master of the Knights Templar, who was burned as a witch in 1314.

Plunges towards nothing, arms and fingers spreading wide
For the embrace of nothing; and I, my wits astray
Because of all that senseless tumult, all but cried
For vengeance on the murderers of Jacques Molay.

Their legs long, delicate and slender, aquamarine their eyes,
Magical unicorns bear ladies on their backs.
The ladies close their musing eyes. No prophecies,
Remembered out of Babylonian almanacs,
Have closed the ladies' eyes, their minds are but a pool
Where even longing drowns under its own excess;
Nothing but stillness can remain when hearts are full
Of their own sweetness, bodies of their loveliness.

The cloud-pale unicorns, the eyes of aquamarine,
The quivering half-closed eyelids, the rags of cloud or of lace,
Or eyes that rage has brightened, arms it has made lean,
Give place to an indifferent multitude, give place
To brazen hawks. Nor self-delighting reverie,
Nor hate of what's to come, nor pity for what's gone,
Nothing but grip of claw, and the eye's complacency,
The innumerable clanging wings that have put out the moon.

I turn away and shut the door, and on the stair
Wonder how many times I could have proved my worth
In something that all others understand or share;
But O! ambitious heart, had such a proof drawn forth
A company of friends, a conscience set at ease,
It had but made us pine the more. The abstract joy,
The half-read wisdom of daemonic images,
Suffice the ageing man as once the growing boy.

1921 1928

Nineteen Hundred and Nineteen

Many ingenious lovely things are gone
That seemed sheer miracle to the multitude,
Protected from the circle of the moon
That pitches common things about. There stood
Amid the ornamental bronze and stone
An ancient image made of olive wood—
And gone are Phidias'[1] famous ivories
And all the golden grasshoppers and bees.

We too had many pretty toys when young;
A law indifferent to blame or praise,
To bribe or threat; habits that made old wrong
Melt down, as it were wax in the sun's rays;
Public opinion ripening for so long

1. A 5th-century B.C.E. Greek sculptor.

We thought it would outlive all future days.
O what fine thought we had because we thought
That the worst rogues and rascals had died out.

All teeth were drawn, all ancient tricks unlearned,
And a great army but a showy thing;
What matter that no cannon had been turned
Into a ploughshare?[2] Parliament and king
Thought that unless a little powder burned
The trumpeters might burst with trumpeting
And yet it lack all glory; and perchance
The guardsmen's drowsy chargers would not prance.

Now days are dragon-ridden, the nightmare
Rides upon sleep: a drunken soldiery
Can leave the mother, murdered at her door,
To crawl in her own blood, and go scot-free;
The night can sweat with terror as before
We pieced our thoughts into philosophy,
And planned to bring the world under a rule,
Who are but weasels fighting in a hole.

He who can read the signs nor sink unmanned
Into the half-deceit of some intoxicant
From shallow wits; who knows no work can stand,
Whether health, wealth or peace of mind were spent
On master-work of intellect or hand,
No honour leave its mighty monument,
Has but one comfort left: all triumph would
But break upon his ghostly solitude.

But is there any comfort to be found?
Man is in love and loves what vanishes,
What more is there to say? That country round
None dared admit, if such a thought were his,
Incendiary or bigot could be found
To burn that stump on the Acropolis,
Or break in bits the famous ivories
Or traffic in the grasshoppers or bees.

2

When Loie Fuller's[3] Chinese dancers enwound
A shining web, a floating ribbon of cloth,
It seemed that a dragon of air
Had fallen among dancers, had whirled them round
Or hurried them off on its own furious path;
So the Platonic Year
Whirls out new right and wrong,

2. Isaiah 2.4: "And they shall beat their swords into ploughshares and their spears into pruninghooks."

3. American dancer (1862–1928).

Whirls in the old instead;
All men are dancers and their tread
Goes to the barbarous clangour of a gong.

3

Some moralist or mythological poet[4]
Compares the solitary soul to a swan;
I am satisfied with that,
Satisfied if a troubled mirror show it,
Before that brief gleam of its life be gone,
An image of its state;
The wings half spread for flight,
The breast thrust out in pride
Whether to play, or to ride
Those winds that clamour of approaching night.
A man in his own secret mediation
Is lost amid the labyrinth that he has made
In art or politics;
Some Platonist affirms that in the station
Where we should cast off body and trade
The ancient habit sticks,
And that if our works could
But vanish with our breath
That were a lucky death,
For triumph can but mar our solitude.

The swan has leaped into the desolate heaven:
That image can bring wildness, bring a rage
To end all things, to end
What my laborious life imagined, even
The half-imagined, the half-written page;
O but we dreamed to mend
Whatever mischief seemed
To afflict mankind, but now
That winds of winter blow
Learn that we were crack-pated when we dreamed.

4

We, who seven years ago
Talked of honour and of truth,
Shriek with pleasure if we show
The weasel's twist, the weasel's tooth.

5

Come let us mock at the great
That had such burdens on the mind
And toiled so hard and late

4. Possibly Shelley in *Prometheus Unbound*, 2.5.72–74.

To leave some monument behind,
Nor thought of the levelling wind.

Come let us mock at the wise;
With all those calendars whereon
They fixed old aching eyes,
They never saw how seasons run,
And now but gape at the sun.

Come let us mock at the good
That fancied goodness might be gay,
And sick of solitude
Might proclaim a holiday:
Wind shrieked—and where are they?

Mock mockers after that
That would not lift a hand maybe
To help good, wise or great
To bar that foul storm out, for we
Traffic in mockery.

6

Violence upon the roads: violence of horses;
Some few have handsome riders, are garlanded
On delicate sensitive ear or tossing mane,
But wearied running round and round in their courses
All break and vanish, and evil gathers head:

Herodias' daughters have returned again,[5]
A sudden blast of dusty wind and after
Thunder of feet, tumult of images,
Their purpose in the labyrinth of the wind;
And should some crazy hand dare touch a daughter
All turn with amorous cries, or angry cries,
According to the wind, for all are blind.
But now wind drops, dust settles; thereupon
There lurches past, his great eyes without thought
Under the shadow of stupid straw-pale locks,
That insolent fiend Robert Artisson[6]
To whom the love-lorn Lady Kyteler brought
Bronzed peacock feathers, red combs of her cocks.

1919

Leda and the Swan[1]

A sudden blow: the great wings beating still
Above the staggering girl, her thighs caressed

5. Herodias told her daughter Salome to ask Herod for the head of John the Baptist on a platter (Matthew 14.8).
6. An evil spirit much run after in Kilkenny at the start of the fourteenth century [Yeats's note]. He was said to have seduced Dame Alice Kyteler, who poisoned her husbands and was accused of sacrificing cocks and peacocks to him.
1. In Greek mythology, Zeus came to Leda in the form of a swan and raped her; Helen of Troy and Clytemnestra were their offspring.

By the dark webs, her nape caught in his bill,
He holds her helpless breast upon his breast.

How can those terrified vague fingers push
The feathered glory from her loosening thighs?
And how can body, laid in that white rush,
But feel the strange heart beating where it lies?

A shudder in the loins engenders there
The broken wall, the burning roof and tower
And Agamemnon[2] dead.
Being so caught up,
So mastered by the brute blood of the air,
Did she put on his knowledge with his power
Before the indifferent beak could let her drop?

1923 1924

Among School Children

1

I walk through the long schoolroom questioning;[1]
A kind old nun in a white hood replies;
The children learn to cipher and to sing,
To study reading-books and history,
To cut and sew, be neat in everything
In the best modern way—the children's eyes
In momentary wonder stare upon
A sixty-year-old smiling public man.

2

I dream of a Ledaean[2] body, bent
Above a sinking fire, a tale that she
Told of a harsh reproof, or trivial event
That changed some childish day to tragedy—
Told, and it seemed that our two natures blent
Into a sphere from youthful sympathy,
Or else, to alter Plato's parable,
Into the yolk and white of the one shell.[3]

3

And thinking of that fit of grief or rage
I look upon one child or t'other there
And wonder if she stood so at that age—
For even daughters of the swan can share
Something of every paddler's heritage—

2. Brother of Menelaus, husband of Helen. When she was abducted by Paris, Agamemnon fought to rescue her. He was murdered by his wife Clytemnestra on his return home.

1. While an Irish senator, Yeats visited St. Otteran's School in Waterford.

2. Of Leda, the mother of Helen of Troy (or Helen herself).

3. According to Plato's parable in the *Symposium*, male and female were once the two halves of a single body; it was subsequently cut in half like a hard-boiled egg.

And had that colour upon cheek or hair,
And thereupon my heart is driven wild:
She stands before me as a living child.

4

Her present image floats into the mind—
Did Quattrocento[4] finger fashion it
Hollow of cheek as though it drank the wind
And took a mess of shadows for its meat?
And I though never of Ledaean kind
Had pretty plumage once—enough of that,
Better to smile on all that smile, and show
There is a comfortable kind of old scarecrow.

5

What youthful mother, a shape upon her lap
Honey of generation had betrayed,
And that must sleep, shriek, struggle to escape
As recollection or the drug decide,
Would think her son, did she but see that shape
With sixty or more winters on its head,
A compensation for the pang of his birth,
Or the uncertainty of his setting forth?

6

Plato thought nature but a spume° that plays *froth*
Upon a ghostly paradigm of things;
Solider Aristotle played the taws[5]
Upon the bottom of a king of kings;
World-famous golden-thighed Pythagoras[6]
Fingered upon a fiddle-stick or strings
What a star sang and careless Muses heard:
Old clothes upon old sticks to scare a bird.

7

Both nuns and mothers worship images,
But those the candles light are not as those
That animate a mother's reveries,
But keep a marble or a bronze repose.
And yet they too break hearts—O Presences
That passion, piety or affection knows,
And that all heavenly glory symbolise—
O self-born mockers of man's enterprise;

8

Labour is blossoming or dancing where
The body is not bruised to pleasure soul,

4. Fifteenth-century artists of Italy's Renaissance.
5. A leather strap, used to spin a top.
6. A 6th-century B.C.E. Greek philosopher who developed a mathematical basis for the universe and music.

Nor beauty born out of its own despair,
Nor blear-eyed wisdom out of midnight oil.
O chestnut tree, great rooted blossomer,
Are you the leaf, the blossom or the bole?
O body swayed to music, O brightening glance,
How can we know the dancer from the dance?

1926 1927

Byzantium

The unpurged images of day recede;
The Emperor's drunken soldiery are abed;
Night resonance recedes, night-walkers' song
After great cathedral gong;
A starlit or a moonlit dome disdains
All that man is,
All mere complexities,
The fury and the mire of human veins.

Before me floats an image, man or shade,
Shade more than man, more image than a shade;
For Hades' bobbin° bound in mummy-cloth *spool*
May unwind the winding path;
A mouth that has no moisture and no breath
Breathless mouths may summon;
I hail the superhuman;
I call it death-in-life and life-in-death.

Miracle, bird or golden handiwork,
More miracle than bird or handiwork,
Planted on the starlit golden bough,
Can like the cocks of Hades crow,
Or, by the moon embittered, scorn aloud
In glory of changeless metal
Common bird or petal
And all complexities of mire or blood.

At midnight on the Emperor's pavement flit
Flames that no faggot° feeds, nor steel has lit, *bundle of sticks*
Nor storm disturbs, flames begotten of flame,
Where blood-begotten spirits come
And all complexities of fury leave,
Dying into a dance,
An agony of trance,
An agony of flame that cannot singe a sleeve.

Astraddle on the dolphin's mire and blood,
Spirit after spirit! The smithies break the flood,
The golden smithies of the Emperor!
Marbles of the dancing floor
Break bitter furies of complexity,
Those images that yet

Fresh images beget,
That dolphin-torn, that gong-tormented sea.

1930 1932

Crazy Jane Talks with the Bishop

I met the Bishop on the road
And much said he and I.
"Those breasts are flat and fallen now
Those veins must soon be dry;
Live in a heavenly mansion,
Not in some foul sty."

"Fair and foul are near of kin,
And fair needs foul," I cried.
"My friends are gone, but that's a truth
Nor grave nor bed denied,
Learned in bodily lowliness
And in the heart's pride.

"A woman can be proud and stiff
When on love intent;
But Love has pitched his mansion in
The place of excrement;
For nothing can be sole or whole
That has not been rent."

1931 1932

Lapis Lazuli[1]

(For Harry Clifton[2])

I have heard that hysterical women say
They are sick of the palette and fiddle-bow,
Of poets that are always gay,
For everybody knows or else should know
That if nothing drastic is done
Aeroplane and Zeppelin will come out,
Pitch like King Billy bomb-balls[3] in
Until the town lie beaten flat.

All perform their tragic play,
There struts Hamlet, there is Lear,
That's Ophelia, that Cordelia;[4]
Yet they, should the last scene be there,
The great stage curtain about to drop,

1. A rich blue mineral producing the pigment ultramarine; used by the ancients for decoration.
2. A friend who gave Yeats a carving in lapis lazuli on his birthday.
3. German bombs; "King Billy" is a nickname for Kaiser Wilhelm II. Yeats may also mean to invoke King William I of England, "William of Orange," whose defeat of King James II at the Battle of the Boyne in 1690 resulted in the Protestant ascendancy in Ireland.
4. Characters from *Hamlet* and *King Lear*.

If worthy their prominent part in the play,
Do not break up their lines to weep.
They know that Hamlet and Lear are gay;
Gaiety transfiguring all that dread.
All men have aimed at, found and lost;
Black out; Heaven blazing into the head:
Tragedy wrought to its uttermost.
Though Hamlet rambles and Lear rages,
And all the drop scenes drop at once
Upon a hundred thousand stages,
It cannot grow by an inch or an ounce.

On their own feet they came, or on shipboard,
Camel-back, horse-back, ass-back, mule-back,
Old civilisations put to the sword.
Then they and their wisdom went to rack:
No handiwork of Callimachus[5]
Who handled marble as if it were bronze,
Made draperies that seemed to rise
When sea-wind swept the corner, stands;
His long lamp chimney shaped like the stem
Of a slender palm, stood but a day;
All things fall and are built again
And those that build them again are gay.

Two Chinamen, behind them a third,
Are carved in Lapis Lazuli,
Over them flies a long-legged bird
A symbol of longevity;
The third, doubtless a serving-man,
Carries a musical instrument.

Every discolouration of the stone,
Every accidental crack or dent
Seems a water-course or an avalanche,
Or lofty slope where it still snows
Though doubtless plum or cherry-branch
Sweetens the little half-way house
Those Chinamen climb towards, and I
Delight to imagine them seated there;
There, on the mountain and the sky,
On all the tragic scene they stare.
One asks for mournful melodies;
Accomplished fingers begin to play.
Their eyes mid many wrinkles, their eyes,
Their ancient, glittering eyes, are gay.

1936

1938

5. Greek poet, grammarian, critic, and sculptor (c. 310–c. 240 B.C.E.).

The Circus Animals' Desertion

1

I sought a theme and sought for it in vain,
I sought it daily for six weeks or so.
Maybe at last being but a broken man
I must be satisfied with my heart, although
Winter and summer till old age began
My circus animals were all on show,
Those stilted boys, that burnished chariot,
Lion and woman and the Lord knows what.

2

What can I but enumerate old themes,
First that sea-rider Oisin[1] led by the nose
Through three enchanted islands, allegorical dreams,
Vain gaiety, vain battle, vain repose,
Themes of the embittered heart, or so it seems,
That might adorn old songs or courtly shows;
But what cared I that set him on to ride,
I, starved for the bosom of his fairy bride.

And then a counter-truth filled out its play,
"The Countess Cathleen"[2] was the name I gave it,
She, pity-crazed, had given her soul away
But masterful Heaven had intervened to save it.
I thought my dear must her own soul destroy
So did fanaticism and hate enslave it,
And this brought forth a dream and soon enough
This dream itself had all my thought and love.

And when the Fool and Blind Man stole the bread
Cuchulain[3] fought the ungovernable sea;
Heart mysteries there, and yet when all is said
It was the dream itself enchanted me:
Character isolated by a deed
To engross the present and dominate memory.
Players and painted stage took all my love
And not those things that they were emblems of.

3

Those masterful images because complete
Grew in pure mind but out of what began?
A mound of refuse or the sweepings of a street,
Old kettles, old bottles, and a broken can,
Old iron, old bones, old rags, that raving slut

1. Mythical Irish poet-warrior, son of the great Finn, who crossed the sea on an enchanted horse; hero of Yeats's early narrative poem *The Wanderings of Oisin*.
2. Yeats's play *Cathleen ní Houlihan* (1902) tells the traditional story of its title character, allegorical symbol of Ireland.
3. Hero of the medieval Irish epic *The Tain*, who single-handedly defended Ulster.

Who keeps the till. Now that my ladder's gone
I must lie down where all the ladders start
In the foul rag and bone shop of the heart.

1939

Under Ben Bulben[1]

1

Swear by what the Sages spoke
Round the Mareotic Lake[2]
That the Witch of Atlas[3] knew,
Spoke and set the cocks a-crow.

Swear by those horsemen, by those women
Complexion and form prove superhuman,
That pale, long-visaged company
That airs an immortality
Completeness of their passions won;
Now they ride the wintry dawn
Where Ben Bulben sets the scene.

Here's the gist of what they mean.

2

Many times man lives and dies
Between his two eternities,
That of race and that of soul,
And ancient Ireland knew it all.
Whether man dies in his bed
Or the rifle knocks him dead,
A brief parting from those dear
Is the worst man has to fear.
Though grave-diggers' toil is long,
Sharp their spades, their muscle strong,
They but thrust their buried men
Back in the human mind again.

3

You that Mitchel's prayer have heard,
"Send war in our time, O Lord!"[4]
Know that when all words are said
And a man is fighting mad,
Something drops from eyes long blind,
He completes his partial mind,
For an instant stands at ease,
Laughs aloud, his heart at peace.

1. A mountain in County Sligo.
2. An ancient region south of Alexandria, Egypt, known as a center of Neoplatonism.
3. *The Witch of Atlas* is the title of a poem by Percy Shelley.
4. John Mitchel, revolutionary patriot, wrote "Give us war in our time, O Lord!" while in prison.

Even the wisest man grows tense
With some sort of violence
Before he can accomplish fate,
Know his work or choose his mate.

4

Poet and sculptor do the work,
Nor let the modish painter shirk
What his great forefathers did,
Bring the soul of man to God,
Make him fill the cradles right.

Measurement began our might:
Forms a stark Egyptian[5] thought,
Forms that gentler Phidias wrought.
Michael Angelo left a proof
On the Sistine Chapel roof,
Where but half-awakened Adam
Can disturb globe-trotting Madam
Till her bowels are in heat,
Proof that there's a purpose set
Before the secret working mind:
Profane perfection of mankind.

Quattrocento[6] put in paint
On backgrounds for a God or Saint
Gardens where a soul's at ease;
Where everything that meets the eye,
Flowers and grass and cloudless sky
Resemble forms that are, or seem
When sleepers wake and yet still dream,
And when it's vanished still declare,
With only bed and bedstead there,
That Heavens had opened.
                                        Gyres run on;
When that greater dream had gone
Calvert and Wilson, Blake and Claude,[7]
Prepared a rest for the people of God,
Palmer's phrase,[8] but after that
Confusion fell upon our thought.

5

Irish poets learn your trade,
Sing whatever is well made,
Scorn the sort now growing up
All out of shape from toe to top,

5. Plotinus, 3rd-century C.E. Egyptian-born philosopher, founder of Neoplatonism.

6. Fifteenth-century artists of Italy's Renaissance.

7. Edward Calvert (1799–1883), English painter and engraver, disciple of William Blake; Richard Wilson (1714–1782), British landscape painter; Claude Lorrain (1600–1682), French landscape painter.

8. Samuel Palmer (1805–1881), English painter of visionary landscapes and admirer of Blake.

Their unremembering hearts and heads
Base-born products of base beds.
Sing the peasantry, and then
Hard-riding country gentlemen,
The holiness of monks, and after
Porter-drinkers' randy° laughter; *lusty*
Sing the lords and ladies gay
That were beaten into the clay
Through seven heroic centuries;[9]
Cast your mind on other days
That we in coming days may be
Still the indomitable Irishry.

6

Under bare Ben Bulben's head
In Drumcliff[1] churchyard Yeats is laid.
An ancestor was rector there
Long years ago; a church stands near,
By the road an ancient cross.
No marble, no conventional phrase,
On limestone quarried near the spot
By his command these words are cut:

Cast a cold eye
On life, on death.
Horseman, pass by!

1938 1939

E. M. Forster
1879–1970

Edward Morgan Forster, fondly referred to by friends as Morgan or "Bunny," had an enormous effect on modern British literature and letters over the course of his long life. Born in 1879, Forster died at 91 in 1970, having traversed the course of British culture from its Victorian and imperial peak to the postimperial world of the Beatles and the waning of the British novel. His prolific output of novels, short stories, literary criticism, travel writing, and political essays had also waned by the time of his death, partly because the subject he most wished to write about—male homosexual love—was the final taboo of British literature he did not live to see broken. His autobiographical novel *Maurice,* describing an upper-class Englishman's finding of true love with a working-class man employed on a friend's estate, was published only in 1971, after Forster's death. The novels of Forster's youth and middle age remain classics of modern British literature—and the basis for several films in recent years. *Howards End* (1910) explores the fault lines between classes in British society, while *A Passage to India* (1924) defines the processes that would lead inexorably to the loss of Britain's empire.

9. I.e., the seven centuries since the conquest of Ireland by Henry II.

1. A village lying on the slopes of Ben Bulben, where Yeats was buried.

Forster had a privileged upbringing, and a private education that led him to King's College, Cambridge, and degrees in classics and history. His family wealth allowed him to live in Greece, Italy, and Egypt after graduation in 1901; he spent part of World War I as a Red Cross volunteer in Alexandria, Egypt. He first traveled to India in 1912–1913, and later served as private secretary to the Maharajah of Dewas in 1921. Observing the tensions of empire firsthand, he became a journalist for the Labor Party's *Daily Herald,* later a radio broadcaster in the cause of Indian independence and a reviewer for the *New Statesman* and *Nation*. After Indian independence was achieved in 1947, he was brought to India in public tribute for his actions on behalf of the political solution to independence.

Forster was close to Virginia Woolf as friend and as literary influence: Woolf's *Mrs Dalloway* (1925) is modeled in part on *A Passage to India,* in that it takes one of its central characters from London to India and back. Like Woolf's novel, *A Passage to India* is notable for its use of multiple perspectives; Forster employed the shifting viewpoints of an elderly British woman, a Muslim Indian physician, and a male British educator and civil servant of empire, writing his story across the lines of difference of race, religion, gender, and culture. *The Life to Come,* coming from a body of work published posthumously, fuses Forster's concern for the expression of homosexual love with his equally distinctive and lifelong focus on the wrongs of Britain's empire and the harsh inequities of imperialism. Set in a nameless colony, the story is an allegory of the costs of suppressing others and the supreme price paid by suppressing oneself. Sexual desire, friendship and love between colonizer and colonized, master and servant, "superior" and "inferior" were the very things that, for Forster, could break down the barriers of empire abroad, and the inequalities of society at home. Reverend Pinmay, a prim, repressed colonial master in a clerical collar, can't accept Chief Vithobai as an equal, but he reaps the destruction he has sown. One of Forster's most famous lines is from an essay on literary form: "Only connect," he wrote, and that call to make connection, whether in narrative form, or between classes, races, sexes, and countries, is the hallmark of his fiction.

For more on Forster, go to *The Longman Anthology of British Literature* Web site at www.myliteraturekit.com.

The Life to Come

1. Night

Love had been born somewhere in the forest, of what quality only the future could decide. Trivial or immortal, it had been born to two human bodies as a midnight cry. Impossible to tell whence the cry had come, so dark was the forest. Or into what worlds it would echo, so vast was the forest. Love had been born for good or evil, for a long life or a short.

There was hidden among the undergrowth of that wild region a small native hut. Here, after the cry had died away, a light was kindled. It shone upon the pagan limbs and the golden ruffled hair of a young man. He, calm and dignified, raised the wick of a lamp which had been beaten down flat, he smiled, lit it, and his surroundings trembled back into his sight. The hut lay against the roots of an aged tree, which undulated[1] over its floor and surged at one place into a natural couch, a sort of throne, where the young man's quilt had been spread. A stream sang outside, a firefly relit its lamp also. A remote, a romantic spot . . . lovely, lovable . . . and then he caught sight of a book on the floor, and he dropped beside it with a dramatic moan as if it was a corpse and he the murderer. For the book in question was his Holy Bible. "Though I speak with the tongues of men and of angels, and have not—" a scarlet flower hid the next word, flowers were everywhere, even round his own neck. Losing his dignity, he sobbed "Oh, what have I done?" and not daring to answer the question he hurled the flowers through the door of the hut and the Bible after them, then rushed to retrieve the latter in an agony of grotesque remorse. All had fallen into the stream, all were carried away by the song.

1. Flowed.

Darkness and beauty, darkness and beauty. "Only one end to this," he thought. And he scuttled back for his pistol. But the pistol was not with him, for he was negligent in his arrangements and had left it over with the servants at the further side of the great tree; and the servants, awoken from slumber, took alarm at his talk of firearms. In spite of all he could say, they concluded that an attack was impending from the neighbouring village, which had already proved unfriendly, and they implored their young master not to resist, but to hide in the brushwood until dawn and slip away as soon as the forest paths were visible. Contrary to his orders, they began packing, and next morning he was riding away from the enchanted hut, and descending the watershed into the next valley. Looking back at the huge and enigmatic masses of the trees, he prayed them to keep his unspeakable secret, to conceal it even from God, and he felt in his unhinged state that they had the power to do this, and that they were not ordinary trees.

When he reached the coast, the other missionaries there saw at once from his face that he had failed. Nor had they expected otherwise. The Roman Catholics, far more expert than themselves, had failed to convert Vithobai, the wildest, strongest, most stubborn of all the inland chiefs. And Paul Pinmay (for this was the young man's name) was at that time a very young man indeed, and had partly been sent in order that he might discover his own limitations. He was inclined to be impatient and headstrong, he knew little of the language and still less of native psychology, and indeed he disdained to study this last, declaring in his naïve way that human nature is the same all over the world. They heard his story with sympathy but without surprise. He related how on his arrival he had asked for an audience, which Vithobai had granted inside his ancestral stockade. There, dictionary in hand, he had put the case for Christ, and at the end Vithobai, not deigning to reply in person, had waved to a retainer and made him answer. The retainer had been duly refuted, but Vithobai remained impassive and unfriendly behind his amulets and robes. So he put the case a second time, and another retainer was put up against him, and the audience continued on these lines until he was so exhausted that he was fain to withdraw. Forbidden to sleep in the village, he was obliged to spend the night all alone in a miserable hut, while the servants kept careful watch before the entrance and reported that an attack might be expected at any moment. He had therefore judged it fitter to come away at sunrise. Such was his story—told in a mixture of missionary jargon and of slang—and towards the close he was looking at his colleagues through his long eyelashes to see whether they suspected anything.

"Do you advise a renewed attempt next week?" asked one of them, who was addicted to irony.

And another: "Your intention, I think, when you left us, was to get into touch with this unapproachable Vithobai personally, indeed you declared that you would not return until you had done so."

And a third: "But you must rest now, you look tired."

He was tired, but as soon as he lay down his secret stole out of its hiding-place beyond the mountains, and lay down by his side. And he recalled Vithobai, Vithobai the unapproachable, coming into his hut out of the darkness and smiling at him. Oh how delighted he had been! Oh how surprised! He had scarcely recognized the sardonic chief in this gracious and bare-limbed boy, whose only ornaments were scarlet flowers. Vithobai had laid all formality aside. "I have come secretly," were his first words. "I wish to hear more about this god whose name is Love." How his heart had leapt after the despondency of the day! "Come to Christ!" he had cried, and Vithobai had said, "Is that your name?" He explained No, his name was not Christ, although he had the fortune to be called Paul after a great apostle, and of course he was no god but a sinful man, chosen to call other sinners to the Mercy Seat. "What is Mercy? I wish to hear more," said Vithobai, and they sat down together upon the couch that was almost a throne. And he had opened the Bible at 1. Cor. 13, and had read and expounded the marvellous chapter, and spoke of the love of Christ and of our love for each other in Christ, very simply but more eloquently than ever before, while Vithobai said, "This is the first time I have heard such words, I like them," and drew closer, his body aglow and smelling sweetly of flowers. And he saw how intelligent the boy was and how handsome, and determining to win him there and then imprinted a kiss on his forehead and drew him to Abraham's bosom.[2] And Vithobai had lain in it gladly—too gladly and too long—and had extinguished the lamp. And God alone saw them after that.

Yes, God saw and God sees. Go down into the depths of the woods and He beholds you, throw His Holy Book into the stream, and you destroy only print and paper, not the Word. Sooner or later, God calls every deed to the light. And so it was with Mr Pinmay. He began, though tardily, to meditate upon his sin. Each time he looked at it its aspect altered. At first he assumed that all the blame was his, because he should have set an example. But this was not the root of the matter, for Vithobai had shown no reluctance to be tempted. On the contrary . . . and it was his hand that beat down the light. And why had he stolen up from the village if not to tempt? . . . Yes, to tempt, to attack the new religion by corrupting its preacher, yes, yes, that was it, and his retainers celebrated his victory now in some cynical orgy. Young Mr Pinmay saw it all. He remembered all that he had heard of the antique[3] power of evil in the country, the tales he had so smilingly dismissed as beneath a Christian's notice, the extraordinary uprushes of energy which certain natives were said to possess and occasionally to employ for unholy purposes. And having reached this point he found that he was able to pray; he confessed his defilement (the very name of which cannot be mentioned among Christians), he lamented that he had postponed, perhaps for a generation, the victory of the Church, and he condemned, with increasing severity, the arts of his seducer. On the last topic he became truly eloquent, he always found something more to say, and having begun by recommending the boy to mercy he ended by asking that he might be damned.

"But perhaps this is going too far," he thought, and perhaps it was, for just as he finished his prayers there was a noise as of horsemen below, and then all his colleagues came dashing into his room. They were in extreme excitement. Cried one: "News from the interior, news from the forest. Vithobai and the entire of his people have embraced Christianity." And the second: "Here we have the triumph of youth, oh it puts us to shame." While the third exclaimed alternately "Praise be to God!" and "I beg your pardon." They rejoiced one with another and rebuked their own hardness of heart and want of faith in the Gospel method, and they thought the more highly of young Pinmay because he was not elated by his success, on the contrary, he appeared to be disturbed, and fell upon his knees in prayer.

2. Evening

Mr Pinmay's trials, doubts and final triumphs are recorded in a special pamphlet, published by his Society and illustrated by woodcuts. There is a picture called "What

2. Forster is using Paul Pinmay's religious rhetoric for double meanings: "drew him to Abraham's bosom" means both that Pinmay tried to convert Vithobai to Christianity, but also that he embraced him.
3. Ancient.

it seemed to be", which shows a hostile and savage potentate threatening him; in another picture, called "What it really was!," a dusky youth in western clothes sits among a group of clergymen and ladies, looking like a waiter, and supported by under-waiters, who line the steps of a building labelled "School." Barnabas (for such was the name that the dusky youth received at his baptism)—Barnabas proved an exemplary convert. He made mistakes, and his theology was crude and erratic, but he never backslid, and he had authority with his own people, so that the missionaries had only to explain carefully what they wanted, and it was carried out. He evinced abundant zeal, and behind it a steadiness of purpose all too rare. No one, not even the Roman Catholics, could point to so solid a success.[4]

Since Mr Pinmay was the sole cause of the victory, the new district naturally fell to his charge. Modest, like all sincere workers, he was reluctant to accept, refusing to go although the chief sent deputation after deputation to escort him, and only going in the end because he was commanded to do so by the Bishop. He was appointed for a term of ten years. As soon as he was installed, he set to work energetically—indeed, his methods provoked criticism, although they were fully justified by their fruits. He who had been wont to lay such stress on the Gospel teaching, on love, kindness, and personal influence, he who had preached that the Kingdom of Heaven is intimacy and emotion, now reacted with violence and treated the new converts and even Barnabas himself with the gloomy severity of the Old Law. He who had ignored the subject of native psychology now became an expert therein, and often spoke more like a disillusioned official[5] than a missionary. He would say: "These people are so unlike ourselves that I much doubt whether they have really accepted Christ. They are pleasant enough when they meet us, yet probably spread all manner of ill-natured gossip when our backs are turned. I cannot wholly trust them." He paid no respect to local customs, suspecting them all to be evil, he undermined the tribal organization, and—most risky of all—he appointed a number of native catechists of low type from the tribe in the adjoining valley. Trouble was expected, for this was an ancient and proud people, but their spirit seemed broken, or Barnabas broke it where necessary. At the end of the ten years the Church was to know no more docile sons.

Yet Mr Pinmay had his anxious moments.

His first meeting with Barnabas was the worst of them.

He had managed to postpone it until the day of his installation by the Bishop, and of the general baptism. The ceremonies were over, and the whole tribe, headed by their chief, had filed past the portable font and been signed on the forehead with the cross of Christ. Mistaking the nature of the rite, they were disposed to gaiety. Barnabas laid his outer garment aside, and running up to the group of missionaries like any young man of his people said, "My brother in Christ, oh come quickly," and stroked Mr Pinmay's flushed face, and tried to kiss his forehead and golden hair.

Mr Pinmay disengaged himself and said in a trembling voice: "In the first place send your people each to his home."

The order was given and obeyed.

"In the second place, let no one come before me again until he is decently clad," he continued, more firmly.

"My brother, like you?"

The missionary was now wearing a suit of ducks[6] with shirt, vest, pants and cholera belt, also sun-helmet, starched collar, blue tie spotted with white, socks, and

4. A number of Christian sects are competing to convert the "heathen."

5. A colonial civil servant.

6. Cotton canvas.

brown boots. "Yes, like me," he said. "And in the third place are you decently clad yourself, Barnabas?"

The chief was wearing but little. A cincture[7] of bright silks supported his dagger and floated in the fresh wind when he ran. He had silver armlets, and a silver necklet, closed by a falcon's head which nestled against his throat. His eyes flashed like a demon, for he was unaccustomed to rebuke, but he submitted and vanished into his stockade.

The suspense of the last few weeks had quite altered Mr Pinmay's character. He was no longer an open-hearted Christian knight[8] but a hypocrite whom a false step would destroy. The retreat of Barnabas relieved him. He saw that he had gained an ascendancy over the chief which it was politic to develop. Barnabas respected him, and would not willingly do harm—had even an affection for him, loathsome as the idea might seem. All this was to the good. But he must strike a second blow. That evening he went in person to the stockade, taking with him two colleagues who had recently arrived and knew nothing of the language.

The chief received them in soiled European clothes—in the interval he had summoned one of the traders who accompanied the baptismal party. He had mastered his anger, and speaking courteously he said: "Christ awaits us in my inner chamber."

Mr Pinmay had thought out his line of action. He dared not explain the hideous error, nor call upon his fellow sinner to repent; the chief must remain in a state of damnation for a time, for a new church depended on it. His reply to the unholy suggestion was "Not yet."

"Why not yet?" said the other, his beautiful eyes filling with tears. "God orders me to love you now."

"He orders me to refrain."

"How can that be, when God *is* Love?"

"I have served him the longer and I know."

"But this is my palace and I am a great chief."

"God is greater than all chiefs."

"As it was in your hut let it here be. Dismiss your companions and the gate will be barred behind them, and we close out the light. My body and the breath in it are yours. Draw me again to your bosom. I give myself, I, Vithobai the King."

"Not yet," repeated Mr Pinmay, covering his eyes with his hand.

"My beloved, I give myself . . . take me . . . I give you my kingdom." And he fell prone.

"Arise, Barnabas. . . . We do not want your kingdom. We have only come to teach you to rule it rightly. And do not speak of what happened in the hut. Never mention the hut, the word hut, the thought, either to me or to anyone. It is my wish and my command."

"Never?"

"Never."

"Come, my gods, come back to me," he cried, leaping up and wrenching at his clothes. "What do I gain by leaving you?"

"No, no, no!" prevaricated Mr Pinmay. "I said Never speak, not that I would never come."

7. Loose belt.

8. A reference to the Crusades, where the Knights Templar killed rather than converted their Muslim enemy.

The boy was reassured. He said: "Yes. I misunderstood. You do come to Christ, but not yet. I must wait. For how long?"

"Until I call you. Meanwhile obey all my orders, whether given directly or through others."

"Very well, my brother. Until you call me."

"And do not call me your brother."

"Very well."

"Or seek my company." Turning to the other missionaries, he said, "Now let us go." He was glad he had brought companions with him, for his repentance was still insecure. The sun was setting, the inner chamber garlanded, the stockade deserted, the boy wild with passion, weeping as if his heart had broken. They might have been so happy together in their sin and no one but God need have known.

3. Day

The next crisis that Mr Pinmay had to face was far less serious, yet it shocked him more, because he was unprepared for it. The occasion was five years later, just before his own marriage. The cause of Christ had progressed greatly in the interval. Dancing had been put down, industry encouraged, inaccurate notions as to the nature of religion had disappeared, nor in spite of espionage had he discovered much secret immorality. He was marrying one of the medical missionaries, a lady who shared his ideals, and whose brother had a mining concession above the village.

As he leant over the veranda, meditating with pleasure on the approaching change in his life, a smart European dogcart[9] drove up, and Barnabas scrambled out of it to pay his congratulations. The chief had developed into an affable and rather weedy[1] Christian with a good knowledge of English. He likewise was about to be married—his bride a native catechist from the adjoining valley, a girl inferior to him by birth, but the missionaries had selected her.

Congratulations were exchanged.

Mr Pinmay's repentance was now permanent, and his conscience so robust that he could meet the chief with ease and transact business with him in private, when occasion required it. The brown hand, lying dead for an instant in his own, awoke no reminiscences of sin.

Wriggling rather awkwardly inside his clothes, Barnabas said with a smile: "Will you take me a short drive in your dog-cart, Mr Pinmay?"

Mr Pinmay replied that he had no dog-cart.

"Excuse me, sir, you have. It stands below. It, and the horse, are my wedding gift to you."

The missionary had long desired a horse and cart, and he accepted them without waiting to ask God's blessing. "You should not have given me such an expensive present," he remarked. For the chief was no longer wealthy; in the sudden advent of civilization he had chanced to lose much of his land.

"My reward is enough if we go one drive, sir."

As a rule he did not choose to be seen pleasuring with a native—it undermined his authority—but this was a special occasion. They moved briskly through the village, Barnabas driving to show the paces of the horse, and presently turned to the

9. Carriage. 1. Shaggy.

woods or to what remained of them; there was a tolerable road, made by the timber-fellers, which wound uphill towards a grove. The scene was uninteresting, and pervaded by a whitish light that seemed to penetrate every recess. They spoke of local affairs.

"How much of the timber is earmarked for the mines?" inquired Mr Pinmay, in the course of the conversation.

"An increasing amount as the galleries extend deeper into the mountain. I am told that the heat down there is now so great that the miners work unclad. Are they to be fined for this?"

"No. It is impossible to be strict about mines. They constitute a special case."

"I understand. I am also told that disease among them increases."

"It does, but then so do our hospitals."

"I do not understand."

"Can't you grasp, Barnabas, that under God's permission certain evils attend civilization, but that if men do God's will the remedies for the evils keep pace? Five years ago you had not a single hospital in this valley."

"Nor any disease. I understand. Then all my people were strong."

"There was abundant disease," corrected the missionary. "Vice and superstition, to mention no others. And intertribal war. Could you have married a lady from another valley five years ago?"

"No. Even as a concubine[2] she would have disgraced me."

"All concubines are a disgrace."

"I understand. In regard to this marriage, sir, there is, however, a promise that you made me once."

"About the mining concession, of course? Exactly. Yes, I never thought you were treated fairly there. I will certainly approach my future brother-in-law to get you some compensation. But you ought to have been more careful at the time. You signed your rights away without consulting me. I am always willing to be consulted."

"It is not the mining concession," said Barnabas patiently; although a good steward for the Church, he had grown careless where his own affairs were concerned. "It is quite another promise." He seemed to be choosing his words. Speaking slowly and without any appearance of emotion, he said at last: "Come to Christ."

"Come to Him indeed," said Mr Pinmay in slightly reproving tones, for he was not accustomed to receive such an invitation from a spiritual inferior.

Barnabas paused again, then said: "In the hut."

"What hut?" He had forgotten.

"The hut with the Mercy Seat."

Shocked and angry, he exclaimed: "Barnabas, Barnabas, this is disgraceful. I forbad you ever to mention this subject."

At that moment the horse drew up at the entrance of the grove. Civilization tapped and clinked behind them, under a garish sun. The road ended, and a path where two could walk abreast continued into the delicate gray and purple recesses of the trees. Tepid, impersonal, as if he still discussed public affairs, the young man said: "Let us both be entirely reasonable, sir. God continues to order me to love you. It is my life, whatever else I seem to do. My body and the breath in it are still yours, though you wither them up with this waiting. Come into the last forest, before it is

2. A formal mistress.

cut down, and I will be kind, and all may end well. But it is now five years since you first said Not yet."

"It is, and now I say Never."

"This time you say Never?"

"I do."

Without replying, Barnabas handed him the reins, and then jerked himself out of the cart. It was a most uncanny movement, which seemed to proceed direct from the will. He scarcely used his hands or rose to his feet before jumping. But his soul uncoiled like a spring, and thrust the cart violently away from it against the ground. Mr Pinmay had heard of such contortions, but never witnessed them; they were startling, they were disgusting. And the descent was equally sinister. Barnabas lay helpless as if the evil uprush had suddenly failed. "Are you ill?" asked the clergyman.

"No."

"Then what ails you?"

"No."

"Do you repent of your words?"

"No."

"Then you must be punished. As the head of the community you are bound to set an example. You are fined one hundred pounds for backsliding."

"No." Then as if to himself he said: "First the grapes of my body are pressed. Then I am silenced. Now I am punished. Night, evening and a day. What remains?"[3]

What should remain? The remark was meaningless. Mr Pinmay drove back alone, rather thoughtful. He would certainly have to return the horse and cart—they had been intended as a bribe—and the hundred pounds must be collected by one of his subordinates. He wished that the whole unsavoury business had not been raked up into the light just before his wedding. Its senselessness alarmed him.

4. Morning

The concluding five years of Mr Pinmay's ministry were less satisfactory than their predecessors. His marriage was happy, his difficulties few, nothing tangible opposed him, but he was haunted by the scene outside the grove. Could it signify that he himself had not been pardoned? Did God, in His mystery, demand from him that he should cleanse his brother's soul before his own could be accepted? The dark erotic perversion that the chief mistook for Christianity—who had implanted it? He had put this question from him in the press of his earlier dangers, but it intruded itself now that he was safe. Day after day he heard the cold voice of the somewhat scraggy and unattractive native inviting him to sin, or saw the leap from the cart that suggested a dislocated soul. He turned to the Christianity of the valley, but he found no consolation there. He had implanted that too: not in sin, but in reaction against sin, and so its fruits were as bitter. If Barnabas distorted Christ, the valley ignored Him. It was hard, it lacked personality and beauty and emotion and all that Paul Pinmay had admired in his youth. It could produce catechists and organizers, but never a saint. What was the cause of the failure? The hut, the hut. In the concluding years of his stay, he ordered it to be pulled down.

3. Barnabas has a seizure in the road, akin to Saul being stricken on the road to Damascus, and becoming Paul, a Christian. Barnabas instead "falls out" of Christianity when Pinmay rejects his love.

He seldom met Barnabas now. There was no necessity for it, since the chief's usefulness decreased as the community developed and new men pushed their way to the top. Though still helpful when applied to, he lost all capacity for initiative. He moved from his old stockaded enclosure with its memories of independence, and occupied a lofty but small modern house at the top of the village, suitable to his straitened[4] circumstances. Here he and his wife and their children (one more every eleven months) lived in the semi-European style. Sometimes he worked in the garden, although menial labour was regarded as degrading, and he was assiduous at prayer meetings, where he frequented the back row. The missionaries called him a true Christian when they called him anything, and congratulated themselves that witchcraft had no rallying-point; he had served their purpose, he began to pass from their talk. Only Mr Pinmay watched him furtively and wondered where his old energies had gone. He would have preferred an outburst to this corrupt acquiescence; he knew now that he could deal with outbursts. He even felt weaker himself, as if the same curse infected them both, and this though he had again and again confessed his own share of the sin to God, and had acquired a natural loathing for it in consequence of his marriage.

He could not really feel much sorrow when he learned that the unfortunate fellow was dying.

Consumption[5] was the cause. One of the imported workers had started an epidemic, and Mr and Mrs Pinmay were busied up to the moment of their own departure, negotiating an extension to the cemetery. They expected to leave the valley before Barnabas did, but during the last week he made, so to speak, a spurt, as if he would outstrip them. His was a very rapid case. He put up no fight. His heart seemed broken. They had little time to devote to individuals, so wide was the scope of their work, still they hurried over to see him one morning, hearing that he had had a fresh haemorrhage, and was not likely to survive the day. "Poor fellow, poor lad, he was an important factor ten years back—times change," murmured Mr Pinmay as he pushed the Holy Communion under the seat of the dog-cart—Barnabas's own cart, as it happened, for Mrs Pinmay, knowing nothing of the incident, had acquired it cheaply at a sale a couple of years back. As he drove it briskly up through the village Mr Pinmay's heart grew lighter, and he thanked God for permitting Barnabas, since die we must, to pass away at this particular moment; he would not have liked to leave him behind, festering, equivocal, and perhaps acquiring some sinister power.

When they arrived, Mrs Barnabas told them that her husband was still alive, and, she thought, conscious, but in such darkness of spirit that he would not open his eyes or speak. He had been carried up onto the roof, on account of the heat in his room, and his gestures had indicated that he would be left alone. "But he must not be left alone," said Mr Pinmay. "We must watch with him through this dark hour. I will prepare him in the first place." He climbed the staircase that led through a trapdoor onto the roof. In the shadow of the parapet lay the dying man, coughing gently, and stark naked.

"Vithobai!" he cried in amazement.

He opened his eyes and said: "Who calls me?"

"You must have some covering, Barnabas," said Mr Pinmay fussily. He looked round, but there was nothing on the roof except a curious skein[6] of blue flowers threaded round a knife. He took them up. But the other said, "Do not lay those upon

4. Reduced.
5. Tuberculosis.
6. Woven or braided.

me yet," and he refrained, remembering that blue is the colour of despair in that valley, just as red is the colour of love. "I'll get you a shawl," he continued. "Why, you are not lying upon a mattress, even."

"It is my own roof. Or I thought it was until now. My wife and household respected my wishes. They laid me here because it is not the custom of my ancestors to die in a bed."

"Mrs Barnabas should have known better. You cannot possibly lie on hard asphalt."

"I have found that I can."

"Vithobai, Vithobai," he cried, more upset than he expected.

"Who calls me?"

"You are not going back to your old false gods?"

"Oh no. So near to the end of my life, why should I make any change? These flowers are only a custom, and they comfort me."

"There is only one comforter. . . ." He glanced around the roof, then fell upon his knees. He could save a soul without danger to himself at last. "Come to Christ," he said, "but not in the way that you suppose. The time has come for me to explain. You and I once sinned together, yes, you and your missionary whom you so reverence. You and I must now repent together, yes, such is God's law." And confusedly, and with many changes of emotion and shiftings of his point of view and reservations, he explained the nature of what had happened ten years ago and its present consequences.

The other made a painful effort to follow, but his eyes kept closing. "What is all this talk?" he said at last. "And why do you wait until I am ill and you old?"

"I waited until I could forgive you and ask your forgiveness. It is the hour of your atonement and mine. Put away all despair, forget those wicked flowers. Let us repent and leave the rest to God."

"I repent, I do not repent . . ." he wailed.

"Hush! Think what you say."

"I forgive you, I do not forgive, both are the same. I am good I am evil I am pure I am foul, I am this or that, I am Barnabas, I am Vithobai. What difference does it make now? It is my deeds that await me, and I have no strength left to add to them. No strength, no time. I lie here empty, but you fill me up with thoughts, and then press me to speak them that you may have words to remember afterwards. . . . But it is deeds, deeds that count, O my lost brother. Mine are this little house instead of my old great one, this valley which other men own, this cough that kills me, those bastards that continue my race; and that deed in the hut, which you say caused all, and which now you call joy, now sin. How can I remember which it was after all these years, and what difference if I could? It was a deed, it has gone before me with the others to be judged."

"Vithobai," he pleaded, distressed because he himself had been called old.

"Who calls me the third time?"

"Kiss me."

"My mouth is down here."

"Kiss my forehead—no more—as a sign that I am forgiven. Do not misunderstand me this time . . . in perfect purity . . . the holy salutation of Christ. And then say with me: Our Father which art in Heaven, hallowed be Thy name. . . . "

"My mouth is down here," he repeated wearily.

Mr Pinmay feared to venture the kiss lest Satan took an advantage. He longed to do something human before he had the sinking man carried down to receive the

Holy Communion, but he had forgotten how. "You have forgiven me, my poor fellow," he worried on. "If you do not, how can I continue my vocation, or hope for the forgiveness of God?"

The lips moved.

"If you forgive me, move your lips once more, as a sign."

He became rigid, he was dying.

"You do still love me?"

"My breast is down here."

"In Christ, I mean." And uncertain of what he ought to do he laid his head hesitatingly upon the poor skeleton. Vithobai shivered, then looked at him with surprise, pity, affection, disdain, with all, but with little of any, for his spirit had mainly departed, and only the ghosts of its activities remained. He was a little pleased. He raised a hand painfully, and stroked the scanty hair, golden no longer. He whispered, "Too late," but he smiled a little.

"It is never too late," said Mr Pinmay, permitting a slow encircling movement of the body, the last it would ever accomplish. "God's mercy is infinite, and endureth for ever and ever. He will give us other opportunities. We have erred in this life but it will not be so in the life to come."

The dying man seemed to find comfort at last. "The life to come," he whispered, but more distinctly. "I had forgotten it. You are sure it is coming?"

"Even your old false religion was sure of that."

"And we shall meet in it, you and I?" he asked, with a tender yet reverent caress.

"Assuredly, if we keep God's commandments."

"Shall we know one another again?"

"Yes, with all spiritual knowledge."

"And will there be love?"

"In the real and true sense, there will."

"Real and true love! Ah, that would be joyful." His voice gained strength, his eyes had an austere beauty as he embraced his friend, parted from him so long by the accidents of earth. Soon God would wipe away all tears. "The life to come," he shouted. "Life, life, eternal life. Wait for me in it." And he stabbed the missionary through the heart.

The jerk the knife gave brought his own fate hurrying upon him. He had scarcely the strength to push the body onto the asphalt or to spread the skein of blue flowers. But he survived for a moment longer, and it was the most exquisite he had ever known. For love was conquered at last and he was again a king, he had sent a messenger before him to announce his arrival in the life to come, as a great chief should. "I served you for ten years," he thought, "and your yoke was hard, but mine will be harder and you shall serve me now for ever and ever." He dragged himself up, he looked over the parapet. Below him were a horse and cart, beyond, the valley which he had once ruled, the site of the hut, the ruins of his old stockade, the schools, the hospital, the cemetery, the stacks of timber, the polluted stream, all that he had been used to regard as signs of his disgrace. But they signified nothing this morning, they were flying like mist, and beneath them, solid and eternal, stretched the kingdom of the dead. He rejoiced as in boyhood, he was expected there now. Mounting on the corpse, he climbed higher, raised his arms over his head, sunlit, naked, victorious, leaving all disease and humilation behind him, and he swooped like a falcon from the parapet in pursuit of the terrified shade.[7]

7. Ghost.

James Joyce

1882–1941

Man Ray (1890–1976), *Portrait of James Joyce,* 1922.

James Joyce was one of the great innovators who brought the novel into the modern era. As T. S. Eliot put it, Joyce made "the modern world possible for art." The poet Edith Sitwell wrote that by the turn of the century, "language had become, not so much an abused medium, as a dead and outworn thing, in which there was no living muscular system. Then came the rebirth of the medium, and this was effected, as far as actual vocabularies were concerned, very largely by such prose writers as Mr. James Joyce and Miss Gertrude Stein." Joyce objected to this flaccidity, citing examples in the work of George Moore, the most important Irish novelist of the first decade of the twentieth century; Moore's novel *The Untilled Field,* Joyce complained to his brother Stanislaus, was "damned stupid," "dull and flat," and "ill written." In a comment that would have pleased Joyce, one critic writing in 1929 declared that Joyce had by that date "conclusively reduced all the pretensions of the realistic novel to absurdity."

James Augustus Aloysius Joyce was born in Rathgar, a middle-class suburb of Dublin; though he was to leave Ireland more or less permanently at age twenty-two, Ireland generally, and "Dear Dirty Dublin" specifically, were never far from his mind and writing. He was the eldest surviving son in a large family consisting, according to his father, of "sixteen or seventeen children." His father, John Stanislaus Joyce, born and raised in Cork, was a tax collector and sometime Parnellite political employee; his mother was Mary Jane Joyce, née Murray. There is no better imaginative guide to the twists and turns of Joyce's family fortunes, and their effect on the young writer, than his first novel, *A Portrait of the Artist as a Young Man;* the life of Joyce's autobiographical hero Stephen Dedalus closely follows Joyce's own. The novel brings young Stephen from his earliest memories, through his Catholic schooling at Clongowes Wood College and Belvedere College, up to his graduation from University College, Dublin, and departure for Paris. Like Stephen, Joyce in these years first considered entering the priesthood, then began regarding Catholicism with increasing skepticism and irony, coming to view religion, family, and nation as three kinds of net or trap. One of the most important events of the early part of Joyce's life was the betrayal and subsequent death of "the uncrowned king of Ireland," Charles Stewart Parnell, the political leader who was working hard to make Home Rule for Ireland a reality; his demise, after his adulterous affair with Kitty O'Shea was discovered, was remembered by Joyce in his first poem, *Et Tu, Healy*—which he wrote at the age of eight—and in a haunting story, *Ivy Day in the Committee Room.* Joyce moved to Paris after graduation in 1902 and began medical studies, but he soon had to return to Dublin, as his mother was dying. Joyce gave up the idea of a medical career, which his father could not afford to finance in any event; he briefly tried teaching school and sought to define himself as a writer.

Like Dedalus, the young Joyce first concentrated on writing poetry. The majority of his early poems were collected in the volume *Chamber Music* (1907); both the strength and weakness of the poems is suggested by the praise of Arthur Symons, who in his review in the *Nation* described the lyrics as "tiny, evanescent things." Poetry was ultimately to prove a dead end for Joyce; though he brought out one more volume of thirteen poems during his lifetime (*Pomes Penyeach,* 1927), and wrote one forgettable play (*Exiles,* 1918), prose fiction is the primary area in which Joyce's influence continues to be felt.

The year 1904 proved to be an absolute watershed in Joyce's development as a writer. In January 1904—indeed, perhaps in the single day 7 January 1904—Joyce wrote an impressionistic prose sketch which would ultimately serve as the manifesto for his first novel. From this beginning, Joyce shaped his novel, which was to have been called *Stephen Hero;* and though he worked on it steadily for more than three years, and the manuscript grew to almost a thousand pages, the novel was not coming together in quite the way Joyce had hoped. Hence in the fall of 1907, he began cutting and radically reshaping the material into what would become *A Portrait of the Artist as a Young Man,* one of the finest examples of the *Künstlerroman* (novel of artistic growth) in English; H. G. Wells called it "by far the most living and convincing picture that exists of an Irish Catholic upbringing."

June 16, 1904, in particular is a crucial day in the Joycean calendar, for it is "Bloomsday"—the day on which the events narrated in *Ulysses* take place—and according to legend, it is the day that Nora Barnacle first agreed to go out walking with Joyce. Joyce's father thought Nora's maiden name a good omen, suggesting that she would "stick to him," and indeed she did; without the benefit of marriage, she agreed to accompany him four months later on his artistic exile to the Continent, and though they were not legally married until 1931, she proved a faithful and devoted partner, a small spot of stability amidst the chaos of Joyce's life. They settled for several years in Trieste, Italy, where Joyce taught English at a Berlitz school and where their two children, Giorgio and Lucia, were born. Joyce returned briefly to Ireland in 1909, seeking unsuccessfully to get work published and to start a movie theater; after another brief visit in 1912, he never returned. He spent most of World War I in Zurich, then moved to Paris, where he eked out an existence with the help of several benefactors as his reputation began to grow.

He had begun his first book in June or July 1904, invited by the Irish man of letters "A.E." (George Russell) to submit a short story to his paper *The Irish Homestead*. Joyce began writing the series of fifteen stories that would be published in 1914 as *Dubliners*. In letters to London publisher Grant Richards about his conception for the short stories, Joyce wrote that he planned the volume to be a chapter of Ireland's "moral history" and that in writing it he had "taken the first step towards the spiritual liberation of my country." Richards, however, objected to the stark realism—or sordidness—of several scenes, and pressed Joyce to eliminate vulgarisms; Joyce refused. Finally, desperate to have the book published, Joyce wrote to Richards: "I seriously believe that you will retard the course of civilisation in Ireland by preventing the Irish people from having one good look at themselves in my nicely polished looking-glass."

During this period, Joyce also experimented with a form of short prose sketch that he called the "epiphany." An epiphany, as it is defined in *Stephen Hero,* is "a sudden spiritual manifestation, whether in the vulgarity of speech or of gesture or in a memorable phase of the mind itself." It consequently falls to the artist to "record these epiphanies with extreme care, seeing that they themselves are the most delicate and evanescent of moments." One benefit of Joyce's experimentation with prose epiphanies is that the searching realism and psychological richness of the stories in *Dubliners* are conveyed with a lucid economy of phrasing—what Joyce called "a style of scrupulous meanness"—and by a similar penchant for understatement on the level of plot. The stories often seem to "stop," rather than end; time and again, Joyce withholds the tidy conclusion that conventional fiction had trained readers to expect. In story after story, characters betray what Joyce termed their "paralysis"—a paralysis of the will that prevents them from breaking out of deadening habit. The final story of the collection, *The Dead*—written after the volume had ostensibly been completed, and comprising a broader scope and larger cast of characters than the other stories—is Joyce's finest work of short fiction, and justly praised as one of the great stories of our time; it was filmed, quite sensitively and beautifully, by director John Huston, the last film project before his death.

A second decisive year for Joyce was 1914. Having completed *Dubliners,* Joyce seems never to have thought seriously about writing short fiction again; and throughout the period he was writing his stories, he continued to work on *A Portrait*. As was the case with *Dubliners,* negotiations for the publication of *A Portrait* were extremely difficult; despite its dazzling

Sackville Street (now O'Connell Street), Dublin, with view of Nelson's Pillar.

language, few editors could get beyond the opening pages, with their references to bedwetting and their use of crude slang. Even though the novel had been published serially in *The Egoist* beginning in 1914, and was praised by influential writers like W. B. Yeats, H. G. Wells, and Ezra Pound, the book was rejected by every publisher in London to whom Joyce offered it, before finally being accepted by B. W. Huebsch in New York, and published in December 1916.

With both his stories and his first novel between hard covers, Joyce was finally able to concentrate his energies on the one novel for which, more than any other, he will be remembered—*Ulysses;* that work, too, had begun in 1914. The novel is structured, loosely, on eighteen episodes from Homer's *Odyssey;* Leopold Bloom, advertising salesman, is a modern-day Ulysses, the streets of Dublin his Aegean Sea, and Molly Bloom his (unfaithful) Penelope. Stephen Dedalus, stuck teaching school and estranged from his real father, is an unwitting Telemachus (Ulysses's son) in search of a father. Critics have disagreed over the years as to how seriously readers should take these Homeric parallels; Eliot understood them to be of the utmost importance—"a way of controlling, of ordering, of giving a shape and a significance to the immense panorama of futility and anarchy which is contemporary history"—while the equally supportive Pound suggested that the parallel structure was merely "the remains of a medieval allegorical culture; it matters little, it is a question of cooking, which does not restrict the action, nor inconvenience it, nor harm the realism, nor the contemporaneity of the action."

Concomitant with the Homeric structure, Joyce sought to give each of his eighteen chapters its own style. Chapter 12, focusing on Bloom's encounter with Dublin's Cyclops, called "the Citizen," is written in a style of "gigantism"—full of mock-epic epithets and catalogues, playfully suggestive of the style of ancient Celtic myth and legend. Chapter 13, which parallels Odysseus's encounter with Nausicaa, is written in the exaggerated style of Victorian women's magazines and sentimental fiction, a style which Joyce characterized as "a namby-pamby jammy marmalady drawersy (alto-là!) style with effects of incense, mariolatry, masturbation, stewed cockles, painter's palette, chitchat, circumlocutions, etc etc." While realist writers sought constantly to flush artifice from their writing, to arrive finally at a style which would be value-neutral, Joyce takes the English language on a voyage in the opposite direction; each chapter, as he wrote to his patron Harriet Shaw Weaver, left behind it "a burnt-up field." It would be difficult to overestimate the influence that *Ulysses* has had on modern writing; Eliot's candid response to the novel, reported in a letter to Joyce, was "I have nothing but admiration; in fact, I wish, for my own sake, that I had not read it."

Other people wanted to make sure that no one else would read it. *Ulysses* was promptly banned as obscene, in Ireland, England, and many other countries. Copies were smuggled into the United States, where a pirated edition was published, paying Joyce no royalties. Finally in 1933, in a landmark decision, a federal judge found that the book's frank language and sexual discussions were fully justified artistically—though he allowed that "*Ulysses* is a rather strong draught to ask some sensitive, though normal, persons to take."

In 1923, with *Ulysses* completed, Joyce suddenly reinvented himself and his writing once again, and turned his attention to the writing of the novel that would occupy him almost until his death—*Finnegans Wake*. If *Ulysses* attacks the novel form at the level of style, *Finnegans Wake* targets the very structures of the English language. The story, in its broad outlines, is adapted from a vaudeville music-hall number, "Finnegan's Wake"; the novel's "protagonist," called by myriad names most of which bear the initials H.C.E. (Humphrey Chimpden Earwicker, Here Comes Everybody), has fallen in a drunken stupor, and the content of his dream is, apparently, the novel we read. But since the book is a night book, so Joyce felt that the language must be a night language, a meeting-place of dream and desire, rather than the straightforward language of the day. The novel's language is a neologismic amalgam of more than a dozen modern and ancient languages—a hybrid that devotees call "Wakese"; when questioned as to the wisdom of such a strategy, Joyce replied that *Ulysses* had proved English to be inadequate. "I'd like a language," he told his friend Stefan Zweig, "which is above all languages, a language to which all will do service. I cannot express myself in English without enclosing myself in a tradition." Though *Finnegans Wake* is of a complexity to frustrate even some of Joyce's most ardent admirers, interest in the novel has, if anything, increased in the wake of poststructuralist criticism, and shows no signs of letting up soon.

On 13 January 1941, Joyce died of a perforated ulcer; his illness and death almost certainly owed something to an adult life of rather heavy drinking and surely to the pain of his self-exile. Though his oeuvre consists largely of one volume of short stories and three novels, his importance for students of modern literature is extraordinary. As Richard Ellmann writes at the opening of his magisterial biography, "We are still learning to be James Joyce's contemporaries, to understand our interpreter."

For additional resources on Joyce, go to *The Longman Anthology of British Literature* Web site at www.myliteraturekit.com.

from DUBLINERS

Araby

North Richmond Street, being blind,[1] was a quiet street except at the hour when the Christian Brothers' School set the boys free. An uninhabited house of two storeys stood at the blind end, detached from its neighbours in a square ground. The other houses of the street, conscious of decent lives within them, gazed at one another with brown imperturbable faces.

The former tenant of our house, a priest, had died in the back drawing-room. Air, musty from having been long enclosed, hung in all the rooms, and the waste room behind the kitchen was littered with old useless papers. Among these I found a few paper-covered books, the pages of which were curled and damp: *The Abbot*, by

1. A dead end.

Walter Scott,[2] *The Devout Communicant*[3] and *The Memoirs of Vidocq*.[4] I liked the last best because its leaves were yellow. The wild garden behind the house contained a central apple-tree and a few straggling bushes under one of which I found the late tenant's rusty bicycle-pump. He had been a very charitable priest; in his will he had left all his money to institutions and the furniture of his house to his sister.

When the short days of winter came dusk fell before we had well eaten our dinners. When we met in the street the houses had grown sombre. The space of sky above us was the colour of ever-changing violet and towards it the lamps of the street lifted their feeble lanterns. The cold air stung us and we played till our bodies glowed. Our shouts echoed in the silent street. The career of our play brought us through the dark muddy lanes behind the houses where we ran the gantlet[5] of the rough tribes from the cottages, to the back doors of the dark dripping gardens where odours arose from the ashpits, to the dark odorous stables where a coachman smoothed and combed the horse or shook music from the buckled harness. When we returned to the street light from the kitchen windows had filled the areas. If my uncle was seen turning the corner we hid in the shadow until we had seen him safely housed. Or if Mangan's sister came out on the doorstep to call her brother in to his tea we watched her from our shadow peer up and down the street. We waited to see whether she would remain or go in and, if she remained, we left our shadow and walked up to Mangan's steps resignedly. She was waiting for us, her figure defined by the light from the half-opened door. Her brother always teased her before he obeyed and I stood by the railings looking at her. Her dress swung as she moved her body and the soft rope of her hair tossed from side to side.

Every morning I lay on the floor in the front parlour watching her door. The blind was pulled down to within an inch of the sash so that I could not be seen. When she came out on the doorstep my heart leaped. I ran to the hall, seized my books and followed her. I kept her brown figure always in my eye and, when we came near the point at which our ways diverged, I quickened my pace and passed her. This happened morning after morning. I had never spoken to her, except for a few casual words, and yet her name was like a summons to all my foolish blood.

Her image accompanied me even in places the most hostile to romance. On Saturday evenings when my aunt went marketing I had to go to carry some of the parcels. We walked through the flaring streets, jostled by drunken men and bargaining women, amid the curses of labourers, the shrill litanies of shop-boys who stood on guard by the barrels of pigs' cheeks, the nasal chanting of street-singers, who sang a *come-all-you*[6] about O'Donovan Rossa,[7] or a ballad about the troubles in our native land. These noises converged in a single sensation of life for me: I imagined that I bore my chalice safely through a throng of foes. Her name sprang to my lips at moments in strange prayers and praises which I myself did not understand. My eyes were often full of tears (I could not tell why) and at times a flood from my heart seemed to pour itself out into my bosom. I thought little of the future. I did not know whether I would ever speak to her or not or, if I spoke to her, how I could tell her of my confused adoration. But my body was like a harp and her words and gestures were like fingers running upon the wires.

2. A romantic novel concerning Mary Queen of Scots, published in 1820.
3. A religious tract written by a Franciscan friar.
4. François Vidocq was chief of detectives with the Paris police in the early 19th century, before being dismissed from the force for falsifying records. He probably did not write the *Memoirs*.
5. Risk; challenge (variation of "gauntlet").
6. A popular type of ballad beginning with the formula, "Come all you Irishmen. . . . "
7. Jeremiah O'Donovan, an Irish nationalist exiled to the United States.

One evening I went into the back drawing-room in which the priest had died. It was a dark rainy evening and there was no sound in the house. Through one of the broken panes I heard the rain impinge upon the earth, the fine incessant needles of water playing in the sodden beds. Some distant lamp or lighted window gleamed below me. I was thankful that I could see so little. All my senses seemed to desire to veil themselves and, feeling that I was about to slip from them, I pressed the palms of my hands together until they trembled, murmuring: *O love! O love!* many times.

At last she spoke to me. When she addressed the first words to me I was so confused that I did not know what to answer. She asked me was I going to *Araby*. I forget whether I answered yes or no. It would be a splendid bazaar, she said; she would love to go.

—And why can't you? I asked.

While she spoke she turned a silver bracelet round and round her wrist. She could not go, she said, because there would be a retreat[8] that week in her convent. Her brother and two other boys were fighting for their caps and I was alone at the railings. She held one of the spikes, bowing her head towards me. The light from the lamp opposite our door caught the white curve of her neck, lit up her hair that rested there and, falling, lit up the hand upon the railing. It fell over one side of her dress and caught the white border of a petticoat, just visible as she stood at ease.

—It's well for you, she said.

—If I go, I said, I will bring you something.

What innumerable follies laid waste my waking and sleeping thoughts after that evening! I wished to annihilate the tedious intervening days. I chafed against the work of school. At night in my bedroom and by day in the classroom her image came between me and the page I strove to read. The syllables of the word *Araby* were called to me through the silence in which my soul luxuriated and cast an Eastern enchantment over me. I asked for leave to go to the bazaar on Saturday night. My aunt was surprised and hoped it was not some Freemason affair.[9] I answered few questions in class. I watched my master's face pass from amiability to sternness; he hoped I was not beginning to idle. I could not call my wandering thoughts together. I had hardly any patience with the serious work of life which, now that it stood between me and my desire, seemed to me child's play, ugly monotonous child's play.

On Saturday morning I reminded my uncle that I wished to go to the bazaar in the evening. He was fussing at the hallstand, looking for the hat-brush, and answered me curtly:

—Yes, boy, I know.

As he was in the hall I could not go into the front parlour and lie at the window. I left the house in bad humour and walked slowly towards the school. The air was pitilessly raw and already my heart misgave me.

When I came home to dinner my uncle had not yet been home. Still it was early. I sat staring at the clock for some time and, when its ticking began to irritate me, I left the room. I mounted the staircase and gained the upper part of the house. The high cold empty gloomy rooms liberated me and I went from room to room singing. From the front window I saw my companions playing below in the street. Their cries reached me weakened and indistinct and, leaning my forehead against the cool glass, I looked over at the dark house where she lived. I may have stood there for an hour,

8. A period of withdrawal for prayer, meditation, and religious study.

9. The Masonic Order was a guild thought to be an enemy of the Catholic Church.

seeing nothing but the brown-clad figure cast by my imagination, touched discreetly by the lamplight at the curved neck, at the hand upon the railings and at the border below the dress.

When I came downstairs again I found Mrs Mercer sitting at the fire. She was an old garrulous woman, a pawnbroker's widow, who collected used stamps for some pious purpose. I had to endure the gossip of the tea-table. The meal was prolonged beyond an hour and still my uncle did not come. Mrs Mercer stood up to go: she was sorry she couldn't wait any longer, but it was after eight o'clock and she did not like to be out late, as the night air was bad for her. When she had gone I began to walk up and down the room, clenching my fists. My aunt said:

—I'm afraid you may put off your bazaar for this night of Our Lord.

At nine o'clock I heard my uncle's latchkey in the halldoor. I heard him talking to himself and heard the hallstand rocking when it had received the weight of his overcoat. I could interpret these signs. When he was midway through his dinner I asked him to give me the money to go to the bazaar. He had forgotten.

—The people are in bed and after their first sleep now, he said.

I did not smile. My aunt said to him energetically:

—Can't you give him the money and let him go? You've kept him late enough as it is.

My uncle said he was very sorry he had forgotten. He said he believed in the old saying: *All work and no play makes Jack a dull boy*. He asked me where I was going and, when I had told him a second time he asked me did I know *The Arab's Farewell to his Steed*.[1] When I left the kitchen he was about to recite the opening lines of the piece to my aunt.

I held a florin[2] tightly in my hand as I strode down Buckingham Street towards the station. The sight of the streets thronged with buyers and glaring with gas recalled to me the purpose of my journey. I took my seat in a third-class carriage of a deserted train. After an intolerable delay the train moved out of the station slowly. It crept onward among ruinous houses and over the twinkling river. At Westland Row Station a crowd of people pressed to the carriage doors; but the porters moved them back, saying that it was a special train for the bazaar. I remained alone in the bare carriage. In a few minutes the train drew up beside an improvised wooden platform. I passed out on to the road and saw by the lighted dial of a clock that it was ten minutes to ten. In front of me was a large building which displayed the magical name.

I could not find any sixpenny entrance and, fearing that the bazaar would be closed, I passed in quickly through a turnstile, handing a shilling to a weary-looking man. I found myself in a big hall girdled at half its height by a gallery. Nearly all the stalls were closed and the greater part of the hall was in darkness. I recognised a silence like that which pervades a church after a service. I walked into the centre of the bazaar timidly. A few people were gathered about the stalls which were still open. Before a curtain, over which the words *Café Chantant*[3] were written in coloured lamps, two men were counting money on a salver.[4] I listened to the fall of the coins.

Remembering with difficulty why I had come I went over to one of the stalls and examined porcelain vases and flowered tea-sets. At the door of the stall a young lady was talking and laughing with two young gentlemen. I remarked their English accents and listened vaguely to their conversation.

1. A sentimental poem by Caroline Norton, in which the speaker imagines his despair upon selling his favorite horse.

2. A coin worth two shillings.

3. A café with musical entertainment.

4. A tray for food and drinks.

—O, I never said such a thing!
—O, but you did!
—O, but I didn't!
—Didn't she say that?
—Yes. I heard her.
—O, there's a. . . fib!

Observing me the young lady came over and asked me did I wish to buy anything. The tone of her voice was not encouraging; she seemed to have spoken to me out of a sense of duty. I looked humbly at the great jars that stood like eastern guards at either side of the dark entrance to the stall and murmured:

—No, thank you.

The young lady changed the position of one of the vases and went back to the two young men. They began to talk of the same subject. Once or twice the young lady glanced at me over her shoulder.

I lingered before her stall, though I knew my stay was useless, to make my interest in her wares seem the more real. Then I turned away slowly and walked down the middle of the bazaar. I allowed the two pennies to fall against the sixpence in my pocket. I heard a voice call from one end of the gallery that the light was out. The upper part of the hall was now completely dark.

Gazing up into the darkness I saw myself as a creature driven and derided by vanity; and my eyes burned with anguish and anger.

Eveline

She sat at the window watching the evening invade the avenue. Her head was leaned against the window curtains and in her nostrils was the odour of dusty cretonne.[1] She was tired.

Few people passed. The man out of the last house passed on his way home; she heard his footsteps clacking along the concrete pavement and afterwards crunching on the cinder path before the new red houses. One time there used to be a field there in which they used to play every evening with other people's children. Then a man from Belfast bought the field and built houses in it—not like their little brown houses but bright brick houses with shining roofs. The children of the avenue used to play together in that field—the Devines, the Waters, the Dunns, little Keogh the cripple, she and her brothers and sisters. Ernest, however, never played: he was too grown up. Her father used often to hunt them in out of the field with his blackthorn stick; but usually little Keogh used to keep *nix*[2] and call out when he saw her father coming. Still they seemed to have been rather happy then. Her father was not so bad then; and besides, her mother was alive. That was a long time ago; she and her brothers and sisters were all grown up; her mother was dead. Tizzie Dunn was dead, too, and the Waters had gone back to England. Everything changes. Now she was going to go away like the others, to leave her home.

Home! She looked round the room, reviewing all its familiar objects which she had dusted once a week for so many years, wondering where on earth all the dust came from. Perhaps she would never see again those familiar objects from which she had never dreamed of being divided. And yet during all those years she had never found out the name of the priest whose yellowing photograph hung on the wall

1. Heavy cotton fabric.
2. To serve as a lookout.

above the broken harmonium[3] beside the coloured print of the promises made to Blessed Margaret Mary Alacoque.[4] He had been a school friend of her father. Whenever he showed the photograph to a visitor her father used to pass it with a casual word:

—He is in Melbourne now.

She had consented to go away, to leave her home. Was that wise? She tried to weigh each side of the question. In her home anyway she had shelter and food; she had those whom she had known all her life about her. Of course she had to work hard both in the house and at business. What would they say of her in the Stores when they found out that she had run away with a fellow? Say she was a fool, perhaps; and her place would be filled up by advertisement. Miss Gavan would be glad. She had always had an edge on her, especially whenever there were people listening.

—Miss Hill, don't you see these ladies are waiting?

—Look lively, Miss Hill, please.

She would not cry many tears at leaving the Stores.

But in her new home, in a distant unknown country, it would not be like that. Then she would be married—she, Eveline. People would treat her with respect then. She would not be treated as her mother had been. Even now, though she was over nineteen, she sometimes felt herself in danger of her father's violence. She knew it was that that had given her the palpitations. When they were growing up he had never gone for her, like he used to go for Harry and Ernest, because she was a girl; but latterly he had begun to threaten her and say what he would do to her only for her dead mother's sake. And now she had nobody to protect her. Ernest was dead and Harry, who was in the church decorating business, was nearly always down somewhere in the country. Besides, the invariable squabble for money on Saturday nights had begun to weary her unspeakably. She always gave her entire wages—seven shillings—and Harry always sent up what he could but the trouble was to get any money from her father. He said she used to squander the money, that she had no head, that he wasn't going to give her his hard-earned money to throw about the streets, and much more, for he was usually fairly bad of a Saturday night. In the end he would give her the money and ask her had she any intention of buying Sunday's dinner. Then she had to rush out as quickly as she could and do her marketing, holding her black leather purse tightly in her hand as she elbowed her way through the crowds and returning home late under her load of provisions. She had hard work to keep the house together and to see that the two young children who had been left to her charge went to school regularly and got their meals regularly. It was hard work—a hard life—but now that she was about to leave it she did not find it a wholly undesirable life.

She was about to explore another life with Frank. Frank was very kind, manly, open-hearted. She was to go away with him by the night-boat to be his wife and to live with him in Buenos Ayres where he had a home waiting for her. How well she remembered the first time she had seen him; he was lodging in a house on the main road where she used to visit. It seemed a few weeks ago. He was standing at the gate, his peaked cap pushed back on his head and his hair tumbled forward over a face of bronze. Then they had come to know each other. He used to meet her outside the

3. A small reed organ.
4. Catholic saint who took a vow of chastity at age four and carved the name "Jesus" into her chest with a knife as an adolescent. In 1673 she experienced a series of revelations; these resulted in the founding of the Devotion to the Sacred Heart of Jesus.

Stores every evening and see her home. He took her to see *The Bohemian Girl*[5] and she felt elated as she sat in an unaccustomed part of the theatre with him. He was awfully fond of music and sang a little. People knew that they were courting and, when he sang about the lass that loves a sailor, she always felt pleasantly confused. He used to call her Poppens out of fun. First of all it had been an excitement for her to have a fellow and then she had begun to like him. He had tales of distant countries. He had started as a deck boy at a pound a month on a ship of the Allan Line going out to Canada. He told her the names of the ships he had been on and the names of the different services. He had sailed through the Straits of Magellan and he told her stories of the terrible Patagonians.[6] He had fallen on his feet in Buenos Ayres, he said, and had come over to the old country just for a holiday. Of course, her father had found out the affair and had forbidden her to have anything to say to him.

—I know these sailor chaps, he said.

One day he had quarrelled with Frank and after that she had to meet her lover secretly.

The evening deepened in the avenue. The white of two letters in her lap grew indistinct. One was to Harry; the other was to her father. Ernest had been her favorite but she liked Harry too. Her father was becoming old lately, she noticed; he would miss her. Sometimes he could be very nice. Not long before, when she had been laid up for a day, he had read her out a ghost story and made toast for her at the fire. Another day, when their mother was alive, they had all gone for a picnic to the Hill of Howth.[7] She remembered her father putting on her mother's bonnet to make the children laugh.

Her time was running out but she continued to sit by the window, leaning her head against the window curtain, inhaling the odour of dusty cretonne. Down far in the avenue she could hear a street organ playing. She knew the air.[8] Strange that it should come that very night to remind her of the promise to her mother, her promise to keep the home together as long as she could. She remembered the last night of her mother's illness; she was again in the close dark room at the other side of the hall and outside she heard a melancholy air of Italy. The organ-player had been ordered to go away and given sixpence. She remembered her father strutting back into the sickroom saying:

—Damned Italians! coming over here!

As she mused the pitiful vision of her mother's life laid its spell on the very quick of her being—that life of commonplace sacrifices closing in final craziness. She trembled as she heard again her mother's voice saying constantly with foolish insistence:

—Derevaun Seraun! Derevaun Seraun![9]

She stood up in a sudden impulse of terror. Escape! She must escape! Frank would save her. He would give her life, perhaps love, too. But she wanted to live. Why should she be unhappy? She had a right to happiness. Frank would take her in his arms, fold her in his arms. He would save her.

She stood among the swaying crowd in the station at the North Wall.[1] He held her hand and she knew that he was speaking to her, saying something about the passage

5. An opera (1843) by Irish composer Michael William Balfe, based on a tale by Cervantes about a rich girl kidnapped by gypsies and an exiled nobleman.
6. Native peoples of Southern Argentina.
7. Northeast of Dublin, the hill dominates Dublin Bay.
8. Tune.
9. Though some commentators have suggested the phrase is Irish, it seems more likely to be incoherent nonsense.
1. A point of embarkation in Dublin for passenger ships—but those, as critic Hugh Kenner points out, heading for Liverpool, not Buenos Aires.

over and over again. The station was full of soldiers with brown baggages. Through the wide doors of the sheds she caught a glimpse of the black mass of the boat, lying in beside the quay wall, with illumined portholes. She answered nothing. She felt her cheek pale and cold and, out of a maze of distress, she prayed to God to direct her, to show her what was her duty. The boat blew a long mournful whistle into the mist. If she went, tomorrow she would be on the sea with Frank, steaming toward Buenos Ayres. Their passage had been booked. Could she still draw back after all he had done for her? Her distress awoke a nausea in her body and she kept moving her lips in silent fervent prayer.

A bell clanged upon her heart. She felt him seize her hand:

—Come!

All the seas of the world tumbled about her heart. He was drawing her into them: he would drown her. She gripped with both hands at the iron railing.

—Come!

No! No! No! It was impossible. Her hands clutched the iron in frenzy. Amid the seas she sent a cry of anguish!

—Eveline! Evvy!

He rushed beyond the barrier and called to her to follow. He was shouted at to go on but he still called to her. She set her white face to him, passive, like a helpless animal. Her eyes gave him no sign of love or farewell or recognition.

Clay

The matron had given her leave to go out as soon as the women's tea was over and Maria looked forward to her evening out. The kitchen was spick and span: the cook said you could see yourself in the big copper boilers. The fire was nice and bright and on one of the side-tables were four very big barmbracks.[1] These barmbracks seemed uncut; but if you went closer you would see that they had been cut into long thick even slices and were ready to be handed round at tea. Maria had cut them herself.

Maria was a very, very small person indeed but she had a very long nose and a very long chin. She talked a little through her nose, always soothingly: *Yes, my dear*, and *No, my dear*. She was always sent for when the women quarrelled over their tubs and always succeeded in making peace. One day the matron had said to her:

—Maria, you are a veritable peace-maker!

And the sub-matron and two of the Board ladies[2] had heard the compliment. And Ginger Mooney was always saying what she wouldn't do to the dummy[3] who had charge of the irons if it wasn't for Maria. Everyone was so fond of Maria.

The women would have their tea at six o'clock and she would be able to get away before seven. From Ballsbridge to the Pillar, twenty minutes; from the Pillar to Drumcondra, twenty minutes; and twenty minutes to buy the things. She would be there before eight. She took out her purse with the silver clasps and read again the words *A Present from Belfast*. She was very fond of that purse because Joe had brought it to her five years before when he and Alphy had gone to Belfast on a Whit-Monday[4] trip. In the purse were two half-crowns and some coppers. She would have five shillings clear after paying tram fare. What a nice evening they would have, all the children singing! Only she hoped that Joe wouldn't come in drunk. He was so different when he took any drink.

1. Speckled cakes or currant buns.
2. Members of the governing board of the Dublin by Lamplight Laundry.
3. Slang for a mute person.
4. Holiday following Whitsunday, the seventh Sunday after Easter.

Often he had wanted her to go and live with them; but she would have felt herself in the way (though Joe's wife was ever so nice with her) and she had become accustomed to the life of the laundry. Joe was a good fellow. She had nursed him and Alphy too; and Joe used often say:

—Mamma is mamma but Maria is my proper mother.

After the break-up at home the boys had got her that position in the *Dublin by Lamplight* laundry,[5] and she liked it. She used to have such a bad opinion of Protestants but now she thought they were very nice people, a little quiet and serious, but still very nice people to live with. Then she had her plants in the conservatory and she liked looking after them. She had lovely ferns and wax-plants and, whenever anyone came to visit her, she always gave the visitor one or two slips from her conservatory. There was one thing she didn't like and that was the tracts[6] on the walls; but the matron was such a nice person to deal with, so genteel.

When the cook told her everything was ready she went into the women's room and began to pull the big bell. In a few minutes the women began to come in by twos and threes, wiping their steaming hands in their petticoats and pulling down the sleeves of their blouses over their red steaming arms. They settled down before their huge mugs which the cook and the dummy filled up with hot tea, already mixed with milk and sugar in huge tin cans. Maria superintended the distribution of the barmbrack and saw that every woman got her four slices. There was a great deal of laughing and joking during the meal. Lizzie Fleming said Maria was sure to get the ring and, though Fleming had said that for so many Hallow Eves, Maria had to laugh and say she didn't want any ring or man either; and when she laughed her grey-green eyes sparkled with disappointed shyness and the tip of her nose nearly met the tip of her chin. Then Ginger Mooney lifted up her mug of tea and proposed Maria's health while all the other women clattered with their mugs on the table, and said she was sorry she hadn't a sup of porter[7] to drink it in. And Maria laughed again till the tip of her nose nearly met the tip of her chin and till her minute body nearly shook itself asunder because she knew that Mooney meant well though, of course, she had the notions of a common woman.

But wasn't Maria glad when the women had finished their tea and the cook and the dummy had begun to clear away the tea-things! She went into her little bedroom and, remembering that the next morning was a mass morning, changed the hand of the alarm from seven to six. Then she took off her working skirt and her house-boots and laid her best skirt out on the bed and her tiny dress-boots beside the foot of the bed. She changed her blouse too and, as she stood before the mirror, she thought of how she used to dress for mass on Sunday morning when she was a young girl; and she looked with quaint affection at the diminutive body which she had so often adorned. In spite of its years she found it a nice tidy little body.

When she got outside the streets were shining with rain and she was glad of her old brown raincloak. The tram was full and she had to sit on the little stool at the end of the car, facing all the people, with her toes barely touching the floor. She arranged in her mind all she was going to do and thought how much better it was to be independent and to have your own money in your pocket. She hoped they would

5. Joyce's invented benevolent society, run by Protestant women, "saves" Dublin's prostitutes from a life on the streets by giving them honest work in a laundry. Maria works for the laundry but appears not to be a reformed prostitute herself.

6. Evangelical religious texts.

7. A heavy, dark brown ale.

have a nice evening. She was sure they would but she could not help thinking what a pity it was Alphy and Joe were not speaking. They were always falling out now but when they were boys together they used to be the best of friends: but such was life.

She got out of her tram at the Pillar and ferreted her way quickly among the crowds. She went into Downes's cakeshop but the shop was so full of people that it was a long time before she could get herself attended to. She bought a dozen of mixed penny cakes, and at last came out of the shop laden with a big bag. Then she thought what else would she buy: she wanted to buy something really nice. They would be sure to have plenty of apples and nuts. It was hard to know what to buy and all she could think of was cake. She decided to buy some plumcake but Downes's plumcake had not enough almond icing on top of it so she went over to a shop in Henry Street. Here she was a long time in suiting herself and the stylish young lady behind the counter, who was evidently a little annoyed by her, asked her was it wedding-cake she wanted to buy. That made Maria blush and smile at the young lady; but the young lady took it all very seriously and finally cut a thick slice of plumcake, parcelled it up and said:

—Two-and-four, please.

She thought she would have to stand in the Drumcondra tram because none of the young men seemed to notice her but an elderly gentleman made room for her. He was a stout gentleman and he wore a brown hard hat; he had a square red face and a greyish moustache. Maria thought he was a colonel-looking gentleman and she reflected how much more polite he was than the young men who simply stared straight before them. The gentleman began to chat with her about Hallow Eve and the rainy weather. He supposed the bag was full of good things for the little ones and said it was only right that the youngsters should enjoy themselves while they were young. Maria agreed with him and favoured him with demure nods and hems. He was very nice with her, and when she was getting out at the Canal Bridge she thanked him and bowed, and he bowed to her and raised his hat and smiled agreeably; and while she was going up along the terrace, bending her tiny head under the rain, she thought how easy it was to know a gentleman even when he has a drop taken.

Everybody said: O, *here's Maria!* when she came to Joe's house. Joe was there, having come home from business, and all the children had their Sunday dresses on. There were two big girls in from next door and games were going on. Maria gave the bag of cakes to the eldest boy, Alphy, to divide and Mrs Donnelly said it was too good of her to bring such a big bag of cakes and made all the children say:

—Thanks, Maria.

But Maria said she had brought something special for papa and mamma, something they would be sure to like, and she began to look for her plumcake. She tried in Downes's bag and then in the pockets of her raincloak and then on the hallstand but nowhere could she find it. Then she asked all the children had any of them eaten it—by mistake, of course—but the children all said no and looked as if they did not like to eat cakes if they were to be accused of stealing. Everybody had a solution for the mystery and Mrs Donnelly said it was plain that Maria had left it behind her in the tram. Maria, remembering how confused the gentleman with the greyish moustache had made her, coloured with shame and vexation and disappointment. At the thought of the failure of her little surprise and of the two and fourpence she had thrown away for nothing she nearly cried outright.

But Joe said it didn't matter and made her sit down by the fire. He was very nice with her. He told her all that went on in his office, repeating for her a smart answer which he had made to the manager. Maria did not understand why Joe laughed so much over the answer he had made but she said that the manager must have been a very overbearing person to deal with. Joe said he wasn't so bad when you knew how to take him, that he was a decent sort so long as you didn't rub him the wrong way. Mrs Donnelly played the piano for the children and they danced and sang. Then the two next-door girls handed round the nuts. Nobody could find the nutcrackers and Joe was nearly getting cross over it and asked how did they expect Maria to crack nuts without a nutcracker. But Maria said she didn't like nuts and that they weren't to bother about her. Then Joe asked would she take a bottle of stout[8] and Mrs Donnelly said there was port wine too in the house if she would prefer that. Maria said she would rather they didn't ask her to take anything: but Joe insisted.

So Maria let him have his way and they sat by the fire talking over old times and Maria thought she would put in a good word for Alphy. But Joe cried that God might strike him stone dead if ever he spoke a word to his brother again and Maria said she was sorry she had mentioned the matter. Mrs Donnelly told her husband it was a great shame for him to speak that way of his own flesh and blood but Joe said that Alphy was no brother of his and there was nearly being a row[9] on the head of it. But Joe said he would not lose his temper on account of the night it was and asked his wife to open some more stout. The two next-door girls had arranged some Hallow Eve games[1] and soon everything was merry again. Maria was delighted to see the children so merry and Joe and his wife in such good spirits. The next-door girls put some saucers on the table and then led the children up to the table, blindfold. One got the prayer-book and the other three got the water; and when one of the next-door girls got the ring Mrs Donnelly shook her finger at the blushing girl as much as to say: *O, I know all about it!* They insisted then on blindfolding Maria and leading her up to the table to see what she would get; and, while they were putting on the bandage, Maria laughed and laughed again till the tip of her nose nearly met the tip of her chin.

They led her up to the table amid laughing and joking and she put her hand out in the air as she was told to do. She moved her hand about here and there in the air and descended on one of the saucers. She felt a soft wet substance with her fingers and was surprised that nobody spoke or took off her bandage. There was a pause for a few seconds; and then a great deal of scuffling and whispering. Somebody said something about the garden, and at last Mrs Donnelly said something very cross to one of the next-door girls and told her to throw it out at once: that was no play. Maria understood that it was wrong that time and so she had to do it over again: and this time she got the prayer-book.

After that Mrs Donnelly played Miss McCloud's Reel for the children and Joe made Maria take a glass of wine. Soon they were all quite merry again and Mrs Donnelly said Maria would enter a convent before the year was out because she had got the prayer-book. Maria had never seen Joe so nice to her as he was that night, so full of pleasant talk and reminiscences. She said they were all very good to her.

At last the children grew tired and sleepy and Joe asked Maria would she not sing some little song before she went, one of the old songs. Mrs Donnelly said *Do, please,*

8. A dark, full-bodied beer.
9. Argument.
1. The primary game that Maria and the girls play is a traditional Irish Halloween game. In its original version, a blindfolded girl would be led to three plates, and would choose one. Choosing the plate with a ring meant that she would soon marry; water meant she would emigrate (probably to America); and soil, or clay, meant she would soon die. In modern times, a prayer book was substituted for this unsavory third option, suggesting that the girl would enter a convent.

Maria! and so Maria had to get up and stand beside the piano. Mrs Donnelly bade the children be quiet and listen to Maria's song. Then she played the prelude and said *Now, Maria!* and Maria, blushing very much, began to sing in a tiny quavering voice. She sang *I Dreamt that I Dwelt*,[2] and when she came to the second verse she sang again:

I dreamt that I dwelt in marble halls
With vassals and serfs at my side
And of all who assembled within those walls
That I was the hope and the pride.
I had riches too great to count, could boast
Of a high ancestral name,
But I also dreamt, which pleased me most,
That you loved me still the same.

But no one tried to show her her mistake;[3] and when she had ended her song Joe was very much moved. He said that there was no time like the long ago and no music for him like poor old Balfe, whatever other people might say; and his eyes filled up so much with tears that he could not find what he was looking for and in the end he had to ask his wife to tell him where the corkscrew was.

The Dead

Lily, the caretaker's daughter, was literally run off her feet. Hardly had she brought one gentleman into the little pantry behind the office on the ground floor and helped him off with his overcoat than the wheezy hall-door bell clanged again and she had to scamper along the bare hallway to let in another guest. It was well for her she had not to attend to the ladies also. But Miss Kate and Miss Julia had thought of that and had converted the bathroom upstairs into a ladies' dressing-room. Miss Kate and Miss Julia were there, gossiping and laughing and fussing, walking after each other to the head of the stairs, peering down over the banisters and calling down to Lily to ask her who had come.

It was always a great affair, the Misses Morkan's annual dance. Everybody who knew them came to it, members of the family, old friends of the family, the members of Julia's choir, any of Kate's pupils that were grown up enough and even some of Mary Jane's pupils too. Never once had it fallen flat. For years and years it had gone off in splendid style as long as anyone could remember; ever since Kate and Julia, after the death of their brother Pat, had left the house in Stoney Batter[1] and taken Mary Jane, their only niece, to live with them in the dark gaunt house on Usher's Island,[2] the upper part of which they had rented from Mr Fulham, the cornfactor on the ground floor. That was a good thirty years ago if it was a day. Mary Jane, who was then a little girl in short clothes, was now the main prop of the household for she had the organ in Haddington Road.[3] She had been through the Academy[4] and gave a pupils' concert every year in the upper room of the Antient Concert Rooms. Many of her pupils belonged to better-class families on the Kingstown and Dalkey line.[5] Old as they were, her aunts also did their share. Julia, though she was quite grey, was still

2. Aria from Act 2 of *The Bohemian Girl*.
3. Maria repeats the first verse rather than singing the second.
1. A district in northwest Dublin.
2. Two adjoining quays on the south side of the river Liffey.
3. Played the organ in a church on the Haddington Road.
4. Royal Academy of Music.
5. The train line connecting Dublin to the affluent suburbs south of the city.

the leading soprano in Adam and Eve's,[6] and Kate, being too feeble to go about much, gave music lessons to beginners on the old square piano in the back room. Lily, the caretaker's daughter, did housemaid's work for them. Though their life was modest they believed in eating well; the best of everything: diamond-bone sirloins, three-shilling tea and the best bottled stout.[7] But Lily seldom made a mistake in the orders so that she got on well with her three mistresses. They were fussy, that was all. But the only thing they would not stand was back answers.

Of course they had good reason to be fussy on such a night. And then it was long after ten o'clock and yet there was no sign of Gabriel and his wife. Besides they were dreadfully afraid that Freddy Malins might turn up screwed.[8] They would not wish for worlds that any of Mary Jane's pupils should see him under the influence; and when he was like that it was sometimes very hard to manage him. Freddy Malins always came late but they wondered what could be keeping Gabriel: and that was what brought them every two minutes to the banisters to ask Lily had Gabriel or Freddy come.

—O, Mr Conroy, said Lily to Gabriel when she opened the door for him, Miss Kate and Miss Julia thought you were never coming. Good-night, Mrs Conroy.

—I'll engage[9] they did, said Gabriel, but they forget that my wife here takes three mortal hours to dress herself.

He stood on the mat, scraping the snow from his goloshes, while Lily led his wife to the foot of the stairs and called out:

—Miss Kate, here's Mrs Conroy.

Kate and Julia came toddling down the dark stairs at once. Both of them kissed Gabriel's wife, said she must be perished alive and asked was Gabriel with her.

—Here I am as right as the mail, Aunt Kate! Go on up. I'll follow, called out Gabriel from the dark.

He continued scraping his feet vigorously while the three women went upstairs, laughing, to the ladies' dressing-room. A light fringe of snow lay like a cape on the shoulders of his overcoat and like toecaps on the toes of his goloshes; and, as the buttons of his overcoat slipped with a squeaking noise through the snow-stiffened frieze, a cold fragrant air from out-of-doors escaped from crevices and folds.

—Is it snowing again, Mr Conroy? asked Lily.

She had preceded him into the pantry to help him off with his overcoat. Gabriel smiled at the three syllables she had given his surname and glanced at her. She was a slim, growing girl, pale in complexion and with hay-coloured hair. The gas in the pantry made her look still paler. Gabriel had known her when she was a child and used to sit on the lowest step nursing a rag doll.

—Yes, Lily, he answered, and I think we're in for a night of it.

He looked up at the pantry ceiling, which was shaking with the stamping and shuffling of feet on the floor above, listened for a moment to the piano and then glanced at the girl, who was folding his overcoat carefully at the end of a shelf.

—Tell me, Lily, he said in a friendly tone, do you still go to school?

—O no, sir, she answered. I'm done schooling this year and more.

—O, then, said Gabriel gaily, I suppose we'll be going to your wedding one of these fine days with your young man, eh?

The girl glanced back at him over her shoulder and said with great bitterness:

6. A Dublin church.
7. An extra-strength ale.
8. Drunk.
9. Wager.

—The men that is now is only all palaver[1] and what they can get out of you.

Gabriel coloured as if he felt he had made a mistake and, without looking at her, kicked off his goloshes and flicked actively with his muffler at his patent-leather shoes.

He was a stout tallish young man. The high colour of his cheeks pushed upwards even to his forehead where it scattered itself in a few formless patches of pale red; and on his hairless face there scintillated restlessly the polished lenses and the bright gilt rims of the glasses which screened his delicate and restless eyes. His glossy black hair was parted in the middle and brushed in a long curve behind his ears where it curled slightly beneath the groove left by his hat.

When he had flicked lustre into his shoes he stood up and pulled his waistcoat down more tightly on his plump body. Then he took a coin rapidly from his pocket.

—O Lily, he said, thrusting it into her hands, it's Christmas-time, isn't it? Just. . . here's a little. . . .

He walked rapidly towards the door.

—O no, sir! cried the girl, following him. Really, sir, I wouldn't take it.

—Christmas-time! Christmas-time! said Gabriel, almost trotting to the stairs and waving his hand to her in deprecation.

The girl, seeing that he had gained the stairs, called out after him:

—Well, thank you, sir.

He waited outside the drawing-room door until the waltz should finish, listening to the skirts that swept against it and to the shuffling of feet. He was still discomposed by the girl's bitter and sudden retort. It had cast a gloom over him which he tried to dispel by arranging his cuffs and the bows of his tie. Then he took from his waistcoat pocket a little paper and glanced at the headings he had made for his speech. He was undecided about the lines from Robert Browning for he feared they would be above the heads of his hearers. Some quotation that they could recognise from Shakespeare or from the Melodies[2] would be better. The indelicate clacking of the men's heels and the shuffling of their soles reminded him that their grade of culture differed from his. He would only make himself ridiculous by quoting poetry to them which they could not understand. They would think that he was airing his superior education. He would fail with them just as he had failed with the girl in the pantry. He had taken up a wrong tone. His whole speech was a mistake from first to last, an utter failure.

Just then his aunts and his wife came out of the ladies' dressing-room. His aunts were two small plainly dressed old women. Aunt Julia was an inch or so taller. Her hair, drawn low over the tops of her ears, was grey; and grey also, with darker shadows, was her large flaccid face. Though she was stout in build and stood erect her slow eyes and parted lips gave her the appearance of a woman who did not know where she was or where she was going. Aunt Kate was more vivacious. Her face, healthier than her sister's, was all puckers and creases, like a shrivelled red apple, and her hair, braided in the same old-fashioned way, had not lost its ripe nut colour.

They both kissed Gabriel frankly. He was their favourite nephew, the son of their dead elder sister, Ellen, who had married T.J. Conroy of the Port and Docks.

—Gretta tells me you're not going to take a cab back to Monkstown[3] to-night, Gabriel, said Aunt Kate.

1. Empty talk.
2. Thomas Moore's *Irish Melodies*, a perennial favorite volume of poetry.
3. An elegant suburb south of Dublin.

—No, said Gabriel, turning to his wife, we had quite enough of that last year, hadn't we. Don't you remember, Aunt Kate, what a cold Gretta got out of it? Cab windows rattling all the way, and the east wind blowing in after we passed Merrion. Very jolly it was. Gretta caught a dreadful cold.

Aunt Kate frowned severely and nodded her head at every word.

—Quite right, Gabriel, quite right, she said. You can't be too careful.

—But as for Gretta there, said Gabriel, she'd walk home in the snow if she were let.

Mrs Conroy laughed.

—Don't mind him, Aunt Kate, she said. He's really an awful bother, what with green shades for Tom's eyes at night and making him do the dumb-bells, and forcing Eva to eat the stirabout.[4] The poor child! And she simply hates the sight of it! . . . O, but you'll never guess what he makes me wear now!

She broke out into a peal of laughter and glanced at her husband, whose admiring and happy eyes had been wandering from her dress to her face and hair. The two aunts laughed heartily too, for Gabriel's solicitude was a standing joke with them.

—Goloshes! said Mrs Conroy. That's the latest. Whenever it's wet underfoot I must put on my goloshes. Tonight even he wanted me to put them on, but I wouldn't. The next thing he'll buy me will be a diving suit.

Gabriel laughed nervously and patted his tie reassuringly while Aunt Kate nearly doubled herself, so heartily did she enjoy the joke. The smile soon faded from Aunt Julia's face and her mirthless eyes were directed towards her nephew's face. After a pause she asked:

—And what are goloshes, Gabriel?

—Goloshes, Julia! exclaimed her sister. Goodness me, don't you know what goloshes are? You wear them over your . . . over your boots, Gretta, isn't it?

—Yes, said Mrs Conroy. Guttapercha[5] things. We both have a pair now. Gabriel says everyone wears them on the continent.

—O, on the continent, murmured Aunt Julia, nodding her head slowly.

Gabriel knitted his brows and said, as if he were slightly angered:

—It's nothing very wonderful but Gretta thinks it very funny because she says the word reminds her of Christy Minstrels.[6]

—But tell me, Gabriel, said Aunt Kate, with brisk tact. Of course, you've seen about the room. Gretta was saying . . .

—O, the room is all right, replied Gabriel. I've taken one in the Gresham.[7]

—To be sure, said Aunt Kate, by far the best thing to do. And the children, Gretta, you're not anxious about them?

—O, for one night, said Mrs Conroy. Besides, Bessie will look after them.

—To be sure, said Aunt Kate again. What a comfort it is to have a girl like that, one you can depend on! There's that Lily, I'm sure I don't know what has come over her lately. She's not the girl she was at all.

Gabriel was about to ask his aunt some questions on this point but she broke off suddenly to gaze after her sister who had wandered down the stairs and was craning her neck over the banisters.

—Now, I ask you, she said, almost testily, where is Julia going? Julia! Julia! Where are you going?

4. Porridge.
5. Rubberized fabric.
6. A 19th-century minstrel show.
7. The most elegant hotel in Dublin.

Julia, who had gone halfway down one flight, came back and announced blandly:

—Here's Freddy.

At the same moment a clapping of hands and a final flourish of the pianist told that the waltz had ended. The drawing-room door was opened from within and some couples came out. Aunt Kate drew Gabriel aside hurriedly and whispered into his ear:

—Slip down, Gabriel, like a good fellow and see if he's all right, and don't let him up if he's screwed. I'm sure he's screwed. I'm sure he is.

Gabriel went to the stairs and listened over the banisters. He could hear two persons talking in the pantry. Then he recognised Freddy Malins' laugh. He went down the stairs noisily.

—It's such a relief, said Aunt Kate to Mrs Conroy, that Gabriel is here. I always feel easier in my mind when he's here. . . . Julia, there's Miss Daly and Miss Power will take some refreshment. Thanks for your beautiful waltz, Miss Daly. It made lovely time.

A tall wizen-faced man, with a stiff grizzled moustache and swarthy skin, who was passing out with his partner said:

—And may we have some refreshment, too, Miss Morkan?

—Julia, said Aunt Kate summarily, and here's Mr Browne and Miss Furlong. Take them in, Julia, with Miss Daly and Miss Power.

—I'm the man for the ladies, said Mr Browne, pursing his lips until his moustache bristled and smiling in all his wrinkles. You know, Miss Morkan, the reason they are so fond of me is—

He did not finish his sentence, but, seeing that Aunt Kate was out of earshot, at once led the three young ladies into the back room. The middle of the room was occupied by two square tables placed end to end, and on these Aunt Julia and the caretaker were straightening and smoothing a large cloth. On the sideboard were arrayed dishes and plates, and glasses and bundles of knives and forks and spoons. The top of the closed square piano served also as a sideboard for viands[8] and sweets. At a smaller sideboard in one corner two young men were standing, drinking hop-bitters.[9]

Mr Browne led his charges thither and invited them all, in jest, to some ladies' punch, hot, strong and sweet. As they said they never took anything strong he opened three bottles of lemonade for them. Then he asked one of the young men to move aside, and, taking hold of the decanter, filled out for himself a goodly measure of whisky. The young men eyed him respectfully while he took a trial sip.

—God help me, he said, smiling, it's the doctor's orders.

His wizened face broke into a broader smile, and the three young ladies laughed in musical echo to his pleasantry, swaying their bodies to and fro, with nervous jerks of their shoulders. The boldest said:

—O, now, Mr Browne, I'm sure the doctor never ordered anything of the kind.

Mr Browne took another sip of his whisky and said, with sidling mimicry:

—Well, you see, I'm like the famous Mrs Cassidy, who is reported to have said: *Now, Mary Grimes, if I don't take it, make me take it, for I feel I want it.*

His hot face had leaned forward a little too confidentially and he had assumed a very low Dublin accent so that the young ladies, with one instinct, received his speech in silence. Miss Furlong, who was one of Mary Jane's pupils, asked Miss Daly what was the name of the pretty waltz she had played; and Mr Browne, seeing that he was ignored, turned promptly to the two young men who were more appreciative.

8. Meats.

9. Dry ale.

A red-faced young woman, dressed in pansy, came into the room, excitedly clapping her hands and crying:

—Quadrilles![1] Quadrilles!

Close on her heels came Aunt Kate, crying:

—Two gentlemen and three ladies, Mary Jane!

—O, here's Mr Bergin and Mr Kerrigan, said Mary Jane. Mr Kerrigan, will you take Miss Power? Miss Furlong, may I get you a partner, Mr Bergin. O, that'll just do now.

—Three ladies, Mary Jane, said Aunt Kate.

The two young gentlemen asked the ladies if they might have the pleasure, and Mary Jane turned to Miss Daly.

—O, Miss Daly, you're really awfully good, after playing for the last two dances, but really we're so short of ladies to-night.

—I don't mind in the least, Miss Morkan.

—But I've a nice partner for you, Mr Bartell D'Arcy, the tenor. I'll get him to sing later on. All Dublin is raving about him.

—Lovely voice, lovely voice! said Aunt Kate.

As the piano had twice begun the prelude to the first figure Mary Jane led her recruits quickly from the room. They had hardly gone when Aunt Julia wandered slowly into the room, looking behind her at something.

—What is the matter, Julia? asked Aunt Kate anxiously. Who is it?

Julia, who was carrying in a column of table-napkins, turned to her sister and said, simply, as if the question had surprised her:

—It's only Freddy, Kate, and Gabriel with him.

In fact right behind her Gabriel could be seen piloting Freddy Malins across the landing. The latter, a young man of about forty, was of Gabriel's size and build, with very round shoulders. His face was fleshy and pallid, touched with colour only at the thick hanging lobes of his ears and at the wide wings of his nose. He had coarse features, a blunt nose, a convex and receding brow, tumid and protruded lips. His heavy-lidded eyes and the disorder of his scanty hair made him look sleepy. He was laughing heartily in a high key at a story which he had been telling Gabriel on the stairs and at the same time rubbing the knuckles of his left fist backwards and forwards into his left eye.

—Good-evening, Freddy, said Aunt Julia.

Freddy Malins bade the Misses Morkan good-evening in what seemed an offhand fashion by reason of the habitual catch in his voice and then, seeing that Mr Browne was grinning at him from the sideboard, crossed the room on rather shaky legs and began to repeat in an undertone the story he had just told to Gabriel.

—He's not so bad, is he? said Aunt Kate to Gabriel.

Gabriel's brows were dark but he raised them quickly and answered:

—O no, hardly noticeable.

—Now, isn't he a terrible fellow! she said. And his poor mother made him take the pledge on New Year's Eve. But come on, Gabriel, into the drawing-room.

Before leaving the room with Gabriel she signalled to Mr Browne by frowning and shaking her forefinger in warning to and fro. Mr Browne nodded in answer and, when she had gone, said to Freddy Malins:

—Now, then, Teddy, I'm going to fill you out a good glass of lemonade just to buck you up.

1. A French square dance.

Freddy Malins, who was nearing the climax of his story, waved the offer aside impatiently but Mr Browne, having first called Freddy Malins' attention to a disarray in his dress, filled out and handed him a full glass of lemonade. Freddy Malins' left hand accepted the glass mechanically, his right hand being engaged in the mechanical readjustment of his dress. Mr Browne, whose face was once more wrinkling with mirth, poured out for himself a glass of whisky while Freddy Malins exploded, before he had well reached the climax of his story, in a kink of high-pitched bronchitic laughter and, setting down his untasted and overflowing glass, began to rub the knuckles of his left fist backwards and forwards into his left eye, repeating words of his last phrase as well as his fit of laughter would allow him.

Gabriel could not listen while Mary Jane was playing her Academy piece, full of runs and difficult passages, to the hushed drawing-room. He liked music but the piece she was playing had no melody for him and he doubted whether it had any melody for the other listeners, though they had begged Mary Jane to play something. Four young men, who had come from the refreshment-room to stand in the door-way at the sound of the piano, had gone away quietly in couples after a few minutes. The only persons who seemed to follow the music were Mary Jane herself, her hands racing along the key-board or lifted from it at the pauses like those of a priestess in momentary imprecation, and Aunt Kate standing at her elbow to turn the page.

Gabriel's eyes, irritated by the floor, which glittered with beeswax under the heavy chandelier, wandered to the wall above the piano. A picture of the balcony scene in *Romeo and Juliet* hung there and beside it was a picture of the two murdered princes[2] in the Tower which Aunt Julia had worked in red, blue and brown wools when she was a girl. Probably in the school they had gone to as girls that kind of work had been taught, for one year his mother had worked for him as a birthday present a waistcoat of purple tabinet,[3] with little foxes' heads upon it, lined with brown satin and having round mulberry buttons. It was strange that his mother had had no musical talent though Aunt Kate used to call her the brains carrier of the Morkan family. Both she and Julia had always seemed a little proud of their serious and matronly sister. Her photograph stood before the pierglass.[4] She held an open book on her knees and was pointing out something in it to Constantine who, dressed in a man-o'-war suit, lay at her feet. It was she who had chosen the names for her sons for she was very sensible of the dignity of family life. Thanks to her, Constantine was now senior curate in Balbriggan[5] and, thanks to her, Gabriel himself had taken his degree in the Royal University.[6] A shadow passed over his face as he remembered her sullen opposition to his marriage. Some slighting phrases she had used still rankled in his memory; she had once spoken of Gretta as being country cute and that was not true of Gretta at all. It was Gretta who had nursed her during all her last long illness in their house at Monkstown.

He knew that Mary Jane must be near the end of her piece for she was playing again the opening melody with runs of scales after every bar and while he waited for the end the resentment died down in his heart. The piece ended with a trill of octaves in the treble and a final deep octave in the bass. Great applause greeted Mary Jane as, blushing and rolling up her music nervously, she escaped from the room. The most vigorous clapping came from the four young men in the doorway who had gone

2. The young sons of Edward IV, murdered in the Tower of London by order of their uncle, Richard III.
3. Silk and wool fabric.
4. A large high mirror.
5. Seaport 19 miles southeast of Dublin.
6. The Royal University of Ireland, established in 1882.

away to the refreshment-room at the beginning of the piece but had come back when the piano had stopped.

Lancers[7] were arranged. Gabriel found himself partnered with Miss Ivors. She was a frank-mannered talkative young lady, with a freckled face and prominent brown eyes. She did not wear a low-cut bodice and the large brooch which was fixed in the front of her collar bore on it an Irish device.

When they had taken their places she said abruptly:

—I have a crow to pluck with you.

—With me? said Gabriel.

She nodded her head gravely.

—What is it? asked Gabriel, smiling at her solemn manner.

—Who is G. C.? answered Miss Ivors, turning her eyes upon him.

Gabriel coloured and was about to knit his brows, as if he did not understand, when she said bluntly:

—O, innocent Amy! I have found out that you write for *The Daily Express*.[8] Now, aren't you ashamed of yourself?

—Why should I be ashamed of myself? asked Gabriel, blinking his eyes and trying to smile.

—Well, I'm ashamed of you, said Miss Ivors frankly. To say you'd write for a rag like that. I didn't think you were a West Briton.[9]

A look of perplexity appeared on Gabriel's face. It was true that he wrote a literary column every Wednesday in *The Daily Express*, for which he was paid fifteen shillings. But that did not make him a West Briton surely. The books he received for review were almost more welcome than the paltry cheque. He loved to feel the covers and turn over the pages of newly printed books. Nearly every day when his teaching in the college was ended he used to wander down the quays to the second-hand booksellers, to Hickey's on Bachelor's Walk, to Webb's or Massey's on Aston's Quay, or to O'Clohissey's in the by-street. He did not know how to meet her charge. He wanted to say that literature was above politics. But they were friends of many years' standing and their careers had been parallel, first at the University and then as teachers: he could not risk a grandiose phrase with her. He continued blinking his eyes and trying to smile and murmured lamely that he saw nothing political in writing reviews of books.

When their turn to cross had come he was still perplexed and inattentive. Miss Ivors promptly took his hand in a warm grasp and said in a soft friendly tone:

—Of course, I was only joking. Come, we cross now.

When they were together again she spoke of the University question[1] and Gabriel felt more at ease. A friend of hers had shown her his review of Browning's poems. That was how she had found out the secret: but she liked the review immensely. Then she said suddenly:

—O, Mr Conroy, will you come for an excursion to the Aran Isles[2] this summer? We're going to stay there a whole month. It will be splendid out in the Atlantic. You

7. A type of quadrille for 8 or 16 people.
8. A conservative paper opposed to the struggle for Irish independence.
9. Disparaging term for people wishing to identify Ireland as British.
1. Ireland's oldest and most prestigious university, Trinity College, was open only to Protestants; the "University question" involved, in part, the provision of quality university education to Catholics.
2. Islands off the west coast of Ireland where the people still retained their traditional culture and spoke Irish.

ought to come. Mr Clancy is coming, and Mr Kilkelly and Kathleen Kearney. It would be splendid for Gretta too if she'd come. She's from Connacht,[3] isn't she?

—Her people are, said Gabriel shortly.

—But you will come, won't you? said Miss Ivors, laying her warm hand eagerly on his arm.

—The fact is, said Gabriel, I have already arranged to go—

—Go where? asked Miss Ivors.

—Well, you know, every year I go for a cycling tour with some fellows and so—

—But where? asked Miss Ivors.

—Well, we usually go to France or Belgium or perhaps Germany, said Gabriel awkwardly.

—And why do you go to France and Belgium, said Miss Ivors, instead of visiting your own land?

—Well, said Gabriel, it's partly to keep in touch with the languages and partly for a change.

—And haven't you your own language to keep in touch with—Irish? asked Miss Ivors.

—Well, said Gabriel, if it comes to that, you know, Irish is not my language.

Their neighbours had turned to listen to the cross-examination. Gabriel glanced right and left nervously and tried to keep his good humour under the ordeal which was making a blush invade his forehead.

—And haven't you your own land to visit, continued Miss Ivors, that you know nothing of, your own people, and your own country?

—O, to tell you the truth, retorted Gabriel suddenly, I'm sick of my own country, sick of it!

—Why? asked Miss Ivors.

Gabriel did not answer for his retort had heated him.

—Why? repeated Miss Ivors.

They had to go visiting together and, as he had not answered her, Miss Ivors said warmly:

—Of course, you've no answer.

Gabriel tried to cover his agitation by taking part in the dance with great energy. He avoided her eyes for he had seen a sour expression on her face. But when they met in the long chain he was surprised to feel his hand firmly pressed. She looked at him from under her brows for a moment quizzically until he smiled. Then, just as the chain was about to start again, she stood on tiptoe and whispered into his ear:

—West Briton!

When the lancers were over Gabriel went away to a remote corner of the room where Freddy Malins' mother was sitting. She was a stout feeble old woman with white hair. Her voice had a catch in it like her son's and she stuttered slightly. She had been told that Freddy had come and that he was nearly all right. Gabriel asked her whether she had had a good crossing. She lived with her married daughter in Glasgow and came to Dublin on a visit once a year. She answered placidly that she had had a beautiful crossing and that the captain had been most attentive to her. She spoke also of the beautiful house her daughter kept in Glasgow, and of all the nice friends they had there. While her tongue rambled on Gabriel tried to banish from his

3. A province on the west coast of Ireland.

mind all memory of the unpleasant incident with Miss Ivors. Of course the girl or woman, or whatever she was, was an enthusiast but there was a time for all things. Perhaps he ought not to have answered her like that. But she had no right to call him a West Briton before people, even in joke. She had tried to make him ridiculous before people, heckling him and staring at him with her rabbit's eyes.

He saw his wife making her way towards him through the waltzing couples. When she reached him she said into his ear:

—Gabriel, Aunt Kate wants to know won't you carve the goose as usual. Miss Daly will carve the ham and I'll do the pudding.

—All right, said Gabriel.

—She's sending in the younger ones first as soon as this waltz is over so that we'll have the table to ourselves.

—Were you dancing? asked Gabriel.

—Of course I was. Didn't you see me? What words had you with Molly Ivors?

—No words. Why? Did she say so?

—Something like that. I'm trying to get that Mr D'Arcy to sing. He's full of conceit, I think.

—There were no words, said Gabriel moodily, only she wanted me to go for a trip to the west of Ireland and I said I wouldn't.

His wife clasped her hands excitedly and gave a little jump.

—O, do go, Gabriel, she cried. I'd love to see Galway again.

—You can go if you like, said Gabriel coldly.

She looked at him for a moment, then turned to Mrs Malins and said:

—There's a nice husband for you, Mrs Malins.

While she was threading her way back across the room Mrs Malins, without adverting to the interruption, went on to tell Gabriel what beautiful places there were in Scotland and beautiful scenery. Her son-in-law brought them every year to the lakes and they used to go fishing. Her son-in-law was a splendid fisher. One day he caught a fish, a beautiful big big fish, and the man in the hotel boiled it for their dinner.

Gabriel hardly heard what she said. Now that supper was coming near he began to think again about his speech and about the quotation. When he saw Freddy Malins coming across the room to visit his mother Gabriel left the chair free for him and retired into the embrasure of the window. The room had already cleared and from the back room came the clatter of plates and knives. Those who still remained in the drawing-room seemed tired of dancing and were conversing quietly in little groups. Gabriel's warm trembling fingers tapped the cold pane of the window. How cool it must be outside! How pleasant it would be to walk out alone, first along by the river and then through the park! The snow would be lying on the branches of the trees and forming a bright cap on the top of the Wellington Monument.[4] How much more pleasant it would be there than at the supper-table!

He ran over the headings of his speech: Irish hospitality, sad memories, the Three Graces, Paris, the quotation from Browning. He repeated to himself a phrase he had written in his review: *One feels that one is listening to a thought-tormented music*. Miss Ivors had praised the review. Was she sincere? Had she really any life of her own behind all her propagandism? There had never been any ill-feeling between them until

4. A monument to the Duke of Wellington, an Irish-born English military hero, located in Phoenix Park, Dublin's major public park.

that night. It unnerved him to think that she would be at the supper-table, looking up at him while he spoke with her critical quizzing eyes. Perhaps she would not be sorry to see him fail in his speech. An idea came into his mind and gave him courage. He would say, alluding to Aunt Kate and Aunt Julia: *Ladies and Gentlemen, the generation which is now on the wane among us may have had its faults but for my part I think it had certain qualities of hospitality, of humour, of humanity, which the new and very serious and hypereducated generation that is growing up around us seems to me to lack.* Very good: that was one for Miss Ivors. What did he care that his aunts were only two ignorant old women?

A murmur in the room attracted his attention. Mr Browne was advancing from the door, gallantly escorting Aunt Julia, who leaned upon his arm, smiling and hanging her head. An irregular musketry of applause escorted her also as far as the piano and then, as Mary Jane seated herself on the stool, and Aunt Julia, no longer smiling, half turned so as to pitch her voice fairly into the room, gradually ceased. Gabriel recognised the prelude. It was that of an old song of Aunt Julia's—*Arrayed for the Bridal.*[5] Her voice, strong and clear in tone, attacked with great spirit the runs which embellish the air and though she sang very rapidly she did not miss even the smallest of the grace notes. To follow the voice, without looking at the singer's face, was to feel and share the excitement of swift and secure flight. Gabriel applauded loudly with all the others at the close of the song and loud applause was borne in from the invisible supper-table. It sounded so genuine that a little colour struggled into Aunt Julia's face as she bent to replace in the music-stand the old leather-bound song-book that had her initials on the cover. Freddy Malins, who had listened with his head perched sideways to hear her better, was still applauding when everyone else had ceased and talking animatedly to his mother who nodded her head gravely and slowly in acquiescence. At last, when he could clap no more, he stood up suddenly and hurried across the room to Aunt Julia whose hand he seized and held in both his hands, shaking it when words failed him or the catch in his voice proved too much for him.

—I was just telling my mother, he said, I never heard you sing so well, never. No, I never heard your voice so good as it is to-night. Now! Would you believe that now? That's the truth. Upon my word and honour that's the truth. I never heard your voice sound so fresh and so . . . so clear and fresh, never.

Aunt Julia smiled broadly and murmured something about compliments as she released her hand from his grasp. Mr Browne extended his open hand towards her and said to those who were near him in the manner of a showman introducing a prodigy to an audience:

—Miss Julia Morkan, my latest discovery!

He was laughing very heartily at this himself when Freddy Malins turned to him and said:

—Well, Browne, if you're serious you might make a worse discovery. All I can say is I never heard her sing half so well as long as I am coming here. And that's the honest truth.

—Neither did I, said Mr. Browne. I think her voice has greatly improved.

Aunt Julia shrugged her shoulders and said with meek pride:

—Thirty years ago I hadn't a bad voice as voices go.

—I often told Julia, said Aunt Kate emphatically, that she was simply thrown away in that choir. But she never would be said by me.

5. A popular but challenging song set to music from Bellini's opera *I Puritani* (1835).

She turned as if to appeal to the good sense of the others against a refractory child while Aunt Julia gazed in front of her, a vague smile of reminiscence playing on her face.

—No, continued Aunt Kate, she wouldn't be said or led by anyone, slaving there in that choir night and day, night and day. Six o'clock on Christmas morning! And all for what?

—Well, isn't it for the honour of God, Aunt Kate? asked Mary Jane, twisting round on the piano-stool and smiling.

Aunt Kate turned fiercely on her niece and said:

—I know all about the honour of God, Mary Jane, but I think it's not at all honourable for the pope to turn out the women out of the choirs that have slaved there all their lives and put little whipper-snappers of boys over their heads. I suppose it is for the good of the Church if the pope does it. But it's not just, Mary Jane, and it's not right.

She had worked herself into a passion and would have continued in defence of her sister for it was a sore subject with her but Mary Jane, seeing that all the dancers had come back, intervened pacifically:

—Now, Aunt Kate, you're giving scandal to Mr Browne who is of the other persuasion.

Aunt Kate turned to Mr Browne, who was grinning at this allusion to his religion, and said hastily:

—O, I don't question the pope's being right. I'm only a stupid old woman and I wouldn't presume to do such a thing. But there's such a thing as common everyday politeness and gratitude. And if I were in Julia's place I'd tell that Father Healy straight up to his face . . .

—And besides, Aunt Kate, said Mary Jane, we really are all hungry and when we are hungry we are all very quarrelsome.

—And when we are thirsty we are also quarrelsome, added Mr Browne.

—So that we had better go to supper, said Mary Jane, and finish the discussion afterwards.

On the landing outside the drawing-room Gabriel found his wife and Mary Jane trying to persuade Miss Ivors to stay for supper. But Miss Ivors, who had put on her hat and was buttoning her cloak, would not stay. She did not feel in the least hungry and she had already overstayed her time.

—But only for ten minutes, Molly, said Mrs Conroy. That won't delay you.

—To take a pick itself, said Mary Jane, after all your dancing.

—I really couldn't, said Miss Ivors.

—I am afraid you didn't enjoy yourself at all, said Mary Jane hopelessly.

—Ever so much, I assure you, said Miss Ivors, but you really must let me run off now.

—But how can you get home? asked Mrs Conroy.

—O, it's only two steps up the quay.

Gabriel hesitated a moment and said:

—If you will allow me, Miss Ivors, I'll see you home if you really are obliged to go.

But Miss Ivors broke away from them.

—I won't hear of it, she cried. For goodness sake go in to your suppers and don't mind me. I'm quite well able to take care of myself.

—Well, you're the comical girl, Molly, said Mrs Conroy frankly.

—*Beannacht libh*,[6] cried Miss Ivors, with a laugh, as she ran down the staircase.

Mary Jane gazed after her, a moody puzzled expression on her face, while Mrs Conroy leaned over the banisters to listen for the hall-door. Gabriel asked himself was he the cause of her abrupt departure. But she did not seem to be in ill humour: she had gone away laughing. He stared blankly down the staircase.

At that moment Aunt Kate came toddling out of the supper-room, almost wringing her hands in despair.

—Where is Gabriel? she cried. Where on earth is Gabriel? There's everyone waiting in there, stage to let, and nobody to carve the goose!

—Here I am, Aunt Kate! cried Gabriel, with sudden animation, ready to carve a flock of geese, if necessary.

A fat brown goose lay at one end of the table and at the other end, on a bed of creased paper strewn with sprigs of parsley, lay a great ham, stripped of its outer skin and peppered over with crust crumbs, a neat paper frill round its shin and beside this was a round of spiced beef. Between these rival ends ran parallel lines of side-dishes: two little minsters of jelly, red and yellow; a shallow dish full of blocks of blancmange and red jam, a large green leaf-shaped dish with a stalk-shaped handle, on which lay bunches of purple raisins and peeled almonds, a companion dish on which lay a solid rectangle of Smyrna figs, a dish of custard topped with grated nutmeg, a small bowl full of chocolates and sweets wrapped in gold and silver papers and a glass vase in which stood some tall celery stalks. In the centre of the table there stood, as sentries to a fruit-stand which upheld a pyramid of oranges and American apples, two squat old-fashioned decanters of cut glass, one containing port and the other dark sherry. On the closed square piano a pudding in a huge yellow dish lay in waiting and behind it were three squads of bottles of stout and ale and minerals, drawn up according to the colours of their uniforms, the first two black, with brown and red labels, the third and smallest squad white, with transverse green sashes.

Gabriel took his seat boldly at the head of the table and, having looked to the edge of the carver, plunged his fork firmly into the goose. He felt quite at ease now for he was an expert carver and liked nothing better than to find himself at the head of a well-laden table.

—Miss Furlong, what shall I send you? he asked. A wing or a slice of the breast?

—Just a small slice of the breast.

—Miss Higgins, what for you?

—O, anything at all, Mr Conroy.

While Gabriel and Miss Daly exchanged plates of goose and plates of ham and spiced beef Lily went from guest to guest with a dish of hot floury potatoes wrapped in a white napkin. This was Mary Jane's idea and she had also suggested apple sauce for the goose but Aunt Kate had said that plain roast goose without apple sauce had always been good enough for her and she hoped she might never eat worse. Mary Jane waited on her pupils and saw that they got the best slices and Aunt Kate and Aunt Julia opened and carried across from the piano bottles of stout and ale for the gentlemen and bottles of minerals for the ladies. There was a great deal of confusion and laughter and noise, the noise of orders and counter-orders, of knives and forks, of

6. Farewell (Irish).

corks and glass-stoppers. Gabriel began to carve second helpings as soon as he had finished the first round without serving himself. Everyone protested loudly so that he compromised by taking a long draught of stout for he had found the carving hot work. Mary Jane settled down quietly to her supper but Aunt Kate and Aunt Julia were still toddling round the table, walking on each other's heels, getting in each other's way and giving each other unheeded orders. Mr Browne begged of them to sit down and eat their suppers and so did Gabriel but they said there was time enough so that, at last, Freddy Malins stood up and, capturing Aunt Kate, plumped her down on her chair amid general laughter.

When everyone had been well served Gabriel said, smiling:

—Now, if anyone wants a little more of what vulgar people call stuffing let him or her speak.

A chorus of voices invited him to begin his own supper and Lily came forward with three potatoes which she had reserved for him.

—Very well, said Gabriel amiably, as he took another preparatory draught, kindly forget my existence, ladies and gentlemen, for a few minutes.

He set to his supper and took no part in the conversation with which the table covered Lily's removal of the plates. The subject of talk was the opera company which was then at the Theatre Royal. Mr Bartell D'Arcy, the tenor, a dark-complexioned young man with a smart moustache, praised very highly the leading contralto of the company but Miss Furlong thought she had a rather vulgar style of production. Freddy Malins said there was a negro chieftain singing in the second part of the Gaiety pantomime who had one of the finest tenor voices he had ever heard.

—Have you heard him? he asked Mr Bartell D'Arcy across the table.

—No, answered Mr Bartell D'Arcy carelessly.

—Because, Freddy Malins explained, now I'd be curious to hear your opinion of him. I think he has a grand voice.

—It takes Teddy to find out the really good things, said Mr Browne familiarly to the table.

—And why couldn't he have a voice too? asked Freddy Malins sharply. Is it because he's only a black?

Nobody answered this question and Mary Jane led the table back to the legitimate opera. One of her pupils had given her a pass for *Mignon*. Of course it was very fine, she said, but it made her think of poor Georgina Burns. Mr Browne could go back farther still, to the old Italian companies that used to come to Dublin—Tietjens, Ilma de Murzka, Campanini, the great Trebelli, Giuglini, Ravelli, Aramburo.[7] Those were the days, he said, when there was something like singing to be heard in Dublin. He told too of how the top gallery of the old Royal used to be packed night after night, of how one night an Italian tenor had sung five encores to *Let Me Like a Soldier Fall*, introducing a high C every time, and of how the gallery boys would sometimes in their enthusiasm unyoke the horses from the carriage of some great *prima donna* and pull her themselves through the streets to her hotel. Why did they never play the grand old operas now, he asked, *Dinorah*, *Lucrezia Borgia?* Because they could not get the voices to sing them: that was why.

—O, well, said Mr Bartell D'Arcy, I presume there are as good singers to-day as there were then.

7. Famous 19th-century operatic singers.

—Where are they? asked Mr Browne defiantly.

—In London, Paris, Milan, said Mr Bartell D'Arcy warmly. I suppose Caruso,[8] for example, is quite as good, if not better than any of the men you have mentioned.

—Maybe so, said Mr Browne. But I may tell you I doubt it strongly.

—O, I'd give anything to hear Caruso sing, said Mary Jane.

—For me, said Aunt Kate, who had been picking a bone, there was only one tenor. To please me, I mean. But I suppose none of you ever heard of him.

—Who was he, Miss Morkan? asked Mr Bartell D'Arcy politely.

—His name, said Aunt Kate, was Parkinson. I heard him when he was in his prime and I think he had then the purest tenor voice that was ever put into a man's throat.

—Strange, said Mr Bartell D'Arcy. I never even heard of him.

—Yes, yes, Miss Morkan is right, said Mr Browne. I remember hearing of old Parkinson but he's too far back for me.

—A beautiful pure sweet mellow English tenor, said Aunt Kate with enthusiasm.

Gabriel having finished, the huge pudding was transferred to the table. The clatter of forks and spoons began again. Gabriel's wife served out spoonfuls of the pudding and passed the plates down the table. Midway down they were held up by Mary Jane, who replenished them with raspberry or orange jelly or with blancmange and jam. The pudding was of Aunt Julia's making and she received praises for it from all quarters. She herself said that it was not quite brown enough.

—Well, I hope, Miss Morkan, said Mr Browne, that I'm brown enough for you because, you know, I'm all brown.

All the gentlemen, except Gabriel, ate some of the pudding out of compliment to Aunt Julia. As Gabriel never ate sweets the celery had been left for him. Freddy Malins also took a stalk of celery and ate it with his pudding. He had been told that celery was a capital thing for the blood and he was just then under doctor's care. Mrs Malins, who had been silent all through the supper, said that her son was going down to Mount Melleray[9] in a week or so. The table then spoke to Mount Melleray, how bracing the air was down there, how hospitable the monks were and how they never asked for a penny-piece from their guests.

—And do you mean to say, asked Mr Browne incredulously, that a chap can go down there and put up there as if it were a hotel and live on the fat of the land and then come away without paying a farthing?

—O, most people give some donation to the monastery when they leave, said Mary Jane.

—I wish we had an institution like that in our Church, said Mr Browne candidly.

He was astonished to hear that the monks never spoke, got up at two in the morning and slept in their coffins. He asked what they did it for.

—That's the rule of the order, said Aunt Kate firmly.

—Yes, but why? asked Mr Browne.

Aunt Kate repeated that it was the rule, that was all. Mr Browne still seemed not to understand. Freddy Malins explained to him, as best he could, that the monks were trying to make up for the sins committed by all the sinners in the outside world. The explanation was not very clear for Mr Browne grinned and said:

8. Enrico Caruso (1874–1921), a famous tenor.

9. Site of a Trappist monastery in the south of Ireland.

—I like that idea very much but wouldn't a comfortable spring bed do them as well as a coffin?

—The coffin, said Mary Jane, is to remind them of their last end.

As the subject had grown lugubrious it was buried in a silence of the table during which Mrs Malins could be heard saying to her neighbour in an indistinct undertone:

—They are very good men, the monks, very pious men.

The raisins and almonds and figs and apples and oranges and chocolates and sweets were now passed about the table and Aunt Julia invited all the guests to have either port or sherry. At first Mr Bartell D'Arcy refused to take either but one of his neighbours nudged him and whispered something to him upon which he allowed his glass to be filled. Gradually as the last glasses were being filled the conversation ceased. A pause followed, broken only by the noise of the wine and by unsettlings of chairs. The Misses Morkan, all three, looked down at the tablecloth. Someone coughed once or twice and then a few gentlemen patted the table gently as a signal for silence. The silence came and Gabriel pushed back his chair and stood up.

The patting at once grew louder in encouragement and then ceased altogether. Gabriel leaned his ten trembling fingers on the tablecloth and smiled nervously at the company. Meeting a row of upturned faces he raised his eyes to the chandelier. The piano was playing a waltz tune and he could hear the skirts sweeping against the drawing-room door. People, perhaps, were standing in the snow on the quay outside, gazing up at the lighted windows and listening to the waltz music. The air was pure there. In the distance lay the park where the trees were weighted with snow. The Wellington Monument wore a gleaming cap of snow that flashed westward over the white field of Fifteen Acres.[1]

He began:

—Ladies and Gentlemen.

—It has fallen to my lot this evening, as in years past, to perform a very pleasing task but a task for which I am afraid my poor powers as a speaker are all too inadequate.

—No, no! said Mr Browne.

—But, however that may be, I can only ask you tonight to take the will for the deed and to lend me your attention for a few moments while I endeavour to express to you in words what my feelings are on this occasion.

—Ladies and Gentlemen. It is not the first time that we have gathered together under this hospitable roof, around this hospitable board. It is not the first time that we have been the recipients—or perhaps, I had better say, the victims—of the hospitality of certain good ladies.

He made a circle in the air with his arm and paused. Everyone laughed or smiled at Aunt Kate and Aunt Julia and Mary Jane who all turned crimson with pleasure. Gabriel went on more boldly:

—I feel more strongly with every recurring year that our country has no tradition which does it so much honour and which it should guard so jealously as that of its hospitality. It is a tradition that is unique as far as my experience goes (and I have visited not a few places abroad) among the modern nations. Some would say, perhaps, that with us it is rather a failing than anything to be boasted of. But granted even that, it is, to my mind, a princely failing, and one that I trust will long be cultivated among us. Of one thing, at least, I am sure. As long as this one roof shelters the good ladies aforesaid—and I wish from my heart it may do so for many and many a

1. A section of Phoenix Park.

long year to come—the tradition of genuine warm-hearted courteous Irish hospitality, which our forefathers have handed down to us and which we in turn must hand down to our descendants, is still alive among us.

A hearty murmur of assent ran round the table. It shot through Gabriel's mind that Miss Ivors was not there and that she had gone away discourteously: and he said with confidence in himself:

—Ladies and Gentlemen.

—A new generation is growing up in our midst, a generation actuated by new ideas and new principles. It is serious and enthusiastic for these new ideas and its enthusiasm, even when it is misdirected, is, I believe, in the main sincere. But we are living in a sceptical and, if I may use the phrase, a thought-tormented age: and sometimes I fear that this new generation, educated or hypereducated as it is, will lack those qualities of humanity, of hospitality, of kindly humour which belonged to an older day. Listening to-night to the names of all those great singers of the past it seemed to me, I must confess, that we were living in a less spacious age. Those days might, without exaggeration, be called spacious days: and if they are gone beyond recall let us hope, at least, that in gatherings such as this we shall still speak of them with pride and affection, still cherish in our hearts the memory of those dead and gone great ones whose fame the world will not willingly let die.

—Hear, hear! said Mr Browne loudly.

—But yet, continued Gabriel, his voice falling into a softer inflection, there are always in gatherings such as this sadder thoughts that will recur to our minds: thoughts of the past, of youth, of changes, of absent faces that we miss here to-night. Our path through life is strewn with many such sad memories: and were we to brood upon them always we could not find the heart to go on bravely with our work among the living. We have all of us living duties and living affections which claim, and rightly claim, our strenuous endeavours.

—Therefore, I will not linger on the past. I will not let any gloomy moralising intrude upon us here to-night. Here we are gathered together for a brief moment from the bustle and rush of our everyday routine. We are met here as friends, in the spirit of good-fellowship, as colleagues, also to a certain extent, in the true spirit of *camaraderie,* and as the guests of—what shall I call them?—the Three Graces[2] of the Dublin musical world.

The table burst into applause and laughter at this sally. Aunt Julia vainly asked each of her neighbors in turn to tell her what Gabriel had said.

—He says we are the Three Graces, Aunt Julia, said Mary Jane.

Aunt Julia did not understand but she looked up, smiling, at Gabriel, who continued in the same vein:

—Ladies and Gentlemen.

—I will not attempt to play to-night the part that Paris[3] played on another occasion. I will not attempt to choose between them. The task would be an invidious one and one beyond my poor powers. For when I view them in turn, whether it be our chief hostess herself, whose good heart, whose too good heart, has become a byword with all who know her, or her sister, who seems to be gifted with perennial youth and whose singing must have been a surprise and a revelation to us all to-night, or, last but not least, when I consider our youngest hostess, talented, cheerful, hard-working and the best of nieces, I confess, Ladies and Gentlemen, that I do not know to which of them I should award the prize.

2. Companions to the Muses in Greek mythology.
3. Paris was the judge of a divine beauty contest in which Hera, Athena, and Aphrodite competed; his selection of Aphrodite was, indirectly, the cause of the Trojan War.

Gabriel glanced down at his aunts and, seeing the large smile on Aunt Julia's face and the tears which had risen to Aunt Kate's eyes, hastened to his close. He raised his glass of port gallantly, while every member of the company fingered a glass expectantly, and said loudly:

—Let us toast them all three together. Let us drink to their health, wealth, long life, happiness and prosperity and may they long continue to hold the proud and self-won position which they hold in their profession and the position of honour and affection which they hold in our hearts.

All the guests stood up, glass in hand, and, turning towards the three seated ladies, sang in unison, with Mr Browne as leader:

For they are jolly gay fellows,
For they are jolly gay fellows,
For they are jolly gay fellows,
Which nobody can deny.

Aunt Kate was making frank use of her handkerchief and even Aunt Julia seemed moved. Freddy Malins beat time with his pudding-fork and the singers turned towards one another, as if in melodious conference, while they sang, with emphasis:

Unless he tells a lie,
Unless he tells a lie.

Then, turning once more towards their hostesses, they sang:

For they are jolly gay fellows,
For they are jolly gay fellows,
For they are jolly gay fellows,
Which nobody can deny.

The acclamation which followed was taken up beyond the door of the supper-room by many of the other guests and renewed time after time, Freddy Malins acting as officer with his fork on high.

The piercing morning air came into the hall where they were standing so that Aunt Kate said:

—Close the door, somebody. Mrs Malins will get her death of cold.

—Browne is out there, Aunt Kate, said Mary Jane.

—Browne is everywhere, said Aunt Kate, lowering her voice.

Mary Jane laughed at her tone.

—Really, she said archly, he is very attentive.

—He has been laid on here like the gas, said Aunt Kate in the same tone, all during the Christmas.

She laughed herself this time good-humouredly and then added quickly:

—But tell him to come in, Mary Jane, and close the door. I hope to goodness he didn't hear me.

At that moment the hall-door was opened and Mr Browne came in from the doorstep, laughing as if his heart would break. He was dressed in a long green overcoat with mock astrakhan cuffs and collar and wore on his head an oval fur cap. He pointed down the snow-covered quay from where the sound of shrill prolonged whistling was borne in.

—Teddy will have all the cabs in Dublin out, he said.

Gabriel advanced from the little pantry behind the office, struggling into his overcoat and looking round the hall, said:

—Gretta not down yet?

—She's getting on her things, Gabriel, said Aunt Kate.

—Who's playing up there? asked Gabriel.

—Nobody. They're all gone.

—O no, Aunt Kate, said Mary Jane. Bartell D'Arcy and Miss O'Callaghan aren't gone yet.

—Someone is strumming at the piano, anyhow, said Gabriel.

Mary Jane glanced at Gabriel and Mr Browne and said with a shiver:

—It makes me feel cold to look at you two gentlemen muffled up like that. I wouldn't like to face your journey home at this hour.

—I'd like nothing better this minute, said Mr Browne stoutly, than a rattling fine walk in the country or a fast drive with a good spanking goer between the shafts.

—We used to have a very good horse and trap at home, said Aunt Julia sadly.

—The never-to-be-forgotten Johnny, said Mary Jane, laughing.

Aunt Kate and Gabriel laughed too.

—Why, what was wonderful about Johnny? asked Mr Browne.

—The late lamented Patrick Morkan, our grandfather, that is, explained Gabriel, commonly known in his later years as the old gentleman, was a glue-boiler.

—O, now, Gabriel, said Aunt Kate, laughing, he had a starch mill.

—Well, glue or starch, said Gabriel, the old gentleman had a horse by the name of Johnny. And Johnny used to work in the old gentleman's mill, walking round and round in order to drive the mill. That was all very well; but now comes the tragic part about Johnny. One fine day the old gentleman thought he'd like to drive out with the quality to a military review in the park.

—The Lord have mercy on his soul, said Aunt Kate compassionately.

—Amen, said Gabriel. So the old gentleman, as I said, harnessed Johnny and put on his very best tall hat and his very best stock collar and drove out in grand style from his ancestral mansion somewhere near Back Lane, I think.

Everyone laughed, even Mrs Malins, at Gabriel's manner and Aunt Kate said:

—O now, Gabriel, he didn't live in Back Lane, really. Only the mill was there.

—Out from the mansion of his forefathers, continued Gabriel, he drove with Johnny. And everything went on beautifully until Johnny came in sight of King Billy's statue:[4] and whether he fell in love with the horse King Billy sits on or whether he thought he was back again in the mill, anyhow he began to walk round the statue.

Gabriel paced in a circle round the hall in his goloshes amid the laughter of the others.

—Round and round he went, said Gabriel, and the old gentleman, who was a very pompous old gentleman, was highly indignant. *Go on, sir! What do you mean, sir? Johnny! Johnny! Most extraordinary conduct! Can't understand the horse!*

The peals of laughter which followed Gabriel's imitation of the incident were interrupted by a resounding knock at the hall-door. Mary Jane ran to open it and let in Freddy Malins. Freddy Malins, with his hat well back on his head and his shoulders humped with cold, was puffing and steaming after his exertions.

4. Statue of William of Orange, who defeated the Irish Catholic forces in the Battle of the Boyne in 1690, which stood in College Green in front of Trinity College in the heart of Dublin. It was seen as a symbol of British imperial oppression.

—I could only get one cab, he said.

—O, we'll find another along the quay, said Gabriel.

—Yes, said Aunt Kate. Better not keep Mrs Malins standing in the draught.

Mrs Malins was helped down the front steps by her son and Mr Browne and, after many manoeuvres, hoisted into the cab. Freddy Malins clambered in after her and spent a long time settling her on the seat, Mr Browne helping him with advice. At last she was settled comfortably and Freddy Malins invited Mr Browne into the cab. There was a good deal of confused talk, and then Mr Browne got into the cab. The cabman settled his rug over his knees, and bent down for the address. The confusion grew greater and the cabman was directed differently by Freddy Malins and Mr Browne, each of whom had his head out through a window of the cab. The difficulty was to know where to drop Mr Browne along the route and Aunt Kate, Aunt Julia and Mary Jane helped the discussion from the doorstep with cross-directions and contradictions and abundance of laughter. As for Freddy Malins he was speechless with laughter. He popped his head in and out of the window every moment, to the great danger of his hat, and told his mother how the discussion was progressing till at last Mr Browne shouted to the bewildered cabman above the din of everybody's laughter:

—Do you know Trinity College?

—Yes, sir, said the cabman.

—Well, drive bang up against Trinity College gates, said Mr Browne, and then we'll tell you where to go. You understand now?

—Yes, sir, said the cabman.

—Make like a bird for Trinity College.

—Right, sir, cried the cabman.

The horse was whipped up and the cab rattled off along the quay amid a chorus of laughter and adieus.

Gabriel had not gone to the door with the others. He was in a dark part of the hall gazing up the staircase, a woman was standing near the top of the first flight, in the shadow also. He could not see her face but he could see the terracotta and salmonpink panels of her skirt which the shadow made appear black and white. It was his wife. She was leaning on the banisters, listening to something. Gabriel was surprised at her stillness and strained his ear to listen also. But he could hear little save the noise of laughter and dispute on the front steps, a few chords struck on the piano and a few notes of a man's voice singing.

He stood still in the gloom of the hall, trying to catch the air that the voice was singing and gazing up at his wife. There was grace and mystery in her attitude as if she were a symbol of something. He asked himself what is a woman standing on the stairs in the shadow, listening to distant music, a symbol of. If he were a painter he would paint her in that attitude. Her blue felt hat would show off the bronze of her hair against the darkness and the dark panels of her skirt would show off the light ones. *Distant Music* he would call the picture if he were a painter.

The hall-door was closed; and Aunt Kate, Aunt Julia and Mary Jane came down the hall, still laughing.

—Well, isn't Freddy terrible? said Mary Jane. He's really terrible.

Gabriel said nothing but pointed up the stairs towards where his wife was standing. Now that the hall-door was closed the voice and the piano could be heard more clearly. Gabriel held up his hand for them to be silent. The song seemed to be in the old Irish tonality and the singer seemed uncertain both of his words and of his voice. The voice, made plaintive by distance and by the singer's hoarseness, faintly illuminated the cadence of the air with words expressing grief:

O, the rain falls on my heavy locks
And the dew wets my skin,
My babe lies cold . . .

—O, exclaimed Mary Jane. It's Bartell D'Arcy singing and he wouldn't sing all the night. O, I'll get him to sing a song before he goes.

—O do, Mary Jane, said Aunt Kate.

Mary Jane brushed past the others and ran to the staircase but before she reached it the singing stopped and the piano was closed abruptly.

—O, what a pity! she cried. Is he coming down, Gretta?

Gabriel heard his wife answer yes and saw her come down towards them. A few steps behind her were Mr Bartell D'Arcy and Miss O'Callaghan.

—O, Mr D'Arcy, cried Mary Jane, it's downright mean of you to break off like that when we were all in raptures listening to you.

—I have been at him all the evening, said Miss O'Callaghan, and Mrs Conroy too and he told us he had a dreadful cold and couldn't sing.

—O, Mr D'Arcy, said Aunt Kate, now that was a great fib to tell.

—Can't you see that I'm as hoarse as a crow? said Mr D'Arcy roughly.

He went into the pantry hastily and put on his overcoat. The others, taken aback by his rude speech, could find nothing to say. Aunt Kate wrinkled her brows and made signs to the others to drop the subject. Mr D'Arcy stood swathing his neck carefully and frowning.

—It's the weather, said Aunt Julia, after a pause.

—Yes, everybody has colds, said Aunt Kate readily, everybody.

—They say, said Mary Jane, we haven't had snow like it for thirty years; and I read this morning in the newspapers that the snow is general all over Ireland.

—I love the look of snow, said Aunt Julia sadly.

—So do I, said Miss O'Callaghan. I think Christmas is never really Christmas unless we have the snow on the ground.

—But poor Mr D'Arcy doesn't like the snow, said Aunt Kate, smiling.

Mr D'Arcy came from the pantry, full swathed and buttoned, and in a repentant tone told them the history of his cold. Everyone gave him advice and said it was a great pity and urged him to be very careful of his throat in the night air. Gabriel watched his wife who did not join in the conversation. She was standing right under the dusty fanlight and the flame of the gas lit up the rich bronze of her hair which he had seen her drying at the fire a few days before. She was in the same attitude and seemed unaware of the talk about her. At last she turned towards them and Gabriel saw that there was colour on her cheeks and that her eyes were shining. A sudden tide of joy went leaping out of his heart.

—Mr D'Arcy, she said, what is the name of that song you were singing?

—It's called *The Lass of Aughrim*, said Mr D'Arcy, but I couldn't remember it properly. Why? Do you know it?

—*The Lass of Aughrim*, she repeated. I couldn't think of the name.

—It's a very nice air, said Mary Jane. I'm sorry you were not in voice to-night.

—Now, Mary Jane, said Aunt Kate, don't annoy Mr D'Arcy. I won't have him annoyed.

Seeing that all were ready to start she shepherded them to the door where good-night was said:

—Well, good-night, Aunt Kate, and thanks for the pleasant evening.

—Good-night, Gabriel. Good-night, Gretta!

—Good-night, Aunt Kate, and thanks ever so much. Good-night, Aunt Julia.

—O, good-night, Gretta, I didn't see you.

—Good-night, Mr D'Arcy. Good-night, Miss O'Callaghan.

—Good-night, Miss Morkan.

—Good-night, again.

—Good-night, all. Safe home.

—Good-night. Good-night.

The morning was still dark. A dull yellow light brooded over the houses and the river; and the sky seemed to be descending. It was slushy underfoot; and only streaks and patches of snow lay on the roofs, on the parapets of the quay and on the area railings. The lamps were still burning redly in the murky air and, across the river, the palace of the Four Courts[5] stood out menacingly against the heavy sky.

She was walking on before him with Mr Bartell D'Arcy, her shoes in a brown parcel tucked under one arm and her hands holding her skirt up from the slush. She had no longer any grace of attitude but Gabriel's eyes were still bright with happiness. The blood went bounding along his veins; and the thoughts went rioting through his brain, proud, joyful, tender, valorous.

She was walking on before him so lightly and so erect that he longed to run after her noiselessly, catch her by the shoulders and say something foolish and affectionate into her ear. She seemed to him so frail that he longed to defend her against something and then to be alone with her. Moments of their secret life together burst like stars upon his memory. A heliotrope envelope was lying beside his breakfast-cup and he was caressing it with his hand. Birds were twittering in the ivy and the sunny web of the curtain was shimmering along the floor: he could not eat for happiness. They were standing on the crowded platform and he was placing a ticket inside the warm palm of her glove. He was standing with her in the cold, looking in through a grated window at a man making bottles in a roaring furnace. It was very cold. Her face, fragrant in the cold air, was quite close to his; and suddenly she called out to the man at the furnace:

—Is the fire hot, sir?

But the man could not hear her with the noise of the furnace. It was just as well. He might have answered rudely.

A wave of yet more tender joy escaped from his heart and went coursing in warm flood along his arteries. Like the tender fires of stars moments of their life together, that no one knew of or would ever know of, broke upon and illumined his memory. He longed to recall to her those moments, to make her forget the years of their dull existence together and remember only their moments of ecstasy. For the years, he felt, had not quenched his soul or hers. Their children, his writing, her household cares had not quenched all their souls' tender fire. In one letter that he had written to her then he had said: *Why is it that words like these seem to me so dull and cold? Is it because there is no word tender enough to be your name?*

Like distant music these words that he had written years before were borne towards him from the past. He longed to be alone with her. When the others had gone away, when he and she were in their room in the hotel, then they would be alone together. He would call her softly:

—Gretta!

5. The Irish law courts.

Perhaps she would not hear at once: she would be undressing. Then something in his voice would strike her. She would turn and look at him. . . .

At the corner of Winetavern Street they met a cab. He was glad of its rattling noise as it saved him from conversation. She was looking out of the window and seemed tired. The others spoke only a few words, pointing out some building or street. The horse galloped along wearily under the murky morning sky, dragging his old rattling box after his heels, and Gabriel was again in a cab with her, galloping to catch the boat, galloping to their honeymoon.

As the cab drove across O'Connell Bridge Miss O'Callaghan said:

—They say you never cross O'Connell Bridge without seeing a white horse.

—I see a white man this time, said Gabriel.

—Where? asked Mr Bartell D'Arcy.

Gabriel pointed to the statue, on which lay patches of snow. Then he nodded familiarly to it and waved his hand.

—Good-night, Dan,[6] he said gaily.

When the cab drew up before the hotel Gabriel jumped out and, in spite of Mr Bartell D'Arcy's protest, paid the driver. He gave the man a shilling over his fare. The man saluted and said:

—A prosperous New Year to you, sir.

—The same to you, said Gabriel cordially.

She leaned for a moment on his arm in getting out of the cab and while standing at the curbstone, bidding the others good-night. She leaned lightly on his arm, as lightly as when she had danced with him a few hours before. He had felt proud and happy then, happy that she was his, proud of her grace and wifely carriage. But now, after the kindling again of so many memories, the first touch of her body, musical and strange and perfumed, sent through him a keen pang of lust. Under cover of her silence he pressed her arm closely to his side; and, as they stood at the hotel door, he felt that they had escaped from their lives and duties, escaped from home and friends and run away together with wild and radiant hearts to a new adventure.

An old man was dozing in a great hooded chair in the hall. He lit a candle in the office and went before them to the stairs. They followed him in silence, their feet falling in soft thuds on the thickly carpeted stairs. She mounted the stairs behind the porter, her head bowed in the ascent, her frail shoulders curved as with a burden, her skirt girt tightly about her. He could have flung his arms about her hips and held her still for his arms were trembling with desire to seize her and only the stress of his nails against the palms of his hands held the wild impulse of his body in check. The porter halted on the stairs to settle his guttering candle. They halted too on the steps below him. In the silence Gabriel could hear the falling of the molten wax into the tray and the thumping of his own heart against his ribs.

The porter led them along a corridor and opened a door. Then he set his unstable candle down on a toilet-table and asked at what hour they were to be called in the morning.

—Eight, said Gabriel.

The porter pointed to the tap of the electric-light and began a muttered apology but Gabriel cut him short.

6. A statue of Daniel O'Connell, 19th-century nationalist leader, stands at the south end of Sackville Street (now called O'Connell Street).

—We don't want any light. We have light enough from the street. And I say, he added, pointing to the candle, you might remove that handsome article, like a good man.

The porter took up his candle again, but slowly for he was surprised by such a novel idea. Then he mumbled good-night and went out. Gabriel shot the lock to.

A ghostly light from the street lamp lay in a long shaft from one window to the door. Gabriel threw his overcoat and hat on a couch and crossed the room towards the window. He looked down into the street in order that his emotion might calm a little. Then he turned and leaned against a chest of drawers with his back to the light. She had taken off her hat and cloak and was standing before a large swinging mirror, unhooking her waist. Gabriel paused for a few moments, watching her, and then said:

—Gretta!

She turned away from the mirror slowly and walked along the shaft of light towards him. Her face looked so serious and weary that the words would not pass Gabriel's lips. No, it was not the moment yet.

—You looked tired, he said.

—I am a little, she answered.

—You don't feel ill or weak?

—No, tired: that's all.

She went on to the window and stood there, looking out. Gabriel waited again and then, fearing that diffidence was about to conquer him, he said abruptly:

—By the way, Gretta!

—What is it?

—You know that poor fellow Malins? he said quickly.

—Yes. What about him?

—Well, poor fellow, he's a decent sort of chap after all, continued Gabriel in a false voice. He gave me back that sovereign I lent him and I didn't expect it really. It's a pity he wouldn't keep away from that Browne, because he's not a bad fellow at heart.

He was trembling now with annoyance. Why did she seem so abstracted? He did not know how he could begin. Was she annoyed, too, about something? If she would only turn to him or come to him of her own accord! To take her as she was would be brutal. No, he must see some ardour in her eyes first. He longed to be master of her strange mood.

—When did you lend him the pound? she asked, after a pause.

Gabriel strove to restrain himself from breaking out into brutal language about the sottish Malins and his pound. He longed to cry to her from his soul, to crush her body against his, to overmaster her. But he said:

—O, at Christmas, when he opened that little Christmas-card shop in Henry Street.

He was in such a fever of rage and desire that he did not hear her come from the window. She stood before him for an instant, looking at him strangely. Then, suddenly raising herself on tiptoe and resting her hands lightly on his shoulders, she kissed him.

—You are a very generous person, Gabriel, she said.

Gabriel, trembling with delight at her sudden kiss and at the quaintness of her phrase, put his hands on her hair and began smoothing it back, scarcely touching it with his fingers. The washing had made it fine and brilliant. His heart was brimming over with happiness. Just when he was wishing for it she had come to him of her own accord. Perhaps her thoughts had been running with his. Perhaps she had felt the impetuous desire that was in him and then the yielding mood had come upon her. Now that she had fallen to him so easily he wondered why he had been so diffident.

He stood, holding her head between his hands. Then, slipping one arm swiftly about her body and drawing her towards him, he said softly:

—Gretta dear, what are you thinking about?

She did not answer nor yield wholly to his arm. He said again, softly:

—Tell me what it is, Gretta. I think I know what is the matter. Do I know?

She did not answer at once. Then she said in an outburst of tears:

—O, I am thinking about that song, *The Lass of Aughrim*.

She broke loose from him and ran to the bed and, throwing her arms across the bed-rail, hid her face. Gabriel stood stock-still for a moment in astonishment and then followed her. As he passed in the way of the cheval-glass he caught sight of himself in full length, his broad, well-filled shirt-front, the face whose expression always puzzled him when he saw it in a mirror and his glimmering gilt-rimmed eyeglasses. He halted a few paces from her and said:

—What about the song? Why does that make you cry?

She raised her head from her arms and dried her eyes with the back of her hand like a child. A kinder note than he had intended went into his voice.

—Why, Gretta? he asked.

—I am thinking about a person long ago who used to sing that song.

—And who was the person long ago? asked Gabriel, smiling.

—It was a person I used to know in Galway when I was living with my grandmother, she said.

The smile passed away from Gabriel's face. A dull anger began to gather again at the back of his mind and the dull fires of his lust began to glow angrily in his veins.

—Someone you were in love with? he asked ironically.

—It was a young boy I used to know, she answered, named Michael Furey. He used to sing that song, *The Lass of Aughrim*. He was very delicate.

Gabriel was silent. He did not wish her to think that he was interested in this delicate boy.

—I can see him so plainly, she said after a moment. Such eyes as he had: big dark eyes! And such an expression in them—an expression!

—O then, you were in love with him? said Gabriel.

—I used to go out walking with him, she said, when I was in Galway.

A thought flew across Gabriel's mind.

—Perhaps that was why you wanted to go to Galway with that Ivors girl? he said coldly.

She looked at him and asked in surprise:

—What for?

Her eyes made Gabriel feel awkward. He shrugged his shoulders and said:

—How do I know? To see him perhaps.

She looked away from him along the shaft of light towards the window in silence.

—He is dead, she said at length. He died when he was only seventeen. Isn't it a terrible thing to die so young as that?

—What was he? asked Gabriel, still ironically.

—He was in the gasworks, she said.

Gabriel felt humiliated by the failure of his irony and by the evocation of this figure from the dead, a boy in the gasworks. While he had been full of memories of their secret life together, full of tenderness and joy and desire, she had been comparing him in her mind with another. A shameful consciousness of his own person assailed him. He saw himself as a ludicrous figure, acting as a pennyboy[7] for his aunts, a nervous well-meaning sentimentalist, orating to vulgarians and idealising his own clownish lusts, the pitiable fatuous fellow he had caught a glimpse of in the mirror. Instinctively he turned his back more to the light lest she might see the shame that burned upon his forehead.

He tried to keep up his tone of cold interrogation but his voice when he spoke was humble and indifferent.

—I suppose you were in love with this Michael Furey, Gretta, he said.

—I was great with him at that time, she said.

Her voice was veiled and sad. Gabriel, feeling now how vain it would be to try to lead her whither he had purposed, caressed one of her hands and said, also sadly:

—And what did he die of so young, Gretta? Consumption, was it?

—I think he died for me, she answered.[8]

A vague terror seized Gabriel at this answer as if, at that hour when he had hoped to triumph, some impalpable and vindictive being was coming against him, gathering forces against him in its vague world. But he shook himself free of it with an effort of reason and continued to caress her hand. He did not question her again for he felt that she would tell him of herself. Her hand was warm and moist: it did not respond to his touch but he continued to caress it just as he had caressed her first letter to him that spring morning.

—It was in the winter, she said, about the beginning of the winter when I was going to leave my grandmother's and come up here to the convent. And he was ill at the time in his lodgings in Galway and wouldn't be let out and his people in Oughterard[9] were written to. He was in decline, they said, or something like that. I never knew rightly.

She paused for a moment and sighed.

—Poor fellow, she said. He was very fond of me and he was such a gentle boy. We used to go out together, walking, you know, Gabriel, like the way they do in the country. He was going to study singing only for his health. He had a very good voice, poor Michael Furey.

—Well; and then? asked Gabriel.

—And then when it came to the time for me to leave Galway and come up to the convent he was much worse and I wouldn't be let see him so I wrote a letter saying I was going up to Dublin and would be back in the summer and hoping he would be better then.

She paused for a moment to get her voice under control and then went on:

—Then the night before I left I was in my grandmother's house in Nuns' Island, packing up, and I heard gravel thrown up against the window. The window was so wet I couldn't see so I ran downstairs as I was and slipped out the back into the garden and there was the poor fellow at the end of the garden, shivering.

7. Errand boy.

8. Gretta here echoes the words of Yeats's Cathleen ní Houlihan: "Singing I am about a man I knew one time, yellow-haired Donough that was hanged in Galway. . . . He died for love of me: many a man has died for love of me." The play was first performed in Dublin on 2 April 1902.

9. A small village in Western Ireland.

—And did you not tell him to go back? asked Gabriel.

—I implored him to go home at once and told him he would get his death in the rain. But he said he did not want to live. I can see his eyes as well as well! He was standing at the end of the wall where there was a tree.

—And did he go home? asked Gabriel.

—Yes, he went home. And when I was only a week in the convent he died and he was buried in Oughterard where his people came from. O, the day I heard that, that he was dead!

She stopped, choking with sobs, and, overcome by emotion, flung herself face downward on the bed, sobbing in the quilt. Gabriel held her hand for a moment longer, irresolutely, and then, shy of intruding on her grief, let it fall gently and walked quietly to the window.

She was fast asleep.

Gabriel, leaning on his elbow, looked for a few moments unresentfully on her tangled hair and half-open mouth, listening to her deep-drawn breath. So she had had that romance in her life: a man had died for her sake. It hardly pained him now to think how poor a part he, her husband, had played in her life. He watched her while she slept as though he and she had never lived together as man and wife. His curious eyes rested long upon her face and on her hair: and, as he thought of what she must have been then, in that time of her first girlish beauty, a strange friendly pity for her entered his soul. He did not like to say even to himself that her face was no longer beautiful but he knew that it was no longer the face for which Michael Furey had braved death.

Perhaps she had not told him all the story. His eyes moved to the chair over which she had thrown some of her clothes. A petticoat string dangled to the floor. One boot stood upright, its limp upper fallen down: the fellow of it lay upon its side. He wondered at his riot of emotions of an hour before. From what had it proceeded? From his aunt's supper, from his own foolish speech, from the wine and dancing, the merry-making when saying good-night in the hall, the pleasure of the walk along the river in the snow. Poor Aunt Julia! She, too, would soon be a shade with the shade of Patrick Morkan and his horse. He had caught that haggard look upon her face for a moment when she was singing *Arrayed for the Bridal*. Soon, perhaps, he would be sitting in that same drawing-room, dressed in black, his silk hat on his knees. The blinds would be drawn down and Aunt Kate would be sitting beside him, crying and blowing her nose and telling him how Julia had died. He would cast about in his mind for some words that might console her, and would find only lame and useless ones. Yes, yes: that would happen very soon.

The air of the room chilled his shoulders. He stretched himself cautiously along under the sheets and lay down beside his wife. One by one they were all becoming shades. Better pass boldly into that other world, in the full glory of some passion, than fade and wither dismally with age. He thought of how she who lay beside him had locked in her heart for so many years that image of her lover's eyes when he had told her that he did not wish to live.

Generous tears filled Gabriel's eyes. He had never felt like that himself towards any woman but he knew that such a feeling must be love. The tears gathered more thickly in his eyes and in the partial darkness he imagined he saw the form of a young man standing under a dripping tree. Other forms were near. His soul had approached that region where dwell the vast hosts of the dead. He was conscious of, but could not apprehend, their wayward and flickering existence. His own identity was fading out into a grey impalpable world: the solid world itself which these dead had one time reared and lived in was dissolving and dwindling.

A few light taps upon the pane made him turn to the window. It had begun to snow again. He watched sleepily the flakes, silver and dark, falling obliquely against the lamplight. The time had come for him to set out on his journey westward. Yes, the newspapers were right: snow was general all over Ireland. It was falling on every part of the dark central plain, on the treeless hills, falling softly upon the Bog of Allen and, farther westward, softly falling into the dark mutinous Shannon waves.[1] It was falling, too, upon every part of the lonely churchyard on the hill where Michael Furey lay buried. It lay thickly drifted on the crooked crosses and headstones, on the spears of the little gate, on the barren thorns. His soul swooned slowly as he heard the snow falling faintly through the universe and faintly falling, like the descent of their last end, upon all the living and the dead.

ULYSSES *Ulysses* boldly announced that modern literature had set itself new tasks and devised new means to "make it new." In his review of the novel, T. S. Eliot wrote that Joyce had discovered "a way of controlling, of ordering, of giving a shape and a significance to the panorama of futility and anarchy which is contemporary history. . . . It is, I seriously believe, a step toward making the modern world possible for art. . . . " The technique with which Joyce shaped his materials Eliot called (at Joyce's suggestion) the mythical method—using ancient myth to suggest "a continuous parallel between contemporaneity and antiquity." Joyce's purposes in using myth—in the case of *Ulysses*, a series of parallels to Homer's *Odyssey*—are open to debate; but he was quite frank about the fact that each of the novel's eighteen chapters was modeled, however loosely, on one of Odysseus's adventures. Thus Leopold Bloom, the novel's advertising-salesman protagonist, is in some sense a modern-day Odysseus; rather than finding his way back from Troy and the Trojan Wars, he simply navigates his way through a very full day in Dublin on 16 June 1904. This day, however, has its perils. Bloom, a Jew, is set upon by anti-Semites, threatened with violence, and driven from the pub where he drinks; much later, in Dublin's red-light district, he rescues a very drunk young poet, Stephen Dedalus, from arrest, and takes him back to his home for a cup of cocoa and conversation. Foremost among Bloom's tests on this particular day, however, is his knowledge that his wife Molly will consummate an affair with the brash, egotistical tenor Blazes Boylan—an affair which, owing to his own shortcomings as a husband, Bloom is unwilling to stop.

The chapter given here is the thirteenth chapter, the "Nausicaa" episode. We find Bloom killing time on the beach at Sandymount, trying to stay away from his home long enough that his wife's new lover, Blazes Boylan, will be gone before his return. He has just narrowly escaped bodily injury at the hands of the unnamed ultra-Nationalist Citizen in Chapter 12, "Cyclops"; finding his way to the seaside for a bit of fresh air and relaxation, Bloom is happy to come across the self-consciously displayed feminine commodity Gerty MacDowell, who, having been stood up by young Reggie Wylie, is willing to suffer Bloom's sensual and sexual gaze. Her poignant fate as a young woman in a country missing half its young men is also clear. In the episode from the *Odyssey* on which this chapter is loosely based, Odysseus finds himself in the land of the seafaring Phaeacians, and in the company of Princess Nausicaa and her ladies, who have come to the water to do the laundry. In the *Odyssey*, Odysseus sheds his disguise, reveals himself to Nausicaa, and begs for her help in returning to home (Ithaca) and wife (Penelope); in Joyce's version, it is Nausicaa who does the revealing, to an admiring Odysseus who is carefully avoiding his return journey home. Joyce uses the scene to comment on the nature of attraction, beauty, and desire, and the ways in which sentimental fiction, commodity culture, and Bloom's own profession of advertising have affected the way we understand and seek to satisfy our deepest desires.

1. Where Ireland's longest river, the Shannon, empties into the sea.

Our text is taken from the April through August, 1920 serial publication of the "Nausicaa" episode in the *Little Review*, published by Margaret Anderson and jane heap. It was this chapter in particular that resulted in seizure of the magazine by the New York Society for the Prevention of Vice, and that led, indirectly, to the obscenity trial in which Judge Woolsey overturned the ban on *Ulysses*. Obvious printing errors have been silently emended in the text.

from Ulysses

[CHAPTER 13. "NAUSICAA"]

The summer evening had begun to fold the world in its mysterious embrace.[1] Far away in the west the sun was setting and the last glow of all too fleeting day lingered lovingly on sea and strand, on the proud promontory of dear old Howth[2] guarding as ever the waters of the bay, on the weedgrown rocks along Sandymount shore and, last but not least, on the quiet church[3] whence there streamed forth at times upon the stillness the voice of prayer to her who is in her pure radiance a beacon ever to the storm-tossed heart of man, Mary, star of the sea.

The three girl friends were seated on the rocks, enjoying the evening scene and the air which was fresh but not too chilly. Many a time and oft were they wont to come there to that favourite nook to have a cosy chat and discuss matters feminine, Cissy Caffrey and Edy Boardman with the baby in the pushcar and Tommy and Jacky Caffrey, two little curly headed boys, dressed in sailor suits with caps to match and the name H. M. S.[4] Belle Isle printed on both. For Tommy and Jacky Caffrey were twins, scarce four years old and very noisy and spoiled twins sometimes but for all that darling little fellows with bright merry faces and endearing ways about them. They were dabbling in the sand with their spades and buckets, building castles as children do, or playing with their big coloured ball, happy as the day was long. And Edy Boardman was rocking the chubby baby to and fro in the pushcar while that young gentleman fairly chuckled with delight. He was but eleven months and nine days old and, though still a tiny toddler, was just beginning to lisp his first babish words. Cissy Caffrey bent over him to tease his fat little plucks and the dainty dimple in his chin.

—Now, baby, Cissy Caffrey said. Say out big, big. I want a drink of water.

And baby prattled after her:

—A jink a jing a jawbo.

Cissy Caffrey cuddled the wee chap for she was awfully fond of children, so patient with little sufferers and Tommy Caffrey could never be got to take his castor oil unless it was Cissy Caffrey that held his nose. But to be sure baby was as good as gold, a perfect little dote in his new fancy bib. None of your spoilt beauties was Cissy Caffrey. A truer-hearted girl never drew the breath of life, always with a laugh in her gipsylike eyes and a frolicsome word on her cherryripe red lips, a girl lovable in the extreme. And Edy Boardman laughed too at the quaint language of little brother.

But just then there was a slight altercation between Master Tommy and Master Jacky. Boys will be boys and our two twins were no exception to this rule. The apple of discord was a certain castle of sand which Master Jacky had built and Master Tommy would have it right or wrong that it was to be architecturally improved by a frontdoor like the Martello tower[5] had. But if Master Tommy was headstrong Master

1. The prose style of the first half of this chapter is to some extent modeled on the overripe prose of sentimental 19th-century "women's" fiction, like Maria Cummins's novel *The Lamplighter* (1854), which Gerty MacDowell has read and which pops up in her thoughts later in the chapter.

2. The northeast headland of Dublin Bay, visible from the shore at Sandymount, where this chapter takes place.

3. The church would be the Roman Catholic Church of Mary, Star of the Sea, near Sandymount Strand.

4. His Majesty's Ship.

5. One of a series of towers on the Irish coast built by the British at the start of the 19th century to protect against a sea invasion by the French during the Napoleonic Wars.

Jacky was selfwilled too and, true to the maxim that every little Irishman's house is his castle, he fell upon his hated rival and to such purpose that the would-be assailant came to grief and (alas to relate!) the coveted castle too. Needless to say the cries of discomfited Master Tommy drew the attention of the girl friends.

—Come here, Tommy, his sister called imperatively, at once! And you, Jacky, for shame to throw poor Tommy in the dirty sand. Wait till I catch you for that.

His eyes misty with unshed tears Master Tommy came at her call for their big sister's word was law with the twins. And in a sad plight he was after his misadventure. His little man-o'-war top and unmentionables were full of sand but Cissy was a past mistress in the art of smoothing over life's tiny troubles and very quickly not one speck of sand was to be seen on his smart little suit. Still the blue eyes were glistening with hot tears that would well up so she shook her hand at Master Jacky the culprit, her eyes dancing in admonition.

—Nasty bold Jacky! she cried.

She put an arm around the little mariner and coaxed winningly:

—What's your name? Butter and cream?

—Tell us who is your sweetheart, spoke Edy Boardman. Is Cissy your sweetheart?

—Nao, tearful Tommy said.

—Is Edy Boardman your sweetheart? Cissy queried.

—Nao, Tommy said.

—I know, Edy Boardman said none too amiably with an arch glance from her shortsighted eyes. I know who is Tommy's sweetheart. Gerty is Tommy's sweetheart.

—Nao, Tommy said on the verge of tears.

Cissy's quick motherwit guessed what was amiss and she whispered to Edy Boardman to take him there behind the pushcar where the gentlemen couldn't see and to mind he didn't wet his new tan shoes.

But who was Gerty?

Gerty MacDowell who was seated near her companions, lost in thought, gazing far away in to the distance was in very truth as fair a specimen of winsome Irish girlhood as one could wish to see. She was pronounced beautiful by all who knew her though, as folks often said, she was more a Giltrap than a MacDowell. Her figure was slight and graceful inclining even to fragility but those iron jelloids she had been taking of late had done her a world of good and she was much better of those discharges she used to get. The waxen pallor of her face was almost spiritual in its ivorylike purity. Her hands were of finely veined alabaster with tapering fingers and as white as lemonjuice and queen of ointments could make them though it was not true that she used to wear kid gloves in bed. Bertha Supple told that once to Edy Boardman when she was black out with Gerty (the girl chums had of course their little tiffs from time to time like the rest of mortals) and she told her not let on whatever she did that it was her that told her or she'd never speak to her again. No. Honour where honour is due. There was an innate refinement, a languid queenly hauteur[6] about Gerty which was unmistakably evidenced in her delicate hands and higharched instep. Had kind fate but willed her to be born a gentlewoman of high degree in her own right and had she only received the benefit of a good education Gerty MacDowell might easily have held her own beside any lady in the land and have seen herself exquisitely gowned with jewels on her brow and patrician[7] suitors at her feet vying with one another to pay their devoirs[8] to her. Mayhap it was this, the love that might have been,

6. Arrogance.
7. Aristocratic.
8. Respects.

that lent to her softly featured face at whiles a look, tense with suppressed meaning, that imparted a strange yearning tendency to the beautiful eyes, a charm few could resist. Why have women such eyes of witchery? Gerty's were of the bluest Irish blue, set off by lustrous lashes and dark expressive brows. Time was when those brows were not so silkily seductive. It was Madame Vera Verity, directress of the Woman Beautiful page of the Princess novelette, who had first advised her to try eyebrowleine which gave that haunting expression to the eyes, so becoming in leaders of fashion, and she had never regretted it. But Gerty's crowning glory was her wealth of hair. It was dark brown with a natural wave in it. She had cut it that very morning on account of the new moon and it nestled about her pretty head in a profusion of luxuriant clusters.[9] And just now at Edy's words as a telltale flush, delicate as the faintest rosebloom, crept into her cheeks she looked so lovely in her sweet girlish shyness that of a surety God's fair land of Ireland did not hold her equal.

For an instant she was silent with rather sad downcast eyes. She was about to retort but something checked the words on her tongue. Inclination prompted her to speak out: dignity told her to be silent. The pretty lips pouted a while but then she glanced up and broke out into a joyous little laugh which had in it all the freshness of a young May morning. She knew right well, no one better, what made squinty Edy say that. As per usual somebody's nose was out of joint about the boy that had the bicycle always riding up and down in front of her window. Only now his father kept him in the evenings studying hard to get an exhibition in the intermediate[1] that was on and he was going to Trinity college to study for a doctor when he left the high school like his brother W. E. Wylie who was racing in the bicycle races in Trinity college university. Little recked[2] he perhaps for what she felt, that dull ache in her heart sometimes, piercing to the core. Yet he was young and perchance he might learn to love her in time. They were protestants in his family and, of course, Gerty knew Who came first and after Him the blessed virgin and then saint Joseph. But he was undeniably handsome and he was what he looked, every inch a gentleman the shape of his head too at the back without his cap on something off the common and the way he turned the bicycle at the lamp with his hands off the bars and also the nice perfume of those good cigarettes and besides they were both of a size and that was why Edy Boardman thought she was so frightfully clever because he didn't go and ride up and down in front of her bit of a garden.

Gerty was dressed simply but with instinctive taste for she felt that there was just a might that he might be out. A neat blouse of electric blue, selftinted by dolly dyes, with a smart vee opening and kerchief pocket (in which she always kept a piece of cottonwool scented with her favourite perfume because the handkerchief spoiled the sit) and a navy threequarter skirt cut to the stride showed off her slim graceful figure to perfection. She wore a coquettish wide-leaved hat of nigger straw with an underbrim of eggblue chenille and at the side a butterfly bow to tone. All Tuesday week afternoon she was hunting to match that chenille but at last she found what she wanted at Clery's[3] summer sales, the very it slightly shopsoiled but you would never notice seven fingers two and a penny. She did it up all by herself and tried it on then smiling at her lovely reflection in the mirror and when she put it on the waterjug to keep the shape she knew that that would take the shine out of some people she knew.

9. Gerty's actions here are suggested by a number of common superstitions and folk beliefs.
1. I.e., to be ranked highly in his class upon graduation, so as to secure a spot at Dublin's protestant university, Trinity College.
2. Cared.
3. The biggest department store in downtown Dublin.

Her shoes were the newest thing in footwear (Edy Boardman prided herself that she was very *petite* but she never had a foot like Gerty MacDowell a five and never would ash oak or elm[4]) with patent toecaps and just one smart buckle. Her wellturned ankle displayed its proportions beneath her skirt and just the proper amount and no more of her shapely leg encased in finespun hose with highspliced heels and wide garter tops. As for undies they were Gerty's chief care and who that knows the fluttering hopes and fears of sweet seventeen (though Gerty would never see seventeen again) can find it in his heart to blame her? She had four dinky sets, three articles and nighties extra, and each set slotted with different coloured ribbons, rosepink, pale blue, mauve and peagreen and she aired them herself and blued them when they came home from the wash and ironed them and she had a brickbat to keep the iron on because she wouldn't trust those washerwomen as far as she'd see them scorching the things. She was wearing the blue for luck, her own colour and the lucky colour too for a bride to have a bit of blue somewhere on her because the green she wore that day week brought grief because his father brought him in to study for the intermediate exhibition and because she thought perhaps he might be out because when she was dressing that morning she nearly slipped up the old pair on her inside out and that was for luck and lovers' meetings if you put those things on inside out so long as it wasn't of a Friday.

And yet—and yet! A gnawing sorrow is there all the time. Her very soul is in her eyes and she would give worlds to be in her own familiar chamber where she could have a good cry and relieve her pentup feelings. The paly light of evening falls upon a face infinitely sad and wistful. Gerty MacDowell yearns in vain. Yes, she had known from the first that it was not to be. He was too young to understand. He would not believe in love. The night of the party long ago in Stoers' (he was still in short trousers) when they were alone and he stole an arm round her waist she went white to the very lips. He called her little one and half kissed her (the first!) but it was only the end of her nose and then he hastened from the room with a remark about refreshments. Impetuous fellow! Strength of character had never been Reggy Wylie's strong point and he who would woo and win Gerty MacDowell must be a man among men. But waiting, always waiting to be asked and it was leap year[5] too and would soon be over. No prince charming is her beau ideal to lay a rare and wondrous love at her feet but rather a manly man with a strong quiet face, perhaps his hair slightly flecked with grey, and who would understand, take her in his sheltering arms, strain her to him in all the strength of his deep passionate nature and comfort her with a long long kiss. For such a one she yearns this balmy summer eve. With all the heart of her she longs to be his only, his affianced bride for riches for poor in sickness in health till death us two part from this to this day forward.

And while Edy Boardman was with little Tommy behind the pushcar she was just thinking would the day ever come when she could call herself his little wife to be. Then they could talk about her, Bertha Supple too, and Edy, the spitfire, because she would be twentytwo in November. She would care for him with creature comforts too for Gerty was womanly wise and knew that a mere man liked that feeling of homeyness. Her griddlecakes and queen Ann's pudding had won golden opinions from all because she had a lucky hand also for lighting a fire, dredge in the fine flour and always stir in the same direction then cream the milk and sugar and whisk well

4. Till the end of time.

5. Traditionally, a woman may propose marriage to a man only during a leap year.

the white of eggs and they would have a nice drawingroom with pictures and chintz covers for the chairs and that silver toastrack in Clery's summer sales like they have in rich houses. He would be tall (she had always admired tall men for a husband) with glistening white teeth under his carefully trimmed sweeping moustache and every morning they would both have brekky[6] for their own two selves and before he went out to business he would give her a good hearty hug and gaze for a moment deep down into her eyes.

Edy Boardman asked Tommy Caffrey was he done and he said yes so then she buttoned up his little knickerbockers for him and told him to run off and play with Jacky and to be good and not to fight. But Tommy said he wanted the ball and Edy told him no that baby was playing with the ball and if he took it there'd be wigs on the green[7] but Tommy said it was his ball and he wanted his ball and he pranced on the ground, if you please. The temper of him! O, he was a man already was little Tommy Caffrey. Edy told him no, no and to be off now with him and she told Cissy Caffrey not to give in to him.

—You're not my sister, naughty Tommy said. It's my ball.

But Cissy Caffrey told baby Boardman to look up, look up high at her finger and she snatched the ball quickly and threw it along the sand and Tommy after it in full career, having won the day.

—Anything for a quiet life, laughed Ciss.

And she tickled baby's two cheeks to make him forget and played here's the lord mayor, here's his two horses, here's his ginger bread carriage and here he walks in, chinchopper, chinchopper, chinchopper chin. But Edy got as cross as two sticks about him getting his own way like that from everyone always petting him.

—I'd like to give him something, she said, so I would, where I won't say.

—On the beeoteetom, laughed Cissy merrily.

Gerty MacDowell bent down her head at the idea of Cissy saying a thing like that out she'd be ashamed of her life to say flushing a deep rosy red and Edy Boardman said she was sure the gentleman opposite heard what she said. But not a pin cared Ciss.

—Let him! she said with a pert toss of her head and a piquant tilt of her nose. Give it to him too on the same place as quick as I'd look at him.

Madcap Ciss. You had to laugh at her sometimes. For instance when she asked you would you have some more Chinese tea and jaspberry ram and when she drew the jugs too and the men's faces make you split your sides or when she said she wanted to run and pay a visit to the miss white. That was just like Cissycums. O, and will you ever forget the evening she dressed up in her father's suit and hat and walked down Tritonville road, smoking a cigarette. But she was sincerity itself, one of the bravest and truest hearts heaven ever made, not one of your twofaced things, too sweet to be wholesome.

And then there came out upon the air the sound of voices and the pealing anthem of the organ. It was the men's temperance retreat conducted by the missioner, the reverend John Hughes S. J.[8] rosary, sermon and benediction of the most blessed sacrament. They were there gathered together without distinction of social class (and a most edifying spectacle it was to see) in that simple fane[9] beside the waves after the storms of this weary world, kneeling before the feet of the immaculate, beseeching

6. Breakfast.
7. A fistfight or altercation.
8. Society of Jesus; the Jesuits.
9. Temple or church.

her to intercede for them, holy Mary, holy virgin of virgins. How sad to poor Gerty's ears! Had her father only avoided the clutches of the demon drink she might now be rolling in her carriage, second to none. Over and over had she told herself that as she mused by the dying embers in a brown study or gazing out of the window dreamily by the hour at the rain falling on the rusty bucket. But that vile decoction which has ruined so many hearts and homes had cast its shadow over her childhood days. Nay, she had even witnessed in the home circle deeds of violence caused by intemperance and had seen her own father, a prey to the fumes of intoxication, forget himself completely for if there was one thing of all things that Gerty knew it was the man who lifts his hand to a woman save in the way of kindness deserves to be branded as the lowest of the low.

And still the voices sang in supplication to the virgin most powerful, virgin most merciful. And Gerty, wrapt in thought, scarce saw or heard her companions or the twins at their boyish gambols[1] or the gentleman off Sandymount green that Cissy Caffrey called the man that was so like himself passing along the strand taking a short walk. You never saw him anyway screwed but still and for all that she would not like him for a father because he was too old or something or on account of his face (it was a palpable case of doctor Fell) or his carbuncly nose with the pimples on it. Poor father! With all his faults she loved him still when he sang *Tell me, Mary, how to woo thee* and they had stewed cockles and lettuce with salad dressing for supper and when he sang *The moon hath raised* with Mr Dignam that died suddenly and was buried, God have mercy on him, from a stroke.[2] Her mother's birthday that was and Charley was home on his holidays and Tom and Mr Dignam and Mrs and Patsy and Freddy Dignam and they were to have had a group[3] taken. No one would have thought the end was so near. Now he was laid to rest. And her mother said to him to let that be a warning to him for the rest of his days and he couldn't even go to the funeral on account of the gout, and she had to go into town to bring him the letters and samples from his office about Catesby's cork lino, artistic designs, fit for a palace, gives tiptop wear and always bright and cheery in the home.

A sterling good daughter was Gerty just like a second mother in the house, a ministering angel too. And when her mother had those splitting headaches who was it rubbed on the menthol cone on her forehead but Gerty though she didn't like her mother taking pinches of snuff and that was the only single thing they ever had words about, taking snuff. It was Gerty who turned off the gas at the main every night and it was Gerty who tacked up on the wall of that place[4] Mr Tunney the grocer's christmas almanac the picture of halcyon days where a young gentleman in the costume they used to wear then with a threecornered hat was offering a bunch of flowers to his ladylove with oldtime chivalry through her lattice window. The colours were done something lovely. She was in a soft clinging white and the gentleman was in chocolate and he looked a thorough aristocrat. She often looked at them dreamily when she went there for a certain purpose and thought about those times because she had found out in Walker's pronouncing dictionary about the halcyon days what they meant.

The twins were now playing in the most approved brotherly fashion, till at last Master Jacky who was really as bold as brass there was no getting behind that deliber-

1. Frolics.
2. The funeral of Patrick ("Paddy") Dignam has taken place this morning, at Glasnevin Cemetery; that he died of a "stroke" is a polite euphemism, since it appears he has died of cirrhosis or another alcohol-related disease.
3. A group photograph.
4. Gerty's euphemism for the outhouse, or outdoor toilet.

ately kicked the ball as hard as ever he could down towards the seaweedy rocks. Needless to say poor Tommy was not slow to voice his dismay but luckily the gentleman in black who was sitting there by himself came to the rescue and intercepted the ball. Our two champions claimed their plaything with lusty cries and to avoid trouble Cissy Caffrey called to the gentleman to throw it to her please. The gentleman aimed the ball once or twice and then threw it up the strand[5] towards Cissy Caffrey but it rolled down the slope and stopped right under Gerty's skirt near the little pool by the rock. The twins clamoured again for it and Cissy told her to kick it way and let them fight for it, so Gerty drew back her foot but she wished their stupid ball hadn't come rolling down to her and she gave a kick but she missed and Edy and Cissy laughed.

—If you fail try again, Edy Boardman said.

Gerty smiled assent. A delicate pink crept into her pretty cheek but she was determined to let them see so she just lifted her skirt a little but just enough and took good aim and gave the ball a jolly good kick and it went ever so far and the two twins after it down towards the shingle. Pure jealousy of course it was nothing else to draw attention on account of the gentleman opposite looking. She felt the warm flush, a danger signal always with Gerty MacDowell, surging and flaming into her cheeks. Till then they had only exchanged glances of the most casual but now under the brim of her new hat she ventured a look at him and the face that met her gaze there in the twilight, wan[6] and strangely drawn, seemed to her the saddest she had ever seen.

Through the open window of the church the fragrant incense was wafted and with it the fragrant names of her who was conceived without stain of original sin, spiritual vessel, pray for us, honourable vessel, pray for us, vessel of singular devotion, pray for us, mystical rose. And careworn hearts were there and toilers for their daily bread and many who had erred and wandered, their eyes wet with contrition but for all that bright with hope for the reverend father Hughes had told them what the great saint Bernard said in his famous prayer of Mary, the most pious virgin's intercessory power that it was not recorded in any age that those who implored her powerful protection were ever abandoned by her.

The twins were now playing again right merrily for the troubles of childhood are but as passing summer showers. Cissy played with baby Boardman till he crowed with glee, clapping baby hands in air. Peep she cried behind the hood of the pushcar and Edy asked where was Cissy gone and then Cissy popped her head and cried ah! and, my word, didn't the little chap enjoy that! And then she told him to say papa.

—Say papa, baby, say pa pa pa pa pa pa pa.

And baby did his level best to say it for he was very intelligent for eleven months everyone said and he would certainly turn out to be something great they said.

—Haja ja ja haja.

Cissy wiped his little mouth with the dribbling bib and wanted him to sit up properly and say pa pa pa but when she undid the strap she cried out, holy saint Denis, that he was possing wet and to double the half blanket the other way under him. Of course his infant majesty was most obstreperous at such toilet formalities and he let everyone know it:

—Habaa baaaahabaaa baaaa.

It was all no use soothering him with no, nono, baby and telling him all about the geegee and where was the puffpuff but Ciss, always readywitted, gave him in his mouth the teat of the suckingbottle and the young heathen was quickly appeased.

5. Seashore.

6. Pale.

Gerty wished to goodness they would take their squalling baby home out of that, no hour to be out, and the little brats of twins. She gazed out towards the distant sea. It was like a picture the evening and the clouds coming out and the Bailey light[7] on Howth and to hear the music like that and the perfume of those incense they burned in the church. And while she gazed her heart went pitapat. Yes, it was her he was looking at and there was meaning in his look. His eyes burned into her as though they would search her through and through, read her very soul. Wonderful eyes they were, superbly expressive, but could you trust them? She could see at once by his dark eyes that he was a foreigner but she could not see whether he had an aquiline nose[8] from where he was sitting. He was in deep mourning,[9] she could see that, and the story of a haunting sorrow was written on his face. She would have given worlds to know what it was. He was looking up so intensely, so still and he saw her kick the ball and perhaps he could see the bright steel buckles of her shoes if she swung them like that thoughtfully. She was glad that something told her to put on the transparent stockings thinking Reggy Wylie might be out but that was far away. Here was that of which she had so often dreamed. The heart of the girl-woman went out to him. If he had suffered, more sinned against than sinning, or even, even, if he had been himself a sinner, a wicked man, she cared not. There were wounds that wanted healing and she just yearned to know all, to forgive all if she could make him fall in love with her, make him forget the memory of the past. Then mayhap he would embrace her gently, crushing her soft body to him and love her for herself alone.

Refuge of sinners. Comfortress of the afflicted. *Ora pro nobis.*[1] Well has it been said that whosoever prays to her with faith and constancy can never be lost or cast away: and fitly is she too a haven of refuge for the afflicted because of the seven dolours[2] which transpierced her own heart. Gerty could picture the whole scene in the church, the stained glass windows lighted up, the candles, the flowers and the blue banner of the blessed virgin's sodality[3] and Father Conroy was helping Canon O'Hanlon at the altar, carrying things in and out with his eyes cast down. He looked almost a saint and his confessionbox was so quiet and clean and dark and his hands were just like white wax. He told her that time when she told him about that in confession crimsoning up to the roots of her hair for fear he could see, not to be troubled because that was only the voice of nature and we were all subject to nature's laws, he said, in this life and that that was no sin because that came from the nature of woman instituted by God, he said, and that Our Blessed Lady herself said to the archangel Gabriel be it done unto me according to Thy Word. He was so kind and holy and often and often she thought could she work an embroidered teacosy[4] for him as a present or a clock but they had a clock she noticed on the mantelpiece white and gold with a canary that came out of a little house to tell the time the day she went there about the flowers for the forty hours' adoration[5] because it was hard to know what sort of a present to give or perhaps an album of illuminated views of Dublin or some place.

The little brats of twins began to quarrel again and Jacky threw the ball out towards the sea and they both ran after it. Little monkeys common as ditch-water.

7. The lighthouse perched at the tip of Howth Head.
8. An aquiline nose is hooked.
9. The as-yet unnamed gentleman on the strand has attended the funeral of Paddy Dignam and is wearing black.
1. From the Litany of Our Lady: "Pray for us."
2. Sorrows.
3. A lay group within a religious order.
4. A padded, lace-edged cover for a teapot, to help keep the tea warm.
5. A period of prayer and devotion instituted by Pope Clement VIII, in memory of the 40 hours Jesus spent in the tomb before the Resurrection.

Someone ought to take them and give them a good hiding for themselves to keep them in their places the both of them. And Cissy and Edy shouted after them to come back because they were afraid the tide might come in on them and be drowned.

—Jacky! Tommy!

Not they! What a great notion they had! So Cissy said it was the very last time she'd ever bring them out. She jumped up and called them and she ran down the slope past him, tossing her hair behind her which had a good enough colour if there had been more of it but with all the thingamerry she was always rubbing in to it she couldn't get it to grow long because it wasn't natural so she could just go and throw her hat at it. She ran with long gandery strides it was a wonder she didn't rip up her skirt at the side that was too tight on her because there was a lot of the tomboy about Cissy Caffrey whenever she thought she had a good opportunity to show off and just because she was a good runner she ran like that so that he could see all the end of her petticoat running, and her skinny shanks up as far as possible. It would have served her just right if she had tripped up over something with her high French heels on her to make her look tall and got a fine tumble. That would have been a very charming expose for a gentleman like that to witness.

Queen of angels, queen of patriarchs, queen of prophets, of all saints, they prayed, queen of the most holy rosary and then Father Conroy handed the thurible[6] to Canon[7] O' Hanlon and he put in the incense and censed the blessed sacrament and Cissy Caffrey caught the two twins and she was itching to give them a good clip on the ear but she didn't because she thought he might be watching but she never made a bigger mistake in her life because Gerty could see without looking that he never took his eyes off of her and then Canon O'Hanlon handed the thurible back to Father Conroy and knelt down looking up at the blessed sacrament and the choir began to sing *Tantum ergo*[8] and she just swung her foot in and out in time to the *Tantumer gosa cramen tum*. Three and eleven she paid for those stockings in Sparrow's of George's street on the Tuesday, no the Monday before easter and there wasn't a brack on them and that was what he was looking at, transparent, and not at hers that had neither shape nor form because he had eyes in his head to see the difference for himself.

Cissy came up along the strand with the two twins and their ball with her hat anyhow on her on one side after her run and she did look like a streel[9] tugging the two kids along with the blouse she bought only a fortnight before like a rag on her back. Gerty just took off her hat for a moment to settle her hair and a prettier, a daintier head of nutbrown tresses was never seen on a girl's shoulder—a radiant little vision, in sooth,[1] almost maddening in its sweetness. You would have to travel many a long mile before you found a head of hair the like of that. She could almost see the swift answering flush of admiration in his eyes that set her tingling in every nerve. She put on her hat so that she could see from underneath the brim and swung her buckled shoe faster for her breath caught as she caught the expression in his eyes. He was eying her as a snake eyes its prey. Her woman's instinct told her that she had raised the devil in him and at the thought a burning scarlet swept from throat to brow till the lovely colour of her face became a glorious rose.

6. A censer; an implement for burning and wafting the smoke of incense in a church service.
7. Title of respect for the member of a religious order.
8. Gerty's rhythmical rendition of the hymn which begins, in Latin, *Tantum ergo Sacramentum*, "So great a sacrament."
9. A loose or disreputable woman.
1. In truth.

Edy Boardman was noticing it too because she was squinting at Gerty, half smiling with her specs, like an old maid, pretending to nurse the baby. Irritable little gnat she was and always would be and that was why no one could get on with her, poking her nose into what was no concern of hers. And she said to Gerty:

—A penny for your thoughts.

—What, laughed Gerty. I was only wondering was it late.

Because she wished to goodness they'd take the snotty-nosed twins and their baby home to the mischief out of that so that was why she just gave a gentle hint about its being late. And when Cissy came up Edy asked her the time and Miss Cissy, as glib as you like, said it was half past kissing time, time to kiss again. But Edy wanted to know because they were told to be in early.

—Wait, said Cissy, I'll ask my uncle Peter over there what's the time by his conundrum.[2]

So over she went and when he saw her coming she could see him take his hand out of his pocket, getting nervous and beginning to play with his watchchain, looking at the church. Passionate nature though he was Gerty could see that he had enormous control over himself. One moment he had been there, fascinated by a loveliness that made him gaze and the next moment it was the quiet gravefaced gentleman, selfcontrol expressed in every line of his distinguished-looking figure.

Cissy said to excuse her would he mind telling her what was the right time and Gerty could see him taking out his watch listening to it and looking up and he said he was very sorry his watch was stopped but he thought it must be after eight because the sun was set. His voice had a cultured ring in it and there was a suspicion of a quiver in the mellow tones. Cissy said thanks and came back with her tongue out and said his water-works were out of order.

Then they sang the second verse of the *Tantum ergo* and Canon O'Hanlon got up again and censed the blessed sacrament and knelt down and he told Father Conroy that one of the candles was just going to set fire to the flowers and Father Conroy got up and settled it all right and she could see the gentleman winding his watch and listening to the works and she swung her leg more in and out in time. It was getting darker but he could see and he was looking all the time that he was winding the watch or whatever he was doing to it and then he put it back and put his hands back into his pockets. She felt a kind of a sensation rushing all over her and she knew by the feel of her scalp and that irritation against her stays that that thing must be coming on because the last time too was when she clipped her hair on account of the moon. His dark eyes fixed themselves on her again, drinking in her every contour, literally worshipping at her shrine. If ever there was undisguised admiration in a man's passionate gaze it was there plain to be seen on that man's face. It is for you, Gertrude MacDowell, and you know it.

Edy began to get ready to go and she noticed that that little hint she gave had the desired effect because it was a long way along the strand to where there was the place to push up the pushcar and Cissy took off the twins' caps and tidied their hair to make herself attractive of course and Canon O'Hanlon stood up with his cope[3] poking up at his neck and Father Conroy handed him the card to read off and he read out *Panem de coelo praestitisti eis*[4] and Edy and Cissy were talking about the time all the time and asking her but Gerty could pay them back in their own coin and she just answered with scathing politeness when Edy asked her was she heart-broken

2. Puzzle (Cissy is using the word nonsensically).
3. A long ecclesiastical mantle.
4. You have given them bread from Heaven (Latin).

about her best boy throwing her over. Gerty winced sharply. A brief cold blaze shot from her eyes that spoke of scorn immeasurable. It hurt—O yes, it cut deep because Edy had her own quiet way of saying things like that she knew would wound like the confounded little cat she was. Gerty's lips parted swiftly but she fought back the sob that rose to her throat, so slim, so flawless, so beautifully moulded it seemed one an artist might have dreamed of. She had loved him better than he knew. Lighthearted deceiver and fickle like all his sex he would never understand what he had meant to her and for an instant there was in the blue eyes a quick stinging of tears. Their eyes were probing her mercilessly but with a brave effort she sparkled back in sympathy as she glanced at her new conquest for them to see.

—O, she laughed and the proud head flashed up. I can throw my cap at who I like because it's leap year.

Her words rang out crystal clear, more musical than the cooing of the ringdove but they cut the silence icily. There was that in her young voice that told that she was not a one to be lightly trifled with. Miss Edy's countenance fell to no slight extent and Gerty could see by her looking as black as thunder that she was simply in a towering rage because that shaft had struck home and they both knew that she was something aloof, apart in another sphere, that she was not of them and never would be and there was somebody else too that knew it and saw it so they could put that in their pipe and smoke it.

Edy straightened up baby Boardman to get ready to go and Cissy tucked in the ball and the spades and buckets and it was high time too because the sandman was on his way for Master Boardman junior and Cissy told him too that Billy Winks was coming and that baby was to go deedaw and baby looked just too ducky, laughing up out of his gleeful eyes, and Cissy poked him like that out of fun in his wee fat tummy and baby, without as much as by your leave, sent up his compliments to all and sundry on to his brand new dribbling bib.

—O my! Puddeny pie! protested Ciss.

The slight contretemps[5] claimed her attention but in two twos she set that little matter to rights.

Gerty stifled a smothered exclamation and Edy asked what and she was just going to tell her to catch it while it was flying but she was ever ladylike in her deportment so she simply passed it off by saying that that was the benediction because just then the bell rang out from the steeple over the quiet seashore because Canon O'Hanlon was up on the altar with the veil that Father Conroy put round him round his shoulders giving the benediction with the blessed sacrament in his hands.

How moving the scene there in the gathering twilight, the last glimpse of Erin, the touching chime of those evening bells and at the same time a bat flew forth from the ivied belfry through the dusk, hither, thither, with a tiny lost cry. And she could see far away the lights of the lighthouses and soon the lamplighter would be going his rounds lighting the lamp near her window where Reggy Wylie used to turn the bicycle like she read in that book *The Lamplighter* by Miss Cummins,[6] author of *Mabel Vaughan* and other tales. For Gerty had her dreams that no one knew of. She loved to read poetry and she got a keepsake from Bertha Supple of that lovely confession album with the coralpink cover to write her thoughts in she laid it in the drawer of her toilettable which though it did not err on the side of luxury, was scrupulously neat and

5. Set to; argument; fight.

6. Maria Cummins's 1854 novel *The Lamplighter* supplies the stylistic template for the first half of this chapter.

clean. It was there she kept her girlish treasures trove the tortoiseshell combs, her child of Mary badge, the whiterose scent, the eyebrowleine, her alabaster pouncetbox and the ribbons to change when her things came home from the wash and there were some beautiful thoughts written in it in violet ink that she bought in Wisdom Hely's for she felt that she too could write poetry if she could only express herself like that poem she had copied out of the newspaper she found one evening round the potherbs[7] *Art thou real, my ideal?* it was called by Louis J. Walsh, Magherafelt,[8] and after there was something about *twilight, wilt thou ever?* and often the beauty of poetry, so sad in its transient loveliness had misted her eyes with silent tears that the years were slipping by for her, one by one, and but for that one shortcoming she knew she need fear no competition and that was an accident coming down the hill and she always tried to conceal it. But it must end she felt. If she saw that magic lure in his eyes there would be no holding back for her. Love laughs at locksmiths. She would make the great sacrifice. Dearer than the whole world would she be to him and gild his days with happiness. There was the all important question and she was dying to know was he a married man or a widower who had lost his wife or some tragedy like the nobleman with the foreign name from the land of song had to have her put into a madhouse, cruel only to be kind. But even if—what then? Would it make a very great difference? From everything in the least indelicate her finebred nature instinctively recoiled. She loathed that sort of person, the fallen woman off the accommodation walk beside the Dodder[9] that went with the soldiers and coarse men, degrading the sex and being taken up to the police station. No, no: not that. They would be just good friends in spite of the conventions of society with a big ess. Perhaps it was an old flame he was in mourning for from the days beyond recall. She thought she understood. She would try to understand him because men were so different. The old love was waiting, waiting with little white hands stretched out, with blue appealing eyes. She would follow the dictates of her heart for love was the master guide. Nothing else mattered. Come what might she would be wild, untrammelled, free.

Canon O'Hanlon put the blessed sacrament back into the tabernacle[1] and the choir sang *Laudate Dominum omnes gentes*[2] and then he locked the tabernacle door because the benediction was over and Father Conroy handed him his hat to put on and Edy asked was she coming but Jacky Caffrey called out:

—O, look, Cissy!

And they all looked was it sheet lightning but Tommy saw it too over the trees beside the church, blue and then green and purple.

—It's fireworks, Cissy Caffrey said.

And they all ran down the strand to see over the houses and the church, helterskelter, Edy with the pushcar with baby Boardman in it and Cissy holding Tommy and Jacky by the hand so they wouldn't fall running.

—Come on, Gerty, Cissy called. It's the bazaar fireworks.

But Gerty was adamant. She had no intention of being at their beck and call. If they could run like rossies[3] she could sit so she said she could see from where she was. The eyes that were fastened upon her set her pulses tingling. She looked at him a moment, meeting his glance, and a light broke in upon her. Whitehot passion was in that face, passion silent as the grave, and it had made her his. At last they were left alone without the others to pry and pass remarks, and she knew he could be trusted to the

7. Herbs or greens cooked in a pot.
8. A small village in northeastern Ireland.
9. One of the four rivers that runs through Dublin.
1. Ceremonial receptacle for the Eucharist.
2. Give praise to the Lord, O ye nations (Latin).
3. A loose or disreputable woman (cf. "streel").

death, steadfast, a man of inflexible honour to his fingertips. She leaned back far to look up where the fireworks were and she caught her knee in her hands so as not to fall back looking up and there was no one to see only him and her when she revealed all her graceful beautifully shaped legs like that, supply soft and delicately rounded, and she seemed to hear the panting of his heart his hoarse breathing, because she knew about the passion of men like that, hotblooded, because Bertha Supple told her once in secret about the gentleman lodger that was staying with them out of the record office that had pictures cut out of papers of those skirtdancers and she said he used to do something not very nice that you could imagine sometimes in the bed. But this was different from a thing like that because there was all the difference because she could almost feel him draw her face to his and the first quick hot touch of his handsome lips. Besides there was absolution[4] so long as you didn't do the other thing before being married and there ought to be women priests that would understand without telling out and Cissy Caffrey too sometimes had that dreamy kind of dreamy look in her eyes so that she too, my dear, and besides it was on account of that other thing coming on the way it did.

And Jacky Caffrey shouted to look, there was another and she leaned back and the garters were blue to match on account of the transparent and they all saw it and shouted to look, look there it was and she leaned back ever so far to see the fireworks and something queer was flying about through the air, a soft thing to and fro, dark. And she saw a long Roman candle going up over the trees up, up, and they were all breathless with excitement as it went higher and higher and she had to lean back more and more to look up after it, high, high, almost out of sight, and her face was suffused with a divine, an entrancing blush from straining back and he could see her other things too, nainsook knickers, four and eleven, on account of being white and she let him and she saw that he saw and then it went so high it went out of sight a moment and she was trembling in every limb from being bent so far back that he could see high up above her knee where no-one ever and she wasn't ashamed and he wasn't either to look in that immodest way like that because he couldn't resist the sight of those skirtdancers behaving so immodest before gentlemen looking and he kept on looking, looking. She would fain have cried to him chokingly, held out her snowy slender arms to him to come, to feel his lips laid on her white brow. And then a rocket sprang and bang shot blind blank and O! then the Roman candle burst and it was like a sigh of O! and everyone cried O! O! and it gushed out of it a stream of rain gold hair threads and they shed and ah! they were all greeny dewy stars falling with golden, O so lovely! O so soft, sweet, soft!

Then all melted away dewily in the grey air: all was silent. Ah! She glanced at him as she bent forward quickly, a glance of piteous protest, of shy reproach under which he coloured like a girl. He was leaning back against the rock behind. Leopold Bloom (for it is he) stands silent, with bowed head before those young guileless eyes. What a brute he had been! At it again? A fair unsullied soul had called to him and, wretch that he was, how had he answered? An utter cad he had been! But there was an infinite store of mercy in those eyes, for him too a word of pardon even though he had erred and sinned and wandered. That was their secret, only theirs, alone in the hiding twilight and there was none to know or tell save the little bat that flew so softly through the evening to and fro and little bats don't tell.

Cissy Caffrey whistled, imitating the boys in the football field to show what a great person she was: and then she cried:

—Gerty Gerty! We're going. Come on. We can see from farther up.

4. A remission of sin.

Gerty had an idea. She slipped a hand into her kerchief pocket and took out the wadding and waved in reply of course without letting him and then slipped it back. Wonder if he's too far to. She rose. She had to go but they would meet again, there, and she would dream of that till then, tomorrow. She drew herself up to her full height. Their souls met in a last lingering glance and the eyes that reached her heart, full of a strange shining, hung enraptured on her sweet flowerlike face. She half smiled at him, a sweet forgiving smile—and then they parted.

Slowly without looking back she went down the uneven strand to Cissy, to Edy, to Jacky and Tommy Caffrey, to little baby Boardman. It was darker now and there were stones and bits of wood on the strand and slippy seaweed. She walked with a certain quiet dignity characteristic of her but with care and very slowly because—because Gerty MacDowell was. . . .

Tight boots? No. She's lame! O![5]

Mr Bloom watched her as she limped away. Poor girl! That's why she's left on the shelf and the others did a sprint. Thought something was wrong by the cut of her jib. Jilted beauty. Glad I didn't know it when she was on show. Hot little devil all the same. Near her monthlies, I expect, makes them feel ticklish. I have such a bad headache today.[6] Where did I put the letter? Yes, all right. All kinds of crazy longings. Girl in Tranquilla convent told me liked to smell rock oil. Sister? That's the moon. But then why don't all women menstruate at the same time with same moon? I mean. Depends on the time they were born, I suppose. Anyhow I got the best of that. Made up for that tramdriver this morning. That gouger M'Coy stopping me to say nothing. And his wife engagement in the country valise voice like a pickaxe. Thankful for small mercies. Cheap too. Yours for the asking. Because they want it themselves. Shoals of them every evening poured out of offices. Catch 'em alive. O. Pity they can't see themselves. A dream of wellfilled hose. Where was that? Ah, yes. Mutoscope[7] pictures in Capel street: for men only. Peeping Tom. Willy's hat and what the girls did with it. Do they snapshot those girls or is it all a fake. *Lingerie* does it. Felt for the curves inside her *deshabille*.[8] Excites them also when they're. Molly.[9] Why I bought her the violet garters. Say a woman loses a charm with every pin she takes out. Pinned together. O Mairy lost the pin of her. Dressed up to the nines for some body. In no hurry either. Always off to a fellow when they are. Out on spec probably. They believe in chance because like themselves. And the others inclined to give her an odd dig. Mary and Martha. Girl friends at school, arms round each other's necks, kissing and whispering secrets about nothing in the convent garden. Nuns with whitewashed faces, cool coifs and their rosaries going up and down, vindictive too for what they can't get. Barbed wire.[1] Be sure now and write to me. And I'll write to you. Now won't you? Molly and Josie Powell. Then meet once in a blue moon. *Tableau!*[2] O, look who it is for the love of God! How are you at all? What have you been doing with yourself? Kiss and delighted to, kiss, to see you. Picking holes in each other's appearance. You're looking splendid. Wouldn't lend each other a pinch of salt.

5. At this point in the chapter, the narrative point of view shifts from primarily Gerty's to Leopold Bloom's.
6. This sentence is remembered by Bloom from the letter he has received earlier in the day from his secret correspondent, Martha Clifford, with whom he is carrying on a postal "affair."
7. A device for viewing sequential stop-action photographs, comprising a primitive motion picture. The mutoscope show Bloom recalls was pornographic.
8. Revealing or inadequately concealing, garment. The word *deshabillé*, along with other phrases like "opulent curves," is remembered in Bloom's interior monologue from the pornographic book *Sweets of Sin* that he has examined and purchased at a second-hand bookseller earlier in the day.
9. Molly is Marion ("Molly") Bloom, Leopold's 33-year-old wife, to whom he has been married for 15 years; Milly is Millicent ("Milly") Bloom, their daughter, who turned 15 the day before that on which the action of the novel is set.
1. Bloom here thinks of the (apocryphal) story that barbed wire was invented by a nun.
2. In a popular parlor game, participants would strike poses to convey scenes or *tableaux*.

Ah.

Devils they are when that's coming on them. Molly often told me feel things a ton weight. Scratch the sole of my foot. O that way! O, that's exquisite! Feel it myself too. Good to rest once in a way. Wonder if it's bad to go with them then. Safe in one way. Something about withering plants I read in a garden. Besides they say if the flower withers she wears she's a flirt. All are. Daresay she felt I. When you feel like that you often meet what you feel. Liked me or what? Dress they look at. Always know a fellow courting: collars and cuffs. Same time might prefer a tie undone or something. Trousers? Suppose I when I was? No. Gently does it. Dislike rough and tumble. Kiss in the dark and never tell. Saw something in me. Wonder what. Sooner have me as I am than some poet chap with bearsgrease plastery hair, lovelock over his dexter optic.[3] To aid gentleman in literary. Ought to attend to my appearance my age. Didn't let her see me in profile. Still, you never know. Pretty girls and ugly men marrying. Beauty and the beast. Besides I can't be so if Molly. Took off her hat to show her hair. Wide brim bought to hide her face, meeting someone might know her, bend down or carry a bunch of flowers to smell. Hair strong in rut. Ten bob I got for Molly's combings when we were on the rocks in Holles street. Why not? Suppose he[4] gave her money. Why not? All a prejudice. She's worth ten, fifteen, more a pound. What? I think so. All that for nothing. Bold hand. Mrs Marion.[5] Did I forget to write address on that letter like the postcard I sent to Flynn. And the day I went to Drimmie's without a necktie. Wrangle with Molly it was put me off. No, I remember. Richie Goulding. He's another. Weighs on his mind. Funny my watch stopped at half past four. Was that just when he, she?[6]

O, he did. Into her. She did. Done.

Ah.

Mr Bloom with careful hand recomposed his wet shirt. O Lord, that little limping devil. Begins to feel cold and clammy. After effect not pleasant. They don't care. Complimented perhaps. Go home and say night prayers with the kiddies. Well, aren't they? Still I feel. The strength it gives a man. That's the secret of it. Good job I let off there behind coming out of Dignam's. Cider that was. Otherwise I couldn't have. Makes you want to sing after. *Lacaus esant tatatara.*[7] Suppose I spoke to her. What about? Bad plan however of you don't know how to end the conversation. Ask them a question they ask you another. Good idea if you're stuck. Gain time. But then you're in a cart. Wonderful of course if you say: Good evening, and you see she's on for it: good evening. Girl in Meath street that night. All the dirty things I made her say. Parrots. Wish she hadn't called me sir. O, her mouth in the dark! And you a married man with a single girl. That's what they enjoy. Taking a man from another woman. French letter still in my pocketbook. But might happen sometime. I don't think. Come in. All is prepared. I dreamt. What? Worst is beginning. How they change the venue when it's not what they like. Ask you do you like mushrooms because she once knew a gentleman who. Yet if I went the whole hog, say: I want to, something like that. Because I did. She too. Offend her. Then make it up.

3. A monocle worn in the right eye (in Bloom's imagination, associated with the stereotypical image of a poet).

4. The masculine pronouns here, and elsewhere in the pages that follow, frequently refer to Hugh "Blazes" Boylan, the Dublin singer and impresario who will be leaving on a musical tour to Belfast with Molly Bloom later in the summer; the two have inaugurated a love affair earlier this same afternoon.

5. The phrases are associated in Bloom's mind with the letter he brought upstairs to Molly that morning, addressed in a "bold hand" by Blazes Boylan to "Mrs. Marion [rather than, as decorum would dictate, Mrs. Leopold] Bloom." The letter probably confirmed the details of their afternoon rendezvous, as Bloom knows all too well.

6. Bloom here wonders if his watch stopped just at the moment that Molly and Boylan were committing their adultery against him (4:30 P.M.). Evidence from elsewhere in the book does suggest that the two events were nearly coincident.

7. Bloom's rhythmical rendition of *La causa è santa*, "The cause is sacred," from the Italian version of Giacomo Meyerbeer's opera, *Les Hugenots* (1836).

Pretend to want something awfully, then cry off for her sake. Flatters them. She must have been thinking of someone else all the time. What harm? Must since she came to the use of reason, he, he and he. First kiss does the trick. Something inside them goes pop. Mushy like, tell by their eye, on the sly. First thoughts are best. Remember that till their dying day. Molly, lieutenant Mulvey that kissed her under the Moorish wall beside the gardens. Fifteen she told me. But her breasts were developed. Fell asleep then. After Glencree dinner that was when we drove home the featherbed mountain. Gnashing her teeth in sleep. Lord mayor had his eye on her too. Val Dillon. Apoplectic.

There she is with them down there for the fireworks. My fireworks. Up like a rocket, down like a stick. And the children, twins they must be, waiting for something to happen. Want to be grownups. Dressing in mother's clothes. Time enough, understand all the ways of the world. And the dark one with the mop head and the nigger mouth. I knew she could whistle. Mouth made for that. Why that high class whore in Jammet's wore her veil only to her nose. Would you mind, please, telling me the right time? I'll tell you the right time up a lane. Say prunes and prisms forty times every morning, cure for fat lips. Caressing the little boy too. Onlookers see most of the game. Of course they understand birds, animals, babies. In their line.

Didn't look back when she was going down the strand. Wouldn't give that satisfaction. Those girls, those girls, those lovely seaside girls.[8] Fine eyes she had, clear. It's the white of the eye brings that out not so much the pupil. Did she know what I? Course. Like a cat sitting beyond a dog's jump. Woman. Never meet one like that Wilkins in the high school drawing a picture of Venus with all his belongings on show. Call that innocence? Poor idiot! His wife has her work cut out for her. Sharp as needles they are. When I said to Molly the man at the corner of Cuffe street was goodlooking, thought she might like, twigged at once he had a false arm. Had too. Where do they get that? Handed down from father to mother to daughter, I mean. Bred in the bone. Milly for example drying her handkerchief on the mirror to save the ironing. And when I sent her for Molly's Paisley shawl to Presscott's by the way that ad I must,[9] carrying home the change in her stocking. Clever little minx! I never told her. Neat way she carries parcels too. Attract men, small thing like that. Holding up her hand, shaking it, to let the blood flow back when it was red. Who did you learn that from? Nobody. Something the nurse taught me. O, don't they know? Three years old she was in front of Molly's dressingtable just before we left Lombard street west. Me have a nice pace. Mullingar. Who knows? Ways of the world. Young student. Straight on her pins anyway not like the other. Still she was game. Lord, I am wet. Devil you are. Swell of her calf. Transparent stockings, stretched to breaking point. Not like that frump today. A. E. Rumpled stockings. Or the one in Grafton street. White. Wow! Beef to the heel.

A monkey puzzle rocket burst, spluttering in darting crackles. Zrads and zrads, zrads, zrads. And Cissy and Tommy ran out to see and Edy after with the pushcar and then Gerty beyond the curve of the rocks. Will she? Watch! Watch! See! Looked round. She smelt an onion. Darling, I saw your. I saw all.

Lord!

Did me good all the same. Off colour after Kiernan's, Dignam's.[1] For this relief much thanks. In *Hamlet*, that is.[2] Lord! It was all things combined. Excitement.

8. From the song of which Milly Bloom's letter to her father makes mention, and which Blazes Boylan is known for singing, "Seaside Girls." The later phrase "Your head it simply swirls" is also from this song.
9. Bloom's profession is advertising canvasser, selling advertising space in newspapers to various retail concerns.
1. Kiernan's is the pub Barney Kiernan's, where Bloom got into a heated argument with a jingoistic Irish nationalist, The Citizen, in the previous chapter; Dignam's is the funeral of Paddy Dignam, recounted in Chapter 6.
2. *Hamlet*, 1.1.8.

When she leaned back felt an ache at the butt of my tongue. Your head it simply swirls. He's right. Might have made a worse fool of myself however. Instead of talking about nothing. Then I will tell you all. Still it was a kind of language between us. It couldn't be? No, Gerty they called her. Might be false name however like my and the address Dolphin's barn a blind.[3]

Her maiden name was Jemima Brown
And she lived with her mother in Irishtown.

Place made me think of that I suppose. All tarred with the same brush. Wiping pens in their stockings. But the ball rolled down to her as if it understood. Every bullet has its billet. Course I never could throw anything straight at school. Crooked as a ram's horn. Sad however because it lasts only a few years till they settle down to potwalloping and fullers' earth[4] for the baby when he does ah ah. No soft job. Saves them. Keeps them out of harm's way. Nature. Washing child, washing corpse. Dignam. Children's hands always round them. Cocoanut skulls, monkeys, not even closed at first, sour milk in their swaddles and tainted curds. Oughtn't to have given that child an empty teat to suck. Fill it up with wind. Mrs Beaufoy, Purefoy. Must call to the hospital.[5] Wonder is nurse Callan there still. And Mrs Breen and Mrs Dignam once like that too, marriageable. Worst of all the night Mrs Diggan told me in the city arms. Husband rolling in drunk, stink of pub off him like a polecat. Have that in your nose all night, whiff of stale boose. Bad policy however to fault the husband. Chickens come home to roost. They stick by one another like glue. Maybe the women's fault also. That's where Molly can knock spots off them. It is the blood of the south. Moorish. Also the form, the figure. Hands felt for the opulent. Just compare for instance those others. Wife locked up at home, skeleton in the cupboard. Allow me to introduce my. Then they trot you out some kind of a nondescript, wouldn't know what to call her. Always see a fellow's weak point in his wife. Still there's destiny in it, falling in love. Have their own secrets between them. Chaps that would go to the dogs if some woman didn't take them in hand. Then little chits of girls, height of a shilling in coppers, with little hubbies. As God made them He matched them. Sometimes children turn out well enough. Twice nought makes one. This wet is very unpleasant.

Ow!

Other hand a sixfooter with a wifey up to his watchpocket. Long and the short of it. Very strange about my watch. Wonder is there any magnetic influence between the person because that was about the time he. Yes, I suppose at once. Cat's away the mice will play. I remember looking in Pill lane. Also that now is magnetism. Back of everything magnetism. Earth for instance pulling this and being pulled. That causes movement. And time? Well that's the time the movement takes. Then if one thing stopped the whole ghesabo would stop bit by bit. Because it's all arranged. Magnetic needle tells you what's going on in the sun, the stars. Little piece of steel iron. When you hold out the fork. Come. Come. Tip. Woman and man that is. Fork and steel. Molly, he. Dress up and look and suggest and let you see and see more and defy you if you're a man to see that and legs, look look and. Tip. Have to let fly.

Wonder how is she feeling in that region. Shame all put on before third person. Molly, her underjaw stuck out, head back, about the farmer in the ridingboots with

3. Bloom here considers for the moment the possibility that this mysterious girl on the beach might be the same mysterious woman, "Martha Clifford," with whom he is carrying on his intrigue by post.

4. Material used for cleaning the grease from clothing.

5. The next chapter of *Ulysses*, known as "Oxen of the Sun," takes place at the Holles Street National Maternity Hospital, where family friend Mina Purefoy is undergoing a long and difficult labor.

the spurs. And when the painters were in Lombard street west. Smell that I did, like flowers. It was too. Violets. Came from the turpentine probably in the paint. Make their own use of everything. Same time doing it scraped her slipper on the floor so they wouldn't hear. But lots of them can't kick the beam, I think. Keep that thing up for hours. Kind of a general all round over me and half down my back.

Wait. Hm. Hm. Yes. That's her perfume. Why she waved her hand. I leave you this to think of me when I'm far away on the pillow. What is it? Heliotrope? No. Hyacinth? Hm. Roses, I think. She'd like scent of that kind. Sweet and cheap: soon sour. Why Molly likes opoponax. Suits her with a little jessamine mixed. Her high notes and her low notes. At the dance night she met him, dance of the hours. Heat brought it out. She was wearing her black and it had the perfume of the time before. Good conductor, is it? Or bad? Light too. Suppose there's some connection. For instance if you go into a cellar where it's dark. Mysterious thing too. Why did I smell it only now? Took its time in coming like herself, slow but sure. Suppose it's ever so many millions of tiny grains blown across. Yes, it is. Because those spice islands, Cinghalese this morning, smell them leagues off. Tell you what it is. It's like a fine fine veil or web they have all over the skin fine like what do you call it gossamer and they're always spinning it out of them, fine as anything, rainbow colours without knowing it. Clings to everything she takes off. Vamp of her stockings. Warm shoe. Stays. Drawers: little kick taking them off. Byby till next time. Also the cat likes to sniff in her shift on the bed. Know her smell in a thousand. Bathwater too. Reminds me of strawberries and cream. Wonder where it is really. There or the armpits or under the neck. Because you get it out of all holes and corners. Hyacinth perfume made of oil or ether or something. Muskrat. Bag under their tails. Dogs at each other behind. Good evening. Evening. How do you sniff? Hm. Hm. Very well, thank you. Animals go by that. Yes now, look at it that way. We're the same. Some women for instance warn you off when they have their period. Come near. Then get a hogo[6] you could hang your hat on. Like what? Potted herrings gone stale or. Boof! Please keep off the grass.

Perhaps they get a man smell off us. What though? Cigary gloves Long John had on his desk the other. Breath? What you eat and drink gives that. No. Mansmell, I mean. Must be connected with that because priests that are supposed to be are different. Women buzz round it like flies round treacle. O father, will you? Let me be the first to. That diffuses itself all through the body, permeates. Source of life. And it's extremely curious the smell. Celery sauce. Let me.

Mr Bloom inserted his nose. Hm. Into the. Hm. Opening of his waistcoat. Almonds or. No. Lemons it is. Ah no, that's the soap.[7]

O by the by that lotion. I knew there was something on my mind. Never went back and the soap not paid. Two and nine. Bad opinion of me he'll have. Call tomorrow. How much do I owe you? Three and nine? Two and nine, sir. Ah. Might stop him giving credit another time. Lose your customers that way. Pubs do. Fellows run up a bill on the slate and then slinking around the back streets into somewhere else.

Here's this nobleman passed before. Blown in from the bay. Just went as far as turn back. Always at home at dinnertime. Looks mangled out: had a good tuck in. Enjoying nature now. Grace after meals. After supper walk a mile. Sure he has a small bank balance somewhere, government sit.[8] Walk after him now makes him

6. Flavor or, in this case, odor.
7. In Chapter 5 ("Lotus Eaters"), Bloom has purchased a bar of lemon soap, which he carries in his pants pocket, and put in an order for hand lotion.
8. Situation, or position.

awkward like those newsboys me today. That's the way to find out. Ask yourself who is he now. *The Man on the Beach*, prize titbit story by Mr Leopold Bloom. Payment at the rate of one guinea per column. And that fellow today at the graveside in the brown mackintosh. Corns on his kismet however. Healthy perhaps absorb all the. Whistle brings rain they say. Must be some somewhere. Salt in the Ormond damp. The body feels the atmosphere. Old Betty's joints are on the rack. Mother Shipton's prophecy that is about ships around they fly in the twinkling. No. Signs of rain it is. The royal reader. And distant hills seem coming nigh.

Howth. Bailey light. Two, four, six, eight, nine. See. People afraid of the dark. Also glowworms, cyclists: lighting up time. Jewels diamonds flash better. Light is a kind of reassuring. Not going to hurt you. Better now of course than long ago. Country roads. Run you through the small guts for nothing. Still two types there are you bob against. Scowl or smile. Not at all. Best time to spray plants too in the shade after the sun. Were those nightclouds there all the time? Land of the setting sun this. Homerule sun setting in the southeast. My native land, goodnight.

Dew falling. Bad for you, dear, to sit on that stone. Brings on white fluxions. Might get piles myself. Sticks too like a summer cold, sore on the mouth. Friction of the position. Like to be that rock she sat on. Also the library today: those girl graduates. Happy chairs under them. But it's the evening influence. They feel all that. Open like flowers, know their hours, sunflowers, Jerusalem artichokes in ballrooms, chandeliers, avenues under the lamps. Nightstock in Mat Dillon's garden where I kissed her shoulder. June that was too I wooed. The year returns. And now? Sad about her lame of course but must be on your guard not to feel too much pity. They take advantage.

All quiet on Howth now. The distant hills seem. Where we. The rhododendrons.[9] I am a fool perhaps. He gets the plums and I the leavings. Where I come in. All that old hill has seen. Names change: that's all. Lovers: yum yum.

Tired I feel now. Drained all the manhood out of me, little wretch. She kissed me. My youth. Never again. Only once it comes. Or hers. Take the train there tomorrow. No. Returning not the same. Like kids your second visit to a house. The new I want. Nothing new under the sun. Care of P. O. Dolphin's barn. Are you not happy in your? Naughty darling. At Dolphin's barn charades in Luke Doyle's house. Mat Dillon and his bevy of daughters: Tiny, Atty, Floey, Sara. Molly too. Eightyseven that was. Year before we. And the old major partial to his drop of spirits. Curious she an only child, I an only child. So it returns. Think you're escaping and run into yourself. Longest way round is the shortest way home. And just when he and she. Circus horse walking in a ring. Rip van Winkle we played. Rip: tear in Henny Doyle's overcoat. Van: bread van delivering. Winkle: cockles and periwinkles. Then I did Rip van Winkle coming back. She leaned on the sideboard watching. Moorish eyes. Twenty years asleep. All changed. Forgotten. The young are old. His gun rusty from the dew.

Ba. What is that flying about? Swallow? Bat probably. Thinks I'm a tree, so blind. Metempsychosis.[1] They believed you could be changed into a tree from grief. Weeping willow. Ba. There he goes. Funny little beggar. Wonder where he lives. Belfry up there. Very likely. Hanging by his heels in the odour of sanctity. Bell scared him out, I suppose.

9. In the closing chapter of *Ulysses*, "Penelope," Molly Bloom recounts in poetic language the early days of her courtship with and marriage to Leopold, including a romantic episode on the rhododendron-covered hillsides of Howth Head.

1. The belief that, after death, the soul is reborn in another body. Molly has earlier asked Leopold to define this term for her in Chapter 4, "Calypso."

Mass seems to be over. Yes, there's the light in the priest's house. Their frugal meal. Remember about the mistake in the valuation when I was in Thom's. Twentyeight it is. Two houses they have. Gabriel Conroy's[2] brother is curate. Ba. Again. Wonder why they come out at night like mice. They're a mixed breed. Birds are like hopping mice. What frightens them, light or noise? Better sit still. All instinct like the bird in drouth got water out of the end of a jar by throwing in pebbles. Like a little man in a cloak he is with tiny hands. Weeny bones. Almost see them shimmering, kind of a bluey white. Colours depend on the light you see. Instance, that cat this morning on the staircase. Colour of brown turf. Howth a while ago amethyst. Glass flashing. That's how that wise man what's his name with the burning glass. Then the heather goes on fire. It can't be tourists' matches. What? Perhaps the sticks dry rub together in the wind and light.

Ba. Who knows what they're always flying for. Insects? That bee last week got into the room playing with his shadow on the ceiling. Birds too never find out what they say. Like our small talk. And says she and says he. Nerve they have to fly over the ocean and back. Lots must be killed in storms, telegraph wires. Dreadful life sailors have too. Big brutes of steamers floundering along in the dark, lowing out like seacows. *Faugh a ballagh.*[3] Out of that, bloody curse to you. Others in vessels, bit of a handkerchief sail, pitched about like snuff at a wake when the stormy winds do blow. Married too. Sometimes away for years at the ends of the earth somewhere. No ends really because it's round. Wife in every port they say. She has a good job if she minds it till Johnny comes marching home again. If ever he does. Smelling the tailend of ports. How can they like the sea? Yet they do. The anchor's weighed. Off he sails with a scapular or a medal on him for luck. Well? And the tephilim[4] poor papa's father had on his door to touch. That brought us out of the land of Egypt and into the house of bondage. Something in all those superstitions because when you go out never know what dangers. Hanging on to a plank for grim life, lifebelt round round him, gulping salt water, and that's the last of his nibs till the sharks catch hold of him. Do fish ever get seasick?

Then you have a beautiful calm without a cloud, smooth sea, placid, crew and cargo in smithereens, Davy Jones' locker. Moon looking down. Not my fault, old cockalorum.

A lost long candle wandered up the sky from Mirus bazaar in search of funds for Mercer's hospital and broke, drooping, and shed a cluster of violet but one white star. They floated, fell: they faded. And among the elms a hoisted lintstock[5] lit the lamp at Leahy's terrace. By the screen of lighted windows, by equal gardens a shrill voice went crying, wailing: Evening Telegraph, extra edition. Result of the Gold Cup races: and from the door of Dignam's house a boy ran out and called. Twittering the bat flew here, flew there. Far out over the sands the coming surf crept, grey. Howth settled for slumber tired of long days, of yumyum rhododendrons (he was old) and felt gladly the night breeze lift, ruffle his many ferns. He lay but opened a red eye unsleeping, deep and slowly breathing, slumberous but awake. And far on Kish bank the anchored lightship twinkled, winked at Mr Bloom.

Life those chaps out there must have, stuck in the same spot. Irish Lights board. Penance for their sins. Day we went out in the Erin's King, throwing them the sack of old papers. Bears in the zoo. Filthy trip. Drunkards out to shake up their livers. Puking overboard to feed the herrings. And the women, fear of God in their faces. Milly, no

2. Gabriel Conroy is the proud protagonist of the great short story that closes *Dubliners*, "The Dead."
3. Irish, "Clear the way" (a battle cry).
4. The *tephilim* is a leather pouch containing passages from the first five books of the Hebrew bible; Bloom is instead thinking of a *mezuzah*, a piece of parchment inscribed with passages from the books of Deuteronomy, affixed to the doorpost of Jewish households.
5. A stake notched at one end to hold a lighted match.

sign of funk. Her blue scarf loose, laughing. Don't know what death is at that age. And then their stomachs clean. But being lost they fear. When we hid behind the tree at Crumlin. I didn't want to. Mamma! Mamma! Frightening them with masks too. Poor kids. Only troubles wildfire and nettlerash. Calomel purge I got her for that. After getting better asleep with Molly. Very same teeth she has. What do they love? Another themselves? But the morning she chased her with the umbrella. Perhaps so as not to hurt. I felt her pulse. Ticking. Little hand it was: now big. Dearest Papli.[6] All that the hand says when you touch. Loved to count my waistcoat buttons. Her first stays I remember. Made me laugh to see. Little paps to begin with. Left one is more sensitive, I think. Mine too. Nearer the heart. Her growing pains at night, calling, wakening me. Frightened she was when her nature came on her first. Poor child! Strange moment for the mother too. Brings back her girlhood. Gibraltar. Looking from Buena Vista. O'Hara's tower. The seabirds screaming. Old Barbary ape that gobbled all his family. Sundown, gunfire for the men to cross the lines. Looking out over the sea she told me. Evening like this, but clear, no clouds. I always thought I'd marry a lord or a gentleman with a private yacht. *Buenas noches, senorita. El hombre ama la muchaha hermosa.*[7] Why me? Because you were so foreign from the others.

Better not stick here all night like an oyster. This weather makes you dull. Must be getting on for nine by the light. Go home. Too late for *Leah, Lily of Killarney*. No. Might be still up. Call to the hospital to see. Hope she's over. Long day I've had. Martha, the bath, funeral, house of keys, Museum with those goddesses, Dedalus' song. Then that brawler in Barney Kiernan's. Got my own back there.[8] Drunken ranters. Ought to go home and laugh at themselves. Always want to be swilling in company. Afraid to be alone like a child of two. Suppose he hit me. Look at it. Other way round. Not so bad then. Perhaps not to hurt he meant. Three cheers for Israel. Three cheers for the sister-in-law he hawked about, three fangs in her mouth. Extremely nice cup of tea. Imagine that in the early morning. Everyone to his taste as Morris said when he kissed the cow. But Dignam's put the boots on it. Houses of mourning so depressing because you never know. Anyhow she wants the money. Must call to those Scottish widows as I promised. Strange name. Takes it for granted we're going to pop off first. That widow on Monday was it outside Cramer's that looked at me. Buried the poor husband but progressing favourably. Well? What do you expect her to do? Must wheedle her way along. Widower I hate to see. Looks so forlorn. Poor man O'Connor wife and five children poisoned by mussels here. The sewage. Hopeless. Some good motherly woman take him in tow, platter face and a large apron. See him sometimes walking about trying to find out who played the trick. U. p: up.[9] Fate that is. He, not me. Also a shop often noticed. Curse seems to dog it. Dreamt last night? Wait. Something confused. She had red slippers on. Turkish. Wore the breeches. Suppose she does. Would I like her in pyjamas? Damned hard to answer. Nannetti's gone. Mailboat.

6. Papli is Milly's affectionate name for her father, with which she opens the letter he has received that morning.
7. Good evening, Miss. The man loves the beautiful young girl (Spanish).
8. Bloom here gives a very brief summary of his day to this point: "Martha," Martha Clifford, his amorous correspondent from whom he has received a letter; "the bath," in which Bloom indulges himself in the "Lotus Eaters" chapter; the "funeral" of Paddy Dignam is recounted in Chapter 6, "Hades"; "house of keys" refers to the motif of an ad he is attempting to sell to Alexander Keyes, Wine & Tea Merchant, in Chapter 7, "Aeolus"; in Chapter 8, "Lestrygonians," Bloom wanders over to the museum to ascertain whether or not Greek statues indeed have anal sphincters; and in Chapter 11, "Sirens," Bloom has heard Simon Dedalus sing "Come, Thou Lost One," from the opera *Martha*. For "that bawler in Barney Kiernan's," see note 1, page 2272.
9. "U.p: up" is the text of a mysterious postcard received by Dennis Breen; he has gone to investigate filing suit against its (anonymous) sender. The message seems to be mocking Breen sexually, suggesting that he is so constantly aroused that he can only urinate upward.

Near Holyhead by now. Must nail that ad of Keyes's. Work Hynes and Crawford. Petticoats for Molly. She has something to put in them. What's that? Might be money.

Mr Bloom stooped and turned over a piece of paper on the strand. He brought it near his eyes and peered. Letter? No. Can't read. Better go. Better. I'm tired to move. Page of an old copybook. Never know what you find. Bottle with story of a treasure in it thrown from a wreck. Parcels post. Children always want to throw things in the sea. Trust? Bread cast on the waters. What's this? Bit of stick.

O! Exhausted that female has me. Not so young now. Will she come here tomorrow? Will I?

Mr Bloom with his stick gently vexed the thick sand at his foot. Write a message for her. Might remain. What?

I.

Some flatfoot tramp on it in the morning. Useless. Tide comes here a pool near her foot. O, those transparent! Besides they don't know. What is the meaning of that other world. I called you naughty boy because I do not like.[1]

AM. A.

No room. Let it go.

Mr Bloom effaced the letters with his slow boot. Hopeless thing sand. Nothing grows in it. All fades. No fear of big vessels coming up here. Except Guinness's barges. Round the Kish in eighty days. Done half by design.

He flung his wooden pen away. The stick fell in silted sand, stuck. Now if you were trying to do that for a week on end you couldn't. Chance. We'll never meet again. But it was lovely. Goodbye, dear. Made me feel so young.

Short snooze now if I had. And she can do the other. Did too. And Belfast. I won't go.[2] Let him. Just close my eyes a moment. Won't sleep though. Bat again. No harm in him. Just a few.

O sweety all your little white I made me do we two naughty darling she him half past the bed met him pike hoses frillies for Raoul de perfume your wife black hair heave under embon senoritayoung eyes Mulvey plump bubs me bread van Winkle red slippers she rusty sleep wander years dreams return tail end Agendath lovey showed me her next year in drawers return next in her next her next.[3]

A bat flew. Here. There. Here. Far in the grey a bell chimed. Mr Bloom with open mouth, his left boot sanded sideways, leaned, breathed. Just for a few.

Cuckoo.
Cuckoo.
Cuckoo.

The clock on the mantelpiece in the priests' house cooed where Canon O'Hanlon and Father Conroy and the reverend John Hughes S. J. were taking tea and sodabread and butter and fried mutton chops with catsup and talking about.

Cuckoo.
Cuckoo.
Cuckoo.

Because it was a bird that came out of its little house to tell the time that Gerty MacDowell noticed the time she was there because she was as quick as anything

1. The preceding two sentences are from Martha Clifford's letter.
2. Bloom is thinking here of Molly's upcoming singing tour, on which she will be accompanied by Blazes Boylan.
3. This paragraph represents the unstructured thought fragments of Bloom as he drifts off to sleep.

about a thing, was Gerty MacDowell, and she noticed at once that that foreign gentleman that was sitting on the rocks looking was.

Cuckoo.
Cuckoo.
Cuckoo.

RESPONSES

Hon. John M. Woolsey: 1933 Decision of the United States District Court Lifting the Ban on Ulysses[1]

UNITED STATES DISTRICT COURT
SOUTHERN DISTRICT OF NEW YORK

United States of America *Libelant* v One Book called "Ulysses" Random House, Inc., *Claimant*	OPINION A. 110-59

On cross motions for a decree in a libel of confiscation, supplemented by a stipulation—hereinafter described—brought by the United States against the book "Ulysses" by James Joyce, under Section 305 of the Tariff Act of 1930, Title 19 United States Code, Section 1305, on the ground that the book is obscene within the meaning of that Section, and, hence, is not importable into the United States, but is subject to seizure, forfeiture and confiscation and destruction.

United States Attorney—by Samuel C. Coleman, Esq., and Nicholas Atlas, Esq., of counsel—for the United States, in support of motion for a decree of forfeiture, and in opposition to motion for a decree dismissing the libel.

Messrs. Greenbaum, Wolff & Ernst,—by Morris L. Ernst, Ésq., and Alexander Lindey, Esq., of counsel—attorneys for claimant Random House, Inc., in support of motion for a decree dismissing the libel, and in opposition to motion for a decree of forfeiture.

WOOLSEY, J.:

The motion for a decree dismissing the libel herein is granted, and, consequently, of course, the Government's motion for a decree of forfeiture and destruction is denied.

Accordingly a decree dismissing the libel without costs may be entered herein.

1. For the first dozen years after its publication, *Ulysses* could not be legally published or purchased in the English-speaking world, for it was declared, first by the U.S. Post Office, to be obscene. The novel was circulated *sub rosa* among those with connections, but it was not a book that was displayed in polite company. Bennett Cerf, the founding publisher of Random House, brought out the first trade edition of *Ulysses;* through a complicated and sometimes comical set of calculations, a French copy was brought through U.S. Customs, seized at the demand of the traveler, and a case then brought to the U.S. District Court where Judge John M. Woolsey cleared the way for the first U.S. publication of *Ulysses* in 1934.

I. The practice followed in this case is in accordance with the suggestion made by me in the case of *United States v. One Book Entitled "Contraception"*, 51 F. (2d) 525, and is as follows:

After issue was joined by the filing of the claimant's answer to the libel for forfeiture against "Ulysses," a stipulation was made between the United States Attorney's office and the attorneys for the claimant providing:

1. That the book "Ulysses" should be deemed to have been annexed to and to have become part of the libel just as if it had been incorporated in its entirety therein.

2. That the parties waived their right to a trial by jury.

3. That each party agreed to move for decree in its favor.

4. That on such cross motions the Court might decide all the questions of law and fact involved and render a general finding thereon.

5. That on the decision of such motions the decree of the Court might be entered as if it were a decree after trial.

It seems to me that a procedure of this kind is highly appropriate in libels for the confiscation of books such as this. It is an especially advantageous procedure in the instant case because on account of the length of "Ulysses" and the difficulty of reading it, a jury trial would have been an extremely unsatisfactory, if not an almost impossible, method of dealing with it.

II. I have read "Ulysses" once in its entirety and I have read those passages of which the Government particularly complains several times. In fact, for many weeks, my spare time has been devoted to the consideration of the decision which my duty would require me to make in this matter.

"Ulysses" is not an easy book to read or to understand. But there has been much written about it, and in order properly to approach the consideration of it it is advisable to read a number of other books which have now become its satellites. The study of "Ulysses" is, therefore, a heavy task.

III. The reputation of "Ulysses" in the literary world, however, warranted my taking such time as was necessary to enable me to satisfy myself as to the intent with which the book was written, for, of course, in any case where a book is claimed to be obscene it must first be determined, whether the intent with which it was written was what is called, according to the usual phrase, pornographic,—that is, written for the purpose of exploiting obscenity.

If the conclusion is that the book is pornographic that is the end of the inquiry and forfeiture must follow.

But in "Ulysses," in spite of its unusual frankness, I do not detect anywhere the leer of the sensualist. I hold, therefore, that it is not pornographic.

IV. In writing "Ulysses," Joyce sought to make a serious experiment in a new, if not wholly novel, literary genre. He takes persons of the lower middle class living in Dublin in 1904 and seeks not only to describe what they did on a certain day early in June of that year as they went about the City bent on their usual occupations, but also to tell what many of them thought about the while.

Joyce has attempted—it seems to me, with astonishing success—to show how the screen of consciousness with its ever-shifting kaleidoscopic impressions carries, as it were on a plastic palimpsest, not only what is in the focus of each man's observation of the actual things about him, but also in a penumbral zone residua of past impressions, some recent and some drawn up by association from the domain of the subsconscious. He shows how each of these impressions affects the life and behavior of the character which he is describing.

What he seeks to get is not unlike the results of a double or, if that is possible, a multiple exposure on a cinema film which would give a clear foreground with a background visible but somewhat blurred and out of focus in varying degrees.

To convey by words an effect which obviously lends itself more appropriately to a graphic technique, accounts, it seems to me, for much of the obscurity which meets a reader of "Ulysses." And it also explains another aspect of the book, which I have further to consider, namely, Joyce's sincerity and his honest effort to show exactly how the minds of his characters operate.

If Joyce did not attempt to be honest in developing the technique which he has adopted in "Ulysses" the result would be psychologically misleading and thus unfaithful to his chosen technique. Such an attitude would be artistically inexcusable.

It is because Joyce has been loyal to his technique and has not funked its necessary implications, but has honestly attempted to tell fully what his characters think about, that he has been the subject of so many attacks and that his purpose has been so often misunderstood and misrepresented. For his attempt sincerely and honestly to realize his objective has required him incidentally to use certain words which are generally considered dirty words and has led at times to what many think is a too poignant preoccupation with sex in the thoughts of his characters.

The words which are criticized as dirty are old Saxon words known to almost all men and, I venture, to many women, and are such words as would be naturally and habitually used, I believe, by the types of folk whose life, physical and mental, Joyce is seeking to describe. In respect of the recurrent emergence of the theme of sex in the minds of his characters, it must always be remembered that his locale was Celtic and his season Spring.

Whether or not one enjoys such a technique as Joyce uses is a matter of taste on which disagreement or argument is futile, but to subject that technique to the standards of some other technique seems to me to be little short of absurd.

Accordingly, I hold that "Ulysses" is a sincere and honest book and I think that the criticisms of it are entirely disposed of by its rationale.

V. Furthermore, "Ulysses" is an amazing *tour de force* when one considers the success which has been in the main achieved with such a difficult objective as Joyce set for himself. As I have stated, "Ulysses" is not an easy book to read. It is brilliant and dull, intelligible and obscure by turns. In many places it seems to me to be disgusting, but although it contains, as I have mentioned above, many words usually considered dirty, I have not found anything that I consider to be dirt for dirt's sake. Each word of the book contributes like a bit of mosaic to the detail of the picture which Joyce is seeking to construct for his readers.

If one does not wish to associate with such folk as Joyce describes, that is one's own choice. In order to avoid indirect contact with them one may not wish to read "Ulysses"; that is quite understandable. But when such a real artist in words, as Joyce undoubtedly is, seeks to draw a true picture of the lower middle class in a European city, ought it to be impossible for the American public legally to see that picture?

To answer this question it is not sufficient merely to find, as I have found above, that Joyce did not write "Ulysses" with what is commonly called pornographic intent, I must endeavor to apply a more objective standard to his book in order to determine its effect in the result, irrespective of the intent with which it was written.

VI. The statute under which the libel is filed only denounces, in so far as we are here concerned, the importation into the United States from any foreign country of "any obscene book." Section 305 of the Tariff Act of 1930, Title 19 United States Code, Section 1305. It does not marshal against books the spectrum of condemnatory adjectives found, commonly, in laws dealing with matters of this kind. I am, therefore, only required to determine whether "Ulysses" is obscene within the legal definition of that word.

The meaning of the word "obscene" as legally defined by the Courts is: tending to stir the sex impulses or to lead to sexually impure and lustful thoughts. *Dunlop* v. *United States*, 165 U. S. 486, 501; *United States* v. *One Book Entitled "Married Love"*, 48 F. (2d) 821, 824; *United States* v. *One Book Entitled "Contraception"*, 51 F. (2d) 525, 528; and compare *Dysart* v. *United States*, 272 U. S. 655, 657; *Swearingen* v. *United States*, 161 U. S. 446, 450; *United States* v. *Dennett*, 39 F. (2d) 564, 568 (C. C. A. 2); *People* v. *Wendling*, 258 N. Y. 451, 453.

Whether a particular book would tend to excite such impulses and thoughts must be tested by the Court's opinion as to its effect on a person with average sex instincts—what the French would call *l'homme moyen sensuel*—who plays, in this branch of legal inquiry, the same role of hypothetical reagent as does the "reasonable man" in the law of torts and "the man learned in the art" on questions of invention in patent law.

The risk involved in the use of such a reagent arises from the inherent tendency of the trier of facts, however fair he may intend to be, to make his reagent too much subservient to his own idiosyncrasies. Here, I have attempted to avoid this, if possible, and to make my reagent herein more objective than he might otherwise be, by adopting the following course:

After I had made my decision in regard to the aspect of "Ulysses," now under consideration, I checked my impressions with two friends of mine who in my opinion answered to the above stated requirement for my reagent.

These literary assessors—as I might properly describe them—were called on separately, and neither knew that I was consulting the other. They are men whose opinion on literature and on life I value most highly. They had both read "Ulysses," and, of course, were wholly unconnected with this cause.

Without letting either of my assessors know what my decision was, I gave to each of them the legal definition of obscene and asked each whether in his opinion "Ulysses" was obscene within that definition.

I was interested to find that they both agreed with my opinion: that reading "Ulysses" in its entirety, as a book must be read on such a test as this, did not tend to excite sexual impulses or lustful thoughts but that its net effect on them was only that of a somewhat tragic and very powerful commentary on the inner lives of men and women.

It is only with the normal person that the law is concerned. Such a test as I have described, therefore, is the only proper test of obscenity in the case of a book like "Ulysses" which is a sincere and serious attempt to devise a new literary method for the observation and description of mankind.

I am quite aware that owing to some of its scenes "Ulysses" is a rather strong draught to ask some sensitive, though normal, persons to take. But my considered opinion, after long reflection, is that whilst in many places the effect of "Ulysses" on the reader undoubtedly is somewhat emetic, nowhere does it tend to be an aphrodisiac.

"Ulysses" may, therefore, be admitted into the United States.

JOHN M. WOOLSEY
UNITED STATES DISTRICT JUDGE

December 6, 1933

Seamus Heaney: from *Station Island*[1]

12

Like a convalescent, I took the hand
stretched down from the jetty, sensed again
an alien comfort as I stepped on ground
to find the helping hand still gripping mine,
fish-cold and bony, but whether to guide
or to be guided I could not be certain

for the tall man in step at my side
seemed blind, though he walked straight as a rush
upon his ash plant, his eyes fixed straight ahead.[2]

Then I knew him in the flesh
out there on the tarmac[3] among the cars,
wintered hard and sharp as a blackthorn bush.

His voice eddying with the vowels of all rivers[4]
came back to me, though he did not speak yet,
a voice like a prosecutor's or a singer's,

cunning, narcotic, mimic, definite
as a steel nib's[5] downstroke, quick and clean,
and suddenly he hit a litter basket

with his stick, saying, 'Your obligation
is not discharged by any common rite.
What you do you must do on your own.

The main thing is to write
for the joy of it. Cultivate a work-lust
that imagines its haven like your hands at night

dreaming the sun in the sunspot of a breast.
You are fasted now, light-headed, dangerous.
Take off from here. And don't be so earnest,

so ready for the sackcloth and the ashes.[6]
Let go, let fly, forget.
You've listened long enough. Now strike your note.'

It was as if I had stepped free into space
alone with nothing that I had not known
already. Raindrops blew in my face

1. *Station Island* is a sequence of dream encounters with familiar ghosts, set on Station Island on Lough Derg in County Donegal. The island is also known as St. Patrick's Purgatory because of a tradition that Patrick was the first to establish the penitential vigil of fasting and praying that still constitutes the basis of the three-day pilgrimage. Each unit of the contemporary pilgrim's exercises is called a "station" and a large part of each station involves walking barefoot and praying round the "beds," stone circles which are said to be the remains of early medieval monastic cells [Heaney's note]. In section 12, the poet meets and wrestles with the shade of Ireland's greatest English-language writer, James Joyce.

2. The speaker alludes to James Joyce, who was nearly blinded by glaucoma and who affected an ashplant walking-stick.

3. Blacktop; pavement.

4. The "Anna Livia Plurabelle" section of Joyce's last novel *Finnegans Wake* is thick with the names of rivers.

5. Penpoint.

6. The dress of repentance and grief.

as I came to and heard the harangue and jeers
going on and on: 'The English language
belongs to us. You are raking at dead fires,

rehearsing the old whinges[7] at your age.
That subject people stuff is a cod's[8] game,
infantile, like this peasant pilgrimage.

You lose more of yourself than you redeem
doing the decent thing. Keep at a tangent.
When they make the circle wide, it's time to swim

out on your own and fill the element
with signatures on your own frequency,
echo-soundings, searches, probes, allurements,

elver-gleams[9] in the dark of the whole sea.'
The shower broke in a cloudburst, the tarmac
fumed and sizzled. As he moved off quickly

the downpour loosed its screens round his straight walk.

T. S. Eliot

1888–1965

Publicity photo from Barry Hyams, *T. S. Eliot,* 1954.

T. S. Eliot was one of the dominant forces in English-language poetry of the twentieth century. When the entire body of Eliot's writing and influence is taken into account—not only his relatively modest poetic and dramatic production, but his literary criticism, his religious and cultural criticism, his editorial work at the British publishing house Faber and Faber, his influence on younger poets coming up in his wake, and quite simply his *presence* as a literary and cultural icon—no one looms larger. As one of those younger poets, Karl Shapiro, has written: "Eliot is untouchable; he is Modern Literature incarnate and an institution unto himself." Eliot's obituary in *Life* magazine declared that "Our age beyond any doubt has been, and will continue to be, the Age of Eliot."

Thomas Stearns Eliot was born in Saint Louis, Missouri. The roots of Eliot's family tree go deep into American, and specifically New England, soil. His ancestor Andrew Eliot was one of the original settlers of the Massachusetts Bay Colony, emigrating from East Coker, in Somerset, England, in the mid-seventeenth century; he later became one of the jurors who tried the Salem "witches." The Eliots became a distinguished New England family; the Eliot family tree includes a president of Harvard University and three U.S. Presidents (John Adams, John Quincy

7. Complaints.
8. Fool's.
9. Young eels, especially those migrating up a stream from the ocean.

Adams, and Rutherford B. Hayes). In 1834 the Reverend William Greenleaf Eliot, the poet's grandfather, graduated from Harvard and moved to Saint Louis, where he established the city's first Unitarian church; he went on to found Washington University, and became its chancellor in 1872. It was into this family environment—redolent of New England, New England religion (Unitarianism), and New England educational tradition (Harvard)—that Eliot was born in 1888. And yet in a 1960 essay, Eliot wrote "My urban imagery was that of Saint Louis, upon which that of Paris and London had been superimposed." The sights and sounds of Saint Louis impressed themselves deeply on Eliot's young imagination, especially the looming figure of the Mississippi River (which he was to call "a strong brown god" in *The Dry Salvages*).

From age ten Eliot attended Smith Academy in Saint Louis—also founded by his grandfather—and spent his last year of secondary school at the Milton Academy in Milton, Massachusetts, in preparation for his entrance into Harvard in 1906. Eliot went on to take his A.B. (1909) and M.A. (1910) degrees from Harvard and largely completed a Ph.D. in philosophy from Harvard, first spending a relatively unstructured year in Paris, attending lectures at the Sorbonne and hearing Henri Bergson lecture at the Collège de France. He wrote a doctoral dissertation on the neo-idealist philosopher F. H. Bradley in 1916, which was accepted by the philosophy department at Harvard, but he never returned to Cambridge to defend the dissertation and take the degree. Eliot's year in Paris was crucial in many ways; in addition to breathing in the vital Parisian intellectual and artistic scene, he soaked up the writing of late-nineteenth-century French poets like Jules Laforgue, Tristan Corbière, and Charles Baudelaire.

Eliot's poems are deeply indebted both to French and to British poets. The poem with which Eliot broke onto the modern poetry scene was *The Love Song of J. Alfred Prufrock*, composed between 1910 and 1911. In a strikingly new and jarring idiom, the poem builds on the dramatic monologues of Robert Browning, breaking up the unified voice at the center of Browning's experiments with startling juxtapositions and transitions, and adding the violent and disturbing imagery of the French symbolist poets. The resulting poem is a heavily ironic "love song" in which neither lover nor beloved exists with any solidity outside the strait-jacket of "a formulated phrase"; Prufrock, like modern European humanity whom he represents, is unable to penetrate the thick husk of habit, custom, and cliché to arrive at something substantial.

Eliot, and the poem, came to the notice of modern literature impresario Ezra Pound; in 1915 Pound saw to it that *Prufrock* was published in Harriet Monroe's influential *Poetry* magazine, as well as in his own *Catholic Anthology*, which brought Eliot to the notice of the (largely hostile) British literary establishment in the person of reviewers like the *Quarterly Review*'s Arthur Waugh. Eliot wrote three other great poems in this early period, *Portrait of a Lady*, *Preludes*, and *Rhapsody on a Windy Night*. Like *Prufrock*, the poems deal unflinchingly with loneliness, alienation, isolation; while isolation is hardly a new theme for poetry, Eliot suggests in a particularly modernist form in these poems that our isolation from others derives from, and tragically mirrors, our isolation from ourselves. This internalized alienation was also one of the themes of Eliot's early and influential review essay *The Metaphysical Poets* (1921); in that piece, he suggested that English poetry had suffered through a long drought, dating from about the time of Milton, caused by what Eliot termed a "dissociation of sensibility." At the time of the metaphysical poets (in the seventeenth century), a poet, or any sensitive thinker, was a unified whole; "A thought to Donne," Eliot writes, "was an experience; it modified his sensibility. . . . the ordinary man's experience is chaotic, irregular, fragmentary." That chaotic consciousness seemed to Eliot especially pronounced in the early decades of the twentieth century; though not sanguine of easy solutions, he did believe that modern poets, writing a poetry that would synthesize the seemingly unrelated sensations and experiences of modern men and women, might show a way out of "the immense panorama of futility and anarchy which is contemporary history," as he wrote in 1923 in a review of Joyce's *Ulysses*.

A collection of Eliot's early poems was published in 1917 as *Prufrock and Other Observations* by the Egoist Press, through the offices of Pound. For the remainder of the decade, however, Eliot's poetic output was small; feeling himself at a creative cul de sac, he wrote a few poems in French in 1917, including *Dans le Restaurant* which later appeared, trimmed and translated, as a part of *The Waste Land.* On Pound's suggestion, Eliot set himself, as a formal exercise, to write several poems modeled on the quatrains of Théophile Gautier. Arguably the most significant and influential of Eliot's early writings, however, were his many critical essays and book reviews; between 1916 and 1921 he wrote nearly a hundred essays and reviews, many of which were published in 1920 as *The Sacred Wood.* Critics still disagree as to whether Eliot's poetry or critical prose has been the more influential; the most important of Eliot's critical precepts, such as the "impersonality" of poetry and the inherent difficulty of modern writing, have entered wholesale into the way that modern literature is studied and taught. Eliot's critical principles, complemented and extended by academics such as I. A. Richards, make up the foundation of what came to be known as the New Criticism, a major mode of reading that emphasizes close attention to verbal textures and to poetic ironies, paradoxes, and tensions between disparate elements—all prominent features of Eliot's own poetry.

Eliot lived in modest circumstances for several years, working as a schoolteacher and then a bank clerk between 1916 and 1922. He then edited an increasingly influential quarterly, *The Criterion* (1922–1939), and became an editor at Faber and Faber, a post he retained until his death. His reputation as a poet was confirmed in 1922 with *The Waste Land,* the epochal work that remains Eliot's best-known and most influential poem; Pound called it "about enough . . . to make the rest of us shut up shop." More than any other text of the century, *The Waste Land* forcibly changed the idiom that contemporary poetry must adopt if it were to remain contemporary. Perhaps the poem's most impressive formal achievement, created in no small part through Ezra Pound's judicious editorial work, is its careful balance between structure and chaos, unity and fragmentation; this poise is created in the poem in equal parts by the mythical structures Eliot used to undergird the contemporary action and the pedantic footnotes he added to the poem, after its periodical publication in the *Dial,* to call the reader's attention to those structures. *The Waste Land*—like *Ulysses, Finnegans Wake,* Pound's *Cantos,* and a number of other important texts—looks unified largely because we readers look for it to be unified. Such a style of reading is one of the great triumphs of modernism, and one Eliot was instrumental in teaching to readers and teachers alike.

The Waste Land is justly celebrated for giving voice to the nearly universal pessimism and alienation of the early decades of the twentieth century Europe—though Eliot maintained to the end that he was not a spokesperson for his generation or for anything else, and that the poem was "only the relief of a personal and wholly insignificant grouse against life; it is just a piece of rhythmical grumbling." Owing to the development of recording technology, to "give voice" in this case is not merely a metaphor, for Eliot's recording of *The Waste Land,* in what Virginia Woolf called Eliot's "sepulchral voice," has been tremendously influential on two generations of poets and students. Eliot's critical principle of "impersonality," however, has sometimes served to obscure how very personal, on one level, the poem is. The poem was completed during Eliot's convalescence at a sanatorium in Margate, England ("On Margate Sands. / I can connect / Nothing with nothing," the speaker despairs in section 3, "The Fire Sermon") and in Lausanne, Switzerland; the speaker, like the poet, is reduced to shoring the fragments of a disappearing civilization against his ruin. The poem also bears painful testimony to the increasingly desperate state of Eliot's wife Vivien Haigh-Wood, whom he had married in 1915; she suffered terribly from what was at the time called "nervousness," and had finally to be institutionalized in 1938. Whole stretches of one-sided "dialogue" from the "A Game of Chess" section would seem to have been taken verbatim from the couple's private conversations: "My nerves are very bad to-night. Yes, bad. Stay with me. / Speak to me. Why do you never speak?

Speak." On the draft of the poem, Pound wrote "photography" alongside this passage. *The Waste Land* remains one of the century's most incisive and insightful texts regarding the breakdown of social, communal, cultural, and personal relationships.

In 1930 Eliot's next important poem, the introspective and confessional *Ash Wednesday*, was published; in the time since the publication of *The Waste Land*, however, Eliot's personal belief system had undergone a sea change. In June 1927 he was baptized into the Anglican church; five months later, he was naturalized as a British citizen. In his 1928 monograph *For Lancelot Andrewes*, Eliot declared himself to be "classicist in literature, royalist in politics, and Anglo-Catholic in religion." His poem *Journey of the Magi*, published as a pamphlet a month after his baptism, addresses the journey Eliot himself had made through death to a rebirth—precisely the rebirth which, in the opening lines of *The Waste Land*, seems an impossibility.

The 1930s also saw Eliot's entry into the theater, with three poetic dramas: *The Rock* (1934), *Murder in the Cathedral* (1935), and *The Family Reunion* (1939). In his later years, these highbrow dramas were complemented with a handful of more popular social dramas, *The Cocktail Party* (1950), *The Confidential Clerk* (1954), and *The Elder Statesman* (1959). Though celebrated by critics at the time for their innovative use of verse and their willingness to wrestle with both modern problems and universal themes, the plays have slipped in popularity in recent years. Nevertheless, as fate would have it, Eliot is the posthumous librettist of one of the most successful musicals in the history of British and American theater: his playful children's book *Old Possum's Book of Practical Cats* (1939), light verse written for the enjoyment of his godchildren, was transformed by Andrew Lloyd Webber in 1980 into the smash-hit musical *Cats*.

Eliot's final poetic achievement—and, for many, his greatest—is the set of four poems published together in 1943 as *Four Quartets*. Eliot believed them to be the best of his writing; "The *Four Quartets:* I rest on those," he told an interviewer in 1959. Structurally—though the analogy is a loose one—Eliot modeled the *Quartets* on the late string quartets of Beethoven, especially the last, the A Minor Quartet; as early as 1931 he had written the poet Stephen Spender, "I have the A Minor Quartet on the gramophone, and I find it quite inexhaustible to study. There is a sort of heavenly or at least more than human gaiety about some of his later things which one imagines might come to oneself as the fruit of reconcilliation and relief after immense suffering; I should like to get something of that into verse before I die."

Eliot's last years were brightened by increasing public accolades, including the Nobel Prize in Literature in 1948; he became a very popular speaker on the public lecture circuit, attracting an audience of 15,000, for instance, at a lecture at the University of Minnesota in 1956, later published as *The Frontiers of Criticism*. These public appearances largely took the place of creative writing after 1960. In January 1947 Vivien Eliot died in an institution; a decade later, he married Esme Valery Fletcher, and enjoyed a fulfilling companionate marriage until his death in January 1965. Like Hardy and Yeats, Eliot expressed his wish to be buried in his ancestors' parish church, in his case at East Coker, the home of his ancestor Andrew Eliot; thus, in his death and burial, the opening of his poem *East Coker* is literalized: "In my beginning is my end."

For additional resources on Eliot, go to *The Longman Anthology of British Literature* Web site at www.myliteraturekit.com.

The Love Song of J. Alfred Prufrock

S'io credessi che mia risposta fosse
a persona che mai tornasse al mondo,
questa fiamma staria senza più scosse.

Ma per ciò che giammai di questo fondo
non tornò vivo alcun, s'i'odo il vero,
senza tema d'infamia ti rispondo.[1]

Let us go then, you and I,
When the evening is spread out against the sky
Like a patient etherised upon a table;
Let us go, through certain half-deserted streets,
The muttering retreats
Of restless nights in one-night cheap hotels
And sawdust restaurants with oyster-shells:
Streets that follow like a tedious argument
Of insidious intent
To lead you to an overwhelming question . . .
Oh, do not ask, "What is it?"
Let us go and make our visit.

In the room the women come and go
Talking of Michelangelo.

The yellow fog that rubs its back upon the window-panes,
The yellow smoke that rubs its muzzle on the window-panes,
Licked its tongue into the corners of the evening,
Lingered upon the pools that stand in drains,
Let fall upon its back the soot that falls from chimneys,
Slipped by the terrace, made a sudden leap,
And seeing that it was a soft October night,
Curled once about the house, and fell asleep.

And indeed there will be time
For the yellow smoke that slides along the street
Rubbing its back upon the window-panes;
There will be time, there will be time
To prepare a face to meet the faces that you meet;
There will be time to murder and create,
And time for all the works and days of hands
That lift and drop a question on your plate;
Time for you and time for me,
And time yet for a hundred indecisions,
And for a hundred visions and revisions,
Before the taking of a toast and tea.

In the room the women come and go
Talking of Michelangelo.

And indeed there will be time
To wonder, "Do I dare?" and, "Do I dare?"
Time to turn back and descend the stair,
With a bald spot in the middle of my hair—

1. From Dante's *Inferno* (27.61–66). Dante asks one of the damned souls for its name, and it replies: "If I thought my answer were for one who could return to the world, I would not reply, but as none ever did return alive from this depth, without fear of infamy I answer thee."

(They will say: "How his hair is growing thin!")
My morning coat, my collar mounting firmly to the chin,
My necktie rich and modest, but asserted by a simple pin—
(They will say: "But how his arms and legs are thin!")
Do I dare
Disturb the universe?
In a minute there is time
For decisions and revisions which a minute will reverse.

For I have known them all already, known them all—
Have known the evenings, mornings, afternoons,
I have measured out my life with coffee spoons;
I know the voices dying with a dying fall
Beneath the music from a farther room.
    So how should I presume?

And I have known the eyes already, known them all—
The eyes that fix you in a formulated phrase,
And when I am formulated, sprawling on a pin,
When I am pinned and wriggling on the wall,
Then how should I begin
To spit out all the butt-ends of my days and ways?
    And how should I presume?

And I have known the arms already, known them all—
Arms that are braceleted and white and bare
(But in the lamplight, downed with light brown hair!)
Is it perfume from a dress
That makes me so digress?
Arms that lie along a table, or wrap about a shawl.
    And should I then presume?
    And how should I begin?

. . .

Shall I say, I have gone at dusk through narrow streets
And watched the smoke that rises from the pipes
Of lonely men in shirt-sleeves, leaning out of windows? . . .

I should have been a pair of ragged claws
Scuttling across the floors of silent seas.

. . .

And the afternoon, the evening, sleeps so peacefully!
Smoothed by long fingers,
Asleep . . . tired . . . or it malingers,
Stretched on the floor, here beside you and me.
Should I, after tea and cakes and ices,
Have the strength to force the moment to its crisis?
But though I have wept and fasted, wept and prayed,
Though I have seen my head (grown slightly bald) brought
    in upon a platter,[2]

2. Cf. Matthew 14. John the Baptist was beheaded by Herod and his head was brought to his wife, Herodias, on a platter.

I am no prophet—and here's no great matter;
I have seen the moment of my greatness flicker,
And I have seen the eternal Footman hold my coat, and snicker,
And in short, I was afraid.

And would it have been worth it, after all,
After the cups, the marmalade, the tea,
Among the porcelain, among some talk of you and me,
Would it have been worth while,
To have bitten off the matter with a smile,
To have squeezed the universe into a ball
To roll it towards some overwhelming question,
To say: "I am Lazarus, come from the dead,
Come back to tell you all, I shall tell you all"[3]—
If one, settling a pillow by her head,
  Should say: "That is not what I meant at all.
  That is not it, at all."

And would it have been worth it, after all,
Would it have been worth while,
After the sunsets and the dooryards and the sprinkled streets,
After the novels, after the teacups, after the skirts that trail
  along the floor—
And this, and so much more?—
It is impossible to say just what I mean!
But as if a magic lantern[4] threw the nerves in patterns on a
  screen:
Would it have been worth while
If one, settling a pillow or throwing off a shawl,
And turning toward the window, should say:
  "That is not it at all,
  That is not what I meant, at all."

. . .

No! I am not Prince Hamlet, nor was meant to be;
Am an attendant lord, one that will do
To swell a progress, start a scene or two,
Advise the prince; no doubt, an easy tool,
Deferential, glad to be of use,
Politic, cautious, and meticulous;
Full of high sentence, but a bit obtuse;
At times, indeed, almost ridiculous—
Almost, at times, the Fool.
I grow old . . . I grow old . . .
I shall wear the bottoms of my trousers rolled.

Shall I part my hair behind? Do I dare to eat a peach?
I shall wear white flannel trousers, and walk upon the beach.
I have heard the mermaids singing, each to each.

3. Cf. John 11. Jesus raised Lazurus from the grave after he had been dead four days.

4. A device that employs a candle to project images, rather like a slide projector.

I do not think that they will sing to me.

I have seen them riding seaward on the waves
Combing the white hair of the waves blown back
When the wind blows the water white and black.

We have lingered in the chambers of the sea
By sea-girls wreathed with seaweed red and brown
Till human voices wake us, and we drown.

RESPONSES

Arthur Waugh:[1] *[Cleverness and the New Poetry]*

Cleverness is, indeed, the pitfall of the New Poetry. There is no question about the ingenuity with which its varying moods are exploited, its elaborate symbolism evolved, and its sudden, disconcerting effect exploded upon the imagination. Swift, brilliant images break into the field of vision, scatter like rockets, and leave a trail of flying fire behind. But the general impression is momentary; there are moods and emotions, but no steady current of ideas behind them. Further, in their determination to surprise and even to puzzle at all costs these young poets are continually forgetting that the first essence of poetry is beauty; and that, however much you may have observed the world around you, it is impossible to translate your observation into poetry, without the intervention of the spirit of beauty, controlling the vision, and reanimating the idea.

The temptations of cleverness may be insistent, but its risks are equally great: how great indeed will, perhaps, be best indicated by the example of the "Catholic Anthology," which apparently represents the very newest of all the new poetic movements of the day. This strange little volume bears upon its cover a geometrical device, suggesting that the material within holds the same relation to the art of poetry as the work of the Cubist school hold to the art of painting and design. The product of the volume is mainly American in origin, only one or two of the contributors being of indisputably English birth. But it appears here under the auspices of a house associated with some of the best poetry of the younger generation, and is prefaced by a short lyric by Mr W. B. Yeats, in which that honoured representative of a very different school of inspiration makes bitter fun of scholars and critics, who

> Edit and annotate the lines
> That young men, tossing on their beds,
> Rhymed out in love's despair
> To flatter beauty's ignorant ear.

The reader will not have penetrated far beyond this warning notice before he finds himself in the very stronghold of literary rebellion, if not of anarchy. Mr Orrick Johns may be allowed to speak for his colleagues, as well as for himself:

> This is the song of youth,
> This is the cause of myself;
> I knew my father well and he was a fool,

1. Influential publisher, editor, and critic (1866–1943); father of novelist Evelyn Waugh. The *Catholic Anthology* (1914), which Waugh attacks in this review from the *Quarterly Review* (London), was edited by Ezra Pound and included Eliot's *The Love Song of J. Alfred Prufrock* and printed W. B. Yeats's *The Scholars* as a preface.

Therefore will I have my own foot in the path before I take a step;
I will go only into new lands,
And I will walk on no plank-walks.
The horses of my family are wind-broken,
And the dogs are old,
And the guns rust;
I will make me a new bow from an ash-tree,
And cut up the homestead into arrows.

And Mr Ezra Pound takes up the parable in turn, in the same wooden prose, cut into battens:

Come, my songs, let us express our baser passions.
Let us express our envy for the man with a steady job and no worry about the future.
You are very idle, my songs;
I fear you will come to a bad end.
You stand about the streets. You loiter at the corners and bus-stops,
You do next to nothing at all.
You do not even express our inner nobility,
You will come to a very bad end.
And I? I have gone half cracked.[2]

It is not for his audience to contradict the poet, who for once may be allowed to pronounce his own literary epitaph. But this, it is to be noted, is the "poetry" that was to say nothing that might not be said "actually in life—under emotion,"[3] the sort of emotion that settles down into the banality of a premature decrepitude:

I grow old. . . . I grow old . . .
I shall wear the bottoms of my trousers rolled.
Shall I part my hair behind? Do I dare to eat a peach?
I shall wear white flannel trousers, and walk upon the beach.
I have heard the mermaids singing, each to each.
I do not think that they will sing to me.

Here, surely, is the reduction to absurdity of that school of literary license which, beginning with the declaration "I knew my father well and he was a fool" naturally proceeds to the convenient assumption that everything which seemed wise and true to the father must inevitably be false and foolish to the son. Yet if the fruits of emancipation are to be recognised in the unmetrical, incoherent banalities of these literary "Cubists," the state of Poetry is indeed threatened with anarchy which will end in something worse even than "red ruin and the breaking up of laws." From such a catastrophe the humour, commonsense, and artistic judgment of the best of the new "Georgians" will assuredly save their generation; nevertheless, a hint of warning may not be altogether out of place. It was a classic custom in the family hall, when the feast was at its height, to display a drunken slave among the sons of the household, to the end that they, being ashamed at the ignominious folly of his gesticulations, might determine never to be tempted into such a pitiable condition themselves. The custom had its advantages; for the wisdom of the younger generation was found to be fostered more surely by a single example than by a world of homily and precept.

2. From Pound's *Further Instructions*.

3. Waugh here paraphrases Wordsworth's prescription in the Preface to *Lyrical Ballads*.

Ezra Pound: Drunken Helots and Mr. Eliot[1]

Genius has I know not what peculiar property, its manifestations are various, but however diverse and dissimilar they may be, they have at least one property in common. It makes no difference in what art, in what mode, whether the most conservative, or the most ribald-revolutionary, or the most diffident; if in any land, or upon any floating deck over the ocean, or upon some newly contrapted craft in the aether, genius manifests itself, at once some elderly gentleman has a flux of bile from his liver; at once from the throne or the easy Cowperian[2] sofa, or from the gutter, or from the oeconomical press room there bursts a torrent of elderly words, splenetic, irrelevant, they form themselves instinctively into large phrases denouncing the inordinate product.

This peculiar kind of *rabbia* [madness] might almost be taken as the test of a work of art, mere talent seems incapable of exciting it. "You can't fool me, sir, you're a scoundrel," bawls the testy old gentleman.

Fortunately the days when "that very fiery particle" could be crushed out by the "Quarterly" are over, but it interests me, as an archaeologist, to note that the firm which no longer produces Byron, but rather memoirs, letters of the late Queen, etc., is still running a review, and that this review is still where it was in 1812, or whatever the year was; and that, not having an uneducated Keats to condemn, a certain Mr. Waugh is scolding about Mr. Eliot.[3]

All I can find out, by asking questions concerning Mr. Waugh, is that he is "a very old chap," "a reviewer." From internal evidence we deduce that he is, like the rest of his generation of English *gens-de-lettres* [men of letters], ignorant of Laforgue; of De Régnier's "Odelettes," of his French contemporaries generally, of De Gourmont's "Litanies," of Tristan Corbière, Laurent Tailhade.[4] This is by no means surprising. We are used to it from his "b'ilin'."[5]

However, he outdoes himself, he calls Mr. Eliot a "drunken helot." So called they Anacreon[6] in the days of his predecessors, but from the context in the "Quarterly" article I judge that Mr. Waugh does not intend the phrase as a compliment, he is trying to be abusive, and moreover, he in his limited way has succeeded.

Let us sample the works of the last "Drunken Helot." I shall call my next anthology "Drunken Helots" if I can find a dozen poems written half so well as the following:

[Quotes *Conversation Galante*]

Our helot has a marvellous neatness. There is a comparable finesse in Laforgue's "Votre âme est affaire d'oculiste," but hardly in English verse.

Let us reconsider this drunkenness:

[Quotes *La Figlia Che Piange*]

And since when have helots taken to reading Dante and Marlowe? Since when have helots made a new music, a new refinement, a new method of turning old phrases into

1. Pound replied to Waugh's review in the *Egoist*, June 1917. A "helot" is a serf or slave.
2. After 18th-century poet William Cowper.
3. Pound is invoking the savage review of Keats that appeared in the *Quarterly Review* and was believed by his friends to have hastened Keats's death.
4. A series of French writers and texts that Pound admired. Jules Laforgue (1860–1887) was a French poet who helped develop free verse; he was an important influence on Eliot's early poetry. Henri de Régnier (1864–1936) was a French symbolist poet; Remy de Gourmont (1858–1915) was an influential French poet, novelist, essayist, publisher, and literary critic; Tristan Corbière, pseudonym for Édouard Joachim Corbière (1854–1919), was a French poet who worked with common speech and slang; and Laurent Tailhade (1854–1919) was a satiric French poet.
5. Byline, identifying the author of a newspaper article.
6. Greek writer of love poems and drinking songs.

new by their aptness? However the "Quarterly," the century old, the venerable, the praeclarus,[7] the voice of Gehova[8] and Co., Sinai and 51A Albemarle Street, London, W. 1, has pronounced this author a helot. They are all for an aristocracy made up of, possibly, Tennyson, Southey and Wordsworth, the flunkey, the dull and the duller. Let us sup with the helots. Or perhaps the good Waugh is a wag,[9] perhaps he hears with the haspirate[1] and wishes to pun on Mr. Heliot's name: a bright bit of syzygy.[2]

I confess his type of mind puzzles me, there is no telling what he is up to.

I do not wish to misjudge him, this theory may be the correct one. You never can tell when old gentlemen grow facetious. He does not mention Mr. Eliot's name; he merely takes his lines and abuses them. The artful dodger,[3] he didn't (*sotto voce*[4]) "he didn't want 'people' to know that Mr. Eliot was a poet".

The poem he chooses for malediction is the title poem, "Prufrock." It is too long to quote entire.

[Quotes portion of *Prufrock*]

Let us leave the silly old Waugh. Mr. Eliot has made an advance on Browning. He has also made his dramatis personae contemporary and convincing. He has been an individual in his poems. I have read the contents of this book over and over, and with continued joy in the freshness, the humanity, the deep quiet culture. "I have tried to write of a few things that really have moved me" is so far as I know, the sum of Mr. Eliot's "poetic theory." His practice has been a distinctive cadence, a personal modus of arrangement, remote origins in Elizabethan English and in the modern French masters, neither origin being sufficiently apparent to affect the personal quality. It is writing without pretence. Mr. Eliot at once takes rank with the five or six living poets whose English one can read with enjoyment.

The "Egoist" has published the best prose writer of my generation. It follows its publication of Joyce by the publication of a "new" poet who is at least unsurpassed by any of his contemporaries, either of his own age or his elders.

It is perhaps "unenglish" to praise a poet whom one can read with enjoyment. Carlyle's generation wanted "improving" literature, Smile's "Self-Help"[5] and the rest of it. Mr. Waugh dates back to that generation, the virus is in his blood, he can't help it. The exactitude of the younger generation gets on his nerves, and so on and so on. He will "fall into line in time" like the rest of the bread-and-butter reviewers. Intelligent people will read "J. Alfred Prufrock"; they will wait with some eagerness for Mr. Eliot's further inspirations. It is 7.30 p.m. I have had nothing alcoholic to-day, nor yet yesterday. I said the same sort of thing about James Joyce's prose over two years ago. I am now basking in the echoes. Only a half-caste rag for the propagation of garden suburbs, and a local gazette in Rochester, N.Y., U.S.A., are left whining in opposition. ***

However, let us leave these bickerings, this stench of the printing-press, weekly and quarterly, let us return to the gardens of the Muses,

Till human voices wake us and we drown,

7. Preeminent.
8. Jehovah.
9. Joker.
1. To aspirate is to add the "h" sound to the begining of a word: thus Eliot becomes "Hel[i]ot."
2. Any two related things (either similar or opposite).
3. The Artful Dodger is the name of Fagan's favorite pickpocket in Dickens's *Oliver Twist*.
4. In a low voice.
5. Samuel Smiles's *Self-Help* (1859) preached the Victorian gospel of self-improvement.

as Eliot has written in conclusion to the poem which the "Quarterly" calls the *reductio ad absurdum*:[6]

> I have seen them riding seaward on the waves
> Combing the white hair of the waves blown back
> When the wind blows the water white and black.
> We have lingered in the chambers of the sea
> By sea-girls wreathed with seaweed red and brown
> Till human voices wake us, and we drown.

The poetic mind leaps the gulf from the exterior world, the trivialities of Mr. Prufrock, diffident, ridiculous, in the drawing-room, Mr. Apollinax's laughter "submarine and profound" transports him from the desiccated new-statesmanly atmosphere of Professor Canning-Cheetah's. Mr. Eliot's melody rushes out like the thought of Fragilion "among the birch-trees."[7] Mr. Waugh is my bitten macaroon at this festival.

Gerontion[1]

Thou hast nor youth nor age
But as it were an after dinner sleep
Dreaming of both.[2]

Here I am, an old man in a dry month,
Being read to by a boy, waiting for rain.
I was neither at the hot gates
Nor fought in the warm rain
Nor knee deep in the salt marsh, heaving a cutlass,
Bitten by flies, fought.
My house is a decayed house,
And the Jew squats on the window sill, the owner,
Spawned in some estaminet° of Antwerp, *café*
Blistered in Brussels, patched and peeled in London.
The goat coughs at night in the field overhead;
Rocks, moss, stonecrop, iron, merds.° *droppings, shit*
The woman keeps the kitchen, makes tea,
Sneezes at evening, poking the peevish gutter.
I an old man,
A dull head among windy spaces.

Signs are taken for wonders. "We would see a sign!"[3]
The word within a word, unable to speak a word,

6. Reduction to absurdity (Latin), the rhetorical technique of pushing the consequences of an idea to the point where it looks ridiculous.

7. The names and images in this sentence not taken from *Prufrock* are from another of Eliot's early poems, Mr. *Apollinax*. The poem ends with the lines, "Of dowager Mrs. Phlaccus, and Professor and Mrs. Cheetah / I remember a slice of lemon, and a bitten macaroon."

1. From the Greek word meaning "old man." While still working on what was to become *The Waste Land*, Eliot had considered printing *Gerontion* as a kind of prelude; Pound disapproved of the idea, and it was dropped.

2. Loosely quoted from Shakespeare's *Measure for Measure* (3.1.32–34).

3. Eliot here echoes the sermon by Anglican theologican Lancelot Andrewes (1555–1626) on Matthew: "An evil and adulterous generation seeketh after a sign; and there shall no sign be given to it, but the sign of the prophet Jonas." (Matthew 12.39).

Swaddled with darkness. In the juvescence° of the year *youth*
Came Christ the tiger

In depraved May, dogwood and chestnut, flowering judas,[4]
To be eaten, to be divided, to be drunk
Among whispers; by Mr. Silvero
With caressing hands, at Limoges[5]
Who walked all night in the next room;
By Hakagawa, bowing among the Titians;[6]
By Madame de Tornquist, in the dark room
Shifting the candles; Fräulein von Kulp
Who turned in the hall, one hand on the door.
Vacant shuttles
Weave the wind. I have no ghosts,
An old man in a draughty house
Under a windy knob.

After such knowledge, what forgiveness? Think now
History has many cunning passages, contrived corridors
And issues, deceives with whispering ambitions,
Guides us by vanities. Think now
She gives when our attention is distracted
And what she gives, gives with such supple confusions
That the giving famishes the craving. Gives too late
What's not believed in, or is still believed,
In memory only, reconsidered passion. Gives too soon
Into weak hands, what's thought can be dispensed with
Till the refusal propagates a fear. Think
Neither fear nor courage saves us. Unnatural vices
Are fathered by our heroism. Virtues
Are forced upon us by our impudent crimes.
These tears are shaken from the wrath-bearing tree.

The tiger springs in the new year. Us he devours. Think at last
We have not reached conclusion, when I
Stiffen in a rented house. Think at last
I have not made this show purposelessly
And it is not by any concitation° *stirring up*
Of the backward devils.
I would meet you upon this honestly.
I that was near your heart was removed therefrom
To lose beauty in terror, terror in inquisition.
I have lost my passion: why should I need to keep it
Since what is kept must be adulterated?
I have lost my sight, smell, hearing, taste and touch:
How should I use them for your closer contact?

4. A flowering shrub-tree, named after Judas Iscariot; according to legend, Judas hanged himself on this type of tree after betraying Jesus.

5. City in France; home of fine china of the same name.

6. Painter of the Italian Renaissance (1477–1576) known for his female nudes.

These with a thousand small deliberations
Protract the profit of their chilled delirium,
Excite the membrane, when the sense has cooled,
With pungent sauces, multiply variety
In a wilderness of mirrors. What will the spider do,
Suspend its operations, will the weevil
Delay? De Bailhache, Fresca, Mrs. Cammel, whirled
Beyond the circuit of the shuddering Bear[7]
In fractured atoms. Gull against the wind, in the windy straits
Of Belle Isle,[8] or running on the Horn.[9]
White feathers in the snow, the Gulf claims,
And an old man driven by the Trades[1]
To a sleepy corner.

Tenants of the house,
Thoughts of a dry brain in a dry season.

The Waste Land Like Conrad's *Heart of Darkness*—from which Eliot had originally planned to take his epigraph, "The horror! the horror!"—*The Waste Land* has become part of the symbolic landscape of twentieth-century Western culture; the text, like Conrad's, has been appropriated by commentators high and low, left and right, as an especially apt description of the psychosocial and interpersonal malaise of modern Europeans. Late in 1921 Eliot, who was suffering under a number of pressures both personal and artistic, took three months' leave from his job at Lloyd's Bank and went for a "rest cure" at a clinic in Lausanne, Switzerland. On his way he passed through Paris and showed the manuscript of the poem—really manuscripts of a number of fragments, whose interrelationship Eliot was trying to work out—to Ezra Pound; Pound and Eliot went through the poem again as Eliot returned to London in January 1922. Pound's editorial work was considerable, as the facsimile edition of the draft reveals; Pound said that he performed the poem's "caesarian operation," and Eliot dedicated *The Waste Land* to Pound—*il miglior fabbro* ("the better craftsman," a phrase from Dante).

The most obvious feature of *The Waste Land* is its difficulty. Eliot was perhaps the first poet and literary critic to argue that such "difficulty" was not just a necessary evil but in fact a constitutive element of poetry that would come to terms with the modern world. In his review of a volume of metaphysical poetry, Eliot implicitly links the complex poetry of Donne and Marvell with the task of the modern poet: "We can only say that it appears likely that poets in our civilization, as it exists at present, must be *difficult*. Our civilization comprehends great variety and complexity, and this variety and complexity, playing upon a refined sensibility, must produce various and complex results." In the case of *The Waste Land,* the difficulty lies primarily in the poem's dense tissue of quotations from and allusions to other texts; as Eliot's own footnotes to the poem demonstrate, the poem draws its strength, and achieves a kind of universality, by making implicit and explicit reference to texts as widely different as Ovid's *Metamorphoses* and a World War I Australian marching song.

Beyond the density of the poem's quotations and allusions, Eliot hoped to suggest the possibilty of an order beneath the chaos. In his review of Joyce's *Ulysses* (published in November 1923) Eliot was to describe the "mythical method," deploying allusions to classical mythology to suggest an

7. The constellation Ursa Major, also called the Great Bear or Big Dipper.
8. The passage between Newfoundland and southern Labrador.
9. Cape Horn, the southernmost point of South America.
1. The trade winds, nearly constant tropical winds.

implicit (and recurring) order beneath contemporary history; and while his use of myth was not so methodical as Joyce's, his use of vegetation myth and romance structures points outside the world of the poem to "another world," where the brokenness of the waste land might be healed. At the time of writing the poem, however, Eliot could not see clearly where that healing might come from.

The Waste Land[1]

"Nam Sibyllam quidem Cumis ego ipse oculis meis vidi in ampulla pendere, et cum illi pueri dicerent: Σίβυλλα τί θέλεις; respondebat illa: ἀποθανειν θέλω."[2]

FOR EZRA POUND
il miglior fabbro.

I. THE BURIAL OF THE DEAD

April is the cruellest month, breeding
Lilacs out of the dead land, mixing
Memory and desire, stirring
Dull roots with spring rain.
Winter kept us warm, covering
Earth in forgetful snow, feeding
A little life with dried tubers.
Summer surprised us, coming over the Starnbergersee[3]
With a shower of rain; we stopped in the colonnade,
And went on in sunlight, into the Hofgarten,[4]
And drank coffee, and talked for an hour.
Bin gar keine Russin, stamm' aus Litauen, echt deutsch.[5]
And when we were children, staying at the arch-duke's,
My cousin's, he took me out on a sled,
And I was frightened. He said, Marie,
Marie, hold on tight. And down we went.
In the mountains, there you feel free.
I read, much of the night, and go south in the winter.

What are the roots that clutch, what branches grow
Out of this stony rubbish? Son of man,[6]
You cannot say, or guess, for you know only

1. Not only the title, but the plan and a good deal of the incidental symbolism of the poem were suggested by Miss Jessie L. Weston's book on the Grail legend: *From Ritual to Romance* (Cambridge). Indeed, so deeply am I indebted, Miss Weston's book will elucidate the difficulties of the poem much better than my notes can do; and I recommend it (apart from the great interest of the book itself) to any who think such elucidation of the poem worth the trouble. To another work of anthropology I am indebted in general, one which has influenced our generation profoundly; I mean *The Golden Bough;* I have used especially the two volumes *Adonis, Attis, Osiris.* Anyone who is acquainted with these works will immediately recognize in the poem certain references to vegetation ceremonies [Eliot's note]. Sir James Frazer (1854–1941) brought out the 12 volumes of *The Golden Bough,* a vast work of anthropology and comparative mythology and religion, between 1890 and 1915, with a supplement published in 1936.

2. From the *Satyricon* of Petronius (first century A.D.). "For once I myself saw with my own eyes the Sybil at Cumae hanging in a cage, and when the boys said to her, 'Sybil, what do you want?' she replied, 'I want to die.'" The Sybil was granted anything she wished by Apollo, if only she would be his; she made the mistake of asking for everlasting life, without asking for eternal youth.

3. A lake near Munich.

4. A public park in Munich, with a zoo and cafés.

5. I'm not a Russian at all; I come from Lithuania, a true German (German).

6. Cf. Ezekiel 2.1 [Eliot's note]. Line 20. Ezekiel 2.1 reads: "But thou, son of man, hear what I say unto thee; Be not thou rebellious like that rebellious house: open thy mouth, and eat that I give thee."

A heap of broken images, where the sun beats,
And the dead tree gives no shelter, the cricket no relief,[7]
And the dry stone no sound of water. Only
There is shadow under this red rock,
(Come in under the shadow of this red rock),
And I will show you something different from either
Your shadow at morning striding behind you
Or your shadow at evening rising to meet you;
I will show you fear in a handful of dust.
Frisch weht der Wind
Der Heimat zu
Mein Irisch Kind,
Wo weilest du?[8]
"You gave me hyacinths first a year ago;
They called me the hyacinth girl."
—Yet when we came back, late, from the hyacinth garden,
Your arms full, and your hair wet, I could not
Speak, and my eyes failed, I was neither
Living nor dead, and I knew nothing,
Looking into the heart of light, the silence.
Oed' und leer das Meer.[9]

Madame Sosostris, famous clairvoyante,
Had a bad cold, nevertheless
Is known to be the wisest woman in Europe,
With a wicked pack of cards.[1] Here, said she,
Is your card, the drowned Phoenician Sailor,
(Those are pearls that were his eyes.[2] Look!)
Here is Belladonna, the Lady of the Rocks,
The lady of situations.
Here is the man with three staves, and here the Wheel,
And here is the one-eyed merchant, and this card,
Which is blank, is something he carries on his back,
Which I am forbidden to see. I do not find
The Hanged Man.[3] Fear death by water.
I see crowds of people, walking round in a ring.

7. Cf. Ecclesiastes 12.5 [Eliot's note]. "They shall be afraid of that which is high, and fears shall be in the way, and the almond tree shall flourish, and the grasshopper shall be a burden, and desire shall fail."

8. *V. Tristan and Isolde*, i, verses 5–8 [Eliot's note]. In Wagner's opera, Tristan sings this about Isolde, the woman he is leaving behind as he sails for home: "Fresh blows the wind to the homeland; my Irish child, where are you waiting?"

9. Id. iii, verse 24 [Eliot's note]. Tristan is dying and waiting for Isolde to come to him, but a shepherd, whom Tristan has hired to keep watch for her ship, reports only "Desolate and empty the sea."

1. I am not familiar with the exact constitution of the Tarot pack of cards, from which I have obviously departed to suit my own convenience. The Hanged Man, a member of the traditional pack, fits my purpose in two ways: because he is associated in my mind with the Hanged God of Frazer, and because I associated him with the hooded figure in the passage of the disciples to Emmaus in Part V. The Phoenician Sailor and the Merchant appear later; also the "crowds of people," and Death by Water is executed in Part IV. The Man with Three Staves (an authentic member of the Tarot pack) I associate, quite arbitrarily, with the Fisher King Himself [Eliot's note].

2. From Ariel's song, in Shakespeare's *The Tempest:* "Full fathom five thy father lies; / Of his bones are coral made; / Those are pearls that were his eyes: / Nothing of him that doth fade, / But doth suffer a sea-change" (1.2.399–403).

3. The tarot card that depicts a man hanging by one foot from a cross.

Thank you. If you see dear Mrs. Equitone,
Tell her I bring the horoscope myself:
One must be so careful these days.

Unreal City,[4]
Under the brown fog of a winter dawn,
A crowd flowed over London Bridge, so many,
I had not thought death had undone so many.[5]
Sighs, short and infrequent, were exhaled,[6]
And each man fixed his eyes before his feet.
Flowed up the hill and down King William Street,
To where Saint Mary Woolnoth kept the hours
With a dead sound on the final stroke of nine.[7]
There I saw one I knew, and stopped him, crying: "Stetson!
You who were with me in the ships at Mylae![8]
That corpse you planted last year in your garden,
Has it begun to sprout? Will it bloom this year?
Or has the sudden frost disturbed its bed?
O keep the Dog far hence, that's friend to men,[9]
Or with his nails he'll dig it up again!
You! hypocrite lecteur!—mon semblable,—mon frère!"[1]

II. A Game of Chess[2]

The Chair she sat in, like a burnished throne,[3]
Glowed on the marble, where the glass
Held up by standards wrought with fruited vines
From which a golden Cupidon peeped out
(Another hid his eyes behind his wing)
Doubled the flames of sevenbranched candelabra
Reflecting light upon the table as
The glitter of her jewels rose to meet it,
From satin cases poured in rich profusion.
In vials of ivory and coloured glass
Unstoppered, lurked her strange synthetic perfumes,
Unguent, powdered, or liquid—troubled, confused
And drowned the sense in odours; stirred by the air
That freshened from the window, these ascended
In fattening the prolonged candle-flames,

4. Cf. Baudelaire: "Fourmillante cité, cité pleine de rêves, / Où le spectre en plein jour raccroche le passant" [Eliot's note].
5. Cf. *Inferno*, iii.55–7: "si lunga tratta / di gente, ch'io non avrei mai creduto / che morte tanta n'avesse disfatta" [Eliot's note]. "Such an endless train, / Of people, it never would have entered in my head / There were so many men whom death had slain."
6. Cf. *Inferno*, iv. 25–7: "Ouivi, secondo che per ascoltare, / non avea pianto, ma' che di sospiri, / che l'aura eterna facevan tremare" [Eliot's note]. "We heard no loud complaint, no crying there, / No sound of grief except the sound of sighing / Quivering forever through the eternal air."
7. A phenomenon which I have often noticed [Eliot's note].
8. The Battle of Mylae (260 B.C.E.) in the First Punic War.
9. Cf. the Dirge in Webster's *White Devil* [Eliot's note].
1. V. Baudelaire, Preface to *Fleurs du Mal* [Eliot's note]. "Hypocrite reader—my double—my brother!"
2. Cf. Thomas Middleton's drama A *Game at Chess* (1625), a political satire.
3. Cf. *Antony and Cleopatra*, II. ii. 190 [Eliot's note].

Flung their smoke into the laquearia,[4]
Stirring the pattern on the coffered ceiling.
Huge sea-wood fed with copper
Burned green and orange, framed by the coloured stone,
In which sad light a carvèd dolphin swam.
Above the antique mantel was displayed
As though a window gave upon the sylvan scene[5]
The change of Philomel, by the barbarous king[6]
So rudely forced; yet there the nightingale[7]
Filled all the desert with inviolable voice
And still she cried, and still the world pursues,
"Jug Jug" to dirty ears.
And other withered stumps of time
Were told upon the walls; staring forms
Leaned out, leaning, hushing the room enclosed.
Footsteps shuffled on the stair.
Under the firelight, under the brush, her hair
Spread out in fiery points
Glowed into words, then would be savagely still.

"My nerves are bad to-night. Yes, bad. Stay with me.
Speak to me. Why do you never speak. Speak.
  What are you thinking of? What thinking? What?
I never know what you are thinking. Think."

I think we are in rats' alley[8]
Where the dead men lost their bones.

"What is that noise?"
                                The wind under the door.[9]
"What is that noise now? What is the wind doing?"
                                Nothing again nothing.
                                                                  "Do
"You know nothing? Do you see nothing? Do you remember
Nothing?"
I remember
Those are pearls that were his eyes.
"Are you alive, or not? Is there nothing in your head?"[1]
                                                                  But

4. "Laquearia. V. *Aeneid*, I.726: "dependent lychni laquearibus aureis / incensi, et noctem flammis funalia vincunt" [Eliot's note]. "Burning lamps hang from the gold-panelled ceiling / And torches dispel the night with their flames"; a *laquearia* is a panelled ceiling. The passage from Virgil's *Aeneid* describes the banquet given by Dido for her lover Aeneas.

5. "Sylvan scene. V. Milton, *Paradise Lost*, iv. 140 [Eliot's note]. "And over head up grew / Insuperable height of loftiest shade, / Cedar, and Pine, and Fir, and branching Palm, / A Silvan Scene, and as the ranks ascend / Shade above shade, a woody Theatre / Of stateliest view" The passage describes the Garden of Eden, as seen through Satan's eyes.

6. V. Ovid, *Metamorphoses*, vi, Philomela [Eliot's note]. Philomela was raped by King Tereus, her sister's husband, and was then changed into a nightingale.

7. Cf. Part III, 1. 204 [Eliot's note].

8. Cf. Part III, 1. 195 [Eliot's note].

9. Cf. Webster: "Is the wind in that door still?" [Eliot's note]. From John Webster's *The Devil's Law Case*, 3.2.162. The doctor asks this question when he discovers that a "murder victim" is still breathing.

1. Cf. Part I, 1. 37, 48 [Eliot's note].

O O O O that Shakespeherian Rag—[2]
It's so elegant
So intelligent
"What shall I do now? What shall I do?"
"I shall rush out as I am, and walk the street
With my hair down, so. What shall we do tomorrow?
What shall we ever do?"
The hot water at ten.
And if it rains, a closed car at four.
And we shall play a game of chess,
Pressing lidless eyes and waiting for a knock upon the door.[3]

When Lil's husband got demobbed,° I said— *demobilized*
I didn't mince my words, I said to her myself,
HURRY UP PLEASE ITS TIME[4]
Now Albert's coming back, make yourself a bit smart.
He'll want to know what you done with that money he gave you
To get yourself some teeth. He did, I was there.
You have them all out, Lil, and get a nice set,
He said, I swear, I can't bear to look at you.
And no more can't I, I said, and think of poor Albert,
He's been in the army four years, he wants a good time,
And if you don't give it him, there's others will, I said.
Oh is there, she said. Something o' that, I said.
Then I'll know who to thank, she said, and give me a straight look.
HURRY UP PLEASE ITS TIME
If you don't like it you can get on with it, I said.
Others can pick and choose if you can't.
But if Albert makes off, it won't be for lack of telling.
You ought to be ashamed, I said, to look so antique.
(And her only thirty-one.)
I can't help it, she said, pulling a long face,
It's them pills I took, to bring it off, she said.
(She's had five already, and nearly died of young George.)
The chemist[5] said it would be all right, but I've never been the same.
You *are* a proper fool, I said.
Well, if Albert won't leave you alone, there it is, I said,
What you get married for if you don't want children?
HURRY UP PLEASE ITS TIME
Well, that Sunday Albert was home, they had a hot gammon,° *ham*
And they asked me in to dinner, to get the beauty of it hot—
HURRY UP PLEASE ITS TIME
HURRY UP PLEASE ITS TIME
Goonight Bill. Goonight Lou. Goonight May. Goonight.

2. Quoting an American ragtime song featured in Ziegfield's Follies of 1912.
3. Cf. the game of chess in Middleton's *Women beware Women* [Eliot's note].
4. A British pub-keeper's call for a last round before closing.
5. Pharmacist.

Ta ta. Goonight. Goonight.
Good night, ladies, good night, sweet ladies, good night, good night.[6]

III. The Fire Sermon

The river's tent is broken; the last fingers of leaf
Clutch and sink into the wet bank. The wind
Crosses the brown land, unheard. The nymphs are departed.
Sweet Thames, run softly, till I end my song.[7]
The river bears no empty bottles, sandwich papers,
Silk handkerchiefs, cardboard boxes, cigarette ends
Or other testimony of summer nights. The nymphs are departed.
And their friends, the loitering heirs of City directors;
Departed, have left no addresses.
By the waters of Leman[8] I sat down and wept . . .
Sweet Thames, run softly till I end my song,
Sweet Thames, run softly, for I speak not loud or long.
But at my back in a cold blast I hear
The rattle of the bones, and chuckle spread from ear to ear.

A rat crept softly through the vegetation
Dragging its slimy belly on the bank
While I was fishing in the dull canal
On a winter evening round behind the gashouse
Musing upon the king my brother's wreck
And on the king my father's death before him.[9]
White bodies naked on the low damp ground
And bones cast in a little low dry garret,
Rattled by the rat's foot only, year to year.
But at my back from time to time I hear[1]
The sound of horns and motors, which shall bring[2]
Sweeney to Mrs. Porter in the spring.
O the moon shone bright on Mrs. Porter[3]
And on her daughter
They wash their feet in soda water
Et O ces voix d'enfants, chantant dans la coupole![4]

Twit twit twit
Jug jug jug jug jug jug

6. Ophelia speaks these words in Shakespeare's *Hamlet*, and they are understood by the King as certain evidence of her insanity: "Good night ladies, good night. Sweet ladies, good night, good night" (4.5.72–73).
7. V. Spenser, *Prothalamion* [Eliot's note]; Spenser's poem (1596) celebrates the double marriage of Lady Elizabeth and Lady Katherine Somerset.
8. Lake Geneva. The line echoes Psalm 137, in which, exiled in Babylon, the Hebrew poets are too full of grief to sing.
9. Cf. *The Tempest*, I. ii [Eliot's note].
1. Cf. Marvell, *To His Coy Mistress* [Eliot's note]. "But at my back I always hear / Time's wingéd chariot hurrying near."
2. Cf. Day, *Parliament of Bees:* "When of the sudden, listening, you shall hear, / A noise of horns and hunting, which shall bring / Actaeon to Diana in the spring, / Where all shall see her naked skin . . . " [Eliot's note].
3. I do not know the origin of the ballad from which these are taken: it was reported to me from Sydney, Australia [Eliot's note]. Sung by Australian soldiers in World War I: "O the moon shone bright on Mrs. Porter / And on the daughter / Of Mrs. Porter / They wash their feet in soda water / And so they oughter / To keep them clean."
4. V. Verlaine, *Parsifal* [Eliot's note]. "And O those children's voices singing in the dome." Paul Verlaine's sonnet describes Parsifal, who keeps himself pure in hopes of seeing the holy grail, and has his feet washed before entering the castle.

So rudely forc'd.
Tereu

Unreal City
Under the brown fog of a winter noon
Mr. Eugenides, the Smyrna[5] merchant
Unshaven, with a pocket full of currants
C.i.f.[6] London: documents at sight,
Asked me in demotic° French *vulgar*
To luncheon at the Cannon Street Hotel[7]
Followed by a weekend at the Metropole.[8]

At the violet hour, when the eyes and back
Turn upward from the desk, when the human engine waits
Like a taxi throbbing waiting,
I Tiresias,[9] though blind, throbbing between two lives,
Old man with wrinkled female breasts, can see
At the violet hour, the evening hour that strives
Homeward, and brings the sailor home from sea,[1]
The typist home at teatime, clears her breakfast, lights
Her stove, and lays out food in tins.
Out of the window perilously spread
Her drying combinations touched by the sun's last rays,
On the divan are piled (at night her bed)
Stockings, slippers, camisoles, and stays.
I Tiresias, old man with wrinkled dugs
Perceived the scene, and foretold the rest—
I too awaited the expected guest.

5. Seaport in western Turkey.

6. The currants were quoted at a price "carriage and insurance free to London"; and the Bill of Lading, etc., were to be handed to the buyer upon payment of the sight draft [Eliot's note].

7. A Hotel in London near the train station used for travel to and from continental Europe.

8. An upscale seaside resort hotel in Brighton.

9. Tiresias, although a mere spectator and not indeed a "character," is yet the most important personage in the poem, uniting all the rest. Just as the one-eyed merchant, seller of currants, melts into the Phoenician Sailor, and the latter is not wholly distinct from Ferdinand Prince of Naples, so all the women are one woman, and the two sexes meet in Tiresias. What Tiresias *sees*, in fact, is the substance of the poem. The whole passage from Ovid is of great anthropological interest: ". . . Cum Iunone iocos et 'maior vestra profecto est / Quam, quae contingit maribus,' dixisse, 'voluptas.' / Illa negat; placuit quae sit sententia docti / Quaerere Tiresiae: venus huic erat utraque nota. / Nam duo magnorum viridi coeuntia silva / Corpora serpentum baculi violaverat ictu / Deque viro factus, mirabile, femina septem / Egerat autumnos; octavo rursus eosdem / Vidit et 'est vestrae si tanta potentia plagae,' / Dixit 'ut auctoris sortem in contraria mutet, / Nunc quoque vos feriam!' percussis anguibus isdem / Forma prior rediit genetivaque venit imago. / Arbiter hic igitur sumptus de lite iocosa / Dicta Iovis firmat; gravius Saturnia iusto / Nec pro materia fertur doluisse suique / Iudicis aeterna damnavit lumina nocte, / At pater omnipotens (neque enim licet inrita cuiquam / Facta dei fecisse deo) pro lumine adempto / Scire futura dedit poenamque levavit honore" [Eliot's note]. This passage from Ovid's *Metamorphoses* describes Tiresias's sex change: "[The story goes that once Jove, having drunk a great deal,] jested with Juno. He said, 'Your pleasure in love is really greater than that enjoyed by men.' She denied it; so they decided to seek the opinion of the wise Tiresias, for he knew both aspects of love. For once, with a blow of his staff, he had committed violence on two huge snakes as they copulated in the green forest; and—wonderful to tell—was turned from a man into a woman and thus spent seven years. In the eighth year he saw the same snakes again and said: 'If a blow struck at you is so powerful that it changes the sex of the giver, I will now strike at you again.' With these words he struck the snakes, and his former shape was restored to him and he became as he had been born. So he was appointed arbitrator in the playful quarrel, and supported Jove's statement. It is said that Saturnia [i.e., Juno] was quite disproportionately upset, and condemned the arbitrator to perpetual blindness. But the almighty father (for no god may undo what has been done by another god), in return for the sight that was taken away, gave him the power to know the future and so lightened the penalty paid by the honor."

1. This may not appear as exact as Sappho's lines but I had in mind the "longshore" or "dory" fisherman, who returns at nightfall [Eliot's note]. "Hesperus, thou bringst home all things bright morning scattered: thou bringest the sheep, the goat, the child to the mother."

He, the young man carbuncular,° arrives, *pimply*
A small house agent's clerk, with one bold stare,
One of the low on whom assurance sits
As a silk hat on a Bradford[2] millionaire.
The time is now propitious, as he guesses,
The meal is ended, she is bored and tired,
Endeavours to engage her in caresses
Which still are unreproved, if undesired.
Flushed and decided, he assaults at once;
Exploring hands encounter no defence;
His vanity requires no response,
And makes a welcome of indifference.
(And I Tiresias have foresuffered all
Enacted on this same divan or bed;
I who have sat by Thebes below the wall
And walked among the lowest of the dead.)
Bestows one final patronising kiss,
And gropes his way, finding the stairs unlit . . .

She turns and looks a moment in the glass,
Hardly aware of her departed lover;
Her brain allows one half-formed thought to pass:
"Well now that's done: and I'm glad it's over."
When lovely woman stoops to folly and[3]
Paces about her room again, alone,
She smoothes her hair with automatic hand,
And puts a record on the gramophone.

"This music crept by me upon the waters"[4]
And along the Strand, up Queen Victoria Street.
O City city, I can sometimes hear
Beside a public bar in Lower Thames Street,
The pleasant whining of a mandoline
And a clatter and a chatter from within
Where fishmen lounge at noon: where the walls
Of Magnus Martyr[5] hold
Inexplicable splendour of Ionian white and gold.

The river sweats[6]
Oil and tar

2. An industrial town in Yorkshire; many of its residents became wealthy during World War I.

3. V. Goldsmith, the song in *The Vicar of Wakefield* [Eliot's note]. Oliver Goldsmith's character Olivia, on returning to the place where she was seduced, sings, "When lovely woman stoops to folly / And finds too late that men betray / What charm can soothe her melancholy, / What art can wash her guilt away? / The only art her guilt to cover, / To hide her shame from every eye, / To give repentance to her lover / And wring his bosom—is to die."

4. V. *The Tempest*, as above [Eliot's note].

5. The interior of St. Magnus Martyr is to my mind one of the finest among Wren's interiors. See *The Proposed Demolition of Nineteen City Churches* (P.S. King & Son, Ltd.) [Eliot's note].

6. The Song of the (three) Thames-daughters begins here. From line 292 to 306 inclusive they speak in turn. V. *Gotterdammerung*, III.I: the Rhine-daughters [Eliot's note]. In Richard Wagner's opera, *Twilight of the Gods*, the Rhine maidens, when their gold is stolen, lament that the beauty of the river is gone.

The barges drift
With the turning tide
Red sails
Wide
To leeward, swing on the heavy spar.
The barges wash
Drifting logs
Down Greenwich reach
Past the Isle of Dogs.[7]
        Weialala leia
        Wallala leialala

Elizabeth and Leicester[8]
Beating oars
The stern was formed
A gilded shell
Red and gold
The brisk swell
Rippled both shores
Southwest wind
Carried down stream
The peal of bells
White towers
        Weialala leia
        Wallala leialala

"Trams and dusty trees.
Highbury bore me. Richmond and Kew[9]
Undid me. By Richmond I raised my knees
Supine on the floor of a narrow canoe."

"My feet are at Moorgate,[1] and my heart
Under my feet. After the event
He wept. He promised 'a new start.'
I made no comment. What should I resent?"

"On Margate Sands.[2]
I can connect
Nothing with nothing.
The broken fingernails of dirty hands.
My people humble people who expect
Nothing."

7. Greenwich is a borough on the south bank of the River Thames; the Isle of Dogs is a peninsula in East London formed by a sharp bend in the Thames called Greenwich Reach.

8. V. Froude, *Elizabeth*, vol. I, Ch. iv, letter of De Quadra to Philip of Spain: "In the afternoon we were in a barge, watching the games on the river. (The Queen) was alone with Lord Robert and myself on the poop, when they began to talk nonsense, and went so far that Lord Robert at last said, as I was on the spot there was no reason why they should not be married if the queen pleased" [Eliot's note].

9. "Cf. *Purgatorio*, V. 133: "Ricorditi di me, che son la Pia; / Siena mi fe', disfecemi Maremma." [Eliot's note]. "Remember me, that I am called Piety; / Sienna made me and Maremma undid me." Highbury, Richmond, and Kew are suburbs of London near the Thames.

1. A slum in East London.

2. A seaside resort in the Thames estuary.

la la
To Carthage then I came[3]

Burning burning burning burning[4]
O Lord Thou pluckest me out[5]
O Lord Thou pluckest

burning

IV. Death by Water

Phlebas the Phoenician, a fortnight dead,
Forgot the cry of gulls, and the deep sea swell
And the profit and loss.
A current under sea
Picked his bones in whispers. As he rose and fell
He passed the stages of his age and youth
Entering the whirlpool.
Gentile or Jew
O you who turn the wheel and look to windward,
Consider Phlebas, who was once handsome and tall as you.

V. What the Thunder Said[6]

After the torchlight red on sweaty faces
After the frosty silence in the gardens
After the agony in stony places
The shouting and the crying
Prison and palace and reverberation
Of thunder of spring over distant mountains
He who was living is now dead
We who were living are now dying
With a little patience

Here is no water but only rock
Rock and no water and the sandy road
The road winding above among the mountains
Which are mountains of rock without water
If there were water we should stop and drink
Amongst the rock one cannot stop or think
Sweat is dry and feet are in the sand
If there were only water amongst the rock
Dead mountain mouth of carious° teeth that cannot spit *rotting*
Here one can neither stand nor lie nor sit

3. V. St. Augustine's *Confessions:* "to Carthage then I came, where a cauldron of unholy loves sang all about mine ears" [Eliot's note].
4. The complete text of the Buddha's Fire Sermon (which corresponds in importance to the Sermon on the Mount) from which these words are taken, will be found translated in the late Henry Clarke Warren's *Buddhism in Translation* (Harvard Oriental Series). Mr. Warren was one of the great pioneers of Buddhist studies in the Occident [Eliot's note].
5. From St. Augustine's *Confessions* again. The collocation of these two representatives of eastern and western asceticism, as the culmination of this part of the poem, is not an accident [Eliot's note]. Augustine writes: "I entangle my steps with these outward beauties, but thou pluckest me out, O Lord, Thou pluckest me out."
6. In the first part of Part V three themes are employed: the journey to Emmaus, the approach to the Chapel Perilous (see Miss Weston's book), and the present decay of eastern Europe [Eliot's note].

There is not even silence in the mountains
But dry sterile thunder without rain
There is not even solitude in the mountains
But red sullen faces sneer and snarl
From doors of mudcracked houses
                                        If there were water
And no rock
If there were rock
And also water
And water
A spring
A pool among the rock
If there were the sound of water only
Not the cicada
And dry grass singing
But sound of water over a rock
Where the hermit-thrush sings in the pine trees
Drip drop drip drop drop drop drop[7]
But there is no water

Who is the third who walks always beside you?
When I count, there are only you and I together[8]
But when I look ahead up the white road
There is always another one walking beside you
Gliding wrapt in a brown mantle, hooded
I do not know whether a man or a woman
—But who is that on the other side of you?

What is that sound high in the air[9]
Murmur of maternal lamentation
Who are those hooded hordes swarming
Over endless plains, stumbling in cracked earth
Ringed by the flat horizon only
What is the city over the mountains
Cracks and reforms and bursts in the violet air
Falling towers
Jerusalem Athens Alexandria
Vienna London
Unreal

7. This is *Turdus aonalaschkae pallasii,* the hermit-thrush which I have heard in Quebec County. Chapman says (*Handbook of Birds of Eastern North America*) "it is most at home in secluded woodland and thickety retreats. . . . Its notes are not remarkable for variety or volume, but in purity and sweetness of tone and exquisite modulation they are unequalled." Its "water-dripping song" is justly celebrated [Eliot's note].

8. The following lines were stimulated by the account of one of the Antarctic expeditions (I forget which, but I think one of Shackleton's): it was related that the party of explorers, at the extremity of their strength, had the constant delusion that there was one more member than could actually be counted [Eliot's note]. There seems also to be an echo of the account of Jesus meeting his disciples on the road to Emmaus: "Jesus himself drew near, and went with them. But their eyes were holden that they should not know him" (Luke 24.13–16).

9. Cf. Hermann Hesse, *Blick ins Chaos:* "Schon ist halb Europa, schon ist zumindest der halbe Osten Europas auf dem Wege zum Chaos, fährt betrunken im heiligen Wahn am Abgrund entlang und singt dazu, singt betrunken und hymnisch wie Dmitri Karamasoff sang. Ueber diese Lieder lacht der Bürger beleidigt, der Heilige und Seher hört sie mit Tränen" [Eliot's note]. "Already half of Europe, already at least half of Eastern Europe, on the way to chaos, drives drunk in sacred infatuation along the edge of the precipice, singing drunkenly, as though singing hymns, as Dmitri Karamazov sang. The offended bourgeois laughs at the songs; the saint and the seer hear them with tears."

A woman drew her long black hair out tight
And fiddled whisper music on those strings
And bats with baby faces in the violet light
Whistled, and beat their wings
And crawled head downward down a blackened wall
And upside down in air were towers
Tolling reminiscent bells, that kept the hours
And voices singing out of empty cisterns and exhausted wells

In this decayed hole among the mountains
In the faint moonlight, the grass is singing
Over the tumbled graves, about the chapel
There is the empty chapel, only the wind's home.
It has no windows, and the door swings,
Dry bones can harm no one.
Only a cock stood on the rooftree
Co co rico co co rico
In a flash of lightning. Then a damp gust
Bringing rain

Ganga[1] was sunken, and the limp leaves
Waited for rain, while the black clouds
Gathered far distant, over Himavant.[2]
The jungle crouched, humped in silence.
Then spoke the thunder
DA
Datta: what have we given?[3]
My friend, blood shaking my heart
The awful daring of a moment's surrender
Which an age of prudence can never retract
By this, and this only, we have existed
Which is not to be found in our obituaries
Or in memories draped by the beneficent spider[4]
Or under seals broken by the lean solicitor
In our empty rooms
DA
Dayadhvam: I have heard the key[5]
Turn in the door once and turn once only
We think of the key, each in his prison

1. The river Ganges.
2. The Himalayas.
3. "Datta, dayadhvam, damyata" (Give, sympathize, control). The fable of the meaning of the Thunder is found in the *Brihadaranyaka—Upanishad*, 5, I. A translation is found in Deussen's *Sechzig Upanishads des Vada*, p. 489 [Eliot's note]. "That very thing is repented even today by the heavenly voice, in the form of thunder, in the form of thunder as 'Da,' 'Da,' 'Da,'. . . . Therefore one should practice these three things: self-control, alms-giving, and compassion."
4. Cf. Webster, *The White Devil*, v. vi: ". . . they'll remarry / Ere the worm pierce your winding-sheet, ere the spider / make a thin curtain for your epitaphs" [Eliot's note].
5. Cf. *Inferno*, xxxiii. 46: "ed io sentii chiavar l'uscio di sotto / all'orrible torre." Also F. H. *Bradley*, *Appearance and Reality*, p. 346: "My external sensations are no less private to myself than are my thoughts or my feelings. In either case my experience falls within my own circle, a circle closed on the outside; and, with all its elements alike, every sphere is opaque to the others which surround it. . . . In brief, regarded as an existence which appears in a soul, the whole world for each is peculiar and private to that soul." [Eliot's note]. In the passage from the *Inferno*, Ugolino tells Dante of his imprisonment and starvation until he became so desperate that he ate his children: "And I heard below me the door of the horrible tower being locked."

Thinking of the key, each confirms a prison
Only at nightfall, aethereal rumours
Revive for a moment a broken Coriolanus[6]
DA
Damyata: The boat responded
Gaily, to the hand expert with sail and oar
The sea was calm, your heart would have responded
Gaily, when invited, beating obedient
To controlling hands
I sat upon the shore
Fishing, with the arid plain behind me[7]
Shall I at least set my lands in order?
London Bridge is falling down falling down falling down
Poi s'ascose nel foco che gli affina[8]
Quando fiam uti chelidon—O swallow swallow[9]
Le Prince d'Aquitaine à la tour abolie[1]
These fragments I have shored against my ruins
Why then Ile fit you. Hieronymo's mad againe.[2]
Datta. Dayadhvam. Damyata.
Shantih shantih shantih[3]

Responses

Fadwa Tuqan: In the Aging City[1]

City streets and pavements receive me
with other people, the human tide rushes
me on. I move in this current, but only on
the surface, remaining by myself.
The tide overflows to sweep
these sidewalks and streets.
Faces, faces, faces rolling on,

6. In Shakespeare's play of the same name, Coriolanus is a Roman general who is exiled and later leads the enemy in an attack against the Romans.
7. V. Weston, *From Ritual to Romance;* chapter on the Fisher King [Eliot's note].
8. V. *Purgatorio,* xxvi.148: "Ara vos prec per aquella valor / que vos condus al som de l'escalina, / sovegna vos a temps de ma dolor." / Poi s'ascose nel foco che gli affina" [Eliot's note]. In this passage, the poet Arnaut Daniel speaks to Dante: "Now I pray you, by the goodness that guides you to the top of this staircase, be mindful in time of my suffering."
9. V. *Pervigilium Veneris.* Cf. Philomela in Parts II and III [Eliot's note]. Philomel asks, "When shall I be a swallow?"
1. V. Gerard de Nerval, Sonnet *El Desdichado* [Eliot's note]. "The Prince of Aquitane in the ruined tower."
2. V. Kyd's *Spanish Tragedy* [Eliot's note]. The subtitle of Kyd's play is, "Hieronymo's Mad Againe." His son having been murdered, Hieronymo is asked to compose a court play, to which he responds "Why then Ile fit you"; his son's murder is revenged in the course of the play.
3. Shantih. Repeated as here, a formal ending to an Upanishad. "The Peace which passeth understanding" is a feeble translation of the content of this word [Eliot's note]. The Upanishads are poetic commentaries on the Hindu Scriptures.

1. Translated by Patricia Alanah Byrne and Naomi Shihab Nye. Fadwa Tuqan (1917–2003) was born in Nablus, Palestine, to a privileged family during the period when Ottoman sovereignty was being replaced by British rule. She began publishing, under a pen name, while in her early twenties; following the establishment of the state of Israel in 1948, she began writing directly political poetry, becoming one of the most prominent Arab-language poets of her generation, noted for a provocatively political use of modernist poetic techniques. *In the Aging City* stems from an extended visit she made to London in 1962—her first major trip away from home, at age 45. Fascinated by life in the great city, she was also consumed with thoughts of home. Both in its images and in its staccato dialogue, now set into relief against memories of her homeland, this poem recalls T. S. Eliot's depiction of London.

dry and grim, they move on the surface,
remaining without human touch.
Here is nearness without being near.
Here is the no-presence in presence.
Here is nothing but the presence of absence!

Traffic light reddens; the tide holds back.
Bats flash across memory:
a tank passes, as I crossed in the Nablus marketplace,
I moved out of its way.
How well I've learned not to disturb
The path of traffic! How well I've memorized
traffic laws!
now here I am, in the London slave market
where they sold my parents and people . . . [2]
Here I stand, a part of the profitable deal,
carrying the brunt of the sin—
Mine was that I am a plant
grown by the mountains of Palestine.
Ah! Those who died yesterday are at rest now.
(I suspect that their corpses cursed me
as I gave way for a tank to pass,
then moved on in the stream.)
Aisha's letter is on my desk,
Nablus is quiet, life flowing on
Like river water . . .
The prison seal is an eloquent silence
(A guard tells her the trees have fallen,
the woods are not set ablaze anymore.
But Aisha insists the forest is thick,
Trees standing like fortresses. She dreams
of the forest she left blazing with fire
five years ago. She heard the thunder
of the wind in her dream, tells the guard:
"I don't believe you, you're one of them,
and you remain the Prophets of the Lie."[3]
Then she crouches in the darkness of prison, dreaming.
Shaded by her standing trees she is joyous at the sound
of the far forest rattling with swords of flame.
And Aisha dreams and dreams.)

The traffic light clicks green, the tide drives on.
My memory flits away, bats fall into a deep well.
A shadow changes direction, follows me,
sends out a bridge.
—Are you a stranger like I am?
Two drops separate from the tide,

2. A reference to the Balfour Declaration, which paved the way for the establishment of the state of Israel; it is seen by the Arabs and the Palestinians as unfairly offering their country to other people.

3. A reference to the Zionists, who claimed that Palestine is a land without people for people without land.

sit removed in a corner of the park.
—Do you like Osborne?[4]
—Who doesn't?
—England's elderly and its officers
setting with the sun of Suez . . . [5]
—Who do you think will plant tomorrow's tree
for this country?
—The hippie youth.
—You are sour, very sour.
The hippie tide passes by,
sweeping the city.
London keeps beat with
the toll of Big Ben.
—Around the-corner
there's a pub and an elegant hotel
with central heating—will you come?
—Impossible!
A London lady passes, complaining to her dog
of arthritis and a pinched sciatic nerve.
—Impossible!
—Aren't you a modern woman?
—I've grown beyond the days of rashness;
sorrow has made me a hundred years old. Impossible!
I remove his arm from my shoulders.
—I'm besieged by loneliness.
—We're all besieged by loneliness;
we're all alone, play along with life alone,
suffer alone, and die by ourselves.
You will remain alone here, even if a hundred
women embrace you!
City streets and sidewalks swallow us with others,
a human tide sweeping us away in waves of faces.
We remain on the surface, touching nothing.

Martin Rowson: from *The Waste Land*

In his graphic novel treatment of *The Waste Land* (1990), British cartoonist Martin Rowson (b. 1959) has created a loving parody of Eliot's poem, underscoring its air of mystery and menace by rendering it in the form of the Raymond Chandler-style film noir of the 1940s. While making light of the gravitas of Eliot's poem, Rowson's frames also manage to retain Eliot's sense of real anguish. The parody extends all the way down to Rowson's footnotes, which poke fun at the ersatz erudition of Eliot's footnotes to *The Waste Land*.

4. John Osborne (1929–1994), the British playwright who started the movement known as "the angry young men."
5. A reference to the Suez crisis of 1956, when Britain, France, and Israel invaded Egypt and were forced by both the United States and the Soviet Union to retreat. This was a blow for England's postwar attempts to retain the remains of its empire, on which it used to be said that the sun never set.

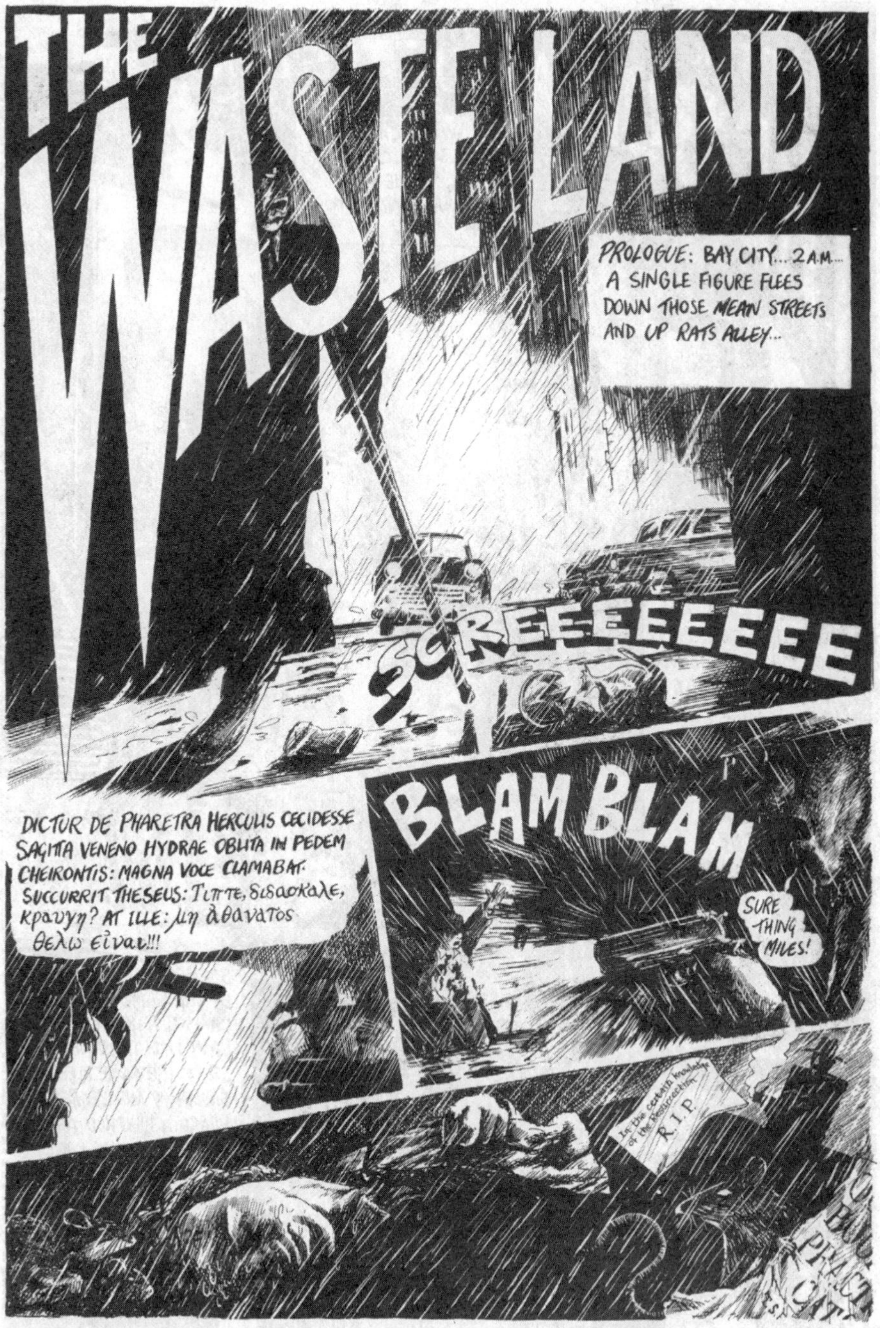

Not only the title but the layout and a good deal of the incidental imagery of the book were suggested by Mr. T. S. Eliot's poem *The Waste Land* (Faber & Faber). Indeed, so heavily am I indebted, Mr. Eliot's poem will illuminate the complexities of the book much better than my notes can; and I recommend it (apart from the intrinsic interest of the poem itself) to anyone who thinks such illumination worth the trouble. To two cinematic works I am indebted in general; I mean *The Big Sleep* and *The Maltese Falcon*. Anyone who is familiar with these works will immediately recognize in the book certain references to Californian private investigators.

The references are listed by chapter and frame number.

PROLOGUE

Frame 2: Varus quoted by Servius in his note to Virgil, *Eclogues*, vi, 42 [Rowson's note].

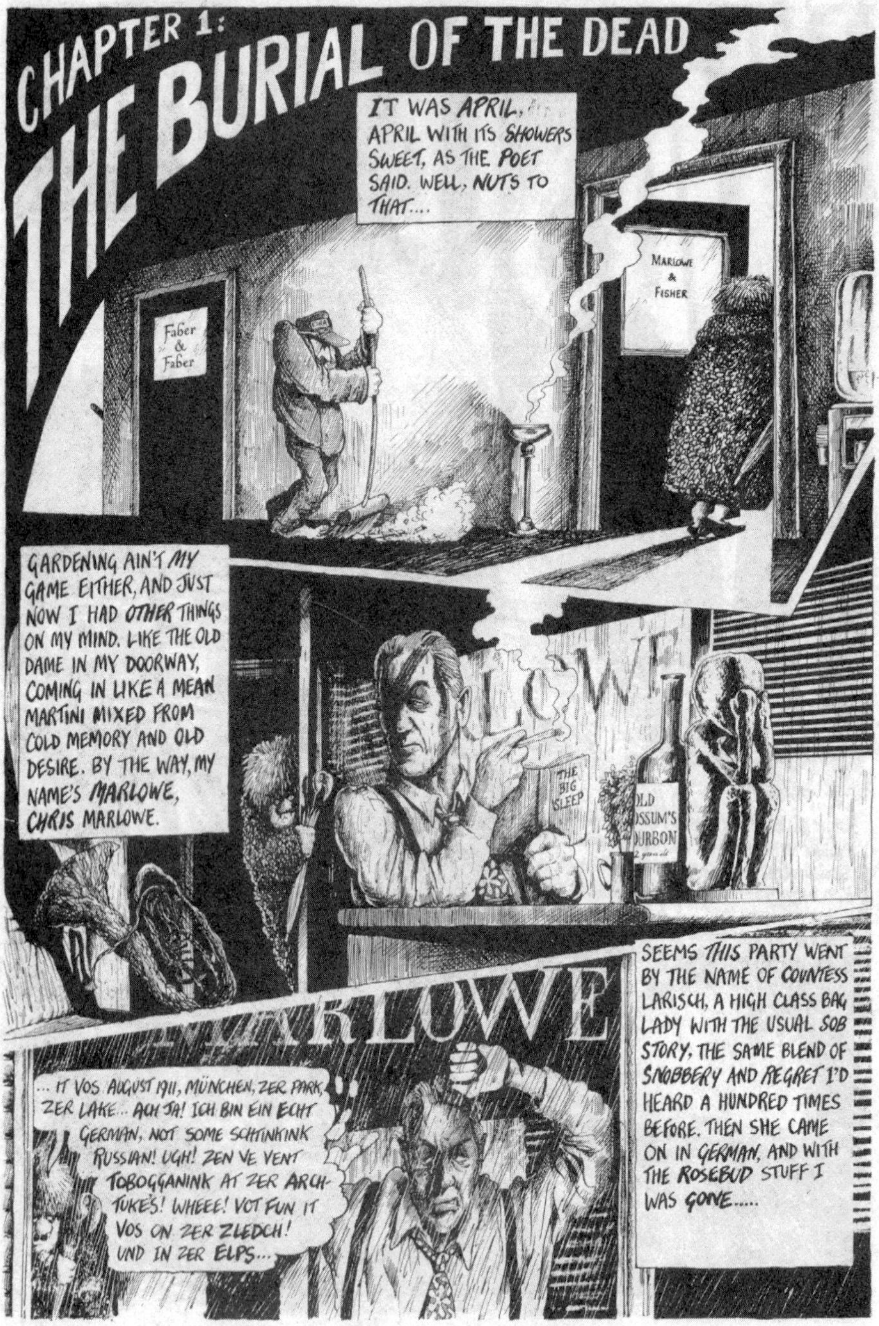

I. THE BURIAL OF THE DEAD

Frame 2: For "dried Tuba," read "dried tuber" throughout [Rowson's note].

...GONE, BACK TO THE LAST TIME I SAW MILES, OVER THE STATE LINE IN NEVADA IN A BURNT-OUT CASINO TORCHED TEN YEARS BACK BY AN EX-BIG SHOT FOR THE INSURANCE. MILES SAID HE HAD TO SHOW ME SOMETHING. MILES WAS MY PARTNER. MILES WAS NOW ON A SLAB IN THE MORGUE.
WELCOME
TO
H-HI CHRIS! HEY, CHRIS! HOW-'RE TH-THINGS IN TH-TH' GARDEN CHRIS? HOW'S THE R-R-R-ROCKERY AN' TH' C-COMPOST HEAP, C-C-CHRIS?
BACK THEN MILES WAS HAVING PROBLEMS. LIKE THE REST OF US, EXCEPT THAT MILES's PROBLEMS LOOKED LIKE GETTING HIM A FITTING FOR A TIGHT JACKET IN A ROOM WITH SOFT WALLS...
I LET HIM TALK. IT SEEMED LIKE THE RIGHT IDEA. IT'S WHAT YOU DO WITH GUYS TAKING A HIKE FROM REALITY...

SO WE WALKED AND HE TALKED AND DANCED AND WHEN HE DECIDED TO ROLL OVER AND PLAY DEAD, IT WAS TIME FOR ME TO WALK AWAY...
FRISCH WEHT DER WIND DER HEIMAT ZU. HERR MARLOWE, MEIN IRISCH KIND, WO WEILEST DU?
BUT THAT WAS THEN. NOW, MILES WASN'T PLAYING DEAD ANYMORE. THE COUNTESS WAS STILL HITTING ME WITH THE KRAUTSPIEL...
SHE GAVE ME TEN BUCKS TO FIND WHATEVER IT WAS SHE SOUGHT. IT WASN'T CLEAR. WAS IT THE SLED, THE ARCHDUKE OR THIS IRISH KID? SHE'D GIVEN ME NOTHING TO GO ON. BUT THERE WAS NOTHING NEW IN THAT. I DECIDED TO WALK THE STREETS AND GET WET...
WHY, HELLO THERE!
AT LEAST I'D BEEN GIVEN A NAME. SOME GREEK DAME DOWNTOWN HAD A LINE IN SEEING THE FUTURE, WHICH WAS USE-FUL IN A CASE LIKE THIS, EVEN IF THE ONLY FUTURE I WAS INTEREST-ED IN WAS LIQUID, GOLDEN WITH A MEAN MESSAGE FOR MARLOWE IN THE TAIL. THE LAST THING I NEEDED WAS A CRAZY KID WITH A BAD MEMORY FOR FACES....
WHERE'S DA BUNCHA FLOWERS YA PROMISED, YA BUM!! DAT WUZ A YEAR BACK AN' I WAN' ARMFULS!!!
OD' UND LEER DAS MEER!
PRUFROCK GALLERY
CLOSE
SEEMS LIKE TODAY WAS BERLITZ LANGUAGE SCHOOL DAY...

The Hollow Men

Mistah Kurtz—he dead.[1]

A penny for the Old Guy[2]

I

We are the hollow men
We are the stuffed men
Leaning together
Headpiece filled with straw. Alas!
Our dried voices, when
We whisper together
Are quiet and meaningless
As wind in dry grass
Or rats' feet over broken glass
In our dry cellar

Shape without form, shade without colour,
Paralysed force, gesture without motion;

Those who have crossed
With direct eyes, to death's other Kingdom
Remember us—if at all—not as lost
Violent souls, but only
As the hollow men
The stuffed men.

II

Eyes I dare not meet in dreams
In death's dream kingdom
These do not appear:
There, the eyes are

Sunlight on a broken column
There, is a tree swinging
And voices are
In the wind's singing
More distant and more solemn
Than a fading star.

Let me be no nearer
In death's dream kingdom
Let me also wear
Such deliberate disguises
Rat's coat, crowskin, crossed staves
In a field
Behaving as the wind behaves
No nearer—

1. from Conrad's *Heart of Darkness*, page 1954.
2. The phrase used by children begging money to buy fireworks to celebrate. Guy Faulkes Day, commemorating Faulkes's execution for plans to blow up the Houses of Parliament in 1605.

Not that final meeting
In the twilight kingdom

III

This is the dead land
This is cactus land
Here the stone images
Are raised, here they receive
The supplication of a dead man's hand
Under the twinkle of a fading star.

Is it like this
In death's other kingdom
Waking alone
At the hour when we are
Trembling with tenderness
Lips that would kiss
Form prayers to broken stone.

IV

The eyes are not here
There are no eyes here
In this valley of dying stars
In this hollow valley
This broken jaw of our lost kingdoms

In this last of meeting places
We grope together
And avoid speech
Gathered on this beach of the tumid river

Sightless, unless
The eyes reappear
As the perpetual star
Multifoliate rose
Of death's twilight kingdom
The hope only
Of empty men.

V

Here we go round the prickly pear
Prickly pear prickly pear
Here we go round the prickly pear
At five o'clock in the morning.[3]

Between the idea
And the reality
Between the motion

3. These lines are a pastiche of the familiar nursery rhyme, "Here We Go Round the Mulberry Bush"; its cadences can be heard as well in the poem's closing stanza.

And the act
Falls the Shadow

For Thine is the Kingdom[4]

Between the conception
And the creation
Between the emotion
And the response
Falls the Shadow

Life is very long

Between the desire
And the spasm
Between the potency
And the existence
Between the essence
And the descent
Falls the Shadow

For Thine is the Kingdom

For Thine is
Life is
For Thine is the

This is the way the world ends
This is the way the world ends
This is the way the world ends
Not with a bang but a whimper.

Journey of the Magi[1]

"A cold coming we had of it,
Just the worst time of the year
For a journey, and such a long journey:
The ways deep and the weather sharp,
The very dead of winter."
And the camels galled, sore-footed, refractory,
Lying down in the melting snow.
There were times we regretted
The summer palaces on slopes, the terraces,
And the silken girls bringing sherbet.
Then the camel men cursing and grumbling
And running away, and wanting their liquor and women,
And the night-fires going out, and the lack of shelters,
And the cities hostile and the towns unfriendly
And the villages dirty and charging high prices:
A hard time we had of it.

4. From the Lord's prayer.
1. The narrative of the poem is based upon the tradition of the three wise men who journeyed to Bethlehem to worship the infant Christ; cf. Matthew 2.1–12.

At the end we preferred to travel all night,
Sleeping in snatches,
With the voices singing in our ears, saying
That this was all folly.

Then at dawn we came down to a temperate valley,
Wet, below the snow line, smelling of vegetation,
With a running stream and a water-mill beating the darkness
And three trees on the low sky.
And an old white horse galloped away in the meadow.
Then we came to a tavern with vine-leaves over the lintel,
Six hands at an open door dicing for pieces of silver,
And feet kicking the empty wine-skins.
But there was no information, and so we continued
And arrived at evening, not a moment too soon
Finding the place; it was (you may say) satisfactory.

All this was a long time ago, I remember,
And I would do it again, but set down
This set down
This: were we led all that way for
Birth or Death? There was a Birth, certainly,
We had evidence and no doubt. I had seen birth and death,
But had thought they were different; this Birth was
Hard and bitter agony for us, like Death, our death.
We returned to our places, these Kingdoms,
But no longer at ease here, in the old dispensation,
With an alien people clutching their gods.
I should be glad of another death.

1927

from Four Quartets

Burnt Norton[1]

τοῦ λόγου δ᾽ ἐόντος ξυνοῦ ζώουσιν οἱ πολλοί ὡς ἰδίαν ἔχοντες φρόνησιν.[2]

I. p. 77. Fr. 2

ὁδὸς ἄνω κάτω μία καὶ ὡυτή.[3]

I. p. 89. Fr. 60

Diels: Die Fragmente der Vorsokratiker (Herakleitos).

1

Time present and time past
Are both perhaps present in time future,

1. A large country house in Gloucestershire, England, named for an earlier house on the site that had burned down in the 17th century.
2. Although the Word governs all things, most people live as though they had wisdom of their own. (From the Greek philosopher Heraclitus, c. 500 B.C.E.)
3. The way up and the way down are the same.

And time future contained in time past.
If all time is eternally present
All time is unredeemable.
What might have been is an abstraction
Remaining a perpetual possibility
Only in a world of speculation.
What might have been and what has been
Point to one end, which is always present.
Footfalls echo in the memory
Down the passage which we did not take
Towards the door we never opened
Into the rose-garden. My words echo
Thus, in your mind.
But to what purpose
Disturbing the dust on a bowl of rose-leaves
I do not know.
Other echoes
Inhabit the garden. Shall we follow?
Quick, said the bird, find them, find them,
Round the corner. Through the first gate,
Into our first world, shall we follow
The deception of the thrush? Into our first world.
There they were, dignified, invisible,
Moving without pressure, over the dead leaves,
In the autumn heat, through the vibrant air,
And the bird called, in response to
The unheard music hidden in the shrubbery,
And the unseen eyebeam crossed, for the roses
Had the look of flowers that are looked at.
There they were as our guests, accepted and accepting.
So we moved, and they, in a formal pattern,
Along the empty alley, into the box circle,
To look down into the drained pool.
Dry the pool, dry concrete, brown edged,
And the pool was filled with water out of sunlight,
And the lotos rose, quietly, quietly,
The surface glittered out of heart of light,
And they were behind us, reflected in the pool.
Then a cloud passed, and the pool was empty.
Go, said the bird, for the leaves were full of children,
Hidden excitedly, containing laughter.
Go, go, go, said the bird: human kind
Cannot bear very much reality.
Time past and time future
What might have been and what has been
Point to one end, which is always present.

2

Garlic and sapphires in the mud
Clot the bedded axle-tree.
The trilling wire in the blood
Sings below inveterate scars
Appeasing long forgotten wars.
The dance along the artery
The circulation of the lymph
Are figured in the drift of stars
Ascend to summer in the tree
We move above the moving tree
In light upon the figured leaf
And hear upon the sodden floor
Below, the boarhound and the boar
Pursue their pattern as before
But reconciled among the stars.
At the still point of the turning world. Neither flesh nor fleshless;
Neither from nor towards; at the still point, there the dance is,
But neither arrest nor movement. And do not call it fixity,
Where past and future are gathered. Neither movement from nor towards,
Neither ascent nor decline. Except for the point, the still point,
There would be no dance, and there is only the dance.
I can only say, *there* we have been: but I cannot say where.
And I cannot say, how long, for that is to place it in time.

The inner freedom from the practical desire,
The release from action and suffering, release from the inner
And the outer compulsion, yet surrounded
By a grace of sense, a white light still and moving,
Erhebung[4] without motion, concentration
Without elimination, both a new world
And the old made explicit, understood
In the completion of its partial ecstasy,
The resolution of its partial horror.
Yet the enchainment of past and future
Woven in the weakness of the changing body,
Protects mankind from heaven and damnation
Which flesh cannot endure.
                                        Time past and time future
Allow but a little consciousness.
To be conscious is not to be in time
But only in time can the moment in the rose-garden,
The moment in the arbour where the rain beat,
The moment in the draughty church at smokefall

4. Lifting up; the German philosopher Hegel's term for a new stage in understanding.

Be remembered; involved with past and future.
Only through time time is conquered.

3

Here is a place of disaffection
Time before and time after
In a dim light: neither daylight
Investing form with lucid stillness
Turning shadow into transient beauty
With slow rotation suggesting permanence
Nor darkness to purify the soul
Emptying the sensual with deprivation
Cleansing affection from the temporal.
Neither plenitude nor vacancy. Only a flicker
Over the strained time-ridden faces
Distracted from distraction by distraction

Filled with fancies and empty of meaning
Tumid apathy with no concentration
Men and bits of paper, whirled by the cold wind
That blows before and after time,
Wind in and out of unwholesome lungs
Time before and time after.
Eructation° of unhealthy souls *belching*
Into the faded air, the torpid
Driven on the wind that sweeps the gloomy hills of London,
Hampstead and Clerkenwell, Campden and Putney,
Highgate, Primrose and Ludgate. Not here
Not here the darkness, in this twittering world.

Descend lower, descend only
Into the world of perpetual solitude,
World not world, but that which is not world,
Internal darkness, deprivation
And destitution of all property,
Desiccation of the world of sense,
Evacuation of the world of fancy,
Inoperancy of the world of spirit;
This is the one way, and the other
Is the same, not in movement
But abstention from movement; while the world moves
In appetency,° on its metalled ways *desire*
Of time past and time future.

4

Time and the bell have buried the day,
The black cloud carries the sun away.
Will the sunflower turn to us, will the clematis
Stray down, bend to us; tendril and spray
Clutch and cling?
Chill

Fingers of yew be curled
Down on us? After the kingfisher's wing
Has answered light to light, and is silent, the light is still
At the still point of the turning world.

5

Words move, music moves
Only in time; but that which is only living
Can only die. Words, after speech, reach
Into the silence. Only by the form, the pattern,
Can words or music reach
The stillness, as a Chinese jar still
Moves perpetually in its stillness.
Not the stillness of the violin, while the note lasts,
Not that only, but the co-existence,
Or say that the end precedes the beginning,
And the end and the beginning were always there
Before the beginning and after the end.
And all is always now. Words strain,
Crack and sometimes break, under the burden,
Under the tension, slip, slide, perish,
Decay with imprecision, will not stay in place,
Will not stay still. Shrieking voices
Scolding, mocking, or merely chattering,
Always assail them. The Word in the desert
Is most attacked by voices of temptation,
The crying shadow in the funeral dance,
The loud lament of the disconsolate chimera.

The detail of the pattern is movement,
As in the figure of the ten stairs.[5]
Desire itself is movement
Not in itself desirable;
Love is itself unmoving,
Only the cause and end of movement,
Timeless, and undesiring
Except in the aspect of time
Caught in the form of limitation
Between un-being and being.
Sudden in a shaft of sunlight
Even while the dust moves
There rises the hidden laughter
Of children in the foliage
Quick now, here, now, always—
Ridiculous the waste sad time
Stretching before and after.

1935 1935, 1943

5. St. John of the Cross used this figure to describe the way to achieve mystical union with God.

Tradition and the Individual Talent

1

In English writing we seldom speak of tradition, though we occasionally apply its name in deploring its absence. We cannot refer to "the tradition" or to "a tradition"; at most, we employ the adjective in saying that the poetry of So-and-so is "traditional" or even "too traditional." Seldom, perhaps, does the word appear except in a phrase of censure. If otherwise, it is vaguely approbative,[1] with the implication, as to the work approved, of some pleasing archaeological reconstruction. You can hardly make the word agreeable to English ears without this comfortable reference to the reassuring science of archaeology.

Certainly the word is not likely to appear in our appreciations of living or dead writers. Every nation, every race, has not only its own creative, but its own critical turn of mind; and is even more oblivious of the shortcomings and limitations of its critical habits than of those of its creative genius. We know, or think we know, from the enormous mass of critical writing that has appeared in the French language the critical method or habit of the French; we only conclude (we are such unconscious people) that the French are "more critical" than we, and sometimes even plume ourselves a little with the fact, as if the French were the less spontaneous. Perhaps they are; but we might remind ourselves that criticism is as inevitable as breathing, and that we should be none the worse for articulating what passes in our minds when we read a book and feel an emotion about it, for criticizing our own minds in their work of criticism. One of the facts that might come to light in this process is our tendency to insist, when we praise a poet, upon those aspects of his work in which he least resembles any one else. In these aspects or parts of his work we pretend to find what is individual, what is the peculiar essence of the man. We dwell with satisfaction upon the poet's difference from his predecessors, especially his immediate predecessors; we endeavour to find something that can be isolated in order to be enjoyed. Whereas if we approach a poet without this prejudice we shall often find that not only the best, but the most individual parts of his work may be those in which the dead poets, his ancestors, assert their immortality most vigorously. And I do not mean the impressionable period of adolescence, but the period of full maturity.

Yet if the only form of tradition, of handing down, consisted in following the ways of the immediate generation before us in a blind or timid adherence to its successes, "tradition" should positively be discouraged. We have seen many such simple currents soon lost in the sand; and novelty is better than repetition. Tradition is a matter of much wider significance. It cannot be inherited, and if you want it you must obtain it by great labour. It involves, in the first place, the historical sense, which we may call nearly indispensable to any one who would continue to be a poet beyond his twenty-fifth year; and the historical sense involves a perception, not only of the pastness of the past, but of its presence; the historical sense compels a man to write not merely with his own generation in his bones, but with a feeling that the whole of the literature of Europe from Homer and within it the whole of the literature of his own country has a simultaneous existence and composes a simultaneous order. This historical sense, which is a sense of the timeless as well as of the temporal and of the timeless and of the temporal together, is what makes a writer traditional.

1. Approving.

And it is at the same time what makes a writer most acutely conscious of his place in time, of his own contemporaneity.

No poet, no artist of any art, has his complete meaning alone. His significance, his appreciation is the appreciation of his relation to the dead poets and artists. You cannot value him alone; you must set him, for contrast and comparison, among the dead. I mean this as a principle of aesthetic, not merely historical, criticism. The necessity that he shall conform, that he shall cohere, is not onesided; what happens when a new work of art is created is something that happens simultaneously to all the works of art which preceded it. The existing monuments form an ideal order among themselves, which is modified by the introduction of the new (the really new) work of art among them. The existing order is complete before the new work arrives; for order to persist after the supervention[2] of novelty, the whole existing order must be, if ever so slightly, altered; and so the relations, proportions, values of each work of art toward the whole are readjusted; and this is conformity between the old and the new. Whoever has approved this idea of order, of the form of European, of English literature will not find it preposterous that the past should be altered by the present as much as the present is directed by the past. And the poet who is aware of this will be aware of great difficulties and responsibilities.

In a peculiar sense he will be aware also that he must inevitably be judged by the standards of the past. I say judged, not amputated, by them; not judged to be as good as, or worse or better than, the dead; and certainly not judged by the canons of dead critics. It is a judgment, a comparison, in which two things are measured by each other. To conform merely would be for the new work not really to conform at all; it would not be new, and would therefore not be a work of art. And we do not quite say that the new is more valuable because it fits in; but its fitting in is a test of its value—a test, it is true, which can only be slowly and cautiously applied, for we are none of us infallible judges of conformity. We say: it appears to conform, and is perhaps individual, or it appears individual, and may conform; but we are hardly likely to find that it is one and not the other.

To proceed to a more intelligible exposition of the relation of the poet to the past: he can neither take the past as a lump, an indiscriminate bolus,[3] nor can he form himself wholly on one or two private admirations, nor can he form himself wholly upon one preferred period. The first course is inadmissible, the second is an important experience of youth, and the third is a pleasant and highly desirable supplement. The poet must be very conscious of the main current, which does not at all flow invariably through the most distinguished reputations. He must be quite aware of the obvious fact that art never improves, but that the material of art is never quite the same. He must be aware that the mind of Europe—the mind of his own country—a mind which he learns in time to be much more important than his own private mind—is a mind which changes, and that this change is a development which abandons nothing *en route*, which does not superannuate either Shakespeare, or Homer, or the rock drawing of the Magdalenian draughtsmen.[4] That this development, refinement perhaps, complication certainly, is not, from the point of view of the artist, any improvement. Perhaps not even an improvement from the point of view of the psychologist or not to the extent which we imagine; perhaps

2. The appearance of something additional.
3. A lump; a mass of chewed food.
4. Drawings of hunting scenes, rendered in caves in France and Spain, c. 13,000–10,000 B.C.E.

only in the end based upon a complication in economics and machinery. But the difference between the present and the past is that the conscious present is an awareness of the past in a way and to an extent which the past's awareness of itself cannot show.

Some one said: "The dead writers are remote from us because we *know* so much more than they did." Precisely, and they are that which we know.

I am alive to a usual objection to what is clearly part of my programme for the *métier* of poetry. The objection is that the doctrine requires a ridiculous amount of erudition (pedantry), a claim which can be rejected by appeal to the lives of poets in any pantheon. It will even be affirmed that much learning deadens or perverts poetic sensibility. While, however, we persist in believing that a poet ought to know as much as will not encroach upon his necessary receptivity and necessary laziness, it is not desirable to confine knowledge to whatever can be put into a useful shape for examinations, drawing-rooms, or the still more pretentious modes of publicity. Some can absorb knowledge, the more tardy must sweat for it. Shakespeare acquired more essential history from Plutarch than most men could from the whole British Museum. What is to be insisted upon is that the poet must develop or procure the consciousness of the past and that he should continue to develop this consciousness throughout his career.

What happens is a continual surrender of himself as he is at the moment to something which is more valuable. The progress of an artist is a continual self-sacrifice, a continual extinction of personality.

There remains to define this process of depersonalization and its relation to the sense of tradition. It is in this depersonalization that art may be said to approach the condition of science. I, therefore, invite you to consider, as a suggestive analogy, the action which takes place when a bit of finely filiated[5] platinum is introduced into a chamber containing oxygen and sulphur dioxide.

2

Honest criticism and sensitive appreciation are directed not upon the poet but upon the poetry. If we attend to the confused cries of the newspaper critics and the *susurrus* [buzzing] of popular repetition that follows, we shall hear the names of poets in great numbers; if we seek not Blue-book[6] knowledge but the enjoyment of poetry, and ask for a poem, we shall seldom find it. I have tried to point out the importance of the relation of the poem to other poems by other authors, and suggested the conception of poetry as a living whole of all the poetry that has ever been written. The other aspect of this Impersonal theory of poetry is the relation of the poem to its author. And I hinted, by an analogy, that the mind of the mature poet differs from that of the immature one not precisely in any valuation of "personality," not being necessarily more interesting, or having "more to say," but rather by being a more finely perfected medium in which special, or very varied, feelings are at liberty to enter into new combinations.

The analogy was that of the catalyst. When the two gases previously mentioned are mixed in the presence of a filament of platinum, they form sulphurous acid. This combination takes place only if the platinum is present; nevertheless the newly formed acid contains no trace of platinum, and the platinum itself is apparently unaffected; has remained inert, neutral, and unchanged. The mind of the poet is the

5. Eliot apparently means "made into filaments."

6. Official government publication.

shred of platinum. It may partly or exclusively operate upon the experience of the man himself; but, the more perfect the artist, the more completely separate in him will be the man who suffers and the mind which creates; the more perfectly will the mind digest and transmute the passions which are its material.

The experience, you will notice, the elements which enter the presence of the transforming catalyst, are of two kinds: emotions and feelings. The effect of a work of art upon the person who enjoys it is an experience different in kind from any experience not of art. It may be formed out of one emotion, or may be a combination of several; and various feelings, inhering for the writer in particular words or phrases or images, may be added to compose the final result. Or great poetry may be made without the direct use of any emotion whatever: composed out of feelings solely. Canto XV of the *Inferno* (Brunetto Latini) is a working up of the emotion evident in the situation; but the effect, though single as that of any work of art, is obtained by considerable complexity of detail. The last quatrain gives an image, a feeling attaching to an image, which "came," which did not develop simply out of what precedes, but which was probably in suspension in the poet's mind until the proper combination arrived for it to add itself to.[7] The poet's mind is in fact a receptacle for seizing and storing up numberless feelings, phrases, images, which remain there until all the particles which can unite to form a new compound are present together.

If you compare several representative passages of the greatest poetry you see how great is the variety of types of combination, and also how completely any semi-ethical criterion of "sublimity" misses the mark. For it is not the "greatness," the intensity, of the emotions, the components, but the intensity of the artistic process, the pressure, so to speak, under which the fusion takes place, that counts. The episode of Paolo and Francesca employs a definite emotion, but the intensity of the poetry is something quite different from whatever intensity in the supposed experience it may give the impression of. It is no more intense, furthermore, than Canto XXVI, the voyage of Ulysses, which has not the direct dependence upon an emotion.[8] Great variety is possible in the process of transmutation of emotion: the murder of Agamemnon,[9] or the agony of Othello, gives an artistic effect apparently closer to a possible original than the scenes from Dante. In the *Agamemnon*, the artistic emotion approximates to the emotion of an actual spectator; in *Othello* to the emotion of the protagonist himself. But the difference between art and the event is always absolute; the combination which is the murder of Agamemnon is probably as complex as that which is the voyage of Ulysses. In either case there has been a fusion of elements. The ode of Keats contains a number of feelings which have nothing particular to do with the nightingale, but which the nightingale, partly, perhaps, because of its attractive name, and partly because of its reputation, served to bring together.

The point of view which I am struggling to attack is perhaps related to the metaphysical theory of the substantial unity of the soul: for my meaning is, that the poet has, not a "personality" to express, but a particular medium, which is only a medium and not a personality, in which impressions and experiences combine in peculiar and unexpected ways. Impressions and experiences which are important for the man may take no place in the poetry, and those which become important in the poetry may play quite a negligible part in the man, the personality.

7. He [Brunetto Latini] turned then, and he seemed, / across that plain, like one of those who run / for the green cloth at Verona; and of those, / more like the one who wins, than those who lose (*Inferno*, 15.119–22).

8. Dante's *Inferno*, Canto 5, tells the story of the lovers Paolo and Francesca; Canto 26 tells of the suffering of Ulysses in hell.

9. In Aeschylus's drama *Agamemnon*, Clytemnestra kills her husband Agamemnon for having sacrificed her daughter, Iphigenia, to the goddess Artemis.

I will quote a passage which is unfamiliar enough to be regarded with fresh attention in the light—or darkness—of these observations:

And now methinks I could e'en chide myself
For doating on her beauty, though her death
Shall be revenged after no common action.
Does the silkworm expend her yellow labours
For thee? For thee does she undo herself?
Are lordships sold to maintain ladyships
For the poor benefit of a bewildering minute?
Why does yon fellow falsify highways,
And put his life between the judge's lips,
To refine such a thing—keeps horse and men
To beat their valours for her? . . .[1]

In this passage (as is evident if it is taken in its context) there is a combination of positive and negative emotions: an intensely strong attraction toward beauty and an equally intense fascination by the ugliness which is contrasted with it and which destroys it. This balance of contrasted emotion is in the dramatic situation to which the speech is pertinent, but that situation alone is inadequate to it. This is, so to speak, the structural emotion, provided by the drama. But the whole effect, the dominant tone, is due to the fact that a number of floating feelings, having an affinity to this emotion by no means superficially evident, have combined with it to give us a new art emotion.

It is not in his personal emotions, the emotions provoked by particular events in his life, that the poet is in any way remarkable or interesting. His particular emotions may be simple, or crude, or flat. The emotion in his poetry will be a very complex thing, but not with the complexity of the emotions of people who have very complex or unusual emotions in life. One error, in fact, of eccentricity in poetry is to seek for new human emotions to express; and in this search for novelty in the wrong place it discovers the perverse. The business of the poet is not to find new emotions, but to use the ordinary ones and, in working them up into poetry, to express feelings which are not in actual emotions at all. And emotions which he has never experienced will serve his turn as well as those familiar to him. Consequently, we must believe that "emotion recollected in tranquillity"[2] is an inexact formula. For it is neither emotion, nor recollection, nor, without distortion of meaning, tranquillity. It is a concentration, and a new thing resulting from the concentration, of a very great number of experiences which to the practical and active person would not seem to be experiences at all; it is a concentration which does not happen consciously or of deliberation. These experiences are not "recollected," and they finally unite in an atmosphere which is "tranquil" only in that it is a passive attending upon the event. Of course this is not quite the whole story. There is a great deal, in the writing of poetry, which must be conscious and deliberate. In fact, the bad poet is usually unconscious where he ought to be conscious, and conscious where he ought to be unconscious. Both errors tend to make him "personal." Poetry is not a turning loose of emotion, but an escape from emotion; it is not the expression of personality, but an escape from personality. But, of course, only those who have personality and emotions know what it means to want to escape from these things.

1. From Cyril Tourneur's *The Revenger's Tragedy* (1607), 3.4; the speaker is addressing the skull of his former beloved, murdered after she refused to respond to an evil duke's advances. The revenger will make up the skull to look alive, putting poison on its lips; the evil Duke then dies when he kisses this supposed maiden in a dusky garden.

2. This is Wordsworth's famous description of poetry in the Preface to *Lyrical Ballads*; see page 394.

3

ὁ δὲ νοῦς ἴσως θειότερόν τι καὶ ἀπαθές ἐστιν.[3]

This essay proposes to halt at the frontier of metaphysics or mysticism, and confine itself to such practical conclusions as can be applied by the responsible person interested in poetry. To divert interest from the poet to the poetry is a laudable aim: for it would conduce to a juster estimation of actual poetry, good and bad. There are many people who appreciate the expression of sincere emotion in verse, and there is a smaller number of people who can appreciate technical excellence. But very few know when there is an expression of *significant* emotion, emotion which has its life in the poem and not in the history of the poet. The emotion of art is impersonal. And the poet cannot reach this impersonality without surrendering himself wholly to the work to be done. And he is not likely to know what is to be done unless he lives in what is not merely the present, but the present moment of the past, unless he is conscious, not of what is dead, but of what is already living.

Virginia Woolf

1882–1941

From New York World-Telegram & Sun Collection, *Virginia Woolf*, 1928.

Virginia Woolf is the foremost woman writer of the twentieth century, writing in any language; within British literature, Woolf is in the company of James Joyce, T. S. Eliot, William Butler Yeats, and few others as a major author, of whatever gender. To take account of the transformations in modern English literature—in language, in style, and in substance—requires reckoning with Virginia Woolf, one of the chief architects of literary modernism. By 1962 Edward Albee could sardonically title a play *Who's Afraid of Virginia Woolf?*, knowing that her name would signify the greatness of modern literature. Woolf wrote luminous and intricate novels, two pivotal books on sexual politics, society, and war, several volumes of short stories and collected essays, reviews and pamphlets, and thirty volumes of a remarkable diary. Woolf was a woman of letters in an almost old-fashioned sense, one of the century's subtlest observers of social and psychic life, and a hauntingly beautiful prose writer.

Woolf's writing career began in childhood but was officially launched in 1915 with the publication of her first novel, *The Voyage Out*, when she was thirty-three. *The Voyage Out* was an emblematic beginning for her public career as a novelist, with its title suggesting the need to venture forth, to make a voyage into the world and out of the imprisonments of life and language. This novel paid special homage to *Heart of Darkness*, Joseph Conrad's story of a voyage through Africa that uncovers the heart of Europe's imperial encounter with the African continent and its exploited people. The theme resonated for Woolf throughout her books, because she too concentrated on the costs—both social and personal—of attempting to gain freedom. With the exception of *Orlando* (1928), a playful and flamboyant novel with a few scenes set in Turkey and Russia, Woolf was never again to set a novel outside the geographical confines of England. Voyaging out had become a matter of voyaging within. Woolf does not turn away from the larger world; she sets that larger world and its history squarely in England.

3. The mind is doubtless something more divine and unimpressionable (from Aristotle's *De Anima* [*On the Soul*]).

Woolf's own roots went deep in Victorian literary culture. She was born in 1882 into a privileged and illustrious British professional family with connections to the world of letters on both sides. She was the third child of the marriage of Leslie Stephen and Julia Duckworth, both of whom had been widowed; Leslie Stephen had married a daughter of the novelist William Thackeray, and Julia had been the wife of a publisher, and was connected to a long line of judges, teachers, and magistrates. Woolf's father, eventually to become Sir Leslie, was a prominent editor and a striving philosopher, who was appointed president of the London Library. His fame was to come not from his philosophical work but from his massive *Dictionary of National Biography*, a book that placed, and ranked, the leading figures of British national life for many centuries. Woolf's *Orlando*, with its subtitle: *A Biography*, spoofed the entire enterprise of the biography of great men by having *her* great man, Orlando, unexpectedly turn into a woman halfway through the novel.

Woolf grew up as an intensely literary child, surrounded by her father's project of arbitrating the greatness of the (mostly) men of letters she nonetheless sought to emulate. Her mother Julia was a famed beauty, whose magical grace was captured in the photographs of her equally famous relative, the photographer Julia Margaret Cameron. Woolf was to provide a haunting portrait of both her mother and father in her novel *To the Lighthouse* (1927), where the beautiful and consummately maternal Mrs. Ramsay ministers to her irascible and intellectually tormented philosopher husband, Mr. Ramsay, until her sudden death deprives the family and its circle of friends of their ballast in life. Julia Stephen's premature death in 1895 had cast just such a pall over her own family, especially over thirteen-year-old Virginia, who had a mental breakdown. Breakdowns would recur at intervals throughout her life.

The death-haunted life characteristic of the Victorian family was Virginia Woolf's own experience. Two years after Julia died, Woolf's beloved half-sister and mother substitute, Stella Duckworth, died in childbirth at the age of twenty-seven. Woolf was also to lose her difficult but immensely loved father in 1904 (not so coincidentally, the same year Virginia was to publish her first essay and review), and her brother Thoby died of typhoid contracted on a trip to Greece with her in 1906. The novel *Jacob's Room* (1922) deals with a young man named Jacob and his college room, as perceived by his sister after his death in World War I. The items in Jacob's room are cloaked in memory and live in the consciousness of the sister as far more than precious objects—memory infuses them with shared life. The dead return again and again in Woolf's imagination and in her imaginative work; her development of the "moment of consciousness" in her writing, her novels' concentration on the binding powers of memory, and her invocation of the spreading, intertwining branches of human relations persisting even after death, may be the effect of her painful tutelage in loss.

As upper-class women, Woolf and her sisters were not given a formal education, while Thoby and Adrian both went to fine schools and ultimately to university. The sense of having been deliberately shut out of education by virtue of her sex was to inflect all of Woolf's writing and thinking. Education is a pervasive issue in her novels, and an enormous issue in her essays on social and political life, *A Room of One's Own* (1929) and *Three Guineas* (1938). Woolf became an autodidact, steeping herself in English literature, history, political theory, and art history, but she never lost the keen anguish nor the self-doubt occasioned by the closed doors of the academy to women. Education became for Woolf perhaps the key to transforming the role and the perception of women in society, and writing became her own mode of entry into the public world.

In 1912, Virginia Stephen married Leonard Woolf, like herself a member of the Bloomsbury group, but unlike her in being a Jew and coming from a commercial and far less illustrious family. Leonard Woolf was an "outsider" in anti-Semitic Britain no less than Virginia, who as a great woman writer was equally outside the norm. An accomplished writer in his own right, a political theorist and an activist in socialist issues and in anti-imperialist causes, Leonard Woolf devoted himself to Virginia and to her writing career. They established and ran the Hogarth Press together, an imprint that was to publish all of Virginia's books, as well as many important works of poetry, prose, and criticism from others. Virginia Woolf's erotic and emotional ties to women, and, in particular, her romance with Vita

Virginia Woolf and T. S. Eliot.

Sackville-West, while not necessarily explicitly sexual—no one seems to know for a certainty—were indubitably of the greatest importance to her life. Despite this, she placed Leonard Woolf and their marriage at the center of her being, and their rich and complex partnership weathered Virginia's numerous mental breakdowns. When she felt another episode of depression overtaking her in 1941, it was partly her reluctance to subject Leonard to what she saw as the burden of her madness, which tragically led her to drown herself in the river near their home and their beloved press.

Woolf's themes and techniques as a writer are all distilled in her gem of a story *The Lady in the Looking-Glass: A Reflection* (1929), which is a parable about the dangers and the transcendence of writing. The lady of the title is absent for most of the brief story; an invisible narrator builds a world around her absence by recounting only what can be seen or sensed in the mirror to be glimpsed above the mantel. One of the oldest metaphors for literary art is the mirror, and with it, the notion that literature "holds up the mirror to nature," or reality. Literary art was long considered to be an imitation of reality, its mirrored reflection, its "re-presentation." Woolf's story takes the garden shears of her missing character and tears representation to pieces, so to speak. Language cannot simply mirror something, her prose tells us, because it is too mysterious and subtle and wayward to do so. No imitation can ever capture subjective reality, and even inanimate objects are, for Woolf, filled with subjectivity. Finally, the story takes a "lady," a woman, as its subject because Woolf indicates that representation which tries to be realistic or real is instead a cruel violation, almost a form of rape. Truth in art is neither a representation nor a reflection: truth can only be gotten at sideways, in fragments, and with the fluidity of consciousness, in a subjective moment. "Examine for a moment an ordinary mind on an ordinary day," Woolf wrote in an essay on *Modern Fiction* in 1925:

> The mind receives a myriad impressions—trivial, fantastic, evanescent, or engraved with the sharpness of steel. From all sides they come, an incessant shower of innumerable atoms; and, as they fall, as they shape themselves into the life of Monday or Tuesday, the accent falls differently from of old; the moment of importance came not here but there; so that, if a writer were a free man and not a slave, if he could write what he chose, not what he must, if he could base his work upon his own feeling and not upon convention, there would be no plot, no comedy, no tragedy, no love interest or catastrophe in the accepted style, and perhaps not a single button sewn on as the Bond Street tailors would have it.

Woolf's stories are written out of her own painfully won freedom of observation; the passages that follow from *A Room of One's Own* and *Three Guineas* meditate on the ways in which society and even human character would have to change in order for such freedom to spread.

For additional resources on Woolf, go to *The Longman Anthology of British Literature* Web site at www.myliteraturekit.com.

The Lady in the Looking-Glass: A Reflection[1]

People should not leave looking-glasses hanging in their rooms any more than they should leave open cheque books or letters confessing some hideous crime. One could not help looking, that summer afternoon, in the long glass that hung outside in the hall. Chance had so arranged it. From the depths of the sofa in the drawing-room one could see reflected in the Italian glass not only the marble-topped table opposite, but a stretch of the garden beyond. One could see a long grass path leading between banks of tall flowers until, slicing off an angle, the gold rim cut it off.

The house was empty, and one felt, since one was the only person in the drawing-room, like one of those naturalists who, covered with grass and leaves, lie watching the shyest animals—badgers, otters, kingfishers—moving about freely, themselves unseen. The room that afternoon was full of such shy creatures, lights and shadows, curtains blowing, petals falling—things that never happen, so it seems, if someone is looking. The quiet old country room with its rugs and stone chimney pieces, its sunken bookcases and red and gold lacquer cabinets, was full of such nocturnal creatures. They came pirouetting across the floor, stepping delicately with high-lifted feet and spread tails and pecking allusive beaks as if they had been cranes or flocks of elegant flamingoes whose pink was faded, or peacocks whose trains were veined with silver. And there were obscure flushes and darkenings too, as if a cuttlefish had suddenly suffused the air with purple; and the room had its passions and rages and envies and sorrows coming over it and clouding it, like a human being. Nothing stayed the same for two seconds together.

But, outside, the looking-glass reflected the hall table, the sunflowers, the garden path so accurately and so fixedly that they seemed held there in their reality unescapably. It was a strange contrast—all changing here, all stillness there. One could not help looking from one to the other. Meanwhile, since all the doors and windows were open in the heat, there was a perpetual sighing and ceasing sound, the voice of the transient and the perishing, it seemed, coming and going like human breath, while in the looking-glass things had ceased to breathe and lay still in the trance of immortality.

Half an hour ago the mistress of the house, Isabella Tyson, had gone down the grass path in her thin summer dress, carrying a basket, and had vanished, sliced off by the gilt rim of the looking-glass. She had gone presumably into the lower garden

1. Published in *Harper's Magazine*, December 1929.

to pick flowers; or as it seemed more natural to suppose, to pick something light and fantastic and leafy and trailing, traveller's joy, or one of those elegant sprays of convolvulus that twine round ugly walls and burst here and there into white and violet blossoms. She suggested the fantastic and the tremulous convolvulus rather than the upright aster, the starched zinnia, or her own burning roses alight like lamps on the straight posts of their rose trees. The comparison showed how very little, after all these years, one knew about her; for it is impossible that any woman of flesh and blood of fifty-five or sixty should be really a wreath or a tendril. Such comparisons are worse than idle and superficial—they are cruel even, for they come like the convolvulus itself trembling between one's eyes and the truth. There must be truth; there must be a wall. Yet it was strange that after knowing her all these years one could not say what the truth about Isabella was; one still made up phrases like this about convolvulus and traveller's joy. As for facts, it was a fact that she was a spinster; that she was rich; that she had bought this house and collected with her own hands—often in the most obscure corners of the world and at great risk from poisonous stings and Oriental diseases—the rugs, the chairs, the cabinets which now lived their nocturnal life before one's eyes. Sometimes it seemed as if they knew more about her than we, who sat on them, wrote at them, and trod on them so carefully, were allowed to know. In each of these cabinets were many little drawers, and each almost certainly held letters, tied with bows of ribbon, sprinkled with sticks of lavender or rose leaves. For it was another fact—if facts were what one wanted—that Isabella had known many people, had had many friends; and thus if one had the audacity to open a drawer and read her letters, one would find the traces of many agitations, of appointments to meet, of upbraidings for not having met, long letters of intimacy and affection, violent letters of jealousy and reproach, terrible final words of parting—for all those interviews and assignations had led to nothing—that is, she had never married, and yet, judging from the mask-like indifference of her face, she had gone through twenty times more of passion and experience than those whose loves are trumpeted forth for all the world to hear. Under the stress of thinking about Isabella, her room became more shadowy and symbolic; the corners seemed darker, the legs of chairs and tables more spindly and hieroglyphic.

Suddenly these reflections were ended violently and yet without a sound. A large black form loomed into the looking-glass; blotted out everything, strewed the table with a packet of marble tablets veined with pink and grey, and was gone. But the picture was entirely altered. For the moment it was unrecognisable and irrational and entirely out of focus. One could not relate these tablets to any human purpose. And then by degrees some logical process set to work on them and began ordering and arranging them and bringing them into the fold of common experience. One realised at last that they were merely letters. The man had brought the post.

There they lay on the marble-topped table, all dripping with light and colour at first and crude and unabsorbed. And then it was strange to see how they were drawn in and arranged and composed and made part of the picture and granted that stillness and immortality which the looking-glass conferred. They lay there invested with a new reality and significance and with a greater heaviness, too, as if it would have needed a chisel to dislodge them from the table. And, whether it was fancy or not, they seemed to have become not merely a handful of casual letters but to be tablets graven with eternal truth—if one could read them, one would know everything there was to be known about Isabella, yes, and about life, too. The pages inside those marble-looking envelopes must be cut deep and scored thick with meaning. Isabella would come in, and take them, one by one, very slowly, and open them, and read them carefully word by word, and then with a profound sigh of comprehension, as if she had seen to the bottom of everything, she would tear the envelopes to little bits and tie the letters together and lock the cabinet drawer in her determination to conceal what she did not wish to be known.

The thought served as a challenge. Isabella did not wish to be known—but she should no longer escape. It was absurd, it was monstrous. If she concealed so much and knew so much one must prize her open with the first tool that came to hand—the imagination. One must fix one's mind upon her at that very moment. One must fasten her down there. One must refuse to be put off any longer with sayings and doings such as the moment brought forth—with dinners and visits and polite conversations. One must put oneself in her shoes. If one took the phrase literally, it was easy to see the shoes in which she stood, down in the lower garden, at this moment. They were very narrow and long and fashionable—they were made of the softest and most flexible leather. Like everything she wore, they were exquisite. And she would be standing under the high hedge in the lower part of the garden, raising the scissors that were tied to her waist to cut some dead flower, some overgrown branch. The sun would beat down on her face, into her eyes; but no, at the critical moment a veil of cloud covered the sun, making the expression of her eyes doubtful—was it mocking or tender, brilliant or dull? One could only see the indeterminate outline of her rather faded, fine face looking at the sky. She was thinking, perhaps, that she must order a new net for the strawberries; that she must send flowers to Johnson's widow; that it was time she drove over to see the Hippesleys in their new house. Those were the things she talked about at dinner certainly. But one was tired of the things that she talked about at dinner. It was her profounder state of being that one wanted to catch and turn to words, the state that is to the mind what breathing is to the body, what one calls happiness or unhappiness. At the mention of those words it became obvious, surely, that she must be happy. She was rich; she was distinguished; she had many friends; she travelled—she bought rugs in Turkey and blue pots in Persia. Avenues of pleasure radiated this way and that from where she stood with her scissors raised to cut the trembling branches while the lacy clouds veiled her face.

Here with a quick movement of her scissors she snipped the spray of traveller's joy and it fell to the ground. As it fell, surely some light came in too, surely one could penetrate a little farther into her being. Her mind then was filled with tenderness and regret. . . . To cut an overgrown branch saddened her because it had once lived, and life was dear to her. Yes, and at the same time the fall of the branch would suggest to her how she must die herself and all the futility and evanescence of things. And then again quickly catching this thought up, with her instant good sense, she thought life had treated her well; even if fall she must, it was to lie on the earth and moulder sweetly into the roots of violets. So she stood thinking. Without making any thought precise—for she was one of those reticent people whose minds hold their thoughts enmeshed in clouds of silence—she was filled with thoughts. Her mind was like her room, in which lights advanced and retreated, came pirouetting and stepping delicately, spread their tails, pecked their way; and then her whole being was suffused, like the room again, with a cloud of some profound knowledge, some unspoken regret, and then she was full of locked drawers, stuffed with letters, like her cabinets. To talk of "prizing her open" as if she were an oyster, to use any but the finest and subtlest and most pliable tools upon her was impious and absurd. One must imagine—here was she in the looking-glass. It made one start.

She was so far off at first that one could not see her clearly. She came lingering and pausing, here straightening a rose, there lifting a pink to smell it, but she never stopped; and all the time she became larger and larger in the looking-glass, more and more completely the person into whose mind one had been trying to penetrate. One verified her by degrees—fitted the qualities one had discovered into this visible body. There were her grey-green dress, and her long shoes, her basket, and something sparkling at her throat. She came so gradually that she did not seem to derange the pattern in the glass, but only to bring in some new element which gently moved and altered the other objects as if asking them, courteously, to make room for her. And the letters and the table and the grass walk and the sunflowers which had been waiting in the looking-glass separated and opened out so that she might be received among them. At last there she was, in the hall. She stopped dead. She stood by the table. She stood perfectly still. At once the looking-glass began to pour over her a light that seemed to fix her; that seemed like some acid to bite off the unessential and superficial and to leave only the truth. It was an enthralling spectacle. Everything dropped from her—clouds, dress, basket, diamond—all that one had called the creeper and convolvulus. Here was the hard wall beneath. Here was the woman herself. She stood naked in that pitiless light. And, there was nothing. Isabella was perfectly empty. She had no thoughts. She had no friends. She cared for nobody. As for her letters, they were all bills. Look, as she stood there, old and angular, veined and lined, with her high nose and her wrinkled neck, she did not even trouble to open them.

People should not leave looking-glasses hanging in their rooms.

Mrs Dalloway From the distance of the twenty-first century, Virginia Woolf's majestic novel *Mrs Dalloway* is a time capsule of modernity. Set on a single day in June in the city of London shortly after the end of World War I, the novel manages to include the whole world and hold it, trembling in the moment, for our inspection. In and through the thoughts of a loosely connected group of friends and acquaintances and strangers on that June day, all the major strands of modernity are woven: war and violence on an unprecedented scale, technology and urbanism, refugees and exile, empire and migration. The divisions between people by virtue of their gender, or their class, their color or their accent, their sexuality and their politics are threads in the fabric of the novel. While there is no long journey or close-up encounter with otherness in *Mrs Dalloway*, it truly is also a modernist work that goes "beyond the pale." Refusing to submit to the acceptable social platitudes about war, women, the poor, empire, violence and suffering, sexual desire and even death, the novel voyages into the heart of darkness Conrad called London: "for it, too, is a heart of darkness." *Mrs Dalloway* rewrites *Heart of Darkness* for twentieth-century Britain spent by World War I, unsure of its values and its traditions, undergoing upheavals by all those dispossessed abroad and at home. It does so through its unlikely heroine Clarissa Dalloway, a middle-aged woman whose name is borrowed from the first major English novel, Samuel Richardson's *Clarissa*, and whose girlhood was spent on an eighteenth-century country estate summoning up a pastoral English tradition now completely disappeared.

Mrs Dalloway was written in part as a response to two very different immediately contemporary modern British novels. Woolf was playing deliberate homage to her friend E. M. Forster's extraordinary *A Passage to India*, a work that approached colonial India and the British who lived there through the prism of multiple consciousness. *Mrs Dalloway*, too, while located in London, uses a narrative that wends its way freely into and out of the minds of its characters, and has only the barest linear plot, since the character Clarissa Dalloway is spending the day making final preparations for the party that closes the novel. The shadow of Joyce's *Ulysses* falls across the novel as well; in response to that colossal and encyclopedic novel of life on 16 June 1904, in Dublin, Woolf crafts a svelte and swift-moving novel, using only one narrative style and taking women and men equally as the momentary home for the roving, nomadic consciousness of the book. Whereas Joyce gave *Ulysses* an epic scale, Woolf was seeking a more intimate form. As she argued three years later in *A Room of One's Own*, "the book has somehow to be adjusted to the body, and at a venture one would say that women's books should be shorter, more concentrated, than those of men." Woolf's smaller canvas is just as open to the world as is *Ulysses*, and there is nothing dainty in her depiction of the horrors of war, of the shock and dazzle of modern consciousness, of the power of desire, and of the violence that courses through human relationships and social institutions alike. Like Dublin for Joyce, London itself becomes the novel's central focus and almost its chief protagonist, a place of surprising encounters and ambiguous possibilities as genders, classes, and nationalities intermingle amid a cityscape replete with centuries of British history and bustling with modern commercial culture.

Mrs Dalloway is centered by the pastoral greensward of Regent's Part, the swathe across which on this day of the party all the major characters cut their path and intersect: Clarissa Dalloway herself; her old friend Peter Walsh, returning from years in India; the mad Septimus Warren Smith, trailing his Italian bride Rezia; Richard Dalloway, plunged in the worries of a civil servant and bureaucrat; a country servant girl who has come to London to try her luck; and an ancient woman who sings a primordial British melody. This green world is sliced and scored by the irresolvable divisions and distinctions that march across it; the park becomes a virtual parade ground for these incommensurable lives. The impossibility of continuing to deny the effects of World War I, with its slaughter of an entire generation and the massive mental and physical illnesses it left in its wake, the difficulty of assimilating the rural and the colonial influx of desperate people, and the intractability of the problem of the urban underclass: all these forces of instability and distance collide across the face of the romantic literary idea of England as a green park writ large, a beautiful island, that once promised to ameliorate those divisions. The people in the book can be united only through shared memories, which it turns out are very different from one another, or in modern moments of spectacle and shopping, for example the sky-writing scene, when the public magic of advertisement unites the scattered onlookers in reading the runic letters Glaxo-Kremo, toffee god of the skies. In a world of conflict and division, Clarissa manages to have her party, and without fully knowing it to draw everyone together.

Modernity has scattered people, tossed them over the globe, scarred them with its violence, wounded them by its social rules and grounded them when they wish to take flight. Against this invisible power that fragments and divides, *Mrs Dalloway* proposes that the frail but potent forces of love and generosity, gathered up as the gift of art, collect the fragments and make them momentarily but preciously whole.

Mrs Dalloway

MRS DALLOWAY said she would buy the flowers herself.

For Lucy had her work cut out for her. The doors would be taken off their hinges; Rumpelmayer's men were coming. And then, thought Clarissa Dalloway, what a morning—fresh as if issued to children on a beach.

What a lark! What a plunge! For so it had always seemed to her, when, with a little squeak of the hinges, which she could hear now, she had burst open the French windows and plunged at Bourton into the open air. How fresh, how calm, stiller than this of course, the air was in the early morning; like the flap of a wave; the kiss of a wave; chill and sharp and yet (for a girl of eighteen as she then was) solemn, feeling as she did, standing there at the open window, that something awful was about to happen; looking at the flowers, at the trees with the smoke winding off them and the rooks rising, falling; standing and looking until Peter Walsh said, "Musing among the vegetables?"—was that it?—"I prefer men to cauliflowers"—was that it? He must have said it at breakfast one morning when she had gone out on to the terrace—Peter Walsh. He would be back from India one of these days, June or July, she forgot which, for his letters were awfully dull; it was his sayings one remembered; his eyes, his pocket-knife, his smile, his grumpiness and, when millions of things had utterly vanished—how strange it was!—a few sayings like this about cabbages.

She stiffened a little on the kerb, waiting for Durtnall's van to pass. A charming woman, Scrope Purvis thought her (knowing her as one does know people who live next door to one in Westminster); a touch of the bird about her, of the jay, blue-green, light, vivacious, though she was over fifty, and grown very white since her illness. There she perched, never seeing him, waiting to cross, very upright.

For having lived in Westminster—how many years now? over twenty,—one feels even in the midst of the traffic, or waking at night, Clarissa was positive, a particular hush, or solemnity; an indescribable pause; a suspense (but that might be her heart, affected, they said, by influenza) before Big Ben strikes. There! Out it boomed. First a warning, musical; then the hour, irrevocable. The leaden circles dissolved in the air. Such fools we are, she thought, crossing Victoria Street. For Heaven only knows why one loves it so, how one sees it so, making it up, building it round one, tumbling it, creating it every moment afresh; but the veriest frumps, the most dejected of miseries sitting on doorsteps (drink their downfall) do the same; can't be dealt with, she felt positive, by Acts of Parliament for that very reason: they love life. In people's eyes, in the swing, tramp, and trudge; in the bellow and the uproar; the carriages, motor cars, omnibuses, vans, sandwich men shuffling and swinging; brass bands; barrel organs; in the triumph and the jingle and the strange high singing of some aeroplane overhead was what she loved; life; London; this moment of June.

For it was the middle of June. The War was over,[1] except for some one like Mrs Foxcroft at the Embassy last night eating her heart out because that nice boy was killed and now the old Manor House must go to a cousin; or Lady Bexborough who opened a bazaar,[2] they said, with the telegram in her hand, John, her favourite, killed; but it was over; thank Heaven—over. It was June. The King and Queen[3] were at the Palace. And everywhere, though it was still so early, there was a beating, a stirring of galloping ponies, tapping of cricket bats; Lords, Ascot, Ranelagh[4] and all the rest of it; wrapped in the soft mesh of the grey-blue morning air, which, as the day wore on, would unwind them, and set down on their lawns and pitches the bouncing ponies, whose forefeet just struck the ground and up they sprung, the whirling young men, and laughing girls in their transparent muslins who, even now, after dancing all night, were taking their absurd woolly dogs for a run; and even now, at this hour, discreet old dowagers were shooting out in their motor cars on errands of mystery; and the shopkeepers were fidgeting in their windows with their paste and diamonds, their lovely old sea-green brooches in eighteenth-century settings to tempt Americans (but one must economise, not buy things rashly for Elizabeth), and she, too, loving it as she did with an absurd and faithful passion, being part of it, since her people were

1. World War I (1914–1918).

2. These street markets, borrowing their exotic name from trading centers in the Middle East, became a fashionable locus of philanthropy in 19th-century London. In the stalls, most often operated by women, were peddled a variety of wares, ostensibly to raise funds for charitable causes. These enterprises also provoked sharp criticism from those, like the *Saturday Review* (June 1872) columnist quoted here, who feared a blurred distinction between the sellers and the goods: "the ladies holding the stalls . . . make a merchandise of their smiles, and drive a roaring trade in their *cartes-de-visite* and autographs, with miserable little coat bouquets made up and fastened in by their own hands, and sold at prices more like the current rates of El Dorado than London . . . " Nor did the ambiguities of the bazaar escape the notice of Woolf's contemporaries, as Joyce's 1916 story *Araby* is in part concerned with the "vanity" of the scene.

3. George V (r. 1910–1936) and Mary.

4. Lord's Cricket Ground, in northwest London, accommodates the headquarters of the game's key organizations and is regarded as the home of cricket in England. Ascot is a premier English racecourse. Ranelagh Gardens were, at one time, one of the most fashionable pleasure gardens of London.

courtiers once in the time of the Georges,[5] she, too, was going that very night to kindle and illuminate; to give her party. But how strange, on entering the Park, the silence; the mist; the hum; the slow-swimming happy ducks; the pouched birds waddling; and who should be coming along with his back against the Government buildings, most appropriately, carrying a despatch box stamped with the Royal Arms,[6] who but Hugh Whitbread; her old friend Hugh—the admirable Hugh!

"Good-morning to you, Clarissa!" said Hugh, rather extravagantly, for they had known each other as children. "Where are you off to?"

"I love walking in London," said Mrs Dalloway. "Really it's better than walking in the country."

They had just come up—unfortunately—to see doctors. Other people came to see pictures; go to the opera; take their daughters out; the Whitbreads came "to see doctors." Times without number Clarissa had visited Evelyn Whitbread in a nursing home. Was Evelyn ill again? Evelyn was a good deal out of sorts, said Hugh, intimating by a kind of pout or swell of his very well-covered, manly, extremely handsome, perfectly upholstered body (he was almost too well dressed always, but presumably had to be, with his little job at Court) that his wife had some internal ailment, nothing serious, which, as an old friend, Clarissa Dalloway would quite understand without requiring him to specify. Ah yes, she did of course; what a nuisance; and felt very sisterly and oddly conscious at the same time of her hat. Not the right hat for the early morning, was that it? For Hugh always made her feel, as he bustled on, raising his hat rather extravagantly and assuring her that she might be a girl of eighteen, and of course he was coming to her party to-night, Evelyn absolutely insisted, only a little late he might be after the party at the Palace to which he had to take one of Jim's boys,—she always felt a little skimpy beside Hugh; schoolgirlish; but attached to him, partly from having known him always, but she did think him a good sort in his own way, though Richard was nearly driven mad by him, and as for Peter Walsh, he had never to this day forgiven her for liking him.

She could remember scene after scene at Bourton—Peter furious; Hugh not, of course, his match in any way, but still not a positive imbecile as Peter made out; not a mere barber's block. When his old mother wanted him to give up shooting or to take her to Bath he did it, without a word; he was really unselfish, and as for saying, as Peter did, that he had no heart, no brain, nothing but the manners and breeding of an English gentleman, that was only her dear Peter at his worst; and he could be intolerable; he could be impossible; but adorable to walk with on a morning like this.

(June had drawn out every leaf on the trees. The mothers of Pimlico gave suck to their young. Messages were passing from the Fleet to the Admiralty. Arlington Street and Piccadilly[7] seemed to chafe the very air in the Park and lift its leaves hotly, brilliantly, on waves of that divine vitality which Clarissa loved. To dance, to ride, she had adored all that.)

For they might be parted for hundreds of years, she and Peter; she never wrote a letter and his were dry sticks; but suddenly it would come over her, If he were with me now what would he say?—some days, some sights bringing him back to her

5. George I (r. 1714–1727), George II (r. 1727–1760), George III (r. 1760–1820) and George IV (r. 1820–1830). It was during these reigns that the East India Company officially ceased to exist as an autonomous entity and was brought under parliamentary supervision/administration, an event that hastened the empire's spread.

6. A visible sign indicating that Hugh Whitbread has been entrusted with official government business.

7. All locations in the vicinity of St. James's Park, in south-central London.

calmly, without the old bitterness; which perhaps was the reward of having cared for people; they came back in the middle of St James's Park on a fine morning—indeed they did. But Peter—however beautiful the day might be, and the trees and the grass, and the little girl in pink—Peter never saw a thing of all that. He would put on his spectacles, if she told him to; he would look. It was the state of the world that interested him; Wagner, Pope's poetry, people's characters eternally, and the defects of her own soul. How he scolded her! How they argued! She would marry a Prime Minister and stand at the top of a staircase; the perfect hostess he called her (she had cried over it in her bedroom), she had the makings of the perfect hostess, he said.

So she would still find herself arguing in St James's Park, still making out that she had been right—and she had too—not to marry him. For in marriage a little licence, a little independence there must be between people living together day in day out in the same house; which Richard gave her, and she him. (Where was he this morning for instance? Some committee, she never asked what.) But with Peter everything had to be shared; everything gone into. And it was intolerable, and when it came to that scene in the little garden by the fountain, she had to break with him or they would have been destroyed, both of them ruined, she was convinced; though she had borne about with her for years like an arrow sticking in her heart the grief, the anguish; and then the horror of the moment when some one told her at a concert that he had married a woman met on the boat going to India! Never should she forget all that! Cold, heartless, a prude, he called her. Never could she understand how he cared. But those Indian women did presumably—silly, pretty, flimsy nincompoops. And she wasted her pity. For he was quite happy, he assured her—perfectly happy, though he had never done a thing that they talked of; his whole life had been a failure. It made her angry still.

She had reached the Park gates. She stood for a moment, looking at the omnibuses in Piccadilly.

She would not say of any one in the world now that they were this or were that. She felt very young; at the same time unspeakably aged. She sliced like a knife through everything; at the same time was outside, looking on. She had a perpetual sense, as she watched the taxi cabs, of being out, out, far out to sea and alone; she always had the feeling that it was very, very dangerous to live even one day. Not that she thought herself clever, or much out of the ordinary. How she had got through life on the few twigs of knowledge Fräulein Daniels gave them she could not think. She knew nothing; no language, no history; she scarcely read a book now, except memoirs in bed; and yet to her it was absolutely absorbing; all this; the cabs passing; and she would not say of Peter, she would not say of herself, I am this, I am that.

Her only gift was knowing people almost by instinct, she thought, walking on. If you put her in a room with some one, up went her back like a cat's; or she purred. Devonshire House, Bath House, the house with the china cockatoo, she had seen them all lit up once; and remembered Sylvia, Fred, Sally Seton—such hosts of people; and dancing all night; and the waggons plodding past to market; and driving home across the Park. She remembered once throwing a shilling into the Serpentine.[8] But every one remembered; what she loved was this, here, now, in front of her; the fat lady in the cab. Did it matter then, she asked herself, walking towards Bond Street,[9] did it matter that she must inevitably cease completely; all this must go on without her; did

8. An artificial pond in Hyde Park, largest of the London parks and site of the 1851 Great Exhibition.

9. Area of fashionable shops in northwest London.

she resent it; or did it not become consoling to believe that death ended absolutely? but that somehow in the streets of London, on the ebb and flow of things, here, there, she survived, Peter survived, lived in each other, she being part, she was positive, of the trees at home; of the house there, ugly, rambling all to bits and pieces as it was; part of people she had never met; being laid out like a mist between the people she knew best, who lifted her on their branches as she had seen the trees lift the mist, but it spread ever so far, her life, herself. But what was she dreaming as she looked into Hatchards' shop window? What was she trying to recover? What image of white dawn in the country, as she read in the book spread open:

Fear no more the heat o' the sun
Nor the furious winter's rages.[1]

This late age of the world's experience had bred in them all, all men and women, a well of tears. Tears and sorrows; courage and endurance; a perfectly upright and stoical bearing. Think, for example, of the woman she admired most, Lady Bexborough, opening the bazaar.

There were Jorrocks' *Jaunts and Jollities;* there were *Soapy Sponge* and Mrs Asquith's *Memoirs* and *Big Game Shooting in Nigeria,*[2] all spread open. Ever so many books there were; but none that seemed exactly right to take to Evelyn Whitbread in her nursing home. Nothing that would serve to amuse her and make that indescribably dried-up little woman look, as Clarissa came in, just for a moment cordial; before they settled down for the usual interminable talk of women's ailments. How much she wanted it—that people should look pleased as she came in, Clarissa thought and turned and walked back towards Bond Street, annoyed, because it was silly to have other reasons for doing things. Much rather would she have been one of those people like Richard who did things for themselves, whereas, she thought, waiting to cross, half the time she did things not simply, not for themselves; but to make people think this or that; perfect idiocy she knew (and now the policeman held up his hand) for no one was ever for a second taken in. Oh if she could have had her life over again! she thought, stepping on to the pavement, could have looked even differently!

She would have been, in the first place, dark like Lady Bexborough, with a skin of crumpled leather and beautiful eyes. She would have been, like Lady Bexborough, slow and stately; rather large; interested in politics like a man; with a country house; very dignified, very sincere. Instead of which she had a narrow pea-stick figure; a ridiculous little face, beaked like a bird's. That she held herself well was true; and had nice hands and feet; and dressed well, considering that she spent little. But often now this body she wore (she stopped to look at a Dutch picture), this body, with all its capacities, seemed nothing—nothing at all. She had the oddest sense of being herself invisible, unseen; unknown; there being no more marrying, no more having of children now, but only this astonishing and rather solemn progress with the rest of them, up Bond Street, this being Mrs Dalloway; not even Clarissa any more; this being Mrs Richard Dalloway.

1. *Cymbeline* 4.2. 258–81. A farewell to the dead, the song is also a reminder that the living must also "come to dust."

2. *Jorrocks' Jaunts and Jollities* (1838) and *Mr Sponge's Sporting Tour* (1853) were comic sporting novels by Robert Smith Surtees (Woolf misattributes authorship of the first of these to its title character). All eight of his books are concerned with characteristic elements of English fox-hunting society. Presumably, the last book mentioned is also of the hunting-adventure ilk. Mrs Emma Alice Margaret (Margot) Asquith (1864–1945) was the second wife of Prime Minister Herbert Asquith. Her autobiography details her prominence in London Society.

Bond Street fascinated her; Bond Street early in the morning in the season; its flags flying; its shops; no splash; no glitter; one roll of tweed in the shop where her father had bought his suits for fifty years; a few pearls; salmon on an iceblock.

"That is all," she said, looking at the fishmonger's. "That is all," she repeated, pausing for a moment at the window of a glove shop where, before the War, you could buy almost perfect gloves. And her old Uncle William used to say a lady is known by her shoes and her gloves. He had turned on his bed one morning in the middle of the War. He had said, "I have had enough." Gloves and shoes; she had a passion for gloves; but her own daughter, her Elizabeth, cared not a straw for either of them.

Not a straw, she thought, going on up Bond Street to a shop where they kept flowers for her when she gave a party. Elizabeth really cared for her dog most of all. The whole house this morning smelt of tar.[3] Still, better poor Grizzle than Miss Kilman; better distemper and tar and all the rest of it than sitting mewed in a stuffy bedroom with a prayer book! Better anything, she was inclined to say. But it might be only a phase, as Richard said, such as all girls go through. It might be falling in love. But why with Miss Kilman? who had been badly treated of course; one must make allowances for that, and Richard said she was very able, had a really historical mind. Anyhow they were inseparable, and Elizabeth, her own daughter, went to Communion; and how she dressed, how she treated people who came to lunch she did not care a bit, it being her experience that the religious ecstasy made people callous (so did causes); dulled their feelings, for Miss Kilman would do anything for the Russians, starved herself for the Austrians, but in private inflicted positive torture, so insensitive was she, dressed in a green mackintosh coat. Year in year out she wore that coat; she perspired; she was never in the room five minutes without making you feel her superiority, your inferiority; how poor she was; how rich you were; how she lived in a slum without a cushion or a bed or a rug or whatever it might be, all her soul rusted with that grievance sticking in it, her dismissal from school during the War—poor embittered unfortunate creature! For it was not her one hated but the idea of her, which undoubtedly had gathered in to itself a great deal that was not Miss Kilman; had become one of those spectres with which one battles in the night; one of those spectres who stand astride us and suck up half our life-blood, dominators and tyrants; for no doubt with another throw of the dice, had the black been uppermost and not the white, she would have loved Miss Kilman! But not in this world. No.

It rasped her, though, to have stirring about in her this brutal monster! to hear twigs cracking and feel hooves planted down in the depths of that leaf-encumbered forest, the soul; never to be content quite, or quite secure, for at any moment the brute would be stirring, this hatred, which, especially since her illness, had power to make her feel scraped, hurt in her spine; gave her physical pain, and made all pleasure in beauty, in friendship, in being well, in being loved and making her home delightful rock, quiver, and bend as if indeed there were a monster grubbing at the roots, as if the whole panoply of content were nothing but self love! this hatred!

Nonsense, nonsense! she cried to herself, pushing through the swing doors of Mulberry's the florists.

3. Used as an agent in dog-grooming products.

She advanced, light, tall, very upright, to be greeted at once by button-faced Miss Pym, whose hands were always bright red, as if they had been stood in cold water with the flowers.

There were flowers: delphiniums, sweet peas, bunches of lilac; and carnations, masses of carnations. There were roses; there were irises. Ah yes—so she breathed in the earthy garden sweet smell as she stood talking to Miss Pym who owed her help, and thought her kind, for kind she had been years ago; very kind, but she looked older, this year, turning her head from side to side among the irises and roses and nodding tufts of lilac with her eyes half closed, snuffing in, after the street uproar, the delicious scent, the exquisite coolness. And then, opening her eyes, how fresh like frilled linen clean from a laundry laid in wicker trays the roses looked; and dark and prim the red carnations, holding their heads up; and all the sweet peas spreading in their bowls, tinged violet, snow white, pale—as if it were the evening and girls in muslin frocks came out to pick sweet peas and roses after the superb summer's day, with its almost blue-black sky, its delphiniums, its carnations, its arum lilies was over; and it was the moment between six and seven when every flower—roses, carnations, irises, lilac—glows; white, violet, red, deep orange; every flower seems to burn by itself, softly, purely in the misty beds; and how she loved the grey-white moths spinning in and out, over the cherry pie, over the evening primroses!

And as she began to go with Miss Pym from jar to jar, choosing, nonsense, nonsense, she said to herself, more and more gently, as if this beauty, this scent, this colour, and Miss Pym liking her, trusting her, were a wave which she let flow over her and surmount that hatred, that monster, surmount it all; and it lifted her up and up when—oh! a pistol shot in the street outside!

"Dear, those motor cars," said Miss Pym, going to the window to look, and coming back and smiling apologetically with her hands full of sweet peas, as if those motor cars, those tyres of motor cars, were all *her* fault.

The violent explosion which made Mrs Dalloway jump and Miss Pym go to the window and apologise came from a motor car which had drawn to the side of the pavement precisely opposite Mulberry's shop window. Passers-by who, of course, stopped and stared, had just time to see a face of the very greatest importance against the dove-grey upholstery, before a male hand drew the blind and there was nothing to be seen except a square of dove grey.

Yet rumours were at once in circulation from the middle of Bond Street to Oxford Street on one side, to Atkinson's scent shop on the other, passing invisibly, inaudibly, like a cloud, swift, veil-like upon hills, falling indeed with something of a cloud's sudden sobriety and stillness upon faces which a second before had been utterly disorderly. But now mystery had brushed them with her wing; they had heard the voice of authority; the spirit of religion was abroad with her eyes bandaged tight and her lips gaping wide. But nobody knew whose face had been seen. Was it the Prince of Wales's, the Queen's, the Prime Minister's? Whose face was it? Nobody knew.

Edgar J. Watkiss, with his roll of lead piping round his arm, said audibly, humorously of course: "The Proime Minister's kyar."

Septimus Warren Smith, who found himself unable to pass, heard him.

Septimus Warren Smith, aged about thirty, palefaced, beak-nosed, wearing brown shoes and a shabby overcoat, with hazel eyes which had that look of apprehension in them which makes complete strangers apprehensive too. The world has raised its whip; where will it descend?

Everything had come to a standstill. The throb of the motor engines sounded like a pulse irregularly drumming through an entire body. The sun became extraordinarily hot because the motor car had stopped outside Mulberry's shop window; old ladies on the tops of omnibuses spread their black parasols; here a green, here a red parasol opened with a little pop. Mrs Dalloway, coming to the window with her arms full of sweet peas, looked out with her little pink face pursed in enquiry. Every one looked at the motor car. Septimus looked. Boys on bicycles sprang off. Traffic accumulated. And there the motor car stood, with drawn blinds, and upon them a curious pattern like a tree, Septimus thought, and this gradual drawing together of everything to one centre before his eyes, as if some horror had come almost to the surface and was about to burst into flames, terrified him. The world wavered and quivered and threatened to burst into flames. It is I who am blocking the way, he thought. Was he not being looked at and pointed at; was he not weighted there, rooted to the pavement, for a purpose? But for what purpose?

"Let us go on, Septimus," said his wife, a little woman, with large eyes in a sallow pointed face; an Italian girl.

But Lucrezia herself could not help looking at the motor car and the tree pattern on the blinds. Was it the Queen in there—the Queen going shopping?

The chauffeur, who had been opening something, turning something, shutting something, got on to the box.[4]

"Come on," said Lucrezia.

But her husband, for they had been married four, five years now, jumped, started, and said, "All right!" angrily, as if she had interrupted him.

People must notice; people must see. People, she thought, looking at the crowd staring at the motor car; the English people, with their children and their horses and their clothes, which she admired in a way; but they were "people" now, because Septimus had said, "I will kill myself"; an awful thing to say. Suppose they had heard him? She looked at the crowd. Help, help! she wanted to cry out to butchers' boys and women. Help! Only last autumn she and Septimus had stood on the Embankment wrapped in the same cloak and, Septimus reading a paper instead of talking, she had snatched it from him and laughed in the old man's face who saw them! But failure one conceals. She must take him away into some park.

"Now we will cross," she said.

She had a right to his arm, though it was without feeling. He would give her, who was so simple, so impulsive, only twenty-four, without friends in England, who had left Italy for his sake, a piece of bone.

The motor car with its blinds drawn and an air of inscrutable reserve proceeded towards Piccadilly, still gazed at, still ruffling the faces on both sides of the street with the same dark breath of veneration whether for Queen, Prince, or Prime Minister nobody knew. The face itself had been seen only once by three people for a few seconds. Even the sex was now in dispute. But there could be no doubt that greatness was seated within; greatness was passing, hidden, down Bond Street, removed only by a hand's-breadth from ordinary people who might now, for the first and last time, be within speaking distance of the majesty of England, of the enduring symbol of the state which will be known to curious antiquaries, sifting the ruins of time, when London is a grass-grown path and all those hurrying along the pavement this Wednesday

4. The car having backfired and stalled, the driver recharges it by cranking the starting handle and returns to his seat.

morning are but bones with a few wedding rings mixed up in their dust and the gold stoppings of innumerable decayed teeth. The face in the motor car will then be known.

It is probably the Queen, thought Mrs Dalloway, coming out of Mulberry's with her flowers; the Queen. And for a second she wore a look of extreme dignity standing by the flower shop in the sunlight while the car passed at a foot's pace, with its blinds drawn. The Queen going to some hospital; the Queen opening some bazaar, thought Clarissa.

The crush was terrific for the time of day. Lords, Ascot, Hurlingham, what was it? she wondered, for the street was blocked. The British middle classes sitting sideways on the tops of omnibuses with parcels and umbrellas, yes, even furs on a day like this, were, she thought, more ridiculous, more unlike anything there has ever been than one could conceive; and the Queen herself held up; the Queen herself unable to pass. Clarissa was suspended on one side of Brook Street; Sir John Buckhurst, the old Judge on the other, with the car between them (Sir John had laid down the law for years and liked a well-dressed woman) when the chauffeur, leaning ever so slightly, said or showed something to the policeman, who saluted and raised his arm and jerked his head and moved the omnibus to the side and the car passed through. Slowly and very silently it took its way.

Clarissa guessed; Clarissa knew of course; she had seen something white, magical, circular, in the footman's hand, a disc inscribed with a name,—the Queen's, the Prince of Wales's, the Prime Minister's?—which, by force of its own lustre, burnt its way through (Clarissa saw the car diminishing, disappearing), to blaze among candelabras, glittering stars, breasts stiff with oak leaves, Hugh Whitbread and all his colleagues, the gentlemen of England, that night in Buckingham Palace. And Clarissa, too, gave a party. She stiffened a little; so she would stand at the top of her stairs.

The car had gone, but it had left a slight ripple which flowed through glove shops and hat shops and tailors' shops on both sides of Bond Street. For thirty seconds all heads were inclined the same way—to the window. Choosing a pair of gloves—should they be to the elbow or above it, lemon or pale grey?—ladies stopped; when the sentence was finished something had happened. Something so trifling in single instances that no mathematical instrument, though capable of transmitting shocks in China, could register the vibration; yet in its fulness rather formidable and in its common appeal emotional; for in all the hat shops and tailors' shops strangers looked at each other and thought of the dead; of the flag; of Empire. In a public house in a back street a Colonial insulted the House of Windsor[5] which led to words, broken beer glasses, and a general shindy, which echoed strangely across the way in the ears of girls buying white underlinen threaded with pure white ribbon for their weddings. For the surface agitation of the passing car as it sunk grazed something very profound.

Gliding across Piccadilly, the car turned down St James's Street. Tall men, men of robust physique, well-dressed men with their tail-coats and their white slips and their hair raked back who, for reasons difficult to discriminate, were standing in the bow window of Brooks's with their hands behind the tails of their coats, looking out, perceived instinctively that greatness was passing, and the pale light of the immortal presence fell upon them as it had fallen upon Clarissa Dalloway. At once they stood even straighter, and removed their hands, and seemed ready to attend their Sovereign, if need be, to the cannon's mouth, as their ancestors had done before them. The

5. The royal house of England since George V so dubbed it in 1917, in abrogation of the nominal German link in the dynastic name Saxe-Coburg-Gotha.

white busts and the little tables in the background covered with copies of the *Tatler* and syphons of soda water seemed to approve; seemed to indicate the flowing corn and the manor houses of England; and to return the frail hum of the motor wheels as the walls of a whispering gallery return a single voice expanded and made sonorous by the might of a whole cathedral. Shawled Moll Pratt with her flowers on the pavement wished the dear boy well (it was the Prince of Wales for certain) and would have tossed the price of a pot of beer—a bunch of roses—into St James's Street out of sheer light-heartedness and contempt of poverty had she not seen the constable's eye upon her, discouraging an old Irishwoman's loyalty. The sentries at St James's saluted; Queen Alexandra's policeman approved.

A small crowd meanwhile had gathered at the gates of Buckingham Palace. Listlessly, yet confidently, poor people all of them, they waited; looked at the Palace itself with the flag flying; at Victoria, billowing on her mound, admired her shelves of running water, her geraniums; singled out from the motor cars in the Mall first this one, then that; bestowed emotion, vainly, upon commoners out for a drive; recalled their tribute to keep it unspent while this car passed and that; and all the time let rumour accumulate in their veins and thrill the nerves in their thighs at the thought of Royalty looking at them; the Queen bowing; the Prince saluting; at the thought of the heavenly life divinely bestowed upon Kings; of the equerries and deep curtsies; of the Queen's old doll's house; of Princess Mary married to an Englishman, and the Prince—ah! the Prince! who took wonderfully, they said, after old King Edward, but was ever so much slimmer. The Prince lived at St James's; but he might come along in the morning to visit his mother.

So Sarah Bletchley said with her baby in her arms, tipping her foot up and down as though she were by her own fender in Pimlico, but keeping her eyes on the Mall, while Emily Coates ranged over the Palace windows and thought of the housemaids, the innumerable housemaids, the bedrooms, the innumerable bedrooms. Joined by an elderly gentleman with an Aberdeen terrier, by men without occupation, the crowd increased. Little Mr Bowley, who had rooms in the Albany and was sealed with wax over the deeper sources of life but could be unsealed suddenly, inappropriately, sentimentally, by this sort of thing—poor women waiting to see the Queen go past—poor women, nice little children, orphans, widows, the War—tut-tut—actually had tears in his eyes. A breeze flaunting ever so warmly down the Mall through the thin trees, past the bronze heroes, lifted some flag flying in the British breast of Mr Bowley and he raised his hat as the car turned into the Mall and held it high as the car approached; and let the poor mothers of Pimlico press close to him, and stood very upright. The car came on.

Suddenly Mrs Coates looked up into the sky. The sound of an aeroplane bored ominously into the ears of the crowd. There it was coming over the trees, letting out white smoke from behind, which curled and twisted, actually writing something! making letters in the sky! Every one looked up.

Dropping dead down the aeroplane soared straight up, curved in a loop, raced, sank, rose, and whatever it did, wherever it went, out fluttered behind it a thick ruffled bar of white smoke which curled and wreathed upon the sky in letters.[6] But what

6. Skywriting was still a fairly cutting-edge phenomenon when Woolf was writing this novel. After the war, aviator Major Jack C. Savage purchased an SE5a airplane, the best British fighter of World War I (then being sold at reduced war-surplus prices) and converted it for skywriting purposes, developing the technique as a form of advertising. By 1922 Savage had sold his services to large companies and drew amazed crowds onto the streets of London and other cities when slogans such as "Persil," "Castrol" and "*Daily Mail*" appeared in the sky.

letters? A C was it? an E, then an L? Only for a moment did they lie still; then they moved and melted and were rubbed out up in the sky, and the aeroplane shot further away and again, in a fresh space of sky, began writing a K, an E, a Y perhaps?

"Glaxo,"[7] said Mrs Coates in a strained, awestricken voice, gazing straight up, and her baby, lying stiff and white in her arms, gazed straight up.

"Kreemo,"[8] murmured Mrs Bletchley, like a sleepwalker. With his hat held out perfectly still in his hand, Mr Bowley gazed straight up. All down the Mall people were standing and looking up into the sky. As they looked the whole world became perfectly silent, and a flight of gulls crossed the sky, first one gull leading, then another, and in this extraordinary silence and peace, in this pallor, in this purity, bells struck eleven times, the sound fading up there among the gulls.

The aeroplane turned and raced and swooped exactly where it liked, swiftly, freely, like a skater—

"That's an E," said Mrs Bletchley—or a dancer—

"It's toffee," murmured Mr Bowley—(and the car went in at the gates and nobody looked at it), and shutting off the smoke, away and away it rushed, and the smoke faded and assembled itself round the broad white shapes of the clouds.

It had gone; it was behind the clouds. There was no sound. The clouds to which the letters E, G, or L had attached themselves moved freely, as if destined to cross from West to East on a mission of the greatest importance which would never be revealed, and yet certainly so it was—a mission of the greatest importance. Then suddenly, as a train comes out of a tunnel, the aeroplane rushed out of the clouds again, the sound boring into the ears of all people in the Mall, in the Green Park, in Piccadilly, in Regent Street, in Regent's Park, and the bar of smoke curved behind and it dropped down, and it soared up and wrote one letter after another—but what word was it writing?

Lucrezia Warren Smith, sitting by her husband's side on a seat in Regent's Park in the Broad Walk, looked up.

"Look, look, Septimus!" she cried. For Dr Holmes had told her to make her husband (who had nothing whatever seriously the matter with him but was a little out of sorts) take an interest in things outside himself.

So, thought Septimus, looking up, they are signalling to me. Not indeed in actual words; that is, he could not read the language yet; but it was plain enough, this beauty, this exquisite beauty, and tears filled his eyes as he looked at the smoke words languishing and melting in the sky and bestowing upon him in their inexhaustible charity and laughing goodness one shape after another of unimaginable beauty and signalling their intention to provide him, for nothing, for ever, for looking merely, with beauty, more beauty! Tears ran down his cheeks.

It was toffee; they were advertising toffee, a nursemaid told Rezia. Together they began to spell t . . . o . . . f . . .

"K . . . R . . . " said the nursemaid, and Septimus heard her say "Kay Arr" close to his ear, deeply, softly, like a mellow organ, but with a roughness in her voice like a grasshopper's, which rasped his spine deliciously and sent running up into his brain waves of sound which, concussing, broke. A marvellous discovery indeed—that the human voice in certain atmospheric conditions (for one must be scientific, above all scientific) can quicken trees into life! Happily Rezia put her hand with a tremendous

7. Glaxo India Limited, a UK pharmaceutical company, incorporated in 1924.

8. Kreemo was a brand of root beer.

View of Regent Street, London, 1927.

weight on his knee so that he was weighted down, transfixed, or the excitement of the elm trees rising and falling, rising and falling with all their leaves alight and the colour thinning and thickening from blue to the green of a hollow wave, like plumes on horses' heads, feathers on ladies', so proudly they rose and fell, so superbly, would have sent him mad. But he would not go mad. He would shut his eyes; he would see no more.

But they beckoned; leaves were alive; trees were alive. And the leaves being connected by millions of fibres with his own body, there on the seat, fanned it up and down; when the branch stretched he, too, made that statement. The sparrows fluttering, rising, and falling in jagged fountains were part of the pattern; the white and blue, barred with black branches. Sounds made harmonies with premeditation; the spaces between them were as significant as the sounds. A child cried. Rightly far away a horn sounded. All taken together meant the birth of a new religion—

"Septimus!" said Rezia. He started violently. People must notice.

"I am going to walk to the fountain and back," she said.

For she could stand it no longer. Dr Holmes might say there was nothing the matter. Far rather would she that he were dead! She could not sit beside him when he stared so and did not see her and made everything terrible; sky and tree, children playing, dragging carts, blowing whistles, falling down; all were terrible. And he would not kill himself; and she could tell no one. "Septimus has been working too hard"—that was all she could say to her own mother. To love makes one solitary, she thought. She could tell nobody, not even Septimus now, and looking back, she saw him sitting in his shabby overcoat alone, on the seat, hunched up, staring. And it was cowardly for a man to say he would kill himself, but Septimus had fought; he was brave; he was not Septimus now. She put on her lace collar. She put on her new hat and he never noticed; and he was happy without her. Nothing could make her happy without him! Nothing! He was selfish. So men are. For he was not ill. Dr Holmes said there was nothing the matter with him. She spread her hand before her. Look! Her wedding ring slipped—she had grown so thin. It was she who suffered—but she had nobody to tell.

Far was Italy and the white houses and the room where her sisters sat making hats, and the streets crowded every evening with people walking, laughing out loud, not half alive like people here, huddled up in Bath chairs, looking at a few ugly flowers stuck in pots!

"For you should see the Milan gardens," she said aloud. But to whom?

There was nobody. Her words faded. So a rocket fades. Its sparks, having grazed their way into the night, surrender to it, dark descends, pours over the outlines of houses and towers; bleak hillsides soften and fall in. But though they are gone, the night is full of them; robbed of colour, blank of windows, they exist more ponderously, give out what the frank daylight fails to transmit—the trouble and suspense of things conglomerated there in the darkness; huddled together in the darkness; reft of the relief which dawn brings when, washing the walls white and grey, spotting each windowpane, lifting the mist from the fields, showing the redbrown cows peacefully grazing, all is once more decked out to the eye; exists again. I am alone; I am alone! she cried, by the fountain in Regent's Park (staring at the Indian and his cross), as perhaps at midnight, when all boundaries are lost, the country reverts to its ancient shape, as the Romans saw it, lying cloudy, when they landed, and the hills had no names and rivers wound they knew not where—such was her darkness; when suddenly, as if a shelf were shot forth and she stood on it, she said how she was his wife, married years ago in Milan, his wife, and would never, never tell that he was mad! Turning, the shelf fell; down, down she dropped. For he was gone, she thought—gone, as he threatened, to kill himself—to throw himself under a cart! But no; there he was; still sitting alone on the seat, in his shabby overcoat, his legs crossed, staring, talking aloud.

Men must not cut down trees. There is a God. (He noted such revelations on the backs of envelopes.) Change the world. No one kills from hatred. Make it known (he wrote it down). He waited. He listened. A sparrow perched on the railing opposite chirped Septimus, Septimus, four or five times over and went on, drawing its notes out, to sing freshly and piercingly in Greek words how there is no crime and, joined by another sparrow, they sang in voices prolonged and piercing in Greek words, from trees in the meadow of life beyond a river where the dead walk, how there is no death.

There was his hand; there the dead. White things were assembling behind the railings opposite. But he dared not look. Evans was behind the railings!

"What are you saying?" said Rezia suddenly, sitting down by him.

Interrupted again! She was always interrupting.

Away from people—they must get away from people, he said (jumping up), right away over there, where there were chairs beneath a tree and the long slope of the park dipped like a length of green stuff with a ceiling cloth of blue and pink smoke high above, and there was a rampart of far irregular houses hazed in smoke, the traffic hummed in a circle, and on the right, duncoloured animals stretched long necks over the Zoo palings, barking, howling. There they sat down under a tree.

"Look," she implored him, pointing at a little troop of boys carrying cricket stumps, and one shuffled, spun round on his heel and shuffled, as if he were acting a clown at the music hall.

"Look," she implored him, for Dr Holmes had told her to make him notice real things, go to a music hall, play cricket—that was the very game, Dr Holmes said, a nice out-of-door game, the very game for her husband.

"Look," she repeated.

Look the unseen bade him, the voice which now communicated with him who was the greatest of mankind, Septimus, lately taken from life to death, the Lord who had come to renew society, who lay like a coverlet, a snow blanket smitten only by the sun, for ever unwasted, suffering for ever, the scapegoat, the eternal sufferer, but he did not want it, he moaned, putting from him with a wave of his hand that eternal suffering, that eternal loneliness.

"Look," she repeated, for he must not talk aloud to himself out of doors.

"Oh look," she implored him. But what was there to look at? A few sheep. That was all.

The way to Regent's Park Tube station—could they tell her the way to Regent's Park Tube station—Maisie Johnson wanted to know. She was only up from Edinburgh two days ago.

"Not this way—over there!" Rezia exclaimed, waving her aside, lest she should see Septimus.

Both seemed queer, Maisie Johnson thought. Everything seemed very queer. In London for the first time, come to take up a post at her uncle's in Leadenhall Street, and now walking through Regent's Park in the morning, this couple on the chairs gave her quite a turn; the young woman seeming foreign, the man looking queer; so that should she be very old she would still remember and make it jangle again among her memories how she had walked through Regent's Park on a fine summer's morning fifty years ago. For she was only nineteen and had got her way at last, to come to London; and now how queer it was, this couple she had asked the way of, and the girl started and jerked her hand, and the man—he seemed awfully odd; quarrelling, perhaps; parting for ever, perhaps; something was up, she knew; and now all these people (for she returned to the Broad Walk), the stone basins, the prim flowers, the old men and women, invalids most of them in Bath chairs—all seemed, after Edinburgh, so queer. And Maisie Johnson, as she joined that gently trudging, vaguely gazing, breeze-kissed company—squirrels perching and preening, sparrow fountains fluttering for crumbs, dogs busy with the railings, busy with each other, while the soft warm air washed over them and lent to the fixed unsurprised gaze with which they received life something whimsical and mollified—Maisie Johnson positively felt she must cry Oh! (For that young man on the seat had given her quite a turn. Something was up, she knew.)

Horror! horror! she wanted to cry. (She had left her people; they had warned her what would happen.)

Why hadn't she stayed at home? she cried, twisting the knob of the iron railing.

That girl, thought Mrs Dempster (who saved crusts for the squirrels and often ate her lunch in Regent's Park), don't know a thing yet; and really it seemed to her better to be a little stout, a little slack, a little moderate in one's expectations. Percy drank. Well, better to have a son, thought Mrs Dempster. She had had a hard time of it, and couldn't help smiling at a girl like that. You'll get married, for you're pretty enough, thought Mrs Dempster. Get married, she thought, and then you'll know. Oh, the cooks, and so on. Every man has his ways. But whether I'd have chosen quite like that if I could have known, thought Mrs Dempster, and could not help wishing to whisper a word to Maisie Johnson; to feel on the creased pouch of her worn old face the kiss of pity. For it's been a hard life, thought Mrs Dempster. What hadn't she given to it? Roses; figure; her feet too. (She drew the knobbed lumps beneath her skirt.)

Roses, she thought sardonically. All trash, m'dear. For really, what with eating, drinking, and mating, the bad days and good, life had been no mere matter of roses, and what was more, let me tell you, Carrie Dempster had no wish to change her lot with any woman's in Kentish Town! But, she implored, pity. Pity, for the loss of roses. Pity she asked of Maisie Johnson, standing by the hyacinth beds.

Ah, but that aeroplane! Hadn't Mrs Dempster always longed to see foreign parts? She had a nephew, a missionary. It soared and shot. She always went on the sea at Margate, not out o' sight of land, but she had no patience with women who were afraid of water. It swept and fell. Her stomach was in her mouth. Up again. There's a fine young feller aboard of it, Mrs Dempster wagered, and away and away it went, fast and fading, away and away the aeroplane shot; soaring over Greenwich and all the masts; over the little island of grey churches, St Paul's and the rest till, on either side of London, fields spread out and dark brown woods where adventurous thrushes hopping boldly, glancing quickly, snatched the snail and tapped him on a stone, once, twice, thrice.

Away and away the aeroplane shot, till it was nothing but a bright spark; an aspiration; a concentration; a symbol (so it seemed to Mr Bentley, vigorously rolling his strip of turf at Greenwich) of man's soul; of his determination, thought Mr Bentley, sweeping round the cedar tree, to get outside his body, beyond his house, by means of thought, Einstein,[9] speculation,[1] mathematics, the Mendelian theory[2]—away the aeroplane shot.

Then, while a seedy-looking nondescript man carrying a leather bag stood on the steps of St Paul's Cathedral, and hesitated, for within was what balm, how great a welcome, how many tombs with banners waving over them, tokens of victories not over armies, but over, he thought, that plaguy spirit of truth seeking which leaves me at present without a situation, and more than that, the cathedral offers company, he thought, invites you to membership of a society; great men belong to it; martyrs have died for it; why not enter in, he thought, put this leather bag stuffed with pamphlets before an altar, a cross, the symbol of something which has soared beyond seeking and questing and knocking of words together and has become all spirit, disembodied, ghostly—why not enter in? he thought and while he hesitated out flew the aeroplane over Ludgate Circus.

It was strange; it was still. Not a sound was to be heard above the traffic. Unguided it seemed; sped of its own free will. And now, curving up and up, straight up, like something mounting in ecstasy, in pure delight, out from behind poured white smoke looping, writing a T, an O, an F.

"What are they looking at?" said Clarissa Dalloway to the maid who opened her door.

The hall of the house was cool as a vault. Mrs Dalloway raised her hand to her eyes, and, as the maid shut the door to, and she heard the swish of Lucy's skirts, she felt like a nun who has left the world and feels fold round her the familiar veils and the response to old devotions. The cook whistled in the kitchen. She heard the click

9. Einstein had just won the Nobel Prize in Physics in 1922 for his general theory of relativity.
1. The practice of speculating in stocks or land.
2. Gregor Mendel (1823–1884), the founder of modern genetics, derived certain basic laws of heredity by observing the occurrence of specific traits over successive generations of pea plants.

of the typewriter. It was her life, and, bending her head over the hall table, she bowed beneath the influence, felt blessed and purified, saying to herself, as she took the pad with the telephone message on it, how moments like this are buds on the tree of life, flowers of darkness they are, she thought (as if some lovely rose had blossomed for her eyes only); not for a moment did she believe in God; but all the more, she thought, taking up the pad, must one repay in daily life to servants, yes, to dogs and canaries, above all to Richard her husband, who was the foundation of it—of the gay sounds, of the green lights, of the cook even whistling, for Mrs Walker was Irish and whistled all day long—one must pay back from this secret deposit of exquisite moments, she thought, lifting the pad, while Lucy stood by her, trying to explain how.

"Mr Dalloway, ma'am"—

Clarissa read on the telephone pad, "Lady Bruton wishes to know if Mr Dalloway will lunch with her to-day."

"Mr Dalloway, ma'am, told me to tell you he would be lunching out."

"Dear!" said Clarissa, and Lucy shared as she meant her to her disappointment (but not the pang); felt the concord between them; took the hint; thought how the gentry love; gilded her own future with calm; and, taking Mrs Dalloway's parasol, handled it like a sacred weapon which a Goddess, having acquitted herself honourably in the field of battle, sheds, and placed it in the umbrella stand.

"Fear no more," said Clarissa. Fear no more the heat o' the sun; for the shock of Lady Bruton asking Richard to lunch without her made the moment in which she had stood shiver, as a plant on the river-bed feels the shock of a passing oar and shivers: so she rocked: so she shivered.

Millicent Bruton, whose lunch parties were said to be extraordinarily amusing, had not asked her. No vulgar jealousy could separate her from Richard. But she feared time itself, and read on Lady Bruton's face, as if it had been a dial cut in impassive stone, the dwindling of life; how year by year her share was sliced; how little the margin that remained was capable any longer of stretching, of absorbing, as in the youthful years, the colours, salts, tones of existence, so that she filled the room she entered, and felt often as she stood hesitating one moment on the threshold of her drawing-room, an exquisite suspense, such as might stay a diver before plunging while the sea darkens and brightens beneath him, and the waves which threaten to break, but only gently split their surface, roll and conceal and encrust as they just turn over the weeds with pearl.

She put the pad on the hall table. She began to go slowly upstairs, with her hand on the bannisters, as if she had left a party, where now this friend now that had flashed back her face, her voice; had shut the door and gone out and stood alone, a single figure against the appalling night, or rather, to be accurate, against the stare of this matter-of-fact June morning; soft with the glow of rose petals for some, she knew, and felt it, as she paused by the open staircase window which let in blinds flapping, dogs barking, let in, she thought, feeling herself suddenly shrivelled, aged, breastless, the grinding, blowing, flowering of the day, out of doors, out of the window, out of her body and brain which now failed, since Lady Bruton, whose lunch parties were said to be extraordinarily amusing, had not asked her.

Like a nun withdrawing, or a child exploring a tower, she went upstairs, paused at the window, came to the bathroom. There was the green linoleum and a tap dripping. There was an emptiness about the heart of life; an attic room. Women must put off their rich apparel. At midday they must disrobe. She pierced the pincushion and laid her feathered yellow hat on the bed. The sheets were clean, tight stretched in a broad white band from side to side. Narrower and narrower would her bed be. The candle was half burnt down and she had read deep in Baron Marbot's *Memoirs*.[3] She had read late at night of the retreat from Moscow. For the House sat so long that Richard insisted, after her illness, that she must sleep undisturbed. And really she preferred to read of the retreat from Moscow. He knew it. So the room was an attic; the bed narrow; and lying there reading, for she slept badly, she could not dispel a virginity preserved through childbirth which clung to her like a sheet. Lovely in girlhood, suddenly there came a moment—for example on the river beneath the woods at Clieveden—when, through some contraction of this cold spirit, she had failed him. And then at Constantinople, and again and again. She could see what she lacked. It was not beauty; it was not mind. It was something central which permeated; something warm which broke up surfaces and rippled the cold contact of man and woman, or of women together. For *that* she could dimly perceive. She resented it, had a scruple picked up Heaven knows where, or, as she felt, sent by Nature (who is invariably wise); yet she could not resist sometimes yielding to the charm of a woman, not a girl, of a woman confessing, as to her they often did, some scrape, some folly. And whether it was pity, or their beauty, or that she was older, or some accident—like a faint scent, or a violin next door (so strange is the power of sounds at certain moments), she did undoubtedly then feel what men felt. Only for a moment; but it was enough. It was a sudden revelation, a tinge like a blush which one tried to check and then, as it spread, one yielded to its expansion, and rushed to the farthest verge and there quivered and felt the world come closer, swollen with some astonishing significance, some pressure of rapture, which split its thin skin and gushed and poured with an extraordinary alleviation over the cracks and sores! Then, for that moment, she had seen an illumination; a match burning in a crocus; an inner meaning almost expressed. But the close withdrew; the hard softened. It was over—the moment. Against such moments (with women too) there contrasted (as she laid her hat down) the bed and Baron Marbot and the candle half-burnt. Lying awake, the floor creaked; the lit house was suddenly darkened, and if she raised her head she could just hear the click of the handle released as gently as possible by Richard, who slipped upstairs in his socks and then, as often as not, dropped his hotwater bottle and swore! How she laughed!

But this question of love (she thought, putting her coat away), this falling in love with women. Take Sally Seton; her relation in the old days with Sally Seton. Had not that, after all, been love?

She sat on the floor—that was her first impression of Sally—she sat on the floor with her arms round her knees, smoking a cigarette. Where could it have been? The Mannings? The Kinloch-Jones's? At some party (where, she could not be certain), for she had a distinct recollection of saying to the man she was with, "Who is *that?*" And he had told her, and said that Sally's parents did not get on (how that shocked her—that one's parents should quarrel!). But all that evening she could not take her eyes off Sally. It was an extraordinary beauty of the kind she most admired, dark, large-eyed, with that quality which, since she hadn't got it herself, she always envied—a sort of abandonment, as if she could say anything, do anything; a quality much commoner in foreigners than in Englishwomen. Sally always said she had French blood in

3. Jean-Baptiste Antoine Marcellin, baron de Marbot (1782–1854). A general in Napoleon's army, his memoirs offer a first-hand account of Napoleon's disastrous Russian campaign and of the decimation of the French army during its retreat from Moscow in 1812.

her veins, an ancestor had been with Marie Antoinette, had his head cut off, left a ruby ring. Perhaps that summer she came to stay at Bourton, walking in quite unexpectedly without a penny in her pocket, one night after dinner, and upsetting poor Aunt Helena to such an extent that she never forgave her. There had been some quarrel at home. She literally hadn't a penny that night when she came to them—had pawned a brooch to come down. She had rushed off in a passion. They sat up till all hours of the night talking. Sally it was who made her feel, for the first time, how sheltered the life at Bourton was. She knew nothing about sex—nothing about social problems. She had once seen an old man who had dropped dead in a field—she had seen cows just after their calves were born. But Aunt Helena never liked discussion of anything (when Sally gave her William Morris,[4] it had to be wrapped in brown paper). There they sat, hour after hour, talking in her bedroom at the top of the house, talking about life, how they were to reform the world. They meant to found a society to abolish private property, and actually had a letter written, though not sent out. The ideas were Sally's, of course—but very soon she was just as excited—read Plato in bed before breakfast; read Morris; read Shelley by the hour.

Sally's power was amazing, her gift, her personality. There was her way with flowers, for instance. At Bourton they always had stiff little vases all the way down the table. Sally went out, picked hollyhocks, dahlias—all sorts of flowers that had never been seen together—cut their heads off, and made them swim on the top of water in bowls. The effect was extraordinary—coming in to dinner in the sunset. (Of course Aunt Helena thought it wicked to treat flowers like that.) Then she forgot her sponge, and ran along the passage naked. That grim old housemaid, Ellen Atkins, went about grumbling—"Suppose any of the gentlemen had seen?" Indeed she did shock people. She was untidy, Papa said.

The strange thing, on looking back, was the purity, the integrity, of her feeling for Sally. It was not like one's feeling for a man. It was completely disinterested, and besides, it had a quality which could only exist between women, between women just grown up. It was protective, on her side; sprang from a sense of being in league together, a presentiment of something that was bound to part them (they spoke of marriage always as a catastrophe), which led to this chivalry, this protective feeling which was much more on her side than Sally's. For in those days she was completely reckless; did the most idiotic things out of bravado; bicycled round the parapet on the terrace; smoked cigars. Absurd, she was—very absurd. But the charm was overpowering, to her at least, so that she could remember standing in her bedroom at the top of the house holding the hot-water can in her hands and saying aloud, "She is beneath this roof. . . . She is beneath this roof!"

No, the words meant absolutely nothing to her now. She could not even get an echo of her old emotion. But she could remember going cold with excitement, and doing her hair in a kind of ecstasy (now the old feeling began to come back to her, as she took out her hairpins, laid them on the dressing-table, began to do her hair), with the rooks flaunting up and down in the pink evening light, and dressing, and going downstairs, and feeling as she crossed the hall "if it were now to die 'twere now to be

4. Morris (1834–1894) was an artist and critic who dedicated himself to increasingly radical political activity beginning in the 1870s. He was an active proponent of the Socialist movement, which he believed was capable of solving the worst problems—poverty, unemployment, the death of art, the growing gap between the upper and lower classes—of industrialized Victorian society. In 1884, he published his *Art and Socialism* and (with Hyndman) *A Summary of the Principles of Socialism*, and until his death, he lectured regularly on art and socialism.

most happy."[5] That was her feeling—Othello's feeling, and she felt it, she was convinced, as strongly as Shakespeare meant Othello to feel it, all because she was coming down to dinner in a white frock to meet Sally Seton!

She was wearing pink gauze—was that possible? She *seemed,* anyhow, all light, glowing, like some bird or air ball that has flown in, attached itself for a moment to a bramble. But nothing is so strange when one is in love (and what was this except being in love?) as the complete indifference of other people. Aunt Helena just wandered off after dinner; Papa read the paper. Peter Walsh might have been there, and old Miss Cummings; Joseph Breitkopf certainly was, for he came every summer, poor old man, for weeks and weeks, and pretended to read German with her, but really played the piano and sang Brahms without any voice.

All this was only a background for Sally. She stood by the fireplace talking, in that beautiful voice which made everything she said sound like a caress, to Papa, who had begun to be attracted rather against his will (he never got over lending her one of his books and finding it soaked on the terrace), when suddenly she said, "What a shame to sit indoors!" and they all went out on to the terrace and walked up and down. Peter Walsh and Joseph Breitkopf went on about Wagner. She and Sally fell a little behind. Then came the most exquisite moment of her whole life passing a stone urn with flowers in it. Sally stopped; picked a flower; kissed her on the lips. The whole world might have turned upside down! The others disappeared; there she was alone with Sally. And she felt that she had been given a present, wrapped up, and told just to keep it, not to look at it—a diamond, something infinitely precious, wrapped up, which, as they walked (up and down, up and down), she uncovered, or the radiance burnt through, the revelation, the religious feeling!—when old Joseph and Peter faced them:

"Star-gazing?" said Peter.

It was like running one's face against a granite wall in the darkness! It was shocking; it was horrible!

Not for herself. She felt only how Sally was being mauled already, maltreated; she felt his hostility; his jealousy; his determination to break into their companionship. All this she saw as one sees a landscape in a flash of lightning—and Sally (never had she admired her so much!) gallantly taking her way unvanquished. She laughed. She made old Joseph tell her the names of the stars, which he liked doing very seriously. She stood there: she listened. She heard the names of the stars.

"Oh this horror!" she said to herself, as if she had known all along that something would interrupt, would embitter her moment of happiness.

Yet, after all, how much she owed to him later. Always when she thought of him she thought of their quarrels for some reason—because she wanted his good opinion so much, perhaps. She owed him words: "sentimental," "civilised"; they started up every day of her life as if he guarded her. A book was sentimental; an attitude to life sentimental. "Sentimental," perhaps she was to be thinking of the past. What would he think, she wondered, when he came back?

That she had grown older? Would he say that, or would she see him thinking when he came back, that she had grown older? It was true. Since her illness she had turned almost white.

5. *Othello* 2.1.87–88.

Laying her brooch on the table, she had a sudden spasm, as if, while she mused, the icy claws had had the chance to fix in her. She was not old yet. She had just broken into her fifty-second year. Months and months of it were still untouched. June, July, August! Each still remained almost whole, and, as if to catch the falling drop, Clarissa (crossing to the dressing-table) plunged into the very heart of the moment, transfixed it, there—the moment of this June morning on which was the pressure of all the other mornings, seeing the glass, the dressing-table, and all the bottles afresh, collecting the whole of her at one point (as she looked into the glass), seeing the delicate pink face of the woman who was that very night to give a party; of Clarissa Dalloway; of herself.

How many million times she had seen her face, and always with the same imperceptible contraction! She pursed her lips when she looked in the glass. It was to give her face point. That was her self—pointed; dart-like; definite. That was her self when some effort, some call on her to be her self, drew the parts together, she alone knew how different, how incompatible and composed so for the world only into one centre, one diamond, one woman who sat in her drawing-room and made a meeting-point, a radiancy no doubt in some dull lives, a refuge for the lonely to come to, perhaps; she had helped young people, who were grateful to her; had tried to be the same always, never showing a sign of all the other sides of her—faults, jealousies, vanities, suspicions, like this of Lady Bruton not asking her to lunch; which, she thought (combing her hair finally), is utterly base! Now, where was her dress?

Her evening dresses hung in the cupboard. Clarissa, plunging her hand into the softness, gently detached the green dress and carried it to the window. She had torn it. Some one had trod on the skirt. She had felt it give at the Embassy party at the top among the folds. By artificial light the green shone, but lost its colour now in the sun. She would mend it. Her maids had too much to do. She would wear it to-night. She would take her silks, her scissors, her—what was it?—her thimble, of course, down into the drawing-room, for she must also write, and see that things generally were more or less in order.

Strange, she thought, pausing on the landing, and assembling that diamond shape, that single person, strange how a mistress knows the very moment, the very temper of her house! Faint sounds rose in spirals up the well of the stairs; the swish of a mop; tapping; knocking; a loudness when the front door opened; a voice repeating a message in the basement; the chink of silver on a tray; clean silver for the party. All was for the party.

(And Lucy, coming into the drawing-room with her tray held out, put the giant candlesticks on the mantelpiece, the silver casket in the middle, turned the crystal dolphin towards the clock. They would come; they would stand; they would talk in the mincing tones which she could imitate, ladies and gentlemen. Of all, her mistress was loveliest—mistress of silver, of linen, of china, for the sun, the silver, doors off their hinges, Rumpelmayer's men, gave her a sense, as she laid the paper-knife on the inlaid table, of something achieved. Behold! Behold! she said, speaking to her old friends in the baker's shop, where she had first seen service at Caterham, prying into the glass. She was Lady Angela, attending Princess Mary, when in came Mrs Dalloway.)

"Oh Lucy," she said, "the silver does look nice!"

"And how," she said, turning the crystal dolphin to stand straight, "how did you enjoy the play last night?" "Oh, they had to go before the end!" she said. "They had to be back at ten!" she said. "So they don't know what happened," she said. "That does seem hard luck," she said (for her servants stayed later, if they asked her). "That does seem rather a shame," she said, taking the old bald-looking cushion in the middle of the sofa and putting it in Lucy's arms, and giving her a little push, and crying:

"Take it away! Give it to Mrs Walker with my compliments! Take it away!" she cried.

And Lucy stopped at the drawing-room door, holding the cushion, and said, very shyly, turning a little pink, Couldn't she help to mend that dress?

But, said Mrs Dalloway, she had enough on her hands already, quite enough of her own to do without that.

"But, thank you, Lucy, oh, thank you," said Mrs Dalloway, and thank you, thank you, she went on saying (sitting down on the sofa with her dress over her knees, her scissors, her silks), thank you, thank you, she went on saying in gratitude to her servants generally for helping her to be like this, to be what she wanted, gentle, generous-hearted. Her servants liked her. And then this dress of hers—where was the tear? and now her needle to be threaded. This was a favourite dress, one of Sally Parker's, the last almost she ever made, alas, for Sally had now retired, living at Ealing, and if ever I have a moment, thought Clarissa (but never would she have a moment any more), I shall go and see her at Ealing. For she was a character, thought Clarissa, a real artist. She thought of little out-of-the-way things; yet her dresses were never queer. You could wear them at Hatfield; at Buckingham Palace. She had worn them at Hatfield; at Buckingham Palace.

Quiet descended on her, calm, content, as her needle, drawing the silk smoothly to its gentle pause, collected the green folds together and attached them, very lightly, to the belt. So on a summer's day waves collect, overbalance, and fall; collect and fall; and the whole world seems to be saying "that is all" more and more ponderously, until even the heart in the body which lies in the sun on the beach says too, That is all. Fear no more, says the heart. Fear no more, says the heart, committing its burden to some sea, which sighs collectively for all sorrows, and renews, begins, collects, lets fall. And the body alone listens to the passing bee; the wave breaking; the dog barking, far away barking and barking.

"Heavens, the front-door bell!" exclaimed Clarissa, staying her needle. Roused, she listened.

"Mrs Dalloway will see me," said the elderly man in the hall. "Oh yes, she will see *me*," he repeated, putting Lucy aside very benevolently, and running upstairs ever so quickly. "Yes, yes, yes," he muttered as he ran upstairs. "She will see me. After five years in India, Clarissa will see me."

"Who can—what can," asked Mrs Dalloway (thinking it was outrageous to be interrupted at eleven o'clock on the morning of the day she was giving a party), hearing a step on the stairs. She heard a hand upon the door. She made to hide her dress, like a virgin protecting chastity, respecting privacy. Now the brass knob slipped. Now the door opened, and in came—for a single second she could not remember what he was called! so surprised she was to see him, so glad, so shy, so utterly taken aback to have Peter Walsh come to her unexpectedly in the morning! (She had not read his letter.)

"And how are you?" said Peter Walsh, positively trembling; taking both her hands; kissing both her hands. She's grown older, he thought, sitting down. I shan't tell her anything about it, he thought, for she's grown older. She's looking at me, he thought, a sudden embarrassment coming over him, though he had kissed her hands. Putting his hand into his pocket, he took out a large pocket-knife and half opened the blade.

Exactly the same, thought Clarissa; the same queer look; the same check suit; a little out of the straight his face is, a little thinner, dryer, perhaps, but he looks awfully well, and just the same.

"How heavenly it is to see you again!" she exclaimed. He had his knife out. That's so like him, she thought.

He had only reached town last night, he said; would have to go down into the country at once; and how was everything, how was everybody—Richard? Elizabeth?

"And what's all this?" he said, tilting his pen-knife towards her green dress.

He's very well dressed, thought Clarissa; yet he always criticises *me*.

Here she is mending her dress; mending her dress as usual, he thought; here she's been sitting all the time I've been in India; mending her dress; playing about; going to parties; running to the House and back and all that, he thought, growing more and more irritated, more and more agitated, for there's nothing in the world so bad for some women as marriage, he thought; and politics; and having a Conservative husband, like the admirable Richard. So it is, so it is, he thought, shutting his knife with a snap.

"Richard's very well. Richard's at a Committee," said Clarissa.

And she opened her scissors, and said, did he mind her just finishing what she was doing to her dress, for they had a party that night?

"Which I shan't ask you to," she said. "My dear Peter!" she said.

But it was delicious to hear her say that—my dear Peter! Indeed, it was all so delicious—the silver, the chairs; all so delicious!

Why wouldn't she ask him to her party? he asked.

Now of course, thought Clarissa, he's enchanting! perfectly enchanting! Now I remember how impossible it was ever to make up my mind—and why did I make up my mind—not to marry him? she wondered, that awful summer?

"But it's so extraordinary that you should have come this morning!" she cried, putting her hands, one on top of another, down on her dress.

"Do you remember," she said, "how the blinds used to flap at Bourton?"

"They did," he said; and he remembered break-fasting alone, very awkwardly, with her father; who had died; and he had not written to Clarissa. But he had never got on well with old Parry, that querulous, weak-kneed old man, Clarissa's father, Justin Parry.

"I often wish I'd got on better with your father," he said.

"But he never liked any one who—our friends," said Clarissa; and could have bitten her tongue for thus reminding Peter that he had wanted to marry her.

Of course I did, thought Peter; it almost broke my heart too, he thought; and was overcome with his own grief, which rose like a moon looked at from a terrace, ghastly beautiful with light from the sunken day. I was more unhappy than I've ever been since, he thought. And as if in truth he were sitting there on the terrace he edged a little towards Clarissa; put his hand out; raised it; let it fall. There above them it hung, that moon. She too seemed to be sitting with him on the terrace, in the moonlight.

"Herbert has it now," she said. "I never go there now," she said.

Then, just as happens on a terrace in the moonlight, when one person begins to feel ashamed that he is already bored, and yet as the other sits silent, very quiet, sadly looking at the moon, does not like to speak, moves his foot, clears his throat, notices some iron scroll on a table leg, stirs a leaf, but says nothing—so Peter Walsh did now. For why go back like this to the past? he thought. Why make him think of it again? Why make him suffer, when she had tortured him so infernally? Why?

"Do you remember the lake?" she said, in an abrupt voice, under the pressure of an emotion which caught her heart, made the muscles of her throat stiff, and contracted her lips in a spasm as she said "lake." For she was a child, throwing bread to the ducks, between her parents, and at the same time a grown woman coming to her parents who stood by the lake, holding her life in her arms which, as she neared them, grew larger and larger in her arms, until it became a whole life, a complete life, which she put down by them and said, "This is what I have made of it! This!" And what had she made of it? What, indeed? sitting there sewing this morning with Peter.

She looked at Peter Walsh; her look, passing through all that time and that emotion, reached him doubtfully; settled on him tearfully; and rose and fluttered away, as a bird touches a branch and rises and flutters away. Quite simply she wiped her eyes.

"Yes," said Peter. "Yes, yes, yes," he said, as if she drew up to the surface something which positively hurt him as it rose. Stop! Stop! he wanted to cry. For he was not old; his life was not over; not by any means. He was only just past fifty. Shall I tell her, he thought, or not? He would like to make a clean breast of it all. But she is too cold, he thought; sewing, with her scissors; Daisy would look ordinary beside Clarissa. And she would think me a failure, which I am in their sense, he thought; in the Dalloways' sense. Oh yes, he had no doubt about that; he was a failure, compared with all this—the inlaid table, the mounted paper-knife, the dolphin and the candlesticks, the chair-covers and the old valuable English tinted prints—he was a failure! I detest the smugness of the whole affair, he thought; Richard's doing, not Clarissa's; save that she married him. (Here Lucy came into the room, carrying silver, more silver, but charming, slender, graceful she looked, he thought, as she stooped to put it down.) And this has been going on all the time! he thought; week after week; Clarissa's life; while I—he thought; and at once everything seemed to radiate from him; journeys; rides; quarrels; adventures; bridge parties; love affairs; work; work, work! and he took out his knife quite openly—his old horn-handled knife which Clarissa could swear he had had these thirty years—and clenched his fist upon it.

What an extraordinary habit that was, Clarissa thought; always playing with a knife. Always making one feel, too, frivolous; empty-minded; a mere silly chatterbox, as he used. But I too, she thought, and, taking up her needle, summoned, like a Queen whose guards have fallen sleep and left her unprotected (she had been quite taken aback by this visit—it had upset her) so that any one can stroll in and have a look at her where she lies with the brambles curving over her, summoned to her help the things she did; the things she liked; her husband; Elizabeth; her self, in short, which Peter hardly knew now, all to come about her and beat off the enemy.

"Well, and what's happened to you?" she said. So before a battle begins, the horses paw the ground; toss their heads; the light shines on their flanks; their necks curve. So Peter Walsh and Clarissa, sitting side by side on the blue sofa, challenged each other. His powers chafed and tossed in him. He assembled from different quarters all sorts of things; praise; his career at Oxford; his marriage, which she knew nothing whatever about; how he had loved; and altogether done his job.

"Millions of things!" he exclaimed, and, urged by the assembly of powers which were now charging this way and that and giving him the feeling at once frightening and extremely exhilarating of being rushed through the air on the shoulders of people he could no longer see, he raised his hands to his forehead.

Clarissa sat very upright; drew in her breath.

"I am in love," he said, not to her however, but to some one raised up in the dark so that you could not touch her but must lay your garland down on the grass in the dark.

"In love," he repeated, now speaking rather dryly to Clarissa Dalloway; "in love with a girl in India." He had deposited his garland. Clarissa could make what she would of it.

"In love!" she said. That he at his age should be sucked under in his little bow-tie by that monster! And there's no flesh on his neck; his hands are red; and he's six months older than I am! her eye flashed back to her; but in her heart she felt, all the same, he is in love. He has that, she felt; he is in love.

But the indomitable egotism which for ever rides down the hosts opposed to it, the river which says on, on, on; even though, it admits, there may be no goal for us whatever, still on, on; this indomitable egotism charged her cheeks with colour; made her look very young; very pink; very bright-eyed as she sat with her dress upon her knee, and her needle held to the end of green silk, trembling a little. He was in love! Not with her. With some younger woman, of course.

"And who is she?" she asked.

Now this statue must be brought from its height and set down between them.

"A married woman, unfortunately," he said; "the wife of a Major in the Indian Army."

And with a curious ironical sweetness he smiled as he placed her in this ridiculous way before Clarissa.

(All the same, he is in love, thought Clarissa.)

"She has," he continued, very reasonably, "two small children; a boy and a girl; and I have come over to see my lawyers about the divorce."

There they are! he thought. Do what you like with them, Clarissa! There they are! And second by second it seemed to him that the wife of the Major in the Indian Army (his Daisy) and her two small children became more and more lovely as Clarissa looked at them; as if he had set light to a grey pellet on a plate and there had risen up a lovely tree in the brisk sea-salted air of their intimacy (for in some ways no one understood him, felt with him, as Clarissa did)—their exquisite intimacy.

She flattered him; she fooled him, thought Clarissa; shaping the woman, the wife of the Major in the Indian Army, with three strokes of a knife. What a waste! What a folly! All his life long Peter had been fooled like that; first getting sent down from Oxford; next marrying the girl on the boat going out to India; now the wife of a Major in the Indian Army—thank Heaven she had refused to marry him! Still, he was in love; her old friend, her dear Peter, he was in love.

"But what are you going to do?" she asked him. Oh the lawyers and solicitors, Messrs. Hooper and Grateley of Lincoln's Inn, they were going to do it, he said. And he actually pared his nails with his pocket-knife.

For Heaven's sake, leave your knife alone! she cried to herself in irrepressible irritation; it was his silly unconventionality, his weakness; his lack of the ghost of a notion what any one else was feeling that annoyed her, had always annoyed her; and now at his age, how silly!

I know all that, Peter thought; I know what I'm up against, he thought, running his finger along the blade of his knife, Clarissa and Dalloway and all the rest of them; but I'll show Clarissa—and then to his utter surprise, suddenly thrown by those uncontrollable forces thrown through the air, he burst into tears; wept; wept without the least shame, sitting on the sofa, the tears running down his cheeks.

And Clarissa had leant forward, taken his hand, drawn him to her, kissed him,—actually had felt his face on hers before she could down the brandishing of silver flashing—plumes like pampas grass in a tropic gale in her breast, which, subsiding, left her holding his hand, patting his knee and, feeling as she sat back extraordinarily at her ease with him and light-hearted, all in a clap it came over her, If I had married him, this gaiety would have been mine all day!

It was all over for her. The sheet was stretched and the bed narrow. She had gone up into the tower alone and left them blackberrying in the sun. The door had shut, and there among the dust of fallen plaster and the litter of birds' nests how distant the view had looked, and the sounds came thin and chill (once on Leith Hill, she remembered), and Richard, Richard! she cried, as a sleeper in the night starts and stretches a hand in the dark for help. Lunching with Lady Bruton, it came back to her. He has left me; I am alone for ever, she thought, folding her hands upon her knee.

Peter Walsh had got up and crossed to the window and stood with his back to her, flicking a bandanna handkerchief from side to side. Masterly and dry and desolate he looked, his thin shoulder-blades lifting his coat slightly; blowing his nose violently. Take me with you, Clarissa thought impulsively, as if he were starting directly upon some great voyage; and then, next moment, it was as if the five acts of a play that had been very exciting and moving were now over and she had lived a lifetime in them and had run away, had lived with Peter, and it was now over.

Now it was time to move, and, as a woman gathers her things together, her cloak, her gloves, her opera-glasses, and gets up to go out of the theatre into the street, she rose from the sofa and went to Peter.

And it was awfully strange, he thought, how she still had the power, as she came tinkling, rustling, still had the power as she came across the room, to make the moon, which he detested, rise at Bourton on the terrace in the summer sky.

"Tell me," he said, seizing her by the shoulders. "Are you happy, Clarissa? Does Richard—"

The door opened.

"Here is my Elizabeth," said Clarissa, emotionally, histrionically, perhaps.

"How d'y do?" said Elizabeth coming forward.

The sound of Big Ben striking the half-hour stuck out between them with extraordinary vigour, as if a young man, strong, indifferent, inconsiderate, were swinging dumb-bells this way and that.

"Hullo, Elizabeth!" cried Peter, stuffing his handkerchief into his pocket, going quickly to her, saying "Good-bye, Clarissa" without looking at her, leaving the room quickly, and running downstairs and opening the hall door.

"Peter! Peter!" cried Clarissa, following him out on to the landing. "My party to-night! Remember my party to-night!" she cried, having to raise her voice against the roar of the open air, and, overwhelmed by the traffic and the sound of all the clocks striking, her voice crying "Remember my party to-night!" sounded frail and thin and very far away as Peter Walsh shut the door.

Remember my party, remember my party, said Peter Walsh as he stepped down the street, speaking to himself rhythmically, in time with the flow of the sound, the direct downright sound of Big Ben striking the half-hour. (The leaden circles dissolved in the air.) Oh these parties, he thought; Clarissa's parties. Why does she give these parties, he thought. Not that he blamed her or this effigy of a man in a tail-coat with a carnation in his button-hole coming towards him. Only one person in the world could be as he was, in love. And there he was, this fortunate man, himself, reflected in the plate-glass window of a motor-car manufacturer in Victoria Street. All India lay behind him; plains, mountains; epidemics of cholera; a district twice as big as Ireland; decisions he had come to alone—he, Peter Walsh; who was now really for the first time in his life, in love. Clarissa had grown hard, he thought; and a trifle sentimental into the bargain, he suspected, looking at the great motor-cars capable of doing—how many miles on how many gallons? For he had a turn for mechanics; had invented a plough in his district, had ordered wheel-barrows from England, but the coolies wouldn't use them, all of which Clarissa knew nothing whatever about.

The way she said "Here is my Elizabeth!"—that annoyed him. Why not "Here's Elizabeth" simply? It was insincere. And Elizabeth didn't like it either. (Still the last tremors of the great booming voice shook the air round him; the half-hour; still early; only half-past eleven still.) For he understood young people; he liked them. There was always something cold in Clarissa, he thought. She had always, even as a girl, a sort of timidity, which in middle age becomes conventionality, and then it's all up, it's all up, he thought, looking rather drearily into the glassy depths, and wondering whether by calling at that hour he had annoyed her; overcome with shame suddenly at having been a fool; wept; been emotional; told her everything, as usual, as usual.

As a cloud crosses the sun, silence falls on London; and falls on the mind. Effort ceases. Time flaps on the mast. There we stop; there we stand. Rigid, the skeleton of habit alone upholds the human frame. Where there is nothing, Peter Walsh said to himself; feeling hollowed out, utterly empty within. Clarissa refused me, he thought. He stood there thinking, Clarissa refused me.

Ah, said St Margaret's,[6] like a hostess who comes into her drawing-room on the very stroke of the hour and finds her guests there already. I am not late. No, it is precisely half-past eleven, she says. Yet, though she is perfectly right, her voice, being the voice of the hostess, is reluctant to inflict its individuality. Some grief for the past holds it back; some concern for the present. It is half-past eleven, she says, and the sound of St Margaret's glides into the recesses of the heart and buries itself in ring after ring of sound, like something alive which wants to confide itself, to disperse itself, to be, with a tremor of delight, at rest—like Clarissa herself, thought Peter Walsh, coming down the stairs on the stroke of the hour in white. It is Clarissa herself, he thought, with a deep emotion, and an extraordinarily clear, yet puzzling, recollection of her, as if this bell had come into the room years ago, where they sat at some moment of great intimacy, and had gone from one to the other and had left, like a bee with honey, laden with the moment. But what room? What moment? And why had he been so profoundly happy when the clock was striking? Then, as the sound of St Margaret's languished, he thought, She has been ill, and the sound expressed languor and suffering. It was her heart, he remembered; and the sudden loudness of the final stroke tolled for death that surprised in the midst of life, Clarissa falling where she stood, in her drawing-room. No! No! he cried. She is not dead! I am not old, he cried, and marched up Whitehall, as if there rolled down to him, vigorous, unending, his future.

He was not old, or set, or dried in the least. As for caring what they said of him—the Dalloways, the Whitbreads, and their set, he cared not a straw—not a straw

6. The parish church for the House of Commons. On 11 November 1918, when the Great War was over, members of both Houses of Parliament attended a service there.

(though it was true he would have, some time or other, to see whether Richard couldn't help him to some job). Striding, staring, he glared at the statue of the Duke of Cambridge. He had been sent down from Oxford—true. He had been a Socialist, in some sense a failure—true. Still the future of civilisation lies, he thought, in the hands of young men like that; of young men such as he was, thirty years ago; with their love of abstract principles; getting books sent out to them all the way from London to a peak in the Himalayas; reading science; reading philosophy. The future lies in the hands of young men like that, he thought.

A patter like the patter of leaves in a wood came from behind, and with it a rustling, regular thudding sound, which as it overtook him drummed his thoughts, strict in step, up Whitehall, without his doing. Boys in uniform, carrying guns, marched with their eyes ahead of them, marched, their arms stiff, and on their faces an expression like the letters of a legend written round the base of a statue praising duty, gratitude, fidelity, love of England.

It is, thought Peter Walsh, beginning to keep step with them, a very fine training. But they did not look robust. They were weedy for the most part, boys of sixteen, who might, to-morrow, stand behind bowls of rice, cakes of soap on counters. Now they wore on them unmixed with sensual pleasure or daily preoccupations the solemnity of the wreath which they had fetched from Finsbury Pavement[7] to the empty tomb. They had taken their vow. The traffic respected it; vans were stopped.

I can't keep up with them, Peter Walsh thought, as they marched up Whitehall, and sure enough, on they marched, past him, past every one, in their steady way, as if one will worked legs and arms uniformly, and life, with its varieties, its irreticences, had been laid under a pavement of monuments and wreaths and drugged into a stiff yet staring corpse by discipline. One had to respect it; one might laugh; but one had to respect it, he thought. There they go, thought Peter Walsh, pausing at the edge of the pavement; and all the exalted statues, Nelson, Gordon, Havelock,[8] the black, the spectacular images of great soldiers stood looking ahead of them, as if they too had made the same renunciation (Peter Walsh felt he too had made it, the great renunciation), trampled under the same temptations, and achieved at length a marble stare. But the stare Peter Walsh did not want for himself in the least; though he could respect it in others. He could respect it in boys. They don't know the troubles of the flesh yet, he thought, as the marching boys disappeared in the direction of the Strand—all that I've been through, he thought, crossing the road, and standing under Gordon's statue, Gordon whom as a boy he had worshipped; Gordon standing lonely with one leg raised and his arms crossed,—poor Gordon, he thought.

And just because nobody yet knew he was in London, except Clarissa, and the earth, after the voyage, still seemed an island to him, the strangeness of standing alone, alive, unknown, at half-past eleven in Trafalgar Square overcame him. What

7. A street near the Armoury House, which housed the Honourable Artillery Company, the oldest regiment in the British Army. The marching boys presumably belong to the Company's London Cadets, who performed ceremonial duties in the city during peacetime. The Cenotaph (empty tomb) in Whitehall was a monument, constructed in 1917 as a temporary memorial and finally completed in stone in 1920, to English soldiers killed in the war.

8. Monumental statuary in Trafalgar Square. Horatio Nelson (1758–1805) was the hero of the Battle of Trafalgar who decisively defeated Napoleon's navy in 1805. Charles George Gordon (1833–1885) served famously as a military leader and administrator in China, Egypt and the Sudan. When he was killed attempting to crush a rebellion in Khartoum, a public outcry was raised against the British government (whose foreign policies he had often criticized publicly) for having been inordinately slow to provide Gordon with relief. General Sir Henry Havelock (1795–1857) distinguished himself in the first Anglo-Burmese war (1824–1826) and the first Afghan war (1839–1842), and also played a significant role in the extremely violent English suppression of the 1857 Indian Mutiny.

is it? Where am I? And why, after all, does one do it? he thought, the divorce seeming all moonshine. And down his mind went flat as a marsh, and three great emotions bowled over him; understanding; a vast philanthropy; and finally, as if the result of the others, an irrepressible, exquisite delight; as if inside his brain by another hand strings were pulled, shutters moved, and he, having nothing to do with it, yet stood at the opening of endless avenues, down which if he chose he might wander. He had not felt so young for years.

He had escaped! was utterly free—as happens in the downfall of habit when the mind, like an unguarded flame, bows and bends and seems about to blow from its holding. I haven't felt so young for years! thought Peter, escaping (only of course for an hour or so) from being precisely what he was, and feeling like a child who runs out of doors, and sees, as he runs, his old nurse waving at the wrong window. But she's extraordinarily attractive, he thought, as, walking across Trafalgar Square in the direction of the Haymarket, came a young woman who, as she passed Gordon's statue, seemed, Peter Walsh thought (susceptible as he was), to shed veil after veil, until she became the very woman he had always had in mind; young, but stately; merry, but discreet; black, but enchanting.

Straightening himself and stealthily fingering his pocket-knife he started after her to follow this woman, this excitement, which seemed even with its back turned to shed on him a light which connected them, which singled him out, as if the random uproar of the traffic had whispered through hollowed hands his name, not Peter, but his private name which he called himself in his own thoughts. "You," she said, only "you," saying it with her white gloves and her shoulders. Then the thin long cloak which the wind stirred as she walked past Dent's shop in Cockspur Street blew out with an enveloping kindness, a mournful tenderness, as of arms that would open and take the tired—

But she's not married; she's young; quite young, thought Peter, the red carnation he had seen her wear as she came across Trafalgar Square burning again in his eyes and making her lips red. But she waited at the kerbstone. There was a dignity about her. She was not worldly, like Clarissa; not rich, like Clarissa. Was she, he wondered as she moved, respectable? Witty, with a lizard's flickering tongue, he thought (for one must invent, must allow oneself a little diversion), a cool waiting wit, a darting wit; not noisy.

She moved; she crossed; he followed her. To embarrass her was the last thing he wished. Still if she stopped he would say "Come and have an ice," he would say, and she would answer, perfectly simply, "Oh yes."

But other people got between them in the street, obstructing him, blotting her out. He pursued; she changed. There was colour in her cheeks; mockery in her eyes; he was an adventurer, reckless, he thought, swift, daring, indeed (landed as he was last night from India) a romantic buccaneer, careless of all these damned proprieties, yellow dressing-gowns, pipes, fishing-rods, in the shop windows; and respectability and evening parties and spruce old men wearing white slips beneath their waistcoats. He was a buccaneer. On and on she went, across Piccadilly, and up Regent Street, ahead of him, her cloak, her gloves, her shoulders combining with the fringes and the laces and the feather boas in the windows to make the spirit of finery and whimsy which dwindled out of the shops on to the pavement, as the light of a lamp goes wavering at night over hedges in the darkness.

Laughing and delightful, she had crossed Oxford Street and Great Portland Street and turned down one of the little streets, and now, and now, the great moment was approaching, for now she slackened, opened her bag, and with one look in his direction, but not at him, one look that bade farewell, summed up the whole situation and dismissed it triumphantly, for ever, had fitted her key, opened the door, and gone! Clarissa's voice saying, Remember my party, Remember my party, sang in his ears. The house was one of those flat red houses with hanging flower-baskets of vague impropriety. It was over.

Well, I've had my fun; I've had it, he thought, looking up at the swinging baskets of pale geraniums. And it was smashed to atoms—his fun, for it was half made up, as he knew very well; invented, this escapade with the girl; made up, as one makes up the better part of life, he thought—making oneself up; making her up; creating an exquisite amusement, and something more. But odd it was, and quite true; all this one could never share—it smashed to atoms.

He turned; went up the street, thinking to find somewhere to sit, till it was time for Lincoln's Inn—for Messrs. Hooper and Grateley. Where should he go? No matter. Up the street, then, towards Regent's Park. His boots on the pavement struck out "no matter"; for it was early, still very early.

It was a splendid morning too. Like the pulse of a perfect heart, life struck straight through the streets. There was no fumbling—no hesitation. Sweeping and swerving, accurately, punctually, noiselessly, there, precisely at the right instant, the motor-car stopped at the door. The girl, silk-stockinged, feathered, evanescent, but not to him particularly attractive (for he had had his fling), alighted. Admirable butlers, tawny chow dogs, halls laid in black and white lozenges with white blinds blowing, Peter saw through the opened door and approved of. A splendid achievement in its own way, after all, London; the season; civilisation. Coming as he did from a respectable Anglo-Indian family which for at least three generations had administered the affairs of a continent (it's strange, he thought, what a sentiment I have about that, disliking India, and empire, and army as he did), there were moments when civilisation, even of this sort, seemed dear to him as a personal possession; moments of pride in England; in butlers; chow dogs; girls in their security. Ridiculous enough, still there it is, he thought. And the doctors and men of business and capable women all going about their business, punctual, alert, robust, seemed to him wholly admirable, good fellows, to whom one would entrust one's life, companions in the art of living, who would see one through. What with one thing and another, the show was really very tolerable; and he would sit down in the shade and smoke.

There was Regent's Park. Yes. As a child he had walked in Regent's Park—odd, he thought, how the thought of childhood keeps coming back to me—the result of seeing Clarissa, perhaps; for women live much more in the past than we do, he thought. They attach themselves to places; and their fathers—a woman's always proud of her father. Bourton was a nice place, a very nice place, but I could never get on with the old man, he thought. There was quite a scene one night—an argument about something or other, what, he could not remember. Politics presumably.

Yes, he remembered Regent's Park; the long straight walk; the little house where one bought air-balls to the left; an absurd statue with an inscription some-where or other. He looked for an empty seat. He did not want to be bothered (feeling a little drowsy as he did) by people asking him the time. An elderly grey nurse, with a baby asleep in its perambulator—that was the best he could do for himself; sit down at the far end of the seat by that nurse.

She's a queer-looking girl, he thought, suddenly remembering Elizabeth as she came into the room and stood by her mother. Grown big; quite grown-up, not exactly pretty; handsome rather; and she can't be more than eighteen. Probably she doesn't get on with Clarissa. "There's my Elizabeth"—that sort of thing—why not "Here's Elizabeth" simply?—trying to make out, like most mothers, that things are what they're not. She trusts to her charm too much, he thought. She overdoes it.

The rich benignant cigar smoke eddied coolly down his throat; he puffed it out again in rings which breasted the air bravely for a moment; blue, circular—I shall try and get a word alone with Elizabeth to-night, he thought—then began to wobble into hour-glass shapes and taper away; odd shapes they take, he thought. Suddenly he closed his eyes, raised his hand with an effort, and threw away the heavy end of his cigar. A great brush swept smooth across his mind, sweeping across it moving branches, children's voices, the shuffle of feet, and people passing, and humming traffic, rising and falling traffic. Down, down he sank into the plumes and feathers of sleep, sank, and was muffled over.

The grey nurse resumed her knitting as Peter Walsh, on the hot seat beside her, began snoring. In her grey dress, moving her hands indefatigably yet quietly, she seemed like the champion of the rights of sleepers, like one of those spectral presences which rise in twilight in woods made of sky and branches. The solitary traveller, haunter of lanes, disturber of ferns, and devastator of great hemlock plants, looking up, suddenly sees the giant figure at the end of the ride.

By conviction an atheist perhaps, he is taken by surprise with moments of extraordinary exaltation. Nothing exists outside us except a state of mind, he thinks; a desire for solace, for relief, for something outside these miserable pigmies, these feeble, these ugly, these craven men and women. But if he can conceive of her, then in some sort she exists, he thinks, and advancing down the path with his eyes upon sky and branches he rapidly endows them with womanhood; sees with amazement how grave they become; how majestically, as the breeze stirs them, they dispense with a dark flutter of the leaves charity, comprehension, absolution, and then, flinging themselves suddenly aloft, confound the piety of their aspect with a wild carouse.

Such are the visions which proffer great cornucopias full of fruit to the solitary traveller, or murmur in his ear like sirens lolloping away on the green sea waves, or are dashed in his face like bunches of roses, or rise to the surface like pale faces which fishermen flounder through floods to embrace.[9]

Such are the visions which ceaselessly float up, pace beside, put their faces in front of, the actual thing; often overpowering the solitary traveller and taking away from him the sense of the earth, the wish to return, and giving him for substitute a general peace, as if (so he thinks as he advances down the forest ride) all this fever of living were simplicity itself; and myriads of things merged in one thing; and this figure, made of sky and branches as it is, had risen from the troubled sea (he is elderly, past fifty now) as a shape might be sucked up out of the waves to shower down from her magnificent hands compassion, comprehension, absolution. So, he thinks, may I never go back to the lamplight; to the sitting-room; never finish my book; never

9. His visions here all allude to powerful female figures in Greek and Roman mythology. The first suggests either Demeter, goddess of the harvest and protectress of women and marriage, often represented holding the cornucopia, or one of the three Graces, with whom the cornucopia (as well as the rose) is associated in some artistic traditions. The synesthetic "visions" which "murmur in his ear" seem to have their origin in Homer's sirens, whose island is littered with the bones of victims lured in by their song, while the "pale faces" connote the popular legend of the mermaid to which Shakespeare alludes in *Comedy of Errors* 3.2: "O, train me not, sweet mermaid, with thy note / To drown in thy sister's flood of tears."

knock out my pipe; never ring for Mrs Turner to clear away; rather let me walk straight on to this great figure, who will, with a toss of her head, mount me on her streamers and let me blow to nothingness with the rest.

Such are the visions. The solitary traveller is soon beyond the wood; and there, coming to the door with shaded eyes, possibly to look for his return, with hands raised, with white apron blowing, is an elderly woman who seems (so powerful is this infirmity) to seek, over a desert, a lost son; to search for a rider destroyed; to be the figure of the mother whose sons have been killed in the battles of the world. So, as the solitary traveller advances down the village street where the women stand knitting and the men dig in the garden, the evening seems ominous; the figures still; as if some august fate, known to them, awaited without fear, were about to sweep them into complete annihilation.

Indoors among ordinary things, the cupboard, the table, the window-sill with its geraniums, suddenly the outline of the landlady, bending to remove the cloth, becomes soft with light, an adorable emblem which only the recollection of cold human contacts forbids us to embrace. She takes the marmalade; she shuts it in the cupboard.

"There is nothing more to-night, sir?"

But to whom does the solitary traveller make reply?

So the elderly nurse knitted over the sleeping baby in Regent's Park. So Peter Walsh snored.

He woke with extreme suddenness, saying to himself, "The death of the soul."

"Lord, Lord!" he said to himself out loud, stretching and opening his eyes. "The death of the soul." The words attached themselves to some scene, to some room, to some past he had been dreaming of. It became clearer; the scene, the room, the past he had been dreaming of.

It was at Bourton that summer, early in the 'nineties, when he was so passionately in love with Clarissa. There were a great many people there, laughing and talking, sitting round a table after tea and the room was bathed in yellow light and full of cigarette smoke. They were talking about a man who had married his housemaid, one of the neighbouring squires, he had forgotten his name. He had married his housemaid, and she had been brought to Bourton to call—an awful visit it had been. She was absurdly over-dressed, "like a cockatoo," Clarissa had said, imitating her, and she never stopped talking. On and on she went, on and on. Clarissa imitated her. Then somebody said—Sally Seton it was—did it make any real difference to one's feelings to know that before they'd married she had had a baby? (In those days, in mixed company, it was a bold thing to say.) He could see Clarissa now, turning bright pink; somehow contracting; and saying, "Oh, I shall never be able to speak to her again!" Whereupon the whole party sitting round the tea-table seemed to wobble. It was very uncomfortable.

He hadn't blamed her for minding the fact, since in those days a girl brought up as she was, knew nothing, but it was her manner that annoyed him; timid; hard; something arrogant; unimaginative; prudish. "The death of the soul." He had said that instinctively, ticketing the moment as he used to do—the death of her soul.

Every one wobbled; every one seemed to bow, as she spoke, and then to stand up different. He could see Sally Seton, like a child who has been in mischief, leaning forward, rather flushed, wanting to talk, but afraid, and Clarissa did frighten people. (She was Clarissa's greatest friend, always about the place, totally unlike her, an attractive creature, handsome, dark, with the reputation in those days of great daring and he used to give her cigars, which she smoked in her bedroom. She had either been engaged to somebody or quarrelled with her family and old Parry disliked them both equally, which was a great bond.) Then Clarissa, still with an air of being offended with them all, got up, made some excuse, and went off, alone. As she opened the door, in came that great shaggy dog which ran after sheep. She flung herself upon him, went into raptures. It was as if she said to Peter—it was all aimed at him, he knew—"I know you thought me absurd about that woman just now; but see how extraordinarily sympathetic I am; see how I love my Rob!"

They had always this queer power of communicating without words. She knew directly he criticised her. Then she would do something quite obvious to defend herself, like this fuss with the dog—but it never took him in, he always saw through Clarissa. Not that he said anything, of course; just sat looking glum. It was the way their quarrels often began.

She shut the door. At once he became extremely depressed. It all seemed useless—going on being in love; going on quarrelling; going on making it up, and he wandered off alone, among outhouses, stables, looking at the horses. (The place was quite a humble one; the Parrys were never very well off; but there were always grooms and stable-boys about—Clarissa loved riding—and an old coachman—what was his name?—an old nurse, old Moody, old Goody, some such name they called her, whom one was taken to visit in a little room with lots of photographs, lots of bird-cages.)

It was an awful evening! He grew more and more gloomy, not about that only; about everything. And he couldn't see her; couldn't explain to her; couldn't have it out. There were always people about—she'd go on as if nothing had happened. That was the devilish part of her—this coldness, this woodenness, something very profound in her, which he had felt again this morning talking to her; an impenetrability. Yet Heaven knows he loved her. She had some queer power of fiddling on one's nerves, turning one's nerves to fiddle-strings, yes.

He had gone in to dinner rather late, from some idiotic idea of making himself felt, and had sat down by old Miss Parry—Aunt Helena—Mr Parry's sister, who was supposed to preside. There she sat in her white Cashmere shawl, with her head against the window—a formidable old lady, but kind to him, for he had found her some rare flower, and she was a great botanist, marching off in thick boots with a black collecting-box slung between her shoulders. He sat down beside her, and couldn't speak. Everything seemed to race past him; he just sat there, eating. And then half-way through dinner he made himself look across at Clarissa for the first time. She was talking to a young man on her right. He had a sudden revelation. "She will marry that man," he said to himself. He didn't even know his name.

For of course it was that afternoon, that very afternoon, that Dalloway had come over; and Clarissa called him "Wickham"; that was the beginning of it all. Somebody had brought him over; and Clarissa got his name wrong. She introduced him to everybody as Wickham. At last he said "My name is Dalloway!"—that was his first view of Richard—a fair young man, rather awkward, sitting on a deck-chair, and blurting out "My name is Dalloway!" Sally got hold of it; always after that she called him "My name is Dalloway!"

He was a prey to revelations at that time. This one—that she would marry Dalloway—was blinding—overwhelming at the moment. There was a sort of—how could he put it?—a sort of ease in her manner to him; something maternal; something gentle. They were talking about politics. All through dinner he tried to hear what they were saying.

Afterwards he could remember standing by old Miss Parry's chair in the drawing-room. Clarissa came up, with her perfect manners, like a real hostess, and wanted to introduce him to some one—spoke as if they had never met before, which enraged him. Yet even then he admired her for it. He admired her courage; her social instinct; he admired her power of carrying things through. "The perfect hostess," he said to her, whereupon she winced all over. But he meant her to feel it. He would have done anything to hurt her after seeing her with Dalloway. So she left him. And he had a feeling that they were all gathered together in a conspiracy against him—laughing and talking—behind his back. There he stood by Miss Parry's chair as though he had been cut out of wood, he talking about wild flowers. Never, never had he suffered so infernally! He must have forgotten even to pretend to listen; at last he woke up; he saw Miss Parry looking rather disturbed, rather indignant, with her prominent eyes fixed. He almost cried out that he couldn't attend because he was in Hell! People began going out of the room. He heard them talking about fetching cloaks; about its being cold on the water, and so on. They were going boating on the lake by moonlight—one of Sally's mad ideas. He could hear her describing the moon. And they all went out. He was left quite alone.

"Don't you want to go with them?" said Aunt Helena—old Miss Parry!—she had guessed. And he turned round and there was Clarissa again. She had come back to fetch him. He was overcome by her generosity—her goodness.

"Come along," she said. "They're waiting."

He had never felt so happy in the whole of his life! Without a word they made it up. They walked down to the lake. He had twenty minutes of perfect happiness. Her voice, her laugh, her dress (something floating, white, crimson), her spirit, her adventurousness; she made them all disembark and explore the island; she startled a hen; she laughed; she sang. And all the time, he knew perfectly well, Dalloway was falling in love with her; she was falling in love with Dalloway; but it didn't seem to matter. Nothing mattered. They sat on the ground and talked—he and Clarissa. They went in and out of each other's minds without any effort. And then in a second it was over. He said to himself as they were getting into the boat, "She will marry that man," dully, without any resentment; but it was an obvious thing. Dalloway would marry Clarissa.

Dalloway rowed them in. He said nothing. But somehow as they watched him start, jumping on to his bicycle to ride twenty miles through the woods, wobbling off down the drive, waving his hand and disappearing, he obviously did feel, instinctively, tremendously, strongly, all that; the night; the romance; Clarissa. He deserved to have her.

For himself, he was absurd. His demands upon Clarissa (he could see it now) were absurd. He asked impossible things. He made terrible scenes. She would have accepted him still, perhaps, if he had been less absurd. Sally thought so. She wrote him all that summer long letters; how they had talked of him; how she had praised him, how Clarissa burst into tears! It was an extraordinary summer—all letters, scenes, telegrams—arriving at Bourton early in the morning, hanging about till the servants were up; appalling *tête-à-têtes* with old Mr Parry at breakfast; Aunt Helena formidable but kind; Sally sweeping him off for talks in the vegetable garden; Clarissa in bed with headaches.

The final scene, the terrible scene which he believed had mattered more than anything in the whole of his life (it might be an exaggeration—but still so it did seem now) happened at three o'clock in the afternoon of a very hot day. It was a trifle that led up to it—Sally at lunch saying something about Dalloway, and calling him "My name is Dalloway"; whereupon Clarissa suddenly stiffened, coloured, in a way she had, and rapped out sharply, "We've had enough of that feeble joke." That was all; but for him it was precisely as if she had said, "I'm only amusing myself with you; I've an understanding with Richard Dalloway." So he took it. He had not slept for nights. "It's got to be finished one way or the other," he said to himself. He sent a note to her by Sally asking her to meet him by the fountain at three. "Something very important has happened," he scribbled at the end of it.

The fountain was in the middle of a little shrubbery, far from the house, with shrubs and trees all round it. There she came, even before the time, and they stood with the fountain between them, the spout (it was broken) dribbling water incessantly. How sights fix themselves upon the mind! For example, the vivid green moss.

She did not move. "Tell me the truth, tell me the truth," he kept on saying. He felt as if his forehead would burst. She seemed contracted, petrified. She did not move. "Tell me the truth," he repeated, when suddenly that old man Breitkopf popped his head in carrying the *Times;* stared at them; gaped; and went away. They neither of them moved. "Tell me the truth," he repeated. He felt that he was grinding against something physically hard; she was unyielding. She was like iron, like flint, rigid up the backbone. And when she said, "It's no use. It's no use. This is the end"—after he had spoken for hours, it seemed, with the tears running down his cheeks—it was as if she had hit him in the face. She turned, she left him, went away.

"Clarissa!" he cried. "Clarissa!" But she never came back. It was over. He went away that night. He never saw her again.

It was awful, he cried, awful, awful!

Still, the sun was hot. Still, one got over things. Still, life had a way of adding day to day. Still, he thought, yawning and beginning to take notice—Regent's Park had changed very little since he was a boy, except for the squirrels—still, presumably there were compensations—when little Elise Mitchell, who had been picking up pebbles to add to the pebble collection which she and her brother were making on the nursery mantelpiece, plumped her handful down on the nurse's knee and scudded off again full tilt into a lady's legs. Peter Walsh laughed out.

But Lucrezia Warren Smith was saying to herself, It's wicked; why should I suffer? she was asking, as she walked down the broad path. No; I can't stand it any longer, she was saying, having left Septimus, who wasn't Septimus any longer, to say hard, cruel, wicked things, to talk to himself, to talk to a dead man, on the seat over there; when the child ran full tilt into her, fell flat, and burst out crying.

That was comforting rather. She stood her upright, dusted her frock, kissed her.

But for herself she had done nothing wrong; she had loved Septimus; she had been happy; she had had a beautiful home, and there her sisters lived still, making hats. Why should *she* suffer?

The child ran straight back to its nurse, and Rezia saw her scolded, comforted, taken up by the nurse who put down her knitting, and the kind-looking man gave her his watch to blow open to comfort her—but why should *she* be exposed? Why not left in Milan? Why tortured? Why?

Slightly waved by tears the broad path, the nurse, the man in grey, the perambulator, rose and fell before her eyes. To be rocked by this malignant torturer was her lot. But why? She was like a bird sheltering under the thin hollow of a leaf, who blinks at the sun when the leaf moves; starts at the crack of a dry twig. She was exposed; she was surrounded by the enormous trees, vast clouds of an indifferent world, exposed; tortured; and why should she suffer? Why?

She frowned; she stamped her foot. She must go back again to Septimus since it was almost time for them to be going to Sir William Bradshaw. She must go back and tell him, go back to him sitting there on the green chair under the tree, talking to himself, or to that dead man Evans, whom she had only seen once for a moment in the shop. He had seemed a nice quiet man; a great friend of Septimus's, and he had been killed in the War. But such things happen to every one. Every one has friends who were killed in the War. Every one gives up something when they marry. She had given up her home. She had come to live here, in this awful city. But Septimus let himself think about horrible things, as she could too, if she tried. He had grown stranger and stranger. He said people were talking behind the bedroom walls. Mrs Filmer thought it odd. He saw things too—he had seen an old woman's head in the middle of a fern. Yet he could be happy when he chose. They went to Hampton Court on top of a bus, and they were perfectly happy. All the little red and yellow flowers were out on the grass, like floating lamps he said, and talked and chattered and laughed, making up stories. Suddenly he said, "Now we will kill ourselves," when they were standing by the river, and he looked at it with a look which she had seen in his eyes when a train went by, or an omnibus—a look as if something fascinated him; and she felt he was going from her and she caught him by the arm. But going home he was perfectly quiet—perfectly reasonable. He would argue with her about killing themselves; and explain how wicked people were; how he could see them making up lies as they passed in the street. He knew all their thoughts, he said; he knew everything. He knew the meaning of the world, he said.

Then when they got back he could hardly walk. He lay on the sofa and made her hold his hand to prevent him from falling down, down, he cried, into the flames! and saw faces laughing at him, calling him horrible disgusting names, from the walls, and hands pointing round the screen. Yet they were quite alone. But he began to talk aloud, answering people, arguing, laughing, crying, getting very excited and making her write things down. Perfect nonsense it was; about death; about Miss Isabel Pole. She could stand it no longer. She would go back.

She was close to him now, could see him staring at the sky, muttering, clasping his hands. Yet Dr Holmes said there was nothing the matter with him. What then had happened—why had he gone, then, why, when she sat by him, did he start, frown at her, move away, and point at her hand, take her hand, look at it terrified?

Was it that she had taken off her wedding ring? "My hand has grown so thin," she said. "I have put it in my purse," she told him.

He dropped her hand. Their marriage was over, he thought, with agony, with relief. The rope was cut; he mounted; he was free, as it was decreed that he, Septimus, the lord of men, should be free; alone (since his wife had thrown away her wedding ring; since she had left him), he, Septimus, was alone, called forth in advance of the mass of men to hear the truth, to learn the meaning, which now at last, after all the toils of civilisation—Greeks, Romans, Shakespeare, Darwin, and now himself—was to be given whole to. . . . "To whom?" he asked aloud. "To the Prime Minister," the voices which rustled above his head replied. The supreme secret must be told to the Cabinet; first that trees are alive; next there is no crime; next love, universal love, he muttered, gasping, trembling, painfully drawing out these profound truths which needed, so deep were they, so difficult, an immense effort to speak out, but the world was entirely changed by them for ever.

No crime; love; he repeated, fumbling for his card and pencil, when a Skye terrier snuffed his trousers and he started in an agony of fear. It was turning into a man!

He could not watch it happen! It was horrible, terrible to see a dog become a man! At once the dog trotted away.

Heaven was divinely merciful, infinitely benignant. It spared him, pardoned his weakness. But what was the scientific explanation (for one must be scientific above all things)? Why could he see through bodies, see into the future, when dogs will become men? It was the heat wave presumably, operating upon a brain made sensitive by eons of evolution. Scientifically speaking, the flesh was melted off the world. His body was macerated until only the nerve fibres were left. It was spread like a veil upon a rock.

He lay back in his chair, exhausted but upheld. He lay resting, waiting, before he again interpreted, with effort, with agony, to mankind. He lay very high, on the back of the world. The earth thrilled beneath him. Red flowers grew through his flesh; their stiff leaves rustled by his head. Music began clanging against the rocks up here. It is a motor horn down in the street, he muttered; but up here it cannoned from rock to rock, divided, met in shocks of sound which rose in smooth columns (that music should be visible was a discovery) and became an anthem, an anthem twined round now by a shepherd boy's piping (That's an old man playing a penny whistle by the public-house, he muttered) which, as the boy stood still came bubbling from his pipe, and then, as he climbed higher, made its exquisite plaint while the traffic passed beneath. This boy's elegy is played among the traffic, thought Septimus. Now he withdraws up into the snows, and roses hang about him—the thick red roses which grow on my bedroom wall, he reminded himself. The music stopped. He has his penny, he reasoned it out, and has gone on to the next public-house.

But he himself remained high on his rock, like a drowned sailor on a rock. I leant over the edge of the boat and fell down, he thought. I went under the sea. I have been dead, and yet am now alive, but let me rest still; he begged (he was talking to himself again—it was awful, awful!); and as, before waking, the voices of birds and the sound of wheels chime and chatter in a queer harmony, grow louder and louder and the sleeper feels himself drawing to the shores of life, so he felt himself drawing towards life, the sun growing hotter, cries sounding louder, something tremendous about to happen.

He had only to open his eyes; but a weight was on them; a fear. He strained; he pushed; he looked; he saw Regent's Park before him. Long streamers of sunlight fawned at his feet. The trees waved, brandished. We welcome, the world seemed to say; we accept; we create. Beauty, the world seemed to say. And as if to prove it (scientifically) wherever he looked at the houses, at the railings, at the antelopes stretching over the palings, beauty sprang instantly. To watch a leaf quivering in the rush of air was an exquisite joy. Up in the sky swallows swooping, swerving, flinging themselves in and out, round and round, yet always with perfect control as if elastics held them; and the flies rising and falling; and the sun spotting now this leaf, now that, in mockery, dazzling it with soft gold in pure good temper; and now and again some chime (it might be a motor horn) tinkling divinely on the grass stalks—all of this, calm and reasonable as it was, made out of ordinary things as it was, was the truth now; beauty, that was the truth now. Beauty was everywhere.[1]

"It is time," said Rezia.

1. Cf. Keats, *Ode on a Grecian Urn*: "Beauty is truth, truth beauty—that is all / Ye know on earth, and all ye need to know."

The word "time" split its husk; poured its riches over him; and from his lips fell like shells, like shavings from a plane, without his making them, hard, white, imperishable words, and flew to attach themselves to their places in an ode to Time; an immortal ode to Time. He sang. Evans answered from behind the tree. The dead were in Thessaly, Evans sang, among the orchids. There they waited till the War was over, and now the dead, now Evans himself—

"For God's sake don't come!" Septimus cried out. For he could not look upon the dead.

But the branches parted. A man in grey was actually walking towards them. It was Evans! But no mud was on him; no wounds; he was not changed. I must tell the whole world, Septimus cried, raising his hand (as the dead man in the grey suit came nearer), raising his hand like some colossal figure who has lamented the fate of man for ages in the desert alone with his hands pressed to his forehead, furrows of despair on his cheeks, and now sees light on the desert's edge which broadens and strikes the iron-black figure (and Septimus half rose from his chair), and with legions of men prostrate behind him he, the giant mourner, receives for one moment on his face the whole—

"But I am so unhappy, Septimus," said Rezia trying to make him sit down.

The millions lamented; for ages they had sorrowed. He would turn round, he would tell them in a few moments, only a few moments more, of this relief, of this joy, of this astonishing revelation—

"The time, Septimus," Rezia repeated. "What is the time?"

He was talking, he was starting, this man must notice him. He was looking at them.

"I will tell you the time," said Septimus, very slowly, very drowsily, smiling mysteriously. As he sat smiling at the dead man in the grey suit the quarter struck—the quarter to twelve.

And that is being young. Peter Walsh thought as he passed them. To be having an awful scene—the poor girl looked absolutely desperate—in the middle of the morning. But what was it about, he wondered, what had the young man in the overcoat been saying to her to make her look like that; what awful fix had they got themselves into, both to look so desperate as that on a fine summer morning? The amusing thing about coming back to England, after five years, was the way it made, anyhow the first days, things stand out as if one had never seen them before; lovers squabbling under a tree; the domestic family life of the parks. Never had he seen London look so enchanting—the softness of the distances; the richness; the greenness; the civilisation, after India, he thought, strolling across the grass.

This susceptibility to impressions had been his undoing no doubt. Still at his age he had, like a boy or a girl even, these alternations of mood; good days, bad days, for no reason whatever, happiness from a pretty face, downright misery at the sight of a frump. After India of course one fell in love with every woman one met. There was a freshness about them; even the poorest dressed better than five years ago surely; and to his eye the fashions had never been so becoming; the long black cloaks; the slimness; the elegance; and then the delicious and apparently universal habit of paint. Every woman, even the most respectable, had roses blooming under glass; lips cut with a knife; curls of Indian ink; there was design, art, everywhere; a change of some sort had undoubtedly taken place. What did the young people think about? Peter Walsh asked himself.

Those five years—1918 to 1923—had been, he suspected, somehow very important. People looked different. Newspapers seemed different. Now for instance there was a man writing quite openly in one of the respectable weeklies about water-closets. That you couldn't have done ten years ago—written quite openly about water-closets in a respectable weekly. And then this taking out a stick of rouge, or a powder-puff and making up in public. On board ship coming home there were lots of young men and girls—Betty and Bertie he remembered in particular—carrying on quite openly; the old mother sitting and watching them with her knitting, cool as a cucumber. The girl would stand still and powder her nose in front of every one. And they weren't engaged; just having a good time; no feelings hurt on either side. As hard as nails she was—Betty What'shername—; but a thorough good sort. She would make a very good wife at thirty—she would marry when it suited her to marry; marry some rich man and live in a large house near Manchester.

Who was it now who had done that? Peter Walsh asked himself, turning into the Broad Walk,—married a rich man and lived in a large house near Manchester? Somebody who had written him a long, gushing letter quite lately about "blue hydrangeas." It was seeing blue hydrangeas that made her think of him and the old days—Sally Seton, of course! It was Sally Seton—the last person in the world one would have expected to marry a rich man and live in a large house near Manchester, the wild, the daring, the romantic Sally!

But of all that ancient lot, Clarissa's friends—Whitbreads, Kinderleys, Cunninghams, Kinloch-Jones's—Sally was probably the best. She tried to get hold of things by the right end anyhow. She saw through Hugh Whitbread anyhow—the admirable Hugh—when Clarissa and the rest were at his feet.

"The Whitbreads?" he could hear her saying. "Who are the Whitbreads? Coal merchants. Respectable tradespeople."

Hugh she detested for some reason. He thought of nothing but his own appearance, she said. He ought to have been a Duke. He would be certain to marry one of the Royal Princesses. And of course Hugh had the most extraordinary, the most natural, the most sublime respect for the British aristocracy of any human being he had ever come across. Even Clarissa had to own that. Oh, but he was such a dear, so unselfish, gave up shooting to please his old mother—remembered his aunts' birthdays, and so on.

Sally, to do her justice, saw through all that. One of the things he remembered best was an argument one Sunday morning at Bourton about women's rights (that antediluvian topic), when Sally suddenly lost her temper, flared up, and told Hugh that he represented all that was most detestable in British middle-class life. She told him that she considered him responsible for the state of "those poor girls in Piccadilly"—Hugh, the perfect gentleman, poor Hugh!—never did a man look more horrified! She did it on purpose she said afterwards (for they used to get together in the vegetable garden and compare notes). "He's read nothing, thought nothing, felt nothing," he could hear her saying in that very emphatic voice which carried so much farther than she knew. The stable-boys had more life in them than Hugh, she said. He was a perfect specimen of the public school type, she said. No country but England could have produced him. She was really spiteful, for some reason; had some grudge against him. Something had happened—he forgot what—in the smoking-room. He had insulted her—kissed her? Incredible! Nobody believed a word against Hugh of course. Who could? Kissing Sally in the smoking-room! If it had been some Honourable Edith or Lady Violet, perhaps; but not that ragamuffin Sally without a penny to her name, and a father or a mother gambling at

Monte Carlo. For of all the people he had ever met Hugh was the greatest snob—the most obsequious—no, he didn't cringe exactly. He was too much of a prig for that. A first-rate valet was the obvious comparison—somebody who walked behind carrying suit cases; could be trusted to send telegrams—indispensable to hostesses. And he'd found his job—married his Honourable Evelyn; got some little post at Court, looked after the King's cellars, polished the Imperial shoe-buckles, went about in knee-breeches and lace ruffles. How remorseless life is! A little job at Court!

He had married this lady, the Honourable Evelyn, and they lived hereabouts, so he thought (looking at the pompous houses overlooking the Park), for he had lunched there once in a house which had, like all Hugh's possessions, something that no other house could possibly have—linen cupboards it might have been. You had to go and look at them—you had to spend a great deal of time always admiring whatever it was—linen cupboards, pillow-cases, old oak furniture, pictures, which Hugh had picked up for an old song. But Mrs Hugh sometimes gave the show away. She was one of those obscure mouse-like little women who admire big men. She was almost negligible. Then suddenly she would say something quite unexpected—something sharp. She had the relics of the grand manner perhaps. The steam coal was a little too strong for her—it made the atmosphere thick. And so there they lived, with their linen cupboards and their old masters and their pillow-cases fringed with real lace at the rate of five or ten thousand a year presumably, while he, who was two years older than Hugh, cadged for a job.

At fifty-three he had to come and ask them to put him into some secretary's office, to find him some usher's job teaching little boys Latin, at the beck and call of some mandarin in an office, something that brought in five hundred a year; for if he married Daisy, even with his pension, they could never do on less. Whitbread could do it presumably; or Dalloway. He didn't mind what he asked Dalloway. He was a thorough good sort; a bit limited; a bit thick in the head; yes; but a thorough good sort. Whatever he took up he did in the same matter-of-fact sensible way; without a touch of imagination, without a spark of brilliancy, but with the inexplicable niceness of his type. He ought to have been a country gentleman—he was wasted on politics. He was at his best out of doors, with horses and dogs—how good he was, for instance, when that great shaggy dog of Clarissa's got caught in a trap and had its paw half torn off, and Clarissa turned faint and Dalloway did the whole thing; bandaged, made splints; told Clarissa not to be a fool. That was what she liked him for perhaps—that was what she needed. "Now, my dear, don't be a fool. Hold this—fetch that," all the time talking to the dog as if it were a human being.

But how could she swallow all that stuff about poetry? How could she let him hold forth about Shakespeare? Seriously and solemnly Richard Dalloway got on his hind legs and said that no decent man ought to read Shakespeare's sonnets because it was like listening at keyholes (besides the relationship was not one that he approved). No decent man ought to let his wife visit a deceased wife's sister. Incredible! The only thing to do was to pelt him with sugared almonds—it was at dinner. But Clarissa sucked it all in; thought it so honest of him; so independent of him; Heaven knows if she didn't think him the most original mind she'd ever met!

That was one of the bonds between Sally and himself. There was a garden where they used to walk, a walled-in place, with rose-bushes and giant cauliflowers—he could remember Sally tearing off a rose, stopping to exclaim at the beauty of the cabbage leaves in the moonlight (it was extraordinary how vividly it all came back to him, things he hadn't thought of for years), while she implored him, half laughing of course, to carry off Clarissa, to save her from the Hughs and the Dalloways and all the other "perfect gentlemen" who would "stifle her soul" (she wrote reams of poetry in those days), make a mere hostess of her, encourage her worldliness. But one must do Clarissa justice. She wasn't going to marry Hugh anyhow. She had a perfectly clear notion of what she wanted. Her emotions were all on the surface. Beneath, she was very shrewd—a far better judge of character than Sally, for instance, and with it all, purely feminine; with that extraordinary gift, that woman's gift, of making a world of her own wherever she happened to be. She came into a room; she stood, as he had often seen her, in a doorway with lots of people round her. But it was Clarissa one remembered. Not that she was striking; not beautiful at all; there was nothing picturesque about her; she never said anything specially clever; there she was, however; there she was.

No, no, no! He was not in love with her any more! He only felt, after seeing her that morning, among her scissors and silks, making ready for the party, unable to get away from the thought of her; she kept coming back and back like a sleeper jolting against him in a railway carriage; which was not being in love, of course; it was thinking of her, criticising her, starting again, after thirty years, trying to explain her. The obvious thing to say of her was that she was worldly; cared too much for rank and society and getting on in the world—which was true in a sense; she had admitted it to him. (You could always get her to own up if you took the trouble; she was honest.) What she would say was that she hated frumps, fogies, failures, like himself presumably; thought people had no right to slouch about with their hands in their pockets; must do something, be something; and these great swells, these Duchesses, these hoary old Countesses one met in her drawing-room, unspeakably remote as he felt them to be from anything that mattered a straw, stood for something real to her. Lady Bexborough, she said once, held herself upright (so did Clarissa herself; she never lounged in any sense of the word; she was straight as a dart, a little rigid in fact). She said they had a kind of courage which the older she grew the more she respected. In all this there was a great deal of Dalloway, of course; a great deal of the public-spirited, British Empire, tariff-reform, governing-class spirit, which had grown on her, as it tends to do. With twice his wits, she had to see things through his eyes—one of the tragedies of married life. With a mind of her own, she must always be quoting Richard—as if one couldn't know to a tittle what Richard thought by reading the *Morning Post* of a morning! These parties for example were all for him, or for her idea of him (to do Richard justice he would have been happier farming in Norfolk). She made her drawing-room a sort of meeting-place; she had a genius for it. Over and over again he had seen her take some raw youth, twist him, turn him, wake him up; set him going. Infinite numbers of dull people conglomerated round her of course. But odd unexpected people turned up; an artist sometimes; sometimes a writer; queer fish in that atmosphere. And behind it all was that network of visiting, leaving cards, being kind to people; running about with bunches of flowers, little presents; So-and-so was going to France—must have an air-cushion; a real drain on her strength; all that interminable traffic that women of her sort keep up; but she did it genuinely, from a natural instinct.

Oddly enough, she was one of the most thorough-going sceptics he had ever met, and possibly (this was a theory he used to make up to account for her, so transparent in some ways, so inscrutable in others), possibly she said to herself, As we are a doomed race, chained to a sinking ship (her favourite reading as a girl was Huxley and Tyndall,[2] and they were fond of these nautical metaphors), as the whole thing is a bad joke, let us, at any rate, do our part; mitigate the sufferings of our fellow-prisoners (Huxley again); decorate the dungeon with flowers and air-cushions; be as decent as we possibly can. Those ruffians, the Gods, shan't have it all their own way,—her notion being that the Gods, who never lost a chance of hurting, thwarting and spoiling human lives were seriously put out if, all the same, you behaved like a lady. That phase came directly after Sylvia's death—that horrible affair. To see your own sister killed by a falling tree (all Justin Parry's fault—all his carelessness) before your very eyes, a girl too on the verge of life, the most gifted of them, Clarissa always said, was enough to turn one bitter. Later she wasn't so positive perhaps; she thought there were no Gods; no one was to blame; and so she evolved this atheist's religion of doing good for the sake of goodness.

And of course she enjoyed life immensely. It was her nature to enjoy (though goodness only knows, she had her reserves; it was a mere sketch, he often felt, that even he, after all these years, could make of Clarissa). Anyhow there was no bitterness in her; none of that sense of moral virtue which is so repulsive in good women. She enjoyed practically everything. If you walked with her in Hyde Park now it was a bed of tulips, now a child in a perambulator, now some absurd little drama she made up on the spur of the moment. (Very likely, she would have talked to those lovers, if she had thought them unhappy.) She had a sense of comedy that was really exquisite, but she needed people, always people, to bring it out, with the inevitable result that she frittered her time away, lunching, dining, giving these incessant parties of hers, talking nonsense, sayings things she didn't mean, blunting the edge of her mind, losing her discrimination. There she would sit at the head of the table taking infinite pains with some old buffer who might be useful to Dalloway—they knew the most appalling bores in Europe—or in came Elizabeth and everything must give way to *her*. She was at a High School, at the inarticulate stage last time he was over, a round-eyed, pale-faced girl, with nothing of her mother in her, a silent stolid creature, who took it all as a matter of course, let her mother make a fuss of her, and then said "May I go now?" like a child of four; going off, Clarissa explained, with that mixture of amusement and pride which Dalloway himself seemed to rouse in her, to play hockey. And now Elizabeth was "out," presumably; thought him an old fogy, laughed at her mother's friends. Ah well, so be it. The compensation of growing old, Peter Walsh thought, coming out of Regent's Park, and holding his hat in hand, was simply this; that the passions remain as strong as ever, but one has gained—at last!—the power which adds the supreme flavour to existence,—the power of taking hold of experience, of turning it round, slowly, in the light.

A terrible confession it was (he put his hat on again), but now, at the age of fifty-three one scarcely needed people any more. Life itself, every moment of it, every drop of it, here, this instant, now, in the sun, in Regent's Park, was enough. Too much indeed. A whole lifetime was too short to bring out, now that one had acquired the power, the full flavour; to extract every ounce of pleasure, every shade of meaning; which both were so much more solid than they used to be, so much less personal. It was impossible that he should ever suffer again as Clarissa had made him suffer. For hours at a time (pray God that one might say these things without being overheard!), for hours and days he never thought of Daisy.

2. Thomas H. Huxley (1825–1895) and John Tyndall (1820–1893) were staunch defenders of Darwin's evolutionary model, as set forth in *On the Origin of Species* (1859).

Could it be that he was in love with her then, remembering the misery, the torture, the extraordinary passion of those days? It was a different thing altogether—a much pleasanter thing—the truth being, of course, that now *she* was in love with *him*. And that perhaps was the reason why, when the ship actually sailed, he felt an extraordinary relief, wanted nothing so much as to be alone; was annoyed to find all her little attentions—cigars, notes, a rug for the voyage—in his cabin. Every one if they were honest would say the same; one doesn't want people after fifty; one doesn't want to go on telling women they are pretty; that's what most men of fifty would say, Peter Walsh thought, if they were honest.

But then these astonishing accesses of emotion—bursting into tears this morning, what was all that about? What could Clarissa have thought of him? thought him a fool presumably, not for the first time. It was jealousy that was at the bottom of it—jealousy which survives every other passion of mankind, Peter Walsh thought, holding his pocket-knife at arm's length. She had been meeting Major Orde, Daisy said in her last letter; said it on purpose he knew; said it to make him jealous; he could see her wrinkling her forehead as she wrote, wondering what she could say to hurt him; and yet it made no difference; he was furious! All this pother of coming to England and seeing lawyers wasn't to marry her, but to prevent her from marrying anybody else. That was what tortured him, that was what came over him when he saw Clarissa so calm, so cold, so intent on her dress or whatever it was; realising what she might have spared him, what she had reduced him to—a whimpering, snivelling old ass. But women, he thought, shutting his pocket-knife, don't know what passion is. They don't know the meaning of it to men. Clarissa was as cold as an icicle. There she would sit on the sofa by his side, let him take her hand, give him one kiss—Here he was at the crossing.

A sound interrupted him; a frail quivering sound, a voice bubbling up without direction, vigour, beginning or end, running weakly and shrilly and with an absence of all human meaning into

ee um fah um so
foo swee too eem oo

the voice of no age or sex, the voice of an ancient spring spouting from the earth; which issued, just opposite Regent's Park Tube station from a tall quivering shape, like a funnel, like a rusty pump, like a wind-beaten tree for ever barren of leaves which lets the wind run up and down its branches singing

ee um fah um so
foo swee too eem oo

and rocks and creaks and moans in the eternal breeze.

Through all ages—when the pavement was grass, when it was swamp, through the age of tusk and mammoth, through the age of silent sunrise, the battered woman—for she wore a skirt—with her right hand exposed, her left clutching at her side, stood singing of love—love which has lasted a million years, she sang, love which prevails, and millions of years ago, her lover, who had been dead these centuries, had walked, she crooned, with her in May; but in the course of ages, long as summer days, and flaming, she remembered, with nothing but red asters, he had gone; death's enormous sickle had swept those tremendous hills, and when at last she laid her hoary and immensely aged head on the earth, now become a mere cinder of ice, she implored the Gods to lay by her side a bunch of purple heather, there on her high burial place which the last rays of the last sun caressed; for then the pageant of the universe would be over.

As the ancient song bubbled up opposite Regent's Park Tube station still the earth seemed green and flowery; still, though it issued from so rude a mouth, a mere hole in the earth, muddy too, matted with root fibres and tangled grasses, still the old bubbling burbling song, soaking through the knotted roots of infinite ages, and skeletons and treasure, streamed away in rivulets over the pavement and all along the Marylebone Road, and down towards Euston, fertilising, leaving a damp stain.

Still remembering how once in some primeval May she had walked with her lover, this rusty pump, this battered old woman with one hand exposed for coppers the other clutching her side, would still be there in ten million years, remembering how once she had walked in May, where the sea flows now, with whom it did not matter—he was a man, oh yes, a man who had loved her. But the passage of ages had blurred the clarity of that ancient May day; the bright petalled flowers were hoar and silver frosted; and she no longer saw, when she implored him (as she did now quite clearly) "look in my eyes with thy sweet eyes intently," she no longer saw brown eyes, black whiskers or sunburnt face but only a looming shape, a shadow shape, to which, with the birdlike freshness of the very aged she still twittered "give me your hand and let me press it gently" (Peter Walsh couldn't help giving the poor creature a coin as he stepped into his taxi), "and if some one should see, what matter they?" she demanded; and her fist clutched at her side, and she smiled, pocketing her shilling, and all peering inquisitive eyes seemed blotted out, and the passing generations—the pavement was crowded with bustling middle-class people—vanished, like leaves, to be trodden under, to be soaked and steeped and made mould of by that eternal spring—

ee um fah um so
foo swee too eem oo

"Poor old woman," said Rezia Warren Smith, waiting to cross.

Oh poor old wretch!

Suppose it was a wet night? Suppose one's father, or somebody who had known one in better days had happened to pass, and saw one standing there in the gutter? And where did she sleep at night?

Cheerfully, almost gaily, the invincible thread of sound wound up into the air like the smoke from a cottage chimney, winding up clean beech trees and issuing in a tuft of blue smoke among the topmost leaves. "And if some one should see, what matter they?"

Since she was so unhappy, for weeks and weeks now, Rezia had given meanings to things that happened, almost felt sometimes that she must stop people in the street, if they looked good, kind people, just to say to them "I am unhappy"; and this old woman singing in the street "if some one should see, what matter they?" made her suddenly quite sure that everything was going to be right. They were going to Sir William Bradshaw; she thought his name sounded nice; he would cure Septimus at once. And then there was a brewer's cart, and the grey horses had upright bristles of straw in their tails; there were newspaper placards. It was a silly, silly dream, being unhappy.

So they crossed, Mr and Mrs Septimus Warren Smith, and was there, after all, anything to draw attention to them, anything to make a passer-by suspect here is a young man who carries in him the greatest message in the world, and is, moreover, the happiest man in the world, and the most miserable? Perhaps they walked more slowly than other people, and there was something hesitating, trailing, in the man's walk, but what more natural for a clerk, who has not been in the West End on a weekday at this hour for years, than to keep looking at the sky, looking at this, that and the other, as if Portland Place were a room he had come into when the family are away, the chandeliers being hung in holland bags, and the caretaker, as she lets in long shafts of dusty light upon deserted, queer-looking armchairs, lifting one corner of the long blinds, explains to the visitors what a wonderful place it is; how wonderful, but at the same time, he thinks, as he looks at chairs and tables, how strange.

To look at, he might have been a clerk, but of the better sort; for he wore brown boots; his hands were educated; so, too, his profile—his angular, big-nosed, intelligent, sensitive profile; but not his lips altogether, for they were loose; and his eyes (as eyes tend to be), eyes merely; hazel, large; so that he was, on the whole, a border case, neither one thing nor the other, might end with a house at Purley and a motor car, or continue renting apartments in back streets all his life; one of those half-educated, self-educated men whose education is all learnt from books borrowed from public libraries, read in the evening after the day's work, on the advice of well-known authors consulted by letter.

As for the other experiences, the solitary ones, which people go through alone, in their bedrooms, in their offices, walking the fields and the streets of London, he had them; had left home, a mere boy, because of his mother; she lied; because he came down to tea for the fiftieth time with his hands unwashed; because he could see no future for a poet in Stroud; and so, making a confidant of his little sister, had gone to London leaving an absurd note behind him, such as great men have written, and the world has read later when the story of their struggles has become famous.

London has swallowed up many millions of young men called Smith; thought nothing of fantastic Christian names like Septimus with which their parents have thought to distinguish them. Lodging off the Euston Road, there were experiences, again experiences, such as change a face in two years from a pink innocent oval to a face lean, contracted, hostile. But of all this what could the most observant of friends have said except what a gardener says when he opens the conservatory door in the morning and finds a new blossom on his plant:—It has flowered; flowered from vanity, ambition, idealism, passion, loneliness, courage, laziness, the usual seeds, which all muddled up (in a room off the Euston Road), made him shy, and stammering, made him anxious to improve himself, made him fall in love with Miss Isabel Pole, lecturing in the Waterloo Road upon Shakespeare.

Was he not like Keats? she asked; and reflected how she might give him a taste of *Antony and Cleopatra* and the rest; lent him books; wrote him scraps of letters; and lit in him such a fire as burns only once in a life-time, without heat, flickering a red gold flame infinitely ethereal and insubstantial over Miss Pole; *Antony and Cleopatra;* and the Waterloo Road. He thought her beautiful, believed her impeccably wise; dreamed of her, wrote poems to her, which, ignoring the subject, she corrected in red ink; he saw her, one summer evening, walking in a green dress in a square. "It has flowered," the gardener might have said, had he opened the door; had he come in, that is to say, any night about this time, and found him writing; found him tearing up his writing; found him finishing a masterpiece at three o'clock in the morning and running out to pace the streets, and visiting churches, and fasting one day, drinking another, devouring Shakespeare, Darwin, *The History of Civilisation,*[3] and Bernard Shaw.[4]

3. The magnum opus of Henry Thomas Buckle (1821–1862), an English historian who gained notoriety by applying the methods of empirical science to historical inquity, and by emphasizing social/intellectual history over more traditional political/military subject matter. (Buckle held, for instance, that the influence of women in any given period was an indicator by which its degree of "civilisation" could be measured.)

4. Irish-born dramatist, journalist, and prominent leader within the socialist Fabian Society. An advocate of major artistic and political reforms, Shaw argued cogently in favor of women's rights, the abolition of private property, and the revitalization of London theater through the performance of works that were imbued with real moral and social weight.

Something was up, Mr Brewer knew; Mr Brewer, managing clerk at Sibleys and Arrowsmiths, auctioneers, valuers, land and estate agents; something was up, he thought, and, being paternal with his young men, and thinking very highly of Smith's abilities, and prophesying that he would, in ten or fifteen years, succeed to the leather arm-chair in the inner room under the skylight with the deed-boxes round him, "if he keeps his health," said Mr Brewer, and that was the danger—he looked weakly; advised football, invited him to supper and was seeing his way to consider recommending a rise of salary, when something happened which threw out many of Mr Brewer's calculations, took away his ablest young fellows, and eventually, so prying and insidious were the fingers of the European War, smashed a plaster cast of Ceres,[5] ploughed a hole in the geranium beds, and utterly ruined the cook's nerves at Mr Brewer's establishment at Muswell Hill.

Septimus was one of the first to volunteer. He went to France to save an England which consisted almost entirely of Shakespeare's plays and Miss Isabel Pole in a green dress walking in a square. There in the trenches the change which Mr Brewer desired when he advised football was produced instantly; he developed manliness; he was promoted; he drew the attention, indeed the affection of his officer, Evans by name. It was a case of two dogs playing on a hearth-rug; one worrying a paper screw, snarling, snapping, giving a pinch, now and then, at the old dog's ear; the other lying somnolent, blinking at the fire, raising a paw, turning and growling good-temperedly. They had to be together, share with each other, fight with each other, quarrel with each other. But when Evans (Rezia who had only seen him once called him "a quiet man," a sturdy red-haired man, undemonstrative in the company of women), when Evans was killed, just before the Armistice, in Italy, Septimus, far from showing any emotion or recognising that here was the end of a friendship, congratulated himself upon feeling very little and very reasonably. The War had taught him. It was sublime. He had gone through the whole show, friendship, European War, death, had won promotion, was still under thirty and was bound to survive. He was right there. The last shells missed him. He watched them explode with indifference. When peace came he was in Milan, billeted in the house of an innkeeper with a courtyard, flowers in tubs, little tables in the open, daughters making hats, and to Lucrezia, the younger daughter, he became engaged one evening when the panic was on him—that he could not feel.

For now that it was all over, truce signed, and the dead buried, he had, especially in the evening, these sudden thunder-claps of fear. He could not feel. As he opened the door of the room where the Italian girls sat making hats, he could see them; could hear them; they were rubbing wires among coloured beads in saucers; they were turning buckram shapes this way and that; the table was all strewn with feathers, spangles, silks, ribbons; scissors were rapping on the table; but something failed him; he could not feel. Still, scissors rapping, girls laughing, hats being made protected him; he was assured of safety; he had a refuge. But he could not sit there all night. There were mo-

5. Roman mythological equivalent of Demeter, Greek goddess of corn and the harvest (cf. Peter Walsh's cornucopia-wielding "vision" on page 2367). According to the myth, when her daughter, Proserpina, was abducted by Pluto, god of the Underworld, Ceres desperately searched the world over for her, and in her grief she allowed the earth to grow barren. Hoping to end the ensuing famine, Jupiter finally intervened with Pluto, and henceforth Proserpina was allowed to leave the underworld for six months each year, during which time Ceres is said annually to restore the earth to a state of fertility. In another story which seems at least tangentially linked to Septimus's postwar "message" ("Men must not cut down trees," page 2350), Ceres is supposed to have punished a man with famine for having cut down a sacred oak. Regardless of how much he had eaten, he always desired to eat as much again; at last he consumed himself and died.

ments of waking in the early morning. The bed was falling; he was falling. Oh for the scissors and the lamplight and the buckram shapes! He asked Lucrezia to marry him, the younger of the two, the gay, the frivolous, with those little artist's fingers that she would hold up and say "It is all in them." Silk, feathers, what not were alive to them.

"It is the hat that matters most," she would say, when they walked out together. Every hat that passed, she would examine; and the cloak and the dress and the way the woman held herself. Ill-dressing, over-dressing she stigmatised, not savagely, rather with impatient movements of the hands, like those of a painter who puts from him some obvious well-meant glaring imposture; and then, generously, but always critically, she would welcome a shopgirl who had turned her little bit of stuff gallantly, or praise, wholly, with enthusiastic and professional understanding, a French lady descending from her carriage, in chinchilla, robes, pearls.

"Beautiful!" she would murmur, nudging Septimus, that he might see. But beauty was behind a pane of glass. Even taste (Rezia liked ices, chocolates, sweet things) had no relish to him. He put down his cup on the little marble table. He looked at people outside; happy they seemed, collecting in the middle of the street, shouting, laughing, squabbling over nothing. But he could not taste, he could not feel. In the teashop among the tables and the chattering waiters the appalling fear came over him—he could not feel. He could reason; he could read, Dante for example, quite easily ("Septimus, do put down your book," said Rezia, gently shutting the *Inferno*), he could add up his bill; his brain was perfect; it must be the fault of the world then—that he could not feel.

"The English are so silent," Rezia said. She liked it, she said. She respected these Englishmen, and wanted to see London, and the English horses, and the tailor-made suits, and could remember hearing how wonderful the shops were, from an Aunt who had married and lived in Soho.

It might be possible, Septimus thought, looking at England from the train window, as they left Newhaven; it might be possible that the world itself is without meaning.

At the office they advanced him to a post of considerable responsibility. They were proud of him; he had won crosses. "You have done your duty; it is up to us—" began Mr Brewer; and could not finish, so pleasurable was his emotion. They took admirable lodgings off the Tottenham Court Road.

Here he opened Shakespeare once more. That boy's business of the intoxication of language—*Antony and Cleopatra*—had shrivelled utterly. How Shakespeare loathed humanity—the putting on of clothes, the getting of children, the sordidity of the mouth and the belly! This was now revealed to Septimus; the message hidden in the beauty of words. The secret signal which one generation passes, under disguise, to the next is loathing, hatred, despair. Dante the same. Aeschylus (translated) the same. There Rezia sat at the table trimming hats. She trimmed hats for Mrs Filmer's friends; she trimmed hats by the hour. She looked pale, mysterious, like a lily, drowned, under water, he thought.

"The English are so serious," she would say, putting her arms round Septimus, her cheek against his.

Love between man and woman was repulsive to Shakespeare. The business of copulation was filth to him before the end. But, Rezia said, she must have children. They had been married five years.

They went to the Tower together; to the Victoria and Albert Museum; stood in the crowd to see the King open Parliament. And there were the shops—hat shops, dress shops, shops with leather bags in the window, where she would stand staring. But she must have a boy.

She must have a son like Septimus, she said. But nobody could be like Septimus; so gentle; so serious; so clever. Could she not read Shakespeare too? Was Shakespeare a difficult author? she asked.

One cannot bring children into a world like this. One cannot perpetuate suffering, or increase the breed of these lustful animals, who have no lasting emotions, but only whims and vanities, eddying them now this way, now that.

He watched her snip, shape, as one watches a bird hop, flit in the grass, without daring to move a finger. For the truth is (let her ignore it) that human beings have neither kindness, nor faith, nor charity beyond what serves to increase the pleasure of the moment. They hunt in packs. Their packs scour the desert and vanish screaming into the wilderness. They desert the fallen. They are plastered over with grimaces. There was Brewer at the office, with his waxed moustache, coral tie-pin, white slip, and pleasurable emotions—all coldness and clamminess within,—his geraniums ruined in the War—his cook's nerves destroyed; or Amelia What'shername, handing round cups of tea punctually at five—a leering, sneering obscene little harpy; and the Toms and Berties in their starched shirt fronts oozing thick drops of vice. They never saw him drawing pictures of them naked at their antics in his notebook. In the street, vans roared past him; brutality blared out on placards; men were trapped in mines; women burnt alive; and once a maimed file of lunatics being exercised or displayed for the diversion of the populace (who laughed aloud), ambled and nodded and grinned past him, in the Tottenham Court Road, each half apologetically, yet triumphantly, inflicting his hopeless woe. And would *he* go mad?

At tea Rezia told him that Mrs Filmer's daughter was expecting a baby. *She* could not grow old and have no children! She was very lonely, she was very unhappy! She cried for the first time since they were married. Far away he heard her sobbing; he heard it accurately, he noticed it distinctly; he compared it to a piston thumping. But he felt nothing.

His wife was crying, and he felt nothing; only each time she sobbed in this profound, this silent, this hopeless way, he descended another step into the pit.

At last, with a melodramatic gesture which he assumed mechanically and with complete consciousness of its insincerity, he dropped his head on his hands. Now he had surrendered; now other people must help him. People must be sent for. He gave in.

Nothing could rouse him. Rezia put him to bed. She sent for a doctor—Mrs Filmer's Dr Holmes. Dr Holmes examined him. There was nothing whatever the matter, said Dr Holmes. Oh, what a relief! What a kind man, what a good man! thought Rezia. When he felt like that he went to the Music Hall, said Dr Holmes. He took a day off with his wife and played golf. Why not try two tabloids of bromide dissolved in a glass of water at bedtime? These old Bloomsbury houses, said Dr Holmes, tapping the wall, are often full of very fine panelling, which the landlords have the folly to paper over. Only the other day, visiting a patient, Sir Somebody Something in Bedford Square—

So there was no excuse; nothing whatever the matter, except the sin for which human nature had condemned him to death; that he did not feel. He had not cared when Evans was killed; that was worst; but all the other crimes raised their heads and shook their fingers and jeered and sneered over the rail of the bed in the early hours of the morning at the prostrate body which lay realising its degradation; how he had married his wife without loving her; had lied to her; seduced her; outraged Miss Isabel Pole, and was so pocked and marked with vice that women shuddered when they saw him in the street. The verdict of human nature on such a wretch was death.

Dr Holmes came again. Large, fresh coloured, handsome, flicking his boots, looking in the glass, he brushed it all aside—headaches, sleeplessness, fears, dreams—nerve symptoms and nothing more, he said. If Dr Holmes found himself even half a pound below eleven stone six, he asked his wife for another plate of porridge at breakfast (Rezia would learn to cook porridge.) But, he continued, health is largely a matter in our own control. Throw yourself into outside interests; take up some hobby. He opened Shakespeare—*Antony and Cleopatra;* pushed Shakespeare aside. Some hobby, said Dr Holmes, for did he not owe his own excellent health (and he worked as hard as any man in London) to the fact that he could always switch off from his patients on to old furniture? And what a very pretty comb, if he might say so, Mrs Warren Smith was wearing!

When the damned fool came again, Septimus refused to see him. Did he indeed? said Dr Holmes, smiling agreeably. Really he had to give that charming little lady, Mrs Smith, a friendly push before he could get past her into her husband's bedroom.

"So you're in a funk," he said agreeably, sitting down by his patient's side. He had actually talked of killing himself to his wife, quite a girl, a foreigner, wasn't she? Didn't that give her a very odd idea of English husbands? Didn't one owe perhaps a duty to one's wife? Wouldn't it be better to do something instead of lying in bed? For he had had forty years' experience behind him; and Septimus could take Dr Holmes's word for it—there was nothing whatever the matter with him. And next time Dr Holmes came he hoped to find Smith out of bed and not making that charming little lady his wife anxious about him.

Human nature, in short, was on him—the repulsive brute, with the blood-red nostrils. Holmes was on him. Dr Holmes came quite regularly every day. Once you stumble, Septimus wrote on the back of a postcard, human nature is on you. Holmes is on you. Their only chance was to escape, without letting Holmes know; to Italy—anywhere, anywhere, away from Dr Holmes.

But Rezia could not understand him. Dr Holmes was such a kind man. He was so interested in Septimus. He only wanted to help them, he said. He had four little children and he had asked her to tea, she told Septimus.

So he was deserted. The whole world was clamouring: Kill yourself, kill yourself, for our sakes. But why should he kill himself for their sakes? Food was pleasant; the sun hot; and this killing oneself, how does one set about it, with a table knife, uglily, with floods of blood,—by sucking a gaspipe? He was too weak; he could scarcely raise his hand. Besides, now that he was quite alone, condemned, deserted, as those who are about to die are alone, there was a luxury in it, an isolation full of sublimity; a freedom which the attached can never know. Holmes had won of course; the brute with the red nostrils had won. But even Holmes himself could not touch this last relic straying on the edge of the world, this outcast, who gazed back at the inhabited regions, who lay, like a drowned sailor, on the shore of the world.

It was at that moment (Rezia gone shopping) that the great revelation took place. A voice spoke from behind the screen. Evans was speaking. The dead were with him.

"Evans, Evans!" he cried.

Mr Smith was talking aloud to himself, Agnes the servant girl cried to Mrs Filmer in the kitchen. "Evans, Evans," he had said as she brought in the tray. She jumped, she did. She scuttled downstairs.

And Rezia came in, with her flowers, and walked across the room, and put the roses in a vase, upon which the sun struck directly, and it went laughing, leaping round the room.

She had had to buy the roses, Rezia said, from a poor man in the street. But they were almost dead already, she said, arranging the roses.

So there was a man outside; Evans presumably; and the roses, which Rezia said were half dead, had been picked by him in the fields of Greece. "Communication is health; communication is happiness, communication—" he muttered.

"What are you saying, Septimus?" Rezia asked, wild with terror, for he was talking to himself.

She sent Agnes running for Dr Holmes. Her husband, she said, was mad. He scarcely knew her.

"You brute! You brute!" cried Septimus, seeing human nature, that is Dr Holmes, enter the room.

"Now what's all this about?" said Dr Holmes in the most amiable way in the world. "Talking nonsense to frighten your wife?" But he would give him something to make him sleep. And if they were rich people, said Dr Holmes, looking ironically round the room, by all means let them go to Harley Street; if they had no confidence in him, said Dr Holmes, looking not quite so kind.

It was precisely twelve o'clock; twelve by Big Ben; whose stroke was wafted over the northern part of London; blent with that of other clocks, mixed in a thin ethereal way with the clouds and wisps of smoke, and died up there among the seagulls—twelve o'clock struck as Clarissa Dalloway laid her green dress on her bed, and the Warren Smiths walked down Harley Street. Twelve was the hour of their appointment. Probably, Rezia thought, that was Sir William Bradshaw's house with the grey motor car in front of it. The leaden circles dissolved in the air.

Indeed it was—Sir William Bradshaw's motor car; low, powerful, grey with plain initials interlocked on the panel, as if the pomps of heraldry were incongruous, this man being the ghostly helper, the priest of science; and, as the motor car was grey, so to match its sober suavity, grey furs, silver grey rugs were heaped in it, to keep her ladyship warm while she waited. For often Sir William would travel sixty miles or more down into the country to visit the rich, the afflicted, who could afford the very large fee which Sir William very properly charged for his advice. Her ladyship waited with the rugs about her knees an hour or more, leaning back, thinking sometimes of the patient, sometimes, excusably, of the wall of gold, mounting minute by minute while she waited; the wall of gold that was mounting between them and all shifts and anxieties (she had borne them bravely; they had had their struggles) until she felt wedged on a calm ocean, where only spice winds blow; respected, admired, envied, with scarcely anything left to wish for, though she regretted her stoutness; large dinner-parties every Thursday night to the profession; an occasional bazaar to be opened; Royalty greeted; too little time, alas, with her husband, whose work grew and grew; a boy doing well at Eton; she would have liked a daughter too; interests she had, however, in plenty; child welfare; the after-care of the epileptic, and photography, so that if there was a church building, or a church decaying, she bribed the sexton, got the key and took photographs, which were scarcely to be distinguished from the work of professionals, while she waited.

Sir William himself was no longer young. He had worked very hard; he had won his position by sheer ability (being the son of a shopkeeper); loved his profession; made a fine figurehead at ceremonies and spoke well—all of which had by the time he was knighted given him a heavy look, a weary look (the stream of patients being so incessant, the responsibilities and privileges of his profession so onerous), which weariness, together with his grey hairs, increased the extraordinary distinction of his presence and gave him the reputation (of the utmost importance in dealing with nerve cases) not merely of lightning skill, and almost infallible accuracy in diagnosis but of sympathy; tact; understanding of the human soul. He could see the first moment they came into the room (the Warren Smiths they were called); he was certain directly he saw the man; it was a case of extreme gravity. It was a case of complete breakdown—complete physical and nervous breakdown, with every symptom in an advanced stage, he ascertained in two or three minutes (writing answers to questions, murmured discreetly, on a pink card).

How long had Dr Holmes been attending him?

Six weeks.

Prescribed a little bromide? Said there was nothing the matter? Ah yes (those general practitioners! thought Sir William. It took half his time to undo their blunders. Some were irreparable).

"You served with great distinction in the War?"

The patient repeated the word "war" interrogatively.

He was attaching meanings to words of a symbolical kind. A serious symptom, to be noted on the card.

"The War?" the patient asked. The European War—that little shindy of schoolboys with gunpowder? Had he served with distinction? He really forgot. In the War itself he had failed.

"Yes, he served with the greatest distinction," Rezia assured the doctor; "he was promoted."

"And they have the very highest opinion of you at your office?" Sir William murmured, glancing at Mr Brewer's very generously worded letter. "So that you have nothing to worry you, no financial anxiety, nothing?"

He had committed an appalling crime and been condemned to death by human nature.

"I have—I have," he began, "committed a crime—"

"He has done nothing wrong whatever," Rezia assured the doctor. If Mr Smith would wait, said Sir William, he would speak to Mrs Smith in the next room. Her husband was very seriously ill, Sir William said. Did he threaten to kill himself?

Oh, he did, she cried. But he did not mean it, she said. Of course not. It was merely a question of rest, said Sir William; of rest, rest, rest; a long rest in bed. There was a delightful home down in the country where her husband would be perfectly looked after. Away from her? she asked. Unfortunately, yes; the people we care for most are not good for us when we are ill. But he was not mad, was he? Sir William said he never spoke of "madness"; he called it not having a sense of proportion. But her husband did not like doctors. He would refuse to go there. Shortly and kindly Sir William explained to her the state of the case. He had threatened to kill himself. There was no alternative. It was a question of law. He would lie in bed in a beautiful house in the country. The nurses were admirable. Sir William would visit him once a week. If Mrs Warren Smith was quite sure she had no more questions to ask—he never hurried his patients—they would return to her husband. She had nothing more to ask—not of Sir William.

So they returned to the most exalted of mankind; the criminal who faced his judges; the victim exposed on the heights; the fugitive; the drowned sailor; the poet of the immortal ode; the Lord who had gone from life to death;[6] to Septimus Warren Smith, who sat in the arm-chair under the skylight staring at a photograph of Lady Bradshaw in Court dress, muttering messages about beauty.

"We have had our little talk," said Sir William.

"He says you are very, very ill," Rezia cried.

"We have been arranging that you should go into a home," said Sir William.

"One of Holmes's homes?" sneered Septimus.

The fellow made a distasteful impression. For there was in Sir William, whose father had been a tradesman, a natural respect for breeding and clothing, which shabbiness nettled; again, more profoundly, there was in Sir William, who had never had time for reading, a grudge, deeply buried, against cultivated people who came into his room and intimated that doctors, whose profession is a constant strain upon all the highest faculties, are not educated men.

"One of *my* homes, Mr Warren Smith," he said, "where we will teach you to rest."

And there was just one thing more.

He was quite certain that when Mr Warren Smith was well he was the last man in the world to frighten his wife. But he had talked of killing himself.

"We all have our moments of depression," said Sir William.

Once you fall, Septimus repeated to himself, human nature is on you. Holmes and Bradshaw are on you. They scour the desert. They fly screaming into the wilderness. The rack and the thumbscrew[7] are applied. Human nature is remorseless.

"Impulses came upon him sometimes?" Sir William asked, with his pencil on a pink card.

That was his own affair, said Septimus.

"Nobody lives for himself alone," said Sir William, glancing at the photograph of his wife in Court dress.

"And you have a brilliant career before you," said Sir William. There was Mr Brewer's letter on the table. "An exceptionally brilliant career."

But if he confessed? If he communicated? Would they let him off then, his torturers?

"I—I—" he stammered.

But what was his crime? He could not remember it.

"Yes?" Sir William encouraged him. (But it was growing late.)

Love, trees, there is no crime—what was his message?

He could not remember it.

"I—I—" Septimus stammered.

"Try to think as little about yourself as possible," said Sir William kindly. Really, he was not fit to be about.

Was there anything else they wished to ask him? Sir William would make all arrangements (he murmured to Rezia) and he would let her know between five and six that evening he murmured.

6. These follow in the series of characterizations which ironize Septimus's sense of his own postwar existence. The drowned sailor must call to mind the corresponding persona in Eliot's *The Waste Land* (1922), Phlebas the Phoenician sailor-merchant, who simultaneously represents the possibility of fertility and renewal, and the failure of this possibility: "As he rose and fell / He passed the stages of his age, and youth / Entering the whirlpool" (316–18). The poet of the immortal ode may refer us back to Keats's *Ode on a Grecian Urn*, in which immortality is both the promise that the lovers figured on the urn will be "forever panting, and forever young," and the similarly everlasting contingency that "never, never, canst [the lovers] kiss." The immortality is as frustrating as it is desired, a thing to "tease us out of thought." The final image before we come to Septimus suggests an unaccomplished version of the Christian resurrection, concluding in death rather than the hope of life.

7. Instruments of torture.

"Trust everything to me," he said, and dismissed them.

Never, never had Rezia felt such agony in her life! She had asked for help and been deserted! He had failed them! Sir William Bradshaw was not a nice man.

The upkeep of that motor car alone must cost him quite a lot, said Septimus, when they got out into the street.

She clung to his arm. They had been deserted.

But what more did she want?

To his patients he gave three-quarters of an hour; and if in this exacting science which has to do with what, after all, we know nothing about—the nervous system, the human brain—a doctor loses his sense of proportion, as a doctor he fails. Health we must have; and health is proportion; so that when a man comes into your room and says he is Christ (a common delusion), and has a message, as they mostly have, and threatens, as they often do, to kill himself, you invoke proportion; order rest in bed; rest in solitude; silence and rest; rest without friends, without books, without messages; six months' rest; until a man who went in weighing seven stone six comes out weighing twelve.

Proportion, divine proportion, Sir William's goddess, was acquired by Sir William walking hospitals, catching salmon, begetting one son in Harley Street by Lady Bradshaw, who caught salmon herself and took photographs scarcely to be distinguished from the work of professionals. Worshipping proportion, Sir William not only prospered himself but made England prosper, secluded her lunatics, forbade childbirth, penalised despair, made it impossible for the unfit to propagate their views until they, too, shared his sense of proportion—his, if they were men, Lady Bradshaw's if they were women (she embroidered, knitted, spent four nights out of seven at home with her son), so that not only did his colleagues respect him, his subordinates fear him, but the friends and relations of his patients felt for him the keenest gratitude for insisting that these prophetic Christs and Christesses, who prophesied the end of the world, or the advent of God, should drink milk in bed, as Sir William ordered; Sir William with his thirty years' experience of these kinds of cases, and his infallible instinct, this is madness, this sense; in fact, his sense of proportion.

But Proportion has a sister, less smiling, more formidable, a Goddess even now engaged—in the heat and sands of India, the mud and swamp of Africa, the purlieus of London, wherever in short the climate or the devil tempts men to fall from the true belief which is her own—is even now engaged in dashing down shrines, smashing idols, and setting up in their place her own stern countenance. Conversion is her name and she feasts on the wills of the weakly, loving to impress, to impose, adoring her own features stamped on the face of the populace. At Hyde Park Corner on a tub she stands preaching; shrouds herself in white and walks penitentially disguised as brotherly love through factories and parliaments; offers help, but desires power; smites out of her way roughly the dissentient, or dissatisfied; bestows her blessing on those who, looking upward, catch submissively from her eyes the light of their own. This lady too (Rezia Warren Smith divined it) had her dwelling in Sir William's heart, though concealed, as she mostly is, under some plausible disguise; some venerable name; love, duty, self sacrifice. How he would work—how toil to raise funds, propagate reforms, initiate institutions! But conversion, fastidious Goddess, loves blood better than brick, and feasts most subtly on the human will. For example, Lady Bradshaw. Fifteen years ago she had gone under. It was nothing you could put your finger on; there had been no scene, no snap; only the slow sinking, water-logged, of her will into his. Sweet was her smile, swift her submission; dinner in Harley Street, numbering eight or nine courses, feeding ten or fifteen guests of the professional classes, was smooth and urbane. Only as the evening wore on a very slight dulness, or uneasiness perhaps, a nervous twitch, fumble, stumble and confusion indicated, what it was really painful to believe—that the poor lady lied. Once, long ago, she had caught salmon freely: now, quick to minister to the craving which lit her husband's eye so oilily for dominion, for power, she cramped, squeezed, pared, pruned, drew back, peeped through; so that without knowing precisely what made the evening disagreeable, and caused this pressure on the top of the head (which might well be imputed to the professional conversation, or the fatigue of a great doctor whose life, Lady Bradshaw said, "is not his own but his patients'") disagreeable it was: so that guests, when the clock struck ten, breathed in the air of Harley Street even with rapture; which relief, however, was denied to his patients.

There in the grey room, with the pictures on the wall, and the valuable furniture, under the ground glass skylight, they learnt the extent of their transgressions; huddled up in arm-chairs, they watched him go through, for their benefit, a curious exercise with the arms, which he shot out, brought sharply back to his hip, to prove (if the patient was obstinate) that Sir William was master of his own actions, which the patient was not. There some weakly broke down; sobbed, submitted; others, inspired by Heaven knows what intemperate madness, called Sir William to his face a damnable humbug; questioned, even more impiously, life itself. Why live? they demanded. Sir William replied that life was good. Certainly Lady Bradshaw in ostrich feathers hung over the mantelpiece, and as for his income it was quite twelve thousand a year. But to us, they protested, life has given no such bounty. He acquiesced. They lacked a sense of proportion. And perhaps, after all, there is no God? He shrugged his shoulders. In short, this living or not living is an affair of our own? But there they were mistaken. Sir William had a friend in Surrey where they taught, what Sir William frankly admitted was a difficult art—a sense of proportion. There were, moreover, family affection; honour; courage; and a brilliant career. All of these had in Sir William a resolute champion. If they failed him, he had to support police and the good of society, which, he remarked very quietly, would take care, down in Surrey, that these unsocial impulses, bred more than anything by the lack of good blood, were held in control. And then stole out from her hiding-place and mounted her throne that Goddess whose lust is to over-ride opposition, to stamp indelibly in the sanctuaries of others the image of herself. Naked, defenceless, the exhausted, the friendless received the impress of Sir William's will. He swooped; he devoured. He shut people up. It was this combination of decision and humanity that endeared Sir William so greatly to the relations of his victims.

But Rezia Warren Smith cried, walking down Harley Street, that she did not like that man.

Shredding and slicing, dividing and subdividing, the clocks of Harley Street nibbled at the June day, counselled submission, upheld authority, and pointed out in chorus the supreme advantages of a sense of proportion, until the mound of time was so far diminished that a commercial clock, suspended above a shop in Oxford Street, announced, genially and fraternally, as if it were a pleasure to Messrs. Rigby and Lowndes to give the information gratis, that it was half-past one.

Looking up, it appeared that each letter of their names stood for one of the hours; subconsciously one was grateful to Rigby and Lowndes for giving one time ratified by Greenwich; and this gratitude (so Hugh Whitbread ruminated, dallying there in front of the shop window), naturally took the form later of buying off Rigby and Lowndes socks or shoes. So he ruminated. It was his habit. He did not go deeply. He brushed surfaces; the dead languages, the living, life in Constantinople, Paris, Rome; riding, shooting, tennis, it had been once. The malicious asserted that he now kept guard at Buckingham Palace, dressed in silk stockings and knee-breeches, over what nobody knew. But he did it extremely efficiently. He had been afloat on the cream of English society for fifty-five years. He had known Prime Ministers. His affections were understood to be deep. And if it were true that he had not taken part in any of the great movements of the time or held important office, one or two humble reforms stood to his credit; an improvement in public shelters was one; the protection of owls in Norfolk another; servant girls had reason to be grateful to him; and his name at the end of letters to the *Times*, asking for funds, appealing to the public to protect, to preserve, to clear up litter, to abate smoke, and stamp out immorality in parks, commanded respect.

A magnificent figure he cut too, pausing for a moment (as the sound of the half hour died away) to look critically, magisterially, at socks and shoes; impeccable, substantial, as if he beheld the world from a certain eminence, and dressed to match; but realised the obligations which size, wealth, health, entail, and observed punctiliously even when not absolutely necessary, little courtesies, old-fashioned ceremonies which gave a quality to his manner, something to imitate, something to remember him by, for he would never lunch, for example, with Lady Bruton, whom he had known these twenty years, without bringing her in his outstretched hand a bunch of carnations and asking Miss Brush, Lady Bruton's secretary, after her brother in South Africa, which, for some reason, Miss Brush, deficient though she was in every attribute of female charm, so much resented that she said "Thank you, he's doing very well in South Africa," when, for half a dozen years, he had been doing badly in Portsmouth.

Lady Bruton herself preferred Richard Dalloway, who arrived at the next moment. Indeed they met on the doorstep.

Lady Bruton preferred Richard Dalloway of course. He was made of much finer material. But she wouldn't let them run down her poor dear Hugh. She could never forget his kindness—he had been really remarkably kind—she forgot precisely upon what occasion. But he had been—remarkably kind. Anyhow, the difference between one man and another does not amount to much. She had never seen the sense of cutting people up, as Clarissa Dalloway did—cutting them up and sticking them together again; not at any rate when one was sixty-two. She took Hugh's carnations with her angular grim smile. There was nobody else coming, she said. She had got them there on false pretences, to help her out of a difficulty—

"But let us eat first," she said.

And so there began a soundless and exquisite passing to and fro through swing doors of aproned white-capped maids, handmaidens not of necessity, but adepts in a mystery or grand deception practised by hostesses in Mayfair from one-thirty to two, when, with a wave of the hand, the traffic ceases, and there rises instead this profound illusion in the first place about the food—how it is not paid for; and then that the table spreads itself voluntarily with glass and silver, little mats, saucers of red fruit; films of brown cream mask turbot; in casseroles severed chickens swim; coloured, undomestic, the fire burns; and with the wine and the coffee (not paid for) rise jocund visions before musing eyes; gently speculative eyes; eyes to whom life appears musical, mysterious; eyes now kindled to observe genially the beauty of the red carnations which Lady Bruton (whose movements were always angular) had laid beside her plate, so that Hugh Whitbread, feeling at peace with the entire universe and at the same time completely sure of his standing, said, resting his fork,

"Wouldn't they look charming against your lace?"

Miss Brush resented this familiarity intensely. She thought him an underbred fellow. She made Lady Bruton laugh.

Lady Bruton raised the carnations, holding them rather stiffly with much the same attitude with which the General held the scroll in the picture behind her; she remained fixed, tranced. Which was she now, the General's great-grand-daughter? great-great-grand-daughter? Richard Dalloway asked himself. Sir Roderick, Sir Miles, Sir Talbot—that was it. It was remarkable how in that family the likeness persisted in the women. She should have been a general of dragoons herself. And Richard would have served under her, cheerfully; he had the greatest respect for her; he cherished these romantic views about well-set-up old women of pedigree, and would have liked, in his good-humoured way, to bring some young hot-heads of his acquaintance to lunch with her; as if a type like hers could be bred of amiable tea-drinking enthusiasts! He knew her country. He knew her people. There was a vine, still bearing, which either Lovelace or Herrick[8]—she never read a word of poetry herself, but so the story ran—had sat under. Better wait to put before them the question that bothered her (about making an appeal to the public; if so, in what terms and so on), better wait until they have had their coffee, Lady Bruton thought; and so laid the carnations down beside her plate.

"How's Clarissa?" she asked abruptly.

Clarissa always said that Lady Bruton did not like her. Indeed, Lady Bruton had the reputation of being more interested in politics than people; of talking like a man; of having had a finger in some notorious intrigue of the eighties, which was now beginning to be mentioned in memoirs. Certainly there was an alcove in her drawing-room, and a table in that alcove, and a photograph upon that table of General Sir Talbot Moore, now deceased, who had written there (one evening in the eighties) in Lady Bruton's presence, with her cognisance, perhaps advice, a telegram ordering the British troops to advance upon an historical occasion. (She kept the pen and told the story.) Thus, when she said in her offhand way "How's Clarissa?" husbands had difficulty in persuading their wives and indeed, however devoted, were secretly doubtful themselves, of her interest in women who often got in their husbands' way, prevented them from accepting posts abroad, and had to be taken to the seaside in the middle of the session to recover from influenza. Nevertheless her inquiry, "How's Clarissa?" was known by women infallibly, to be a signal from a well-wisher, from an almost silent companion, whose utterances (half a dozen perhaps in the course of a lifetime) signified recognition of some feminine comradeship which went beneath masculine lunch parties and united Lady Bruton and Mrs Dalloway, who seldom met, and appeared when they did meet indifferent and even hostile, in a singular bond.

"I met Clarissa in the Park this morning," said Hugh Whitbread, diving into the casserole, anxious to pay himself this little tribute, for he had only to come to London and he met everybody at once; but greedy, one of the greediest men she had ever known, Milly Brush thought, who observed men with unflinching rectitude, and was

8. Both were Cavalier poets of the 17th century; with others in this school, Lovelace and Herrick were influenced primarily by Ben Jonson and John Donne. The Cavaliers were characterized by their treatment of sophisticated and whimsical themes alike in a witty yet colloquial and straightforward style.

capable of everlasting devotion, to her own sex in particular, being knobbed, scraped, angular, and entirely without feminine charm.

"D'you know who's in town?" said Lady Bruton suddenly bethinking her. "Our old friend, Peter Walsh."

They all smiled. Peter Walsh! And Mr Dalloway was genuinely glad, Milly Brush thought; and Mr Whitbread thought only of his chicken.

Peter Walsh! All three, Lady Bruton, Hugh Whitbread, and Richard Dalloway, remembered the same thing—how passionately Peter had been in love; been rejected; gone to India; come a cropper; made a mess of things; and Richard Dalloway had a very great liking for the dear old fellow too. Milly Brush saw that; saw a depth in the brown of his eyes; saw him hesitate; consider; which interested her, as Mr Dalloway always interested her, for what was he thinking, she wondered, about Peter Walsh?

That Peter Walsh had been in love with Clarissa; that he would go back directly after lunch and find Clarissa; that he would tell her, in so many words, that he loved her. Yes, he would say that.

Milly Brush once might almost have fallen in love with these silences; and Mr Dalloway was always so dependable; such a gentleman too. Now, being forty, Lady Bruton had only to nod, or turn her head a little abruptly, and Milly Brush took the signal, however deeply she might be sunk in these reflections of a detached spirit, of an uncorrupted soul whom life could not bamboozle, because life had not offered her a trinket of the slightest value; not a curl, smile, lip, cheek, nose; nothing whatever; Lady Bruton had only to nod, and Perkins was instructed to quicken the coffee.

"Yes; Peter Walsh has come back," said Lady Bruton. It was vaguely flattering to them all. He had come back, battered, unsuccessful, to their secure shores. But to help him, they reflected, was impossible; there was some flaw in his character. Hugh Whitbread said one might of course mention his name to So-and-so. He wrinkled lugubriously, consequentially, at the thought of the letters he would write to the heads of Government offices about "my old friend, Peter Walsh," and so on. But it wouldn't lead to anything—not to anything permanent, because of his character.

"In trouble with some woman," said Lady Bruton. They had all guessed that *that* was at the bottom of it.

"However," said Lady Bruton, anxious to leave the subject, "we shall hear the whole story from Peter himself."

(The coffee was very slow in coming.)

"The address?" murmured Hugh Whitbread; and there was at once a ripple in the grey tide of service which washed round Lady Bruton day in, day out, collecting, intercepting, enveloping her in a fine tissue which broke concussions, mitigated interruptions, and spread round the house in Brook Street a fine net where things lodged and were picked out accurately, instantly, by grey-haired Perkins, who had been with Lady Bruton these thirty years and now wrote down the address; handed it to Mr Whitbread, who took out his pocketbook, raised his eyebrows, and slipping it in among documents of the highest importance, said that he would get Evelyn to ask him to lunch.

(They were waiting to bring the coffee until Mr Whitbread had finished.)

Hugh was very slow, Lady Bruton thought. He was getting fat, she noticed. Richard always kept himself in the pink of condition. She was getting impatient; the whole of her being was setting positively, undeniably, domineeringly brushing aside all this unnecessary trifling (Peter Walsh and his affairs) upon that subject which engaged her attention, and not merely her attention, but that fibre which was the ramrod of her soul, that essential part of her without which Millicent Bruton would not have been Millicent Bruton; that project for emigrating young people[9] of both sexes born of respectable parents and setting them up with a fair prospect of doing well in Canada. She exaggerated. She had perhaps lost her sense of proportion. Emigration was not to others the obvious remedy, the sublime conception. It was not to them (not to Hugh, or Richard, or even to devoted Miss Brush) the liberator of the pent egotism, which a strong martial woman, well nourished, well descended, of direct impulses, downright feelings, and little introspective power (broad and simple—why could not every one be broad and simple? she asked) feels rise within her, once youth is past, and must eject upon some object—it may be Emigration, it may be Emancipation; but whatever it be, this object round which the essence of her soul is daily secreted, becomes inevitably prismatic, lustrous, half looking-glass, half precious stone; now carefully hidden in case people should sneer at it; now proudly displayed. Emigration had become, in short, largely Lady Bruton.

But she had to write. And one letter to the *Times*, she used to say to Miss Brush, cost her more than to organise an expedition to South Africa (which she had done in the war). After a morning's battle beginning, tearing up, beginning again, she used to feel the futility of her own womanhood as she felt it on no other occasion, and would turn gratefully to the thought of Hugh Whitbread who possessed—no one could doubt it—the art of writing letters to the *Times*.

A being so differently constituted from herself, with such a command of language; able to put things as editors like them put; had passions which one could not call simply greed. Lady Bruton often suspended judgement upon men in deference to the mysterious accord in which they, but no woman, stood to the laws of the universe; knew how to put things; knew what was said; so that if Richard advised her, and Hugh wrote for her, she was sure of being somehow right. So she let Hugh eat his soufflé; asked after poor Evelyn; waited until they were smoking, and then said,

"Milly, would you fetch the papers?"

And Miss Brush went out, came back; laid papers on the table; and Hugh produced his fountain pen; his silver fountain pen, which had done twenty years' service, he said, unscrewing the cap. It was still in perfect order; he had shown it to the makers; there was no reason, they said, why it should ever wear out; which was somehow to Hugh's credit, and to the credit of the sentiments which his pen expressed (so Richard Dalloway felt) as Hugh began carefully writing capital letters with rings round them in the margin, and thus marvellously reduced Lady Bruton's tangles to sense, to grammar such as the editor of the *Times*, Lady Bruton felt, watching the marvellous transformation, must respect. Hugh was slow. Hugh was pertinacious. Richard said one must take risks. Hugh proposed modifications in deference to people's feelings, which, he said rather tartly when Richard laughed, "had to be considered," and read out "how, therefore, we are of opinion that the times are ripe . . . the superfluous youth of our ever-increasing population . . . what we owe to the dead . . . " which Richard thought all stuffing and bunkum, but no harm in it, of course, and Hugh went on drafting sentiments in alphabetical order of the highest nobility, brushing the cigar ash from his waistcoat, and summing up now and

9. Assisted emigration, particularly of children and women, to the colonies was one solution proposed to the problems posed by surplus labor and unemployment in England. Between 1869 and the early 1930s, various philanthropic organizations sent over 100,000 children to Canada from Great Britain during the child emigration movement.

then the progress they had made until, finally, he read out the draft of a letter which Lady Bruton felt certain was a masterpiece. Could her own meaning sound like that?

Hugh could not guarantee that the editor would put it in; but he would be meeting somebody at luncheon.

Whereupon Lady Bruton, who seldom did a graceful thing, stuffed all Hugh's carnations into the front of her dress, and flinging her hands out called him "My Prime Minister!" What she would have done without them both she did not know. They rose. And Richard Dalloway strolled off as usual to have a look at the General's portrait, because he meant, whenever he had a moment of leisure, to write a history of Lady Bruton's family.

And Millicent Bruton was very proud of her family. But they could wait, they could wait, she said, looking at the picture; meaning that her family, of military men, administrators, admirals, had been men of action, who had done their duty; and Richard's first duty was to his country, but it was a fine face, she said; and all the papers were ready for Richard down at Aldmixton whenever the time came; the Labour Government she meant. "Ah, the news from India!" she cried.

And then, as they stood in the hall taking yellow gloves from the bowl on the malachite table and Hugh was offering Miss Brush with quite unnecessary courtesy some discarded ticket or other compliment, which she loathed from the depths of her heart and blushed brick red, Richard turned to Lady Bruton, with his hat in his hand, and said,

"We shall see you at our party to-night?" whereupon Lady Bruton resumed the magnificence which letter-writing had shattered. She might come; or she might not come. Clarissa had wonderful energy. Parties terrified Lady Bruton. But then, she was getting old. So she intimated, standing at her doorway; handsome; very erect; while her chow stretched behind her, and Miss Brush disappeared into the background with her hands full of papers.

And Lady Bruton went ponderously, majestically, up to her room, lay, one arm extended, on the sofa. She sighed, she snored, not that she was asleep, only drowsy and heavy, drowsy and heavy, like a field of clover in the sunshine this hot June day, with the bees going round and about and the yellow butterflies. Always she went back to those fields down in Devonshire, where she had jumped the brooks on Patty, her pony, with Mortimer and Tom, her brothers. And there were the dogs; there were the rats; there were her father and mother on the lawn under the trees, with the tea-things out, and the beds of dahlias, the hollyhocks, the pampas grass; and they, little wretches, always up to some mischief! stealing back through the shrubbery, so as not to be seen, all bedraggled from some roguery. What old nurse used to say about her frocks!

Ah dear, she remembered—it was Wednesday in Brook Street. Those kind good fellows, Richard Dalloway, Hugh Whitbread, had gone this hot day through the streets whose growl came up to her lying on the sofa. Power was hers, position, income. She had lived in the forefront of her time. She had had good friends; known the ablest men of her day. Murmuring London flowed up to her, and her hand, lying on the sofa back, curled upon some imaginary baton such as her grandfathers might have held, holding which she seemed, drowsy and heavy, to be commanding battalions marching to Canada, and those good fellows walking across London, that territory of theirs, that little bit of carpet, Mayfair.

And they went further and further from her, being attached to her by a thin thread (since they had lunched with her) which would stretch and stretch, get thinner and thinner as they walked across London; as if one's friends were attached to one's body, after lunching with them, by a thin thread, which (as she dozed there) became hazy with the sound of bells, striking the hour or ringing to service, as a single spider's thread is blotted with rain-drops, and, burdened, sags down. So she slept.

And Richard Dalloway and Hugh Whitbread hesitated at the corner of Conduit Street at the very moment that Millicent Bruton, lying on the sofa, let the thread snap; snored. Contrary winds buffeted at the street corner. They looked in at a shop window; they did not wish to buy or to talk but to part, only with contrary winds buffeting the street corner, with some sort of lapse in the tides of the body, two forces meeting in a swirl, morning and afternoon, they paused. Some newspaper placard went up in the air, gallantly, like a kite at first, then paused, swooped, fluttered; and a lady's veil hung. Yellow awnings trembled. The speed of the morning traffic slackened, and single carts rattled carelessly down half-empty streets. In Norfolk, of which Richard Dalloway was half thinking, a soft warm wind blew back the petals; confused the waters; ruffled the flowering grasses. Haymakers, who had pitched beneath hedges to sleep away the morning toil, parted curtains of green blades; moved trembling globes of cow parsley to see the sky; the blue, the steadfast, the blazing summer sky.

Aware that he was looking at a silver two-handled Jacobean mug, and that Hugh Whitbread admired condescendingly with airs of connoisseurship a Spanish necklace which he thought of asking the price of in case Evelyn might like it—still Richard was torpid; could not think or move. Life had thrown up this wreckage; shop windows full of coloured paste, and one stood stark with the lethargy of the old, stiff with the rigidity of the old, looking in. Evelyn Whitbread might like to buy this Spanish necklace—so she might. Yawn he must. Hugh was going into the shop.

"Right you are!" said Richard, following.

Goodness knows he didn't want to go buying necklaces with Hugh. But there are tides in the body. Morning meets afternoon. Borne like a frail shallop[1] on deep, deep floods, Lady Bruton's great-grandfather and his memoir and his campaigns in North America were whelmed and sunk. And Millicent Bruton too. She went under. Richard didn't care a straw what became of Emigration; about that letter, whether the editor put it in or not. The necklace hung stretched between Hugh's admirable fingers. Let him give it to a girl, if he must buy jewels—any girl, any girl in the street. For the worthlessness of this life did strike Richard pretty forcibly—buying necklaces for Evelyn. If he'd had a boy he'd have said, Work, work. But he had his Elizabeth; he adored his Elizabeth.

"I should like to see Mr Dubonnet," said Hugh in his curt worldly way. It appeared that this Dubonnet had the measurements of Mrs Whitbread's neck, or, more strangely still, knew her views upon Spanish jewellery and the extent of her possessions in that line (which Hugh could not remember). All of which seemed to Richard Dalloway awfully odd. For he never gave Clarissa presents, except a bracelet two or three years ago, which had not been a success. She never wore it. It pained him to remember that she never wore it. And as a single spider's thread after wavering here and there attaches itself to the point of a leaf, so Richard's mind, recovering from its lethargy, set now on his wife, Clarissa, whom Peter Walsh had loved so passionately; and Richard had had a sudden vision of her there at luncheon; of himself and Clarissa; of their life together; and he drew the tray of old jewels towards him,

1. A small open boat fitted with sails or oars.

and taking up first this brooch then that ring, "How much is that?" he asked, but doubted his own taste. He wanted to open the drawing-room door and come in holding out something; a present for Clarissa. Only what? But Hugh was on his legs again. He was unspeakably pompous. Really, after dealing here for thirty-five years he was not going to be put off by a mere boy who did not know his business. For Dubonnet, it seemed, was out, and Hugh would not buy anything until Mr Dubonnet chose to be in; at which the youth flushed and bowed his correct little bow. It was all perfectly correct. And yet Richard couldn't have said that to save his life! Why these people stood that damned insolence he could not conceive. Hugh was becoming an intolerable ass. Richard Dalloway could not stand more than an hour of his society. And, flicking his bowler hat by way of farewell, Richard turned at the corner of Conduit Street eager, yes, very eager, to travel that spider's thread of attachment between himself and Clarissa; he would go straight to her, in Westminster.

But he wanted to come in holding something. Flowers? Yes, flowers, since he did not trust his taste in gold; any number of flowers, roses, orchids, to celebrate what was, reckoning things as you will, an event; this feeling about her when they spoke of Peter Walsh at luncheon; and they never spoke of it; not for years had they spoken of it; which, he thought, grasping his red and white roses together (a vast bunch in tissue paper), is the greatest mistake in the world. The time comes when it can't be said; one's too shy to say it, he thought, pocketing his sixpence or two of change, setting off with his great bunch held against his body to Westminster to say straight out in so many words (whatever she might think of him), holding out his flowers, "I love you." Why not? Really it was a miracle thinking of the War, and thousands of poor chaps, with all their lives before them, shovelled together, already half forgotten; it was a miracle. Here he was walking across London to say to Clarissa in so many words that he loved her. Which one never does say, he thought. Partly one's lazy; partly one's shy. And Clarissa—it was difficult to think of her; except in starts, as at luncheon, when he saw her quite distinctly; their whole life. He stopped at the crossing; and repeated—being simple by nature, and undebauched, because he had tramped, and shot; being pertinacious and dogged, having championed the down-trodden and followed his instincts in the House of Commons; being preserved in his simplicity yet at the same time grown rather speechless, rather stiff—he repeated that it was a miracle that he should have married Clarissa; a miracle—his life had been a miracle, he thought; hesitating to cross. But it did make his blood boil to see little creatures of five or six crossing Piccadilly alone. The police ought to have stopped the traffic at once. He had no illusions about the London police. Indeed, he was collecting evidence of their malpractices; and those costermongers,[2] not allowed to stand their barrows in the streets; and prostitutes, good Lord, the fault wasn't in them, nor in young men either, but in our detestable social system and so forth; all of which he considered, could be seen considering, grey, dogged, dapper, clean, as he walked across the Park to tell his wife that he loved her.

For he would say it in so many words, when he came into the room. Because it is a thousand pities never to say what one feels, he thought, crossing the Green Park and observing with pleasure how in the shade of the trees whole families, poor families, were sprawling; children kicking up their legs; sucking milk; paper bags thrown about, which could easily be picked up (if people objected) by one of those fat gentlemen in livery; for he was of opinion that every park, and every square, during the

2. Merchants who sell produce out of a cart or street stand.

summer months should be open to children (the grass of the park flushed and faded, lighting up the poor mothers of Westminster and their crawling babies, as if a yellow lamp were moved beneath). But what could be done for female vagrants like that poor creature, stretched on her elbow (as if she had flung herself on the earth, rid of all ties, to observe curiously, to speculate boldly, to consider the whys and the wherefores, impudent, loose-lipped, humorous), he did not know. Bearing his flowers like a weapon, Richard Dalloway approached her; intent he passed her; still there was time for a spark between them—she laughed at the sight of him, he smiled good-humouredly, considering the problem of the female vagrant; not that they would ever speak. But he would tell Clarissa that he loved her, in so many words. He had, once upon a time, been jealous of Peter Walsh; jealous of him and Clarissa. But she had often said to him that she had been right not to marry Peter Walsh; which, knowing Clarissa, was obviously true; she wanted support. Not that she was weak; but she wanted support.

As for Buckingham Palace (like an old prima donna facing the audience all in white) you can't deny it a certain dignity, he considered, nor despise what does, after all, stand to millions of people (a little crowd was waiting at the gate to see the King drive out) for a symbol, absurd though it is; a child with a box of bricks could have done better, he thought; looking at the memorial to Queen Victoria (whom he could remember in her horn spectacles driving through Kensington), its white mound, its billowing motherliness; but he liked being ruled by the descendant of Horsa; he liked continuity; and the sense of handing on the traditions of the past. It was a great age in which to have lived. Indeed, his own life was a miracle; let him make no mistake about it; here he was, in the prime of life, walking to his house in Westminster to tell Clarissa that he loved her. Happiness is this, he thought.

It is this, he said, as he entered Dean's Yard. Big Ben was beginning to strike, first the warning, musical; then the hour, irrevocable. Lunch parties waste the entire afternoon, he thought, approaching his door.

The sound of Big Ben flooded Clarissa's drawing-room, where she sat, ever so annoyed, at her writing-table; worried; annoyed. It was perfectly true that she had not asked Ellie Henderson to her party; but she had done it on purpose. Now Mrs Marsham wrote "she had told Ellie Henderson she would ask Clarissa—Ellie so much wanted to come."

But why should she invite all the dull women in London to her parties? Why should Mrs Marsham interfere? And there was Elizabeth closeted all this time with Doris Kilman. Anything more nauseating she could not conceive. Prayer at this hour with that woman. And the sound of the bell flooded the room with its melancholy wave; which receded, and gathered itself together to fall once more, when she heard, distractingly, something fumbling, something scratching at the door. Who at this hour? Three, good Heavens! Three already! For with overpowering directness and dignity the clock struck three; and she heard nothing else; but the door handle slipped round and in came Richard! What a surprise! In came Richard, holding out flowers. She had failed him, once at Constantinople; and Lady Bruton, whose lunch parties were said to be extraordinarily amusing, had not asked her. He was holding out flowers—roses, red and white roses. (But he could not bring himself to say he loved her; not in so many words.)

But how lovely, she said, taking his flowers. She understood; she understood without his speaking; his Clarissa. She put them in vases on the mantelpiece. How lovely they looked! she said. And was it amusing, she asked? Had Lady Bruton asked after her? Peter Walsh was back. Mrs Marsham had written. Must she ask Ellie Henderson? That woman Kilman was upstairs.

"But let us sit down for five minutes," said Richard.

It all looked so empty. All the chairs were against the wall. What had they been doing? Oh, it was for the party; no, he had not forgotten, the party. Peter Walsh was back. Oh yes; she had had him. And he was going to get a divorce; and he was in love with some woman out there. And he hadn't changed in the slightest. There she was, mending her dress. . . .

"Thinking of Bourton," she said.

"Hugh was at lunch," said Richard. She had met him too! Well, he was getting absolutely intolerable. Buying Evelyn necklaces; fatter than ever, an intolerable ass.

"And it came over me 'I might have married you,'" she said, thinking of Peter sitting there in his little bow-tie; with that knife, opening it, shutting it. "Just as he always was, you know."

They were talking about him at lunch, said Richard. (But he could not tell her he loved her. He held her hand. Happiness is this, he thought.) They had been writing a letter to the *Times* for Millicent Bruton. That was about all Hugh was fit for.

"And our dear Miss Kilman?" he asked. Clarissa thought the roses absolutely lovely; first bunched together; now of their own accord starting apart.

"Kilman arrives just as we've done lunch," she said. "Elizabeth turns pink. They shut themselves up. I suppose they're praying."

Lord! He didn't like it; but these things pass over if you let them.

"In a mackintosh with an umbrella," said Clarissa.

He had not said "I love you"; but he held her hand. Happiness is this, is this, he thought.

"But why should I ask all the dull women in London to my parties?" said Clarissa. And if Mrs Marsham gave a party, did *she* invite her guests?

"Poor Ellie Henderson," said Richard—it was a very odd thing how much Clarissa minded about her parties, he thought.

But Richard had no notion of the look of a room. However—what was he going to say?

If she worried about these parties he would not let her give them. Did she wish she had married Peter? But he must go.

He must be off, he said, getting up. But he stood for a moment as if he were about to say something; and she wondered what? Why? There were the roses.

"Some Committee?" she asked, as he opened the door.

"Armenians," he said; or perhaps it was "Albanians."

And there is a dignity in people; a solitude; even between husband and wife a gulf; and that one must respect, thought Clarissa, watching him open the door; for one would not part with it oneself, or take it, against his will, from one's husband, without losing one's independence, one's self-respect—something, after all, priceless.

He returned with a pillow and a quilt.

"An hour's complete rest after luncheon," he said. And he went.

How like him! He would go on saying "An hour's complete rest after luncheon" to the end of time, because a doctor had ordered it once. It was like him to take what doctors said literally; part of his adorable, divine simplicity, which no one had to the same extent; which made him go and do the thing while she and Peter frittered their time away bickering. He was already halfway to the House of Commons, to his Armenians, his Albanians, having settled her on the sofa, looking at his roses. And people would say, "Clarissa Dalloway is spoilt." She cared much more for her roses than for the Armenians. Hunted out of existence, maimed, frozen, the victims of cruelty and injustice (she had heard Richard say so over and over again)—no, she could feel nothing for the Albanians, or was it the Armenians? but she loved her roses (didn't that help the Armenians?)—the only flowers she could bear to see cut. But Richard was already at the House of Commons; at his Committee, having settled all her difficulties. But no; alas, that was not true. He did not see the reasons against asking Ellie Henderson. She would do it, of course, as he wished it. Since he had brought the pillows, she would lie down. . . . But—but—why did she suddenly feel, for no reason that she could discover, desperately unhappy? As a person who has dropped some grain of pearl or diamond into the grass and parts the tall blades very carefully, this way and that, and searches here and there vainly, and at last spies it there at the roots, so she went through one thing and another; no, it was not Sally Seton saying that Richard would never be in the Cabinet because he had a second-class brain (it came back to her); no, she did not mind that; nor was it to do with Elizabeth either and Doris Kilman; those were facts. It was a feeling, some unpleasant feeling, earlier in the day perhaps; something that Peter had said, combined with some depression of her own, in her bedroom, taking off her hat; and what Richard had said had added to it, but what had he said? There were his roses. Her parties! That was it! Her parties! Both of them criticised her very unfairly, laughed at her very unjustly, for her parties. That was it! That was it!

Well, how was she going to defend herself? Now that she knew what it was, she felt perfectly happy. They thought, or Peter at any rate thought, that she enjoyed imposing herself; liked to have famous people about her; great names; was simply a snob in short. Well, Peter might think so. Richard merely thought it foolish of her to like excitement when she knew it was bad for her heart. It was childish, he thought. And both were quite wrong. What she liked was simply life.

"That's what I do it for," she said, speaking aloud, to life.

Since she was lying on the sofa, cloistered, exempt, the presence of this thing which she felt to be so obvious became physically existent; with robes of sound from the street, sunny, with hot breath, whispering, blowing out the blinds. But suppose Peter said to her, "Yes, yes, but your parties—what's the sense of your parties?" all she could say was (and nobody could be expected to understand): They're an offering; which sounded horribly vague. But who was Peter to make out that life was all plain sailing?—Peter always in love, always in love with the wrong woman? What's your love? she might say to him. And she knew his answer; how it is the most important thing in the world and no woman possibly understood it. Very well. But could any man understand what she meant either? about life? She could not imagine Peter or Richard taking the trouble to give a party for no reason whatever.

But to go deeper, beneath what people said (and these judgements, how superficial, how fragmentary they are!) in her own mind now, what did it mean to her, this thing she called life? Oh, it was very queer. Here was So-and-so in South Kensington; some one up in Bayswater; and somebody else, say, in Mayfair. And she felt quite continuously a sense of their existence; and she felt what a waste; and she felt what a pity; and she felt if only they could be brought together; so she did it. And it was an offering; to combine, to create; but to whom?

An offering for the sake of offering, perhaps. Anyhow, it was her gift. Nothing else had she of the slightest importance; could not think, write, even play the piano. She muddled Armenians and Turks; loved success; hated discomfort; must be liked; talked oceans of nonsense: and to this day, ask her what the Equator was, and she did not know.

All the same, that one day should follow another; Wednesday, Thursday, Friday, Saturday; that one should wake up in the morning; see the sky; walk in the park;

meet Hugh Whitbread; then suddenly in came Peter; then these roses; it was enough. After that, how unbelievable death was!—that it must end; and no one in the whole world would know how she had loved it all; how, every instant . . .

The door opened. Elizabeth knew that her mother was resting. She came in very quietly. She stood perfectly still. Was it that some Mongol had been wrecked on the coast of Norfolk (as Mrs Hilbery said), had mixed with the Dalloway ladies, perhaps, a hundred years ago? For the Dalloways, in general, were fairhaired; blue-eyed; Elizabeth, on the contrary, was dark; had Chinese eyes in a pale face; an Oriental mystery; was gentle, considerate, still. As a child, she had had a perfect sense of humour; but now at seventeen, why, Clarissa could not in the least understand, she had become very serious; like a hyacinth, sheathed in glossy green, with buds just tinted, a hyacinth which has had no sun.

She stood quite still and looked at her mother; but the door was ajar, and outside the door was Miss Kilman, as Clarissa knew; Miss Kilman in her mackintosh, listening to whatever they said.

Yes, Miss Kilman stood on the landing, and wore a mackintosh; but had her reasons. First, it was cheap; second, she was over forty; and did not, after all, dress to please. She was poor, moreover; degradingly poor. Otherwise she would not be taking jobs from people like the Dalloways; from rich people, who liked to be kind. Mr Dalloway, to do him justice, had been kind. But Mrs Dalloway had not. She had been merely condescending. She came from the most worthless of all classes—the rich, with a smattering of culture. They had expensive things everywhere; pictures, carpets, lots of servants. She considered that she had a perfect right to anything that the Dalloways did for her.

She had been cheated. Yes, the word was no exaggeration, for surely a girl has a right to some kind of happiness? And she had never been happy, what with being so clumsy and so poor. And then, just as she might have had a chance at Miss Dolby's school, the War came; and she had never been able to tell lies. Miss Dolby thought she would be happier with people who shared her views about the Germans. She had had to go. It was true that the family was of German origin; spelt the name Kiehlman in the eighteenth century; but her brother had been killed. They turned her out because she would not pretend that the Germans were all villains—when she had German friends, when the only happy days of her life had been spent in Germany! And after all, she could read history. She had had to take whatever she could get. Mr Dalloway had come across her working for the Friends.[3] He had allowed her (and that was really generous of him) to teach his daughter history. Also she did a little Extension[4] lecturing and so on. Then Our Lord had come to her (and here she always bowed her head). She had seen the light two years and three months ago. Now she did not envy women like Clarissa Dalloway; she pitied them.

She pitied and despised them from the bottom of her heart, as she stood on the soft carpet, looking at the old engraving of a little girl with a muff. With all this luxury going on, what hope was there for a better state of things? Instead of lying on a sofa—"My mother is resting," Elizabeth had said—she should have been in a factory; behind a counter; Mrs Dalloway and all the other fine ladies!

3. The Quakers, known as the Society of Friends, are a Protestant sect devoted to the practice and promotion of pacifism, as well as philanthropic causes such as prison reform and the improvement of conditions for the institutionalized insane.

4. Extension lectures were a mode of higher education available to students who were unable to attend the university proper. The extension lecture was an important transitional development in the struggle for equal education for women in England in the later 19th century; due to the efforts of local Ladies Educational Associations and similar organizations, the lecture circuit continued to grow even after women began to gain admission to universities.

Bitter and burning, Miss Kilman had turned in to a church two years three months ago. She had heard the Rev. Edward Whittaker preach; the boys sing; had seen the solemn lights descend, and whether it was the music, or the voices (she herself when alone in the evening found comfort in a violin; but the sound was excruciating; she had no ear), the hot and turbulent feelings which boiled and surged in her had been assuaged as she sat there, and she had wept copiously, and gone to call on Mr Whittaker at his private house in Kensington. It was the hand of God, he said. The Lord had shown her the way. So now, whenever the hot and painful feelings boiled within her, this hatred of Mrs Dalloway, this grudge against the world, she thought of God. She thought of Mr Whittaker. Rage was succeeded by calm. A sweet savour filled her veins, her lips parted, and, standing formidable upon the landing in her mackintosh, she looked with steady and sinister serenity at Mrs Dalloway, who came out with her daughter.

Elizabeth said she had forgotten her gloves. That was because Miss Kilman and her mother hated each other. She could not bear to see them together. She ran upstairs to find her gloves.

But Miss Kilman did not hate Mrs Dalloway. Turning her large gooseberry-coloured eyes upon Clarissa, observing her small pink face, her delicate body, her air of freshness and fashion, Miss Kilman felt, Fool! Simpleton! You who have known neither sorrow nor pleasure; who have trifled your life away! And there rose in her an overmastering desire to overcome her; to unmask her. If she could have felled her it would have eased her. But it was not the body; it was the soul and its mockery that she wished to subdue; make feel her mastery. If only she could make her weep; could ruin her; humiliate her; bring her to her knees crying, You are right! But this was God's will, not Miss Kilman's. It was to be a religious victory. So she glared; so she glowered.

Clarissa was really shocked. This a Christian—this woman! This woman had taken her daughter from her! She in touch with invisible presences! Heavy, ugly, commonplace, without kindness or grace, she know the meaning of life!

"You are taking Elizabeth to the Stores?" Mrs Dalloway said.

Miss Kilman said she was. They stood there. Miss Kilman was not going to make herself agreeable. She had always earned her living. Her knowledge of modern history was thorough in the extreme. She did out of her meagre income set aside so much for causes she believed in; whereas this woman did nothing, believed nothing; brought up her daughter—but here was Elizabeth, rather out of breath, the beautiful girl.

So they were going to the Stores. Odd it was, as Miss Kilman stood there (and stand she did, with the power and taciturnity of some prehistoric monster armoured for primeval warfare), how, second by second, the idea of her diminished, how hatred (which was for ideas, not people) crumbled, how she lost her malignity, her size, became second by second merely Miss Kilman, in a mackintosh, whom Heaven knows Clarissa would have liked to help.

At this dwindling of the monster, Clarissa laughed. Saying good-bye, she laughed.

Off they went together, Miss Kilman and Elizabeth, downstairs.

With a sudden impulse, with a violent anguish, for this woman was taking her daughter from her, Clarissa leant over the bannisters and cried out, "Remember the party! Remember our party to-night!"

But Elizabeth had already opened the front door; there was a van passing; she did not answer.

Love and religion! thought Clarissa, going back into the drawing-room, tingling all over. How detestable, how destestable they are! For now that the body of Miss Kilman was not before her, it overwhelmed her—the idea. The cruelest things in the world, she thought, seeing them clumsy, hot, domineering, hypocritical, eavesdropping, jealous, infinitely cruel and unscrupulous, dressed in a mackintosh coat, on the landing; love and religion. Had she ever tried to convert any one herself? Did she not wish everybody merely to be themselves? And she watched out of the window the old lady opposite climbing upstairs. Let her climb upstairs if she wanted to; let her stop; then let her, as Clarissa had often seen her, gain her bedroom, part her curtains, and disappear again into the background. Somehow one respected that—that old woman looking out of the window, quite unconscious that she was being watched. There was something solemn in it—but love and religion would destroy that, whatever it was, the privacy of the soul. The odious Kilman would destroy it. Yet it was a sight that made her want to cry.

Love destroyed too. Everything that was fine, everything that was true went. Take Peter Walsh now. There was a man, charming, clever, with ideas about everything. If you wanted to know about Pope, say, or Addison, or just to talk nonsense, what people were like, what things meant, Peter knew better than any one. It was Peter who had helped her; Peter who had lent her books. But look at the women he loved—vulgar, trivial, commonplace. Think of Peter in love—he came to see her after all these years, and what did he talk about? Himself. Horrible passion! she thought. Degrading passion! she thought, thinking of Kilman and her Elizabeth walking to the Army and Navy Stores.

Big Ben struck the half-hour.

How extraordinary it was, strange, yes, touching, to see the old lady (they had been neighbours ever so many years) move away from the window, as if she were attached to that sound, that string. Gigantic as it was, it had something to do with her. Down, down, into the midst of ordinary things the finger fell making the moment solemn. She was forced, so Clarissa imagined, by that sound, to move, to go—but where? Clarissa tried to follow her as she turned and disappeared, and could still just see her white cap moving at the back of the bedroom. She was still there moving about at the other end of the room. Why creeds and prayers and mackintoshes? when, thought Clarissa, that's the miracle, that's the mystery; that old lady, she meant, whom she could see going from chest of drawers to dressing-table. She could still see her. And the supreme mystery which Kilman might say she had solved, or Peter might say he had solved, but Clarissa didn't believe either of them had the ghost of an idea of solving, was simply this: here was one room; there another. Did religion solve that, or love?

Love—but here the other clock, the clock which always struck two minutes after Big Ben, came shuffling in with its lap full of odds and ends, which it dumped down as if Big Ben were all very well with his majesty laying down the law, so solemn, so just, but she must remember all sorts of little things besides—Mrs Marsham, Ellie Henderson, glasses for ices—all sorts of little things came flooding and lapping and dancing in on the wake of that solemn stroke which lay flat like a bar of gold on the sea. Mrs Marsham, Ellie Henderson, glasses for ices. She must telephone now at once.

Volubly, troublously, the late clock sounded, coming in on the wake of Big Ben, with its lap full of trifles. Beaten up, broken up by the assault of carriages, the brutality of vans, the eager advance of myriads of angular men, of flaunting women, the domes and spires of offices and hospitals, the last relics of this lap full of odds and ends seemed to break, like the spray of an exhausted wave, upon the body of Miss Kilman standing still in the street for a moment to mutter "It is the flesh."

It was the flesh that she must control. Clarissa Dalloway had insulted her. That she expected. But she had not triumphed; she had not mastered the flesh. Ugly, clumsy, Clarissa Dalloway had laughed at her for being that; and had revived the fleshly desires, for she minded looking as she did beside Clarissa. Nor could she talk as she did. But why wish to resemble her? Why? She despised Mrs Dalloway from the bottom of her heart. She was not serious. She was not good. Her life was a tissue of vanity and deceit. Yet Doris Kilman had been over-come. She had, as a matter of fact, very nearly burst into tears when Clarissa Dalloway laughed at her. "It is the flesh, it is the flesh," she muttered (it being her habit to talk aloud) trying to subdue this turbulent and painful feeling as she walked down Victoria Street. She prayed to God. She could not help being ugly; she could not afford to buy pretty clothes. Clarissa Dalloway had laughed—but she would concentrate her mind upon something else until she had reached the pillar-box. At any rate she had got Elizabeth. But she would think of something else; she would think of Russia; until she reached the pillar-box.

How nice it must be, she said, in the country, struggling, as Mr Whittaker had told her, with that violent grudge against the world which had scorned her, sneered at her, cast her off, beginning with this indignity—the infliction of her unlovable body which people could not bear to see. Do her hair as she might, her forehead remained like an egg, bald, white. No clothes suited her. She might buy anything. And for a woman, of course, that meant never meeting the opposite sex. Never would she come first with any one. Sometimes lately it had seemed to her that, except for Elizabeth, her food was all that she lived for; her comforts; her dinner, her tea; her hot-water bottle at night. But one must fight; vanquish; have faith in God. Mr Whittaker had said she was there for a purpose. But no one knew the agony! He said, pointing to the crucifix, that God knew. But why should she have to suffer when other women, like Clarissa Dalloway, escaped? Knowledge comes through suffering, said Mr Whittaker.

She had passed the pillar-box, and Elizabeth had turned into the cool brown tobacco department of the Army and Navy Stores while she was still muttering to herself what Mr Whittaker had said about knowledge coming through suffering and the flesh. "The flesh," she muttered.

What department did she want? Elizabeth interrupted her.

"Petticoats," she said abruptly, and stalked straight on to the lift.

Up they went. Elizabeth guided her this way and that; guided her in her abstraction as if she had been a great child, an unwieldy battleship. There were the petticoats, brown, decorous, striped, frivolous, solid, flimsy; and she chose, in her abstraction, portentously, and the girl serving thought her mad.

Elizabeth rather wondered, as they did up the parcel, what Miss Kilman was thinking. They must have their tea, said Miss Kilman, rousing, collecting herself. They had their tea.

Elizabeth rather wondered whether Miss Kilman could be hungry. It was her way of eating, eating with intensity, then looking, again and again, at a plate of sugared cakes on the table next them; then, when a lady and a child sat down and the child took the cake, could Miss Kilman really mind it? Yes, Miss Kilman did mind it. She had wanted that cake—the pink one. The pleasure of eating was almost the only pure pleasure left her, and then to be baffled even in that!

When people are happy, they have a reserve, she had told Elizabeth, upon which to draw, whereas she was like a wheel without a tyre (she was fond of such metaphors), jolted by every pebble, so she would say staying on after the lesson standing by the fire-place with her bag of books, her "satchel," she called it, on a Tuesday morning, after the lesson was over. And she talked too about the War. After all, there were people who did not think the English invariably right. There were books. There were meetings. There were other points of view. Would Elizabeth like to come with her to listen to So-and-so (a most extraordinary looking old man)? Then Miss Kilman took her to some church in Kensington and they had tea with a clergyman. She had lent her books. Law, medicine, politics, all professions are open to women of your generation, said Miss Kilman. But for herself, her career was absolutely ruined and was it her fault? Good gracious, said Elizabeth, no.

And her mother would come calling to say that a hamper had come from Bourton and would Miss Kilman like some flowers? To Miss Kilman she was always very, very nice, but Miss Kilman squashed the flowers all in a bunch, and hadn't any small talk, and what interested Miss Kilman bored her mother, and Miss Kilman and she were terrible together; and Miss Kilman swelled and looked very plain. But then Miss Kilman was frightfully clever. Elizabeth had never thought about the poor. They lived with everything they wanted,—her mother had breakfast in bed every day; Lucy carried it up; and she liked old women because they were Duchesses, and being descended from some Lord. But Miss Kilman said (one of those Tuesday mornings when the lesson was over), "My grandfather kept an oil and colour shop in Kensington." Miss Kilman made one feel so small.

Miss Kilman took another cup of tea. Elizabeth, with her oriental bearing, her inscrutable mystery, sat perfectly upright; no, she did not want anything more. She looked for her gloves—her white gloves. They were under the table. Ah, but she must not go! Miss Kilman could not let her go! this youth, that was so beautiful, this girl, whom she genuinely loved! Her large hand opened and shut on the table.

But perhaps it was a little flat somehow, Elizabeth felt. And really she would like to go.

But said Miss Kilman, "I've not quite finished yet."

Of course, then, Elizabeth would wait. But it was rather stuffy in here.

"Are you going to the party to-night?" Miss Kilman said. Elizabeth supposed she was going; her mother wanted her to go. She must not let parties absorb her, Miss Kilman said, fingering the last two inches of a chocolate éclair.

She did not much like parties, Elizabeth said. Miss Kilman opened her mouth, slightly projected her chin, and swallowed down the last inches of the chocolate éclair, then wiped her fingers, and washed the tea round in her cup.

She was about to split asunder, she felt. The agony was so terrific. If she could grasp her, if she could clasp her, if she could make her hers absolutely and forever and then die; that was all she wanted. But to sit here, unable to think of anything to say; to see Elizabeth turning against her; to be felt repulsive even by her—it was too much; she could not stand it. The thick fingers curled inwards.

"I never go to parties," said Miss Kilman, just to keep Elizabeth from going. "People don't ask me to parties"—and she knew as she said it that it was this egotism that was her undoing; Mr Whittaker had warned her; but she could not help it. She had suffered so horribly. "Why should they ask me?" she said. "I'm plain, I'm unhappy." She knew it was idiotic. But it was all those people passing—people with parcels who despised her, who made her say it. However, she was Doris Kilman. She had her degree. She was a woman who had made her way in the world. Her knowledge of modern history was more than respectable.

"I don't pity myself," she said. "I pity"—she meant to say "your mother" but no, she could not, not to Elizabeth. "I pity other people," she said, "more."

Like some dumb creature who has been brought up to a gate for an unknown purpose, and stands there longing to gallop away, Elizabeth Dalloway sat silent. Was Miss Kilman going to say anything more?

"Don't quite forget me," said Doris Kilman; her voice quivered. Right away to the end of the field the dumb creature galloped in terror.

The great hand opened and shut.

Elizabeth turned her head. The waitress came. One had to pay at the desk, Elizabeth said, and went off, drawing out, so Miss Kilman felt, the very entrails in her body, stretching them as she crossed the room, and then, with a final twist, bowing her head very politely, she went.

She had gone. Miss Kilman sat at the marble table among the éclairs, stricken once, twice, thrice by shocks of suffering. She had gone. Mrs Dalloway had triumphed. Elizabeth had gone. Beauty had gone, youth had gone.

So she sat. She got up, blundered off among the little tables, rocking slightly from side to side, and somebody came after her with her petticoat, and she lost her way, and was hemmed in by trunks specially prepared for taking to India; next got among the accouchement sets, and baby linen; through all the commodities of the world, perishable and permanent, hams, drugs, flowers, stationery, variously smelling, now sweet, now sour she lurched; saw herself thus lurching with her hat askew, very red in the face, full length in a looking-glass; and at last came out into the street.

The tower of Westminster Cathedral rose in front of her, the habitation of God. In the midst of the traffic, there was the habitation of God. Doggedly she set off with her parcel to that other sanctuary, the Abbey, where, raising her hands in a tent before her face, she sat beside those driven into shelter too; the variously assorted worshippers, now divested of social rank, almost of sex, as they raised their hands before their faces; but once they removed them, instantly reverent, middle class, English men and women, some of them desirous of seeing the wax works.

But Miss Kilman held her tent before her face. Now she was deserted; now rejoined. New worshippers came in from the street to replace the strollers, and still, as people gazed round and shuffled past the tomb of the Unknown Warrior, still she barred her eyes with her fingers and tried in this double darkness, for the light in the Abbey was bodiless, to aspire above the vanities, the desires, the commodities, to rid herself both of hatred and of love. Her hands twitched. She seemed to struggle. Yet to others God was accessible and the path to Him smooth. Mr Fletcher, retired, of the Treasury, Mrs Gorham, widow of the famous K.C., approached Him simply, and having done their praying, leant back, enjoyed the music (the organ pealed sweetly), and saw Miss Kilman at the end of the row, praying, praying, and, being still on the threshold of their underworld, thought of her sympathetically as a soul haunting the same territory; a soul cut out of immaterial substance; not a woman, a soul.

But Mr Fletcher had to go. He had to pass her, and being himself neat as a new pin, could not help being a little distressed by the poor lady's disorder; her hair down; her parcel on the floor. She did not at once let him pass. But, as he stood gazing about him, at the white marbles, grey window panes, and accumulated treasures (for he was extremely proud of the Abbey), her largeness, robustness, and power as she sat there shifting her knees from time to time (it was so rough the approach to her God—so tough her desires) impressed him, as they had impressed Mrs Dalloway (she could not get the thought of her out of her mind that afternoon), the Rev. Edward Whittaker, and Elizabeth too.

And Elizabeth waited in Victoria Street for an omnibus. It was so nice to be out of doors. She thought perhaps she need not go home just yet. It was so nice to be out in the air. So she would get on to an omnibus. And already, even as she stood there, in her very well cut clothes, it was beginning. . . . People were beginning to compare her to poplar trees, early dawn, hyacinths, fawns, running water, and garden lilies, and it made her life a burden to her, for she so much preferred being left alone to do what she liked in the country, but they would compare her to lilies, and she had to go to parties, and London was so dreary compared with being alone in the country with her father and the dogs.

Buses swooped, settled, were off-garish caravans, glistening with red and yellow varnish. But which should she get on to? She had no preferences. Of course, she would not push her way. She inclined to be passive. It was expression she needed, but her eyes were fine, Chinese, oriental, and, as her mother said, with such nice shoulders and holding herself so straight, she was always charming to look at; and lately, in the evening especially, when she was interested, for she never seemed excited, she looked almost beautiful, very stately, very serene. What could she be thinking? Every man fell in love with her, and she was really awfully bored. For it was beginning. Her mother could see that—the compliments were beginning. That she did not care more about it—for instance for her clothes—sometimes worried Clarissa, but perhaps it was as well with all those puppies and guinea pigs about having distemper, and it gave her a charm. And now there was this odd friendship with Miss Kilman. Well, thought Clarissa about three o'clock in the morning, reading Baron Marbot for she could not sleep, it proves she has a heart.

Suddenly Elizabeth stepped forward and most competently boarded the omnibus, in front of everybody. She took a seat on top. The impetuous creature—a pirate—started forward, sprang away; she had to hold the rail to steady herself, for a pirate it was, reckless, unscrupulous, bearing down ruthlessly, circumventing dangerously, boldly snatching a passenger, or ignoring a passenger, squeezing eel-like and arrogant in between, and then rushing insolently all sails spread up Whitehall. And did Elizabeth give one thought to poor Miss Kilman who loved her without jealousy, to whom she had been a fawn in the open, a moon in a glade? She was delighted to be free. The fresh air was so delicious. It had been so stuffy in the Army and Navy Stores. And now it was like riding, to be rushing up Whitehall; and to each movement of the omnibus the beautiful body in the fawn-coloured coat responded freely like a rider, like the figure-head of a ship, for the breeze slightly disarrayed her; the heat gave her cheeks the pallor of white painted wood; and her fine eyes, having no eyes to meet, gazed ahead, blank, bright, with the staring incredible innocence of sculpture.

It was always talking about her own sufferings that made Miss Kilman so difficult. And was she right? If it was being on committees and giving up hours and hours every day (she hardly ever saw him in London) that helped the poor, her father did that, goodness knows,—if that was what Miss Kilman meant about being a Christian; but it was so difficult to say. Oh, she would like to go a little further. Another penny was it to the Strand? Here was another penny then. She would go up the Strand.

She liked people who were ill. And every profession is open to the women of your generation, said Miss Kilman. So she might be a doctor. She might be a farmer.

Animals are often ill. She might own a thousand acres and have people under her. She would go and see them in their cottages. This was Somerset[5] House. One might be a very good farmer—and that, strangely enough though Miss Kilman had her share in it, was almost entirely due to Somerset House. It looked so splendid, so serious, that great grey building. And she liked the feeling of people working. She liked those churches, like shapes of grey paper, breasting the stream of the Strand. It was quite different here from Westminster, she thought, getting off at Chancery Lane. It was so serious; it was so busy. In short, she would like to have a profession. She would become a doctor, a farmer, possibly go into Parliament, if she found it necessary, all because of the Strand.

The feet of those people busy about their activities, hands putting stone to stone, minds eternally occupied not with trivial chatterings (comparing women to poplars—which was rather exciting, of course, but very silly), but with thoughts of ships, of business, of law, of administration, and with it all so stately (she was in the Temple), gay (there was the river), pious (there was the Church), made her quite determined, whatever her mother might say, to become either a farmer or a doctor. But she was, of course, rather lazy.

And it was much better to say nothing about it. It seemed so silly. It was the sort of thing that did sometimes happen, when one was alone—buildings without architects' names, crowds of people coming back from the city having more power than single clergymen in Kensington, than any of the books Miss Kilman had lent her, to stimulate what lay slumbrous, clumsy, and shy on the mind's sandy floor to break surface, as a child suddenly stretches its arms; it was just that, perhaps, a sigh, a stretch of the arms, an impulse, a revelation, which has its effects for ever, and then down again it went to the sandy floor. She must go home. She must dress for dinner. But what was the time?—where was a clock?

She looked up Fleet Street. She walked just a little way towards St Paul's, shyly, like some one penetrating on tiptoe, exploring a strange house by night with a candle, on edge lest the owner should suddenly fling wide his bedroom door and ask her business, nor did she dare wander off into queer alleys, tempting bye-streets, any more than in a strange house open doors which might be bedroom doors, or sitting-room doors, or lead straight to the larder.[6] For no Dalloways came down the Strand daily; she was a pioneer, a stray, venturing, trusting.

In many ways, her mother felt, she was extremely immature, like a child still, attached to dolls, to old slippers; a perfect baby; and that was charming. But then, of course, there was in the Dalloway family the tradition of public service. Abbesses, principals, head mistresses, dignitaries, in the republic of women—without being brilliant, any of them, they were that. She penetrated a little further in the direction of St Paul's. She liked the geniality, sisterhood, motherhood, brotherhood of this uproar. It seemed to her good. The noise was tremendous; and suddenly there were trumpets (the unemployed) blaring, rattling about in the uproar; military music; as if people were marching; yet had they been dying—had some woman breathed her last and whoever was watching, opening the window of the room where she had just brought off that act of supreme dignity, looked down on Fleet Street, that uproar, that military music would have come triumphing up to him, consolatory, indifferent.

5. Somerset House is a huge neoclassical building located between the Strand and river Thames; it primarily housed government offices.

6. Where the food supplies of a household are kept; a pantry.

It was not conscious. There was no recognition in it of one's fortune, or fate, and for that very reason even to those dazed with watching for the last shivers of consciousness on the faces of the dying, consoling. Forgetfulness in people might wound, their ingratitude corrode, but this voice, pouring endlessly, year in year out, would take whatever it might be; this vow; this van; this life; this procession, would wrap them all about and carry them on, as in the rough stream of a glacier the ice holds a splinter of bone, a blue petal, some oak trees, and rolls them on.

But it was later than she thought. Her mother would not like her to be wandering off alone like this. She turned back down the Strand.

A puff of wind (in spite of the heat, there was quite a wind) blew a thin black veil over the sun and over the Strand. The faces faded; the omnibuses suddenly lost their glow. For although the clouds were of mountainous white so that one could fancy hacking hard chips off with a hatchet, with broad golden slopes, lawns of celestial pleasure gardens, on their flanks, and had all the appearance of settled habitations assembled for the conference of gods above the world, there was a perpetual movement among them. Signs were interchanged, when, as if to fulfil some scheme arranged already, now a summit dwindled, now a whole block of pyramidal size which had kept its station inalterably advanced into the midst or gravely led the procession to fresh anchorage. Fixed though they seemed at their posts, at rest in perfect unanimity, nothing could be fresher, freer, more sensitive superficially than the snow-white or gold-kindled surface; to change, to go, to dismantle the solemn assemblage was immediately possible; and in spite of the grave fixity, the accumulated robustness and solidity, now they struck light to the earth, now darkness.

Calmly and competently, Elizabeth Dalloway mounted the Westminster omnibus.

Going and coming, beckoning, signalling, so the light and shadow which now made the wall grey, now the bananas bright yellow, now made the Strand grey, now made the omnibuses bright yellow, seemed to Septimus Warren Smith lying on the sofa in the sitting-room; watching the watery gold glow and fade with the astonishing sensibility of some live creature on the roses, on the wall-paper. Outside the trees dragged their leaves like nets through the depths of the air; the sound of water was in the room and through the waves came the voices of birds singing. Every power poured its treasures on his head, and his hand lay there on the back of the sofa, as he had seen his hand lie when he was bathing, floating, on the top of the waves, while far away on shore he heard dogs barking and barking far away. Fear no more, says the heart in the body; fear no more.

He was not afraid. At every moment Nature signified by some laughing hint like that gold spot which went round the wall—there, there, there—her determination to show, by brandishing her plumes, shaking her tresses, flinging her mantle this way and that, beautifully, always beautifully, and standing close up to breathe through her hollowed hands Shakespeare's words, her meaning.

Rezia, sitting at the table twisting a hat in her hands, watched him; saw him smiling. He was happy then. But she could not bear to see him smiling. It was not marriage; it was not being one's husband to look strange like that, always to be starting, laughing, sitting hour after hour silent, or clutching her and telling her to write. The table drawer was full of those writings; about war; about Shakespeare; about great discoveries; how there is no death. Lately he had become excited suddenly for no reason (and both Dr Holmes and Sir William Bradshaw said excitement was the worst thing for him), and waved his hands and cried out that he knew the truth! He knew everything! That man, his friend who was killed, Evans, had come, he said. He was singing behind the screen. She wrote it down just as he spoke it. Some things were very beautiful; others sheer nonsense. And he was always stopping in the middle, changing his mind; wanting to add something; hearing something new; listening with his hand up.

But she heard nothing.

And once they found the girl who did the room reading one of these papers in fits of laughter. It was a dreadful pity. For that made Septimus cry out about human cruelty—how they tear each other to pieces. The fallen, he said, they tear to pieces. "Holmes is on us," he would say, and he would invent stories about Holmes; Holmes eating porridge; Holmes reading Shakespeare—making himself roar with laughter or rage, for Dr Holmes seemed to stand for something horrible to him. "Human nature," he called him. Then there were the visions. He was drowned, he used to say, and lying on a cliff with the gulls screaming over him. He would look over the edge of the sofa down into the sea. Or he was hearing music. Really it was only a barrel organ or some man crying in the street. But "Lovely!" he used to cry, and the tears would run down his cheeks, which was to her the most dreadful thing of all, to see a man like Septimus, who had fought, who was brave, crying. And he would lie listening until suddenly he would cry that he was falling down, down into the flames! Actually she would look for flames, it was so vivid. But there was nothing. They were alone in the room. It was a dream, she would tell him and so quiet him at last, but sometimes she was frightened too. She sighed as she sat sewing.

Her sigh was tender and enchanting, like the wind outside a wood in the evening. Now she put down her scissors; now she turned to take something from the table. A little stir, a little crinkling, a little tapping built up something on the table there, where she sat sewing. Through his eyelashes he could see her blurred outline; her little black body; her face and hands; her turning movements at the table, as she took up a reel, or looked (she was apt to lose things) for her silk. She was making a hat for Mrs Filmer's married daughter, whose name was—he had forgotten her name.

"What is the name of Mrs Filmer's married daughter?" he asked.

"Mrs Peters," said Rezia. She was afraid it was too small, she said, holding it before her. Mrs Peters was a big woman; but she did not like her. It was only because Mrs Filmer had been so good to them. "She gave me grapes this morning," she said—that Rezia wanted to do something to show that they were grateful. She had come into the room the other evening and found Mrs Peters, who thought they were out, playing the gramophone.

"Was it true?" he asked. She was playing the gramophone? Yes; she had told him about it at the time; she had found Mrs Peters playing the gramophone.

He began, very cautiously, to open his eyes, to see whether a gramophone was really there. But real things—real things were too exciting. He must be cautious. He would not go mad. First he looked at the fashion papers on the lower shelf, then, gradually at the gramophone with the green trumpet. Nothing could be more exact. And so, gathering courage, he looked at the sideboard; the plate of bananas; the engraving of Queen Victoria and the Prince Consort; at the mantelpiece, with the jar of roses. None of these things moved. All were still; all were real.

"She is a woman with a spiteful tongue," said Rezia.

"What does Mr Peters do?" Septimus asked.

"Ah," said Rezia, trying to remember. She thought Mrs Filmer had said that he travelled for some company. "Just now he is in Hull," she said.

"Just now!" She said that with her Italian accent. She said that herself. He shaded his eyes so that he might see only a little of her face at a time, first the chin, then the nose, then the forehead, in case it were deformed, or had some terrible mark on it. But no, there she was, perfectly natural, sewing, with the pursed lips that women have, the set, the melancholy expression, when sewing. But there was nothing terrible about it, he assured himself, looking a second time, a third time at her face, her hands, for what was frightening or disgusting in her as she sat there in broad daylight, sewing? Mrs Peters had a spiteful tongue. Mr Peters was in Hull. Why then rage and prophesy? Why fly scourged and outcast? Why be made to tremble and sob by the clouds? Why seek truths and deliver messages when Rezia sat sticking pins into the front of her dress, and Mr Peters was in Hull? Miracles, revelations, agonies, loneliness, falling through the sea, down, down into the flames, all were burnt out, for he had a sense, as he watched Rezia trimming the straw hat for Mrs Peters, of a coverlet of flowers.

"It's too small for Mrs Peters," said Septimus.

For the first time for days he was speaking as he used to do! Of course it was—absurdly small, she said. But Mrs Peters had chosen it.

He took it out of her hands. He said it was an organ grinder's monkey's hat.

How it rejoiced her that! Not for weeks had they laughed like this together, poking fun privately like married people. What she meant was that if Mrs Filmer had come in, or Mrs Peters or anybody they would not have understood what she and Septimus were laughing at.

"There," she said, pinning a rose to one side of the hat. Never had she felt so happy! Never in her life!

But that was still more ridiculous, Septimus said. Now the poor woman looked like a pig at a fair. (Nobody ever made her laugh as Septimus did.)

What had she got in her work-box? She had ribbons and beads, tassels, artificial flowers. She tumbled them out on the table. He began putting odd colours together—for though he had no fingers, could not even do up a parcel, he had a wonderful eye, and often he was right, sometimes absurd, of course, but sometimes wonderfully right.

"She shall have a beautiful hat!" he murmured, taking up this and that, Rezia kneeling by his side, looking over his shoulder. Now it was finished—that is to say the design; she must stitch it together. But she must be very, very careful, he said, to keep it just as he had made it.

So she sewed. When she sewed, he thought, she made a sound like a kettle on the hob; bubbling, murmuring, always busy, her strong little pointed fingers pinching and poking; her needle flashing straight. The sun might go in and out, on the tassels, on the wallpaper, but he would wait, he thought, stretching out his feet, looking at his ringed sock at the end of the sofa; he would wait in this warm place, this pocket of still air, which one comes on at the edge of a wood sometimes in the evening, when, because of a fall in the ground, or some arrangement of the trees (one must be scientific above all, scientific), warmth lingers, and the air buffets the cheek like the wing of a bird.

"There it is," said Rezia, twirling Mrs Peters' hat on the tips of her fingers. "That'll do for the moment. Later . . . " her sentence bubbled away drip, drip, drip, like a contented tap left running.

It was wonderful. Never had he done anything which made him feel so proud. It was so real, it was so substantial, Mrs Peters' hat.

"Just look at it," he said.

Yes, it would always make her happy to see that hat. He had become himself then, he had laughed then. They had been alone together. Always she would like that hat.

He told her to try it on.

"But I must look so queer!" she cried, running over to the glass and looking first this side then that. Then she snatched it off again, for there was a tap at the door. Could it be Sir William Bradshaw? Had he sent already?

No! it was only the small girl with the evening paper.

What always happened, then happened—what happened every night of their lives. The small girl sucked her thumb at the door; Rezia went down on her knees; Rezia cooed and kissed; Rezia got a bag of sweets out of the table drawer. For so it always happened. First one thing, then another. So she built it up, first one thing and then another. Dancing, skipping, round and round the room they went. He took the paper. Surrey was all out, he read. There was a heat wave. Rezia repeated: Surrey was all out. There was a heat wave, making it part of the game she was playing with Mrs Filmer's grandchild, both of them laughing, chattering at the same time, at their game. He was very tired. He was very happy. He would sleep. He shut his eyes. But directly he saw nothing the sounds of the game became fainter and stranger and sounded like the cries of people seeking and not finding, and passing further and further away. They had lost him!

He started up in terror. What did he see? The plate of bananas on the sideboard. Nobody was there (Rezia had taken the child to its mother. It was bedtime). That was it: to be alone forever. That was the doom pronounced in Milan when he came into the room and saw them cutting out buckram shapes with their scissors; to be alone forever.

He was alone with the sideboard and the bananas. He was alone, exposed on this bleak eminence, stretched out—but not on a hill-top; not on a crag; on Mrs Filmer's sitting-room sofa. As for the visions, the faces, the voices of the dead, where were they? There was a screen in front of him, with black bulrushes and blue swallows. Where he had once seen mountains, where he had seen faces, where he had seen beauty, there was a screen.

"Evans!" he cried. There was no answer. A mouse had squeaked, or a curtain rustled. Those were the voices of the dead. The screen, the coal-scuttle, the sideboard remained to him. Let him then face the screen, the coal-scuttle and the sideboard . . . but Rezia burst into the room chattering.

Some letter had come. Everybody's plans were changed. Mrs Filmer would not be able to go to Brighton after all. There was no time to let Mrs Williams know, and really Rezia thought it very, very annoying, when she caught sight of the hat and thought . . . perhaps . . . she . . . might just make a little. . . . Her voice died out in contented melody.

"Ah, damn!" she cried (it was a joke of theirs, her swearing), the needle had broken. Hat, child, Brighton, needle. She built it up; first one thing, then another, she built it up, sewing.

She wanted him to say whether by moving the rose she had improved the hat. She sat on the end of the sofa.

They were perfectly happy now, she said, suddenly, putting the hat down. For she could say anything to him now. She could say whatever came into her head. That was almost the first thing she had felt about him, that night in the café when he had come in with his English friends. He had come in, rather shyly, looking round him, and his hat had fallen when he hung it up. That she could remember. She knew he was English, though not one of the large Englishmen her sister admired, for he was always thin; but he had a beautiful fresh colour; and with his big nose, his bright eyes, his way of sitting a little hunched made her think, she had often told him, of a young hawk, that first evening she saw him, when they were playing dominoes, and he had come in—of a young hawk; but with her he was always very gentle. She had never seen him wild or drunk, only suffering sometimes through this terrible war, but even so, when she came in, he would put it all away. Anything, anything in the whole world, any little bother with her work, anything that struck her to say she would tell him, and he understood at once. Her own family even were not the same. Being older than she was and being so clever—how serious he was, wanting her to read Shakespeare before she could even read a child's story in English!—being so much more experienced, he could help her. And she too could help him.

But this hat now. And then (it was getting late) Sir William Bradshaw.

She held her hands to her head, waiting for him to say did he like the hat or not, and as she sat there, waiting, looking down, he could feel her mind, like a bird, falling from branch to branch, and always alighting, quite rightly; he could follow her mind, as she sat there in one of those loose lax poses that came to her naturally and, if he should say anything, at once she smiled, like a bird alighting with all its claws firm upon the bough.

But he remembered Bradshaw said, "The people we are most fond of are not good for us when we are ill." Bradshaw said, he must be taught to rest. Bradshaw said they must be separated.

"Must," "must," why "must"? What power had Bradshaw over him? "What right has Bradshaw to say 'must' to me?" he demanded.

"It is because you talked of killing yourself," said Rezia. (Mercifully, she could now say anything to Septimus.)

So he was in their power! Holmes and Bradshaw were on him! The brute with the red nostrils was snuffing into every secret place! "Must" it could say! Where were his papers? the things he had written?

She brought him his papers, the things he had written, things she had written for him. She tumbled them out on to the sofa. They looked at them together. Diagrams, designs, little men and women brandishing sticks for arms, with wings—were they?—on their backs; circles traced round shillings and sixpences—the suns and stars; zigzagging precipices with mountaineers ascending roped together, exactly like knives and forks; sea pieces with little faces laughing out of what might perhaps be waves: the map of the world. Burn them! he cried. Now for his writings; how the dead sing behind rhododendron bushes; odes to Time; conversations with Shakespeare; Evans, Evans, Evans—his messages from the dead; do not cut down trees; tell the Prime Minister. Universal love: the meaning of the world. Burn them! he cried.

But Rezia laid her hands on them. Some were very beautiful, she thought. She would tie them up (for she had no envelope) with a piece of silk.

Even if they took him, she said, she would go with him. They could not separate them against their wills, she said.

Shuffling the edges straight, she did up the papers, and tied the parcel almost without looking, sitting beside him, he thought, as if all her petals were about her. She was a flowering tree; and through her branches looked out the face of a lawgiver, who had reached a sanctuary where she feared no one; not Holmes; not Bradshaw; a miracle, a triumph, the last and greatest. Staggering he saw her mount the appalling staircase, laden with Holmes and Bradshaw, men who never weighed less than eleven stone six, who sent their wives to Court, men who made ten thousand a year and talked of proportion; who different in their verdicts (for Holmes said one thing, Bradshaw another), yet judges they were; who mixed the vision and the sideboard; saw nothing clear, yet ruled, yet inflicted. "Must" they said. Over them she triumphed.

"There!" she said. The papers were tied up. No one should get at them. She would put them away.

And, she said, nothing should separate them. She sat down beside him and called him by the name of that hawk or crow which being malicious and a great destroyer of crops was precisely like him. No one could separate them, she said.

Then she got up to go into the bedroom to pack their things, but hearing voices downstairs and thinking that Dr Holmes had perhaps called, ran down to prevent him coming up.

Septimus could hear her talking to Holmes on the staircase.

"My dear lady, I have come as a friend," Holmes was saying.

"No. I will not allow you to see my husband," she said.

He could see her, like a little hen, with her wings spread barring his passage. But Holmes persevered.

"My dear lady, allow me . . . " Holmes said, putting her aside (Holmes was a powerfully built man).

Holmes was coming upstairs. Holmes would burst open the door. Holmes would say "In a funk, eh?" Holmes would get him. But no; not Holmes; not Bradshaw. Getting up rather unsteadily, hopping indeed from foot to foot, he considered Mrs Filmer's nice clean bread knife with "Bread" carved on the handle. Ah, but one mustn't spoil that. The gas fire? But it was too late now. Holmes was coming. Razors he might have got, but Rezia, who always did that sort of thing, had packed them. There remained only the window, the large Bloomsbury-lodging house window, the tiresome, the troublesome, and rather melodramatic business of opening the window and throwing himself out. It was their idea of tragedy, not his or Rezia's (for she was with him). Holmes and Bradshaw like that sort of thing. (He sat on the sill.) But he would wait till the very last moment. He did not want to die. Life was good. The sun hot. Only human beings—what did *they* want? Coming down the staircase opposite an old man stopped and stared at him. Holmes was at the door. "I'll give it you!" he cried, and flung himself vigorously, violently down on to Mrs Filmer's area railings.

"The coward!" cried Dr Holmes, bursting the door open. Rezia ran to the window, she saw; she understood. Dr Holmes and Mrs Filmer collided with each other. Mrs Filmer flapped her apron and made her hide her eyes in the bedroom. There was a great deal of running up and down stairs. Dr Holmes came in—white as a sheet, shaking all over, with a glass in his hand. She must be brave and drink something, he said (What was it? Something sweet), for her husband was horribly mangled, would not recover consciousness, she must not see him, must be spared as much as possible, would have the inquest to go through, poor young woman. Who could have foretold it? A sudden impulse, no one was in the least to blame (he told Mrs Filmer). And why the devil he did it, Dr Holmes could not conceive.

It seemed to her as she drank the sweet stuff that she was opening long windows, stepping out into some garden. But where? The clock was striking—one, two, three: how sensible the sound was; compared with all this thumping and whispering; like Septimus himself. She was falling asleep. But the clock went on striking, four, five, six and Mrs Filmer waving her apron (they wouldn't bring the body in here, would they?) seemed part of that garden; or a flag. She had once seen a flag slowly rippling out from a mast when she stayed with her aunt at Venice. Men killed in battle were thus saluted, and Septimus had been through the War. Of her memories, most were happy.

She put on her hat, and ran through cornfields—where could it have been?—on to some hill, somewhere near the sea, for there were ships, gulls, butterflies, they sat on a cliff. In London too, there they sat, and, half dreaming, came to her through the bedroom door, rain falling, whisperings, stirrings among dry corn, the caress of the sea, as it seemed to her, hollowing them in its arched shell and murmuring to her laid on shore, strewn she felt, like flying flowers over some tomb.

"He is dead," she said, smiling at the poor old woman who guarded her with her honest light-blue eyes fixed on the door. (They wouldn't bring him in here, would they?) But Mrs Filmer pooh-poohed. Oh no, oh no! They were carrying him away now. Ought she not to be told? Married people ought to be together, Mrs Filmer thought. But they must do as the doctor said.

"Let her sleep," said Dr Holmes, feeling her pulse. She saw the large outline of his body standing dark against the window. So that was Dr Holmes.

One of the triumphs of civilisation, Peter Walsh thought. It is one of the triumphs of civilisation, as the light high bell of the ambulance sounded. Swiftly, cleanly the ambulance sped to the hospital, having picked up instantly, humanely, some poor devil; some one hit on the head, struck down by disease, knocked over perhaps a minute or so ago at one of these crossings, as might happen to oneself. That was civilisation. It struck him coming back from the East—the efficiency, the organisation, the communal spirit of London. Every cart or carriage of its own accord drew aside to let the ambulance pass. Perhaps it was morbid; or was it not touching rather, the respect which they showed this ambulance with its victim inside—busy men hurrying home yet instantly bethinking them as it passed of some wife; or presumably how easily it might have been them there, stretched on a shelf with a doctor and a nurse. . . . Ah, but thinking became morbid, sentimental, directly one began conjuring up doctors, dead bodies; a little glow of pleasure, a sort of lust too over the visual impression warned one not to go on with that sort of thing any more—fatal to art, fatal to friendship. True. And yet, thought Peter Walsh, as the ambulance turned the corner though the light high bell could be heard down the next street and still farther as it crossed the Tottenham Court Road, chiming constantly, it is the privilege of loneliness; in privacy one may do as one chooses. One might weep if no one saw. It had been his undoing—this susceptibility—in Anglo-Indian society; not weeping at the right time, or laughing either. I have that in me, he thought standing by the pillar-box, which could now dissolve in tears. Why, Heaven knows. Beauty of some sort probably, and the weight of the day, which beginning with that visit to Clarissa had exhausted him with its heat, its intensity, and the drip, drip, of one impression after another down into that cellar where they stood, deep, dark, and no one would ever know. Partly for that reason, its secrecy, complete and inviolable, he had found life like an unknown garden, full of turns and corners, surprising, yes; really it took one's breath away, these moments; there coming to him by the pillar-box opposite the British Museum one of them, a moment, in which things came together; this ambulance; and life and death. It was as if he were sucked up to some very high roof by that rush of emotion and the rest of him, like a white shell-sprinkled beach, left bare. It had been his undoing in Anglo-Indian society—this susceptibility.

Clarissa once, going on top of an omnibus with him somewhere, Clarissa superficially at least, so easily moved, now in despair, now in the best of spirits, all aquiver in those days and such good company, spotting queer little scenes, names, people from the top of a bus, for they used to explore London and bring back bags full of treasures from the Caledonian market—Clarissa had a theory in those days—they had heaps of theories, always theories, as young people have. It was to explain the feeling they had of dissatisfaction; not knowing people; not being known. For how could they know each other? You met every day; then not for six months, or years. It was unsatisfactory, they agreed, how little one knew people. But she said, sitting on the bus going up Shaftesbury Avenue, she felt herself everywhere; not "here, here, here"; and she tapped the back of the seat; but everywhere. She waved her hand, going up Shaftesbury Avenue. She was all that. So that to know her, or any one, one must seek out the people who completed them; even the places. Odd affinities she had with people she had never spoken to, some woman in the street, some man behind a counter—even trees, or barns. It ended in a transcendental theory which, with her horror of death, allowed her to believe, or say that she believed (for all her scepticism), that since our apparitions, the part of us which appears, are so momentary compared with the other, the unseen part of us, which spreads wide, the unseen might survive, be recovered somehow attached to this person or that, or even haunting certain places after death . . . perhaps—perhaps.

Looking back over that long friendship of almost thirty years her theory worked to this extent. Brief, broken, often painful as their actual meetings had been what with his absences and interruptions (this morning, for instance, in came Elizabeth, like a long-legged colt, handsome, dumb, just as he was beginning to talk to Clarissa) the effect of them on his life was immeasurable. There was a mystery about it. You were given a sharp, acute, uncomfortable grain—the actual meeting; horribly painful as often as not; yet in absence, in the most unlikely places, it would flower out, open, shed its scent, let you touch, taste, look about you, get the whole feel of it and understanding, after years of lying lost. Thus she had come to him; on board ship; in the Himalayas; suggested by the oddest things (so Sally Seton, generous, enthusiastic goose! thought of *him* when she saw blue hydrangeas). She had influenced him more than any person he had ever known. And always in this way coming before him without his wishing it, cool, ladylike, critical; or ravishing, romantic, recalling some field or English harvest. He saw her most often in the country, not in London. One scene after another at Bourton. . . .

He had reached his hotel. He crossed the hall, with its mounds of reddish chairs and sofas, its spike-leaved, withered-looking plants. He got his key off the hook. The young lady handed him some letters. He went upstairs—he saw her most often at Bourton, in the late summer, when he stayed there for a week, or fortnight even, as people did in those days. First on top of some hill there she would stand, hands clapped to her hair, her cloak blowing out, pointing, crying to them—she saw the Severn[7] beneath. Or in a wood, making the kettle boil—very ineffective with her fingers; the smoke curtseying, blowing in their faces; her little pink face showing through; begging water from an old woman in a cottage, who came to the door to watch them go. They walked always; the others drove. She was bored driving, disliked all animals, except that dog. They tramped miles along roads. She would break off to get her bearings, pilot him back across country; and all the time they argued, discussed poetry, discussed people, discussed politics (she was a Radical then); never noticing a thing except when she stopped, cried out at a view or a tree, and made him

7. River flowing from central Wales through England and into the Bristol Channel.

look with her; and so on again, through stubble fields, she walking ahead, with a flower for her aunt, never tired of walking for all her delicacy; to drop down on Bourton in the dusk. Then, after dinner, old Breitkopf would open the piano and sing without any voice, and they would lie sunk in arm-chairs, trying not to laugh, but always breaking down and laughing laughing—laughing at nothing. Breitkopf was supposed not to see. And then in the morning, flirting up and down like a wagtail in front of the house. . . .

Oh it was a letter from her! This blue envelope; that was her hand. And he would have to read it. Here was another of those meetings, bound to be painful! To read her letter needed the devil of an effort. "How heavenly it was to see him. She must tell him that." That was all.

But it upset him. It annoyed him. He wished she hadn't written it. Coming on top of his thoughts, it was like a nudge in the ribs. Why couldn't she let him be? After all, she had married Dalloway, and lived with him in perfect happiness all these years.

These hotels are not consoling places. Far from it. Any number of people had hung up their hats on those pegs. Even the flies, if you thought of it, had settled on other people's noses. As for the cleanliness which hit him in the face, it wasn't cleanliness, so much as bareness, frigidity; a thing that had to be. Some arid matron made her rounds at dawn sniffing, peering, causing blue-nosed maids to scour, for all the world as if the next visitor were a joint of meat to be served on a perfectly clean platter. For sleep, one bed; for sitting in, one arm-chair; for cleaning one's teeth and shaving one's chin, one tumbler, one looking-glass. Books, letters, dressing-gown, slipped about on the impersonality of the horsehair like incongruous impertinences. And it was Clarissa's letter that made him see all this. "Heavenly to see you. She must say so!" He folded the paper; pushed it away; nothing would induce him to read it again!

To get that letter to him by six o'clock she must have sat down and written it directly he left her; stamped it; sent somebody to the post. It was, as people say, very like her. She was upset by his visit. She had felt a great deal; had for a moment, when she kissed his hand, regretted, envied him even, remembered possibly (for he saw her look it) something he had said—how they would change the world if she married him perhaps; whereas, it was this; it was middle age; it was mediocrity; then forced herself with her indomitable vitality to put all that aside, there being in her a thread of life which for toughness, endurance, power to overcome obstacles, and carry her triumphantly through he had never known the like of. Yes; but there would come a reaction directly he left the room. She would be frightfully sorry for him; she would think what in the world she could do to give him pleasure (short always of the one thing) and he could see her with the tears running down her cheeks going to her writing-table and dashing off that one line which he was to find greeting him. . . . "Heavenly to see you!" And she meant it.

Peter Walsh had now unlaced his boots.

But it would not have been a success, their marriage. The other thing, after all, came so much more naturally.

It was odd; it was true; lots of people felt it. Peter Walsh, who had done just respectably, filled the usual posts adequately, was liked, but thought a little cranky, gave himself airs—it was odd that *he* should have had, especially now that his hair was grey, a contented look; a look of having reserves. It was this that made him attractive to women who liked the sense that he was not altogether manly. There was something unusual about him, or something behind him. It might be that he was bookish—never came to see you without taking up the book on the table (he was now reading, with his bootlaces trailing on the floor); or that he was a gentleman, which showed itself in the way he knocked the ashes out of his pipe, and in his manners of course to women. For it was very charming and quite ridiculous how easily some girl without a grain of sense could twist him round her finger. But at her own risk. That is to say, though he might be ever so easy, and indeed with his gaiety and good-breeding fascinating to be with, it was only up to a point. She said something—no, no; he saw through that. He wouldn't stand that—no, no. Then he could shout and rock and hold his sides together over some joke with men. He was the best judge of cooking in India. He was a man. But not the sort of man one had to respect—which was a mercy; not like Major Simmons, for instance; not in the least like that, Daisy thought, when, in spite of her two small children, she used to compare them.

He pulled off his boots. He emptied his pockets. Out came with his pocket-knife a snapshot of Daisy on the verandah; Daisy all in white, with a fox-terrier on her knee; very charming, very dark; the best he had ever seen of her. It did come, after all so naturally; so much more naturally than Clarissa. No fuss. No bother. No finicking and fidgeting. All plain sailing. And the dark, adorably pretty girl on the verandah exclaimed (he could hear her). Of course, of course she would give him everything! she cried (she had no sense of discretion) everything he wanted! she cried, running to meet him, whoever might be looking. And she was only twenty-four. And she had two children. Well, well!

Well indeed he had got himself into a mess at his age. And it came over him when he woke in the night pretty forcibly. Suppose they did marry? For him it would be all very well, but what about her? Mrs Burgess, a good sort and no chatterbox, in whom he had confided, thought this absence of his in England, ostensibly to see lawyers might serve to make Daisy reconsider, think what it meant. It was a question of her position, Mrs Burgess said; the social barrier; giving up her children. She'd be a widow with a past one of these days, draggling about in the suburbs, or more likely, indiscriminate (you know, she said, what such women get like, with too much paint). But Peter Walsh pooh-poohed all that. He didn't mean to die yet. Anyhow she must settle for herself; judge for herself, he thought, padding about the room in his socks, smoothing out his dress-shirt, for he might go to Clarissa's party, or he might go to one of the Halls, or he might settle in and read an absorbing book written by a man he used to know at Oxford. And if he did retire, that's what he'd do—write books. He would go to Oxford and poke about in the Bodleian. Vainly the dark, adorably pretty girl ran to the end of the terrace; vainly waved her hand; vainly cried she didn't care a straw what people said. There he was, the man she thought the world of, the perfect gentleman, the fascinating, the distinguished (and his age made not the least difference to her), padding about a room in an hotel in Bloomsbury, shaving, washing, continuing, as he took up cans, put down razors, to poke about in the Bodleian, and get at the truth about one or two little matters that interested him. And he would have a chat with whoever it might be, and so come to disregard more and more precise hours for lunch, and miss engagements, and when Daisy asked him, as she would, for a kiss, a scene, fail to come up to the scratch (though he was genuinely devoted to her)—in short it might be happier, as Mrs Burgess said, that she should forget him, or merely remember him as he was in August 1922, like a figure standing at the cross roads at dusk, which grows more and more remote as the dog-cart spins away, carrying her securely fastened to the back seat, though her arms are outstretched, and as she sees the figure dwindle and disappear still she cries out how she would do anything in the world, anything, anything, anything. . . .

He never knew what people thought. It became more and more difficult for him to concentrate. He became absorbed; he became busied with his own concerns; now surly, now gay; dependent on women, absent-minded, moody, less and less able (so he thought as he shaved) to understand why Clarissa couldn't simply find them a lodging and be nice to Daisy; introduce her. And then he could just—just do what? just haunt and hover (he was at the moment actually engaged in sorting out various keys, papers), swoop and taste, be alone, in short, sufficient to himself; and yet nobody of course was more dependent upon others (he buttoned his waistcoat); it had been his undoing. He could not keep out of smoking-rooms, liked colonels, liked golf, liked bridge, and above all women's society, and the fineness of their companionship, and their faithfulness and audacity and greatness in loving which though it had its drawbacks seemed to him (and the dark, adorably pretty face was on top of the envelopes) so wholly admirable, so splendid a flower to grow on the crest of human life, and yet he could not come up to the scratch, being always apt to see round things (Clarissa had sapped something in him permanently), and to tire very easily of mute devotion and to want variety in love, though it would make him furious if Daisy loved anybody else, furious! for he was jealous, uncontrollably jealous by temperament. He suffered tortures! But where was his knife; his watch; his seals, his note-case, and Clarissa's letter which he would not read again but liked to think of, and Daisy's photograph? And now for dinner.

They were eating.

Sitting at little tables round vases, dressed or not dressed, with their shawls and bags laid beside them, with their air of false composure, for they were not used to so many courses at dinner, and confidence, for they were able to pay for it, and strain, for they had been running about London all day shopping, sightseeing; and their natural curiosity, for they looked round and up as the nice-looking gentleman in horn-rimmed spectacles came in, and their good nature, for they would have been glad to do any little service, such as lend a time-table or impart useful information, and their desire, pulsing in them, tugging at them subterraneously, somehow to establish connections if it were only a birth-place (Liverpool, for example) in common or friends of the same name; with their furtive glances, odd silences, and sudden withdrawals into family jocularity and isolation; there they sat eating dinner when Mr Walsh came in and took his seat at a little table by the curtain.

It was not that he said anything, for being solitary he could only address himself to the waiter; it was his way of looking at the menu, of pointing his forefinger to a particular wine, of hitching himself up to the table, of addressing himself seriously, not gluttonously to dinner, that won him their respect; which, having to remain unexpressed for the greater part of the meal, flared up at the table where the Morrises sat when Mr Walsh was heard to say at the end of the meal, "Bartlett pears." Why he should have spoken so moderately yet firmly, with the air of a disciplinarian well within his rights which are founded upon justice, neither young Charles Morris, nor old Charles, neither Miss Elaine nor Mrs Morris knew. But when he said, "Bartlett pears," sitting alone at his table, they felt that he counted on their support in some lawful demand; was champion of a cause which immediately became their own, so that their eyes met his eyes sympathetically, and when they all reached the smoking-room simultaneously, a little talk between them became inevitable.

It was not very profound—only to the effect that London was crowded; had changed in thirty years; that Mr Morris preferred Liverpool; that Mrs Morris had been to the Westminster flower-show, and that they had all seen the Prince of Wales. Yet, thought Peter Walsh, no family in the world can compare with the Morrises; none whatever; and their relations to each other are perfect, and they don't care a hang for the upper classes, and they like what they like, and Elaine is training for the family business, and the boy has won a scholarship at Leeds, and the old lady (who is about his own age) has three more children at home; and they have two motor cars, but Mr Morris still mends the boots on Sunday: it is superb, it is absolutely superb, thought Peter Walsh, swaying a little backwards and forwards with his liqueur glass in his hand among the hairy red chairs and ash-trays, feeling very well pleased with himself, for the Morrises liked him. Yes, they liked a man who said, "Bartlett pears." They liked him, he felt.

He would go to Clarissa's party. (The Morrises moved off; but they would meet again.) He would go to Clarissa's party, because he wanted to ask Richard what they were doing in India—the conservative duffers. And what's being acted? And music. . . . Oh yes, and mere gossip.

For this is the truth about our soul, he thought, our self, who fish-like inhabits deep seas and plies among obscurities threading her way between the boles of giant weeds, over sun-flickered spaces and on and on into gloom, cold, deep, inscrutable; suddenly she shoots to the surface and sports on the wind-wrinkled waves; that is, has a positive need to brush, scrape, kindle herself, gossiping. What did the Government mean—Richard Dalloway would know—to do about India?

Since it was a very hot night and the paper boys went by with placards proclaiming in huge red letters that there was a heat-wave, wicker chairs were placed on the hotel steps and there, sipping, smoking, detached gentlemen sat. Peter Walsh sat there. One might fancy that day, the London day, was just beginning. Like a woman who had slipped off her print dress and white apron to array herself in blue and pearls, the day changed, put off stuff, took gauze, changed to evening, and with the same sigh of exhilaration that a woman breathes, tumbling petticoats on the floor, it too shed dust, heat, colour; the traffic thinned; motor cars, tinkling, darting, succeeded the lumber of vans; and here and there among the thick foliage of the squares an intense light hung. I resign, the evening seemed to say, as it paled and faded above the battlements and prominences, moulded, pointed, of hotel, flat, and block of shops, I fade, she was beginning, I disappear, but London would have none of it, and rushed her bayonets into the sky, pinioned her, constrained her to partnership in her revelry.

For the great revolution of Mr Willett's summer time had taken place since Peter Walsh's last visit to England. The prolonged evening was new to him. It was inspiriting, rather. For as the young people went by with their despatch-boxes, awfully glad to be free, proud too, dumbly, of stepping this famous pavement, joy of a kind, cheap, tinselly, if you like, but all the same rapture, flushed their faces. They dressed well too; pink stockings; pretty shoes. They would now have two hours at the pictures. It sharpened, it refined them, the yellow-blue evening light; and on the leaves in the square shone lurid, livid—they looked as if dipped in sea water—the foliage of a submerged city. He was astonished by the beauty; it was encouraging too, for where the returned Anglo-Indian sat by rights (he knew crowds of them) in the Oriental Club biliously summing up the ruin of the world, here was he, as young as ever; envying young people their summer time and the rest of it, and more than suspecting from the words of a girl, from a housemaid's laughter—intangible things you couldn't lay your hands on—that shift in the whole pyramidal accumulation which in his youth had seemed immovable. On top of them it had pressed; weighed them down, the women especially, like those flowers Clarissa's Aunt Helena used to press between sheets of grey blotting-paper with Littré's dictionary on top, sitting under the lamp after dinner. She was dead now.

He had heard of her, from Clarissa, losing the sight of one eye. It seemed so fitting—one of nature's masterpieces—that old Miss Parry should turn to glass. She would die like some bird in a frost gripping her perch. She belonged to a different age, but being so entire, so complete, would always stand up on the horizon, stone-white, eminent, like a lighthouse marking some past stage on this adventurous, long, long voyage, this interminable (he felt for a copper to buy a paper and read about Surrey and Yorkshire—he had held out that copper millions of times. Surrey was all out once more)—this interminable life. But cricket was no mere game. Cricket was important. He could never help reading about cricket. He read the scores in the stop press first, then how it was a hot day; then about a murder case. Having done things millions of times enriched them, though it might be said to take the surface off. The past enriched, and experience, and having cared for one or two people, and so having acquired the power which the young lack, of cutting short, doing what one likes, not caring a rap what people say and coming and going without any very great expectations (he left his paper on the table and moved off), which however (and he looked for his hat and coat) was not altogether true of him, not to-night, for here he was starting to go to a party, at his age, with the belief upon him that he was about to have an experience. But what?

Beauty anyhow. Not the crude beauty of the eye. It was not beauty pure and simple—Bedford Place leading into Russell Square. It was straightness and emptiness of course; the symmetry of a corridor; but it was also windows lit up, a piano, a gramophone sounding; a sense of pleasure-making hidden, but now and again emerging when, through the uncurtained window, the window left open, one saw parties sitting over tables, young people slowly circling, conversations between men and women, maids idly looking out (a strange comment theirs, when work was done), stockings drying on top ledges, a parrot, a few plants. Absorbing, mysterious, of infinite richness, this life. And in the large square where the cabs shot and swerved so quick, there were loitering couples, dallying, embracing, shrunk up under the shower of a tree; that was moving; so silent, so absorbed, that one passed, discreetly, timidly, as if in the presence of some sacred ceremony to interrupt which would have been impious. That was interesting. And so on into the flare and glare.

His light overcoat blew open, he stepped with indescribable idiosyncrasy, leant a little forward, tripped, with his hands behind his back and his eyes still a little hawk-like; he tripped through London, towards Westminster, observing.

Was everybody dining out, then? Doors were being opened here by a footman to let issue a high-stepping old dame, in buckled shoes, with three purple ostrich feathers in her hair. Doors were being opened for ladies wrapped like mummies in shawls with bright flowers on them, ladies with bare heads. And in respectable quarters with stucco pillars through small front gardens lightly swathed with combs in their hair (having run up to see the children), women came; men waited for them, with their coats blowing open, and the motor started. Everybody was going out. What with these doors being opened, and the descent and the start, it seemed as if the whole of London were embarking in little boats moored to the bank, tossing on the waters, as if the whole place were floating off in carnival. And Whitehall was skated over, silver beaten as it was, skated over by spiders, and there was a sense of midges[8] round the arc lamps; it was so hot that people stood about talking. And here in Westminster was a retired Judge, presumably, sitting four square at his house door dressed all in white. An Anglo-Indian presumably.

8. Tiny, gnatlike flying insects.

And here a shindy of brawling women, drunken women; here only a policeman and looming houses, high houses, domed houses, churches, parliaments, and the hoot of a steamer on the river, a hollow misty cry. But it was her street, this, Clarissa's; cabs were rushing round the corner, like water round the piers of a bridge, drawn together, it seemed to him because they bore people going to her party, Clarissa's party.

The cold stream of visual impressions failed him now as if the eye were a cup that overflowed and let the rest run down its china walls unrecorded. The brain must wake now. The body must contract now, entering the house, the lighted house, where the door stood open, where the motor cars were standing, and bright women descending: the soul must brave itself to endure. He opened the big blade of his pocket-knife.

Lucy came running full tilt downstairs, having just nipped in to the drawing-room to smooth a cover, to straighten a chair, to pause a moment and feel whoever came in must think how clean, how bright, how beautifully cared for, when they saw the beautiful silver, the brass fire-irons, the new chair-covers, and the curtains of yellow chintz: she appraised each; heard a roar of voices; people already coming up from dinner; she must fly!

The Prime Minister was coming, Agnes said: so she had heard them say in the dining-room, she said, coming in with a tray of glasses. Did it matter, did it matter in the least, one Prime Minister more or less? It made no difference at this hour of the night to Mrs Walker among the plates, saucepans, cullenders, frying-pans, chicken in aspic, ice-cream freezers, pared crusts of bread, lemons, soup tureens, and pudding basins which, however hard they washed up in the scullery seemed to be all on top of her, on the kitchen table, on chairs, while the fire blared and roared, the electric lights glared, and still supper had to be laid. All she felt was, one Prime Minister more or less made not a scrap of difference to Mrs Walker.

The ladies were going upstairs already, said Lucy; the ladies were going up, one by one, Mrs Dalloway walking last and almost always sending back some message to the kitchen, "My love to Mrs Walker," that was it one night. Next morning they would go over the dishes—the soup, the salmon; the salmon, Mrs Walker knew, as usual underdone, for she always got nervous about the pudding and left it to Jenny; so it happened, the salmon was always underdone. But some lady with fair hair and silver ornaments had said, Lucy said, about the entrée, was it really made at home? But it was the salmon that bothered Mrs Walker, as she spun the plates round and round, and pulled in dampers[9] and pulled out dampers; and there came a burst of laughter from the dining-room; a voice speaking; then another burst of laughter—the gentlemen enjoying themselves when the ladies had gone. The tokay, said Lucy running in. Mr Dalloway had sent for the tokay, from the Emperor's cellars, the Imperial Tokay.[1]

It was borne through the kitchen. Over her shoulder Lucy reported how Miss Elizabeth looked quite lovely; she couldn't take her eyes off her; in her pink dress, wearing the necklace Mr Dalloway had given her. Jenny must remember the dog, Miss Elizabeth's fox-terrier, which, since it bit, had to be shut up and might, Elizabeth thought, want something. Jenny must remember the dog. But Jenny was not going upstairs with all those people about. There was a motor at the door already! There was a ring at the bell—and the gentlemen still in the dining-room, drinking tokay!

9. Movable plates or valves that control the draft in a stove or furnace.

1. A sweet or dry wine made in the vicinity of Tokay, a town in northern Hungary.

There, they were going upstairs; that was the first to come, and now they would come faster and faster, so that Mrs Parkinson (hired for parties) would leave the hall door ajar, and the hall would be full of gentlemen waiting (they stood waiting, sleeking down their hair) while the ladies took their cloaks off in the room along the passage; where Mrs Barnet helped them, old Ellen Barnet, who had been with the family for forty years, and came every summer to help the ladies, and remembered mothers when they were girls, and though very unassuming did shake hands; said "milady" very respectfully, yet had a humorous way with her, looking at the young ladies, and ever so tactfully helping Lady Lovejoy, who had some trouble with her underbodice. And they could not help feeling, Lady Lovejoy and Miss Alice, that some little privilege in the matter of brush and comb, was awarded them having known Mrs Barnet—"thirty years, milady," Mrs Barnet supplied her. Young ladies did not use to rouge, said Lady Lovejoy, when they stayed at Bourton in the old days. And Miss Alice didn't need rouge, said Mrs Barnet, looking at her fondly. There Mrs Barnet would sit, in the cloakroom, patting down the furs, smoothing out the Spanish shawls, tidying the dressing-table, and knowing perfectly well, in spite of the furs and the embroideries, which were nice ladies, which were not. The dear old body, said Lady Lovejoy, mounting the stairs, Clarissa's old nurse.

And then Lady Lovejoy stiffened. "Lady and Miss Lovejoy," she said to Mr Wilkins (hired for parties). He had an admirable manner, as he bent and straightened himself, bent and straightened himself and announced with perfect impartiality "Lady and Miss Lovejoy . . . Sir John and Lady Needham . . . Miss Weld . . . Mr Walsh." His manner was admirable; his family life must be irreproachable, except that it seemed impossible that a being with greenish lips and shaven cheeks could ever have blundered into the nuisance of children.

"How delightful to see you!" said Clarissa. She said it to every one. How delightful to see you! She was at her worst—effusive, insincere. It was a great mistake to have come. He should have stayed at home and read his book, thought Peter Walsh; should have gone to a music hall; he should have stayed at home, for he knew no one.

Oh dear, it was going to be a failure; a complete failure, Clarissa felt it in her bones as dear old Lord Lexham stood there apologising for his wife who had caught cold at the Buckingham Palace garden party. She could see Peter out of the tail of her eye, criticising her, there, in that corner. Why, after all, did she do these things? Why seek pinnacles and stand drenched in fire? Might it consume her anyhow! Burn her to cinders! Better anything, better brandish one's torch and hurl it to earth than taper and dwindle away like some Ellie Henderson! It was extraordinary how Peter put her into these states just by coming and standing in a corner. He made her see herself; exaggerate. It was idiotic. But why did he come, then, merely to criticise? Why always take, never give? Why not risk one's one little point of view? There he was wandering off, and she must speak to him. But she would not get the chance. Life was that—humiliation, renunciation. What Lord Lexham was saying was that his wife would not wear her furs at the garden party because "my dear, you ladies are all alike"—Lady Lexham being seventy-five at least! It was delicious, how they petted each other, that old couple. She did like old Lord Lexham. She did think it mattered, her party, and it made her feel quite sick to know that it was all going wrong, all falling flat. Anything, any explosion, any horror was better than people wandering aimlessly, standing in a bunch at a corner like Ellie Henderson, not even caring to hold themselves upright.

Gently the yellow curtain with all the birds of Paradise blew out and it seemed as if there were a flight of wings into the room, right out, then sucked back. (For the windows were open.) Was it draughty, Ellie Henderson wondered? She was subject to chills. But it did not matter that she should come down sneezing tomorrow; it was the girls with their naked shoulders she thought of, being trained to think of others by an old father, an invalid, late vicar of Bourton, but he was dead now; and her chills never went to her chest, never. It was the girls she thought of, the young girls with their bare shoulders, she herself having always been a wisp of a creature, with her thin hair and meagre profile; though now, past fifty, there was beginning to shine through some mild beam, something purified into distinction by years of self-abnegation but obscured again, perpetually, by her distressing gentility, her panic fear, which arose from three hundred pounds' income, and her weaponless state (she could not earn a penny) and it made her timid, and more and more disqualified year by year to meet well-dressed people who did this sort of thing every night of the season, merely telling their maids "I'll wear so and so," whereas Ellie Henderson ran out nervously and bought cheap pink flowers, half a dozen, and then threw a shawl over her old black dress. For her invitation to Clarissa's party had come at the last moment. She was not quite happy about it. She had a sort of feeling that Clarissa had not meant to ask her this year.

Why should she? There was no reason really, except that they had always known each other. Indeed, they were cousins. But naturally they had rather drifted apart, Clarissa being so sought after. It was an event to her, going to a party. It was quite a treat just to see the lovely clothes. Wasn't that Elizabeth, grown up, with her hair done in the fashionable way, in the pink dress? Yet she could not be more than seventeen. She was very, very handsome. But girls when they first came out didn't seem to wear white as they used. (She must remember everything to tell Edith.) Girls wore straight frocks, perfectly tight, with skirts well above the ankles. It was not becoming, she thought.

So, with her weak eyesight, Ellie Henderson craned rather forward, and it wasn't so much she who minded not having any one to talk to (she hardly knew anybody there), for she felt that they were all such interesting people to watch; politicians presumably; Richard Dalloway's friends; but it was Richard himself who felt that he could not let the poor creature go on standing there all the evening by herself.

"Well, Ellie, and how's the world treating *you?*" he said in his genial way, and Ellie Henderson, getting nervous and flushing and feeling that it was extraordinarily nice of him to come and talk to her, said that many people really felt the heat more than the cold.

"Yes, they do," said Richard Dalloway. "Yes."

But what more did one say?

"Hullo, Richard," said somebody, taking him by the elbow, and, good Lord, there was old Peter, old Peter Walsh. He was delighted to see him—ever so pleased to see him! He hadn't changed a bit. And off they went together walking right across the room, giving each other little pats, as if they hadn't met for a long time, Ellie Henderson thought, watching them go, certain she knew that man's face. A tall man, middle aged, rather fine eyes, dark, wearing spectacles, with a look of John Burrows. Edith would be sure to know.

The curtain with its flight of birds of Paradise blew out again. And Clarissa saw—she saw Ralph Lyon beat it back, and go on talking. So it wasn't a failure after all! it was going to be all right now—her party. It had begun. It had started. But it was still touch and go. She must stand there for the present. People seemed to come in a rush.

Colonel and Mrs Garrod . . . Mr Hugh Whitbread . . . Mr Bowley . . . Mrs Hilbery . . . Lady Mary Maddox . . . Mr Quin . . . intoned Wilkin. She had six or seven words with each, and they went on, they went into the rooms; into something now, not nothing, since Ralph Lyon had beat back the curtain.

And yet for her own part, it was too much of an effort. She was not enjoying it. It was too much like being—just anybody, standing there; anybody could do it; yet this anybody she did a little admire, couldn't help feeling that she had, anyhow, made this happen, that it marked a stage, this post that she felt herself to have become, for oddly enough she had quite forgotten what she looked like, but felt herself a stake driven in at the top of her stairs. Every time she gave a party she had this feeling of being something not herself, and that every one was unreal in one way; much more real in another. It was, she thought, partly their clothes, partly being taken out of their ordinary ways, partly the background, it was possible to say things you couldn't say anyhow else, things that needed an effort; possible to go much deeper. But not for her; not yet anyhow.

"How delightful to see you!" she said. Dear old Sir Harry! He would know every one.

And what was so odd about it was the sense one had as they came up the stairs one after another, Mrs Mount and Celia, Herbert Ainsty, Mrs Dakers—oh and Lady Bruton!

"How awfully good of you to come!" she said, and she meant it—it was odd how standing there one felt them going on, going on, some quite old, some . . . .

What name? Lady Rosseter? But who on earth was Lady Rosseter?

"Clarissa!" That voice! It was Sally Seton! Sally Seton! after all these years! She loomed through a mist. For she hadn't looked like *that*, Sally Seton, when Clarissa grasped the hot water can, to think of her under this roof, under this roof! Not like that!

All on top of each other, embarrassed, laughing, words tumbled out—passing through London; heard from Clara Haydon; what a chance of seeing you! So I thrust myself in—without an invitation. . . .

One might put down the hot water can quite composedly. The lustre had gone out of her. Yet it was extraordinary to see her again, older, happier, less lovely. They kissed each other, first this cheek then that, by the drawing-room door, and Clarissa turned, with Sally's hand in hers, and saw her rooms full, heard the roar of voices, saw the candlesticks, the blowing curtains, and the roses which Richard had given her.

"I have five enormous boys," said Sally.

She had the simplest egotism, the most open desire to be thought first always, and Clarissa loved her for being still like that. "I can't believe it!" she cried, kindling all over with pleasure at the thought of the past.

But alas, Wilkins; Wilkins wanted her; Wilkins was emitting in a voice of commanding authority as if the whole company must be admonished and the hostess reclaimed from frivolity, one name:

"The Prime Minister," said Peter Walsh.

The Prime Minister? Was it really? Ellie Henderson marvelled. What a thing to tell Edith!

One couldn't laugh at him. He looked so ordinary. You might have stood him behind a counter and bought biscuits—poor chap, all rigged up in gold lace. And to be fair, as he went his rounds, first with Clarissa then with Richard escorting him, he did it very well. He tried to look somebody. It was amusing to watch. Nobody looked at him. They just went on talking, yet it was perfectly plain that they all knew, felt to the marrow of their bones, this majesty passing; this symbol of what they all stood for,

English society. Old Lady Bruton, and she looked very fine too, very stalwart in her lace, swam up, and they withdrew into a little room which at once became spied upon, guarded, and a sort of stir and rustle rippled through every one, openly: the Prime Minister!

Lord, lord, the snobbery of the English! thought Peter Walsh, standing in the corner. How they loved dressing up in gold lace and doing homage! There! That must be, by Jove it was, Hugh Whitbread, snuffing round the precincts of the great, grown rather fatter, rather whiter, the admirable Hugh!

He looked always as if he were on duty, thought Peter, a privileged, but secretive being, hoarding secrets which he would die to defend, though it was only some little piece of tittle-tattle dropped by a court footman, which would be in all the papers to-morrow. Such were his rattles, his baubles, in playing with which he had grown white, come to the verge of old age, enjoying the respect and affection of all who had the privilege of knowing this type of the English public school man. Inevitably one made up things like that about Hugh; that was his style; the style of those admirable letters which Peter had read thousands of miles across the sea in the *Times*, and had thanked God he was out of that pernicious hubble-bubble if it were only to hear baboons chatter and coolies beat their wives. An olive-skinned youth from one of the Universities stood obsequiously by. Him he would patronise, initiate, teach how to get on. For he liked nothing better than doing kindnesses, making the hearts of old ladies palpitate with the joy of being thought of in their age, their affliction, thinking themselves quite forgotten, yet here was dear Hugh driving up and spending an hour talking of the past, remembering trifles, praising the homemade cake, though Hugh might eat cake with a Duchess any day of his life, and, to look at him, probably did spend a good deal of time in that agreeable occupation. The All-judging, the All-merciful, might excuse. Peter Walsh had no mercy. Villains there must be, and God knows the rascals who get hanged for battering the brains of a girl out in a train do less harm on the whole than Hugh Whitbread and his kindness. Look at him now, on tiptoe, dancing forward, bowing and scraping, as the Prime Minister and Lady Bruton emerged, intimating for all the world to see that he was privileged to say something, something private, to Lady Bruton as she passed. She stopped. She wagged her fine old head. She was thanking him presumably for some piece of servility. She had her toadies, minor officials in Government offices who ran about putting through little jobs on her behalf, in return for which she gave them luncheon. But she derived from the eighteenth century. She was all right.

And now Clarissa escorted her Prime Minister down the room, prancing, sparkling, with the stateliness of her grey hair. She wore ear-rings, and a silver-green mermaid's dress. Lolloping on the waves and braiding her tresses she seemed, having that gift still; to be; to exist; to sum it all up in the moment as she passed; turned, caught her scarf in some other woman's dress, unhitched it, laughed, all with the most perfect ease and air of a creature floating in its element. But age had brushed her; even as a mermaid might behold in her glass the setting sun on some very clear evening over the waves. There was a breath of tenderness; her severity, her prudery, her woodenness were all warmed through now, and she had about her as she said good-bye to the thick gold-laced man who was doing his best, and good luck to him, to look important, an inexpressible dignity; an exquisite cordiality; as if she wished the whole world well, and must now, being on the very verge and rim of things, take her leave. So she made him think. (But he was not in love.)

Indeed, Clarissa felt, the Prime Minister had been good to come. And, walking down the room with him, with Sally there and Peter there and Richard very pleased, with all those people rather inclined, perhaps, to envy, she had felt that intoxication of the moment, that dilatation of the nerves of the heart itself till it seemed to quiver, steeped, upright;—yes, but after all it was what other people felt, that; for, though she loved it and felt it tingle and sting, still these semblances, these triumphs (dear old Peter, for example, thinking her so brilliant), had a hollowness; at arm's length they were, not in the heart; and it might be that she was growing old but they satisfied her no longer as they used; and suddenly, as she saw the Prime Minister go down the stairs, the gilt rim of the Sir Joshua picture of the little girl with a muff brought back Kilman with a rush; Kilman her enemy. That was satisfying; that was real. Ah, how she hated her—hot, hypocritical, corrupt; with all that power; Elizabeth's seducer; the woman who had crept in to steal and defile (Richard would say, What nonsense!). She hated her: she loved her. It was enemies one wanted, not friends—not Mrs Durrant and Clara, Sir William and Lady Bradshaw, Miss Truelock and Eleanor Gibson (whom she saw coming upstairs). They must find her if they wanted her. She was for the party!

There was her old friend Sir Harry.

"Dear Sir Harry!" she said, going up to the fine old fellow who had produced more bad pictures than any other two Academicians in the whole of St John's Wood (they were always of cattle, standing in sunset pools absorbing moisture, or signifying, for he had a certain range of gesture, by the raising of one foreleg and the toss of the antlers, "the Approach of the Stranger"—all his activities, dining out, racing, were founded on cattle standing absorbing moisture in sunset pools).

"What are you laughing at?" she asked him. For Willie Titcomb and Sir Harry and Herbert Ainsty were all laughing. But no. Sir Harry could not tell Clarissa Dalloway (much though he liked her; of her type he thought her perfect, and threatened to paint her) his stories of the music hall stage. He chaffed her about her party. He missed his brandy. These circles, he said, were above him. But he liked her; respected her, in spite of her damnable, difficult upper-class refinement, which made it impossible to ask Clarissa Dalloway to sit on his knee. And up came that wandering will-o'-the-wisp, that vagulous phosphorescence, old Mrs Hilbery, stretching her hands to the blaze of his laughter (about the Duke and the Lady), which, as she heard it across the room, seemed to reassure her on a point which sometimes bothered her if she woke early in the morning and did not like to call her maid for a cup of tea; how it is certain we must die.

"They won't tell us their stories," said Clarissa.

"Dear Clarissa!" exclaimed Mrs Hilbery. She looked to-night, she said, so like her mother as she first saw her walking in a garden in a grey hat.

And really Clarissa's eyes filled with tears. Her mother, walking in a garden! But alas, she must go.

For there was Professor Brierly, who lectured on Milton, talking to little Jim Hutton (who was unable even for a party like this to compass both tie and waist-coat or make his hair lie flat), and even at this distance they were quarrelling, she could see. For Professor Brierly was a very queer fish. With all those degrees, honours, lectureships between him and the scribblers he suspected instantly an atmosphere not favourable to his queer compound; his prodigious learning and timidity; his wintry charm without cordiality; his innocence blent with snobbery; he quivered if made conscious by a lady's unkempt hair, a youth's boots, of an underworld, very creditable doubtless, of rebels, of ardent young people; of would-be geniuses, and intimated with a little toss of the head, with a sniff—Humph!—the value of moderation; of some slight training in the classics in order to appreciate Milton. Professor Brierly (Clarissa could see) wasn't hitting it off with little Jim Hutton (who wore red socks, his black being at the laundry) about Milton. She interrupted.

She said she loved Bach. So did Hutton. That was the bond between them, and Hutton (a very bad poet) always felt that Mrs Dalloway was far the best of the great ladies who took an interest in art. It was odd how strict she was. About music she was purely impersonal. She was rather a prig. But how charming to look at! She made her house so nice if it weren't for her Professors. Clarissa had half a mind to snatch him off and set him down at the piano in the back room. For he played divinely.

"But the noise!" she said. "The noise!"

"The sign of a successful party." Nodding urbanely, the Professor stepped delicately off.

"He knows everything in the whole world about Milton," said Clarissa.

"Does he indeed?" said Hutton, who would imitate the Professor throughout Hampstead; the Professor on Milton; the Professor on moderation; the Professor stepping delicately off.

But she must speak to that couple, said Clarissa, Lord Gayton and Nancy Blow.

Not that *they* added perceptibly to the noise of the party. They were not talking (perceptibly) as they stood side by side by the yellow curtains. They would soon be off elsewhere, together; and never had very much to say in any circumstances. They looked; that was enough. They looked so clean, so sound, she with an apricot bloom of powder and paint, but he scrubbed, rinsed, with the eyes of a bird, so that no ball could pass him or stroke surprise him. He struck, he leapt, accurately, on the spot. Ponies' mouths quivered at the end of his reins. He had his honours, ancestral monuments, banners hanging in the church at home. He had his duties; his tenants; a mother and sisters; had been all day at Lords, and that was what they were talking about—cricket, cousins, the movies—when Mrs Dalloway came up. Lord Gayton liked her most awfully. So did Miss Blow. She had such charming manners.

"It is angelic—it is delicious of you to have come!" she said. She loved Lords; she loved youth, and Nancy, dressed at enormous expense by the greatest artists in Paris, stood there looking as if her body had merely put forth, of its own accord, a green frill.

"I had meant to have dancing," said Clarissa.

For the young people could not talk. And why should they? Shout, embrace, swing, be up at dawn; carry sugar to ponies; kiss and caress the snouts of adorable chows; and then all tingling and streaming, plunge and swim. But the enormous resources of the English language, the power it bestows, after all, of communicating feelings (at their age, she and Peter would have been arguing all the evening), was not for them. They would solidify young. They would be good beyond measure to the people on the estate, but alone, perhaps, rather dull.

"What a pity!" she said. "I had hoped to have dancing."

It was so extraordinarily nice of them to have come! But talk of dancing! The rooms were packed.

There was old Aunt Helena in her shawl. Alas, she must leave them—Lord Gayton and Nancy Blow. There was old Miss Parry, her aunt.

For Miss Helena Parry was not dead: Miss Parry was alive. She was past eighty. She ascended staircases slowly with a stick. She was placed in a chair (Richard had seen to it). People who had known Burma in the 'seventies were always led up to her. Where had Peter got to? They used to be such friends. For at the mention of India, or even Ceylon, her eyes (only one was glass) slowly deepened, became blue, beheld, not human beings—she had no tender memories, no proud illusions about Viceroys, Generals, Mutinies—it was orchids she saw, and mountain passes and herself carried on the backs of coolies in the 'sixties over solitary peaks; or descending to uproot orchids (startling blossoms, never beheld before) which she painted in water-colour; an indomitable Englishwoman, fretful if disturbed by the War, say, which dropped a bomb at her very door, from her deep meditation over orchids and her own figure journeying in the 'sixties in India—but here was Peter.

"Come and talk to Aunt Helena about Burma," said Clarissa.

And yet he had not had a word with her all the evening!

"We will talk later," said Clarissa, leading him up to Aunt Helena, in her white shawl, with her stick.

"Peter Walsh," said Clarissa.

That meant nothing.

Clarissa had asked her. It was tiring; it was noisy; but Clarissa had asked her. So she had come. It was a pity that they lived in London—Richard and Clarissa. If only for Clarissa's health it would have been better to live in the country. But Clarissa had always been fond of society.

"He has been in Burma," said Clarissa.

Ah. She could not resist recalling what Charles Darwin had said about her little book on the orchids of Burma.

(Clarissa must speak to Lady Bruton.)

No doubt it was forgotten now, her book on the orchids of Burma, but it went into three editions before 1870, she told Peter. She remembered him now. He had been at Bourton (and he had left her, Peter Walsh remembered, without a word in the drawing-room that night when Clarissa had asked him to come boating).

"Richard so much enjoyed his lunch party," said Clarissa to Lady Bruton.

"Richard was the greatest possible help," Lady Bruton replied. "He helped me to write a letter. And how are you?"

"Oh, perfectly well!" said Clarissa. (Lady Bruton detested illness in the wives of politicians.)

"And there's Peter Walsh!" said Lady Bruton (for she could never think of anything to say to Clarissa; though she liked her. She had lots of fine qualities; but they had nothing in common—she and Clarissa. It might have been better if Richard had married a woman with less charm, who would have helped him more in his work. He had lost his chance of the Cabinet). "There's Peter Walsh!" she said, shaking hands with that agreeable sinner, that very able fellow who should have made a name for himself but hadn't (always in difficulties with women), and, of course, old Miss Parry. Wonderful old lady!

Lady Bruton stood by Miss Parry's chair, a spectral grenadier, draped in black, inviting Peter Walsh to lunch; cordial; but without small talk, remembering nothing whatever about the flora or fauna of India. She had been there, of course; had stayed with three Viceroys; thought some of the Indian civilians uncommonly fine fellows; but what a tragedy it was—the state of India! The Prime Minister had just been telling her (old Miss Parry huddled up in her shawl, did not care what the Prime Minister had just been telling her), and Lady Bruton would like to have Peter Walsh's opinion, he being fresh from the centre, and she would get Sir Sampson to meet him, for really it prevented her from sleeping at night, the folly of it, the wickedness she might say, being a soldier's daughter. She was an old woman now, not good for much. But her house, her servants, her good friend Milly Brush—did he remember her?—were all there only asking to be used if—if they could be of help, in short. For she never spoke of England, but this isle of men, this dear, dear land, was in her blood (without reading Shakespeare),[2] and if ever a woman could have worn the helmet and shot the arrow, could have led troops to attack, ruled with indomitable justice barbarian hordes and lain under a shield noseless in a church, or made a green grass mound on some primeval hillside, that woman was Millicent Bruton. Debarred by her sex and some truancy, too, of the logical faculty (she found it impossible to write a letter to the *Times*), she had the thought of Empire always at hand, and had acquired from her association with that armoured goddess her ramrod bearing, her robustness of demeanour, so that one could not figure her even in death parted from the earth or roaming territories over which, in some spiritual shape, the Union Jack had ceased to fly. To be not English even among the dead—no, no! Impossible!

But was it Lady Bruton (whom she used to know)? Was it Peter Walsh grown grey? Lady Rosseter asked herself (who had been Sally Seton). It was old Miss Parry certainly—the old aunt who used to be so cross when she stayed at Bourton. Never should she forget running along the passage naked, and being sent for by Miss Parry! And Clarissa! oh Clarissa! Sally caught her by the arm.

Clarissa stopped beside them.

"But I can't stay," she said. "I shall come later. Wait," she said, looking at Peter and Sally. They must wait, she meant, until all these people had gone.

"I shall come back," she said, looking at her old friends, Sally and Peter, who were shaking hands, and Sally, remembering the past no doubt, was laughing.

But her voice was wrung of its old ravishing richness; her eyes not aglow as they used to be, when she smoked cigars, when she ran down the passage to fetch her sponge bag, without a stitch of clothing on her, and Ellen Atkins asked, What if the gentlemen had met her? But everybody forgave her. She stole a chicken from the larder because she was hungry in the night; she smoked cigars in her bedroom; she left a priceless book in the punt.[3] But everybody adored her (except perhaps Papa). It was her warmth; her vitality—she would paint, she would write. Old women in the village never to this day forgot to ask after "your friend in the red cloak who seemed so bright." She accused Hugh Whitbread, of all people (and there he was, her old friend Hugh, talking to the Portuguese Ambassador), of kissing her in the smoking-room to punish her for saying that women should have votes. Vulgar men did, she said. And Clarissa remembered having to persuade her not to denounce him at family prayers—which she was capable of doing with her daring, her recklessness, her melodramatic love of being the centre of everything and creating scenes, and it was bound, Clarissa used to think, to end in some awful tragedy; her death; her martyrdom; instead of which she had married, quite unexpectedly, a bald man with a large buttonhole who owned, it was said, cotton mills at Manchester. And she had five boys!

She and Peter had settled down together. They were talking: it seemed so familiar—that they should be talking. They would discuss the past. With the two of them (more even than with Richard) she shared her past; the garden; the trees; old Joseph

2. Lady Bruton intuitively refers to John of Gaunt's extravagant catalogue of patriotic descriptors in *Richard II* 2.1:

This royal throne of kings, this sceptred isle . . .
This happy breed of men, this little world . . .
This blessed plot, this earth, this realm, this England . . .
This land of such dear souls, this dear dear land. . . .

That she incorporates these terms into her celebration of empire is ironic given the grim prophecy with which Gaunt concludes: "That England that was wont to conquer others / Hath made a shameful conquest of itself."

3. A flat-bottomed boat with broad, square ends, usually propelled using a long pole.

Breitkopf singing Brahms without any voice; the drawing-room wall-paper; the smell of the mats. A part of this Sally must always be; Peter must always be. But she must leave them. There were the Bradshaws, whom she disliked. She must go up to Lady Bradshaw (in grey and silver, balancing like a sea-lion at the edge of its tank, barking for invitations, Duchesses, the typical successful man's wife), she must go up to Lady Bradshaw and say . . .

But Lady Bradshaw anticipated her.

"We are shockingly late, dear Mrs Dalloway, we hardly dared to come in," she said.

And Sir William, who looked very distinguished, with his grey hair and blue eyes, said yes; they had not been able to resist the temptation. He was talking to Richard about that Bill probably, which they wanted to get through the Commons. Why did the sight of him, talking to Richard, curl her up? He looked what he was, a great doctor. A man absolutely at the head of his profession, very powerful, rather worn. For think what cases came before him—people in the uttermost depths of misery; people on the verge of insanity; husbands and wives. He had to decide questions of appalling difficulty. Yet—what she felt was, one wouldn't like Sir William to see one unhappy. No; not that man.

"How is your son at Eton?" she asked Lady Bradshaw.

He had just missed his eleven, said Lady Bradshaw, because of the mumps. His father minded even more than he did, she thought "being," she said, "nothing but a great boy himself."

Clarissa looked at Sir William, talking to Richard. He did not look like a boy—not in the least like a boy. She had once gone with some one to ask his advice. He had been perfectly right; extremely sensible. But Heavens—what a relief to get out to the street again! There was some poor wretch sobbing, she remembered, in the waiting-room. But she did not know what it was—about Sir William; what exactly she disliked. Only Richard agreed with her, "didn't like his taste, didn't like his smell." But he was extraordinarily able. They were talking about this Bill. Some case, Sir William was mentioning, lowering his voice. It had its bearing upon what he was saying about the deferred effects of shell shock. There must be some provision in the Bill.

Sinking her voice, drawing Mrs Dalloway into the shelter of a common femininity, a common pride in the illustrious qualities of husbands and their sad tendency to overwork, Lady Bradshaw (poor goose—one didn't dislike her) murmured how, "just as we were starting, my husband was called up on the telephone, a very sad case. A young man (that is what Sir William is telling Mr Dalloway) had killed himself. He had been in the army." Oh! thought Clarissa, in the middle of my party, here's death, she thought.

She went on, into the little room where the Prime Minister had gone with Lady Bruton. Perhaps there was somebody there. But there was nobody. The chairs still kept the impress of the Prime Minister and Lady Bruton, she turned deferentially, he sitting four-square, authoritatively. They had been talking about India. There was nobody. The party's splendour fell to the floor, so strange it was to come in alone in her finery.

What business had the Bradshaws to talk of death at her party? A young man had killed himself. And they talked of it at her party—the Bradshaws, talked of death. He had killed himself—but how? Always her body went through it first, when she was told, suddenly, of an accident; her dress flamed, her body burnt. He had thrown himself from a window. Up had flashed the ground; through him, blundering, bruising, went the rusty spikes. There he lay with a thud, thud, thud in his brain, and then a suffocation of blackness. So she saw it. But why had he done it? And the Bradshaws talked of it at her party!

She had once thrown a shilling into the Serpentine, never anything more. But he had flung it away. They went on living (she would have to go back; the rooms were still crowded; people kept on coming). They (all day she had been thinking of Bourton, of Peter, of Sally), they would grow old. A thing there was that mattered; a thing, wreathed about with chatter, defaced, obscured in her own life, let drop every day in corruption, lies, chatter. This he had preserved. Death was defiance. Death was an attempt to communicate; people feeling the impossibility of reaching the centre which, mystically, evaded them; closeness drew apart; rapture faded, one was alone. There was an embrace in death.

But this young man who had killed himself—had he plunged holding his treasure? "If it were now to die, 'twere now to be most happy," she had said to herself once, coming down in white.

Or there were the poets and thinkers. Suppose he had had that passion, and had gone to Sir William Bradshaw, a great doctor yet to her obscurely evil, without sex or lust, extremely polite to women, but capable of some indescribable outrage—forcing your soul, that was it—if this young man had gone to him, and Sir William had impressed[4] him, like that, with his power, might he not then have said (indeed she felt it now), Life is made intolerable; they make life intolerable, men like that?

Then (she had felt it only this morning) there was the terror; the overwhelming incapacity, one's parents giving it into one's hands, this life, to be lived to the end, to be walked with serenely; there was in the depths of her heart an awful fear. Even now, quite often if Richard had not been there reading the *Times*, so that she could crouch like a bird and gradually revive, send roaring up that immeasurable delight, rubbing stick to stick, one thing with another, she must have perished. But that young man had killed himself.

Somehow it was her disaster—her disgrace. It was her punishment to see sink and disappear here a man, there a woman, in this profound darkness, and she forced to stand here in her evening dress. She had schemed; she had pilfered. She was never wholly admirable. She had wanted success. Lady Bexborough and the rest of it. And once she had walked on the terrace at Bourton.

It was due to Richard; she had never been so happy. Nothing could be slow enough; nothing last too long. No pleasure could equal, she thought, straightening the chairs, pushing in one book on the shelf, this having done with the triumphs of youth, lost herself in the process of living, to find it, with a shock of delight, as the sun rose, as the day sank. Many a time had she gone, at Bourton when they were all talking, to look at the sky; or seen it between people's shoulders at dinner; seen it in London when she could not sleep. She walked to the window.

It held, foolish as the idea was, something of her own in it, this country sky, this sky above Westminster. She parted the curtains; she looked. Oh, but how surprising!—in the room opposite the old lady stared straight at her! She was going to bed. And the sky. It will be a solemn sky, she had thought, it will be a dusky sky, turning away its cheek in beauty. But there it was—ashen pale, raced over quickly by

4. Given the cause of Septimus's condition, "impress" here may suggest both the usual meaning of the word (i.e., that Sir William had a marked effect on Septimus) and, figuratively, an older sense of it, meaning "to force a person into public, especially military service."

tapering vast clouds. It was new to her. The wind must have risen. She was going to bed, in the room opposite. It was fascinating to watch her, moving about, that old lady, crossing the room, coming to the window. Could she see her? It was fascinating, with people still laughing and shouting in the drawing-room, to watch that old woman, quite quietly, going to bed. She pulled the blind now. The clock began striking. The young man had killed himself; but she did not pity him; with the clock striking the hour, one, two, three, she did not pity him, with all this going on. There! the old lady had put out her light! the whole house was dark now with this going on, she repeated, and the words came to her, Fear no more the heat of the sun. She must go back to them. But what an extraordinary night! She felt somehow very like him—the young man who had killed himself. She felt glad that he had done it; thrown it away. The clock was striking. The leaden circles dissolved in the air. He made her feel the beauty; made her feel the fun. But she must go back. She must assemble. She must find Sally and Peter. And she came in from the little room.

"But where is Clarissa?" said Peter. He was sitting on the sofa with Sally. (After all these years he really could not call her "Lady Rosseter.") "Where's the woman gone to?" he asked. "Where's Clarissa?"

Sally supposed, and so did Peter for the matter of that, that there were people of importance, politicians, whom neither of them knew unless by sight in the picture papers, whom Clarissa had to be nice to, had to talk to. She was with them. Yet there was Richard Dalloway not in the Cabinet. He hadn't been a success, Sally supposed? For herself, she scarcely ever read the papers. She sometimes saw his name mentioned. But then—well, she lived a very solitary life, in the wilds, Clarissa would say, among great merchants, great manufacturers, men, after all, who did things. She had done things too!

"I have five sons!" she told him.

Lord, Lord, what a change had come over her! the softness of motherhood; its egotism too. Last time they met, Peter remembered, had been among the cauliflowers in the moonlight, the leaves "like rough bronze" she had said, with her literary turn; and she had picked a rose. She had marched him up and down that awful night, after the scene by the fountain; he was to catch the midnight train. Heavens, he had wept!

That was his old trick, opening a pocket-knife, thought Sally, always opening and shutting a knife when he got excited. They had been very, very intimate, she and Peter Walsh, when he was in love with Clarissa, and there was that dreadful, ridiculous scene over Richard Dalloway at lunch. She had called Richard "Wickham." Why not call Richard "Wickham"? Clarissa had flared up! and indeed they had never seen each other since, she and Clarissa, not more than half a dozen times perhaps in the last ten years. And Peter Walsh had gone off to India, and she had heard vaguely that he had made an unhappy marriage, and she didn't know whether he had any children, and she couldn't ask him, for he had changed. He was rather shrivelled-looking, but kinder, she felt, and she had a real affection for him, for he was connected with her youth, and she still had a little Emily Brontë he had given her, and he was to write, surely? In those days he was to write.

"Have you written?" she asked him, spreading her hand, her firm and shapely hand, on her knee in a way he recalled.

"Not a word!" said Peter Walsh, and she laughed.

She was still attractive, still a personage, Sally Seton. But who was this Rosseter? He wore two camellias on his wedding day—that was all Peter knew of him. "They have myriads of servants, miles of conservatories," Clarissa wrote; something like that. Sally owned it with a shout of laughter.

"Yes, I have ten thousand a year"—whether before the tax was paid or after, she couldn't remember, for her husband, "whom you must meet," she said, "whom you would like," she said, did all that for her.

And Sally used to be in rags and tatters. She had pawned her grandmother's ring which Marie Antoinette had given her great-grandfather to come to Bourton.

Oh yes, Sally remembered; she had it still, a ruby ring which Marie Antoinette had given her great-grandfather. She never had a penny to her name in those days, and going to Bourton always meant some frightful pinch. But going to Bourton had meant so much to her—had kept her sane, she believed, so unhappy had she been at home. But that was all a thing of the past—all over now, she said. And Mr Parry was dead; and Miss Parry was still alive. Never had he had such a shock in his life! said Peter. He had been quite certain she was dead. And the marriage had been, Sally supposed, a success? And that very handsome, very self-possessed young woman was Elizabeth, over there, by the curtains, in red.

(She was like a poplar, she was like a river, she was like a hyacinth, Willie Titcomb was thinking. Oh how much nicer to be in the country and do what she liked! She could hear her poor dog howling, Elizabeth was certain.) She was not a bit like Clarissa, Peter Walsh said.

"Oh, Clarissa!" said Sally.

What Sally felt was simply this. She had owed Clarissa an enormous amount. They had been friends, not acquaintances, friends, and she still saw Clarissa all in white going about the house with her hands full of flowers—to this day tobacco plants made her think of Bourton. But—did Peter understand?—she lacked something. Lacked what was it? She had charm; she had extraordinary charm. But to be frank (and she felt that Peter was an old friend, a real friend—did absence matter? did distance matter? She had often wanted to write to him, but torn it up, yet felt he understood, for people understand without things being said, as one realises growing old, and old she was, had been that afternoon to see her sons at Eton, where they had the mumps), to be quite frank then, how could Clarissa have done it?—married Richard Dalloway? a sportsman, a man who cared only for dogs. Literally, when he came into the room he smelt of the stables. And then all this? She waved her hand.

Hugh Whitbread it was, strolling past in his white waistcoat, dim, fat, blind, past everything he looked, except self-esteem and comfort.

"He's not going to recognise *us*," said Sally, and really she hadn't the courage—so that was Hugh! the admirable Hugh!

"And what does he do?" she asked Peter.

He blacked the King's boots or counted bottles at Windsor, Peter told her. Peter kept his sharp tongue still! But Sally must be frank, Peter said. That kiss now, Hugh's.

On the lips, she assured him, in the smoking-room one evening. She went straight to Clarissa in a rage. Hugh didn't do such things! Clarissa said, the admirable Hugh! Hugh's socks were without exception the most beautiful she had ever seen—and now his evening dress. Perfect! And had he children?

"Everybody in the room has six sons at Eton," Peter told her, except himself. He, thank God, had none. No sons, no daughters, no wife. Well, he didn't seem to mind, said Sally. He looked younger, she thought, than any of them.

But it had been a silly thing to do, in many ways, Peter said, to marry like that; "a perfect goose she was," he said, but, he said, "we had a splendid time of it," but how could that be? Sally wondered; what did he mean? and how odd it was to know him and yet not know a single thing that had happened to him. And did he say it out of pride? Very likely, for after all it must be galling for him (though he was an oddity, a sort of sprite, not at all an ordinary man), it must be lonely at his age to have no home, nowhere to go to. But he must stay with them for weeks and weeks. Of course he would; he would love to stay with them, and that was how it came out. All these years the Dalloways had never been once. Time after time they had asked them. Clarissa (for it was Clarissa of course) would not come. For, said Sally, Clarissa was at heart a snob—one had to admit it, a snob. And it was that that was between them, she was convinced. Clarissa thought she had married beneath her, her husband being—she was proud of it—a miner's son. Every penny they had he had earned. As a little boy (her voice trembled) he had carried great sacks.

(And so she would go on, Peter felt, hour after hour; the miner's son; people thought she had married beneath her; her five sons; and what was the other thing—plants, hydrangeas, syringas, very, very rare hibiscus lilies that never grow north of the Suez Canal, but she, with one gardener in a suburb near Manchester, had beds of them, positively beds! Now all that Clarissa had escaped, unmaternal as she was.)

A snob was she? Yes, in many ways. Where was she, all this time? It was getting late.

"Yet," said Sally, "when I heard Clarissa was giving a party, I felt I couldn't *not* come—must see her again (and I'm staying in Victoria Street, practically next door). So I just came without an invitation. But," she whispered, "tell me, do. Who is this?"

It was Mrs Hilbery, looking for the door. For how late it was getting! And, she murmured, as the night grew later, as people went, one found old friends; quiet nooks and corners; and the loveliest views. Did they know, she asked, that they were surrounded by an enchanted garden? Lights and trees and wonderful gleaming lakes and the sky. Just a few fairy lamps, Clarissa Dalloway had said, in the back garden! But she was a magician! It was a park. . . . And she didn't know their names, but friends she knew they were, friends without names, songs without words, always the best. But there were so many doors, such unexpected places, she could not find her way.

"Old Mrs Hilbery," said Peter; but who was that? that lady standing by the curtain all the evening, without speaking? He knew her face; connected her with Bourton. Surely she used to cut up underclothes at the large table in the window? Davidson, was that her name?

"Oh, that is Ellie Henderson," said Sally. Clarissa was really very hard on her. She was a cousin, very poor. Clarissa *was* hard on people.

She was rather, said Peter. Yet, said Sally, in her emotional way, with a rush of that enthusiasm which Peter used to love her for, yet dreaded a little now, so effusive she might become—how generous to her friends Clarissa was! and what a rare quality one found it, and how sometimes at night or on Christmas Day, when she counted up her blessings, she put that friendship first. They were young; that was it. Clarissa was pure-hearted; that was it. Peter would think her sentimental. So she was. For she had come to feel that it was the only thing worth saying—what one felt. Cleverness was silly. One must say simply what one felt.

"But I do not know," said Peter Walsh, "what I feel."

Poor Peter, thought Sally. Why did not Clarissa come and talk to them? That was what he was longing for. She knew it. All the time he was thinking only of Clarissa, and was fidgeting with his knife.

He had not found life simple, Peter said. His relations with Clarissa had not been simple. It had spoilt his life, he said. (They had been so intimate—he and Sally Seton, it was absurd not to say it.) One could not be in love twice, he said. And what could she say? Still, it is better to have loved (but he would think her sentimental—he used to be so sharp). He must come and stay with them in Manchester. That is all very true, he said. All very true. He would love to come and stay with them, directly he had done what he had to do in London.

And Clarissa had cared for him more than she had ever cared for Richard. Sally was positive of that.

"No, no, no!" said Peter (Sally should not have said that—she went too far). That good fellow—there he was at the end of the room, holding forth, the same as ever, dear old Richard. Who was he talking to? Sally asked, that very distinguished-looking man? Living in the wilds as she did, she had an insatiable curiosity to know who people were. But Peter did not know. He did not like his looks, he said, probably a Cabinet Minister. Of them all, Richard seemed to him the best, he said—the most disinterested.

"But what has he done?" Sally asked. Public work, she supposed. And were they happy together? Sally asked (she herself was extremely happy); for, she admitted, she knew nothing about them, only jumped to conclusions, as one does, for what can one know even of the people one lives with every day? she asked. Are we not all prisoners? She had read a wonderful play about a man who scratched on the wall of his cell,[5] and she had felt that was true of life—one scratched on the wall. Despairing of human relationships (people were so difficult), she often went into her garden and got from her flowers a peace which men and women never gave her. But no; he did not like cabbages; he preferred human beings, Peter said. Indeed, the young are beautiful, Sally said, watching Elizabeth cross the room. How unlike Clarissa at her age! Could he make anything of her? She would not open her lips. Not much, not yet, Peter admitted. She was like a lily, Sally said, a lily by the side of a pool. But Peter did not agree that we know nothing. We know everything, he said; at least he did.

But these two, Sally whispered, these two coming now (and really she must go, if Clarissa did not come soon), this distinguished-looking man and his rather common-looking wife who had been talking to Richard—what could one know about people like that?

"That they're damnable humbugs," said Peter, looking at them casually. He made Sally laugh.

But Sir William Bradshaw stopped at the door to look at a picture. He looked in the corner for the engraver's name. His wife looked too. Sir William Bradshaw was so interested in art.

When one was young, said Peter, one was too much excited to know people. Now that one was old, fifty-two to be precise (Sally was fifty-five, in body, she said, but her heart was like a girl's of twenty); now that one was mature then, said Peter, one could watch, one could understand, and one did not lose the power of feeling, he said. No, that is true, said Sally. She felt more deeply, more passionately, every year. It increased, he said, alas, perhaps, but one should be glad of it—it went on increasing in his experience. There was some one in India. He would like to tell Sally about her. He would like Sally to know her. She was married, he said. She had two small children. They must all come to Manchester, said Sally—he must promise before they left.

5. Perhaps another reference to *Richard II*. See 5.5.19–21: "how these vain weak nails / May tear a passage through the flinty ribs / Of this hard world, my ragged prison walls."

There's Elizabeth, he said, she feels not half what we feel, not yet. But, said Sally, watching Elizabeth go to her father, one can see they are devoted to each other. She could feel it by the way Elizabeth went to her father.

For her father had been looking at her, as he stood talking to the Bradshaws, and he had thought to himself, Who is that lovely girl? And suddenly he realised that it was his Elizabeth, and he had not recognised her, she looked so lovely in her pink frock! Elizabeth had felt him looking at her as she talked to Willie Titcomb. So she went to him and they stood together, now that the party was almost over, looking at the people going, and the rooms getting emptier and emptier, with things scattered on the floor. Even Ellie Henderson was going, nearly last of all, though no one had spoken to her, but she had wanted to see everything, to tell Edith. And Richard and Elizabeth were rather glad it was over, but Richard was proud of his daughter. And he had not meant to tell her, but he could not help telling her. He had looked at her, he said, and he had wondered, Who is that lovely girl? and it was his daughter! That did make her happy. But her poor dog was howling.

"Richard has improved. You are right," said Sally. "I shall go and talk to him. I shall say good-night. What does the brain matter," said Lady Rosseter, getting up, "compared with the heart?"

"I will come," said Peter, but he sat on for a moment. What is this terror? what is this ecstasy? he thought to himself. What is it that fills me with extraordinary excitement?

It is Clarissa, he said.

For there she was.

RESPONSE

Sigrid Nunez: On Rereading Mrs. Dalloway[1]

HERE IS MY COPY OF THE PAPERBACK EDITION OF *MRS. DALLOWAY* that I read for the first time more than thirty years ago. It has my name in it because at that time I wrote my name in all my books. Tucked inside the front cover is the stub from a ticket to the play *Vita & Virginia* (Union Square Theatre, December 21, 1994), which I saw with a friend with whom I have since fallen out. In that play the role of Vita Sackville-West was played by Vanessa Redgrave, who was to play the role of Clarissa Dalloway in the movie version of *Mrs. Dalloway* that was made several years later. (The movie was a bore, the play great fun.) Also tucked inside my copy of *Mrs. Dalloway* is a clipping from the *New York Times Book Review*, which reprinted a letter from Vita to Virginia dated Wednesday, December 1, 1926. ("Last night I went to bed very early and read *Mrs. Dalloway*. It was a very curious sensation: I thought you were in the room——") It is a letter that was clearly written under the influence of Woolf's prose, and it is a love letter. My copy of *Mrs. Dalloway* has tiny notches at the top of the spine; these were inflicted by Percival, the very large brown-and-white rabbit I used to live with who had the awful habit of gnawing books. Every time I see such tooth marks (his taste was not limited to Woolf) I miss Percival; and, seeing the ticket stub, I miss my friend with whom I had

1. Sigrid Nunez is a Fellow of the American Academy of Arts and Sciences, and lives in New York City. Her novel *Mitz: The Marmoset of Bloomsbury* (1998) is a fictionalized treatment of Virginia and Leonard Woolf's pet monkey.

the falling out and who, as it happens, once wrote a poem about that rabbit and his habit of gnawing books. No, I did not name the rabbit after the character in *The Waves*.

Mrs. Dalloway was the first novel by Virginia Woolf that I read. It would not be my favorite. *To the Lighthouse* and *The Waves* are better novels, and *Between the Acts* is her best. Around the same time I read *Mrs. Dalloway*, I also read *A Room of One's Own*, *A Writer's Diary*, and the Quentin Bell biography whose publication the year I graduated from college was drawing huge attention to Bloomsbury, to which, of course, much attention had been paid already. In those days of Women's Liberation, it meant a great deal that Woolf was a feminist. It mattered deeply that this indisputably first-rate mind had concerned itself with, among other things, what it meant not only to be a writer but also to be a woman and a woman writer. It mattered so much partly because so many contemporary women who were writers, including feminists, did not want that label "woman writer" pinned to their breast for any reason. (Still true.) And it mattered that she was not the kind of feminist who would *ever* give up reading men.

Long before reading *Mrs. Dalloway* I knew that I wanted to be a writer and that I wanted to write fiction. Now I thought I had discovered the kind of fiction I might try to write. To begin with, Woolf had broken certain rules that I had begun to find irksome. Here was proof that a novel—a great novel—could "show" nothing, in the conventional sense; could be all "tell." Repetition, rather than being something always conscientiously to avoid, could be used lavishly, to sublime effect. Plot could be forsaken, the development of character ignored. One day in the life of an ordinary middle-aged woman—thoughts of an intense, perceptive, sensitive mind—this in itself could make a narrative. Form, style—beautiful sentences—were what mattered most. It was a revelation: A novel could be like a poem. Certainly, this was what Woolf was after in *Mrs. Dalloway*, and there was no doubt in my mind that she had succeeded. To read her as a young woman who hoped to write novels one day was to be a disciple. Everything I wrote during this time was some sort of feeble imitation of Woolf. And here is a question I don't remember ever asking myself: If the beauty of the writing was all that mattered, why should I have been hurt when people said of some story of mine, as they often did, It's beautifully written, *but* . . . ?

Time passed. I read the other novels, I read the essays. Now came the years when the complete diaries and letters began to be published, and I read each new volume the moment it appeared, and I could hardly wait for the next one. There were long periods when I read so much Woolf and so hungrily that it often felt as though I were feeding off her as much as reading her. And many readers—writers especially, women writers above all—have fed off Woolf in this same way. With the publication of so much "life-writing," to use her own phrase for the genre (her favorite genre, according to her diary), the private world stood fully revealed. It was now possible to know more or less what Virginia Woolf had done almost every day of her adult life. It was possible to imagine that you knew her better than you knew your own friends. There was, most importantly, the detailed record of the painstaking efforts she put into her writing, the challenges she set herself with each new work, the depth and breadth of her reading, her formidable self-discipline, her stoical attitude toward criticism. And that she was not merely able to carry on but to triumph, over and over, her whole life long, despite bouts of psychosis and paralyzing depression, made her almost superhuman. She was a genius in art and a heroine in life. She was the Goddess of Literature. I was at her feet.

In the beginning I must have taken it for granted that everyone I admired—every writer, anyway—must love Woolf as I did, unconditionally. But it was not so among those I would meet just out of school, working at the *New York Review of Books*. I am talking about people whose opinions could not have been more important to me. Susan Sontag suggested that my passion for Woolf was something I would outgrow. Joseph Brodsky placed her well below such moderns as Proust and Joyce. Elizabeth Hardwick, with whom I had taken college courses in writing, published in the *Review* an essay, "Bloomsbury and Virginia Woolf," that came to the conclusion that "in a sense her novels aren't interesting." For Hardwick, this was "part of the risk of setting a goal in fiction, of having an idea about it, an abstract idea." Hardwick also had serious questions about the character Doris Kilman: "the object of the author's" (and not merely Mrs. Dalloway's) "insolent loathing." She accuses Woolf of "bad taste" and even sadism in her portrait of the embittered, perspiring, greedy, ugly-green-mackintosh-wearing, lower-class Kilman. "It doesn't matter to us that she hates a woman like Miss Kilman; we'd rather not be told."

I don't remember exactly when I read *Mrs. Dalloway* a second time. I know I had yet to accomplish anything as a writer myself, but by then a significant change had occurred in my life. Like Septimus Warren Smith, I had lost "a sense of proportion." I had had a total breakdown. I had been confined unwillingly to a quiet place (where it was no longer "You must rest in bed" but "You must take your medication"). Reading the novel for the second time, I remember thinking that, for all she knew what she was talking about, Woolf had not succeeded in making madness . . . *interesting*. By then I was also aware of the judgment of Louise Bogan, who records in one of her own journals her response to *A Writer's Diary*. Woolf is "a monster of egotism." And: "How I have always disliked *Mrs. Dalloway*, with its attempt to *care* for the poor young man." But Woolf did not "care," in the way I take Bogan to mean, about any of her characters. Bogan, who also suffered breakdowns and had experience of mental homes and psychiatrists, also disliked *Mrs. Dalloway* for "its hatred of doctors." Surely Holmes and Bradshaw, the doctors who treat the psychologically damaged war veteran Septimus, are cartoon villains, indeed no more than targets for Woolf's hatred and scorn, and surely it strains belief to have Dr. Holmes cry "The coward!" at the moment Septimus has thrown himself from a window to his death—and in the presence of the victim's poor wife, no less. But much of *Mrs. Dalloway* strains belief. We know that realism was not what Woolf was after. *Reality*, however, was a different matter. To dig beneath the surface, to get at what lies behind the appearance of things, was always her aim as a novelist, and we feel that she succeeds so well because so much of her writing has the ring of truth.

So: Here is my old copy with its two mementoes, ticket stub and newspaper clipping. And what do I remember of this novel I have read already twice? That it was one of the most beautiful books I had ever read, that it gave me goose bumps, that it was like no other book I had read, that it made me want to read everything its author had written, that it made me want to write. Some sentences had stayed with me from my first reading. The famous opening: "Mrs. Dalloway said she would buy the flowers herself." The famous last words: "For there she was." The early description of Big Ben chiming—"The leaden circles dissolved in the air"—which is repeated three more times in the book. How people are often described as sitting or standing "upright" or "very upright" or "perfectly upright." Punctuation: extravagant use of parentheses; semicolons where the reader might reasonably expect commas (doubtless to achieve the desired beat). I remember all this. But Mrs. Dalloway? She does not live in the memory the way many other literary characters do: Anna Karenina, for example, or Daniel Deronda. It is the language I remember (and wasn't this, after all, what the author said she wanted?); it is the imagery (birds, skies, flowers, London gardens, London streets), the lovely, haunting cadences. And, always with Woolf, the death's-head showing through the fine lace. Not the people, not what does or does not happen to them, but the piercing beauty and sadness of the Woolfian vision is what lives on. It is like remembering a performance of Schubert.

I often thought I might someday write something about Woolf, and if I ever did it must be some kind of homage.

I had published two novels. I had read *Flush*, the least known of Woolf's novels, a mock biography of Elizabeth Barrett Browning's cocker spaniel. Remembering that the Woolfs had owned a pet monkey that had lived and traveled with them for several years in the 1930s, I made it the subject of a Life. Writing *Mitz: The Marmoset of Bloomsbury* meant many hours of rereading letters and diaries and researching other Bloomsbury documents. As it happened, the year I began doing this work was not a happy one for me; it was another period of personal upheaval, and retreating to the Bloomsbury sanctuary for a few hours each day was both a distraction and a solace.

Reading *Mrs. Dalloway* for the third and, I would say, probably the last time, I am struck by the book's artifice: specifically, the coincidences that bring Peter Walsh and Sally Seton, those major figures from Clarissa Dalloway's past—the two great loves of her life, neither of whom she has seen in years and both of whom just happen to be dominating her thoughts this very day—back to London, back into Clarissa's life, and, of course, to her party. And how the moment we see Septimus fling himself to his gruesome death we can be sure that some other character (it turns out to be Peter Walsh) will just happen to pass by, thinking some elevated thought (in this case, that the ambulance is "one of the triumphs of civilisation"). I don't recall being struck, much less troubled, by this kind of manipulation before (it is pure Woolf, after all). But there is something else that strikes and troubles me more, and it is this: moving constantly with the narrative from the mind of one character to another and, within the mind of each, back and forth in time as the character muses on his or her past, the present moment, or the future, why—no matter the character's age, sex, class, level of education, occupation, personality type, degree of sanity—why do I find these minds all more or less the same? This is true for the most part even of the very minor characters, such as Maisie Johnson ("only up from Edinburgh two days ago"), who happens to cross paths with Septimus and his wife in Regent's Park. In general (and not just in this novel), Woolf's characters tend to notice the same kind of things, to draw the same conclusions about what they see, and to be emotionally affected in the same way. All are obsessive and easily stirred. They all talk to themselves, usually with the same oracular blue streak; they all repeat little phrases such as "Fear no more" or "The death of the soul" or "It is the flesh." They are all highly susceptible to impressions; they are all terribly sensitive to nature; they all seem to have read Shelley and Shakespeare and Plato; they are all aesthetes; they are all mystics; they all have the same nostalgic relationship to the past; and they all use the same elaborate metaphors to interpret life and the human condition. Everyone is death-haunted, everyone is a poet, everyone is neurotic, everyone is a genius, everyone is Virginia Woolf.

And so, again and again, the reader has the uneasy feeling that the streams of thoughts sent gushing through the minds of the characters, from Mrs. Dalloway to Maisie Johnson, are too sophisticated for them. We do not believe these brilliant, original thoughts except as having come from the brilliant, original mind of the author. This might be less of a problem were the characters shown a little more from the outside, but Woolf will not give us this. It is strange. We know that she was a keen observer of other people, unusually perceptive about human nature and behavior (just read the letters); yet it is almost as if she were incapable of imagining any character that was not herself.

Perhaps one could argue that the language of consciousness is universal. Do not most people believe that all of us when we sleep, no matter how different we are, dream alike? Is there any reason to think we do not? Perhaps Woolf would argue that her goal (her duty, even) was to express her characters' inner lives as purely and eloquently and articulately as the characters themselves would express them, had they a novelist's gifts. Perhaps. But I remain unconvinced that people so various would wear such similar, interchangeable heads. If I have exaggerated above, it has not been by much, and on this reading it struck me full force: Mrs. Dalloway is not a character; she is a medium.

And not all the writing is good. "It was her punishment to see sink and disappear here a man, there a woman, in this profound darkness, and she forced to stand here in her evening dress. She had schemed; she had pilfered." (It is remarkable that no one has thought to initiate a bad Woolf contest, like the bad Hemingway contest.)

One more thing Louise Bogan disliked about *Mrs. Dalloway:* "Its frightful sentimentality." Bogan may have been thinking specifically of Woolf's romantic treatment of insanity, but the criticism could be made about much of this effusive book.

Flannery O'Connor thought Woolf had been compelled to use the novel as a laboratory. Elizabeth Hardwick calls Woolf "a theorist of fiction" and speaks admiringly of "the risk . . . of the bravest and most daring insistence that she would make something new." But for Bogan, Woolf "was not an innovator, in any true sense."

"Her work was the first definitive expression in the English novel of the whole, self-tortured modern consciousness, together with the precise idiom in which it does its thinking. . . . She masters her subject not by analyzing it from a strategic angle, but by achieving complete identity with it throughout."

Who else could these words be about but Virginia Woolf? Haven't we heard one version or another of them a hundred times? But, of course, these words were written not about Virginia Woolf but about Dorothy Richardson. They are the words of Wilson Follett, and they are quoted by Louise Bogan in a paper on women writers that she gave at Bennington College in 1962. And it is to Richardson, novelist and feminist, born the same year as Woolf and dying unknown sixteen years after Woolf's death, that Bogan awards the palm for true innovation, reminding us that it was Richardson who invented the stream-of-consciousness technique that Woolf was to use to such splendid effect.

Returning the much-read, rabbit-eaten *Mrs. Dalloway* to the bookshelf, I make a prediction: In future when I want to read Woolf, more likely I will go to the nonfiction.

And here is another hunch I have, not about the future but about the past. Had she wished to, in addition to her immortal achievements in other genres, Woolf could have written the greatest children's books of the age. There is much to suggest this, beginning, of course, with her extraordinary powers of imagination and verbal invention, the vividness and clarity of her prose, and the hushed, distilled quality that makes you bring the book a little closer to your nose. But there is also her love of animals, her high spirits, her playful and affectionate nature, her sense of comedy, the rocking-horse rhythm she sometimes gets into (*she rocks!*), her ability to cast a spell, and her child's sense of wonder about even the most ordinary things, which she herself never lost and which, with the generosity of the artist of genius, she keeps giving back to you. Of the thousands of letters Woolf wrote, some as beautiful as anything in her fiction, I do not love any one of them more than No. 3313, written to six-year-old Elaine Robson and quoted here in full.

> *I liked your poem and your story very much indeed. I have not seen a rabbit washing his ceiling but yesterday I saw a hare who was making a warm bed for his winter lodging in the marsh. He had just laid down a nice blanket made of thistledown when he saw me and ran away. His bed was quite hot, and I put a mushroom there for him to eat. The marsh is full of mushrooms. I wish you and Daddy and Mummie were all here to pick them and then we would cook them and have them for supper. I also saw a kingfisher. His bed is in the bank of the river but I have never found it. Sally has had a thorn in her paw and we have had to poultice it. At last the thorn came out and her paw is only as big as a penny bun. It was as big as a soup plate. Mitzi had a macaroon for breakfast this morning. When you are in London will you come to tea with us and make a binding for your lovely poem and story. Do you like writing prose or poetry best. This typewriter cannot spell and sometimes uses the wrong type. xxxxxx Uncle Leonard sends his love: Sally has just barked her love also and Mitz bit me in the ear which means she sends you her love too.*
>
> *Your affectionate Aunt Virginia*

June 2003

A Room of One's Own *A Room of One's Own* is difficult to categorize—it is a long essay, a nonfiction novella, a political pamphlet, and a philosophical discourse all in one. Its effects have not been so difficult to categorize—Virginia Woolf's idiosyncratic text has been recognized as a classic from the time of its publication in 1929. The book was a departure from Woolf's output until then; she was a major literary figure, having already published such key novels as *Jacob's Room, Mrs Dalloway, To the Lighthouse*, and *Orlando*, and she was an established essayist with a formidable reputation as an arbiter of the literary tradition. One way of characterizing this book is to see that it represents Woolf's scrutiny of her own position as a woman writer, a self-examination of her public position that inevitably became a political document. The focus is not on Woolf's life or her work per se, but rather on the social and psychological conditions that would make such a life generally possible. The book creates a microcosm of such possibility in the "room" of its title; the book itself is a room within which its author contemplates and analyzes the dimensions of social space for women. Woolf recognizes that seemingly neutral social space, the room of cultural agency just as the room of writing, is in truth a gendered space. She directs her political inquiry toward the making and remaking of such rooms.

A Room of One's Own comes from established traditions of writing as well. It draws on the conversational tone and novelistic insight of the literary essay as perfected in the nineteenth century by such writers as Charles Lamb—whose *Oxford in the Vacation* (see page 990) was certainly in Woolf's mind when she wrote the opening chapter of her essay. At the same time, Woolf's book joins a lineage of feminist political philosophy, whose most eloquent exponent prior to Woolf herself was Mary Wollstonecraft, who joined the rhetorical ranks of Rousseau and John Stuart Mill with the publication of *A Vindication of the Rights of Woman*, her passionately reasoned exhortation for the equal and universal human rights of women. (Selections from Wollstonecraft's *Vindication* can be found on pages 288–310.) The century and a half since Wollstonecraft had produced a rich history of feminist agitation and feminist thought. Virginia Woolf draws on this less-known tradition, invoking nineteenth-century figures from the women's movement like Emily Davies, Josephine Butler, and Octavia Hill. She also places her deliberations in the context of the suffragist movement and its fraught history in Britain. Virginia Woolf was strongly engaged in the debates of the suffrage movement, and its divisions over radical action or more conciliatory political approaches. Much of Woolf's long essay is devoted to demonstrating the subversive quality of occupying the blank page and wielding the printed word.

As politically motivated as *A Room of One's Own* is, it is equally a literary text. Woolf draws on all the intricacies of literary tropes and figures to mount her argument for women's education, women's equality, and women's social presence. Not the least of her strategies is her manipulation of the rhetoric of address—in other words, the audience implied by the language of a text. Woolf creates an ironic space, or room, in which she is a playfully ambiguous speaker addressing an uncertain audience: women at the colleges where she has been invited to speak, but also men and women alike who will read her printed text. By doing so, she keeps an ironic tension in play, holding at bay her anger at being censored or silenced by male readers by creating a sense of privacy and secrecy among women. This underscores Woolf's primary argument, the need for autonomy and self-determination. Her modest proposal, although faintly ironic, is also eminently pragmatic—the room of one's own that is her metaphor for the college classroom or the blank canvas or the book's page is at the same time the actual room, paid for and unintruded upon by domestic worries or social codes, whose possession permits a woman to find out who she may be.

from A Room of One's Own
Chapter 1

But, you may say, we asked you to speak about women and fiction—what has that got to do with a room of one's own?[1] I will try to explain. When you asked me to speak about women and fiction I sat down on the banks of a river and began to wonder what the words meant. They might mean simply a few remarks about Fanny Burney; a few more about Jane Austen; a tribute to the Brontës and a sketch of Haworth Parsonage under snow; some witticisms if possible about Miss Mitford; a respectful allusion to George Eliot; a reference to Mrs Gaskell and one would have done.[2] But at second sight the words seemed not so simple. The title women and fiction might mean, and you may have meant it to mean, women and what they are like; or it might mean women and the fiction that they write; or it might mean women and the fiction that is written about them; or it might mean that somehow all three are inextricably mixed together and you want me to consider them in that light. But when I began to consider the subject in this last way, which seemed the most interesting, I soon saw that it had one fatal drawback. I should never be able to come to a conclusion. I should never be able to fulfil what is, I understand, the first duty of a lecturer—to hand you after an hour's discourse a nugget of pure truth to wrap up between the pages of your notebooks and keep on the mantelpiece for ever. All I could do was to offer you an opinion upon one minor point—a woman must have money and a room of her own if she is to write fiction; and that, as you will see, leaves the great problem of the true nature of woman and the true nature of fiction unsolved. I have shirked the duty of coming to a conclusion upon these two questions—women and fiction remain, so far as I am concerned, unsolved problems. But in order to make some amends I am going to do what I can to show you how I arrived at this opinion about the room and the money. I am going to develop in your presence as fully and freely as I can the train of thought which led me to think this. Perhaps if I lay bare the ideas, the prejudices, that lie behind this statement you will find that they have some bearing upon women and some upon fiction. At any rate, when a subject is highly controversial—and any question about sex is that—one cannot hope to tell the truth. One can only show how one came to hold whatever opinion one does hold. One can only give one's audience the chance of drawing their own

1. Woolf delivered her essay in a shorter version to meetings first at two women's colleges, Newnham and Girton College, Cambridge University, in October 1928.
2. Important 19th-century novelists.

conclusions as they observe the limitations, the prejudices, the idiosyncrasies of the speaker. Fiction here is likely to contain more truth than fact. Therefore I propose, making use of all the liberties and licences of a novelist, to tell you the story of the two days that preceded my coming here—how, bowed down by the weight of the subject which you have laid upon my shoulders, I pondered it, and made it work in and out of my daily life. I need not say that what I am about to describe has no existence; Oxbridge is an invention; so is Fernham;[3] "I" is only a convenient term for somebody who has no real being. Lies will flow from my lips, but there may perhaps be some truth mixed up with them; it is for you to seek out this truth and to decide whether any part of it is worth keeping. If not, you will of course throw the whole of it into the wastepaper basket and forget all about it.

Here then was I (call me Mary Beton, Mary Seton, Mary Carmichael[4] or by any name you please—it is not a matter of any importance) sitting on the banks of a river a week or two ago in fine October weather, lost in thought. That collar I have spoken of, women and fiction, the need of coming to some conclusion on a subject that raises all sorts of prejudices and passions, bowed my head to the ground. To the right and left bushes of some sort, golden and crimson, glowed with the colour, even it seemed burnt with the heat, of fire. On the further bank the willows wept in perpetual lamentation, their hair about their shoulders. The river reflected whatever it chose of sky and bridge and burning tree, and when the undergraduate had oared his boat through the reflections they closed again, completely, as if he had never been. There one might have sat the clock round lost in thought. Thought—to call it by a prouder name than it deserved—had let its line down into the stream. It swayed, minute after minute, hither and thither among the reflections and the weeds, letting the water lift it and sink it, until—you know the little tug—the sudden conglomeration of an idea at the end of one's line: and then the cautious hauling of it in, and the careful laying of it out? Alas, laid on the grass how small, how insignificant this thought of mine looked; the sort of fish that a good fisherman puts back into the water so that it may grow fatter and be one day worth cooking and eating. I will not trouble you with that thought now, though if you look carefully you may find it for yourselves in the course of what I am going to say.

But however small it was, it had, nevertheless, the mysterious property of its kind—put back into the mind, it became at once very exciting, and important; and as it darted and sank, and flashed hither and thither, set up such a wash and tumult of ideas that it was impossible to sit still. It was thus that I found myself walking with extreme rapidity across a grass plot. Instantly a man's figure rose to intercept me. Nor did I at first understand that the gesticulations of a curious-looking object, in a cut-away coat and evening shirt, were aimed at me. His face expressed horror and indignation. Instinct rather than reason came to my help; he was a Beadle; I was a woman. This was the turf; there was the path. Only the Fellows and Scholars are allowed here; the gravel is the place for me.[5] Such thoughts were the work of a moment. As I regained the path the arms of the Beadle sank, his face assumed its usual repose, and though turf is better walking than gravel, no very great harm was done. The only charge I could bring against the Fellows and Scholars of whatever the college might happen to be was that in protection of their turf, which has been rolled for 300 years in succession, they had sent my little fish into hiding.

3. "Oxbridge" was in fact the common slang term for Oxford and Cambridge universities. "Fernham" suggests Newnham College.

4. Three of the four Marys who by tradition were attendants to Mary Queen of Scots (executed in 1567), and who figure in many Scottish ballads; the fourth was Mary Hamilton.

5. A beadle is a disciplinary officer. The fellows of Oxbridge colleges typically tutor the undergraduates, who are divided into scholars and commoners. The commoners form the majority of the student body.

What idea it had been that had sent me so audaciously trespassing I could not now remember. The spirit of peace descended like a cloud from heaven, for if the spirit of peace dwells anywhere, it is in the courts and quadrangles of Oxbridge on a fine October morning. Strolling through those colleges past those ancient halls the roughness of the present seemed smoothed away; the body seemed contained in a miraculous glass cabinet through which no sound could penetrate, and the mind, freed from any contact with facts (unless one trespassed on the turf again), was at liberty to settle down upon whatever meditation was in harmony with the moment. As chance would have it, some stray memory of some old essay about revisiting Oxbridge in the long vacation brought Charles Lamb to mind—Saint Charles, said Thackeray,[6] putting a letter of Lamb's to his forehead. Indeed, among all the dead (I give you my thoughts as they came to me), Lamb is one of the most congenial; one to whom one would have liked to say, Tell me then how you wrote your essays? For his essays are superior even to Max Beerbohm's, I thought, with all their perfection, because of that wild flash of imagination, that lightning crack of genius in the middle of them which leaves them flawed and imperfect, but starred with poetry. Lamb then came to Oxbridge perhaps a hundred years ago. Certainly he wrote an essay—the name escapes me—about the manuscript of one of Milton's poems which he saw here.[7] It was *Lycidas* perhaps, and Lamb wrote how it shocked him to think it possible that any word in *Lycidas* could have been different from what it is. To think of Milton changing the words in that poem seemed to him a sort of sacrilege. This led me to remember what I could of *Lycidas* and to amuse myself with guessing which word it could have been that Milton had altered, and why. It then occurred to me that the very manuscript itself which Lamb had looked at was only a few hundred yards away, so that one could follow Lamb's footsteps across the quadrangle to that famous library where the treasure is kept. Moreover, I recollected, as I put this plan into execution, it is in this famous library that the manuscript of Thackeray's *Esmond* is also preserved. The critics often say that *Esmond* is Thackeray's most perfect novel. But the affectation of the style, with its imitation of the eighteenth century, hampers one, so far as I remember; unless indeed the eighteenth-century style was natural to Thackeray—a fact that one might prove by looking at the manuscript and seeing whether the alterations were for the benefit of the style or of the sense. But then one would have to decide what is style and what is meaning, a question which—but here I was actually at the door which leads into the library itself. I must have opened it, for instantly there issued, like a guardian angel barring the way with a flutter of black gown instead of white wings, a deprecating, silvery, kindly gentleman, who regretted in a low voice as he waved me back that ladies are only admitted to the library if accompanied by a Fellow of the College or furnished with a letter of introduction.

That a famous library has been cursed by a woman is a matter of complete indifference to a famous library. Venerable and calm, with all its treasures safe locked within its breast, it sleeps complacently and will, so far as I am concerned, so sleep for ever. Never will I wake those echoes, never will I ask for that hospitality again, I vowed as I descended the steps in anger. Still an hour remained before luncheon, and what was one to do? Stroll on the meadows? sit by the river? Certainly it was a lovely autumn morning; the leaves were fluttering red to the ground; there was no great

6. William Makepeace Thackeray (1811–1863), novelist and journalist, Woolf's father's first father-in-law.

7. Lamb's *Oxford in the Vacation* (see page 990)—describing the locales Lamb himself was too poor to attend in term time. The manuscript of Milton's elegy *Lycidas* (1638) is in the Wren Library of Trinity College, Cambridge, together with that of Thackeray's novel *The History of Henry Esmond* (1852).

hardship in doing either. But the sound of music reached my ear. Some service or celebration was going forward. The organ complained magnificently as I passed the chapel door. Even the sorrow of Christianity sounded in that serene air more like the recollection of sorrow than sorrow itself; even the groanings of the ancient organ seemed lapped in peace. I had no wish to enter had I the right, and this time the verger might have stopped me, demanding perhaps my baptismal certificate, or a letter of introduction from the Dean. But the outside of these magnificent buildings is often as beautiful as the inside. Moreover, it was amusing enough to watch the congregation assembling, coming in and going out again, busying themselves at the door of the chapel like bees at the mouth of a hive. Many were in cap and gown; some had tufts of fur on their shoulders; others were wheeled in bath-chairs; others, though not past middle age, seemed creased and crushed into shapes so singular that one was reminded of those giant crabs and crayfish who heave with difficulty across the sand of an aquarium. As I leant against the wall the University indeed seemed a sanctuary in which are preserved rare types which would soon be obsolete if left to fight for existence on the pavement of the Strand.[8] Old stories of old deans and old dons came back to mind, but before I had summoned up courage to whistle—it used to be said that at the sound of a whistle old Professor——instantly broke into a gallop—the venerable congregation had gone inside. The outside of the chapel remained. As you know, its high domes and pinnacles can be seen, like a sailing-ship always voyaging never arriving, lit up at night and visible for miles, far away across the hills. Once, presumably, this quadrangle with its smooth lawns, its massive buildings, and the chapel itself was marsh too, where the grasses waved and the swine rootled. Teams of horses and oxen, I thought, must have hauled the stone in wagons from far countries, and then with infinite labour the grey blocks in whose shade I was now standing were poised in order one on top of another, and then the painters brought their glass for the windows, and the masons were busy for centuries up on that roof with putty and cement, spade and trowel. Every Saturday somebody must have poured gold and silver out of a leathern purse into their ancient fists, for they had their beer and skittles presumably of an evening. An unending stream of gold and silver, I thought, must have flowed into this court perpetually to keep the stones coming and the masons working; to level, to ditch, to dig and to drain. But it was then the age of faith, and money was poured liberally to set these stones on a deep foundation, and when the stones were raised, still more money was poured in from the coffers of kings and queens and great nobles to ensure that hymns should be sung here and scholars taught. Lands were granted; tithes were paid. And when the age of faith was over and the age of reason had come, still the same flow of gold and silver went on; fellowships were founded; lectureships endowed; only the gold and silver flowed now, not from the coffers of the king, but from the chests of merchants and manufacturers, from the purses of men who had made, say, a fortune from industry, and returned, in their wills, a bounteous share of it to endow more chairs, more lectureships, more fellowships in the university where they had learnt their craft. Hence the libraries and laboratories; the observatories; the splendid equipment of costly and delicate instruments which now stands on glass shelves, where centuries ago the grasses waved and the swine rootled. Certainly, as I strolled round the court, the foundation of gold and silver seemed deep enough; the pavement laid solidly over the wild grasses. Men with

8. A thoroughfare in central London.

trays on their heads went busily from staircase to staircase. Gaudy blossoms flowered in window-boxes. The strains of the gramophone blared out from the rooms within. It was impossible not to reflect—the reflection whatever it may have been was cut short. The clock struck. It was time to find one's way to luncheon.

It is a curious fact that novelists have a way of making us believe that luncheon parties are invariably memorable for something very witty that was said, or for something very wise that was done. But they seldom spare a word for what was eaten. It is part of the novelist's convention not to mention soup and salmon and ducklings, as if soup and salmon and ducklings were of no importance whatsoever, as if nobody ever smoked a cigar or drank a glass of wine. Here, however, I shall take the liberty to defy that convention and to tell you that the lunch on this occasion began with soles, sunk in a deep dish, over which the college cook had spread a counterpane of the whitest cream, save that it was branded here and there with brown spots like the spots on the flanks of a doe. After that came the partridges, but if this suggests a couple of bald, brown birds on a plate you are mistaken. The partridges, many and various, came with all their retinue of sauces and salads, the sharp and the sweet, each in its order; their potatoes, thin as coins but not so hard; their sprouts, foliated as rosebuds but more succulent. And no sooner had the roast and its retinue been done with than the silent serving-man, the Beadle himself perhaps in a milder manifestation, set before us, wreathed in napkins, a confection which rose all sugar from the waves. To call it pudding and so relate it to rice and tapioca would be an insult. Meanwhile the wineglasses had flushed yellow and flushed crimson; had been emptied; had been filled. And thus by degrees was lit, halfway down the spine, which is the seat of the soul, not that hard little electric light which we call brilliance, as it pops in and out upon our lips, but the more profound, subtle and subterranean glow, which is the rich yellow flame of rational intercourse. No need to hurry. No need to sparkle. No need to be anybody but oneself. We are all going to heaven and Vandyck[9] is of the company—in other words, how good life seemed, how sweet its rewards, how trivial this grudge or that grievance, how admirable friendship and the society of one's kind, as, lighting a good cigarette, one sunk among the cushions in the window-seat.

If by good luck there had been an ash-tray handy, if one had not knocked the ash out of the window in default, if things had been a little different from what they were, one would not have seen, presumably, a cat without a tail. The sight of that abrupt and truncated animal padding softly across the quadrangle changed by some fluke of the subconscious intelligence the emotional light for me. It was as if some one had let fall a shade. Perhaps the excellent hock was relinquishing its hold. Certainly, as I watched the Manx cat pause in the middle of the lawn as if it too questioned the universe, something seemed lacking, something seemed different. But what was lacking, what was different, I asked myself, listening to the talk. And to answer that question I had to think myself out of the room, back into the past, before the war indeed,[1] and to set before my eyes the model of another luncheon party held in rooms not very far distant from these; but different. Everything was different. Meanwhile the talk went on among the guests, who were many and young, some of this sex, some of that; it went on swimmingly, it went on agreeably, freely, amusingly. And as it went on I set it against the background of that other talk, and as I matched the two together I had no doubt that one was the descendant, the legitimate heir of the other. Nothing was

9. Sir Anthony Van Dyck, prominent 17th-century society painter.

1. World War I.

changed; nothing was different save only—here I listened with all my ears not entirely to what was being said, but to the murmur or current behind it. Yes, that was it—the change was there. Before the war at a luncheon party like this people would have said precisely the same things but they would have sounded different, because in those days they were accompanied by a sort of humming noise, not articulate, but musical, exciting, which changed the value of the words themselves. Could one set that humming noise to words? Perhaps with the help of the poets one could. A book lay beside me and, opening it, I turned casually enough to Tennyson. And here I found Tennyson was singing:

There has fallen a splendid tear
From the passion-flower at the gate.
She is coming, my dove, my dear;
She is coming, my life, my fate;
The red rose cries, "She is near, she is near";
And the white rose weeps, "She is late";
The larkspur listens, "I hear, I hear";
And the lily whispers, "I wait."[2]

Was that what men hummed at luncheon parties before the war? And the women?

My heart is like a singing bird
Whose nest is in a water'd shoot;
My heart is like an apple tree
Whose boughs are bent with thick-set fruit;
My heart is like a rainbow shell
That paddles in a halcyon sea;
My heart is gladder than all these
Because my love is come to me.[3]

Was that what women hummed at luncheon parties before the war?

There was something so ludicrous in thinking of people humming such things even under their breath at luncheon parties before the war that I burst out laughing, and had to explain my laughter by pointing at the Manx cat, who did look a little absurd, poor beast, without a tail, in the middle of the lawn. Was he really born so, or had he lost his tail in an accident? The tailless cat, though some are said to exist in the Isle of Man, is rarer than one thinks. It is a queer animal, quaint rather than beautiful. It is strange what a difference a tail makes—you know the sort of things one says as a lunch party breaks up and people are finding their coats and hats.

This one, thanks to the hospitality of the host, had lasted far into the afternoon. The beautiful October day was fading and the leaves were falling from the trees in the avenue as I walked through it. Gate after gate seemed to close with gentle finality behind me. Innumerable beadles were fitting innumerable keys into well-oiled locks; the treasure-house was being made secure for another night. After the avenue one comes out upon a road—I forget its name—which leads you, if you take the right turning, along to Fernham.[4] But there was plenty of time. Dinner was not till half-past seven. One could almost do without dinner after such a luncheon. It is strange

2. From Tennyson's *Maud* (1855), lines 908–15.
3. The first stanza of Christina Rossetti's poem *A Birthday* (1857); see page 1648.
4. Both Girton and Newnham Colleges, established only in the late 19th century, are outside the old university area of Cambridge.

how a scrap of poetry works in the mind and makes the legs move in time to it along the road. Those words—

There has fallen a splendid tear
From the passion-flower at the gate.
She is coming, my dove, my dear—

sang in my blood as I stepped quickly along towards Headingley. And then, switching off into the other measure, I sang, where the waters are churned up by the weir:

My heart is like a singing bird
Whose nest is in a water'd shoot;
My heart is like an apple tree—

What poets, I cried aloud, as one does in the dusk, what poets they were!

In a sort of jealousy, I suppose, for our own age, silly and absurd though these comparisons are, I went on to wonder if honestly one could name two living poets now as great as Tennyson and Christina Rossetti were then. Obviously it is impossible, I thought, looking into those foaming waters, to compare them. The very reason why the poetry excites one to such abandonment, such rapture, is that it celebrates some feeling that one used to have (at luncheon parties before the war perhaps), so that one responds easily, familiarly, without troubling to check the feeling, or to compare it with any that one has now. But the living poets express a feeling that is actually being made and torn out of us at the moment. One does not recognize it in the first place; often for some reason one fears it; one watches it with keenness and compares it jealously and suspiciously with the old feeling that one knew. Hence the difficulty of modern poetry; and it is because of this difficulty that one cannot remember more than two consecutive lines of any good modern poet. For this reason—that my memory failed me—the argument flagged for want of material. But why, I continued, moving on towards Headingley, have we stopped humming under our breath at luncheon parties? Why has Alfred ceased to sing

She is coming, my dove, my dear?

Why has Christina ceased to respond

My heart is gladder than all these
Because my love is come to me?

Shall we lay the blame on the war? When the guns fired in August 1914, did the faces of men and women show so plain in each other's eyes that romance was killed? Certainly it was a shock (to women in particular with their illusions about education, and so on) to see the faces of our rulers in the light of the shell-fire. So ugly they looked—German, English, French—so stupid. But lay the blame where one will, on whom one will, the illusion which inspired Tennyson and Christina Rossetti to sing so passionately about the coming of their loves is far rarer now than then. One has only to read, to look, to listen, to remember. But why say "blame"? Why, if it was an illusion, not praise the catastrophe, whatever it was, that destroyed illusion and put truth in its place? For truth . . . those dots mark the spot where, in search of truth, I missed the turning up to Fernham. Yes indeed, which was truth and which was illusion, I asked myself. What was the truth about these houses, for example, dim and festive now with their red windows in the dusk, but raw and red and squalid, with their sweets and their boot-laces, at nine o'clock in the morning? And the willows and the river and the gardens that run down to the river, vague now with the mist stealing over them, but gold and red in the sunlight—which was the truth, which was the illusion about them? I spare you the twists and turns of my cogitations, for no conclusion was found on the road to Headingley, and I ask you to suppose that I soon found out my mistake about the turning and retraced my steps to Fernham.

As I have said already that it was an October day, I dare not forfeit your respect and imperil the fair name of fiction by changing the season and describing lilacs hanging over garden walls, crocuses, tulips and other flowers of spring. Fiction must stick to facts, and the truer the facts the better the fiction—so we are told. Therefore it was still autumn and the leaves were still yellow and falling, if anything, a little faster than before, because it was now evening (seven twenty-three to be precise) and a breeze (from the south-west to be exact) had risen. But for all that there was something odd at work:

My heart is like a singing bird
Whose nest is in a water'd shoot;
My heart is like an apple tree
Whose boughs are bent with thick-set fruit—

perhaps the words of Christina Rossetti were partly responsible for the folly of the fancy—it was nothing of course but a fancy—that the lilac was shaking its flowers over the garden walls, and the brimstone butterflies were scudding hither and thither, and the dust of the pollen was in the air. A wind blew, from what quarter I know not, but it lifted the half-grown leaves so that there was a flash of silver grey in the air. It was the time between the lights when colours undergo their intensification and purples and golds burn in window-panes like the beat of an excitable heart; when for some reason the beauty of the world revealed and yet soon to perish (here I pushed into the garden, for, unwisely, the door was left open and no beadles seemed about), the beauty of the world which is so soon to perish, has two edges, one of laughter, one of anguish, cutting the heart asunder. The gardens of Fernham lay before me in the spring twilight, wild and open, and in the long grass, sprinkled and carelessly flung, were daffodils and bluebells, not orderly perhaps at the best of times, and now wind-blown and waving as they tugged at their roots. The windows of the building, curved like ships' windows among generous waves of red brick, changed from lemon to silver under the flight of the quick spring clouds. Somebody was in a hammock, somebody, but in this light they were phantoms only, half guessed, half seen, raced across the grass—would no one stop her?—and then on the terrace, as if popping out to breathe the air, to glance at the garden, came a bent figure, formidable yet humble, with her great forehead and her shabby dress—could it be the famous scholar, could it be J—— H—— herself?[5] All was dim, yet intense too, as if the scarf which the dusk had flung over the garden were torn asunder by star or sword—the flash of some terrible reality leaping, as its way is, out of the heart of the spring. For youth——

Here was my soup. Dinner was being served in the great dining-hall. Far from being spring it was in fact an evening in October. Everybody was assembled in the big dining-room. Dinner was ready. Here was the soup. It was a plain gravy soup. There

5. Jane Harrison, a famous classical scholar.

was nothing to stir the fancy in that. One could have seen through the transparent liquid any pattern that there might have been on the plate itself. But there was no pattern. The plate was plain. Next came beef with its attendant greens and potatoes—a homely trinity, suggesting the rumps of cattle in a muddy market, and sprouts curled and yellowed at the edge, and bargaining and cheapening, and women with string bags on Monday morning. There was no reason to complain of human nature's daily food, seeing that the supply was sufficient and coal-miners doubtless were sitting down to less. Prunes and custard followed. And if any one complains that prunes, even when mitigated by custard, are an uncharitable vegetable (fruit they are not), stringy as a miser's heart and exuding a fluid such as might run in misers' veins who have denied themselves wine and warmth for eighty years and yet not given to the poor, he should reflect that there are people whose charity embraces even the prune. Biscuits and cheese came next, and here the water-jug was liberally passed round, for it is the nature of biscuits to be dry, and these were biscuits to the core. That was all. The meal was over. Everybody scraped their chairs back; the swing-doors swung violently to and fro; soon the hall was emptied of every sign of food and made ready no doubt for breakfast next morning. Down corridors and up staircases the youth of England went banging and singing. And was it for a guest, a stranger (for I had no more right here in Fernham than in Trinity or Somerville or Girton or Newnham or Christchurch),[6] to say, "The dinner was not good," or to say (we were now, Mary Seton and I, in her sitting-room), "Could we not have dined up here alone?" for if I had said anything of the kind I should have been prying and searching into the secret economies of a house which to the stranger wears so fine a front of gaiety and courage. No, one could say nothing of the sort. Indeed, conversation for a moment flagged. The human frame being what it is, heart, body and brain all mixed together, and not contained in separate compartments as they will be no doubt in another million years, a good dinner is of great importance to good talk. One cannot think well, love well, sleep well, if one has not dined well. The lamp in the spine does not light on beef and prunes. We are all *probably* going to heaven, and Vandyck is, we *hope*, to meet us round the next corner—that is the dubious and qualifying state of mind that beef and prunes at the end of the day's work breed between them. Happily my friend, who taught science, had a cupboard where there was a squat bottle and little glasses—(but there should have been sole and partridge to begin with)—so that we were able to draw up to the fire and repair some of the damages of the day's living. In a minute or so we were slipping freely in and out among all those objects of curiosity and interest which form in the mind in the absence of a particular person, and are naturally to be discussed on coming together again—how somebody has married, another has not; one thinks this, another that; one has improved out of all knowledge, the other most amazingly gone to the bad—with all those speculations upon human nature and the character of the amazing world we live in which spring naturally from such beginnings. While these things were being said, however, I became shamefacedly aware of a current setting in of its own accord and carrying everything forward to an end of its own. One might be talking of Spain or Portugal, of book or racehorse, but the real interest of whatever was said was none of those things, but a scene of masons on a high roof some five centuries ago. Kings and nobles brought treasure in huge sacks and poured it under the earth. This scene was for

6. Trinity, Girton, and Newnham are colleges of Cambridge University; Somerville and Christchurch are at Oxford.

ever coming alive in my mind and placing itself by another of lean cows and a muddy market and withered greens and the stringy hearts of old men—these two pictures, disjointed and disconnected and nonsensical as they were, were for ever coming together and combating each other and had me entirely at their mercy. The best course, unless the whole talk was to be distorted, was to expose what was in my mind to the air, when with good luck it would fade and crumble like the head of the dead king when they opened the coffin at Windsor. Briefly, then, I told Miss Seton about the masons who had been all those years on the roof of the chapel, and about the kings and queens and nobles bearing sacks of gold and silver on their shoulders, which they shovelled into the earth; and then how the great financial magnates of our own time came and laid cheques and bonds, I suppose, where the others had laid ingots and rough lumps of gold. All that lies beneath the colleges down there, I said; but this college, where we are now sitting, what lies beneath its gallant red brick and the wild unkempt grasses of the garden? What force is behind the plain china off which we dined, and (here it popped out of my mouth before I could stop it) the beef, the custard and the prunes?

Well, said Mary Seton, about the year 1860—Oh, but you know the story, she said, bored, I suppose, by the recital. And she told me—rooms were hired. Committees met. Envelopes were addressed. Circulars were drawn up. Meetings were held; letters were read out; so-and-so has promised so much; on the contrary, Mr——won't give a penny. The *Saturday Review* has been very rude. How can we raise a fund to pay for offices? Shall we hold a bazaar? Can't we find a pretty girl to sit in the front row? Let us look up what John Stuart Mill said on the subject.[7] Can any one persuade the editor of the——to print a letter? Can we get Lady——to sign it? Lady——is out of town. That was the way it was done, presumably, sixty years ago, and it was a prodigious effort, and a great deal of time was spent on it. And it was only after a long struggle and with the utmost difficulty that they got thirty thousand pounds together.[8] So obviously we cannot have wine and partridges and servants carrying tin dishes on their heads, she said. We cannot have sofas and separate rooms. "The amenities," she said, quoting from some book or other, "will have to wait."[9]

At the thought of all those women working year after year and finding it hard to get two thousand pounds together, and as much as they could do to get thirty thousand pounds, we burst out in scorn at the reprehensible poverty of our sex. What had our mothers been doing then that they had no wealth to leave us? Powdering their noses? Looking in at shop windows? Flaunting in the sun at Monte Carlo? There were some photographs on the mantel-piece. Mary's mother—if that was her picture—may have been a wastrel in her spare time (she had thirteen children by a minister of the church), but if so her gay and dissipated life had left too few traces of its pleasures on her face. She was a homely body; an old lady in a plaid shawl which was fastened by a large cameo; and she sat in a basket-chair, encouraging a spaniel to look at the camera, with the amused, yet strained expression of one who is sure that the dog will move directly the bulb is pressed. Now if she had gone into business; had become a

7. In 1869 Mill published his essay *The Subjection of Women*, which argued forcefully for women's suffrage and their right to equality with men.

8. "We are told that we ought to ask for £ 30,000 at least. . . . It is not a large sum, considering that there is to be but one college of this sort for Great Britain, Ireland and the Colonies, and considering how easy it is to raise immense sums for boys' schools. But considering how few people really wish women to be educated, it is a good deal."—Lady Stephen, *Life of Miss Emily Davies* [Woolf's note].

9. Every penny which could be scraped together was set aside for building, and the amenities had to be postponed.—R. Strachey, *The Cause* [Woolf's note].

manufacturer of artificial silk or a magnate on the Stock Exchange; if she had left two or three hundred thousand pounds to Fernham, we could have been sitting at our ease tonight and the subject of our talk might have been archaeology, botany, anthropology, physics, the nature of the atom, mathematics, astronomy, relativity, geography. If only Mrs Seton and her mother and her mother before her had learnt the great art of making money and had left their money, like their fathers and their grandfathers before them, to found fellowships and lectureships and prizes and scholarships appropriated to the use of their own sex, we might have dined very tolerably up here alone off a bird and a bottle of wine; we might have looked forward without undue confidence to a pleasant and honourable lifetime spent in the shelter of one of the liberally endowed professions. We might have been exploring or writing; mooning about the venerable places of the earth; sitting contemplative on the steps of the Parthenon, or going at ten to an office and coming home comfortably at half-past four to write a little poetry. Only, if Mrs Seton and her like had gone into business at the age of fifteen, there would have been—that was the snag in the argument—no Mary. What, I asked, did Mary think of that? There between the curtains was the October night, calm and lovely, with a star or two caught in the yellowing trees. Was she ready to resign her share of it and her memories (for they had been a happy family, though a large one) of games and quarrels up in Scotland, which she is never tired of praising for the fineness of its air and the quality of its cakes, in order that Fernham might have been endowed with fifty thousand pounds or so by a stroke of the pen? For, to endow a college would necessitate the suppression of families altogether. Making a fortune and bearing thirteen children—no human being could stand it. Consider the facts, we said. First there are nine months before the baby is born. Then the baby is born. Then there are three or four months spent in feeding the baby. After the baby is fed there are certainly five years spent in playing with the baby. You cannot, it seems, let children run about the streets. People who have seen them running wild in Russia say that the sight is not a pleasant one. People say, too, that human nature takes its shape in the years between one and five. If Mrs Seton, I said, had been making money, what sort of memories would you have had of games and quarrels? What would you have known of Scotland, and its fine air and cakes and all the rest of it? But it is useless to ask these questions, because you would never have come into existence at all. Moreover, it is equally useless to ask what might have happened if Mrs Seton and her mother and her mother before her had amassed great wealth and laid it under the foundations of college and library, because, in the first place, to earn money was impossible for them, and in the second, had it been possible, the law denied them the right to possess what money they earned. It is only for the last forty-eight years that Mrs Seton has had a penny of her own. For all the centuries before that it would have been her husband's property—a thought which, perhaps, may have had its share in keeping Mrs Seton and her mothers off the Stock Exchange.[1] Every penny I earn, they may have said, will be taken from me and disposed of according to my husband's wisdom—perhaps to found a scholarship or to endow a fellowship in Balliol or Kings,[2] so that to earn money, even if I could earn money, is not a matter that interests me very greatly. I had better leave it to my husband.

1. The late 19th century saw the passage of legislation designed to improve the legal status of women. In 1870 the Married Women's Property Act allowed women to retain £200 of their own earnings (which previously had automatically become the property of her husband); in 1884 a further act gave married women the same rights over property as unmarried women, and allowed them to carry on trades or businesses using their property.

2. Balliol is a college of Oxford University; King's is at Cambridge.

At any rate, whether or not the blame rested on the old lady who was looking at the spaniel, there could be no doubt that for some reason or other our mothers had mismanaged their affairs very gravely. Not a penny could be spared for "amenities"; for partridges and wine, beadles and turf, books and cigars, libraries and leisure. To raise bare walls out of the bare earth was the utmost they could do.

So we talked standing at the window and looking, as so many thousands look every night, down on the domes and towers of the famous city beneath us. It was very beautiful, very mysterious in the autumn moonlight. The old stone looked very white and venerable. One thought of all the books that were assembled down there; of the pictures of old prelates and worthies hanging in the panelled rooms; of the painted windows that would be throwing strange globes and crescents on the pavement; of the tablets and memorials and inscriptions; of the fountains and the grass; of the quiet rooms looking across the quiet quadrangles. And (pardon me the thought) I thought, too, of the admirable smoke and drink and the deep armchairs and the pleasant carpets: of the urbanity, the geniality, the dignity which are the offspring of luxury and privacy and space. Certainly our mothers had not provided us with anything comparable to all this—our mothers who found it difficult to scrape together thirty thousand pounds, our mothers who bore thirteen children to ministers of religion at St Andrews.

So I went back to my inn, and as I walked through the dark streets I pondered this and that, as one does at the end of the day's work. I pondered why it was that Mrs Seton had no money to leave us; and what effect poverty has on the mind; and what effect wealth has on the mind; and I thought of the queer old gentlemen I had seen that morning with tufts of fur upon their shoulders; and I remembered how if one whistled one of them ran; and I thought of the organ booming in the chapel and of the shut doors of the library; and I thought how unpleasant it is to be locked out; and I thought how it is worse perhaps to be locked in; and, thinking of the safety and prosperity of the one sex and of the poverty and insecurity of the other and of the effect of tradition and of the lack of tradition upon the mind of a writer, I thought at last that it was time to roll up the crumpled skin of the day, with its arguments and its impressions and its anger and its laughter, and cast it into the hedge. A thousand stars were flashing across the blue wastes of the sky. One seemed alone with an inscrutable society. All human beings were laid asleep—prone, horizontal, dumb. Nobody seemed stirring in the streets of Oxbridge. Even the door of the hotel sprang open at the touch of an invisible hand—not a boots was sitting up to light me to bed, it was so late.

from *Chapter 3*

It would have been impossible, completely and entirely, for any woman to have written the plays of Shakespeare in the age of Shakespeare. Let me imagine, since facts are so hard to come by, what would have happened had Shakespeare had a wonderfully gifted sister, called Judith, let us say. Shakespeare himself went, very probably—his mother was an heiress—to the grammar school, where he may have learnt Latin—Ovid, Virgil, and Horace—and the elements of grammar and logic. He was, it is well known, a wild boy who poached rabbits, perhaps shot a deer, and had, rather sooner than he should have done, to marry a woman in the neighbourhood, who bore him a child rather quicker than was right. That escapade sent him to seek his fortune in London. He had, it seemed, a taste for the theatre; he began by holding horses at the stage door. Very soon he got work in the theatre, became a successful actor, and lived at the hub of the universe, meeting everybody, knowing everybody, practising his art on the boards, exercising his wits in the streets, and even getting access to the palace of the queen. Meanwhile his extraordinarily gifted sister, let us suppose, remained at home. She was as adventurous, as imaginative, as agog to see the world as he was. But she was not sent to school. She had no chance of learning grammar and logic, let alone of reading Horace and Virgil. She picked up a book now and then, one of her brother's perhaps, and read a few pages. But then her parents came in and told her to mend the stockings or mind the stew and not moon about with books and papers. They would have spoken sharply but kindly, for they were substantial people who knew the conditions of life for a woman and loved their daughter—indeed, more likely than not she was the apple of her father's eye. Perhaps she scribbled some pages up in an apple loft on the sly, but was careful to hide them or set fire to them. Soon, however, before she was out of her teens, she was to be betrothed to the son of a neighbouring wool-stapler. She cried out that marriage was hateful to her, and for that she was severely beaten by her father. Then he ceased to scold her. He begged her instead not to hurt him, not to shame him in this matter of her marriage. He would give her a chain of beads or a fine petticoat, he said; and there were tears in his eyes. How could she disobey him? How could she break his heart? The force of her own gift alone drove her to it. She made up a small parcel of her belongings, let herself down by a rope one summer's night and took the road to London. She was not seventeen. The birds that sang in the hedge were not more musical than she was. She had the quickest fancy, a gift like her brother's, for the tune of words. Like him, she had a taste for the theatre. She stood at the stage door; she wanted to act, she said. Men laughed in her face. The manager—a fat, loose-lipped man—guffawed. He bellowed something about poodles dancing and women acting—no woman, he said, could possibly be an actress. He hinted—you can imagine what. She could get no training in her craft. Could she even seek her dinner in a tavern or roam the streets at midnight? Yet her genius was for fiction and lusted to feed abundantly upon the lives of men and women and the study of their ways. At last—for she was very young, oddly like Shakespeare the poet in her face, with the same grey eyes and rounded brows—at last Nick Greene the actor-manager took pity on her; she found herself with child by that gentleman and so—who shall measure the heat and violence of the poet's heart when caught and tangled in a woman's body?—killed herself one winter's night and lies buried at some cross-roads where the omnibuses now stop outside the Elephant and Castle.[3]

That, more or less, is how the story would run, I think, if a woman in Shakespeare's day had had Shakespeare's genius. But for my part, I agree with the deceased bishop, if such he was—it is unthinkable that any woman in Shakespeare's day should have had Shakespeare's genius. For genius like Shakespeare's is not born among labouring, uneducated, servile people. It was not born in England among the Saxons and the Britons. It is not born today among the working classes. How, then, could it have been born among women whose work began, according to Professor Trevelyan,[4] almost before they were out of the nursery, who were forced to it by their parents and held to it by all the power of law and custom? Yet genius of a sort must have existed among women as it must have existed among the working classes. Now and again an Emily Brontë or a Robert Burns blazes out and proves its presence. But

3. A tavern on the outskirts of South London.

4. George Trevelyan (1876–1962), historian.

certainly it never got itself on to paper. When, however, one reads of a witch being ducked, of a woman possessed by devils, of a wise woman selling herbs, or even of a very remarkable man who had a mother, then I think we are on the track of a lost novelist, a suppressed poet, of some mute and inglorious Jane Austen, some Emily Brontë who dashed her brains out on the moor or mopped and mowed about the highways crazed with the torture that her gift had put her to. Indeed, I would venture to guess that Anon, who wrote so many poems without signing them, was often a woman. It was a woman Edward Fitzgerald,[5] I think, suggested who made the ballads and the folk-songs, crooning them to her children, beguiling her spinning with them, or the length of the winter's night.

This may be true or it may be false—who can say?—but what is true in it, so it seemed to me, reviewing the story of Shakespeare's sister as I had made it, is that any woman born with a great gift in the sixteenth century would certainly have gone crazed, shot herself, or ended her days in some lonely cottage outside the village, half witch, half wizard, feared and mocked at. For it needs little skill in psychology to be sure that a highly gifted girl who had tried to use her gift for poetry would have been so thwarted and hindered by other people, so tortured and pulled asunder by her own contrary instincts, that she must have lost her health and sanity to a certainty. No girl could have walked to London and stood at a stage door and forced her way into the presence of actor-managers without doing herself a violence and suffering an anguish which may have been irrational—for chastity may be a fetish invented by certain societies for unknown reasons—but were none the less inevitable. Chastity had then, it has even now, a religious importance in a woman's life, and has so wrapped itself round with nerves and instincts that to cut it free and bring it to the light of day demands courage of the rarest. To have lived a free life in London in the sixteenth century would have meant for a woman who was poet and playwright a nervous stress and dilemma which might well have killed her. Had she survived, whatever she had written would have been twisted and deformed, issuing from a strained and morbid imagination. And undoubtedly, I thought, looking at the shelf where there are no plays by women, her work would have gone unsigned. That refuge she would have sought certainly. It was the relic of the sense of chastity that dictated anonymity to women even so late as the nineteenth century. Currer Bell, George Eliot, George Sand,[6] all the victims of inner strife as their writings prove, sought ineffectively to veil themselves by using the name of a man. Thus they did homage to the convention, which if not implanted by the other sex was liberally encouraged by them (the chief glory of a woman is not to be talked of, said Pericles, himself a much-talked-of man), that publicity in women is detestable.[7] Anonymity runs in their blood. The desire to be veiled still possesses them. They are not even now as concerned about the health of their fame as men are, and, speaking generally, will pass a tombstone or a signpost without feeling an irresistible desire to cut their names on it, as Alf, Bert or Chas. must do in obedience to their instinct, which murmurs if it sees a fine woman go by, or even a dog, Ce chien est à moi [that dog is mine]. And, of course, it may not be a dog, I thought, remembering Parliament Square, the Sieges Allee[8] and other avenues; it may be a piece of land or a man with curly black hair. It is one of the great

5. Poet and translator (1809–1883).
6. Currer Bell, pen name of Charlotte Brontë; George Eliot, pen name of Mary Ann Evans; George Sand, pen name of Amandine Aurore Lucille Dupin (1804–1876).
7. The Athenian statesman Pericles was reported by the historian Thucydides to have said, "That woman is most praiseworthy whose name is least bandied about on men's lips, whether for praise or dispraise."
8. Victory Road, a thoroughfare in Berlin.

advantages of being a woman that one can pass even a very fine negress without wishing to make an Englishwoman of her.

That woman, then, who was born with a gift of poetry in the sixteenth century, was an unhappy woman, a woman at strife against herself. All the conditions of her life, all her own instincts, were hostile to the state of mind which is needed to set free whatever is in the brain. But what is the state of mind that is most propitious to the act of creation, I asked. Can one come by any notion of the state that furthers and makes possible that strange activity? Here I opened the volume containing the Tragedies of Shakespeare. What was Shakespeare's state of mind, for instance, when he wrote *Lear* and *Antony and Cleopatra?* It was certainly the state of mind most favourable to poetry that there has ever existed. But Shakespeare himself said nothing about it. We only know casually and by chance that he "never blotted a line." Nothing indeed was ever said by the artist himself about his state of mind until the eighteenth century perhaps. Rousseau perhaps began it.[9] At any rate, by the nineteenth century self-consciousness had developed so far that it was the habit for men of letters to describe their minds in confessions and autobiographies. Their lives also were written, and their letters were printed after their deaths. Thus, though we do not know what Shakespeare went through when he wrote *Lear,* we do know what Carlyle went through when he wrote the *French Revolution;* what Flaubert went through when he wrote *Madame Bovary;* what Keats was going through when he tried to write poetry against the coming of death and the indifference of the world.

And one gathers from this enormous modern literature of confession and self-analysis that to write a work of genius is almost always a feat of prodigious difficulty. Everything is against the likelihood that it will come from the writer's mind whole and entire. Generally material circumstances are against it. Dogs will bark; people will interrupt; money must be made; health will break down. Further, accentuating all these difficulties and making them harder to bear is the world's notorious indifference. It does not ask people to write poems and novels and histories; it does not need them. It does not care whether Flaubert finds the right word or whether Carlyle scrupulously verifies this or that fact. Naturally, it will not pay for what it does not want. And so the writer, Keats, Flaubert, Carlyle, suffers, especially in the creative years of youth, every form of distraction and discouragement. A curse, a cry of agony, rises from those books of analysis and confession. "Mighty poets in their misery dead"—that is the burden of their song. If anything comes through in spite of all this, it is a miracle, and probably no book is born entire and uncrippled as it was conceived.

But for women, I thought, looking at the empty shelves, these difficulties were infinitely more formidable. In the first place, to have a room of her own, let alone a quiet room or a sound-proof room, was out of the question, unless her parents were exceptionally rich or very noble, even up to the beginning of the nineteenth century. Since her pin money, which depended on the good will of her father, was only enough to keep her clothed, she was debarred from such alleviations as came even to Keats or Tennyson or Carlyle, all poor men, from a walking tour, a little journey to France, from the separate lodging which, even if it were miserable enough, sheltered them from the claims and tyrannies of their families. Such material difficulties were formidable; but much worse were the immaterial. The indifference of the world

9. Jean-Jacques Rousseau, 18th-century political philosopher and novelist, author of a famous memoir, *Confessions*.

which Keats and Flaubert and other men of genius have found so hard to bear was in her case not indifference but hostility. The world did not say to her as it said to them, Write if you choose; it makes no difference to me. The world said with a guffaw, Write? What's the good of your writing? Here the psychologists of Newnham and Girton might come to our help, I thought, looking again at the blank spaces on the shelves. For surely it is time that the effect of discouragement upon the mind of the artist should be measured, as I have seen a dairy company measure the effect of ordinary milk and Grade A milk upon the body of the rat. They set two rats in cages side by side, and of the two one was furtive, timid and small, and the other was glossy, bold and big. Now what food do we feed women as artists upon? I asked, remembering, I suppose, that dinner of prunes and custard. To answer that question I had only to open the evening paper and to read that Lord Birkenhead is of opinion—but really I am not going to trouble to copy out Lord Birkenhead's opinion upon the writing of women. What Dean Inge says I will leave in peace.[1] The Harley Street specialist may be allowed to rouse the echoes of Harley Street with his vociferations without raising a hair on my head. I will quote, however, Mr Oscar Browning,[2] because Mr Oscar Browning was a great figure in Cambridge at one time, and used to examine the students at Girton and Newnham. Mr Oscar Browning was wont to declare "that the impression left on his mind, after looking over any set of examination papers, was that, irrespective of the marks he might give, the best woman was intellectually the inferior of the worst man." After saying that Mr Browning went back to his rooms—and it is this sequel that endears him and makes him a human figure of some bulk and majesty—he went back to his rooms and found a stable-boy lying on the sofa—"a mere skeleton, his cheeks were cavernous and sallow, his teeth were black, and he did not appear to have the full use of his limbs. . . . 'That's Arthur' [said Mr Browning]. 'He's a dear boy really and most high-minded.'" The two pictures always seem to me to complete each other. And happily in this age of biography the two pictures often do complete each other, so that we are able to interpret the opinions of great men not only by what they say, but by what they do.

But though this is possible now, such opinions coming from the lips of important people must have been formidable enough even fifty years ago. Let us suppose that a father from the highest motives did not wish his daughter to leave home and become writer, painter or scholar. "See what Mr Oscar Browning says," he would say; and there was not only Mr Oscar Browning; there was the *Saturday Review;* there was Mr Greg[3]—the "essentials of a woman's being," said Mr Greg emphatically, "are that *they are supported by, and they minister to, men*"—there was an enormous body of masculine opinion to the effect that nothing could be expected of women intellectually. Even if her father did not read out loud these opinions, any girl could read them for herself; and the reading, even in the nineteenth century, must have lowered her vitality, and told profoundly upon her work. There would always have been that assertion—you cannot do this, you are incapable of doing that—to protest against, to overcome. Probably for a novelist this germ is no longer of much effect; for there have been women novelists of merit. But for painters it must still have some sting in it; and for musicians, I imagine, is even now active and poisonous in the extreme. The woman composer stands where the actress stood in the time of Shakespeare. Nick Greene, I

1. F. E. Smith, Lord Birkenhead (1872–1930), British statesman; William Ralph Inge (1860–1954), Dean of St. Paul's Cathedral in London.

2. Cambridge historian (1837–1923).

3. Sir Walter Greg (1879–1959), scholar and bibliographer.

thought, remembering the story I had made about Shakespeare's sister, said that a woman acting put him in mind of a dog dancing. Johnson repeated the phrase two hundred years later of women preaching.[4] And here, I said, opening a book about music, we have the very words used again in this year of grace, 1928, of women who try to write music. "Of Mlle. Germaine Tailleferre one can only repeat Dr. Johnson's dictum concerning a woman preacher, transposed into terms of music. 'Sir, a woman's composing is like a dog's walking on his hind legs. It is not done well, but you are surprised to find it done at all.'"[5] So accurately does history repeat itself.

Thus, I concluded, shutting Mr Oscar Browning's life and pushing away the rest, it is fairly evident that even in the nineteenth century a woman was not encouraged to be an artist. On the contrary, she was snubbed, slapped, lectured and exhorted. Her mind must have been strained and her vitality lowered by the need of opposing this, of disproving that. For here again we come within range of that very interesting and obscure masculine complex which has had so much influence upon the woman's movement; that deep-seated desire, not so much that she shall be inferior as that he shall be superior, which plants him wherever one looks, not only in front of the arts, but barring the way to politics too, even when the risk to himself seems infinitesimal and the suppliant humble and devoted. Even Lady Bessborough, I remembered, with all her passion for politics, must humbly bow herself and write to Lord Granville Leveson-Gower:[6] ". . . notwithstanding all my violence in politics and talking so much on that subject, I perfectly agree with you that no woman has any business to meddle with that or any other serious business, farther than giving her opinion (if she is ask'd)." And so she goes on to spend her enthusiasm where it meets with no obstacle whatsoever upon that immensely important subject, Lord Granville's maiden speech in the House of Commons. The spectacle is certainly a strange one, I thought. The history of men's opposition to women's emancipation is more interesting perhaps than the story of that emancipation itself. An amusing book might be made of it if some young student at Girton or Newnham would collect examples and deduce a theory—but she would need thick gloves on her hands, and bars to protect her of solid gold.

But what is amusing now, I recollected, shutting Lady Bessborough, had to be taken in desperate earnest once. Opinions that one now pastes in a book labelled cock-a-doodle-dum and keeps for reading to select audiences on summer nights once drew tears, I can assure you. Among your grandmothers and great-grandmothers there were many that wept their eyes out. Florence Nightingale shrieked aloud in her agony.[7] Moreover, it is all very well for you, who have got yourselves to college and enjoy sitting-rooms—or is it only bed-sitting-rooms?—of your own to say that genius should disregard such opinions; that genius should be above caring what is said of it. Unfortunately, it is precisely the men or women of genius who mind most what is said of them. Remember Keats. Remember the words he had cut on his tombstone. Think of Tennyson; think—but I need hardly multiply instances of the undeniable, if very unfortunate, fact that it is the nature of the artist to mind excessively what is said about him. Literature is strewn with the wreckage of men who have minded beyond reason the opinions of others.

4. Samuel Johnson (1709–1784), poet and man of letters.
5. A *Survey of Contemporary Music*, Cecil Gray, page 246 [Woolf's note].
6. Lady Bessborough (1761–1821), correspondent of the British statesman Lord Granville.
7. See *Cassandra*, by Florence Nightingale, printed in *The Cause*, by R. Strachey [Woolf's note]; see page 1510.

And this susceptibility of theirs is doubly unfortunate, I thought, returning again to my original enquiry into what state of mind is most propitious for creative work, because the mind of an artist, in order to achieve the prodigious effort of freeing whole and entire the work that is in him, must be incandescent, like Shakespeare's mind, I conjectured, looking at the book which lay open at *Antony and Cleopatra*. There must be no obstacle in it, no foreign matter unconsumed.

For though we say that we know nothing about Shakespeare's state of mind, even as we say that, we are saying something about Shakespeare's state of mind. The reason perhaps why we know so little of Shakespeare—compared with Donne or Ben Jonson or Milton—is that his grudges and spites and antipathies are hidden from us. We are not held up by some "revelation" which reminds us of the writer. All desire to protest, to preach, to proclaim an injury, to pay off a score, to make the world the witness of some hardship or grievance was fired out of him and consumed. Therefore his poetry flows from him free and unimpeded. If ever a human being got his work expressed completely, it was Shakespeare. If ever a mind was incandescent, unimpeded, I thought, turning again to the bookcase, it was Shakespeare's mind.

from *Chapter 4*

The extreme activity of mind which showed itself in the later eighteenth century among women—the talking, and the meeting, the writing of essays on Shakespeare, the translating of the classics—was founded on the solid fact that women could make money by writing. Money dignifies what is frivolous if unpaid for. It might still be well to sneer at "blue stockings with an itch for scribbling," but it could not be denied that they could put money in their purses. Thus, towards the end of the eighteenth century a change came about which, if I were rewriting history, I should describe more fully and think of greater importance than the Crusades or the Wars of the Roses. The middle-class woman began to write. For if *Pride and Prejudice* matters, and *Middlemarch* and *Villette* and *Wuthering Heights* matter,[8] then it matters far more than I can prove in an hour's discourse that women generally, and not merely the lonely aristocrat shut up in her country house among her folios and her flatterers, took to writing. Without those forerunners, Jane Austen and the Brontës and George Eliot could no more have written than Shakespeare could have written without Marlowe, or Marlowe without Chaucer, or Chaucer without those forgotten poets who paved the ways and tamed the natural savagery of the tongue. For masterpieces are not single and solitary births; they are the outcome of many years of thinking in common, of thinking by the body of the people, so that the experience of the mass is behind the single voice. Jane Austen should have laid a wreath upon the grave of Fanny Burney, and George Eliot done homage to the robust shade of Eliza Carter—the valiant old woman who tied a bell to her bedstead in order that she might wake early and learn Greek. All women together ought to let flowers fall upon the tomb of Aphra Behn[9] which is, most scandalously but rather appropriately, in Westminster Abbey, for it was she who earned them the right to speak their minds. It is she—shady and amorous as she was—who makes it not quite fantastic for me to say to you tonight: Earn five hundred a year by your wits.

8. *Pride and Prejudice* (1813), a novel by Jane Austen; *Middlemarch* (1871–1872) by George Eliot; *Villette* (1853) by Charlotte Brontë; *Wuthering Heights* (1847) by Emily Brontë.

9. A dramatist and the first English woman to earn a living by writing (1640–1689). Westminster Abbey, in central London, is the burial place of many of the English kings and queens, as well as of famous poets and statesmen.

Here, then, one had reached the early nineteenth century. And here, for the first time, I found several shelves given up entirely to the works of women. But why, I could not help asking, as I ran my eyes over them, were they, with very few exceptions, all novels? The original impulse was to poetry. The "supreme head of song" was a poetess. Both in France and in England the women poets precede the women novelists. Moreover, I thought, looking at the four famous names, what had George Eliot in common with Emily Brontë? Did not Charlotte Brontë fail entirely to understand Jane Austen? Save for the possibly relevant fact that not one of them had a child, four more incongruous characters could not have met together in a room—so much so that it is tempting to invent a meeting and a dialogue between them. Yet by some strange force they were all compelled, when they wrote, to write novels. Had it something to do with being born of the middle class, I asked; and with the fact, which Miss Emily Davies a little later was so strikingly to demonstrate,[1] that the middle-class family in the early nineteenth century was possessed only of a single sitting-room between them? If a woman wrote, she would have to write in the common sitting-room. And, as Miss Nightingale was so vehemently to complain,—"women never have an half hour . . . that they can call their own"—she was always interrupted. Still it would be easier to write prose and fiction there than to write poetry or a play. Less concentration is required. Jane Austen wrote like that to the end of her days. "How she was able to effect all this," her nephew writes in his Memoir, "is surprising, for she had no separate study to repair to, and most of the work must have been done in the general sitting-room, subject to all kinds of casual interruptions. She was careful that her occupation should not be suspected by servants or visitors or any persons beyond her own family party."[2] Jane Austen hid her manuscripts or covered them with a piece of blotting-paper. Then, again, all the literary training that a woman had in the early nineteenth century was training in the observation of character, in the analysis of emotion. Her sensibility had been educated for centuries by the influences of the common sitting-room. People's feelings were impressed on her; personal relations were always before her eyes. Therefore, when the middle-class woman took to writing, she naturally wrote novels, even though, as seems evident enough, two of the four famous women here named were not by nature novelists. Emily Brontë should have written poetic plays; the overflow of George Eliot's capacious mind should have spread itself when the creative impulse was spent upon history or biography. They wrote novels, however; one may even go further, I said, taking *Pride and Prejudice* from the shelf, and say that they wrote good novels. Without boasting or giving pain to the opposite sex, one may say that *Pride and Prejudice* is a good book. At any rate, one would not have been ashamed to have been caught in the act of writing *Pride and Prejudice*. Yet Jane Austen was glad that a hinge creaked, so that she might hide her manuscript before any one came in. To Jane Austen there was something discreditable in writing *Pride and Prejudice*. And, I wondered, would *Pride and Prejudice* have been a better novel if Jane Austen had not thought it necessary to hide her manuscript from visitors? I read a page or two to see; but I could not find any signs that her circumstances had harmed her work in the slightest. That, perhaps, was the chief miracle about it. Here was a woman about the year 1800 writing without hate, without bitterness, without fear, without protest, without preaching. That was how Shakespeare wrote, I thought, looking at *Antony and Cleopatra*;

1. (Sarah) Emily Davies was prominent in the movement to secure university education for women in the 19th century and was chief founder of Girton College, Cambridge (1873).

2. *Memoir of Jane Austen*, by her nephew, James Edward Austen-Leigh [Woolf's note].

and when people compare Shakespeare and Jane Austen, they may mean that the minds of both had consumed all impediments; and for that reason we do not know Jane Austen and we do not know Shakespeare, and for that reason Jane Austen pervades every word that she wrote, and so does Shakespeare. If Jane Austen suffered in any way from her circumstances it was in the narrowness of life that was imposed upon her. It was impossible for a woman to go about alone. She never travelled; she never drove through London in an omnibus or had luncheon in a shop by herself. But perhaps it was the nature of Jane Austen not to want what she had not. Her gift and her circumstances matched each other completely. But I doubt whether that was true of Charlotte Brontë, I said, opening *Jane Eyre* and laying it beside *Pride and Prejudice*.[3]

I opened it at chapter twelve and my eye was caught by the phrase, "Anybody may blame me who likes." What were they blaming Charlotte Brontë for, I wondered? And I read how Jane Eyre used to go up on to the roof when Mrs Fairfax was making jellies and looked over the fields at the distant view. And then she longed—and it was for this that they blamed her—that "then I longed for a power of vision which might overpass that limit; which might reach the busy world, towns, regions full of life I had heard of but never seen: that then I desired more of practical experience than I possessed; more of intercourse with my kind, of acquaintance with variety of character than was here within my reach. I valued what was good in Mrs Fairfax, and what was good in Adèle; but I believed in the existence of other and more vivid kinds of goodness, and what I believed in I wished to behold.

"Who blames me? Many, no doubt, and I shall be called discontented. I could not help it: the restlessness was in my nature; it agitated me to pain sometimes. . . .

"It is vain to say human beings ought to be satisfied with tranquillity: they must have action; and they will make it if they cannot find it. Millions are condemned to a stiller doom than mine, and millions are in silent revolt against their lot. Nobody knows how many rebellions ferment in the masses of life which people earth. Women are supposed to be very calm generally: but women feel just as men feel; they need exercise for their faculties and a field for their efforts as much as their brothers do; they suffer from too rigid a restraint, too absolute a stagnation, precisely as men would suffer; and it is narrow-minded in their more privileged fellow-creatures to say that they ought to confine themselves to making puddings and knitting stockings, to playing on the piano and embroidering bags. It is thoughtless to condemn them, or laugh at them, if they seek to do more or learn more than custom has pronounced necessary for their sex.

"When thus alone I not unfrequently heard Grace Poole's laugh. . . . "

That is an awkward break, I thought. It is upsetting to come upon Grace Poole all of a sudden. The continuity is disturbed. One might say, I continued, laying the book down beside *Pride and Prejudice*, that the woman who wrote those pages had more genius in her than Jane Austen; but if one reads them over and marks that jerk in them, that indignation, one sees that she will never get her genius expressed whole

3. Woolf goes on to describe parts of the plot of *Jane Eyre*; Jane Eyre, a penniless orphan, having suffered greatly during her schooling, takes up the post of governess to Adele, the daughter of Mr. Rochester, a man of strange moods. Rochester falls in love with Jane, who agrees to marry him; however this is prevented by Rochester's mad wife—whom Rochester has locked in the attic, concealing her existence from Jane—who tears Jane's wedding veil on the eve of the marriage. Rochester at first tells Jane that Grace Poole, a servant, had been responsible for this and other strange events, including the uncanny laughter occasionally heard in the house.

and entire. Her books will be deformed and twisted. She will write in a rage where she should write calmly. She will write foolishly where she should write wisely. She will write of herself where she should write of her characters. She is at war with her lot. How could she help but die young, cramped and thwarted?

One could not but play for a moment with the thought of what might have happened if Charlotte Brontë had possessed say three hundred a year—but the foolish woman sold the copyright of her novels outright for fifteen hundred pounds; had somehow possessed more knowledge of the busy world, and towns and regions full of life; more practical experience, and intercourse with her kind and acquaintance with a variety of character. In those words she puts her finger exactly not only upon her own defects as a novelist but upon those of her sex at that time. She knew, no one better, how enormously her genius would have profited if it had not spent itself in solitary visions over distant fields; if experience and intercourse and travel had been granted her. But they were not granted; they were withheld; and we must accept the fact that all those good novels, *Villette*, *Emma*, *Wuthering Heights*, *Middlemarch*, were written by women without more experience of life than could enter the house of a respectable clergyman; written too in the common sitting-room of that respectable house and by women so poor that they could not afford to buy more than a few quires of paper at a time upon which to write *Wuthering Heights* or *Jane Eyre*. One of them, it is true, George Eliot, escaped after much tribulation, but only to a secluded villa in St John's Wood. And there she settled down in the shadow of the world's disapproval.[4] "I wish it to be understood," she wrote, "that I should never invite any one to come and see me who did not ask for the invitation"; for was she not living in sin with a married man and might not the sight of her damage the chastity of Mrs Smith or whoever it might be that chanced to call? One must submit to the social convention, and be "cut off from what is called the world." At the same time, on the other side of Europe, there was a young man living freely with this gipsy or with that great lady; going to the wars; picking up unhindered and uncensored all that varied experience of human life which served him so splendidly later when he came to write his books. Had Tolstoi lived at the Priory in seclusion with a married lady "cut off from what is called the world," however edifying the moral lesson, he could scarcely, I thought, have written *War and Peace*.

But one could perhaps go a little deeper into the question of novel-writing and the effect of sex upon the novelist. If one shuts one's eyes and thinks of the novel as a whole, it would seem to be a creation owning a certain looking-glass likeness to life, though of course with simplifications and distortions innumerable. At any rate, it is a structure leaving a shape on the mind's eye, built now in squares, now pagoda shaped, now throwing out wings and arcades, now solidly compact and domed like the Cathedral of Saint Sofia at Constantinople.[5] This shape, I thought, thinking back over certain famous novels, starts in one the kind of emotion that is appropriate to it. But that emotion at once blends itself with others, for the "shape" is not made by the relation of stone to stone, but by the relation of human being to human being. Thus a novel starts in us all sorts of antagonistic and opposed emotions. Life conflicts with something that is not life. Hence the difficulty of coming to any agreement about

4. Following a strictly religious childhood, the novelist George Eliot lost her faith and eloped with G. H. Lewes, a married man, with whom she lived for the rest of his life; her family never forgave her.

5. The Hagia Sophia, a domed basilica completed in 537 C.E., named for the female personification of Wisdom in the Bible.

novels, and the immense sway that our private prejudices have upon us. On the one hand, we feel, You—John the hero—must live, or I shall be in the depths of despair. On the other, we feel, Alas, John, you must die, because the shape of the book requires it. Life conflicts with something that is not life. Then since life it is in part, we judge it as life. James is the sort of man I most detest, one says. Or, This is a farrago of absurdity. I could never feel anything of the sort myself. The whole structure, it is obvious, thinking back on any famous novel, is one of infinite complexity, because it is thus made up of so many different judgments, of so many different kinds of emotion. The wonder is that any book so composed holds together for more than a year or two, or can possibly mean to the English reader what it means for the Russian or the Chinese. But they do hold together occasionally very remarkably. And what holds them together in these rare instances of survival (I was thinking of *War and Peace*) is something that one calls integrity, though it has nothing to do with paying one's bills or behaving honourably in an emergency. What one means by integrity, in the case of the novelist, is the conviction that he gives one that this is the truth. Yes, one feels, I should never have thought that this could be so; I have never known people behaving like that. But you have convinced me that so it is, so it happens. One holds every phrase, every scene to the light as one reads—for Nature seems, very oddly, to have provided us with an inner light by which to judge of the novelist's integrity or disintegrity. Or perhaps it is rather that Nature, in her most irrational mood, has traced in invisible ink on the walls of the mind a premonition which these great artists confirm; a sketch which only needs to be held to the fire of genius to become visible. When one so exposes it and sees it come to life one exclaims in rapture, But this is what I have always felt and known and desired! And one boils over with excitement, and, shutting the book even with a kind of reverence as if it were something very precious, a stand-by to return to as long as one lives, one puts it back on the shelf, I said, taking *War and Peace* and putting it back in its place. If, on the other hand, these poor sentences that one takes and tests rouse first a quick and eager response with their bright colouring and their dashing gestures but there they stop: something seems to check them in their development: or if they bring to light only a faint scribble in that corner and a blot over there, and nothing appears whole and entire, then one heaves a sigh of disappointment and says, Another failure. This novel has come to grief somewhere.

And for the most part, of course, novels do come to grief somewhere. The imagination falters under the enormous strain. The insight is confused; it can no longer distinguish between the true and the false; it has no longer the strength to go on with the vast labour that calls at every moment for the use of so many different faculties. But how would all this be affected by the sex of the novelist, I wondered, looking at *Jane Eyre* and the others. Would the fact of her sex in any way interfere with the integrity of a woman novelist—that integrity which I take to be the backbone of the writer? Now, in the passages I have quoted from *Jane Eyre*, it is clear that anger was tampering with the integrity of Charlotte Brontë the novelist. She left her story, to which her entire devotion was due, to attend to some personal grievance. She remembered that she had been starved of her proper due of experience—she had been made to stagnate in a parsonage mending stockings when she wanted to wander free over the world. Her imagination swerved from indignation and we feel it swerve. But there were many more influences than anger tugging at her imagination and deflecting it from its path. Ignorance, for instance. The portrait of Rochester is drawn in the dark. We feel the influence of fear in it; just as we constantly feel an acidity which is the result of oppression, a buried suffering smouldering beneath her passion, a rancour which contracts those books, splendid as they are, with a spasm of pain.

And since a novel has this correspondence to real life, its values are to some extent those of real life. But it is obvious that the values of women differ very often from the values which have been made by the other sex; naturally, this is so. Yet it is the masculine values that prevail. Speaking crudely, football and sport are "important"; the worship of fashion, the buying of clothes "trivial." And these values are inevitably transferred from life to fiction. This is an important book, the critic assumes, because it deals with war. This is an insignificant book because it deals with the feelings of women in a drawing-room. A scene in a battlefield is more important than a scene in a shop—everywhere and much more subtly the difference of value persists. The whole structure, therefore, of the early nineteenth-century novel was raised, if one was a woman, by a mind which was slightly pulled from the straight, and made to alter its clear vision in deference to external authority. One has only to skim those old forgotten novels and listen to the tone of voice in which they are written to divine that the writer was meeting criticism; she was saying this by way of aggression, or that by way of conciliation. She was admitting that she was "only a woman," or protesting that she was "as good as a man." She met that criticism as her temperament dictated, with docility and diffidence, or with anger and emphasis. It does not matter which it was; she was thinking of something other than the thing itself. Down comes her book upon our heads. There was a flaw in the centre of it. And I thought of all the women's novels that lie scattered, like small pock-marked apples in an orchard, about the secondhand book shops of London. It was the flaw in the centre that had rotted them. She had altered her values in deference to the opinion of others.

But how impossible it must have been for them not to budge either to the right or to the left. What genius, what integrity it must have required in face of all that criticism, in the midst of that purely patriarchal society, to hold fast to the thing as they saw it without shrinking. Only Jane Austen did it and Emily Brontë. It is another feather, perhaps the finest, in their caps. They wrote as women write, not as men write. Of all the thousand women who wrote novels then, they alone entirely ignored the perpetual admonitions of the eternal pedagogue—write this, think that. They alone were deaf to that persistent voice, now grumbling, now patronising, now domineering, now grieved, now shocked, now angry, now avuncular, that voice which cannot let women alone, but must be at them, like some too conscientious governess, adjuring them, like Sir Egerton Brydges,[6] to be refined; dragging even into the criticism of poetry criticism of sex; admonishing them, if they would be good and win, as I suppose, some shiny prize, to keep within certain limits which the gentleman in question thinks suitable:[7] ". . . female novelists should only aspire to excellence by courageously acknowledging the limitations of their sex."[8] That

6. Scholar and editor (1762–1837), Brydges had criticized the writings of Margaret Cavendish, Duchess of Newcastle (1623–1674), for what he considered to be their coarse language.

7. "[She] has a metaphysical purpose, and that is a dangerous obsession, especially with a woman, for women rarely posses men's healthy love of rhetoric. It is a strange lack in the sex which is in other things more primitive and more materialistic."—*New Criterion,* June 1928 [Woolf's note].

8. "If, like the reporter, you believe that female novelists should only aspire to excellence by courageously acknowledging the limitations of their sex (Jane Austen [has] demonstrated how gracefully this gesture can be accomplished). . . ."—*Life and Letters,* August 1928 [Woolf's note].

puts the matter in a nutshell, and when I tell you, rather to your surprise, that this sentence was written not in August 1828 but in August 1928, you will agree, I think, that however delightful it is to us now, it represents a vast body of opinion—I am not going to stir those old pools, I take only what chance has floated to my feet—that was far more vigorous and far more vocal a century ago. It would have needed a very stalwart young woman in 1828 to disregard all those snubs and chidings and promises of prizes. One must have been something of a firebrand to say to oneself, Oh, but they can't buy literature too. Literature is open to everybody. I refuse to allow you, Beadle though you are, to turn me off the grass. Lock up your libraries if you like; but there is no gate, no lock, no bolt that you can set upon the freedom of my mind.

But whatever effect discouragement and criticism had upon their writing—and I believe that they had a very great effect—that was unimportant compared with the other difficulty which faced them (I was still considering those early nineteenth-century novelists) when they came to set their thoughts on paper—that is that they had no tradition behind them, or one so short and partial that it was of little help. For we think back through our mothers if we are women. It is useless to go to the great men writers for help, however much one may go to them for pleasure. Lamb, Browne, Thackeray, Newman, Sterne, Dickens, De Quincey—whoever it may be—never helped a woman yet, though she may have learnt a few tricks of them and adapted them to her use. The weight, the pace, the stride of a man's mind are too unlike her own for her to lift anything substantial from him successfully. The ape is too distant to be sedulous. Perhaps the first thing she would find, setting pen to paper, was that there was no common sentence ready for her use. All the great novelists like Thackeray and Dickens and Balzac have written a natural prose, swift but not slovenly, expressive but not precious, taking their own tint without ceasing to be common property. They have based it on the sentence that was current at the time. The sentence that was current at the beginning of the nineteenth century ran something like this perhaps: "The grandeur of their works was an argument with them, not to stop short, but to proceed. They could have no higher excitement or satisfaction than in the exercise of their art and endless generations of truth and beauty. Success prompts to exertion; and habit facilitates success." That is a man's sentence; behind it one can see Johnson, Gibbon[9] and the rest. It was a sentence that was unsuited for a woman's use. Charlotte Brontë, with all her splendid gift for prose, stumbled and fell with that clumsy weapon in her hands. George Eliot committed atrocities with it that beggar description. Jane Austen looked at it and laughed at it and devised a perfectly natural, shapely sentence proper for her own use and never departed from it. Thus, with less genius for writing than Charlotte Brontë, she got infinitely more said. Indeed, since freedom and fullness of expression are of the essence of the art, such a lack of tradition, such a scarcity and inadequacy of tools, must have told enormously upon the writing of women. Moreover, a book is not made of sentences laid end to end, but of sentences built, if an image helps, into arcades or domes. And this shape too has been made by men out of their own needs for their own uses. There is no reason to think that the form of the epic or of the poetic plays suits a woman any more than the sentence suits her. But all the older forms of literature were hardened and set by the time she became a writer. The

9. Edward Gibbon, author of *The History of the Decline and Fall of the Roman Empire* (1776–1788).

novel alone was young enough to be soft in her hands—another reason, perhaps, why she wrote novels. Yet who shall say that even now "the novel" (I give it inverted commas to mark my sense of the words' inadequacy), who shall say that even this most pliable of all forms is rightly shaped for her use? No doubt we shall find her knocking that into shape for herself when she has the free use of her limbs; and providing some new vehicle, not necessarily in verse, for the poetry in her. For it is the poetry that is still denied outlet. And I went on to ponder how a woman nowadays would write a poetic tragedy in five acts—would she use verse—would she not use prose rather?

But these are difficult questions which lie in the twilight of the future. I must leave them, if only because they stimulate me to wander from my subject into trackless forests where I shall be lost and, very likely, devoured by wild beasts. I do not want, and I am sure that you do not want me, to broach that very dismal subject, the future of fiction, so that I will only pause here one moment to draw your attention to the great part which must be played in that future so far as women are concerned by physical conditions. The book has somehow to be adapted to the body, and at a venture one would say that women's books should be shorter, more concentrated, than those of men, and framed so that they do not need long hours of steady and uninterrupted work. For interruptions there will always be. Again, the nerves that feed the brain would seem to differ in men and women, and if you are going to make them work their best and hardest, you must find out what treatment suits them—whether these hours of lectures, for instance, which the monks devised, presumably, hundreds of years ago, suit them—what alternations of work and rest they need, interpreting rest not as doing nothing but as doing something but something that is different; and what should that difference be? All this should be discussed and discovered; all this is part of the question of women and fiction. And yet, I continued, approaching the bookcase again, where shall I find that elaborate study of the psychology of women by a woman? If through their incapacity to play football women are not going to be allowed to practise medicine——

Happily my thoughts were now given another turn.

Chapter 6

Next day the light of the October morning was falling in dusty shafts through the uncurtained windows, and the hum of traffic rose from the street. London then was winding itself up again; the factory was astir; the machines were beginning. It was tempting, after all this reading, to look out of the window and see what London was doing on the morning of the twenty-sixth of October 1928. And what was London doing? Nobody, it seemed, was reading *Antony and Cleopatra*. London was wholly indifferent, it appeared, to Shakespeare's plays. Nobody cared a straw—and I do not blame them—for the future of fiction, the death of poetry or the development by the average woman of a prose style completely expressive of her mind. If opinions upon any of these matters had been chalked on the pavement, nobody would have stooped to read them. The nonchalance of the hurrying feet would have rubbed them out in half an hour. Here came an errand-boy; here a woman with a dog on a lead. The fascination of the London street is that no two people are ever alike; each seems bound on some private affair of his own. There were the business-like, with their little bags; there were the drifters rattling sticks upon area railings; there were affable characters to whom the streets serve for clubroom, hailing men in carts and giving information without being asked for it. Also there were funerals to which men, thus suddenly reminded of the passing of their own bodies, lifted their hats. And then a very distinguished gentleman came slowly down a doorstep and paused to avoid collision with a bustling lady who had, by some means or other, acquired a splendid fur coat and a bunch of Parma violets. They all seemed separate, self-absorbed, on business of their own.

At this moment, as so often happens in London, there was a complete lull and suspension of traffic. Nothing came down the street; nobody passed. A single leaf detached itself from the plane tree at the end of the street, and in that pause and suspension fell. Somehow it was like a signal falling, a signal pointing to a force in things which one had overlooked. It seemed to point to a river, which flowed past, invisibly, round the corner, down the street, and took people and eddied them along, as the stream at Oxbridge had taken the undergraduate in his boat and the dead leaves. Now it was bringing from one side of the street to the other diagonally a girl in patent leather boots, and then a young man in a maroon overcoat; it was also bringing a taxi-cab; and it brought all three together at a point directly beneath my window; where the taxi stopped; and the girl and the young man stopped; and they got into the taxi; and then the cab glided off as if it were swept on by the current elsewhere.

The sight was ordinary enough; what was strange was the rhythmical order with which my imagination had invested it; and the fact that the ordinary sight of two people getting into a cab had the power to communicate something of their own seeming satisfaction. The sight of two people coming down the street and meeting at the corner seems to ease the mind of some strain, I thought, watching the taxi turn and make off. Perhaps to think, as I had been thinking these two days, of one sex as distinct from the other is an effort. It interferes with the unity of the mind. Now that effort had ceased and that unity had been restored by seeing two people come together and get into a taxi-cab. The mind is certainly a very mysterious organ, I reflected, drawing my head in from the window, about which nothing whatever is known, though we depend upon it so completely. Why do I feel that there are severances and oppositions in the mind, as there are strains from obvious causes on the body? What does one mean by "the unity of the mind," I pondered, for clearly the mind has so great a power of concentrating at any point at any moment that it seems to have no single state of being. It can separate itself from the people in the street, for example, and think of itself as apart from them, at an upper window looking down on them. Or it can think with other people spontaneously, as, for instance, in a crowd waiting to hear some piece of news read out. It can think back through its fathers or through its mothers, as I have said that a woman writing thinks back through her mothers. Again if one is a woman one is often surprised by a sudden splitting off of consciousness, say in walking down Whitehall,[1] when from being the natural inheritor of that civilisation, she becomes, on the contrary, outside of it, alien and critical. Clearly the mind is always altering its focus, and bringing the world into different perspectives. But some of these states of mind seem, even if adopted spontaneously, to be less comfortable than others. In order to keep oneself continuing in them one is unconsciously holding something back, and gradually the repression becomes an ef-

1. A main thoroughfare in central London and site of government offices.

fort. But there may be some state of mind in which one could continue without effort because nothing is required to be held back. And this perhaps, I thought, coming in from the window, is one of them. For certainly when I saw the couple get into the taxi-cab the mind felt as if, after being divided, it had come together again in a natural fusion. The obvious reason would be that it is natural for the sexes to co-operate. One has a profound, if irrational, instinct in favour of the theory that the union of man and woman makes for the greatest satisfaction, the most complete happiness. But the sight of the two people getting into the taxi and the satisfaction it gave me made me also ask whether there are two sexes in the mind corresponding to the two sexes in the body, and whether they also require to be united in order to get complete satisfaction and happiness. And I went on amateurishly to sketch a plan of the soul so that in each of us two powers preside, one male, one female; and in the man's brain, the man predominates over the woman, and in the woman's brain, the woman predominates over the man. The normal and comfortable state of being is that when the two live in harmony together, spiritually co-operating. If one is a man, still the woman part of the brain must have effect; and a woman also must have intercourse with the man in her. Coleridge perhaps meant this when he said that a great mind is androgynous.[2] It is when this fusion takes place that the mind is fully fertilised and uses all its faculties. Perhaps a mind that is purely masculine cannot create, any more than a mind that is purely feminine, I thought. But it would be well to test what one meant by man-womanly, and conversely by woman-manly, by pausing and looking at a book or two.

Coleridge certainly did not mean, when he said that a great mind is androgynous, that it is a mind that has any special sympathy with women; a mind that takes up their cause or devotes itself to their interpretation. Perhaps the androgynous mind is less apt to make these distinctions than the single-sexed mind. He meant, perhaps, that the androgynous mind is resonant and porous; that it transmits emotion without impediment; that it is naturally creative, incandescent and undivided. In fact one goes back to Shakespeare's mind as the type of the androgynous, of the man-womanly mind, though it would be impossible to say what Shakespeare thought of women. And if it be true that it is one of the tokens of the fully developed mind that it does not think specially or separately of sex, how much harder it is to attain that condition now than ever before. Here I came to the books by living writers, and there paused and wondered if this fact were not at the root of something that had long puzzled me. No age can ever have been as stridently sex-conscious as our own; those innumerable books by men about women in the British Museum are a proof of it. The Suffrage campaign was no doubt to blame.[3] It must have roused in men an extraordinary desire for self-assertion; it must have made them lay an emphasis upon their own sex and its characteristics which they would not have troubled to think about had they not been challenged. And when one is challenged, even by a few women in black bonnets, one retaliates, if one has never been challenged before, rather excessively. That perhaps accounts for some of the characteristics that I remember to have found here, I thought, taking down a new

2. The poet Samuel Taylor Coleridge made the remark in September 1832—"a great mind must be androgynous"—and it was duly recorded in his *Table Talk*.

3. The campaign for women's suffrage, which had been steadily gaining support during the 19th century, resorted to unconstitutional methods following the founding of the Women's Social and Political Union in 1903.

novel by Mr A, who is in the prime of life and very well thought of, apparently, by the reviewers. I opened it. Indeed, it was delightful to read a man's writing again. It was so direct, so straightforward after the writing of women. It indicated such freedom of mind, such liberty of person, such confidence in himself. One had a sense of physical well-being in the presence of this well-nourished, well-educated, free mind, which had never been thwarted or opposed, but had had full liberty from birth to stretch itself in whatever way it liked. All this was admirable. But after reading a chapter or two a shadow seemed to lie across the page. It was a straight dark bar, a shadow shaped something like the letter "I." One began dodging this way and that to catch a glimpse of the landscape behind it. Whether that was indeed a tree or a woman walking I was not quite sure. Back one was always hailed to the letter "I." One began to be tired of "I." Not but what this "I" was a most respectable "I"; honest and logical; as hard as a nut, and polished for centuries by good teaching and good feeding. I respect and admire that "I" from the bottom of my heart. But—here I turned a page or two, looking for something or other—the worst of it is that in the shadow of the letter "I" all is shapeless as mist. Is that a tree? No, it is a woman. But . . . she has not a bone in her body, I thought, watching Phoebe, for that was her name, coming across the beach. Then Alan got up and the shadow of Alan at once obliterated Phoebe. For Alan had views and Phoebe was quenched in the flood of his views. And then Alan, I thought, has passions; and here I turned page after page very fast, feeling that the crisis was approaching, and so it was. It took place on the beach under the sun. It was done very openly. It was done very vigorously. Nothing could have been more indecent. But . . . I had said "but" too often. One cannot go on saying "but." One must finish the sentence somehow, I rebuked myself. Shall I finish it, "But . . . I am bored!" But why was I bored? Partly because of the dominance of the letter "I" and the aridity, which, like the giant beech tree, it casts within its shade. Nothing will grow there. And partly for some more obscure reason. There seemed to be some obstacle, some impediment of Mr A's mind which blocked the fountain of creative energy and shored it within narrow limits. And remembering the lunch party at Oxbridge, and the cigarette ash and the Manx cat and Tennyson and Christina Rossetti all in a bunch, it seemed possible that the impediment lay there. As he no longer hums under his breath, "There has fallen a splendid tear from the passion-flower at the gate," when Phoebe crosses the beach, and she no longer replies, "My heart is like a singing bird whose nest is in a water'd shoot," when Alan approaches what can he do? Being honest as the day and logical as the sun, there is only one thing he can do. And that he does, to do him justice, over and over (I said, turning the pages) and over again. And that, I added, aware of the awful nature of the confession, seems somehow dull. Shakespeare's indecency uproots a thousand other things in one's mind, and is far from being dull. But Shakespeare does it for pleasure; Mr A, as the nurses say, does it on purpose. He does it in protest. He is protesting against the equality of the other sex by asserting his own superiority. He is therefore impeded and inhibited and self-conscious as Shakespeare might have been if he too had known Miss Clough[4] and Miss Davies. Doubtless Elizabethan literature would have been very different from what it is if the woman's movement had begun in the sixteenth century and not in the nineteenth.

4. Anne Jemima Clough (1820–1892), feminist and first Principal of Newnham College, Cambridge.

What, then, it amounts to, if this theory of the two sides of the mind holds good, is that virility has now become self-conscious—men, that is to say, are now writing only with the male side of their brains. It is a mistake for a woman to read them, for she will inevitably look for something that she will not find. It is the power of suggestion that one most misses, I thought, taking Mr B the critic in my hand and reading, very carefully and very dutifully, his remarks upon the art of poetry. Very able they were, acute and full of learning; but the trouble was, that his feelings no longer communicated; his mind seemed separated into different chambers; not a sound carried from one to the other. Thus, when one takes a sentence of Mr B into the mind it falls plump to the ground—dead; but when one takes a sentence of Coleridge into the mind, it explodes and gives birth to all kinds of other ideas, and that is the only sort of writing of which one can say that it has the secret of perpetual life.

But whatever the reason may be, it is a fact that one must deplore. For it means—here I had come to rows of books by Mr Galsworthy and Mr Kipling—that some of the finest works of our greatest living writers fall upon deaf ears. Do what she will a woman cannot find in them that fountain of perpetual life which the critics assure her is there. It is not only that they celebrate male virtues, enforce male values and describe the world of men; it is that the emotion with which these books are permeated is to a woman incomprehensible. It is coming, it is gathering, it is about to burst on one's head, one begins saying long before the end. That picture will fall on old Jolyon's head;[5] he will die of the shock; the old clerk will speak over him two or three obituary words; and all the swans on the Thames will simultaneously burst out singing. But one will rush away before that happens and hide in the gooseberry bushes, for the emotion which is so deep, so subtle, so symbolical to a man moves a woman to wonder. So with Mr Kipling's officers who turn their backs; and his Sowers who sow the Seed; and his Men who are alone with their Work; and the Flag—one blushes at all these capital letters as if one had been caught eavesdropping at some purely masculine orgy. The fact is that neither Mr Galsworthy nor Mr Kipling has a spark of the woman in him. Thus all their qualities seem to a woman, if one may generalise, crude and immature. They lack suggestive power. And when a book lacks suggestive power, however hard it hits the surface of the mind it cannot penetrate within.

And in that restless mood in which one takes books out and puts them back again without looking at them I began to envisage an age to come of pure, of self-assertive virility, such as the letters of professors (take Sir Walter Raleigh's letters, for instance) seem to forebode, and the rulers of Italy have already brought into being.[6] For one can hardly fail to be impressed in Rome by the sense of unmitigated masculinity; and whatever the value of unmitigated masculinity upon the state, one may question the effect of it upon the art of poetry. At any rate, according to the newspapers, there is a certain anxiety about fiction in Italy. There has been a meeting of academicians whose object it is "to develop the Italian novel." "Men famous by birth, or in finance, industry or the Fascist corporations" came together the other day and discussed the matter, and a telegram was sent to the Duce expressing the hope "that the Fascist era would soon give birth to a poet worthy of it." We may all join in that pious hope, but it is doubtful whether poetry can come out of an incubator. Poetry ought to have a mother as well as a father. The Fascist poem, one may fear, will be a horrid lit-

5. A climactic moment in John Galsworthy's novel sequence *The Forsyte Saga* (1906–1929).
6. Sir Walter Raleigh was Professor of English Literature at Oxford; his *Letters* were published in 1926. Woolf refers to the nascent Italian Fascist state.

tle abortion such as one sees in a glass jar in the museum of some county town. Such monsters never live long, it is said; one has never seen a prodigy of that sort cropping grass in a field. Two heads on one body do not make for length of life.

However, the blame for all this, if one is anxious to lay blame, rests no more upon one sex than upon the other. All seducers and reformers are responsible, Lady Bessborough when she lied to Lord Granville; Miss Davies when she told the truth to Mr Greg. All who have brought about a state of sex-consciousness are to blame, and it is they who drive me, when I want to stretch my faculties on a book, to seek it in that happy age, before Miss Davies and Miss Clough were born, when the writer used both sides of his mind equally. One must turn back to Shakespeare then, for Shakespeare was androgynous; and so was Keats and Sterne and Cowper and Lamb and Coleridge. Shelley perhaps was sexless. Milton and Ben Jonson had a dash too much of the male in them. So had Wordsworth and Tolstoi. In our time Proust was wholly androgynous, if not perhaps a little too much of a woman. But that failing is too rare for one to complain of it, since without some mixture of the kind the intellect seems to predominate and the other faculties of the mind harden and become barren. However, I consoled myself with the reflection that this is perhaps a passing phase; much of what I have said in obedience to my promise to give you the course of my thoughts will seem out of date; much of what flames in my eyes will seem dubious to you who have not yet come of age.

Even so, the very first sentence that I would write here, I said, crossing over to the writing-table and taking up the page headed Women and Fiction, is that it is fatal for any one who writes to think of their sex. It is fatal to be a man or woman pure and simple; one must be woman-manly or man-womanly. It is fatal for a woman to lay the least stress on any grievance; to plead even with justice any cause; in any way to speak consciously as a woman. And fatal is no figure of speech; for anything written with that conscious bias is doomed to death. It ceases to be fertilised. Brilliant and effective, powerful and masterly, as it may appear for a day or two, it must wither at nightfall; it cannot grow in the minds of others. Some collaboration has to take place in the mind between the woman and the man before the act of creation can be accomplished. Some marriage of opposites has to be consummated. The whole of the mind must lie wide open if we are to get the sense that the writer is communicating his experience with perfect fullness. There must be freedom and there must be peace. Not a wheel must grate, not a light glimmer. The curtains must be close drawn. The writer, I thought, once his experience is over, must lie back and let his mind celebrate its nuptials in darkness. He must not look or question what is being done. Rather, he must pluck the petals from a rose or watch the swans float calmly down the river. And I saw again the current which took the boat and the undergraduate and the dead leaves; and the taxi took the man and the woman, I thought, seeing them come together across the street, and the current swept them away, I thought, hearing far off the roar of London's traffic, into that tremendous stream.

Here, then, Mary Beton ceases to speak. She has told you how she reached the conclusion—the prosaic conclusion—that it is necessary to have five hundred a year and a room with a lock on the door if you are to write fiction or poetry. She has tried to lay bare the thoughts and impressions that led her to think this. She has asked you to follow her flying into the arms of a Beadle, lunching here, dining there, drawing pictures in the British Museum, taking books from the shelf, looking out of the window. While she has been doing all these things, you no doubt have been observing her failings and foibles and deciding what effect they have had on her opinions. You have been contradicting her and making whatever additions and deductions seem good to you. That is all as it should be, for in a question like this truth is only to be had by laying together many varieties of error. And I will end now in my own person by anticipating two criticisms, so obvious that you can hardly fail to make them.

No opinion has been expressed, you may say, upon the comparative merits of the sexes even as writers. That was done purposely, because, even if the time had come for such a valuation—and it is far more important at the moment to know how much money women had and how many rooms than to theorise about their capacities—even if the time had come I do not believe that gifts, whether of mind or character, can be weighed like sugar and butter, not even in Cambridge, where they are so adept at putting people into classes and fixing caps on their heads and letters after their names. I do not believe that even the Table of Precedency which you will find in Whitaker's *Almanac*[7] represents a final order of values, or that there is any sound reason to suppose that a Commander of the Bath will ultimately walk in to dinner behind a Master in Lunacy. All this pitting of sex against sex, of quality against quality; all this claiming of superiority and imputing of inferiority, belong to the private-school stage of human existence where there are "sides," and it is necessary for one side to beat another side, and of the utmost importance to walk up to a platform and receive from the hands of the Headmaster himself a highly ornamental pot. As people mature they cease to believe in sides or in Headmasters or in highly ornamental pots. At any rate, where books are concerned, it is notoriously difficult to fix labels of merit in such a way that they do not come off. Are not reviews of current literature a perpetual illustration of the difficulty of judgment? "This great book," "this worthless book," the same book is called by both names. Praise and blame alike mean nothing. No, delightful as the pastime of measuring may be, it is the most futile of all occupations, and to submit to the decrees of the measurers the most servile of attitudes. So long as you write what you wish to write, that is all that matters; and whether it matters for ages or only for hours, nobody can say. But to sacrifice a hair of the head of your vision, a shade of its colour, in deference to some Headmaster with a silver pot in his hand or to some professor with a measuring-rod up his sleeve, is the most abject treachery, and the sacrifice of wealth and chastity which used to be said to be the greatest of human disasters, a mere flea-bite in comparison.

Next I think that you may object that in all this I have made too much of the importance of material things. Even allowing a generous margin for symbolism, that five hundred a year stands for the power to contemplate, that a lock on the door means the power to think for oneself, still you may say that the mind should rise above such things; and that great poets have often been poor men. Let me then quote to you the words of your own Professor of Literature, who knows better than I do what goes to the making of a poet. Sir Arthur Quiller-Couch writes:[8]

7. A compendium of general information first published in 1868.

8. *The Art of Writing*, by Sir Arthur Quiller-Couch [Woolf's note]. Quiller-Couch was then Professor of English Literature at Cambridge University.

"What are the great poetical names of the last hundred years or so? Coleridge, Wordsworth, Byron, Shelly, Landor, Keats, Tennyson, Browning, Arnold, Morris, Rossetti, Swinburne . . . we may stop there. Of these, all but Keats, Browning, Rossetti were University men; and of these three, Keats, who died young, cut off in his prime, was the only one not fairly well to do. It may seem a brutal thing to say, and it is a sad thing to say: but, as a matter of hard fact, the theory that poetical genius bloweth where it listeth, and equally in poor and rich, holds little truth. As a matter of hard fact, nine out of those twelve were University men: which means that somehow or other they procured the means to get the best education England can give. As a matter of hard fact, of the remaining three you know that Browning was well to do, and I challenge you that, if he had not been well to do, he would no more have attained to write *Saul* or *The Ring and the Book* than Ruskin would have attained to writing *Modern Painters* if his father had not dealt prosperously in business. Rossetti had a small private income; and, moreover, he painted. There remains but Keats; whom Atropos[9] slew young, as she slew John Clare in a mad-house, and James Thomson by the laudanum he took to drug disappointment. These are dreadful facts, but let us face them. It is—however dishonouring to us as a nation—certain that, by some fault in our commonwealth, the poor poet has not in these days, nor has had for two hundred years, a dog's chance. Believe me—and I have spent a great part of ten years in watching some three hundred and twenty elementary schools—we may prate of democracy, but actually, a poor child in England has little more hope than had the son of an Athenian slave to be emancipated into that intellectual freedom of which great writings are born."

Nobody could put the point more plainly. "The poor poet has not in these days, nor has had for two hundred years, a dog's chance . . . a poor child in England has little more hope than had the son of an Athenian slave to be emancipated into that intellectual freedom of which great writings are born." That is it. Intellectual freedom depends upon material things. Poetry depends upon intellectual freedom. And women have always been poor, not for two hundred years merely, but from the beginning of time. Women have had less intellectual freedom than the sons of Athenian slaves. Women, then, have not had a dog's chance of writing poetry. That is why I have laid so much stress on money and a room of one's own. However, thanks to the toils of those obscure women in the past, of whom I wish we knew more, thanks, curiously enough, to two wars, the Crimean which let Florence Nightingale out of her drawing-room, and the European War which opened the doors to the average woman some sixty years later, these evils are in the way to be bettered. Otherwise you would not be here tonight, and your chance of earning five hundred pounds a year, precarious as I am afraid that it still is, would be minute in the extreme.

Still, you may object, why do you attach so much importance to this writing of books by women when, according to you, it requires so much effort, leads perhaps to the murder of one's aunts, will make one almost certainly late for luncheon, and may bring one into very grave disputes with certain very good fellows? My motives, let me admit, are partly selfish. Like most uneducated Englishwomen, I like reading—I like reading books in the bulk. Lately my diet has become a trifle monotonous; history is too much about wars; biography too much about great men; poetry has shown, I think, a tendency to sterility, and fiction—but I have sufficiently exposed my disabilities as a critic of modern fiction and will say no more about it. Therefore I would ask

9. One of the three Fates in Greek mythology.

you to write all kinds of books, hesitating at no subject however trivial or however vast. By hook or by crook, I hope that you will possess yourselves of money enough to travel and to idle, to contemplate the future or the past of the world, to dream over books and loiter at street corners and let the line of thought dip deep into the stream. For I am by no means confining you to fiction. If you would please me—and there are thousands like me—you would write books of travel and adventure, and research and scholarship, and history and biography, and criticism and philosophy and science. By so doing you will certainly profit the art of fiction. For books have a way of influencing each other. Fiction will be much the better for standing cheek by jowl with poetry and philosophy. Moreover, if you consider any great figure of the past, like Sappho, like the Lady Murasaki,[1] like Emily Brontë, you will find that she is an inheritor as well as an originator, and has come into existence because women have come to have the habit of writing naturally; so that even as a prelude to poetry such activity on your part would be invaluable.

But when I look back through these notes and criticise my own train of thought as I made them, I find that my motives were not altogether selfish. There runs through these comments and discursions the conviction—or is it the instinct?—that good books are desirable and that good writers, even if they show every variety of human depravity, are still good human beings. Thus when I ask you to write more books I am urging you to do what will be for your good and for the good of the world at large. How to justify this instinct or belief I do not know, for philosophic words, if one has not been educated at a university, are apt to play one false. What is meant by "reality"? It would seem to be something very erratic, very undependable—now to be found in a dusty road, now in a scrap of newspaper in the street, now in a daffodil in the sun. It lights up a group in a room and stamps some casual saying. It overwhelms one walking home beneath the stars and makes the silent world more real than the world of speech—and then there it is again in an omnibus in the uproar of Piccadilly.[2] Sometimes, too, it seems to dwell in shapes too far away for us to discern what their nature is. But whatever it touches, it fixes and makes permanent. That is what remains over when the skin of the day has been cast into the hedge; that is what is left of past time and of our loves and hates. Now the writer, as I think, has the chance to live more than other people in the presence of this reality. It is his business to find it and collect it and communicate it to the rest of us. So at least I infer from reading *Lear* or *Emma* or *La Recherche du Temps Perdu*. For the reading of these books seems to perform a curious couching operation on the senses; one sees more intensely afterwards; the world seems bared of its covering and given an intenser life. Those are the enviable people who live at enmity with unreality; and those are the pitiable who are knocked on the head by the thing done without knowing or caring. So that when I ask you to earn money and have a room of your own, I am asking you to live in the presence of reality, an invigorating life, it would appear, whether one can impart it or not.

Here I would stop, but the pressure of convention decrees that every speech must end with a peroration. And a peroration addressed to women should have something, you will agree, particularly exalting and ennobling about it. I should implore you to

1. Sappho (c. mid-7th century B.C.E.), Greek woman poet; Shikibu Murasaki (978–1014) wrote *The Tale of Genji*, a major early work of Japanese literature.
2. A district of London.

remember your responsibilities, to be higher, more spiritual; I should remind you how much depends upon you, and what an influence you can exert upon the future. But those exhortations can safely, I think, be left to the other sex, who will put them, and indeed have put them, with far greater eloquence than I can compass. When I rummage in my own mind I find no noble sentiments about being companions and equals and influencing the world to higher ends. I find myself saying briefly and prosaically that it is much more important to be oneself than anything else. Do not dream of influencing other people, I would say, if I knew how to make it sound exalted. Think of things in themselves.

And again I am reminded by dipping into newspapers and novels and biographies that when a woman speaks to women she should have something very unpleasant up her sleeve. Women are hard on women. Women dislike women. Women . . . but are you not sick to death of the word? I can assure you that I am. Let us agree, then, that a paper read by a woman to women should end with something particularly disagreeable.

But how does it go? What can I think of? The truth is, I often like women. I like their unconventionality. I like their subtlety. I like their anonymity. I like—but I must not run on in this way. That cupboard there,—you say it holds clean table-napkins only; but what if Sir Archibald Bodkin were concealed among them?[3] Let me then adopt a sterner tone. Have I, in the preceding words, conveyed to you sufficiently the warnings and reprobation of mankind? I have told you the very low opinion in which you were held by Mr Oscar Browning. I have indicated what Napoleon once thought of you and what Mussolini thinks now. Then, in case any of you aspire to fiction, I have copied out for your benefit the advice of the critic about courageously acknowledging the limitations of your sex. I have referred to Professor X and given prominence to his statement that women are intellectually, morally and physically inferior to men. I have handed on all that has come my way without going in search of it, and here is a final warning—from Mr John Langdon Davies.[4] Mr John Langdon Davies warns women "that when children cease to be altogether desirable, women cease to be altogether necessary." I hope you will make a note of it.

How can I further encourage you to go about the business of life? Young women, I would say, and please attend, for the peroration is beginning, you are, in my opinion, disgracefully ignorant. You have never made a discovery of any sort of importance. You have never shaken an empire or led an army into battle. The plays of Shakespeare are not by you, and you have never introduced a barbarous race to the blessings of civilisation. What is your excuse? It is all very well for you to say, pointing to the streets and squares and forests of the globe swarming with black and white and coffee-coloured inhabitants, all busily engaged in traffic and enterprise and love-making, we have had other work on our hands. Without our doing, those seas would be unsailed and those fertile lands a desert. We have borne and bred and washed and taught, perhaps to the age of six or seven years,

3. Sir Archibald Bodkin was then Director of Public Prosecutions; his office had been responsible for the 1928 prosecution of Radclyffe Hall's novel *The Well of Loneliness* on a charge of obscenity. It was subsequently banned. Woolf had wanted to give evidence in the book's defense at the trial, but expert witnesses were not allowed by the presiding magistrate.

4. *A Short History of Women*, by John Langford Davies [Woolf's note].

the one thousand six hundred and twenty-three million human beings who are, according to statistics, at present in existence, and that, allowing that some had help, takes time.

There is truth in what you say—I will not deny it. But at the same time may I remind you that there have been at least two colleges for women in existence in England since the year 1866; that after the year 1880 a married woman was allowed by law to possess her own property; and that in 1919—which is a whole nine years ago—she was given a vote? May I also remind you that the most of the professions have been open to you for close on ten years now? When you reflect upon these immense privileges and the length of time time during which they have been enjoyed, and the fact that there must be at this moment some two thousand women capable of earning over five hundred a year in one way or another, you will agree that the excuse of lack of opportunity, training, encouragement, leisure and money no longer holds good. Moreover, the economists are telling us that Mrs Seton has had too many children. You must, of course, go on bearing children, but, so they say, in twos and threes, not in tens and twelves.

Thus, with some time on your hands and with some book learning in your brains—you have had enough of the other kind, and are sent to college partly, I suspect, to be uneducated—surely you should embark upon another stage of your very long, very laborious and highly obscure career. A thousand pens are ready to suggest what you should do and what effect you will have. My own suggestion is a little fantastic, I admit; I prefer, therefore, to put it in the form of fiction.

I told you in the course of this paper that Shakespeare had a sister; but do not look for her in Sir Sidney Lee's life of the poet. She died young–alas, she never wrote a word. She lies buried where the omnibuses now stop, opposite the Elephant and Castle. Now my belief is that this poet who never wrote a word and was buried at the crossroads still lives. She lives in you and in me, and in many other women who are not here tonight, for they are washing up the dishes and putting the children to bed. But she lives; for great poets do not die; they are continuing presences; they need only the opportunity to walk among us in the flesh. This opportunity, as I think, it is now coming within your power to give her. For my belief is that if we live another century or so—I am talking of the common life which is the real life and not of the little separate lives which we live as individuals—and have five hundred a year each of us and rooms of our own; if we have the habit of freedom and the courage to write exactly what we think; if we escape a little from the common sitting-room and see human beings not always in their relation to each other but in relation to reality; and the sky, too, and the trees or whatever it may be in themselves; if we look past Milton's bogey, for no human being should shut out the view; if we face the fact, for it is a fact, that there is no arm to cling to, but that we go alone and that our relation is to the world of reality and not only to the world of men and women, then the opportunity will come and the dead poet who was Shakespeare's sister will put on the body which she has so often laid down. Drawing her life from the lives of the unknown who were her forerunners, as her brother did before her, she will be born. As for her coming without that preparation, without that effort on our part, without that determination that when she is born again she shall find it possible to live and write her poetry, that we cannot expect, for that would be impossible. But I maintain that she would come if we worked for her, and that so to work, even in poverty and obscurity, is worth while.

Katherine Mansfield

1888–1923

Katherine Mansfield was one of the twentieth century's most gifted writers of short fiction. As Elizabeth Bowen has written, Mansfield realized that "the short story . . . is not intended to be the medium either for exploration or long-term development of character. Character cannot be more than *shown*. . . . " Mansfield thus turned the short story away from contrived plot conventions, and toward the illumination of small events as they reveal the fabric of a life, making of short fiction an almost dramatic form.

Mansfield was born in Wellington, New Zealand. She moved to England more or less permanently before her twentieth birthday, but many of her most successful stories return to her childhood and her homeland for their subject. The path to this mature fiction was complicated, however; when she arrived in London in 1908, Mansfield was pregnant. She quickly married and the same day left her husband, who was not the child's father; she went to a German spa, where she miscarried. This tumultuous background is reflected in the bitter stories of her first volume, *In a German Pension*. In 1911 Mansfield met John Middleton Murray, editor and man of letters, with whom she remained until the end of her life.

Paradoxically, the horrors of World War I (in which her brother Leslie was killed) had an uplifting effect on Mansfield's writing. The result of the war, she wrote, is that "Now we know ourselves for what we are. In a way its a tragic knowledge. Its as though, even while we live again we face death. But *through Life:* thats the point. We see death in life as we see death in a flower that is fresh unfolded. Our hymn is to the flower's beauty—we would make that beauty immortal because we *know*."

One important element of Mansfield's "tragic knowledge" was the awareness that she was dying; she suffered her first tubercular hemorrhage in 1918, and never regained her health. She remained dedicated to her art until the very end, however, producing nineteen major stories during the last nineteen months of her life; Virginia Woolf, who admired and even envied Mansfield's talent, wrote that "No one felt more seriously the importance of writing than she did." The story included here, *The Daughters of the Late Colonel*, diagnoses with both tenderness and horror the spiritual death that Mansfield saw around her. It invokes a theme that has been important in twentieth-century literature from Henry James's *The Beast in the Jungle* to Samuel Beckett's *Waiting for Godot*, and beyond: that, as John Lennon put it, "Life is what happens to you / While you're busy making other plans."

For additional resources on Mansfield, go to *The Longman Anthology of British Literature* Web site at www.myliteraturekit.com.

The Daughters of the Late Colonel

1

The week after was one of the busiest weeks of their lives. Even when they went to bed it was only their bodies that lay down and rested; their minds went on, thinking things out, talking things over, wondering, deciding, trying to remember where. . .

Constantia lay like a statue, her hands by her sides, her feet just overlapping each other, the sheet up to her chin. She stared at the ceiling.

"Do you think father would mind if we gave his top-hat to the porter?"

"The porter?" snapped Josephine. "Why ever the porter? What a very extraordinary idea!"

"Because," said Constantia slowly, "he must often have to go to funerals. And I noticed at—at the cemetery that he only had a bowler." She paused. "I thought then how very much he'd appreciate a top-hat. We ought to give him a present, too. He was always very nice to father."

"But," cried Josephine, flouncing on her pillow and staring across the dark at Constantia, "father's head!" And suddenly, for one awful moment, she nearly giggled. Not, of course, that she felt in the least like giggling. It must have been habit. Years ago, when they had stayed awake at night talking, their beds had simply heaved. And now the porter's head, disappearing, popped out, like a candle, under father's hat. . . . The giggle mounted, mounted; she clenched her hands; she fought it down; she frowned fiercely at the dark and said "Remember" terribly sternly.

"We can decide to-morrow," she sighed.

Constantia had noticed nothing; she sighed.

"Do you think we ought to have our dressing-gowns dyed as well?"

"Black?" almost shrieked Josephine.

"Well, what else?" said Constantia. "I was thinking—it doesn't seem quite sincere, in a way, to wear black out of doors and when we're fully dressed, and then when we're at home—"

"But nobody sees us," said Josephine. She gave the bedclothes such a twitch that both her feet became uncovered, and she had to creep up the pillows to get them well under again.

"Kate does," said Constantia. "And the postman very well might."

Josephine thought of her dark-red slippers, which matched her dressing-gown, and of Constantia's favourite indefinite green ones which went with hers. Black! Two black dressing-gowns and two pairs of black woolly slippers, creeping off to the bathroom like black cats.

"I don't think it's absolutely necessary," said she.

Silence. Then Constantia said, "We shall have to post the papers with the notice in them to-morrow to catch the Ceylon mail. . . . How many letters have we had up till now?"

"Twenty-three."

Josephine had replied to them all, and twenty-three times when she came to "We miss our dear father so much" she had broken down and had to use her handkerchief, and on some of them even to soak up a very light-blue tear with an edge of blotting-paper. Strange! She couldn't have put it on—but twenty-three times. Even now, though, when she said over to herself sadly. "We miss our dear father so much" she could have cried if she'd wanted to.

"Have you got enough stamps?" came from Constantia.

"Oh, how can I tell?" said Josephine crossly. "What's the good of asking me that now?"

"I was just wondering," said Constantia mildly.

Silence again. There came a little rustle, a scurry, a hop.

"A mouse," said Constantia.

"It can't be a mouse because there aren't any crumbs," said Josephine.

"But it doesn't know there aren't," said Constantia.

A spasm of pity squeezed her heart. Poor little thing! She wished she'd left a tiny piece of biscuit on the dressing-table. It was awful to think of it not finding anything. What would it do?

"I can't think how they manage to live at all," she said slowly.

"Who?" demanded Josephine.

And Constantia said more loudly than she meant to, "Mice."

Josephine was furious. "Oh, what nonsense, Con!" she said. "What have mice got to do with it? You're asleep."

"I don't think I am," said Constantia. She shut her eyes to make sure. She was.

Josephine arched her spine, pulled up her knees, folded her arms so that her fists came under her ears, and pressed her cheek hard against the pillow.

2

Another thing which complicated matters was they had Nurse Andrews staying on with them that week. It was their own fault; they had asked her. It was Josephine's idea. On the morning—well, on the last morning, when the doctor had gone, Josephine had said to Constantia, "Don't you think it would be rather nice if we asked Nurse Andrews to stay on for a week as our guest?"

"Very nice," said Constantia.

"I thought," went on Josephine quickly, "I should just say this afternoon, after I've paid her, 'My sister and I would be very pleased, after all you've done for us, Nurse Andrews, if you would stay on for a week as our guest.' I'd have to put that in about being our guest in case—"

"Oh, but she could hardly expect to be paid!" cried Constantia.

"One never knows," said Josephine sagely.

Nurse Andrews had, of course, jumped at the idea. But it was a bother. It meant they had to have regular sit-down meals at the proper times, whereas if they'd been alone they could just have asked Kate if she wouldn't have minded bringing them a tray wherever they were. And meal-times now that the strain was over were rather a trial.

Nurse Andrews was simply fearful about butter. Really they couldn't help feeling that about butter, at least, she took advantage of their kindness. And she had that maddening habit of asking for just an inch more bread to finish what she had on her plate, and then, at the last mouthful, absent-mindedly—of course it wasn't absent-mindedly—taking another helping. Josephine got very red when this happened, and she fastened her small, beadlike eyes on the tablecloth as if she saw a minute strange insect creeping through the web of it. But Constantia's long, pale face lengthened and set, and she gazed away—away—far over the desert, to where that line of camels unwound like a thread of wool. . . .

"When I was with Lady Tukes," said Nurse Andrews, "she had such a dainty little contrayvance for the buttah. It was a silvah Cupid balanced on the—on the bordah of a glass dish, holding a tayny fork. And when you wanted some buttah you simply pressed his foot and he bent down and speared you a piece. It was quite a gayme."

Josephine could hardly bear that. But "I think those things are very extravagant" was all she said.

"But whey?" asked Nurse Andrews, beaming through her eye-glasses. "No one, surely, would take more buttah than one wanted—would one?"

"Ring, Con," cried Josephine. She couldn't trust herself to reply.

And proud young Kate, the enchanted princess, came in to see what the old tabbies wanted now. She snatched away their plates of mock something or other and slapped down a white, terrified blancmange.

"Jam, please, Kate," said Josephine kindly.

Kate knelt and burst open the sideboard, lifted the lid of the jam-pot, saw it was empty, put it on the table, and stalked off.

"I'm afraid," said Nurse Andrews a moment later, "there isn't any."

"Oh, what a bother!" said Josephine. She bit her lip. "What had we better do?"

Constantia looked dubious. "We can't disturb Kate again," she said softly.

Nurse Andrews waited, smiling at them both. Her eyes wandered, spying at everything behind her eye-glasses. Constantia in despair went back to her camels. Josephine frowned heavily—concentrated. If it hadn't been for this idiotic woman she and Con would, of course, have eaten their blancmange without. Suddenly the idea came.

"I know," she said. "Marmalade. There's some marmalade in the sideboard. Get it, Con."

"I hope," laughed Nurse Andrews, and her laugh was like a spoon tinkling against a medicine-glass—"I hope it's not very bittah marmalayde."

3

But, after all, it was not long now, and then she'd be gone for good. And there was no getting over the fact that she had been very kind to father. She had nursed him day and night at the end. Indeed, both Constantia and Josephine felt privately she had rather overdone the not leaving him at the very last. For when they had gone in to say good-bye Nurse Andrews had sat beside his bed the whole time, holding his wrist and pretending to look at her watch. It couldn't have been necessary. It was so tactless, too. Supposing father had wanted to say something—something private to them. Not that he had. Oh, far from it! He lay there, purple, a dark, angry purple in the face, and never even looked at them when they came in. Then, as they were standing there, wondering what to do, he had suddenly opened one eye. Oh, what a difference it would have made, what a difference to their memory of him, how much easier to tell people about it, if he had only opened both! But no—one eye only. It glared at them a moment and then. . . went out.

4

It had made it very awkward for them when Mr Farolles, of St John's, called the same afternoon.

"The end was quite peaceful, I trust?" were the first words he said as he glided towards them through the dark drawing-room.

"Quite," said Josephine faintly. They both hung their heads. Both of them felt certain that eye wasn't at all a peaceful eye.

"Won't you sit down?" said Josephine.

"Thank you, Miss Pinner," said Mr Farolles gratefully. He folded his coat-tails and began to lower himself into father's armchair, but just as he touched it he almost sprang up and slid into the next chair instead.

He coughed. Josephine clasped her hands; Constantia looked vague.

"I want you to feel, Miss Pinner," said Mr Farolles, "and you, Miss Constantia, that I'm trying to be helpful. I want to be helpful to you both, if you will let me. These are the times," said Mr Farolles, very simply and earnestly, "when God means us to be helpful to one another."

"Thank you very much, Mr Farolles," said Josephine and Constantia.

"Not at all," said Mr Farolles gently. He drew his kid gloves through his fingers and leaned forward. "And if either of you would like a little Communion, either or both of you, here *and* now, you have only to tell me. A little Communion is often very help—a great comfort," he added tenderly.

But the idea of a little Communion terrified them. What! In the drawing-room by themselves—with no—no altar or anything! The piano would be much too high, thought Constantia, and Mr Farolles could not possibly lean over it with the chalice. And Kate would be sure to come bursting in and interrupt them, thought Josephine. And supposing the bell rang in the middle? It might be somebody important—about their mourning. Would they get up reverently and go out, or would they have to wait . . . in torture?

"Perhaps you will send round a note by your good Kate if you would care for it later," said Mr Farolles.

"Oh yes, thank you very much!" they both said.

Mr Farolles got up and took his black straw hat from the round table.

"And about the funeral," he said softly. "I may arrange that—as your dear father's old friend and yours, Miss Pinner—and Miss Constantia?"

Josephine and Constantia got up too.

"I should like it to be quite simple," said Josephine firmly, "and not too expensive. At the same time, I should like—"

"A good one that will last," thought dreamy Constantia, as if Josephine were buying a nightgown. But of course Josephine didn't say that. "One suitable to our father's position." She was very nervous.

"I'll run round to our good friend Mr Knight," said Mr Farolles soothingly. "I will ask him to come and see you. I am sure you will find him very helpful indeed."

5

Well, at any rate, all that part of it was over, though neither of them could possibly believe that father was never coming back. Josephine had had a moment of absolute terror at the cemetery, while the coffin was lowered, to think that she and Constantia had done this thing without asking his permission. What would father say when he found out? For he was bound to find out sooner or later. He always did. "Buried. You two girls had me *buried!*" She heard his stick thumping. Oh, what would they say? What possible excuse could they make? It sounded such an appalling heartless thing to do. Such a wicked advantage to take of a person because he happened to be helpless at the moment. The other people seemed to treat it all as a matter of course. They were strangers; they couldn't be expected to understand that father was the very last person for such a thing to happen to. No, the entire blame for it all would fall on her and Constantia. And the expense, she thought, stepping into the tight-buttoned cab. When she had to show him the bills. What would he say then?

She heard him absolutely roaring, "And do you expect me to pay for this gimcrack excursion of yours?"

"Oh," groaned poor Josephine aloud, "we shouldn't have done it, Con!"

And Constantia, pale as a lemon in all that blackness, said in a frightened whisper, "Done what, Jug?"

"Let them bu-bury father like that," said Josephine, breaking down and crying into her new, queer-smelling mourning handkerchief.

"But what else could we have done?" asked Constantia wonderingly. "We couldn't have kept him, Jug—we couldn't have kept him unburied. At any rate, not in a flat that size."

Josephine blew her nose; the cab was dreadfully stuffy.

"I don't know," she said forlornly. "It is all so dreadful. I feel we ought to have tried to, just for a time at least. To make perfectly sure. One thing's certain"—and her tears sprang out again—"father will never forgive us for this—never!"

6

Father would never forgive them. That was what they felt more than ever when, two mornings later, they went into his room to go through his things. They had discussed it quite calmly. It was even down on Josephine's list of things to be done. *Go through father's things and settle about them.* But that was a very different matter from saying after breakfast:

"Well, are you ready, Con?"

"Yes, Jug—when you are."

"Then I think we'd better get it over."

It was dark in the hall. It had been a rule for years never to disturb father in the morning, whatever happened. And now they were going to open the door without knocking even. . . . Constantia's eyes were enormous at the idea; Josephine felt weak in the knees.

"You—you go first," she gasped, pushing Constantia.

But Constantia said, as she always had said on those occasions, "No, Jug, that's not fair. You're eldest."

Josephine was just going to say—what at other times she wouldn't have owned to for the world—what she kept for her very last weapon, "But you're tallest," when they noticed that the kitchen door was open, and there stood Kate. . . .

"Very stiff," said Josephine, grasping the door-handle and doing her best to turn it. As if anything ever deceived Kate!

It couldn't be helped. That girl was . . . Then the door was shut behind them, but—but they weren't in father's room at all. They might have suddenly walked through the wall by mistake into a different flat altogether. Was the door just behind them? They were too frightened to look. Josephine knew that if it was it was holding itself tight shut; Constantia felt that, like the doors in dreams, it hadn't any handle at all. It was the coldness which made it so awful. Or the whiteness—which? Everything was covered. The blinds were down, a cloth hung over the mirror, a sheet hid the bed; a huge fan of white paper filled the fireplace. Constantia timidly put out her hand; she almost expected a snowflake to fall. Josephine felt a queer tingling in her nose, as if her nose was freezing. Then a cab klop-klopped over the cobbles below, and the quiet seemed to shake into little pieces.

"I had better pull up a blind," said Josephine bravely.

"Yes, it might be a good idea," whispered Constantia.

They only gave the blind a touch, but it flew up and the cord flew after, rolling round the blindstick, and the little tassel tapped as if trying to get free. That was too much for Constantia.

"Don't you think—don't you think we might put it off for another day?" she whispered.

"Why?" snapped Josephine, feeling, as usual, much better now that she knew for certain that Constantia was terrified. "It's got to be done. But I do wish you wouldn't whisper, Con."

"I didn't know I was whispering," whispered Constantia.

"And why do you keep on staring at the bed?" said Josephine, raising her voice almost defiantly. "There's nothing *on* the bed."

"Oh, Jug, don't say so!" said poor Connie. "At any rate, not so loudly."

Josephine felt herself that she had gone too far. She took a wide swerve over to the chest of drawers, put out her hand, but quickly drew it back again.

"Connie!" she gasped, and she wheeled round and leaned with her back against the chest of drawers.

"Oh, Jug—what?"

Josephine could only glare. She had the most extraordinary feeling that she had just escaped something simply awful. But how could she explain to Constantia that father was in the chest of drawers? He was in the top drawer with his handkerchiefs and neckties, or in the next with his shirts and pyjamas, or in the lowest of all with his suits. He was watching there, hidden away—just behind the door-handle—ready to spring.

She pulled a funny old-fashioned face at Constantia, just as she used to in the old days when she was going to cry.

"I can't open," she nearly wailed.

"No, don't, Jug," whispered Constantia earnestly. "It's much better not to. Don't let's open anything. At any rate, not for a long time."

"But—but it seems so weak," said Josephine, breaking down.

"But why not be weak for once, Jug?" argued Constantia, whispering quite fiercely. "If it is weak." And her pale stare flew from the locked writing-table—so safe—to the huge glittering wardrobe, and she began to breathe in a queer, panting way. "Why shouldn't we be weak for once in our lives, Jug? It's quite excusable. Let's be weak—be weak, Jug. It's much nicer to be weak than to be strong."

And then she did one of those amazingly bold things that she'd done about twice before in their lives; she marched over to the wardrobe, turned the key, and took it out of the lock. Took it out of the lock and held it up to Josephine, showing Josephine by her extraordinary smile that she knew what she'd done, she'd risked deliberately father being in there among his overcoats.

If the huge wardrobe had lurched forward, had crashed down on Constantia, Josephine wouldn't have been surprised. On the contrary, she would have thought it the only suitable thing to happen. But nothing happened. Only the room seemed quieter than ever, and bigger flakes of cold air fell on Josephine's shoulders and knees. She began to shiver.

"Come, Jug," said Constantia, still with that awful callous smile, and Josephine followed just as she had that last time, when Constantia had pushed Benny into the round pond.

7

But the strain told on them when they were back in the dining-room. They sat down, very shaky, and looked at each other.

"I don't feel I can settle to anything," said Josephine, "until I've had something. Do you think we could ask Kate for two cups of hot water?"

"I really don't see why we shouldn't," said Constantia carefully. She was quite normal again. "I won't ring. I'll go to the kitchen door and ask her."

"Yes, do," said Josephine, sinking down into a chair. "Tell her, just two cups, Con, nothing else—on a tray."

"She needn't even put the jug on, need she?" said Constantia, as though Kate might very well complain if the jug had been there.

"Oh no, certainly not! The jug's not at all necessary. She can pour it direct out of the kettle," cried Josephine, feeling that would be a labour-saving indeed.

Their cold lips quivered at the greenish brims. Josephine curved her small red hands round the cup; Constantia sat up and blew on the wavy stream, making it flutter from one side to the other.

"Speaking of Benny," said Josephine.

And though Benny hadn't been mentioned Constantia immediately looked as though he had.

"He'll expect us to send him something of father's, of course. But it's so difficult to know what to send to Ceylon."

"You mean things get unstuck so on the voyage," murmured Constantia.

"No, lost," said Josephine sharply. "You know there's no post. Only runners."

Both paused to watch a black man in white linen drawers running through the pale fields for dear life, with a large brown-paper parcel in his hands. Josephine's black man was tiny; he scurried along glistening like an ant. But there was something blind and tireless about Constantia's tall, thin fellow, which made him, she decided, a very unpleasant person indeed. . . . On the veranda, dressed all in white and wearing a cork helmet, stood Benny. His right hand shook up and down, as father's did when he was impatient. And behind him, not in the least interested, sat Hilda, the unknown sister-in-law. She swung in a cane rocker and flicked over the leaves of the *Tatler*.

"I think his watch would be the most suitable present," said Josephine.

Constantia looked up; she seemed surprised.

"Oh, would you trust a gold watch to a native?"

"But of course I'd disguise it," said Josephine. "No one would know it was a watch." She liked the idea of having to make a parcel such a curious shape that no one could possibly guess what it was. She even thought for a moment of hiding the watch in a narrow cardboard corset-box that she'd kept by her for a long time, waiting for it to come in for something. It was such beautiful firm cardboard. But, no, it wouldn't be appropriate for this occasion. It had lettering on it: *Medium Women's 28. Extra Firm Busks*. It would be almost too much of a surprise for Benny to open that and find father's watch inside.

"And of course it isn't as though it would be going—ticking, I mean," said Constantia, who was still thinking of the native love of jewellery. "At least," she added, "it would be very strange if after all that time it was."

8

Josephine made no reply. She had flown off on one of her tangents. She had suddenly thought of Cyril. Wasn't it more usual for the only grandson to have the watch? And then dear Cyril was so appreciative, and a gold watch meant so much to a young man. Benny, in all probability, had quite got out of the habit of watches; men so seldom wore waistcoats in those hot climates. Whereas Cyril in London wore them from year's end to year's end. And it would be so nice for her and Constantia, when he came to tea, to know it was there. "I see you've got on grandfather's watch, Cyril." It would be somehow so satisfactory.

Dear boy! What a blow his sweet, sympathetic little note had been! Of course they quite understood; but it was most unfortunate.

"It would have been such a point, having him," said Josephine.

"And he would have enjoyed it so," said Constantia, not thinking what she was saying.

However, as soon as he got back he was coming to tea with his aunties. Cyril to tea was one of their rare treats.

"Now, Cyril, you mustn't be frightened of our cakes. Your Auntie Con and I bought them at Buszard's this morning. We know what a man's appetite is. So don't be ashamed of making a good tea."

Josephine cut recklessly into the rich dark cake that stood for her winter gloves or the soling and heeling of Constantia's only respectable shoes. But Cyril was most unmanlike in appetite.

"I say, Aunt Josephine, I simply can't. I've only just had lunch, you know."

"Oh, Cyril, that can't be true! It's after four," cried Josephine. Constantia sat with her knife poised over the chocolate-roll.

"It is, all the same," said Cyril. "I had to meet a man at Victoria, and he kept me hanging about till . . . there was only time to get lunch and to come on here. And he gave me—phew"—Cyril put his hand to his forehead—"a terrific blow-out," he said.

It was disappointing—to-day of all days. But still he couldn't be expected to know.

"But you'll have a meringue, won't you, Cyril?" said Aunt Josephine. "These meringues were bought specially for you. Your dear father was so fond of them. We were sure you are, too."

"I *am*, Aunt Josephine," cried Cyril ardently. "Do you mind if I take half to begin with?"

"Not at all, dear boy; but we mustn't let you off with that."

"Is your dear father still so fond of meringues?" asked Auntie Con gently. She winced faintly as she broke through the shell of hers.

"Well, I don't quite know, Auntie Con," said Cyril breezily. At that they both looked up.

"Don't know?" almost snapped Josephine. "Don't know a thing like that about your own father, Cyril?"

"Surely," said Auntie Con softly.

Cyril tried to laugh it off. "Oh, well," he said, "it's such a long time since—" He faltered. He stopped. Their faces were too much for him.

"Even *so*," said Josephine.

And Auntie Con looked.

Cyril put down his teacup. "Wait a bit," he cried. "Wait a bit, Aunt Josephine. What am I thinking of?"

He looked up. They were beginning to brighten. Cyril slapped his knee.

"Of course," he said, "it was meringues. How could I have forgotten? Yes, Aunt Josephine, you're perfectly right. Father's most frightfully keen on meringues."

They didn't only beam. Aunt Josephine went scarlet with pleasure; Auntie Con gave a deep, deep sigh.

"And now, Cyril, you must come and see father," said Josephine. "He knows you were coming to-day."

"Right," said Cyril, very firmly and heartily. He got up from his chair; suddenly he glanced at the clock.

"I say, Auntie Con, isn't your clock a bit slow? I've got to meet a man at—at Paddington just after five. I'm afraid I shan't be able to stay very long with grandfather."

"Oh, he won't expect you to stay *very* long!" said Aunt Josephine.

Constantia was still gazing at the clock. She couldn't make up her mind if it was fast or slow. It was one or the other, she felt almost certain of that. At any rate, it had been.

Cyril still lingered. "Aren't you coming along, Auntie Con?"

"Of course," said Josephine, "we shall all go. Come on, Con."

9

They knocked at the door, and Cyril followed his aunts into grandfather's hot, sweetish room.

"Come on," said Grandfather Pinner. "Don't hang about. What is it? What've you been up to?"

He was sitting in front of a roaring fire, clasping his stick. He had a thick rug over his knees. On his lap there lay a beautiful pale yellow silk handkerchief.

"It's Cyril, father," said Josephine shyly. And she took Cyril's hand and led him forward.

"Good afternoon, grandfather," said Cyril, trying to take his hand out of Aunt Josephine's. Grandfather Pinner shot his eyes at Cyril in the way he was famous for. Where was Auntie Con? She stood on the other side of Aunt Josephine; her long arms hung down in front of her; her hands were clasped. She never took her eyes off grandfather.

"Well," said Grandfather Pinner, beginning to thump, "what have you got to tell me?"

What had he, what had he got to tell him? Cyril felt himself smiling like a perfect imbecile. The room was stifling, too.

But Aunt Josephine came to his rescue. She cried brightly, "Cyril says his father is still very fond of meringues, father dear."

"Eh?" said Grandfather Pinner, curving his hand like a purple meringue-shell over one ear.

Josephine repeated, "Cyril says his father is still very fond of meringues."

"Can't hear," said old Colonel Pinner. And he waved Josephine away with his stick, then pointed with his stick to Cyril. "Tell me what she's trying to say," he said.

(My God!) "Must I?" said Cyril, blushing and staring at Aunt Josephine.

"Do, dear," she smiled. "It will please him so much."

"Come on, out with it!" cried Colonel Pinner testily, beginning to thump again.

And Cyril leaned forward and yelled, "Father's still very fond of meringues."

At that Grandfather Pinner jumped as though he had been shot.

"Don't shout!" he cried. "What's the matter with the boy? *Meringues!* What about 'em?"

"Oh, Aunt Josephine, must we go on?" groaned Cyril desperately.

"It's quite all right, dear boy," said Aunt Josephine, as though he and she were at the dentist's together. "He'll understand in a minute." And she whispered to Cyril, "He's getting a bit deaf, you know." Then she leaned forward and really bawled at Grandfather Pinner, "Cyril only wanted to tell you, father dear, that *his* father is still very fond of meringues."

Colonel Pinner heard that time, heard and brooded, looking Cyril up and down.

"What an esstrordinary thing!" said old Grandfather Pinner. "What an esstrordinary thing to come all this way here to tell me!"

And Cyril felt it *was*.

"Yes, I shall send Cyril the watch," said Josephine.

"That would be very nice," said Constantia. "I seem to remember last time he came there was some little trouble about the time."

10

They were interrupted by Kate bursting through the door in her usual fashion, as though she had discovered some secret panel in the wall.

"Fried or boiled?" asked the bold voice.

Fried or boiled? Josephine and Constantia were quite bewildered for the moment. They could hardly take it in.

"Fried or boiled what, Kate?" asked Josephine, trying to begin to concentrate. Kate gave a loud sniff. "Fish."

"Well, why didn't you say so immediately?" Josephine reproached her gently. "How could you expect us to understand, Kate? There are a great many things in this world, you know, which are fried or boiled." And after such a display of courage she said quite brightly to Constantia, "Which do you prefer, Con?"

"I think it might be nice to have it fried," said Constantia. "On the other hand, of course boiled fish is very nice. I think I prefer both equally well . . . Unless you . . . In that case—"

"I shall fry it," said Kate, and she bounced back, leaving their door open and slamming the door of her kitchen.

Josephine gazed at Constantia; she raised her pale eyebrows until they rippled away into her pale hair. She got up. She said in a very lofty, imposing way, "Do you mind following me into the drawing-room, Constantia? I've something of great importance to discuss with you."

For it was always to the drawing-room they retired when they wanted to talk over Kate.

Josephine closed the door meaningly. "Sit down, Constantia," she said, still very grand. She might have been receiving Constantia for the first time. And Con looked round vaguely for a chair, as though she felt indeed quite a stranger.

"Now the question is," said Josephine, bending forward, "whether we shall keep her or not."

"That is the question," agreed Constantia.

"And this time," said Josephine firmly, "we must come to a definite decision."

Constantia looked for a moment as though she might begin going over all the other times, but she pulled herself together and said, "Yes, Jug."

"You see, Con," explained Josephine, "everything is so changed now." Constantia looked up quickly. "I mean," went on Josephine, "we're not dependent on Kate as we were." And she blushed faintly. "There's not father to cook for."

"That is perfectly true," agreed Constantia. "Father certainly doesn't want any cooking now, whatever else—"

Josephine broke in sharply. "You're not sleepy, are you, Con?"

"Sleepy, Jug?" Constantia was wide-eyed.

"Well, concentrate more," said Josephine sharply, and she returned to the subject. "What it comes to is, if we did"—and this she barely breathed, glancing at the door—"give Kate notice"—she raised her voice again—"we could manage our own food."

"Why not?" cried Constantia. She couldn't help smiling. The idea was so exciting. She clasped her hands. "What should we live on, Jug?"

"Oh, eggs in various forms!" said Jug, lofty again. "And, besides, there are all the cooked foods."

"But I've always heard," said Constantia, "they are considered so very expensive."

"Not if one buys them in moderation," said Josephine. But she tore herself away from this fascinating bypath and dragged Constantia after her.

"What we've got to decide now, however, is whether we really do trust Kate or not."

Constantia leaned back. Her flat little laugh flew from her lips.

"Isn't it curious, Jug," said she, "that just on this one subject I've never been able to quite make up my mind?"

11

She never had. The whole difficulty was to prove anything. How did one prove things, how could one? Suppose Kate had stood in front of her and deliberately made a face. Mightn't she very well have been in pain? Wasn't it impossible, at any rate, to ask Kate if she was making a face at her? If Kate answered "No"—and of course she would say "No"—what a position! How undignified! Then again Constantia suspected, she was almost certain that Kate went to her chest of drawers when she and Josephine were out, not to take things but to spy. Many times she had come back to find her amethyst cross in the most unlikely places, under her lace ties or on top of her evening Bertha. More than once she had laid a trap for Kate. She had arranged things in a special order and then called Josephine to witness.

"You see, Jug?"

"Quite, Con."

"Now we shall be able to tell."

But, oh dear, when she did go to look, she was as far off from a proof as ever! If anything was displaced, it might so very well have happened as she closed the drawer; a jolt might have done it so easily.

"You come, Jug, and decide. I really can't. It's too difficult."

But after a pause and a long glare Josephine would sigh, "Now you've put the doubt into my mind, Con, I'm sure I can't tell myself."

"Well, we can't postpone it again," said Josephine. "If we postpone it this time—"

12

But at that moment in the street below a barrel-organ struck up. Josephine and Constantia sprang to their feet together.

"Run, Con," said Josephine. "Run quickly. There's sixpence on the—"

Then they remembered. It didn't matter. They would never have to stop the organ-grinder again. Never again would she and Constantia be told to make that monkey take his noise somewhere else. Never would sound that loud, strange bellow when father thought they were not hurrying enough. The organ-grinder might play there all day and the stick would not thump.

It never will thump again,
It never will thump again,

played the barrel-organ.

What was Constantia thinking? She had such a strange smile; she looked different. She couldn't be going to cry.

"Jug, Jug," said Constantia softly, pressing her hands together. "Do you know what day it is? It's Saturday. It's a week to-day, a whole week."

A week since father died,
A week since father died,

cried the barrel-organ. And Josephine, too, forgot to be practical and sensible; she smiled faintly, strangely. On the Indian carpet there fell a square of sunlight, pale red; it came and went and came—and stayed, deepened—until it shone almost golden.

"The sun's out," said Josephine, as though it really mattered.

A perfect fountain of bubbling notes shook from the barrel-organ, round, bright notes, carelessly scattered.

Constantia lifted her big, cold hands as if to catch them, and then her hands fell again. She walked over to the mantelpiece to her favourite Buddha. And the stone and gilt image, whose smile always gave her such a queer feeling, almost a pain and yet a pleasant pain, seemed to-day to be more than smiling. He knew something; he had a secret. "I know something that you don't know," said her Buddha. Oh, what was it, what could it be? And yet she had always felt there was . . . something.

The sunlight pressed through the windows, thieved its way in, flashed its light over the furniture and the photographs. Josephine watched it. When it came to mother's photograph, the enlargement over the piano, it lingered as though puzzled to find so little remained of mother, except the earrings shaped like tiny pagodas and a black feather boa. Why did the photographs of dead people always fade so? wondered Josephine. As soon as a person was dead their photograph died too. But, of course, this one of mother was very old. It was thirty-five years old. Josephine remembered standing on a chair and pointing out that feather boa to Constantia and telling her that it was a snake that had killed their mother in Ceylon. . . . Would everything have been different if mother hadn't died? She didn't see why. Aunt Florence had lived with them until they had left school, and they had moved three times and had their yearly holiday and . . . and there'd been changes of servants, of course.

Some little sparrows, young sparrows they sounded, chirped on the window-ledge. *Yeep-eyeep-yeep*. But Josephine felt they were not sparrows, not on the window-ledge. It was inside her, that queer little crying noise. *Yeep-eyeep-yeep*. Ah, what was it crying, so weak and forlorn?

If mother had lived, might they have married? But there had been nobody for them to marry. There had been father's Anglo-Indian friends before he quarreled with them. But after that she and Constantia never met a single man except clergymen. How did one meet men? Or even if they'd met them, how could they have got to know men well enough to be more than strangers? One read of people having adventures, being followed, and so on. But nobody had ever followed Constantia and her. Oh yes, there had been one year at Eastbourne a mysterious man at their boarding-house who had put a note on the jug of hot water outside their bedroom door! But by the time Connie had found it the steam had made the writing too faint to read; they couldn't even make out to which of them it was addressed. And he had left next day. And that was all. The rest had been looking after father, and at the same time keeping out of father's way. But now? But now? The thieving sun touched Josephine gently. She lifted her face. She was drawn over to the window by gentle beams. . . .

Until the barrel-organ stopped playing Constantia stayed before the Buddha, wondering, but not as usual, not vaguely. This time her wonder was like longing. She remembered the times she had come in here, crept out of bed in her nightgown when the moon was full, and lain on the floor with her arms outstretched, as though she was crucified. Why? The big, pale moon had made her do it. The horrible dancing figures on the carved screen had leered at her and she hadn't minded. She remembered too how, whenever they were at the seaside, she had gone off by herself and got as close to the sea as she could, and sung something, something she had made up, while she gazed all over that restless water. There had been this other life, running out, bringing things home in bags, getting things on approval, discussing them with Jug, and taking them back to get more things on approval, and arranging father's trays and trying not to annoy father. But it all seemed to have happened in a kind of tunnel. It wasn't real. It was only when she came out of the tunnel into the moonlight or by the sea or into a thunderstorm that she really felt herself. What did it mean? What was it she was always wanting? What did it all lead to? Now? Now?

She turned away from the Buddha with one of her vague gestures. She went over to where Josephine was standing. She wanted to say something to Josephine, something frightfully important, about—about the future and what . . .

"Don't you think perhaps—" she began.

But Josephine interrupted her. "I was wondering if now—" she murmured. They stopped; they waited for each other.

"Go on, Con," said Josephine.

"No, no, Jug; after you," said Constantia.

"No, say what you were going to say. You began," said Josephine.

"I . . . I'd rather hear what you were going to say first," said Constantia.

"Don't be absurd, Con."

"Really, Jug."

"Connie!"

"Oh, *Jug!*"

A pause. Then Constantia said faintly, "I can't say what I was going to say, Jug, because I've forgotten what it was . . . that I was going to say."

Josephine was silent for a moment. She stared at a big cloud where the sun had been. Then she replied shortly, "I've forgotten too."

D. H. Lawrence

1885–1930

D. H. Lawrence's meteoric literary life ended in Venice, Italy, in 1930, where he died at the age of forty-five, far from his birthplace in Nottinghamshire, the coal-mining heart of England. If Lawrence was something of a comet in British literature, arcing across its skies with vibrant energy and controversy while he lived, he was equally visible after his death in the excitement and danger that persisted like a halo around his texts. A formidable poet, an exceptional essayist and literary critic, and a major novelist, Lawrence created works that were pioneering in their defiant eroticism, their outspoken treatment of class politics, and their insistence on seeing British literature as part of world literature in a time of global crisis. Many of his writings were censored and unavailable in England until long after his death, or published in expurgated versions or in private printings. Their frank concentration on sexuality, and on female as well as male desire, continues to make Lawrence's novels provocative and even controversial today.

David Herbert Lawrence was the son of a coal miner. As a primarily self-educated writer who studied and taught at Nottingham University College, instead of Oxford or Cambridge, he was unlike many of his literary peers in being lower-class and outside the privileged literary and social circles they moved in. He essentially invented himself, drawing on the support and encouragement of his mother, and nurturing a clear-eyed and furious analysis of British class structure that pervades many of his novels. The sexual frankness of his work is accompanied by its economic frankness, its willingness to point out all the ways that culture and taste are fashioned by income as much as by ideas. The sense of being an outsider to the gentlemanly world of letters fed Lawrence's need to live and work outside Britain, and he traveled restlessly to Europe and America, to Australia and Mexico. Lawrence is deeply associated with many of the countries and places he lived in; with Italy, above all, in the power of his writing about Italian culture and landscape; with the United States, in classic analysis of American literature, and in works set in New Mexico and San Francisco; with France, Germany, and Switzerland as backdrops for his literary works and their cultural theorizing; with

Australia for his commentary on this distant British colony and its indigenous peoples, in novels like *Kangaroo*; with Mexico and the primitivism and exoticism he explored in *The Plumed Serpent* and *Aaron's Rod*.

As peripatetic and as open to experience as Lawrence was, his great writing begins with novels and stories set in England. Some of his early and most exceptional works are, in fact, modernist versions of a central nineteenth-century literary genre, the *bildungsroman*, or the story of a personal education. Lawrence's *Sons and Lovers* (1912) has the autobiographical overtones that often accompany a coming-of-age narrative. Written after the death of his devoted mother Lydia Lawrence in 1910, the book delineates the experience of a young man who was as socially and economically disadvantaged as Lawrence himself, and the almost incestuous love between mother and son that allows him to break free from the crushing life in the mines that might have been his only option, and to follow his deep need for love, imagination, and poetry into the writing of literature. His later novel *The Rainbow* (published in an expurgated version in 1915) is also a *bildungsroman*, but featuring as its protagonist a female character and specifically feminine issues of education and freedom. In a preface to the novel, Lawrence wrote that he insisted on portraying characters that were not the old-fashioned character portraits of the past, relying on "the old stable ego." For Lawrence, people were internally fragmented, not completely self-aware, and above all governed by sexual currents that exceeded their conscious knowledge and control. In this Lawrence was profoundly influenced by Freud's discovery of the prominence and power of the unconscious. All of Lawrence's writing engages with the invisible and largely silent realm of the unconscious, whose wishes and impulses are a kind of dynamic dance running under the surface of the conscious sense of self.

To this dance of the unconscious rhythms of life Lawrence added an abiding fascination with myth. He joined most modernist writers in his interest in showing the persistence of myth in modern culture: Joyce, Woolf, Eliot, and Faulkner all structured work around mythic parallels or mythic figures. For Lawrence, myth loomed importantly because it allowed for the discussion of hidden patterns and cycles in human action and human relationships, patterns that are much larger than the individual human being. Our personalities are illusions, Lawrence's fiction claims, because they mask deeper mythic forms. In *The Rainbow*, Lawrence draws his mythic structure from the Bible, and the cycles of birth, death, and rebirth in the story of Noah and the flood, with the rainbow of God's promise starting the cycle of rebirth over and over again.

One of Lawrence's greatest novels is *Women in Love*, a story of two sisters confronting modern life as they move out of their country's orbit and take on independence, sexual freedom, and careers in the world. He began writing it in 1916, during World War I. The war was as shattering to Lawrence as it was to every other British writer; for Lawrence, it was the apotheosis and the logical conclusion of the machine culture he hated for having spoiled England even before the war wreaked its devastation. Lawrence sharply criticized industrial capitalism, but not from the vantage point of an aristocratic worldview that regretted the loss of the landed estates. He thought and wrote as the son of a worker whose life was maimed by industrial toil in the mines, and as a school teacher of the impoverished children of miners and laborers who had lost their self-sufficient way of life on the land. Lawrence did not dream of a return to a golden feudal age, but he did dissect the ravages of industry and the connections between world war, capital, and modernization. *Women in Love* embraces these themes and more, as it turns to Europe and its classical culture to try to find a way out of the cultural impasse and sterility Lawrence saw around him. However, in this novel and others Lawrence writes of a death instinct visible for him in European culture, including its philosophy and art. At times, Lawrence's intense hatred of modernity led him to flirt with fascism, which occasionally seemed to him to promise a way out of the dead end of modern society and its hideous conflagrations in war. In order to rescue the life-affirming capacities of human society Lawrence sought out exotic and foreign cultures, and what he termed "primitive" cultures around the world—ostensibly unspoiled agricultural societies still predicated on myth rather than machine. These exotic alternatives, as Lawrence saw, were hardly utopian either, and most such societies were contaminated by colonization and Western influences. Lawrence did seek a less rationalized and less materialistic perspective in the "primitive" or archaic worlds he explored, and found that these cultures were more open to the life-giving force of sexuality. At once intense and engaging, his travel writing gives a sense of immediacy mingled with deep reflection.

Sexuality is the force in human life that most clearly derives from unconscious fantasies and desires, and on that basis it is at the heart of Lawrence's writing. Lawrence's work was thought shocking because it takes for granted the erotic elements hidden in the family—what Freud had called the "family romance." The alliances and the divisions between family members have an erotic component for Lawrence; in addition, relations to friends and to all others one encounters are sexualized in mysterious ways, often involving a powerful homoerotic current. Much of Lawrence's fiction seems to idealize a sexual state beyond words and beyond conscious understanding, and to depict this Lawrence draws on a beautiful incantatory style, filled with a highly musical repetition and rhythm.

Lawrence's own erotic career is as famous as his writing. The passion and frustrations of his marriage to the formidable Frieda Weekely (born Frieda von Richthofen) remained a hidden presence in all his writing after their marriage in 1914. When they met, Frieda was a married woman with an impressive erotic career behind her; she became a close partner in his political and cultural essay writing, and in his restless travels. They lived in Germany, Italy, and in Taos, New Mexico, among other locales. After his death in Italy, she and her then lover transported Lawrence's ashes back to Taos, and the two built a kind of shrine to Lawrence on the grounds of what had been his home with Frieda. It was in this region that they had explored Hispanic and Indian cultures under the sponsorship of a patron of the avant-garde, Mabel Dodge Luhan. Up until the mid-1980s it was possible to pay a dollar to the manager of the Taos Hotel and be admitted into his office, where numerous paintings by D. H. Lawrence were on display. Lawrence was a fascinating, if not a major, painter; the exhibits of his paintings in England were subject to the same censorship and public outrage as his novels. A viewer of the paintings could read them as an allegory for many of the disquieting themes of his literary work: the majority of them depict a couple, usually male and female, locked in an embrace that is as urgent as it is suffocating; around the edges of these couplings Lawrence painted menacing wolves and dogs, often with teeth bared or fangs dripping with blood, emblematic of the intensity and even the destructiveness of erotic relationships.

In his 1923 essay *Surgery for the Novel—or a Bomb*, Lawrence expresses his impatience with the endlessly refined analyses of modernists like Proust and Joyce. "What is the underlying impulse in us," he asks, "that will provide the motive power for a new state of things, when this democratic-industrial-lovey-dovey-darling-take-me-to-mama state of things is bust? *What next?*" His own efforts to forge a new mythic realism can be seen in his novella *The Fox*, also from 1923, which explores the interpenetration of human and animal, nature and social constraint, masculinity and feminity, sexual desire and deep aggression. The story's rural setting becomes a place at once of poverty and of beauty, in which Lawrence can counterpoint pursuits and entrapments on several levels, giving symbolic resonance to sharply observed naturalistic detail.

Lawrence's poetry explores related concerns. Like Thomas Hardy before him, Lawrence was equally gifted in both literary endeavors. Lawrence's poetry emanates from the same image-suffused, musically rhythmic, and tautly modern space as his prose works. Like Lawrence himself, his art desires to move *beyond*—beyond the old stable fictions of the ego in his prose, and beyond the old stable fiction of the lyric voice. In his poetry he accomplishes this by a preternatural immediacy, an intensity of "thereness" that includes what might in the past have seemed to be incoherent elements or fragmentary perspectives. What has been silent, veiled, or unconscious, in personal and in public life, rears up and announces itself in Lawrence's writing, appears on the page and defies silencing.

For additional resources on Lawrence, go to *The Longman Anthology of British Literature* Web site at www.myliteraturekit.com.

Piano

Softly, in the dusk, a woman is singing to me;
Taking me back down the vista of years, till I see
A child sitting under the piano, in the boom of the tingling strings
And pressing the small, poised feet of a mother who smiles as she sings.

In spite of myself, the insidious mastery of song
Betrays me back, till the heart of me weeps to belong
To the old Sunday evenings at home, with winter outside
And hymns in the cosy parlour, the tinkling piano our guide.

So now it is vain for the singer to burst into clamour
With the great black piano appassionato. The glamour
Of childish days is upon me, my manhood is cast
Down in the flood of remembrance, I weep like a child for the past.

1908 1913

Song of a Man Who Has Come Through

Not I, not I, but the wind that blows through me!
A fine wind is blowing the new direction of Time.
If only I let it bear me, carry me, if only it carry me!
If only I am sensitive, subtle, oh, delicate, a winged gift!
If only, most lovely of all, I yield myself and am borrowed
By the fine, fine wind that takes its course through the chaos of the world
Like a fine, an exquisite chisel, a wedge-blade inserted;
If only I am keen and hard like the sheer tip of a wedge
Driven by invisible blows,
The rock will split, we shall come at the wonder, we shall find the Hesperides.[1]

Oh, for the wonder that bubbles into my soul,
I would be a good fountain, a good well-head,
Would blur no whisper, spoil no expression.

What is the knocking?
What is the knocking at the door in the night?
It is somebody wants to do us harm.

No, no, it is the three strange angels.[2]
Admit them, admit them.

1917

Tortoise Shout

I thought he was dumb,
I said he was dumb,
Yet I've heard him cry.
First faint scream,

1. Three sisters who guard a tree with golden apples at the end of the world; Hercules (Heracles) steals the apples as the eleventh of his twelve labors.

2. Probably the three angels who appeared to Abraham in Genesis 18, prior to the destruction of the cities of Sodom and Gomorrah.

Out of life's unfathomable dawn,
Far off, so far, like a madness, under the horizon's dawning rim,
Far, far off, far scream.

Tortoise *in extremis*.

Why were we crucified into sex?
Why were we not left rounded off, and finished in ourselves,
As we began,
As he certainly began, so perfectly alone?

A far, was-it-audible scream,
Or did it sound on the plasm direct?

Worse than the cry of the new-born,
A scream,
A yell,
A shout,
A paean,
A death-agony,
A birth-cry,
A submission,
All tiny, tiny, far away, reptile under the first dawn.
War-cry, triumph, acute-delight, death-scream reptilian,
Why was the veil torn?
The silken shriek of the soul's torn membrane?
The male soul's membrane
Torn with a shriek half music, half horror.

Crucifixion.
Male tortoise, cleaving behind the hovel-wall of that dense female,
Mounted and tense, spread-eagle, out-reaching out of the shell
In tortoise-nakedness,
Long neck, and long vulnerable limbs extruded, spread-eagle over her house-roof,
And the deep, secret, all-penetrating tail curved beneath her walls,
Reaching and gripping tense, more reaching anguish in uttermost tension
Till suddenly, in the spasm of coition, tupping like a jerking leap, and oh!
Opening its clenched face from his outstretched neck
And giving that fragile yell, that scream,
Super-audible,
From his pink, cleft, old-man's mouth,
Giving up the ghost,
Or screaming in Pentecost,[1] receiving the ghost.

His scream, and his moment's subsidence,
The moment of eternal silence,
Yet unreleased, and after the moment, the sudden, startling jerk of coition, and at once

1. The day the Holy Spirit descended on Christ's disciples, which marked the beginning of the Christian church's mission to the world.

The inexpressible faint yell—
And so on, till the last plasm of my body was melted back
To the primeval rudiments of life, and the secret.

So he tups, and screams
Time after time that frail, torn scream
After each jerk, the longish interval,
The tortoise eternity,
Age-long, reptilian persistence,
Heart-throb, slow heart-throb, persistent for the next spasm.

I remember, when I was a boy,
I heard the scream of a frog, which was caught with his foot in the mouth of an up-starting snake;
I remember when I first heard bull-frogs break into sound in the spring;
I remember hearing a wild goose out of the throat of night
Cry loudly, beyond the lake of waters;
I remember the first time, out of a bush in the darkness, a nightingale's piercing cries and gurgles startled the depths of my soul;
I remember the scream of a rabbit as I went through a wood at midnight;
I remember the heifer in her heat, blorting and blorting through the hours, persistent and irrepressible;
I remember my first terror hearing the howl of weird, amorous cats;
I remember the scream of a terrified, injured horse, the sheet-lightning,
And running away from the sound of a woman in labour, something like an owl whooing,
And listening inwardly to the first bleat of a lamb,
The first wail of an infant,
And my mother singing to herself,
And the first tenor singing of the passionate throat of a young collier,[2] who has long since drunk himself to death,
The first elements of foreign speech
On wild dark lips.

And more than all these,
And less than all these,
This last,
Strange, faint coition yell
Of the male tortoise at extremity,
Tiny from under the very edge of the farthest far-off horizon of life.

The cross,
The wheel on which our silence first is broken,
Sex, which breaks up our integrity, our single inviolability, our deep silence,
Tearing a cry from us.

Sex, which breaks us into voice, sets us calling across the deeps, calling, calling for the complement,
Singing, and calling, and singing again, being answered, having found.

2. A coal miner.

Torn, to become whole again, after long seeking for what is lost,
The same cry from the tortoise as from Christ, the Osiris-cry of
    abandonment,[3]
That which is whole, torn asunder,
That which is in part, finding its whole again throughout the universe.

1921

Snake[1]

A snake came to my water-trough
On a hot, hot day, and I in pyjamas for the heat,
To drink there.

In the deep, strange-scented shade of the great dark carob tree
I came down the steps with my pitcher
And must wait, must stand and wait, for there he was at the trough before me.

He reached down from a fissure in the earth-wall in the gloom
And trailed his yellow-brown slackness soft-bellied down, over the edge of
    the stone trough
And rested his throat upon the stone bottom,
And where the water had dripped from the tap, in a small clearness,
He sipped with his straight mouth,
Softly drank through his straight gums, into his slack long body,
Silently.
Someone was before me at my water-trough,
And I, like a second comer, waiting.

He lifted his head from his drinking, as cattle do,
And looked at me vaguely, as drinking cattle do,
And flickered his two-forked tongue from his lips, and mused a moment,
And stooped and drank a little more,
Being earth-brown, earth-golden from the burning bowels of the earth
On the day of Sicilian July, with Etna smoking.

The voice of my education said to me
He must be killed,
For in Sicily the black, black snakes are innocent, the gold are venomous.

And voices in me said, If you were a man
You would take a stick and break him now, and finish him off.

But must I confess how I liked him,
How glad I was he had come like a guest in quiet, to drink at my water-trough
And depart peaceful, pacified, and thankless,
Into the burning bowels of this earth?

Was it cowardice, that I dared not kill him?
Was it perversity, that I longed to talk to him?

3. Osiris was a major god of ancient Egypt; he was slain and fragments of his corpse scattered; these were found and buried, and Osiris became ruler of the underworld.

1. Lawrence had an encounter with a snake drinking from a water trough while living in Taormina, Sicily, in July 1912.

Was it humility, to feel so honoured?
I felt so honoured.

And yet those voices:
If you were not afraid, you would kill him!

And truly I was afraid, I was most afraid,
But even so, honoured still more
That he should seek my hospitality
From out the dark door of the secret earth.

He drank enough
And lifted his head, dreamily, as one who has drunken,
And flickered his tongue like a forked night on the air, so black,
Seeming to lick his lips,
And looked around like a god, unseeing, into the air,
And slowly turned his head,
And slowly, very slowly, as if thrice adream,
Proceeded to draw his slow length curving round
And climb again the broken bank of my wall-face.

And as he put his head into that dreadful hole,
And as he slowly drew up, snake-easing his shoulders, and entered farther,
A sort of horror, a sort of protest against his withdrawing into that horrid
black hole,
Deliberately going into the blackness, and slowly drawing himself after,
Overcame me now his back was turned.
I looked round, I put down my pitcher,
I picked up a clumsy log
And threw it at the water-trough with a clatter.
I think it did not hit him,
But suddenly that part of him that was left behind convulsed in
undignified haste,
Writhed like lightning, and was gone
Into the black hole, the earth-lipped fissure in the wall front,
At which, in the intense still noon, I stared with fascination.

And immediately I regretted it.
I thought how paltry, how vulgar, what a mean act!
I despised myself and the voices of my accursed human education.

And I thought of the albatross,
And I wished he would come back, my snake.

For he seemed to me again like a king,
Like a king in exile, uncrowned in the underworld,
Now due to be crowned again.

And so, I missed my chance with one of the lords
Of life.
And I have something to expiate;
A pettiness.

1923

Bavarian Gentians

Not every man has gentians in his house
in soft September, at slow, sad Michaelmas.[1]

Bavarian gentians, big and dark, only dark
darkening the day-time, torch-like with the smoking blueness of Pluto's gloom,
ribbed and torch-like, with their blaze of darkness spread blue
down flattening into points, flattened under the sweep of white day
torch-flower of the blue-smoking darkness, Pluto's dark-blue daze,[2]
black lamps from the halls of Dis, burning dark blue,
giving off darkness, blue darkness, as Demeter's pale lamps give off light,
lead me then, lead the way.

Reach me a gentian, give me a torch!
let me guide myself with the blue, forked torch of this flower
down the darker and darker stairs, where blue is darkened on blueness
even where Persephone goes, just now, from the frosted September
to the sightless realm where darkness is awake upon the dark
and Persephone herself is but a voice
or a darkness invisible enfolded in the deeper dark
of the arms Plutonic, and pierced with the passion of dense gloom,
among the splendour of torches of darkness, shedding darkness on the lost
bride and her groom.

1923, 1929 1932

Cypresses[1]

Tuscan cypresses,
What is it?

Folded in like a dark thought
For which the language is lost,
Tuscan cypresses,
Is there a great secret?
Are our words no good?

The undeliverable secret,
Dead with a dead race and a dead speech, and yet
Darkly monumental in you,
Etruscan[2] cypresses.

Ah, how I admire your fidelity,
Dark cypresses!

1. The feast of St. Michael the Archangel, 29 September.
2. Persephone was a daughter of Zeus and Demeter, goddess of agriculture; she was abducted by Hades, king of the Underworld (also known as Pluto or Dis), causing Demeter such sorrow that the land became barren. Zeus commanded Hades to release Persephone, which he did, though she was able to emerge from the Underworld each spring, returning in the fall to her husband. The story offers an explanation of seasonal change.

1. An evergreen tree traditionally associated with mourning.
2. A native or inhabitant of Etruria, an ancient country of Italy in modern Tuscany, conquered by the Romans. The Etruscan language is extinct.

Is it the secret of the long-nosed Etruscans?
The long-nosed, sensitive-footed, subtly-smiling Etruscans,
Who made so little noise outside the cypress groves?

Among the sinuous, flame-tall cypresses
That swayed their length of darkness all around
Etruscan-dusky, wavering men of old Etruria:
Naked except for fanciful long shoes,
Going with insidious, half-smiling quietness
And some of Africa's imperturbable sang-froid[3]
About a forgotten business.

What business, then?
Nay, tongues are dead, and words are hollow as hollow seed-pods,
Having shed their sound and finished all their echoing
Etruscan syllables,
That had the telling.

Yet more I see you darkly concentrate,
Tuscan cypresses,
On one old thought:
On one old slim imperishable thought, while you remain
Etruscan cypresses;
Dusky, slim marrow-thought of slender, flickering men of Etruria,
Whom Rome called vicious.

Vicious, dark cypresses:
Vicious, you supple, brooding, softly-swaying pillars of dark flame.
Monumental to a dead, dead race
Embowered in you!

Were they then vicious, the slender, tender-footed
Long-nosed men of Etruria?
Or was their way only evasive and different, dark, like cypress-trees in a wind?
They are dead, with all their vices,
And all that is left
Is the shadowy monomania[4] of some cypresses
And tombs.

The smile, the subtle Etruscan smile still lurking
Within the tombs,
Etruscan cypresses.
He laughs longest who laughs last;
Nay, Leonardo only bungled the pure Etruscan smile.

What would I not give
To bring back the rare and orchid-like
Evil-yclept[5] Etruscan?
For as to the evil

3. Composure.
4. Obsession with one idea.
5. Named (Middle English).

We have only Roman word for it,
Which I, being a little weary of Roman virtue,
Don't hang much weight on.

For oh, I know, in the dust where we have buried
The silenced races and all their abominations,
We have buried so much of the delicate magic of life.

There in the deeps
That churn the frankincense and ooze the myrrh,
Cypress shadowy,
Such an aroma of lost human life!

They say the fit survive,
But I invoke the spirits of the lost.
Those that have not survived, the darkly lost,
To bring their meaning back into life again,
Which they have taken away
And wrapt inviolable in soft cypress-trees,
Etruscan cypresses.

Evil, what is evil?
There is only one evil, to deny life
As Rome denied Etruria
And mechanical America Montezuma still.

Fiesole.
1923

Odour of Chrysanthemums

1

The small locomotive engine Number 4, came clanking, stumbling down from Selston[1] with seven full wagons. It appeared round the corner with loud threats of speed, but the colt that it startled from among the gorse,[2] which still flickered indistinctly in the raw afternoon, out-distanced it at a canter. A woman, walking up the railway line to Underwood,[3] drew back into the hedge, held her basket aside, and watched the footplate of the engine advancing. The trucks thumped heavily past, one by one, with slow inevitable movement, as she stood insignificantly trapped between the jolting black wagons and the hedge; then they curved away towards the coppice where the withered oak leaves dropped noiselessly, while the birds, pulling at the scarlet hips beside the track, made off into the dusk that had already crept into the spinney.[4] In the open, the smoke from the engine sank and cleaved to the rough grass. The fields were dreary and forsaken, and in the marshy strip that led to the whimsey, a reedy pit-pond, the fowls had already abandoned their run among the alders, to roost in the tarred fowl-house. The pit-bank loomed up beyond the pond, flames like red sores licking its ashy sides, in the afternoon's stagnant light. Just beyond rose the tapering chimneys and the clumsy black headstocks of Brinsley Colliery. The two wheels were spinning fast up against the sky, and the winding engine rapped out its little spasms. The miners were being turned up.

1. Mining village in Nottinghamshire, central England.
2. Wild, yellow-flowered shrub.
3. Small village in central England.
4. A small thicket.

The engine whistled as it came into the wide bay of railway lines beside the colliery, where rows of trucks stood in harbour.

Miners, single, trailing and in groups, passed like shadows diverging home. At the edge of the ribbed level of sidings squat a low cottage, three steps down from the cinder track. A large bony vine clutched at the house, as if to claw down the tiled roof. Round the bricked yard grew a few wintry primroses. Beyond, the long garden sloped down to a bushcovered brook course. There were some twiggy apple trees, winter-crack trees, and ragged cabbages. Beside the path hung dishevelled pink chrysanthemums, like pink cloths hung on bushes. A woman came stooping out of the felt-covered fowl-house, half-way down the garden. She closed and padlocked the door, then drew herself erect, having brushed some bits from her white apron.

She was a tall woman of imperious mien, handsome, with definite black eyebrows. Her smooth black hair was parted exactly. For a few moments she stood steadily watching the miners as they passed along the railway: then she turned towards the brook course. Her face was calm and set, her mouth was closed with disillusionment. After a moment she called:

"John!" There was no answer. She waited, and then said distinctly:

"Where are you?"

"Here!" replied a child's sulky voice from among the bushes. The woman looked piercingly through the dusk.

"Are you at that brook?" she asked sternly.

For answer the child showed himself before the raspberrycanes that rose like whips. He was a small, sturdy boy of five. He stood quite still, defiantly.

"Oh!" said the mother, conciliated. "I thought you were down at that wet brook—and you remember what I told you——"

The boy did not move or answer.

"Come, come on in," she said more gently, "it's getting dark. There's your grandfather's engine coming down the line!"

The lad advanced slowly, with resentful, taciturn movement. He was dressed in trousers and waistcoat of cloth that was too thick and hard for the size of the garments. They were evidently cut down from a man's clothes.

As they went slowly towards the house he tore at the ragged wisps of chrysanthemums and dropped the petals in handfuls among the path.

"Don't do that—it does look nasty," said his mother. He refrained, and she, suddenly pitiful, broke off a twig with three or four wan flowers and held them against her face. When mother and son reached the yard her hand hesitated, and instead of laying the flower aside, she pushed it in her apron-band. The mother and son stood at the foot of the three steps looking across the bay of lines at the passing home of the miners. The trundle of the small train was imminent. Suddenly the engine loomed past the house and came to a stop opposite the gate.

The engine-driver, a short man with round grey beard, leaned out of the cab high above the woman.

"Have you got a cup of tea?" he said in a cheery, hearty fashion.

It was her father. She went in, saying she would mash.[5] Directly, she returned.

"I didn't come to see you on Sunday," began the little greybearded man.

"I didn't expect you," said his daughter.

5. Separate tea from the leaves.

The engine-driver winced; then, reassuming his cheery, airy manner, he said:

"Oh, have you heard then? Well, and what do you think——?"

"I think it is soon enough," she replied.

At her brief censure the little man made an impatient gesture, and said coaxingly, yet with dangerous coldness:

"Well, what's a man to do? It's no sort of life for a man of my years, to sit at my own hearth like a stranger. And if I'm going to marry again it may as well be soon as late—what does it matter to anybody?"

The woman did not reply, but turned and went into the house. The man in the engine-cab stood assertive, till she returned with a cup of tea and a piece of bread and butter on a plate. She went up the steps and stood near the footplate of the hissing engine.

"You needn't 'a' brought me bread an' butter," said her father. "But a cup of tea"—he sipped appreciatively—"it's very nice." He sipped for a moment or two, then: "I hear as Walter's got another bout on," he said.

"When hasn't he?" said the woman bitterly.

"I heerd tell of him in the 'Lord Nelson' braggin' as he was going to spend that b——afore he went: half a sovereign that was."

"When?" asked the woman.

"A' Sat'day night—I know that's true."

"Very likely," she laughed bitterly. "He gives me twenty-three shillings."

"Aye, it's a nice thing, when a man can do nothing with his money but make a beast of himself!" said the grey-whiskered man. The woman turned her head away. Her father swallowed the last of his tea and handed her the cup.

"Aye," he sighed, wiping his mouth. "It's a settler, it is——"

He put his hand on the lever. The little engine strained and groaned, and the train rumbled towards the crossing. The woman again looked across the metals. Darkness was settling over the spaces of the railway and trucks: the miners, in grey sombre groups, were still passing home. The winding engine pulsed hurriedly, with brief pauses. Elizabeth Bates looked at the dreary flow of men, then she went indoors. Her husband did not come.

The kitchen was small and full of firelight; red coals piled glowing up the chimney mouth. All the life of the room seemed in the white, warm hearth and the steel fender reflecting the red fire. The cloth was laid for tea; cups glinted in the shadows. At the back, where the lowest stairs protruded into the room, the boy sat struggling with a knife and a piece of white wood. He was almost hidden in the shadow. It was half-past four. They had but to await the father's coming to begin tea. As the mother watched her son's sullen little struggle with the wood, she saw herself in his silence and pertinacity; she saw the father in her child's indifference to all but himself. She (seemed to be) occupied by her husband. He had probably gone past his home, slunk past his own door, to drink before he came in, while his dinner spoiled and wasted in waiting. She glanced at the clock, then took the potatoes to strain them in the yard. The garden and fields beyond the brook were closed in uncertain darkness. When she rose with the saucepan, leaving the drain steaming into the night behind her, she saw the yellow lamps were lit along the high road that went up the hill away beyond the space of the railway lines and the field.

Then again she watched the men trooping home, fewer now and fewer.

Indoors the fire was sinking and the room was dark red. The woman put her saucepan on the hob, and set a batter-pudding near the mouth of the oven. Then she stood unmoving. Directly, gratefully, came quick young steps to the door. Someone hung on the latch a moment, then a little girl entered and began pulling off her outdoor things, dragging a mass of curls, just ripening from gold to brown, over her eyes with her hat.

Her mother chid her for coming late from school, and said she would have to keep her at home the dark winter days.

"Why, mother, it's hardly a bit dark yet. The lamp's not lighted, and my father's not home."

"No, he isn't. But it's a quarter to five! Did you see anything of him?"

The child became serious. She looked at her mother with large, wistful blue eyes.

"No, mother, I've never seen him. Why? Has he come up an' gone past, to Old Brinsley? He hasn't, mother, 'cos I never saw him."

"He'd watch that," said the mother bitterly, "he'd take care as you didn't see him. But you may depend upon it, he's seated in the 'Prince o' Wales.' He wouldn't be this late."

The girl looked at her mother piteously.

"Let's have our teas, mother, should we?" said she.

The mother called John to table. She opened the door once more and looked out across the darkness of the lines. All was deserted: she could not hear the winding-engines.

"Perhaps," she said to herself, "he's stopped to get some ripping[6] done."

They sat down to tea. John, at the end of the table near the door, was almost lost in the darkness. Their faces were hidden from each other. The girl crouched against the fender slowly moving a thick piece of bread before the fire. The lad, his face a dusky mark on the shadow, sat watching her who was transfigured in the red glow.

"I do think it's beautiful to look in the fire," said the child.

"Do you?" said her mother. "Why?"

"It's so red, and full of little caves—and it feels so nice, and you can fair smell it."

"It'll want mending directly," replied her mother, "and then if your father comes he'll carry on and say there never is a fire when a man comes home sweating from the pit. A public-house[7] is always warm enough."

There was silence till the boy said complainingly: "Make haste, our Annie."

"Well, I am doing! I can't make the fire do it no faster, can I?"

"She keeps wafflin' it about so's to make 'er slow," grumbled the boy.

"Don't have such an evil imagination, child," replied the mother.

Soon the room was busy in the darkness with the crisp sound of crunching. The mother ate very little. She drank her tea determinedly, and sat thinking. When she rose her anger was evident in the stern unbending of her head. She looked at the pudding in the fender, and broke out:

"It is a scandalous thing as a man can't even come home to his dinner! If it's crozzled up to a cinder I don't see why I should care. Past his very door he goes to get to a public-house, and here I sit with his dinner waiting for him——"

She went out. As she dropped piece after piece of coal on the red fire, the shadows fell on the walls, till the room was almost in total darkness.

"I canna see," grumbled the invisible John. In spite of herself, the mother laughed.

6. Tearing a vein of coal from the earth.

7. Pub; tavern.

"You know the way to your mouth," she said. She set the dust-pan outside the door. When she came again like a shadow on the hearth, the lad repeated, complaining sulkily:

"I canna see."

"Good gracious!" cried the mother irritably, "you're as bad as your father if it's a bit dusk!"

Nevertheless, she took a paper spill from a sheaf on the mantelpiece and proceeded to light the lamp that hung from the ceiling in the middle of the room. As she reached up, her figure displayed itself just rounding with maternity.

"Oh, mother——!" exclaimed the girl.

"What?" said the woman, suspended in the act of putting the lamp-glass over the flame. The copper reflector shone handsomely on her, as she stood with uplifted arm, turning to face her daughter.

"You've got a flower in your apron!" said the child, in a little rapture at this unusual event.

"Goodness me!" exclaimed the woman, relieved. "One would think the house was afire." She replaced the glass and waited a moment before turning up the wick. A pale shadow was seen floating vaguely on the floor.

"Let me smell!" said the child, still rapturously, coming forward and putting her face to her mother's waist.

"Go along, silly!" said the mother, turning up the lamp. The light revealed their suspense so that the woman felt it almost unbearable. Annie was still bending at her waist. Irritably, the mother took the flowers out from her apron-band.

"Oh, mother—don't take them out!" Annie cried, catching her hand and trying to replace the sprig.

"Such nonsense!" said the mother, turning away. The child put the pale chrysanthemums to her lips, murmuring:

"Don't they smell beautiful!"

Her mother gave a short laugh.

"No," she said, "not to me. It was chrysanthemums when I married him, and chrysanthemums when you were born, and the first time they ever brought him home drunk, he'd got brown chrysanthemums in his button-hole."

She looked at the children. Their eyes and their parted lips were wondering. The mother sat rocking in silence for some time. Then she looked at the clock.

"Twenty minutes to six!" In a tone of fine bitter carelessness she continued: "Eh, he'll not come now till they bring him. There he'll stick! But he needn't come rolling in here in his pit-dirt, for *I* won't wash him. He can lie on the floor——Eh, what a fool I've been, what a fool! And this is what I came here for, to this dirty hole, rats and all, for him to slink past his very door. Twice last week—he's begun now——"

She silenced herself, and rose to clear the table.

While for an hour or more the children played, subduedly intent, fertile of imagination, united in fear of the mother's wrath, and in dread of their father's home-coming, Mrs. Bates sat in her rocking-chair making a 'singlet' of thick cream-coloured flannel, which gave a dull wounded sound as she tore off the grey edge. She worked at her sewing with energy, listening to the children, and her anger wearied itself, lay down to rest, opening its eyes from time to time and steadily watching, its ears raised to listen. Sometimes even her anger quailed and shrank, and the mother suspended her sewing, tracing the footsteps that thudded along the sleepers outside; she would lift her head sharply to bid the children 'hush', but she recovered herself in time, and the footsteps went past the gate, and the children were not flung out of their play-world.

But at last Annie sighed, and gave in. She glanced at her wagon of slippers, and loathed the game. She turned plaintively to her mother.

"Mother!"—but she was inarticulate.

John crept out like a frog from under the sofa. His mother glanced up.

"Yes," she said, "just look at those shirt-sleeves!"

The boy held them out to survey them, saying nothing. Then somebody called in a hoarse voice away down the line, and suspense bristled in the room, till two people had gone by outside, talking.

"It is time for bed," said the mother.

"My father hasn't come," wailed Annie plaintively. But her mother was primed with courage.

"Never mind. They'll bring him when he does come—like a log." She meant there would be no scene. "And he may sleep on the floor till he wakes himself. I know he'll not go to work to-morrow after this!"

The children had their hands and faces wiped with a flannel. They were very quiet. When they had put on their night-dresses, they said their prayers, the boy mumbling. The mother looked down at them, at the brown silken bush of intertwining curls in the nape of the girl's neck, at the little black head of the lad, and her heart burst with anger at their father, who caused all three such distress. The children hid their faces in her skirts for comfort.

When Mrs. Bates came down, the room was strangely empty, with a tension of expectancy. She took up her sewing and stitched for some time without raising her head. Meantime her anger was tinged with fear.

2

The clock struck eight and she rose suddenly, dropping her sewing on her chair. She went to the stair-foot door, opened it, listening. Then she went out, locking the door behind her.

Something scuffled in the yard, and she started, though she knew it was only the rats with which the place was over-run. The night was very dark. In the great bay of railway lines, bulked with trucks, there was no trace of light, only away back she could see a few yellow lamps at the pit-top, and the red smear of the burning pit-bank on the night. She hurried along the edge of the track, then, crossing the converging lines, came to the stile by the white gates, whence she emerged on the road. Then the fear which had led her shrank. People were walking up to New Brinsley; she saw the lights in the houses; twenty yards farther on were the broad windows of the 'Prince of Wales', very warm and bright, and the loud voices of men could be heard distinctly. What a fool she had been to imagine that anything had happened to him! He was merely drinking over there at the 'Prince of Wales'. She faltered. She had never yet been to fetch him, and she never would go. So she continued her walk towards the long straggling line of houses, standing back on the highway. She entered a passage between the dwellings.

"Mr. Rigley?—Yes! Did you want him? No, he's not in at this minute."

The raw-boned woman leaned forward from her dark scullery and peered at the other, upon whom fell a dim light through the blind of the kitchen window.

"Is it Mrs. Bates?" she asked in a tone tinged with respect.

"Yes. I wondered if your Master was at home. Mine hasn't come yet."

"'Asn't 'e! Oh, Jack's been 'ome an' 'ad 'is dinner an' gone out. 'E's just gone for 'alf an hour afore bed-time. Did you call at the 'Prince of Wales'?"

"No——"

"No, you didn't like——! It's not very nice." The other woman was indulgent. There was an awkward pause. "Jack never said nothink about—about your Master," she said.

"No!—I expect he's stuck in there!"

Elizabeth Bates said this bitterly, and with recklessness. She knew that the woman across the yard was standing at her door listening, but she did not care. As she turned:

"Stop a minute! I'll just go an' ask Jack if 'e knows anythink," said Mrs. Rigley.

"Oh no—I wouldn't like to put——!"

"Yes, I will, if you'll just step inside an' see as th' childer doesn't come downstairs and set theirselves afire."

Elizabeth Bates, murmuring a remonstrance,[8] stepped inside. The other woman apologised for the state of the room.

The kitchen needed apology. There were little frocks and trousers and childish undergarments on the squab and on the floor, and a litter of playthings everywhere. On the black American cloth of the table were pieces of bread and cake, crusts, slops, and a teapot with cold tea.

"Eh, ours is just as bad," said Elizabeth Bates, looking at the woman, not at the house. Mrs. Rigley put a shawl over her head and hurried out, saying:

"I shanna be a minute."

The other sat, noting with faint disapproval the general untidiness of the room. Then she fell to counting the shoes of various sizes scattered over the floor. There were twelve. She sighed and said to herself: "No wonder!"—glancing at the litter. There came the scratching of two pairs of feet on the yard, and the Rigleys entered. Elizabeth Bates rose. Rigley was a big man, with very large bones. His head looked particularly bony. Across his temple was a blue scar, caused by a wound got in the pit, a wound in which the coal-dust remained blue like tattooing.

"'Asna 'e come whoam yit?" asked the man, without any form of greeting, but with deference and sympathy. "I couldna say wheer he is—'e's non ower theer!"—he jerked his head to signify the 'Prince of Wales'.

"'E's 'appen[9] gone up to th' 'Yew'," said Mrs. Rigley.

There was another pause. Rigley had evidently something to get off his mind:

"Ah left 'im finishin' a stint,"[1] he began. "Loose-all 'ad bin gone about ten minutes when we com'n away, an' I shouted: 'Are ter comin', Walt?' an' 'e said: 'Go on, Ah shanna be but a'ef a minnit,' so we com'n ter th' bottom, me an' Bowers, thinkin' as 'e wor just behint, an' 'ud come up i' th' next bantle[2]——"

He stood perplexed, as if answering a charge of deserting his mate. Elizabeth Bates, now again certain of disaster, hastened to reassure him:

"I expect 'e's gone up to th' 'Yew Tree', as you say. It's not the first time. I've fretted myself into a fever before now. He'll come home when they carry him."

"Ay, isn't it too bad!" deplored the other woman.

8. Protestation or objection.
9. Perhaps, maybe.
1. Amount of work to be done.
2. Carload.

"I'll just step up to Dick's an' see if 'e *is* theer," offered the man, afraid of appearing alarmed, afraid of taking liberties.

"Oh, I wouldn't think of bothering you that far," said Elizabeth Bates, with emphasis, but he knew she was glad of his offer.

As they stumbled up the entry, Elizabeth Bates heard Rigley's wife run across the yard and open her neighbour's door. At this, suddenly all the blood in her body seemed to switch away from her heart.

"Mind!" warned Rigley. "Ah've said many a time as Ah'd fill up them ruts in this entry, sumb'dy 'll be breakin' their legs yit."

She recovered herself and walked quickly along with the miner.

"I don't like leaving the children in bed, and nobody in the house," she said.

"No, you dunna!" he replied courteously. They were soon at the gate of the cottage.

"Well, I shanna be many minnits, Dunna you be frettin' now, 'e'll be all right," said the butty.[3]

"Thank you very much, Mr. Rigley," she replied.

"You're welcome!" he stammered, moving away. "I shanna be many minnits."

The house was quiet. Elizabeth Bates took off her hat and shawl, and rolled back the rug. When she had finished, she sat down. It was a few minutes past nine. She was startled by the rapid chuff of the winding-engine at the pit, and the sharp whirr of the brakes on the rope as it descended. Again she felt the painful sweep of her blood, and she put her hand to her side, saying aloud: "Good gracious!—it's only the nine o'clock deputy going down," rebuking herself.

She sat still, listening. Half an hour of this, and she was wearied out.

"What am I working myself up like this for?" she said pitiably to herself, "I s'll only be doing myself some damage."

She took out her sewing again.

At a quarter to ten there were footsteps. One person! She watched for the door to open. It was an elderly woman, in a black bonnet and a black woollen shawl—his mother. She was about sixty years old, pale, with blue eyes, and her face all wrinkled and lamentable. She shut the door and turned to her daughter-in-law peevishly.

"Eh, Lizzie, whatever shall we do, whatever shall we do!" she cried.

Elizabeth drew back a little, sharply.

"What is it, mother?" she said.

The elder woman seated herself on the sofa.

"I don't know, child, I can't tell you!"—she shook her head slowly. Elizabeth sat watching her, anxious and vexed.

"I don't know," replied the grandmother, sighing very deeply. "There's no end to my troubles, there isn't. The things I've gone through, I'm sure it's enough——!" She wept without wiping her eyes, the tears running.

"But, mother," interrupted Elizabeth, "what do you mean? What is it?"

The grandmother slowly wiped her eyes. The fountains of her tears were stopped by Elizabeth's directness. She wiped her eyes slowly.

"Poor child! Eh, you poor thing!" she moaned. "I don't know what we're going to do, I don't—and you as you are—it's a thing, it is indeed!"

Elizabeth waited.

3. Fellow coal miner.

"Is he dead?" she asked, and at the words her heart swung violently, though she felt a slight flush of shame at the ultimate extravagance of the question. Her words sufficiently frightened the old lady, almost brought her to herself.

"Don't say so, Elizabeth! We'll hope it's not as bad as that; no, may the Lord spare us that, Elizabeth. Jack Rigley came just as I was sittin' down to a glass afore going to bed, an' 'e said: ''Appen you'll go down th' line, Mrs. Bates. Walt's had an accident. 'Appen you'll go an' sit wi' 'er till we can get him home.' I hadn't time to ask him a word afore he was gone. An' I put my bonnet on an' come straight down, Lizzie. I thought to myself: 'Eh, that poor blessed child, if anybody should come an' tell her of a sudden, there's no knowin' what'll 'appen to 'er.' You mustn't let it upset you, Lizzie—or you know what to expect. How long is it, six months—or is it five, Lizzie? Ay!"—the old woman shook her head—"time slips on, it slips on! Ay!"

Elizabeth's thoughts were busy elsewhere. If he was killed—would she be able to manage on the little pension and what she could earn?—she counted up rapidly. If he was hurt—they wouldn't take him to the hospital—how tiresome he would be to nurse!—but perhaps she'd be able to get him away from the drink and his hateful ways. She would—while he was ill. The tears offered to come to her eyes at the picture. But what sentimental luxury was this she was beginning? She turned to consider the children. At any rate she was absolutely necessary for them. They were her business.

"Ay!" repeated the old woman, "it seems but a week or two since he brought me his first wages. Ay—he was a good lad, Elizabeth, he was, in his way. I don't know why he got to be such a trouble, I don't. He was a happy lad at home, only full of spirits. But there's no mistake he's been a handful of trouble, he has! I hope the Lord'll spare him to mend his ways. I hope so, I hope so. You've had a sight o' trouble with him, Elizabeth, you have indeed. But he was a jolly enough lad wi' me, he was, I can assure you. I don't know how it is. . . ."

The old woman continued to muse aloud, a monotonous irritating sound, while Elizabeth thought concentratedly, startled once, when she heard the winding-engine chuff quickly, and the brakes skirr with a shriek. Then she heard the engine more slowly, and the brakes made no sound. The old woman did not notice. Elizabeth waited in suspense. The mother-in-law talked, with lapses into silence.

"But he wasn't your son, Lizzie, an' it makes a difference. Whatever he was, I remember him when he was little, an' I learned to understand him and to make allowances. You've got to make allowances for them——"

It was half-past ten, and the old woman was saying: "But it's trouble from beginning to end; you're never too old for trouble, never too old for that——" when the gate banged back, and there were heavy feet on the steps.

"I'll go, Lizzie, let me go," cried the old woman, rising. But Elizabeth was at the door. It was a man in pit-clothes.

"They're bringin' 'im, Missis," he said. Elizabeth's heart halted a moment. Then it surged on again, almost suffocating her.

"Is he—is it bad?" she asked.

The man turned away, looking at the darkness:

"The doctor says 'e'd been dead hours. 'E saw 'im i' th' lamp-cabin."

The old woman, who stood just behind Elizabeth, dropped into a chair, and folded her hands, crying: "Oh, my boy, my boy!"

"Hush!" said Elizabeth, with a sharp twitch of a frown. "Be still, mother, don't waken th' children: I wouldn't have them down for anything!"

The old woman moaned softly, rocking herself. The man was drawing away. Elizabeth took a step forward.

"How was it?" she asked.

"Well, I couldn't say for sure," the man replied, very ill at ease. "'E wor finishin' a stint an' th' butties 'ad gone, an' a lot o' stuff come down atop 'n 'im."

"And crushed him?" cried the widow, with a shudder.

"No," said the man, "it fell at th' back of 'im. 'E wor under th' face, an' it niver touched 'im. It shut 'im in. It seems 'e wor smothered."

Elizabeth shrank back. She heard the old woman behind her cry:

"What?—what did 'e say it was?"

The man replied, more loudly: "'E wor smothered!"

Then the old woman wailed aloud, and this relieved Elizabeth.

"Oh, mother," she said, putting her hand on the old woman, "don't waken th' children, don't waken th' children."

She wept a little, unknowing, while the old mother rocked herself and moaned. Elizabeth remembered that they were bringing him home, and she must be ready. "They'll lay him in the parlour," she said to herself, standing a moment pale and perplexed.

Then she lighted a candle and went into the tiny room. The air was cold and damp, but she could not make a fire, there was no fireplace. She set down the candle and looked round. The candlelight glittered on the lustre-glasses, on the two vases that held some of the pink chrysanthemums, and on the dark mahogany. There was a cold, deathly smell of chrysanthemums in the room. Elizabeth stood looking at the flowers. She turned away, and calculated whether there would be room to lay him on the floor, between the couch and the chiffonier.[4] She pushed the chairs aside. There would be room to lay him down and to step round him. Then she fetched the old red tablecloth, and another old cloth, spreading them down to save her bit of carpet. She shivered on leaving the parlour; so, from the dresser drawer she took a clean shirt and put it at the fire to air. All the time her mother-in-law was rocking herself in the chair and moaning.

"You'll have to move from there, mother," said Elizabeth. "They'll be bringing him in. Come in the rocker."

The old mother rose mechanically, and seated herself by the fire, continuing to lament. Elizabeth went into the pantry for another candle, and there, in the little pent-house under the naked tiles, she heard them coming. She stood still in the pantry doorway, listening. She heard them pass the end of the house, and come awkwardly down the three steps, a jumble of shuffling footsteps and muttering voices. The old woman was silent. The men were in the yard.

Then Elizabeth heard Matthews, the manager of the pit, say: "You go in first, Jim. Mind!"

The door came open, and the two women saw a collier backing into the room, holding one end of a stretcher, on which they could see the nailed pit-boots of the dead man. The two carriers halted, the man at the head stooping to the lintel of the door.

"Wheer will you have him?" asked the manager, a short, white-bearded man.

Elizabeth roused herself and came from the pantry carrying the unlighted candle.

"In the parlour," she said.

4. Chest of drawers.

"In there, Jim!" pointed the manager, and the carriers backed round into the tiny room. The coat with which they had covered the body fell off as they awkwardly turned through the two doorways, and the women saw their man, naked to the waist, lying stripped for work. The old woman began to moan in a low voice of horror.

"Lay th' stretcher at th' side," snapped the manager, "an' put 'im on th' cloths. Mind now, mind! Look you now——!"

One of the men had knocked off a vase of chrysanthemums. He stared awkwardly, then they set down the stretcher. Elizabeth did not look at her husband. As soon as she could get in the room, she went and picked up the broken vase and the flowers.

"Wait a minute!" she said.

The three men waited in silence while she mopped up the water with a duster.

"Eh, what a job, what a job, to be sure!" the manager was saying, rubbing his brow with trouble and perplexity. "Never knew such a thing in my life, never! He'd no busines to ha' been left. I never knew such a thing in my life! Fell over him clean as a whistle, an' shut him in. Not four foot of space, there wasn't—yet it scarce bruised him."

He looked down at the dead man, lying prone, half naked, all grimed with coal-dust.

" 'Sphyxiated', the doctor said. It *is* the most terrible job I've ever known. Seems as if it was done o' purpose. Clean over him, an' shut 'im in, like a mouse-trap"—he made a sharp, descending gesture with his hand.

The colliers standing by jerked aside their heads in hopeless comment.

The horror of the thing bristled upon them all.

Then they heard the girl's voice upstairs calling shrilly: "Mother, mother—who is it? Mother, who is it?"

Elizabeth hurried to the foot of the stairs and opened the door:

"Go to sleep!" she commanded sharply. "What are you shouting about? Go to sleep at once—there's nothing—"

Then she began to mount the stairs. They could hear her on the boards, and on the plaster floor of the little bedroom. They could hear her distinctly:

"What's the matter now?—what's the matter with you, silly thing?"—her voice was much agitated, with an unreal gentleness.

"I thought it was some men come," said the plaintive voice of the child. "Has he come?"

"Yes, they've brought him. There's nothing to make a fuss about. Go to sleep now, like a good child."

They could hear her voice in the bedroom, they waited whilst she covered the children under the bedclothes.

"Is he drunk?" asked the girl, timidly, faintly.

"No! No—he's not! He—he's asleep."

"Is he asleep downstairs?"

"Yes—and don't make a noise."

There was silence for a moment, then the men heard the frightened child again:

"What's that noise?"

"It's nothing, I tell you, what are you bothering for?"

The noise was the grandmother moaning. She was oblivious of everything, sitting on her chair rocking and moaning. The manager put his hand on her arm and bade her "Sh—sh!!"

The old woman opened her eyes and looked at him. She was shocked by this interruption, and seemed to wonder.

"What time is it?" the plaintive thin voice of the child, sinking back unhappily into sleep, asked this last question.

"Ten o'clock," answered the mother more softly. Then she must have bent down and kissed the children.

Matthews beckoned to the men to come away. They put on their caps and took up the stretcher. Stepping over the body, they tiptoed out of the house. None of them spoke till they were far from the wakeful children.

When Elizabeth came down she found her mother alone on the parlour floor, leaning over the dead man, the tears dropping on him.

"We must lay him out," the wife said. She put on the kettle, then returning knelt at the feet, and began to unfasten the knotted leather laces. The room was clammy and dim with only one candle, so that she had to bend her face almost to the floor. At last she got off the heavy boots and put them away.

"You must help me now," she whispered to the old woman. Together they stripped the man.

When they arose, saw him lying in the naïve dignity of death, the women stood arrested in fear and respect. For a few moments they remained still, looking down, the old mother whimpering. Elizabeth felt countermanded.[5] She saw him, how utterly inviolable he lay in himself. She had nothing to do with him. She could not accept it. Stooping, she laid her hand on him, in claim. He was still warm, for the mine was hot where he had died. His mother had his face between her hands, and was murmuring incoherently. The old tears fell in succession as drops from wet leaves; the mother was not weeping, merely her tears flowed. Elizabeth embraced the body of her husband, with cheek and lips. She seemed to be listening, inquiring, trying to get some connection. But she could not. She was driven away. He was impregnable.

She rose, went into the kitchen, where she poured warm water into a bowl, brought soap and flannel and a soft towel.

"I must wash him," she said.

Then the old mother rose stiffly, and watched Elizabeth as she carefully washed his face, carefully brushing the big blond moustache from his mouth with the flannel. She was afraid with a bottomless fear, so she ministered to him. The old woman, jealous, said:

"Let me wipe him!"—and she kneeled on the other side drying slowly as Elizabeth washed, her big black bonnet sometimes brushing the dark head of her daughter-in-law. They worked thus in silence for a long time. They never forgot it was death, and the touch of the man's dead body gave them strange emotions, different in each of the women; a great dread possessed them both, the mother felt the lie was given to her womb, she was denied; the wife felt the utter isolation of the human soul, the child within her was a weight apart from her.

At last it was finished. He was a man of handsome body, and his face showed no traces of drink. He was blond, full-fleshed, with fine limbs. But he was dead.

"Bless him," whispered his mother, looking always at his face, and speaking out of sheer terror. "Dear lad—bless him!" She spoke in a faint, sibilant ecstasy of fear and mother love.

Elizabeth sank down again to the floor, and put her face against his neck, and trembled and shuddered. But she had to draw away again. He was dead, and her living flesh had no place against his. A great dread and weariness held her: she was so unavailing. Her life was gone like this.

5. Overruled, contradicted.

"White as milk he is, clear as a twelve-month baby, bless him, the darling!" the old mother murmured to herself. "Not a mark on him, clear and clean and white, beautiful as ever a child was made," she murmured with pride. Elizabeth kept her face hidden.

"He went peaceful, Lizzie—peaceful as sleep. Isn't he beautiful, the lamb? Ay—he must ha' made his peace, Lizzie. 'Appen he made it all right, Lizzie, shut in there. He'd have time. He wouldn't look like this if he hadn't made his peace. The lamb, the dear lamb. Eh, but he had a hearty laugh. I loved to hear it. He had the heartiest laugh, Lizzie, as a lad——"

Elizabeth looked up. The man's mouth was fallen back, slightly open under the cover of the moustache. The eyes, half shut, did not show glazed in the obscurity. Life with its smoky burning gone from him, had left him apart and utterly alien to her. And she knew what a stranger he was to her. In her womb was ice of fear, because of this separate stranger with whom she had been living as one flesh. Was this what it all meant—utter, intact separateness, obscured by heat of living? In dread she turned her face away. The fact was too deadly. There had been nothing between them, and yet they had come together, exchanging their nakedness repeatedly. Each time he had taken her, they had been two isolated beings, far apart as now. He was no more responsible than she. The child was like ice in her womb. For as she looked at the dead man, her mind, cold and detached, said clearly: "Who am I? What have I been doing? I have been fighting a husband who did not exist. He existed all the time. What wrong have I done? What was that I have been living with? There lies the reality, this man." And her soul died in her for fear: she knew she had never seen him, he had never seen her, they had met in the dark and had fought in the dark, not knowing whom they met nor whom they fought. And now she saw, and turned silent in seeing. For she had been wrong. She had said he was something he was not; she had felt familiar with him. Whereas he was apart all the while, living as she never lived, feeling as she never felt.

In fear and shame she looked at his naked body, that she had known falsely. And he was the father of her children. Her soul was torn from her body and stood apart. She looked at his naked body and was ashamed, as if she had denied it. After all, it was itself. It seemed awful to her. She looked at his face, and she turned her own face to the wall. For his look was other than hers, his way was not her way. She had denied him what he was—she saw it now. She had refused him as himself. And this had been her life, and his life. She was grateful to death, which restored the truth. And she knew she was not dead.

And all the while her heart was bursting with grief and pity for him. What had he suffered? What stretch of horror for this helpless man! She was rigid with agony. She had not been able to help him. He had been cruelly injured, this naked man, this other being, and she could make no reparation. There were the children—but the children belonged to life. This dead man had nothing to do with them. He and she were only channels through which life had flowed to issue in the children. She was a mother—but how awful she knew it now to have been a wife. And he, dead now, how awful he must have felt it to be a husband. She felt that in the next world he would be a stranger to her. If they met there, in the beyond, they would only be ashamed of what had been before. The children had come, for some mysterious reason, out of both of them. But the children did not unite them. Now he was dead, she knew how eternally he was apart from her, how eternally he had nothing more to do with her. She saw this episode of her life closed. They had denied each other in life. Now he had withdrawn. An anguish came over her. It was finished then: it had become hopeless between them long before he died. Yet he had been her husband. But how little!

"Have you got his shirt, 'Lizabeth?"

Elizabeth turned without answering, though she strove to weep and behave as her mother-in-law expected. But she could not, she was silenced. She went into the kitchen and returned with the garment.

"It is aired," she said, grasping the cotton shirt here and there to try. She was almost ashamed to handle him; what right had she or anyone to lay hands on him; but her touch was humble on his body. It was hard work to clothe him. He was so heavy and inert. A terrible dread gripped her all the while: that he could be so heavy and utterly inert, unresponsive, apart. The horror of the distance between them was almost too much for her—it was so infinite a gap she must look across.

At last it was finished. They covered him with a sheet and left him lying, with his face bound. And she fastened the door of the little parlour, lest the children should see what was lying there. Then, with peace sunk heavy on her heart, she went about making tidy the kitchen. She knew she submitted to life, which was her immediate master. But from death, her ultimate master, she winced with fear and shame.

Surgery for the Novel—or a Bomb

You talk about the future of the baby, little cherub, when he's in the cradle cooing; and it's a romantic, glamorous subject. You also talk, with the parson, about the future of the wicked old grandfather who is at last lying on his death-bed. And there again you have a subject for much vague emotion, chiefly of fear this time.

How do we feel about the novel? Do we bounce with joy thinking of the wonderful novelistic days ahead? Or do we grimly shake our heads and hope the wicked creature will be spared a little longer? Is the novel on his death-bed, old sinner? Or is he just toddling round his cradle, sweet little thing? Let us have another look at him before we decide this rather serious case.

There he is, the monster with many faces, many branches to him, like a tree: the modern novel. And he is almost dual, like Siamese twins. On the one hand, the pale-faced, high-browed, earnest novel, which you have to take seriously; on the other, that smirking, rather plausible hussy, the popular novel.

Let us just for the moment feel the pulses of *Ulysses* and of Miss Dorothy Richardson and M. Marcel Proust, on the earnest side of Briareus;[1] on the other, the throb of *The Sheik* and Mr Zane Grey, and, if you will, Mr Robert Chambers and the rest.[2] Is *Ulysses* in his cradle? Oh, dear! What a grey face! And *Pointed Roofs*, are they a gay little toy for nice little girls? And M. Proust? Alas! You can hear the death-rattle in their throats. They can hear it themselves. They are listening to it with acute interest, trying to discover whether the intervals are minor thirds or major fourths. Which is rather infantile, really.

So there you have the "serious" novel, dying in a very long-drawn-out fourteen-volume death-agony, and absorbedly, childishly interested in the phenomenon. "Did I feel a twinge in my little toe, or didn't I?" asks every character of Mr Joyce or of Miss Richardson or M. Proust. Is my aura a blend of frankincense and orange pekoe and boot-blacking, or is it myrrh and bacon-fat and Shetland tweed? The audience round the death-bed gapes for the answer. And when, in a sepulchral tone, the answer comes

1. Briareus aided Zeus in fighting the Titans, here represented by the epic modernist novels of Joyce, Proust, and Dorothy Richardson (author of a 12-volume sequence of novels, *Pilgrimage* [1915–1938], of which *Pointed Roofs* was the first).

2. *The Sheik* (1919) was a lurid best-seller by Edith Maude Hull; Zane Grey (1875–1939), popular American writer of westerns; Robert Chalmers (1865–1933), prolific American novelist.

at length, after hundreds of pages: "It is none of these, it is abysmal chloro-coryambasis,"[3] the audience quivers all over, and murmurs: "That's just how I feel myself."

Which is the dismal, long-drawn-out comedy of the death-bed of the serious novel. It is self-consciousness picked into such fine bits that the bits are most of them invisible, and you have to go by smell. Through thousands and thousands of pages Mr Joyce and Miss Richardson tear themselves to pieces, strip their smallest emotions to the finest threads, till you feel you are sewed inside a wool mattress that is being slowly shaken up, and you are turning to wool along with the rest of the woolliness.

It's awful. And it's childish. It really is childish, after a certain age, to be absorbedly self-conscious. One has to be self-conscious at seventeen: still a little self-conscious at twenty-seven; but if we are going it strong at thirty-seven, then it is a sign of arrested development, nothing else. And if it is still continuing at forty-seven, it is obvious senile precocity.

And there's the serious novel: senile-precocious. Absorbedly, childishly concerned with *what I am*. "I am this, I am that, I am the other. My reactions are such, and such, and such. And, oh, Lord, if I liked to watch myself closely enough, if I liked to analyse my feelings minutely, as I unbutton my gloves, instead of saying crudely I unbuttoned them, then I could go on to a million pages instead of a thousand. In fact, the more I come to think of it, it is gross, it is uncivilized bluntly to say: I unbuttoned my gloves. After all, the absorbing adventure of it! Which button did I begin with?" etc.

The people in the serious novels are so absorbedly concerned with themselves and what they feel and don't feel, and how they react to every mortal button; and their audience as frenziedly absorbed in the application of the author's discoveries to their own reactions: "That's me! That's exactly it! I'm just finding myself in this book!" Why, this is more than death-bed, it is almost post-mortem behaviour.

Some convulsion or cataclysm will have to get this serious novel out of its self-consciousness. The last great war made it worse. What's to be done? Because, poor thing, it's really young yet. The novel has never become fully adult. It has never quite grown to years of discretion. It has always youthfully hoped for the best, and felt rather sorry for itself on the last page. Which is just childish. The childishness has become very long-drawn-out. So very many adolescents who drag their adolescence on into their forties and their fifties and their sixties! There needs some sort of surgical operation, somewhere.

Then the popular novels—the *Sheiks* and *Babbitts* and Zane Grey novels. They are just as self-conscious, only they do have more illusions about themselves. The heroines do think they are lovelier, and more fascinating, and purer. The heroes do see themselves more heroic, braver, more chivalrous, more fetching. The mass of the populace "find themselves" in the popular novels. But nowadays it's a funny sort of self they find. A Sheik with a whip up his sleeve, and a heroine with weals on her back, but adored in the end, adored, the whip out of sight, but the weals still faintly visible.

It's a funny sort of self they discover in the popular novels. And the essential moral of *If Winter Comes*, for example, is so shaky. "The gooder you are, the worse it is for you, poor you, oh, poor you. Don't you be so blimey good, it's not good enough." Or *Babbitt*:[4] "Go on, you make your pile, and then pretend you're too good for it. Put it over the rest of the grabbers that way. They're only pleased with themselves when they've made their pile. You go one better."

3. A word of Lawrence's invention.
4. *If Winter Comes* (1915), a novel by American author A. S. M. Hutchinson; *Babbitt* (1922) by American author Sinclair Lewis.

Always the same sort of baking-powder gas to make you rise: the soda counteracting the cream of tartar, and the tartar counteracted by the soda. Sheik heroines, duly whipped, wildly adored. Babbitts with solid fortunes, weeping from self-pity. Winter-Comes heroes as good as pie, hauled off to jail. *Moral:* Don't be too good, because you'll go to jail for it. *Moral:* Don't feel sorry for yourself till you've made your pile and don't need to feel sorry for yourself. *Moral:* Don't let him adore you till he's whipped you into it. Then you'll be partners in mild crime as well as in holy matrimony.

Which again is childish. Adolescence which *can't* grow up. Got into the self-conscious rut and going crazy, quite crazy in it. Carrying on their adolescence into middle age and old age, like the looney Cleopatra in *Dombey and Son*,[5] murmuring "Rose-coloured curtains" with her dying breath.

The future of the novel? Poor old novel, it's in a rather dirty, messy tight corner. And it's either got to get over the wall or knock a hole through it. In other words, it's got to grow up. Put away childish things like: "Do I love the girl, or don't I?"—"Am I pure and sweet, or am I not?"—"Do I unbutton my right glove first, or my left?"—"Did my mother ruin my life by refusing to drink the cocoa which my bride had boiled for her?" These questions and their answers don't really interest me any more, though the world still goes sawing them over. I simply don't care for any of these things now, though I used to. The purely emotional and self-analytical stunts are played out in me. I'm finished. I'm deaf to the whole band. But I'm neither *blasé* nor cynical, for all that. I'm just interested in something else.

Supposing a bomb were put under the whole scheme of things, what would we be after? What feelings do we want to carry through into the next epoch? What feelings will carry us through? What is the underlying impulse in us that will provide the motive power for a new state of things, when this democratic-industrial-lovey-dovey-darling-take-me-to-mamma state of things is bust?

What next? That's what interests me. "What now?" is no fun any more.

If you wish to look into the past for what-next books, you can go back to the Greek philosophers. Plato's Dialogues are queer little novels. It seems to me it was the greatest pity in the world, when philosophy and fiction got split. They used to be one, right from the days of myth. Then they went and parted, like a nagging married couple, with Aristotle and Thomas Aquinas and that beastly Kant.[6] So the novel went sloppy, and philosophy went abstract-dry. The two should come together again—in the novel.

You've got to find a new impulse for new things in mankind, and it's really fatal to find it through abstraction. No, no; philosophy and religion, they've both gone too far on the algebraical tack: Let X stand for sheep and Y for goats: then X minus Y equals Heaven, and X plus Y equals Earth, and Y minus X equals Hell. Thank you! But what coloured shirt does X have on?

The novel has a future. It's got to have the courage to tackle new propositions without using abstractions; it's got to present us with new, really new feelings, a whole line of new emotion, which will get us out of the emotional rut. Instead of snivelling about what is and has been, or inventing new sensations in the old line, it's got to break a way through, like a hole in the wall. And the public will scream and say it is sacrilege: because, of course, when you've been jammed for a long time in a tight corner, and you get really used to its stuffiness and its tightness, till you find it

5. In Dickens's novel *Dombey and Son* (1847–1848), the second wife of Mr. Dombey is known as "Cleopatra."

6. All systematic philosophers who wrote syllogistically; in a letter of 1928, Lawrence included Immanuel Kant in a list of "grand perverts."

suffocatingly cozy; then, of course, you're horrified when you see a new glaring hole in what was your cosy wall. You're horrified. You back away from the cold stream of fresh air as if it were killing you. But gradually, first one and then another of the sheep filters through the gap, and finds a new world outside.

Graham Greene

1904–1991

In a 1945 essay on the French Catholic novelist François Mauriac, Graham Greene wrote that "a disaster overtook the English novel" with the death of Henry James; the cause of that disaster, Greene goes on to explain, was that "the religious sense was lost to the English novel, and with the religious sense went the sense of the importance of the human act." It is this importance of the human act that comprises the recurrent theme of Greene's own writing, and makes his voice a unique one in twentieth-century fiction.

Greene was one of six children born to Charles Henry Greene, the headmaster of Berkhamstead School, and his wife Marion R. Greene. Graham matriculated at his father's school in 1915 and graduated in 1921, when he went to Oxford, taking his degree in history. Like Evelyn Waugh, whom he would later befriend, Greene became a Roman Catholic convert in his twenties (he joined the church in 1926); after a few years as a literary journalist and an editor for the *Times* of London, Greene published his first novel, *The Man Within*, in 1929. His first self-consciously Catholic novel was *Brighton Rock* (1938); the religious framework through which Greene had come to view the world was now pressed into service as a framework for fictional narrative, and with impressive success. The novel makes clear the pattern that was to emerge in the majority of Greene's later fiction: that of "perfect evil walking the world where perfect good can never walk again"—a theme amply illustrated in his chilling 1936 story *A Chance for Mr Lever*.

Three novels of the 1940s and 1950s are today generally recognized as Greene's greatest: *The Power and the Glory* (1940), set in Mexico; *The Heart of the Matter* (1948), set, like *A Chance for Mr Lever*, in West Africa; and *The End of the Affair* (1951), which takes place back home in London during the Blitz. In all of Greene's most powerful work, his protagonist suffers a fall—a fall which, as the critic Richard Hauer Costa writes, often comes to seem a fortunate fall, stripping him of all disguises and pretense and hurling him headlong into a state of unmerited grace. The narrator who tells of Mr. Lever's fall, though, doubts that the hand of Providence has been at work.

A Chance for Mr Lever

Mr Lever knocked his head against the ceiling and swore. Rice was stored above, and in the dark the rats began to move. Grains of rice fell between the slats on to his Revelation suitcase, his bald head, his cases of tinned food, the little square box in which he kept his medicines. His boy had already set up the camp-bed and mosquito-net, and outside in the warm damp dark his folding table and chair. The thatched pointed huts streamed away towards the forest and a woman went from hut to hut carrying fire. The glow lit her old face, her sagging breasts, her tattooed diseased body.

It was incredible to Mr Lever that five weeks ago he had been in London.

He couldn't stand upright; he went down on hands and knees in the dust and opened his suitcase. He took out his wife's photograph and stood it on the chop-box; he took out a writing-pad and an indelible pencil: the pencil had softened in the heat and left mauve stains on his pyjamas. Then, because the light of the hurricane lamp disclosed cockroaches the size of black-beetles flattened against the mud wall, he carefully closed the suitcase. Already in ten days he had learnt that they'd eat anything—socks, shirts, the laces out of your shoes.

Mr Lever went outside; moths beat against his lamp, but there were no mosquitoes; he hadn't seen or heard one since he landed. He sat in a circle of light carefully observed. The blacks squatted outside their huts and watched him; they were friendly, interested, amused, but their strict attention irritated Mr Lever. He could feel the small waves of interest washing round him, when he began to write, when he stopped writing, when he wiped his damp hands with a handkerchief. He couldn't touch his pocket without a craning of necks.

Dearest Emily, he wrote, *I've really started now. I'll send this letter back with a carrier when I've located Davidson. I'm very well. Of course everything's a bit strange. Look after yourself, my dear, and don't worry*.

"Massa buy chicken," his cook said, appearing suddenly between the huts. A small stringy fowl struggled in his hands.

"Well," Mr Lever said, "I gave you a shilling, didn't I?"

"They no like," the cook said. "These low bush people."

"Why don't they like? It's good money."

"They want king's money," the cook said, handing back the Victorian shilling. Mr Lever had to get up, go back into his hut, grope for his money-box, search through twenty pounds of small change: there was no peace.

He had learnt that very quickly. He had to economize (the whole trip was a gamble which scared him); he couldn't afford hammock carriers. He would arrive tired out after seven hours of walking at a village of which he didn't know the name and not for a minute could he sit quietly and rest. He must shake hands with the chief, he must see about a hut, accept presents of palm wine he was afraid to drink, buy rice and palm oil for the carriers, give them salts and aspirin, paint their sores with iodine. They never left him alone for five minutes on end until he went to bed. And then the rats began, rushing down the walls like water when he put out the light, gambolling[1] among his cases.

I'm too old, Mr Lever told himself, I'm too old, writing damply, indelibly, *I hope to find Davidson tomorrow. If I do, I may be back almost as soon as this letter. Don't economize on the stout and milk, dear, and call in the doctor if you feel bad. I've got a premonition this trip's going to turn out well. We'll take a holiday, you need a holiday*, and staring ahead past the huts and the black faces and the banana trees towards the forest from which he had come, into which he would sink again next day, he thought, Eastbourne,[2] Eastbourne would do her a world of good; and he continued to write the only kind of lies he had ever told Emily, the lies which comforted. *I ought to draw at least three hundred in commission and expenses*. But it wasn't the sort of place where he'd been accustomed to sell heavy machinery; thirty years of it, up and down Europe and in the States, but never anything like this. He could hear his filter dripping in the hut, and somewhere somebody was playing something (he was so lost he hadn't got the simplest terms to his hands), something monotonous, melancholy, superficial, a twanging of palm fibres which seemed to convey that you weren't happy, but it didn't matter, everything would always be the same.

Look after yourself, Emily, he repeated. It was almost the only thing he found himself capable of writing to her; he couldn't describe the narrow, steep, lost paths,

1. Frolicking.

2. A seaport in Sussex, England.

the snakes sizzling away like flames, the rats, the dust, the naked diseased bodies. He was unbearably tired of nakedness. *Don't forget*—It was like living with a lot of cows.

"The chief," his boy whispered, and between the huts under a waving torch came an old stout man wearing a robe of native cloth and a battered bowler hat. Behind him his men carried six bowls of rice, a bowl of palm oil, two bowls of broken meat. "Chop for the labourers," the boy explained, and Mr Lever had to get up and smile and nod and try to convey without words that he was pleased, that the chop was excellent, that the chief would get a good dash[3] in the morning. At first the smell had been almost too much for Mr Lever.

"Ask him," he said to his boy, "if he's seen a white man come through here lately. Ask him if a white man's been digging around here. Damn it," Mr Lever burst out, the sweat breaking on the backs of his hands and on his bald head, "ask him if he's seen Davidson?"

"Davidson?"

"Oh, hell," Mr Lever said, "you know what I mean. The white man I'm looking for."

"White man?"

"What do you imagine I'm here for, eh? White man? Of course white man. I'm not here for my health." A cow coughed, rubbed its horns against the hut and two goats broke through between the chief and him, upsetting the bowls of meat scraps; nobody cared, they picked the meat out of the dust and dung.

Mr Lever sat down and put his hands over his face, fat white well-cared-for hands with wrinkles of flesh over the rings. He felt too old for this.

"Chief say no white man been here long time."

"How long?"

"Chief say not since he pay hut tax."

"How long's that?"

"Long long time."

"Ask him how far is it to Greh, tomorrow."

"Chief say too far."

"Nonsense," Mr Lever said.

"Chief say too far. Better stay here. Fine town. No humbug."

Mr Lever groaned. Every evening there was the same trouble. The next town was always too far. They would invent any excuse to delay him, to give themselves a rest.

"Ask the chief how many hours—?"

"Plenty, plenty." They had no idea of time.

"This fine chief. Fine chop. Labourers tired. No humbug."

"We are going on," Mr Lever said.

"This fine town. Chief say—"

He thought: if this wasn't the last chance, I'd give up. They nagged him so, and suddenly he longed for another white man (not Davidson, he daren't say anything to Davidson) to whom he could explain the desperation of his lot. It wasn't fair that a man, after thirty years' commercial travelling, should need to go from door to door asking for a job. He had been a good traveller, he had made money for many people, his references were excellent, but the world had moved on since his day. He wasn't streamlined; he certainly wasn't streamlined. He had been ten years retired when he lost his money in the depression.

3. Tip.

Mr Lever walked up and down Victoria Street showing his references. Many of the men knew him, gave him cigars, laughed at him in a friendly way for wanting to take on a job at his age ("I can't somehow settle at home. The old warhorse you know. . . "), cracked a joke or two in the passage, went back that night to Maidenhead silent in the first-class carriage, shut in with age and ruin and how bad things were and poor devil his wife's probably sick.

It was in the rather shabby little office off Leadenhall Street that Mr Lever met his chance. It called itself an engineering firm, but there were only two rooms, a typewriter, a girl with gold teeth and Mr Lucas, a thin narrow man with a tic in one eyelid. All through the interview the eyelid flickered at Mr Lever. Mr Lever had never before fallen so low as this.

But Mr Lucas struck him as reasonably honest. He put "all his cards on the table." He hadn't got any money, but he had expectations; he had the handling of a patent. It was a new crusher. There was money in it. But you couldn't expect the big trusts to change over their machinery now. Things were too bad. You'd got to get in at the start, and that was where—why, that was where this chief, the bowls of chop, the nagging and the rats and the heat came in. They called themselves a republic, Mr Lucas said, he didn't know anything about that, they were not as black as they were painted, he supposed (ha, ha, nervously, ha, ha); anyway, this company had slipped agents over the border and grabbed a concession: gold and diamonds. He could tell Mr Lever in confidence that the trust was frightened of what they'd found. Now an enterprising man could just slip across (Mr Lucas liked the word slip, it made everything sound easy and secret) and introduce this new crusher to them: it would save them thousands when they started work, there'd be a fat commission, and afterwards, with that start. . . There was a fortune for them all.

"But can't you fix it up in Europe?"

Tic, tic, went Mr Lucas's eyelid. "A lot of Belgians; they are leaving all decisions to the man on the spot. An Englishman called Davidson."

"How about expenses?"

"That's the trouble," Mr Lucas said. "We are only beginning. What we want is a partner. We can't afford to send a man. But if you like a gamble. . . Twenty per cent commission."

"Chief say excuse him." The carriers squatted round the basins and scooped up the rice in their left hands. "Of course. Of course," Mr Lever said absent-mindedly. "Very kind, I'm sure."

He was back out of the dust and dark, away from the stink of goats and palm oil and whelping bitches, back among the rotarians and lunch at Stone's, "the pint of old," and the trade papers; he was a good fellow again, finding his way back to Golders Green just a bit lit;[4] his masonic emblem rattled on his watch-chain, and he bore with him from the tube station to his house in Finchley Road a sense of companionship, of broad stories and belches, a sense of bravery.

He needed all his bravery now; the last of his savings had gone into the trip. After thirty years he knew a good thing when he saw it, and he had no doubts about the new crusher. What he doubted was his ability to find Davidson. For one thing there weren't any maps; the way you travelled in the Republic was to write down a list of names and trust that someone in the villages you passed would understand and know the route. But they always said "Too far." Good fellowship wilted before the phrase.

4. Tipsy.

"Quinine,"[5] Mr Lever said. "Where's my quinine?" His boy never remembered a thing; they just didn't care what happened to you; their smiles meant nothing, and Mr Lever, who knew better than anyone the value of a meaningless smile in business, resented their heartlessness, and turned towards the dilatory boy an expression of disappointment and dislike.

"Chief say white man in bush five hours away."

"That's better," Mr Lever said. "It must be Davidson. He's digging for gold?"

"Ya. White man dig for gold in bush."

"We'll be off early tomorrow," Mr Lever said.

"Chief say better stop this town. Fever humbug white man."

"Too bad," Mr Lever said, and he thought with pleasure: my luck's changed. He'll want help. He won't refuse me a thing. A friend in need is a friend indeed, and his heart warmed towards Davidson, seeing himself arrive like an answer to prayer out of the forest, feeling quite biblical and vox humana.[6] He thought: Prayer. I'll pray tonight, that's the kind of thing a fellow gives up, but it pays, there's something in it, remembering the long agonizing prayer on his knees, by the sideboard, under the decanters, when Emily went to hospital.

"Chief say white man dead."

Mr Lever turned his back on them and went into his hut. His sleeve nearly overturned the hurricane lamp. He undressed quickly, stuffing his clothes into a suitcase away from the cockroaches. He wouldn't believe what he had been told; it wouldn't pay him to believe. If Davidson were dead, there was nothing he could do but return; he had spent more than he could afford; he would be a ruined man. He supposed that Emily might find a home with her brother, but he could hardly expect her brother—he began to cry, but you couldn't have told in the shadowy hut the difference between sweat and tears. He knelt down beside his camp-bed and mosquito-net and prayed on the dust of the earth floor. Up till now he had always been careful never to touch ground with his naked feet for fear of jiggers;[7] there were jiggers everywhere, they only waited an opportunity to dig themselves in under the toe-nails, lay their eggs and multiply.

"O God," Mr Lever prayed, "don't let Davidson be dead; let him be just sick and glad to see me." He couldn't bear the idea that he might not any longer be able to support Emily. "O God, there's nothing I wouldn't do." But that was an empty phrase; he had no real notion as yet of what he would do for Emily. They had been happy together for thirty-five years; he had never been more than momentarily unfaithful to her when he was lit after a rotarian dinner and egged on by the boys; whatever skirt he'd been with in his time, he had never for a moment imagined that he could be happy married to anyone else. It wasn't fair if, just when you were old and needed each other most, you lost your money and couldn't keep together.

But of course Davidson wasn't dead. What would he have died of? The blacks were friendly. People said the country was unhealthy, but he hadn't so much as heard a mosquito. Besides, you didn't die of malaria; you just lay between the blankets and took quinine and felt like death and sweated it out of you. There was dysentery, but Davidson was an old campaigner; you were safe if you boiled and filtered the water. The water was poison even to touch; it was unsafe to wet your feet because of guinea worm,[8] but you didn't die of guinea worm.

5. Chemical compound taken to fight off malaria.
6. A type of pipe organ.
7. A tropical flea that burrows under the skin.
8. A worm, growing up to several feet long, which lives under the skin.

Mr Lever lay in bed and his thoughts went round and round and he couldn't sleep. He thought: you don't die of a thing like guinea worm. It makes a sore on your foot, and if you put your foot in water you can see the eggs dropping out. You have to find the end of the worm, like a thread of cotton, and wind it round a match and wind it out of your leg without breaking; it stretches as high as the knee. I'm too old for this country, Mr Lever thought.

Then his boy was beside him again. He whispered urgently to Mr Lever through the mosquito-net. "Massa, the labourers say they go home."

"Go home?" Mr Lever asked wearily; he had heard it so often before. "Why do they want to go home? What is it now?" but he didn't really want to hear the latest squabble: that the Bande men were never sent to carry water because the headman was a Bande, that someone had stolen an empty treacle tin and sold it in the village for a penny, that someone wasn't made to carry a proper load, that the next day's journey was "too far." He said, "Tell 'em they can go home. I'll pay them off in the morning. But they won't get any dash. They'd have got a good dash if they'd stayed." He was certain it was just another try-on; he wasn't as green as all that.

"Yes, massa. They no want dash."

"What's that?"

"They frightened fever humbug them like white man."

"I'll get carriers in the village. They can go home."

"Me too, massa."

"Get out," Mr Lever said; it was the last straw; "get out and let me sleep." The boy went at once, obedient even though a deserter, and Mr Lever thought: sleep, what a hope. He lifted the net and got out of bed (barefooted again: he didn't care a damn about the jiggers) and searched for his medicine box. It was locked, of course, and he had to open his suitcase and find the key in a trouser pocket. His nerves were more on edge than ever by the time he found the sleeping tablets and he took three of them. That made him sleep, heavily and dreamlessly, though when he woke he found that something had made him fling out his arms and open the net. If there had been a single mosquito in the place, he'd have been bitten, but of course there wasn't one.

He could tell at once that the trouble hadn't blown over. The village—he didn't know its name—was perched on a hilltop; east and west the forest flowed out beneath the little plateau; to the west it was a dark unfeatured mass like water, but in the east you could already discern the unevenness, the great grey cotton trees lifted above the palms. Mr Lever was always called before dawn, but no one had called him. A few of his carriers sat outside a hut sullenly talking; his boy was with them. Mr Lever went back inside and dressed; he thought all the time, I must be firm, but he was scared, scared of being deserted, scared of being made to return.

When he came outside again the village was awake: the women were going down the hill to fetch water, winding silently past the carriers, past the flat stones where the chiefs were buried, the little grove of trees where the rice birds, like green and yellow canaries, nested. Mr Lever sat down on his folding chair among the chickens and whelping bitches and cow dung and called his boy. He took "a strong line"; but he didn't know what was going to happen. "Tell the chief I want to speak to him," he said.

There was some delay; the chief wasn't up yet, but presently he appeared in his blue and white robe, setting his bowler hat straight. "Tell him," Mr Lever said, "I want carriers to take me to the white man and back. Two days."

"Chief no agree," the boy said.

Mr Lever said furiously, "Damn it, if he doesn't agree, he won't get any dash from me, not a penny." It occurred to him immediately afterwards how hopelessly dependent he was on these people's honesty. There in the hut for all to see was his money-box; they had only to take it. This wasn't a British or French colony; the blacks on the coast wouldn't bother, could do nothing if they did bother, because a stray Englishman had been robbed in the interior.

"Chief say how many?"

"It's only for two days," Mr Lever said. "I can do with six."

"Chief say how much?"

"Sixpence a day and chop."

"Chief no agree."

"Ninepence a day then."

"Chief say too far. A shilling."

"All right, all right," Mr Lever said, "A shilling then. You others can go home if you want to. I'll pay you off now, but you won't get any dash, not a penny."

He had never really expected to be left, and it gave him a sad feeling of loneliness to watch them move sullenly away (they were ashamed of themselves) down the hill to the west. They hadn't any loads, but they weren't singing; they drooped silently out of sight, his boy with them, and he was alone with his pile of boxes and the chief who couldn't talk a word of English. Mr Lever smiled tremulously.

It was ten o'clock before his new carriers were chosen; he could tell that none of them wanted to go, and they would have to walk through the heat of the middle day if they were to find Davidson before it was dark. He hoped the chief had explained properly where they were going; he couldn't tell; he was completely shut off from them, and when they started down the eastward slope, he might just as well have been alone.

They were immediately caught up in the forest. Forest conveys a sense of wildness and beauty, of an active natural force, but this Liberian forest was simply a dull green wilderness. You passed, on the path a foot or so wide, through an endless back garden of tangled weeds; it didn't seem to be growing round you, so much as dying. There was no life at all, except for a few large birds whose wings creaked overhead through the invisible sky like an unoiled door. There was no view, no way out for the eyes, no change of scene. It wasn't the heat that tired, so much as the boredom; you had to think of things to think about; but even Emily failed to fill the mind for more than three minutes at a time. It was a relief, a distraction, when the path was flooded and Mr Lever had to be carried on a man's back. At first he had disliked the strong bitter smell (it reminded him of a breakfast food he was made to eat as a child), but he soon got over that. Now he was unaware that they smelt at all; any more than he was aware that the great swallow-tailed butterflies, which clustered at the water's edge and rose in green clouds round his waist, were beautiful. His senses were dulled and registered very little except his boredom.

But they did register a distinct feeling of relief when his leading carrier pointed to a rectangular hole dug just off the path. Mr Lever understood. Davidson had come this way. He stopped and looked at it. It was like a grave dug for a small man, but it went down deeper than graves usually do. About twelve feet below there was black water, and a few wooden props which held the sides from slipping were beginning to rot; the hole must have been dug since the rains. It didn't seem enough, that hole, to have brought out Mr Lever with his plans and estimates for a new crusher. He was used to big industrial concerns, the sight of pitheads, the smoke of chimneys, the dingy rows of cottages back to back, the leather armchair in the office, the good cigar, the masonic hand-grips, and again it seemed to him, as it had seemed in Mr Lucas's office, that he had fallen very low. It was as if he was expected to do business beside a hole a child had dug in an overgrown and abandoned back garden; percentages wilted in the hot damp air. He shook his head; he mustn't be discouraged; this was an old hole. Davidson had probably done better since. It was only common sense to suppose that the gold rift which was mined at one end in Nigeria, at the other in Sierra Leone, would pass through the republic. Even the biggest mines had to begin with a hole in the ground. The company (he had talked to the directors in Brussels) were quite confident: all they wanted was the approval of the man on the spot that the crusher was suitable for local conditions. A signature, that was all he had to get, he told himself, staring down into the puddle of black water.

Five hours, the chief had said, but after six hours they were still walking. Mr Lever had eaten nothing; he wanted to get to Davidson first. All through the heat of the day he walked. The forest protected him from the direct sun, but it shut out the air, and the occasional clearings, shrivelled though they were in the vertical glare, seemed cooler than the shade because there was a little more air to breathe. At four o'clock the heat diminished, but he began to fear they wouldn't reach Davidson before dark. His foot pained him; he had caught a jigger the night before; it was as if someone were holding a lighted match to his toe. Then at five they came on a dead black.

Another rectangular hole in a small cleared space among the dusty greenery had caught Mr Lever's eye. He peered down and was shocked to see a face return his stare, white eyeballs like phosphorus in the black water. The black had been bent almost double to fit him in; the hole was really too small to be a grave, and he had swollen. His flesh was like a blister you could prick with a needle. Mr Lever felt sick and tired; he might have been tempted to return if he could have reached the village before dark, but now there was nothing to do but go on; the carriers luckily hadn't seen the body. He waved them forward and stumbled after them among the roots, fighting his nausea. He fanned himself with his sun helmet; his wide fat face was damp and pale. He had never seen an uncared-for body before; his parents he had seen carefully laid out with closed eyes and washed faces; they "fell asleep" quite in accordance with their epitaphs, but you couldn't think of sleep in connexion with the white eyeballs and the swollen face. Mr Lever would have liked very much to say a prayer, but prayers were out of place in the dead drab forest; they simply didn't "come."

With the dusk a little life did waken: something lived in the dry weeds and brittle trees, if only monkeys. They chattered and screamed all round you, but it was too dark to see them; you were like a blind man in the centre of a frightened crowd who wouldn't say what scared them. The carriers too were frightened. They ran under their fifty-pound loads behind the dipping light of the hurricane lamp, their huge flat carriers' feet flapping in the dust like empty gloves. Mr Lever listened nervously for mosquitoes; you would have expected them to be out by now, but he didn't hear one.

Then at the top of a rise above a small stream they came on Davidson. The ground had been cleared in a square of twelve feet and a small tent pitched; he had dug another hole; the scene came dimly into view as they climbed the path; the chop-boxes piled outside the tent, the syphon of soda water, the filter, an enamel basin. But there wasn't a light, there wasn't a sound, the flaps of the tent were not closed, and Mr Lever had to face the possibility that after all the chief might have told the truth.

Mr Lever took the lamp and stooped inside the tent. There was a body on the bed. At first Mr Lever thought Davidson was covered with blood, but then he realized it was a black vomit which stained his shirt and khaki shorts, the fair stubble on his chin. He put out a hand and touched Davidson's face, and if he hadn't felt a slight breath on his palm he would have taken him for dead; his skin was so cold. He moved the lamp closer, and now the lemon-yellow face told him all he wanted to know: he hadn't thought of that when his boy said fever. It was quite true that a man didn't die of malaria, but an odd piece of news read in New York in '98 came back to mind: there had been an outbreak of yellow jack[9] in Rio and ninety-four per cent of the cases had been fatal. It hadn't meant anything to him then, but it did now. While he watched, Davidson was sick, quite effortlessly; he was like a tap out of which something flowed.

It seemed at first to Mr Lever to be the end of everything, of his journey, his hopes, his life with Emily. There was nothing he could do for Davidson, the man was unconscious, there were times when his pulse was so low and irregular that Mr Lever thought that he was dead until another black stream spread from his mouth; it was no use even cleaning him. Mr Lever laid his own blankets over the bed on top of Davidson's because he was so cold to the touch, but he had no idea whether he was doing the right, or even the fatally wrong, thing. The chance of survival, if there were any chance at all, depended on neither of them. Outside his carriers had built a fire and were cooking the rice they had brought with them. Mr Lever opened his folding chair and sat by the bed. He wanted to keep awake: it seemed right to keep awake. He opened his case and found his unfinished letter to Emily. He sat by Davidson's side and tried to write, but he could think of nothing but what he had already written too often: *Look after yourself. Don't forget that stout and milk.*

He fell asleep over his pad and woke at two and thought that Davidson was dead. But he was wrong again. He was very thirsty and missed his boy. Always the first thing his boy did at the end of a march was to light a fire and put on a kettle; after that, by the time his table and chair were set up, there was water ready for the filter. Mr Lever found half a cup of soda water left in Davidson's syphon; if it had been only his health at stake he would have gone down to the stream, but he had Emily to remember. There was a typewriter by the bed, and it occurred to Mr Lever that he might just as well begin to write his report of failure now; it might keep him awake; it seemed disrespectful to the dying man to sleep. He found paper under some letters which had been typed and signed but not sealed. Davidson must have been taken ill very suddenly. Mr Lever wondered whether it was he who had crammed the black into the hole; his boy perhaps, for there was no sign of a servant. He balanced the typewriter on his knee and headed the letter "In Camp near Greh."

It seemed to him unfair that he should have come so far, spent so much money, worn out a rather old body to meet his inevitable ruin in a dark tent beside a dying man, when he could have met it just as well at home with Emily in the plush parlour. The thought of the prayers he had uselessly uttered on his knees by the camp-bed among the jiggers, the rats and the cockroaches made him rebellious. A mosquito, the first he had heard, went humming round the tent. He slashed at it savagely; he wouldn't have recognized himself among the rotarians. He was lost and he was set free. Moralities were what enabled a man to live happily and successfully with his fellows, but Mr Lever wasn't happy and he wasn't successful, and his only fellow in the little stuffy tent wouldn't be troubled by Untruth in Advertising or by Mr Lever coveting his neighbour's oxen. You couldn't keep your ideas intact when you discovered their geographical nature. The Solemnity of Death: death wasn't solemn; it was a lemon-yellow skin and a black vomit. Honesty is the Best Policy: he saw quite suddenly how false that was. It was an anarchist who sat happily over the typewriter, an anarchist

9. Yellow fever, a tropical disease transmitted by mosquitoes.

who recognized nothing but one personal relationship, his affection for Emily. Mr Lever began to type: *I have examined the plans and estimates of the new Lucas crusher* . . .

Mr Lever thought with savage happiness: I win. This letter would be the last the company would hear from Davidson. The junior partner would open it in the dapper Brussels office; he would tap his false teeth with a Waterman pen and go in to talk to M. Golz. *Taking all these factors into consideration I recommend acceptance*. . . . They would telegraph to Lucas. As for Davidson, that trusted agent of the company would have died of yellow fever at some never accurately determined date. Another agent would come out, and the crusher . . . Mr Lever carefully copied Davidson's signature on a spare sheet of paper. He wasn't satisfied. He turned the original upside-down and copied it that way, so as not to be confused by his own idea of how a letter should be formed. That was better, but it didn't satisfy him. He searched until he found Davidson's own pen and began again to copy and copy the signature. He fell asleep copying it and woke again an hour later to find the lamp was out; it had burnt up all the oil. He sat there beside Davidson's bed till daylight; once he was bitten by a mosquito in the ankle and clapped his hand to the place too late: the brute went humming out. With the light Mr Lever saw that Davidson was dead. "Dear, dear," he said. "Poor fellow." He spat out with the words, quite delicately in a corner, the bad morning taste in his mouth. It was like a little sediment of his conventionality.

Mr Lever got two of his carriers to cram Davidson tidily into his hole. He was no longer afraid of them or of failure or of separation. He tore up his letter to Emily. It no longer represented his mood in its timidity, its secret fear, its gentle fussing phrases, *Don't forget the stout. Look after yourself*. He would be home as soon as the letter, and they were going to do things together now they'd never dreamt of doing. The money for the crusher was only the beginning. His ideas stretched farther now than Eastbourne, they stretched as far as Switzerland; he had a feeling that, if he really let himself go, they'd stretch as far as the Riviera. How happy he was on what he thought of as "the trip home." He was freed from what had held him back through a long pedantic career, the fear of a conscious fate that notes the dishonesty, notes the skirt in Piccadilly, notes the glass too many of Stone's special. Now he had said Boo to that goose . . .

But you who are reading this, who know so much more than Mr Lever, who can follow the mosquito's progress from the dead swollen black to Davidson's tent, to Mr Lever's ankle, you may possibly believe in God, a kindly god tender towards human frailty, ready to give Mr Lever three days of happiness, three days off the galling chain, as he carried back through the forest his amateurish forgeries and the infection of yellow fever in the blood. The story might very well have encouraged my faith in that loving omniscience if it had not been shaken by personal knowledge of the drab forest through which Mr Lever now went so merrily, where it is impossible to believe in any spiritual life, in anything outside the nature dying round you, the shrivelling of the weeds. But of course, there are two opinions about everything; it was Mr Lever's favourite expression, drinking beer in the Ruhr, Pernod[1] in Lorraine, selling heavy machinery.

1936

1. A licorice-flavored liqueur.

PERSPECTIVES

World War II and the End of Empire

World War I had been a catastrophe of unprecedented proportions. Never before in world history had a preponderance of national powers joined together into two warring alliances; never before had the theater of war included such a wide expanse of the globe. But for Great Britain, at least, the war was foreign rather than domestic; as demoralizing and bleak as the fighting was, it was "over there," and never touched the British Isles. World War II would be a very different story.

World War II started, technically, with Hitler's invasion of Poland on 1 September 1939; as is the case with all world-historical conflicts, however, the war's genesis can be traced further back—in this case, back two decades to the peace treaties with which World War I was uneasily concluded. The victors of World War I never quite got what they hoped for, and the defeated nations had their defeat transformed into ritual diplomatic humiliation. Meanwhile, a worldwide economic depression had begun in the United States in 1929 and spread to Europe by the early 1930s, weakening democratic governments and lending a seductive edge to the rhetoric of political extremists. As a result, when Hitler began to rise to power in a beleaguered Germany during the 1930s, his message of empowerment was one that many Germans wanted to hear. Beginning with Poland, Hitler overran Denmark, Luxembourg, the Netherlands, Belgium, and Norway in quick succession, and by June 1940 had conquered even France. Britain was next on Hitler's list, as the major remaining obstacle to the domination of Europe.

Hitler hoped to paralyze and demoralize the British by a devastating series of attacks by air. This drew out to become the ten-month long Battle of Britain, in which the German Luftwaffe (air force) engaged Britain's Royal Air Force in the previously inviolable air space over England's green and pleasant land. The battle brought enormous costs—especially during the eight months of nightly air raids over British metropolitan centers known as the Blitz. The bombing caused great destruction to London, which was bombed every night between 7 September and 2 November 1940; more than 15,000 civilians were killed in London (30,000 nationwide), over half a million left homeless, and important cultural and architectural treasures, such as the House of Commons and Buckingham Palace, were damaged or destroyed. This violation of England's homeland was costly in psychological and emotional terms as well; one poignant register of the broad impact of the air raids can be seen in Virginia Woolf's final novel *Between the Acts*, where the sound of bombs falling on distant London unnerves the residents and guests of Pointz Hall. As Woolf's diaries and letters make clear, the sound of those bombs was also a crucial factor in her decision to take her own life in March 1941.

In May 1941, Germany finally gave up its attempt to conquer Britain from the air. With the bombing of Pearl Harbor by the Japanese in December 1941, the United States entered the war on the side of the Allies; with their help, Britain was able to mount an offensive against Germany on the European mainland and retake land that had been invaded by Germany. In 1942, Britain and the United States began to plan an invasion across the English Channel. The first attempt, a raid staged at the French port of Dieppe in the summer of 1942, was a disappointing failure. The Allies regrouped, however, and planned the offensive known as D-Day. On 6 June 1944, Allied troops, under the command of General Dwight D. Eisenhower, crossed the channel with 2,700 ships and 176,000 soldiers and overcame German defenses; by the end of the month, about a million Allied troops were on the ground in France, and the tide of the war had turned. In April 1945 Hitler committed suicide; one week later, Germany signed a statement of unconditional surrender, with Japan following suit on 2 September.

World War II was over; in some important arenas, however, its influence had just begun to be felt. With such a great proportion of its able-bodied young men going off to war, millions of women in both Britain and the United States took employment outside the home for the first time; that trend, once started, was only to gain momentum in the years that followed. The economic and personal freedom ceded to women during the wartime emergency laid the groundwork for the contemporary women's movement in Great Britain; Margaret Thatcher, Britain's first woman Prime Minister (1979–1990), was a postwar inheritor of Winston Churchill's legacy.

At the same time, the United States and the Soviet Union emerged from the war as the preeminent world powers; Britain, although on the winning side, saw its global prestige in eclipse, and found itself in the midst of an economic crisis. At the height of the war, Britain was devoting 54 percent of its gross national product to the war effort; by the war's end it had expended practically all of its foreign financial resources and was several billion pounds in debt to its wartime allies. In short, Britain was bankrupt. As its colonial possessions increased their protests against British rule, Britain had neither the military nor the economic power to control them; India, which had begun its independence movement during World War I, finally won full independence on 15 August 1947, and Burma and Ceylon (now Sri Lanka) quickly followed suit in early 1948. At about the same time, Britain was forced to withdraw from Palestine, and from all of Egypt except for the Suez Canal; the Canal itself was nationalized by Egypt in the summer of 1956. The 1960s saw increased Irish Republican activity in Northern Ireland, degenerating into armed sectarian violence in 1968; recent years have seen periodic waves of IRA violence in support of independence for Ulster, alternating with largely unsuccessful diplomatic attempts to forge a lasting peace in Northern Ireland. In the spring of 1982 Prime Minister Thatcher sent British troops to liberate the Falkland Islands, a small self-governing British colony off the coast of Argentina, from an Argentinian occupying force; Thatcher won a resounding reelection the following year on the strength of the British success, suggesting that pride in the British Empire, while diminishing in importance, was by no means yet extinct.

For additional resources on World War II and the End of Empire, go to *The Longman Anthology of British Literature* Web site at www.myliteraturekit.com.

Sir Winston Churchill

1874–1965

British historian A. J. P. Taylor has written of a unique paradox of World War II: though it was a time of unprecedented stress and anxiety for the British people, "Great Britain was never so free from political controversy." The reason? Winston Churchill's ability to forge a partnership between himself and the British people. "There have been many great British leaders," Taylor continues; "There has only been one whom everyone recognized as the embodiment of the national will." The pictures of Churchill—watch-chain draped across his waistcoat, cigar drooping from his jowly face (above his bow tie and beneath his homburg), index and middle fingers raised in the V of Victory—is perhaps the most familiar and bouyant icon of Allied victory in the war.

Winston Churchill was born at Blenheim Palace, the ancestral home of his grandfather, the seventh duke of Marlborough; his father, Lord Randolph Churchill, had a distinguished career as a Conservative member of Parliament. Young Winston proved not to be an outstanding scholar, however, and instead of university, was sent to the Royal Military Academy. This military training, and his subsequent combat experience on the Western Front and in the Sudan, was to prove invaluable as he led his country as prime minister through the darkest days of World War II. Equally important to Churchill the statesman was his early work as a journalist and essayist; the economist John Kenneth Galbraith suggested that Churchill's power as an orator derived from his "fearsome certainty that he was completely right," a certainty made manifest in "his use of language as a weapon." In Churchill's well-known phrases, like "blood, toil, tears and sweat," a nation at war found its rallying cries.

Winston Churchill, June 1943. Returning to 10 Downing Street after meeting with American president Franklin Roosevelt in Washington, D.C., and visiting Allied armies in North Africa, the Prime Minister flashes his famous "V for Victory" sign to reporters.

Two Speeches Before the House of Commons

["Blood, Toil, Tears and Sweat"][1]

I beg to move,

> That this House welcomes the formation of a Government representing the united and inflexible resolve of the nation to prosecute the war with Germany to a victorious conclusion.

On Friday evening last I received His Majesty's Commission to form a new Administration. It was the evident wish and will of Parliament and the nation that this should be conceived on the broadest possible basis and that it should include all parties, both those who supported the late Government and also the parties of the Opposition. I have completed the most important part of this task. A War Cabinet has been formed of five Members, representing, with the Opposition Liberals, the unity of the nation. The three party Leaders have agreed to serve, either in the War Cabinet or in high executive office. The three Fighting Services have been filled. It was necessary that this should be done in one single day, on account of the extreme ur-

1. Delivered in the House of Commons, 13 May 1940.

gency and rigour of events. A number of other positions, key positions, were filled yesterday, and I am submitting a further list to His Majesty to-night. I hope to complete the appointment of the principal Ministers during to-morrow. The appointment of the other Ministers usually takes a little longer, but I trust that, when Parliament meets again, this part of my task will be completed, and that the administration will be complete in all respects.

I considered it in the public interest to suggest that the House should be summoned to meet to-day. Mr Speaker agreed, and took the necessary steps, in accordance with the powers conferred upon him by the Resolution of the House. At the end of the proceedings to-day, the Adjournment of the House will be proposed until Tuesday, 21st May, with, of course, provision for earlier meeting, if need be. The business to be considered during that week will be notified to Members at the earliest opportunity. I now invite the House, by the Motion which stands in my name, to record its approval of the steps taken and to declare its confidence in the new Government.

To form an Administration of this scale and complexity is a serious undertaking in itself, but it must be remembered that we are in the preliminary stage of one of the greatest battles in history, that we are in action at many other points in Norway and in Holland, that we have to be prepared in the Mediterranean, that the air battle is continuous and that many preparations, such as have been indicated by my hon. Friend below the Gangway, have to be made here at home. In this crisis I hope I may be pardoned if I do not address the House at any length to-day. I hope that any of my friends and colleagues, or former colleagues, who are affected by the political reconstruction, will make allowance, all allowance, for any lack of ceremony with which it has been necessary to act. I would say to the House, as I said to those who have joined this Government: "I have nothing to offer but blood, toil, tears and sweat."

We have before us an ordeal of the most grievous kind. We have before us many, many long months of struggle and of suffering. You ask, what is our policy? I can say: It is to wage war, by sea, land and air, with all our might and with all the strength that God can give us; to wage war against a monstrous tyranny, never surpassed in the dark, lamentable catalogue of human crime. That is our policy. You ask, what is our aim? I can answer in one word: It is victory, victory at all costs, victory in spite of all terror, victory, however long and hard the road may be; for without victory, there is no survival. Let that be realised; no survival for the British Empire, no survival for all that the British Empire has stood for, no survival for the urge and impulse of the ages, that mankind will move forward towards its goal. But I take up my task with buoyancy and hope. I feel sure that our cause will not be suffered to fail among men. At this time I feel entitled to claim the aid of all, and I say, "Come then, let us go forward together with our united strength."

["WARS ARE NOT WON BY EVACUATIONS"][1]

From the moment that the French defenses at Sedan and on the Meuse[2] were broken at the end of the second week of May, only a rapid retreat to Amiens[3] and the south could have saved the British and French Armies who had entered Belgium at the

1. Delivered in the Hosue of Commons 4 June 1940. This speech exemplifies Churchill's ability to rally his people amid the greatest difficulties—here, the disastrous defeat of the British and French armies in April–May 1940. What might have been seen as the humiliation of the British army becomes, in Churchill's stirring account, the heroic achievement of a successful evacuation against all odds.

2. A river flowing through France, Belgium, and the Netherlands.

3. A city located on the Somme River in northern France.

appeal of the Belgian King; but this strategic fact was not immediately realized. The French High Command hoped they would be able to close the gap, and the Armies of the north were under their orders. Moreover, a retirement of this kind would have involved almost certainly the destruction of the fine Belgian Army of over 20 divisions and the abandonment of the whole of Belgium. Therefore, when the force and scope of the German penetration were realized and when a new French Generalissimo,[4] General Weygand, assumed command in place of General Gamelin, an effort was made by the French and British Armies in Belgium to keep on holding the right hand of the Belgians and to give their own right hand to the newly created French Army which was to have advanced across the Somme[5] in great strength to grasp it.

However, the German eruption swept like a sharp scythe around the right and rear of the Armies of the north. Eight or nine armored divisions, each of about four hundred armored vehicles of different kinds, but carefully assorted to be complementary and divisible into small self-contained units, cut off all communications between us and the main French Armies. It severed our own communications for food and ammunition, which ran first to Amiens and afterwards through Abbeville, and it shore its way up the coast to Boulogne and Calais, and almost to Dunkirk.[6] Behind this armored and mechanized onslaught came a number of German divisions in lorries, and behind them again there plodded comparatively slowly the dull brute mass of the ordinary German Army and German people, always so ready to be led to the trampling down in other lands of liberties and comforts which they have never known in their own.

I have said this armored scythe-stroke almost reached Dunkirk—almost but not quite. Boulogne and Calais were the scenes of desperate fighting. The Guards defended Boulogne for a while and were then withdrawn by orders from this country. The Rifle Brigade, the 60th Rifles, and the Queen Victoria's Rifles, with a battalion of British tanks and 1,000 Frenchmen, in all about four thousand strong, defended Calais to the last. The British Brigadier was given an hour to surrender. He spurned the offer, and four days of intense street fighting passed before silence reigned over Calais, which marked the end of a memorable resistance. Only 30 unwounded survivors were brought off by the Navy, and we do not know the fate of their comrades. Their sacrifice, however, was not in vain. At least two armored divisions, which otherwise would have been turned against the British Expeditionary Force, had to be sent to overcome them. They have added another page to the glories of the light divisions, and the time gained enabled the Graveline water lines to be flooded and to be held by the French troops.

Thus it was that the port of Dunkirk was kept open. When it was found impossible for the Armies of the north to reopen their communications to Amiens with the main French Armies, only one choice remained. It seemed, indeed, forlorn. The Belgian, British and French Armies were almost surrounded. Their sole line of retreat was to a single port and to its neighboring beaches. They were pressed on every side by heavy attacks and far outnumbered in the air.

When, a week ago today, I asked the House to fix this afternoon as the occasion for a statement, I feared it would be my hard lot to announce the greatest military disaster in our long history. I thought—and some good judges agreed with me—that

4. Supreme commander of the French forces.
5. A river in northern France.
6. Seaports in northern France.

perhaps 20,000 or 30,000 men might be re-embarked. But it certainly seemed that the whole of the French First Army and the whole of the British Expeditionary Force north of the Amiens-Abbeville gap would be broken up in the open field or else would have to capitulate for lack of food and ammunition. These were the hard and heavy tidings for which I called upon the House and the nation to prepare themselves a week ago. The whole root and core and brain of the British Army, on which and around which we were to build, and are to build, the great British Armies in the later years of the war, seemed about to perish upon the field or to be led into an ignominious and starving capacity.

That was the prospect a week ago. But another blow which might well have proved final was yet to fall upon us. The King of the Belgians[7] had called upon us to come to his aid. Had not this Ruler and his Government severed themselves from the Allies, who rescued their country from extinction in the late war, and had they not sought refuge in what was proved to be a fatal neutrality, the French and British Armies might well at the outset have saved not only Belgium but perhaps even Poland. Yet at the last moment, when Belgium was already invaded, King Leopold called upon us to come to his aid, and even at the last moment we came. He and his brave, efficient Army, nearly half a million strong, guarded our left flank and thus kept open our only line of retreat to the sea. Suddenly, without prior consultation, with the least possible notice, without the advice of his Ministers and upon his own personal act, he sent a plenipotentiary[8] to the German Command, surrendered his Army, and exposed our whole flank and means of retreat.

I asked the House a week ago to suspend its judgment because the facts were not clear, but I do not feel that any reason now exists why we should not form our own opinions upon this pitiful episode. The surrender of the Belgian Army compelled the British at the shortest notice to cover a flank to the sea more than 30 miles in length. Otherwise all would have been cut off, and all would have shared the fate to which King Leopold had condemned the finest Army his country had ever formed. So in doing this and in exposing this flank, as anyone who followed the operations on the map will see, contact was lost between the British and two out of the three corps forming the First French Army, who were still farther from the coast than we were, and it seemed impossible that any large number of Allied troops could reach the coast.

The enemy attacked on all sides with great strength and fierceness, and their main power, the power of their far more numerous Air Force, was thrown into the battle or else concentrated upon Dunkirk and the beaches. Pressing in upon the narrow exit, both from the east and from the west, the enemy began to fire with cannon upon the beaches by which alone the shipping could approach or depart. They sowed magnetic mines in the channels and seas; they sent repeated waves of hostile aircraft, sometimes more than a hundred strong in one formation, to cast their bombs upon the single pier that remained, and upon the sand dunes upon which the troops had their eyes for shelter. Their U-boats, one of which was sunk, and their motor launches took their toll of the vast traffic which now began. For four or five days an intense struggle reigned. All their armored divisions—or what was left of them—together with great masses of infantry and artillery, hurled themselves in vain upon the ever-narrowing, ever-contracting appendix within which the British and French Armies fought.

7. Leopold III (1901–1983).

8. Diplomatic agent.

Meanwhile, the Royal Navy, with the willing help of countless merchant seamen, strained every nerve to embark the British and Allied troops; 220 light warships and 650 other vessels were engaged. They had to operate upon the difficult coast, often in adverse weather, under an almost ceaseless hail of bombs and an increasing concentration of artillery fire. Nor were the seas, as I have said, themselves free from mines and torpedoes. It was in conditions such as these that our men carried on, with little or no rest, for days and nights on end, making trip after trip across the dangerous waters, bringing with them always men whom they had rescued. The numbers they have brought back are the measure of their devotion and their courage. The hospital ships, which brought off many thousands of British and French wounded, being so plainly marked were a special target for Nazi bombs; but the men and women on board them never faltered in their duty.

Meanwhile, the Royal Air Force, which had already been intervening in the battle, so far as its range would allow, from home bases, now used part of its main metropolitan fighter strength, and struck at the German bombers and at the fighters which in large numbers protected them. This struggle was protracted and fierce. Suddenly the scene has cleared, the crash and thunder has for the moment—but only for the moment—died away. A miracle of deliverance, achieved by valor, by perseverance, by perfect discipline, by faultless service, by resource, by skill, by unconquerable fidelity, is manifest to us all. The enemy was hurled back by the retreating British and French troops. He was so roughly handled that he did not hurry their departure seriously. The Royal Air Force engaged the main strength of the German Air Force, and inflicted upon them losses of at least four to one; and the Navy, using nearly 1,000 ships of all kinds, carried over 335,000 men, French and British, out of the jaws of death and shame, to their native land and to the tasks which lie immediately ahead. We must be very careful not to assign to this deliverance the attributes of a victory. Wars are not won by evacuations. But there was a victory inside this deliverance, which should be noted. It was gained by the Air Force. Many of our soldiers coming back have not seen the Air Force at work; they saw only the bombers which escaped its protective attack. They underrate its achievements. I have heard much talk of this; that is why I go out of my way to say this. I will tell you about it.

This was a great trial of strength between the British and German Air Forces. Can you conceive a greater objective for the Germans in the air than to make evacuation from these beaches impossible, and to sink all these ships which were displayed, almost to the extent of thousands? Could there have been an objective of greater military importance and significance for the whole purpose of the war than this? They tried hard, and they were beaten back; they were frustrated in their task. We got the Army away; and they have paid fourfold for any losses which they have inflicted. Very large formations of German aeroplanes—and we know that they are a very brave race—have turned on several occasions from the attack of one-quarter of their number of the Royal Air Force, and have dispersed in different directions. Twelve aeroplanes have been hunted by two. One aeroplane was driven into the water and cast away by the mere charge of a British aeroplane, which had no more ammunition. All of our types—the Hurricane, the Spitfire and the new Defiant—and all our pilots have been vindicated as superior to what they have at present to face.

When we consider how much greater would be our advantage in defending the air above this Island against an overseas attack, I must say that I find in these facts a sure basis upon which practical and reassuring thoughts may rest. I will pay my tribute to these young airmen. The great French Army was very largely, for the time being, cast back and disturbed by the onrush of a few thousands of armored vehicles. May it not also be that the cause of civilization itself will be defended by the skill and devotion of a few thousand airmen? There never has been, I suppose, in all the world, in all the history of war, such an opportunity for youth. The Knights of the Round Table, the Crusaders, all fall back into the past—not only distant but prosaic; these young men, going forth every morn to guard their native land and all that we stand for, holding in their hands these instruments of colossal and shattering power, of whom it may be said that

> Every morn brought forth a noble chance
> And every chance brought forth a noble knight,[9]

deserve our gratitude, as do all the brave men who, in so many ways and on so many occasions, are ready, and continue ready to give life and all for their native land.

I return to the Army. In the long series of very fierce battles, now on this front, now on that, fighting on three fronts at once, battles fought by two or three divisions against an equal or somewhat larger number of the enemy, and fought fiercely on some of the old grounds that so many of us knew so well—in these battles our losses in men have exceeded 30,000 killed, wounded and missing. I take occasion to express the sympathy of the House to all who have suffered bereavement or who are still anxious. The President of the Board of Trade [Sir Andrew Duncan] is not here today. His son has been killed, and many in the House have felt the pangs of affliction in the sharpest form. But I will say this about the missing: We have had a large number of wounded come home safely to this country, but I would say about the missing that there may be very many reported missing who will come back home, some day, in one way or another. In the confusion of this fight it is inevitable that many have been left in positions where honor required no further resistance from them.

Against this loss of over 30,000 men, we can set a far heavier loss certainly inflicted upon the enemy. But our losses in materiel are enormous. We have perhaps lost one-third of the men we lost in the opening days of the battle of 21st March, 1918, but we have lost nearly as many guns—nearly one thousand—and all our transport, all the armored vehicles that were with the Army in the north. This loss will impose a further delay on the expansion of our military strength. That expansion had not been proceeding as far as we had hoped. The best of all we had to give had gone to the British Expeditionary Force, and although they had not the numbers of tanks and some articles of equipment which were desirable, they were a very well and finely equipped Army. They had the first-fruits of all that our industry had to give, and that is gone. And now here is this further delay. How long it will be, how long it will last, depends upon the exertions which we make in this Island. An effort the like of which has never been seen in our records is now being made. Work is proceeding everywhere, night and day, Sundays and week days. Capital and Labor have cast aside their interests, rights, and customs and put them into the common stock. Already the flow of munitions has leaped forward. There is no reason why we should not in a few months overtake the sudden and serious loss that has come upon us, without retarding the development of our general program.

Nevertheless, our thankfulness at the escape of our Army and so many men, whose loved ones have passed through an agonizing week, must not blind us to the

9. Churchill misquotes slightly Tennyson's poem *Morte d'Arthur*, lines 280–81.

fact that what has happened in France and Belgium is a colossal military disaster. The French Army has been weakened, the Belgian Army has been lost, a large part of those fortified lines upon which so much faith had been reposed is gone, many valuable mining districts and factories have passed into the enemy's possession, the whole of the Channel ports are in his hands, with all the tragic consequences that follow from that, and we must expect another blow to be struck almost immediately at us or at France. We are told that Herr Hitler has a plan for invading the British Isles. This has often been thought of before. When Napoleon lay at Boulogne for a year with his flat-bottomed boats and his Grand Army, he was told by someone. "There are bitter weeds in England." There are certainly a great many more of them since the British Expeditionary Force returned.

The whole question of home defense against invasion is, of course, powerfully affected by the fact that we have for the time being in this Island incomparably more powerful military forces than we have ever had at any moment in this war or the last. But this will not continue. We shall not be content with a defensive war. We have our duty to our Ally. We have to reconstitute and build up the British Expeditionary Force once again, under its gallant Commander-in-Chief, Lord Gort. All this is in train; but in the interval we must put our defenses in this Island into such a high state of organization that the fewest possible numbers will be required to give effective security and that the largest possible potential of offensive effort may be realized. On this we are now engaged. It will be very convenient, if it be the desire of the House, to enter upon this subject in a secret Session. Not that the government would necessarily be able to reveal in very great detail military secrets, but we like to have our discussions free, without the restraint imposed by the fact that they will be read the next day by the enemy; and the Government would benefit by views freely expressed in all parts of the House by Members with their knowledge of so many different parts of the country. I understand that some request is to be made upon this subject, which will be readily acceded to by His Majesty's Government.

We have found it necessary to take measures of increasing stringency, not only against enemy aliens and suspicious characters of other nationalities, but also against British subjects who may become a danger or a nuisance should the war be transported to the United Kingdom. I know there are a great many people affected by the orders which we have made who are the passionate enemies of Nazi Germany. I am very sorry for them, but we cannot, at the present time and under the present stress, draw all the distinctions which we should like to do. If parachute landings were attempted and fierce fighting attendant upon them followed, these unfortunate people would be far better out of the way, for their own sakes as well as for ours. There is, however, another class, for which I feel not the slightest sympathy. Parliament has given us the powers to put down Fifth Column[1] activities with a strong hand, and we shall use those powers subject to the supervision and correction of the House, without the slightest hesitation until we are satisfied, and more than satisfied, that this malignancy in our midst has been effectively stamped out.

Turning once again, and this time more generally, to the question of invasion, I would observe that there has never been a period in all these long centuries of which we boast when an absolute guarantee against invasion, still less against serious raids, could have been given to our people. In the days of Napoleon the same wind which

1. Traitorous: a term coined by a Spanish fascist general in 1936, who attacked Madrid with four columns of troops, and later boasted that he had been aided by a "fifth column" of secret fascist supporters inside the city.

would have carried his transports across the Channel might have driven away the blockading fleet. There was always the chance, and it is that chance which has excited and befooled the imaginations of many Continental tyrants. Many are the tales that are told. We are assured that novel methods will be adopted, and when we see the originality of malice, the ingenuity of aggression, which our enemy displays, we may certainly prepare ourselves for every kind of novel stratagem and every kind of brutal and treacherous maneuver. I think that no idea is so outlandish that it should not be considered and viewed with a searching, but at the same time, I hope, with a steady eye. We must never forget the solid assurances of sea power and those which belong to air power if it can be locally exercised.

I have, myself, full confidence that if all do their duty, if nothing is neglected, and if the best arrangements are made, as they are being made, we shall prove ourselves once again able to defend our Island home, to ride out the storm of war, and to outlive the menace of tyranny, if necessary for years, if necessary alone. At any rate, that is what we are going to try to do. That is the resolve of His Majesty's Government—every man of them. That is the will of Parliament and the nation. The British Empire and the French Republic, linked together in their cause and in their need, will defend to the death their native soil, aiding each other like good comrades to the utmost of their strength. Even though large tracts of Europe and many old and famous States have fallen or may fall into the grip of the Gestapo and all the odious apparatus of Nazi rule, we shall not flag or fail. We shall go on to the end, we shall fight in France, we shall fight on the seas and oceans, we shall fight with growing confidence and growing strength in the air, we shall defend our Island, whatever the cost may be, we shall fight on the beaches, we shall fight on the landing grounds, we shall fight in the fields and in the streets, we shall fight in the hills; we shall never surrender, and even if, which I do not for a moment believe, this Island or a large part of it were subjugated and starving, then our Empire beyond the seas, armed and guarded by the British Fleet, would carry on the struggle, until, in God's good time, the New World, with all its power and might, steps forth to the rescue and the liberation of the old.

Stephen Spender
1909–1995

Stephen Spender was an important member of the group of poets writing in the wake of World War I and in the rising shadow of fascism and the approach of World War II. World War I, Spender said, "knocked the ballroom-floor from under middle-class English life"; his first important volume, *Poems,* was published in 1933—the year that Hitler rose to the chancellorship of the Third Reich. Thus the turn toward politics that characterizes the poetry of Spender and the other young Oxford poets who allied themselves with W. H. Auden—the so-called "Auden Generation"—seems in retrospect not so much a decision as an inevitability. Spender speaks this way, too, about his brief affiliation with communism, suggesting that the embrace of communism by British intellectuals in the 1930s was not a matter of economic theory but of conscience. For Spender, Auden, Cecil Day-Lewis and others, fascism was such an obvious, and obviously powerful, evil that only communism appeared strong enough to keep it at bay.

The complex energies and tensions of the 1930s drew forth from Spender his most idealistic and passionate poetry; he will be remembered primarily for the poetry he wrote in his twenties. Some of the energy of his writing derives from his sense of exclusion from English society; his mixed German-Jewish-English ancestry and his bisexuality led him to find, as he wrote, that "my feeling for the English was at times almost like being in love with an alien race". After World War II, Spender wrote little poetry, but continued to work in literary and cultural criticism. His *Collected Poems* was published in 1985.

Icarus[1]

He will watch the hawk with an indifferent eye
Or pitifully;
Nor on those eagles that so feared him, now
Will strain his brow;
Weapons men use, stone, sling and strong-thewed° bow *strong-muscled*
He will not know.

This aristocrat, superb of all instinct,
With death close linked
Had paced the enormous cloud, almost had won
War on the sun;
Till now, like Icarus mid-ocean-drowned,
Hands, wings, are found.

1929

What I Expected

What I expected, was
Thunder, fighting,
Long struggles with men
And climbing.
After continual straining
I should grow strong;
Then the rocks would shake
And I rest long.

What I had not foreseen
Was the gradual day
Weakening the will
Leaking the brightness away,
The lack of good to touch,
The fading of body and soul
Smoke before wind,
Corrupt, unsubstantial.

The wearing of Time,
And the watching of cripples pass
With limbs shaped like questions
In their odd twist,
The pulverous° grief *dusty*
Melting the bones with pity,
The sick falling from earth—

1. In Greek mythology, Icarus was the son of Daedalus, the inventor. To escape from Crete, Daedalus fashioned wings for his son and himself out of wax. Daedalus warned Icarus not to fly too high, for the heat of the sun would melt the wax wings; but Icarus, intoxicated by the power of flight, ignored his father's warning and plunged to his death in the sea.

These, I could not foresee.
Expecting always
Some brightness to hold in trust
Some final innocence
Exempt from dust,
That, hanging solid,
Would dangle through all
Like the created poem,
Or the faceted crystal.

1933

The Express

After the first powerful plain manifesto
The black statement of pistons, without more fuss
But gliding like a queen, she leaves the station.
Without bowing and with restrained unconcern
She passes the houses which humbly crowd outside,
The gasworks, and at last the heavy page
Of death, printed by gravestones in the cemetery.
Beyond the town, there lies the open country
Where, gathering speed, she acquires mystery,
The luminous self-possession of ships on ocean.
It is now she begins to sing—at first quite low
Then loud, and at last with a jazzy madness—
The song of her whistle screaming at curves,
Of deafening tunnels, brakes, innumerable bolts.
And always light, aerial underneath
Retreats the elate metre of her wheels.
Steaming through metal landscape on her lines,
She plunges new eras of white happiness
Where speed throws up strange shapes, broad curves
And parallels clean like trajectories from guns.
At last, further than Edinburgh or Rome,
Beyond the crest of the world, she reaches night
Where only a low stream-line brightness
Of phosphorus, on the tossing hills is white.
Ah, like a comet through flame, she moves entranced
Wrapt in her music no bird-song, no, nor bough,
Breaking with honey buds, shall ever equal.

1933

The Pylons

The secret of these hills was stone, and cottages
Of that stone made,
And crumbling roads
That turned on sudden hidden villages.

Now over these small hills, they have built the concrete
That trails black wire;
Pylons, those pillars
Bare like nude, giant girls that have no secret.

The valley with its gilt and evening look
And the green chestnut
Of customary root,
Are mocked dry like the parched bed of a brook.

But far above and far as sight endures
Like whips of anger
With lightning's danger
There runs the quick perspective of the future.

This dwarfs our emerald country by its trek
So tall with prophecy:
Dreaming of cities
Where often clouds shall lean their swan-white neck.

1933

Elizabeth Bowen
1899–1973

Elizabeth Bowen was born into a world that was, at the turn of the century, on the verge of disappearing forever: the world of the Anglo-Irish ascendancy, the privileged world of the Protestant "big house" tradition. Bowen's Court, an estate in County Cork, had been in her family since an ancestor in the service of Oliver Cromwell had come to Ireland in 1749; the estate passed out of the family in 1960, when Elizabeth could no longer afford to maintain the property, and it was torn down by its new owner in 1963.

In stark contrast to her proud Anglo-Irish heritage, Bowen's childhood was rootless in the extreme. As a young child, the family's time was split between Bowen's Court, in the country, and Dublin, where her father was a barrister; in 1906, he suffered a nervous breakdown, and Elizabeth moved to London with her mother. Bowen's mother died of cancer in 1912, and Elizabeth was shuttled between various relatives. During World War I, she returned to neutral Ireland, where she worked in a hospital with veterans suffering from "shell shock"; she returned to London in 1918 to attend art school and lived primarily in London for the rest of her life.

Bowen was in London during the Blitz. She again volunteered her services to the victims of war, working for the Ministry of Information as an air-raid warden. She wrote a number of vivid, powerful stories about the ravages of war in London during the Blitz—among them *Mysterious Kôr* (1946), which the American novelist and short-story writer Eudora Welty has called the "most extraordinary story of those she wrote out of her life in wartime London."

Bowen's writing was not confined to short fiction; in addition to her more than eighty short stories, she was the author of ten novels—the most popular of which are *The Death of the Heart* (1938) and *The Heat of the Day* (1949)—as well as a great deal of newspaper and magazine writing and a history of her ancestral home, *Bowen's Court* (1964), published the year after it was demolished.

Mysterious Kôr

Full moonlight drenched the city and searched it; there was not a niche left to stand in. The effect was remorseless: London looked like the moon's capital—shallow, cratered, extinct. It was late, but not yet midnight; now the buses had stopped the polished roads and streets in this region sent for minutes together a ghostly unbroken reflection up. The soaring new flats and the crouching old shops and houses looked equally brittle under the moon, which blazed in windows that looked its way. The futility of the black-out[1] became laughable: from the sky, presumably, you could see every slate in the roofs, every whited kerb, every contour of the naked winter flowerbeds in the park; and the lake, with its shining twists and tree-darkened islands would be a landmark for miles, yes, miles, overhead.

However, the sky, in whose glassiness floated no clouds but only opaque balloons, remained glassy-silent. The Germans no longer came by the full moon. Something more immaterial seemed to threaten, and to be keeping people at home. This day between days, this extra tax, was perhaps more than senses and nerves could bear. People stayed indoors with a fervour that could be felt: the buildings strained with battened-down human life, but not a beam, not a voice, not a note from a radio escaped. Now and then under streets and buildings the earth rumbled: the Underground[2] sounded loudest at this time.

Outside the now gateless gates of the park, the road coming downhill from the north-west turned south and became a street, down whose perspective the traffic lights went through their unmeaning performance of changing colour. From the promontory of pavement outside the gates you saw at once up the road and down the street: from behind where you stood, between the gateposts, appeared the lesser strangeness of grass and water and trees. At this point, at this moment, three French soldiers, directed to a hostel[3] they could not find, stopped singing to listen derisively to the waterbirds wakened up by the moon. Next, two wardens coming off duty emerged from their post and crossed the road diagonally, each with an elbow cupped inside a slung-on tin hat. The wardens turned their faces, mauve in the moonlight, towards the Frenchmen with no expression at all. The two sets of steps died in opposite directions, and, the birds subsiding, nothing was heard or seen until, a little way down the street, a trickle of people came out of the Underground, around the anti-panic brick wall. These all disappeared quickly, in an abashed way, or as though dissolved in the street by some white acid, but for a girl and a soldier who, by their way of walking, seemed to have no destination but each other and to be not quite certain even of that. Blotted into one shadow he tall, she little, these two proceeded towards the park. They looked in, but did not go in; they stood there debating without speaking. Then, as though a command from the street behind them had been received by their synchronized bodies, they faced round to look back the way they had come.

His look up the height of a building made his head drop back, and she saw his eyeballs glitter. She slid her hand from his sleeve, stepped to the edge of the pavement and said: "Mysterious Kôr."

"What is?" he said, not quite collecting himself.

"This is—

1. During the Blitz, all lights were ordered concealed or extinguished at night so that enemy planes would have difficulty locating their targets.

2. The London subway system.

3. An inn.

Mysterious Kôr thy walls forsaken stand,
Thy lonely towers beneath a lonely moon—

—this is Kôr."[4]

"Why," he said, "it's years since I've thought of that."

She said: "I think of it all the time—"

Not in the waste beyond the swamps and sand,
The fever-haunted forest and lagoon,
Mysterious Kôr thy walls———

—a completely forsaken city, as high as cliffs and as white as bones, with no history———"

"But something must once have happened: why had it been forsaken?"

"How could anyone tell you when there's nobody there?"

"Nobody there since how long?"

"Thousands of years."

"In that case, it would have fallen down."

"No, not Kôr," she said with immediate authority. "Kôr's altogether different; it's very strong; there is not a crack in it anywhere for a weed to grow in; the corners of stones and the monuments might have been cut yesterday, and the stairs and arches are built to support themselves."

"You know all about it," he said, looking at her.

"I know, I know all about it."

"What, since you read that book?"

"Oh, I didn't get much from that; I just got the name. I knew that must be the right name; it's like a cry."

"Most like the cry of a crow to me." He reflected, then said: "But the poem begins with 'Not'—'*Not in the waste beyond the swamps and sand—*' And it goes on, as I remember, to prove Kôr's not really anywhere. When even a poem says there's no such place—"

"What it tries to say doesn't matter: I see what it makes me see. Anyhow, that was written some time ago, at that time when they thought they had got everything taped, because the whole world had been explored, even the middle of Africa. Every thing and place had been found and marked on some map; so what wasn't marked on any map couldn't be there at all. So *they* thought: that was why he wrote the poem. '*The world is disenchanted,*' it goes on. That was what set me off hating civilization."

"Well, cheer up," he said; "there isn't much of it left."

"Oh, yes, I cheered up some time ago. This war shows we've by no means come to the end. If you can blow whole places out of existence, you can blow whole places into it. I don't see why not. They say we can't say what's come out since the bombing started. By the time we've come to the end, Kôr may be the one city left: the abiding city. I should laugh."

"No, you wouldn't," he said sharply. "*You* wouldn't—at least, I hope not. I hope you don't know what you're saying—does the moon make you funny?"

"Don't be cross about Kôr; please don't, Arthur," she said.

4. Kôr is the lost city of H. Rider Haggard's 1887 adventure novel *She*. These lines are from a poem by Andrew Lang (1844–1912). The central character Ayesha, whose name means *She-who-must-be-obeyed*, is incessantly described as "mysterious." One of Ayesha's statements—"My empire is of the imagination"—may have had an ironic resonance for Bowen, writing about the condition of England during World War II.

"I thought girls thought about people."

"What, these days?" she said. "Think about people? How can anyone think about people if they've got any heart? I don't know how other girls manage: I always think about Kôr."

"Not about me?" he said. When she did not at once answer, he turned her hand over, in anguish, inside his grasp. "Because I'm not there when you want me—is that my fault?"

"But to think about Kôr is to think about you and me."

"In that dead place?"

"No, ours—we'd be alone here."

Tightening his thumb on her palm while he thought this over, he looked behind them, around them, above them—even up at the sky. He said finally: "But we're alone here."

"That was why I said 'Mysterious Kôr.' "

"What, you mean we're there now, that here's there, that now's then? . . . *I* don't mind," he added, letting out as a laugh the sigh he had been holding in for some time. "You ought to know the place, and for all I could tell you we might be anywhere: I often do have it, this funny feeling, the first minute or two when I've come up out of the Underground. Well, well: join the Army and see the world." He nodded towards the perspective of traffic lights and said, a shade craftily: "What are those, then?"

Having caught the quickest possible breath, she replied: "Inexhaustible gases; they bored through to them and lit them as they came up; by changing colour they show the changing of minutes; in Kôr there is no sort of other time."

"You've got the moon, though: that can't help making months."

"Oh, and the sun, of course; but those two could do what they liked; we should not have to calculate when they'd come or go."

"We might not have to," he said, "but I bet I should."

"I should not mind what you did, so long as you never said, 'What next?' "

"I don't know about 'next,' but I do know what we'd do first."

"What, Arthur?"

"Populate Kôr."

She said: "I suppose it would be all right if our children were to marry each other?"

But her voice faded out; she had been reminded that they were homeless on this his first night of leave. They were, that was to say, in London without any hope of any place of their own. Pepita shared a two-roomed flatlet with a girl friend, in a by-street off the Regent's Park Road, and towards this they must make their halfhearted way. Arthur was to have the sitting-room divan, usually occupied by Pepita, while she herself had half of her girl friend's bed. There was really no room for a third, and least of all for a man, in those small rooms packed with furniture and the two girls' belongings: Pepita tried to be grateful for her friend Callie's forbearance—but how could she be, when it had not occurred to Callie that she would do better to be away tonight? She was more slow-witted than narrow-minded—but Pepita felt she owed a kind of ruin to her. Callie, not yet known to be home later than ten, would be now waiting up, in her house-coat, to welcome Arthur. That would mean three-sided chat, drinking cocoa, then turning in: that would be that, and that would be all. That was London, this war—they were lucky to have a roof—London, full enough before the Americans came. Not a place: they would even grudge you sharing a grave—that was what even married couples complained. Whereas in Kôr . . .

In Kôr . . . Like glass, the illusion shattered: a car hummed like a hornet towards them, veered, showed its scarlet tail-light, streaked away up the road. A woman edged round a front door and along the area railings timidly called her cat; meanwhile a clock near, then another set further back in the dazzling distance, set about striking midnight. Pepita, feeling Arthur release her arm with an abruptness that was the inverse of passion, shivered; whereat he asked brusquely: "Cold? Well, which way?—we'd better be getting on."

Callie was no longer waiting up. Hours ago she had set out the three cups and saucers, the tins of cocoa and household milk and, on the gas-ring, brought the kettle to just short of the boil. She had turned open Arthur's bed, the living-room divan, in the neat inviting way she had learnt at home—then, with a modest impulse, replaced the cover. She had, as Pepita foresaw, been wearing her cretonne[5] housecoat, the nearest thing to a hostess gown that she had; she had already brushed her hair for the night, rebraided it, bound the braids in a coronet round her head. Both lights and the wireless[6] had been on, to make the room both look and sound gay: all alone, she had come to that peak moment at which company should arrive—but so seldom does. From then on she felt welcome beginning to wither in her, a flower of the heart that had bloomed too early. There she had sat like an image, facing the three cold cups, on the edge of the bed to be occupied by an unknown man.

Callie's innocence and her still unsought-out state had brought her to take a proprietary pride in Arthur; this was all the stronger, perhaps, because they had not yet met. Sharing the flat with Pepita, this last year, she had been content with reflecting the heat of love. It was not, surprisingly, that Pepita seemed very happy—there were times when she was palpably on the rack, and this was not what Callie could understand. "Surely you owe it to Arthur," she would then say, "to keep cheerful? So long as you love each other———" Callie's calm brow glowed—one might say that it glowed in place of her friend's; she became the guardian of that ideality which for Pepita was constantly lost to view. It was true, with the sudden prospect of Arthur's leave, things had come nearer to earth: he became a proposition, and she would have been as glad if he could have slept somewhere else. Physically shy, a brotherless virgin, Callie shrank from sharing this flat with a young man. In this flat you could hear everything: what was once a three-windowed Victorian drawing-room had been partitioned, by very thin walls, into kitchenette, living-room, Callie's bedroom. The living-room was in the centre; the two others open off it. What was once the conservatory, half a flight down, was now converted into a draughty bathroom, shared with somebody else on the girl's floor. The flat, for these days, was cheap—even so, it was Callie, earning more than Pepita, who paid the greater part of the rent: it thus became up to her, more or less, to express good will as to Arthur's making a third. "Why, it will be lovely to have him here," Callie said. Pepita accepted the good will without much grace—but then, had she ever much grace to spare?—she was as restlessly secretive, as self-centred, as a little half-grown black cat. Next came a puzzling moment: Pepita seemed to be hinting that Callie should fix herself up somewhere else. "But where would I go?" Callie marvelled when this was at last borne in on her. "You know what London's like now. And, anyway"—here she laughed, but hers was a forehead that coloured as easily as it glowed—"it wouldn't be

5. Cotton fabric with a printed pattern. 6. Radio.

proper, would it, me going off and leaving just you and Arthur; I don't know what your mother would say to me. No, we may be a little squashed, but we'll make things ever so homey. I shall not mind playing gooseberry, really, dear."

But the hominess by now was evaporating, as Pepita and Arthur still and still did not come. At half-past ten, in obedience to the rule of the house, Callie was obliged to turn off the wireless, whereupon silence out of the stepless street began seeping into the slighted room. Callie recollected the fuel target and turned off her dear little table lamp, gaily painted with spots to make it look like a toadstool, thereby leaving only the hanging light. She laid her hand on the kettle, to find it gone cold again and sigh for the wasted gas if not for her wasted thought. Where are they? Cold crept up her out of the kettle; she went to bed.

Callie's bed lay along the wall under the window: she did not like sleeping so close up under glass, but the clearance that must be left for the opening of door and cupboards made this the only possible place. Now she got in and lay rigidly on the bed's inner side, under the hanging hems of the window curtains, training her limbs not to stray to what would be Pepita's half. This sharing of her bed with another body would not be the least of her sacrifice to the lovers' love; tonight would be the first night—or at least, since she was an infant—that Callie had slept with anyone. Child of a sheltered middle-class household, she had kept physical distances all her life. Already repugnance and shyness ran through her limbs; she was preyed upon by some more obscure trouble than the expectation that she might not sleep. As to *that*, Pepita was restless; her tossings on the divan, her broken-off exclamations and blurred pleas had been to be heard, most nights, through the dividing wall.

Callie knew, as though from a vision, that Arthur would sleep soundly, with assurance and majesty. Did they not all say, too, that a soldier sleeps like a log? With awe she pictured, asleep, the face that she had not yet, awake, seen—Arthur's man's eyelids, cheekbones and set mouth turned up to the darkened ceiling. Wanting to savour darkness herself, Callie reached out and put off her bedside lamp.

At once she knew that something was happening—outdoors, in the street, the whole of London, the world. An advance, an extraordinary movement was silently taking place; blue-white beams overflowed from it, silting, dropping round the edges of the muffling black-out curtains. When, starting up, she knocked a fold of the curtain, a beam like a mouse ran across her bed. A searchlight, the most powerful of all time, might have been turned full and steady upon her defended window; finding flaws in the blackout stuff, it made veins and stars. Once gained by this idea of pressure she could not lie down again; she sat tautly, drawn-up knees touching her breasts, and asked herself if there were anything she should do. She parted the curtains, opened them slowly wider, looked out—and was face to face with the moon.

Below the moon, the houses opposite her window blazed back in transparent shadow; and something—was it a coin or a ring?—glittered half-way across the chalk-white street. Light marched in past her face, and she turned to see where it went: out stood the curves and garlands of the great white marble Victorian mantelpiece of that lost drawing-room; out stood, in the photographs turned her way, the thoughts with which her parents had faced the camera, and the humble puzzlement of her two dogs at home. Of silver brocade, just faintly purpled with roses, became her housecoat hanging over the chair. And the moon did more: it exonerated and beautified the lateness of the lovers' return. No wonder, she said herself, no wonder—if this was the world they walked in, if this was whom they were with. Having drunk in the white explanation, Callie lay down again. Her half of the bed was in shadow, but she allowed one hand to lie, blanched, in what would be Pepita's place. She lay and looked at the hand until it was no longer her own.

Callie woke to the sound of Pepita's key in the latch. But no voices? What had happened? Then she heard Arthur's step. She heard his unslung equipment dropped with a weary, dull sound, and the plonk of his tin hat on a wooden chair. "Sssh-sssh!" Pepita exclaimed, "she *might* be asleep!"

Then at last Arthur's voice: "But I thought you said—"

"I'm not asleep; I'm just coming!" Callie called out with rapture, leaping out from her form in shadow into the moonlight, zipping on her enchanted house-coat over her nightdress, kicking her shoes on, and pinning in place, with a trembling firmness, her plaits in their coronet round her head. Between these movements of hers she heard not another sound. Had she only dreamed they were there? Her heart beat: she stepped through the living-room, shutting her door behind her.

Pepita and Arthur stood on the other side of the table; they gave the impression of being lined up. Their faces, at different levels—for Pepita's rough, dark head came only an inch above Arthur's khaki shoulder—were alike in abstention from any kind of expression; as though, spiritually, they both still refused to be here. Their features looked faint, weathered—was this the work of the moon? Pepita said at once: "I suppose we are very late?"

"I don't wonder," Callie said, "on this lovely night."

Arthur had not raised his eyes; he was looking at the three cups. Pepita now suddenly jogged his elbow, saying, "Arthur, wake up; say something; this is Callie—well, Callie, this is Arthur, of course."

"Why, yes of course this is Arthur," returned Callie, whose candid eyes since she entered had not left Arthur's face. Perceiving that Arthur did not know what to do, she advanced round the table to shake hands with him. He looked up, she looked down, for the first time: she rather beheld than felt his red-brown grip on what still seemed her glove of moonlight. "Welcome, Arthur," she said. "I'm so glad to meet you at last. I hope you will be comfortable in the flat."

"It's been kind of you," he said after consideration.

"Please do not feel that," said Callie. "This is Pepita's home, too, and we both hope—don't we, Pepita?—that you'll regard it as yours. Please feel free to do just as you like. I am sorry it is so small."

"Oh, I don't know," Arthur said, as though hypnotized; "it seems a nice little place."

Pepita, meanwhile, glowered and turned away.

Arthur continued to wonder, though he had once been told, how these two unalike girls had come to set up together—Pepita so small, except for her too-big head, compact of childish brusqueness and of unchildish passion, and Callie, so sedate, waxy and tall—an unlit candle. Yes, she was like one of those candles on sale outside a church; there could be something votive even in her demeanour. She was unconscious that her good manners, those of an old fashioned country doctor's daughter, were putting the other two at a disadvantage. He found himself touched by the grave good faith with which Callie was wearing that tartish house-coat, above which her face kept the glaze of sleep; and, as she knelt to relight the gas-ring under the kettle, he marked the strong, delicate arch of one bare foot, disappearing into the arty green shoe. Pepita was now too near him ever again to be seen as he now saw Callie—in a sense, he never *had* seen Pepita for the first time: she had not been, and still sometimes was not, his type. No, he had not thought of her twice; he had not remembered her until he began to remember her with passion. You might say he had not seen Pepita coming: their love had been a collision in the dark.

Callie, determined to get this over, knelt back and said: "Would Arthur like to wash his hands?" When they had heard him stumble down the half-flight of stairs, she said to Pepita: "Yes, I was so glad you had the moon."

"Why?" said Pepita. She added: "There was too much of it."

"You're tired. Arthur looks tired, too."

"How would you know? He's used to marching about. But it's all this having no place to go."

"But, Pepita, you——"

But at this point Arthur came back: from the door he noticed the wireless, and went direct to it. "Nothing much on now, I suppose?" he doubtfully said.

"No; you see it's past midnight; we're off the air. And, anyway, in this house they don't like the wireless late. By the same token," went on Callie, friendly smiling, "I'm afraid I must ask you, Arthur, to take your boots off, unless, of course, you mean to stay sitting down. The people below us——"

Pepita flung off, saying something under her breath, but Arthur, remarking, "No, I don't mind," both sat down and began to take off his boots. Pausing, glancing to left and right at the divan's fresh cotton spread, he said: "It's all right is it, for me to sit on this?"

"That's my bed," said Pepita. "You are to sleep in it."

Callie then made the cocoa, after which they turned in. Preliminary trips to the bathroom having been worked out, Callie was first to retire, shutting the door behind her so that Pepita and Arthur might kiss each other good night. When Pepita joined her, it was without knocking: Pepita stood still in the moon and began to tug off her clothes. Glancing with hate at the bed, she asked: "Which side?"

"I expected you'd like the outside."

"What are you standing about for?"

"I don't really know: as I'm inside I'd better get in first."

"Then why not get in?"

When they had settled rigidly, side by side, Callie asked: "Do you think Arthur's got all he wants?"

Pepita jerked her head up. "We can't sleep in all this moon."

"Why, you don't believe the moon does things, actually?"

"Well, it couldn't hope to make some of us *much* more screwy."

Callie closed the curtains, then said: "What do you mean? And—didn't you hear?—I asked if Arthur's got all he wants."

"That's what I meant—have you got a screw loose, really?"

"Pepita, I won't stay here if you're going to be like this."

"In that case, you had better go in with Arthur."

"What about me?" Arthur loudly said through the wall. "I can hear practically all you girls are saying."

They were both startled—rather that than abashed. Arthur, alone in there, had thrown off the ligatures[7] of his social manner: his voice held the whole authority of his sex—he was impatient, sleepy, and he belonged to no one.

"Sorry," the girls said in unison. Then Pepita laughed soundlessly, making their bed shake, till to stop herself she bit the back of her hand, and this movement made

7. Restrictions.

her elbow strike Callie's cheek. "Sorry," she had to whisper. No answer: Pepita fingered her elbow and found, yes, it was quite true, it was wet. "Look, shut up crying, Callie: what have I done?"

Callie rolled right round, in order to press her forehead closely under the window, into the curtains, against the wall. Her weeping continued to be soundless: now and then, unable to reach her handkerchief, she staunched her eyes with a curtain, disturbing slivers of moon. Pepita gave up marvelling, and soon slept: at least there is something in being dog-tired.

A clock struck four as Callie woke up again—but something else had made her open her swollen eyelids. Arthur, stumbling about on his padded feet, could be heard next door attempting to make no noise. Inevitably, he bumped the edge of the table. Callie sat up: by her side Pepita lay like a mummy rolled half over, in forbidding, tenacious sleep. Arthur groaned. Callie caught a breath, climbed lightly over Pepita, felt for her torch[8] on the mantelpiece, stopped to listen again. Arthur groaned again: Callie, with movements soundless as they were certain, opened the door and slipped through to the living-room. "What's the matter?" she whispered. "Are you ill?"

"No; I just got a cigarette. Did I wake you up?"

"But you groaned."

"I'm sorry; I'd no idea."

"But do you often?"

"I've no idea, really, I tell you," Arthur repeated. The air of the room was dense with his presence, overhung by tobacco. He must be sitting on the edge of his bed, wrapped up in his overcoat—she could smell the coat, and each time he pulled on the cigarette his features appeared down there, in the fleeting, dull reddish glow. "Where are you?" he said. "Show a light."

Her nervous touch on her torch, like a reflex to what he said, made it flicker up for a second. "I am just by the door; Pepita's asleep; I'd better go back to bed."

"Listen. Do you two get on each other's nerves?"

"Not till tonight," said Callie, watching the uncertain swoops of the cigarette as he reached across to the ashtray on the edge of the table. Shifting her bare feet patiently, she added: "You don't see us as we usually are."

"She's a girl who shows things in funny ways—I expect she feels bad at our putting you out like this—I know I do. But then we'd got no choice, had we?"

"It is really I who am putting you out," said Callie.

"Well, that can't be helped either, can it? You had the right to stay in your own place. If there'd been more time, we might have gone to the country, though I still don't see where we'd have gone there. It's one harder when you're not married, unless you've got the money. Smoke?"

"No, thank you. Well, if you're all right, I'll go back to bed."

"I'm glad she's asleep—funny the way she sleeps, isn't it? You can't help wondering where she is. You haven't got a boy, have you, just at present?"

"No. I've never had one."

"I'm not sure in one way that you're not better off. I can see there's not so much in it for a girl these days. It makes me feel cruel the way I unsettle her: I don't know how much it's me myself or how much it's something the matter that I can't help. How are any of us to know how things could have been? They forget war's not just

8. Flashlight.

only war; it's years out of people's lives that they've never had before and won't have again. Do you think she's fanciful?"

"Who, Pepita?"

"It's enough to make her—tonight was the pay-off. We couldn't get near any movie or any place for sitting; you had to fight into the bars, and she hates the staring in bars, and with all that milling about, every street we went, they kept on knocking her even off my arm. So then we took the tube to that park down there, but the place was as bad as daylight, let alone it was cold. We hadn't the nerve—well, that's nothing to do with you."

"I don't mind."

"Or else you don't understand. So we began to play—we were off in Kôr."

"Core of what?"

"Mysterious Kôr—ghost city."

"Where?"

"You may ask. But I could have sworn she saw it, and from the way she saw it I saw it, too. A game's a game, but what's a hallucination? You begin by laughing, then it gets in you and you can't laugh it off. I tell you, I woke up just now not knowing where I'd been; and I had to get up and feel round this table before I even knew where I was. It wasn't till then that I thought of a cigarette. Now I see why she sleeps like that, if that's where she goes."

"But she is just as often restless; I often hear her."

"Then she doesn't always make it. Perhaps it takes me, in some way—Well, I can't see any harm: when two people have got no place, why not want Kôr, as a start? There are no restrictions on wanting, at any rate."

"But, oh, Arthur, can't wanting want what's human?"

He yawned. "To be human's to be at a dead loss." Stopping yawning, he ground out his cigarette: the china tray skidded at the edge of the table. "Bring that light here a moment—that is, will you? I think I've messed ash all over these sheets of hers."

Callie advanced with the torch alight, but at arm's length: now and then her thumb made the beam wobble. She watched the lit-up inside of Arthur's hand as he brushed the sheet; and once he looked up to see her white-nightgowned figure curving above and away from him, behind the arc of light. "What's that swinging?"

"One of my plaits of hair. Shall I open the window wider?"

"What, to let the smoke out? Go on. And how's your moon?"

"Mine?" Marvelling over this, as the first sign that Arthur remembered that she was Callie, she uncovered the window, pushed up the sash, then after a minute said: "Not so strong."

Indeed, the moon's power over London and the imagination had now declined. The siege of light had relaxed; the search was over; the street had a look of survival and no more. Whatever had glittered there, coin or ring, was now invisible or had gone. To Callie it seemed likely that there would never be such a moon again; and on the whole she felt this was for the best. Feeling air reach in like a tired arm round her body, she dropped the curtains against it and returned to her own room.

Back by her bed, she listened; Pepita's breathing still had the regular sound of sleep. At the other side of the wall the divan creaked as Arthur stretched himself out again. Having felt ahead of her lightly, to make sure her half was empty, Callie climbed over Pepita and got in. A certain amount of warmth had travelled between the sheets from Pepita's flank, and in this Callie extended her sword-cold body: she tried to compose her limbs; even they quivered after Arthur's words in the dark, words to the dark. The loss of her own mysterious expectation, of her love for love, was a small thing beside the war's total of unlived lives. Suddenly Pepita flung out one hand: its back knocked Callie lightly across the face.

Pepita had now turned over and lay with her face up. The hand that had struck Callie must have lain over the other, which grasped the pyjama collar. Her eyes, in the dark, might have been either shut or open, but nothing made her frown more or less steadily: it became certain, after another moment, that Pepita's act of justice had been unconscious. She still lay, as she had lain, in an avid dream, of which Arthur had been the source, of which Arthur was not the end. With him she looked this way, that way, down the wide, void, pure streets, between statues, pillars and shadows, through archways and colonnades. With him she went up the stairs down which nothing but moon came; with him trod the ermine[9] dust of the endless halls, stood on terraces, mounted the extreme tower, looked down on the statued squares, the wide, void, pure streets. He was the password, but not the answer: it was to Kôr's finality that she turned.

Evelyn Waugh

1903–1966

Few writers have demonstrated Evelyn Waugh's keen eye for the foibles and pretensions of the British aristocracy, while at the same time creating a gallery of vivid and memorable characters. He made a name for himself with his first novel *Decline and Fall* (1928), which is a thinly veiled autobiographical novel detailing Waugh's experiences at Oxford (which he left after three years without graduating) and as a schoolteacher (Waugh was fired from three schools in two years). The novel reveals a considerable gift as a social critic and satirist; all of the important writing Waugh would do for the next three and a half decades works in a similar vein.

Evelyn Waugh was born the son of Arthur Waugh, an influential late-Victorian literary critic and publisher (whose savage review of Eliot's *The Love Song of J. Alfred Prufrock* is reprinted on page 2291); reading and writing were central to Evelyn's childhood experience, as was an Anglican religious training. For a time, Waugh attempted to renounce both his religious faith and writing vocation; the publication of *Decline and Fall*, however, and his conversion to Catholicism (following the breakup of his brief first marriage) in 1930, confirmed both aspects of his calling. He went on to write a long string of critically and popularly successful novels, including *Vile Bodies* (1930), *Black Mischief* (1932), *A Handful of Dust* (1934), and *Put Out More Flags* (1942). His most enduringly popular novel (owing in part to its serialization by the BBC in 1980), is *Brideshead Revisited* (1945); a good deal of its interest lies in Waugh's vivid picture of the effete, aestheticist, homoerotic atmosphere of Oxford during his time there. His story *Cruise* (1936) is classic Waugh: biliously funny and sharply observant, mocking the idle British tourist who can see nothing new under the exotic Mediterranean sun.

Far less comically, Waugh's story *The Man Who Liked Dickens* is a cautionary tale of what might happen to an ordinary, if wealthy, Englishman venturing "beyond the pale" of European civilization in a disastrous journey to the Amazon. Waugh adapted the chilling ending of his

9. White.

story to serve as the equally disturbing ending of his great novel *A Handful of Dust*. Like Graham Greene's *A Chance for Mr Lever*, Waugh's story and novel are in dialogue with modernism, re-creating Conrad by undertaking a journey to the heart of darkness, a heart found to the dismay of the main character to contain the very England he had futilely tried to escape. Waugh's work has a satiric modernism at its heart.

The Man Who Liked Dickens

Although Mr McMaster had lived in Amazonas for nearly sixty years, no one except a few families of Shiriana Indians was aware of his existence. His house stood in a small savannah,[1] one of those little patches of sand and grass that crop up occasionally in that neighbourhood, three miles or so across, bounded on all sides by forest.

The stream which watered it was not marked on any map; it ran through rapids, always dangerous and at most seasons of the year impassable, to join the upper waters of the River Uraricoera, whose course, though boldly delineated in every school atlas, is still largely conjectural. None of the inhabitants of the district, except Mr McMaster, had ever heard of the republic of Colombia, Venezuela, Brazil or Bolivia, each of whom had at one time or another claimed its possession.

Mr McMaster's house was larger than those of his neighbours, but similar in character—a palm thatch roof, breast high walls of mud and wattle, and a mud floor. He owned the dozen or so head of puny cattle which grazed in the savannah, a plantation of cassava, some banana and mango trees, a dog, and, unique in the neighbourhood, a single-barrelled, breech-loading shotgun. The few commodities which he employed from the outside world came to him through a long succession of traders, passed from hand to hand, bartered for in a dozen languages at the extreme end of one of the longest threads in the web of commerce that spreads from Manáos into the remote fastness of the forest.

One day while Mr McMaster was engaged in filling some cartridges, a Shiriana came to him with the news that a white man was approaching through the forest, alone and very sick. He closed the cartridge and loaded his gun with it, put those that were finished into his pocket and set out in the direction indicated.

The man was already clear of the bush when Mr McMaster reached him, sitting on the ground, clearly in a very bad way. He was without hat or boots, and his clothes were so torn that it was only by the dampness of his body that they adhered to it; his feet were cut and grossly swollen, every exposed surface of skin was scarred by insect and bat bites; his eyes were wild with fever. He was talking to himself in delirium, but stopped when Mr McMaster approached and addressed him in English.

"I'm tired," the man said; then: "Can't go any farther. My name is Henty and I'm tired. Anderson died. That was a long time ago. I expect you think I'm very odd."

"I think you are ill, my friend."

"Just tired. It must be several months since I had anything to eat."

Mr McMaster hoisted him to his feet and, supporting him by the arm, led him across the hummocks of grass towards the farm.

"It is a very short way. When we get there I will give you something to make you better."

"Jolly kind of you." Presently he said: "I say, you speak English. I'm English, too. My name is Henty."

1. Field.

"Well, Mr Henty, you aren't to bother about anything more. You're ill and you've had a rough journey. I'll take care of you."

They went very slowly, but at length reached the house.

"Lie there in the hammock. I will fetch something for you."

Mr McMaster went into the back room of the house and dragged a tin canister from under a heap of skins. It was full of a mixture of dried leaf and bark. He took a handful and went outside to the fire. When he returned he put one hand behind Henty's head and held up the concoction of herbs in a calabash for him to drink. He sipped, shuddering slightly at the bitterness. At last he finished it. Mr McMaster threw out the dregs on the floor. Henty lay back in the hammock sobbing quietly. Soon he fell into a deep sleep.

* * * * *

"Ill-fated" was the epithet applied by the press to the Anderson expedition to the Parima and upper Uraricoera region of Brazil. Every stage of the enterprise from the preliminary arrangements in London to its tragic dissolution in Amazonas was attacked by misfortune. It was due to one of the early setbacks that Paul Henty became connected with it.

He was not by nature an explorer; an even-tempered, good-looking young man of fastidious tastes and enviable possessions, unintellectual, but appreciative of fine architecture and the ballet, well travelled in the more accessible parts of the world, a collector though not a connoisseur, popular among hostesses, revered by his aunts. He was married to a lady of exceptional charm and beauty, and it was she who upset the good order of his life by confessing her affection for another man for the second time in the eight years of their marriage. The first occasion had been a short-lived infatuation with a tennis professional, the second was a captain in the Coldstream Guards, and more serious.

Henty's first thought under the shock of this revelation was to go out and dine alone. He was a member of four clubs, but at three of them he was liable to meet his wife's lover. Accordingly he chose one which he rarely frequented, a semi-intellectual company composed of publishers, barristers, and men of scholarship awaiting election to the Athenaeum.[2]

Here, after dinner, he fell into conversation with Professor Anderson and first heard of the proposed expedition to Brazil. The particular misfortune that was retarding arrangements at that moment was the defalcation[3] of the secretary with two-thirds of the expedition's capital. The principals were ready—Professor Anderson, Dr Simmons the anthropologist, Mr Necher the biologist, Mr Brough the surveyor, wireless operator and mechanic—the scientific and sporting apparatus was packed up in crates ready to be embarked, the necessary facilities had been stamped and signed by the proper authorities, but unless twelve hundred pounds was forthcoming the whole thing would have to be abandoned.

Henty, as has been suggested, was a man of comfortable means; the expedition would last from nine months to a year; he could shut his country house—his wife, he reflected, would want to remain in London near her young man—and cover more than the sum required. There was a glamour about the whole journey which might, he felt, move even his wife's sympathies. There and then, over the club fire, he decided to accompany Professor Anderson.

2. The Athenaeum was a prestigious, intellectual society and men's club.

3. Disappearance.

When he went home that evening he announced to his wife: "I have decided what I shall do."

"Yes, darling?"

"You are certain that you no longer love me?"

"*Darling*, you *know*, I *adore* you."

"But you are certain you love this guardsman, Tony whatever-his-name-is, more?"

"Oh, yes, *ever* so much more. Quite a different thing altogether."

"Very well, then. I do not propose to do anything about a divorce for a year. You shall have time to think it over. I am leaving next week for the Uraricoera."

"Golly, where's that?"

"I am not perfectly sure. Somewhere in Brazil, I think. It is unexplored. I shall be away a year."

"But darling, how ordinary! Like people in books—big game, I mean, and all that."

"You have obviously already discovered that I am a very ordinary person."

"Now, Paul, don't be disagreeable—oh, there's the telephone. It's probably Tony. If it is, d'you mind terribly if I talk to him alone for a bit?"

But in the ten days of preparation that followed she showed greater tenderness, putting off her soldier twice in order to accompany Henty to the shops where he was choosing his equipment and insisting on his purchasing a worsted cummerbund.[4] On his last evening she gave a supper party for him at the Embassy to which she allowed him to ask any of his friends he liked; he could think of no one except Professor Anderson, who looked oddly dressed, danced tirelessly and was something of a failure with everyone. Next day Mrs Henty came with her husband to the boat train and presented him with a pale blue, extravagantly soft blanket, in a suède case of the same colour furnished with a zip fastener and monogram. She kissed him good-bye and said, "Take care of yourself in wherever it is."

Had she gone as far as Southampton she might have witnessed two dramatic passages. Mr Brough got no farther than the gangway before he was arrested for debt—a matter of £32; the publicity given to the dangers of the expedition was responsible for the action. Henty settled the account.

The second difficulty was not to be overcome so easily. Mr Necher's mother was on the ship before them; she carried a missionary journal in which she had just read an account of the Brazilian forests. Nothing would induce her to permit her son's departure; she would remain on board until he came ashore with her. If necessary, she would sail with him, but go into those forests alone he should not. All argument was unavailing with the resolute old lady, who eventually, five minutes before the time of embarkation, bore her son off in triumph, leaving the company without a biologist.

Nor was Mr Brough's adherence long maintained. The ship in which they were travelling was a cruising liner taking passengers on a round voyage. Mr Brough had not been on board a week and had scarcely accustomed himself to the motion of the ship before he was engaged to be married; he was still engaged, although to a different lady, when they reached Manáos and refused all inducements to proceed farther, borrowing his return fare from Henty and arriving back in Southampton engaged to the lady of his first choice, whom he immediately married.

4. A cummerbund wraps around the waist and is usually worn with a tuxedo; Henty's wife encouraged him to buy a woolen (worsted) one, impractical for the tropics.

In Brazil the officials to whom their credentials were addressed were all out of power. While Henty and Professor Anderson negotiated with the new administrators, Dr Simmons proceeded up river to Boa Vista where he established a base camp with the greater part of the stores. These were instantly commandeered by the revolutionary garrison, and he himself imprisoned for some days and subjected to various humiliations which so enraged him that, when released, he made promptly for the coast, stopping at Manáos only long enough to inform his colleagues that he insisted on leaving his case personally before the central authorities at Rio.

Thus, while they were still a month's journey from the start of their labours, Henty and Professor Anderson found themselves alone and deprived of the greater part of their supplies. The ignominy of immediate return was not to be borne. For a short time they considered the advisability of going into hiding for six months in Madeira or Tenerife, but even there detection seemed probable; there had been too many photographs in the illustrated papers before they left London. Accordingly, in low spirits, the two explorers at last set out alone for the Uraricoera with little hope of accomplishing anything of any value to anyone.

For seven weeks they paddled through green, humid tunnels of forest. They took a few snapshots of naked, misanthropic Indians; bottled some snakes and later lost them when their canoe capsized in the rapids; they overtaxed their digestions, imbibing nauseous intoxicants at native galas; they were robbed of the last of their sugar by a Guianese prospector. Finally, Professor Anderson fell ill with malignant malaria, chattered feebly for some days in his hammock, lapsed into coma and died, leaving Henty alone with a dozen Maku oarsmen, none of whom spoke a word of any language known to him. They reversed their course and drifted down stream with a minimum of provisions and no mutual confidence.

One day, a week or so after Professor Anderson's death, Henty awoke to find that his boys and his canoe had disappeared during the night, leaving him with only his hammock and pajamas some two or three hundred miles from the nearest Brazilian habitation. Nature forbade him to remain where he was although there seemed little purpose in moving. He set himself to follow the course of the stream, at first in the hope of meeting a canoe. But presently the whole forest became peopled for him with frantic apparitions, for no conscious reason at all. He plodded on, now wading in the water, now scrambling through the bush.

Vaguely at the back of his mind he had always believed that the jungle was a place full of food; that there was danger of snakes and savages and wild beasts, but not of starvation. But now he observed that this was far from being the case. The jungle consisted solely of immense tree trunks, embedded in a tangle of thorn and vine rope, all far from nutritious. On the first day he suffered hideously. Later he seemed anaesthetized and was chiefly embarrassed by the behaviour of the inhabitants who came out to meet him in footman's livery, carrying his dinner, and then irresponsibly disappeared or raised the covers of their dishes and revealed live tortoises. Many people who knew him in London appeared and ran round him with derisive cries, asking him questions to which he could not possibly know the answer. His wife came, too, and he was pleased to see her, assuming that she had got tired of her guardsman and was there to fetch him back; but she soon disappeared, like all the others.[5]

It was then that he remembered that it was imperative for him to reach Manàos; he redoubled his energy, stumbling against boulders in the stream and getting caught

5. Henty is obviously delirious.

up among the vines. "But I mustn't waste my strength," he reflected. Then he forgot that, too, and was conscious of nothing more until he found himself lying in a hammock in Mr McMaster's house.

His recovery was slow. At first, days of lucidity alternated with delirium; then his temperature dropped and he was conscious even when most ill. The days of fever grew less frequent, finally occurring in the normal system of the tropics, between long periods of comparative health. Mr McMaster dosed him regularly with herbal remedies.

"It's very nasty," said Henty, "but it does do good."

"There is medicine for everything in the forest," said Mr McMaster; "to make you well and to make you ill. My mother was an Indian and she taught me many of them. I have learned others from time to time from my wives. There are plants to cure you and give you fever, to kill you and send you mad, to keep away snakes, to intoxicate fish so that you can pick them out of the water with your hands like fruit from a tree. There are medicines even I do not know. They say that it is possible to bring dead people to life after they have begun to stink, but I have not seen it done."

"But surely you are English?"

"My father was—at least a Barbadian. He came to British Guiana as a missionary. He was married to a white woman but he left her in Guiana to look for gold. Then he took my mother. The Shiriana women are ugly but very devoted. I have had many. Most of the men and women living in this savannah are my children. That is why they obey—for that reason and because I have the gun. My father lived to a great age. It is not twenty years since he died. He was a man of education. Can you read?"

"Yes, of course."

"It is not everyone who is so fortunate. I cannot."

Henty laughed apologetically. "But I suppose you haven't much opportunity here."

"Oh yes, that is just it. I have a great many books. I will show you when you are better. Until five years ago there was an Englishman—at least a black man, but he was well educated in Georgetown. He died. He used to read to me every day until he died. You shall read to me when you are better."

"I shall be delighted to."

"Yes, you shall read to me," Mr McMaster repeated, nodding over the calabash.

During the early days of his convalescence Henty had little conversation with his host; he lay in the hammock staring up at the thatched roof and thinking about his wife, rehearsing over and over again different incidents in their life together, including her affairs with the tennis professional and the soldier. The days, exactly twelve hours each, passed without distinction. Mr McMaster retired to sleep at sundown, leaving a little lamp burning—a hand-woven wick drooping from a pot of beef fat—to keep away vampire bats.

The first time that Henty left the house Mr McMaster took him for a little stroll around the farm.

"I will show you the black man's grave," he said, leading him to a mound between the mango trees. "He was very kind to me. Every afternoon until he died, for two hours, he used to read to me. I think I will put up a cross—to commemorate his death and your arrival—a pretty idea. Do you believe in God?"

"I've never really thought about it much."

"You are perfectly right. I have thought about it a *great* deal and I still do not know . . . Dickens did."

"I suppose so."

"Oh yes, it is apparent in all his books. You will see."

That afternoon Mr McMaster began the construction of a head-piece for the Negro's grave. He worked with a large spokeshave in a wood so hard that it grated and rang like metal.

At last when Henty had passed six or seven consecutive days without fever, Mr McMaster said, "Now I think you are well enough to see the books."

At one end of the hut there was a kind of loft formed by a rough platform erected up in the eaves of the roof. Mr McMaster propped a ladder against it and mounted. Henty followed, still unsteady after his illness. Mr McMaster sat on the platform and Henty stood at the top of the ladder looking over. There was a heap of small bundles there, tied up with rag, palm leaf and rawhide.

"It has been hard to keep out the worms and ants. Two are practically destroyed. But there is an oil the Indians know how to make that is useful."

He unwrapped the nearest parcel and handed down a calf-bound book. It was an early American edition of *Bleak House*.

"It does not matter which we take first."

"You are fond of Dickens?"

"Why, yes, of course. More than fond, far more. You see, they are the only books I have ever heard. My father used to read them and then later the black man . . . and now you. I have heard them all several times by now but I never get tired; there is always more to be learned and noticed, so many characters, so many changes of scene, so many words . . . I have all Dickens's books except those that the ants devoured. It takes a long time to read them all—more than two years."

"Well," said Henty lightly. "they will well last out my visit."

"Oh, I hope not. It is delightful to start again. Each time I think I find more to enjoy and admire."

They took down the first volume of *Bleak House* and that afternoon Henty had his first reading.

He had always rather enjoyed reading aloud and in the first year of marriage had shared several books in this way with his wife, until one day, in one of her rare moments of confidence, she remarked that it was torture to her. Sometimes after that he had thought it might be agreeable to have children to read to. But Mr McMaster was a unique audience.

The old man sat astride his hammock opposite Henty, fixing him throughout with his eyes, and following the words, soundlessly, with his lips. Often when a new character was introduced he would say, "Repeat the name, I have forgotten him," or, "Yes, yes, I remember her well. She dies, poor woman." He would frequently interrupt with questions; not as Henty would have imagined about the circumstances of the story—such things as the procedure of the Lord Chancellor's Court or the social conventions of the time, though they must have been unintelligible, did not concern him—but always about the characters. "Now, why does she say that? Does she really mean it? Did she feel faint because of the heat of the fire or of something in that paper?" He laughed loudly at all the jokes and at some passages which did not seem humorous to Henty, asking him to repeat them two or three times; and later at the description of the sufferings of the outcasts in "Tom-all-Alone's" tears ran down his cheeks into his beard. His comments on the story were usually simple. "I think that Dedlock is a very proud man," or, "Mrs Jellyby does not take enough care of her children." Henty enjoyed the readings almost as much as he did.

At the end of the first day the old man said, "You read beautifully, with a far better accent than the black man. And you explain better. It is almost as though my father were here again." And always at the end of a session he thanked his guest courteously. "I enjoyed that very much. It was an extremely distressing chapter. But, if I remember rightly, it will all turn out well."

By the time that they were well into the second volume, however, the novelty of the old man's delight had begun to wane, and Henty was feeling strong enough to be restless. He touched more than once on the subject of his departure, asking about canoes and rains and the possibility of finding guides. But Mr McMaster seemed obtuse and paid no attention to these hints.

One day, running his thumb through the pages of *Bleak House* that remained to be read, Henty said, "We still have a lot to get through. I hope I shall be able to finish it before I go."

"Oh yes," said Mr McMaster. "Do not disturb yourself about that. You will have time to finish it, my friend."

For the first time Henty noticed something slightly menacing in his host's manner. That evening at supper, a brief meal of farine[6] and dried beef eaten just before sundown, Henty renewed the subject.

"You know, Mr McMaster, the time has come when I must be thinking about getting back to civilization. I have already imposed myself on your hospitality for too long."

Mr McMaster bent over his plate, crunching mouthfuls of farine, but made no reply. "How soon do you think I shall be able to get a boat? . . . I said how soon do you think I shall be able to get a boat? I appreciate all your kindness to me more than I can say, but . . ."

"My friend, any kindness I may have shown is amply repaid by your reading of Dickens. Do not let us mention the subject again."

"Well, I'm very glad you have enjoyed it. I have, too. But I really must be thinking of getting back . . ."

"Yes," said Mr McMaster. "The black man was like that. He thought of it all the time. But he died here . . ."

Twice during the next day Henty opened the subject but his host was evasive. Finally he said, "Forgive me, Mr McMaster, but I really must press the point. When can I get a boat?"

"There is no boat."

"Well, the Indians can build one."

"You must wait for the rains. There is not enough water in the river now."

"How long will that be?"

"A month . . . two months . . ."

They had finished *Bleak House* and were nearing the end of *Dombey and Son* when the rain came.

"Now it is time to make preparations to go."

"Oh, that is impossible. The Indians will not make a boat during the rainy season—it is one of their superstitions."

"You might have told me."

"Did I not mention it? I forgot."

6. Grain.

Next morning Henty went out alone while his host was busy, and, looking as aimless as he could, strolled across the savannah to the group of Indian houses. There were four or five Shirianas sitting in one of the doorways. They did not look up as he approached them. He addressed them in the few words of Maku he had acquired during the journey but they made no sign whether they understood him or not. Then he drew a sketch of a canoe in the sand, he went through some vague motions of carpentry, pointed from them to him, then made motions of giving something to them and scratched out the outlines of a gun and a hat and a few other recognizable articles of trade. One of the women giggled, but no one gave any sign of comprehension, and he went away unsatisfied.

At their midday meal Mr McMaster said, "Mr Henty, the Indians tell me that you have been trying to speak with them. It is easier that you say anything you wish through me. You realize, do you not, that they would do nothing without my authority. They regard themselves, quite rightly in most cases, as my children."

"Well, as a matter of fact, I was asking them about a canoe."

"So they gave me to understand . . . and now if you have finished your meal perhaps we might have another chapter. I am quite absorbed in the book."

They finished *Dombey and Son;* nearly a year had passed since Henty had left England, and his gloomy foreboding of permanent exile became suddenly acute when, between the pages of *Martin Chuzzlewit,* he found a document written in pencil in irregular characters.

> Year 1919
>
> I James McMaster of Brazil do swear to Barnabas Washington of Georgetown that if he finish this book in fact Martin Chuzzlewit I will let him go away back as soon as finished.

There followed a heavy pencil X, and after it: *Mr McMaster made this mark signed Barnabas Washington.*

"Mr McMaster," said Henty. "I must speak frankly. You saved my life, and when I get back to civilization I will reward you to the best of my ability. I will give you anything within reason. But at present you are keeping me here against my will. I demand to be released."

"But, my friend, what is keeping you? You are under no restraint. Go when you like."

"You know very well that I can't get away without your help."

"In that case you must humour an old man. Read me another chapter."

"Mr McMaster, I swear by anything you like that when I get to Manáos I will find someone to take my place. I will pay a man to read to you all day."

"But I have no need of another man. You read so well."

"I have read for the last time."

"I hope not," said Mr McMaster politely.

That evening at supper only one plate of dried meat and farine was brought in and Mr McMaster ate alone. Henty lay without speaking, staring at the thatch.

Next day at noon a single plate was put before Mr McMaster, but with it lay his gun, cocked, on his knee, as he ate. Henty resumed the reading of *Martin Chuzzlewit* where it had been interrupted.

Weeks passed hopelessly. They read *Nicholas Nickleby* and *Little Dorrit* and *Oliver Twist.* Then a stranger arrived in the savannah, a half-caste prospector, one of that lonely order of men who wander for a lifetime through the forests, tracing the little streams, sifting the gravel and, ounce by ounce, filling the little leather sack of gold dust, more often than not dying of exposure and starvation with five hundred dollars' worth of gold hung around their necks. Mr McMaster was vexed at his arrival, gave him farine and *passo* and sent him on his journey within an hour of his arrival, but in that hour Henty had time to scribble his name on a slip of paper and put it into the man's hand.

From now on there was hope. The days followed their unvarying routine; coffee at sunrise, a morning of inaction while Mr McMaster pottered about on the business of the farm, farine and *passo* at noon. Dickens in the afternoon, farine and *passo* and sometimes some fruit for supper, silence from sunset to dawn with the small wick glowing in the beef fat and the palm thatch overhead dimly discernible; but Henty lived in quiet confidence and expectation.

Some time, this year or the next, the prospector would arrive at a Brazilian village with news of his discovery. The disasters to the Anderson expedition would not have passed unnoticed. Henty could imagine the headlines that must have appeared in the popular press; even now probably there were search parties working over the country he had crossed; any day English voices might sound over the savannah and a dozen friendly adventurers come crashing through the bush. Even as he was reading, while his lips mechanically followed the printed pages, his mind wandered away from his eager, crazy host opposite, and he began to narrate to himself incidents of his homecoming—the gradual re-encounters with civilization; he shaved and bought new clothes at Manáos, telegraphed for money, received wires of congratulation; he enjoyed the leisurely river journey to Belem, the big liner to Europe; savoured good claret and fresh meat and spring vegetables; he was shy at meeting his wife and uncertain how to address . . . "*Darling*, you've been much longer than you said. I quite thought you were lost . . . "

And then Mr McMaster interrupted. "May I trouble you to read that passage again? It is one I particularly enjoy."

The weeks passed; there was no sign of rescue, but Henty endured the day for hope of what might happen on the morrow; he even felt a slight stirring of cordiality towards his gaoler[7] and was therefore quite willing to join him when, one evening after a long conference with an Indian neighbour, he proposed a celebration.

"It is one of the local feast days," he explained, "and they have been making *piwari*. You may not like it, but you should try some. We will go across to this man's home tonight."

Accordingly after supper they joined a party of Indians that were assembled round the fire in one of the huts at the other side of the savannah. They were singing in an apathetic, monotonous manner and passing a large calabash of liquid from mouth to mouth. Separate bowls were brought for Henty and Mr McMaster, and they were given hammocks to sit in.

"You must drink it all without lowering the cup. That is the etiquette."

Henty gulped the dark liquid, trying not to taste it. But it was not unpleasant, hard and muddy on the palate like most of the beverages he had been offered in Brazil, but with a flavour of honey and brown bread. He leant back in the hammock feeling unusually contented. Perhaps at that very moment the search party was in camp a few hours' journey from them. Meanwhile he was warm and drowsy. The cadence of song rose and fell interminably, liturgically. Another calabash of *piwari* was offered him and he handed it back empty. He lay full length watching the play of shadows on the thatch as the Shirianas began to dance. Then he shut his eyes and thought of England and his wife and fell asleep.

He awoke, still in the Indian hut, with the impression that he had outslept his usual hour. By the position of the sun he knew it was late afternoon. No one else was

7. Jailer.

about. He looked for his watch and found to his surprise that it was not on his wrist. He had left it in the house, he supposed, before coming to the party.

"I must have been tight last night," he reflected. "Treacherous drink, that." He had a headache and feared a recurrence of fever. He found when he set his feet to the ground that he stood with difficulty; his walk was unsteady and his mind confused as it had been during the first weeks of his convalescence. On the way across the savannah he was obliged to stop more than once, shutting his eyes and breathing deeply. When he reached the house he found Mr McMaster sitting there.

"Ah, my friend, you are late for the reading this afternoon. There is scarcely another half hour of light. How do you feel?"

"Rotten. That drink doesn't seem to agree with me."

"I will give you something to make you better. The forest has remedies for everything; to make you awake and to make you sleep."

"You haven't seen my watch anywhere?"

"You have missed it?"

"Yes. I thought I was wearing it. I say, I've never slept so long."

"Not since you were a baby. Do you know how long? Two days."

"Nonsense. I can't have."

"Yes, indeed. It is a long time. It is a pity because you missed our guests."

"Guests?"

"Why, yes. I have been quite gay while you were asleep. Three men from outside. Englishmen. It is a pity you missed them. A pity for them, too, as they particularly wished to see you. But what could I do? You were so sound asleep. They had come all the way to find you, so—I thought you would not mind—as you could not greet them yourself I gave them a little souvenir, your watch. They wanted something to take home to your wife who is offering a great reward for news of you. They were very pleased with it. And they took some photographs of the little cross I put up to commemorate your coming. They were pleased with that, too. They were very easily pleased. But I do not suppose they will visit us again, our life here is so retired . . . no pleasures except reading . . . I do not suppose we shall ever have visitors again . . . well, well, I will get you some medicine to make you feel better. Your head aches, does it not . . . We will not have any Dickens today . . . but tomorrow, and the day after that, and the day after that. Let us read *Little Dorrit* again. There are passages in that book I can never hear without the temptation to weep."

Cruise

LETTERS FROM A YOUNG LADY OF LEISURE

S.S. *Glory of Greece*

Darling,

Well I said I would write and so I would have only goodness it was rough so didnt. Now everything is a bit more alright so I will tell you. Well as you know the cruise started at Monte Carlo[1] and when papa and all of us went to Victoria[2] we found that the tickets didnt include the journey there so Goodness how furious he was and said he wouldnt go but Mum said of course we must go and we said that too only papa had changed all his money into Liri or Franks on account of foreigners being so dishonest but he kept a shilling for the porter at Dover being methodical so

1. Gambling resort in southeast France.

2. London train station.

then he had to change it back again and that set him wrong all the way to Monte Carlo and he wouldnt get me and Bertie a sleeper and wouldnt sleep himself in his through being so angry Goodness how Sad.

Then everything was much more alright the purser called him Colonel and he likes his cabin so he took Bertie to the casino and he lost and Bertie won and I think Bertie got a bit plastered at least he made a noise going to bed he's in the next cabin as if he were being sick and that was before we sailed. Bertie has got some books on Baroque art on account of his being at Oxford.

Well the first day it was rough and I got up and felt odd in the bath and the soap wouldnt work on account of salt water you see and came into breakfast and there was a list of so many things including steak and onions and there was a corking young man who said we are the only ones down may I sit here and it was going beautifully and he had steak and onions but it was no good I had to go back to bed just when he was saying there was nothing he admired so much about a girl as her being a good sailor goodness how sad.

The thing is not to have a bath and to be very slow in all movements. So next day it was Naples and we saw some Bertie churches and then that bit that got blown up in an earthquake and a poor dog killed they have a plaster cast of him goodness how sad.[3] Papa and Bertie saw some pictures we weren't allowed to see and Bill drew them for me afterwards and Miss P. tried to look too. I havent told you about Bill and Miss P. have I? Well Bill is rather old but clean looking and I dont suppose hes very old not really I mean and he's had a very disillusionary life on account of his wife who he says I wont say a word against but she gave him the raspberry with a foreigner and that makes him hate foreigners. Miss P. is called Miss Phillips and is lousy[4] she wears a yachting cap and is a bitch. And the way she makes up to the second officer is no ones business and its clear to the meanest intelligence he hates her but its part of the rules that all the sailors have to pretend to fancy the passengers. Who else is there? Well a lot of old ones. Papa is having a walk out with one called Lady Muriel something or other who knew uncle Ned. And there is a honeymoon couple very embarrassing. And a clergyman and a lovely pansy with a camera and white suit and lots of families from the industrial north.

So Bertie sends his love too. XXXXXX etc.

Mum bought a shawl and an animal made of lava.

POST-CARD

This is a picture of Taormina.[5] Mum bought a shawl here. V. funny because Miss P. got left as shed made chums only with second officer and he wasnt allowed ashore so when it came to getting into cars Miss P. had to pack in with a family from the industrial north.

S.S. *Glory of Greece*

Darling,

Hope you got P.C. from Sicily. The moral of that was not to make chums with sailors though who I've made a chum of is the purser who's different on account he leads a very cynical life with a gramophone in his cabin and as many cocktails as he

3. Pompeii is being described, a city on the Bay of Naples buried by the eruption of Mount Vesuvius in 79 C.E. Much of the city has been excavated, including several erotic frescoes.

4. Lousy with money; rich.

5. Coastal town on the island of Sicily.

likes and welsh rabbits[6] sometimes and I said but do you pay for all these drinks but he said no that's all right.

So we have three days at sea which the clergyman said is a good thing as it makes us all friendly but it hasn't made me friendly with Miss P. who won't leave poor Bill alone not taking any more chances of being left alone when she goes ashore. The purser says theres always someone like her on board in fact he says that about everyone except me who he says quite rightly is different goodness how decent.

So there are deck games they are hell. And the day before we reach Haifa[7] there is to be a fancy dress dance. Papa is very good at the deck games expecially one called shuffle board and eats more than he does in London but I daresay its alright. You have to hire dresses for the ball from the barber I mean we do not you. Miss P. has brought her own. So I've thought of a v. clever thing at least the purser suggested it and that is to wear the clothes of one of the sailors I tried his on and looked a treat. Poor Miss P.

Bertie is madly unpop. he wont play any of the games and being plastered the other night too and tried to climb down a ventilator and the second officer pulled him out and the old ones at the captains table look *askance* at him. New word that. Literary yes? No?

So I think the pansy is writing a book he has a green fountain pen and green ink but I couldnt see what it was. XXXX Pretty good about writing you will say and so I am.

POST-CARD

This is a photograph of the Holyland and the famous sea of Gallillee. It is all v. Eastern with camels. I have a lot to tell you about the ball. *Such* goings on and will write very soon. Papa went off for the day with Lady M. and came back saying enchanting woman Knows the world.

S.S. *Glory of Greece*

Darling,

Well the Ball we had to come in to dinner in our clothes and everyone clapped as we came downstairs. So I was pretty late on account of not being able to make up my mind whether to wear the hat and in the end did and looked a corker. Well it was rather a faint clap for me considering so when I looked about there were about twenty girls and some women all dressed like me so how cynical the purser turns out to be. Bertie looked horribly dull as an apache. Mum and Papa were sweet. Miss P. had a ballet dress from the Russian ballet which couldnt have been more unsuitable so we had champagne for dinner and were jolly and they threw paper streamers and I threw mine before it was unrolled and hit Miss P. on the nose. Ha ha. So feeling matey I said to the steward isnt this fun and he said yes for them who hasnt got to clear it up goodness how Sad.

Well of course Bertie was plastered and went a bit far particularly in what he said to Lady M. then he sat in the cynical pursers cabin in the dark and cried so Bill and I found him and Bill gave him some drinks and what you do think he went off with

6. Welsh rabbit (or rarebit): English muffins covered with a sauce of melted cheese, beer, and mustard.

7. Port city in Palestine, now Israel.

Miss P. and we didnt see either of them again it only shows into what degradation the Demon Drink can drag you him I mean.

Then who should I meet but the young man who had steak and onions on the first morning and is called Robert and said I have been trying to meet you again all the voyage. Then I bitched him a bit goodness how Decent.

Poor Mum got taken up by Bill and he told her all about his wife and how she had disillusioned him with the foreigner so to-morrow we reach Port Said d.v.[8] which is latin in case you didn't know meaning God Willing and all go up the nile and to Cairo for a week.

Will send P.C. of Sphinx.

XXXXXX

POST-CARD

This is the Sphinx. Goodness how Sad.

POST-CARD

This is temple of someone. Darling I cant wait to tell you I'm engaged to Arthur. Arthur is the one I thought was a pansy. Bertie thinks egyptian art is v. inartistic.

POST-CARD

This is Tutankhamens v. famous Tomb. Bertie says it is vulgar and is engaged to Miss P. so hes not one to speak and I call her Mabel now. G how S. Bill wont speak to Bertie Robert wont speak to me Papa and Lady M. seem to have had a row there was a man with a snake in a bag also a little boy who told my fortune which was v. prosperous Mum bought a shawl.

POST-CARD

Saw this Mosque today. Robert is engaged to a new girl called something or other who is lousy.

S.S. *Glory of Greece*

Darling,

Well so we all came back from Egypt pretty excited and the cynical purser said what *news* and I said news well Im engaged to Arthur and Bertie is engaged to Miss P. and she is called Mabel now which is hardest of all to bear I said and Robert to a lousy girl and Papa has had a row with Lady M. and Bill has had a row with Bertie and Roberts lousy girl was awful to me and Arthur was sweet but the cynical purser wasnt a bit surprised on account he said people always get engaged and have quarrels on the Egyptian trip every cruise so I said I wasnt in the habit of getting engaged lightly thank you and he said I wasnt apparently in the habit of going to Egypt so I wont speak to him again nor will Arthur.

All love.

8. *Deo volente:* God willing.

S.S. *Glory of Greece*

Sweet,

This is Algiers[9] not very eastern in fact full of frogs.[1] So it is all off with Arthur I was right about him at the first but who I am engaged to is Robert which is *much* better for all concerned really particularly Arthur on account of what I said originally first impressions always right. Yes? No? Robert and I drove about all day in the Botanic gardens and Goodness he was Decent. Bertie got plastered and had a row with Mabel—Miss P. again—so thats all right too and Robert's lousy girl spent all day on board with second officer. Mum bought shawl. Bill told Lady M. about his disillusionment and she told Robert who said yes we all know so Lady M. said it was very unreticent of Bill and she had very little respect for him and didnt blame his wife or the foreigner.

Love.

POST-CARD

I forget what I said in my last letter but if I mentioned a lousy man called Robert you can take it as unsaid. This is still Algiers and Papa ate *dubious oysters* but is all right. Bertie went to a house full of tarts when he was plastered and is pretty unreticent about it as Lady M. would say.

POST-CARD

So now we are back and sang old lang syne is that how you spell it and I kissed Arthur but wont speak to Robert and he cried not Robert I mean Arthur so then Bertie apologised to most of the people hed insulted but Miss P. walked away pretending not to hear. Goodness what a bitch.

RESPONSE

Monty Python:[1] *Travel Agent*

Fade up on close up of picture of Everest. Pull back to reveal travel agent's office.

BOUNDER: Mount Everest, forbidding, aloof, terrifying. The highest place on earth. No I'm sorry we don't go there. No.

By the time Bounder is saying his last sentence the camera has revealed the office and Bounder himself sitting at a desk. Bounder now replaces the telephone into which he has been speaking. After a pause the tourist—Mr Smoke-Too-Much—enters the office and approaches Mr Bounder's secretary.

9. Capital of Algeria, port city on the Mediterranean Sea.

1. Frenchmen.

1. A popular British comedy troupe, made famous through their weekly BBC television series *Monty Python's Flying Circus* (1969–1974), as well as feature films such as *Monty Python and the Holy Grail* (1974) and *The Life of Brian* (1979). The performers in this skit, as presented on their television program, are Michael Palin (Bounder), Eric Idle (Tourist) and Carol Cleveland (Secretary). In its exploration of the burgeoning British tourist industry, the Python sketch, like the Waugh story, suggests that tourism and imperialism are separated by a sometimes fine line.

TOURIST: Good morning.
SECRETARY: Oh good morning. [*Sexily*.] Do you want to go upstairs?
TOURIST: What?
SECRETARY [*sexily*]: Do you want to go upstairs? [*Brightly*.] Or have you come to arrange a holiday?
TOURIST: Er. . . to arrange a holiday.
SECRETARY: Oh, sorry.
TOURIST: What's all this about going upstairs?
SECRETARY: Oh, nothing, nothing. Now, where were you thinking of going?
TOURIST: India.
SECRETARY: Ah one of our adventure holidays!
TOURIST: Yes!
SECRETARY: Well you'd better speak to Mr Bounder about that. Mr Bounder, this gentleman is interested in the India Overland.

[*Walks over to Bounder's desk where he is greeted by Bounder*.]

BOUNDER: Ah. Good morning. I'm Bounder of Adventure.
TOURIST: My name is Smoke-Too-Much.
BOUNDER: What?
TOURIST: My name is Smoke-Too-Much. Mr Smoke-Too-Much.
BOUNDER: Well, you'd better cut down a bit then.
TOURIST: What?
BOUNDER: You'd better cut down a bit then.
TOURIST: Oh I see! Cut down a bit, for Smoke-Too-Much.
BOUNDER: Yes, ha ha. . . I expect you get people making jokes about your name all the time, eh?
TOURIST: No, no actually. Actually, it never struck me before. Smoke. . . too. . . much!
BOUNDER: Anyway, you're interested in one of our adventure holidays, eh?
TOURIST: Yes. I saw your advert in the bolour supplement.
BOUNDER: The what?
TOURIST: The bolour supplement.
BOUNDER: The colour supplement?[2]
TOURIST: Yes. I'm sorry I can't say the letter "B."
BOUNDER: C?
TOURIST: Yes that's right. It's all due to a trauma I suffered when I was a spoolboy. I was attacked by a bat.
BOUNDER: A cat?
TOURIST: No a bat.
BOUNDER: Can you say the letter "K."
TOURIST: Oh yes. Khaki, king, kettle, Kuwait, Keble Bollege Oxford.
BOUNDER: Why don't you say the letter "K" instead of the letter "C?"
TOURIST: What you mean. . . spell bolour with a "K?"
BOUNDER: Yes.
TOURIST: Kolour. Oh, that's very good, I never thought of that.
BOUNDER: Anyway, about the holiday.
TOURIST: Well I saw your adverts in the paper and I've been on package tours several times, you see, and I decided that this was for me.

2. A photo insert in the Sunday newspaper.

BOUNDER: Ah good.

TOURIST: Yes I quite agree with you, I mean what's the point of being treated like a sheep, I mean I'm fed up going abroad and being treated like sheep, what's the point of being carted round in buses, surrounded by sweaty mindless oafs from Kettering and Boventry in their cloth caps and their cardigans and their transistor radios and their "Sunday Mirrors," complaining about the tea, "Oh they don't make it properly here do they not like at home" stopping at Majorcan bodegas,[3] selling fish and chips and Watney's Red Barrel[4] and calamares[5] and two veg and sitting in cotton sun frocks squirting Timothy White's suncream all over their puffy raw swollen purulent flesh cos they "overdid it on the first day!"

BOUNDER [*agreeing patiently*]: Yes. Absolutely, yes, I quite agree. . .

TOURIST: And being herded into endless Hotel Miramars and Bellevueses and Bontinentals with their international luxury modern roomettes and their Watney's Red Barrel and their swimming pools full of fat German businessmen pretending to be acrobats and forming pyramids and frightening the children and barging in to the queues and if you're not at your table spot on seven you miss your bowl of Campbell's Cream of Mushroom soup, the first item on the menu of International Cuisine, and every Thursday night there's bloody cabaret in the bar featuring some tiny emaciated dago with nine-inch hips and some big fat bloated tart with her hair Brylcreemed down and a big arse presenting Flamenco for Foreigners.

BOUNDER [*beginning to get fed up*]: Yes, yes, now. . .

TOURIST: And then some adenoidal typists from Birmingham with diarrhoea and flabby white legs and hairy bandy-legged wop waiters called Manuel, and then, once a week there's an excursion to the local Roman ruins where you can buy cherryade and melted ice cream and bleedin' Watney's Red Barrel, and then one night they take you to a local restaurant with local colour and colouring and they show you there and you sit next to a party of people from Rhyl[6] who keeps singing "Torremolinos, Torremolinos," and complaining about the food, "Oh! It's so greasy isn't it?" and then you get cornered by some drunken greengrocer from Luton with an Instamatic and Dr Scholl sandals and Tuesday's "Daily Express" and he drones on and on and on about how Mr Smith should be running this country and how many languages Enoch Powell can speak and then he throws up all over the Cuba Libres.[7]

BOUNDER: Will you be quiet please.

TOURIST: And sending tinted postcards of places they don't know they haven't even visited, "to all at number 22, weather wonderful our room is marked with an "X." Wish you were here."

BOUNDER: Shut up.

TOURIST: "Food very greasy but we have managed to find this marvellous little place hidden away in the back streets."

BOUNDER: Shut up!

TOURIST: "Where you can even get Watney's Red Barrel and cheese and onion. . ."

BOUNDER: Shut up!!!

TOURIST: ". . . crisps[8] and the accordionist plays 'Maybe its because I'm a Londoner'" and spending four days on the tarmac at Luton[9] airport on a five-day package tour with nothing to eat but dried Watney's sandwiches. . .

3. Grocery stores on the island of Majorca, off the coast of Spain.
4. A popular English beer.
5. Squid.
6. A small town in Wales.
7. A drink made with rum and cola.
8. Potato chips.
9. Small city northwest of London.

BOUNDER: Shut your bloody gob! I've had enough of this, I'm going to ring the police. [*He dials and waits. Cut to a corner of a police station. One* policeman *is knitting, another is making a palm tree out of old newspapers. The phone rings.*]

KNITTING POLICEMAN: Oh. . . take it off the hook. [*They do so.*]

Cut back to travel agent's office. The man is still going on, the travel agent looks crossly at the phone and puts it down. Then picks it up and dials again.

BOUNDER: Hello operator, operator. . . I'm trying to get the police. . . the police yes, what? [*Takes his shoe off and looks inside.*] nine and a half, nine and a half, yes, yes. . . I see. . . well can you keep trying please. . .

Through all this the tourist is still going on:

TOURIST: . . . and there's nowhere to sleep and the kids are vomiting and throwing up on the plastic flowers and they keep telling you it'll only be another hour although your plane is still in Iceland waiting to take some Swedes to Yugoslavia before it can pick you up on the tarmac at 3 a.m. in the bloody morning and you sit on the tarmac till six because of "unforeseen difficulties," i.e. the permanent strike of Air Traffic Control in Paris, and nobody can go to the lavatory until you take off at eight, and when you get to Malaga airport everybody's swallowing Enterovioform tablets[1] and queuing for the toilets and when you finally get to the hotel there's no water in the taps, there's no water in the pool, there's no water in the bog and there's only a bleeding lizard in the bidet, and half the rooms are double-booked and you can't sleep anyway . . .

George Orwell

1903–1950

The critic Irving Howe called George Orwell (pseudonym of Eric Arthur Blair) "the greatest moral force in English letters during the past several decades," as well as "the best English essayist since Hazlitt." He was one of the most consistently provocative British writers of the 1930s and 1940s; his characteristic mode was the polemic, whether that polemic was cloaked in the form of an essay or literary criticism, a novel or even travel writing.

Orwell was born in India into a lower-middle-class family, his father a British civil servant working as an administrator in the Opium Department of the Government of India. His mother managed to gain his entrance into Eton, an elite preparatory school, on a scholarship. The snobbism of his more affluent classmates was to leave a permanent mark. Unable to afford college, Orwell followed in his father's footsteps and enlisted in the Indian Imperial Police. Unlike his father, however, he was disgusted by the inhumanity of colonial rule that he witnessed while stationed in Burma; his revulsion is vividly depicted in essays like *Shooting an Elephant* and *A Hanging*, as well as in his early novel *Burmese Days* (1934). His distaste for police work caused Orwell to leave after five years, determined to establish himself as a writer; he became convinced of the importance of establishing an art of political writing. His 1945 political allegory *Animal Farm* is most specifically an indictment of the Soviet Union during the Cold War, but it conveys timeless larger lessons—that totalitarianism lurks just below the surface of every civil government, that absolute power in the hands of any government leads to the abolition of

1. Antidiarrheal medicine.

personal freedoms. Students in both the United Kingdom and the United States are familiar with the novel's famous slogan: "All animals are equal . . . but some are more equal than others." These same themes are explored in Orwell's dystopian novel *Nineteen Eighty-Four* (1949), which has entered the contemporary imagination through its images of tyranny and oppression, through phrases like "newspeak" and "double-think," and through the foreboding, forbidding image of Big Brother, who is always "watching you."

Before his untimely death from tuberculosis, Orwell did important work in literary and cultural criticism. His criticism, Evelyn Waugh complained, insisted that the critic ask of every text: "What kind of man wrote or painted this? What were his motives, conscious or unconscious? What sort of people like his work? Why?" They were questions under which, as his disparaging mention of Waugh in *Inside the Whale* suggests, most of the fiction written during the 1930s did not fare well. He also became a defender of British popular culture in the 1940s; his essays on such "subliterary" forms as boys' magazines, seaside resort postcards, and personal ads, for instance, anticipate the recent interest in material culture at the center of British and American cultural studies. Almost half a century after his death, Orwell's enduring importance would seem to be his thoroughgoing distrust of "smelly little orthodoxies," be they literary, aesthetic, political, or linguistic.

Shooting an Elephant

In Moulmein, in Lower Burma,[1] I was hated by large numbers of people—the only time in my life that I have been important enough for this to happen to me. I was sub-divisional police officer of the town, and in an aimless, petty kind of way anti-European feeling was very bitter. No one had the guts to raise a riot, but if a European woman went through the bazaars alone somebody would probably spit betel[2] juice over her dress. As a police officer I was an obvious target and was baited whenever it seemed safe to do so. When a nimble Burman tripped me up on the football field and the referee (another Burman) looked the other way, the crowd yelled with hideous laughter. This happened more than once. In the end the sneering yellow faces of young men that met me everywhere, the insults hooted after me when I was at a safe distance, got badly on my nerves. The young Buddhist priests were the worst of all. There were several thousands of them in the town and none of them seemed to have anything to do except stand on street corners and jeer at Europeans.

All this was perplexing and upsetting. For at that time I had already made up my mind that imperialism was an evil thing and the sooner I chucked up my job and got out of it the better. Theoretically—and secretly, of course—I was all for the Burmese and all against their oppressors, the British. As for the job I was doing, I hated it more bitterly than I can perhaps make clear. In a job like that you see the dirty work of Empire at close quarters. The wretched prisoners huddling in the stinking cages of the lock-ups, the grey, cowed faces of the long-term convicts, the scarred buttocks of the men who had been flogged with bamboos—all these oppressed me with an intolerable sense of guilt. But I could get nothing into perspective. I was young and ill-educated and I had had to think out my problems in the utter silence that is imposed on every Englishman in the East. I did not even know that the British Empire is dying, still less did I know that it is a great deal better than the younger empires that are going to supplant it. All I knew was that I was stuck between my hatred of the empire I served and my rage against the evil-spirited little beasts who tried to make my job

1. Republic in southeast Asia, bordered by Bangladesh, India, China, Laos, and Thailand.

2. An East Indian pepper plant, the leaves of which are chewed.

impossible. With one part of my mind I thought of the British Raj[3] as an unbreakable tyranny, as something clamped down, *in saecula saeculorum*,[4] upon the will of prostrate peoples; with another part I thought that the greatest joy in the world would be to drive a bayonet into a Buddhist priest's guts. Feelings like these are the normal by-products of imperialism; ask any Anglo-Indian official, if you can catch him off duty.

One day something happened which in a roundabout way was enlightening. It was a tiny incident in itself, but it gave me a better glimpse than I had had before of the real nature of imperialism—the real motives for which despotic governments act. Early one morning the sub-inspector at a police station the other end of the town rang me up on the phone and said that an elephant was ravaging the bazaar. Would I please come and do something about it? I did not know what I could do, but I wanted to see what was happening and I got on to a pony and started out. I took my rifle, an old 44 Winchester and much too small to kill an elephant, but I thought the noise might be useful *in terrorem*.[5] Various Burmans stopped me on the way and told me about the elephant's doings. It was not, of course, a wild elephant, but a tame one which had gone "must."[6] It had been chained up as tame elephants always are when their attack of "must" is due, but on the previous night it had broken its chain and escaped. Its mahout,[7] the only person who could manage it when it was in that state, had set out in pursuit, but he had taken the wrong direction and was now twelve hours' journey away, and in the morning the elephant had suddenly reappeared in the town. The Burmese population had no weapons and were quite helpless against it. It had already destroyed somebody's bamboo hut, killed a cow and raided some fruit-stalls and devoured the stock; also it had met the municipal rubbish van, and, when the driver jumped out and took to his heels, had turned the van over and inflicted violence upon it.

The Burmese sub-inspector and some Indian constables were waiting for me in the quarter where the elephant had been seen. It was a very poor quarter, a labyrinth of squalid bamboo huts, thatched with palm-leaf, winding all over a steep hillside. I remember that it was a cloudy stuffy morning at the beginning of the rains. We began questioning the people as to where the elephant had gone, and, as usual, failed to get any definite information. That is invariably the case in the East; a story always sounds clear enough at a distance, but the nearer you get to the scene of events the vaguer it becomes. Some of the people said that the elephant had gone in one direction, some said that he had gone in another, some professed not even to have heard of any elephant. I had almost made up my mind that the whole story was a pack of lies, when we heard yells a little distance away. There was a loud, scandalised cry of "Go away, child! Go away this instant!" and an old woman with a switch in her hand came round the corner of a hut, violently shooing away a crowd of naked children. Some more women followed, clicking their tongues and exclaiming; evidently there was something there that the children ought not to have seen. I rounded the hut and saw a man's dead body sprawling in the mud. He was an Indian, a black Dravidian[8] coolie,[9] almost naked, and he could not have been dead many minutes. The people said that the elephant had come suddenly upon him round the corner of the hut, caught him with its trunk, put its foot on his

3. "Rule" (Hindi).
4. Forever and ever (Latin).
5. To frighten it (Latin).
6. A period of heightened aggressiveness and sexual activity in male elephants, during which violent frenzies occur.
7. Elephant driver (Hindi).
8. Native of southeast India or Sri Lanka.
9. A derogatory term for an unskilled Asian laborer.

back and ground him into the earth. This was the rainy season and the ground was soft, and his face had scored a trench a foot deep and a couple of yards long. He was lying on his belly with arms crucified and head sharply twisted to one side. His face was coated with mud, the eyes wide open, the teeth bared and grinning with an expression of unendurable agony. (Never tell me, by the way, that the dead look peaceful. Most of the corpses I have seen looked devilish.) The friction of the great beast's foot had stripped the skin from his back as neatly as one skins a rabbit. As soon as I saw the dead man I sent an orderly to a friend's house nearby to borrow an elephant rifle. I had already sent back the pony, not wanting it to go mad with fright and throw me if it smelled the elephant.

The orderly came back in a few minutes with a rifle and five cartridges, and meanwhile some Burmans had arrived and told us that the elephant was in the paddy fields below, only a few hundred yards away. As I started forward practically the whole population of the quarter flocked out of their houses and followed me. They had seen the rifle and were all shouting excitedly that I was going to shoot the elephant. They had not shown much interest in the elephant when he was merely ravaging their homes, but it was different now that he was going to be shot. It was a bit of fun to them, as it would be to an English crowd; besides, they wanted the meat. It made me vaguely uneasy. I had no intention of shooting the elephant—I had merely sent for the rifle to defend myself if necessary—and it is always unnerving to have a crowd following you. I marched down the hill, looking and feeling a fool, with the rifle over my shoulder and an ever-growing army of people jostling at my heels. At the bottom, when you got away from the huts, there was a metalled road and beyond that a miry waste of paddy fields a thousand yards across, not yet ploughed but soggy from the first rains and dotted with coarse grass. The elephant was standing eighty yards from the road, his left side towards us. He took not the slightest notice of the crowd's approach. He was tearing up bunches of grass, beating them against his knees to clean them and stuffing them into his mouth.

I had halted on the road. As soon as I saw the elephant I knew with perfect certainty that I ought not to shoot him. It is a serious matter to shoot a working elephant—it is comparable to destroying a huge and costly piece of machinery—and obviously one ought not to do it if it can possibly be avoided. And at that distance, peacefully eating, the elephant looked no more dangerous than a cow. I thought then and I think now that his attack of "must" was already passing off; in which case he would merely wander harmlessly about until the mahout came back and caught him. Moreover, I did not in the least want to shoot him. I decided that I would watch him for a little while to make sure that he did not turn savage again, and then go home.

But at that moment I glanced round at the crowd that had followed me. It was an immense crowd, two thousand at the least and growing every minute. It blocked the road for a long distance on either side. I looked at the sea of yellow faces above the garish clothes—faces all happy and excited over this bit of fun, all certain that the elephant was going to be shot. They were watching me as they would watch a conjuror about to perform a trick. They did not like me, but with the magical rifle in my hands I was momentarily worth watching. And suddenly I realised that I should have to shoot the elephant after all. The people expected it of me and I had got to do it; I could feel their two thousand wills pressing me forward, irresistibly. And it was at this moment, as I stood there with the rifle in my hands, that I first grasped the hollowness, the futility of the white man's dominion in the East. Here was I, the white man with his gun, standing in front of the unarmed native crowd—seemingly the leading actor of the piece; but in reality I was only an absurd puppet pushed to and fro by the will of those yellow faces behind. I perceived in this moment that when the white man turns tyrant it is his own freedom that he destroys. He becomes a sort of hollow, posing dummy, the conventionalised figure of a sahib.[1] For it is the condition of his rule that he shall spend his life in trying to impress the "natives" and so in every crisis he has got to do what the "natives" expect of him. He wears a mask, and his face grows to fit it. I had got to shoot the elephant. I had committed myself to doing it when I sent for the rifle. A sahib has got to act like a sahib; he has got to appear resolute, to know his own mind and do definite things. To come all that way, rifle in hand, with two thousand people marching at my heels, and then to trail feebly away, having done nothing—no, that was impossible. The crowd would laugh at me. And my whole life, every white man's life in the East, was one long struggle not to be laughed at.

But I did not want to shoot the elephant. I watched him beating his bunch of grass against his knees, with that preoccupied grandmotherly air that elephants have. It seemed to me that it would be murder to shoot him. At that age I was not squeamish about killing animals, but I had never shot an elephant and never wanted to. (Somehow it always seems worse to kill a *large* animal.) Besides, there was the beast's owner to be considered. Alive, the elephant was worth at least a hundred pounds; dead, he would only be worth the value of his tusks—five pounds, possibly. But I had got to act quickly. I turned to some experienced-looking Burmans who had been there when we arrived, and asked them how the elephant had been behaving. They all said the same thing: he took no notice of you if you left him alone, but he might charge if you went too close to him.

It was perfectly clear to me what I ought to do. I ought to walk up to within, say, twenty-five yards of the elephant and test his behaviour. If he charged I could shoot, if he took no notice of me it would be safe to leave him until the mahout came back. But also I knew that I was going to do no such thing. I was a poor shot with a rifle and the ground was soft mud into which one would sink at every step. If the elephant charged and I missed him, I should have about as much chance as a toad under a steam-roller. But even then I was not thinking particularly of my own skin, only the watchful yellow faces behind. For at that moment, with the crowd watching me, I was not afraid in the ordinary sense, as I would have been if I had been alone. A white man mustn't be frightened in front of "natives"; and so, in general, he isn't frightened. The sole thought in my mind was that if anything went wrong those two thousand Burmans would see me pursued, caught, trampled on and reduced to a grinning corpse like that Indian up the hill. And if that happened it was quite probable that some of them would laugh. That would never do. There was only one alternative. I shoved the cartridges into the magazine and lay down on the road to get a better aim.

The crowd grew very still, and a deep, low, happy sigh, as of people who see the theatre curtain go up at last, breathed from innumerable throats. They were going to have their bit of fun after all. The rifle was a beautiful German thing with cross-hair sights. I did not then know that in shooting an elephant one should shoot to cut an imaginary bar running from ear-hole to ear-hole. I ought therefore, as the elephant was sideways on, to have aimed straight at his ear-hole; actually I aimed several inches in front of this, thinking the brain would be further forward.

1. White gentleman (Urdu).

When I pulled the trigger I did not hear the bang or feel the kick—one never does when a shot goes home—but I heard the devilish roar of glee that went up from the crowd. In that instant, in too short a time, one would have thought, even for the bullet to get there, a mysterious, terrible change had come over the elephant. He neither stirred nor fell, but every line of his body had altered. He looked suddenly stricken, shrunken, immensely old, as though the frightful impact of the bullet had paralysed him without knocking him down. At last, after what seemed a long time—it might have been five seconds, I dare say—he sagged flabbily to his knees. His mouth slobbered. An enormous senility seemed to have settled upon him. One could have imagined him thousands of years old. I fired again into the same spot. At the second shot he did not collapse but climbed with desperate slowness to his feet and stood weakly upright, with legs sagging and head drooping. I fired a third time. That was the shot that did for him. You could see the agony of it jolt his whole body and knock the last remnant of strength from his legs. But in falling he seemed for a moment to rise, for as his hind legs collapsed beneath him he seemed to tower upwards like a huge rock toppling, his trunk reaching skyward like a tree. He trumpeted, for the first and only time. And then down he came, his belly towards me, with a crash that seemed to shake the ground even where I lay.

I got up. The Burmans were already racing past me across the mud. It was obvious that the elephant would never rise again, but he was not dead. He was breathing very rhythmically with long rattling gasps, his great mound of a side painfully rising and falling. His mouth was wide open—I could see far down into caverns of pale pink throat. I waited a long time for him to die, but his breathing did not weaken. Finally I fired my two remaining shots into the spot where I thought his heart must be. The thick blood welled out of him like red velvet, but still he did not die. His body did not even jerk when the shots hit him, the tortured breathing continued without a pause. He was dying, very slowly and in great agony, but in some world remote from me where not even a bullet could damage him further. I felt that I had got to put an end to that dreadful noise. It seemed dreadful to see the great beast lying there, powerless to move and yet powerless to die, and not even to be able to finish him. I sent back for my small rifle and poured shot after shot into his heart and down his throat. They seemed to make no impression. The tortured gasps continued as steadily as the ticking of a clock.

In the end I could not stand it any longer and went away. I heard later that it took him half an hour to die. Burmans were arriving with dahs[2] and baskets even before I left, and I was told they had stripped his body almost to the bones by the afternoon.

Afterwards, of course, there were endless discussions about the shooting of the elephant. The owner was furious, but he was only an Indian and could do nothing. Besides, legally I had done the right thing, for a mad elephant has to be killed, like a mad dog, if its owner fails to control it. Among the Europeans opinion was divided. The older men said I was right, the younger men said it was a damn shame to shoot an elephant for killing a coolie, because an elephant was worth more than any damn Coringhee[3] coolie. And afterwards I was very glad that the coolie had been killed; it put me legally in the right and it gave me a sufficient pretext for shooting the elephant. I often wondered whether any of the others grasped that I had done it solely to avoid looking a fool.

END OF PERSPECTIVES: WORLD WAR II AND THE END OF EMPIRE

2. Large knives.

3. Burmese place-name.

Dylan Thomas

1914–1953

One of the most important facts of Dylan Thomas's biography is his birthplace: Swansea, South Wales. Thomas was Welsh first, English second. Although Wales is entirely contained within the borders of England, it has its own language, unrelated to English. The Welsh language is a living and thriving one, and it is visible in Wales in place names, street signs, church music, and a host of other daily manifestations. Thomas uses the words of the English language in making his poems, plays, and stories, but these words are defamiliarized, are made strange, by virtue of their having been laid on top, as it were, of absent Welsh words and phrasings that echo nonetheless through the English lines. A common criticism made about Dylan Thomas's poetry by English critics who were his contemporaries was that the poetry was overly emotional and excessively musical, and that it lacked "rigor." These charges against the poems sound all too familiarly like the complaints against the Welsh and the Irish peoples—too emotional, too lyrical, too irrational. The innovative and densely lyrical patterns of Thomas's poetry and his prose style come partially out of his "Welshification" of English, a process that has effects on both the style and the subject matter of his work. In another register, he can be seen as the last of the Romantic poets, writing precocious lyrics infused with an intense sense of self.

Dylan Thomas's earliest volume, *18 Poems*, appeared in 1934 when Thomas was twenty years old, a suite of poems based on the cycle of life, birth, childhood, and death in Swansea. It caused a sensation for the magic of its wordplay and the intensely personal focus of the poems. The book was received ecstatically in Britain, but not so in Wales, whose provincial proprieties Thomas always viewed with a half-affectionate sarcasm. Like James Joyce, Thomas felt the necessity of escape; at the age of twenty-one he moved to the metropolitan center, to London, to pursue his hopes of a literary career. There he worked for the BBC as a writer and a performer on radio broadcasts. The short stories of his collection *Portrait of the Artist as a Young Dog* (1940) wittily recount, in obvious homage and parody of Joyce's *Portrait of the Artist as a Young Man*, the travails of the would-be writer who hopes to break through the barriers of class and nation. He spent the years of World War II in London as well, but as a conscientious objector, not a combatant, and, as a Welshman, to a certain degree as an outsider within. The war was traumatizing for him as for so many others, and Thomas's pacifism and despair led to the superb poetry of his volume *Deaths and Entrances*.

Poetry alone could not pay the bills and allow Thomas and his young family to live in London. After the war he turned to screenplays and to short stories. The haunting radio play *Return Journey* gives a medley of voices encountered by the poet returning to a Swansea inhabited by the ghost of his youthful self. It can be compared to some of Hardy's memory-filled poetic landscapes and to stories like *Ivy Day in the Committee Room* in Joyce's *Dubliners;* it also anticipates the spare, ironic dramas that Samuel Beckett would write in the 1960s and 1970s.

In the late 1940s, Thomas returned to his poetry, this time less as a poet than as a performer or public reader of his own work. His vibrant and sonorous Welsh-accented voice (akin to that of the Welsh actor Richard Burton), melded with the incantatory lyricism of his poetic language, proved to be irresistible to the public, both in England and in the United States. His brilliant poetry readings instigated a new popularity for poetry itself on both sides of the Atlantic, and his captivating talents as a reader and indeed an actor created for him the persona of Dylan Thomas, Bohemian poet, which he wore until his early death in New York City, after an overdose of whiskey following a poetry reading. He was on his way to California to stay with Igor Stravinsky, with whom he planned to write an epic opera.

The great American poet John Berryman described certain recurrent words as the "unmistakable signature" of Dylan Thomas's poetry. Berryman chose a list of forty "key words" in Thomas's work, including among them: blood, sea, ghost, grave, death, light, time, sun, night, wind, love, and rain. Berryman noted the symbolic value Thomas made these seemingly simple words carry across the span of many poems. Thomas's themes were agreed by most critics to be simple and elemental ones—related to the cycles of life, to nature and childhood, to life's meaning. Berryman argued fiercely that while these were simple themes on the surface, what a poem means *is* its imagery, the way its words are put into relation to one another: "A poem that works well demonstrates an insight, and the insight may consist, not in the theme, but in the image-relations or the structure-relations." Thomas himself aimed at using wordplay and fractured syntax to create sound as a "verbal music." The musicality of his poems and his prose is stunningly evident, and rarely more so than in his play *Under Milk Wood,* a kind of oratorio for disembodied voices. In the play, published posthumously in 1954, Thomas gives voice to the inhabitants of the Welsh village of Llaregyub, whose voices weave together the actions of nature and humans on one single rural day. There is no "plot," and the actors simply stand on stage and read, taking on many voices as these ebb and flow musically through them.

Oral speech and song are more important than written language in rural countries and cultures, especially when one's written language is officially discouraged or even forbidden. Social memory is passed on in story and song; tales and jokes and sermons and performances loom larger in the society of a country town than do written artifacts. Dylan Thomas was very much a writer, yet his poetry and prose are written to be heard, to exist in the ear of the listener as much as the eye of the reader. The lush richness of Thomas's poetic voice is a verbal music that passes on a tradition of oral culture and its precious gifts. The spoken or sung word is a word accompanied by breath; breath is related in most cultures, but certainly in those of Wales and Ireland, to the spirit. One collection of Dylan Thomas's poetry and sketches he titled *The World I Breathe*. This title could as easily be *The Word I Breathe*.

For additional resources on Thomas, go to *The Longman Anthology of British Literature* Web site at www.myliteraturekit.com.

The Force That Through the Green Fuse Drives the Flower

The force that through the green fuse drives the flower
Drives my green age; that blasts the roots of trees
Is my destroyer.
And I am dumb to tell the crooked rose
My youth is bent by the same wintry fever.

The force that drives the water through the rocks
Drives my red blood; that dries the mouthing streams
Turns mine to wax.
And I am dumb to mouth unto my veins
How at the mountain spring the same mouth sucks.

The hand that whirls the water in the pool
Stirs the quicksand; that ropes the blowing wind
Hauls my shroud sail.
And I am dumb to tell the hanging man
How of my clay is made the hangman's lime.

The lips of time leech to the fountain head;
Love drips and gathers, but the fallen blood
Shall calm her sores.
And I am dumb to tell a weather's wind
How time has ticked a heaven round the stars.

And I am dumb to tell the lover's tomb
How at my sheet goes the same crooked worm.

1933

Fern Hill

Now as I was young and easy under the apple boughs
About the lilting house and happy as the grass was green,
The night above the dingle° starry, *cart*
Time let me hail and climb
Golden in the heydays of his eyes,
And honoured among wagons I was prince of the apple towns
And once below a time I lordly had the trees and leaves
Trail with daisies and barley
Down the rivers of the windfall light.

And as I was green and carefree, famous among the barns
About the happy yard and singing as the farm was home,
In the sun that is young once only,
Time let me play and be
Golden in the mercy of his means,
And green and golden I was huntsman and herdsman, the calves
Sang to my horn, the foxes on the hills barked clear and cold,
And the sabbath rang slowly
In the pebbles of the holy streams.

All the sun long it was running, it was lovely, the hay
Fields high as the house, the tunes from the chimneys, it was air
And playing, lovely and watery
And fire green as grass.
And nightly under the simple stars
As I rode to sleep the owls were bearing the farm away,
All the moon long I heard, blessed among stables, the nightjars.° *birds*
Flying with the ricks,° and the horses *straw*
Flashing into the dark.

And then to awake, and the farm, like a wanderer white
With the dew, come back, the cock on his shoulder: it was all
Shining, it was Adam and maiden,
The sky gathered again
And the sun grew round that very day.
So it must have been after the birth of the simple light
In the first, spinning place, the spellbound horses walking warm
Out of the whinnying green stable
On to the fields of praise.

And honoured among foxes and pheasants by the gay house
Under the new made clouds and happy as the heart was long,
In the sun born over and over,
I ran my heedless ways,
My wishes raced through the house high hay

And nothing I cared, at my sky blue trades, that time allows
In all his tuneful turning so few and such morning songs
Before the children green and golden
Follow him out of grace,

Nothing I cared, in the lamb white days, that time would take me
Up to the swallow thronged loft by the shadow of my hand,
In the moon that is always rising,
Nor that riding to sleep
I should hear him fly with the high fields
And wake to the farm forever fled from the childless land.
Oh as I was young and easy in the mercy of his means,
Time held me green and dying
Though I sang in my chains like the sea.

Poem in October

It was my thirtieth year to heaven
Woke to my hearing from harbour and neighbour wood
And the mussel° pooled and the heron *shellfish*
Priested° shore *presided over*
The morning beckon
With water praying and call of seagull and rook
And the knock of sailing boats on the net webbed wall
Myself to set foot
That second
In the still sleeping town and set forth.

My birthday began with the water-
Birds and the birds of the winged trees flying my name
Above the farms and the white horses
And I rose
In the rainy autumn
And walked abroad in a shower of all my days.
High tide and the heron dived when I took the road
Over the border
And the gates
Of the town closed as the town awoke.

A springful of larks in a rolling
Cloud and the roadside bushes brimming with whistling
Blackbirds and the sun of October
Summery
On the hill's shoulder,
Here were fond climates and sweet singers suddenly
Come in the morning where I wandered and listened
To the rain wringing
Wind blow cold
In the wood faraway under me.

Pale rain over the dwindling harbour
And over the sea wet church the size of a snail
With its horns through mist and the castle
Brown as owls
But all the gardens
Of spring and summer were blooming in the tall tales
Beyond the border and under the lark full cloud.
There could I marvel
My birthday
Away but the weather turned around.

It turned away from the blithe° country *lighthearted*
And down the other air and the blue altered sky
Streamed again a wonder of summer
With apples
Pears and red currants
And I saw in the turning so clearly a child's
Forgotten mornings when he walked with his mother
Through the parables° *religious fables*
Of sun light
And the legends of the green chapels

And the twice told fields of infancy
That his tears burned my cheeks and his heart moved in mine.
These were the woods the river and sea
Where a boy
In the listening
Summertime of the dead whispered the truth of his joy
To the trees and the stones and the fish in the tide.
And the mystery
Sang alive
Still in the water and singingbirds.

And there could I marvel my birthday
Away but the weather turned around. And the true
Joy of the long dead child sang burning
In the sun.
It was my thirtieth
Year to heaven stood there then in the summer noon
Though the town below lay leaved with October blood.
O may my heart's truth
Still be sung
On this high hill in a year's turning.

Do Not Go Gentle into That Good Night

Do not go gentle into that good night,
Old age should burn and rave at close of day;
Rage, rage against the dying of the light.

Though wise men at their end know dark is right,
Because their words had forked no lightning they
Do not go gentle into that good night.

Good men, the last wave by, crying how bright
Their frail deeds might have danced in a green bay,
Rage, rage against the dying of the light.

Wild men who caught and sang the sun in flight,
And learn, too late, they grieved it on its way,
Do not go gentle into that good night.

Grave men, near death, who see with blinding sight
Blind eyes could blaze like meteors and be gay,
Rage, rage against the dying of the light.

And you, my father, there on the sad height,
Curse, bless, me now with your fierce tears, I pray.
Do not go gentle into that good night.
Rage, rage against the dying of the light.

1951

Samuel Beckett

1906–1989

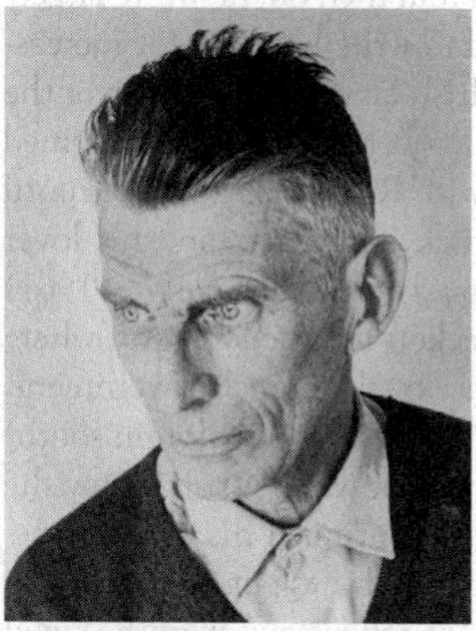

Samuel Beckett, 1971.

On January 5, 1953, *En Attendant Godot* (*Waiting for Godot*) premiered at the Théâtre de Babylone, Paris—and the shape of twentieth-century drama was permanently changed. *Godot* helped to strip the modern stage of everything but its essentials: two characters, seemingly without past or future or worldly possessions, and a spare stage: "A country road. A tree. Evening." Critics would subsequently find in Beckett's bleak stage suggestions of a postnuclear holocaust landscape, as they would in the later *Fin de partie* (*Endgame*, 1957); and for the remainder of his long and productive career, Beckett would continue to explore, with unparalleled honesty and courage, that realm of being that he called in one story *Sans*—"lessness."

April 13, 1906—Good Friday—is the date usually given for Samuel Barclay Beckett's birth, though the birth certificate shows May 13. He was born in the family home of Cooldrinagh in Foxrock, an upper-class Protestant suburb south of Dublin, to William Beckett, surveyor, and Mary (May) Roe, the daughter of a wealthy Kildare family. "You might say I had a happy childhood," Beckett later recalled; "my father did not beat me, nor did my mother run away from home." Beckett attended private academies in Dublin, then in 1920 was enrolled in Portora Royal School in Enniskillen, Northern Ireland, where he excelled more in sports than studies as star bowler on the cricket team, captain of rugby and swimming, and light-heavyweight champion in boxing. In 1923 Beckett entered Trinity College, Dublin, studying modern languages; he also enjoyed the freedom of the city, frequenting the Gate Theatre (for the drama of Pirandello and O'Casey), the music hall, and the movies (especially Charlie Chaplin,

Laurel and Hardy, Buster Keaton, and the Marx Brothers). All would prove formative influences on his later drama and fiction.

In 1927 Beckett received his B.A. degree, first in his class in modern languages, and went off on fellowship to France to teach for two years at the École Normale Supérieure in Paris. While in Paris he became a friend of James Joyce, who influenced him profoundly. Besides aiding Joyce in various ways with his work, Beckett wrote an important essay, *Dante . . . Bruno . . . Vico . . . Joyce*, on *Finnegans Wake*—for a volume of critical writing published before the novel itself was completed. With characteristic understatement, Beckett has said that "Paris in the twenties was a good place for a young man to be"; at the same time, learning the craft of writing in Paris under the shadow of fellow Irish expatriate James Joyce would be enough to provoke the anxiety of influence in even the best of writers. However, Beckett's respect and admiration for Joyce were boundless and never wavered. In 1969 Beckett admitted that Joyce had become "an ethical ideal" for him: "Joyce had a moral effect on me. He made me realize artistic integrity."

The term of his fellowship in Paris having run out, Beckett returned to Dublin to assume teaching at Trinity College. That he was ill-suited to this role was immediately apparent to students, colleagues, and Beckett himself. "I saw that in teaching," Beckett later said, "I was talking of something I knew little about, to people who cared nothing about it. So I behaved very badly." The bad behavior to which Beckett refers was his resignation by mail while on spring holidays in Germany during his second year. Beckett returned briefly to Paris, where it became clear that the unwelcome attentions of Joyce's daughter Lucia were straining Beckett's relationship with the elder writer. He returned to the family home for a time in 1933, where he worked on his first published fiction, the Joycean collection of short stories *More Pricks than Kicks*.

The 1930s found Beckett shuttling back and forth between poverty in London and the frustrating comforts of home in Dublin; Paris seemed to him forbidden, owing to the break with Joyce. In spite of his difficult living circumstances, however, and occasional crippling attacks of clinical depression, Beckett managed to complete his first novel, *Murphy*. The manuscript was rejected by forty-one publishers before being accepted by Routledge in 1937. At the end of 1937, Beckett overcame his reluctance and moved back to Paris. From then on, he wrote largely in French. During the early years of World War II, he attempted to write but found it increasingly difficult to maintain the neutrality required of him by his Irish citizenship in light of the German invasion of France. He abandoned that neutrality in October 1940, when he joined one of the earliest French Resistance groups; he helped in Paris with Resistance activities until his group had been penetrated and betrayed, and just in the nick of time he and his lover Suzanne Deschevaux-Dumesnil (the two had met in 1938, and would eventually marry in 1961) were smuggled into Unoccupied France. At the end of the war Beckett returned to Paris, where he was awarded the *Croix de Guerre* and the *Médaille de la Résistance* by the French government.

While hiding from the Germans from 1942 to 1945 in the village of Roussillon in southeast France, Beckett wrote *Watt*, a complex and aridly witty novel that was never to enjoy the attention devoted to Beckett's other fiction. Meanwhile, Beckett continued his experiments with drama. Though it is drama for which Beckett is best known, he always put more stock in his fiction; "I turned to writing plays," he once said dismissively, "to relieve myself of the awful depression the prose led me into."

At an impasse in the writing of what would prove to be his greatest novels, the trilogy *Molloy*, *Malone Dies*, and *The Unnameable* (1951–1953), Beckett took off three months to write *Waiting for Godot*; it took four years to get the play produced. It is easy enough, in retrospect, to understand the producers' reservations: *Godot* breaks with the conventions of the well-made play at just about every turn, even down to its symmetrical, mirror-image two-act structure. The Irish critic Vivian Mercier wittily described *Godot* as a play in which "nothing happens, twice." *Endgame* (1958) may well be Beckett's bleakest stage production: from its suggestion of Shakespeare's *King Lear*, from which all possibility of heroism and grandeur has been drained away, to its vaguely post-apocalyptic mood and *mise-on-scène*, *Endgame* replicates the despair of *Waiting for Godot* without the earlier play's gallows humor. Beckett's play *Krapp's Last Tape*

(1960) uses a tape recorder (which, at the time of writing, Beckett had never seen) as a stage metaphor for the struggle over memory.

After the success of his plays of the fifties and early sixties, Beckett turned to shorter and shorter forms, both in drama and fiction; he produced a number of very powerful, very short plays (*Not I*, 1973; *Footfalls*, 1976; *Rockabye*, 1981) and short, poetic texts that he called by a variety of self-deprecating names ("fizzles," "residua," "texts for nothing"). He sought an intensified power in the increasing economy of his works. In 1969 Beckett was awarded the Nobel Prize in Literature, for "a body of work," as the citation declares, "that, in new forms of fiction and the theatre, has transmuted the destitution of modern man into exaltation."

For additonal resources on Beckett, go to *The Longman Anthology of British Literature* Web site at www.myliteraturekit.com.

Endgame[1]

A Play in One Act

Characters

NAGG
NELL
HAMM
CLOV

Bare interior.

Grey light.

Left and right back, high up, two small windows, curtains drawn. Front right, a door. Hanging near door, its face to wall, a picture. Front left, touching each other, covered with an old sheet, two ashbins. Center, in an armchair on castors, covered with an old sheet, Hamm. Motionless by the door, his eyes fixed on Hamm, Clov. Very red face. Brief tableau.

Clov goes and stands under window left. Stiff, staggering walk. He looks up at window left. He turns and looks at window right. He goes and stands under window right. He looks up at window right. He turns and looks at window left. He goes out, comes back immediately with a small step-ladder, carries it over and sets it down under window left, gets up on it, draws back curtain. He gets down, takes six steps (for example) towards window right, goes back for ladder, carries it over and sets it down under window right, gets up on it, draws back curtain. He gets down, takes three steps towards window left, goes back for ladder, carries it over and sets it down under window left, gets up on it, looks out of window. Brief laugh. He gets down, takes one step towards window right, goes back for ladder, carries it over and sets it down under window right, gets up on it, looks out of window. Brief laugh. He gets down, goes with ladder towards ashbins, halts, turns, carries back ladder and sets it down under window right, goes to ashbins, removes sheet covering them, folds it over his arm. He raises one lid, stoops and looks into bin. Brief laugh. He closes lid. Same with other bin. He goes to Hamm, removes sheet covering him, folds it over his arm. In a dressing-gown, a stiff toque[2] on his head, a large blood-stained handkerchief over his face, a whistle hanging from his neck, a rug over his knees, thick socks on his feet, Hamm seems to be asleep. Clov looks him over. Brief laugh. He goes to door, halts, turns towards auditorium.

CLOV [*fixed gaze, tonelessly*]: Finished, it's finished, nearly finished, it must be nearly finished. [*Pause.*] Grain upon grain, one by one, and one day, suddenly,

1. Written in French, then translated into English by Beckett himself. Beckett dedicated the play to its first director, Roger Blin.

2. A round brimless hat.

there's a heap, a little heap, the impossible heap. [*Pause.*] I can't be punished any more. [*Pause.*] I'll go now to my kitchen, ten feet by ten feet by ten feet, and wait for him to whistle me. [*Pause.*] Nice dimensions, nice proportions, I'll lean on the table, and look at the wall, and wait for him to whistle me.

[*He remains a moment motionless, then goes out. He comes back immediately, goes to window right, takes up the ladder and carries it out. Pause. Hamm stirs. He yawns under the handkerchief. He removes the handkerchief from his face. Very red face. Black glasses.*]

HAMM: Me—[*he yawns*]—to play. [*He holds the handkerchief spread out before him.*]

Old stancher! [*He takes off his glasses, wipes his eyes, his face, the glasses, puts them on again, folds the handkerchief and puts it back neatly in the breast-pocket of his dressing-gown. He clears his throat, joins the tips of his fingers.*]

Can there be misery—[*he yawns*]—loftier than mine? No doubt. Formerly. But now? [*Pause.*] My father? [*Pause.*] My mother? [*Pause.*] My . . . dog? [*Pause.*] Oh I am willing to believe they suffer as much as such creatures can suffer. But does that mean their sufferings equal mine? No doubt. [*Pause.*] No, all is a—[*he yawns*]—bsolute, [*proudly*] the bigger a man is the fuller he is. [*Pause. Gloomily.*] And the emptier. [*He sniffs.*] Clov! [*Pause.*] No, alone. [*Pause.*] What dreams! Those forests! [*Pause.*] Enough, it's time it ended, in the shelter too. [*Pause.*] And yet I hesitate, I hesitate to . . . to end. Yes, there it is, it's time it ended and yet I hesitate to—[*he yawns*]—to end. [*Yawns.*] God, I'm tired, I'd be better off in bed.

[*He whistles. Enter Clov immediately. He halts beside the chair.*]

You pollute the air! [*Pause.*] Get me ready, I'm going to bed.

CLOV: I've just got you up.

HAMM: And what of it?

CLOV: I can't be getting you up and putting you to bed every five minutes, I have things to do. [*Pause.*]

HAMM: Did you ever see my eyes?

CLOV: No.

HAMM: Did you never have the curiosity, while I was sleeping, to take off my glasses and look at my eyes?

CLOV: Pulling back the lids? [*Pause.*] No.

HAMM: One of these days I'll show them to you. [*Pause.*] It seems they've gone all white. [*Pause.*] What time is it?

CLOV: The same as usual.

HAMM [*gesture towards window right*]: Have you looked?

CLOV: Yes.

HAMM: Well?

CLOV: Zero.

HAMM: It'd need to rain.

CLOV: It won't rain. [*Pause.*]

HAMM: Apart from that, how do you feel?

CLOV: I don't complain.

HAMM: You feel normal?

CLOV [*irritably*]: I tell you I don't complain.

HAMM: I feel a little queer. [*Pause.*] Clov!

CLOV: Yes.
HAMM: Have you not had enough?
CLOV: Yes! [*Pause.*] Of what?
HAMM: Of this . . . this . . . thing.
CLOV: I always had. [*Pause.*] Not you?
HAMM [*gloomily*]: Then there's no reason for it to change.
CLOV: It may end. [*Pause.*] All life long the same questions, the same answers.
HAMM: Get me ready.

[*Clov does not move.*]

Go and get the sheet.

[*Clov does not move.*]

Clov!
CLOV: Yes.
HAMM: I'll give you nothing more to eat.
CLOV: Then we'll die.
HAMM: I'll give you just enough to keep you from dying. You'll be hungry all the time.
CLOV: Then we won't die. [*Pause.*] I'll go and get the sheet.

[*He goes towards the door.*]

HAMM: No!

[*Clov halts.*]

I'll give you one biscuit per day. [*Pause.*] One and a half. [*Pause.*] Why do you stay with me?
CLOV: Why do you keep me?
HAMM: There's no one else.
CLOV: There's nowhere else. [*Pause.*]
HAMM: You're leaving me all the same.
CLOV: I'm trying.
HAMM: You don't love me.
CLOV: No.
HAMM: You loved me once.
CLOV: Once!
HAMM: I've made you suffer too much. [*Pause.*] Haven't I?
CLOV: It's not that.
HAMM [*shocked*]: I haven't made you suffer too much?
CLOV: Yes!
HAMM [*relieved*]: Ah you gave me a fright! [*Pause. Coldly.*] Forgive me. [*Pause. Louder.*] I said, Forgive me.
CLOV: I heard you. [*Pause.*] Have you bled?
HAMM: Less. [*Pause.*] Is it not time for my pain-killer?
CLOV: No. [*Pause.*]
HAMM: How are your eyes?
CLOV: Bad.
HAMM: How are your legs?
CLOV: Bad.

HAMM: But you can move.
CLOV: Yes.
HAMM [*violently*]: Then move!

[*Clov goes to back wall, leans against it with his forehead and hands.*]

Where are you?
CLOV: Here.
HAMM: Come back!

[*Clov returns to his place beside the chair.*]

Where are you?
CLOV: Here.
HAMM: Why don't you kill me?
CLOV: I don't know the combination of the cupboard. [*Pause.*]
HAMM: Go and get two bicycle-wheels.
CLOV: There are no more bicycle-wheels.
HAMM: What have you done with your bicycle?
CLOV: I never had a bicycle.
HAMM: The thing is impossible.
CLOV: When there were still bicycles I wept to have one. I crawled at your feet. You told me to go to hell. Now there are none.
HAMM: And your rounds? When you inspected my paupers. Always on foot?
CLOV: Sometimes on horse.

[*The lid of one of the bins lifts and the hands of Nagg appear, gripping the rim. Then his head emerges. Nightcap. Very white face. Nagg yawns, then listens.*]

I'll leave you, I have things to do.
HAMM: In your kitchen?
CLOV: Yes.
HAMM: Outside of here it's death. [*Pause.*] All right, be off.

[*Exit Clov. Pause.*]

We're getting on.
NAGG: Me pap!
HAMM: Accursed progenitor!
NAGG: Me pap!
HAMM: The old folks at home! No decency left! Guzzle, guzzle, that's all they think of.

[*He whistles. Enter Clov. He halts beside the chair.*]

Well! I thought you were leaving me.
CLOV: Oh not just yet, not just yet.
NAGG: Me pap!
HAMM: Give him his pap.
CLOV: There's no more pap.
HAMM [*to Nagg*]: Do you hear that? There's no more pap. You'll never get any more pap.
NAGG: I want me pap!
HAMM: Give him a biscuit.

[*Exit Clov.*]

Accursed fornicator! How are your stumps?

NAGG: Never mind me stumps.

[*Enter Clov with biscuit.*]

CLOV: I'm back again, with the biscuit.

[*He gives biscuit to Nagg who fingers it, sniffs it.*]

NAGG [*plaintively*]: What is it?

CLOV: Spratt's medium.

NAGG [*as before*]: It's hard! I can't!

HAMM: Bottle him!

[*Clov pushes Nagg back into the bin, closes the lid.*]

CLOV [*returning to his place beside the chair*]: If age but knew!

HAMM: Sit on him!

CLOV: I can't sit.

HAMM: True. And I can't stand.

CLOV: So it is.

HAMM: Every man his speciality. [*Pause.*] No phone calls? [*Pause.*] Don't we laugh?

CLOV [*after reflection*]: I don't feel like it.

HAMM [*after reflection*]: Nor I. [*Pause.*] Clov!

CLOV: Yes.

HAMM: Nature has forgotten us.

CLOV: There's no more nature.

HAMM: No more nature! You exaggerate.

CLOV: In the vicinity.

HAMM: But we breathe, we change! We lose our hair, our teeth! Our bloom! Our ideals!

CLOV: Then she hasn't forgotten us.

HAMM: But you say there is none.

CLOV [*sadly*]: No one that ever lived ever thought so crooked as we.

HAMM: We do what we can.

CLOV: We shouldn't. [*Pause.*]

HAMM: You're a bit of all right, aren't you?

CLOV: A smithereen. [*Pause.*]

HAMM: This is slow work. [*Pause.*] Is it not time for my pain-killer?

CLOV: No. [*Pause.*] I'll leave you, I have things to do.

HAMM: In your kitchen?

CLOV: Yes.

HAMM: What, I'd like to know.

CLOV: I look at the wall.

HAMM: The wall! And what do you see on your wall? Mene, mene?[3] Naked bodies?

3. A phrase that appears written by a supernatural hand on a wall of the Babylonian king Belshazzar's palace in the book of Daniel. The inscription, "mene, mene, tekel, upharsin," is translated by the prophet Daniel as "God has numbered the days of your kingdom and brought it to an end" (Daniel 5.26); Belshazzar is killed the same night.

CLOV: I see my light dying.

HAMM: Your light dying! Listen to that! Well, it can die just as well here, *your* light. Take a look at me and then come back and tell me what you think of *your* light. [*Pause.*]

CLOV: You shouldn't speak to me like that. [*Pause.*]

HAMM [*coldly*]: Forgive me. [*Pause. Louder.*] I said, Forgive me.

CLOV: I heard you.

[*The lid of Nagg's bin lifts. His hands appear, gripping the rim. Then his head emerges. In his mouth the biscuit. He listens.*]

HAMM: Did your seeds come up?

CLOV: No.

HAMM: Did you scratch round them to see if they had sprouted?

CLOV: They haven't sprouted.

HAMM: Perhaps it's still too early.

CLOV: If they were going to sprout they would have sprouted. [*Violently.*] They'll never sprout!

[*Pause. Nagg takes biscuit in his hand.*]

HAMM: This is not much fun. [*Pause.*] But that's always the way at the end of the day, isn't it, Clov?

CLOV: Always.

HAMM: It's the end of the day like any other day, isn't it, Clov?

CLOV: Looks like it. [*Pause.*]

HAMM [*anguished*]: What's happening, what's happening?

CLOV: Something is taking its course. [*Pause.*]

HAMM: All right, be off.

[*He leans back in his chair, remains motionless. Clov does not move, heaves a great groaning sigh. Hamm sits up.*]

I thought I told you to be off.

CLOV: I'm trying.

[*He goes to door, halts.*]

Ever since I was whelped.

[*Exit Clov.*]

HAMM: We're getting on.

[*He leans back in his chair, remains motionless. Nagg knocks on the lid of the other bin. Pause. He knocks harder. The lid lifts and the hands of Nell appear, gripping the rim. Then her head emerges. Lace cap. Very white face.*]

NELL: What is it, my pet? [*Pause.*] Time for love?

NAGG: Were you asleep?

NELL: Oh no!

NAGG: Kiss me.

NELL: We can't:

NAGG: Try.

[*Their heads strain towards each other, fail to meet, fall apart again.*]

NELL: Why this farce, day after day? [*Pause.*]
NAGG: I've lost me tooth.
NELL: When?
NAGG: I had it yesterday.
NELL [*elegiac*]: Ah yesterday!

[*They turn painfully towards each other.*]

NAGG: Can you see me?
NELL: Hardly. And you?
NAGG: What?
NELL: Can you see me?
NAGG: Hardly.
NELL: So much the better, so much the better.
NAGG: Don't say that. [*Pause.*] Our sight has failed.
NELL: Yes.

[*Pause. They turn away from each other.*]

NAGG: Can you hear me?
NELL: Yes. And you?
NAGG: Yes. [*Pause.*] Our hearing hasn't failed.
NELL: Our what?
NAGG: Our hearing.
NELL: No. [*Pause.*] Have you anything else to say to me?
NAGG: Do you remember—
NELL: No.
NAGG: When we crashed on our tandem and lost our shanks.

[*They laugh heartily.*]

NELL: It was in the Ardennes.

[*They laugh less heartily.*]

NAGG: On the road to Sedan.[4]

[*They laugh still less heartily.*]

Are you cold?
NELL: Yes, perished. And you?
NAGG: [*Pause.*] I'm freezing. [*Pause.*] Do you want to go in?
NELL: Yes.
NAGG: Then go in.

[*Nell does not move.*]

Why don't you go in?
NELL: I don't know. [*Pause.*]
NAGG: Has he changed your sawdust?
NELL: It isn't sawdust. [*Pause. Wearily.*] Can you not be a little accurate, Nagg?

4. A town in the Ardennes, a wooded region in northern France.

NAGG: Your sand then. It's not important.

NELL: It is important. [*Pause.*]

NAGG: It was sawdust once.

NELL: Once!

NAGG: And now it's sand. [*Pause.*] From the shore. [*Pause. Impatiently.*] Now it's sand he fetches from the shore.

NELL: Now it's sand.

NAGG: Has he changed yours?

NELL: No.

NAGG: Nor mine. [*Pause.*] I won't have it! [*Pause. Holding up the biscuit.*] Do you want a bit?

NELL: No. [*Pause.*] Of what?

NAGG: Biscuit. I've kept you half. [*He looks at the biscuit. Proudly.*] Three quarters. For you. Here. [*He proffers the biscuit.*] No? [*Pause.*] Do you not feel well?

HAMM [*wearily*]: Quiet, quiet, you're keeping me awake. [*Pause.*] Talk softer. [*Pause.*] If I could sleep I might make love. I'd go into the woods. My eyes would see . . . the sky, the earth. I'd run, run, they wouldn't catch me. [*Pause.*] Nature! [*Pause.*] There's something dripping in my head. [*Pause.*] A heart, a heart in my head. [*Pause.*]

NAGG [*soft*]: Do you hear him? A heart in his head! [*He chuckles cautiously.*]

NELL: One mustn't laugh at those things, Nagg. Why must you always laugh at them?

NAGG: Not so loud!

NELL [*without lowering her voice*]: Nothing is funnier than unhappiness, I grant you that. But—

NAGG [*shocked*]: Oh!

NELL: Yes, yes, it's the most comical thing in the world. And we laugh, we laugh, with a will, in the beginning. But it's always the same thing. Yes, it's like the funny story we have heard too often, we still find it funny, but we don't laugh any more. [*Pause.*] Have you anything else to say to me?

NAGG: No.

NELL: Are you quite sure? [*Pause.*] Then I'll leave you.

NAGG: Do you not want your biscuit? [*Pause.*] I'll keep it for you. [*Pause.*] I thought you were going to leave me.

NELL: I am going to leave you.

NAGG: Could you give me a scratch before you go?

NELL: No. [*Pause.*] Where?

NAGG: In the back.

NELL: No. [*Pause.*] Rub yourself against the rim.

NAGG: It's lower down. In the hollow.

NELL: What hollow?

NAGG: The hollow! [*Pause.*] Could you not? [*Pause.*] Yesterday you scratched me there.

NELL [*elegiac*]: Ah yesterday!

NAGG: Could you not? [*Pause.*] Would you like me to scratch you? [*Pause.*] Are you crying again?

NELL: I was trying. [*Pause.*]

HAMM: Perhaps it's a little vein. [*Pause.*]

NAGG: What was that he said?

NELL: Perhaps it's a little vein.
NAGG: What does that mean? [*Pause.*] That means nothing. [*Pause.*] Will I tell you the story of the tailor?
NELL: No. [*Pause.*] What for?
NAGG: To cheer you up.
NELL: It's not funny.
NAGG: It always made you laugh. [*Pause.*] The first time I thought you'd die.
NELL: It was on Lake Como.[5] [*Pause.*] One April afternoon. [*Pause.*] Can you believe it?
NAGG: What?
NELL: That we once went out rowing on Lake Como. [*Pause.*] One April afternoon.
NAGG: We had got engaged the day before.
NELL: Engaged!
NAGG: You were in such fits that we capsized. By rights we should have been drowned.
NELL: It was because I felt happy.
NAGG [*indignant*]: It was not, it was not, it was my story and nothing else. Happy! Don't you laugh at it still? Every time I tell it. Happy!
NELL: It was deep, deep. And you could see down to the bottom. So white. So clean.
NAGG: Let me tell it again. [*Raconteur's*[6] *voice.*] An Englishman, needing a pair of striped trousers in a hurry for the New Year festivities, goes to his tailor who takes his measurements.

[*Tailor's voice.*]

"That's the lot, come back in four days, I'll have it ready."
Good. Four days later.

[*Tailor's voice.*]

"So sorry, come back in a week, I've made a mess of the seat." Good, that's all right, a neat seat can be very ticklish. A week later.

[*Tailor's voice.*]

"Frightfully sorry, come back in ten days, I've made a hash of the crotch." Good, can't be helped, a snug crotch is always a teaser. Ten days later.

[*Tailor's voice.*]

"Dreadfully sorry, come back in a fortnight, I've made a balls of the fly." Good, at a pinch, a smart fly is a stiff proposition. [*Pause. Normal voice.*] I never told it worse. [*Pause. Gloomy.*] I tell this story worse and worse.

[*Pause. Raconteur's voice.*]

Well, to make it short, the bluebells are blowing and he ballockses the buttonholes.

[*Customer's voice.*]

5. A scenic lake in northern Italy.

6. A talented storyteller.

"God damn you to hell, Sir, no, it's indecent, there are limits! In six days, do you hear me, six days, God made the world. Yes Sir, no less Sir, the WORLD! And you are not bloody well capable of making me a pair of trousers in three months!"

[*Tailor's voice, scandalized.*]

"But my dear Sir, my dear Sir, look—[*disdainful gesture, disgustedly*]—at the world—[*pause*] and look—[*loving gesture, proudly*]—at my TROUSERS!"

[*Pause. He looks at Nell who has remained impassive, her eyes unseeing, breaks into a high forced laugh, cuts it short, pokes his head towards Nell, launches his laugh again.*]

HAMM: Silence!

[*Nagg starts, cuts short his laugh.*]

NELL: You could see down to the bottom.

HAMM [*exasperated*]: Have you not finished? Will you never finish? [*With sudden fury.*] Will this never finish?

[*Nagg disappears into his bin, closes the lid behind him. Nell does not move. Frenziedly.*]

My kingdom for a nightman![7]

[*He whistles. Enter Clov.*]

Clear away this muck! Chuck it in the sea!

[*Clov goes to bins, halts.*]

NELL: So white.

HAMM: What? What's she blathering about?

[*Clov stoops, takes Nell's hand, feels her pulse.*]

NELL [*to Clov*]: Desert!

[*Clov lets go her hand, pushes her back in the bin, closes the lid.*]

CLOV [*returning to his place beside the chair*]: She has no pulse.

HAMM: What was she drivelling about?

CLOV: She told me to go away, into the desert.

HAMM: Damn busybody! Is that all?

CLOV: No.

HAMM: What else?

CLOV: I didn't understand.

HAMM: Have you bottled her?

CLOV: Yes.

HAMM: Are they both bottled?

CLOV: Yes.

HAMM: Screw down the lids.

[*Clov goes towards door.*]

7. Someone who empties outhouses. Hamm's phrasing alludes to Richard III's call, "My kingdom for a horse!" in Shakespeare's tragedy *Richard III* 5.4.

Time enough.

[*Clov halts*.]

My anger subsides, I'd like to pee.

CLOV [*with alacrity*]: I'll go and get the catheter.

[*He goes towards door*.]

HAMM: Time enough.

[*Clov halts*.]

Give me my pain-killer.

CLOV: It's too soon. [*Pause*.] It's too soon on top of your tonic, it wouldn't act.

HAMM: In the morning they brace you up and in the evening they calm you down. Unless it's the other way round. [*Pause*.] That old doctor, he's dead naturally?

CLOV: He wasn't old.

HAMM: But he's dead?

CLOV: Naturally. [*Pause*.] *You* ask *me* that? [*Pause*.]

HAMM: Take me for a little turn.

[*Clov goes behind the chair and pushes it forward*.]

Not too fast!

[*Clov pushes chair*.]

Right round the world!

[*Clov pushes chair*.]

Hug the walls, then back to the center again.

[*Clov pushes chair*.]

I was right in the center, wasn't I?

CLOV [*pushing*]: Yes.

HAMM: We'd need a proper wheel-chair. With big wheels. Bicycle wheels! [*Pause*.] Are you hugging?

CLOV [*pushing*]: Yes.

HAMM [*groping for wall*]: It's a lie! Why do you lie to me?

CLOV [*bearing closer to wall*]: There! There!

HAMM: Stop!

[*Clov stops chair close to back wall. Hamm lays his hand against wall*.]

Old wall! [*Pause*.] Beyond is the . . . other hell. [*Pause. Violently*.] Closer! Closer! Up against!

CLOV: Take away your hand.

[*Hamm withdraws his hand. Clov rams chair against wall*.]

There!

[*Hamm leans towards wall, applies his ear to it*.]

HAMM: Do you hear?

[*He strikes the wall with his knuckles*.]

Do you hear? Hollow bricks!

[*He strikes again*.]

All that's hollow! [*Pause. He straightens up. Violently*.] That's enough. Back!

CLOV: We haven't done the round.

HAMM: Back to my place!

[*Clov pushes chair back to center*.]

Is that my place?

CLOV: Yes, that's your place.

HAMM: Am I right in the center?

CLOV: I'll measure it.

HAMM: More or less! More or less!

CLOV [*moving chair slightly*]: There!

HAMM: I'm more or less in the center?

CLOV: I'd say so.

HAMM: You'd say so! Put me right in the center!

CLOV: I'll go and get the tape.

HAMM: Roughly! Roughly!

[*Clov moves chair slightly*.]

Bang in the center!

CLOV: There! [*Pause*.]

HAMM: I feel a little too far to the left.

[*Clov moves chair slightly*.]

Now I feel a little too far to the right.

[*Clov moves chair slightly*.]

I feel a little too far forward.

[*Clov moves chair slightly*.]

Now I feel a little too far back.

[*Clov moves chair slightly*.]

Don't stay there [*i.e. behind the chair*], you give me the shivers.

[*Clov returns to his place beside the chair*.]

CLOV: If I could kill him I'd die happy. [*Pause*.]

HAMM: What's the weather like?

CLOV: As usual.

HAMM: Look at the earth.

CLOV: I've looked.

HAMM: With the glass?

CLOV: No need of the glass.

HAMM: Look at it with the glass.

CLOV: I'll go and get the glass

[*Exit Clov.*]

HAMM: No need for the glass!

[*Enter Clov with telescope.*]

CLOV: I'm back again, with the glass.

[*He goes to window right, looks up at it.*]

I need the steps.

HAMM: Why? Have you shrunk?

[*Exit Clov with telescope.*]

I don't like that, I don't like that.

[*Enter Clov with ladder, but without telescope.*]

CLOV: I'm back again, with the steps.

[*He sets down ladder under window right, gets up on it, realizes he has not the telescope, gets down.*]

I need the glass.

[*He goes towards door.*]

HAMM [*violently*]: But you have the glass!

CLOV [*halting, violently*]: No, I haven't the glass!

[*Exit Clov.*]

HAMM: This is deadly.

[*Enter Clov with telescope. He goes towards ladder.*]

CLOV: Things are livening up.

[*He gets up on the ladder, raises the telescope, lets it fall.*]

I did it on purpose.

[*He gets down, picks up the telescope, turns it on auditorium.*]

I see . . . a multitude . . . in transports . . . of joy. [*Pause.*] That's what I call a magnifier.

[*He lowers the telescope, turns towards Hamm.*]

Well? Don't we laugh?

HAMM [*after reflection*]: I don't.

CLOV [*after reflection*]: Nor I.

[*He gets up on ladder, turns the telescope on the without.*]

Let's see.

[*He looks, moving the telescope.*]

Zero . . . [*he looks*] . . . zero . . . [*he looks*] . . . and zero.

HAMM: Nothing stirs. All is—

CLOV: Zer—

HAMM [*violently*]: Wait till you're spoken to! [*Normal voice.*] All is . . . all is . . . all is what? [*Violently.*] All is what?

CLOV: What all is? In a word? Is that what you want to know? Just a moment.

[*He turns the telescope on the without, looks, lowers the telescope, turns towards Hamm.*]

Corpsed. [*Pause.*] Well? Content?

HAMM: Look at the sea.

CLOV: It's the same.

HAMM: Look at the ocean!

[*Clov gets down, takes a few steps towards window left, goes back for ladder, carries it over and sets it down under window left, gets up on it, turns the telescope on the without, looks at length. He starts, lowers the telescope, examines it, turns it again on the without.*]

CLOV: Never seen anything like that!

HAMM [*anxious*]: What? A sail? A fin? Smoke?

CLOV [*looking*]: The light is sunk.

HAMM [*relieved*]: Pah! We all knew that.

CLOV [*looking*]: There was a bit left.

HAMM: The base.

CLOV [*looking*]: Yes.

HAMM: And now?

CLOV [*looking*]: All gone.

HAMM: No gulls?

CLOV [*looking*]: Gulls!

HAMM: And the horizon? Nothing on the horizon?

CLOV [*lowering the telescope, turning towards Hamm, exasperated*]: What in God's name could there be on the horizon? [*Pause.*]

HAMM: The waves, how are the waves?

CLOV: The waves?

[*He turns the telescope on the waves.*]

Lead.

HAMM: And the sun?

CLOV [*looking*]: Zero.

HAMM: But it should be sinking. Look again.

CLOV [*looking*]: Damn the sun.

HAMM: Is it night already then?

CLOV [*looking*]: No.

HAMM: Then what is it?

CLOV [*looking*]: Gray.

[*Lowering the telescope, turning towards Hamm, louder.*]

Gray! [*Pause. Still louder.*] GRRAY! [*Pause. He gets down, approaches Hamm from behind, whispers in his ear.*]

HAMM [*starting*]: Gray! Did I hear you say gray?

CLOV: Light black. From pole to pole.

HAMM: You exaggerate. [*Pause.*] Don't stay there, you give me the shivers.

[*Clov returns to his place beside the chair*.]

CLOV: Why this farce, day after day?
HAMM: Routine. One never knows. [*Pause*.] Last night I saw inside my breast. There was a big sore.
CLOV: Pah! You saw your heart.
HAMM: No, it was living. [*Pause. Anguished.*] Clov!
CLOV: Yes.
HAMM: What's happening?
CLOV: Something is taking its course. [*Pause*.]
HAMM: Clov!
CLOV [*impatiently*]: What is it?
HAMM: We're not beginning to . . . to . . . mean something?
CLOV: Mean something! You and I, mean something! [*Brief laugh*.] Ah that's a good one!
HAMM: I wonder. [*Pause*.] Imagine if a rational being came back to earth, wouldn't he be liable to get ideas into his head if he observed us long enough. [*Voice of rational being*.] Ah, good, now I see what it is, yes, now I understand what they're at!

[*Clov starts, drops the telescope and begins to scratch his belly with both hands. Normal voice*.]

And without going so far as that, we ourselves . . . [*with emotion*] . . . we ourselves . . . at certain moments . . . [*Vehemently*.] To think perhaps it won't all have been for nothing!
CLOV [*anguished, scratching himself*]: I have a flea!
HAMM: A flea! Are there still fleas?
CLOV: On me there's one. [*Scratching*.] Unless it's a crablouse.
HAMM [*very perturbed*]: But humanity might start from there all over again! Catch him, for the love of God!
CLOV: I'll go and get the powder.

[*Exit Clov*.]

HAMM: A flea! This is awful! What a day!

[*Enter Clov with a sprinkling-tin*.]

CLOV: I'm back again, with the insecticide.
HAMM: Let him have it!

[*Clov loosens the top of his trousers, pulls it forward and shakes powder into the aperture. He stoops, looks, waits, starts, frenziedly shakes more powder, stoops, looks, waits*.]

CLOV: The bastard!
HAMM: Did you get him?
CLOV: Looks like it.

[*He drops the tin and adjusts his trousers*.]

Unless he's laying doggo.
HAMM: Laying! Lying you mean. Unless he's *lying* doggo.
CLOV: Ah? One says lying? One doesn't say laying?

HAMM: Use your head, can't you. If he was laying we'd be bitched.
CLOV: Ah. [*Pause.*] What about that pee?
HAMM: I'm having it.
CLOV: Ah that's the spirit, that's the spirit! [*Pause.*]
HAMM [*with ardour*]: Let's go from here, the two of us! South! You can make a raft and the currents will carry us away, far away, to other . . . mammals!
CLOV: God forbid!
HAMM: Alone, I'll embark alone! Get working on that raft immediately. Tomorrow I'll be gone for ever.
CLOV [*hastening towards door*]: I'll start straight away.
HAMM: Wait!

[*Clov halts.*]

Will there be sharks, do you think?
CLOV: Sharks? I don't know. If there are there will be.

[*He goes towards door.*]

HAMM: Wait!

[*Clov halts.*]

Is it not yet time for my pain-killer?
CLOV [*violently*]: No!

[*He goes towards door.*]

HAMM: Wait!

[*Clov halts.*]

How are your eyes?
CLOV: Bad.
HAMM: But you can see.
CLOV: All I want.
HAMM: How are your legs?
CLOV: Bad.
HAMM: But you can walk.
CLOV: I come . . . and go.
HAMM: In my house. [*Pause. With prophetic relish.*] One day you'll be blind, like me. You'll be sitting there, a speck in the void, in the dark, for ever, like me. [*Pause.*] One day you'll say to yourself, I'm tired, I'll sit down, and you'll go and sit down. Then you'll say, I'm hungry, I'll get up and get something to eat. But you won't get up. You'll say, I shouldn't have sat down, but since I have I'll sit on a little longer, then I'll get up and get something to eat. But you won't get up and you won't get anything to eat. [*Pause.*] You'll look at the wall a while, then you'll say, I'll close my eyes, perhaps have a little sleep, after that I'll feel better, and you'll close them. And when you open them again there'll be no wall any more. [*Pause.*] Infinite emptiness will be all around you, all the resurrected dead of all the ages wouldn't fill it, and there you'll be like a little bit of grit in the middle of the steppe. [*Pause.*] Yes, one day you'll know what it is, you'll be like me, except that you won't have anyone with you, because you won't have had pity on anyone and because there won't be anyone left to have pity on. [*Pause.*]

CLOV: It's not certain. [*Pause*.] And there's one thing you forget.
HAMM: Ah?
CLOV: I can't sit down.
HAMM [*impatiently*]: Well you'll lie down then, what the hell! Or you'll come to a standstill, simply stop and stand still, the way you are now. One day you'll say, I'm tired, I'll stop. What does the attitude matter? [*Pause*.]
CLOV: So you all want me to leave you.
HAMM: Naturally.
CLOV: Then I'll leave you.
HAMM: You can't leave us.
CLOV: Then I won't leave you. [*Pause*.]
HAMM: Why don't you finish us? [*Pause*.] I'll tell you the combination of the cupboard if you promise to finish me.
CLOV: I couldn't finish you.
HAMM: Then you won't finish me. [*Pause*.]
CLOV: I'll leave you, I have things to do.
HAMM: Do you remember when you came here?
CLOV: No. Too small, you told me.
HAMM: Do you remember your father.
CLOV [*wearily*]: Same answer. [*Pause*.] You've asked me these questions millions of times.
HAMM: I love the old questions. [*With fervour*.] Ah the old questions, the old answers, there's nothing like them! [*Pause*.] It was I was a father to you.
CLOV: Yes. [*He looks at Hamm fixedly*.] You were that to me.
HAMM: My house a home for you.
CLOV: Yes. [*He looks about him*.] This was that for me.
HAMM [*proudly*]: But for me, [*gesture towards himself*] no father. But for Hamm, [*gesture towards surroundings*] no home. [*Pause*.]
CLOV: I'll leave you.
HAMM: Did you ever think of one thing?
CLOV: Never.
HAMM: That here we're down in a hole. [*Pause*.] But beyond the hills? Eh? Perhaps it's still green. Eh? [*Pause*.] Flora! Pomona! [*Ecstatically*.] Ceres![8] [*Pause*.] Perhaps you won't need to go very far.
CLOV: I can't go very far. [*Pause*.] I'll leave you.
HAMM: Is my dog ready?
CLOV: He lacks a leg.
HAMM: Is he silky?
CLOV: He's a kind of Pomeranian.
HAMM: Go and get him.
CLOV: He lacks a leg.
HAMM: Go and get him!

[*Exit Clov*.]

We're getting on.

8. Flora, Pomona, and Ceres: the Roman goddesses of flowering plants, fruits, and grains.

[*Enter Clov holding by one of its three legs a black toy dog.*]

CLOV: Your dogs are here.

[*He hands the dog to Hamm who feels it, fondles it.*]

HAMM: He's white, isn't he?
CLOV: Nearly.
HAMM: What do you mean, nearly? Is he white or isn't he?
CLOV: He isn't. [*Pause.*]
HAMM: You've forgotten the sex.
CLOV [*vexed*]: But he isn't finished. The sex goes on at the end. [*Pause.*]
HAMM: You haven't put on his ribbon.
CLOV [*angrily*]: But he isn't finished, I tell you! First you finish your dog and then you put on his ribbon! [*Pause.*]
HAMM: Can he stand?
CLOV: I don't know.
HAMM: Try.

[*He hands the dog to Clov who places it on the ground.*]

Well?
CLOV: Wait!

[*He squats down and tries to get the dog to stand on its three legs, fails, lets it go. The dog falls on its side.*]

HAMM [*impatiently*]: Well?
CLOV: He's standing.
HAMM [*groping for the dog*]: Where? Where is he?

[*Clov holds up the dog in a standing position.*]

CLOV: There.

[*He takes Hamm's hand and guides it towards the dog's head.*]

HAMM [*his hand on the dog's head*]: Is he gazing at me?
CLOV: Yes.
HAMM [*proudly*]: As if he were asking me to take him for a walk?
CLOV: If you like.
HAMM [*as before*]: Or as if he were begging me for a bone.

[*He withdraws his hand.*]

Leave him like that, standing there imploring me.

[*Clov straightens up. The dog falls on its side.*]

CLOV: I'll leave you.
HAMM: Have you had your visions?
CLOV: Less.
HAMM: Is Mother Pegg's light on?
CLOV: Light! How could anyone's light be on?
HAMM: Extinguished!
CLOV: Naturally it's extinguished. If it's not on it's extinguished.

HAMM: No, I mean Mother Pegg.
CLOV: But naturally she's extinguished! [*Pause*.] What's the matter with you today?
HAMM: I'm taking my course. [*Pause*.] Is she buried?
CLOV: Buried! Who would have buried her?
HAMM: You.
CLOV: Me! Haven't I enough to do without burying people?
HAMM: But you'll bury me.
CLOV: No I won't bury you. [*Pause*.]
HAMM: She was bonny once, like a flower of the field. [*With reminiscent leer*.] And a great one for the men!
CLOV: We too were bonny—once. It's a rare thing not to have been bonny—once. [*Pause*.]
HAMM: Go and get the gaff.[9]

[*Clov goes to door, halts*.]

CLOV: Do this, do that, and I do it. I never refuse. Why?
HAMM: You're not able to.
CLOV: Soon I won't do it any more.
HAMM: You won't be able to any more.

[*Exit Clov*.]

Ah the creatures, the creatures, everything has to be explained to them.

[*Enter Clov with gaff*.]

CLOV: Here's your gaff. Stick it up.

[*He gives the gaff to Hamm who, wielding it like a puntpole, tries to move his chair*.]

HAMM: Did I move?
CLOV: No.

[*Hamm throws down the gaff*.]

HAMM: Go and get the oilcan.
CLOV: What for?
HAMM: To oil the castors.
CLOV: I oiled them yesterday.
HAMM: Yesterday! What does that mean? Yesterday!
CLOV [*violently*]: That means that bloody awful day, long ago, before this bloody awful day. I use the words you taught me. If they don't mean anything any more, teach me others. Or let me be silent. [*Pause*.]
HAMM: I once knew a madman who thought the end of the world had come. He was a painter—and engraver. I had a great fondness for him. I used to go and see him, in the asylum. I'd take him by the hand and drag him to the window. Look! There! All that rising corn! And there! Look! The sails of the herring fleet! All that loveliness! [*Pause*.] He'd snatch away his hand and go back into his corner. Appalled. All he had seen was ashes. [*Pause*.] He alone had been spared. [*Pause*.] Forgotten. [*Pause*.] It appears the case is . . . was not so . . . so unusual.

9. A fishing pole designed for catching large fish.

CLOV: A madman? When was that?
HAMM: Oh way back, way back, you weren't in the land of the living.
CLOV: God be with the days!

[*Pause. Hamm raises his toque.*]

HAMM: I had a great fondness for him.

[*Pause. He puts on his toque again.*]

He was a painter—and engraver.
CLOV: There are so many terrible things.
HAMM: No, no, there are not so many now. [*Pause.*] Clov!
CLOV: Yes.
HAMM: Do you not think this has gone on long enough?
CLOV: Yes! [*Pause.*] What?
HAMM: This . . . this . . . thing.
CLOV: I've always thought so. [*Pause.*] You not?
HAMM [*gloomily*]: Then it's a day like any other day.
CLOV: As long as it lasts. [*Pause.*] All life long the same inanities.
HAMM: I can't leave you.
CLOV: I know. And you can't follow me. [*Pause.*]
HAMM: If you leave me how shall I know?
CLOV [*briskly*]: Well you simply whistle me and if I don't come running it means I've left you. [*Pause.*]
HAMM: You won't come and kiss me goodbye?
CLOV: Oh I shouldn't think so. [*Pause.*]
HAMM: But you might be merely dead in your kitchen.
CLOV: The result would be the same.
HAMM: Yes, but how would I know, if you were merely dead in your kitchen?
CLOV: Well . . . sooner or later I'd start to stink.
HAMM: You stink already. The whole place stinks of corpses.
CLOV: The whole universe.
HAMM [*angrily*]: To hell with the universe. [*Pause.*] Think of something.
CLOV: What?
HAMM: An idea, have an idea. [*Angrily.*] A bright idea!
CLOV: Ah good.

[*He starts pacing to and fro, his eyes fixed on the ground, his hands behind his back. He halts.*]

The pains in my legs! It's unbelievable! Soon I won't be able to think any more.
HAMM: You won't be able to leave me.

[*Clov resumes his pacing.*]

What are you doing?
CLOV: Having an idea.

[*He paces.*]

Ah!

[*He halts.*]

HAMM: What a brain! [*Pause*.] Well?

CLOV: Wait! [*He meditates. Not very convinced.*] Yes . . . [*Pause. More convinced.*] Yes! [*He raises his head.*] I have it! I set the alarm. [*Pause.*]

HAMM: This is perhaps not one of my bright days, but frankly—

CLOV: You whistle me. I don't come. The alarm rings. I'm gone. It doesn't ring. I'm dead. [*Pause.*]

HAMM: Is it working? [*Pause. Impatiently.*] The alarm, is it working?

CLOV: Why wouldn't it be working?

HAMM: Because it's worked too much.

CLOV: But it's hardly worked at all.

HAMM [*angrily*]: Then because it's worked too little!

CLOV: I'll go and see.

[*Exit Clov. Brief ring of alarm off. Enter Clov with alarm-clock. He holds it against Hamm's ear and releases alarm. They listen to it ringing to the end. Pause.*]

Fit to wake the dead! Did you hear it?

HAMM: Vaguely.

CLOV: The end is terrific!

HAMM: I prefer the middle. [*Pause.*] Is it not time for my pain-killer?

CLOV: No! [*He goes to door, turns.*] I'll leave you.

HAMM: It's time for my story. Do you want to listen to my story?

CLOV: No.

HAMM: Ask my father if he wants to listen to my story.

[*Clov goes to bins, raises the lid of Nagg's, stoops, looks into it. Pause. He straightens up.*]

CLOV: He's asleep.

HAMM: Wake him.

[*Clov stoops, wakes Nagg with the alarm. Unintelligible words. Clov straightens up.*]

CLOV: He doesn't want to listen to your story.

HAMM: I'll give him a bon-bon.

[*Clov stoops. As before.*]

CLOV: He wants a sugar-plum.

HAMM: He'll get a sugar-plum.

[*Clov stoops. As before.*]

CLOV: It's a deal.

[*He goes towards door. Nagg's hands appear, gripping the rim. Then the head emerges. Clov reaches door, turns.*]

Do you believe in the life to come?

HAMM: Mine was always that.

[*Exit Clov.*]

Got him that time!

NAGG: I'm listening.

HAMM: Scoundrel! Why did you engender me?

NAGG: I didn't know.
HAMM: What? What didn't you know?
NAGG: That it'd be you. [*Pause.*] You'll give me a sugar-plum?
HAMM: After the audition.
NAGG: You swear?
HAMM: Yes.
NAGG: On what?
HAMM: My honor. [*Pause. They laugh heartily.*]
NAGG: Two.
HAMM: One.
NAGG: One for me and one for—
HAMM: One! Silence! [*Pause.*] Where was I? [*Pause. Gloomily.*] It's finished, we're finished. [*Pause.*] Nearly finished. [*Pause.*] There'll be no more speech. [*Pause.*] Something dripping in my head, ever since the fontanelles.[1] [*Stifled hilarity of Nagg.*] Splash, splash, always on the same spot. [*Pause.*] Perhaps it's a little vein. [*Pause.*] A little artery. [*Pause. More animated.*] Enough of that, it's story time, where was I? [*Pause. Narrative tone.*] The man came crawling towards me, on his belly. Pale, wonderfully pale and thin, he seemed on the point of—[*Pause. Normal tone.*] No, I've done that bit. [*Pause. Narrative tone.*] I calmly filled my pipe—the meerschaum, lit it with . . . let us say a vesta,[2] drew a few puffs. Aah! [*Pause.*] Well, what is it *you* want? [*Pause.*] It was an extra-ordinarily bitter day, I remember, zero by the thermometer. But considering it was Christmas Eve there was nothing . . . extra-ordinary about that. Seasonable weather, for once in a way. [*Pause.*] Well, what ill wind blows you my way? He raised his face to me, black with mingled dirt and tears. [*Pause. Normal tone.*] That should do it.

[*Narrative tone.*]

No no, don't look at me, don't look at me. He dropped his eyes and mumbled something, apologies I presume. [*Pause.*] I'm a busy man, you know, the final touches, before the festivities, you know what it is. [*Pause. Forcibly.*] Come on now, what is the object of this invasion? [*Pause.*] It was a glorious bright day, I remember, fifty by the heliometer, but already the sun was sinking down into the . . . down among the dead.

[*Normal tone.*]

Nicely put, that.

[*Narrative tone.*]

Come on now, come on, present your petition and let me resume my labors.

[*Pause. Normal tone.*]

There's English for you. Ah well . . .

[*Narrative tone.*]

It was then he took the plunge. It's my little one, he said. Tsstss, a little one, that's bad. My little boy, he said, as if the sex mattered. Where did he come from? He named the hole. A good half-day, on horse. What are you insinuating? That the

1. Soft gaps between an infant's skull bones.
2. A match.

place is still inhabited? No no, not a soul, except himself and the child—assuming he existed. Good. I enquired about the situation at Kov, beyond the gulf. Not a sinner. Good. And you expect me to believe you have left your little one back there, all alone, and alive into the bargain? Come now! [*Pause.*] It was a howling wild day, I remember, a hundred by the anenometer.[3] The wind was tearing up the dead pines and sweeping them . . . away.

[*Pause. Normal tone.*]

A bit feeble, that.

[*Narrative tone.*]

Come on, man, speak up, what is it you want from me, I have to put up my holly. [*Pause.*]

Well to make it short it finally transpired that what he wanted from me was . . . bread for his brat? Bread? But I have no bread, it doesn't agree with me. Good. Then perhaps a little corn?

[*Pause. Normal tone.*]

That should do it.

[*Narrative tone.*]

Corn, yes, I have corn, it's true, in my granaries. But use your head. I give you some corn, a pound, a pound and a half, you bring it back to your child and you make him—if he's still alive—a nice pot of porridge, [*Nagg reacts*] a nice pot and a half of porridge, full of nourishment. Good. The colors come back into his little cheeks—perhaps. And then? [*Pause.*] I lost patience. [*Violently.*] Use your head, can't you, use your head, you're on earth, there's no cure for that! [*Pause.*] It was an exceedingly dry day, I remember, zero by the hygrometer. Ideal weather, for my lumbago. [*Pause. Violently.*] But what in God's name do you imagine? That the earth will awake in spring? That the rivers and seas will run with fish again? That there's manna in heaven still for imbeciles like you? [*Pause.*] Gradually I cooled down, sufficiently at least to ask him how long he had taken on the way. Three whole days. Good. In what condition he had left the child. Deep in sleep. [*Forcibly.*] But deep in what sleep, deep in what sleep already? [*Pause.*] Well to make it short I finally offered to take him into my service. He had touched a chord. And then I imagined already that I wasn't much longer for this world. [*He laughs. Pause.*] Well? [*Pause.*] Well? Here if you were careful you might die a nice natural death, in peace and comfort. [*Pause.*] Well? [*Pause.*] In the end he asked me would I consent to take in the child as well—if he were still alive. [*Pause.*] It was the moment I was waiting for. [*Pause.*] Would I consent to take in the child . . . [*Pause.*] I can see him still, down on his knees, his hands flat on the ground, glaring at me with his mad eyes, in defiance of my wishes. [*Pause. Normal tone.*] I'll soon have finished with this story. [*Pause.*] Unless I bring in other characters. [*Pause.*] But where would I find them? [*Pause.*] Where would I look for them? [*Pause. He whistles. Enter Clov.*] Let us pray to God.

NAGG: Me sugar-plum!

CLOV: There's a rat in the kitchen!

3. An instrument used to measure wind speed.

HAMM: A rat! Are there still rats?
CLOV: In the kitchen there's one.
HAMM: And you haven't exterminated him?
CLOV: Half. You disturbed us.
HAMM: He can't get away?
CLOV: No.
HAMM: You'll finish him later. Let us pray to God.
CLOV: Again!
NAGG: Me sugar-plum!
HAMM: God first! [*Pause.*] Are you right?
CLOV [*resigned*]: Off we go.
HAMM [*to Nagg*]: And you?
NAGG [*clasping his hands, closing his eyes, in a gabble*]: Our Father which art—
HAMM: Silence! In silence! Where are your manners? [*Pause.*] Off we go. [*Attitudes of prayer. Silence. Abandoning his attitude, discouraged.*] Well?
CLOV [*abandoning his attitude*]: What a hope! And you?
HAMM: Sweet damn all! [*To Nagg.*] And you?
NAGG: Wait! [*Pause. Abandoning his attitude.*] Nothing doing!
HAMM: The bastard! He doesn't exist!
CLOV: Not yet.
NAGG: Me sugar-plum!
HAMM: There are no more sugar-plums! [*Pause.*]
NAGG: It's natural. After all I'm your father. It's true if it hadn't been me it would have been someone else. But that's no excuse. [*Pause.*] Turkish Delight, for example, which no longer exists, we all know that, there is nothing in the world I love more. And one day I'll ask you for some, in return for a kindness, and you'll promise it to me. One must live with the times. [*Pause.*] Whom did you call when you were a tiny boy, and were frightened, in the dark? Your mother? No. Me. We let you cry. Then we moved you out of earshot, so that we might sleep in peace. [*Pause.*] I was asleep, as happy as a king, and you woke me up to have me listen to you. It wasn't indispensable, you didn't really need to have me listen to you. Besides I didn't listen to you. [*Pause.*] I hope the day will come when you'll really need to have me listen to you, and need to hear my voice, any voice. [*Pause.*] Yes, I hope I'll live till then, to hear you calling me like when you were a tiny boy, and were frightened, in the dark, and I was your only hope. [*Pause. Nagg knocks on lid of Nell's bin. Pause.*] Nell! [*Pause. He knocks louder. Pause. Louder.*] Nell! [*Pause. Nagg sinks back into his bin, closes the lid behind him. Pause.*]
HAMM: Our revels now are ended.[4]

[*He gropes for the dog.*]

The dog's gone.
CLOV: He's not a real dog, he can't go.
HAMM [*groping*]: He's not there.
CLOV: He's lain down.
HAMM: Give him up to me.

4. Quoting the exiled magician Prospero in Shakespeare's *The Tempest* (4.1): "Our revels are now ended. These our actors / As I foretold you, were all spirits, and / Are melted into air, into thin air."

[*Clov picks up the dog and gives it to Hamm. Hamm holds it in his arms. Pause. Hamm throws away the dog.*]

Dirty brute!

[*Clov begins to pick up the objects lying on the ground.*]

What are you doing?

CLOV: Putting things in order. [*He straightens up. Fervently.*] I'm going to clear everything away! [*He starts picking up again.*]

HAMM: Order!

CLOV [*straightening up*]: I love order. It's my dream. A world where all would be silent and still and each thing in its last place, under the last dust. [*He starts picking up again.*]

HAMM [*exasperated*]: What in God's name do you think you are doing?

CLOV [*straightening up*]: I'm doing my best to create a little order.

HAMM: Drop it!

[*Clov drops the objects he has picked up.*]

CLOV: After all, there or elsewhere. [*He goes towards door.*]

HAMM [*irritably*]: What's wrong with your feet?

CLOV: My feet?

HAMM: Tramp! Tramp!

CLOV: I must have put on my boots.

HAMM: Your slippers were hurting you? [*Pause.*]

CLOV: I'll leave you.

HAMM: No!

CLOV: What is there to keep me here?

HAMM: The dialogue. [*Pause.*] I've got on with my story. [*Pause.*] I've got on with it well. [*Pause. Irritably.*] Ask me where I've got to.

CLOV: Oh, by the way, your story?

HAMM [*surprised*]: What story?

CLOV: The one you've been telling yourself all your days.

HAMM: Ah you mean my chronicle?

CLOV: That's the one. [*Pause.*]

HAMM [*angrily*]: Keep going, can't you, keep going!

CLOV: You've got on with it, I hope.

HAMM [*modestly*]: Oh not very far, not very far. [*He sighs.*] There are days like that, one isn't inspired. [*Pause.*] Nothing you can do about it, just wait for it to come. [*Pause.*] No forcing, no forcing, it's fatal. [*Pause.*] I've got on with it a little all the same. [*Pause.*] Technique, you know. [*Pause. Irritably.*] I say I've got on with it a little all the same.

CLOV [*admiringly*]: Well I never! In spite of everything you were able to get on with it!

HAMM [*modestly*]: Oh not very far, you know, not very far, but nevertheless, better than nothing.

CLOV: Better than nothing! Is it possible?

HAMM: I'll tell you how it goes. He comes crawling on his belly—

CLOV: Who?

HAMM: What?

CLOV: Who do you mean, he?
HAMM: Who do I mean! Yet another.
CLOV: Ah him! I wasn't sure.
HAMM: Crawling on his belly, whining for bread for his brat. He's offered a job as gardener. Before—

[*Clov bursts out laughing.*]

What is there so funny about that?
CLOV: A job as gardener!
HAMM: Is that what tickles you?
CLOV: It must be that.
HAMM: It wouldn't be the bread?
CLOV: Or the brat. [*Pause.*]
HAMM: The whole thing is comical, I grant you that. What about having a good guffaw the two of us together?
CLOV [*after reflection*]: I couldn't guffaw again today.
HAMM [*after reflection*]: Nor I. [*Pause.*] I continue then. Before accepting with gratitude he asks if he may have his little boy with him.
CLOV: What age?
HAMM: Oh tiny.
CLOV: He would have climbed the trees.
HAMM: All the little odd jobs.
CLOV: And then he would have grown up.
HAMM: Very likely. [*Pause.*]
CLOV: Keep going, can't you, keep going!
HAMM: That's all. I stopped there. [*Pause.*]
CLOV: Do you see how it goes on.
HAMM: More or less.
CLOV: Will it not soon be the end?
HAMM: I'm afraid it will.
CLOV: Pah! You'll make up another.
HAMM: I don't know. [*Pause.*] I feel rather drained. [*Pause.*] The prolonged creative effort. [*Pause.*] If I could drag myself down to the sea! I'd make a pillow of sand for my head and the tide would come.
CLOV: There's no more tide. [*Pause.*]
HAMM: Go and see is she dead.

[*Clov goes to bins, raises the lid of Nell's, stoops, looks into it. Pause.*]

CLOV: Looks like it.

[*He closes the lid, straightens up. Hamm raises his toque. Pause. He puts it on again.*]

HAMM [*with his hand to his toque*]: And Nagg?

[*Clov raises lid of Nagg's bin, stoops, looks into it. Pause.*]

CLOV: Doesn't look like it. [*He closes the lid, straightens up.*]
HAMM [*letting go his toque*]: What's he doing?

[*Clov raises lid of Nagg's bin, stoops, looks into it. Pause.*]

CLOV: He's crying. [*He closes lid, straightens up.*]

HAMM: Then he's living. [*Pause.*] Did you ever have an instant of happiness?
CLOV: Not to my knowledge. [*Pause.*]
HAMM: Bring me under the window.

[*Clov goes towards chair.*]

I want to feel the light on my face.

[*Clov pushes chair.*]

Do you remember, in the beginning, when you took me for a turn? You used to hold the chair too high. At every step you nearly tipped me out. [*With senile quaver.*] Ah great fun, we had, the two of us, great fun. [*Gloomily.*] And then we got into the way of it.

[*Clov stops the chair under window right.*]

There already? [*Pause. He tilts back his head.*] Is it light?
CLOV: It isn't dark.
HAMM [*angrily*]: I'm asking you is it light.
CLOV: Yes. [*Pause.*]
HAMM: The curtain isn't closed?
CLOV: No.
HAMM: What window is it?
CLOV: The earth.
HAMM: I knew it! [*Angrily.*] But there's no light there! The other!

[*Clov pushes chair towards window left.*]

The earth!

[*Clov stops the chair under window left. Hamm tilts back his head.*]

That's what I call light! [*Pause.*] Feels like a ray of sunshine. [*Pause.*] No?
CLOV: No.
HAMM: It isn't a ray of sunshine I feel on my face?
CLOV: No. [*Pause.*]
HAMM: Am I very white? [*Pause. Angrily.*] I'm asking you am I very white!
CLOV: Not more so than usual. [*Pause.*]
HAMM: Open the window.
CLOV: What for?
HAMM: I want to hear the sea.
CLOV: You wouldn't hear it.
HAMM: Even if you opened the window?
CLOV: No.
HAMM: Then it's not worth while opening it?
CLOV: No.
HAMM [*violently*]: Then open it!

[*Clov gets up on the ladder, opens the window. Pause.*]

Have you opened it?
CLOV: Yes. [*Pause.*]
HAMM: You swear you've opened it?
CLOV: Yes. [*Pause.*]

HAMM: Well . . . ! [*Pause.*] It must be very calm. [*Pause. Violently.*] I'm asking you is it very calm!

CLOV: Yes.

HAMM: It's because there are no more navigators. [*Pause.*] You haven't much conversation all of a sudden. Do you not feel well?

CLOV: I'm cold.

HAMM: What month are we? [*Pause.*] Close the window, we're going back.

[*Clov closes the window, gets down, pushes the chair back to its place, remains standing behind it, head bowed.*]

Don't stay there, you give me the shivers!

[*Clov returns to his place beside the chair.*]

Father! [*Pause. Louder.*] Father! [*Pause.*] Go and see did he hear me.

[*Clov goes to Nagg's bin, raises the lid, stoops. Unintelligible words. Clov straightens up.*]

CLOV: Yes.

HAMM: Both times?

[*Clov stoops. As before.*]

CLOV: Once only.

HAMM: The first time or the second?

[*Clov stoops. As before.*]

CLOV: He doesn't know.

HAMM: It must have been the second.

CLOV: We'll never know.

[*He closes lid.*]

HAMM: Is he still crying?

CLOV: No.

HAMM: The dead go fast. [*Pause.*] What's he doing?

CLOV: Sucking his biscuit.

HAMM: Life goes on.

[*Clov returns to his place beside the chair.*]

Give me a rug, I'm freezing.

CLOV: There are no more rugs. [*Pause.*]

HAMM: Kiss me. [*Pause.*] Will you not kiss me?

CLOV: No.

HAMM: On the forehead.

CLOV: I won't kiss you anywhere. [*Pause.*]

HAMM [*holding out his hand*]: Give me your hand at least. [*Pause.*] Will you not give me your hand?

CLOV: I won't touch you. [*Pause.*]

HAMM: Give me the dog.

[*Clov looks round for the dog.*]

No!

CLOV: Do you not want your dog?
HAMM: No.
CLOV: Then I'll leave you.
HAMM [*head bowed, absently*]: That's right.

[*Clov goes to door, turns.*]

CLOV: If I don't kill that rat he'll die.
HAMM [*as before*]: That's right.

[*Exit Clov. Pause.*]

Me to play.

[*He takes out his handkerchief, unfolds it, holds it spread out before him.*]

We're getting on. [*Pause.*] You weep, and weep, for nothing, so as not to laugh, and little by little . . . you begin to grieve.

[*He folds the handkerchief, puts it back in his pocket, raises his head.*]

All those I might have helped. [*Pause.*] Helped! [*Pause.*] Saved. [*Pause.*] Saved! [*Pause.*] The place was crawling with them! [*Pause. Violently.*] Use your head, can't you, use your head, you're on earth, there's no cure for that! [*Pause.*] Get out of here and love one another! Lick your neighbor as yourself! [*Pause. Calmer.*] When it wasn't bread they wanted it was crumpets. [*Pause. Violently.*] Out of my sight and back to your petting parties! [*Pause.*] All that, all that! [*Pause.*] Not even a real dog! [*Calmer.*] The end is in the beginning and yet you go on. [*Pause.*] Perhaps I could go on with my story, end it and begin another. [*Pause.*] Perhaps I could throw myself out on the floor.

[*He pushes himself painfully off his seat, falls back again.*]

Dig my nails into the cracks and drag myself forward with my fingers. [*Pause.*] It will be the end and there I'll be, wondering what can have brought it on and wondering what can have . . . [*he hesitates*] . . . why it was so long coming. [*Pause.*] There I'll be, in the old shelter, alone against the silence and . . . [*he hesitates*] . . . the stillness. If I can hold my peace, and sit quiet, it will be all over with sound, and motion, all over and done with. [*Pause.*] I'll have called my father and I'll have called my . . . [*he hesitates*] . . . my son. And even twice, or three times, in case they shouldn't have heard me, the first time, or the second. [*Pause.*] I'll say to myself, He'll come back. [*Pause.*] And then? [*Pause.*] And then? [*Pause.*] He couldn't, he has gone too far. [*Pause.*] And then? [*Pause. Very agitated.*] All kinds of fantasies! That I'm being watched! A rat! Steps! Breath held and then . . . [*He breathes out.*] Then babble, babble, words, like the solitary child who turns himself into children, two, three, so as to be together, and whisper together, in the dark. [*Pause.*] Moment upon moment, pattering down, like the millet grains of . . . [*he hesitates*] . . . that old Greek, and all life long you wait for that to mount up to a life.[5] [*Pause. He opens his mouth to continue, renounces.*] Ah let's get it over!

5. Hamm is referring to Zeno of Elea (5th century B.C.E.), who is known for his philosophical paradoxes. One of them is based on the sound a bushel of millet makes when it falls on the floor: since this sound is caused by the grains, each grain must make a sound when striking the ground. This sound, however, can't be heard, so the apparent sound is really an accumulation of silences.

[*He whistles. Enter Clov with alarm-clock. He halts beside the chair.*]

What? Neither gone nor dead?

CLOV: In spirit only.

HAMM: Which?

CLOV: Both.

HAMM: Gone from me you'd be dead.

CLOV: And vice versa.

HAMM: Outside of here it's death! [*Pause.*] And the rat?

CLOV: He's got away.

HAMM: He can't go far. [*Pause. Anxious.*] Eh?

CLOV: He doesn't need to go far. [*Pause.*]

HAMM: Is it not time for my pain-killer?

CLOV: Yes.

HAMM: Ah! At last! Give it to me! Quick! [*Pause.*]

CLOV: There's no more pain-killer. [*Pause.*]

HAMM [*appalled*]: Good . . . ! [*Pause.*] No more pain-killer!

CLOV: No more pain-killer. You'll never get any more pain-killer. [*Pause.*]

HAMM: But the little round box. It was full!

CLOV: Yes. But now it's empty.

[*Pause. Clov starts to move about the room. He is looking for a place to put down the alarm-clock.*]

HAMM [*soft*]: What'll I do? [*Pause. In a scream.*] What'll I do?

[*Clov sees the picture, takes it down, stands it on the floor with its face to the wall, hangs up the alarm-clock in its place.*]

What are you doing?

CLOV: Winding up.

HAMM: Look at the earth.

CLOV: Again!

HAMM: Since it's calling to you.

CLOV: Is your throat sore? [*Pause.*] Would you like a lozenge? [*Pause.*] No. [*Pause.*] Pity.

[*Clov goes, humming, towards window right, halts before it, looks up at it.*]

HAMM: Don't sing.

CLOV [*turning towards Hamm*]: One hasn't the right to sing any more?

HAMM: No.

CLOV: Then how can it end?

HAMM: You want it to end?

CLOV: I want to sing.

HAMM: I can't prevent you.

[*Pause. Clov turns towards window right.*]

CLOV: What did I do with that steps? [*He looks around for ladder.*] You didn't see that steps? [*He sees it.*] Ah, about time. [*He goes towards window left.*] Sometimes I wonder if I'm in my right mind. Then it passes over and I'm as lucid as before. [*He gets up on ladder, looks out of window.*] Christ, she's under water! [*He looks.*] How can that be? [*He pokes forward his head, his hand above his eyes.*] It hasn't rained. [*He wipes the pane, looks. Pause.*] Ah what a fool I am! I'm on the wrong side! [*He gets down, takes a few steps towards window right.*] Under water! [*He goes back for ladder.*] What a fool I am! [*He carries ladder towards window right.*] Sometimes I wonder if I'm in my right senses. Then it passes off and I'm as intelligent as ever.

[*He sets down ladder under window right, gets up on it, looks out of window. He turns towards Hamm.*]

Any particular sector you fancy? Or merely the whole thing?

HAMM: Whole thing.

CLOV: The general effect? Just a moment. [*He looks out of window. Pause.*]

HAMM: Clov.

CLOV [*absorbed*]: Mmm.

HAMM: Do you know what it is?

CLOV [*as before*]: Mmm.

HAMM: I was never there. [*Pause.*] Clov!

CLOV [*turning towards Hamm, exasperated*]: What is it?

HAMM: I was never there.

CLOV: Lucky for you. [*He looks out of window.*]

HAMM: Absent, always. It all happened without me. I don't know what's happened. [*Pause.*] Do you know what's happened? [*Pause.*] Clov!

CLOV [*turning towards Hamm, exasperated*]: Do you want me to look at this muck-heap, yes or no?

HAMM: Answer me first.

CLOV: What?

HAMM: Do you know what's happened?

CLOV: When? Where?

HAMM [*violently*]: When! What's happened? Use your head, can't you! What has happened?

CLOV: What for Christ's sake does it matter? [*He looks out of window.*]

HAMM: I don't know. [*Pause. Clov turns towards Hamm.*]

CLOV [*harshly*]: When old Mother Pegg asked you for oil for her lamp and you told her to get out to hell, you knew what was happening then, no? [*Pause.*] You know what she died of, Mother Pegg? Of darkness.

HAMM [*feebly*]: I hadn't any.

CLOV [*as before*]: Yes, you had. [*Pause.*]

HAMM: Have you the glass?

CLOV: No, it's clear enough as it is.

HAMM: Go and get it.

[*Pause. Clov casts up his eyes, brandishes his fists. He loses balance, clutches on to the ladder. He starts to get down, halts.*]

CLOV: There's one thing I'll never understand. [*He gets down.*] Why I always obey you. Can you explain that to me?

HAMM: No .... Perhaps it's compassion. [*Pause.*] A kind of great compassion. [*Pause.*] Oh you won't find it easy, you won't find it easy.

[*Pause. Clov begins to move about the room in search of the telescope.*]

CLOV: I'm tired of our goings on, very tired. [*He searches.*] You're not sitting on it?

[*He moves the chair, looks at the place where it stood, resumes his search.*]

HAMM [*anguished*]: Don't leave me there! [*Angrily Clov restores the chair to its place.*] Am I right in the center?

CLOV: You'd need a microscope to find this—[*He sees the telescope.*] Ah, about time.

[*He picks up the telescope, gets up on the ladder, turns the telescope on the without.*]

HAMM: Give me the dog.

CLOV [*looking*]: Quiet!

HAMM [*angrily*]: Give me the dog!

[*Clov drops the telescope, clasps his hands to his head. Pause. He gets down precipitately, looks for the dog, sees it, picks it up, hastens towards Hamm and strikes him violently on the head with the dog.*]

CLOV: There's your dog for you!

[*The dog falls to the ground. Pause.*]

HAMM: He hit me!

CLOV: You drive me mad, I'm mad!

HAMM: If you must hit me, hit me with the axe. [*Pause.*] Or with the gaff, hit me with the gaff. Not with the dog. With the gaff. Or with the axe.

[*Clov picks up the dog and gives it to Hamm who takes it in his arms.*]

CLOV [*imploringly*]: Let's stop playing!

HAMM: Never! [*Pause.*] Put me in my coffin.

CLOV: There are no more coffins.

HAMM: Then let it end!

[*Clov goes towards ladder.*]

With a bang!

[*Clov gets up on ladder, gets down again, looks for telescope, sees it, picks it up, gets up ladder, raises telescope.*]

Of darkness! And me? Did anyone ever have pity on me?

CLOV [*lowering the telescope, turning towards Hamm*]: What? [*Pause.*] Is it me you're referring to?

HAMM [*angrily*]: An aside, ape! Did you never hear an aside before? [*Pause.*] I'm warming up for my last soliloquy.

CLOV: I warn you. I'm going to look at this filth since it's an order. But it's the last time. [*He turns the telescope on the without.*] Let's see. [*He moves the telescope.*] Nothing . . . nothing . . . good . . . good . . . nothing . . . goo—[*He starts, lowers the telescope, examines it, turns it again on the without. Pause.*] Bad luck to it!

HAMM: More complications!

[*Clov gets down.*]

Not an underplot, I trust.

[*Clov moves ladder nearer window, gets up on it, turns telescope on the without.*]

CLOV [*dismayed*]: Looks like a small boy!
HAMM [*sarcastic*]: A small . . . boy!
CLOV: I'll go and see.

[*He gets down, drops the telescope, goes towards door, turns.*]

I'll take the gaff.

[*He looks for the gaff, sees it, picks it up, hastens towards door.*]

HAMM: No!

[*Clov halts.*]

CLOV: No? A potential procreator?
HAMM: If he exists he'll die there or he'll come here. And if he doesn't . . . [*Pause.*]
CLOV: You don't believe me? You think I'm inventing? [*Pause.*]
HAMM: It's the end, Clov, we've come to the end. I don't need you any more. [*Pause.*]
CLOV: Lucky for you. [*He goes towards door.*]
HAMM: Leave me the gaff.

[*Clov gives him the gaff, goes towards door, halts, looks at alarm-clock, takes it down, looks round for a better place to put it, goes to bins, puts it on lid of Nagg's bin. Pause.*]

CLOV: I'll leave you. [*He goes towards door.*]
HAMM: Before you go . . .

[*Clov halts near door.*]

. . . say something.
CLOV: There is nothing to say.
HAMM: A few words . . . to ponder . . . in my heart.
CLOV: Your heart!
HAMM: Yes. [*Pause. Forcibly.*] Yes! [*Pause.*] With the rest, in the end, the shadows, the murmurs, all the trouble, to end up with. [*Pause.*] Clov . . . . He never spoke to me. Then, in the end, before he went, without my having asked him, he spoke to me. He said . . .
CLOV [*despairingly*]: Ah . . . !
HAMM: Something . . . from your heart.
CLOV: My heart!
HAMM: A few words . . . from your heart. [*Pause.*]
CLOV [*fixed gaze, tonelessly, towards auditorium*]: They said to me, That's love, yes, yes, not a doubt, now you see how—
HAMM: Articulate!
CLOV [*as before*]: How easy it is. They said to me, That's friendship, yes, yes, no question, you've found it. They said to me, Here's the place, stop, raise your head and look at all that beauty. That order! They said to me, Come now, you're not a brute

beast, think upon these things and you'll see how all becomes clear. And simple! They said to me, What skilled attention they get, all these dying of their wounds.

HAMM: Enough!

CLOV [*as before*]: I say to myself—sometimes, Clov, you must learn to suffer better than that if you want them to weary of punishing you—one day. I say to myself—sometimes, Clov, you must be there better than that if you want them to let you go—one day. But I feel too old, and too far, to form new habits. Good, it'll never end, I'll never go. [*Pause.*] Then one day, suddenly, it ends, it changes, I don't understand, it dies, or it's me, I don't understand, that either. I ask the words that remain—sleeping, waking, morning, evening. They have nothing to say. [*Pause.*] I open the door of the cell and go. I am so bowed I only see my feet, if I open my eyes, and between my legs a little trail of black dust. I say to myself that the earth is extinguished, though I never saw it lit. [*Pause.*] It's easy going. [*Pause.*] When I fall I'll weep for happiness. [*Pause. He goes towards door.*]

HAMM: Clov!

[*Clov halts, without turning.*]

Nothing.

[*Clov moves on.*]

Clov!

[*Clov halts, without turning.*]

CLOV: This is what we call making an exit.

HAMM: I'm obliged to you, Clov. For your services.

CLOV [*turning, sharply*]: Ah pardon, it's I am obliged to you.

HAMM: It's we are obliged to each other.

[*Pause. Clov goes towards door.*]

One thing more.

[*Clov halts.*]

A last favor.

[*Exit Clov.*]

Cover me with the sheet. [*Long pause.*] No? Good. [*Pause.*] Me to play. [*Pause. Wearily.*] Old endgame lost of old, play and lose and have done with losing. [*Pause. More animated.*] Let me see. [*Pause.*] Ah yes!

[*He tries to move the chair, using the gaff as before. Enter Clov, dressed for the road. Panama hat, tweed coat, raincoat over his arm, umbrella, bag. He halts by the door and stands there, impassive and motionless, his eyes fixed on Hamm, till the end. Hamm gives up.*]

Good. [*Pause.*] Discard. [*He throws away the gaff, makes to throw away the dog, thinks better of it.*] Take it easy. [*Pause.*] And now? [*Pause.*] Raise hat. [*He raises his toque.*] Peace to our . . . arses. [*Pause.*] And put on again. [*He puts on his toque.*] Deuce. [*Pause. He takes off his glasses.*] Wipe. [*He takes out his handkerchief and, without *unfolding it, wipes his glasses.*] And put on again. [*He puts on his glasses, puts back the handkerchief in his pocket.*] We're coming. A few more squirms like that and I'll call. [*Pause.*] A little poetry. [*Pause.*] You prayed—[*Pause. He corrects himself.*] You CRIED for night; it comes—[*Pause. He corrects himself.*] It FALLS: now cry in darkness. [*He repeats, chanting.*] You cried for night; it falls: now cry in darkness. [*Pause.*] Nicely put, that. [*Pause.*] And now? [*Pause.*] Moments for nothing, now as always, time was never and time is over, reckoning closed and story ended. [*Pause. Narrative tone.*] If he could have his child with him. . . . [*Pause.*] It was the moment I was waiting for. [*Pause.*] You don't want to abandon him? You want him to bloom while you are withering? Be there to solace your last million last moments? [*Pause.*] He doesn't realize, all he knows is hunger, and cold, and death to crown it all. But you! You ought to know what the earth is like, nowadays. Oh I put him before his responsibilities! [*Pause. Normal tone.*] Well, there we are, there I am, that's enough. [*He raises the whistle to his lips, hesitates, drops it. Pause.*] Yes, truly! [*He whistles. Pause. Louder. Pause.*] Good. [*Pause.*] Father! [*Pause. Louder.*] Father! [*Pause.*] Good. [*Pause.*] We're coming. [*Pause.*] And to end up with? [*Pause.*] Discard. [*He throws away the dog. He tears the whistle from his neck.*] With my compliments.

[*He throws whistle towards auditorium. Pause. He sniffs. Soft.*]

Clov!

[*Long pause.*]

No? Good.

[*He takes out the handkerchief.*]

Since that's the way we're playing it . . .

[*He unfolds handkerchief.*]

. . . let's play it that way . . .

[*He unfolds.*]

. . . and speak no more about it . . .

[*He finishes unfolding.*]

. . . speak no more.

[*He holds handkerchief spread out before him.*]

Old stancher!

[*Pause.*]

You . . . remain.

[*Pause. He covers his face with handkerchief, lowers his arms to armrests, remains motionless.*]

[*Brief tableau.*]

Curtain

POSTWAR ENGLISH VOICES

W. H. Auden

1907–1973

Wystan Hugh Auden's fantastically wrinkled face is a familiar icon from photographs taken in his later years. Often depicting Auden posing with his ever-present cigarette against a cityscape or airport, the photographs reveal part of Auden's continuing allure, which is that he was a witness, in his writing and in his person, to the changing scene of life and letters in the middle decades of the twentieth century. Auden came to embody a British literary Golden Age that lived on after the conditions that had brought it into being had changed utterly. His imperturbable face, looking much older than it was, had a sagelike quality of wisdom and the measurement of time passing: a map of modern experience.

Born in York, England, Auden had a pampered childhood, and was too young to see service in World War I. He was of the postwar generation, a group of gifted poets and writers who sought to replace the terrible losses of the war, its literary as well as its human casualties. Auden attended Christ Church College, Oxford, where his precocious literary career began in 1928 with the private publication of his *Poems*, thirty copies of which were put together by his friend and fellow writer Stephen Spender at Oxford. Auden joined a number of his friends and peers in heading to Berlin; his friend Christopher Isherwood's *I Am a Camera* (later the basis for the musical *Cabaret*) documented the phenomenon of these expatriate British writers spending their youthful careers in a decadent and exciting Berlin. Like many of the rest—though some died fighting fascism in Spain—Auden returned to England; he became a teacher in Scotland and England while writing feverishly. The cultural ferment of the thirties led Auden in many directions: chiefly, he wrote poetry, but he also became a noted literary critic, and he collaborated with Isherwood and others on plays and screenplays.

Auden's literary and political wanderlust took him to Iceland in 1936, where he wrote *Letters from Iceland* with Louis MacNeice; to Spain, which resulted in much poetry and occasional writing; to China, Japan, and the United States, culminating in the book *On the Frontier*. In 1939 he took an epochal step: he settled in the United States, where he became a citizen in 1946. In this he was a reverse T. S. Eliot—Eliot was an American who became a British citizen and is usually included as a premier writer of British, not American, literature. Auden was an American citizen who is always included in British anthologies, and rarely, if ever, in American collections. Part of Auden's desire to live in America had to do with his need to escape a stifling set of expectations for him that obtained in England—social, literary, and even personal expectations. In 1935, he had married Thomas Mann's daughter Erika, largely to protect her from political persecution in Germany, since Auden was a homosexual and lived for most of his adult life with the poet Chester Kallman, whom he met in 1939.

It was during Auden's teaching and fellowship years in the United States that he began to produce the large oeuvre of his poetry and his criticism. He taught and lectured at many colleges and universities, and read widely, taking a particular interest in the existentialist theology of Søren Kierkegaard. Increasingly impatient with Marxist materialism, Auden found a renewed commitment to Christianity in his later decades. During these years he published such notable milestones as his *Collected Shorter Poems*, *The Age of Anxiety*, and the critical work *The Enchafèd Flood*. In 1958 his definitive *Selected Poetry* was published, followed in 1962 by his magisterial work of criticism, *The Dyer's Hand.* His peripatetic and sometimes difficult teaching life led him to accept an offer from Oxford in 1956, to spend summers in Italy and in Austria, and to make a final move to Oxford and Christ Church College in 1972. However, he died shortly thereafter in 1973, in Austria, where he shared a summer house with Kallman.

The title of one of Auden's major long poems, *The Age of Anxiety*, summons up a reigning motif of Auden's poetic writing. Auden's poetry is edgy, tense, worried, psychoanalytic and yet despondent of the powers of psychoanalysis to allay anxiety. Anxiety is in some ways Auden's muse. This arises from the seriousness with which Auden had gauged the world political situation. Having witnessed the depression, the rise of Nazism, totalitarianism, World War II, the Holocaust, the atomic bomb, and the Cold War, Auden's political realism is tinged inevitably with disillusionment. Modern history is one primary source for Auden's poetry; in poems like *Spain 1937* and *September 1, 1939,* he makes no retreat to purely aesthetic subject matter, or to the past, or to pure experimentation. Auden's is a poetry of waiting rooms, radio broadcasts, armed battalions, and of snatched pleasures treasured all the more for their fleeting magic.

Paradoxically, Auden's moral and political engagements coexist with an anarchic streak, a wry wit, and a love of leisure and play. Auden developed one of the most seductively varied voices in modern poetry, creating an endlessly inventive style that draws at will on Latin elegy, Anglo-Saxon alliterative verse forms, Norse runes and "kennings," technical scientific discourse, and the meters and language of British music hall songs and of American blues singers. All these elements can be present in a single stanza, to sometimes dizzying effect; in other poems, these radically different materials are blended and modulated into a deceptively plain style of great power.

A topic of special concern for Auden was the survival of literary language. How would poetry make claims for its relevance, given that it was now surrounded by so many other voices, from those of mass culture to the exigent rhetoric of war? Auden often compared himself poetically to William Butler Yeats, as another political poet in a time when poetry was seen as largely irrelevant or even antithetical to politics.

Auden's poetry remains a profoundly lyric poetry: that is, it celebrates the singular human voice that sings its lines. It is not surprising that he wrote opera librettos, notably *The Rake's Progress*, which he wrote with Chester Kallman for Igor Stravinsky. Auden was an intellectual inheritor of Freud and Marx—he knew the ways that the self could remain unknown to itself, and the ways that history could relentlessly rush on oblivious of the human lives swept up in its current. Still, the human voice of poetry goes on, even in the age of anxiety, framing its lyric songs. In the late phase of his poetry, Auden had despaired of systems, and returned even more to the meticulous versification he was so well versed in. His poems become almost defiant vehicles of traditional rhyme and meter, lodged in the modern, everyday world, where "in the deserts of the heart," Auden would "let the healing fountain start."

"Sir, no man's enemy, forgiving all"

Sir, no man's enemy, forgiving all
But will his negative inversion, be prodigal:
Send to us power and light, a sovereign touch
Curing the intolerable neural itch,
The exhaustion of weaning, the liar's quinsy,° *tonsillitis*
And the distortions of ingrown virginity.
Prohibit sharply the rehearsed response
And gradually correct the coward's stance;
Cover in time with beams those in retreat
That, spotted, they turn though the reverse were great;
Publish each healer that in city lives

Or country houses at the end of drives;
Harrow the house of the dead; look shining at
New styles of architecture, a change of heart.

October 1929

Lullaby

Lay your sleeping head, my love,
Human on my faithless arm;
Time and fevers burn away
Individual beauty from
Thoughtful children, and the grave
Proves the child ephemeral:
But in my arms till break of day
Let the living creature lie,
Mortal, guilty, but to me
The entirely beautiful.

Soul and body have no bounds:
To lovers as they lie upon
Her tolerant enchanted slope
In their ordinary swoon,
Grave the vision Venus sends
Of supernatural sympathy,
Universal love and hope;
While an abstract insight wakes
Among the glaciers and the rocks
The hermit's carnal ecstasy.

Certainty, fidelity
On the stroke of midnight pass
Like vibrations of a bell
And fashionable madmen raise
Their pedantic boring cry:
Every farthing of the cost,
All the dreaded cards foretell,
Shall be paid, but from this night
Not a whisper, not a thought,
Not a kiss nor look be lost.

Beauty, midnight, vision dies:
Let the winds of dawn that blow
Softly round your dreaming head
Such a day of welcome show
Eye and knocking heart may bless,
Find our mortal world enough;
Noons of dryness find you fed
By the involuntary powers,
Nights of insult let you pass
Watched by every human love.

1937 1940

Spain[1]

Yesterday all the past. The language of size
Spreading to China along the trade-routes; the diffusion
Of the counting-frame and the cromlech;[2]
Yesterday the shadow-reckoning in the sunny climates.
Yesterday the assessment of insurance by cards,
The divination of water; yesterday the invention
Of cart-wheels and clocks, the taming of
Horses; yesterday the bustling world of the navigators.
Yesterday the abolition of fairies and giants;
The fortress like a motionless eagle eyeing the valley,
The chapel built in the forest;
Yesterday the carving of angels and of frightening gargoyles.

The trial of heretics among the columns of stone;
Yesterday the theological feuds in the taverns
And the miraculous cure at the fountain;
Yesterday the Sabbath of Witches. But today the struggle.

Yesterday the installation of dynamos and turbines;
The construction of railways in the colonial desert;
Yesterday the classic lecture
On the origin of Mankind. But today the struggle.

Yesterday the belief in the absolute value of Greek;
The fall of the curtain upon the death of a hero;
Yesterday the prayer to the sunset,
And the adoration of madmen. But today the struggle.

As the poet whispers, startled among the pines
Or, where the loose waterfall sings, compact, or upright
On the crag by the leaning tower:
"O my vision. O send me the luck of the sailor."

And the investigator peers through his instruments
At the inhuman provinces, the virile bacillus
Or enormous Jupiter finished:
"But the lives of my friends. I inquire, I inquire."
And the poor in their fireless lodgings dropping the sheets
Of the evening paper: "Our day is our loss. O show us
History the operator, the
Organiser, Time the refreshing river."

And the nations combine each cry, invoking the life
That shapes the individual belly and orders
The private nocturnal terror:
"Did you not found once the city state of the sponge,

1. Auden visited Spain between January and March 1937, when the civil war between the Spanish government and military-backed Fascist insurgents was at its height. Many foreigners (the so-called "International Brigade") went to Spain at this time to aid the republican forces.
2. Prehistoric stone circle.

"Raise the vast military empires of the shark
And the tiger, establish the robin's plucky canton?
Intervene. O descend as a dove or
A furious papa or a mild engineer: but descend."

And the life, if it answers at all, replies from the heart
And the eyes and the lungs, from the shops and squares of the city:
"O no, I am not the Mover,
Not today, not to you. To you I'm the

"Yes-man, the bar-companion, the easily-duped:
I am whatever you do; I am your vow to be
Good, your humorous story;
I am your business voice; I am your marriage.

"What's your proposal? To build the Just City? I will.
I agree. Or is it the suicide pact, the romantic
Death? Very well, I accept, for
I am your choice, your decision: yes, I am Spain."

Many have heard it on remote peninsulas,
On sleepy plains, in the aberrant fishermen's islands,
In the corrupt heart of the city;
Have heard and migrated like gulls or the seeds of a flower.

They clung like burrs to the long expresses that lurch
Through the unjust lands, through the night, through the alpine tunnel;
They floated over the oceans;
They walked the passes: they came to present their lives.

On that arid square, that fragment nipped off from hot
Africa, soldered so crudely to inventive Europe,
On that tableland scored by rivers,
Our fever's menacing shapes are precise and alive.

Tomorrow, perhaps, the future: the research on fatigue
And the movements of packers; the gradual exploring of all the
Octaves of radiation;
Tomorrow the enlarging of consciousness by diet and breathing.

Tomorrow the rediscovery of romantic love;
The photographing of ravens; all the fun under
Liberty's masterful shadow;
Tomorrow the hour of the pageant-master and the musician.

Tomorrow, for the young, the poets exploding like bombs,
The walks by the lake, the winter of perfect communion;
Tomorrow the bicycle races
Through the suburbs on summer evenings: but today the struggle.

Today the inevitable increase in the chances of death;
The conscious acceptance of guilt in the fact of murder;
Today the expending of powers
On the flat ephemeral pamphlet and the boring meeting.

Today the makeshift consolations; the shared cigarette;
The cards in the candle-lit barn and the scraping concert,
The masculine jokes; today the
Fumbled and unsatisfactory embrace before hurting.

The stars are dead; the animals will not look:
We are left alone with our day, and the time is short and
History to the defeated
May say Alas but cannot help or pardon.

1937

September 1, 1939[1]

I sit in one of the dives
On Fifty-Second Street
Uncertain and afraid
As the clever hopes expire
Of a low dishonest decade:
Waves of anger and fear
Circulate over the bright
And darkened lands of the earth,
Obsessing our private lives;
The unmentionable odour of death
Offends the September night.

Accurate scholarship can
Unearth the whole offence
From Luther[2] until now
That has driven a culture mad,
Find what occurred at Linz,[3]
What huge imago made
A psychopathic god:[4]
I and the public know
What all schoolchildren learn,
Those to whom evil is done
Do evil in return.

Exiled Thucydides[5] knew
All that a speech can say
About Democracy,

1. Auden arrived in New York City, where he was to spend World War II and much of the rest of his life, in January 1939. German forces marched into Poland on 1 September 1939; Britain and France declared war on 3 September.

2. Martin Luther, German religious reformer (1483–1546), whose criticisms of Roman Catholic doctrine sparked the Protestant Reformation in Europe.

3. Linz, Austria, was Adolf Hitler's birthplace.

4. In the psychological terminology developed by C. G. Jung (1875–1961), an *imago* is an idealized mental image of self or others, especially parental figures.

5. Fifth-century Athenian historian and general in the Peloponnesian War between Athens and Sparta (431–404 B.C.E.). In his famous *History of the Peloponnesian War*, which follows events until 411 B.C.E., Thucydides records the Athenian statesman Pericles's *Funeral Oration*, given at the end of the first year of the war. In it, Pericles describes the benefits and possible dangers of democratic government as it was then practiced at Athens. Thucydides himself was exiled from Athens in 424 B.C.E., following a military defeat incurred under his leadership.

And what dictators do,
The elderly rubbish they talk
To an apathetic grave;
Analysed all in his book,
The enlightenment driven away,
The habit-forming pain,
Mismanagement and grief:
We must suffer them all again.

Into this neutral air
Where blind skyscrapers use
Their full height to proclaim
The strength of Collective Man,
Each language pours its vain
Competitive excuse:
But who can live for long
In an euphoric dream;
Out of the mirror they stare,
Imperialism's face
And the international wrong.

Faces along the bar
Cling to their average day:
The lights must never go out,
The music must always play,
All the conventions conspire
To make this fort assume
The furniture of home;
Lest we should see where we are,
Lost in a haunted wood,
Children afraid of the night
Who have never been happy or good.

The windiest militant trash
Important Persons shout
Is not so crude as our wish:
What mad Nijinsky wrote
About Diaghilev
Is true of the normal heart;[6]
For the error bred in the bone
Of each woman and each man
Craves what it cannot have,
Not universal love
But to be loved alone.

From the conservative dark
Into the ethical life

6. Vaslav Nijinsky (1890–1950), principal male dancer in the Ballets Russes company under the direction of Sergei Pavlovich Diaghilev (1872–1929). The company revolutionized the world of dance, causing a sensation on its visit to Paris in 1909. Auden borrowed the following lines from Nijinsky's (1937) *Diary*: "Diaghilev does not want universal love, but to be loved alone."

The dense commuters come,
Repeating their morning vow,
"I *will* be true to the wife,
I'll concentrate more on my work,"
And helpless governors wake
To resume their compulsory game:
Who can release them now,
Who can reach the deaf,
Who can speak for the dumb?

All I have is a voice
To undo the folded lie,
The romantic lie in the brain
Of the sensual man-in-the-street
And the lie of Authority
Whose buildings grope the sky:
There is no such thing as the State
And no one exists alone;
Hunger allows no choice
To the citizen or the police;
We must love one another or die.

Defenceless under the night
Our world in stupor lies;
Yet, dotted everywhere,
Ironic points of light
Flash out wherever the Just
Exchange their messages:
May I, composed like them
Of Eros and of dust,
Beleaguered by the same
Negation and despair,
Show an affirming flame.

1939 1940

Musée des Beaux Arts[1]

About suffering they were never wrong,
The Old Masters: how well they understood
Its human position; how it takes place
While someone else is eating or opening a window or just walking dully along;
How, when the aged are reverently, passionately waiting
For the miraculous birth, there always must be
Children who did not specially want it to happen, skating
On a pond at the edge of the wood:
They never forgot

1. The Musées Royaux des Beaux-Arts in Brussels contain a collection of paintings by the Flemish painter Pieter Brueghel (1525–1569) that includes *The Fall of Icarus;* Brueghel is famous for his acute observation of ordinary life. A figure from Greek mythology, Icarus had wings of wax and feathers but flew too close to the sun, which melted the wax and caused him to fall into the sea.

That even the dreadful martyrdom must run its course
Anyhow in a corner, some untidy spot
Where the dogs go on with their doggy life and the torturer's horse
Scratches its innocent behind on a tree.

In Brueghel's *Icarus*, for instance: how everything turns away
Quite leisurely from the disaster; the ploughman may
Have heard the splash, the forsaken cry,
But for him it was not an important failure; the sun shone
As it had to on the white legs disappearing into the green
Water; and the expensive delicate ship that must have seen
Something amazing, a boy falling out of the sky,
Had somewhere to get to and sailed calmly on.

1938 1940

In Memory of W. B. Yeats

(d. January 1939)

1

He disappeared in the dead of winter:
The brooks were frozen, the air-ports almost deserted,
And snow disfigured the public statues;
The mercury sank in the mouth of the dying day.
O all the instruments agree
The day of his death was a dark cold day.

Far from his illness
The wolves ran on through the evergreen forests,
The peasant river was untempted by the fashionable quays;
By mourning tongues
The death of the poet was kept from his poems.

But for him it was his last afternoon as himself,
An afternoon of nurses and rumours;
The provinces of his body revolted,
The squares of his mind were empty,
Silence invaded the suburbs,
The current of his feeling failed: he became his admirers.

Now he is scattered among a hundred cities
And wholly given over to unfamiliar affections;
To find his happiness in another kind of wood
And be punished under a foreign code of conscience.
The words of a dead man
Are modified in the guts of the living.

But in the importance and noise of to-morrow
When the brokers are roaring like beasts on the floor of the Bourse,[1]
And the poor have the sufferings to which they are fairly accustomed,

1. Stock exchange.

And each in the cell of himself is almost convinced of his freedom;
A few thousand will think of this day
As one thinks of a day when one did something slightly unusual.
O all the instruments agree
The day of his death was a dark cold day.

2

You were silly like us: your gift survived it all;
The parish of rich women, physical decay,
Yourself; mad Ireland hurt you into poetry.
Now Ireland has her madness and her weather still,
For poetry makes nothing happen: it survives
In the valley of its saying where executives
Would never want to tamper; it flows south
From ranches of isolation and the busy griefs,
Raw towns that we believe and die in; it survives,
A way of happening, a mouth.

3

Earth, receive an honoured guest;
William Yeats is laid to rest:
Let the Irish vessel lie
Emptied of its poetry.

Time that is intolerant
Of the brave and innocent,
And indifferent in a week
To a beautiful physique,

Worships language and forgives
Everyone by whom it lives;
Pardons cowardice, conceit,
Lays its honours at their feet.

Time that with this strange excuse
Pardoned Kipling and his views,
And will pardon Paul Claudel,[2]
Pardons him for writing well.

In the nightmare of the dark
All the dogs of Europe bark,
And the living nations wait,
Each sequestered in its hate;

Intellectual disgrace
Stares from every human face,
And the seas of pity lie
Locked and frozen in each eye.

2. Rudyard Kipling (1865–1936), short-story writer, poet, and novelist remembered for his celebration of British imperialism; Paul Claudel (1868–1955), French poet and diplomat noted for his conservative views.

Follow, poet, follow right
To the bottom of the night,
With your unconstraining voice
Still persuade us to rejoice;

With the farming of a verse
Make a vineyard of the curse,
Sing of human unsuccess
In a rapture of distress;

In the deserts of the heart
Let the healing fountain start,
In the prison of his days
Teach the free man how to praise.

February 1939 1940

Law Like Love

Law, say the gardeners, is the sun,
Law is the one
All gardeners obey
To-morrow, yesterday, to-day.

Law is the wisdom of the old,
The impotent grandfathers feebly scold;
The grandchildren put out a treble tongue,
Law is the senses of the young.

Law, says the priest with a priestly look,
Expounding to an unpriestly people,
Law is the words in my priestly book,
Law is my pulpit and my steeple.

Law, says the judge as he looks down his nose,
Speaking clearly and most severely,
Law is as I've told you before,
Law is as you know I suppose,
Law is but let me explain it once more,
Law is The Law.

Yet law-abiding scholars write:
Law is neither wrong nor right,
Law is only crimes
Punished by places and by times,
Law is the clothes men wear
Anytime, anywhere,
Law is Good morning and Good night.

Others say, Law is our Fate;
Others say, Law is our State;
Others say, others say
Law is no more,
Law has gone away.

And always the loud angry crowd,
Very angry and very loud,
Law is We,
And always the soft idiot softly Me.

If we, dear, know we know no more
Than they about the Law,
If I no more than you
Know what we should and should not do
Except that all agree
Gladly or miserably
That the Law is
And that all know this,
If therefore thinking it absurd
To identify Law with some other word,
Unlike so many men
I cannot say Law is again,
No more than they can we suppress
The universal wish to guess
Or slip out of our own position
Into an unconcerned condition.

Although I can at least confine
Your vanity and mine
To stating timidly
A timid similarity,
We shall boast anyway:
Like love I say.

Like love we don't know where or why,
Like love we can't compel or fly,
Like love we often weep,
Like love we seldom keep.

September 1939

In Memory of Sigmund Freud[1]

When there are so many we shall have to mourn,
when grief has been made so public, and exposed
to the critique of a whole epoch
the frailty of our conscience and anguish,

of whom shall we speak? For every day they die
among us, those who were doing us some good,
who knew it was never enough but
hoped to improve a little by living.

Such was this doctor: still at eighty he wished
to think of our life from whose unruliness

1. Founder of psychoanalysis and modern psychiatry.

so many plausible young futures
with threats or flattery ask obedience,

but his wish was denied him: he closed his eyes
upon that last picture, common to us all,
of problems like relatives gathered
puzzled and jealous about our dying.

For about him till the very end were still
those he had studied, the fauna of the night,
and shades that still waited to enter
the bright circle of his recognition

turned elsewhere with their disappointment as he
was taken away from his life interest
to go back to the earth in London,
an important Jew who died in exile.[2]

Only Hate was happy, hoping to augment
his practice now, and his dingy clientele
who think they can be cured by killing
and covering the gardens with ashes.

They are still alive, but in a world he changed
simply by looking back with no false regrets;
all he did was to remember
like the old and be honest like children.

He wasn't clever at all: he merely told
the unhappy Present to recite the Past
like a poetry lesson till sooner
or later it faltered at the line where

long ago the accusations had begun,
and suddenly knew by whom it had been judged,
how rich life had been and how silly,
and was life-forgiven and more humble,

able to approach the Future as a friend
without a wardrobe of excuses, without
a set mask of rectitude or an
embarrassing over-familiar gesture.

No wonder the ancient cultures of conceit
in his technique of unsettlement foresaw
the fall of princes, the collapse of
their lucrative patterns of frustration:

if he succeeded, why, the Generalised Life
would become impossible, the monolith
of State be broken and prevented
the co-operation of avengers.

2. Freud died in London, having fled his native Austria during its annexation by the Nazis.

Of course they called on God, but he went his way
down among the lost people like Dante,[3] down
to the stinking fosse° where the injured *ditch or moat*
lead the ugly life of the rejected,

and showed us what evil is, not, as we thought,
deeds that must be punished, but our lack of faith,
our dishonest mood of denial,
the concupiscence° of the oppressor. *lust*

If some traces of the autocratic pose,
the paternal strictness he distrusted, still
clung to his utterance and features,
it was a protective coloration

for one who'd lived among enemies so long:
if often he was wrong and, at times, absurd,
to us he is no more a person
now but a whole climate of opinion

under whom we conduct our different lives:
Like weather he can only hinder or help,
the proud can still be proud but find it
a little harder, the tyrant tries to

make do with him but doesn't care for him much:
he quietly surrounds all our habits of growth
and extends, till the tired in even
the remotest miserable duchy° *area ruled by a duke or duchess*

have felt the change in their bones and are cheered,
till the child, unlucky in his little State,
some hearth where freedom is excluded,
a hive whose honey is fear and worry,

feels calmer now and somehow assured of escape,
while, as they lie in the grass of our neglect,
so many long-forgotten objects
revealed by his undiscouraged shining

are returned to us and made precious again;
games we had thought we must drop as we grew up,
little noises we dared not laugh at,
faces we made when no one was looking.

But he wishes us more than this. To be free
is often to be lonely. He would unite
the unequal moieties° fractured *halves or portions*
by our own well-meaning sense of justice,

would restore to the larger the wit and will
the smaller possesses but can only use

3. Dante Alighieri (1265–1321), poet of the *Divine Comedy*, in which the poet descends and visits the souls of the dead.

for arid disputes, would give back to
the son the mother's richness of feeling:

but he would have us remember most of all
to be enthusiastic over the night,
not only for the sense of wonder
it alone has to offer, but also

because it needs our love. With large sad eyes
its delectable creatures look up and beg
us dumbly to ask them to follow:
they are exiles who long for the future

that lies in our power, they too would rejoice
if allowed to serve enlightenment like him,
even to bear our cry of "Judas,"
as he did and all must bear who serve it.

One rational voice is dumb. Over his grave
the household of Impulse mourns one dearly loved:
sad is Eros, builder of cities,
and weeping anarchic Aphrodite.

November 1939

The Hidden Law

The Hidden Law does not deny
Our laws of probability,
But takes the atom and the star
And human beings as they are,
And answers nothing when we lie.

It is the only reason why
No government can codify,
And legal definitions mar
The Hidden Law.

Its utter patience will not try
To stop us if we want to die:
When we escape It in a car,
When we forget It in a bar,
These are the ways we're punished by
The Hidden Law.

1940

In Praise of Limestone[1]

If it form the one landscape that we, the inconstant ones,
Are consistently homesick for, this is chiefly

1. This poem is set in the landscape of Yorkshire, where Auden was born.

Because it dissolves in water. Mark these rounded slopes
With their surface fragrance of thyme and, beneath,
A secret system of caves and conduits; hear the springs
That spurt out everywhere with a chuckle,
Each filling a private pool for its fish and carving
Its own little ravine whose cliffs entertain
The butterfly and the lizard; examine this region
Of short distances and definite places:
What could be more like Mother or a fitter background
For her son, the flirtatious male who lounges
Against a rock in the sunlight, never doubting
That for all his faults he is loved; whose works are but
Extensions of his power to charm? From weathered outcrop
To hill-top temple, from appearing waters to
Conspicuous fountains, from a wild to a formal vineyard,
Are ingenious but short steps that a child's wish
To receive more attention than his brothers, whether
By pleasing or teasing, can easily take.

Watch, then, the band of rivals as they climb up and down
Their steep stone gennels[2] in twos and threes, at times
Arm in arm, but never, thank God, in step; or engaged
On the shady side of a square at midday in
Voluble discourse, knowing each other too well to think
There are any important secrets, unable
To conceive a god whose temper-tantrums are moral
And not to be pacified by a clever line
Or a good lay: for, accustomed to a stone that responds,
They have never had to veil their faces in awe
Of a crater whose blazing fury could not be fixed;
Adjusted to the local needs of valleys
Where everything can be touched or reached by walking,
Their eyes have never looked into infinite space
Through the lattice-work of a nomad's comb; born lucky,
Their legs have never encountered the fungi
And insects of the jungle, the monstrous forms and lives
With which we have nothing, we like to hope, in common.
So, when one of them goes to the bad, the way his mind works
Remains comprehensible: to become a pimp
Or deal in fake jewellery or ruin a fine tenor voice
For effects that bring down the house, could happen to all
But the best and worst of us . . .
That is why, I suppose,
The best and worst never stayed here long but sought
Immoderate soils where the beauty was not so external,
The light less public and the meaning of life
Something more than a mad camp. "Come!" cried the granite wastes,
"How evasive is your humour, how accidental

2. Channels.

Your kindest kiss, how permanent is death." (Saints-to-be
Slipped away sighing.) "Come!" purred the clays and gravels.
"On our plains there is room for armies to drill; rivers
Wait to be tamed and slaves to construct you a tomb
In the grand manner: soft as the earth is mankind and both
Need to be altered." (Intendant Caesars rose and
Left, slamming the door.) But the really reckless were fetched
By an older colder voice, the oceanic whisper:
"I am the solitude that asks and promises nothing;
That is how I shall set you free. There is no love;
There are only the various envies, all of them sad."
They were right, my dear, all those voices were right
And still are; this land is not the sweet home that it looks,
Nor its peace the historical calm of a site
Where something was settled once and for all: A backward
And dilapidated province, connected
To the big busy world by a tunnel, with a certain
Seedy appeal, is that all it is now? Not quite:
It has a worldly duty which in spite of itself
It does not neglect, but calls into question
All the Great Powers assume; it disturbs our rights. The poet,
Admired for his earnest habit of calling
The sun the sun, his mind Puzzle, is made uneasy
By these marble statues which so obviously doubt
His antimythological myth; and these gamins,[3]
Pursuing the scientist down the tiled colonnade
With such lively offers, rebuke his concern for Nature's
Remotest aspects: I, too, am reproached, for what
And how much you know. Not to lose time, not to get caught,
Not to be left behind, not, please! to resemble
The beasts who repeat themselves, or a thing like water
Or stone whose conduct can be predicted, these
Are our Common Prayer, whose greatest comfort is music
Which can be made anywhere, is invisible,
And does not smell. In so far as we have to look forward
To death as a fact, no doubt we are right: But if
Sins can be forgiven, if bodies rise from the dead,
These modifications of matter into
Innocent athletes and gesticulating fountains,
Made solely for pleasure, make a further point:
The blessed will not care what angle they are regarded from,
Having nothing to hide. Dear, I know nothing of
Either, but when I try to imagine a faultless love
Or the life to come, what I hear is the murmur
Of underground streams, what I see is a limestone landscape.

1948

3. Street urchins.

Philip Larkin

1922–1985

Philip Larkin's lifetime production of poems was quite small, but highly influential; he is best known for his three last volumes, *The Less Deceived* (1955), *The Whitsun Weddings* (1964), and *High Windows* (1974), which together collect fewer than one hundred poems. During his lifetime, however, he fulfilled the role—a role that every society seems to require—of the crotchety traditionalist poet, becoming famous for what the poet and critic Donald Hall has called a "genuine, uncultivated, sincere philistinism."

Born in Coventry, Larkin completed a BA and MA at Oxford (where he was a friend of the novelist Kingsley Amis), and became a professional librarian, working at the University of Hull from 1955 until his death. After two modestly successful novels (*Jill* and *A Girl in Winter*) and two undistinguished volumes of poetry (*The North Ship* and *XX Poems*), Larkin established himself as a new and important voice in British poetry with his collection *The Less Deceived*. According to most critics, the influence of Thomas Hardy's poetry was decisive; Seamus Heaney writes that the "slips and excesses" of his first two volumes—consisting, primarily, of embarrassing echoes of W. B. Yeats—led Larkin "to seek the antidote of Thomas Hardy."

Larkin was attracted to Hardy's bleak outlook on life, as well as his skilled versification and spare language. Larkin's dark vision remained unremitting as late as *Aubade*, the last poem to be published during his lifetime:

> I work all day, and get half-drunk at night.
> Waking at four to soundless dark, I stare.
> In time the curtain-edges will grow light.
> Till then I see what's really always there:
> Unresting death, a whole day nearer now,
> Making all thought impossible but how
> And where and when I shall myself die.

Like the most famous postwar British playwright, Samuel Beckett, the most important postwar British poet was not above having a laugh at his own despair; in an oft-repeated remark, Larkin told an interviewer that "deprivation is for me what daffodils were for Wordsworth."

Larkin is one of the most English of modern British poets; he refused to read "foreign" literature—including most American poetry—or to travel abroad; Hull became the center and circumference of his poetic world. He kept to himself to an extraordinary degree; he never married, nor did he maintain any longstanding intimate relationship. In his obituary for Larkin, Kingsley Amis described him as "a man much driven in upon himself, with increasing deafness from early middle age cruelly emphasizing his seclusion."

Even in his solitude, though, Larkin kept up a running dialogue with the outside world, not only as a poet but as a jazz reviewer for many years. His encyclopedic knowledge of jazz provides the basis for his probing, dyspeptic account of modernity in the opening essay of his collection *All What Jazz*. In this essay as in his verse, Larkin's writing is pointed, skeptical, acerbic—and always self-consciously English.

Church Going

Once I am sure there's nothing going on
I step inside, letting the door thud shut.

Another church: matting, seats, and stone,
And little books; sprawlings of flowers, cut
For Sunday, brownish now; some brass and stuff
Up at the holy end; the small neat organ;
And a tense, musty, unignorable silence,
Brewed God knows how long. Hatless, I take off
My cycle-clips in awkward reverence,
Move forward, run my hand around the font.
From where I stand, the roof looks almost new—
Cleaned, or restored? Someone would know: I don't.
Mounting the lectern, I peruse a few
Hectoring large-scale verses, and pronounce
"Here endeth" much more loudly than I'd meant.
The echoes snigger briefly. Back at the door
I sign the book, donate an Irish sixpence,
Reflect the place was not worth stopping for.

Yet stop I did: in fact I often do,
And always end much at a loss like this,
Wondering what to look for; wondering, too,
When churches fall completely out of use
What we shall turn them into, if we shall keep
A few cathedrals chronically on show,
Their parchment, plate and pyx[1] in locked cases,
And let the rest rent-free to rain and sheep.
Shall we avoid them as unlucky places?

Or, after dark, will dubious women come
To make their children touch a particular stone;
Pick simples° for a cancer; or on some *medicinal plants*
Advised night see walking a dead one?
Power of some sort or other will go on
In games, in riddles, seemingly at random;
But superstition, like belief, must die,
And what remains when disbelief has gone?
Grass, weedy pavement, brambles, buttress, sky,

A shape less recognisable each week,
A purpose more obscure. I wonder who
Will be the last, the very last, to seek
This place for what it was; one of the crew
That tap and jot and know what rood-lofts[2] were?
Some ruin-bibber, randy for antique,
Or Christmas-addict, counting on a whiff
Of gown-and-bands and organ-pipes and myrrh?
Or will he be my representative,

1. The vessel in which the consecrated bread of the Eucharist is kept.

2. Loft at the top of a carved wood or stone screen, separating the nave from the chancel of a church.

Bored, uninformed, knowing the ghostly silt
Dispersed, yet tending to this cross of ground
Through suburb scrub because it held unspilt
So long and equably what since is found
Only in separation—marriage, and birth,
And death, and thoughts of these—for which was built
This special shell? For, though I've no idea
What this accoutred frowsty° barn is worth, *stuffy*
It pleases me to stand in silence here;

A serious house on serious earth it is,
In whose blent air all our compulsions meet,
Are recognised, and robed as destinies.
And that much never can be obsolete,
Since someone will forever be surprising
A hunger in himself to be more serious,
And gravitating with it to this ground,
Which, he once heard, was proper to grow wise in,
If only that so many dead lie round.

1954 1955

The Importance of Elsewhere

Lonely in Ireland, since it was not home,
Strangeness made sense. The salt rebuff of speech,
Insisting so on difference, made me welcome:
Once that was recognised, we were in touch.

Their draughty streets, end-on to hills, the faint
Archaic smell of dockland, like a stable,
The herring-hawker's cry, dwindling, went
To prove me separate, not unworkable.

Living in England has no such excuse:
These are my customs and establishments
It would be much more serious to refuse.
Here no elsewhere underwrites my existence.

13 June 1955

MCMXIV[1]

Those long uneven lines
Standing as patiently
As if they were stretched outside
The Oval or Villa Park,
The crowns of hats, the sun
On moustached archaic faces

1. The year 1914, in the style of a monument to the war dead.

Grinning as if it were all
An August Bank Holiday lark;

And the shut shops, the bleached
Established names on the sunblinds,
The farthings and sovereigns,
And dark-clothed children at play
Called after kings and queens,
The tin advertisements
For cocoa and twist, and the pubs
Wide open all day;

And the countryside not caring:
The place-names all hazed over
With flowering grasses, and fields
Shadowing Domesday[2] lines
Under wheat's restless silence;
The differently-dressed servants
With tiny rooms in huge houses,
The dust behind limousines;

Never such innocence,
Never before or since,
As changed itself to past
Without a word—the men
Leaving the gardens tidy,
The thousands of marriages
Lasting a little while longer:
Never such innocence again.

1960 1964

Talking in Bed

Talking in bed ought to be easiest,
Lying together there goes back so far,
An emblem of two people being honest.

Yet more and more time passes silently.
Outside, the wind's incomplete unrest
Builds and disperses clouds about the sky,

And dark towns heap up on the horizon.
None of this cares for us. Nothing shows why
At this unique distance from isolation

It becomes still more difficult to find
Words at once true and kind,
Or not untrue and not unkind.

1960 1964

2. The Domesday Book is the medieval record of the extent, value, and ownership of lands in England.

High Windows

When I see a couple of kids
And guess he's fucking her and she's
Taking pills or wearing a diaphragm,
I know this is paradise

Everyone old has dreamed of all their lives—
Bonds and gestures pushed to one side
Like an outdated combine harvester,
And everyone young going down the long slide

To happiness, endlessly. I wonder if
Anyone looked at me, forty years back,
And thought, *That'll be the life;*
No God any more, or sweating in the dark

About hell and that, or having to hide
What you think of the priest. He
And his lot will all go down the long slide
Like free bloody birds. And immediately

Rather than words comes the thought of high windows:
The sun-comprehending glass,
And beyond it, the deep blue air, that shows
Nothing, and is nowhere, and is endless.

1967 1974

Annus Mirabilis°

year of wonders

Sexual intercourse began
In nineteen sixty-three
(Which was rather late for me)—
Between the end of the *Chatterley* ban
And the Beatles' first LP.[1]

Up till then there'd only been
A sort of bargaining,
A wrangle for a ring,
A shame that started at sixteen
And spread to everything.

Then all at once the quarrel sank:
Everyone felt the same,
And every life became
A brilliant breaking of the bank,
A quite unlosable game.

1. The British obscenity ban against D.H. Lawrence's novel *Lady Chatterly's Lover* was lifted on November 2, 1960; the Beatles's first LP, *Please Please Me*, was released in the UK on March 22, 1963.

So life was never better than
In nineteen sixty-three
(Though just too late for me)—
Between the end of the *Chatterley* ban
And the Beatles' first LP.

16 June 1967

Homage to a Government

Next year we are to bring the soldiers home
For lack of money, and it is all right.
Places they guarded, or kept orderly,
Must guard themselves, and keep themselves orderly.
We want the money for ourselves at home
Instead of working. And this is all right.

It's hard to say who wanted it to happen,
But now it's been decided nobody minds.
The places are a long way off, not here,
Which is all right, and from what we hear
The soldiers there only made trouble happen.
Next year we shall be easier in our minds.

Next year we shall be living in a country
That brought its soldiers home for lack of money.
The statues will be standing in the same
Tree-muffled squares, and look nearly the same.
Our children will not know it's a different country.
All we can hope to leave them now is money.

10 January 1969

Aubade

I work all day, and get half-drunk at night.
Waking at four to soundless dark, I stare.
In time the curtain-edges will grow light.
Till then I see what's really always there:
Unresting death, a whole day nearer now,
Making all thought impossible but how
And where and when I shall myself die.
Arid interrogation: yet the dread
Of dying, and being dead,
Flashes afresh to hold and horrify.

The mind blanks at the glare. Not in remorse
—The good not done, the love not given, time
Torn off unused—nor wretchedly because
An only life can take so long to climb
Clear of its wrong beginnings, and may never;

But at the total emptiness for ever,
The sure extinction that we travel to
And shall be lost in always. Not to be here,
Not to be anywhere,
And soon; nothing more terrible, nothing more true.

This is a special way of being afraid
No trick dispels. Religion used to try,
That vast moth-eaten musical brocade
Created to pretend we never die,
And specious stuff that says *No rational being*
Can fear a thing it will not feel, not seeing
That this is what we fear—no sight, no sound,
No touch or taste or smell, nothing to think with,
Nothing to love or link with,
The anaesthetic from which none come round.

And so it stays just on the edge of vision,
A small unfocused blur, a standing chill
That slows each impulse down to indecision.
Most things may never happen: this one will,
And realisation of it rages out
In furnace-fear when we are caught without
People or drink. Courage is no good:
It means not scaring others. Being brave
Lets no one off the grave.
Death is no different whined at than withstood.

Slowly light strengthens, and the room takes shape.
It stands plain as a wardrobe, what we know,
Have always known, know that we can't escape,
Yet can't accept. One side will have to go.
Meanwhile telephones crouch, getting ready to ring
In locked-up offices, and all the uncaring
Intricate rented world begins to rouse.
The sky is white as clay, with no sun.
Work has to be done.
Postmen like doctors go from house to house.

29 November 1977

Thom Gunn

b. 1929

Another of the twentieth-century's celebrated Anglo-American poets, Thom Gunn continues to be identified in the public mind as English, while he has lived almost exclusively in California since his first book was published in 1954. In the case of Gunn's poetry, this transatlantic identity is largely channeled through the medium of a popular culture that knows no national boundaries: growing up in post–World War II England and later San Francisco, Gunn is a poet who early chose to write about the most lowbrow of topics (motorcycle gangs, surfing, Elvis Presley, the leather scene) in classically trained and restrained high-verse forms. Though not the most celebrated of his generation, Gunn's will be the body of poetry, as the critic Blake Morrison has remarked, to which "future social historians and cultural anthropologists wanting to learn about the texture of our times" will turn in years to come. This observation seems even more accurate now than when it was written, as Gunn's poems about the AIDS crisis have poignantly demonstrated.

Gunn grew up in Hampstead, a well-heeled neighborhood of London, and was from his earliest years both a voracious reader and precocious writer. He studied English at Trinity College, Cambridge, and published his first book of poems, *Fighting Terms*, shortly after his graduation in 1954. These early poems were characterized by a youthful enthusiasm for strong authority figures, especially countercultural ones; the homosexuality that Gunn recognized in his Cambridge days would not be acknowledged openly in his poetry until *The Passages of Joy* (1982), and it is not difficult to see an unacknowledged homoeroticism energizing many of the poems of his early volumes. After receiving his B.A., Gunn moved to California, where he studied at Stanford; he soon established a home base in San Francisco, reveling in the countercultural scene that flourished there in the 1960s.

Early in his career, Gunn was identified with the group of young British poets known as The Movement; but a literary or political movement is always a somewhat fixed, stable, and inflexible thing, whereas Gunn's poetry—as his punning 1957 volume title suggests—is rather about "the sense of movement." He has explored many poetic and geographic terrains, and inhabited many different poetic *personae*, during his half-century as a public poet; perhaps the most vital of all came in 1992, when his volume *The Man with Night Sweats* (from which the poems *The Hug*, *Patch Work*, and *The Missing* are taken) was published. Though writing of course as a gay man for whom the tragedy of AIDS had been a particularly personal one, Gunn succeeds in these poems in bringing the implications and repercussions of the pandemic home for one and all.

Lines for a Book

I think of all the toughs through history
And thank heaven they lived, continually.
I praise the overdogs from Alexander
To those who would not play with Stephen Spender.[1]
Their pride exalted some, some overthrew,
But was not vanity at last: they knew
That though the mind has also got a place
It's not in marvelling at its mirrored face
And evident sensibility. It's better
To go and see your friend than write a letter;
To be a soldier than to be a cripple;
To take an early weaning from the nipple
Than think your mother is the only girl;
To be insensitive, to steel the will,
Than sit irresolute all day at stool
Inside the heart; and to despise the fool,
Who may not help himself and may not choose,
Than give him pity which he cannot use.

1. British poet of the generation preceding Gunn's; see page 2536.

I think of those exclusive by their action,
For whom mere thought could be no satisfaction–
The athletes lying under tons of dirt
Or standing gelded so they cannot hurt
The pale curators and the families
By calling up disturbing images.
I think of all the toughs through history
And thank heaven they lived, continually.

Elvis Presley

Two minutes long it pitches through some bar:
Unreeling from a corner box, the sigh
Of this one, in his gangling finery
And crawling sideburns, wielding a guitar.

The limitations where he found success
Are ground on which he, panting, stretches out
In turn, promiscuously, by every note.
Our idiosyncrasy and our likeness.

We keep ourselves in touch with a mere dime:
Distorting hackneyed words in hackneyed songs
He turns revolt into a style, prolongs
The impulse to a habit of the time.

Whether he poses or is real, no cat
Bothers to say: the pose held is a stance,
Which, generation of the very chance
It wars on, may be posture for combat.

A Map of the City

I stand upon a hill and see
A luminous country under me,
Through which at two the drunk must weave;
The transient's pause, the sailor's leave.

I notice, looking down the hill,
Arms braced upon a window sill;
And on the web of fire escapes
Move the potential, the grey shapes.

I hold the city here, complete:
And every shape defined by light
Is mine, or corresponds to mine,
Some flickering or some steady shine.

This map is ground of my delight.
Between the limits, night by night,
I watch a malady's advance,
I recognize my love of chance.

By the recurrent lights I see
Endless potentiality,

The crowded, broken, and unfinished!
I would not have the risk diminished.

Black Jackets

In the silence that prolongs the span
Rawly of music when the record ends,
The red-haired boy who drove a van
In weekday overalls but, like his friends,

Wore cycle boots and jacket here
To suit the Sunday hangout he was in,
Heard, as he stretched back from his beer,
Leather creak softly round his neck and chin.

Before him, on a coal-black sleeve
Remote exertion had lined, scratched, and burned
Insignia that could not revive
The heroic fall or climb where they were earned.

On the other drinkers bent together,
Concocting selves for their impervious kit,
He saw it as no more than leather
Which, taut across the shoulders grown to it,

Sent through the dimness of a bar
As sudden and anonymous hints of light
As those that shipping give, that are
Now flickers in the Bay, now lost in night.

He stretched out like a cat, and rolled
The bitterish taste of beer upon his tongue,
And listened to a joke being told:
The present was the things he stayed among.

If it was only loss he wore,
He wore it to assert, with fierce devotion,
Complicity and nothing more.
He recollected his initiation,

And one especially of the rites.
For on his shoulders they had put tattoos:
The group's name on the left, The Knights,
And on the right the slogan Born To Lose.

From the Wave

It mounts at sea, a concave wall
Down-ribbed with shine,
And pushes forward, building tall
Its steep incline.

Then from their hiding rise to sight
Black shapes on boards

Bearing before the fringe of white
    It mottles towards.

Their pale feet curl, they poise their weight
    With a learn'd skill.
It is the wave they imitate
    Keeps them so still.

The marbling bodies have become
    Half wave, half men,
Grafted it seems by feet of foam
    Some seconds, then,

Late as they can, they slice the face
    In timed procession:
Balance is triumph in this place,
    Triumph possession.

The mindless heave of which they rode
    A fluid shelf
Breaks as they leave it, falls and, slowed,
    Loses itself.

Clear, the sheathed bodies slick as seals
    Loosen and tingle;
And by the board the bare foot feels
    The suck of shingle.

They paddle in the shallows still;
    Two splash each other;
Then all swim out to wait until
    The right waves gather.

The Hug

It was your birthday, we had drunk and dined
  Half of the night with our old friend
    Who'd showed us in the end
  To a bed I reached in one drunk stride.
    Already I lay snug,
And drowsy with the wine dozed on one side.

I dozed, I slept. My sleep broke on a hug,
    Suddenly, from behind,
In which the full lengths of our bodies pressed:
    Your instep to my heel,
  My shoulder-blades against your chest.
  It was not sex, but I could feel
  The whole strength of your body set,
      Or braced, to mine,
    And locking me to you
  As if we were still twenty-two
  When our grand passion had not yet
    Become familial.

My quick sleep had deleted all
Of intervening time and place.
I only knew
The stay of your secure firm dry embrace.

Patch Work

The bird book says, common, conspicuous.
This time of year all day
The mocking bird
Sweeps at a moderate height
Above the densely flowering
Suburban plots of May,
The characteristic shine
Of white patch cutting through the curved ash-grey
That bars each wing;
Or it appears to us
Perched on the post that ends a washing-line
To sing there, as in flight,
A repertoire of songs that it has heard
–From other birds, and others of its kind–
Which it has recombined
And made its own, especially one
With a few separate plangent[1] notes begun
Then linking trills[2] as a long confident run
Toward the immediate distance,
Repeated all day through
In the sexual longings of the spring
(Which also are derivative)
And almost mounting to
Fulfilment, thus to give
Such muscular vigour to a note so strong,
Fulfilment that does not destroy
The original, still-unspent
Longings that led it where it went
But links them in a bird's inhuman joy
Lifted upon the wing
Of that patched body, that insistence
Which fills the gardens up with headlong song.

The Missing

Now as I watch the progress of the plague,[1]
The friends surrounding me fall sick, grow thin,
And drop away. Bared, is my shape less vague
–Sharply exposed and with a sculpted skin?

I do not like the statue's chill contour,
Not nowadays. The warmth investing me

1. Loud; striking.

2. Tremulous sounds, or the rapid alteration of two tones.

Led outward through mind, limb, feeling, and more
In an involved increasing family.

Contact of friend led to another friend,
Supple entwinement through the living mass
Which for all that I knew might have no end,
Image of an unlimited embrace.

I did not just feel ease, though comfortable:
Aggressive as in some ideal of sport,
With ceaseless movement thrilling through the whole,
Their push kept me as firm as their support.

But death–Their deaths have left me less defined:
It was their pulsing presence made me clear.
I borrowed from it, I was unconfined,
Who tonight balance unsupported here,

Eyes glaring from raw marble, in a pose
Languorously part-buried in the block,
Shins perfect and no calves, as if I froze
Between potential and a finished work.

–Abandoned incomplete, shape of a shape,
In which exact detail shows the more strange,
Trapped in unwholeness, I find no escape
Back to the play of constant give and change.

August 1987

Ted Hughes

1930–1998

Ted Hughes can be called a "nature" poet—a somewhat unfortunate label with which he is often tagged—only in a complex and rather dark sense of the word. Critical of Western scientific discourse as leading to nuclear destruction, and finding Christianity depleted of spiritual sustenance, Hughes invokes the "bigger energy" of the natural world—not as a place of tranquil repose or a medium to the sublime, but as a fierce and virile life-force, driven solely by its own relentless will for survival, Tennyson's "nature red in tooth and claw." And yet this force, long neglected by modern humanity, is the source of creativity and regeneration.

Because of their supposed unsevered relationship with nature—their reliance on instinct rather than consciousness—animals, often predatory, provide the subject matter for many of Hughes's poems. Jaguars, crows, foxes, and wolves dominate their respective texts, as Hughes traces through their physicality a deep undercurrent of both human and nonhuman existence. In the much celebrated *Hawk Roosting* (*Lupercal* 1960), the beast provides a voice for nature, in a language as poised and powerful as its speaker: "I kill where I please because it is all mine. / There is no sophistry in my body." In subsequent volumes Hughes's creatures assume complex identities that blur the demarcations of "otherness." *Gog* and *Wodwo*, for instance (*Wodwo* 1967), introduce characters as enigmatic as their names, struggling to understand themselves in relation to their environment. In 1971 Hughes published *Crow*, a poetic-mythology that, among other things, reexamines biblical narratives in light of its grisly protagonist.

Like his modernist predecessors, Hughes was influenced by turn-of-the-century anthropological studies (including Sir James George Frazer's *The Golden Bough*) that infused ancient cultural practices with new meaning and provided disillusioned writers with an alternative symbolic system. Adopting to some extent the model of Robert Graves's *The White Goddess*, Hughes maps out a mythology that places at the center of divinity an earth goddess, the source of true poetry, who has been tragically usurped by patriarchal ideology.

Just as Hughes peers deep into the past for a better understanding of man and nature, his language maintains a toughness and a vitality that harken back to more primitive verse forms. That language was shaped early on by the farms and soggy moors of Mytholmroyd, where he grew up. The torments of war were not eluded there; Hughes's father, after serving four years in Flanders during World War I, brought home the emotional scarring of trench warfare. After working two years as a radio mechanic for the RAF, Hughes went on to study anthropology at Cambridge. There, he met Sylvia Plath, whom he married in 1956, and the tragic relationship that ensued has kindled much interest in both popular and critical circles. *The Birthday Letters*, in which Hughes retrospectively addresses Plath's suicide, met with immediate success after its publication in 1998. Hughes died that same year, after serving fourteen years as Poet Laureate.

Wind

This house has been far out at sea all night,
The woods crashing through darkness, the booming hills,
Winds stampeding the fields under the window
Floundering black astride and blinding wet

Till day rose; then under an orange sky
The hills had new places, and wind wielded
Blade-light, luminous black and emerald,
Flexing like the lens of a mad eye.

At noon I scaled along the house-side as far as
The coal-house door. Once I looked up—
Through the brunt wind that dented the balls of my eyes
The tent of the hills drummed and strained its guyrope,[1]

The fields quivering, the skyline a grimace,
At any second to bang and vanish with a flap:
The wind flung a magpie away and a black-
Back gull bent like an iron bar slowly. The house

Rang like some fine green goblet in the note
That any second would shatter it. Now deep
In chairs, in front of the great fire, we grip
Our hearts and cannot entertain book, thought,

Or each other. We watch the fire blazing,
And feel the roots of the house move, but sit on,

1. Guide or anchoring rope on a ship or, as here, a tent.

Seeing the window tremble to come in,
Hearing the stones cry out under the horizons.

Relic

I found this jawbone at the sea's edge:
There, crabs, dogfish, broken by the breakers or tossed
To flap for half an hour and turn to a crust
Continue the beginning. The deeps are cold:
In that darkness camaraderie does not hold;
Nothing touches but, clutching, devours. And the jaws,
Before they are satisfied or their stretched purpose
Slacken, go down jaws; go gnawn bare. Jaws
Eat and are finished and the jawbone comes to the beach:
This is the sea's achievement; with shells,
Vertebrae, claws, carapaces,[1] skulls.

Time in the sea eats its tail, thrives, casts these
Indigestibles, the spars of purposes
That failed far from the surface. None grow rich
In the sea. This curved jawbone did not laugh
But gripped, gripped and is now a cenotaph.[2]

Theology

No, the serpent did not
Seduce Eve to the apple.
All that's simply
Corruption of the facts.

Adam ate the apple.
Eve ate Adam.
The serpent ate Eve.
This is the dark intestine.

The serpent, meanwhile,
Sleeps his meal off in Paradise—
Smiling to hear
God's querulous calling.

Dust As We Are

My post-war father was so silent
He seemed to be listening. I eavesdropped
On the hot line. His lonely sittings
Mangled me, in secret—like TV
Watched too long, my nerves lasered.
Then, an after-image of the incessant

1. A bony shell or shield, such as a turtle's shell.

2. A monument erected in memory of a deceased person whose body is buried elsewhere.

Mowing passage of machine-gun effects,
What it filled a trench with. And his laugh
(How had that survived—so nearly intact?)
Twitched the curtain never quite deftly enough
Over the hospital wards
Crowded with his (photographed) shock-eyed pals.

I had to use up a lot of spirit
Getting over it. I was helping him.
I was his supplementary convalescent.
He took up his pre-war *joie de vivre*.[1]
But his displays of muscular definition
Were a bleached montage—lit landscapes:
Swampquakes of the slime of puddled soldiers
Where bones and bits of equipment
Showered from every shell-burst.
Naked men
Slithered staring where their mothers and sisters
Would never have to meet their eyes, or see
Exactly how they sprawled and were trodden.

So he had been salvaged and washed.
His muscles very white—marble white.
He had been heavily killed. But we had revived him.
Now he taught us a silence like prayer.
There he sat, killed but alive—so long
As we were very careful. I divined,
With a comb,
Under his wavy, golden hair, as I combed it,
The fragility of skull. And I filled
With his knowledge.
After mother's milk
This was the soul's food. A soap-smell spectre
Of the massacre of innocents. So the soul grew.
A strange thing, with rickets[2]—a hyena.
No singing—that kind of laughter.

Leaf Mould[1]

In Hardcastle Crags, that echoey museum,
Where she dug leaf mould for her handfuls of garden
And taught you to walk, others are making poems.

Between finger and thumb roll a pine-needle,
Feel the chamfer,[2] *feel how they threaded*
The sewing machines.

1. Enjoyment of life (French).
2. Disease caused by vitamin D deficiency, resulting in soft bones.

1. British variant of "mold."
2. A beveled cut, usually in wood.

And
Billy Holt invented a new shuttle[3]
As like an ant's egg, with its folded worker,
As every other.
You might see an ant carrying one.

And
The cordite[4] *conscripts tramped away. But the cenotaphs*[5]
Of all the shells that got their heads blown off
And their insides blown out
Are these beech-bole[6] *stalwarts.*
And oak, birch,

Holly, sycamore, pine.

The lightest air-stir
Released their love-whispers when she walked
The needles weeping, singing, dedicating
Your spectre-double, still in her womb,
To this temple of her *Missa Solemnis*.[7]

White-faced, brain-washed by her nostalgias,
You were her step-up transformer.
She grieved for her girlhood and the fallen.
You mourned for Paradise and its fable.

Giving you the kiss of life
She hung round your neck her whole valley
Like David's harp.[8]
Now, whenever you touch it, God listens
Only for her voice.

Leaf mould. Blood-warm. Fibres crumbled alive
Between thumb and finger.
Feel again
The clogs twanging your footsoles, on the street's steepness,
As you escaped.

Telegraph Wires

Take telegraph wires, a lonely moor,
And fit them together. The thing comes alive in your ear.

Towns whisper to towns over the heather.
But the wires cannot hide from the weather.

So oddly, so daintily made
It is picked up and played.

3. A device that carries thread in a sewing machine.
4. A smokeless explosive powder.
5. A monument erected in memory of a deceased person whose body is buried elsewhere.
6. Trunk of a beech tree.
7. The "solemn mass," op. 123 by Ludwig van Beethoven.
8. In the Old Testament book of Psalms, King David plays his harp before the Lord.

Such unearthly airs
The ear hears, and withers!

In the revolving ballroom of space,
Bowed over the moor, a bright face

Draws out of telegraph wires the tones
That empty human bones.

Carol Ann Duffy

b. 1955

During an era in which the center of gravity for British writing seemed to have moved decisively away from England, Carol Ann Duffy has created a body of poetry that gives voice to the sense of strangeness and disaffection we might have otherwise thought exclusively the province of the former colonies.

Duffy was born in Glasgow, Scotland, but started her schooling in Staffordshire, attended university in Liverpool, and now serves as Creative Director of the Writing School at Manchester Metropolitan University. Her work ranges across a number of genres, including drama and children's literature; she is probably best known, however, for two distinct poetic modes she has cultivated to perfection. One is the lover's voice, most luxuriously on display in the 2006 volume *Rapture*, and in poems such as the sonnet *You* ("Falling in love / is glamorous hell: the crouched, parched heart / like a tiger, ready to kill; a flame's fierce licks under the skin. / into my life, larger than life, you strolled in"). The other encompasses the multiple, distinct voices of the dramatic monologue, represented in the poems *Little Red-Cap* and *Elvis's Twin Sister*, which were published in the 1999 volume *The World's Wife*, a thematic collection of poems spoken from the point of view of the women whose voices have been muted by the powerful men of history. Duffy explains that she set out to look for the "missing or hidden or unspoken truths in old stories," in much the same way that Jean Rhys restored a "speaking role" to the first Mrs. Rochester of Charlotte Brontë's 1847 novel *Jane Eyre* in her 1966 rewrite, *Wide Sargasso Sea*. In a knotty/naughty sonnet called *Frau Freud*, for instance, the wife of the founder of psychoanalysis dismisses the concept of "penis envy" with a wave: "I suppose what I mean is, / ladies, dear ladies, the average penis—not pretty . . . / the squint of its envious solitary eye . . . one's feeling of pity."

In awarding her the T. S. Eliot prize for poetry in 2006 (for *Rapture*), the panel wrote that their unanimous decision marked "a rare moment of agreement between the critics and the booksellers as to what constitutes great poetry"; in her ability to span the critical and popular taste, Duffy has been compared with midcentury poets Ted Hughes and Philip Larkin, and like those two, has risen to prominence at a historical moment in which responsibility for reimagining what "British" might mean has fallen to the arts.

Originally

We came from our own country in a red room
which fell through the fields, our mother singing
our father's name to the turn of the wheels.
My brothers cried, one of them bawling *Home*,
Home, as the miles rushed back to the city,
the street, the house, the vacant rooms
where we didn't live any more. I stared
at the eyes of a blind toy, holding its paw.

All childhood is an emigration. Some are slow,
leaving you standing, resigned, up an avenue
where no one you know stays. Others are sudden.
Your accent wrong. Corners, which seem familiar,
leading to unimagined, pebble-dashed estates, big boys
eating worms and shouting words you don't understand.
My parents' anxiety stirred like a loose tooth
in my head. *I want our own country*, I said.

But then you forget, or don't recall, or change,
and, seeing your brother swallow a slug, feel only
a skelf° of shame. I remember my tongue — *splinter*
shedding its skin like a snake, my voice
in the classroom sounding just like the rest. Do I only think
I lost a river, culture, speech, sense of first space
and the right place? Now, *Where do you come from?*
strangers ask. *Originally*? And I hesitate.

1990

Translating the English, 1989

". . . and much of the poetry, alas, is lost in translation. . ."

Welcome to my country! We have here Edwina Currie[1]
and The Sun newspaper.[2] Much excitement.
Also the weather has been most improving
even in February. Daffodils. (Wordsworth. Up North.) If
you like
Shakespeare or even Opera we have too the Black Market.
For two hundred quids we are talking Les Miserables,
nods being as good as winks. Don't eat the eggs.
Wheel-clamp. Dogs. Vagrants. A tour of our wonderful
capital city is not to be missed. The Fergie,[3]
The Princess Di and the football hooligan, truly you will
like it here, Squire. Also we can be talking crack, smack
and Carling Black Label if we are so inclined. Don't
drink the H_2O. All very proud we now have
a green Prime Minister. What colour yours? Binbags.° — *disposable trash bags*
You will be knowing of Charles Dickens and
Terry Wogan° — *BBC radio broadcaster*
and Scotland. All this can be arranged for cash no questions.
Ireland not on. Fish and chips and the Official Secrets Act[4]
second to none. Here we go. We are liking
a smashing good time like estate agents° and Neighbours,[5] — *realtors*
also Brookside for we are allowed four Channels.

1. Outspoken and often outrageous Conservative member of Parliament.
2. Scandal-loving British tabloid.
3. Nickname of the popular Duchess of York, Sarah Ferguson (b. 1959). "Princess Di": Diana Spenser (1961–1997), Princess of Wales.
4. British national security legislation.
5. Neighbours was an Australian, Brookside a Liverpool, soap opera.

How many you have? Last night of Proms. Andrew
Lloyd-Webber.[6] Jeffrey Archer. Plenty culture you will be agreeing.
Also history and buildings. The Houses of Lords. Docklands.
Many thrills and high interest rates for own good. Muggers.
Much lead in petrol. Filth. Rule Britannia and child abuse.
Electronic tagging, Boss, ten pints and plenty rape. Queen Mum.
Channel Tunnel. You get here fast no problem to my country
my country my country welcome welcome welcome.

1990

Little Red-Cap

At childhood's end, the houses petered out
into playing fields, the factory, allotments
kept, like mistresses, by kneeling married men,
the silent railway line, the hermit's caravan,
till you came at last to the edge of the woods.
It was there that I first clapped eyes on the wolf.

He stood in a clearing, reading his verse out loud
in his wolfy drawl, a paperback in his hairy paw,
red wine staining his bearded jaw. What big ears
he had! What big eyes he had! What teeth!
In the interval, I made quite sure he spotted me,
sweet sixteen, never been, babe, waif, and bought me a drink,

my first. You might ask why. Here's why. Poetry.
The wolf, I knew, would lead me deep into the woods,
away from home, to a dark tangled thorny place
lit by the eyes of owls. I crawled in his wake,
my stockings ripped to shreds, scraps of red from my blazer
snagged on twig and branch, murder clues. I lost both shoes
but got there, wolf's lair, better beware. Lesson one that night,

breath of the wolf in my ear, was the love poem.
I clung till dawn to his thrashing fur, for
what little girl doesn't dearly love a wolf?
Then I slid from between his heavy matted paws
and went in search of a living bird—white dove—
which flew, straight, from my hands to his open mouth.
One bite, dead. How nice, breakfast in bed, he said,
licking his chops. As soon as he slept, I crept to the back
of the lair, where a whole wall was crimson, gold, aglow with books.
Words, words were truly alive on the tongue, in the head,
warm, beating, frantic, winged; music and blood.

But then I was young—and it took ten years
in the woods to tell that a mushroom

6. Composer of such popular musicals as *Phantom of the Opera*, *Evita*, and *Cats*; Jeffrey Archer: popular novelist, and later Member of Parliament; he served a prison term for obstruction of justice.

stoppers the mouth of a buried corpse, that birds
are the uttered thought of trees, that a greying wolf
howls the same old song at the moon, year in, year out,
season after season, same rhyme, same reason. I took an axe

to a willow to see how it wept. I took an axe to a salmon
to see how it leapt. I took an axe to the wolf
as he slept, one chop, scrotum to throat, and saw
the glistening, virgin white of my grandmother's bones.
I filled his old belly with stones. I stitched him up.
Out of the forest I come with my flowers, singing, all alone.

Elvis's Twin Sister

Are you lonesome tonight? Do you miss me tonight?[1]
Elvis is alive and she's female: Madonna

In the convent, y'all,
I tend the gardens,
watch things grow,
pray for the immortal soul
of rock 'n' roll.

They call me
Sister Presley here.
The Reverend Mother
digs the way I move my hips
just like my brother.

Gregorian chant
drifts out across the herbs,
Pascha nostrum immolatus est . . .[2]
I wear a simple habit,
darkish hues,

a wimple° with a novice-sewn *nun's headcloth*
lace band, a rosary,
a chain of keys,
a pair of good and sturdy
blue suede shoes.[3]

I think of it
as Graceland[4] here,
a land of grace.
It puts my trademark slow lopsided smile
back on my face.

1. From Elvis Presley's 1961 hit, "Are You Lonesome Tonight?"
2. Title of a Latin hymn (Gregorian chant), trans. "Our passover is sacrificed."
3. Refers to the Carl Perkins hit, "Blue Suede Shoes" (1955), covered by Elvis in 1956.
4. Elvis's Memphis mansion.

Lawdy.
I'm alive and well.
Long time since I walked
down Lonely Street
towards Heartbreak Hotel.[5]

1999

The Diet

The diet worked like a dream. No sugar,
salt, dairy, fat, protein, starch or alcohol.
By the end of week one, she was half a stone[1]
shy of ten and shrinking, skipping breakfast,
lunch, dinner, thinner; a fortnight° in, she was *two weeks*
eight stone; by the end of the month, she was skin
and bone.

She starved on, stayed in, stared in
the mirror, svelter, slimmer. The last apple
aged in the fruit bowl, untouched. The skimmed milk
soured in the fridge, unsupped. Her skeleton preened
under its tight flesh dress. She was all eyes,
all cheekbones, had guns for hips. Not a stitch
in the wardrobe fitted.

What passed her lips? Air,
water. She was Anorexia's true daughter, a slip
of a girl, a shadow, dwindling away. One day,
the width of a stick, she started to grow smaller—
child-sized, doll-sized, the height of a thimble.
She sat at her open window and the wind
blew her away.

Seed small, she was out and about,
looking for home. An empty beer bottle rolled
in the gutter. She crawled in, got drunk on the dregs,
started to sing, down, out, nobody's love. Tiny others
joined in. They raved all night. She woke alone,
head splitting, mouth dry, hungry and cold, and made
for the light.

She found she could fly on the wind,
could breathe, if it rained, underwater. That night,
she went to a hotel bar that she knew and floated into
the barman's eye. She slept for hours, left at dawn
in a blink, in a wink, drifted away on a breeze.
Minute, she could suit herself from here on in, go
where she pleased.

5. Refers to another 1956 Elvis hit, "Heartbreak Hotel"

1. 133 lbs. (one stone = 14 lbs.)

She stayed near people,
lay in the tent of a nostril like a germ, dwelled
in the caves of an ear. She lived in a tear, swam
clear, moved south to a mouth, kipped° in the chap *slept*
of a lip. She loved flesh and blood, wallowed
in mud under fingernails, dossed° in a fold of fat *slept*
on a waist.

But when she squatted the tip of a tongue,
she was gulped, swallowed, sent down the hatch
in a river of wine, bottoms up, cheers, fetched up
in a stomach just before lunch. She crouched
in the lining, hearing the avalanche munch of food,
then it was carrots, peas, courgettes,° potatoes, *zucchini*
gravy and meat.

Then it was sweet. Then it was stilton,
roquefort, weisslacker-käse, gex;° it was smoked salmon *varieties of cheese*
with scrambled eggs, hot boiled ham, plum flan, frogs'
legs. She knew where she was all right, clambered
onto the greasy breast of a goose, opened wide, then
chomped and chewed and gorged; inside the Fat Woman now,
trying to get out.

2002

Anon

If she were here
she'd forget who she was,
it's been so long,
maybe a nurse, a nanny,
maybe a nun—
Anon.

A girl I met
was willing to bet
that she still lived on—
Anon—
but had packed it all in,
the best verb, the right noun,
for a life in the sun.

A woman I knew
kept her skull
on a shelf in a room—
Anon's—
And swore that one day
as she worked at her desk
it cleared its throat
as though it had something
to get off its chest.

But I know best—
how she passed on her pen
like a baton
down through the years,
with a hey nonny
hey nonny
hey nonny no—
Anon.

2002

[END OF POSTWAR POETS: ENGLISH VOICES]

Nadine Gordimer

b. 1923

Nadine Gordimer was born in South Africa to Jewish emigrant parents from London. Thus her childhood, like those of the children of countless middle-class colonial families, was somewhat complex and contradictory. In an interview, Gordimer offers this explanation: "I think when you're born white in South Africa, you're peeling like an orange. You're sloughing off all the conditioning that you've had since you were a child." In Gordimer's case, that "sloughing off" of white, British prejudices and habits of mind has been thorough; the novelist Paul Theroux, for instance, suggests that "Gordimer's vision of Africa is the most complete one we have, and in time to come, when we want to know everything there is to know about a newly independent black African country, it is to this white South African woman . . . that we will turn."

Since Gordimer published her first collection of short stories in 1949 her writing has been praised for its evenhanded and scrupulously honest treatment of the political terrain of South Africa; over the years she has become, in the words of one critic, "the literary voice and conscience of her society." Among her gifts are an ear sensitive to the cadences and idiosyncrasies of spoken English, and a gift for social satire in service of a finally moral purpose. The longstanding subject of Gordimer's writing—her great theme—is, as critic Michiko Kakutani describes it, "the consequences of apartheid on the daily lives of men and women, the distortions it produces in relationships among both blacks and whites." In Gordimer's writing, these distortions are always shown rather than explained; her presentation is essentially dramatic, a trait she shares with modern masters of short fiction like Chekhov and Joyce.

Gordimer has been faulted for the emphasis in politics in her writing. Her response to this charge is eloquent: "The real influence of politics on my writing is the influence of politics on people. Their lives, and I believe their very personalities, are changed by the extreme political circumstances one lives under in South Africa. I am dealing with people; here are people who are shaped and changed by politics. In that way my material is profoundly influenced by politics." To date, Gordimer has published more than ten novels, including the celebrated *A Guest of Honour* (1970) and *The Conservationist* (1974; cowinner of the Booker McConnell Prize), and nine collections of short stories. *Jump and Other Stories*, which includes *What Were You Dreaming?*, was published in 1991, the same year Gordimer was awarded the Nobel Prize in Literature. In this story, the disjunction between black and white South African English is the starting-point for an exploration of blocked communication between races and genders alike. Her thirteenth novel, *Get a Life*, was published in 2005.

For additional resources on Gordimer, go to *The Longman Anthology of British Literature* Web site at www.myliteraturekit.com.

What Were You Dreaming?

I'm standing here by the road long time, yesterday, day before, today. Not the same road but it's the same—hot, hot like today. When they turn off where they're going, I must get out again, wait again. Some of them they just pretend there's nobody there, they don't want to see nobody. Even go a bit faster, *ja*. Then they past, and I'm waiting. I combed my hair; I don't want to look like a *skollie* [ruffian]. Don't smile because they think you being too friendly, you think you good as them. They go and they go. Some's got the baby's napkin hanging over the back window to keep out this sun. Some's not going on holiday with their kids but is alone; all alone in a big car. But they'll never stop, the whites, if they alone. Never. Because these *skollies* and that kind've spoilt it all for us, sticking a gun in the driver's neck, stealing his money, beating him up and taking the car. Even killing him. So it's buggered up for us. No white wants some guy sitting behind his head. And the blacks—when they stop for you, they ask for money. They want you must pay, like for a taxi! The blacks!

But then these whites: they stopping; I'm surprised, because it's only two—empty in the back—and the car it's a beautiful one. The windows are that special glass, you can't see in if you outside, but the woman has hers down and she's calling me over with her finger. She ask me where I'm going and I say the next place because they don't like to have you for too far, so she say get in and lean into the back to move along her stuff that's on the back seat to make room. Then she say, lock the door, just push that button down, we don't want you to fall out, and it's like she's joking with someone she know. The man driving smiles over his shoulder and say something—I can't hear it very well, it's the way he talk English. So anyway I say what's all right to say, yes master, thank you master, I'm going to Warmbad. He ask again, but man, I don't get it—*Ekskuus?* Please? And she chips in—she's a lady with grey hair and he's a young chap—My friend's from England, he's asking if you've been waiting a long time for a lift. So I tell them—A long time? Madam! And because they white, I tell them about the blacks, how when they stop they ask you to pay. This time I understand what the young man's saying, he say, And most whites don't stop? And I'm careful what I say, I tell them about the blacks, how too many people spoil it for us, they robbing and killing, you can't blame white people. Then he ask where I'm from. And she laugh and look round where I'm behind her. I see she know I'm from the Cape, although she ask me. I tell her I'm from the Cape Flats[1] and she say she suppose I'm not born there, though, and she's right, I'm born in Wynberg, right there in Cape Town. So she say, And they moved you out?

Then I catch on what kind of white she is; so I tell her, yes, the government kicked us out from our place, and she say to the young man, You see?

He want to know why I'm not in the place in the Cape Flats, why I'm so far away here. I tell them I'm working in Pietersburg.[2] And he keep on, why? Why? What's my job, everything, and if I don't understand the way he speak, she chips in again all the time and ask me for him. So I tell him, panel beater.[3] And I tell him, the pay is very low in the Cape. And then I begin to tell them lots of things, some things is real and some things I just think of, things that are going to make them like me, maybe they'll take me all the way there to Pietersburg.

1. A small town near Cape Town.
2. A city in northeastern South Africa.
3. A person who does bodywork on automobiles.

I tell them I'm six days on the road. I not going to say I'm sick as well, I been home because I was sick—because *she's* not from overseas, I suss that, she know that old story. I tell them I had to take leave because my mother's got trouble with my brothers and sisters, we seven in the family and no father. And s'true's God, it seem like what I'm saying. When do you ever see him except he's drunk. And my brother is trouble, trouble, he hangs around with bad people and my other brother doesn't help my mother. And that's no lie, neither, how can he help when he's doing time; but they don't need to know that, they only get scared I'm the same kind like him, if I tell about him, assault and intent to do bodily harm. The sisters are in school and my mother's only got the pension. *Ja.* I'm working there in Pietersburg and every week, madam, I swear to you, I send my pay for my mother and sisters. So then he say, Why get off here? Don't you want us to take you to Pietersburg? And she say, of course, they going that way.

And I tell them some more. They listening to me so nice, and I'm talking, talking. I talk about the government, because I hear she keep saying to him, telling about this law and that law. I say how it's not fair we had to leave Wynberg and go to the Flats. I tell her we got sicknesses—she say what kind, is it unhealthy there? And I don't have to think what, I just say it's *bad, bad*, and she say to the man, *As I told you.* I tell about the house we had in Wynberg, but it's not my grannie's old house where we was all living together so long, the house I'm telling them about is more the kind of house they'll know, they wouldn't like to go away from, with a tiled bathroom, electric stove, everything. I tell them we spend three thousand rands fixing up that house—my uncle give us the money, that's how we got it. He give us his savings, three thousand rands. (I don't know why I say three; old Uncle Jimmy never have three or two or one in his life. I just say it.) And then we just kicked out. And panel beaters getting low pay there; it's better in Pietersburg.

He say, but I'm far from my home? And I tell her again, because she's white but she's a woman too, with that grey hair she's got grown-up kids—Madam. I send my pay home every week, s'true's God, so's they can eat, there in the Flats. I'm saying, *six days on the road.* While I'm saying it, I'm thinking; then I say, look at me, I got only these clothes, I sold my things on the way, to have something to eat. *Six days on the road.* He's from overseas and she isn't one of those who say you're a liar, doesn't trust you—right away when I got in the car, I notice she doesn't take her stuff over to the front like they usually do in case you pinch something of theirs. Six days on the road, and am I tired, tired! When I get to Pietersburg I must try borrow me a rand to get a taxi there to where I live. He say, Where do you live? Not in town? And she laugh, because he don't know nothing about this place, where whites live and where we must go—but I know they both thinking and I know what they thinking; I know I'm going to get something when I get out, don't need to worry about that. They feeling bad about me, now. Bad. Anyhow it's God's truth that I'm tired, tired, that's true.

They've put up her window and he's pushed a few buttons, now it's like in a supermarket, cool air blowing, and the windows like sunglasses: that sun can't get me here.

The Englishman glances over his shoulder as he drives.

"Taking a nap."

"I'm sure it's needed."

All through the trip he stops for everyone he sees at the roadside. Some are not hitching at all, never expecting to be given a lift anywhere, just walking in the heat outside with an empty plastic can to be filled with water or paraffin or whatever it is they buy in some country store, or standing at some point between departure and destination, small children and bundles linked on either side, baby on back. She hasn't said anything to him. He would only misunderstand if she explained why one doesn't give lifts in this country; and if she pointed out that in spite of this, she doesn't mind him breaking the sensible if unfortunate rule, he might misunderstand that, as well—think she was boasting of her disregard for personal safety weighed in the balance against decent concern for fellow beings.

He persists in making polite conversation with these passengers because he doesn't want to be patronizing; picking them up like so many objects and dropping them off again, silent, smelling of smoke from open cooking fires, sun and sweat, there behind his head. They don't understand his Englishman's English and if he gets an answer at all it's a deaf man's guess at what's called for. Some grin with pleasure and embarrass him by showing it the way they've been taught is acceptable, invoking him as *baas* and *master* when they get out and give thanks. But although he doesn't know it, being too much concerned with those names thrust into his hands like whips whose purpose is repugnant to him, has nothing to do with him, she knows each time that there is a moment of annealment[4] in the air-conditioned hired car belonging to nobody—a moment like that on a no-man's-land bridge in which an accord between warring countries is signed—when there is no calling of names, and all belong in each other's presence. He doesn't feel it because he has no wounds, neither has inflicted, nor will inflict any.

This one standing at the roadside with his transistor radio in a plastic bag was actually thumbing a lift like a townee; his expectation marked him out. And when her companion to whom she was showing the country inevitably pulled up, she read the face at the roadside immediately: the lively, cajoling, performer's eyes, the salmon-pinkish cheeks and nostrils, and as he jogged over smiling, the unselfconscious gap of gum between the canines.

A sleeper is always absent; although present, there on the back seat.

"The way he spoke about black people, wasn't it surprising? I mean—he's black himself."

"Oh no he's not. Couldn't you see the difference? He's a Cape Coloured. From the way he speaks English—couldn't you hear he's not like the Africans you've talked to?"

But of course he hasn't seen, hasn't heard: the fellow is dark enough, to those who don't know the signs by which you're classified, and the melodramatic, long-vowelled English is as difficult to follow if more fluent than the terse, halting responses of blacker people.

"Would he have a white grandmother or even a white father, then?"

She gives him another of the little history lessons she has been supplying along the way. The Malay slaves brought by the Dutch East India Company[5] to their supply station, on the route to India, at the Cape in the seventeenth century; the Khoikhoi who were the indigenous inhabitants of that part of Africa; add Dutch, French, English, German settlers whose back-yard progeniture with these and other blacks began a people who are all the people in the country mingled in one bloodstream. But encounters along the road teach him more than her history lessons, or the political analyses in which they share the same ideological approach although he does not share responsibility for the experience to which the ideology is being applied. She has explained Acts, Proclamations, Amendments. The Group Areas Act, Resettlement

4. Tempering by heating.

5. Occupied South Africa from 1652–1795 while it was a Dutch Cape Colony.

Act, Orderly Movement and Settlement of Black Persons Act. She has translated these statute-book euphemisms: people as movable goods. People packed onto trucks along with their stoves and beds while front-end loaders scoop away their homes into rubble. People dumped somewhere else. Always somewhere else. People as the figures, decimal points and multiplying zero-zero-zeros into which individual lives—Black Persons Orderly-Moved, -Effluxed, -Grouped—coagulate and compute. Now he has here in the car the intimate weary odour of a young man to whom these things happen.

"Half his family sick . . . it must be pretty unhealthy, where they've been made to go."

She smiles. "Well, I'm not too sure about that. I had the feeling, some of what he said . . . they're theatrical by nature. You must take it with a pinch of salt."

"You mean about the mother and sisters and so on?"

She's still smiling, she doesn't answer.

"But he couldn't have made up about taking a job so far from home—and the business of sending his wages to his mother? That too?"

He glances at her.

Beside him, she's withdrawn as the other one, sleeping behind him. While he turns his attention back to the road, she is looking at him secretly, as if somewhere in his blue eyes registering the approaching road but fixed on the black faces he is trying to read, somewhere in the lie of his inflamed hand and arm that on their travels have been plunged in the sun as if in boiling water, there is the place through which the worm he needs to be infected with can find a way into him, so that he may host it and become its survivor, himself surviving through being fed on. Become like her. Complicity is the only understanding.

"Oh it's true, it's all true. . . not in the way he's told about it. Truer than the way he told it. All these things happen to them. And other things. Worse. But why burden us? Why try to explain to us? Things so far from what we know, how will they ever explain? How will we react? Stop our ears? Or cover our faces? Open the door and throw him out? They don't know. But sick mothers and brothers gone to the bad—these are the staples of misery, mmh? Think of the function of charity in the class struggles in your own country in the nineteenth century; it's all there in your literature. The lord-of-the-manor's compassionate daughter carrying hot soup to the dying cottager on her father's estate. The "advanced" upper-class woman comforting her cook when the honest drudge's daughter takes to whoring for a living. *Shame,* we say here. Shame. You must've heard it? We think it means, what a pity; we think we are expressing sympathy—for them. *Shame.* I don't know what we're saying about ourselves." She laughs.

"So you think it would at least be true that his family were kicked out of their home, sent away?"

"Why would anyone of them need to make that up? It's an everyday affair."

"What kind of place would they get, where they were moved?"

"Depends. A tent, to begin with. And maybe basic materials to build themselves a shack. Perhaps a one-room prefab. Always a tin toilet set down in the veld,[6] if nothing else. Some industrialist must be making a fortune out of government contracts for those toilets. You build your new life round that toilet. His people are Coloured, so it could be they were sent where there were houses of some sort already built for them; Coloureds usually get something a bit better than blacks are given."

6. Plains.

"And the house would be more or less as good as the one they had? People as poor as that—and they'd spent what must seem a fortune to them, fixing it up."

"I don't know what kind of house they had. We're not talking about slum clearance, my dear; we're talking about destroying communities because they're black, and white people want to build houses or factories for whites where blacks live. I told you. We're talking about loading up trucks and carting black people out of sight of whites."

"And even where he's come to work—Pietersburg, whatever-it's-called—he doesn't live in the town."

"Out of sight." She has lost the thought for a moment, watching to make sure the car takes the correct turning. "Out of sight. Like those mothers and grannies and brothers and sisters far away on the Cape Flats."

"I don't think it's possible he actually sends all his pay. I mean how would one eat?"

"Maybe what's left doesn't buy anything he really wants."

Not a sound, not a sigh in sleep behind them. They can go on talking about him as he always has been discussed, there and yet not there.

Her companion is alert to the risk of gullibility. He verifies the facts, smiling, just as he converts, mentally, into pounds and pence any sum spent in foreign coinage. "He didn't sell the radio. When he said he'd sold all his things on the road, he forgot about that."

"When did he say he'd last eaten?"

"Yesterday. He said."

She repeats what she has just been told: "Yesterday." She is looking through the glass that takes the shine of heat off the landscape passing as yesterday passed, time measured by the ticking second hand of moving trees, rows of crops, country-store stoeps,[7] filling stations, spiny crook'd fingers of giant euphorbia.[8] Only the figures by the roadside waiting, standing still.

Personal remarks can't offend someone dead-beat in the back. "How d'you think such a young man comes to be without front teeth?"

She giggles whisperingly and keeps her voice low, anyway. "Well, you may not believe me if I tell you . . . "

"Seems odd . . . I suppose he can't afford to have them replaced."

"It's—how shall I say—a sexual preference. Most usually you see it in their young girls, though. They have their front teeth pulled when they're about seventeen."

She feels his uncertainty, his not wanting to let comprehension lead him to a conclusion embarrassing to an older woman. For her part, she is wondering whether he won't find it distasteful if—at her de-sexed age—she should come out with it: for cock-sucking. "No one thinks the gap spoils a girl's looks, apparently. It's simply a sign she knows how to please. Same significance between men, I suppose? A form of beauty. So everyone says. We've always been given to understand that's the reason."

"Maybe it's just another sexual myth. There are so many."

She's in agreement. "Black girls. Chinese girls. Jewish girls."

"And black men?"

"Oh my goodness, you bet. But we white ladies don't talk about that, we only dream, you know! Or have nightmares."

They're laughing. When they are quiet, she flexes her shoulders against the seat-back and settles again. The streets of a town are flickering their text across her eyes. "He might have had a car accident. They might have been knocked out in a fight."

7. Verandas.

8. An African shrub.

They have to wake him because they don't know where he wants to be set down. He is staring at her lined white face (turned to him, calling him gently), stunned for a moment at this evidence that he cannot be anywhere he ought to be; and now he blinks and smiles his empty smile caught on either side by a canine tooth, and gulps and gives himself a shake like someone coming out of water. "Sorry! Sorry! Sorry madam!"

What about, she says, and the young man glances quickly, his blue eyes coming round over his shoulder: "Had a good snooze?"

"Ooh I was finished, master, finished, God bless you for the rest you give me. And with an empty stummick, you know, you dreaming so real. I was dreaming, dreaming, I didn't know nothing about I'm in the car!"

It comes from the driver's seat with the voice (a real Englishman's from overseas) of one who is hoping to hear something that will explain everything. "What were you dreaming?"

But there is only hissing, spluttery laughter between the two white pointed teeth. The words gambol. "Ag, nothing, master, nothing, all *non*-sunce—"

The sense is that if pressed, he will produce for them a dream he didn't dream, a dream put together from bloated images on billboards, discarded calendars picked up, scraps of newspapers blown about—but they interrupt, they're asking where he'd like to get off.

"No, anywhere. Here it's all right. Fine. Just there by the corner. I must go look for someone who'll praps give me a rand for the taxi, because I can't walk so far, I haven't eaten nothing since yesterday . . . just here, the master can please stop just here—"

The traffic light is red, anyway, and the car is in the lane nearest the kerb. Her thin, speckled white arm with a skilled flexible hand, but no muscle with which to carry a load of washing or lift a hoe, feels back to release the lock he is fumbling at. "Up, up, pull it up." She has done it for him. "Can't you take a bus?"

"There's no buses Sunday, madam, this place is ve-ery bad for us for transport, I must tell you, we can't get nowhere Sundays, only work-days." He is out, the plastic bag with the radio under his arm, his feet in their stained, multi-striped jogging sneakers drawn neatly together like those of a child awaiting dismissal. "Thank you madam, thank you master, God bless you for what you done."

The confident dextrous hand is moving quickly down in the straw bag bought from a local market somewhere along the route. She brings up a pale blue note (the Englishman recognizes the two-rand denomination of this currency that he has memorized by colour) and turns to pass it, a surreptitious message, through the open door behind her. *Goodbye master madam*. The note disappears delicately as a tit-bit finger-fed. He closes the door, he's keeping up the patter, *goodbye master, goodbye madam,* and she instructs—"No, bang it. Harder. That's it." *Goodbye master, goodbye madam*—but they don't look back at him now, they don't have to see him thinking he must keep waving, keep smiling, in case they should look back.

She is the guide and mentor; she's the one who knows the country. She's the one—she knows that too—who is accountable. She must be the first to speak again. "At least if he's hungry he'll be able to buy a bun or something. And the bars are closed on Sunday."

1991

Derek Walcott

b. 1930

Over the last five decades, Derek Walcott has articulated the tensions of living between two worlds—the competing claims and traditions of the West Indies, his home, and Europe. A concern with issues of national identity runs throughout Walcott's large body of poetry and drama; his poetry exploits the resources of a European literary tradition in the service of Caribbean themes and concerns. No poet, as T. S. Eliot insisted, can write important poetry without tapping into some cultural or literary tradition; in the poem *Forest of Europe,* Walcott puts the question this way:

> What's poetry, if it is worth its salt,
> but a phrase men can pass from hand to mouth?
> From hand to mouth, across the centuries,
> the bread that lasts when systems have decayed.

Walcott was born in Castries, Saint Lucia, an isolated, volcanic island in the West Indies. Saint Lucia is a former British colony, and Walcott's education there was thoroughly British. In the introduction to *Dream on Monkey Mountain and Other Plays* (1970), Walcott writes, "The writers of my generation were natural assimilators. We knew the literature of Empires, Greek, Roman, British, through their essential classics; and both the patois of the street and the language of the classroom hid the elation of discovery." Empire and slavery left their impress on the Walcott family; both of his grandmothers were said to be descended from slaves. Walcott attended University College of the West Indies in Jamaica on a British government scholarship; he completed a degree in English in 1953, and from 1954 until 1957 taught in West Indian schools. In 1958 a Rockefeller Fellowship allowed him to spend a year in New York studying theater; the following year he moved to Trinidad and founded the Little Carib Theatre Workshop. It was in his playwriting that Walcott first accomplished the fusion of native and European elements he sought; his 1958 play *Drums and Colours,* for instance, employs calypso music, mime, and carnival masks to "carnivalize" the smooth surface of European drama, creating a literary form which, while written in English, is uniquely Caribbean in character. *O Babylon!* (1976), his most popular play, focuses on the Rastafarians of Jamaica. He is also a talented painter, and his poems are notable for the vivid clarity of their images.

Walcott has written more than fifteen volumes of poetry as well as a dozen plays. His first important poetry collection was *In a Green Night* (1962), which includes his best-known poem, *A Far Cry from Africa.* Africa and Britain serve as the double setting for his trenchant portrait of a foreign aid bureaucrat in *The Fortunate Traveller.* Walcott himself has never settled in one place for long, and for many years he has split his time between his home in Trinidad and a teaching post at Boston University. Walcott's poems create a landscape of historical and personal memory, overlaying empires, centuries, continents, and stages of his own life. He developed his themes most expansively in his verse novel *Omeros* (1991), which rewrites Homer's *Iliad* as a Caribbean story, interspersed with scenes of the poet's own life and travels in Boston, London, and Dublin. Walcott has declared that his 2004 book-length poem, *The Prodigal,* prompted by the death of his twin brother Roderick, will be his last. Walcott was awarded the Nobel Prize in literature in 1992, "for a poetic oeuvre of great luminosity, sustained by a historical vision, the outcome of a multicultural commitment."

A Far Cry from Africa

A wind is ruffling the tawny pelt
Of Africa. Kikuyu,[1] quick as flies,
Batten° upon the bloodstreams of the veldt.° *fasten / open country*
Corpses are scattered through a paradise.
Only the worm, colonel of carrion, cries:
"Waste no compassion on these separate dead!"
Statistics justify and scholars seize
The salients of colonial policy.
What is that to the white child hacked in bed?
To savages, expendable as Jews?

Threshed out by beaters, the long rushes break
In a white dust of ibises[2] whose cries
Have wheeled since civilization's dawn
From the parched river or beast-teeming plain.
The violence of beast on beast is read
As natural law, but upright man
Seeks his divinity by inflicting pain.
Delirious as these worried beasts, his wars
Dance to the tightened carcass of a drum,
While he calls courage still that native dread
Of the white peace contracted by the dead.

Again brutish necessity wipes its hands
Upon the napkin of a dirty cause, again
A waste of our compassion, as with Spain,
The gorilla wrestles with the superman.
I who am poisoned with the blood of both,
Where shall I turn, divided to the vein?
I who have cursed
The drunken officer of British rule, how choose
Between this Africa and the English tongue I love?
Betray them both, or give back what they give?
How can I face such slaughter and be cool?
How can I turn from Africa and live?

1962

Volcano

Joyce was afraid of thunder,
but lions roared at his funeral
from the Zurich zoo.
Was it Zurich or Trieste?
No matter. These are legends, as much
as the death of Joyce is a legend,
or the strong rumour that Conrad
is dead, and that *Victory* is ironic.

1. Indigenous people of Kenya.
2. Wading birds resembling storks.

On the edge of the night-horizon
from this beach house on the cliffs
there are now, till dawn,
two glares from the miles-out-
at-sea derricks; they are like
the glow of the cigar
and the glow of the volcano
at *Victory*'s end.
One could abandon writing
for the slow-burning signals
of the great, to be, instead,
their ideal reader, ruminative,
voracious, making the love of masterpieces
superior to attempting
to repeat or outdo them,
and be the greatest reader in the world.
At least it requires awe,
which has been lost to our time;
so many people have seen everything,
so many people can predict,
so many refuse to enter the silence
of victory, the indolence
that burns at the core,
so many are no more than
erect ash, like the cigar,
so many take thunder for granted.
How common is the lightning,
how lost the leviathans
we no longer look for!
There were giants in those days.
In those days they made good cigars.
I must read more carefully.

1976

Wales
for Ned Thomas

Those white flecks cropping the ridges of Snowdon[1]
will thicken their fleece and come wintering down
through the gap between alliterative hills,
through the caesura[2] that let in the Legions,
past the dark disfigured mouths of the chapels,
till a white silence comes to green-throated Wales.
Down rusty gorges, cold rustling gorse,[3]
over rocks hard as consonants, and rain-vowelled shales
sang the shallow-buried axe, helmet, and baldric° *sword belt*
before the wet asphalt sibilance of tires.
A plump raven, Plantagenet,[4] unfurls its heraldic

1. The highest peak in Wales.
2. A break or pause in the middle of a line of verse.
3. Spiny shrub with yellow leaves.
4. English royal house between 1154 and 1485.

caw over walls that held the cult of the horse.
In blackened cottages with their stony hatred
of industrial fires, a language is shared
like bread to the mouth, white flocks to dark byres° *sheds*

1981

The Fortunate Traveller[1]

for Susan Sontag

And I heard a voice in the midst of the four beasts say,
A measure of wheat for a penny,
and three measures of barley for a penny;
and see thou hurt not the oil and the wine.

—*Revelation* 6.6[2]

1

It was in winter. Steeples, spires
congealed like holy candles. Rotting snow
flaked from Europe's ceiling. A compact man,
I crossed the canal in a grey overcoat,
on one lapel a crimson buttonhole
for the cold ecstasy of the assassin.
In the square coffin manacled to my wrist:
small countries pleaded through the mesh of graphs,
in treble-spaced, Xeroxed forms to the World Bank
on which I had scrawled the one word, MERCY;

I sat on a cold bench
under some skeletal lindens.
Two other gentlemen, black skins gone grey
as their identical, belted overcoats,
crossed the white river.
They spoke the stilted French
of their dark river,
whose hooked worm, multiplying its pale sickle,
could thin the harvest of the winter streets.
"Then we can depend on you to get us those tractors?"
"I gave my word."
"May my country ask you why you are doing this, sir?"
Silence.
"You know if you betray us, you cannot hide?"
A tug. Smoke trailing its dark cry.

At the window in Haiti, I remember
a gecko[3] pressed against the hotel glass,
with white palms, concentrating head.
With a child's hands. Mercy, monsieur. Mercy.

1. Walcott's title invokes Thomas Nashe's tale *The Unfortunate Traveller* (1594). Susan Sontag (b. 1933–2004), American cultural critic and novelist.
2. One of the Four Horsemen of the Apocalypse is decreeing the famine and inflation that accompany wars as the end of the world approaches.
3. A small lizard.

Famine sighs like a scythe
across the field of statistics and the desert
is a moving mouth. In the hold of this earth
10,000,000 shoreless souls are drifting.
Somalia: 765,000, their skeletons will go under the tidal sand.
"We'll meet you in Bristol to conclude the agreement?"
Steeples like tribal lances, through congealing fog
the cries of wounded church bells wrapped in cotton,
grey mist enfolding the conspirator
like a sealed envelope next to its heart.

No one will look up now to see the jet
fade like a weevil through a cloud of flour.
One flies first-class, one is so fortunate.
Like a telescope reversed, the traveller's eye
swiftly screws down the individual sorrow
to an oval nest of antic numerals,
and the iris, interlocking with this globe,
condenses it to zero, then a cloud.
Beetle-black taxi from Heathrow[4] to my flat.
We are roaches,
riddling the state cabinets, entering the dark holes
of power, carapaced in topcoats,
scuttling around columns, signalling for taxis,
with frantic antennae, to other huddles with roaches;
we infect with optimism, and when
the cabinets crack, we are the first
to scuttle, radiating separately
back to Geneva, Bonn, Washington, London.

Under the dripping planes of Hampstead Heath,
I read her letter again, watching the drizzle
disfigure its pleading like mascara. Margo,
I cannot bear to watch the nations cry.
Then the phone: "We will pay you in Bristol."
Days in fetid bedclothes swallowing cold tea,
the phone stifled by the pillow. The telly
a blue storm with soundless snow.
I'd light the gas and see a tiger's tongue.
I was rehearsing the ecstasies of starvation
for what I had to do. *And have not charity*.[5]

I found my pity, desperately researching
the origins of history, from reed-built communes
by sacred lakes, turning with the first sprocketed
water-driven wheels. I smelled imagination
among bestial hides by the gleam of fat,
seeking in all races a common ingenuity.
I envisaged an Africa flooded with such light

4. London's primary airport.
5. "Though I speak with the tongues of men and of angels, and have not charity, I am become as sounding brass, or a tinkling cymbal" (1 Corinthians 13.1).

as alchemized the first fields of emmer wheat and barley,
when we savages dyed our pale dead with ochre,
and bordered our temples
with the ceremonial vulva of the conch
in the grey epoch of the obsidian adze.
I sowed the Sahara with rippling cereals,
my charity fertilized these aridities.

What was my field? Late sixteenth century.
My field was a dank acre. A Sussex don,
I taught the Jacobean anxieties: *The White Devil*.[6]
Flamineo's torch startles the brooding yews.
The drawn end comes in strides. I loved my Duchess,
the white flame of her soul blown out between
the smoking cypresses. Then I saw children pounce
on green meat with a rat's ferocity.

I called them up and took the train to Bristol,
my blood the Severn's[7] dregs and silver.
On Severn's estuary the pieces flash,
Iscariot's salary,[8] patron saint of spies.
I thought, who cares how many million starve?
Their rising souls will lighten the world's weight
and level its gull-glittering waterline;
we left at sunset down the estuary.

England recedes. The forked white gull
screeches, circling back.
Even the birds are pulled back by their orbit,
even mercy has its magnetic field.
                                        Back in the cabin,
I uncap the whisky, the porthole
mists with glaucoma. By the time I'm pissed,[9]
England, England will be
that pale serrated indigo on the sea-line.
"You are so fortunate, you get to see the world—"
Indeed, indeed, sirs, I have seen the world.
Spray splashes the portholes and vision blurs.

Leaning on the hot rail, watching the hot sea,
I saw them far off, kneeling on hot sand
in the pious genuflections of the locust,
as Ponce's armoured knees crush Florida
to the funereal fragrance of white lilies.

2

Now I have come to where the phantoms live,
I have no fear of phantoms, but of the real.
The Sabbath benedictions of the islands.

6. Revenge tragedy (c. 1612) by John Webster.
7. A river running through Wales and England.
8. For betraying Jesus Christ, Judas Iscariot was paid 30 pieces of silver by the Roman authorities.
9. Drunk.

Treble clef of the snail on the scored leaf,
the Tantum Ergo[1] of black choristers
soars through the organ pipes of coconuts.
Across the dirty beach surpliced with lace,
they pass a brown lagoon behind the priest,
pale and unshaven in his frayed soutane,[2]
into the concrete church at Canaries;
as Albert Schweitzer[3] moves to the harmonium
of morning, and to the pluming chimneys,
the groundswell lifts *Lebensraum, Lebensraum.*[4]

Black faces sprinkled with continual dew—
dew on the speckled croton,[5] dew
on the hard leaf of the knotted plum tree,
dew on the elephant ears of the dasheen.[6]
Through Kurtz's teeth, white skull in elephant grass,
the imperial fiction sings. Sunday
wrinkles downriver from the Heart of Darkness.
The heart of darkness is not Africa.
The heart of darkness is the core of fire
in the white center of the holocaust.
The heart of darkness is the rubber claw
selecting a scalpel in antiseptic light,
the hills of children's shoes outside the chimneys,
the tinkling nickel instruments on the white altar;
Jacob, in his last card, sent me these verses:
"Think of a God who doesn't lose His sleep
if trees burst into tears or glaciers weep.
So, aping His indifference, I write now,
not Anno Domini: After Dachau."[7]

3

The night maid brings a lamp and draws the blinds.
I stay out on the verandah with the stars.
Breakfast congealed to supper on its plate.

There is no sea as restless as my mind.
The promontories snore. They snore like whales.
Cetus, the whale, was Christ.
The ember dies, the sky smokes like an ash heap.
Reeds wash their hands of guilt and the lagoon
is stained. Louder, since it rained,
a gauze of sand flies hisses from the marsh.

Since God is dead,[8] and these are not His stars,
but man-lit, sulphurous, sanctuary lamps,
it's in the heart of darkness of this earth

1. A hymn sung after the Blessed Sacrament has been exposed in the mass.
2. Black robe.
3. German physician, missionary, and musician in Africa; winner of the Nobel Peace Prize in 1952.
4. Space to live in; the term is especially associated with Nazi Germany's territorial expansion.
5. A tropical plant.
6. The taro plant of tropical Asia.
7. Site of the notorious Nazi concentration camp.
8. So the German philosopher Friedrich Nietzsche declared in his 1882 text *The Gay Science*.

that backward tribes keep vigil of His Body,
in deya, lampion,[9] and this bedside lamp.
Keep the news from their blissful ignorance.
Like lice, like lice, the hungry of this earth
swarm to the tree of life. If those who starve
like these rain-flies who shed glazed wings in light
grew from sharp shoulder blades their brittle vans
and soared towards that tree, how it would seethe—
ah, Justice! But fires
drench them like vermin, quotas
prevent them, and they remain
compassionate fodder for the travel book,
its paragraphs like windows from a train,
for everywhere that earth shows its rib cage
and the moon goggles with the eyes of children,
we turn away to read. Rimbaud[1] learned that.
Rimbaud, at dusk,

idling his wrist in water past temples
the plumed dates still protect in Roman file,
knew that we cared less for one human face
than for the scrolls in Alexandria's ashes,
that the bright water could not dye his hand
any more than poetry. The dhow's[2] silhouette
moved through the blinding coinage of the river
that, endlessly, until we pay one debt,
shrouds, every night, an ordinary secret.

4

The drawn sword comes in strides.
It stretches for the length of the empty beach;
the fishermen's huts shut their eyes tight.
A frisson[3] shakes the palm trees.
and sweats on the traveller's tree.
They've found out my sanctuary. Philippe, last night:
"It had two gentlemen in the village yesterday, sir,
asking for you while you was in town.
I tell them you was in town. They send to tell you,
there is no hurry. They will be coming back."

In loaves of cloud, *and have not charity*,
the weevil will make a sahara of Kansas,
the ant shall eat Russia.
Their soft teeth shall make, *and have not charity*,
the harvest's desolation,
and the brown globe crack like a begging bowl,
and though you fire oceans of surplus grain,
and have not charity,

9. A small oil lamp with tinted glass.
1. Arthur Rimbaud (1854–1891), French poet. After abandoning poetry at the age of 20, he traveled in Egypt and the Sudan, later settling in Ethiopia as a trader and arms dealer.
2. A sailing vessel used by Arabs.
3. Sudden passing excitement.

still, through thin stalks,
the smoking stubble, stalks
grasshopper: third horseman,
the leather-helmed locust.[4]

1981

from Midsummer

50

I once gave my daughters, separately, two conch shells
that were dived from the reef, or sold on the beach, I forget.
They use them as doorstops or bookends, but their wet
pink palates are the soundless singing of angels.
I once wrote a poem called "The Yellow Cemetery,"
when I was nineteen. Lizzie's age. I'm fifty-three.
These poems I heaved aren't linked to any tradition
like a mossed cairn;[1] each goes down like a stone
to the seabed, settling, but let them, with luck, lie
where stones are deep, in the sea's memory.
Let them be, in water, as my father, who did watercolours,
entered his work. He became one of his shadows,
wavering and faint in the midsummer sunlight.
His name is Warwick Walcott. I sometimes believe
that his father, in love or bitter benediction,
named him for Warwickshire.[2] Ironies
are moving. Now, when I rewrite a line,
or sketch on the fast-drying paper the coconut fronds
that he did so faintly, my daughters' hands move in mine.
Conches move over the sea-floor. I used to move
my father's grave from the blackened Anglican headstones
in Castries[3] to where I could love both at once—
the sea and his absence. Youth is stronger than fiction.

52

I heard them marching the leaf-wet roads of my head,
the sucked vowels of a syntax trampled to mud,
a division of dictions, one troop black, barefooted,
the other in redcoats bright as their sovereign's blood;
their feet scuffled like rain, the bare soles with the shod.
One fought for a queen, the other was chained in her service,
but both, in bitterness, travelled the same road.
Our occupation and the Army of Occupation
are born enemies, but what mortar can size
the broken stones of the barracks of Brimstone Hill
to the gaping brick of Belfast? Have we changed sides
to the moustached sergeants and the horsy gentry

4. The locust, eater of crops, is here identified with the horseman of the Apocalypse quoted in the poem's epigraph.

1. A heap of stones marking a trail.

2. Birthplace of Shakespeare. Warwick Walcott, journalist, occasional poet, and printer, died when his son was a young child.

3. Port and capital of Saint Lucia.

because we serve English, like a two-headed sentry
guarding its borders? No language is neutral;
the green oak of English is a murmurous cathedral
where some took umbrage,[4] some peace, but every shade, all,
helped widen its shadow. I used to haunt the arches
of the British barracks of Vigie.[5] There were leaves there,
bright, rotting like revers of epaulettes,[6] and the stenches
of history and piss. Leaves piled like the dropped aitches
of soldiers from rival shires, from the brimstone trenches
of Agincourt to the gas of the Somme.[7] On Poppy Day[8]
our schools bought red paper flowers. They were for Flanders.[9]
I saw Hotspur cursing the smoke through which a popinjay
minced from the battle. Those raging commanders
from Thersites to Percy,[1] their rant is our model.
I pinned the poppy to my blazer. It bled like a vowel.

54

The midsummer sea, the hot pitch road, this grass, these shacks that made me,
jungle and razor grass shimmering by the roadside, the edge of art;
wood lice are humming in the sacred wood,
nothing can burn them out, they are in the blood;
their rose mouths, like cherubs, sing of the slow science
of dying—all heads, with, at each ear, a gauzy wing.
Up at Forest Reserve, before branches break into sea,
I looked through the moving, grassed window and thought "pines,"
or conifers of some sort. I thought, they must suffer
in this tropical heat with their child's idea of Russia.
Then suddenly, from their rotting logs, distracting signs
of the faith I betrayed, or the faith that betrayed me—
yellow butterflies rising on the road to Valencia[2]
stuttering "yes" to the resurrection; "yes, yes is our answer,"
the gold-robed Nunc Dimittis[3] of their certain choir.
Where's my child's hymnbook, the poems edged in gold leaf,
the heaven I worship with no faith in heaven,
as the Word turned toward poetry in its grief?
Ah, bread of life, that only love can leaven!
Ah, Joseph, though no man ever dies in his own country,[4]
the grateful grass will grow thick from his heart.

1984

4. In two senses: offense, shade.
5. Vigie Beach near Castries, Saint Lucia.
6. Turned-up edges of ornamental shoulder pieces worn on uniforms.
7. French sites of important battles in 1415 and in World War I.
8. Veterans Day.
9. Scene of a disastrous World War I offensive—"the battle of the mud"—in which the British lost 324,000 soldiers.
1. The headstrong Sir Henry Percy (1364–1403) became known as "Hotspur"; he serves as rival to Prince Hal in Shakespeare's *Henry IV*. Thersites accuses Achilles of cowardice in Homer's *Iliad*.
2. A seaport in Eastern Spain.
3. "Lord, now let thy servant depart in peace," sung at the end of Mass.
4. The line echoes Jesus's comment that no prophet is honored in his own country (Mark 6.4). On one level, Joseph may be Jesus's father, mourning his son's early death. *Midsummer* as a whole is addressed to Walcott's friend Joseph Brodsky, the exiled Russian poet.

V. S. Naipaul

b. 1932

V. S. Naipaul has been called "the world's writer," and his Nobel Prize in Literature in 2001 confirms his global significance. Naipaul is a British citizen, and he writes in English; he was educated at Oxford University, and he currently resides in Wiltshire, England. All the elements lend themselves to imagining an almost cozy British writer, happily ensconced within British society. And yet Naipaul's novels, stories, and essays are anything but complacent, rooted in place, or, for that matter, cozy. In major novels from *A House for Mr. Biswas* (1961) to *The Mimic Men* (1967), *In a Free State* (1971), *Guerillas* (1973), and *The Enigma of Arrival* (1987), Naipaul has addressed the most volatile, violent, and despairing aspects of life in the developing world, from India to Africa to the Caribbean. Naipaul has referred to himself as "rootless," in spite of his present rootedness in the British countryside, and as "content to be a colonial, without a past, without ancestors."

Born in Chaguanas, Trinidad, Vidiadhar Surajprasad Naipaul grew up amid the complexities of a still-colonial environment, as the British government presided over the Caribbean islands of Trinidad and Tobago. His father was a journalist and writer; both his parents were part of the West Indian community in Trinidad, a community that was created as the British brought laborers from the then-British colony of India to work in other colonies in Africa and the Caribbean. Naipaul has always described himself as estranged from India where he has never lived, yet his family carried on many Indian traditions in Trinidad. Trinidad was and is a poor country, still suffering from the effects of its colonial dependence and underdevelopment. As Naipaul's semiautobiographical novel *A House for Mr. Biswas* depicts it, jobs were almost nonexistent. Naipaul attended Queen's Royal College in Trinidad from 1943 to 1948; at that point, like many other intellectuals from Caribbean nations, he left for England and Oxford University, from which he received his BA in 1953.

Naipaul writes of places that are on the brink of national independence or experiencing its aftermath, places that must try to construct a national identity out of the flimsy leavings of colonial power and superiority. Part of Naipaul's force as a writer derives from his unsparing examination of such societies, whether Caribbean, Indian, African, or even, in his travel memoir *A Turn in the South* (1988), the southern United States. Naipaul is noteworthy for his refusal to exempt the developing world from criticism for the failures he detects in its societies, even though he fully grants the harsh struggles of these nations and regions emerging from colonial rule into independence. In fact, Naipaul has himself been criticized for the harshness of his judgments of the efforts of postcolonial societies, which his essays have excoriated for their corruption, ineptitude, and political oppressiveness. Even the drive for political justice Naipaul often represents as turning into a desperate and futile fanaticism—the tragedy of conquest having devolved into farcical attempts at revolution. He also extends this pessimism to Britain itself, tracing the bitter legacy of empire, and the permanent scars it caused in British culture and politics.

Naipaul can be compared to his great precursor Joseph Conrad, also a novelist of the world, an exile and a rootless man. Conrad was never fully part of British society, and his first language was Polish, yet he remains a consummate British writer. Naipaul is something of a reverse Conrad, in that, also a self-imposed exile, he came back to the heart of England from one of the "ends of the earth" Conrad writes about. Naipaul's prose style is as elegantly British as the most rooted of British native writers; he uses chiseled cadences to construct compelling narratives about the strangest thing of all—the ordinariness of the extraordinary in modern times. He deals with specific themes: the loss of home in postcolonial Britain, the loss of the past that is a consequence of these forced migrations, and the unalterable void that remains behind.

Naipaul's *In a Free State* was awarded the Booker Prize, England's major literary award, in 1971. The novella presents three intertwined stories of displacement and homelessness: the first, *One Out of Many*, describes a Bombay-born domestic servant who finds himself transplanted to Washington, D.C.; the middle story, *Tell Me Who to Kill*, focuses on a frustrated young West Indian man transported to London; and the final story, *In a Free State*, turns the tables, throwing two white Englishmen into the middle of an African state in upheaval. The novella is framed within two passages from Naipaul's journal writing, reprinted here; the tramp in the first selection, who considers himself "a citizen of the world," poses the question, "what's nationality these days?"—a question with real resonance for Naipaul's writing; the closing piece presents a circus as a symbol of postwar Europe, in which the old geopolitical and racial boundaries no longer make sense.

For additional resources on Naipaul, go to *The Longman Anthology of British Literature* Web site at www.myliteraturekit.com.

from In a Free State

Prologue, from a Journal

The Tramp at Piraeus

It was only a two-day crossing from Piraeus to Alexandria,[1] but as soon as I saw the dingy little Greek steamer I felt I ought to have made other arrangements. Even from the quay it looked overcrowded, like a refugee ship; and when I went aboard I found there wasn't enough room for everybody.

There was no deck to speak of. The bar, open on two sides to the January wind, was the size of a cupboard. Three made a crowd there, and behind his little counter the little Greek barman, serving bad coffee, was in a bad mood. Many of the chairs in the small smoking-room, and a good deal of the floor space, had been seized by overnight passengers from Italy, among them a party of overgrown American schoolchildren in their mid-teens, white and subdued but watchful. The only other public room was the dining-room, and that was being got ready for the first of the lunch sittings by stewards who were as tired and bad-tempered as the barman. Greek civility was something we had left on shore; it belonged perhaps to idleness, unemployment and pastoral despair.

But we on the upper part of the ship were lucky. We had cabins and bunks. The people on the lower deck didn't. They were deck passengers; night and day they required only sleeping room. Below us now they sat or lay in the sun, sheltering from the wind, humped figures in Mediterranean black among the winches and orange-coloured bulkheads.

They were Egyptian Greeks. They were travelling to Egypt, but Egypt was no longer their home. They had been expelled; they were refugees. The invaders had left Egypt; after many humiliations Egypt was free; and these Greeks, the poor ones, who by simple skills had made themselves only just less poor than Egyptians, were the casualties of that freedom.[2] Dingy Greek ships like ours had taken them out of Egypt.

1. Piraeus is the port of Athens, Greece; Alexandria is a major port on Egypt's Mediterranean coast.

2. Since antiquity, there had been a strong Greek presence in Egypt, especially in Alexandria. In the 19th century, however, there was a renewed influx of Greek immigrants, most of whom retained their Greek nationality. This community played major roles in business, finance, shipping, and the professions, and Alexandria became noted for its flourishing Greek cultural life. From the 1930s on, however, with the rise of Egyptian nationalism and the end of many features of colonial rule, Greek numbers declined; following the 1952 revolution, the end of British colonial power in the region, and the later advent of "Arab Socialism," events to which Naipaul here refers, this decline became an exodus; today there are few Greeks in Egypt.

Now, briefly, they were going back, with tourists like ourselves, who were neutral, travelling only for the sights; with Lebanese businessmen; a troupe of Spanish night-club dancers; fat Egyptian students returning from Germany.

The tramp, when he appeared on the quay, looked very English; but that might only have been because we had no English people on board. From a distance he didn't look like a tramp. The hat and the rucksack, the lovat tweed jacket, the grey flannels and the boots might have belonged to a romantic wanderer of an earlier generation; in that rucksack there might have been a book of verse, a journal, the beginnings of a novel.

He was slender, of medium height, and he moved from the knees down, with short springy steps, each foot lifted high off the ground. It was a stylish walk, as stylish as his polka-dotted saffron neck-scarf. But when he came nearer we saw that all his clothes were in ruin, that the knot on his scarf was tight and grimy; that he was a tramp. When he came to the foot of the gangway he took off his hat, and we saw that he was an old man, with a tremulous worn face and wet blue eyes.

He looked up and saw us, his audience. He raced up the gangway, not using the hand-ropes. Vanity! He showed his ticket to the surly Greek; and then, not looking about him, asking no questions, he continued to move briskly, as though he knew his way around the ship. He turned into a passageway that led nowhere. With comical abruptness he swung right round on one heel and brought his foot down hard.

"Purser," he said to the deck-boards, as though he had just remembered something. "I'll go and see the purser."

And so he picked his way to his cabin and bunk.

Our sailing was delayed. While their places in the smoking-room were being watched over, some of the American schoolchildren had gone ashore to buy food; we were waiting for them to come back. As soon as they did—no giggles: the girls were plain, pale and abashed—the Greeks became especially furious and rushed. The Greek language grated like the anchor chain. Water began to separate us from the quay and we could see, not far from where we had been, the great black hulk of the liner *Leonardo da Vinci,* just docked.

The tramp reappeared. He was without his hat and rucksack and looked less nervous. Hands in trouser-pockets already stuffed and bulging, legs apart, he stood on the narrow deck like an experienced sea-traveller exposing himself to the first sea breeze of a real cruise. He was also assessing the passengers; he was looking for company. He ignored people who stared at him; when others, responding to his own stare, turned to look at him he swivelled his head away.

In the end he went and stood beside a tall blond young man. His instinct had guided him well. The man he had chosen was a Yugoslav who, until the day before, had never been out of Yugoslavia. The Yugoslav was willing to listen. He was baffled by the tramp's accent but he smiled encouragingly; and the tramp spoke on.

"I've been to Egypt six or seven times. Gone around the world about a dozen times. Australia, Canada, all those countries. Geologist, or used to be. First went to Canada in 1923. Been there about eight times now. I've been travelling for thirty-eight years. Youth-hostelling, that's how I do it. Not a thing to be despised. New Zealand, have you been there? I went there in 1934. Between you and me, they're a cut above the Australians. But what's nationality these days? I myself, I think of myself as a citizen of the world."

His speech was like this, full of dates, places and numbers, with sometimes a simple opinion drawn from another life. But it was mechanical, without conviction; even the vanity made no impression; those quivering wet eyes remained distant.

The Yugoslav smiled and made interjections. The tramp neither saw nor heard. He couldn't manage a conversation; he wasn't looking for conversation; he didn't even require an audience. It was as though, over the years, he had developed this way of swiftly explaining himself to himself, reducing his life to names and numbers. When the names and numbers had been recited he had no more to say. Then he just stood beside the Yugoslav. Even before we had lost sight of Piraeus and the *Leonardo da Vinci* the tramp had exhausted that relationship. He hadn't wanted company; he wanted only the camouflage and protection of company. The tramp knew he was odd.

At lunch I sat with two Lebanese. They were both overnight passengers from Italy and were quick to explain that it was luggage, not money, that had prevented them travelling by air. They looked a good deal less unhappy with the ship than they said they were. They spoke in a mixture of French, English and Arabic and were exciting and impressing each other with talk of the money other people, mainly Lebanese, were making in this or that unlikely thing.

They were both under forty. One was pink, plump and casually dressed, with a canary pullover; his business in Beirut was, literally, money. The other Lebanese was dark, well-built, with moustached Mediterranean good looks, and wore a three-piece check suit. He made reproduction furniture in Cairo and he said that business was bad since the Europeans had left. Commerce and culture had vanished from Egypt; there was no great demand among the natives for reproduction furniture; and there was growing prejudice against Lebanese like himself. But I couldn't believe in his gloom. While he was talking to us he was winking at one of the Spanish dancers.

At the other end of the room a fat Egyptian student with thick-lensed glasses was being raucous in German and Arabic. The German couple at his table were laughing. Now the Egyptian began to sing an Arabic song.

The man from Beirut said in his American accent, "You should go modern."

"Never," the furniture-maker said. "I will leave Egypt first. I will close my factory. It is a horror, the modern style. It is grotesque, totally grotesque. *Mais le style Louis Seize, ah, voilà l'âme*[3]—" He broke off to applaud the Egyptian and to shout his congratulations in Arabic. Wearily then, but without malice, he said under his breath, "Ah, these natives." He pushed his plate from him, sank in his chair, beat his fingers on the dirty tablecloth. He winked at the dancer and the tips of his moustache flicked upwards.

The steward came to clear away. I was eating, but my plate went as well.

"You were dining, monsieur?" the furniture-maker said. "You must be *calme*. We must all be *calme*."

Then he raised his eyebrows and rolled his eyes. There was something he wanted us to look at.

It was the tramp, standing in the doorway, surveying the room. Such was the way he held himself that even now, at the first glance, his clothes seemed whole. He came to the cleared table next to ours, sat on a chair and shifted about in it until he was settled. Then he leaned right back, his arms on the rests, like the head of a household at the head of his table, like a cruise-passenger waiting to be served. He sighed and moved his jaws, testing his teeth. His jacket was in an appalling state. The pockets bulged; the flaps were fastened with safety pins.

3. But in Louis XVI style—now there is the soul (French).

The furniture-maker said something in Arabic and the man from Beirut laughed. The steward shooed us away and we followed the Spanish girls to the windy little bar for coffee.

Later that afternoon, looking for privacy, I climbed some steep steps to the open railed area above the cabins. The tramp was standing there alone, stained trouser-legs swollen, turn-ups shredded, exposed to the cold wind and the smuts from the smoke-stack. He held what looked like a little prayer-book. He was moving his lips and closing and opening his eyes, like a man praying hard. How fragile that face was, worked over by distress; how frail that neck, below the tight knot of the polka-dotted scarf. The flesh around his eyes seemed especially soft; he looked close to tears. It was strange. He looked for company but needed solitude; he looked for attention, and at the same time wanted not to be noticed.

I didn't disturb him. I feared to be involved with him. Far below, the Greek refugees sat or lay in the sun.

In the smoking-room after dinner the fat young Egyptian shouted himself hoarse, doing his cabaret act. People who understood what he was saying laughed all the time. Even the furniture-maker, forgetting his gloom about the natives, shouted and clapped with the rest. The American schoolchildren lay in their own promiscuous seasick heap and looked on, like people helplessly besieged; when they spoke among themselves it was in whispers.

The non-American part of the room was predominantly Arab and German and had its own cohesion. The Egyptian was our entertainer, and there was a tall German girl we could think of as our hostess. She offered us chocolate and had a word for each of us. To me she said: "You are reading a very good English book. These Penguin books are very good English books." She might have been travelling out to join an Arab husband; I wasn't sure.

I was sitting with my back to the door and didn't see when the tramp came in. But suddenly he was there before me, sitting on a chair that someone had just left. The chair was not far from the German girl's, but it stood in no intimate relationship to that chair or any other group of chairs. The tramp sat squarely on it, straight up against the back. He faced no one directly, so that in that small room he didn't become part of the crowd but appeared instead to occupy the centre of a small stage within it.

He sat with his old man's legs wide apart, his weighted jacket sagging over his bulging trouser-pockets. He had come with things to read, a magazine, the little book which I had thought was a prayer-book. I saw now that it was an old pocket diary with many loose leaves. He folded the magazine in four, hid it under his thigh, and began to read the pocket diary. He laughed, and looked up to see whether he was being noticed. He turned a page, read and laughed again, more loudly. He leaned towards the German girl and said to her over his shoulder, "I say, do you read Spanish?"

She said, carefully, "No."

"These Spanish jokes are awfully funny."

But though he read a few more, he didn't laugh again.

The Egyptian continued to clown; that racket went on. Soon the German girl was offering chocolate once more. "*Bitte?*" [would you like some] Her voice was soft.

The tramp was unfolding his magazine. He stopped and looked at the chocolate. But there was none for him. He unfolded his magazine. Then, unexpectedly, he began to destroy it. With nervous jigging hands he tore at a page, once, twice. He turned some pages, began to tear again; turned back, tore. Even with the raucousness around the Egyptian the sound of tearing paper couldn't be ignored. Was he tearing out pictures—sport, women, advertisements—that offended him? Was he hoarding toilet paper for Egypt?

The Egyptian fell silent and looked. The American schoolchildren looked. Now, too late after the frenzy, and in what was almost silence, the tramp made a show of reason. He opened the tattered magazine wide out, turned it around angrily, as though the right side up hadn't been easy to find, and at last pretended to read. He moved his lips; he frowned; he tore and tore. Strips and shreds of paper littered the floor around his chair. He folded the loose remains of the magazine, stuffed it into his jacket pocket, pinned the flaps down, and went out of the room, looking like a man who had been made very angry.

"I will kill him," the furniture-maker said at breakfast the next morning.

He was in his three-piece suit but he was unshaven and the dark rings below his eyes were like bruises. The man from Beirut, too, looked tired and crumpled. They hadn't had a good night. The third bunk in their cabin was occupied by an Austrian boy, a passenger from Italy, with whom they were on good terms. They had seen the rucksack and the hat on the fourth bunk; but it wasn't until it was quite late, all three in their bunks, that they had discovered that the tramp was to be the fourth among them.

"It was pretty bad," the man from Beirut said. He felt for delicate words and added, "The old guy's like a child."

"Child! If the English pig comes in now"—the furniture-maker raised his arm and pointed at the door—"I will *kill* him. *Now*."

He was pleased with the gesture and the words; he repeated them, for the room. The Egyptian student, hoarse and hungover after the evening's performance, said something in Arabic. It was obviously witty, but the furniture-maker didn't smile. He beat his fingers on the table, stared at the door and breathed loudly through his nose.

No one was in a good mood. The drumming and the throbbing and bucking of the ship had played havoc with stomachs and nerves; the cold wind outside irritated as much as it refreshed; and in the dining-room the air was stale, with a smell as of hot rubber. There was no crowd, but the stewards, looking unslept and unwashed, even their hair not well combed, were as rushed as before.

The Egyptian shrieked.

The tramp had come in, benign and rested and ready for his coffee and rolls. He had no doubts about his welcome now. He came without hesitation or great speed to the table next to ours, settled himself in his chair and began to test his teeth. He was quickly served. He chewed and drank with complete relish.

The Egyptian shrieked again.

The furniture-maker said to him, "I will send him to your room tonight."

The tramp didn't see or hear. He was only eating and drinking. Below the tight knot of his scarf his Adam's apple was very busy. He drank noisily, sighing afterwards; he chewed with rabbit-like swiftness, anxious to be free for the next mouthful; and between mouthfuls he hugged himself, rubbing his arms and elbows against his sides, in pure pleasure at food.

The fascination of the furniture-maker turned to rage. Rising, but still looking at the tramp, he called, "Hans!"

The Austrian boy, who was at the table with the Egyptian, got up. He was about sixteen or seventeen, square and chunky, enormously well-developed, with a broad smiling face. The man from Beirut also got up, and all three went outside.

The tramp, oblivious of this, and of what was being prepared for him, continued to eat and drink until, with a sigh which was like a sigh of fatigue, he was finished.

It was to be like a tiger-hunt, where bait is laid out and the hunter and spectators watch from the security of a platform. The bait here was the tramp's own rucksack. They placed that on the deck outside the cabin door, and watched it. The furniture-maker still pretended to be too angry to talk. But Hans smiled and explained the rules of the game as often as he was asked.

The tramp, though, didn't immediately play. After breakfast he disappeared. It was cold on the deck, even in the sunshine, and sometimes the spray came right up. People who had come out to watch didn't stay, and even the furniture-maker and the man from Beirut went from time to time to rest in the smoking-room among the Germans and Arabs and the Spanish girls. They were given chairs; there was sympathy for their anger and exhaustion. Hans remained at his post. When the cold wind made him go inside the cabin he watched through the open door, sitting on one of the lower bunks and smiling up at people who passed.

Then the news came that the tramp had reappeared and had been caught according to the rules of the game. Some of the American schoolchildren were already on deck, studying the sea. So were the Spanish girls and the German girl. Hans blocked the cabin door. I could see the tramp holding the strap of his rucksack; I could hear him complaining in English through the French and Arabic shouts of the furniture-maker, who was raising his arms and pointing with his right hand, the skirts of his jacket dancing.

In the dining-room the furniture-maker's anger had seemed only theatrical, an aspect of his Mediterranean appearance, the moustache, the wavy hair. But now, in the open, with an expectant audience and a victim so nearly passive, he was working himself into a frenzy.

"Pig! Pig!"

"It's not true," the tramp said, appealing to people who had only come to watch.

"Pig!"

The grotesque moment came. The furniture-maker, so strongly built, so elegant in his square-shouldered jacket, lunged with his left hand at the old man's head. The tramp swivelled his head, the way he did when he refused to acknowledge a stare. And he began to cry. The furniture-maker's hand went wide and he stumbled forward against the rails into a spatter of spray. Putting his hands to his breast, feeling for pen and wallet and other things, he cried out, like a man aggrieved and desperate, "Hans! Hans!"

The tramp stooped; he stopped crying; his blue eyes popped. Hans had seized him by the polka-dotted scarf, twisting it, jerking it down. Kicking the rucksack hard, Hans at the same time flung the tramp forward by the knotted scarf. The tramp stumbled over Hans's kicking foot. The strain went out of Hans's smiling face and all that was left was the smile. The tramp could have recovered from his throw and stumble. But he preferred to fall and then to sit up. He was still holding the strap of his rucksack. He was crying again.

"It's not true. These remarks they've been making, it's not true."

The young Americans were looking over the rails.

"Hans!" the furniture-maker called.

The tramp stopped crying.

"Ha-ans!"

The tramp didn't look round. He got up with his rucksack and ran.

The story was that he had locked himself in one of the lavatories. But he reappeared among us, twice.

About an hour later he came into the smoking-room, without his rucksack, with no sign of distress on his face. He was already restored. He came in, in his abrupt way, not looking to right or left. Just a few steps brought him right into the small room and almost up against the legs of the furniture-maker, who was stretched out in an upholstered chair, exhausted, one hand over his half-closed eyes. After surprise, anger and contempt filled the tramp's eyes. He started to swivel his head away.

"Hans!" the furniture-maker called, recovering from his astonishment, drawing back his legs, leaning forward. "Ha-ans!"

Swivelling his head, the tramp saw Hans rising with some playing cards in his hands. Terror came to the tramp's eyes. The swivelling motion of his head spread to the rest of his body. He swung round on one heel, brought the other foot down hard, and bolted. Entry, advance, bandy-legged swivel and retreat had formed one unbroken movement.

"Hans!"

It wasn't a call to action. The furniture-maker was only underlining the joke. Hans, understanding, laughed and went back to his cards.

The tramp missed his lunch. He should have gone down immediately, to the first sitting, which had begun. Instead, he went into hiding, no doubt in one of the lavatories, and came out again only in time for the last sitting. It was the sitting the Lebanese and Hans had chosen. The tramp saw from the doorway.

"Ha-ans!"

But the tramp was already swivelling.

Later he was to be seen with his rucksack, but without his hat, on the lower deck, among the refugees. Without him, and then without reference to him, the joke continued, in the bar, on the narrow deck, in the smoking-room. "Hans! Ha-ans!" Towards the end Hans didn't laugh or look up; when he heard his name he completed the joke by giving a whistle. The joke lived; but by nightfall the tramp was forgotten.

At dinner the Lebanese spoke again in their disinterested way about money. The man from Beirut said that because of certain special circumstances in the Middle East that year, there was a fortune to be made from the well-judged exporting of Egyptian shoes; but not many people knew. The furniture-maker said the fact had been known to him for months. They postulated an investment, vied with each other in displaying knowledge of hidden, local costs, and calmly considered the staggering profits. But they weren't really exciting one another any longer. The game was a game; each had taken the measure of the other. And they were both tired.

Something of the lassitude of the American schoolchildren had come over the other passengers on this last evening. The Americans themselves were beginning to thaw out. In the smoking-room, where the lights seemed dimmer, their voices were raised in friendly boy-girl squabbles; they did a lot more coming and going; especially active was a tall girl in a type of ballet-dancer's costume, all black from neck to wrist to ankle. The German girl, our hostess of the previous evening, looked quite ill. The Spanish girls were flirting with nobody. The Egyptian, whose hangover had been compounded by seasickness, was playing bridge. Gamely from time to time he croaked out a witticism or a line of a song, but he got smiles rather than laughs. The furniture-maker and Hans were also playing cards. When a good card or a disappointing one was played the furniture-maker said in soft exclamation, expecting no response, "Hans, Hans." It was all that remained of the day's joke.

The man from Beirut came in and watched. He stood beside Hans. Then he stood beside the furniture-maker and whispered to him in English, their secret language. "The guy's locked himself in the cabin."

Hans understood. He looked at the furniture-maker. But the furniture-maker was weary. He played his hand, then went out with the man from Beirut.

When he came back he said to Hans, "He says that he will set fire to the cabin if we try to enter. He says that he has a quantity of paper and a quantity of matches. I believe that he will do it."

"What do we do?" the man from Beirut asked.

"We will sleep here. Or in the dining-room."

"But those Greek stewards sleep in the dining-room. I saw them this morning."

"That proves that it is possible," the furniture-maker said.

Later, the evening over, I stopped outside the tramp's cabin. At first I heard nothing. Then I heard paper being crumpled: the tramp's warning. I wonder how long he stayed awake that night, listening for footsteps, waiting for the assault on the door and the entry of Hans.

In the morning he was back on the lower deck, among the refugees. He had his hat again; he had recovered it from the cabin.

Alexandria was a long shining line on the horizon: sand and the silver of oil-storage tanks. The sky clouded over; the green sea grew choppier. We entered the breakwater in cold rain and stormlight.

Long before the immigration officials came on board we queued to meet them. Germans detached themselves from Arabs, Hans from the Lebanese, the Lebanese from the Spanish girls. Now, as throughout the journey since his meeting with the tramp, the tall blond Yugoslav was a solitary. From the lower deck the refugees came up with their boxes and bundles, so that at last they were more than their emblematic black wrappings. They had the slack bodies and bad skins of people who ate too many carbohydrates. Their blotched faces were immobile, distant, but full of a fierce, foolish cunning. They were watching. As soon as the officials came aboard the refugees began to push and fight their way towards them. It was a factitious frenzy, the deference of the persecuted to authority.

The tramp came up with his hat and rucksack. There was no nervousness in his movements but his eyes were quick with fear. He took his place in the queue and pretended to frown at its length. He moved his feet up and down, now like a man made impatient by officials, now like someone only keeping out the cold. But he was of less interest than he thought. Hans, mountainous with his own rucksack, saw him and then didn't see him. The Lebanese, shaved and rested after their night in the dining room, didn't see him. That passion was over.

Epilogue, from a Journal

The Circus at Luxor

I was going to Egypt, this time by air, and I broke my journey at Milan. I did so for business reasons. But it was Christmas week, not a time for business, and I had to stay in Milan over the holidays. The weather was bad, the hotel empty and desolate.

Returning through the rain to the hotel one evening, after a restaurant dinner, I saw two Chinese men in dark-blue suits come out of the hotel dining-room. Fellow Asiatics, the three of us, I thought, wanderers in industrial Europe. But they didn't glance at me. They had companions: three more Chinese came out of the dining-room, two young men in suits, a fresh-complexioned young woman in a flowered tunic and slacks. Then five more Chinese came out, healthy young men and women; then about a dozen. Then I couldn't count. Chinese poured out of the dining-room and swirled about the spacious carpeted lobby before moving in a slow, softly chattering mass up the steps.

There must have been about a hundred Chinese. It was minutes before the lobby emptied. The waiters, serving-napkins in hand, stood in the door of the dining-room and watched, like people able at last to acknowledge an astonishment. Two more Chinese came out of the dining-room; they were the last. They were both short, elderly men, wrinkled and stringy, with glasses. One of them held a fat wallet in his small hand, but awkwardly, as though the responsibility made him nervous. The waiters straightened up. Not attempting style, puzzling over the Italian notes, the old Chinese with the wallet tipped, thanked and shook hands with each waiter. Then both the Chinese bowed and got into the lift. And the hotel lobby was desolate again.

"They are the circus," the dark-suited desk-clerk said. He was as awed as the waiters. "*Vengono dalla Cina rossa*. They come from Red China."

I left Milan in snow. In Cairo, in the derelict cul-de-sac behind my hotel, children in dingy jibbahs,[1] feeble from their day-long Ramadan fasting, played football in the white, warm dust.[2] In cafés, shabbier than I remembered, Greek and Lebanese businessmen in suits read the local French and English newspapers and talked with sullen excitement about the deals that might be made in Rhodesian tobacco, now that it was outlawed. The Museum was still haunted by Egyptian guides possessing only native knowledge. And on the other bank of the Nile there was a new Hilton hotel.

But Egypt still had her revolution. Street signs were now in Arabic alone; people in tobacco kiosks reacted sharply, as to an insult, when they were asked for *Egyptian* cigarettes; and in the railway station, when I went to get the train south, there was a reminder of the wars that had come with the revolution. Sunburnt soldiers, back from duty in Sinai,[3] crouched and sprawled on the floor of the waiting-room. These men with shrunken faces were the guardians of the land and the revolution; but to Egyptians they were only common soldiers, peasants, objects of a disregard that was older and more rooted than the revolution.

All day the peasant land rolled past the windows of the train: the muddy river, the green fields, the desert, the black mud, the *shadouf*,[4] the choked and crumbling flat-roofed towns the colour of dust: the Egypt of the school geography book. The sun set in a smoky sky; the land felt old. It was dark when I left the train at Luxor. Later that evening I went to the temple of Karnak.[5] It was a good way of seeing it for the first time, in the darkness, separate from the distress of Egypt: those extravagant columns, ancient in ancient times, the work of men of this Nile Valley.

There was no coin in Egypt that year, only paper money. All foreign currencies went far; and Luxor,[6] in recent imperial days a winter resort of some style, was accommodating itself to simpler tourists. At the Old Winter Palace Hotel, where fat Negro servants in

1. A long outer garment, open at the front, with wide sleeves.
2. During the month of Ramadan in the Islamic calendar, Muslims fast from sunrise to sunset.
3. The Sinai Peninsula, stretching from the Suez Canal to the Israeli border, was occupied by Israel during the 1967 war between Israel and several Arab countries including Egypt; it was restored to Egypt in 1982 following almost a decade of negotiations.
4. A mechanism for raising irrigation water.
5. Luxor is a city in southern Egypt; north of it are ruins of the temple-complex of Karnak, which mostly dates back to the New Kingdom (1550–1069 B.C.E.).
6. A favorite winter resort for European tourists when the Ottoman province and later Kingdom of Egypt was a British "protectorate" and British troops were stationed in the country. Following the coup d'etat in 1952, the subsequent declaration of a republic and British evacuation, their numbers dropped.

long white gowns stood about in the corridors, they told me they were giving me the room they used to give the Aga Khan.[7] It was an enormous room, overfurnished in a pleasing old-fashioned way. It had a balcony and a view of the Nile and low desert hills on the other bank.

In those hills were the tombs.[8] Not all were of kings and not all were solemn. The ancient artist, recording the life of a lesser personage, sometimes recorded with a freer hand the pleasures of that life: the pleasures of the river, full of fish and birds, the pleasures of food and drink. The land had been studied, everything in it categorized, exalted into design. It was the special vision of men who knew no other land and saw what they had as rich and complete. The muddy Nile was only water: in the paintings, a blue-green chevron: recognizable, but remote, a river in fairyland.

It could be hot in the tombs. The guide, who was also sometimes the watchman, crouched and chattered in Arabic, earning his paper piastres,[9] pointing out every symbol of the goddess Hathor, rubbing a grimy finger on the paintings he was meant to protect. Outside, after the darkness and the bright visions of the past, there was only rubbled white sand; the sunlight stunned; and sometimes there were beggar boys in jibbahs.

To me these boys, springing up expectantly out of rock and sand when men approached, were like a type of sand animal. But my driver knew some of them by name; when he shooed them away it was with a languid gesture which also contained a wave. He was a young man, the driver, of the desert himself, and once no doubt he had been a boy in a jibbah. But he had grown up differently. He wore trousers and shirt and was vain of his good looks. He was reliable and correct, without the frenzy of the desert guide. Somehow in the desert he had learned boredom. His thoughts were of Cairo and a real job. He was bored with the antiquities, the tourists and the tourist routine.

I was spending the whole of that day in the desert, and now it was time for lunch. I had a Winter Palace lunchbox, and I had seen somewhere in the desert the new government rest-house where tourists could sit at tables and eat their sandwiches and buy coffee. I thought the driver was taking me there. But we went by unfamiliar ways to a little oasis with palm trees and a large, dried-up timber hut. There were no cars, no minibuses, no tourists, only anxious Egyptian serving-people in rough clothes. I didn't want to stay. The driver seemed about to argue, but then he was only bored. He drove to the new rest-house, set me down and said he would come back for me later.

The rest-house was crowded. Sunglassed tourists, exploring their cardboard lunch-boxes, chattered in various European languages. I sat on the terrace at a table with two young Germans. A brisk middle-aged Egyptian in Arab dress moved among the tables and served coffee. He had a camel-whip at his waist, and I saw, but only slowly, that for some way around the rest-house the hummocked sand was alive with little desert children. The desert was clean, the air was clean; these children were very dirty.

The rest-house was out of bounds to them. When they came close, tempted by the offer of a sandwich or an apple, the man with the camel-whip gave a camel-frightening shout. Sometimes he ran out among them, beating the sand with his

7. The *Imam,* or spiritual leader, of a sect within Islam.
8. Across from Luxor, on the western bank of the Nile, are the mountains that enclose the Valley of the Kings, where many Egyptian pharoahs were buried.
9. There are 100 piastres in one Egyptian pound.

whip, and they skittered away, thin little sand-smoothed legs frantic below swinging jibbahs. There was no rebuke for the tourists who had offered the food; this was an Egyptian game with Egyptian rules.

It was hardly a disturbance. The young Germans at my table paid no attention. The English students inside the rest-house, behind glass, were talking competitively about Carter and Lord Carnarvon.[1] But the middle-aged Italian group on the terrace, as they understood the rules of the game, became playful. They threw apples and made the children run far. Experimentally they broke up sandwiches and threw the pieces out onto the sand; and they got the children to come up quite close. Soon it was all action around the Italians; and the man with the camel-whip, like a man understanding what was required of him, energetically patrolled that end of the terrace, shouting, beating the sand, earning his paper piastres.

A tall Italian in a cerise jersey stood up and took out his camera. He laid out food just below the terrace and the children came running. But this time, as though it had to be real for the camera, the camel-whip fell not on sand but on their backs, with louder, quicker camel-shouts. And still, among the tourists in the rest-house and among the Egyptian drivers standing about their cars and minibuses, there was no disturbance. Only the man with the whip and the children scrabbling in the sand were frantic. The Italians were cool. The man in the cerise jersey was opening another packet of sandwiches. A shorter, older man in a white suit had stood up and was adjusting his camera. More food was thrown out; the camel-whip continued to fall; the shouts of the man with the whip turned to resonant grunts.

Still the Germans at my table didn't notice; the students inside were still talking. I saw that my hand was trembling. I put down the sandwich I was eating on the metal table; it was my last decision. Lucidity, and anxiety, came to me only when I was almost on the man with the camel-whip. I was shouting. I took the whip away, threw it on the sand. He was astonished, relieved. I said, "I will report this to Cairo." He was frightened; he began to plead in Arabic. The children were puzzled; they ran off a little way and stood up to watch. The two Italians, fingering cameras, looked quite calm behind their sunglasses. The women in the party leaned back in their chairs to consider me.

I felt exposed, futile, and wanted only to be back at my table. When I got back I took up my sandwich. It had happened quickly; there had been no disturbance. The Germans stared at me. But I was indifferent to them now as I was indifferent to the Italian in the cerise jersey. The Italian women had stood up, the group was leaving; and he was ostentatiously shaking out lunch-boxes and sandwich wrappers onto the sand.

The children remained where they were. The man from whom I had taken the whip came to give me coffee and to plead again in Arabic and English. The coffee was free; it was his gift to me. But even while he was talking the children had begun to come closer. Soon they would be back, raking the sand for what they had seen the Italian throw out.

I didn't want to see that. The driver was waiting, leaning against the car door, his bare arms crossed. He had seen all that had happened. From him, an emancipated young man of the desert in belted trousers and sports shirt, with his thoughts of Cairo, I was expecting some gesture, some sign of approval. He smiled at me with the

1. Funded by Lord Carnarvon, the British Egyptologist Howard Carter discovered the tomb of Tutankhamen in the Valley of the Kings at Luxor in 1922.

corners of his wide mouth, with his narrow eyes. He crushed his cigarette in the sand and slowly breathed out smoke through his lips; he sighed. But that was his way of smoking. I couldn't tell what he thought. He was as correct as before, he looked as bored.

Everywhere I went that afternoon I saw the pea-green Volkswagen minibus of the Italian group. Everywhere I saw the cerise jersey. I learned to recognize the plump, squiffy, short-stepped walk that went with it, the dark glasses, the receding hairline, the little stiff swing of the arms. At the ferry I thought I had managed to escape; but the minibus arrived, the Italians got out. I thought we would separate on the Luxor bank. But they too were staying at the Winter Palace. The cerise jersey bobbed confidently through bowing Egyptian servants in the lobby, the bar, the grand dining-room with fresh flowers and intricately folded napkins. In Egypt that year there was only paper money.

I stayed for a day or two on the Luxor bank. Dutifully, I saw Karnak by moonlight. When I went back to the desert I was anxious to avoid the rest-house. The driver understood. Without any show of triumph he took me when the time came to the timber hut among the palm trees. They were doing more business that day. There were about four or five parked minibuses. Inside, the hut was dark, cool and uncluttered. A number of tables had been joined together; and at this central dining-board there were about forty or fifty Chinese, men and women, chattering softly. They were part of the circus I had seen in Milan.

The two elderly Chinese sat together at one end of the long table, next to a small, finely made lady who looked just a little too old to be an acrobat. I had missed her in the crowd in Milan. Again, when the time came to pay, the man with the fat wallet used his hands awkwardly. The lady spoke to the Egyptian waiter. He called the other waiters and they all formed a line. For each waiter the lady had a handshake and gifts, money, something in an envelope, a medal. The ragged waiters stood stiffly, with serious averted faces, like soldiers being decorated. Then all the Chinese rose and, chattering, laughing softly, shuffled out of the echoing hut with their relaxed, slightly splayed gait. They didn't look at me; they appeared scarcely to notice the hut. They were as cool and well-dressed in the desert, the men in suits, the girls in slacks, as they had been in the rain of Milan. So self-contained, so handsome and healthy, so silently content with one another: it was hard to think of them as sightseers.

The waiter, his face still tense with pleasure, showed the medal on his dirty striped jibbah. It had been turned out from a mould that had lost its sharpness; but the ill-defined face was no doubt Chinese and no doubt that of the leader. In the envelope were pretty coloured postcards of Chinese peonies.

Peonies, China! So many empires had come here. Not far from where we were was the colossus on whose shin the Emperor Hadrian had caused to be carved verses in praise of himself, to commemorate his visit.[2] On the other bank, not far from the Winter Palace, was a stone with a rougher Roman inscription marking the southern limit of the Empire, defining an area of retreat.[3] Now another, more remote empire was announcing itself. A medal, a postcard; and all that was asked in return was anger and a sense of injustice.

2. The Roman emperor Hadrian (r. 117–138 C.E.) was noted for his interest in Egypt, traveling extensively there.

3. Egypt became a personal estate of the Roman emperor following the defeat of Cleopatra at the hands of Roman forces in 30 B.C.E.; the border with Nubia was set some 50 miles south of the first cataract of the Nile (some distance south of Luxor).

Perhaps that had been the only pure time, at the beginning, when the ancient artist, knowing no other land, had learned to look at his own and had seen it as complete. But it was hard, travelling back to Cairo, looking with my stranger's eye at the fields and the people who worked in them, the dusty towns, the agitated peasant crowds at railway stations, it was hard to believe that there had been such innocence. Perhaps that vision of the land, in which the Nile was only water, a blue-green chevron, had always been a fabrication, a cause for yearning, something for the tomb.

The air-conditioning in the coach didn't work well; but that might have been because the two Negro attendants, still with the habits of the village, preferred to sit before the open doors to chat. Sand and dust blew in all day; it was hot until the sun set and everything went black against the red sky. In the dimly lit waiting-room of Cairo station there were more sprawled soldiers from Sinai, peasants in bulky woollen uniforms going back on leave to their villages. Seventeen months later these men, or men like them, were to know total defeat in the desert; and news photographs taken from helicopters flying down low were to show them lost, trying to walk back home, casting long shadows on the sand.

August 1969–October 1970

Tom Stoppard

b. 1937

Tom Stoppard's route to British knighthood (C.B.E., 1997) was a very improbable one—as unlikely, perhaps, as Rosencrantz's flipping a coin "heads" eighty-five times in a row at the opening of Stoppard's Tony-winning play, *Rosencrantz & Guildenstern Are Dead* (1966). In the more than four decades since the triumphant debut of his first major play at the venerable Old Vic theater in London, Stoppard has gone on to dominate the British stage in the second half of the twentieth, and the opening years of the twenty-first, centuries.

Stoppard was born Tomáš Straussler in Zlin, Czechoslovakia; his Jewish family was forced to flee the Nazi invasion in 1941, relocating in Singapore. Just two years later, the Strausslers were on the run again, this time to Darjeeling, India, ahead of the Japanese invasion of Singapore. From before the age of two, then, Stoppard was a temporary resident of the eastern outposts of the British Empire. His British schooling was begun in India, but after his widowed mother remarried, and as India gained its independence from Great Britain, Stoppard (his stepfather's name) moved to England, completing his secondary schooling in Nottinghamshire and Devonshire.

Stoppard began his career as a journalist, and eventually was made drama critic at the *Bristol Evening World;* this entrée into the theater proved fateful, as it had for the theater and music critic Bernard Shaw before him, and Stoppard completed his first play in 1960 (though it was not staged until 1968, in a much revised version). *Rosencrantz & Guildenstern* followed a few years later, and captured the attention of the British and American theater world: "In one bound," wrote the influential *New York Times* theater critic Clive Barnes, "Mr. Stoppard is asking to be considered as among the finest English-speaking writers of our stage." Revisiting *Hamlet* from the perspective of two childhood friends of the prince, the play helped to inaugurate, along with Jean Rhys's novel *Wide Sargasso Sea* published in the same year (and based on Charlotte Brontë's *Jane Eyre*), the postmodern penchant for interrogating the great works of the Western tradition from the perspective of characters whose stories remain untold in the originals.

What has followed from Stoppard's pen is a string of critical and popular successes, most notable among them *The Real Inspector Hound* (1968), *Jumpers* (1972), *Travesties* (1974), *The Real Thing* (1982), and *Arcadia* (1993). *The Invention of Love* (1997) explores the life of poet and classics scholar A. E. Housman, interweaving what is known of his biography with the life and work of another British sexual outlaw, Oscar Wilde. Each man dealt with his sexuality differently; Wilde's homosexuality, famously put on trial in 1895, resulted in a prison term that effectively put an end to his life, while Housman's struggles remained more private. Both men, however, sought in their own way a new language for "the love," as Wilde famously dubbed it, "that dare not speak its name." Most recently, *Rock 'n' Roll* (2006) demonstrates Stoppard's increasing engagement with political causes, especially that of international human rights; the play is dedicated to Stoppard's friend, the Czech playwright and dissident—as well as the last president of Czechoslovakia and first president of the Czech Republic—Václav Havel. In 2004, Stoppard was recognized in the United States with the Presidential Medal of Freedom.

The Invention of Love

Characters

AEH, *A. E. Housman, aged 77*
HOUSMAN, *A. E. Housman, aged from 18 to 26*
ALFRED WILLIAM POLLARD, *aged from 18 to 26*
MOSES JOHN JACKSON, *aged from 19 to 27*
CHARON, *ferryman of the Underworld*

IN ACT ONE:

MARK PATTISON, *Rector of Lincoln College, aged 64 a classical scholar*
WALTER PATER, *critic, essayist, scholar, fellow of Brasenose, aged 38*
JOHN RUSKIN, *pre-eminent art critic, aged 58*
BENJAMIN JOWETT, *Master of Balliol, aged 60*
ROBINSON ELLIS, *a Latin scholar, aged 45*

In addition, the VICE-CHANCELLOR OF OXFORD UNIVERSITY and a BALLIOL STUDENT

IN ACT TWO:

KATHARINE HOUSMAN, *sister of AEH, at the ages of 19 and 35*
HENRY LABOUCHERE, *Liberal MP and journalist, at the ages of 54 and 64*
FRANK HARRIS, *writer and journalist, at the ages of 29 and about 40*
W. T. STEAD, *editor and journalist, at the ages of 36 and 46*
CHAMBERLAIN, *a clerk in his 20s, then 30s*
JOHN PERCIVAL POSTGATE, *a Latin scholar, aged about 40*
JEROME K. JEROME, *humourist and editor, aged 38*
OSCAR WILDE, *aged 41*

In addition, BUNTHORNE, a character in *Patience* by Gilbert and Sullivan, and the CHAIRMAN and MEMBERS OF THE SELECTION COMMITTEE

The two groups of characters appearing only in Act One or Act Two, respectively, may be played by the same group of actors.
References in the stage directions to river, boats, garden, etc., need not be taken at face value.

ACT ONE[1]

AEH, aged seventy-seven and getting no older, wearing a buttoned-up dark suit and neat black boots, stands on the bank of the Styx watching the approach of the ferryman, Charon[2]

AEH: I'm dead, then. Good. And this is the Stygian gloom[3] one has heard so much about.

CHARON: Belay the painter[4] there, sir!

AEH: "Belay the painter!" The tongues of men and of angels!

CHARON: See the cleat. I trust you had grieving friends and family, sir, to give you a decent burial.

AEH: Cremation, but very decent I believe: a service at Trinity College[5] and the ashes laid to rest—for fathomable reasons—in Shropshire,[6] a county where I never lived and seldom set foot.

CHARON: So long as the wolves and bears don't dig you up.

AEH: No fear of that. The jackals are another matter. One used to say, "After I'm dead." The consolation is not as complete as one had supposed. There—the painter is belayed. I heard Ruskin[7] lecture in my first term at Oxford. Painters belayed on every side. He died mad. As you may have noticed. Are we waiting for someone?

CHARON: He's late. I hope nothing's happened to him. What do they call you, sir?

AEH: Alfred Housman is my name. My friends call me Housman. My enemies call me Professor Housman. Now you're going to ask me for a coin, and, regrettably, the custom of putting a coin in the mouth of the deceased is foreign to the Evelyn Nursing Home and probably against the rules. [*Looking out.*] Doubly late. Are you sure?

CHARON: A poet and a scholar is what I was told.

AEH: I think that must be me.

CHARON: Both of them?

AEH: I'm afraid so.

CHARON: It sounded like two different people.

AEH: I know.

CHARON: Give him a minute.

AEH: To collect myself. Ah, look, I've found a sixpence. Mint. 1936 Anno Domini.

CHARON: You know Latin.

AEH: I should say I do. I am—I was, for twenty-five years, Benjamin Hall Kennedy Professor of Latin at Cambridge. Is Kennedy here? I should like to meet him.

CHARON: Everyone is here, and those that aren't will be. Sit in the middle.

AEH: Of course. Well, I don't suppose I'll have time to meet everybody.

CHARON: Yes, you will, but Benjamin Hall Kennedy isn't usually first choice.

AEH: I didn't mean to suggest that he is mine. He imputed to the practice of translation into Greek and Latin verse a value which it does not really possess, at least not as an insight into the principles of ancient metre. It stands to reason that you are not likely to discover the laws of metre by composing verses in which you occasionally break those laws because you have not yet discovered them. But

1. Many of the foreign words and phrases of the play are translated in the play itself; much of the play is about the activity of translation. Latin and Greek passages are translated only where their meanings are not clear from the context.

2. Boatman who ferries the dead across the River Styx into the underworld in Greek mythology.

3. The dark of Hades ("Stygian" means "of the River Styx"); a tag from Dante's *Inferno.*

4. Moor the boat.

5. One of the Cambridge colleges.

6. Housman's first book of poems was titled, *A Shropshire Lad* (1896).

7. See page 1492 in volume 2B.

Kennedy was a schoolmaster, a schoolmaster of genius but a schoolmaster. It was only in an outbreak of sentimentality that Cambridge named a chair after him. I would have countenanced a small inkpot. Even so, let it be said, it is to Kennedy, or more directly to his *Sabrinae Corolla*,[8] the third edition, which I received as a school prize when I was seventeen, that I owe my love of Latin and Greek. In Greek I am, as it were, an amateur, and know hardly more than the professors: well, a great deal more than Pearson, who knew more than Jowett and Jebb[9] (knew)[1] combined. As Regius Professor of Greek when I was at Oxford, Jowett was contaminated by a misplaced enthusiasm for classical education, which to him meant supplying the governing classes with Balliol men who had read some Plato, or with Oxford men who had read some Plato when Balliol men who had read some Plato were not available. In my first week, which was in October 1877, I heard Jowett pronounce "*akribos*"[2] with the accent on the first syllable, and I thought, "Well! So much for Jowett!" With Jebb it was Sophocles. There are places in Jebb's Sophocles where the responsibility for reading the metre seems to have been handed over to the Gas, Light and Coke[3] Company.

CHARON: Could you keep quiet for a bit?

AEH: Yes, I expect so. My life was marked by long silences.

[*Charon unties the painter and starts to pole.*]

Who *is* usually first choice?

CHARON: Helen of Troy. You'll see a three-headed dog when we've crossed over. If you don't take any notice of him he won't take any notice of you.

[*Voices off-stage—yapping dog, splashing oars.*]

HOUSMAN: . . . yea, we have been forsaken in the wilderness to gather grapes of thorns and figs of thistles![4]

POLLARD: Pull on your right, Jackson.

JACKSON: Do you want to take the oars?

POLLARD: No, you're doing splendidly.

[*Three men in a boat*[5] *row into view, small dog yapping. Housman in the bow (holding the dog), Jackson rowing, Pollard in the stern. The dog is played realistically by a toy (stuffed) dog.*]

JACKSON: Hous hasn't done any work since Iffley.[6]

AEH: Mo!

HOUSMAN: The nerve of it—who brought you up from Hades?—to say nothing of the dog.

POLLARD: The dog says nothing of you. The dog loves Jackson.

HOUSMAN: Jackson loves the dog.

8. A nineteenth-century anthology of English and European poetry translated into Greek and Latin, used for teaching the classical languages in the schools.

9. Benjamin Jowett (1817–1893), classicist at Balliol College, Oxford; Sir Richard Claverhouse Jebb (1841–1905), Regius Professor of Greek at Cambridge.

1. Parentheses within characters' speeches indicate changes to the text introduced by Stoppard after the Royal National Theatre production.

2. Greek, "exactly"; the accent properly falls on the last syllable.

3. Coal.

4. Matt. 7.16, KJV: "Ye shall know them by their fruits. Do men gather grapes of thorns, or figs of thistles?"

5. *Three Men in a Boat (To Say Nothing of the Dog)* (1889) by Jerome K. Jerome, is a pervasive subtext in the play; Jerome himself is a character in Act Two.

6. Village within the city limits of Oxford.

POLLARD: The uninflected dog the uninfected Jackson loves, that's the beauty of it. Good dog.
HOUSMAN: The uninflected dog can't be good, dogs have no soul.
JACKSON: What did he say?
POLLARD: He said your dog has no soul.
JACKSON: What a cheek!
POLLARD: It just goes to show you don't know much about dogs, and nothing at all about Jackson's dog whose soul is already bespoke for the Elysian Fields, where it is eagerly awaited by many of his friends who are not gone but only sleeping.
AEH: Not dead, only dreaming!

[The three men row out of view, arguing "Pull on your right!" . . . "Is anybody hungry?"]

CHARON: Well, I never! Brought their own boat, whatever next?
AEH: I had only to stretch out my hand!—*ripae ulterioris amore!* [*Cries out.*] Oh, Mo! Mo! I would have died for you but I never had the luck![7]
CHARON: The dog?
AEH: My greatest friend and comrade Moses Jackson. "*Nec Lethaea valet Theseus abrumpere caro vincula Pirithoo.*"[8]
CHARON: That's right, I remember him—Theseus—trying to break the chains that held fast his friend, to take him back with him from the Underworld. But it can't be done, sir. It can't be done.

[*Charon poles the ferry into the mist. Light on Vice-Chancellor in robes of office. His voice is echoing. Alternatively, he is heard only.*]

VICE-CHANCELLOR: Alfredus Edvardus Housman.

[Housman, aged eighteen, comes forward and receives a "book" from him]

Alfredus Guilielmus Pollard . . . Moses Johannus Jackson . . .

[Light on Pollard, eighteen, and Jackson, nineteen, with their statute books.]

JACKSON: What is "*trochum*"?
POLLARD: A hoop, in the accusative.
JACKSON: "*Neque volvere . . .*"
POLLARD: Yes, we are forbidden by the statutes to trundle a hoop. I'm Pollard. I believe we have the two open scholarships this year. May I offer my congratulations.
JACKSON: How do you do? Well, congratulations to you, too.
POLLARD: Where were you at school?
JACKSON: The Vale Academy. It's in Ramsgate. Actually my father is the Principal. But I haven't come from school, I've been two years at University College, London. I did a bit of rowing there, actually. And you?
POLLARD: King's College School.
JACKSON: You play rugby, don't you?
POLLARD: Yes. Not personally.
JACKSON: I prefer rugby football to Association rules.[9] I wonder if the College turns out a strong side. I don't count myself a serious cricketer though I can put in

7. Echoes Housman's "Poem XX," "For I was luckless aye / And shall not die for you."
8. "Diffugere Nives" from the *Odes* of Horace (4.3). In Housman's translation: "And Theseus leaves Pirithous in the chain / The love of comrades cannot take away."
9. Rugby football, which bears resemblance to a game played in ancient Greece, allows players to pick up the ball, whereas FA (football association) rules football—known to Americans as "soccer"—does not.

a useful knock on occasion. Field athletics is probably what I'll concentrate on in the Easter term.

POLLARD: Ah. So long as it's not trundling a hoop.

JACKSON: No, I'm a runner first and foremost, I suppose. The quarter-mile and the half-mile are my best distances.

POLLARD: So you're keen on sport.

JACKSON: One is at Oxford to work, of course, but as the poet said—all work and no play . . .

POLLARD [*overlapping*]: *Orandum est ut sit mens sana in corpore sano*.[1]

JACKSON: . . . makes Jack a dull boy.

POLLARD: I didn't realize that the classics scholarship was open to university men.

JACKSON: Classics? No, that's not me. I have the science scholarship.

POLLARD [*happily*]: Oh . . . *Science!* Sorry! How do you do?

JACKSON: I'm Jackson.

POLLARD: Pollard. Congratulations. That explains it.

JACKSON: What?

POLLARD: I don't know. Yes, *trochus* comes into Ovid,[2] or Horace[3] somewhere, the *Satires*.

[*Housman joins*.]

HOUSMAN: The *Odes*. Sorry. *Odes Three*, 24, "*ludere doctior seu Graeco iubeas trocho*"—it's where he's saying everything's gone to the dogs.

POLLARD: That's it! Highborn young men can't sit on a horse and are afraid to hunt, they're better at playing with the Greek hoop!

HOUSMAN: Actually, "*trochos*" *is* Greek, it's the Greek word for hoop, so when Horace uses "*Graecus trochus*" it's rather like saying "French *chapeau*." I mean he's laying it on thick, isn't he?

JACKSON: Is he? What?

HOUSMAN: Well, to a Roman, to call something *Greek* meant—very often—sissy-like, or effeminate. In fact, a hoop, a *trochos*, was a favourite gift given by a Greek man to the boy he, you know, to his favourite boy.

JACKSON: Oh, beastliness,[4] you mean?

POLLARD: This is Mr Jackson, by the way.

HOUSMAN: How do you do, sir?

JACKSON: I say, I'm a freshman too, you know. Have you seen there's a board where you put your name down? I'm going to try for the Torpids[5] next term. Perhaps I'll see you at the river.

POLLARD [*overlapping*]: —at dinner—*river*.

[*Jackson goes*.]

A science scholar.

HOUSMAN: Seems quite decent, though.

POLLARD: I'm Pollard.

HOUSMAN: Housman. We're on the same staircase.

POLLARD: Oh, spiffing[6] Where were you at school?

1. A tag from Satire X of the Roman poet Juvenal: pray for a healthy mind in a healthy body.
2. Publius Ovidius Naso (43 B.C.E.–17 C.E.), Roman poet.
3. Quintus Horatius Flaccus (65 B.C.E.–8 B.C.E.), Roman poet.
4. Homosexuality.
5. Oxford crew races on the River Thames.
6. "Spiffy"; fantastic.

HOUSMAN: Bromsgrove. It's in, well, Bromsgrove, in fact. It's a place in Worcestershire.

POLLARD: I was at King's College School—that's in London.

HOUSMAN: I've been to London. I went to the Albert Hall and the British Museum. The best thing was the Guards, though. You were right about Ovid, by the way. *Trochus* is in *Ars. Am.*[7]

[*An Oxford garden, a river, a garden seat. An invisible "croquet ball" rolls on, followed by Pattison with a croquet mallet.*]

PATTISON: My young friends, I am very grieved to tell you that if you have come up to Oxford with the idea of getting knowledge, you must give that up at once. We have bought you, and we're running you in two plates,[8] Mods[9] and the Finals.

POLLARD: Yes, sir.

PATTISON: The curriculum is designed on the idle plan that all of knowledge will be found inside the covers of four Latin and four Greek books, though not the same four each year.

HOUSMAN: Thank you, sir.

PATTISON: A genuine love of learning is one of the two delinquencies which cause blindness and lead a young man to ruin.

POLLARD/HOUSMAN [*leaving*]: Yes, sir, thank you, sir.

PATTISON: Hopeless.

[*Pattison knocks his croquet ball off-stage and follows it.*
Pater[1] *enters attended by a Balliol Student. The Student is handsome and debonair. Pater is short, unhandsome, a dandy: top hat, yellow gloves, blue cravat.*]

PATER: Thank you for sending me your sonnet, dear boy. And also for your photograph, of course. But why do you always write poetry? Why don't you write prose? Prose is so much more difficult.

STUDENT: No one has written the poetry I wish to write, Mr Pater, but you have already written the prose.

PATER: That is charmingly said. I will look at your photograph more carefully when I get home.

[*They leave.*
Ruskin and Jowett enter, playing croquet.]

RUSKIN: I was seventeen when I came up to Oxford. That was in 1836, and the word "Aesthete" was unknown. Aesthetics was newly arrived from Germany but there was no suggestion that it involved dressing up, as it might be the London Fire Brigade; nor that it was connected in some way with that excessive admiration for male physical beauty which conduced to the fall of Greece. It was not until the 1860s that moral degeneracy came under the baleful protection of artistic licence and advertised itself as aesthetic. Before that, unnatural behaviour was generally left behind at school, like football . . .

7. Ovid's *Ars Amatoria*, "The Art of Love," a poem in three books.
8. Races.
9. Short for Moderations, the first public exam for an Oxford B.A. degree; Finals are the last exams.
1. Walter Pater (1839–1894), British literary and art critic; inspiration for the Aesthetic movement. See [page 1693].

JOWETT: Alas, I was considered very beautiful at school. I had golden curls. The other boys called me Miss Jowett. How I dreaded that ghastly ritual!—the torment!—the humiliation!—my body ached from the indignities, I used to run away whenever the ball came near me . . .

[*As they leave.*]

No one now, I think, calls me Miss Jowett . . . or Mistress of Balliol.

[*Housman, Pollard and Jackson enter in a boat, Jackson rowing.*]

HOUSMAN: False quantities in all around I see, yea we have been forsaken in the wilderness to gather grapes of thorns and figs of thistles.

POLLARD: That's possibly why the College is named for John the Baptist.

JACKSON: John the Baptist was locusts and wild honey, actually. Pollard.

POLLARD: It's the Baptist School of Hard Knocks. First the Wilderness, then the head on the platter.

HOUSMAN: It was clear something was amiss from the day we matriculated. The statutes warned us against drinking, gambling and hoop-trundling but not a word about Jowett's translation of Plato. The Regius Professor can't even pronounce the Greek language and there is no one at Oxford to tell him.

POLLARD: Except you, Housman.

HOUSMAN: I will take his secret to the grave, telling people I meet on the way. Betrayal is no sin if it's whimsical.

JACKSON: We did the new pronunciation,[2] you know. As an Englishman I never took to the speaking of it. *Veni, vidi, vici* [3] . . . It was never natural to my mind.

[*Latin pronunciation: "wayny, weedy, weeky."*]

POLLARD: That was Latin, actually, Jackson.

JACKSON: And "Wennus" the Goddess of Love. I mean to say!

POLLARD: Perhaps I don't make myself plain. Latin and Greek are two entirely separate languages spoken by distinct peoples living in different parts of the ancient world. Some inkling of this must have got through to you, Jackson, at the Vale Academy, Ramsgate, surely.

HOUSMAN: But "'Wennus' the Goddess of Love," for a man of Jackson's venereal pursuits, is a strong objection to the new pronunciation—where is the chemistry in Wennus?

JACKSON: I know you and Pollard look down on science.

POLLARD: Is it a science? Ovid said it was an art.

JACKSON: Oh—*love!* You're just ragging me because you've never kissed a girl.

POLLARD: Well, what's it like, Jackson?

JACKSON: Kissing girls is not like science, nor is it like sport. It is the third thing when you thought there were only two.

POLLARD: Gosh.

HOUSMAN: *Da mi basia mille, deinde centum.*

2. The "new pronunciation," meant more closely to resemble classical Roman usage, was introduced into English classrooms in 1907.

3. Traditionally attributed to Julius Caesar: "I came, I saw, I conquered."

POLLARD: Catullus! Give me a thousand kisses, and then a hundred! Then another thousand, then a second hundred!—yes, Catullus is Jackson's sort of poet.
JACKSON: How does it go? Is it suitable for sending to Miss Liddell as my own work?
POLLARD: That depends on which Miss Liddell. Does she go dum-di-di?
JACKSON: I very much doubt it. She's the daughter of the Dean of Christ Church.[4]
POLLARD: You misunderstand. She has to scan with Lesbia. All Catullus's love poems are written to Lesbia, or about her "*Vivamus, mea Lesbia, atque amemus* . . ."
JACKSON: I mean in English. Girls who kiss don't know Latin.
POLLARD: Oh, in English. Come on, Housman. "Let us live, my Lesbia, and let us love, and value at one penny the murmurs of disapproving old men . . ."
HOUSMAN: "And not give tuppence for the mutterence of old men's tut-tutterence."
POLLARD: He's such a show-off.
HOUSMAN:

"Suns can set and rise again: when our brief light
is gone we sleep the sleep of perpetual night.
Give me a thousand kisses, and then a hundred more,
and then another thousand, and add five score . . ."

JACKSON: But what happens in the end?
HOUSMAN: In the end they're both dead and Catullus is set for Moderations. *Nox est perpetua*.[5]
POLLARD: It's not perpetual if he's set for Mods.
HOUSMAN: Is that Church of England?
JACKSON: Did they get married?
POLLARD: No. They loved, and quarrelled, and made up, and loved, and fought, and were true to each other and untrue. She made him the happiest man in the whole world and the most wretched, and after a few years she died, and then, when he was thirty, he died, too. But by that time Catullus had invented the love poem.
JACKSON: He *invented* it? Did he, Hous?
POLLARD: You don't have to ask *him*. Like everything else, like clocks and trousers and algebra, the love poem had to be invented. After millenniums of sex and centuries of poetry, the love poem as understood by Shakespeare and Donne, and by Oxford undergraduates—the true-life confessions of the poet in love, immortalizing the mistress, who is actually *the cause of the poem—that* was invented in Rome in the first century before Christ.
JACKSON: Gosh.
HOUSMAN: *Basium* is a point of interest. A kiss was always *osculum*[6] until Catullus.
POLLARD: Now, Hous, concentrate—is that the point of interest in the kiss?
HOUSMAN: Yes.
POLLARD: Pull on your right.
JACKSON: Do you want to take the oars?
POLLARD: No, you're doing splendidly.
JACKSON: Hous hasn't done any work since below Iffley.

4. Alice Liddell, the inspiration for Lewis Carroll's "Alice" books, was the daughter of Henry Liddell, Dean of Christ Church, Oxford.
5. From Catullus 5: "night is everlasting."
6. Literally, "little mouth."

HOUSMAN: The nerve of it! Who brought us up from Hades?

[*They row out of sight*.

The croquet game returns—Pattison, followed in series by Jowett, Pater and Ruskin. The game accounts for the entrances, actions and exits of Pattison, Pater, Jowett and Ruskin.]

PATTISON: I was not quite seventeen when I first saw Oxford. That was in 1830 and Oxford was delightful then, not the overbuilt slum it has become. The town teems with people who have no business here, which is to say business is all they have. The University held off the London and Birmingham Railway until the forties, and I said at the time "If the Birmingham train comes, can the London train be far behind?"

PATER: I don't think that can be quite right, Dr Pattison.

JOWETT: Posting ten miles to Steventon for the Paddington train was never anything to cherish. Personally, I thank God for the branch line, and hope His merciful bounty is not exhausted by changing at Didcot.

RUSKIN: When I am at Paddington I feel I am in hell.

JOWETT: You must not go about telling everyone, Dr Ruskin. It will not do for the moral education of Oxford undergraduates that the wages of sin may be no more than the sense of being stranded at one of the larger railway stations.

RUSKIN: To be morally educated is to realize that such would be a terrible price. Mechanical advance is the slack taken up of our failing humanity. Hell is very likely to be modernization infinitely extended. There is a rocky valley between Buxton and Bakewell where once you may have seen at first and last light the Muses dance for Apollo and heard the pan-pipes play. But its rocks were blasted away for the railway, and now every fool in Buxton can be at Bakewell in half an hour, and every fool in Bakewell at Buxton.

PATER [*at croquet*]: First-class return.

JOWETT: Mind the gap.

PATTISON: Personally I am in favour of education but a university is not the place for it. A university exists to seek the meaning of life by the pursuit of scholarship.

RUSKIN: I have announced the meaning of life in my lectures. There is nothing beautiful which is not good, and nothing good which has no moral purpose. I had my students up at dawn building a flower-bordered road across a swamp at Ferry Hinksey. There was an Irish exquisite, a great slab of a youth with white hands and long poetical hair who said he was glad to say he had never seen a shovel, but I made him a navvy for one term and taught him that the work of one's hands is the beginning of virtue. Then I went sketching to Venice and the road sank into the swamp. My protégé rose at noon to smoke cigarettes and read French novels, and Oxford reverted to a cockney watering-place for learning to row.

[*Housman and Pollard enter along the river bank,*
Housman intent on an unseen boat race.]

HOUSMAN: Come on, St John's!

POLLARD: Ruskin said, when he's at Paddington he feels he is in hell—and this man Oscar Wilde said, "Ah, but—"

HOUSMAN: "—when he's in hell he'll think he's only at Paddington." It'll be a pity if inversion is all he is known for. Row up, St John's!

POLLARD: You *hate* sport.

HOUSMAN: Keep the stroke!

POLLARD: Wilde is reckoned the wittiest man at Oxford. His rooms at Magdalen are said to be completely bare except for a lily in a blue vase.

HOUSMAN: No furniture?

POLLARD: Well, of course there is *furniture* . . . I suppose there is furniture.

HOUSMAN: Come on, St John's!

POLLARD: He went to the Morrell's ball in a Prince Rupert costume which he has absentmindedly put on every morning since, and has been seen wearing it in the High.[7] Everyone is repeating his remark that he finds it harder and harder every day to live up to his blue china. Don't you think that's priceless?

HOUSMAN: We have a blue china butterdish at Bromsgrove, we never take any notice of it.

Well rowed! Bad luck, St John's!

JOWETT: I was eighteen when I came up to Oxford. That was in 1835, and Oxford was an utter disgrace. Education rarely interfered with the life of the University. Learning was carried on in nooks and corners, like Papism[8] in an Elizabethan manor house. The fellows were socially negligible, and perfectly astonished by the historical process that had placed the teaching of undergraduates into the hands of amiable clergymen waiting for preferment to a country parsonage. I say nothing against the undergraduates, a debauched and indolent rabble as it happens. The great reform of the fifties[9] laid the foundation of the educated class that has spread moral and social order to parts of the world where, to take one example, my Plato was formerly quite unknown.

PATTISON: The great reform made us into a cramming shop. The railway brings in the fools and takes them away with their tickets punched for the world outside.

JOWETT: The modern university exists by consent of the world outside. We must send out men fitted for that world. What better example can we show them than classical antiquity? Nowhere was the ideal of morality, art and social order realized more harmoniously than in Greece in the age of the great philosophers.

RUSKIN: Buggery[1] apart.

JOWETT: Buggery apart.

PATER: Actually, Italy in the late-fifteenth century . . . Nowhere was the ideal of art, morality and social order realized more harmoniously, morality and social order apart.

RUSKIN: The Medieval Gothic! The Medieval Gothic cathedrals which were the great engines of art, morality and social order!

PATTISON [*at croquet*]: Check. Play the advantage.

PATER: I have been touched by the medieval but its moment has passed, and now I wouldn't return the compliment with a barge-pole. As for arts-and-crafts, it is very well for the people; without it, Liberty's would be at risk, in fact it would be closed, but the true Aesthetic spirit goes back to Florence, Venice, Rome—Japanese apart. One sees it plain in Michelangelo's *David*—legs apart.[2] The blue of my very necktie declares that we are still living in that revolution whereby man regained possession of his nature and produced the Italian Tumescence.[3]

7. High Street, or (in American English) Main Street.

8. Derogatory Protestant term for Catholicism.

9. Reforms following in the wake of the Oxford Movement, a reaction against theological liberalism; these reforms included opening Oxford to the influence of German scholarship.

1. Sodomy; male homosexuality.

2. For this deplorable image the author gratefully acknowledges the actor playing Pater, Robin Soans [Stoppard's note].

3. Tumescence: swelling.

PATTISON: Renaissance, surely. Deuce.

PATER: On the frescoed walls of Santa Maria della Grazie and the painted ceiling of St Pancras—

PATTISON: Peter's, surely. Leg-before unless I'm much mistaken.

[*Jackson comes, in rowing kit.*]

HOUSMAN: Well rowed, Jackson! I'm afraid they had the measure of us.

JACKSON: Extraordinary thing. Fellow in velvet knickerbockers like something from the halls came up and said he wished to compliment me on my race. I replied with dignity, "Thank you, but although my first name happens to be Moses I am not Jewish and can take no merit from it." He said, "Allow me to do the jokes, it's what I'm at Oxford for—I saw you in the Torpids and your left leg is a poem."

POLLARD: What did you say?

JACKSON: Naturally, I asked him if he was a rowing man. He said he tried out for an oar in the Magdalen boat but couldn't see the use of going backwards down to Iffley every evening so he gave it up and now plays no outdoor games at all, except dominoes: he has sometimes played dominoes outside French cafés. Do you know what I think he is?

POLLARD: What?

JACKSON: I think he's one of those Aesthetes.[4]

[*They go.*]

RUSKIN: Conscience, faith, disciplined restraint, fidelity to nature—all the Christian virtues that gave us the cathedral at Chartres, the paintings of Giotto,[5] the poetry of Dante—have been tricked out in iridescent rags to catch the attention of the moment.

PATER: In the young Raphael, in the sonnets of Michelangelo, in Correggio's lily-bearer in the cathedral at Parma, and ever so faintly in my necktie, we feel the touch of a, what shall I say?—

PATTISON: Barge-pole?

PATER: Barge-pole? . . . No . . . the touch of a refined and comely paganism that rescued beauty from the charnel house[6] of the Christian conscience. The Renaissance teaches us that the book of knowledge is not to be learned by rote but is to be written anew in the ecstasy of living each moment for the moment's sake. Success in life is to maintain this ecstasy, to burn always with this hard gemlike flame. Failure is to form habits. To burn with a gemlike flame is to capture the awareness of each moment; and for that moment only. To form habits is to be absent from those moments. How may we always be present for them?—to garner not the fruits of experience but experience itself?—

[*At a distance, getting no closer, Jackson is seen as a runner running towards us. The game takes Ruskin and Pattison out.*]

. . . to catch at the exquisite passion, the strange flower, or art—or the face of one's friend? For, not to do so in our short day of frost and sun is to sleep before evening. The conventional morality which requires of us the sacrifice of any one

4. Aesthetes: the "art for art's sake" movement that took Pater's *Studies in the Renaissance* (1873) as a kind of manifesto.

5. Giotto di Bondone (c. 1267–1337), Italian painter.

6. Storage area for human remains.

of those moments has no real claim on us. The love of art for art's sake seeks nothing in return except the highest quality to the moments of your life, and simply for those moments' sake.

JOWETT: Mr Pater, can you spare a moment?

PATER: Certainly! As many as you like!

[Jackson arrives out of breath. Housman meets him, holding a watch. Jackson sits exhausted on the seat. Housman has a home-made "laurel crown".[7] *He crowns Jackson—a lighthearted gesture.]*

HOUSMAN: One minute, fifty-eight seconds.

JACKSON: What. . . ?

HOUSMAN: One fifty-eight, exactly.

JACKSON: That's nonsense.

HOUSMAN: Or two fifty-eight.

JACKSON: That's nonsense the other way. What was the first quarter?

HOUSMAN: I'm afraid I forgot to look.

JACKSON: What were you doing?

HOUSMAN: Watching you.

JACKSON: You duffer!

HOUSMAN: Why can't it be one fifty-eight?

JACKSON: The world record for the half is over two minutes.

HOUSMAN: Oh, well . . . congratulations, Jackson.

JACKSON: What will become of you, Hous?

[Jackson takes off the laurel and leaves it on the seat, as he leaves. Housman picks up the book.]

HOUSMAN: It has become of me.

PATER: The story has been grossly exaggerated, it has, if you will, accrued grossness in the telling, but when all's said and done, a letter signed "Yours lovingly"—

JOWETT: Several letters, and addressed to an undergraduate.

PATER: Several letters signed "Yours lovingly" and addressed to an undergraduate—

JOWETT: Of Balliol.

PATER: Even of Balliol, do not prove beastliness—would hardly support a suggestion of spooniness,[8] in fact—

JOWETT: From a *tutor*, sir, a fellow not even of his own College, thanking him for a *disgusting sonnet!*

PATER: You feel, in short, Dr Jowett, that I have overstepped the mark.

JOWETT: I feel, Mr Pater, that letters to an undergraduate signed "Yours lovingly," thanking him for a sonnet on the honeyed mouth and lissome thighs of Ganymede[9] would be capable of a construction fatal to the ideals of higher learning even if the undergraduate in question were not colloquially known as the Balliol bugger.[1]

PATER: You astonish me.

7. Alludes to Housman's best-known poem, "To an Athlete Dying Young": "And round that early-laurelled head / Will flock to gaze the strengthless dead. . . ."
8. Foolishness; sentimentality.
9. In Greek mythology, a Trojan prince, the most handsome of all mortals.
1. Sodomist; male homosexual.

JOWETT: The Balliol bugger, I am assured.

PATER: No, no, I am astonished that you should take exception to an obviously Platonic enthusiasm.

JOWETT: A Platonic enthusiasm as far as Plato was concerned meant an enthusiasm of the kind that would empty the public schools and fill the prisons where it is not nipped in the bud. In my translation of the Phaedrus[2] it required all my ingenuity to rephrase his depiction of paederastia,[3] into the affectionate regard as exists between an Englishman and his wife. Plato would have made the transposition himself if he had had the good fortune to be a Balliol man.

PATER: And yet, Master, no amount of ingenuity can dispose of boy-love as the distinguishing feature of a society which we venerate as one of the most brilliant in the history of human culture, raised far above its neighbours in moral and mental distinction.

JOWETT: You are very kind but one undergraduate is hardly a distinguishing feature, and I have written to his father to remove him. [*To Housman, who is arriving with a new book.*] Pack your bags, sir, and be gone! The canker that brought low the glory that was Greece shall not prevail over Balliol!

PATER [*leaving, to Housman*]: It's a long story, but there is a wash and it will all come out in it.

HOUSMAN: I am Housman, sir, of St John's.

JOWETT: Then I am at a loss to understand why I should be addressing you. Who is your tutor?

HOUSMAN: I go to Mr Warren at Magdalen three times a week.

JOWETT: That must be it. Warren is a Balliol man, he has spoken of you, he believes you capable of great things.

HOUSMAN: Really, sir?

JOWETT: If you can rid yourself of your levity and your cynicism, and find another way to dissimulate your Irish provincialism than by making affected remarks about your blue china and going about in plum-coloured velvet breeches, which you don't, and cut your hair—you're not him at all, are you? Never mind, what have you got there? Oh, Munro's *Catullus*.[4] I glanced at it in Blackwell's. A great deal of Munro and precious little of Catullus. It's amazing what people will pay four shillings and sixpence for. Is Catullus on your reading list?

HOUSMAN: Yes, sir, "The Marriage of Peleus and Thetis."

JOWETT: Catullus 64! Lord Leighton should paint that opening scene! The flower of the young men of Argos hot for the capture of the Golden Fleece, churning the waves with their blades of pine, the first ship ever to plough the ocean! "And the wild faces of the sea-nymphs emerged from the white foaming waters—*emersere feri candenti e gurgite vultus aequoreae*—staring in amazement at the sight—*monstrum Nereides admirantes*."

HOUSMAN: Yes, sir. *Freti*, actually, sir.

JOWETT: What?

HOUSMAN: Munro concurs that *feri* is a mistake for *freti*, sir, because *vultus* must be accusative.

JOWETT: Concurs with whom?

HOUSMAN: Concurs with, well, everybody.

2. One of Plato's dialogues.
3. Greek, "love of boys."
4. Gaius Valerius Catullus (c. 84 B.C.E.—c. 54 B.C.E.), Roman poet.

JOWETT: Everybody but Catullus. The textual critics have spoken. Death to wild faces emerging in the nominative. Long live the transitive *emersere* raising up the accusative unqualified faces from the white foaming waters, of the *freti*, something watery like channel. Never mind that we already have so many watery words that the last thing we need is another—here we are: "*freti* for *feri* is an easy correction, as r, t, tr, rt are among the letters most frequently confounded in the manuscripts." Well, Munro is entitled to concur with everybody who amends the manuscripts of Catullus according to his taste and calls his taste his conjectures—it's a futile business suitable to occupy the leisure of professors of Cambridge University. But you, sir, have not been put on earth with an Oxford scholarship so that you may bother your head with whether Catullus in such-and-such place wrote *ut* or *et* or *aut* or none of them or whether such-and-such line is spurious or corrupt or on the contrary an example of Catullus's peculiar genius. You are here to take the ancient authors as they come from a reputable English printer, and to study them until you can write in the metre. If you cannot write Latin and Greek verse how can you hope to be of any use in the world?

HOUSMAN: But isn't it of use to establish what the ancient authors really wrote?

JOWETT: It would be on the whole desirable rather than undesirable and the job was pretty well done, where it could be done, by good scholars dead these hundred years and more. For the rest, certainty could only come from recovering the autograph. This morning I had cause to have typewritten an autograph letter I wrote to the father of a certain undergraduate. The copy as I received it asserted that the Master of Balliol had a solemn duty to stamp out unnatural mice. In other words, anyone with a secretary knows that what Catullus really wrote was already corrupt by the time it was copied twice, which was about the time of the first Roman invasion of Britain: and the earliest copy that has come down to *us* was written about 1,500 years after that. Think of all those secretaries!—corruption breeding corruption from papyrus to papyrus, and from the last disintegrating scrolls to the first new-fangled parchment books, with a thousand years of copying-out still to come, running the gauntlet of changing forms of script and spelling, and absence of punctuation—not to mention mildew and rats and fire and flood and Christian disapproval to the brink of extinction as what Catullus really wrote passed from scribe to scribe, this one drunk, that one sleepy, another without scruple, and of those sober, wide-awake and scrupulous, some ignorant of Latin and some, even worse, fancying themselves better Latinists than Catullus—until!—finally and at long last—mangled and tattered like a dog that has fought its way home, there falls across the threshold of the Italian Renaissance the sole surviving witness to thirty generations of carelessness and stupidity: the *Verona Codex* of Catullus; which was almost immediately lost again, but not before being copied with one last opportunity for error. And there you have the foundation of the poems of Catullus as they went to the printer for the first time, in Venice 400 years ago.

HOUSMAN: Where, sir?

JOWETT [*pointing*]: In there.

HOUSMAN: Do you mean, sir, that it's here in Oxford?

JOWETT: Why, yes. That is why it is called the *Codex Oxoniensis*. Only recently was its importance recognized, by a German scholar who made the *Oxoniensis* the foundation of his edition of the poet. Mr Robinson Ellis of Trinity College discovered its existence several years before but, unluckily, not its importance, and *his* edition of Catullus has the singular distinction of vitiating itself by ignoring the discovery of its own editor.

[*Ellis enters as a child with a lollipop, on a scooter; but not dressed as a child.*]

Awfully hard cheese, Ellis! Ignoring your *Oxoniensis!*

ELLIS: Didn't ignore it.

JOWETT: Did.

ELLIS: Didn't.

JOWETT: Did.

ELLIS: Didn't!

[*They continue thuswise as AEH and Charon pole into view on the river*.]

JOWETT: Did.

ELLIS: Didn't.

JOWETT [*leaving*]: Did, did, did!

ELLIS: Didn't! And anyway, Baehrens overvalued it, so there!

AEH: That's Bobby Ellis! He's somewhat altered in demeanour, but the intellect is unmistakable.

ELLIS: Young man, they tell me you are an absolutely safe First. I am proposing to form a class next term to read the Monobiblos. The fee will be one pound.

HOUSMAN: The Monobiblos?

AEH: I've seen *him* before, too.

ELLIS: Dear me. Propertius Book One.

HOUSMAN: Propertius.[5]

ELLIS: The greatest of the Roman love elegists, and the most corrupt.

HOUSMAN: Oh.

ELLIS: Only Catullus has a later text, but I would say Propertius is the more corrupt.

HOUSMAN: Oh—*corrupt*. Yes. Thank you, sir.

[*They go*.]

AEH: Do you know Propertius?

CHARON: You mean personally?

AEH: I mean the poems.

CHARON: Ah. No, then. Here we are. Elysium.

AEH: Elysium! Where else?! I was eighteen when I first saw Oxford, and Oxford was charming then, not the trippery emporium it has become. There were horse-buses at the station to meet the Birmingham train; and not a brick to be seen, before the Kinema and Kardomah.[6] The Oxford of my dreams, re-dreamt. The desire to urinate, combined with a sense that it would not be a good idea, usually means we are asleep.

CHARON: Or in a boat. That happened to me once.

AEH: Were you asleep?

CHARON: No, I was in a play.

AEH: That needs thinking about.

CHARON: Aristophanes, *The Frogs*.[7]

5. Sextus Aurelius Propertius (c. 50 B.C.E.–15 B.C.E.), Latin elegiac poet.

6. A chain of coffee houses; kinema: "cinema," in its faux-Greek spelling.

7. Late fifth-century B.C.E. Greek comedy.

AEH: You speak the truth. I saw you.

CHARON: I had that Dionysus[8] in the back of my boat.

AEH: You were very good.

CHARON: No, I was just in it. I was caught short. Good stuff, *The Frogs*, don't you think?

AEH: Not particularly. But it quotes from Aeschylus.

CHARON: Ah, now that was a play.

AEH: What was?

CHARON: Aeschylus, *Myrmidones*.[9] Do you know it?

AEH: It didn't survive; only the title and some fragments. I would join Sisyphus[1] in Hades and gladly push my boulder up the slope if only, each time it rolled back down, I were given a line of Aeschylus.

CHARON: I think I can remember some of it.

AEH: Oh my goodness.

CHARON: Give me a minute.

AEH: Oh my Lord.

CHARON: Achilles is in his tent.

AEH: Oh please don't let it be a dream!

CHARON: The chorus is his clansmen, the Myrmidons.

AEH: Yes.

CHARON: They tell him off for sulking in his—

AEH: Tent, yes, but can you remember an actual line that Aeschylus *wrote?*

CHARON: I'm coming to it. First Achilles compares himself to an eagle hit by an arrow fledged with one of its own feathers, do you know that one?

AEH: The words, the words.

CHARON: Achilles is in his—

AEH: Tent.

CHARON: Tent—am I telling this or are you?—he's playing dice with himself when news comes that Patroclus has been killed. Achilles goes mad, blaming him, you see, for being dead. Now for the line. "Does it mean nothing to you," he says, "the unblemished thighs I worshipped and the showers of kisses you had from me."

AEH:

σέβας δὲ μηρῶν ἁγνὸν οὐκ έπηδέσω,
ὦ δυσχάριοτε τῶν πυκνῶν φιλημάτων.

CHARON: There you go.

AEH: Yes, I see.

CHARON: No good?

AEH: Very good. It's one of the fragments that has come down to us. Also the metaphor of the eagle, but not Aeschylus's own words, which I dare say you can't recall.

CHARON: It's maddening, isn't it?

AEH: Quite so. All is plain. I may as well wet the bed, the night nurse will change the sheets and tuck me up without reproach. They are very kind to me here in the Evelyn Nursing Home.

8. Greek god of wine.
9. The first in a trilogy of plays by Aeschylus, the *Achilleis*; only 54 verses remain. The Myrmidones were brave warriors described in Homer's *Illiad*.
1. In Greek mythology, punished by the gods by being forced to roll a boulder uphill, only to watch it roll back down, for eternity.

JACKSON [*off-stage*]: Housman!
POLLARD [*off-stage*]: Housman!
CHARON: Look alive, then! Get it?
AEH: Indeed yes.
CHARON: I've got dozens of them like that.
AEH: Perhaps next time.
CHARON: I'm afraid not.
AEH: Ah yes. Where is thy sting?[2]

[*Charon poles AEH to the shore.*]

POLLARD [*off-stage*]: Hous!—Picnic!
JACKSON [*off-stage*]: Locusts! Honey!

[*Housman enters with a pile of books which he puts down on the seat.*]

HOUSMAN: I say, can I give you a hand?
AEH [*to Charon*]: Who's that?
CHARON: Who's that, he says.
AEH [*to Housman*]: Thank you!
CHARON: Dead on time.

[*Housman helps AEH ashore.*]

AEH: Most opportune.
CHARON: Dead on time!—there's no end to them! [*He poles himself away.*]
AEH: Don't mind him. What are you doing here, may one ask?
HOUSMAN: Classics, sir. I'm studying for Greats.
AEH: Are you? I did Greats, too. Of course, that was more than fifty years ago, when Oxford was still the sweet city of dreaming spires.
HOUSMAN: It must have been delightful then.
AEH: It was. I felt as if I had come up from the plains of Moab to the top of Mount Pisgah like Moses when the Lord showed him all the land of Judah unto the utmost sea.[3]
HOUSMAN: There's a hill near our house where I live in Worcestershire which I and my brothers and sisters call Mount Pisgah. I used to climb it often, and look out towards Wales, to what I thought was a kind of Promised Land, though it was only the Clee Hills really—Shropshire was our western horizon.
AEH: Oh . . . excellent. You are . . .
HOUSMAN: Housman, sir, of St John's.
AEH: Well, this is an unexpected development. Where can we sit down before philosophy finds us out. I'm not as young as I was. Whereas you, of course, are.

[*They sit.*]

Classical studies, eh?
HOUSMAN: Yes, sir.
AEH: You are to be a rounded man, fit for the world, a man of taste and moral sense.
HOUSMAN: Yes, sir.

2. 1 Cor. 15.55: "O death, where is thy sting? O grave, where is thy victory?"
3. Cf. Deut. 34.1–2, KJV: "And Moses went up from the plains of Moab unto the mountain of Nebo, to the top of Pisgah, that is over against Jericho. And the LORD shewed him all the land of Gilead, unto Dan, and all Naphtali, and the land of Ephraim, and Manasseh, and all the land of Judah, unto the utmost sea."

AEH: Science for our material improvement, classics for our inner nature. The beautiful and the good. Culture. Virtue. The ideas and moral influence of the ancient philosophers.
HOUSMAN: Yes, sir.
AEH: Humbug.
HOUSMAN: Oh.
AEH: Looking about you, does it appear to you that the classical fellows are the superior in sense, morality, taste, or even amiability, to the scientists?
HOUSMAN: I'm acquainted with only one person in the Science School, and he is the finest man I know.
AEH: And he knows more than the ancient philosophers.
HOUSMAN: (Oh—!)
AEH: They made the best use of the knowledge they had. They were the best minds. The French are the best cooks, and during the Siege of Paris I'm sure rats never tasted better, but that is no reason to continue eating rat now that *coq au vin* is available. The only reason to consider what the ancient philosophers meant about anything is if it's relevant to settling corrupt or disputed passages in the text. With the poets there may be other reasons for reading them; I wouldn't discount it—it may even improve your inner nature, if the miraculous collusion of sound and sense in, let us say, certain poems by Horace, teaches humility in regard to adding to the store of available literature poems by, let us say, yourself. But the effect is not widespread. Are these your books?
HOUSMAN: Yes, sir.
AEH: What have we here? [*He looks at Housman's books, reading the spines. He never opens them.*] Propertius! And . . . Propertius! And, of course, Propertius.
HOUSMAN [*eagerly*]: Do you know him?
AEH: No, not as yet.
HOUSMAN: He's difficult—tangled-up thoughts, or, anyway, tangled-up Latin—
AEH: Oh—know him.
HOUSMAN:—if you can believe the manuscripts—which you can't because they all come from the same one, and *that* was about as far removed from Propertius as we are from Alfred burning the cakes![4] He just scraped through to the invention of printing—a miracle!—the first of the Roman love elegists.
AEH: Not the first, I think, strictly speaking.
HOUSMAN: Oh, yes. Really and truly. Catullus was earlier but he used all sorts of metres for his Lesbia poems.
AEH: Ah.
HOUSMAN: Propertius's mistress was called Cynthia—"Cynthia who first took me captive with her eyes."
AEH: *Cynthia prima suis miserum me cepit ocellis*. You mustn't forget *miserum*.
HOUSMAN: Yes—*poor* me. You do know him.
AEH: Oh, yes. When I was a young man at Oxford my edition of Propertius was going to replace all its forerunners and require no successor.
HOUSMAN: Wouldn't that be something! I have been thinking of it, too. You see, Propertius is so corrupt (that) it seems to me, even today, *here* is a poet on which the work has not been done. All those editors!, each with his own Propertius,

4. Legend maintains that Alfred (849–99), King of Wessex, having been asked by the peasant woman who had taken him in to watch the cakes, allowed them to burn.

right up to Baehrens hot from the press!—and still (there's) the feeling that between the natural chaos of his writing and the whole hit-or-miss of the manuscripts, nobody has got the text anywhere near right. Baehrens should make everyone obsolete—isn't that why one edits Propertius? It's certainly why *I* would edit Propertius!—but one has hardly settled down with Baehrens before one is jolted out of one's chair by something like *cunctas*[5] in one-one-five.

AEH: Yes, *cunctas* for *castas* is intolerable.

HOUSMAN: Well, exactly!—and he's *Baehrens*, who found the *Catullus Oxoniensis* in the Bodleian library!

AEH: Baehrens is overenamoured with the manuscripts overlooked by everyone but himself. He's only human, and that's an impediment to editing a classic. To defend the credit of a scribe he'll impute any idiocy to a poet. His *conjectures*, on the other hand, are despicable trifling or barbarous depravations; yet on the whole his vanity and arrogance have deprived Baehrens of the esteem his Propertius is due.

HOUSMAN [*confused*]: Oh . . . so is he good or bad?

AEH: On that, you'll have to ask his mother. [*He picks up the next book.*] And here is Paley with *et* for *aut* in one-one-twenty-five. He overestimates Propertius as a poet, in my opinion, yet he has no scruple in making Propertius pray that Cynthia may love him *and also* that he may cease to love Cynthia! [*Puts the book aside.*] Some of it may be read without mirth or disgust.

HOUSMAN [*shocked*]: *Paley?!*

AEH [*next book*]: And Palmer. Palmer is a different case. He is more singularly and eminently gifted by nature than any English Latinist since Markland.

HOUSMAN [*eagerly*]: Really? Palmer, then?

AEH: With all his genius, in precision of thought and stability of judgement many excel him.

HOUSMAN: Oh.

AEH: Munro most of all.

HOUSMAN: Oh, yes—Munro!

AEH: And Munro you wouldn't rely on for settling a text. But Palmer has no intellectual power. Sustained thought is beyond him, so he shuns it.

HOUSMAN: But I thought you said—

AEH: He trusts to his felicity of instinct. When that fails him, no one can defend more stubbornly a plain corruption, or advocate more confidently an incredible conjecture, and to these defects he adds a calamitous propensity to reckless assertion.

HOUSMAN: Oh! So, really, Palmer . . .

AEH [*next book*]: Oh, yes. A liar and a slave, [*Next book.*] And him: I could teach a dog to edit Propertius like *him*. [*Next book.*] Oh, dear . . . well, his idea of editing a text is to change a letter or two and see what happens. If what happens can by the warmest goodwill be mistaken for sense and grammar he calls it an emendation. This is not scholarship, it is not even a sport, like hopscotch or marbles, which requires a degree of skill. It is simply a pastime, like leaning against a wall and spitting.

HOUSMAN: But that's Mr Ellis!—I *went* to him for Propertius!

AEH: Indeed, yes, I saw him. I thought he looked well, dangerously well. [*Next book.*] Ah!—Mueller! [*Next book.*] And Haupt! [*Next book.*] Rosberg! Really there's no need for you to read anything published in German in the last fifty years. Or the next fifty.

5. Whole; entire.

[*AEH picks up Housman's notebook casually. Housman takes it from him, a little awkwardly.*]

HOUSMAN: Oh—that's only . . .

AEH: Oh—of course. You *do* write poetry.

HOUSMAN: Well, I've written poems, as one does, you know . . .

AEH: One does.

HOUSMAN: . . . for the poetry prize at school—quite speakable, I think—

AEH: Good for you, mine were quite unspeakable.

HOUSMAN: Actually, I was thinking of going in for the Newdigate—I thought the poem that won it last year was not so—how may one put it?

AEH: Not such a poem as to suggest that your attempt would be a piece of impudence.

HOUSMAN: But I don't know, I don't feel enough of a swell to carry off the Newdigate. Oscar Wilde of Magdalen, who went down with the Newdigate and a First in Greats, used to have tea with Ruskin. *Pater* used to have tea with *him*, in his rooms, and talk of lilies perhaps, and Michelangelo, and the French novel. The year before Wilde, it was won by a Balliol man who sent poems to Pater in the manner of the early Greek lyrics treating of matters that get you sacked at Oxford, and was duly sacked by Dr Jowett, which is rather grand behaviour in itself and almost excusable as a miscalculation of the limits of the Aesthetic. How am I to leave my mark?, a monument more lasting than bronze as Horace boasted, higher than the pyramids of kings, unyielding to wind and weather and the passage of time?

AEH: Do you mean as a poet or a scholar?

HOUSMAN: I don't mind.

AEH: I think it helps to mind.

HOUSMAN: Can't one be both?

AEH: No. Not of the first rank. Poetical feelings are a peril to scholarship. There are always poetical people ready to protest that a corrrupt line is exquisite. Exquisite to whom? The Romans were foreigners writing for foreigners two millenniums ago; and for people whose gods we find quaint, whose savagery we abominate, whose private habits we don't like to talk about, but whose idea of what is exquisite is, we flatter ourselves, mysteriously identical with ours.

HOUSMAN: But it *is*, isn't it? We catch our breath at the places where the breath was always caught. The poet writes to his mistress how she's killed his love—"fallen like a flower at the field's edge where the plough touched it and passed on by." He answers a friend's letter—"so you won't think your letter got forgotten like a lover's apple forgotten in a good girl's lap till she jumps up for her mother and spills it to the floor blushing crimson over her sorry face." Two thousand years in the tick of a clock—oh, forgive me, I . . .

AEH: No (need), we're never too old to learn.

HOUSMAN: I could weep when I think how nearly lost it was, that apple, and that flower, lying among the rubbish under a wine-vat, the last, corrupt, copy of Catullus left alive in the wreck of ancient literature. It's a cry that cannot be ignored. Do you know Munro?

AEH: I corresponded with him once.

HOUSMAN: I'm going to write to him. Do you think he'd send me his photograph?

AEH: No. What a strange thing is a young man. You had better be a poet. Literary enthusiasm never made a scholar, and unmade many. Taste is not knowledge. A scholar's business is to add to what is known. That is all. But it is capable of giving the very greatest satisfaction, because knowledge is good. It does not have to look good or sound good or even do good. It is good just by being knowledge. And the only thing that makes it knowledge is that it is true. You can't have too much of it and there is no little too little to be worth having. There is truth and falsehood in a comma. In your text of "The Marriage of Peleus and Thetis," Catullus says that Peleus is the protector of the power or Emathia: *Emathiae tutamen opis,* comma, *carissime nato:* how can Peleus be *carissime nato,* most dear to his son, when his son has not yet been born?

HOUSMAN: I don't know.

AEH: To be a scholar is to strike your finger on the page and say, "Thou ailest here, and here."

HOUSMAN: The comma has got itself in the wrong place, hasn't it?, because there aren't any commas in the *Oxoniensis,* any more than there are capital letters—which is the other thing—

AEH: Not now, nurse, let him finish.

HOUSMAN: So *opis* isn't *power* with a small "o," it's the genitive of Ops who was the mother of Jupiter. Everything comes clear when you put the comma back one place.

AEH: *Emathiae tutamen,* comma, *Opis* with a capital "O," *carissime nato.* Protector of Emathia, most dear to the son of Ops.

HOUSMAN: Is that right?

AEH: Oh, yes. It's right because it's true—Peleus, the protector of Emathia, *was* most dear to Jupiter the son of Ops. By taking out a comma and putting it back in a different place, sense is made out of nonsense in a poem that has been read continuously since it was first misprinted four hundred years ago. A small victory over ignorance and error. A scrap of knowledge to add to our stock. What does this remind you of? Science, of course. Textual criticism is a science whose subject is literature, as botany is the science of flowers and zoology of animals and geology of rocks. Flowers, animals and rocks being the work of nature, their sciences are exact sciences, and must answer to the authority of what can be seen and measured. Literature, however, being the work of the human mind with all its frailty and aberration, and of human fingers which make mistakes, the science of textual criticism must aim for degrees of likelihood, and the only authority it might answer to is an author who has been dead for hundreds or thousands of years. But it is a science none the less, not a sacred mystery. Reason and common sense, a congenial intimacy with the author, a comprehensive familiarity with the language, a knowledge of ancient script for those fallible fingers, concentration, integrity, mother wit and repression of self-will—these are a good start for the textual critic. In other words, almost anybody can be a botanist or a zoologist. Textual criticism is the crown and summit of scholarship. Most people, though not enough, find it dry and dull, but it is the only reason for existence for a Latin professor. I tell you this because you would not know it from the way it is conducted in the English universities. The fudge and flim-flam, the hocus-pocus and plain dishonesty that parade as scholarship in the journals would excite the professional admiration of a hawker of patent medicines. In the German universities the situation is different. Most German scholars I would put up for the Institute of Mechanics; the remainder, the Institute of Statisticians. Except for Wilamowitz who is the greatest European scholar since Richard Bentley. There are people who say that I am but they would not know it if I were. Wilamowitz, I should add, is dead. Or will be. Or will have been dead. I think it must be time for my tablet, it orders my tenses. The future perfect I have always regarded as an oxymoron. I wouldn't worry so much about your monument, if I were you. If I had my time again, I would pay more regard to those poems of Horace which tell you you will not have your time again. Life is brief and death kicks at the door impartially. Who knows how many tomorrows the gods will grant us? Now is the time, when you are young, to deck your hair with myrtle, drink the best of the wine, pluck the fruit. Seasons and moons renew themselves but neither noble name nor eloquence, no, nor righteous deeds will restore us. Night holds Hippolytus the pure of stain, Diana steads him nothing, he must stay; and Theseus leaves Pirithous in the chain the love of comrades cannot take away.

HOUSMAN: What is that?

AEH: A lapse.

HOUSMAN: It's "*Diffugere nives.*" *Nec Lethaea valet Theseus abrumpere caro vincula Pirithoo*. And Theseus has not the strength to break the Lethean bonds of his beloved Pirithous.

AEH: Your translation is closer.

HOUSMAN: Were they comrades—Theseus and Pirithous?

AEH: (Yes), companions in adventure.

HOUSMAN: Companions in adventure! *There* is something to stir the soul! Was there ever a love like the love of comrades ready to lay down their lives for each other?

AEH: Oh, dear.

HOUSMAN: I don't mean spooniness, you know.

AEH: Oh—not the love of comrades that gets you sacked at Oxford—

HOUSMAN: (No!—)

AEH: —not as in the lyric poets—"when thou art kind I spend the day like a god: when thy face is turned away, it is very dark with me"[6]—

HOUSMAN: No—I mean friendship—virtue—like the Greek heroes.

AEH: The Greek heroes—of course.

HOUSMAN: The Argonauts[7] . . . Achilles and Patroclus[8] . . .

AEH: Oh, yes, Achilles would get his Blue[9] for single combat. Jason and the Argonauts would make an impression on Eights Week.[1]

HOUSMAN: Is it something to be made fun of, then?

AEH: No. No.

HOUSMAN: Oh, I know very well there are things not spoken of foursquare at Oxford. The passion for truth is the faintest of all human passions. In the translation of Tibullus[2] in my College library, the *he* loved by the poet is turned into a *she:* and then when you come to the bit where this "she" goes off with somebody's wife, the translator is equal to the crisis—he leaves it out. Horace must have been a god when he wrote "*Diffugere nives*"—the snows fled, and the seasons rolling round each year but for us, when we've had our turn, it's over!—you can't order words in English to get near it—

AEH:

But oh, whate'er the sky-led seasons mar,
Moon upon moon rebuilds it with her beams:

6. From the *Phaedrus*, Jowett's translation.
7. In Greek mythology, the men who accompanied Jason in quest of the Golden Fleece.
8. In the *Illiad*, Achilles's dear friend.
9. Distinction at Oxford.
1. An annual rowing competition akin to the Torpids.
2. Albius Tibullus (c. 54–19 B.C.E.), Latin poet and elegist.

Come *we* where Tullus and where Ancus are,
And good Aeneas, we are dust and dreams.[3]

HOUSMAN: [*cheerfully*]:—yes, it's hopeless, isn't it?—one can only fall dumb, caught between your life that's gone and going! Then turn a few pages back, and Horace is in tears over some athlete, running after him in his dreams, across the Field of Mars and into the rolling waves of the Tiber!— . . . Horace!, who has lots of girls in his poems; and that's tame compared to Catullus—*he's* madly in love with Lesbia, and in between—well, the least of it is stealing kisses from—frankly—a boy who'd still be in the junior dorm at Bromsgrove.

AEH: Catullus 99—*vester* for *tuus*[4] is the point of interest there.

HOUSMAN: No, it isn't!

AEH: I'm sorry.

HOUSMAN: The point of interest is—what is virtue?, what is the good and the beautiful really and truly?

[*AEH notices the laurel on the seat. He picks it up, negligently.*]

AEH: You think there is an answer: the lost autograph copy of life's meaning, which we might recover from the corruptions that have made it nonsense. But if there is no such copy, really and truly there is no answer. It's all in the timing. In Homer, Achilles and Patroclus were comrades, brave and pure of stain. Centuries later in a play now lost, Aeschylus brought in Eros, which I suppose we may translate as extreme spooniness; showers of kisses, and unblemished thighs. Sophocles, too; he wrote *The Loves of Achilles:* more spooniness than you'd find in a cutlery drawer, I shouldn't wonder. Also lost.

HOUSMAN: How is it known, if the plays were lost?

AEH: They were mentioned by critics.

HOUSMAN: There were critics?

AEH: Naturally—it was the cradle of democracy. Euripides wrote a *Pirithous*, the last copy having passed through the intestines of an unknown rat probably a thousand years ago if it wasn't burned by bishops—the Church's idea of the good and the beautiful excludes sexual aberration, apart from chastity, I suppose because it's the rarest. What is this? [*He holds up the laurel crown.*]

HOUSMAN: It's actually mine.

AEH: You'd better take it, then.

To be the fastest runner, the strongest wrestler, the best at throwing the javelin—this was virtue when Horace in his dreams ran after Ligurinus across the Field of Mars, and Ligurinus didn't lose his virtue by being caught. Virtue was practical: the athletic field was named after the god of war. If only an army should be made up of lovers and their loves!—that's not me, that's Plato, or rather Phaedrus in the Master of Balliol's nimble translation: "although a mere handful, they would overcome the world, for each would rather die a thousand deaths than be seen by his beloved to abandon his post or throw away his arms, the veriest coward would be inspired by love." Oh, one can sneer—the sophistry of dirty old men ogling beautiful young ones; then as now, ideals become debased. But there was such an army, a hundred and fifty pairs of lovers, the Sacred Band of Theban

3. From Housman's translation of Horace's Ode 4.7.
4. I.e., the singular, masculine "your" is replaced with the plural. Stoppard seems to have modeled these scholarly quarrels on Housman's 1921 paper before the Cambridge Classical Society, "The Application of Thought to Textual Criticism."

youths, and they were never beaten till Greek liberty died for good at the battle of Chaeronea. At the end of that day, says Plutarch, the victorious Philip of Macedon went forth to view the slain, and when he came to that place where the three hundred fought and lay dead together, he wondered, and understanding that it was the band of lovers, he shed tears and said, whoever suspects baseness in anything these men did, let him perish.

HOUSMAN: I would be such a friend to someone.

AEH: To dream of taking the sword in the breast, the bullet in the brain—

HOUSMAN: I would.

AEH: —and wake up to find the world goes wretchedly on and you will die of age and not of pain.

HOUSMAN: (Well—)

AEH: But lay down your life for your comrade—good lad!—lay it down like a doormat—

HOUSMAN: (Oh—!)

AEH: Lay it down like a card on a card-table for a kind word and a smile—lay it down like a bottle of the best to drink when your damnfool life is all but done: any more laying-downs we can think of?—oh, above all—*above all*—lay down your life like a pack on the roadside though your days of march are numbered and end with the grave. Love will not be deflected from its mischief by being called comradeship or anything else.

HOUSMAN: I don't know what love is.

AEH: Oh, but you do. In the Dark Ages, in Macedonia, in the last guttering light from classical antiquity, a man copied out bits from old books for his young son, whose name was Septimius; so we have one sentence from *The Loves of Achilles*.[5] Love, said Sophocles, is like the ice held in the hand by children. A piece of ice held fast in the fist. I wish I could help you, but it's not in my gift.

HOUSMAN: Love it is, then, and I will make the best of it. I'm sorry that it made you unhappy, but it's not my fault, and it can't be made good by unhappiness in another. Will you shake hands?

AEH: Gladly. [*He shakes Housman's offered hand.*]

HOUSMAN: What happened to Theseus and Pirithous in the end?

AEH: That was the end—their last adventure was down to Hades and they were caught, bound in invisible chains. Theseus was rescued finally but he had to leave his friend behind. In the chain the love of comrades cannot take away.

HOUSMAN: That's not right for *abrumpere*. If it were me I'd have put "break away."

AEH: If it were you, you wouldn't win the Newdigate either.

HOUSMAN: Oh, I don't expect I will. The subject this year is from Catullus—the lament for the Golden Age when the gods still came down to visit us, before we went to the bad.

AEH: An excellent topic for a poem. False nostalgia. Ruskin said you could see the Muses dance for Apollo in Derbyshire before the railways.

HOUSMAN: Where did he say that?

AEH [*points*]: There.

Is there a chamberpot under this seat?

HOUSMAN: A . . . ? No.

AEH: Well, it probably isn't a good idea.

5. Lost play of Sophocles.

We're always living in someone's golden age, it turns out: even Ruskin who takes it all so hard. A hard nut: he looks hard at everything he looks at, and everything he looks at looks hard back at him, it would drive anybody mad. In no time at all, life is like a street accident, with Ruskin raving for doctors, diverting the traffic and calling for laws to control the highway—and that's just his art criticism.

HOUSMAN: I heard Ruskin lecture in mv first term. Painters belayed on every side.

AEH: I think we're in danger of going round again.

[*He stands up. Houstman picks up his books. Pater and the Balliol Student enter as before.*]

PATER: That is charmingly said. I will look at your photograph more carefully when I get home.

[*They leave.*]

AEH: Yes, we are.

Pater doesn't meddle, minds his business, steps aside. When *he* looks at a thing, it melts: tone, resonance, complexity, a moment's rapture and for him alone. Life is not there to be understood, only endured and ameliorated. You'll be all right one way or the other. I was an absolutely safe First, too.

HOUSMAN: Didn't you get it?

AEH: No. Nor a Second, nor a Third, nor even a pass degree.

HOUSMAN: You were *ploughed?*[6]

AEH: Yes.

HOUSMAN: But how?

AEH: That's what they all wanted to know.

HOUSMAN: Oh . . .

JACKSON [*off-stage*]: Housman!

POLLARD [*off-stage*]: Housman!

HOUSMAN: What happened after that?

AEH: I became a clerk and lived in lodgings in Bayswater.

POLLARD [*off-stage*]: Hous! Picnic!

JACKSON [*off-stage*]: Locusts! Honey!

HOUSMAN: I'm sorry, they're calling me. Did you finish your Propertius?

AEH: No.

HOUSMAN: Have you still got it?

AEH: Oh, yes. It's in a box of papers I've arranged to be burned when I'm dead.

[*Jackson and Pollard arrive in the boat.*]

HOUSMAN: [*to the boat*]: I'm here.

AEH: Mo . . . !

POLLARD: It's time to go.

[*Housman goes to the boat and gets in.*]

AEH: I would have died for you but I never had the luck!

HOUSMAN: Where are we going?

POLLARD: Hades. I've brought my Plato—will you con[7] him with me?—

6. Dismissed from the college. 7. Study.

HOUSMAN: I haven't looked at it. Plato is useless to explain anything except what Plato thought.
JACKSON: Why study him, then?
POLLARD: We study the ancient authors to draw lessons for our age.
HOUSMAN: That's all humbug.
POLLARD: Is it? So it is. We study the ancient authors to get a First and a life of learned ease.
HOUSMAN: We need *science* to explain the world. Jackson knows more than Plato. The only reason to consider what Plato meant about anything is if it's relevant to settling the text. Which is classical scholarship, which is a science, the science of textual criticism, Jackson—we will be scientists together. I mean we will both be scientists. Pollard will be what passes as a classical scholar at Oxford, which is to be a literary critic in dead languages.
POLLARD: I say, did you see in the *Sketch*—Oscar Wilde's latest? "Oh, I have worked hard all day—in the morning I put in a comma, and in the afternoon I took it out again!" Isn't that priceless?
HOUSMAN: Why?
POLLARD: What?
HOUSMAN: Oh, I see. It was a joke, you mean?
POLLARD: Oh—really, Housman!

[*The boat takes them away.*
Housman tosses the laurel wreath on the water.]

Pull on your right, Jackson.
JACKSON: Do you want to take the oars?
AEH: *Parce, precor, precor.* Odes Four, one. Ah me, Venus, you old bawd. Where were we? Oh!—we're all here. Good. Open your Horace. Book Four, Ode One, a prayer to the Goddess of Love:

Intermissa, Venus, diu
rursus bella moves? Parce precor, precor!

—mercy, I pray, I pray!, or perhaps better: spare me, I beg you, I beg you!—the very words I spoke when I saw that Mr Fry was determined that *bella* is the adjective and very likely to mean beautiful, and that as eggs go with bacon it goes with Venus.

Intermissa Venus diu
rursus bella moves?

Beautiful Venus having been interrupted do you move again?, he has Horace enquire in a rare moment of imbecility, and Horace is dead as we will all be dead but while I live I will report his cause aright. It's *war*, Mr Fry!, and so is *bella*. Venus do you move *war?*, set in motion war, shall we say?, or start up the war, or better: Venus are you calling me to arms, *rursus*, again, *diu*, after a long time, *intermissa*, having been interrupted, or suspended if you like, and what is it that has been suspended? Two centuries ago Bentley read *intermissa* with *bella*, *war* having been suspended, not Venus, Mr Fry, and—yes—Mr Carsen—and also Miss Frobisher, good morning, you'll forgive us for starting without you—and now all is clear, is it not? Ten years after announcing in Book Three that he was giving up love, the poet feels desire stirring once more and begs for mercy: "Venus, are you calling me to arms again after this long time of truce? Spare me, I beg you, I beg you!" Miss

Frobisher smiles, with little cause that I know of. If Jesus of Nazareth had had before him the example of Miss Frobisher getting through the Latin degree papers of the London University Examinations Board he wouldn't have had to fall back on camels and the eyes of needles, and Miss Frobisher's name would be a delightful surprise to encounter in Matthew, Chapter 19; as would, even more surprisingly, the London University Examinations Board. Your name is not Miss Frobisher? What is your name? Miss Burton. I'm very sorry. I stand corrected. If Jesus of Nazareth had had before him the example of Miss Burton getting through the . . . Oh, dear, I hope it is not I who have made you cry. You don't mind? You don't mind when I make you cry? Oh, Miss Burton, you must try to mind a little. Life is in the minding. Here is Horace at the age of fifty pretending not to mind, verse 29, *me nec femina nec puer, iam nec spes animi credula mutui*—where's the verb? anyone? *iuvat*, thank you, it delights me not, what doesn't?—neither woman nor boy, nor the *spes credula*, the credulous hope, *animi mutui*—the trusting hope of love returned, *nec*, nor, that's four *necs* and a fifth to come before the "but," that's why we call it poetry—*nec certare iuvat mero*—yes, to compete in wine, that'll do for the moment, and *nec*—what?—*nec vincire novis tempora floribus*, rendered by Mr Howard as to tie new flowers to my head, Tennyson would hang himself—never mind, here is Horace not minding: I take no pleasure in woman or boy, nor the trusting hope of love returned, nor matching drink for drink, nor binding fresh-cut flowers around my brow—*but—sed—cur heu, Ligurine, cur—*

[*Jackson is seen as a runner running towards us from the dark, getting no closer.*]

—but why, Ligurinus, alas why this unaccustomed tear trickling down my cheek?—why does my glib tongue stumble to silence as I speak? At night I hold you fast in my dreams, I run after you across the Field of Mars, I follow you into the tumbling waters, and you show no pity.

BLACKOUT

ACT TWO

The summit of "Mount Pisgah" at sunset, Housman, aged twenty-two, and Katharine Housman, aged nineteen, looking out to the west. Some breeze.

HOUSMAN: . . . All the land of Gilead, unto Dan, and all Naphtali, and the land of Ephraim, and Manasseh, and all the land of Judah unto the utmost sea, but not including Wales which I give to the Methodists.

KATE: But what happened, Alfred?

HOUSMAN: That's what they all wanted to know.

KATE: It's the end of fun. We're all frightened of you now, except me, and I am, too. Father feels the blow, in the rain of blows. We're a house of scrimping and tip-toeing and only one fire allowed in winter. Clemence does the books to a halfpenny. Mr Millington always said if she'd been a boy he'd have been glad to have her in his Sixth Form.

HOUSMAN: Millington thought the worst thing that could happen to me was that I'd get a Second. Well, he was wrong about that. He's asked me to take the Sixth for classics from time to time, an act of charity. I'll be teaching young Basil.

KATE: I wish I'd had you to teach me, I wouldn't be the dunce. You put us all on the lawn once to be the sun and planets. I was the earth, and did pirouettes round

Laurence while you skipped around me for my moonlight. That's all the astronomy I ever knew. Will you be a schoolmaster, then?

HOUSMAN: Only while I'm waiting to take the Civil Service exam.

KATE: The Civil Service?

HOUSMAN: A Servant of the Crown.

KATE: Like a diplomat?

HOUSMAN: Yes, exactly. Or a postman. My friend Jackson has got himself into Her Majesty's Patent Office. That would be convenient for the Reading Room of the British Museum. I'm going to carry on with classics. Look at Clee now—how blue it gets when the sun goes down!

KATE: Oh, yes!—our Promised Land!

HOUSMAN: I stopped believing in God, by the way.

KATE: Oh, that's just Oxford.

HOUSMAN: I was waiting by the river for my friends Jackson and Pollard. You don't know Jackson. Pollard is the one who came to stay once. Mamma disapproved of his letting her see him approach the door of the lavatory. He lacked the proper furtiveness . . . Well, I was waiting for them on a bench by the river and it came upon me that I was alone, and there was no help for anything.

KATE: Mamma would die if she could hear you.

HOUSMAN: I won't mention it at family prayers.

KATE: Oxford has made you smart. Do you remember what our real mother was like?

HOUSMAN: Oh, yes: when she was ill I sat with her all the time. We used to pray together for her to get better, and she talked to me as if I were grown up.

KATE: *She* can hear you.

HOUSMAN: I stopped believing in *that* part when I was thirteen.

KATE: That was only to punish Him for mother dying.

HOUSMAN: And by God, He stayed punished.

[*Darkness.*

In a spotlight, "Bunthorne" in Patience *by Gilbert and Sullivan,*[8] *is singing.*]

BUNTHORNE [*sings*]:

"Though the Philistines may jostle,
you may rank as an apostle
in the high aesthetic band,
if you walk down Piccadilly
with a poppy or a lily
in your medieval hand . . ."

[*Bunthorne exits.*

A station platform at night, the "Underground—Overground" Steam Railway.

Housman, aged twenty-three, and Jackson, aged twenty-four, dressed as for "the office," are waiting for the train. Housman has a Journal of Philology, *Jackson an evening paper.*]

JACKSON: Wasn't it magnificent? A landmark, Hous!

HOUSMAN: I thought it was . . . quite jolly . . .

JACKSON: Quite jolly? It was a watershed! D'Oyly Carte has made the theatre *modern.*

HOUSMAN [*surprised*]: You mean Gilbert and Sullivan?

8. Librettist W. S. Gilbert (1836–1911) and composer Arthur Sullivan (1842–1900), comic opera writers.

JACKSON: What? No. No, the *theatre*.
HOUSMAN: (Oh, I see.)
JACKSON: The first theatre lit entirely by electricity!
HOUSMAN: Dear old Mo . . .
JACKSON: D'Oyly Carte's new Savoy is a triumph.
HOUSMAN: . . . you're the only London theatre critic worthy of the name. "The new electrified Savoy is a triumph. The contemptible flickering gas-lit St James's—"
JACKSON [*overlapping*]: Oh, I know you're ragging me . . .
HOUSMAN: ". . . the murky malodorous Haymarket . . . the unscientific Adelphi . . . "
JACKSON: But it was exciting, wasn't it, Hous? Every age thinks it's the modern age, but this one really is. Electricity is going to change everything. Everything! We had an electric corset sent in today.
HOUSMAN: One that lights up?
JACKSON: I've never thought of it before, but in a way the Patent Office is the gatekeeper to the new age.
HOUSMAN: An Examiner of Electrical Specifications may be, but it's not the same with us toiling down in Trade Marks. I had sore throat lozenges today, an application to register a wonderfully woebegone giraffe—raised rather a subtle point in Trade Marks regulation, actually: it seems there is already a giraffe at large, wearing twelve styles of celluloid collar, but, and here's the nub, a *happy* giraffe, in fact a preening self-satisfied giraffe. The question arises—is the registered giraffe Platonic?, are all God's giraffes *in esse et in posse*[9] to be rendered unto the Houndsditch Novelty Collar Company?
JACKSON: It's true, then—a classical education fits a fellow for anything.
HOUSMAN: Well, I consulted my colleague Chamberlain—he's compiling the new Index—I don't think he's altogether sound, Chamberlain, he put John the Baptist under Mythological Characters—
JACKSON: Do you know what someone said?
HOUSMAN: —and a monk holding a tankard under Biblical Subjects.
JACKSON: Will you tell me what happened?
HOUSMAN: Oh, we found for the lozenges.
JACKSON: Someone said you ploughed yourself on purpose.
HOUSMAN: Pollard?
JACKSON: No. But they had him in to ask about you.
HOUSMAN: I saw Pollard in the Reading Room.
JACKSON: What did *he* have to say?
HOUSMAN: Nothing. It was the Reading Room. We adjusted our expressions briefly.
JACKSON: We got what we wanted, Pollard at the British Museum and here's me with an Examinership and three hundred a year with prospects . . . You were cleverer than any of us, Hous!
HOUSMAN: I didn't get what I wanted, that's true, but I want what I've got.
JACKSON: Pushing a pen at thirty-eight shillings a week.
HOUSMAN: But here we are, you and I, we eat the same meals in the same digs, catch the same train to work in the same office, and the work is easy, I've got time to do classics . . . and friendship is all, sometimes I'm so happy, it makes me dizzy—and,

9. Actual and potential.

look, I have prospects, too!, I'm published! [*He shows Jackson the journal.*] I was saving it for cocoa.

JACKSON: I say!—

HOUSMAN: *The Journal of Philology*. See?

JACKSON: "Horatiana" . . . "A. E. Housman"—I say! . . . What is it?

HOUSMAN: It's putting people right about what Horace really wrote.

JACKSON: Horace!

HOUSMAN: Only bits. I'm working on Propertius really.

JACKSON: Well done, Hous! We must celebrate!

HOUSMAN: But we have—that's why I. . .

JACKSON [*reminded*]: Oh, but I still owe you for . . .

HOUSMAN: No, it was my idea, and anyway you thought the electricians were the best thing in it.

JACKSON: The girls were pretty, and the tunes, it was only the story.

HOUSMAN: The whole thing was silly.

JACKSON: *Jolly*, you said. You don't have to agree with me all the time.

HOUSMAN: I don't!

JACKSON: Well, you do, you know, Hous—you should stick to your own opinions more.

HOUSMAN: Well, that's a bit thick when I've just told Richard Bentley (that) his "securesque" in three twenty-six won't do!

JACKSON: Who?—Oh, *veni, vidi, vici* . . .
What gets *my* goat, actually, if you want to know, is that the fellow isn't worth the fuss, none of them are—I mean, what *use* is he to anyone?

HOUSMAN: *Use?* . . . I know it's not useful like electricity, but it's exciting, really and truly, to spot something—

JACKSON: What?

HOUSMAN: —to be the first person for thousands of years to read the verse as it was written—What?

JACKSON: I mean these Aesthetes—the show . . .

HOUSMAN: (Oh—!)

JACKSON: What gets *me* is all this attention—you can't open a newspaper (without . . .), and cartoons in *Punch* every time he opens his mouth being aesthetic and better than ordinary people working at proper things . . . I mean what's he ever *done?*, and now an operetta, for heaven's sake, to make him the talk of the town twice over—*what has he ever done?*, that's what I'd like to know.

HOUSMAN: Well, I . . . He's had a book of poems . . .

JACKSON: I've got nothing against poetry, don't think I have, I like a good poem as well as the next man, but you don't find Tennyson flouncing about Piccadilly and trying to be witty, do you?—and all that posing and dressing up, it's not manly, if you ask me, Hous.

HOUSMAN: It wasn't him with the electric corset, was it?

JACKSON: There were several at Oxford, I remember.

HOUSMAN: Do you remember he said your leg was a poem?

JACKSON: Which one?

HOUSMAN: Left. Oh—Wilde. Oscar Wilde.

JACKSON: Oscar Wilde was at Oxford with *us?*

HOUSMAN: In our first year, he went down with a First in Greats. I went to Warren, his tutor at Magdalen. You don't remember?

JACKSON: There was a Wyld who bowled a bit, left arm round the wicket . . .
HOUSMAN: No, no . . . Blue china . . .
JACKSON: Wait a minute. Velvet knickerbockers! Well, I'm damned! I knew he wasn't the full shilling!

[*Noise and lights: arriving train. Darkness.*

A room—the billiard room, perhaps—in a London club, 1885, at night.

Labouchere and Harris,[1] *in full evening dress—perhaps—with brandy and cigars—for example—are playing billiards, or not.*

A third man, Stead,[2] *wears an almost shabby office suit. He has a full beard and the fanatical gleam of a prophet. He is scanning a newspaper in a professional manner.*

LABOUCHERE: We invented Oscar, we bodied him forth. Then we floated him. Then we kited the stock. When D'Oyly Carte took *Patience* to New York, he had the idea of bringing Oscar to America and exhibiting him as the original aesthetic article for purposes of publicity, and Oscar did him proud before he was off the boat—"Mr Wilde Disappointed by Atlantic"—remember that, Stead?, you gave it space in the *Gazette*, and I printed the Atlantic's reply in *Truth*—"Atlantic Disappointed by Mr Wilde." I wrote him up nicely, and Oscar, who didn't know it was all a ramp,[3] told people over there, "Henry Labouchere is one of my heroes" . . . all in all, most satisfactory, a job well done. But now he's got away from us. No matter where we cut the string, the kite won't fall. The ramp is over and the stock keeps rising. When he came home and had the cheek to lecture in Piccadilly on his impressions of America, I filled three columns under the heading "Exit Oscar." I dismissed him, no doubt to his surprise, as an effeminate phrase-maker. I counted up the number of times he used the word "beautiful," "lovely" or "charming," and it came to eighty-six. You'd think that would sink anybody, but not at all . . . He went off round the provinces and people paid good money to be told they were provincial . . . their houses were ugly inside and out, their dress dowdy, their husbands dull, their wives plain, and their opinions on art worthless. Meanwhile, Oscar himself has never done anything.
HARRIS: You were on the wrong end of the string, Labby.
LABOUCHERE: Up, up, up . . . It shakes one's faith in the operation of a moral universe by journalism.
STEAD: It's the aimless arrow that brings us down, the arrow fledged with one of our own feathers.
HARRIS: You really ought to edit the Old Testament, old man.
LABOUCHERE: He does.
STEAD: The *Pall Mall Gazette* is testament enough that the Lord is at my elbow, and was there today when I—yes, I!—forced Parliament to pass the Criminal Law Amendment Act.[4]

1. Frank Harris: (1856–1931), Irish author and journalist, editor of the *Saturday Review*.
2. William Thomas Stead (1849–1912), reformer journalist; he caused a stir by purchasing the thirteen-year-old daughter of a chimney sweep, a publicity stunt for which he was imprisoned.
3. Swindle.
4. Outlawing acts of "gross indecency" between men.

HARRIS: You know, Stead, most people think you're mad. They thought so even before you bought a thirteen-year-old virgin for £5 to prove a point. A wonderful stunt, I wouldn't deny—I doff my hat. When I took over the *Evening News* I edited the paper with the best in me at twenty-eight. The circulation wouldn't budge. So, I edited the paper as a boy of fourteen. The circulation started to rise and never looked back.

STEAD: No, by heavens, Harris! In the right hands the editor's pen is the sceptre of power! For us, life can once more be brilliant as in the heroic days. In my first campaign, when I was still a young man in the provinces, I roused the north against Lord Beaconsfield's Russian Policy[5] and the Turkish atrocities in Bulgaria[6] "The honour of the Bulgarian virgins," I told my readers, "is in the hands of the electors of Darlington." I heard the clear call of the voice of God in 1876: I heard it again last year when I forced the government to send General Gordon to Khartoum; and I heard it in my campaign which today has given thirteen-, fourteen-, and fifteen-year-old British virgins the protection of Parliament.

HARRIS: General Gordon got his head cut off.

STEAD: Whether he did or not—

HARRIS: He did.

STEAD: —we journalists have a divine mission to be the tribunes of the people.

HARRIS: The Turko-Russia war was my blooding as a journalist. I was with General Skobeleff at the battle of Plevna.

LABOUCHERE [*To Stead*]: I'm a Member of Parliament, I don't have to be a journalist to be a tribune of the people. [To *Harris*.] No, you weren't, Frank. You were at Brighton. [*To Stead.*] The Criminal Law Amendment Act is badly drawn up and will do more harm than good, as I said in my paper. [*To Harris.*] In '76 you were a French tutor at Brighton College, or so you told Hattie during the interval at *Phedre*.

HARRIS: That was a flight of fancy.

LABOUCHERE [*To Stead*]: The Bill should have been referred to a Select Committee, and would have been but for the government being stampeded by your disgusting articles.

HARRIS: Traditionally, Parliament has always been the protector of the British virgin, but usually on a first come first served basis.

LABOUCHERE: You have made the *Pall Mall Gazette* look sensational even when there's nothing sensational in it, but the Maiden Tribute campaign was a disgrace to decency—you had errand boys reading about filthy goings-on which concerned nobody but their sisters.

HARRIS: Is it true you caught a mouse in the *Gazette* office and ate it on toast?

STEAD: Perfectly true.
[*To Labouchere.*] When I came down from Darlington to join the *Gazette*—

HARRIS: Up.

STEAD: —it never sold more than 13,000 copies and never deserved to—it kept the reader out.

HARRIS: Up from Darlington.

STEAD: I introduced the crosshead in '81, the illustration in '82, the interview in '83, the personal note, the signed article—

LABOUCHERE: Why did you eat a mouse?

5. Benjamin Disraeli (1804–1881), Prime Minister of Britain, made Lord Beaconsfield in 1876; he promoted policies to contain Russia's influence in Central Asia.

6. Suppression of Bulgarian rebellion against the Ottoman Empire, April 1876.

STEAD: I wanted to know what it tasted like.

LABOUCHERE: You should have asked me. I ate them in Paris during the Siege, and rats and cats.

STEAD: I invented the New Journalism![7]

LABOUCHERE: We didn't eat the rats till we'd eaten all the cats.

STEAD: I gave virtue a voice Parliament couldn't ignore.

LABOUCHERE: Then we ate the dogs. When there were no dogs left we ate the animals in the zoo.

STEAD: Item! The age of consent raised from thirteen to sixteen.

LABOUCHERE: I sent my despatches out by balloon and made my name. I suppose you were in the Siege of Paris, too, Frank.

HARRIS: No, in 1870 I was building the Brooklyn Bridge.

STEAD: Item! Girls in moral danger may be removed from their parents by the courts.

LABOUCHERE: *That'll* be a dead letter.

STEAD: But it was your Amendment.

LABOUCHERE: Anybody with any sense on the backbenches was pitch-forking Amendments in to get the government to admit it had a pig's breakfast on its hands and withdraw it. I forced a division on raising the age of consent to twenty-one!, and two people voted for it. My final effort was the Amendment on indecency between male persons, and God help me, it went through on the nod—(it had) nothing to do with the Bill we were supposed to be debating; normally it would have been ruled out of order, but everyone wanted to be shot of the business, prorogue Parliament, and get on to the General Election.

STEAD: But—but surely—you *intended* the Bill to address a contemporary evil—?

LABOUCHERE: Nothing of the sort. I intended to make the Bill absurd to any sensible person left in what by then was a pretty thin House . . . but that one got away, so now a French kiss and what-you-fancy between two chaps safe at home with the door shut is good for two years with or without hard labour. It's a funny old world.

STEAD: Then your mischief was timely. London shows all the indications of falling into the abyss of perverse eroticism that encompassed the fall of Greece and Rome.

LABOUCHERE: What indications are they?

STEAD: There is a scepticism of what is morally elevating, a taste for the voluptuous and the forbidden in French literature. Our Aesthetes look to Paris for their sins, which I will not name, which are so odious they should never have been allowed to leave France.

HARRIS: Actually, in Greece and Rome sodomy was rarely associated with a taste for French novels, it was the culture of the athletic ground and the battlefield; as in Sparta, for example, or the Sacred Band of Thebes. It so happens that I was wandering through Greece in October of 1880, travelling sometimes on foot, sometimes on horse, putting up at monasteries or with shepherds in their huts, and I arrived finally at Thebes. There was a German archaeologist there who said his name was Schliemann—

LABOUCHERE: Harris, do you *ever* tell the truth?

HARRIS: —who told us that a young Greek lad had just discovered a very large grave at Chaeronea near by, right under the stone lion erected by Philip of Macedon to commemorate his victory there in 338 BC. It was at the battle of Chaeronea, you

7. New style of tabloid journalism arising in Britain in the second half of the nineteenth century, responding to rising literacy rates and relaxed libel statutes.

remember, where, according to Plutarch, a hundred and fifty pairs of lovers pledged to defend Thebes from the invader fought and died to the last man. Well, I stayed on there until we had uncovered 297 skeletons, buried together.

LABOUCHERE: So it was you!

HARRIS: They were in two layers, packed like sardines. You could still see where the Macedonian lances smashed arms, ribs, skulls . . . Most extraordinary thing I've ever seen.

[*Open ground. Summer afternoon, 1885.*

Housman, aged twenty-six, is comfortable on the grass, reading the Journal of Philology. *Chamberlain, a contemporary, is sitting up, reading the* Daily Telegraph *or similar. They are inattentive spectators at a suburban athletics meeting, the sounds of which are now some feeble applause, a few random shouts, perhaps a bandstand; all of these at a distance. A bag containing bottled beer and sandwiches lies by them.*]

CHAMBERLAIN: What do you think, Housman? Five pounds for a virgin. Would that mean one go? . . .

HOUSMAN: You can't have two goes at the same virgin.

CHAMBERLAIN: . . . or do you get her to keep?, I mean. What *are* the parliamentary reports coming to?

HOUSMAN: Is that the quarter-mile lining up? I can't see Jackson.

CHAMBERLAIN: It probably isn't, then.

HOUSMAN [*anxious*]: Are you sure? We haven't come all the way out to Ealing to miss it.

CHAMBERLAIN: "Mr Labouchere, Lib., Northampton . . ." *he* has a way with him.

HOUSMAN: Or is that the half?

CHAMBERLAIN: There's no way of telling at the start, it all depends on where they stop. "Mr Labouchere's Amendment . . ." Oh dear oh dear oh dear, well, that's opened up the north-west passage for every blackmailer in town; you'd think they'd know, wouldn't you? Educated at Eton and Trinity, too, so what's he got left to be shocked about?

HOUSMAN: I do believe it is the quarter-mile, you know. [*He stands up as a distant starting pistol is heard.*] Can you see him?

[*Chamberlain finally looks up from his paper.*]

CHAMBERLAIN: The quarter-mile is a flat race, isn't it?—that's hurdles. [*He returns to his paper.*]

HOUSMAN [*relieved*]: Oh, yes . . . it's after the 220 hurdles.

CHAMBERLAIN: Running late.

HOUSMAN: (No, 220 yards . . .)

CHAMBERLAIN: Sit down, you're like a nervous girl.

[*Distant shouts, some applause. Chamberlain studies his newspaper.*]

No offence, old chap. I like you more than anyone I know. I even like you for the way you stick to Jackson. But he'll never want what you want. You'll have to find it somewhere else or you'll be unhappy, even unhappier. I know whereof I speak. I don't mind you knowing. I know you won't tell on me at the office. You're the straightest, kindest man I know and I'm sorry for you, that's all. I'm sorry if I spoke out of turn.

[*A distant starting pistol. Chamberlain stands up. They watch the progress of the runners, for form's sake, silent, separate, remote from the fact. The race takes nearly a minute: the pauses and speeches are in real time.*
Long pause.]

He'll be in the first three if he keeps it up.

[*Long pause.*]

HOUSMAN [*watching the runners*]: What do I want?

CHAMBERLAIN: Nothing which you'd call indecent, though I don't see what's wrong with it myself. You want to be brothers-in-arms, to have him to yourself . . . to be shipwrecked together, (to) perform valiant deeds to earn his admiration, to save him from certain death, to die for him—to die in his arms, like a Spartan, kissed once on the lips . . . or just run his errands in the meanwhile. You want him to know what cannot be spoken, and to make the perfect reply, in the same language. [*Pause. Still without inflection.*] He's going to win it. [*Finally he warms into excitement as the race passes in front of them.*] By God, he is! Come on, Jackson! Up the Patent Office! . . .
. . . He's won it!

[*Chamberlain slaps Housman on the back in unaffected joy. Housman thaws, catching up.*]

HOUSMAN: He won!

CHAMBERLAIN: We should have brought champagne!

HOUSMAN: No, he likes his bottle of Biblical Subject. [*Embarrassed.*] Well . . .

CHAMBERLAIN: Come on, then—I'm thirsty with all that running.

[*Pollard, aged twenty-six, arrives hot and bothered, in office dress, carrying a* Pink 'Un[8] *edition of the Saturday afternoon newspaper.*]

POLLARD: Housman!—there you are! Was that the quarter?

HOUSMAN: Pollard—you duffer! You've missed it! He won!

POLLARD: Damn! I mean—you know what I mean. I couldn't get here a minute sooner. I bet I ran faster from the station than Jackson.

[*To Chamberlain.*] How do you do?

HOUSMAN: Chamberlain, this is Pollard; Pollard, this is Chamberlain.

CHAMBERLAIN: Very pleased to meet you.

HOUSMAN: He's at the British Museum.

POLLARD [*to Chamberlain*]: Not an exhibit, I work at the library.

HOUSMAN: You are an exhibit . . . [*He tidies Pollard's collar and tie.*] Here, look. There. We've got a picnic.

POLLARD: Ah, locusts and honey.

HOUSMAN: The three of us used to take a boat down to Hades, with a picnic—where's Mo?

POLLARD: It was only once.

HOUSMAN: We were chums together at St John's—

CHAMBERLAIN: (Hades . . .?)

8. Newspaper sports supplement.

HOUSMAN: —oh!—Chamberlain is an expert on the Baptist, that well-known mythological character.

POLLARD: Really?

CHAMBERLAIN: He was a water-biscuit. Yes, it's confusing but we keep an open mind at the Trade Marks Registry.

HOUSMAN: Here he is—*victor ludorum*.[9]

[*Jackson joins them.*]

POLLARD: *Ave, Ligurine!*

HOUSMAN: Jolly well done, Mo!

CHAMBERLAIN: I say! What was your time?

JACKSON: Oh, I don't know, it's only a race, don't make a fuss. Fifty-four, apparently. Hello, Pollard, [*accepting a bottle of beer from Housman.*] Thanks. This is sporting of you. And sandwiches!

CHAMBERLAIN [*offering sandwiches*]: Age before beauty.

JACKSON [*declining*]: I'll get changed first. [*To Pollard.*] Got the *Pink 'Un?* Good man. [*Taking it.*] How were the Australians doing?

POLLARD: At what?

JACKSON: Oh, *really*, Pollard! [*He laughs, leaving with his beer and the* Pink 'Un.]

POLLARD: The paper is full of white-slave traffic today. Apparently we lead the world in exporting young women to Belgium.

CHAMBERLAIN: It's disgusting, the way the papers have been hashing it up.

POLLARD: Hushing it up?

CHAMBERLAIN: Not *hushing* it up. *Hashing* it up.

POLLARD: Oh . . .

[*Pollard and Housman catch each other's eye and laugh at the same thought.*]

CHAMBERLAIN [*after a pause*]: Well, we'll never know.

HOUSMAN: It's nothing much to know anyway. Before books were printed, often you'd have one person dictating to two or three copyists . . .

POLLARD: . . . then, hundreds of years later, there'd be a manuscript in one place that's got "hushing it up" and one in another place that's got "hashing it up," only in Latin, of course, and people like Housman here arguing about which the author really wrote. Have you got something in there (the *Journal)?*

CHAMBERLAIN: Why?

HOUSMAN: (No.)

POLLARD: And, of course, the copies get copied, so then you can argue about which copies come first and which scribes had bad habits—oh, the fun is endless.

CHAMBERLAIN: But there's no way to tell if they both make sense.

HOUSMAN: One of them always makes the better sense if you can get into the writer's mind, without prejudices.

POLLARD: And then you publish your article insisting it was really "lashing it up."

CHAMBERLAIN: Why?

POLLARD: Why? So that other people can write articles insisting it was "mashing it up" or "washing it up."

9. Winner of the games.

CHAMBERLAIN: Toss a coin—I would.

POLLARD: That's another good method. (I'm) only teasing, Housman, don't look so down in the mouth.

CHAMBERLAIN [*gets up*]: I'm off, apologize for me to Jackson. I've got to meet someone in the West End at five.

POLLARD: There's still plenty of trains.

CHAMBERLAIN: I came on my bicycle.

POLLARD: Goodness!

CHAMBERLAIN: It was very nice to meet you.

POLLARD: Likewise. Yes, don't keep the lady waiting!

CHAMBERLAIN: Oh, you've guessed my secret. Thanks, Housman. I'll see you on Monday.

HOUSMAN: I'm sorry you have to go. Thank you.

CHAMBERLAIN: Wouldn't have missed it.

POLLARD: Nor I.

CHAMBERLAIN: But you did.

POLLARD: Oh, that.

[*Chamberlain goes.*]

HOUSMAN: No need to tell Jackson—he'd be disappointed. Why did you call him Ligurinus?

POLLARD: Wasn't it Ligurinus?—running over the Campus Martius? [*From his pocket he takes about twenty handwritten pages.*] Thanks for this.

HOUSMAN: What did you think?

POLLARD: You won't expect me to judge it. I'm no Propertius scholar.

HOUSMAN: But you've read him.

POLLARD: I read a few of the elegies in my third year but Propertius is too rough-cornered for my taste.

HOUSMAN: Yes—mine, too.

POLLARD: (But—?!)

HOUSMAN: To be a scholar, the first thing you have to learn is that scholarship is nothing to do with taste; speaking, of course, as a Higher Division Clerk in Her Majesty's Patent Office. Propertius looked to me like a garden gone to wilderness, and not a very interesting garden either, but what an opportunity!—it was begging to be put back in order. Better still, various nincompoops thought they had already done it . . . hacking about, to make room for their dandelions. So far, I've improved the vulgate in about two hundred places.

[*Pollard laughs.*]

But I have.

POLLARD: I'm sure you have.

HOUSMAN: What worries you about it?

POLLARD: Well, the tone of some of it, it's a bit breathtaking. It's all right me reading it, because I know what a soft old thing you are underneath, but it isn't the way scholars generally deal with each other, is it?

HOUSMAN [*lightly*]: Oh, Bentley and Scaliger were far ruder.

POLLARD: But that was centuries ago, and you're not Bentley, not yet anyway. Who is Postgate?

HOUSMAN: Oh, he's a good man, one of the best of the younger Propertius critics—

POLLARD: (What—?!) [*He finds his place, on the last page*.]
HOUSMAN: —he's a professor at UCL.[1]
POLLARD [*reading*]: " . . . makes nonsense of the whole elegy from beginning to end . . ."
HOUSMAN: Well, he does. "*Voces*" in verse 33 is an emendation to frighten children in their beds.
POLLARD: ". . . But I imagine these considerations will have occurred to Mr Postgate himself ere now, or will have been pointed out to him by his friends.". . . It's so disrespectful.
HOUSMAN: Your point being that I'm a clerk in the Patent Office.
POLLARD [*hotly*]: No!—I'm *not* saying that!
HOUSMAN: I'm sorry. Let's not fall out. Have another Biblical Subject.

[*They open two bottles of beer*.]

POLLARD [*explaining*]: I was only thinking suppose one day you put in for a lectureship at University College and your Mr Postgate was on the selection committee.
HOUSMAN: I'd only apply for a Chair[2] at UCL.
POLLARD [*laughs*]: Oh . . . Housman, what will become of you?
HOUSMAN: You're my only friend who might understand, don't let me down. If I'm disrespectful it's because it's important and not a game anyone can play. I could have given Chamberlain a proper answer. Scholarship doesn't need to wriggle out of it with a joke. It's where we're nearest to our humanness. Unless knowledge for its own sake. Useful knowledge is good, too, but it's for the faint-hearted, an elaboration of the real thing, which is only to shine some light, it doesn't matter where on what, it's the light itself, against the darkness, it's what's left of God's purpose when you take away God. It doesn't mean I don't care about the poetry. I do. *Diffugere nives* goes through me like a spear. Nobody makes it stick like Horace that you're a long time dead—dust and shadow, and no good deeds, no eloquence, will bring you back. I think it's the most beautiful poem in Latin or Greek there ever was; but in verse 15 Horace never wrote "*dives*" which is in all the texts, and I'm pretty sure I know what he did write. Anyone who says "So what?" got left behind five hundred years ago when we became modern, that's why it's called Humanism. The recovery of ancient texts is the highest task of all—Erasmus, bless him. It is work to be done. Posterity has a brisk way with manuscripts: scholarship is a small redress against the vast unreason of what is taken from us—it's not just the worthless that perish, Jesus doesn't save.
POLLARD: Stop—stop it, Housman!—the sun is shining, it's Saturday afternoon!—I'm happy! The best survives because it is the best.
HOUSMAN: Oh . . . Pollard. Have you ever seen a cornfield after the reaping? Laid flat to stubble, and here and there, unaccountably, miraculously spared, a few stalks still upright. Why those? There is no reason. Ovid's Medea, the Thyestes of Varius who was Virgil's friend and considered by some his equal, the lost Aeschylus trilogy of the Trojan war . . . gathered to oblivion in *sheaves*, along with hundreds of Greek and Roman authors known only for fragments or their names alone—and here and there a cornstalk, a thistle, a poppy, still standing, but as to purpose, signifying nothing.
POLLARD: I know what you want.

1. University College, London.

2. A more prestigious position than the "lectureship" for which Pollard suggests he might apply.

HOUSMAN: What do I want?
POLLARD: A monument. Housman was here.
HOUSMAN: Oh, you've guessed my secret.
POLLARD: A mud pie against the incoming tide.
HOUSMAN: (Oh, that's) a fine way to speak of my edition of Propertius.
POLLARD [*toasting*]: To you and your Propertius. Who's that with Jackson?, do you know her?
HOUSMAN: No. Yes. She came to the office.
POLLARD: Well, don't stare.
HOUSMAN: I'm not.
POLLARD [*toasting*]: Coupled with the British Museum library! The aggregate of human progress made stackable!
HOUSMAN [*toasting*]: Making a stand against the natural and merciful extinction of the unreadable! How very British of it. Bring back the manuscript . . .
POLLARD: Is it over?, people seem to be leaving.

[*Housman starts packing up the picnic.*]

HOUSMAN: When you consider the ocean of bilge brought forth by the invention of printing, it does make you wonder about this boon of civilization. I wonder about it every time I open the *Journal of Philology*.
No. They're gathering . . . Oh!—they're giving out the trophies! Come on!

[*They go. Housman taking the picnic bag.*]

[*Elsewhere—night.*
Jackson, in his pyjamas and dressing-gown, reads aloud from a handwritten page; a modest silver trophy-cup perhaps in evidence.]

JACKSON:

"Blest as one of the gods is he,
The Youth who fondly sits by thee,
And hears and sees thee all the while
Softly speak and sweetly smile.
For while I gaze with trembling heart[3] . . . "

Mmm. Did you write this?

[*Housman comes with two mugs of cocoa. He is wearing day-clothes.*]

HOUSMAN: Well, Sappho, really, more or less.
JACKSON [*ponders*]: Mmm. What's that one you used to have about kisses?
HOUSMAN: Catullus. "Give me a thousand kisses and then a hundred more."
JACKSON: Yes. She might think that's a bit hot, though. It should really be about me being unhappy and ticking her off for her unfaithfulness, and at the same time willing to forgive. Where's the one again where I'm carving her name on trees?
HOUSMAN: Propertius. But honestly, that's bit raving—she's only said she's staying in to wash her hair.
JACKSON: But I'd got tickets and everything! After being at her beck and call . . .
HOUSMAN: *Quinque tibi potui servire (fidelitur annos)*.

3. From Catullus's Ode 51, "Ad Lesbiam," in imitation of Sappho's fragment 2.

JACKSON: What?

HOUSMAN: Five years your faithful slave.

JACKSON: Exactly. Two weeks anyway.

HOUSMAN: The problem we're up against here is that the ticking-off ones make her out to be a harlot, and the happy ones make her out to be, well, *your* harlot . . . so I think the way to go is more *carpe diem*, gather ye rosebuds while you may, the grave's a fine and private place but none I think do there embrace.[4]

JACKSON: She'd never believe I wrote that.

HOUSMAN: Dear old Mo, what will become of you?

JACKSON: Orchestra stalls, too.

HOUSMAN: Oh, *well!*—"If that's the price for kisses due, it's the last kiss I steal from *you*"[5]—written to a boy, but never mind—interesting poem, by the way: *vester* for *tuus*—

JACKSON: She thinks you're sweet on me.

HOUSMAN: —plural for singular, the first use. What?

JACKSON: Rosa said you're sweet on me.

HOUSMAN: What did she mean?

JACKSON: Well, you know.

HOUSMAN: What did you say?

JACKSON: I said it was nonsense. We're chums. We've been chums since Oxford, you, me and Pollard.

HOUSMAN: Did she think Pollard was sweet on you?

JACKSON: She didn't talk about Pollard. You're not, are you, Hous?

HOUSMAN: You're my best friend.

JACKSON: That's what I said, like . . .

HOUSMAN: Theseus and Pirithous.

JACKSON: The Three Musketeers.

HOUSMAN: What did she say?

JACKSON: She hasn't read it.

HOUSMAN: I don't understand. You mean, just from Saturday, just from going home together on the train from Ealing?

JACKSON: I suppose so. Yes. It was odd Chamberlain being there that day.

HOUSMAN: Why?

JACKSON: Well, it was just odd. An odd coincidence. I was going to mention it.

HOUSMAN: Mention what?

JACKSON: Mention that perhaps you shouldn't get to be pals with him too much, it may be misunderstood.

HOUSMAN: You think Chamberlain is sweet on me?

JACKSON: No, of course not. But one has heard things about Chamberlain at the office. I'am sorry now I mentioned him! I know I'm all hobnails but you're all right about it, aren't you, Hous? You see, I'm awfully strong on Rosa, she's not like other girls, she's not what I'd call a *girl* at all, you saw that for yourself, she's a woman, we love each other.

HOUSMAN: I'm glad for you, Mo. I liked her very much.

4. Combines famous lines from Robert Herrick's "To the Virgins, To Make Much of Time" and Andrew Marvell's "To His Coy Mistress."

5. A loose translation of Catullus 99.

JACKSON [*pleased*]: Did you? I knew you would. You're a good pal to me and I hope I am to you. I knew I only had to ask you and that would be the end of it. I'll tell her she's a cuckoo. Shake hands?

[*Jackson puts out his hand, Housman takes it.*]

HOUSMAN: Gladly.
JACKSON: Still pals.
HOUSMAN: Comrades.
JACKSON: Like whoever they were.
HOUSMAN: Theseus and Pirithous. They were kings. They met on the field of battle to fight to the death, but when they saw each other, each was struck in admiration for his adversary, so they became comrades instead and had many adventures together. Theseus was never so happy as when he was with his friend. They weren't sweet on each other. They loved each other, as men loved each other in the heroic age, in virtue, paired together in legend and poetry as the pattern of comradeship, the chivalric ideal of virtue in the ancient world. Virtue! What happened to it? It had a good run—centuries!—it was still virtue in Socrates to admire a beautiful youth, virtue to be beautiful and admired, it was still there, grubbier and a shadow of itself but still there, for my Roman poets who competed for women and boys as fancy took them; virtue in Horace to shed tears of love over Ligurinus on the athletic field. Well, not any more, eh, Mo? Virtue is what women have to lose, the rest is vice. Pollard thinks I'm sweet on you, too, though he hardly knows he thinks it. Will you mind if I go to live somewhere but close by?
JACKSON: Why?
Oh . . .
HOUSMAN: We'll still be friends, won't we?
JACKSON: Oh!
HOUSMAN: Of *course* Rosa knew!—of *course* she'd know!
JACKSON: Oh!
HOUSMAN: Did you really not know even for a minute?
JACKSON: How could I know? You seem just like . . . you know, normal. You're not one of those Aesthete types or anything—(*angrily*) how could I know?!
HOUSMAN: You mean if I dressed like the Three Musketeers you'd have suspected? You're half my life.

We took a picnic down to Hades. There was a dog on the island there, a friendly lost dog and not even wet, a mystery, he jumped into the boat to be rescued. Do you remember the dog? Pollard and I were arguing about English or Latin being best for poetry—the dog was subjoined: lost dog loves young man—dog young lost man loves, loves lost young man dog, you can't beat Latin: shuffle the words to suit, the endings tell you which loves what, who's young, who lost, if you can't read Latin go home, you've missed it! You kissed the dog. After that day, everything else seemed futile and ridiculous: the ridiculous idea that one's life was poised on the reading course . . .

JACKSON [*puzzled*]: Dog?
HOUSMAN [*cries out*]: Oh, if only you hadn't said anything! We could have carried on the same!
JACKSON: [*an announcement*]: It's not your fault. That's what I say. It's terrible but it's not your fault. You won't find me casting the first stone. [*Pause.*] We'll be just like before.

HOUSMAN: Do you mean it, Mo?
JACKSON: No one will know it from me. We've been pals a long time.
HOUSMAN: Thank you.
JACKSON: It's rotten luck but it'll be our secret. You'll easily find some decent digs round here—we'll catch the same train to work as always, and I bet before you know it you'll meet the right girl and we'll all three be chuckling over this—Rosa, I mean. What about that? I dare say I've surprised you! All right? Shake on it?

[Jackson puts out his hand.
Darkness, except on Housman.]

HOUSMAN:
He would not stay for me; and who can wonder?
He would not stay for me to stand and gaze.
I shook his hand and tore my heart in sunder

[Light on AEH.]

And went with half my life about my ways.[6]

[Darkness on Housman.
AEH is at a desk among books, inkpot and pen.
Elsewhere, simultaneously, a Selection Committee meets, comprising "several" men. They include a Chairman, two or more speakers, designated "Committee," and Postgate. They wear academic gowns.]

AEH: Am I asleep or awake? We arrive at evening upon a field of battle, where lie 200 corpses. 197 of them have no beards: the 198th has a beard on the chin; the 199th has a false beard slewed round under the left ear; the 200th has been decapitated and the head is nowhere to be found. Problem: Had it a beard, a false beard, or no beard at all? Mr Buecheler can tell you. It had a beard, a beard on the chin. I only say, look at the logic. Because a manuscript has suffered loss, therefore the lost portion contained something which Mr Buecheler wishes it to have contained: and scholars have been unable to detect any error in his reasoning.
CHAIRMAN *[reading from a letter]*: "During the last ten years, the study of the Classics has been the chief occupation of my leisure . . ."
AEH: But I have long dwelt among men.
CHAIRMAN: Copies of Mr Housman's testimonials are tabled.
AEH: Conjectures, to Mr Marx's eyes, are arranged in a three-fold order of merit: first, the conjectures of Mr Marx; second, the conjectures of mankind in general; third, the conjectures of certain odious persons.
COMMITTEE: A Post Office clerk?
CHAIRMAN: Patent Office . . . supported by the Professors of Latin at Oxford and Cambridge, of Latin *and* Greek at Dublin—the editor of the *Classical Review* . . . Warren, the President of Magdalen . . .
AEH: The width and variety of Francken's ignorance are wonderful. For stupidity of plan and slovenliness of execution, his *apparatus criticus*[7] is worse than Breiter's *apparatus* to Manilius, and I never saw another of which that could be said.

6. Housman's poem, "He Would Not Stay For Me, and Who Can Wonder?"
7. "Critical apparatus"; explanation of critical procedures used in establishing a scholarly text.

CHAIRMAN [*to Postgate*]: Is he well liked?

AEH: Confronted with two manuscripts of equal merit, he is like a donkey between two bundles of hay, and confusedly imagines that if one bundle were removed he would cease to be a donkey.

POSTGATE: He is . . . well remarked.

AEH: The notes are vicious to a degree which well nigh protects them from refutation, so intricate is the tangle of every imaginable kind of blunder, and his main purpose in withholding useful information is to make room for a long record of conjectures which dishonour the human intellect.

COMMITTEE [*reading*]: "When Mr Housman took my Sixth Form he proved himself a thorough and sympathetic teacher . . ."

AEH: Having small literary culture, he is not revolted by illiteracy or dismayed by the hideous and has a relish for the uncouth; yet would defend *pronos* against Bentley's *privos* as being very poetical, although Bentley never denied it was poetical, he only denied it was Latin.

COMMITTEE [*reading*]: ". . . the sagacity and closeness desiderated[8] by Bentley . . ." That's Warren. ". . . one of the most interesting and attractive pupils I can remember . . ."

CHAIRMAN: . . . and Robinson Ellis of Trinity . . .
"Personally I have always found Mr Housman an amiable and modest man."

AEH: No word is safe from Ellis if he can think of a similar one which is not much worse. Trying to follow his thoughts is like being in perpetual contact with an idiot child. Here is the born hater of science who fills his pages to half their height with the dregs of the Italian renaissance, and by appeals to his reader's superstition persuade him that he will gather grapes of thorns and figs of thistles.

CHAIRMAN: Well . . . Professor Postgate?

POSTGATE: Mmm.

AEH: But Mr Postgate's morbid alertness is cast into deep sleep at *modo* in verse II, and it's goodnight to grammatical science.

COMMITTEE: Yes. What do *you* say, Postgate?

AEH: Of Mr Postgate's "*voces*" for "*noctes*" in 33, I am at a loss to know *what* to say.

POSTGATE: I have to declare an interest.

AEH [*continuing*]: The alteration makes nonsense of the whole elegy from beginning to end.

POSTGATE: Mr Housman is applying for this post at my urging. He is, in my view, very likely the best classical scholar in England.
Though he is not always right on Propertius.

CHAIRMAN [*closing the meeting*]: *Tempus fugit. Nunc est bibendum.*[9]

[*Light fades on Committee.*]

AEH: When I with some thought and some pains have got this rather uninteresting garden into decent order, here is Dr Postgate hacking at the fence in a spirited attempt to re-establish chaos amongst Propertius manuscripts. All the tools he employs are two-edged, though to be sure both edges are blunt. I feel it a hardship, but I suppose it is a duty, (to). . .

[*Light on Postgate.*]

8. Desiderated: desired.

9. Time flees. Now is the time for drinking. (From Horace, Odes.)

POSTGATE [*angry*]: Your *stemma codicum*[1] is fundamentally flawed—not to mince words, it is almost totally wrong. Your reliance on Baehrens's dating of the Neapolitanus was a blunder.
AEH: Have you seen the paper?
POSTGATE: I am in the act of replying to it. I intend to make you ashamed.
AEH: The paper.
POSTGATE: Oh . . .
AEH: Oscar Wilde has been arrested.[2]
POSTGATE: Oh . . .
AEH: I had no idea I had offended you, Postgate.

[*Postgate goes.*

Light on Stead, Labouchere and Harris with open newspapers. Perhaps in a railway carriage.]

STEAD: Guilty and sentenced to two years with hard labour!
LABOUCHERE [*reading*]: "The aesthetic cult, in its nasty form, is now over."
HARRIS [*reading*]: "Open the windows! Let in the fresh air! . . . By our Dramatic Critic."
LABOUCHERE: Convicted under the Labouchere Amendment clause!
AEH:

Oh who is that young sinner with the handcuffs on his wrists?
And what has he been after that they groan and shake their fists?
And wherefore is he wearing such a conscience-stricken air?
Oh they're taking him to prison for the colour of his hair.[3]

HARRIS: I begged him to leave the country. I had a closed cab waiting at Hyde Park Corner and a steam-yacht at Gravesend to take him to France . . .
LABOUCHERE [*To Stead*]: Two years is totally inadequate. [*To Harris.*] No, you didn't, Frank. You told him to brazen it out at the Café Royal.

[*To Stead.*] I wanted a maximum of *seven* years.

HARRIS: . . . With a lobster supper on board and a bottle of Pommery, and a small library of French and English books.
LABOUCHERE: Look, it wasn't a yacht, it was a table at the Café Royal.

[*To Stead.*] The Attorney General of the day persuaded me that two years was more likely to secure a conviction from a hesitant jury.

HARRIS: You did it to scupper the Bill—that's what you told me.
LABOUCHERE: Who's going to believe *you*?
STEAD: If Oscar Wilde's taste had been for fresh young innocent virgins of, say, sixteen, no one would have laid a finger on him.
LABOUCHERE: I did it because Stead happened to tell me just before the debate that in certain parts of London the problem of indecency between men was as serious as with virgins.
HARRIS: There's no serious problem with virgins in certain parts of London.

1. A "family tree" of manuscripts from which one has derived a scholarly edition.
2. On April 5, 1895, after the failure of his prosecution of Lord Queensberry for libel, Wilde was arrested for "gross indecency" under the Labouchére amendment.
3. Housman's poem "The Colour of His Hair," written on the occasion of Wilde's arrest.

STEAD: With virgins, there are tastes in certain parts best left to the obscurity of a learned tongue.

HARRIS: My point.

[*Light fades on them.*]

AEH:

Now 'tis oakum for his fingers and the treadmill for his feet
And the quarry-gang at Portland in the cold and in the heat,
And between his spells of labour in the time he has to spare
He can curse the God that made him for the colour of his hair.

[*Three Men in a Boat row into view. Jerome has the oars, Chamberlain (George) is trying to play a banjo. (Frank) Harris has a first edition of* A Shropshire Lad.

Chamberlain, eleven years older, with a moustache, wears a blazer striped in violent colours. Jerome and Harris wear tweed jackets with their "cricket trousers."]

CHAMBERLAIN: Ta-ra-ra . . . pull on your right, J. Ta-ra-ra-boom[4]—

JEROME: Do you want to take the oars?

CHAMBERLAIN: No, you're doing splendidly . . . boom-di-ay . . .

HARRIS/JEROME: Shut up, George!

HARRIS: Anybody hungry?

CHAMBERLAIN: Harris hasn't done any work since we left Henley.

HARRIS: When Chamberlain said take a boat up the river, I understood him to mean a boat which takes passengers from one place to another, not an arrangement where the passengers take the boat. Personally I had no reason to want this boat removed from where it was; as far as I (was concerned)—

CHAMBERLAIN/JEROME: Shut up, Harris!

CHAMBERLAIN: Where are we, J?

JEROME: Getting towards Reading.

CHAMBERLAIN: Reading!

[*They look up-river*]

Will we pass the gaol?[5]

JEROME: Perhaps Oscar will see us going by . . . he always asked for the river view at the Savoy.

HARRIS [*solemnly*]: The prostitutes danced in the streets.

CHAMBERLAIN: So did J.

JEROME: I did not. It's true that as the editor of a popular newspaper I had a duty to speak out, but I take no pride in the fact that it was I as much as anybody, I suppose, who was indirectly responsible for the tragic unfolding of—

CHAMBERLAIN/HARRIS: Shut up, J!

JEROME: I'm not sorry. I might have been sorry, if he'd kept his misfortune to himself like a gentleman.[6]

CHAMBERLAIN: Posing as a gentleman.

4. "Ta-ra-ra Boom-de-ay," a music hall song made famous in London by Lottie Collins in the 1890s.

5. British, "jail." Wilde was imprisoned, after his conviction, in Reading Gaol, and wrote there "The Ballad of Reading Gaol."

6. Chamberlain plays on the wording of the calling card Lord Douglas's father, the Marquess of Queensberry, left for Wilde at his club: "For Oscar Wilde, posing as a Somdomite" [sic].

JEROME: Exactly. His work won't last either. Decadence was a blind alley in English life and letters. Wholesome humour has always been our strength. Wholesome humour and a rattling good yarn. Look at Shakespeare.
CHAMBERLAIN: Or your own work.
JEROME: That's not for me to say.
CHAMBERLAIN: Right, Harris, take his legs.
HARRIS: Robbie Ross[7] gave me this man's poems. He got several off by heart to tell them to Oscar when he went to see him in prison.
JEROME: Oh, yes—Gosse[8] said to me, who is this Houseboat person Robbie likes?
HARRIS: Not Houseboat. A. E. Housman.
CHAMBERLAIN: Alfred Housman?
HARRIS: I think he stayed with the wrong people in Shropshire. I never read such a book for telling you you're better off dead.
CHAMBERLAIN: That's him!
HARRIS: No one gets off; if you're not shot, hanged or stabbed, you kill yourself. Life's a curse, love's a blight, God's a blaggard,[9] cherry blossom is quite nice.
CHAMBERLAIN: He's a Latin prof.
JEROME: But of the Greek persuasion,[1] would you say, George?
CHAMBERLAIN: Three or four years ago he was just one of us in the office.
JEROME: Uranian[2] persuasion, I mean.
CHAMBERLAIN: How can one tell?
JEROME: I could. Is there something eye-catching about the way he dresses?
HARRIS: As opposed to George, you mean?
JEROME: That's a point, eh, George?!
CHAMBERLAIN: Pull the other one, J.
JEROME: Do you want to take the oars?

[*The boat goes.*

AEH alone under a starry night sky. Distant bonfires. Jubilee Night, June 1897.]

AEH:

"The thoughts of others
Were light and fleeting,
Of lovers' meeting
Or luck or fame,
Mine were of trouble
And mine were steady,
So I was ready
When trouble came.[3]"

[*Chamberlain, at the age we saw him but in street clothes, has joined him on the hilltop.*

CHAMBERLAIN [*simultaneous with AEH*]:

"So I was ready
When trouble came."

Pull the other one.

7. Robert Baldwin "Robbie" Ross (1869–1918), lifelong friend of Wilde and executor of his estate.
8. Edmund Gosse (1849–1928), English writer and man of letters.
9. Blackguard; scoundrel.
1. I.e., homosexual.
2. Homosexual.
3. Housman, *More Poems*, VI: "I to my perils."

AEH [*pleased*]: Chamberlain! I haven't thought about you for years! You've got a moustache.

CHAMBERLAIN: Hello, old chap. I'm not sure about it, but it's growing on me.

AEH: Oh, I say, that's a good one.

CHAMBERLAIN: Fancy you living to a ripe old age, I wouldn't have put a tanner on it the way you looked.

AEH: When?

CHAMBERLAIN: Most of the time. Happy days, I don't think. When Jackson went off to be a headmaster in India. No—worse before. No—worse after, when he came home on leave to be married. No, before—that time no one could find you for a week. I thought: the river, and no two ways about it. But you turned up again, dry as a stick. I did tell you, didn't I?

AEH: Tell me what? Oh . . . yes, you did tell me.

CHAMBERLAIN: Still, you probably wouldn't have written the poems.

AEH: This is true.

CHAMBERLAIN: So it's an ill wind from yon far country blows through holt and hanger.[4]

AEH: If I might give you a piece of advice, Chamberlain, mangling a chap's poems isn't the way to show you've read them.

CHAMBERLAIN: I'm word perfect. "Oh were he and I together, shipmates on the fleeted main, sailing through the summer weather[5] . . ." What happened to Jackson?

AEH: He retired, settled in British Columbia, died of cancer.

CHAMBERLAIN: Well, early though the laurel grows, it withers quicker than the rose.[6]

AEH: This is a revolting habit, Chamberlain—I forbid you.

CHAMBERLAIN: Oh, I like them, I really do. Holt and hanger. Cumber. Thews. Lovely old words. Never knew what they meant. But proper poetry, no question about that. You old slyboots. You must have been writing poetry all the time you were in Trade Marks.

AEH: Not so much. It was a couple of years after, something overcame me, at the beginning of '95, a ferment. I wrote half the book in the first five months of that year, before I started to calm down. It was a time of strange excitement.

CHAMBERLAIN: The Oscar Wilde trials.

AEH: Oh, really, Chamberlain. You should take up biography.

CHAMBERLAIN: Yes, what about those ploughboys and village lads dropping like flies all over Shropshire?—those that didn't take the Queen's shilling and get shot in foreign parts.

AEH: The landscape of the imagination.

CHAMBERLAIN: "Because I liked you better than suits a man to say . . ."[7]

AEH: Could you contain yourself?

CHAMBERLAIN:

"But this unlucky love should last.
When answered passions thin to air.[8]"

Did you send them to Jackson, the ones you didn't put in the book?

4. From *A Shropshire Lad*, XXXI: "On Wenlock Edge the wood's in trouble."

5. From *Additional Poems*, II: "O were he and I together."

6. From "To an Athlete Dying Young."

7. From *More Poems*, XXI: "Because I liked you better."

8. From *More Poems*, XII: "I promise nothing: friends will part."

AEH: No.

CHAMBERLAIN: Saving them till you're dead?

AEH: It's a courtesy. Confession is an act of violence against the unoffending. Can you see the bonfires? It's the old Queen's Diamond Jubilee. I was a Victorian poet, don't forget.

[*Katharine joins, aged thirty-five. Chamberlain stays.*]

KATE: From Clee to Heaven the beacon burns!

AEH: It was a grand sight. I counted fifty-two fires just to the south and west. Malvern had the biggest but it burned out in an hour.

KATE: The Clent fire is a good one. The boys are here.

AEH: Do I know them?

KATE: Your nephews, Alfred!

AEH: Oh, your boys, of course I know *them*.

KATE: And the Millingtons. Mrs M. says you're no guide to Shropshire—she went to look at Hughley church and it doesn't even *have* a steeple!, never mind a graveyard full of suicides.

AEH: That can surely be rectified. I never expected a two-and-six-penny book which couldn't sell out an edition of 500 copies to draw pilgrims to Hughley. I was never there, I just liked the name.

KATE: Laurence thought *he* was the poet in the family, and now he knows your book by heart and recites his favourites. He met someone who told him *A Shropshire Lad* was his best yet.

AEH: I hope no one is attributing *his* poems to *me*.

KATE: It's sweet of him to be proud.

AEH: It is, yes.

KATE: We're all proud, and astonished. Clem said, "Alfred has a heart!"

AEH: No, not at all, I was depressed because of a sore throat which wouldn't leave me. I might have gone on writing poems for years, but luckily I remembered a brand of lozenges and was cured.

KATE: A sore throat!?

AEH: (A) punishment for a disagreeable controversy in the journals. You were clever to be a dunce, Kate, before it found you out.

KATE: Oh—listen!—The larks think it's daybreak.

AEH: Or the end of the world.

KATE: Oh, you! Same old Alfred. [*She goes.*]

AEH: But I intend to change. The day nurse will get the benefit of my transformation into "a character," the wag of the Evelyn. I have been practising a popular style of lecture, as yet confused with memories of University College, but it's based on noticing that there are students present. I shall cause a sensation by addressing a remark to my neighbour at dinner in Hall. I am trying to think of a remark. My reputation at Trinity is for censoriousness and misanthropy. Some people say it's only shyness—impudent fools. Nevertheless, I am determined. Affability is only suffering the fools gladly, and Cambridge affords endless scope for this peculiar joy. I introduced crème brulée to Trinity, but if that isn't enough I'll talk to people. Do you still ride a bicycle?

CHAMBERLAIN: Yes, a Robertson. I know your brother Laurence. We belong to a sort of secret society, the Order of Chaeronea, like the Sacred Band of Thebes. Actually it's more like a discussion group. We discuss what we should call ourselves. "Homosexuals" has been suggested.

AEH: Homosexuals?

CHAMBERLAIN: We aren't anything till there's a word for it.

AEH: Homosexuals? Who is responsible for this barbarity?

CHAMBERLAIN: What's wrong with it?

AEH: It's half Greek and half Latin!

CHAMBERLAIN: That sounds about right. What happened to me, by the way?

AEH: How should I know? I suppose you became a sort of footnote. [*Listening.*] Listen!

[*The "Marseillaise" is faintly heard.*]

CHAMBERLAIN: The "Marseillaise.[9]" That's unusual, isn't it?—for the Queen's Jubilee.

AEH: Oscar Wilde was in France, on the coast near Dieppe. I'd sent him my book when he came out of prison.

[*Darkness on Chamberlain.*

The faint sound of children singing the "Marseillaise" is overtaken by Oscar Wilde's strong fluting voice reciting.

Wilde, aged forty-one, is reading aloud from his copy of A Shropshire Lad. *He is drinking brandy, and smoking a cigarette.*

Around him is the debris of a Diamond Jubilee children's party. There is bunting, Union Jacks and Tricolours, and the remains of a large decorated cake.]

WILDE:

"Shot? So quick, so clean an ending?
Oh, that was right, lad, that was brave:
Yours was not an ill for mending,
T'was best to take it to the grave.[1]"

This is not one of the ones Robbie learned for me, but your poems, when I opened your parcel, were not all strangers.

"Oh, you had forethought, you could reason,
And saw your road and where it led,
And early wise and brave in season—"

AEH: To me, they're importunate friends when they take the floor.

WILDE:

"And early wise and brave in season
Put the pistol to your head."

Poor, silly boy!

AEH: I read a report of the inquest in the *Evening Standard*.

WILDE: Oh, thank goodness! That explains why I never believed a word of it.

AEH: But it's all true.

WILDE: On the contrary, it's only fact. Truth is quite another thing and is the work of the imagination.

AEH: I assure you. It was not long after your trial. He was a Woolwich cadet. He blew his brains out so that he wouldn't live to shame himself, or bring shame on others. He left a letter for the coroner.

9. National anthem of France.

1. From *A Shropshire Lad*, XLIV. "Shot? so quick, so clean an ending?" Wilde continues to quote from this poem in his next two speeches.

WILDE: Of course he did, and you should have sent your poem to the coroner, too. Art deals with exceptions, not with types. Facts deal only with types. Here was the type of young man who shoots himself. He read about someone shooting himself in the *Evening News*, so he shot himself in the *Evening Standard*.

AEH: Oh, I say—!

WILDE:

> "Oh, soon, and better so than later
> After long disgrace and scorn,
> You shot dead the household traitor,
> The soul that should not have been born."

Still, if he hadn't shot himself before reading your poem, he would have shot himself after. I am not unfeeling. I dare say I would have wept if I'd read the newspaper. But that does not make a newspaper poetry. Art cannot be subordinate to its subject, otherwise it is not art but biography, and biography is the mesh through which our real life escapes. I was said to have walked down Piccadilly with a lily in my hand. There was no need. To do it is nothing, to be said to have done it is everything. It is the truth about me. Shakespeare's Dark Lady probably had bad breath—almost everybody did until my third year at Oxford—but sincerity is the enemy of art. This is what Pater taught me, and what Ruskin never learned. Ruskin made a vice out of virtue. Poor Pater might have made a virtue out of vice but, like your cadet, he lacked the courage to act. I breakfasted with Ruskin. Pater came to tea. The one impotent, the other terrified, they struggled for my artistic soul. But I caught syphilis from a prostitute, and the mercury cure blackened my teeth. Did we meet at Oxford?

AEH: No. We once had a poem in the same magazine. Mine was for my dead mother. Yours was about the Turkish atrocities in Bulgaria.

WILDE: Oh, yes, I swore never to touch Turkish champagne, and eat only Bulgarian Delight. Do you eat cake? I invited fifteen children from the village to celebrate Jubilee Day. We toasted the Queen and the President of the Republic, and the children shouted, "*Vive Monsieur Melmoth!*[2]" I am Monsieur Melmoth. We had strawberries and chocolates and grenadine syrup, and the cake, and everyone received a present. It was one of my most successful parties. Did you come to any of my parties in London? No? But we must have had friends in common. Bernard Shaw[3]? Frank Harris? Beardsley[4]? Labouchere? Whistler[5]? W. T Stead? Did you know Henry Irving[6]? Lily Langtry[7]? No? The Prince of Wales? You did *have* friends?

AEH: I had colleagues.

WILDE: Once, I bought a huge armful of lilies in Covent Garden to give to Miss Langtry, and as I waited to put them in a cab, a small boy said to me, "Oh, how rich you are!" . . . "Oh, how rich you are!" [*He weeps.*] Oh—forgive me. I'm somewhat the worse for—cake. I have tried to give it up, whenever I feel myself weakening I take a glass of cognac, often I don't eat cake for days at a time; but the Jubilee broke my will, I allowed myself a social eclair out of politeness to my guests, and remember nothing more until I woke up in a welter of patisseries. Oh—Bosie![8] [*He weeps.*] I have to go

2. After his release from Reading Gaol and emigration to Paris, Wilde started to use the pseudonym "Sebastian Melmoth," combining the persecuted Saint Sebastian and the character in Charles Robert Maturin's gothic novel *Melmoth the Wanderer* (1820).
3. Irish playwright George Bernard Shaw (1856–1950); see page 2026.
4. Aubrey Beardsley (1872–1898), graphic artist of the Aesthetic movement.
5. James McNeill Whistler (1834–1903), American painter celebrated by the Aesthetic movement.
6. Sir Henry Irving (1838–1905), English stage actor.
7. Lillie Langtry (1853–1929), English actress and "media personality."
8. Wilde's nickname for Alfred Douglas, whose relationship with Wilde led to Queensberry's accusations and Wilde's trial and downfall.

back to him, you know. Robbie will be furious but it can't be helped. The betrayal of one's friends is a bagatelle in the stakes of love, but the betrayal of oneself is lifelong regret. Bosie is what became of me. He is spoiled, vindictive, utterly selfish and not very talented, but these are merely the facts. The truth is he was Hyacinth when Apollo loved him,[9] he is ivory and gold, from his red rose-leaf lips comes music that fills me with joy, he is the only one who understands me. "Even as a teething child throbs with ferment, so does the soul of him who gazes upon the boy's beauty; he can neither sleep at night nor keep still by day," and a lot more besides, but before Plato could describe love, the loved one had to be invented. We would never love anybody if we could see past our invention. Bosie is my creation, my poem. In the mirror of invention, love discovered itself. Then we saw what we had made—the piece of ice in the fist you cannot hold or let go. [*He weeps.*] You are kind to listen.

AEH: No. My life is marked by long silences. The first conjecture I ever published was on Horace. Six ears later I withdrew it. Propertius I put aside nearly fifty years ago to wait for the discovery of a better manuscript, which seemed to me essential if there were the slightest hope of recovering the text. So far, silence. Meanwhile I defended the classical authors from the conjectures of idiots, and produced editions of books by Ovid, Juvenal[1] and Lucan,[2] and finally of Manilius, which I dedicated to my comrade Moses Jackson, and that will have to do, my sandcastle against the confounding sea. Classics apart, my life was not short enough for me to not do the things I wanted to not do, but they were few and the jackals will find it hard scavenging. I moved house four times, once, it was said, because a stranger spoke to me on my train to work. It wasn't so, but it was the truth about me. In Diamond Jubilee year I went abroad for the first time.

WILDE: There's my boatman. It was he who told me you were a Latin professor, but he's profligate with titles and often confers professorships on quite unsuitable people—many of whom turn out to have chairs at our older universities.

AEH: I'm very sorry. Your life is a terrible thing. A chronological error. The choice was not always between renunciation and folly. You should have lived in Megara when Theognis[3] was writing and made his lover a song sung unto all posterity . . . and not *now*!—when disavowal and endurance are in honour, and a nameless luckless love has made notoriety your monument.

WILDE: My dear fellow, a hundred francs would have done just as well. Better a fallen rocket than never a burst of light. Dante reserved a place in his Inferno for those who wilfully live in sadness—sullen in the sweet air, he says. Your "honour" is all shame and timidity and compliance. Pure of stain! But the artist is the secret criminal in our midst. He is the agent of progress against authority. You are right to be a scholar. A scholar is all scruple, an artist is none. The artist must lie, cheat, deceive, be untrue to nature and contemptuous of history. I made my life into my art and it was an unqualified success. The blaze of my immolation threw its light into every corner of the land where uncounted young men sat each in his own darkness. What would I have done in Megara!?—think what I would have missed! I awoke the imagination of the century. I banged Ruskin's and Pater's heads together, and from the moral severity of one and the aesthetic soul of the other I made art a philosophy that can look the twentieth century in the eye. I had genius, brilliancy, daring, I took charge of my own myth. I dipped my staff into the comb of wild

9. In Greek mythology, Hyacinth was a young man whose beauty captured Apollo.
1. Decimus Iunius Iuvenalis, first and second century Roman poet, author of the *Satires*.
2. Marcus Annaeus Lucanus (39 C.E.–65 C.E.), Roman poet.
3. Theognis of Megara (c. 6th century B.C.E.), Greek poet, elegist.

honey.[4] I tasted forbidden sweetness and drank the stolen waters. I lived at the turning point of the world where everything was waking up new—the New Drama, the New Novel, New Journalism, New Hedonism, New Paganism, even the New Woman. Where were you when all this was happening?

AEH: At home.

WILDE: Couldn't you at least have got a New Tailor? Are we going together?

AEH: No. I will be coming later.

WILDE: You didn't mention your poems. How can you be unhappy when you know you wrote them? They are all that will still matter.

[*The Boatman helps Wilde aboard.*]

But you are not my boatman! Sebastian Melmoth *à votre service*.

BOATMAN: Sit in the middle.

WILDE: Of course.

[*The Boatman poles Wilde away.*

Housman is sitting on the bench by the river with a couple of books.]

AEH: What are you doing here, may I ask?

HOUSMAN: Classics, sir.

AEH: Ah.

Of course.

What year are you in now?

HOUSMAN: My final year.

AEH: So am I, indeed for all practical purposes I'm dead. And how are *you?* [*He picks up Housman's book.*]

HOUSMAN: I'm quite well, thank you, sir.

AEH: Propertius!

HOUSMAN: The first of the Roman love elegists. Actually, Propertius is not set for Finals. I should be cramming, everybody expects me to get a First, you see. My family, too. I'm the eldest and I've always been . . . a scholarship boy . . . I ought to put Propertius aside now, but we're already all of us so late!—and there's someone with his Propertius coming out next year, Postgate he's called. Who knows how many of my conjectures he'll anticipate?

AEH: Yes, who knows? Before you publish, by the way, the first of the Roman love elegists was not Propertius, strictly speaking. It was Cornelius Gallus.[5]

HOUSMAN: Gallus?

AEH: Really and truly.

HOUSMAN: But I've not read him.

AEH: Nor I. Only one line of Gallus survived. The rest perished.

HOUSMAN: Oh!

AEH: But strictly speaking—which I do in my sleep—he was first.

HOUSMAN: One line for his monument!

AEH: Virgil wrote a poem for him: how much immortality does a man need?—his own poetry, all but a line, as if he had never been, but his memory alive in a garden in the northernmost province of an empire that disappeared fifteen hundred years ago. To do as much for a friend would be no small thing.

4. cf. 1 Samuel 14.27 "But Jonathan heard not when his father charged the people with the oath: wherefore he put forth the end of the rod that was in his hand, and dipped it in an honeycomb, and put his hand to his mouth; and his eyes were enlightened." Jonathan's father Saul had forbidden the people to eat, and Jonathan unwittingly violated that prohibition. The people ultimately ensured his safety.

5. Gaius Cornelius Gallus (c. 70 B.C.E.–26 B.C.E.), Roman poet.

HOUSMAN: Yes. [*Pause.*] Was it a good line?

AEH: Quite suggestive, as it happens. I'm not sure about dead for love, though. He fought on the winning side against Antony and Cleopatra, and afterwards was put in charge of Egypt, which is not bad going for a poet. But he got above himself and was admonished by the Emperor: whereupon he killed himself. But by then he'd invented the love elegy.

HOUSMAN: Propertius mentions him. "And lately how many wounds has Gallus bathed in the waters of the Underworld, dead for love of beautiful Lycoris!" *Lately. Modo. Just recently*. They were real people to each other, that's the thing. They knew each other's poems. They knew each other's girls. Virgil puts it all in a Golden Age with pan-pipes and goatherds, and Apollo there in person—but you can trust it, that's what I mean. Real people in real love, baring their souls in poetry that made their mistresses immortal!—and it all happened in such a short span. As if all the poetry till then had to pass through a bottleneck where a handful of poets were waiting to see what could be done with it. And then it was over, the love poem complete, love as it really is.

AEH: Oh, yes, there'd been songs . . . valentines—mostly in Greek, often charming . . . but the self-advertisement of farce and folly, love as abject slavery and all-out war—madness, disease, the whole catastrophe owned up to and written in the metre—no; that was new.

HOUSMAN: (Oh—!)

JACKSON [*off-stage*]: Housman!

POLLARD [*off-stage*]: Housman!

HOUSMAN: I'm sorry, they're calling me.

POLLARD [*off-stage*]: Hous! Picnic!

JACKSON [*off-stage*]: Locusts! Honey!

[*Jackson and Pollard arrive in the boat.*]

HOUSMAN [*to the boat*]: I'm here.

AEH: Mo . . . !

POLLARD: It's time to go.

[*Housman goes to the boat and gets in.*]

AEH: I would have died for you but I never had the luck!

HOUSMAN: Where are we going?

POLLARD: Hades.

Pull on your right, Jackson.

JACKSON: Do you want to take the oars?

HOUSMAN: *Tendebantque manus ripae ulterioris amore.*

[*The boat goes.*]

AEH: "And they stretched out their hands in desire of the further shore." Cleverboots was usually good for a tag. Thus Virgil, Aeneas in the Underworld, the souls of the dead reaching out across the water *ripae ulterioris amore*, you couldn't do better with a Kodak, and those who were unburied were made to wait a hundred years. I could wait a hundred if I had to. Seventy-seven go quick enough. Which is not to say I have remembered it right, messing about in a boat with Moses and dear old young Pollard on a summer's day in '79 or '80 or '81; but not impossible, not so out of court as to count as an untruth in the dream-warp of the ultimate room, though the dog is still in question. And yet not dreaming either, wide awake to all the risks—archaism, anachronism, the wayward inconsequence that only hindsight can acquit of *non sequitur, quietus interruptus* by monologue incontinent in the hind leg of a donkey class (you're too kind but I'm not there yet), and the unities out of the window without so much as a window to be out of: still shaky, too, from that first plummet into bathos, Greek for depth but in rhetoric a ludicrous descent from the elevated to the commonplace, as it might be from Virgil to Jerome K. Jerome if that is even a downward slope at time of speaking, and when is for *that*?—for walking on water is not among my party tricks, the water and the walking work it out between them. Neither dead nor dreaming, then, but in between, not short on fact, or fiction, and suitably attired in leather boots, the very ones I was too clever for, which—here comes the fact—I left in my will to my college servant. They were too small for him but it's the thought that counts, and here is one to be going on with: In December 1894 Jerome K. Jerome, the celebrated author of *Three Men in a Boat (To Say Nothing of the Dog)*, made an attack on an Oxford magazine, *The Chameleon*—which, he wrote, appeared to be nothing more or less than an advocacy for indulgence in the cravings of an unnatural disease. It was, he said, a case for the police. Oscar Wilde had contributed a page or two of epigrams, to oblige an Oxford student he'd befriended, Lord Alfred Douglas. Douglas himself had a poem—the one which ended "I am the love that dare not speak its name." Jerome's article goaded Douglas's father into leaving a card at the Albermarle Club, "to Oscar Wilde, posing as a Sodomite." From which all that followed, followed. Which goes to show, I know what I'm doing even when I don't know I'm doing it, in the busy hours between the tucking up and the wakey-wakey thermometer faintly antiseptic under the tongue from its dainty gauze-stoppered vase on the bedside cabinet.

[*Light on Jackson, then Housman.*]

JACKSON: What will become of you, Hous?

HOUSMAN:

Κὤτα μὲν σὺ θέλεις, μακάρεσσιν ἴσαν ἄγω
ἀμέραν· ὄτα δ' οὐκ ἐθέλησθα, μάλ' ἐν σκότω

JACKSON: I never took to it, you know—all that *veni, vidi, vici* . . .

HOUSMAN: When thou art kind I spend the day like a god, when thy face is turned aside, it is very dark with me. I shall give thee wings. Thou shalt be a song sung unto posterity so long as earth and sun abide. And when thou comest to go down to the lamentable house of Hades, never—albeit thou be dead—shalt thou lose thy fame.

[*Darkness on Housman and Jackson.*
Dimly, Charon is seen poling Wilde across the Styx.]

WILDE: Wickedness is a myth invented by good people to account for the curious attractiveness of others.

One should always be a little improbable.

Nothing that actually occurs is of the smallest importance.

AEH: Oxford in the Golden Age!—the hairshirts versus the Aesthetes: the neo-Christians versus the neo-pagans: the study of classics for advancement in the fair of the world versus the study of classics for the advancement of classical studies—what emotional storms, and oh what a tiny teacup. You should have been here last night when I did Hades properly—Furies, Harpies, Gorgons, and the snake-haired Medusa, to say nothing of the Dog. But now I really do have to go. How lucky to find myself standing on this empty shore, with the indifferent waters at my feet.

FADE OUT

Seamus Heaney

b. 1939

More prominently than any poet since Yeats, Seamus Heaney has put Irish poetry back at the center of British literary studies. His first full-length collection, *Death of a Naturalist* (1966), ushered in a period of renewed interest in Irish poetry generally, and Ulster poetry in particular; the subsequent attention to poets like Derek Mahon, Michael Longley, Medbh McGuckian, and Paul Muldoon owes a great deal to the scope of Heaney's popularity.

As a great number of Heaney's early poems bear poignant witness, he spent his childhood in rural County Derry, Northern Ireland; his family was part of the Catholic minority in Ulster, and his experiences growing up were for that reason somewhat atypical. The critic Irvin Ehrenpreis maps the matrix of Heaney's contradictory position as an Irish poet: "Speech is never simple, in Heaney's conception. He grew up as an Irish Catholic boy in a land governed by Protestants whose tradition is British. He grew up on a farm in his country's northern, industrial region. As a person, therefore, he springs from the old divisions of his nation." His experience was split not only along religious lines, then, but also national and linguistic ones; in some of his early poetry Heaney suggests the split through the paired names—"Mossbawn" (the very English name of his family's fifty-acre farm) and "Anahorish" (Irish *anach fhior uisce*, "place of clear water," where he attended primary school). As a result, Heaney's is a liminal poetry—a "door into the dark"—and Heaney stands in the doorway, with one foot in each world. Heaney makes brilliant use of the linguistic resources of both the traditions he inherited, drawing on the heritage of English Romanticism while also relying heavily on Irish-language assonance in lines like "There were dragon-flies, spotted butterflies, / But best of all was the warm thick slobber / of frogspawn that grew like clotted water / In the shade of the banks" (*Death of a Naturalist*).

When he was twelve, Heaney won a scholarship to a Catholic boarding school in Londonderry (now Derry) then went on to Queen's University, Belfast, which was the center of a vital new poetic movement in the 1960s. He was influenced by poets who were able to transform the local into the universal, especially Ted Hughes and Robert Frost. As an "Ulster poet," it has fallen to Heaney to use his voice and his position to comment on Northern Ireland's sectarian violence; ironically enough, however, his most explicitly "political" poems were published before the flare-up of the Troubles that began in 1969, and his most self-conscious response to Ulster's strife, the volume *North* (1975), uses historical and mythological frameworks to address the current political situation obliquely. The Irish critic Seamus Deane has written, "Heaney is very much in the Irish tradition in that he has learned, more successfully than most, to conceive of his personal experience in terms of his country's history"; for Heaney, as the popular saying has it, the personal is the political, and the political the personal. His most successful poems dealing with Ulster's political and religious situation are probably those treating neolithic bodies found preserved in peat bogs. Heaney was living in Belfast, lecturing at Queen's University, at the inception of the Troubles; as a Catholic, he felt a need to convey the urgency of the situation without falling into the easy Republican—or Unionist, for that matter—rhetoric. It was at this point that Heaney discovered the anthropologist P. V. Glob's *The Bog People* (1969), which documents (with riveting photographs) the discovery of sacrificial victims preserved in bogs for 2,000 years. Heaney intuitively knew that he had found his "objective correlative"—what he has called his "emblems of adversity"—with which to explore the Troubles.

Like Yeats, Heaney has, from the very start, enjoyed both popular and critical acclaim. His poems have a surface simplicity; his early poetry especially relishes the carefully observed detail of rural Irish life.

Personal Helicon[1]

For Michael Longley

As a child, they could not keep me from wells
And old pumps with buckets and windlasses.
I loved the dark drop, the trapped sky, the smells
Of waterweed, fungus and dank moss.

One, in a brickyard, with a rotted board top.
I savoured the rich crash when a bucket
Plummeted down at the end of a rope.
So deep you saw no reflection in it.

A shallow one under a dry stone ditch
Fructified like any aquarium.
When you dragged out long roots from the soft mulch
A white face hovered over the bottom.

Others had echoes, gave back your own call
With a clean new music in it. And one
Was scaresome, for there, out of ferns and tall
Foxgloves, a rat slapped across my reflection.

Now, to pry into roots, to finger slime,
To stare, big-eyed Narcissus, into some spring
Is beneath all adult dignity. I rhyme
To see myself, to set the darkness echoing.

1965

Requiem for the Croppies[2]

The pockets of our greatcoats full of barley–
No kitchens on the run, no striking camp–
We moved quick and sudden in our own country.
The priest lay behind ditches with the tramp.
A people, hardly marching—on the hike–
We found new tactics happening each day:
We'd cut through reins and rider with the pike
And stampede cattle into infantry,
Then retreat through hedges where cavalry must be thrown.
Until, on Vinegar Hill,[3] the fatal conclave.
Terraced thousands died, shaking scythes at cannon.
The hillside blushed, soaked in our broken wave.
They buried us without shroud or coffin
And in August the barley grew up out of the grave.

Punishment[4]

I can feel the tug
of the halter at the nape

1. Home of the Muses in Greek mythology.
2. Irish rebels in the 1798 Irish uprising against British rule.
3. Site of the last stand of the United Irishmen against the British in 1798.
4. A young girl's body, dating from the first century C.E., was recovered from a German bog in 1951. The body exhibited various punishments bestowed upon adulterous women by ancient Germanic peoples.

of her neck, the wind
on her naked front.

It blows her nipples
to amber beads,
it shakes the frail rigging
of her ribs.

I can see her drowned
body in the bog,
the weighing stone,
the floating rods and boughs.

Under which at first
she was a barked sapling
that is dug up
oak-bone, brain-firkin:[2]

her shaved head
like a stubble of black corn,
her blindfold a soiled bandage,
her noose a ring

to store
the memories of love.
Little adulteress,
before they punished you

you were flaxen-haired,
undernourished, and your
tar-black face was beautiful.
My poor scapegoat,

I almost love you
but would have cast, I know,
the stones of silence.
I am the artful voyeur

of your brain's exposed
and darkened combs,
your muscles' webbing
and all your numbered bones:

I who have stood dumb
when your betraying sisters,
cauled[3] in tar,
wept by the railings,[4]

2. A wooden container.
3. Capped.
4. In Belfast, women may still be shaven, stripped, tarred and handcuffed to railings by the Irish Republican Army for keeping company with British soldiers [Heaney's note].

who would connive
in civilized outrage
yet understand the exact
and tribal, intimate revenge.

1975

Act of Union

1

To-night, a first movement, a pulse,
As if the rain in bogland gathered head
To slip and flood: a bog-burst,
A gash breaking open the ferny bed.
Your back is a firm line of eastern coast
And arms and legs are thrown
Beyond your gradual hills. I caress
The heaving province where our past has grown.
I am the tall kingdom over your shoulder
That you would neither cajole nor ignore.
Conquest is a lie. I grow older
Conceding your half-independent shore
Within whose borders now my legacy
Culminates inexorably.

2

And I am still imperially
Male, leaving you with the pain,
The rending process in the colony,
The battering ram, the boom burst from within.
The act sprouted an obstinate fifth column
Whose stance is growing unilateral.
His heart beneath your heart is a wardrum
Mustering force. His parasitical
And ignorant little fists already
Beat at your borders and I know they're cocked
At me across the water. No treaty
I foresee will salve completely your tracked
And stretchmarked body, the big pain
That leaves you raw, like opened ground, again.

1975

The Skunk

Up, black, striped and damasked like the chasuble[1]
At a funeral Mass, the skunk's tail
Paraded the skunk. Night after night
I expected her like a visitor.

1. A sleeveless vest worn by priests.

The refrigerator whinnied into silence.
My desk light softened beyond the verandah.
Small oranges loomed in the orange tree.
I began to be tense as a voyeur.

After eleven years I was composing
Love-letters again, broaching the word "wife"
Like a stored cask, as if its slender vowel
Had mutated into the night earth and air

Of California. The beautiful, useless
Tang of eucalyptus spelt your absence.
The aftermath of a mouthful of wine
Was like inhaling you off a cold pillow.

And there she was, the intent and glamorous,
Ordinary, mysterious skunk,
Mythologized, demythologized.
Snuffing the boards five feet beyond me.

It all came back to me last night, stirred
By the sootfall of your things at bedtime,
Your head-down, tail-up hunt in a bottom drawer
For the black plunge-line nightdress.

Hear it calling out to every creature.
And they drink these waters, although it is dark here
    because it is the night.

I am repining for this living fountain.
Within this bread of life I see it plain
    although it is the night.

1978

The Toome Road

One morning early I met armoured cars
In convoy, warbling along on powerful tyres,
All camouflaged with broken alder branches,
And headphoned soldiers standing up in turrets.
How long were they approaching down my roads
As if they owned them? The whole country was sleeping.
I had rights-of-way, fields, cattle in my keeping,
Tractors hitched to buckrakes in open sheds,
Silos, chill gates, wet slates, the greens and reds
Of outhouse roofs. Whom should I run to tell
Among all of those with their back doors on the latch
For the bringer of bad news, that small-hours visitant
Who, by being expected, might be kept distant?
Sowers of seed, erectors of headstones. . .

O charioteers, above your dormant guns,
It stands here still, stands vibrant as you pass,
The invisible, untoppled omphalos.[1]

1979

The Singer's House

When they said Carrickfergus[1] I could hear
the frosty echo of saltminers' picks.
I imagined it, chambered and glinting,
a township built of light.

What do we say any more
to conjure the salt of our earth?
So much comes and is gone
that should be crystal and kept,

and amicable weathers
that bring up the grain of things,
their tang of season and store,
are all the packing we'll get.

So I say to myself *Gweebarra*[2]
and its music hits off the place
like water hitting off granite.
I see the glittering sound

framed in your window,
knives and forks set on oilcloth,[3]
and the seals' heads, suddenly outlined,
scanning everything.

People here used to believe
that drowned souls lived in the seals.
At spring tides they might change shape.
They loved music and swam in for a singer

who might stand at the end of summer
in the mouth of a whitewashed turf-shed,
his shoulder to the jamb, his song
a rowboat far out in evening.

When I came here first you were always singing,
a hint of the clip of the pick
in your winnowing climb and attack.
Raise it again, man. We still believe what we hear.

1979

1. The navel, or central point (Greek).

1. Seaport just north of Belfast on the northeast coast of Ireland.

2. Bay in County Donegal, in the northwest of Ireland.

3. Stiff, waterproof cloth often used as tablecloth.

In Memoriam Francis Ledwidge[1]

Killed in France 31 July 1917

The bronze soldier hitches a bronze cape
That crumples stiffly in imagined wind
No matter how the real winds buff and sweep
His sudden hunkering run, forever craned

Over Flanders.[2] Helmet and haversack,
The gun's firm slope from butt to bayonet,
The loyal, fallen names on the embossed plaque—
It all meant little to the worried pet

I was in nineteen forty-six or seven,
Gripping my Aunt Mary by the hand
Along the Portstewart prom, then round the crescent[3]
To thread the Castle Walk out to the strand.

The pilot from Coleraine sailed to the coal-boat.
Courting couples rose out of the scooped dunes.
A farmer stripped to his studs and shiny waistcoat
Rolled the trousers down on his timid shins.

Francis Ledwidge, you courted at the seaside
Beyond Drogheda[4] one Sunday afternoon.
Literary, sweet-talking, countrified,
You pedalled out the leafy road from Slane[5]

Where you belonged, among the dolorous
And lovely: the May altar of wild flowers,
Easter water sprinkled in outhouses,
Mass-rocks and hill-top raths and raftered byres.[6]

I think of you in your Tommy's uniform,[7]
A haunted Catholic face, pallid and brave,
Ghosting the trenches like a bloom of hawthorn
Or silence cored from a Boyne passage-grave.[8]

It's summer, nineteen-fifteen. I see the girl
My aunt was then, herding on the long acre.
Behind a low bush in the Dardanelles
You suck stones to make your dry mouth water.

It's nineteen-seventeen. She still herds cows
But a big strafe[9] puts the candles out in Ypres:

1. Francis Ledwidge (1891–1917) was friendly with some of the leaders of the 1916 Rising yet, like thousands of Irishmen of the time, felt himself constrained to enlist in the British Army to defend "the rights of small nations" [Heaney's note].
2. Much trench warfare took place here during World War I.
3. Promenade; crescent: curved row of houses.
4. Seaport near the mouth of the Boyne River.
5. The Hill of Slane rises above Slane village, with a commanding view of the Boyne River.
6. Rocks where persecuted Roman Catholics celebrated mass in secret; raths: old circular forts; byres: cow sheds.
7. Uniform of a British soldier in World War I.
8. An underground burial chamber entered through a long tunnel; the Boyne is a river in east Ireland where William III defeated James II.
9. A close-range airplane attack; Ypres: site of three World War I battles.

"My soul is by the Boyne, cutting new meadows . . .
My country wears her confirmation dress."

"To be called a British soldier while my country
Has no place among nations . . ." You were rent
By shrapnel six weeks later. "I am sorry
That party politics should divide our tents."

In you, our dead enigma, all the strains
Criss-cross in useless equilibrium
And as the wind tunes through this vigilant bronze
I hear again the sure confusing drum

You followed from Boyne water to the Balkans
But miss the twilit note your flute should sound.
You were not keyed or pitched like these true-blue ones
Though all of you consort now underground.

1979

Postscript

And some time make the time to drive out west
Into County Clare,[1] along the Flaggy Shore,
In September or October, when the wind
And the light are working off each other
So that the ocean on one side is wild
With foam and glitter, and inland among stones
The surface of a slate-grey lake is lit
By the earthed lightning of a flock of swans,
Their feathers roughed and ruffling, white on white,
Their fully grown headstrong-looking heads
Tucked or cresting or busy underwater.
Useless to think you'll park and capture it
More thoroughly. You are neither here nor there,
A hurry through which known and strange things pass
As big soft buffetings come at the car sideways
And catch the heart off guard and blow it open.

1996

A Call

"Hold on," she said, "I'll just run out and get him.
The weather here's so good, he took the chance
To do a bit of weeding."

So I saw him
Down on his hands and knees beside the leek rig,
Touching, inspecting, separating one
Stalk from the other, gently pulling up
Everything not tapered, frail and leafless,

1. County in western Ireland.

Pleased to feel each little weed-root break,
But rueful also . . .

Then found myself listening to
The amplified grave ticking of hall clocks
Where the phone lay unattended in a calm
Of mirror glass and sunstruck pendulums . . .

And found myself then thinking: if it were nowadays,
This is how Death would summon Everyman.

Next thing he spoke and I nearly said I loved him.

1996

The Errand

"On you go now! Run, son, like the devil
And tell your mother to try
To find me a bubble for the spirit level
And a new knot for this tie."

But still he was glad, I know, when I stood my ground,
Putting it up to him
With a smile that trumped his smile and his fool's errand,
Waiting for the next move in the game.

1996

The Gaeltacht[1]

I wish, *mon vieux*,[2] that you and Barlo and I
Were back in Rosguill,[3] on the Atlantic Drive,
And that it was again nineteen sixty
And Barlo was alive

And Paddy Joe and Chips Rafferty and Dicky
Were there talking Irish, for I believe
In that case Aoibheann[4] Marren and Margaret Conway
And M. and M. and Deirdre Morton and Niamh[5]

Would be there as well. And it would be great too
If we could see ourselves, if the people we are now
Could hear what we were saying, and if this sonnet

In imitation of Dante's, where he's set free
In a boat with Lapo and Guido,[6] with their girlfriends in it,
Could be the wildtrack of our gabble above the sea.

1. The majority Irish-speaking portion of western Ireland.
2. Pal, old friend.
3. (Irish, *Ros Goill*), peninsula in northwest Donegal.
4. Eavan in its Angelicized form, cf. the poet Eavan Boland.
5. Pronounced "Neev."
6. Heaney refers to Dante's poem "Guido, i' vorrei che tu e Lapo ed io." Guide Cavalcante (1255–1300), and Lapo Gianni (d. circa 1328), Italian poets.

Salman Rushdie

b. 1947

Salman Rushdie, c. 1999–2000

Born in Bombay in the heady days leading up to India's independence from Britain, Salman Rushdie was raised in Pakistan after the partition of the subcontinent. He then settled in England, where he soon became one of the most noted writers about the aftermath of empires. His magisterial novel *Midnight's Children* was awarded not only the prestigious Booker McConnell Prize for the best British novel of 1981 but later the "Booker of Bookers," as the best novel in the first twenty-five years of the prize's history. Like Saleem Sinai, the protagonist and narrator of *Midnight's Children*, Rushdie delights in telling its story, in a mixture of history, fantasy, fable, and sheer stylistic exuberance that has come to be known (through the works of Latin American writers like Gabriel Garcia Marquez) as magic realism. At once an Indian and a British writer, Rushdie enjoys a double status as both insider and outsider that allows him to comment both on the history of his native land and on the contemporary politics of Britain with savage and comic incisiveness.

Unfortunately, most who do not know Rushdie's writing well know his name from the publicity surrounding his 1988 novel *The Satanic Verses;* the novel was judged to be an affront to Islam, and on Valentine's Day in 1989 the late Iranian leader Ayatollah Ruhollah Khomeini issued a *fatwa,* or death threat, against both Rushdie and his publisher, carrying a multimillion dollar bounty. As a result, Rushdie was forced to go underground; for nearly ten years he moved from place to place protected by full-time bodyguards, making but unable to receive phone calls, and generally staying out of the public eye and out of harm's way. Under Islamic law, a *fatwa* can be lifted only by the man who imposed it; since Khomeini died with the *fatwa* still in effect, it technically will remain in effect until Rushdie's death, although subsequent Iranian leaders have suggested that the edict would not be enforced. Rushdie has, in recent years, begun a boldly public life in England and the United States.

It is both appalling and intriguing that the written word still has this much power. The book that followed *The Satanic Verses* was *Haroun and the Sea of Stories,* a tale often (mistakenly) labeled "juvenile." It is in fact an allegory of the power of language—its power to liberate, and the desperate attempts of what political philosopher Louis Althusser calls the "ideological state apparatus" to silence this free, anarchic speech. The story did indeed begin as a bath-time entertainment for Rushdie's son Zafar; but as the affair over the *Satanic Verses* grew and festered, the story matured into a parable of the responsibility of the artist to speak from the heart and conscience, regardless of the political consequences. "Chekov and Zulu," playfully but with sinister overtones, adopts the narrative frame of television's *Star Trek* to speak of international terrorism and political violence. "The Courter," one of Rushdie's most tender stories, closes his 1994 volume *East, West,* emphasizing two of his perennial themes: the (sometimes benevolent) influence of transnational popular culture, and the creative magic of everyday language.

For additional resources on Rushdie, go to *The Longman Anthology of British Literature* Web site at www.myliteraturekit.com.

Chekov and Zulu

I

On 4th November, 1984, Zulu disappeared in Birmingham, and India House sent his old schoolfriend Chekov to Wembley[1] to see the wife.

"Adaabarz, Mrs Zulu. Permission to enter?"

"Of course come in, Dipty sahib, why such formality?"

"Sorry to disturb you on a Sunday, Mrs Zulu, but Zulu-tho hasn't been in touch this morning?"

"With me? Since when he contacts me on official trip? Why to hit a telephone call when he is probably enjoying?"

"Whoops, sore point, excuse *me*. Always been the foot-in-it blunderbuss type."

"At least sit, take tea-shee."

"Fixed the place up damn fine, Mrs Zulu, wah-wah.[2] Tasteful decor, in spades, I must say. So much cut-glass! That bounder Zulu must be getting too much pay, more than yours truly, clever dog."

"No, how is it possible? Acting Dipty's tankha[3] must be far in excess of Security Chief."

"No suspicion intended, ji.[4] Only to say what a bargain-hunter you must be."

"Some problem but there is, na?"

"Beg pardon?"

"Arré,[5] Jaisingh! Where have you been sleeping? Acting Dipty Sahib is thirsting for his tea. And biscuits and jalebis, can you not keep two things in your head? Jump, now, guest is waiting."

"Truly, Mrs Zulu, please go to no trouble."

"No trouble is there, Diptyji, only this chap has become lazy since coming from home. Days off, TV in room, even pay in pounds sterling, he expects all. So far we brought him but no gratitude, what to tell you, noth-*thing*."

"Ah, Jaisingh; why not? Excellent jalebi, Mrs Z. Thanking you."

Assembled on top of the television and on shelf units around it was the missing man's collection of *Star Trek* memorabilia: Captain Kirk and Spock dolls, spaceship models—a Klingon Bird of Prey, a Romulan vessel, a space station, and of course the Starship *Enterprise*. In pride of place were large figurines of two of the series's supporting cast.

"These old Doon School nicknames," Chekov exclaimed heartily. "They stay put like stuck records. Dumpy, Stumpy, Grumpy, Humpy. They take over from our names. As in our case our intrepid cosmonaut aliases."

"I don't like. This 'Mrs Zulu' I am landed with! It sounds like a blackie."

"Wear the name with pride, begum sahib.[6] We're old comrades-in-arms, your husband and I; since boyhood days, perhaps he was good enough to mention? Intrepid diplonauts. Our umpteen-year mission to explore new worlds and new civilisations. See there, our alter egos standing on your TV, the Asiatic-looking Russky and the Chink. Not the leaders, as you'll appreciate, but the ultimate professional servants. 'Course laid in!' 'Hailing frequencies open!' 'Warp factor three!' What would that strutting Captain have been without his top-level staffers? Likewise with the good ship Hindustan.[7] We are servants also, you see, just like your fierce Jaisingh

1. Birmingham is a city in West Midlands, central England; Wembley is a London suburb.
2. Excellent.
3. Wages.
4. Term of respect added to ends of sentences or words.
5. Exclamation of surprise.
6. High-ranking Muslim woman.
7. Persian name for India.

here. Never more important than in a moment like the present sad crisis, when an even keel must be maintained, jalebis must be served and tea poured, no matter what. We do not lead, but we enable. Without us, no course can be laid, no hailing frequency opened. No factors can be warped."

"Is he in difficulties, then, your Zulu? As if it wasn't bad enough, this terrible time."

On the wall behind the TV was a framed photograph of Indira Gandhi,[8] with a garland hung around it. She had been dead since Wednesday. Pictures of her cremation had been on the TV for hours. The flower-petals, the garish, unbearable flames.

"Hard to believe it. Indiraji! Words fail one. She was our mother. Hai, hai! Cut down in her prime."

"And on radio-TV, such-such stories are coming about Delhi goings-on. So many killings, Dipty Sahib. So many of our decent Sikh[9] people done to death, as if all were guilty for the crimes of one-two badmash guards."

"The Sikh community has always been thought loyal to the nation," Chekov reflected. "Backbone of the Army, to say nothing of the Delhi taxi service. Super-citizens, one might say, seemingly wedded to the national idea. But such ideas are being questioned now, you must admit; there are those who would point to the comb, bangle, dagger et cetera as signs of the enemy within."

"Who would dare say such a thing about us? Such an evil thing."

"I know. I know. But you take Zulu. The ticklish thing is, he's not on any official business that we know of. He's dropped off the map, begum sahib. AWOL[1] ever since the assassination. No contact for two days plus."

"O God."

"There is a view forming back at HQ that he may have been associated with the gang. Who have in all probability long-established links with the community over here."

"O God."

"Naturally I am fighting strenuously against the proponents of this view. But his absence is damning, you must see. We have no fear of these tinpot Khalistan wallahs.[2] But they have a ruthless streak. And with Zulu's inside knowledge and security background . . . They have threatened further attacks, as you know. As you must know. As some would say you must know all too well."

"O God."

"It is possible," Chekov said, eating his jalebi, "that Zulu has boldly gone where no Indian diplonaut has gone before."

The wife wept. "Even the stupid name you could never get right. It was with S. 'Sulu.' So-so many episodes I have been made to see, you think I don't know? Kirk Spock McCoy Scott Uhura Chekov *Sulu*."

"But Zulu is a better name for what some might allege to be a wild man," Chekov said. "For a suspected savage. For a putative traitor. Thank you for excellent tea."

2

In August, Zulu, a shy, burly giant, had met Chekov off the plane from Delhi. Chekov at thirty-three was a small, slim, dapper man in grey flannels, stiff-collared shirt and a double-breasted navy blue blazer with brass buttons. He had

8. Prime minister of India between 1966 and 1977 and 1980 and 1984; assassinated in 1984.
9. Community in the Punjab whose religion attempts to combine Hinduism and Islam.
1. Absent without leave.
2. Sikh military who call for a separate Sikh state called Khalistan; *wallah* means boy or man.

bat's-wing eyebrows and a prominent and pugnacious jaw, so that his cultivated tones and habitual soft-spokenness came as something of a surprise, disarming those who had been led by the eyebrows and chin to expect an altogether more aggressive personality. He was a high flyer, with one small embassy already notched up. The Acting Number Two job in London, while strictly temporary, was his latest plum.

"What-ho, Zools! Years, yaar,[3] years," Chekov said, thumping his palm into the other man's chest. "So," he added, "I see you've become a hairy fairy." The young Zulu had been a modern Sikh in the matter of hair—sporting a fine moustache at eighteen, but beardless, with a haircut instead of long tresses wound tightly under a turban. Now, however, he had reverted to tradition.

"Hullo, ji," Zulu greeted him cautiously. "So then is it OK to utilise the old modes of address?"

"Utilise away! Wouldn't hear of anything else," Chekov said, handing Zulu his bags and baggage tags. "Spirit of the *Enterprise* and all that jazz."

In his public life the most urbane of men, Chekov when letting his hair down in private enjoyed getting interculturally hot under the collar. Soon after his taking up his new post he sat with Zulu one lunchtime on a bench in Embankment Gardens and jerked his head in the direction of various passers-by.

"Crooks," he said, *sotto voce*.

"Where?" shouted Zulu, leaping athletically to his feet. "Should I pursue?"

Heads turned. Chekov grabbed the hem of Zulu's jacket and pulled him back on to the bench. "Don't be such a hero," he admonished fondly. "I meant all of them, generally; thieves, every last one. God, I love London! Theatre, ballet, opera, restaurants! The Pavilion at Lord's on the Saturday of the Test Match![4] The royal ducks on the royal pond in royal St James's Park! Decent tailors, a decent mixed grill when you want it, decent magazines to read! I see the remnants of greatness and I don't mind telling you I am impressed. The Athenaeum, Buck House, the lions in Trafalgar Square. *Damn* impressive. I went to a meeting with the junior Minister at the F. & C.O. and realised I was in the old India Office. All that John Company black teak, those tuskers rampant on the old bookcases. Gave me quite a turn. I applaud them for their success: hurrah! But then I look at my own home, and I see that it has been plundered by burglars. I can't deny there is a residue of distress."

"I am sorry to hear of your loss," Zulu said, knitting his brows. "But surely the culpables are not in the vicinity."

"Zulu, Zulu, a figure of speech, my simpleton warrior prince. Their museums are full of our treasures, I meant. Their fortunes and cities, built on the loot they took. So on, so forth. One forgives, of course; that is our national nature. One need not forget."

Zulu pointed at a tramp, sleeping on the next bench in a ragged hat and coat. "Did he steal from us, too?" he asked.

"Never forget," said Chekov, wagging a finger, "that the British working class collaborated for its own gain in the colonial project. Manchester cotton workers, for instance, supported the destruction of our cotton industry. As diplomats we must never draw attention to such facts; but facts, nevertheless, they remain."

3. Friend, buddy.

4. A group of cricket games played between international all-star teams.

"But a beggarman is not in the working class," objected Zulu, reasonably. "Surely this fellow at least is not our oppressor."

"Zulu," Chekov said in exasperation, "don't be so bleddy difficult."

Chekov and Zulu went boating on the Serpentine, and Chekov got back on his hobby-horse. "They have stolen us," he said, reclining boatered and champagned on striped cushions while mighty Zulu rowed. "And now we are stealing ourselves back. It is an Elgin marbles[5] situation."

"You should be more content," said Zulu, shipping oars and gulping cola. "You should be less hungry, less cross. See how much you have! It is enough. Sit back and enjoy. I have less, and it suffices for me. The sun is shining. The colonial period is a closed book."

"If you don't want that sandwich, hand it over," said Chekov. "With my natural radicalism I should not have been a diplomat. I should have been a terrorist."

"But then we would have been enemies, on opposite sides," protested Zulu, and suddenly there were real tears in his eyes. "Do you care nothing for our friendship? For my responsibilities in life?"

Chekov was abashed. "Quite right, Zools old boy. Too bleddy true. You can't imagine how delighted I was when I learned we would be able to join forces like this in London. Nothing like the friendships of one's boyhood, eh? Nothing in the world can take their place. Now listen, you great lummox, no more of that long face. I won't permit it. Great big chap like you shouldn't look like he's about to blub. Blood brothers, old friend, what do you say? All for one and one for all."

"Blood brothers," said Zulu, smiling a shy smile.

"Onward, then," nodded Chekov, settling back on his cushions. "Impulse power only."

The day Mrs Gandhi was murdered by her Sikh bodyguards, Zulu and Chekov played squash in a private court in St John's Wood. In the locker-room after showering, prematurely-greying Chekov still panted heavily with a towel round his softening waist, reluctant to expose his exhaustion-shrivelled purple penis to view; Zulu stood proudly naked, thick-cocked, tossing his fine head of long black hair, caressing and combing it with womanly sensuality, and at last twisting it swiftly into a knot.

"Too good, Zulu yaar. Fataakh! Fataakh! What shots! Too bleddy good for me."

"You desk-pilots, ji. You lose your edge. Once you were ready for anything."

"Yeah, yeah, I'm over the hill. But you were only one year junior."

"I have led a purer life, ji—action, not words."

"You understand we will have to blacken your name," Chekov said softly.

Zulu turned slowly in Charles Atlas pose in front of a full-length mirror.

"It has to look like a maverick stunt. If anything goes wrong, deniability is essential. Even your wife must not suspect the truth."

Spreading his arms and legs, Zulu made his body a giant X, stretching himself to the limit. Then he came to attention. Chekov sounded a little frayed.

"Zools? What do you say?"

"Is the transporter ready?"

"Come on, yaar, don't arse around."

"Respectfully, Mister Chekov, sir, it's my arse. Now then: is the transporter ready?"

5. A group of sculptures removed from the Acropolis in Athens by Lord Elgin between 1801 and 1803 and purchased by the British Museum in 1816. Rightful ownership of the marbles is a matter of ongoing controversy between the British and Greek governments.

"Transporter ready. Aye."

"Then, energise."

Chekov's memorandum, classified top-secret, eyes-only, and addressed to "JTK" [James T. Kirk):

> My strong recommendation is that Operation Startrek be aborted. To send a Federation employee of Klingon origin unarmed into a Klingon cell to spy is the crudest form of loyalty test. The operative in question has never shown ideological deviation of any sort and deserves better, even in the present climate of mayhem, hysteria and fear. If he fails to persuade the Klingons of his *bona fides* he can expect to be treated with extreme prejudice. These are not hostage takers.
>
> The entire undertaking is misconceived. The locally settled Klingon population is not the central problem. Even should we succeed, such intelligence as can be gleaned about more important principals back home will no doubt be of dubious accuracy and limited value. We should advise Star Fleet Headquarters to engage urgently with the grievances and aspirations of the Klingon people. Unless these are dealt with fair and square there cannot be a lasting peace.

The reply from JTK:

> Your closeness to the relevant individual excuses what is otherwise an explosively communalist document. It is not for you to define the national interest nor to determine what undercover operations are to be undertaken. It is for you to enable such operations to occur and to provide back-up as and when required to do so. As a personal favour to you and in the name of my long friendship with your eminent Papaji I have destroyed your last without keeping a copy and suggest you do the same. Also destroy this.

Chekov asked Zulu to drive him up to Stratford for a performance of *Coriolanus*.[6]

"How many kiddiwinks by now? Three?"

"Four," said Zulu. "All boys."

"By the grace of God. She must be a good woman."

"I have a full heart," said Zulu, with sudden feeling. "A full house, a full belly, a full bed."

"Lucky so and so," said Chekov. "Always were warm-blooded. I, by contrast, am not. Reptiles, certain species of dinosaur, and me. I am in the wife market, by the way, if you know any suitable candidates. Bachelordom being, after a certain point, an obstacle on the career path."

Zulu was driving strangely. In the slow lane of the motorway, as they approached an exit lane, he accelerated towards a hundred miles an hour. Once the exit was behind them, he slowed. Chekov noticed that he varied his speed and lane constantly. "Doesn't the old rattletrap have cruise control?" he asked. "Because, sport, this kind of performance would not do on the bridge of the flagship of the United Federation of Planets."

"Anti-surveillance," said Zulu. "Dry-cleaning." Chekov, alarmed, looked out of the back window.

"Have we been rumbled, then?"

"Nothing to worry about," grinned Zulu. "Better safe than sorry is all. Always anticipate the worst-case scenario."

Chekov settled back in his seat. "You liked toys and games," he said. Zulu had been a crack rifle shot, the school's champion wrestler, and an expert fencer. "Every

6. Shakespeare's bloodiest tragedy; its themes are civil unrest and revolt.

Speech Day," Zulu said, "I would sit in the hall and clap, while you went up for all the work prizes. English Prize, History Prize, Latin Prize, Form Prize. Clap, clap, clap, term after term, year after year. But on Sports Day I got my cups. And now also I have my area of expertise."

"Quite a reputation you're building up, if what I hear is anything to go by."

There was a silence. England passed by at speed.

"Do you like Tolkien?" Zulu asked.

"I wouldn't have put you down as a big reader," said Chekov, startled. "No offence."

"J.R.R. Tolkien," said Zulu. "*The Lord of the Rings*."[7]

"Can't say I've read the gentleman. Heard of him, of course. Elves and pixies. Not your sort of thing at all, I'd have thought."

"It is about a war to the finish between Good and Evil," said Zulu intently. "And while this great war is being fought there is one part of the world, the Shire, in which nobody even knows it's going on. The hobbits who live there work and squabble and make merry and they have no fucking clue about the forces that threaten them, and those that save their tiny skins." His face was red with vehemence.

"Meaning me, I suppose," Chekov said.

"I am a soldier in that war," said Zulu. "If you sit in an office you don't have one small idea of what the real world is like. The world of action, ji. The world of deeds, of things that are done and maybe undone too. The world of life and death."

"Only in the worst case," Chekov demurred.

"Do I tell you how to apply your smooth-tongued musca-polish to people's behinds?" stormed Zulu. "Then do not tell me how to ply my trade."

Soldiers going into battle pump themselves up, Chekov knew. This chest-beating was to be expected, it must not be misunderstood. "When will you vamoose?" he quietly asked.

"Chekov ji, you won't see me go."

Stratford approached. "Did you know, ji," Zulu offered, "that the map of Tolkien's Middle-earth fits quite well over central England and Wales? Maybe all fairylands are right here, in our midst."

"You're a deep one, old Zools," said Chekov. "Full of revelations today."

Chekov had a few people over for dinner at his modern-style official residence in a private road in Hampstead: a Very Big Businessman he was wooing, journalists he liked, prominent India-lovers, noted Non-Resident Indians. The policy was business as usual. The dreadful event must not be seen to have derailed the ship of State: whose new captain, Chekov mused, was a former pilot himself. As if a Sulu, a Chekov had been suddenly promoted to the skipper's seat.

Damned difficult doing all this without a lady wife to act as hostess, he grumbled inwardly. The best golden plates with the many-headed lion at the centre, the finest crystal, the menu, the wines. Personnel had been seconded from India House to help him out, but it wasn't the same. The secrets of good evenings, like God, were in the details. Chekov meddled and fretted.

The evening went off well. Over brandy, Chekov even dared to introduce a blacker note. "England has always been a breeding ground for our revolutionists," he

7. Tolkien's trilogy (1954–1955), written during and just after World War II, concerns a war for control of Middle Earth, in which men, elves, dwarfs, and a few British-like hobbits band together to defeat the evil eastern empire of Sauron.

said. "What would Pandit Nehru[8] have been without Harrow?[9] Or Gandhiji without his formative experiences here? Even the Pakistan idea was dreamt up by young radicals at college in what we then were asked to think of as the Mother Country. Now that England's status has declined, I suppose it is logical that the quality of the revolutionists she breeds has likewise fallen. The Kashmiris![1] Not a hope in hell. And as for these Khalistan types, let them not think that their evil deed has brought their dream a day closer. On the contrary. On the contrary. We will root them out and smash them to—what's the right word?—to *smithereens*."

To his surprise he had begun speaking loudly and had risen to his feet. He sat down hard and laughed. The moment passed.

"The funny thing about this blasted nickname of mine," he said quickly to his dinner-table neighbour, the septuagenarian Very Big Businessman's improbably young and attractive wife, "is that back then we never saw one episode of the TV series. No TV to see it on, you see. The whole thing was just a legend wafting its way from the US and UK to our lovely hill-station of Dehra Dun.

"After a while we got a couple of cheap paperback novelisations and passed them round as if they were naughty books like *Lady* C or some such. Lots of us tried the names on for size but only two of them stuck; probably because they seemed to go together, and the two of us got on pretty well, even though he was younger. A lovely boy. So just like Laurel and Hardy we were Chekov and Zulu."

"Love and marriage," said the woman.

"Beg pardon?"

"*You* know," she said. "Go together like is it milk and porridge. Or a car and garage, that's right. I love old songs. La-la-la-something-brother, you can't have fun without I think it's your mother."[2]

"Yes, now I do recall," said Chekov.

3

Three months later Zulu telephoned his wife.

"O my God where have you vanished are you dead?"

"Listen please my bivi. Listen carefully my wife, my only love."

"Yes. OK. I am calm. Line is bad, but."

"Call Chekov and say condition red."

"Arré! What is wrong with your condition?"

"Please. Condition red."

"Yes. OK. Red."

"Say the Klingons may be smelling things."

"Clingers-on may be smelly things. Means what?"

"My darling, I beg you."

"I have it all right here only. With this pencil I have written it, both."

"Tell him, get Scotty to lock on to my signal and beam me up at once."

"What rubbish! Even now you can't leave off that stupid game."

"Bivi. It is urgent. *Beam me up*."

8. Jawaharlal Nehru, first prime minister of the Republic of India (1947–1964), father of Indira Gandhi.
9. An exclusive English preparatory school.
1. Residents of Kashmir, a territory in dispute between India and Pakistan since 1947.
2. She is mangling the lyrics of Sammy Cahn's 1955 song *Love and Marriage*: "Love and marriage, love and marriage / Go together like a horse and carriage / This I tell you brother / You can't have one without the other."

Chekov dropped everything and drove. He went via the dry-cleaners as instructed; he drove round roundabouts twice, jumped red lights, deliberately took a wrong turning, stopped and turned round, made as many right turns as possible to see if anything followed him across the stream of traffic, and, on the motorway, mimicked Zulu's techniques. When he was as certain as he could be that he was clean, he headed for the rendezvous point. "Roll over Len Deighton," he thought, "and tell le Carré the news."[3]

He turned off the motorway and pulled into a lay-by. A man stepped out of the trees, looking newly bathed and smartly dressed, with a sheepish smile on his face. It was Zulu.

Chekov jumped out of the car and embraced his friend, kissing him on both cheeks. Zulu's bristly beard pricked his lips. "I expected you'd have an arm missing, or blood pouring from a gunshot wound, or some black eyes at least," he said. "Instead here you are dressed for the theatre, minus only an opera cloak and cane."

"Mission accomplished," said Zulu, patting his breast pocket. "All present and correct."

"Then what was that 'condition red' bakvaas?"

"The worst-case scenario," said Zulu, "does not always materialise."

In the car, Chekov scanned the names, places, dates in Zulu's brown envelope. The information was better than anyone had expected. From this anonymous Midlands lay-by a light was shining on certain remote villages and urban back-alleys in Punjab[4] There would be a round-up, and, for some big badmashes at least, there would no longer be shadows in which to hide.

He gave a little, impressed whistle.

Zulu in the passenger seat inclined his head. "Better move off now," he said. "Don't tempt fate."

They drove south through Middle-earth.

Not long after they came off the motorway, Zulu said, "By the way, I quit."

Chekov stopped the car. The two towers of Wembley Stadium were visible through a gap in the houses to the left.

"What's this? Did those extremists manage to turn your head or what?"

"Chekov, ji, don't be a fool. Who needs extremists when there are the killings in Delhi? Hundreds, maybe thousands. Sikh men scalped and burned alive in front of their families. Boy-children, too."

"We know this."

"Then, ji, we also know who was behind it."

"There is not a shred of evidence," Chekov repeated the policy line.

"There are eyewitnesses and photographs," said Zulu. "We know this."

"There are those who think," said Chekov slowly, "that after Indiraji the Sikhs deserved what they got."

Zulu stiffened.

"You know me better than that, I hope," said Chekov.

"Zulu, for God's sake, come on. All our bleddy lives."

"No Congress workers have been indicted," said Zulu. "In spite of all the evidence of complicity. Therefore, I resign. You should quit, too."

"If you have gone so damn radical," cried Chekov, "why hand over these lists at all? Why go only half the bleddy hog?"

3. Len Deighton and John le Carré are two popular contemporary writers of espionage fiction. The line refers to the popular song lyric, "Roll over, Beethoven."

4. Province divided between India and Pakistan.

"I am a security wallah," said Zulu, opening the car door. "Terrorists of all sorts are my foes. But not, apparently, in certain circumstances, yours."

"Zulu, get in, damn it," Chekov shouted. "Don't you care for your career? A wife and four kiddiwinks to support. What about your old chums? Are you going to turn your back on me?"

But Zulu was already too far away.

Chekov and Zulu never met again. Zulu settled in Bombay and as the demand for private-sector protection increased in that cash-rich boom-town, so his Zulu Shield and Zulu Spear companies prospered and grew. He had three more children, all of them boys, and remains happily married to this day.

As for Chekov, he never did take a wife. In spite of this supposed handicap, however, he did well in his chosen profession. His rapid rise continued. But one day in May 1991 he was, by chance, a member of the entourage accompanying Mr Rajiv Gandhi[5] to the South Indian village of Sriperumbudur, where Rajiv was to address an election rally. Security was lax, intentionally so. In the previous election, Rajivji felt, the demands of security had placed an alienating barrier between himself and the electorate. On this occasion, he decreed, the voters must be allowed to feel close.

After the speeches, the Rajiv group descended from the podium. Chekov, who was just a few feet behind Rajiv, saw a small Tamil[6] woman come forward, smiling. She shook Rajiv's hand and did not let go. Chekov understood what she was smiling about, and the knowledge was so powerful that it stopped time itself.

Because time had stopped, Chekov was able to make a number of private observations. "These Tamil revolutionists are not England-returned," he noted. "So, finally, we have learned to produce the goods at home, and no longer need to import. Bang goes that old dinner-party standby; so to speak." And, less dryly: "The tragedy is not how one dies," he thought. "It is how one has lived."

The scene around him vanished, dissolving in a pool of light, and was replaced by the bridge of the Starship *Enterprise*. All the leading figures were in their appointed places. Zulu sat beside Chekov at the front.

"Shields no longer operative," Zulu was saying. On the main screen, they could see the Klingon Bird of Prey uncloaking, preparing to strike.

"One direct hit and we're done for," cried Dr McCoy. "For God's sake, Jim, get us out of here!"

"Illogical," said First Officer Spock. "The degradation of our dilithium crystal drive means that warp speed is unavailable. At impulse power only, we would make a poor attempt indeed to flee the Bird of Prey. Our only logical course is unconditional surrender."

"Surrender to a Klingon!" shouted McCoy. "Damn it, you cold-blooded, pointy-eared adding-machine, don't you know how they treat their prisoners?"

"Phaser banks completely depleted," said Zulu. "Offensive capability nil."

"Should I attempt to contact the Klingon captain, sir?" Chekov inquired. "They could fire at any moment."

"Thank you, Mr Chekov," said Captain Kirk. "I'm afraid that won't be necessary. On this occasion, the worst-case scenario is the one we are obliged to play out. Hold your position. Steady as she goes."

5. Prime minister of India (1984–1989), assassinated in May 1991, son of Indira Gandhi.
6. Member of a people of southern India and Sri Lanka. The government of India had been aiding the Sri Lankan government in suppressing violent protest by Tamil separatists in Sri Lanka.

"The Bird of Prey has fired, sir," said Zulu.

Chekov took Zulu's hand and held it firmly, victoriously, as the speeding balls of deadly light approached.

1994

The Courter

I

Certainly-Mary was the smallest woman Mixed-Up the hall porter had come across, dwarfs excepted, a tiny sixty-year-old Indian lady with her greying hair tied behind her head in a neat bun, hitching up her red-hemmed white sari[1] in the front and negotiating the apartment block's front steps as if they were Alps. "No," he said aloud, furrowing his brow. What would be the right peaks. Ah, good, that was the name. "Ghats," he said proudly. Word from a schoolboy atlas long ago, when India felt as far away as Paradise. (Nowadays Paradise seemed even further away but India, and Hell, had come a good bit closer.) "Western Ghats, Eastern Ghats, and now Kensington[2] Ghats," he said, giggling. "Mountains."

She stopped in front of him in the oak-panelled lobby. "But ghats in India are also stairs," she said. "Yes yes certainly. For instance in Hindu holy city of Varanasi, where the Brahmins sit taking the filgrims' money is called Dasashwamedh-ghat. Broad-broad staircase down to River Ganga. O, most certainly! Also Manikarnika-ghat. They buy fire from a house with a tiger leaping from the roof—yes certainly, a statue tiger, coloured by Technicolor, what are you thinking?—and they bring it in a box to set fire to their loved ones' bodies. Funeral fires are of sandal. Photographs not allowed; no, certainly not."

He began thinking of her as Certainly-Mary because she never said plain yes or no; always this O-yes-certainly or no-certainly-not. In the confused circumstances that had prevailed ever since his brain, his one sure thing, had let him down, he could hardly be certain of anything any more; so he was stunned by her sureness, first into nostalgia, then envy, then attraction. And attraction was a thing so long forgotten that when the churning started he thought for a long time it must be the Chinese dumplings he had brought home from the High Street carry-out.

English was hard for Certainly-Mary, and this was a part of what drew damaged old Mixed-Up towards her. The letter p was a particular problem, often turning into an f or a c; when she proceeded through the lobby with a wheeled wicker shopping basket, she would say, "Going shocking," and when, on her return, he offered to help lift the basket up the front ghats, she would answer, "Yes, fleas." As the elevator lifted her away, she called through the grille: "Oé, courter! Thank you, courter. O, yes, certainly." (In Hindi and Konkani,[3] however, her p's knew their place.)

So: thanks to her unexpected, somehow stomach-churning magic, he was no longer porter, but courter. "Courter," he repeated to the mirror when she had gone. His breath made a little dwindling picture of the word on the glass. "Courter courter caught." Okay. People called him many things, he did not mind. But this name, this courter, this he would try to be.

1. Traditional Indian woman's wrap dress.
2. Fashionable London neighborhood.
3. Two of India's indigenous languages.

2

For years now I've been meaning to write down the story of Certainly-Mary, our ayah,[4] the woman who did as much as my mother to raise my sisters and me, and her great adventure with her "courter" in London, where we all lived for a time in the early Sixties in a block called Waverley House; but what with one thing and another I never got round to it.

Then recently I heard from Certainly-Mary after a longish silence. She wrote to say that she was ninety-one, had had a serious operation, and would I kindly send her some money, because she was embarrassed that her niece, with whom she was now living in the Kurla district of Bombay, was so badly out of pocket.

I sent the money, and soon afterwards received a pleasant letter from the niece, Stella, written in the same hand as the letter from "Aya"—as we had always called Mary, palindromically[5] dropping the "h." Aya had been so touched, the niece wrote, that I remembered her after all these years. "I have been hearing the stories about you folks all my life," the letter went on, "and I think of you a little bit as family. Maybe you recall my mother, Mary's sister. She unfortunately passed on. Now it is I who write Mary's letters for her. We all wish you the best."

This message from an intimate stranger reached out to me in my enforced exile from the beloved country of my birth and moved me, stirring things that had been buried very deep. Of course it also made me feel guilty about having done so little for Mary over the years. For whatever reason, it has become more important than ever to set down the story I've been carrying around unwritten for so long, the story of Aya and the gentle man whom she renamed—with unintentional but prophetic overtones of romance—"the courter." I see now that it is not just their story, but ours, mine, as well.

3

His real name was Mecir: you were supposed to say Mishirsh because it had invisible accents on it in some Iron Curtain language in which the accents had to be invisible, my sister Durré said solemnly, in case somebody spied on them or rubbed them out or something. His first name also began with an m but it was so full of what we called Communist consonants, all those z's and c's and w's walled up together without vowels to give them breathing space, that I never even tried to learn it.

At first we thought of nicknaming him after a mischievous little comic-book character, Mr Mxyztplk from the Fifth Dimension, who looked a bit like Elmer Fudd and used to make Superman's life hell until ole Supe could trick him into saying his name backwards, Klptzyxm, whereupon he disappeared back into the Fifth Dimension; but because we weren't too sure how to say Mxyztplk (not to mention Klptzyxm) we dropped that idea. "We'll just call you Mixed-Up," I told him in the end, to simplify life. "Mishter Mikshed-Up Mishirsh." I was fifteen then and bursting with unemployed cock and it meant I could say things like that right into people's faces, even people less accommodating than Mr Mecir with his stroke.

What I remember most vividly are his pink rubber washing-up gloves, which he seemed never to remove, at least not until he came calling for Certainly-Mary . . . At any rate, when I insulted him, with my sisters Durré and Muneeza cackling in the lift,[6] Mecir just

4. Hindi, "nanny."
5. A palindrome is a word that reads the same forwards and backwards.
6. Elevator.

grinned an empty good-natured grin, nodded, "You call me what you like, okay," and went back to buffing and polishing the brasswork. There was no point teasing him if he was going to be like that, so I got into the lift and all the way to the fourth floor we sang *I Can't Stop Loving You* at the top of our best Ray Charles voices, which were pretty awful. But we were wearing our dark glasses, so it didn't matter.

4

It was the summer of 1962, and school was out. My baby sister Scheherazade was just one year old. Durré was a beehived fourteen; Muneeza was ten, and already quite a handful. The three of us—or rather Durré and me, with Muneeza trying desperately and unsuccessfully to be included in our gang—would stand over Scheherazade's cot and sing to her. "No nursery rhymes," Durré had decreed, and so there were none, for though she was a year my junior she was a natural leader. The infant Scheherazade's lullabies were our cover versions of recent hits by Chubby Checker, Neil Sedaka, Elvis and Pat Boone.

"Why don't you come home, Speedy Gonzales?"[7] we bellowed in sweet disharmony: but most of all, and with actions, we would jump down, turn around and pick a bale of cotton. We would have jumped down, turned around and picked those bales all day except that the Maharaja of B— in the flat below complained, and Aya Mary came in to plead with us to be quiet.

"Look, see, it's Jumble-Aya[8] who's fallen for Mixed-Up," Durré shouted, and Mary blushed a truly immense blush. So naturally we segued right into a quick me-oh-my-oh; son of a gun, we had big fun. But then the baby began to yell, my father came in with his head down bull-fashion and steaming from both ears, and we needed all the good luck charms we could find.

I had been at boarding school in England for a year or so when Abba took the decision to bring the family over. Like all his decisions, it was neither explained to nor discussed with anyone, not even my mother. When they first arrived he rented two adjacent flats in a seedy Bayswater[9] mansion block called Graham Court, which lurked furtively in a nothing street that crawled along the side of the ABC Queensway cinema towards the Porchester Baths. He commandeered one of these flats for himself and put my mother, three sisters and Aya in the other; also, on school holidays, me. England, where liquor was freely available, did little for my father's *bonhomie*,[1] so in a way it was a relief to have a flat to ourselves.

Most nights he emptied a bottle of Johnnie Walker Red Label and a soda-siphon. My mother did not dare to go across to "his place" in the evenings. She said: "He makes faces at me."

Aya Mary took Abba his dinner and answered all his calls (if he wanted anything, he would phone us up and ask for it). I am not sure why Mary was spared his drunken rages. She said it was because she was nine years his senior, so she could tell him to show due respect.

After a few months, however, my father leased a three-bedroom fourth-floor apartment with a fancy address. This was Waverley House in Kensington Court, W8.

7. "Speedy Gonzales" was a hit in the United States for Pat Boone in 1962.
8. "Jumble-aya" invokes "jambalaya," a cajun stew, but also the title of a Hank Williams song, later recorded by Pat Boone, and a hit for Fats Domino in 1961, and again for John Fogerty (formerly of Creedence Clearwater Revival) in 1973.
9. London neighborhood.
1. Good nature.

Among its other residents were not one but two Indian Maharajas, the sporting Prince P— as well as the old B— who has already been mentioned. Now we were jammed in together, my parents and Baby Scare-zade (as her siblings had affectionately begun to call her) in the master bedroom, the three of us in a much smaller room, and Mary, I regret to admit, on a straw mat laid on the fitted carpet in the hall. The third bedroom became my father's office, where he made phone-calls and kept his *Encyclopaedia Britannica*, his *Reader's Digests*, and (under lock and key) the television cabinet. We entered it at our peril. It was the Minotaur's[2] lair.

One morning he was persuaded to drop in at the corner pharmacy and pick up some supplies for the baby. When he returned there was a hurt, schoolboyish look on his face that I had never seen before, and he was pressing his hand against his cheek.

"She hit me," he said plaintively.

"Hai! Allah-tobah! Darling!" cried my mother, fussing. "Who hit you? Are you injured? Show me, let me see."

"I did nothing," he said, standing there in the hall with the pharmacy bag in his other hand and a face as pink as Mecir's rubber gloves. "I just went in with your list. The girl seemed very helpful. I asked for baby compound, Johnson's powder, teething jelly, and she brought them out. Then I asked did she have any nipples, and she slapped my face."

My mother was appalled. "Just for that?" And Certainly-Mary backed her up. "What is this nonsense?" she wanted to know. "I have been in that chemist's[3] shock, and they have flenty nickels, different sizes, all on view."

Durré and Muneeza could not contain themselves. They were rolling round on the floor, laughing and kicking their legs in the air.

"You both shut your face at once," my mother ordered. "A madwoman has hit your father. Where is the comedy?"

"I don't believe it," Durré gasped. "You just went up to that girl and said," and here she fell apart again, stamping her feet and holding her stomach, " '*have you got any nipples?*' "

My father grew thunderous, empurpled. Durré controlled herself. "But Abba," she said, at length, "here they call them teats."

Now my mother's and Mary's hands flew to their mouths, and even my father looked shocked. "But how shameless!" my mother said. "The same word as for what's on your bosoms?" She coloured, and stuck out her tongue for shame.

"These English," sighed Certainly-Mary. "But aren't they the limit? Certainly-yes; they are."

I remember this story with delight, because it was the only time I ever saw my father so discomfited, and the incident became legendary and the girl in the pharmacy was installed as the object of our great veneration. (Durré and I went in there just to take a look at her—she was a plain, short girl of about seventeen, with large, unavoidable breasts—but she caught us whispering and glared so fiercely that we fled.) And also because in the general hilarity I was able to conceal the shaming truth that I, who had been in England for so long, would have made the same mistake as Abba did.

It wasn't just Certainly-Mary and my parents who had trouble with the English language. My schoolfellows tittered when in my Bombay way I said "brought-up" for

2. The Minotaur was the monster of Greek myth, slain by Theseus; his lair lay in the center of the famous labyrinth on Crete.

3. Pharmacists.

upbringing (as in "where was your brought-up?") and "thrice" for three times and "quarter-plate" for side-plate and "macaroni" for pasta in general. As for learning the difference between nipples and teats, I really hadn't had any opportunities to increase my word power in that area at all.

5

So I was a little jealous of Certainly-Mary when Mixed-Up came to call. He rang our bell, his body quivering with deference in an old suit grown too loose, the trousers tightly gathered by a belt; he had taken off his rubber gloves and there were roses in his hand. My father opened the door and gave him a withering look. Being a snob, Abba was not pleased that the flat lacked a separate service entrance, so that even a porter had to be treated as a member of the same universe as himself.

"Mary," Mixed-Up managed, licking his lips and pushing back his floppy white hair. "I, to see Miss Mary, come, am."

"Wait on," Abba said, and shut the door in his face.

Certainly-Mary spent all her afternoons off with old Mixed-Up from then on, even though that first date was not a complete success. He took her "up West" to show her the visitors' London she had never seen, but at the top of an up escalator at Piccadilly Circus, while Mecir was painfully enunciating the words on the posters she couldn't read—*Unzip a banana,* and *Idris when I's dri*—she got her sari stuck in the jaws of the machine, and as the escalator pulled at the garment it began to unwind. She was forced to spin round and round like a top, and screamed at the top of her voice, "O BAAP! BAAPU-RÉ! BAAP-RÉ-BAAP-RÉ-BAAP!" It was Mixed-Up who saved her by pushing the emergency stop button before the sari was completely unwound and she was exposed in her petticoat for all the world to see.

"O, courter!" she wept on his shoulder. "O, no more escaleater, courter, nevermore, surely not!"

My own amorous longings were aimed at Durré's best friend, a Polish girl called Rozalia, who had a holiday job at Faiman's shoe shop on Oxford Street. I pursued her pathetically throughout the holidays and, on and off, for the next two years. She would let me have lunch with her sometimes and buy her a Coke and a sandwich, and once she came with me to stand on the terraces at White Hart Lane to watch Jimmy Greaves's first game for the Spurs. "Come on you whoi-oites," we both shouted dutifully. "Come on you *Lily-whoites*." After that she even invited me into the back room at Faiman's, where she kissed me twice and let me touch her breast, but that was as far as I got.

And then there was my sort-of-cousin Chandni, whose mother's sister had married my mother's brother, though they had since split up. Chandni was eighteen months older than me, and so sexy it made you sick. She was training to be an Indian classical dancer, Odissi as well as Natyam, but in the meantime she dressed in tight black jeans and a clinging black polo-neck jumper and took me, now and then, to hang out at Bunjie's, where she knew most of the folk-music crowd that frequented the place, and where she answered to the name of Moonlight, which is what *chandni* means. I chain-smoked with the folkies and then went to the toilet to throw up.

Chandni was the stuff of obsessions. She was a teenage dream, the Moon River come to Earth like the Goddess Ganga, dolled up in slinky black. But for her I was just the young greenhorn cousin to whom she was being nice because he hadn't learned his way around.

She-E-rry, won't you come out tonight? yodelled the Four Seasons. I knew exactly how they felt. *Come, come, come out toni-yi-yight*. And while you're at it, love me do.[4]

6

They went for walks in Kensington Gardens. "Pan," Mixed-Up said, pointing at a statue. "Los' boy. Nev' grew up." They went to Barkers and Pontings and Derry & Toms and picked out furniture and curtains for imaginary homes. They cruised supermarkets and chose little delicacies to eat. In Mecir's cramped lounge they sipped what he called "chimpanzee tea" and toasted crumpets in front of an electric bar fire.

Thanks to Mixed-Up, Mary was at last able to watch television. She liked children's programmes best, especially *The Flintstones*. Once, giggling at her daring, Mary confided to Mixed-Up that Fred and Wilma reminded her of her Sahib and Begum Sahiba upstairs; at which the courter, matching her audaciousness, pointed first at Certainly-Mary and then at himself, grinned a wide gappy smile and said, "Rubble."

Later, on the news, a vulpine Englishman with a thin moustache and mad eyes declaimed a warning about immigrants, and Certainly-Mary flapped her hand at the set: "Khali-pili bom marta," she objected, and then, for her host's benefit translated: "For nothing he is shouting shouting. Bad life! Switch it off."

They were often interrupted by the Maharajas of B— and P—, who came downstairs to escape their wives and ring other women from the call-box in the porter's room.

"Oh, baby, forget that guy," said sporty Prince P—, who seemed to spend all his days in tennis whites, and whose plump gold Rolex was almost lost in the thick hair on his arm. "I'll show you a better time than him, baby; step into my world."

The Maharaja of B— was older, uglier, more matter-of-fact. "Yes, bring all appliances. Room is booked in name of Mr Douglas Home. Six forty-five to seven fifteen. You have printed rate card? Please. Also a two-foot ruler, must be wooden. Frilly apron, plus."

This is what has lasted in my memory of Waverley House, this seething mass of bad marriages, booze, philanderers and unfulfilled young lusts; of the Maharaja of P— roaring away towards London's casinoland every night, in a red sports car with fitted blondes, and of the Maharaja of B— skulking off to Kensington High Street wearing dark glasses in the dark, and a coat with the collar turned up even though it was high summer; and at the heart of our little universe were Certainly-Mary and her courter, drinking chimpanzee tea and singing along with the national anthem of Bedrock.

But they were not really like Barney and Betty Rubble at all. They were formal, polite. They were . . . courtly. He courted her, and, like a coy, ringleted ingénue with a fan, she inclined her head, and entertained his suit.

7

I spent one half-term weekend in 1963 at the home in Beccles, Suffolk of Field Marshal Sir Charles Lutwidge-Dodgson,[5] an old India hand and a family friend who was supporting my application for British citizenship. "The Dodo," as he was known, invited me down by myself, saying he wanted to get to know me better.

4. Hits, respectively, for Frankie Valli and the Four Seasons (1962) and the Beatles (1962).

5. Charles Lutwidge Dodgson was the birth name of the writer better known as Lewis Carroll, author of *Alice's Adventures in Wonderland* and *Through the Looking Glass*; the latter book uses the game of chess as a structural device. Dodgson was familiarly called "Dodo" by his young companion, Alice Liddell.

He was a huge man whose skin had started hanging too loosely on his face, a giant living in a tiny thatched cottage and forever bumping his head. No wonder he was irascible at times; he was in Hell, a Gulliver trapped in that rose-garden Lilliput of croquet hoops, church bells, sepia photographs and old battle-trumpets.

The weekend was fitful and awkward until the Dodo asked if I played chess. Slightly awestruck at the prospect of playing a Field Marshal, I nodded; and ninety minutes later, to my amazement, won the game.

I went into the kitchen, strutting somewhat, planning to boast a little to the old soldier's long-time housekeeper, Mrs Liddell. But as soon as I entered she said: "Don't tell me. You never went and won?"

"Yes," I said, affecting nonchalance. "As a matter of fact, yes, I did."

"Gawd," said Mrs Liddell. "Now there'll be hell to pay. You go back in there and ask him for another game, and this time make sure you lose."

I did as I was told, but was never invited to Beccles again.

Still, the defeat of the Dodo gave me new confidence at the chessboard, so when I returned to Waverley House after finishing my O levels, and was at once invited to play a game by Mixed-Up (Mary had told him about my victory in the Battle of Beccles with great pride and some hyperbole), I said: "Sure, I don't mind." How long could it take to thrash the old duffer, after all?

There followed a massacre royal. Mixed-Up did not just beat me; he had me for breakfast, over easy. I couldn't believe it—the canny opening, the fluency of his combination play, the force of his attacks, my own impossibly cramped, strangled positions—and asked for a second game. This time he tucked into me even more heartily. I sat broken in my chair at the end, close to tears. *Big girls don't cry*, I reminded myself, but the song went on playing in my head: *That's just an alibi*.[6]

"Who are you?" I demanded, humiliation weighing down every syllable. "The devil in disguise?"

Mixed-Up gave his big, silly grin. "Grand Master," he said. "Long time. Before head."

"You're a Grand Master," I repeated, still in a daze. Then in a moment of horror I remembered that I had seen the name Mecir in books of classic games. "Nimzo-Indian," I said aloud. He beamed and nodded furiously.

"That Mecir?" I asked wonderingly.

"That," he said. There was saliva dribbling out of a corner of his sloppy old mouth. This ruined old man was in the books. He was in the books. And even with his mind turned to rubble he could still wipe the floor with me.

"Now play lady," he grinned. I didn't get it. "Mary lady," he said. "Yes yes certainly."

She was pouring tea, waiting for my answer. "Aya, you can't play," I said, bewildered.

"Learning, baba," she said. "What is it, na? Only a game."

And then she, too, beat me senseless, and with the black pieces, at that. It was not the greatest day of my life.

8

From *100 Most Instructive Chess Games* by Robert Reshevsky, 1961:

M. Mecir—M. Najdorf
Dallas 1950, Nimzo-Indian Defense

6. "Big Girl's Don't Cry" was another falsetto hit for Frankie Valli and the Four Seasons in 1962.

> The attack of a tactician can be troublesome to meet—that of a strategist even more so. Whereas the tactician's threats may be unmistakable, the strategist confuses the issue by keeping things in abeyance. He threatens to threaten!
>
> Take this game for instance: Mecir posts a Knight at Q6 to get a grip on the center. Then he establishes a passed Pawn on one wing to occupy his opponent on the Queen side. Finally he stirs up the position on the King-side. What does the poor bewildered opponent do? How can he defend everything at once? Where will the blow fall?
>
> Watch Mecir keep Najdorf on the run, as he shifts the attack from side to side!

Chess had become their private language. Old Mixed-Up, lost as he was for words, retained, on the chess-board, much of the articulacy and subtlety which had vanished from his speech. As Certainly-Mary gained in skill—and she had learned with astonishing speed, I thought bitterly, for someone who couldn't read or write or pronounce the letter p—she was better able to understand, and respond to, the wit of the reduced maestro with whom she had so unexpectedly forged a bond.

He taught her with great patience, showing-not-telling, repeating openings and combinations and endgame techniques over and over until she began to see the meaning in the patterns. When they played, he handicapped himself, he told her her best moves and demonstrated their consequences, drawing her, step by step, into the infinite possibilities of the game.

Such was their courtship. "It is like an adventure, baba," Mary once tried to explain to me. "It is like going with him to his country, you know? What a place, baap-ré! Beautiful and dangerous and funny and full of fuzzles. For me it is a big-big discovery. What to tell you? I go for the game. It is a wonder."

I understood, then, how far things had gone between them. Certainly-Mary had never married, and had made it clear to old Mixed-Up that it was too late to start any of that monkey business at her age. The courter was a widower, and had grown-up children somewhere, lost long ago behind the ever-higher walls of Eastern Europe. But in the game of chess they had found a form of flirtation, and endless renewal that precluded the possibility of boredom, a courtly wonderland of the ageing heart.

What would the Dodo have made of it all? No doubt it would have scandalised him to see chess, chess of all games, the great formalisation of war, transformed into an art of love.

As for me: my defeats by Certainly-Mary and her courter ushered in further humiliations. Durré and Muneeza went down with the mumps, and so, finally, in spite of my mother's efforts to segregate us, did I. I lay terrified in bed while the doctor warned me not to stand up and move around if I could possibly help it. "If you do," he said, "your parents won't need to punish you. You will have punished yourself quite enough."

I spent the following few weeks tormented day and night by visions of grotesquely swollen testicles and a subsequent life of limp impotence—finished before I'd even started, it wasn't fair—which were made much worse by my sisters' quick recovery and incessant gibes. But in the end I was lucky; the illness didn't spread to the deep South. "Think how happy your hundred and one girlfriends will be, bhai," sneered Durré, who knew all about my continued failures in the Rozalia and Chandni departments.

On the radio, people were always singing about the joys of being sixteen years old. I wondered where they were, all those boys and girls of my age having the time of their lives. Were they driving around America in Studebaker convertibles? They certainly weren't in my neighbourhood. London, W8 was Sam Cooke country that summer. *Another Saturday night* . . .[7] There might be a mop-top love-song stuck at number one, but I was down with lonely Sam in the lower depths of the charts, how-I-wishing I had someone, etc., and generally feeling in a pretty goddamn dreadful way.

9

"Baba, come quick."

It was late at night when Aya Mary shook me awake. After many urgent hisses, she managed to drag me out of sleep and pull me, pajama'ed and yawning, down the hall. On the landing outside our flat was Mixed-Up the courter, huddled up against a wall, weeping. He had a black eye and there was dried blood on his mouth.

"What happened?" I asked Mary, shocked.

"Men," wailed Mixed-Up. "Threaten. Beat."

He had been in his lounge earlier that evening when the sporting Maharaja of P— burst in to say, "If anybody comes looking for me, okay, any tough-guy type guys, okay, I am out, okay? Oh you tea. Don't let them go upstairs, okay? Big tip, okay?"

A short time later, the old Maharaja of B— also arrived in Mecir's lounge, looking distressed.

"Suno, listen on," said the Maharaja of B—. "You don't know where I am, samajh liya? Understood? Some low persons may inquire. You don't know. I am abroad, achha? On extended travels abroad. Do your job, porter. Handsome recompense."

Late at night two tough-guy types did indeed turn up. It seemed the hairy Prince P— had gambling debts. "Out," Mixed-Up grinned in his sweetest way. The tough-guy types nodded, slowly. They had long hair and thick lips like Mick Jagger's. "He's a busy gent. We should of made an appointment," said the first type to the second. "Didn't I tell you we should of called?"

"You did," agreed the second type. "Got to do these things right, you said, he's royalty. And you was right, my son, I put my hand up, I was dead wrong. I put my hand up to that."

"Let's leave our card," said the first type. "Then he'll know to expect us."

"Ideal," said the second type, and smashed his fist into old Mixed-Up's mouth. "You tell him," the second type said, and struck the old man in the eye. "When he's in. You mention it."

He had locked the front door after that; but much later, well after midnight, there was a hammering. Mixed-Up called out, "Who?"

"We are close friends of the Maharaja of B—" said a voice. "No, I tell a lie. Acquaintances."

"He calls upon a lady of our acquaintance," said a second voice. "To be precise."

"It is in that connection that we crave audience," said the first voice.

"Gone," said Mecir. "Jet plane. Gone."

There was a silence. Then the second voice said, "Can't be in the jet set if you never jump on a jet, eh? Biarritz, Monte, all of that."

"Be sure and let His Highness know," said the first voice, "that we eagerly await his return."

"With regard to our mutual friend," said the second voice. "Eagerly."

7. "Another Saturday Night" was a hit for R&B singer Sam Cooke in 1963.

What does the poor bewildered opponent do? The words from the chess book popped unbidden into my head. *How can he defend everything at once? Where will the blow fall? Watch Mecir keep Najdorf on the run, as he shifts the attack from side to side!*

Mixed-Up returned to his lounge and on this occasion, even though there had been no use of force, he began to weep. After a time he took the elevator up to the fourth floor and whispered through our letter-box to Certainly-Mary sleeping on her mat.

"I didn't want to wake Sahib," Mary said. "You know his trouble, na? And Begum Sahiba is so tired at end of the day. So now you tell, baba, what to do?"

What did she expect me to come up with? I was sixteen years old. "Mixed-Up must call the police," I unoriginally offered.

"No, no, baba," said Certainly-Mary emphatically. "If the courter makes a scandal for Maharaja-log, then in the end it is the courter only who will be out on his ear."

I had no other ideas. I stood before them feeling like a fool, while they both turned upon me their frightened, supplicant eyes.

"Go to sleep," I said. "We'll think about it in the morning." *The first pair of thugs were tacticians,* I was thinking. *They were troublesome to meet. But the second pair were scarier; they were strategists. They threatened to threaten.*

Nothing happened in the morning, and the sky was clear. It was almost impossible to believe in fists, and menacing voices at the door. During the course of the day both Maharajas visited the porter's lounge and stuck five-pound notes in Mixed-Up's waistcoat pocket. "Held the fort, good man," said Prince P—, and the Maharaja of B— echoed those sentiments: "Spot on. All handled now, achha? Problem over."

The three of us—Aya Mary, her courter, and me—held a council of war that afternoon and decided that no further action was necessary. The hall porter was the front line in any such situation, I argued, and the front line had held. And now the risks were past. Assurances had been given. End of story.

"End of story," repeated Certainly-Mary doubtfully, but then, seeking to reassure Mecir, she brightened. "Correct," she said. "Most certainly! All-done, finis." She slapped her hands against each other for emphasis. She asked Mixed-Up if he wanted a game of chess; but for once the courter didn't want to play.

10

After that I was distracted, for a time, from the story of Mixed-Up and Certainly-Mary by violence nearer home.

My middle sister Muneeza, now eleven, was entering her delinquent phase a little early. She was the true inheritor of my father's black rage, and when she lost control it was terrible to behold. That summer she seemed to pick fights with my father on purpose; seemed prepared, at her young age, to test her strength against his. (I intervened in her rows with Abba only once, in the kitchen. She grabbed the kitchen scissors and flung them at me. They cut me on the thigh. After that I kept my distance.)

As I witnessed their wars I felt myself coming unstuck from the idea of family itself. I looked at my screaming sister and thought how brilliantly self-destructive she was, how triumphantly she was ruining her relations with the people she needed most.

And I looked at my choleric, face-pulling father and thought about British citizenship. My existing Indian passport permitted me to travel only to a very few countries, which were carefully listed on the second right-hand page. But I might soon have a British passport and then, by hook or by crook, I would get away from him. I would not have this face-pulling in my life.

At sixteen, you still think you can escape from your father. You aren't listening to his voice speaking through your mouth, you don't see how your gestures already mirror his; you don't see him in the way you hold your body, in the way you sign your name. You don't hear his whisper in your blood.

On the day I have to tell you about, my two-year-old sister Chhoti Scheherazade, Little Scare-zade, started crying as she often did during one of our family rows. Amma and Aya Mary loaded her into her push-chair and made a rapid getaway. They pushed her to Kensington Square and then sat on the grass, turned Scheherazade loose and made philosophical remarks while she tired herself out. Finally, she fell asleep, and they made their way home in the fading light of the evening. Outside Waverley House they were approached by two well-turned-out young men with Beatle haircuts and the buttoned-up, collarless jackets made popular by the band. The first of these young men asked my mother, very politely, if she might be the Maharani of B—.

"No," my mother answered, flattered.

"Oh, but you are, madam," said the second Beatle, equally politely. "For you are heading for Waverley House and that is the Maharaja's place of residence."

"No, no," my mother said, still blushing with pleasure. "We are a different Indian family."

"Quite so," the first Beatle nodded understandingly, and then, to my mother's great surprise, placed a finger alongside his nose, and winked. "Incognito, eh. Mum's the word."

"Now excuse us," my mother said, losing patience. "We are not the ladies you seek."

The second Beatle tapped a foot lightly against a wheel of the push-chair. "Your husband seeks ladies, madam, were you aware of that fact? Yes, he does. Most assiduously, may I add."

"Too assiduously," said the first Beatle, his face darkening.

"I tell you I am not the Maharani Begum," my mother said, growing suddenly alarmed. "Her business is not my business. Kindly let me pass."

The second Beatle stepped closer to her. She could feel his breath, which was minty. "One of the ladies he sought out was our ward, as you might say," he explained. "That would be the term. Under our protection, you follow. Us, therefore, being responsible for her welfare."

"Your husband," said the first Beatle, showing his teeth in a frightening way, and raising his voice one notch, "damaged the goods. Do you hear me, Queenie? He damaged the fucking goods."

"Mistaken identity, fleas," said Certainly-Mary. "Many Indian residents in Waverley House. We are decent ladies; *fleas*."

The second Beatle had taken out something from an inside pocket. A blade caught the light. "Fucking wogs,"[8] he said. "You fucking come over here, you don't fucking know how to fucking behave. Why don't you fucking fuck off to fucking Wogistan? Fuck your fucking wog arses. Now then," he added in a quiet voice, holding up the knife, "unbutton your blouses."

8. Derisive term for a dark-skinned foreigner, especially Indian or Pakistani.

Just then a loud noise emanated from the doorway of Waverley House. The two women and the two men turned to look, and out came Mixed-Up, yelling at the top of his voice and windmilling his arms like a mad old loon.

"Hullo," said the Beatle with the knife, looking amused. "Who's this, then? Oh oh fucking seven?"

Mixed-Up was trying to speak, he was in a mighty agony of effort, but all that was coming out of his mouth was raw, unshaped noise. Scheherazade woke up and joined in. The two Beatles looked displeased. But then something happened inside old Mixed-Up; something popped, and in a great rush he gabbled, "Sirs sirs no sirs these not B—women sirs B—women upstairs on floor three sirs Maharaja of B—also sirs God's truth mother's grave swear."

It was the longest sentence he had spoken since the stroke that had broken his tongue long ago.

And what with his torrent and Scheherazade's squalls there were suddenly heads poking out from doorways, attention was being paid, and the two Beatles nodded gravely. "Honest mistake," the first of them said apologetically to my mother, and actually bowed from the waist. "Could happen to anyone," the knife-man added, ruefully. They turned and began to walk quickly away. As they passed Mecir, however, they paused. "I know you, though," said the knife-man. " '*Jet plane. Gone.*' " He made a short movement of the arm, and then Mixed-Up the courter was lying on the pavement with blood leaking from a wound in his stomach. "All okay now," he gasped, and passed out.

II

He was on the road to recovery by Christmas; my mother's letter to the landlords, in which she called him a "knight in shining armour," ensured that he was well looked after, and his job was kept open for him. He continued to live in his little ground-floor cubby-hole, while the hall porter's duties were carried out by shift-duty staff. "Nothing but the best for our very own hero," the landlords assured my mother in their reply.

The two Maharajas and their retinues had moved out before I came home for the Christmas holidays, so we had no further visits from the Beatles or the Rolling Stones. Certainly-Mary spent as much time as she could with Mecir; but it was the look of my old Aya that worried me more than poor Mixed-Up. She looked older, and powdery, as if she might crumble away at any moment into dust.

"We didn't want to worry you at school," my mother said. "She has been having heart trouble. Palpitations. Not all the time, but."

Mary's health problems had sobered up the whole family. Muneeza's tantrums had stopped, and even my father was making an effort. They had put up a Christmas tree in the sitting-room and decorated it with all sorts of baubles. It was so odd to see a Christmas tree at our place that I realised things must be fairly serious.

On Christmas Eve my mother suggested that Mary might like it if we all sang some carols. Amma had made song-sheets, six copies, by hand. When we did *O come, all ye faithful* I showed off by singing from memory in Latin. Everybody behaved perfectly. When Muneeza suggested that we should try *Swinging on a Star* or *I Wanna Hold Your Hand* instead of this boring stuff, she wasn't really being serious. So this is family life, I thought. This is it.

But we were only play-acting.

A few weeks earlier, at school, I'd come across an American boy, the star of the school's Rugby football team, crying in the Chapel cloisters. I asked him what the matter was and he told me that President Kennedy had been assassinated. "I don't believe you," I said, but I could see that it was true. The football star sobbed and sobbed. I took his hand.

"When the President dies, the nation is orphaned," he eventually said, broken-heartedly parroting a piece of cracker-barrel wisdom he'd probably heard on Voice of America.[9]

"I know how you feel," I lied. "My father just died, too."

Mary's heart trouble turned out to be a mystery; unpredictably, it came and went. She was subjected to all sorts of tests during the next six months, but each time the doctors ended up by shaking their heads: they couldn't find anything wrong with her. Physically, she was right as rain; except that there were these periods when her heart kicked and bucked in her chest like the wild horses in *The Misfits*,[1] the ones whose roping and tying made Marilyn Monroe so mad.

Mecir went back to work in the spring, but his experience had knocked the stuffing out of him. He was slower to smile, duller of eye, more inward. Mary, too, had turned in upon herself. They still met for tea, crumpets and *The Flintstones*, but something was no longer quite right.

At the beginning of the summer Mary made an announcement.

"I know what is wrong with me," she told my parents, out of the blue. "I need to go home."

"But, Aya," my mother argued, "homesickness is not a real disease."

"God knows for what-all we came over to this country," Mary said. "But I can no longer stay. No. Certainly not." Her determination was absolute.

So it was England that was breaking her heart, breaking it by not being India. London was killing her, by not being Bombay. And Mixed-Up? I wondered. Was the courter killing her, too, because he was no longer himself? Or was it that her heart, roped by two different loves, was being pulled both East and West, whinnying and rearing, like those movie horses being yanked this way by Clark Gable and that way by Montgomery Clift, and she knew that to live she would have to choose?

"I must go," said Certainly-Mary. "Yes, certainly. *Bas*. Enough."

That summer, the summer of '64, I turned seventeen. Chandni went back to India. Durré's Polish friend Rozalia informed me over a sandwich in Oxford Street that she was getting engaged to a "real man," so I could forget about seeing her again, because this Zbigniew was the jealous type. Roy Orbison sang *It's Over* in my ears as I walked away to the Tube, but the truth was that nothing had really begun.

Certainly-Mary left us in mid-July. My father bought her a one-way ticket to Bombay, and that last morning was heavy with the pain of ending. When we took her bags down to the car, Mecir the hall porter was nowhere to be seen. Mary did not knock on the door of his lounge, but walked straight out through the freshly polished oak-panelled lobby, whose mirrors and brasses were sparkling brightly; she climbed into the back seat of our Ford Zodiac and sat there stiffly with her carry-on grip on her lap, staring straight ahead. I had known and loved her all my life. *Never mind your damned courter*, I wanted to shout at her, *what about me?*

9. Radio service established by the U.S. government in 1942 for the dissemination of news and information in occupied Europe during World War II.

1. *The Misfits*, a 1961 John Huston western starring Clark Gable, Marilyn Monroe, and Montgomery Clift.

As it happened, she was right about the homesickness. After her return to Bombay, she never had a day's heart trouble again; and, as the letter from her niece Stella confirmed, at ninety-one she was still going strong.

Soon after she left, my father told us he had decided to "shift location" to Pakistan. As usual, there were no discussions, no explanations, just the simple fiat. He gave up the lease on the flat in Waverley House at the end of the summer holidays, and they all went off to Karachi,[2] while I went back to school.

I became a British citizen that year. I was one of the lucky ones, I guess, because in spite of that chess game I had the Dodo on my side. And the passport did, in many ways, set me free. It allowed me to come and go, to make choices that were not the ones my father would have wished. But I, too, have ropes around my neck, I have them to this day, pulling me this way and that, East and West, the nooses tightening, commanding, *choose, choose*.

I buck, I snort, I whinny, I rear, I kick. Ropes, I do not choose between you. Lassoes, lariats, I choose neither of you, and both. Do you hear? I refuse to choose.

A year or so after we moved out I was in the area and dropped in at Waverley House to see how the old courter was doing. Maybe, I thought, we could have a game of chess, and he could beat me to a pulp. The lobby was empty, so I knocked on the door of his little lounge. A stranger answered.

"Where's Mixed-Up?" I cried, taken by surprise. I apologised at once, embarrassed. "Mr Mecir, I meant, the porter."

"I'm the porter, sir," the man said. "I don't know anything about any mix-up."

PERSPECTIVES

Whose Language?

Though Britain's last major overseas colony, Hong Kong, rejoined China in 1997, at least one important reminder of British rule remains in countries as far-flung as India, South Africa, and New Zealand: the English language itself. Twentieth-century linguists, following on the pioneering work of Benjamin Lee Whorf and Edward Sapir, are nearly unanimous in their belief that languages do not merely serve to describe the world but in fact help to create that world, establishing both a set of possibilities and a set of limits.

The politics of language thus becomes important for writers, especially writers in colonial and postcolonial cultures. In an episode from Joyce's *A Portrait of the Artist as a Young Man*, the Irish protagonist Stephen Dedalus converses with the English-born Dean of Studies at University College, Dublin, where Stephen is a student. In the course of the conversation it becomes clear that Stephen is already a more supple and cunning user of the English language than his teacher, and yet he feels himself at a disadvantage in having to use the language of the invader; he muses: "The language in which we are speaking is his before it is mine. How different are the words *home*, *Christ*, *ale*, *master*, on his lips and on mine! I cannot speak or write these words without unrest of spirit. His language, so familiar and so foreign, will always be for me an acquired speech. I have not made or accepted its words. My voice holds them at bay. My soul frets in the shadow of his language." The Penal Acts of 1695 and 1696 had made the Irish language illegal in Ireland; after 500 years of trying to subdue the "wild Irish," British lawmakers realized that the Irish natives would never be brought under English rule until their tongues were bound. In his poem *Traditions*, Seamus Heaney meditates on the enduring cost of what he has called elsewhere "the government of the tongue":

> Our guttural muse
> was bulled long ago
> by the alliterative tradition,
> her uvula grows
> vestigial, forgotten.

In much colonial and postcolonial writing, however, the confusion of tongues inflicted by British rule has been seen by the writers of Empire as a positive linguistic resource. Salman Rushdie, explaining his decision to use English rather than his native Hindi, writes: "Those of us who do use English do so in spite of our ambiguity towards it, or perhaps because of that, perhaps because we can find in that linguistic struggle a reflection of other struggles taking place in the real world, struggles between the cultures within ourselves and the influences working upon our societies. To conquer English may be to complete the process of making ourselves free." Thus a great deal of contemporary English-language writing—especially in countries where English was once the language of the conqueror (such as Ireland, Scotland, Wales, South Africa, India, and Kenya)—meditates on the blindnesses and insights inherent in using English. Some writers, like the Irish poet Nuala Ní Dhomhnaill, write in defiance of English; if one's native tongue is a minority language like Irish, this decision necessarily narrows a writer's potential audience. More common is the decision made by Rushdie, and by James Joyce before him: to write English as an "outsider," attesting to an alien's perspective on the majority language.

Ngũgĩ wa Thiong'o

b. 1938

The great novelist and postcolonial theorist Ngũgĩ wa Thiong'o is a crucial figure to bring into the debate about the ownership of English. Like Nuala Ní Dhomhnaill, the Irish poet who has decided to write in Irish and have her work translated by others into English, even though English is her first language, Ngũgĩ has political reasons for questioning the use of English by African writers who, as he once did, write the literature of modern Africa in European languages. Ngũgĩ achieved prominence in Africa and in Britain and America for his English-language novels of the African struggle for self-determination, especially the revolution in Kenya that led to its independence from Great Britain. After two years of imprisonment by the Kenyan government in 1977 for what it considered a subversive play, Ngũgĩ made the decision to stop writing in English and has since done his creative work in Gĩkũyũ, offering English translations, while continuing to write critical works and political essays in English for world-wide audiences. Despite his love of English and the global impact of his novels, Ngũgĩ wa Thiong'o believes English can never be one of Africa's true languages of liberation and cultural creation.

A Kenyan of the Gĩkũyũ tribe, Ngũgĩ was born James Ngũgĩ, one of twenty-eight children of a peasant farmer who squatted on the land of an African landlord. Kenya was under British colonial rule then, and James's early education was at missionary-run primary schools. Political agitation for independence reached a peak in the 1950s, and when a "State of Emergency" was declared in Kenya in 1952 by the British, English became the official language of instruction. Ngũgĩ won a place at the prestigious Alliance High School and received a thorough training in English literature. The struggle for independence powerfully affected him and his community; upon arriving home on a school vacation, for example, Ngũgĩ found his home destroyed by the colonial soldiers, whose policy of "protecting" villages from insurgency was actually designed to cut off the supply of food the villagers gave to the freedom fighters. This trauma is registered at the heart of Ngũgĩ's writing; his novels almost all contain the motif of a thwarted attempt to return home.

Ngũgĩ graduated from Makerere University College in Kampala with an honors degree in English; in the heady postcolonial atmosphere he read not only English classics but was also exposed to the new literature of Africa and the Caribbean by writers like Chinua Achebe and George Lamming. By 1966 James Ngũgĩ had gone to England to study for an M.A. in English at Leeds University, although his main subject was to be Caribbean literature. Ngũgĩ never finished his thesis, which was ironically a boon to world literature, because he was immersed in completing his important novel *A Grain of Wheat* (1966). Two novels had preceded it, the autobiographical *Weep Not, Child* (1964) and *The River Between* (1965). Throughout this time Ngũgĩ continued to write plays; the last work he published as James Ngũgĩ was a collection of short plays *This Time Tomorrow* (1970). While teaching as a visiting professor at several universities, Ngũgĩ wa Thiong'o wrote one of his most impressive novels, *Petals of Blood* (1977). As its title suggests, the novel also treats the bloody trauma of breaking away as a new nation, a nation inevitably haunted by its former colonial existence.

The two years Ngũgĩ spent in prison crystallized his thoughts about decolonization, which he had come to see was not merely a political event but demanded an entire change in the minds of those who had been dominated. The price of becoming free and establishing a viable culture entailed giving up the language of the colonizer. The then-President of Kenya, Daniel arap Moi, has permanently banned Ngũgĩ from Kenya as a political threat. From the time of his sentence on, although living in exile and far from his Gĩkũyũ roots in Kenya, Ngũgĩ's fiction, plays, and poetry have been written in the Gĩkũyũ language. His first post-English novel, *Caitaani Muthara-ini* (*Devil on the Cross*, 1980), was written in jail on sheets of the coarse toilet paper provided him in his prison cell and smuggled out by a sympathetic guard. With the strokes of his worn pencil on that rough and precious paper, Ngũgĩ proved his dedication to creating an African literature in its indigenous tongues and ceased to be what he now calls an Afro-European writer. Ngũgĩ has not been back to Kenya since 1982, and his books are banned in his homeland. He has written several novels in the past decade, as well as screenplays for African cinema and many more plays; he founded and edited the first Gĩkũyũ language literary journal *Mutiri*. Ngũgĩ taught all over the world as a visiting professor at such institutions as Beyreuth University, Auckland University, Yale University, and New York University, among others; he is currently a distinguised professor of comparative literature at the University of California, Irvine.

Paradoxically, perhaps, Ngũgĩ wrote his great theoretical analysis of the political and spiritual process of decolonization, *Decolonizing the Mind* (1980), in English, and it has circulated globally as a worldwide touchstone of liberation. An excerpt chosen from this lasting book represents Ngũgĩ's uncompromising answer to the question "whose language?" English can never belong to Africans until the languages of Africa create a literary home where English is not the master, but only an invited guest.

from DECOLONIZING THE MIND

Native African Languages

3

I was born into a large peasant family: father, four wives and about twenty-eight children. I also belonged, as we all did in those days, to a wider extended family and to the community as a whole.

We spoke Gĩkũyũ as we worked in the fields. We spoke Gĩkũyũ in and outside the home. I can vividly recall those evenings of story-telling around the fireside. It was mostly the grown-ups telling the children but everybody was interested and involved. We children would re-tell the stories the following day to other children who worked in the fields picking the pyrethrum flowers, tea-leaves or coffee beans of our European and African landlords.

The stories, with mostly animals as the main characters, were all told in Gĩkũyũ. Hare, being small, weak but full of innovative wit and cunning, was our hero. We identified with him as he struggled against the brutes of prey like Lion, Leopard, Hyena. His victories were our victories and we learnt that the apparently weak can outwit the strong. We followed the animals in their struggle against hostile nature—drought, rain, sun, wind—a confrontation often forcing them to search for forms of co-operation. But we were also interested in their struggles amongst themselves, and particularly between the beasts and the victims of prey. These twin struggles, against nature and other animals, reflected real-life struggles in the human world.

Not that we neglected stories with human beings as the main characters. There were two types of characters in such human-centred narratives: the species of truly human beings with qualities of courage, kindness, mercy, hatred of evil, concern for others; and a man-eat-man two-mouthed species with qualities of greed, selfishness, individualism and hatred of what was good for the larger co-operative community. Co-operation as the ultimate good in a community was a constant theme. It could unite human beings with animals against ogres and beasts of prey, as in the story of how Dove, after being fed with castoroil seeds, was sent to fetch a smith working far away from home and whose pregnant wife was being threatened by these man-eating two-mouthed ogres.

There were good and bad story-tellers. A good one could tell the same story over and over again, and it would always be fresh to us, the listeners. He or she could tell a story told by someone else and make it more alive and dramatic. The differences really were in the use of words and images and the inflexion of voices to effect different tones.

We therefore learnt to value words for their meaning and nuances. Language was not a mere string of words. It had a suggestive power well beyond the immediate and lexical meaning. Our appreciation of the suggestive magical power of language was reinforced by the games we played with words through riddles, proverbs, transpositions of syllables, or through nonsensical but musically arranged words. So we learnt the music of our language on top of the content. The language, through images and symbols, gave us a view of the world, but it had a beauty of its own. The home and the field were then our pre-primary school but what is important, for this discussion, is that the language of our evening teach-ins, and the language of our immediate and wider community, and the language of our work in the fields were one.

And then I went to school, a colonial school, and this harmony was broken. The language of my education was no longer the language of my culture. I first went to Kamaandura, missionary run, and then to another called Maanguuũ run by nationalists grouped around the Gĩkũyũ Independent and Karinga Schools Association. Our language of education was still Gĩkũyũ. The very first time I was ever given an ovation for my writing was over a composition in Gĩkũyũ. So for my first four years there was still harmony between the language of my formal education and that of the Limuru peasant community.

It was after the declaration of a state of emergency over Kenya in 1952 that all the schools run by patriotic nationalists were taken over by the colonial regime and were placed under District Education Boards chaired by Englishmen. English became the language of my formal education. In Kenya, English became more than a language: it was *the* language, and all the others had to bow before it in deference.

Thus one of the most humiliating experiences was to be caught speaking Gĩkũyũ in the vicinity of the school. The culprit was given corporal punishment—three to five strokes of the cane on bare buttocks—or was made to carry a metal plate around the neck with inscriptions such as I AM STUPID or I AM A DONKEY. Sometimes the culprits were fined money they could hardly afford. And how did the teachers catch the culprits? A button was initially given to one pupil who was supposed to hand it over to whoever was caught speaking his mother tongue. Whoever had the button at the end of the day would sing who had given it to him and the ensuing process would bring out all the culprits of the day. Thus children were turned into witch-hunters and in the process were being taught the lucrative value of being a traitor to one's immediate community.

The attitude to English was the exact opposite: any achievement in spoken or written English was highly rewarded; prizes, prestige, applause; the ticket to higher realms. English became the measure of intelligence and ability in the arts, the sciences, and all the other branches of learning. English became *the* main determinant of a child's progress up the ladder of formal education.

As you may know, the colonial system of education in addition to its apartheid racial demarcation had the structure of a pyramid: a broad primary base, a narrowing secondary middle, and an even narrower university apex. Selections from primary into secondary were through an examination, in my time called Kenya African Preliminary Examination, in which one had to pass six subjects ranging from Maths to Nature Study and Kiswahili. All the papers were written in English. Nobody could pass the exam who failed the English language paper no matter how brilliantly he had done in the other subjects. I remember one boy in my class of 1954 who had distinctions in all subjects except English, which he had failed. He was made to fail the entire exam. He went on to become a turn boy in a bus company. I who had only passes but a credit in English got a place at the Alliance High School, one of the most elitist institutions for Africans in colonial Kenya. The requirements for a place at the University, Makerere University College, were broadly the same: nobody could go on to wear the undergraduate red gown, no matter how brilliantly they had performed in all the other subjects unless they had a credit—not even a simple pass!—in English. Thus the most coveted place in the pyramid and in the system was only available to the holder of an English language credit card. English was the official vehicle and the magic formula to colonial elitedom.

Literary education was now determined by the dominant language while also reinforcing that dominance. Orature (oral literature) in Kenyan languages stopped. In primary school I now read simplified Dickens and Stevenson alongside Rider Haggard. Jim Hawkins, Oliver Twist, Tom Brown—not Hare, Leopard and Lion—were now my daily companions in the world of imagination. In secondary school, Scott and G. B. Shaw vied with more Rider Haggard, John Buchan, Alan Paton, Captain W. E. Johns. At Makerere I read English: from Chaucer to T. S. Eliot with a touch of Graham Greene.

Thus language and literature were taking us further and further from ourselves to other selves, from our world to other worlds.

What was the colonial system doing to us Kenyan children? What were the consequences of, on the one hand, this systematic suppression of our languages and the literature they carried, and on the other the elevation of English and the literature it carried?

9

I started writing in Gĩkũyũ language in 1977 after seventeen years of involvement in Afro-European literature, in my case Afro-English literature. It was then that I collaborated with Ngũgĩ wa Mĩriĩ in the drafting of the playscript, *Ngaahika Ndeenda* (the English translation was *I Will Marry When I Want*). I have since published a novel in Gĩkũyũ, *Caitaani Mũtharabainĩ* (English translation: *Devil on the Cross*) and completed a musical drama, *Maitũ Njugĩra*, (English translation: *Mother Sing for Me*); three books for children, *Njamba Nene na Mbaathi i Mathagu, Bathitoora ya Njamba Nene, Njamba Nene na Cibũ Kĩng'ang'i*, as well as another novel manuscript: *Matigari Ma Njirũũngi*. Wherever I have gone, particularly in Europe, I have been confronted with the question: why are you now writing in Gĩkũyũ? Why do you now write in an African language? In some academic quarters I have been confronted with the rebuke, "Why have you abandoned us?" It was almost as if, in choosing to write in Gĩkũyũ, I was doing something abnormal. But Gĩkũyũ is my mother tongue! The very fact that what common sense dictates in the literary practice of other cultures is being questioned in an African writer is a measure of how far imperialism has distorted the view of African realities. It has turned reality upside down: the abnormal is viewed as normal and the normal is viewed as abnormal. Africa actually enriches Europe: but Africa is made to believe that it needs Europe to rescue it from poverty. Africa's natural and human resources continue to develop Europe and America: but Africa is made to feel grateful for aid from the same quarters that still sit on the back of the continent. Africa even produces intellectuals who now rationalise this upside-down way of looking at Africa.

I believe that my writing in Gĩkũyũ language, a Kenyan language, an African language, is part and parcel of the anti-imperialist struggles of Kenyan and African peoples. In schools and universities our Kenyan languages—that is the languages of the many nationalities which make up Kenya—were associated with negative qualities of backwardness, underdevelopment, humiliation and punishment. We who went through that school system were meant to graduate with a hatred of the people and the culture and the values of the language of our daily humiliation and punishment. I do not want to see Kenyan children growing up in that imperialist-imposed tradition of contempt for the tools of communication developed by their communities and their history. I want them to transcend colonial alienation.

* * *

Chinua Achebe once decried the tendency of African intellectuals to escape into abstract universalism in the words that apply even more to the issue of the language of African literature:

> Africa has had such a fate in the world that the very adjective *African* can call up hideous fears of rejection. Better then to cut all the links with this homeland, this liability, and become in one giant leap the universal man. Indeed I understand this anxiety. *But running away from oneself seems to me a very inadequate way of dealing with an anxiety* [italics mine]. And if writers should opt for such escapism, who is to meet the challenge?

Who indeed?

We African writers are bound by our calling to do for our languages what Spenser, Milton and Shakespeare did for English; what Pushkin and Tolstoy did for Russian; indeed what all writers in world history have done for their languages by meeting the challenge of creating a literature in them, which process later opens the languages for philosophy, science, technology and all the other areas of human creative endeavours.

Eavan Boland

b. 1944

The question posed by this section of the anthology—"whose language?"—asks to whom the English language belongs. The poet Eavan Boland puts a special spin on this question throughout her work. As an Irish writer, she has a complex relationship to the language and the literary tradition shared with England, of course. But the thrust of Boland's questioning is directed more toward Irish literature in English and above all to modern Irish poetry. In that rich poetic tradition, Boland sees an absence, hears a silence: the woman poet in Ireland has been, she argues, shut out of poetry in a distinctive way.

The *Field Day Anthology of Irish Literature* was a monumental undertaking; published to wide acclaim in the early 1990s, and edited by Seamus Heaney and Brian Friel among others, the anthology had an ambitious scope, intending to collect all the major writing in the Irish tradition up to the present day. Eavan Boland made a bold stand in print and in person after its publication, declaring that the absence of more female editors and more works by women was evidence of a long-standing gender problem in Irish literature, even today. Ireland was traditionally represented in poetry and fiction by the figure of a suffering woman, whether she was an old country crone, "the old sow that eats its farrow" in Joyce's *Ulysses*, the beautiful Countess Cathleen Ní Houlihan in Yeats's play, the grieving mother of the famine literature, or the magical ancient Queen Mab. Poetry was written about these metaphorical women, standing in for Ireland and symbolizing the country, but almost never, Boland asserts, in a woman's voice. Women had been sidelined in Irish history altogether, despite having played many active roles, turned by poetic language into beautiful icons or sorrowing mothers in the literature that articulated Irish independence. All of Eavan Boland's complex and distinguished poetry before and since her quarrel with the *Field Day* anthology has been devoted to supplying those absent women's voices. Boland's eloquent poetry is regarded as among the finest women's writing of our time.

Eavan Boland was born in Dublin in 1944; since her father was a diplomat, she spent considerable time outside Ireland growing up, in London when her father was Ambassador to the Court of St. James's from 1950 to 1956, and in New York City from 1956 to 1964 when he served as the Irish ambassador to the United Nations. She returned to Ireland and Dublin for college, receiving a first-class honors degree in English from Trinity College. She spent a year at Trinity as a junior lecturer, but then left the academic life to write full time, raise a family of two children with her novelist husband, and teach sporadically at the School of Irish Studies in Dublin. Her first full-length book of poems, *New Territory*, came out in 1967, followed eight years later by *The War Horse*.

Boland's third collection was a watershed for her: *In Her Own Image* (1980) inaugurated her concentration on bringing the inner lives of women to poetic voice. A fountain of volumes has emerged since then, as well as awards to match them. Among the books are *The Journey and Other Poems* (1983), *Selected Poems 1980–1990* (1990), *In a Time of Violence* (1994), *An Origin Like Water: Collected Poems* (1996), and *The Lost Land* (1998); the awards include a Lannan Foundation Award in Poetry and the American Ireland Fund Literary Award. Eavan Boland is currently almost as well known for her essays and reviews, and for her cultural journalism in the *Irish Times*, as for her prominence as a reader of her own poetry. And she has come full circle since leaving academe; Boland is currently a professor of English at Stanford University.

The poems by Boland collected for this anthology are diverse and complicated, yet each works to restore missing voices, missing narratives, most of them female. *Anorexic* voices the paradoxical self-destruction of starving for love and power; *The Pomegranate* is a beautiful rewriting of the myth of Persephone, the Greek maiden whose mother, Ceres, the goddess of fertility, was forced to let her daughter spend the winter each year underground with Hades, the god of the underworld, in order to let spring come again. Narrated in the voice of a contemporary mother gazing at her own teenage daughter, separated from her by the girl's need to acquire independence, the poem modernizes the cycle of human seasons and probes the nature of maternal regret. Boland brings the intimacy of such feelings to her meditations on history, violence, and Ireland itself. *The Journey* evokes a mother's grief for her children of war and catastrophe, yet is far from passive—the woman is the traveler. *Mise Eire* is a dazzling play on words from its title onward; a defiant female voice repudiates Ireland, rejects it for naming her "the woman" in its poetry, not seeing beyond that designation to the real woman who once stood on the deck of the *Mary Belle*, headed to America, a half-dead infant in her arms. "A new language is a scar," the poem tells us. Eavan Boland's poetic task has been to heal those scars by uncovering them, to give voice to the absent throng of women in the Irish past.

Anorexic

Flesh is heretic.
My body is a witch.
I am burning it.

Yes I am torching
her curves and paps[1] and wiles.
They scorch in my self-denials.

1. Breasts.

How she meshed my head
in the half-truths
of her fevers till I renounced
milk and honey
and the taste of lunch.

I vomited
her hungers.
Now the bitch is burning.

I am starved and curveless.
I am skin and bone.
She has learned her lesson.

Thin as a rib
I turn in sleep.
My dreams probe

a claustrophobia
a sensuous enclosure.
How warm it was and wide

once by a warm drum,
once by the song of his breath
and in his sleeping side.[2]

Only a little more,
only a few more days
sinless, foodless.

I will slip
back into him again
as if I have never been away.

Caged so
I will grow
angular and holy

past pain
keeping his heart
such company

as will make me forget
in a small space
the fall

into forked dark,
into python needs
heaving to hips and breasts
and lips and heat
and sweat and fat and greed.

1987

2. These verses recall God's creation of Eve from one of Adam's ribs as he sleeps (Genesis 2.21).

Mise Eire[1]

I won't go back to it—

my nation displaced
into old dactyls,[2]
oaths made
by the animal tallows
of the candle—

land of the Gulf Stream,
the small farm,
the scalded memory,
the songs
that bandage up the history,
the words
that make a rhythm of the crime

where time is time past.
A palsy of regrets.
No. I won't go back.
My roots are brutal:

I am the woman—
a sloven's mix
of silk at the wrists,
a sort of dove-strut
in the precincts of the garrison—

who practices
the quick frictions,
the rictus[3] of delight
and gets cambric for it,
rice-colored silks.

I am the woman
in the gansy-coat[4]
on board the *Mary Belle*,
in the huddling cold,

holding her half-dead baby to her
as the wind shifts East
and North over the dirty
water of the wharf

mingling the immigrant
guttural with the vowels
of homesickness who neither
knows nor cares that

a new language
is a kind of scar

1. I am Ireland (Gaelic). Mise Eire also reads as "misery," a pun.
2. The English adapted "Eire" to "Ireland," drawing the word out into dactylic meter.
3. Frozen smile.
4. A cheap cloth coat.

and heals after a while
into a passable imitation
of what went before.

1987

The Pomegranate

The only legend I have ever loved is
The story of a daughter lost in hell.
And found and rescued there.
Love and blackmail are the gist of it.
Ceres and Persephone the names.
And the best thing about the legend is
I can enter it anywhere. And have.
As a child in exile in
A city of fogs and strange consonants,
I read it first and at first I was
An exiled child in the crackling dusk of
The underworld, the stars blighted. Later
I walked out in a summer twilight
Searching for my daughter at bedtime.
When she came running I was ready
To make any bargain to keep her.
I carried her back past whitebeams.
And wasps and honey-scented buddleias.
But I was Ceres then and I knew
Winter was in store for every leaf
On every tree on that road.
Was inescapable for each one we passed.
And for me.
It is winter
And the stars are hidden.
I climb the stairs and stand where I can see
My child asleep beside her teen magazines,
Her can of Coke, her plate of uncut fruit.
The pomegranate! How did I forget it?
She could have come home and been safe
And ended the story and all
Our heartbroken searching but she reached
Out a hand and plucked a pomegranate.[1]
She put out her hand and pulled down
The French sound for apple and
The noise of stone and the proof
That even in the place of death,
At the heart of legend, in the midst
Of rocks full of unshed tears
Ready to be diamonds by the time
The story was told, a child can be

1. In the classical myth, Persephone would have emerged from the underworld unharmed except for the fact that she broke a command to bring nothing back: by plucking a pomegranate, she became liable to death. The next lines recall the derivation of the term "pomegranate" from Old French *pomme granade*, "seeded apple."

Hungry. I could warn her. There is still a chance.
The rain is cold. The road is flint-coloured.
The suburb has cars and cable television.
The veiled stars are above ground.
It is another world. But what else
Can a mother give her daughter but such
Beautiful rifts in time?
If I defer the grief I will diminish the gift.
The legend must be hers as well as mine.
She will enter it. As I have.
She will wake up. She will hold
The papery, flushed skin in her hand.
And to her lips. I will say nothing.

1994

A Woman Painted on a Leaf

I found it among curios and silver.
in the pureness of wintry light.

A woman painted on a leaf.

Fine lines drawn on a veined surface
in a handmade frame.

This is not my face. Neither did I draw it.

A leaf falls in a garden.
The moon cools its aftermath of sap.
The pith of summer dries out in starlight.

A woman is inscribed there.

This is not death. It is the terrible
suspension of life.

I want a poem
I can grow old in. I want a poem I can die in.

I want to take
this dried-out face,
as you take a starling from behind iron,
and return it to its element of air, of ending—
so that autumn
which was once
the hard look of stars,
the frown on a gardener's face,
a gradual bronzing of the distance,
will be,
from now on,
a crisp tinder underfoot. Cheekbones. Eyes. Will be
a mouth crying out. Let me.

Let me die.

1994

Paul Muldoon

b. 1951

If reading poetry sometimes appears to be a simple process of translation—a kind of verbal puzzle to be solved—the work of Paul Muldoon should disabuse readers of that notion. Muldoon's poetry celebrates and bears witness to a sense of the mysterious at the heart of everyday existence—the sense, which for Muldoon is a reason to celebrate rather than despair, that life will always elude our attempts to make it all make sense. Indeed, Muldoon's poetry often seems to adopt the motto of one of the bands he writes about in *Sleeve Notes*, the Talking Heads: "Stop making sense."

Like Seamus Heaney, who was later to be his tutor at Queen's University, Belfast, Muldoon was raised Catholic in protestant Northern Ireland. He was born and raised in Portadown, County Armagh; in grammar school his teachers introduced him to poetry, music, and the Irish language. Muldoon's first poems were written in Irish; but when he went to university he switched and began writing in English, fearing that his knowledge of Irish wasn't sufficiently sound. (He has, nevertheless, made English translations of some Irish poetry, including that of Nuala Ní Dhomhnaill.) Queen's University was a crucible of new poetry at the time, with Heaney and Michael Longley the group's established poets, and Medbh McGuckian and Ciaran Carson among his classmates. His first poetry collection, *New Weather*, was published by the prestigious British publisher Faber and Faber while Muldoon was still a student.

Muldoon's now substantial body of poetry—the poems of his first eight collections published with Faber were collected in *Poems 1968–1998* (2001)—covers a very wide geographic and imaginative terrain. His subjects range from ancient Irish legends and sagas, to detective fiction, to popular movies and song; his tastes are, in the lowercase sense of the word, truly catholic.

Since 1990, Muldoon has directed the creative writing program at Princeton University; in 1999 he was elected Professor of Poetry at Oxford. His Clarendon lectures in English literature, delivered at Oxford, were published as *To Ireland, I* in 1998. His most recent poetry collection is *Wayside Shrines* (2009).

Cuba[1]

My eldest sister arrived home that morning
In her white muslin evening dress.
"Who the hell do you think you are,
Running out to dances in next to nothing?
As though we hadn't enough bother
With the world at war, if not at an end."
My father was pounding the breakfast-table.

"Those Yankees were touch and go as it was—
If you'd heard Patton[2] in Armagh[3]—
But this Kennedy's nearly an Irishman

1. The background for the poem is the Cuban Missile Crisis of October 1962, to which the Irish felt some connection through the Irish-American president, John Fitzgerald Kennedy.

2. General George S. Patton (1885–1945), fiery and controversial American military leader in World Wars I and II.

3. An urban district of Northern Ireland.

So he's not much better than ourselves.
And him with only to say the word.
If you've got anything on your mind
Maybe you should make your peace with God."

I could hear May from beyond the curtain.
"Bless me, Father, for I have sinned.
I told a lie once, I was disobedient once.
And, Father, a boy touched me once."
"Tell me, child. Was this touch immodest?
Did he touch your breast, for example?"
"He brushed against me, Father. Very gently."

1980

Aisling[1]

I was making my way home late one night
this summer, when I staggered
into a snow drift.

Her eyes spoke of a sloe-year,
her mouth a year of haws.[2]

Was she Aurora, or the goddess Flora,
Artemidora, or Venus bright,[3]
or Anorexia[4] who left
a lemon stain on my flannel sheet?

It's all much of a muchness.
In Belfast's Royal Victoria Hospital
a kidney machine
supports the latest hunger-striker
to have called off his fast, a saline
drip into his bag of brine.

A lick and a promise. Cuckoo spittle.
I hand my sample to Doctor Maw.
She gives me back a confident *All Clear*.

1983

Meeting the British

We met the British in the dead of winter.
The sky was lavender

1. The *aisling* (pron. "ashling") is a traditional Irish poetic form, in which the poet goes out walking and meets a beautiful lady; he learns that she is the personification of Ireland, and she promises him early deliverance from the yoke of foreign oppressors.

2. Both sloes and haws are shrubs (the blackthorn and hawthorn, respectively); both words have also been used to indicate something of little or no value, as in "not worth a haw."

3. Goddesses of classical mythology, representing, respectively, the morning, vegetation, the hunt and beauty.

4. Anorexia is no goddess, of course, but the medical condition *anorexia nervosa* in which a young woman (most commonly) denies herself food, sometimes to the point of death. Muldoon here likens the 1981 hunger strikes of the Irish Republican Army "blanket men" in British prisons (like Bobby Sands) to anorexia.

and the snow lavender-blue.
I could hear, far below,

the sound of two streams coming together
(both were frozen over)

and, no less strange,
myself calling out in French

across that forest—
clearing. Neither General Jeffrey Amherst

nor Colonel Henry Bouquet[1]
could stomach our willow-tobacco.

As for the unusual
scent when the Colonel shook out his hand—

kerchief: *C'est la lavande,*
une fleur mauve comme le ciel.[2]

They gave us six fishhooks
and two blankets embroidered with smallpox.

1987

Sleeve Notes

MICK JAGGER: *Rock music was a completely new musical form. It hadn't been around for ten years when we started doing it. Now it's forty years old.*
JANN S. WENNER: *What about your own staying power?*
MICK JAGGER: *I have a lot of energy, so I don't see it as an immediate problem.*
JANN S. WENNER: *How's your hearing?*
MICK JAGGER: *My hearing's all right. Sometimes I use earplugs because it gets too loud on my left ear.*
JANN S. WENNER: *Why your left ear?*
MICK JAGGER: *Because Keith's*[1] *standing on my left.*

—"JAGGER REMEMBERS," *Rolling Stone*, MARCH 1996

THE JIMI HENDRIX EXPERIENCE: *Are You Experienced?*[2]

"Like being driven over by a truck"
was how Pete Townshend[3] described the effect
of the wah-wah on "I Don't Live Today."

This predated by some months the pedal
Clapton used on "Tales of Brave Ulysses"[4]
And I'm taken aback (jolt upon jolt)
to think that Hendrix did it all "by hand."

1. General Jeffrey Amherst and Colonel Henry Bouquet: 18th-century British officers who served in the colonial United States.
2. It is lavender, a flower purple like the sky (French).
1. Keith Richards, the Rolling Stones' guitarist.
2. *Are You Experienced?* (1967) was Jimi Hendrix's first album; its best-known tracks are "Purple Haze" and "Fire."
3. Lead guitarist of The Who.
4. Track on the Cream album *Disraeli Gears* (see next page).

To think, moreover, that he used *four*-track
one-inch tape has (jolt upon jolt) evoked
the long, long view from the Senior Study
through the smoke, yes sir, the smoke of battle
on the fields of Laois, yes sir, and Laos.[5]

Then there was the wah-wah on "Voodoo Child
(Slight Return)" from *Electric Ladyland*.[6]

CREAM: *Disraeli Gears*[7]

As I labored over the "Georgiks and Bukolikis"[8]
I soon learned to tell thunder from dynamite.

THE BEATLES: *The Beatles*[9]

Though that was the winter when late each night
I'd put away Cicero or Caesar
and pour new milk into an old saucer
for the hedgehog which, when it showed up right

on cue, would set its nose down like that flight
back from the U.S. . . . back from the, yes sir.
back from the . . . back from the U.S.S.R. . . .
I'd never noticed the play on "*album*" and "white."[1]

THE ROLLING STONES: *Beggar's Banquet*[2]

Thanks to Miss Latimore,
I was "coming along nicely" at piano

while, compared to the whoops and wild halloos
of the local urchins,

my diction
was im-pecc-a-ble.

In next to no time I would be lost
to the milk bars

and luncheonettes
of smoky Belfast,

5. Laois is a county and a town (Portlaois) in the midlands of Ireland; Laos is a country in Southeast Asia, in which the United States conducted bombing raids during the Vietnam War (about the time that *Are You Experienced?* was released).

6. *Electric Ladyland* (1968) was Hendrix's third album and featured the tracks "All Along the Watchtower" and "Crosstown Traffic."

7. *Disraeli Gears* (1967) was the second album from British "supergroup" Cream, featuring Eric Clapton on lead guitar. The record featured "Sunshine of Your Love" and "Tales of Brave Ulysses."

8. A georgic is a poem on an agricultural theme; a bucolic is a pastoral poem.

9. The Beatles's 1968 double-album release, officially titled *The Beatles* but known colloquially as "The White Album," for its unadorned white cover. Best-known tracks: "While My Guitar Gently Weeps" (on which Eric Clapton plays an uncredited guitar solo), "Blackbird," "Helter Skelter," "Back in the USSR."

1. In the romance languages, the root *alb-* means "white."

2. *Beggar's Banquet* (1968) opens with "Sympathy for the Devil" and also features "Street Fighting Man."

where a troubadour
such as the frontman of Them[3]

had long since traded in the lute
for bass and blues harmonica.

VAN MORRISON: *Astral Weeks*[4]

Not only had I lived on Fitzroy Avenue,
I'd lived there with Madame Georgie Hyde Lees,[5]
to whom I would rather shortly be wed.
Georgie would lose out to The George and El Vino's
when I "ran away to the BBC"
as poets did, so Dylan Thomas said.

ERIC CLAPTON: *461 Ocean Boulevard*[6]

It's the house in all its whited sepulchritude[7]
(not the palm tree against which dogs piddle
as they make their way back from wherever
it was they were all night) that's really at a list.

Through the open shutters his music, scatty, skewed,
skids and skites from the neck of a bottle[8]
that might turn on him, might turn and sever
an artery, the big one that runs through his wrist.

ELVIS COSTELLO AND THE ATTRACTIONS: *My Aim Is True*[9]

Even the *reductio ad absurdum*[1]
of the *quid pro quo*[2] or "tit for tat"
killing (For "Eilis" read "Alison")

that now took over from the street riot
was not without an old-fashioned
sense of decorum, an unseemly seemliness.

WARREN ZEVON: *Excitable Boy*[3]

Somewhere between *Ocean Boulevard* and *Slowhand*[4]
I seemed to have misplaced my wedding band

3. "Them" was the name of Van Morrison's band before he left to go solo.
4. *Astral Weeks* (1968) is generally considered Morrison's greatest album, although it did not produce any hits (like his earlier "Brown-Eyed Girl" and later "Moondance").
5. Georgiana ("Georgie") Hyde-Lees married William Butler Yeats in 1917.
6. *461 Ocean Boulevard* (1974) produced the hit "I Shot the Sheriff" (his cover of a Bob Marley song). The cover shows Clapton standing in front of a whitewashed stucco house next to a wind-bent palm tree.
7. Muldoon's coinage, combining "sepulchre" (tomb) and "pulchritude" (beauty). In *Heart of Darkness*, the narrator Marlow says that the city from which he embarks, and to which he returns at the end of his journey, always reminded him of "a whited sepulchre," a phrase Jesus used to describe the Pharisees in the New Testament.
8. The smoothed neck of a bottle is often used as a "slide" in playing slide guitar; Muldoon here also probably alludes to Clapton's severe substance abuse problems of this period (including heroin addiction), although by the release of *461 Ocean Boulevard* Clapton had kicked heroin.
9. *My Aim Is True* was Costello's first album in 1977, featuring "Alison" and "Less Than Zero."
1. Reduction to absurdity (Latin), a rhetorical strategy.
2. This for that (Latin), or as Muldoon puts it, "tit for tat."
3. *Excitable Boy* (1978) features Zevon's only brush with pop success, the song "Werewolves of London."
4. Two Clapton albums: *461 Ocean Boulevard* was released in 1974 and *Slowhand* in 1977.

and taken up with waitresses and usherettes
who drank straight gins and smoked crooked cheroots.[5]

Since those were still the days when more meant less
Georgie was herself playing fast and loose
with the werewolf who, not so very long before,
had come how-howling round our kitchen door

and introduced me to Warren Zevon, whose hymns
to booty, to beasts, to bimbos, boom boom,
are inextricably part of the warp and woof
of the wild and wicked poems in *Quoof*.[6]

DIRE STRAITS: *Dire Straits*[7]

There was that time the archangel ran his thumb along the shelf
and anointed, it seemed, his own brow with soot.

BLONDIE: *Parallel Lines*[8]

It had taken all morning to rehearse
a tracking shot

with an Arriflex[9]
mounted on a gurney.

The dream of rain
on the face of a well.

"Ready when you are, Mr. DeMilledoon."[1]
Another small crowd

on the horizon.
We should have rented a Steadicam.[2]

BRUCE SPRINGSTEEN: *The River*[3]

So it was I gave up the Oona for the Susquehanna,[4]
the Shannon for the Shenandoah.

LLOYD COLE AND THE COMMOTIONS: *Easy Pieces*[5]

Though not before I'd done my stint on the Cam.
The ceilings taller than the horizon.

The in-crowd
on the outs with the likes of Milton

5. Cigars.
6. Muldoon's 1983 volume of poetry, including the poem *Aisling*.
7. Dire Straits's debut album was released in 1978 and featured their first hit, "Sultans of Swing."
8. *Parallel Lines* (1978) featured Blondie's only venture into "disco," "Heart of Glass," as well as the hit "One Way or Another."
9. A professional movie camera.

1. Muldoon here merges his name with that of legendary Hollywood director Cecil B. DeMille.
2. A consumer-oriented videocamera.
3. *The River* (1980) is seen by many purists as a "sellout," containing the pop-oriented single "Hungry Heart."
4. Muldoon replaces two Irish with two American rivers.
5. *Easy Pieces* (1985) was the title of the American release of Cole's first album (*Rattlesnakes*, 1984, in the UK).

and Spenser while Cromwell
still walked through the pouring rain.

In graveyards from Urney
to Ardglass, my countrymen laying down some *Lex*

talionis:[6] "Only the guy who's shot
gets to ride in the back of the hearse."

TALKING HEADS: *True Stories*[7]

You can take the man out of Armagh but, you may ask yourself,
can you take the Armagh out of the man in the big Armani suit?[8]

U2: *The Joshua Tree*[9]

When I went to hear them in Giants Stadium
a year or two ago, the whiff
of kef[1]
brought back the night we drove all night from Palm

Springs to Blythe.[2] No Irish lad and his lass
were so happy as we who roared
and soared
through yucca-scented air. Dawn brought a sense of loss,

faint at first, that would deepen and expand
as our own golden chariot
was showered
with Zippo[3] spears from the upper tiers of the stands.

PINK FLOYD: *A Momentary Lapse of Reason*[4]

We stopped in at a roadhouse on the way back from Lyonesse
and ordered a Tom Collins and an Old-Fashioned.
As we remounted the chariot

the poplars' synthesized alamo-alamo-eleison
was counterpointed by a redheaded woodpecker's rat-tat-tat
on a snare, a kettledrum's de dum de dum.

PAUL SIMON: *Negotiations and Love Songs*[5]

Little did I think as I knelt by a pothole

6. The principle of "an eye for an eye, a tooth for a tooth."
7. *True Stories* (1986) was the "soundtrack" for the 1986 David Byrne–directed film of the same title; it yielded the hit "Wild Wild Life."
8. In Jonathan Demme's wonderful 1984 documentary about the band, *Stop Making Sense*, David Byrne wears an enormously oversized ecru Georgio Armani suit.
9. The enduringly popular *The Joshua Tree* (1987) yielded the U2 hits, "With or Without You" and "I Still Haven't Found What I'm Looking For."
1. Marijuana.
2. A town in the Mohave Desert in southern California.
3. Disposable lighters.
4. A 1987 album featuring the track, "The Dogs of War."
5. A 1988 greatest-hits compilation of Simon's solo work, including "Mother and Child Reunion," "Still Crazy After All These Years," and many other familiar hits.

to water my elephant with the other elephant drivers,
little did I think as I chewed on some betel[6]

that I might one day be following the river
down the West Side Highway[7] in his smoke-glassed
limo complete with bodyguard-cum-chauffeur

and telling him that his lyrics must surely last:
little did I think as I chewed and chewed
that my own teeth and tongue would be eaten by rust.

LEONARD COHEN: *I'm Your Man*[8]

When I turn up the rickety old gramophone
the wow and flutter[9] from a scratched LP
summons up white walls, the table, the single bed
where Lydia Languish will meet her Le Fanu
his songs have meant far more to me
than most of the so-called poems I've read.

NIRVANA: *Bleach*[1]

I went there, too, with Mona, or Monica.
Another shot of Absolut.

"The Wild Rover" or some folk anthem
on the jukebox. Some dour

bartender. I, too, have been held fast
by those snares and nets

off the Zinc Coast, the coast of Zanzibar,
lost
able
addiction
"chin-chins"
loos,[2]
"And it's no,
nay, never, no never no more . . . "

BOB DYLAN: *Oh Mercy*[3]

All great artists are their own greatest threat,
as when they aim an industrial laser
at themselves and cut themselves back to the root

6. An East Indian pepper plant, the leaves of which are chewed.
7. The West Side Highway in Manhattan, running along the Hudson River.
8. A 1988 album featuring the title cut and "First We Take Manhattan."
9. The distortion introduced in playback by a phonograph.
1. *Bleach*, Nirvana's first record, was released on Seattle independent label Sub Pop in 1989 and features the hit single "About a Girl."
2. Toilets.
3. *Oh Mercy* (1989) is thought by many to be Dylan's best album of a rather weak decade for him. It includes the track "Ring Them Bells."

so that, with spring, we can never ever be sure
if they shake from head to foot
from an orgasm, you see, sir, or a seizure.

R.E.M.: *Automatic for the People*[4]

Like the grasping for air by an almighty mite
who's suffering from a bad case of the colic.

THE ROLLING STONES: *Voodoo Lounge*[5]

Giants Stadium again . . . Again the scent of drugs
struggling through rain so heavy some young Turks
would feel obliged to butt-hole
surf[6] across those vast puddles

on the field. Some might have burned damp faggots[7]
on a night like this, others faked
the ho-ho-hosannas and the hallelujahs
with their "*Tout passe, tout casse, tout lasse.*"[8]

The Stones, of course, have always found the way
of setting a burning brand
to a petrol-soaked stack of hay

and making a "Thou Shalt"
of a "Thou Shalt Not." The sky over the Meadowlands[9]
was still aglow as I drove home to my wife and child.

1998

Nuala Ní Dhomhnaill
b. 1952

Nuala Ní Dhomhnaill was born in a coal mining region in England, to Irish parents; she was sent at the age of five, however, to live with relatives in the Gaeltacht (Irish-speaking area) on the Dingle Peninsula in West Kerry—"dropped into it cold-turkey," she says. She thus grew up bilingual, speaking English in the home, Irish out of it. Ní Dhomhnaill quickly learned that translation always picks up and leaves behind meaning; she tells this story: "I recall as a child someone asking my name in Irish. The question roughly translates as 'Who do you belong to?' Still most fluent in English, I replied, 'I don't belong to anybody. I belong to myself.' That became quite a joke in the village." In some ways, Ní Dhomhnaill's poetic career has been the process of discovering who, and whose, she is—and making those discoveries through the medium of the Irish language; her name itself, pronounced *nu-AH-la ne GOE-ne*, sounds different than it looks to English eyes.

4. *Automatic for the People* (1992) was R.E.M.'s biggest critical and popular success; it contained the hits "Everybody Hurts," "Drive," and "Man on the Moon," about the late comedian Andy Kaufmann.
5. *Voodoo Lounge* (1994) marked the thirtieth anniversary of the Rolling Stone's career as a rock band.
6. Muldoon plays on the name of the Texas-based band Butthole Surfers.
7. Cigarettes.
8. Everything passes; everything breaks; everything tires ("all is vanity") (French).
9. The Meadowlands is a popular sports complex and rock venue in New Jersey.

"The individual psyche is a rather puny thing," she has said; "One's interior life dries up without the exchange with tradition." Ní Dhomhnaill's fruitful exchange with the Irish literary tradition has resulted in a poetry rich in the imagery of Irish folklore and mythology, and pregnant with the sense of contradiction and irony that undergirds Irish writing ("We [Celts] are truly comfortable only with ambiguity," she says). Ní Dhomhnaill's poetry in Irish includes the prize-winning volumes *An Dealg Droighin* (1981) and *Féar Suaithinseach* (1984), as well as a selection of poems from her volume *Feis* translated into English by the poet Paul Muldoon. The *Irish Literary Supplement* has called her "the most widely known and acclaimed Gaelic poet of the century"; by continuing to write in Irish, she has helped make it a viable language for modern poetry. Ní Dhomhnaill lives in Dublin and has taught at University College, Cork.

Feeding a Child[1]

From honey-dew of milking
from cloudy heat of beestings
the sun rises up the back
of bare hills,
a guinea gold
to put in your hand,
my own.
You drink your fill from my breast
and fall back asleep
into a lasting dream
laughter in your face.
What is going through your head
you who are but
a fortnight on earth?

Do you know day from night
that the great early ebb
announces spring tide?
That the boats
are on deep ocean,
where live the seals and fishes
and the great whales,
and are coming hand over hand
each by seven oars manned?
That your small boats swims
óró[2] in the bay
with the flippered peoples
and the small sea-creatures
she slippery-sleek
from stem to bow
stirring sea-sand up
sinking sea-foam down.

Of all these things are you
ignorant?
As my breast is explored

1. Translated by Michael Hartnett.

2. Soothing nonsense sound in Irish.

by your small hand
you grunt with pleasure
smiling and senseless.
I look into your face child
not knowing if you know
your herd of cattle
graze in the land of giants
trespassing and thieving
and that soon you will hear
the fee-fie-fo-fum
sounding in your ear.

You are my piggy
who went to market
who stayed at home
who got bread and butter
who got none.
There's one good bite in you
but hardly two—
I like your flesh
but not the broth thereof.
And who are the original patterns
of the heroes and giants
if not you and I?

1986

Parthenogenesis[1]

Once, a lady of the Ó Moores
(married seven years without a child)
swam in the sea in summertime.
She swam well, and the day
was fine as Ireland ever saw
not even a puff of wind in the air
all the bay calm, all the sea smooth—
a sheet of glass—supple, she struck out
with strength for the breaking waves
and frisked, elated by the world.
She ducked beneath the surface and there saw
what seemed a shadow, like a man's.
And every twist and turn she made
the shadow did the same
and came close enough to touch.
Heart jumped and sound stopped in her mouth
her pulses ran and raced, sides near burst.
The lower currents with their ice
pierced her to the bone

1. Translated by Michael Hartnett. "Parthenogenesis" is the scientific term for virgin birth.

and the noise of the abyss numbed all her limbs
then scales grew on her skin. . .
the lure of the quiet dreamy undersea. . .
desire to escape to sea and shells. . .
the seaweed tresses where at last
her bones changed into coral
and time made atolls of her arms,
pearls of her eyes in deep long sleep,
at rest in a nest of weed,
secure as feather beds. . .
But stop!
Her heroic heritage was there,
she rose with speedy, threshing feet
and made in desperation for the beach:
with nimble supple strokes she made the sand.
Near death until the day,
some nine months later
she gave birth to a boy.
She and her husband so satisfied,
so full of love for this new son
forgot the shadow in the sea
and did not see what only the midwife saw—
stalks of sea-tangle in the boy's hair
small shellfish and sea-ribbons
and his two big eyes
as blue and limpid as lagoons.
A poor scholar passing by
who found lodging for the night
saw the boy's eyes never closed
in dark or light and when all the world slept
he asked the boy beside the fire
"Who are your people?" Came the prompt reply
"Sea People."

This same tale is told in the West
but the woman's an Ó Flaherty
and tis the same in the South
where the lady's called Ó Shea:
this tale is told on every coast.
But whoever she was I want to say
that the fear she felt
when the sea-shadow followed her
is the same fear that vexed
the young heart of the Virgin
when she heard the angels' sweet bell
and in her womb was made flesh
by all accounts
the Son of the Living God.

1986

Labasheedy (The Silken Bed)[1]

I'd make a bed for you
in Labasheedy
in the tall grass
under the wrestling trees
where your skin
would be silk upon silk
in the darkness
when the moths are coming down.

Skin which glistens
shining over your limbs
like milk being poured
from jugs at dinnertime;
your hair is a herd of goats
moving over rolling hills,
hills that have high cliffs
and two ravines.

And your damp lips
would be as sweet as sugar
at evening and we walking
by the riverside
with honeyed breezes
blowing over the Shannon
and the fuchsias bowing down to you
one by one.

The fuchsias bending low
their solemn heads
in obeisance to the beauty
in front of them
I would pick a pair of flowers
as pendant earrings
to adorn you
like a bride in shining clothes.

O I'd make a bed for you
in Labasheedy,
in the twilight hour
with evening falling slow
and what a pleasure it would be
to have our limbs entwine
wrestling
while the moths are coming down.

1986

1. Translated by the author.

As for the Quince[1]

There came this bright young thing
with a Black & Decker
and cut down my quince-tree.
I stood with my mouth hanging open
while one by one
she trimmed off the branches.

When my husband got home that evening
and saw what had happened
he lost the rag,
as you might imagine.
"Why didn't you stop her?
What would she think
if I took the Black & Decker
round to her place
and cut down a quince-tree
belonging to her?
What would she make of that?"

Her ladyship came back next morning
while I was at breakfast.
She enquired about his reaction.
I told her straight
that he was wondering how she'd feel
if he took a Black & Decker
round to her house
and cut down a quince-tree of hers,
etcetera etcetera.

"O," says she, "that's very interesting."
There was a stress on the "very."
She lingered over the "ing."
She was remarkably calm and collected.

These are the times that are in it, so,
all a bit topsy-turvy.
The bottom falling out of my belly
as if I had got a kick up the arse
or a punch in the kidneys.
A fainting-fit coming over me
that took the legs from under me
and left me so zonked
I could barely lift a finger
till Wednesday.

As for the quince, it was safe and sound
and still somehow holding its ground.

1988

1. Translated by Paul Muldoon.

Why I Choose to Write in Irish, The Corpse That Sits Up and Talks Back[1]

Not so long ago I telephoned my mother about some family matter. "So what are you writing these days?" she asked, more for the sake of conversation than anything else. "Oh, an essay for *The New York Times*," I said, as casually as possible. "What is it about?" she asked. "About what it is like to write in Irish," I replied. There was a good few seconds' pause on the other end of the line; then, "Well, I hope you'll tell them that it is mad." End of conversation. I had got my comeuppance. And from my mother, who was the native speaker of Irish in our family, never having encountered a single word of English until she went to school at the age of 6, and well up in her teens before she realized that the name they had at home for a most useful item was actually two words—"safety pin"—and that they were English. Typical.

But really not so strange. Some time later I was at a reception at the American Embassy in Dublin for two of their writers, Toni Morrison and Richard Wilbur. We stood in line and took our buffet suppers along to the nearest available table. An Irishwoman across from me asked what I did. Before I had time to open my mouth her partner butted in: "Oh, Nuala writes poetry in Irish." And what did I write about? she asked. Again before I had time to reply he did so for me: "She writes poems of love and loss, and I could quote you most of them by heart." This was beginning to get up my nose, and so I attempted simultaneously to deflate him and to go him one better. "Actually," I announced, "I think the only things worth writing about are the biggies: birth, death and the most important thing in between, which is sex." "Oh," his friend said to me archly, "and is there a word for sex in Irish?"

I looked over at the next table, where Toni Morrison was sitting, and I wondered if a black writer in America had to put up with the likes of that, or its equivalent. Here I was in my own country, having to defend the official language of the state from a compatriot who obviously thought it was an accomplishment to be ignorant of it. Typical, and yet maybe not so strange.

Let me explain. Irish (as it is called in the Irish Constitution; to call it Gaelic is not P.C. at the moment, but seen as marginalizing) is the Celtic language spoken by a small minority of native speakers principally found in rural pockets on the western seaboard. These Irish-speaking communities are known as the "Gaeltacht," and are the last remnants of an earlier historical time when the whole island was Irish-speaking, or one huge "Gaeltacht." The number of Irish speakers left in these areas who use the language in most of their daily affairs is a hotly debated point, and varies from 100,000 at the most optimistic estimate to 20,000 at the most conservative. For the sake of a round number let us take it to be 60,000, or about 2 percent of the population of the Republic of Ireland.

Because of the effort of the Irish Revival movement, and of the teaching of Irish in the school system, however, the language is also spoken with varying degrees of frequency and fluency by a considerably larger number of people who have learned it as a second language. So much so that census figures over the last few decades have consistently indicated that up to one million people, or 30 percent of the population of the Republic, claim to be speakers of Irish. To this can be added the 146,000 peo-

1. Published in the *New York Times Book Review*, January 1995.

ple in the Six Counties of Northern Ireland who also are competent in Irish. This figure of one million speakers is, of course, grossly misleading and in no way reflects a widespread use of the language in everyday life. Rather it can be seen as a reflection of general good will toward the language, as a kind of wishful thinking. Nevertheless that good will is important.

The fact that the Irish language, and by extension its literature, has a precarious status in Ireland at the moment is a development in marked contrast to its long and august history. I believe writing in Irish is the oldest continuous literary activity in Western Europe, starting in the fifth century and flourishing in a rich and varied manuscript tradition right down through the Middle Ages. During this time the speakers of any invading language, such as Norse, Anglo-Norman and English, were assimilated, becoming "more Irish than the Irish themselves." But the Battle of Kinsale in 1601, in which the British routed the last independent Irish princes, and the ensuing catastrophes of the turbulent 17th century, including forced population transfers, destroyed the social underpinning of the language. Its decline was much accelerated by the great famine of the mid-19th century; most of the one million who died of starvation and the millions who left on coffin ships for America were Irish speakers. The fact that the fate of emigration stared most of the survivors in the eye further speeded up the language change to English—after all, "What use was your Irish to you over in Boston?"

The indigenous high culture became the stuff of the speech of fishermen and small farmers, and this is the language that I learned in West Kerry in the 1950's at the age of 5 in a situation of total immersion, when I was literally and figuratively farmed out to my aunt in the parish of Ventry. Irish is a language of enormous elasticity and emotional sensitivity; of quick and hilarious banter and a welter of references both historical and mythological; it is an instrument of imaginative depth and scope, which has been tempered by the community for generations until it can pick up and sing out every hint of emotional modulation that can occur between people. Many international scholars rhapsodize that this speech of ragged peasants seems always on the point of bursting into poetry. The pedagogical accident that had me learn this language at an early age can only be called a creative one.

The Irish of the Revival, or "book Irish," was something entirely different, and I learned it at school. Although my first literary love affair was with the Munster poets, Aodhagán Ó Rathaille and Eoghan Rua Ó Suilleabháin, and I had learned reams and reams of poetry that wasn't taught at school, when I myself came to write it didn't dawn on me that I could possibly write in Irish. The overriding ethos had got even to me. Writing poetry in Irish somehow didn't seem to be intellectually credible. So my first attempts, elegies on the deaths of Bobby Kennedy and Martin Luther King published in the school magazine, were all in English. They were all right, but even I could see that there was something wrong with them.

Writing Irish poetry in English suddenly seemed a very stupid thing to be doing. So I switched language in mid-poem and wrote the very same poem in Irish, and I could see immediately that it was much better. I sent it in to a competition in *The Irish Times*, where it won a prize, and that was that. I never looked back.

I had chosen my language, or more rightly, perhaps, at some very deep level, the language had chosen me. If there is a level to our being that for want of any other word for it I might call "soul" (and I believe there is), then for some reason that I can never understand, the language that my soul speaks, and the place it comes from, is Irish. At 16 I had made my choice. And that was that. It still is. I have no other.

But if the actual choice to write poetry in Irish was easy, then nothing else about it actually is, especially the hypocritical attitude of the state. On the one hand, Irish is enshrined as a nationalistic token (the ceremonial *cúpla focal*—"few words"—at the beginning and end of speeches by politicians, broadcasters and even airline crews is an example). On the other hand, it would not be an exaggeration to speak of the state's indifference, even downright hostility, to Irish speakers in its failure to provide even the most basic services in Irish for those who wish to go about their everyday business in that language.

"The computer cannot understand Irish" leads the excuses given by the state to refuse to conduct its business in Irish, even in the Gaeltacht areas. Every single service gained by Irish speakers has been fought for bitterly. Thus the "Gaelscoileanna," or Irish schools, have been mostly started by groups of parents, often in the very teeth of fierce opposition from the Department of Education. And the only reason we have a single Irish radio station is that a civil rights group started a pirate station 20 years ago in the West and shamed the Government into establishing this vital service. An Irish television channel is being mooted[2] at present, but I'll believe it when I see it.

You might expect at least the cultural nationalists and our peers writing in English to be on our side. Not so. A recent television documentary film about Thomas Kinsella begins with the writer intoning the fact that history has been recorded in Irish from the fifth century to the 19th. Then there is a pregnant pause. We wait for a mention of the fact that life, experience, sentient consciousness, even history is being recorded in literature in Irish in the present day. We wait in vain. By an antiquarian sleight of hand it is implied that Irish writers in English are now the natural heirs to a millennium and a half of writing in Irish. The subtext of the film is that Irish is dead.

So what does that make me, and the many other writers of the large body of modern literature in Irish? A walking ghost? A linguistic specter?

Mind you, it is invidious of me to single out Thomas Kinsella; this kind of insidious "bad faith" about modern literature in Irish is alive and rampant among many of our fellow writers in English. As my fellow poet in Irish, Biddy Jenkinson, has said, "We have been pushed into an ironic awareness that by our passage we would convenience those who will be uneasy in their Irishness as long as there is a living Gaelic tradition to which they do not belong." Now let them make their peace with the tradition if they wish to, I don't begrudge them a line of it. But I'll be damned if their cultural identity is procured at the expense of my existence, or of that of my language.

I can well see how it suits some people to see Irish-language literature as the last rictus[3] of a dying beast. As far as they are concerned, the sooner the language lies down and dies, the better, so they can cannibalize it with greater equanimity, peddling their "ethnic chic" with nice little translations "from the Irish." Far be it from them to make the real effort it takes to learn the living language. I dare say they must be taken somewhat aback when the corpse that they have long since consigned to choirs of angels, like a certain Tim Finnegan,[4] sits up and talks back to them.

2. Debated.
3. Gasp.
4. In the vaudeville song *Tim Finnegan's Wake,* the hero takes a drunken fall and dies. At his wake, however, whiskey is spilled over his body and he comes back to life. James Joyce uses this story as the central structure for *Finnegans Wake*.

The fault is not always one-sided. The Gaels (Irish-language writers) often fell prey to what Terence Browne, a literary historian, has called an "atmosphere of national self-righteousness and cultural exclusiveness," and their talent did not always equal the role imposed on them. Nevertheless, long after the emergence of a high standard of literature in Irish with Seán Ó Riordáin, Máirtin Ó Direáin and Máire Mhac an tSaoi in poetry, and Máirtin Ó Cadhain in prose, writing in Irish was conspicuously absent from anthologies in the 1950's and 60's. Even as late as the 70's one of our "greats," Seán Ó Riordáin, could hear on the radio two of his co-writers in English saying how "poetry in Ireland had been quiescent in the 50's," thus consigning to nothingness the great work that he and his fellow poets in Irish had produced during that very decade. After a lifetime devoted to poetry, is it any wonder that he died in considerable grief and bitterness?

As for the cultural nationalists, Irish was never the language of nationalist mobilization. Unlike other small countries where nationalism rose throughout the 19th century, in Ireland it was religion rather than language that mostly colored nationalism. Daniel O'Connell, the Liberator, a native-Irish-speaking Kerryman, used to address his monster mass meetings from the 1820's to the 40's in English, even though this language was not understood by 70 percent of the people he was addressing. Why? Because it was at the reporters over from *The Times* of London and their readers that his words were being primarily directed. It is particularly painful to recall that while nationalism was a major motivator in developing modern literary languages out of such varied tongues as Norwegian, Hungarian, Finnish and Estonian, during that very same period the high literary culture of Irish was being reduced to the language of peasants. By the time the revival began, the damage had already been done, and the language was already in irreversible decline (spoken by only 14.5 percent in 1880). The blatant myopia of the cultural nationalists is still alive and glaringly obvious in the disgraceful underrepresentation of Irish in the recently published three-volume *Field Day Anthology of Irish Writing*.

It should not be surprising, then, that we poets and fiction writers in Irish who are included in the anthology feel as if we are being reduced to being exotic background, like Irish Muzak. Thus the cultural nationalists, without granting Irish the intellectual credibility of rational discourse or the popular base of the oral tradition, enshrine it instead as the repository of their own utopian fantasies; pristine, changeless, "creative," but otherwise practically useless.

How does all this affect me, as a poet writing in Irish? Well, inasmuch as I am human and frail and prone to vanity and clamoring for attention, of course it disturbs me to be misunderstood, misrepresented and finally all but invisible in my own country. I get depressed, I grumble and complain, I stand around in rooms muttering darkly. Still and all, at some very deep and fundamental level it matters not one whit. All I ever wanted was to be left alone so that I could go on writing poetry in Irish. I still remember a time when I had an audience I could count on the fingers of one hand. I was perfectly prepared for that. I still am.

But it has been gratifying to reach a broader audience through the medium of translations, especially among the one million who profess some knowledge of Irish. Many of them probably had good Irish when they left school but have had no chance of using it since for want of any functional context where it would make sense to use the language. I particularly like it when my poetry in English translation sends them back to the originals in Irish, and when they then go on to pick up the long-lost threads of the language that is so rightly theirs. I also find it pleasant and vivifying to make an occasional trip abroad and to reach a wider audience by means of dual-language readings and publications.

But my primary audience is those who read my work in Irish only. A print run for a book of poems in Irish is between 1,000 and 1,500 copies. That doesn't sound like much until you realize that that number is considered a decent run by many poets in English in Ireland, or for that matter even in Britain or America, where there's a much larger population.

The very ancientness of the Irish literary tradition is also a great source of strength to me as a writer. This works at two levels, one that is mainly linguistic and prosodic and another that is mainly thematic and inspirational. At the linguistic level, Old Irish, though undoubtedly very difficult, is much closer to Modern Irish than, say, Anglo-Saxon is to Modern English. Anyone like me with a basic primary degree in the language and a bit of practice can make a fair job of reading most of the medieval texts in the original.

Thematically too, the older literature is a godsend, though I am only now slowly beginning to assess its unique possibilities to a modern writer. There are known to be well over 4,000 manuscripts in Ireland and elsewhere of material from Old to Modern Irish. Apart from the great medieval codices, only about 50 other manuscripts date from before 1650. Nevertheless, the vast majority of the manuscripts painstakingly copied down after this time are exemplars of much earlier manuscripts that have since been lost. A lot of this is catalogued in ways that are unsatisfactory for our time.

Many items of enormous psychological and sexual interest, for example, are described with the bias of the last century as "indecent and obscene tales, unsuitable for publication." On many such manuscripts human eye has not set sight since they were so described. In addition, most scholarly attention has been paid to pre-Norman-Conquest material as the repository of the unsullied wellsprings of the native soul (those cultural nationalists again!), with the result that the vast area of post-Conquest material has been unfairly neglected. The main advantage of all this material to me is that it is proof of the survival until even a very late historical date of a distinct *Weltanschauung* [worldview] radically different from the Anglo mentality that has since eclipsed it.

Because of a particular set of circumstances, Irish fell out of history just when the modern mentality was about to take off. So major intellectual changes like the Reformation, the Renaissance, the Enlightenment, Romanticism and Victorian prudery have never occurred in it, as they did in the major European languages.

One consequence is that the attitude to the body enshrined in Irish remains extremely open and uncoy. It is almost impossible to be "rude" or "vulgar" in Irish. The body, with its orifices and excretions, is not treated in a prudish manner but is accepted as *an nádúir*, or "nature," and becomes a source of repartee and laughter rather than anything to be ashamed of. Thus little old ladies of quite impeccable and unimpeachable moral character tell risqué stories with gusto and panache. Is there a word for sex in Irish, indeed! Is there an Eskimo word for snow?

By now I must have spent whole years of my life burrowing in the department of folklore at University College, Dublin, and yet there are still days when my hands shake with emotion holding manuscripts. Again, this material works on me on two levels. First is when I revel in the well-turned phrase or nuance or retrieve a word that may have fallen into disuse. To turn the pages of these manuscripts is to hear the voices of my neighbors and my relatives—all the fathers and grandfathers and uncles come to life again. The second interest is more thematic. This material is genuinely ineffable, like nothing else on earth.

Indeed, there is a drawer in the index entitled "Neacha neamhbeo agus nithe nach bhfuil ann" ("Unalive beings and things that don't exist"). Now I am not the greatest empiricist in the world but this one has even me stumped. Either they exist or they don't exist. But if they don't exist why does the card index about them stretch the length of my arm? Yet that is the whole point of this material and its most enduring charm. Do these beings exist? Well, they do and they don't. You see, they are beings from *an saol eile*, the "otherworld," which in Irish is a concept of such impeccable intellectual rigor and credibility that it is virtually impossible to translate into English, where it all too quickly becomes fey and twee and "fairies-at-the-bottom-of-the-garden."

The way so-called depth psychologists go on about the subconscious nowadays you'd swear they had invented it, or at the very least stumbled on a ghostly and ghastly continent where mankind had never previously set foot. Even the dogs in the street in West Kerry know that the "otherworld" exists, and that to be in and out of it constantly is the most natural thing in the world.

This constant tension between reality and fantasy, according to Jeffrey Gantz, the translator of *Early Irish Myths and Sagas*, is characteristic of all Celtic art, but manifests itself particularly in the literature of Ireland. Mr Gantz believes that it is not accidental to the circumstances of the literary transmission but is rather an innate characteristic, a gift of the Celts. It means that the "otherworld" is not simply an anticipated joyful afterlife; it is also—even primarily—an alternative to reality.

This easy interaction with the imaginary means that you don't have to have a raving psychotic breakdown to enter the "otherworld." The deep sense in the language that something exists beyond the ego-envelope is pleasant and reassuring, but it is also a great source of linguistic and imaginative playfulness, even on the most ordinary and banal of occasions.

Let's say I decide some evening to walk up to my aunt's house in West Kerry. She hears me coming. She knows it is me because she recognizes my step on the cement pavement. Still, as I knock lightly on the door she calls out, "An de bheoaibh nó de mhairbh thu?" ("Are you of the living or of the dead?") Because the possibility exists that you could be either, and depending on which category you belong to, an entirely different protocol would be brought into play. This is all a joke, of course, but a joke that is made possible by the imaginative richness of the language itself.

I am not constructing an essentialist argument here, though I do think that because of different circumstances, mostly historical, the strengths and weaknesses of Irish are different from those of English, and the imaginative possibilities of Irish are, from a poet's perspective, one of its greatest strengths. But this is surely as true of, say, Bengali as it is of Irish. It is what struck me most in the Nobel Prize acceptance speech made by the Yiddish writer Isaac Bashevis Singer. When often asked why he wrote in a dead language, Singer said he was wont to reply that he wrote mostly about ghosts, and that is what ghosts speak, a dead language.

Singer's reply touched a deep chord with his Irish audience. It reminded us that the precariousness of Irish is not an Irish problem alone. According to the linguist Michael Krause in *Language* magazine, minority languages in the English language sphere face a 90 percent extinction rate between now and some time in the next century. Therefore, in these days when a major problem is the growth of an originally Anglo-American, but now genuinely global, pop monoculture that reduces everything to the level of the most stupendous boredom, I would think that the preservation of minority languages like Irish, with their unique and unrepeatable way of looking at the world, would be as important for human beings as the preservation of the remaining tropical rain forests is for biological diversity.

Recently, on a short trip to Kerry with my three daughters, I stayed with my brother and his wife in the old house he is renovating on the eastern end of the Dingle peninsula, under the beetling brow of Cathair Chonroi promontory fort. My brother said he had something special to show us, so one day we trooped up the mountain to Derrymore Glen. Although the area is now totally denuded of any form of growth other than lichens and sphagnum moss, the name itself is a dead giveaway: Derrymore from *Doire Mór* in Irish, meaning "Large Oak Grove."

A more desolate spot you cannot imagine, yet halfway up the glen, in the crook of a hanging valley, intricate and gnarled, looking for all the world like a giant bonsai, was a single survivor, one solitary oak tree. Only the top branches were producing leaves, it was definitely on its last legs and must have been at least 200 to 300 years old. How it had survived the massive human and animal depredation of the countryside that occurred during that time I do not know, but somehow it had.

It was very much a *bile*, a sacred tree, dear to the Celts. A fairy tree. A magic tree. We were all very moved by it. Not a single word escaped us, as we stood in the drizzle. At last Ayse, my 10-year-old, broke the silence. "It would just give you an idea," she said, "of what this place was like when it really was a '*Doire Mór*' and covered with oak trees." I found myself humming the air of *Cill Cais*, that lament for both the great woods of Ireland and the largess of the Gaelic order that they had come to symbolize:

Cad a dhéanfaimid feasta gan adhmad?
Tá deireadh na gcoillte ar lár.
Níl trácht ar Chill Cais ná a theaghlach
is ní chlingfear a chling go brách.

What will we do now without wood
Now that the woods are laid low?
Cill Cais or its household are not mentioned
and the sound of its bell is no more.

A week later, back in Dublin, that question is still ringing in the air. I am waiting for the children to get out of school and writing my journal in Irish in a modern shopping mall in a Dublin suburb. Not a single word of Irish in sight on sign or advertisement, nor a single sound of it in earshot. All around me are well-dressed and articulate women. I am intrigued by snatches of animated conversation, yet I am conscious of a sense of overwhelming loss. I think back to the lonely hillside, and to Ayse. This is the answer to the question in the song. This is what we will do without wood.

At some level, it doesn't seem too bad. People are warm and not hungry. They are expressing themselves without difficulty in English. They seem happy. I close my notebook with a snap and set off in the grip of that sudden pang of despair that is always lurking in the ever-widening rents of the linguistic fabric of minority languages. Perhaps my mother is right. Writing in Irish is mad. English is a wonderful language, and it also has the added advantage of being very useful for putting bread on the table. Change is inevitable, and maybe it is part of the natural order of things that some languages should die while others prevail.

And yet, and yet . . . I know this will sound ridiculously romantic and sentimental. Yet not by bread alone. . . . We raise our eyes to the hills. . . . We throw our bread upon the waters.[5] There are mythical precedents. Take for instance Moses' mother, consider her predicament. She had the choice of giving up her son to the Egyptian soldiery, to have him cleft in two before her very eyes, or to send him down the Nile in a basket, a tasty dinner for crocodiles. She took what under the circumstances must have seemed very much like *rogha an dá dhiogha* ("the lesser of two evils") and Exodus and the annals of Jewish history tell the rest of the story, and are the direct results of an action that even as I write is still working out its inexorable destiny. I know it is wrong to compare small things with great, yet my final answer to why I write in Irish is this:

Ceist 'na Teangan

Cuirim mo dhóchas ar snámh
i mbáidn' teangan
faoi mar a leagfá naíonán
i gcliabhán
a bheadh fite fuaite
de dhuilleoga feileastraim
is bitiúman agus pic
bheith cuimilte lena thóin

ansan é a leagadh síos
i measc na ngiolcach
is coigeal na mban sí
le taobh na habhann,
féachaint n'fheadaráis
cá dtabharfaidh an sruth é,
féachaint, dála Mhaoise,
an bhfóirfidh iníon Fharoinn?

The Language Issue

I place my hope on the water
in this little boat
of the language, the way a body might put
an infant

in a basket of intertwined
iris leaves,
its underside proofed
with bitumen and pitch,

then set the whole thing down amidst
the sedge
and bulrushes by the edge
of a river

5. Echoing three biblical affirmations of the need to look beyond immediate material wants (Matthew 4.4, Psalm 121.1, Ecclesiastes 11.1). In the first passage cited, Jesus is fasting in the wilderness and rejects Satan's tempting suggestion that he turn stones into bread: "he answered, 'It is written, "Man shall not live by bread alone, but by every word that proceeds from the mouth of God." ' "

only to have it borne hither and thither,
not knowing where it might end up;
in the lap, perhaps,
of some Pharaoh's daughter.[6]

1996

Gwyneth Lewis
b. 1959

Born in Cardiff, Wales, Gwyneth Lewis attended a bilingual school in Pontypridd and went on to Cambridge University, where she studied English. She continued her studies in the United States at Harvard and Columbia, and worked as a freelance journalist in New York before returning to Britain to write for television. Lewis writes in Welsh, her first language, as well as English, and she has published five volumes of poetry in both languages. Her first collection in English, *Parables and Faxes* (1995), won the Aldeburgh Poetry Festival Prize and was short-listed for the Forward Prize for Best First Collection. Her second book, *Zero Gravity* (1998), was short-listed for the Forward Poetry Prize for Best Poetry Collection of the Year, and was inspired in part by the work of astronaut Joe Tanner, Lewis's cousin, in repairing the Hubble telescope in 1997. *Y Llofrudd Iaith* (*The Language Murderer*, 2000) was awarded the Arts Council of Wales Book of the Year Award. In 2002, Lewis published her first nonfiction book, *Sunbathing in the Rain: A Cheerful Book on Depression*, an autobiographical account of her struggle with and triumph over depression. She is a fellow of the Royal Society of Literature. Her latest book of poetry is *Keeping Mum* (2003), and she is currently using a grant from the National Endowment for Science, Technology, and the Arts to conduct research on ports historically linked with Cardiff. In 2004, Lewis was named the first National Poet of Wales.

Therapy

Did you hear the one about the shrink
who let obsessive-compulsives clean his house
as if their illnesses were his?
They made good caretakers, stayed up all night
rattling doorknobs, testing locks,
domesticated poltergeists.

He started an amateur dramatics group
with the psychotics, who had a ball
in togas, till they burnt down the hall.
Chronic depressives are always apart,
so he'd check them through his telescope,
placed them in poses from classical art
and, of course, they'd hardly ever move,
added a certain style to the grounds.

6. As happened with Moses when the Israelites were enslaved in Egypt (Exodus 2). Fearing their growing numbers, Pharaoh had ordered all male Hebrew infants to be drowned in the Nile; Moses's mother instead set him adrift in a reed basket, which was found by the Pharaoh's daughter, who adopted him and raised him as an Egyptian. As an adult, Moses led the Israelites out of Egypt to the Promised Land.

He recorded Tourette patients' sounds,
sold them to pop groups as backing tracks.
Whenever possible, he'd encourage love
between staff and patients. He had a knack

with manics, whom he sent out to shop
for all his parties, gave tarot cards
to schizoids so they could read their stars.
Perhaps he was flip with other people's pain
but his patients loved him and his hope
that two or three madnesses might make one sane.

2002

Mother Tongue

"I started to translate in seventy-three
in the schoolyard. For a bit of fun
to begin with—the occasional 'fuck'
for the bite of another language's smoke
at the back of my throat, its bitter chemicals.
Soon I was hooked on whole sentences
behind the shed, and lessons in Welsh
seemed very boring. I started on printed,
Jeeves & Wooster, Dick Francis, James Bond,
in Welsh covers. That worked for a while
until Mam discovered Jean Plaidy inside
a Welsh concordance one Sunday night.
There were ructions: a language, she screamed,
should be for a lifetime. Too late for me.
I was snorting Simenon
and Flaubert. Had to read much more
for any effect. One night I OD'd
after reading far too much Proust.
I came to, but it scared me. For a while
I went Welsh-only but it was bland
and my taste was changing. Before too long
I was back on translating, found that three
languages weren't enough. The 'ch'
in German was easy, Rilke a buzz. . .
For a language fetishist like me
sex is part of the problem. Umlauts make me sweat,
so I need a multilingual man
but they're rare in West Wales and tend to be
married already. If only I'd kept
myself much purer, with simpler tastes,
the Welsh might be living. . .
Detective, you speak
Russian, I hear, and Japanese.
Could you whisper some softly?
I'm begging you. Please. . . ."

2003

Robert Crawford

b. 1959

Born in Bellshill, Scotland, Robert Crawford grew up in and around Glasgow. He studied English at the University of Glasgow and went on to do his postgraduate work at Balliol College, Oxford. He is currently a professor of modern Scottish literature and head of the School of English at the University of St. Andrews. Crawford has published several volumes of poetry, including *Talkies* (1994), *Spirit Machines* (1999), and *The Tip of My Tongue* (2003); his most recent is *Full Volume* (2008). In addition, he has written a number of critical works, among them *The Savage and the City in the Works of T. S. Eliot* (1987) and *Devolving English Literature* (1992). Much of Crawford's earlier verse is written in Scots, demonstrating his interest in reclaiming Scots as a language suitable for poetry. Through his poetry, he looks at Scotland as it must appear to tourists and adds to the picture of a lovely, wild country the image of a postindustrial Scotland, where connection to the Internet has made the country's small physical size unimportant. In his later work, Crawford considers communication beyond language, as influenced by gender, aging, and awareness of death, and the inescapable physicality of one's body.

The Saltcoats Structuralists

(for Douglas Cairns)

They found the world's new structure was a binary
Gleaming opposition of two rails

That never crossed but ran on parallel
Straight out of Cairo. From small boys

On Platform One who listened to the great
Schola cantorum[1] of connecting rods

Dreamed-up by Scots-tongued engineers, they went on
To tame the desert, importing locomotives

From a distant Firth. New wives came out, and one,
Shipwrecked off Ailsa Craig, returned to Glasgow,

Caught the next boat; her servants had her wardrobe
Replaced in just four hours from the city shops.

Scotsmen among colonial expats
They learned RP, embarrassing their families

In Ayrshire villages where they talked non-stop
About biggah boilahs, crankshawfts. Nicknamed "The Pharaohs,"

They never understood the deconstruction
Visited on Empire when their reign in Egypt

Ran out of steam. They first-classed back to Saltcoats,
Post-Nasser,[2] on slow commuter diesels

1. Singing school (Latin).

2. Gamel Abdel-Nasser, President of Egypt, 1956–1970.

They passed the bare brick shells of loco-sheds
Like great robbed tombs. They eyed the proud slave faces

Of laid-off engineering workers, lost
In the electronics revolution. Along the prom

They'd holidayed on in childhood, with exotic walking sticks,
History in Residence, they moved

In Sophoclean raincoats. People laughed
At a world still made from girders, an Iron Age

Of Queen Elizabeths, pea-soupers, footplates,
And huge black toilet cisterns named "St Mungo."

Kids zapped the videogames in big arcades
Opposite Arran. Local people found

New energy sources, poems didn't rhyme.
The Pharaohs' grandchildren's accents sounded to them

Wee hell-taught ploughmen's. In slow seafront caffs
They felt poststructuralism, tanged with salt.

1990

Alba Einstein

When proof of Einsten's Glaswegian[1] birth
First hit the media everything else was dropped:
Logie Baird,[2] Dundee painters, David Hume[3]—all
Got the big E. Physics documentaries
Became peak-viewing; Scots publishers hurled awa
MacDiarmid[4] like an overbaked potato, and swooped
On the memorabilia: *Einstein Used My Fruitshop*,
Einstein in Old Postcards, *Einstein's Bearsden Relatives*.
Hot on their heels came the A. E. Fun Park,
Quantum Court, Glen Einstein Highland Malt.
Glasgow was booming. Scotland rose to its feet
At Albert Suppers where The Toast to the General Theory
Was given by footballers, panto-dames, or restaurateurs.
In the US an ageing lab-technician recorded
How the Great Man when excited showed a telltale glottal stop.
He'd loved fiddlers' rallies. His favourite sport was curling.[5]
Thanks to this, Scottish business expanded
Endlessly. His head grew toby-jug-shaped,
Ideal for keyrings. He'd always worn brogues.[6]
Ate bannocks[7] in exile. As a wee boy he'd read *The Beano*.[8]

1. Native of Glasgow, Scotland.
2. Scottish inventor who first publically demonstrated a working television in 1926.
3. Eighteenth-century Scottish philosopher and historian.
4. Hugh MacDiarmid, pen name of Christopher Murray Grieve, Scottish modernist poet.
5. A game played on ice, in which large stones are slid toward a target, developed in Scotland in the sixteenth century.
6. Traditional Scottish shoes.
7. Scottish oatmeal or barley cakes.
8. A popular British comic book series; since 1984 it has been edited by Euan Kerr, a Scotsman.

His name brought new energy: our culture was solidly based
On pride in our hero, The Universal Scot.

1990

W. N. Herbert

b. 1961

Born in Dundee, Scotland, W. N. Herbert received his doctorate from Brasenose College, Oxford, and has served as Northern Arts Literary Fellow at the universities of Newcastle and Durham, Writer in Residence on Cumbria Arts in the Education Skylines project, and Writing Fellow for the Wordsworth Trust in Grasmere. He has taught creative writing at Lancaster University, and currently holds a post in creative writing and contemporary Scottish poetry at the University of Newcastle, Tyne. His dissertation on the Scottish poet Hugh MacDiarmid's work was published in 1992 as *To Circumjack MacDiarmid*. His collections include *Dundee Doldrums* (1991), *The Testament of the Reverend Thomas Dick* (1994), *Forked Tongue* (1994), *Cabaret McGonagall* (1996), *The Laurelude* (1998), and *The Bumper Book of Troy* (2002). He has edited various collections and anthologies, including *Strong Words: Modern Poets on Modern Poetry* with Matthew Hollis (2000), and he edits the poetry webzine *Frank's Casket*. Much of his work is in Scots, a language he appreciates for its stanza forms and for its sense of otherness, which helps to hold a reader's attention. He currently lives in a converted lighthouse on the Tyne estuary.

Cabaret McGonagall

Come as ye dottilt,[1] brain-deid lunks,
ye hibernatin cyber-punks,
gadget-gadjies, comics-gecks,
guys wi perfick rat's physiques,
fowk wi fuck-aa social skills,
fowk that winnae tak thir pills:
gin ye cannae even pley fuitball
treh thi Cabaret McGonagall.

Thi decor pits a cap oan oorie,[2]
ut's puke-n-flock a la Tandoori;
there's a sculpture made frae canine stools,
there's a robot armadillo drools
when shown a phone o thi Pope,
and a salad spinner cerved fae dope:
gin ye cannae design a piss oan thi mall
trek thi Cabaret McGonagall.

We got: Clangers, Blimpers, gowks[3] in mohair jimpers,
Bangers, Whimpers, cats wi stupit simpers—
Ciamar a thu,[4] how are you, and hoozit gaun pal,

1. Daft, confused [Herbert's gloss].
2. Dirty, tasteless [Herbert's gloss].
3. Fools [Herbert's gloss].
4. "How are you" (Gaelic) [Herbert's gloss].

welcome to thi Cabaret Guillaume McGonagall
We got: Dadaists,[5] badass gits, shits wi RADA[6] voices,
Futurists wi sutured wrists and bygets o James Joyce's—
Bienvenue, wha thi fuck are you, let's drink thi nicht away,
come oan yir own, or oan thi phone, or to thi Cabaret.

Come as ye bards that cannae scan,
fowk too scared tae get a tan,
come as ye anxious-chicken tykes
wi stabilisers oan yir bikes,
fowk whas mithers waash thir pants,
fowk wha drink deodorants:
fowk that think they caused thi Fall
like thi Cabaret McGonagall.

Fur as that's cheesy, static, stale,
this place gaes sae faur aff thi scale
o ony Wigwam Bam-meter
mimesis wad brak thi pentameter;
in oarder tae improve thi species' genes,
t'e'll find self-oaperatin guillotines:
bring yir knittin, bring yir shawl
tae thi Cabaret McGonagall.

We got: Berkoffs, jerk-offs, noodles wi nac knickers,
Ubuists,[7] tubes wi zits, poodles dressed as vicars—
Gutenaben Aiberdeen, wilkommen Cumbernauld,
thi dregs o Scoatlan gaither at Chez McGonagall.
We got: mimes in tights, a MacDiarmidite that'iz ainsel contradicts,
kelpies,[8] selkies,[9] grown men that think they're Picts—[1]
Buonaserra Oban and Ola! tae as Strathsprey,
come in disguise fist tae despise thi haill damn Cabaret.

Panic-attack Mac is oor DJ,
thi drugs he tuke werr as Class A,
sae noo he cannae laive thi bog;
thon ambient soond's him layin a log.
Feelin hungry? sook a plook;
thi son o Sawney Bean's oor cook:
gin consumin humans diz not appal
treh thi Bistro de McGonagall.

Waatch Paranoia Pete pit speed
intil auld Flaubert's parrot's feed,[2]
and noo ut's squaakin oot in leids
naebody kens till uts beak bleeds
and when ut faas richt aff uts perch,

5. Avant-garde artistic movement of the early twentieth century.
6. Royal Academy of Dramatic Arts.
7. After Alfred Jarry's surrealist play *Ubu Roi* (1896).
8. River spirits in the shape of horses [Herbert's gloss].
9. Seals which can take on human form [Herbert's gloss].
1. Ancient inhabitants of Scotland.
2. Languages [Herbert's gloss].

Pete gees himsel a boady search:
thi evidence is there fur all
at thi Cabaret McGonagall.

We got: weirdos, beardos, splutniks, fools,
Culdees,[3] bauldies, Trekkies, ghouls—
Airheids fae thi West Coast, steely knives and all,
welcome to thi Hotel Guillaume McGonagall.
We got: Imagists, bigamists, fowk dug up wi beakers,
lit.mag.eds, shit-thir-beds, and fans o thi New Seekers—[4]
Doric loons wi Bothy tunes[5] that ploo[6] yir wits tae clay;
ut's open mike fur ony shite doon at thi Cabaret.

Alpha males ur no allowed
amang this outre-foutery[7] crowd
tho gin they wear thir alphaboots
there's nane o us can keep thum oot,
and damn-aa wimmen care tae visit,
and nane o thum iver seem tae miss it:
gin you suspeck yir dick's too small
treh thi Cabaret McGonagall.

There's dum-dum boys wi wuiden heids
and Myrna Loy[8] is snoggin[9] Steed[1]
there's wan drunk wearin breeks[2] he's peed—
naw—thon's thi Venerable Bede;[3]
in fack thon auld scribe smells lyk ten o um,
he's no cheenged'iz habit i thi last millenium:
gin thi wits ye werr bourn wi hae stertit tae stall
treh thi Cabaret McGonagall.

We got: Loplops and robocops and Perry Comatose,
Cyclops and ZZ Top and fowk that pick thir nose—
Fare ye-weel and cheery-bye and bonne nuit tae you all,
thi booncirs think we ought tae leave thi Club McGonagall.
But we got: Moptops and bebop bats and Krapp's Last Tapeworm friends,
Swap-Shop vets and neurocrats, but damn-aa sapiens—
Arrevederchi Rothesay, atque vale tae thi Tay,
Eh wish that Eh hud ne'er set eye upon this Cabaret.

1996

Smirr

The leaves flick past the windows of the train
like feeding swifts: they're scooping up small mouth-

3. Members of the Columban church [Herbert's gloss], named for Scottish St. Columbanus.
4. Ersatz folk-music group formed in 1969.
5. Ballads from the rural North-East [Herbert's gloss].
6. Plough [Herbert's gloss].
7. Excessively fussy [Herbert's gloss].
8. Early American film star (one of whose grandmothers was Scottish).
9. Kissing.
1. Possibly John Steed, secret agent from the television series *The Avengers* which ran through the 1960s.
2. Pants.
3. Seventh/eighth century churchman; author, *Ecclesiastical History of the English People*.

fuls of the midge-like autumn, fleeing south
with the train's hot wake: their feathers are small rain.
'Serein' they could say, where I'm passing through,
then just a sound could link rain with the leaves'
symptom, of being sere. But who deceives
themselves such rhyming leaps knit seasons now?
Some alchemist would get the point at once;
why I, against the leaves' example, try—
migrating to my cold roots like a dunce.
Thicker than needles sticking to a fir,
Winter is stitching mists of words with chance,
like smears of myrrh, like our small rain, our smirr.

1996

END OF PERSPECTIVES: WHOSE LANGUAGE?

CONTEMPORARY BRITISH FICTION

Alan Moore and David Lloyd

b. 1953 b. 1950

Alan Moore was born in Northampton, a city of 185,000 approximately midway between London and Birmingham in the East Midlands, the son of working-class parents. His schooling ended abruptly when he was expelled at seventeen for selling drugs; he has since described himself as "one of the world's most inept LSD dealers."

His career as a cartoonist began in earnest in the late 1970s. He began working in the music press in the magazines *Sounds* and *NME* (*New Musical Express*), and began writing and drawing his first long-running strip, *Maxwell the Magic Cat*, in 1979. He gradually moved away from drawing to focus on writing, contributing scripts to the comics *2000 AD*, *Marvel UK*, and *Warrior*. The success of his work for these British publishers, especially the work he did for *Warrior* (including *V for Vendetta*), brought him to the attention of American powerhouse DC Comics, for whom he wrote *Swamp Thing* and *Hellboy*, among many other projects. Eventually Moore brought *V for Vendetta* to DC, who published the entire series as a color graphic novel; the original *Warrior* serials had been in black and white, as they are reproduced here.

Watchmen, as much as any other single title, established Moore's place as the British master of the graphic novel, though the number and range of Moore's comics projects is mind-boggling. After the completion of *V for Vendetta*, Moore left DC and spent a period as an independent comics writer working on *From Hell* and *Lost Girls*, among other projects. Another of his best-known franchises, *The League of Extraordinary Gentlemen*, was launched under the auspices of the America's Best Comics imprint of Wildstorm Comics in 1999. Many of Moore's projects, including *The League of Extraordinary Gentlemen*, *From Hell*, *Watchmen*, and *V for Vendetta*, have been produced as big-budget Hollywood films.

David Lloyd started drawing comics for Marvel UK in the late 1970s, where he met Alan Moore; the two had worked together on an issue of *The Hulk*, and on *Dr. Who*. They collaborated closely on *V for Vendetta*; V's Guy Fawkes disguise, for instance, was Lloyd's suggestion. He has also collaborated with writer Steve Parkhouse on *Night Raven*.

V FOR VENDETTA
GOOD EVENING, LONDON. IT'S NINE O'CLOCK AND THIS IS THE VOICE OF FATE BROADCASTING ON 275 AND 285 IN THE MEDIUM WAVE... IT IS THE FIFTH OF THE ELEVENTH, NINETEEN-NINETY-SEVEN
THE WEATHER WILL BE FINE UNTIL 12:07 A.M. WHEN A SHOWER WILL COMMENCE, LASTING UNTIL 1:30 A.M...
FOR YOUR PROTECTION
THE TEMPERATURE WILL VARY BETWEEN 13 AND 14 DEGREES CENTIGRADE THROUGHOUT THE NIGHT.
FOR YOUR PROTECTION
THE PEOPLE OF LONDON ARE ADVISED THAT THE BRIXTON AND STREATHAM AREAS ARE QUARANTINE ZONES AS OF TODAY. IT IS SUGGESTED THAT THESE AREAS BE AVOIDED FOR REASONS OF HEALTH AND SAFETY.
PRODUCTIVITY REPORTS FROM HEREFORDSHIRE INDICATE A POSSIBLE END TO MEAT RATIONING STARTING FROM MID-FEBRUARY, 1998...
THIS GOOD NEWS FOLLOWS SIMILAR ANNOUNCEMENTS CONCERNING THE INCREASED PRODUCTION OF BOTH EGGS AND POTATOES.
SON OF FRANKENSTEIN
ALL CAGNEY
AT THE STRAND
TOMORROW!
WHITE HEAT
Murders in the Rue Morgue
POLICE RAIDED SEVENTEEN HOMES IN THE BIRMINGHAM AREA EARLY THIS MORNING, UNCOVERING WHAT IS BELIEVED TO BE A MAJOR TERRORIST RING.
TWENTY PEOPLE, EIGHT OF THEM WOMEN, ARE CURRENTLY IN DETENTION AWAITING TRIAL.

QUEEN ZARA TODAY APPEARED AT THE OPENING OF A NEW WASTE-RECLAMATION PLANT IN PLAISTOW. THIS WAS THE QUEEN'S FIRST PUBLIC APPEARANCE SINCE HER SIXTEENTH BIRTHDAY IN JUNE.
THE QUEEN WAS WEARING A SUIT OF PEACH SILK CREATED SPECIALLY FOR THE OCCASION BY THE ROYAL COUTURIER.
IN A SPEECH TODAY MR. ADRIAN KAREL, PARTY MINISTER FOR INDUSTRY, STATED THAT BRITAIN'S INDUSTRIAL PROSPECTS ARE BRIGHTER THAN AT ANY TIME SINCE THE LAST WAR.
MR. KAREL WENT ON TO SAY THAT IT IS THE DUTY OF EVERY MAN IN THIS COUNTRY TO SEIZE THE INITIATIVE AND MAKE BRITAIN GREAT AGAIN.
...AND THAT IS THE FACE OF LONDON TONIGHT. WE REMIND YOU THAT TOMORROW IS THE FINAL DATE FOR THE COMPLETION OF YOUR CENSUS FORMS...
...AND THE TARGET DATE FOR THE CONCLUSION OF THE DEPTFORD MARSH-CLEARANCE PROJECT. THIS IS THE VOICE OF FATE SIGNING OFF.
HAVE A PLEASANT EVENING.
ARNER BROS
Chapter One
THE VILLAIN
PARLIAMENT'S COLD SHADOW FALLS ON WESTMINSTER BRIDGE, AND SHE SHIVERS. THERE WAS POWER HERE ONCE, POWER THAT DECIDED THE DESTINY OF MILLIONS.
HER TRANSACTIONS, HER DECISIONS, ARE INSIGNIFICANT. THEY AFFECT NO ONE...
MISTER?
...EXCEPT HER.
...UH... WOULD... WOULD YOU LIKE TO... UH... SLEEP WITH ME OR ANYTHING?
...I MEAN ...UH... FOR MONEY?

THAT'S THE CLUMSIEST PIECE OF PROPOSITIONING I'VE EVER HEARD. YOU'VE NOT BEEN DOING THIS VERY LONG, HAVE YOU?
OH GOD. I MUST BE REALLY TERRIBLE.
YEAH, YOU'RE RIGHT. IT'S MY FIRST NIGHT. YOU'RE MY FIRST...
... CUSTOMER?
CUSTOMER. YEAH.
I... I'VE GOT A JOB IN MUNITIONS, BUT THE MONEY IS, YOU KNOW, IT ISN'T ENOUGH... LOOK MISTER, I REALLY NEED THAT MONEY. I'D BE OK. I MEAN, I'M SIXTEEN. I KNOW WHAT I'M DOING...
NO, YOU DON'T KNOW WHAT YOU'RE DOING.
...BECAUSE IF YOU DID YOU WOULDN'T HAVE PICKED A VICE DETAIL ON STAKE-OUT.
OH CHRIST. YOU'RE A FINGERMAN.
THAT'S RIGHT. AND THESE ARE MY COLLEAGUES.
YOU KNOW THE LAWS ON PROSTITUTION. THAT'S A CLASS-H OFFENCE. THAT MEANS WE GET TO DECIDE WHAT HAPPENS TO YOU. THAT'S OUR PREROGATIVE.
OH NO. LOOK, PLEASE, MISTER, IT WAS MY FIRST TIME. I'LL DO ANYTHING YOU WANT.
PLEASE DON'T KILL ME.
STRENGTH THROUGH PURITY PURITY THROUGH FAITH
YOU'VE GOT IT WRONG, MISS. YOU'LL DO ANYTHING WE WANT AND THEN WE'LL KILL YOU.
THAT'S OUR PREROGATIVE.
OH PLEASE DON'T OH JESUS NO PLEASE.
"THE MULTIPLYING VILLAINIES OF NATURE DO SWARM UPON HIM..."
WHO THE HELL..

"AND FORTUNE, ON HIS DAMNED QUARREL, SMILING, SHOWED LIKE A REBEL'S WHORE."
WHO'S HE?
I DUNNO. MUST BE SOME KINDA RETARD GOT OUT OF A HOSPITAL. HEY YOU!
"BUT ALL'S TOO WEAK; FOR BRAVE MACBETH... WELL HE DESERVES THAT NAME..."
WHAT ARE YOU DOING?
YOU'RE IN TROUBLE, CHUM. BIG TROUBLE. THIS WOMAN IS A CRIMINAL. WE'RE POLICE OFFICERS.
SHE'S WANTED FOR INTERROGATION, SO KEEP YOUR...
...HANDS OFF?
"DISDAINING FORTUNE, WITH HIS BRANDISHED STEEL,
"WHICH SMOKED WITH BLOODY EXECUTION.
"LIKE VALOUR'S MINION, CARVED OUT HIS PASSAGE...
"...TILL HE FACED THE SLAVE;
OH.
"WHICH NE'ER SHOOK HANDS,
"NOR BADE FAREWELL TO HIM."
TEAR GAS! COUGH! HOLY CHRIST, IT'S TEAR GAS!

I GOT HIS HAND. WHAT SHALL I DO WITH HIS
OH JESUS...
WHAT THE HELL HAPPENED?? HE JUST CAME OUT OF NOWHERE AND...JUST WHAT THE HELL HAPPENED?!?
FRANK'S DEAD. THEY'RE ALL DEAD. OH CHRIST, WHAT ARE WE GOING TO DO??
FIND HIM. WE'VE GOT TO FIND HIM OR THE HEAD WILL HAVE OUR GUTS...
HOW DID HE DO IT? I NEVER SEEN ANYBODY MOVE SO FAST. HE KILLED FRANK...
THAT BASTARD. WE'VE GOT TO FIND HIM...
YOU...YOU RESCUED ME! LIKE IN A STORY! I DON'T BELIEVE IT.
WH-WHO ARE YOU?
ME? I'M THE KING OF THE TWENTIETH CENTURY. I'M THE BOGEYMAN. THE VILLAIN.
...THE BLACK SHEEP OF THE FAMILY.
UH...YEAH. BUT WHAT WERE YOU DOING AROUND HERE? I DIDN'T THINK ANYBODY CAME TO WESTMINSTER AT NIGHT EXCEPT. YOU KNOW...
...WOMEN.
AHH, BUT TONIGHT IS SPECIAL. TONIGHT IS A CELEBRATION. A GRAND OPENING. WERE YOU NEVER TAUGHT THE RHYME?

"REMEMBER, REMEMBER THE FIFTH OF NO-VEMBER, THE GUN-POWDER TREASON AND PLOT. I KNOW OF NO REASON WHY THE GUN-POWDER TREASON...
...SHOULD EVER BE FORGOT."
OH. OH. THE HOUSES OF PARLIAMENT! THEY'VE... THEY'VE BEEN... DID YOU DO THAT?
I DID THAT.
BUT THAT... THAT'S AGAINST THE LAW! THEY'LL KILL YOU.. THEY'LL...
DID YOU REALLY DO THAT?
I REALLY DID THAT. NOW HUSH. THERE'S MORE...
THE RUMBLE OF THE EXPLOSION HAS NOT YET DIED AWAY AS FROM FAR BELOW COMES THE RATTLE OF SMALLER REPORTS...
AND SUDDENLY THE SKY IS ALIGHT WITH...
FIREWORKS! REAL FIREWORKS!
OH GOD, THEY'RE SO BEAUTIFUL!
...AND ALL OVER LONDON WINDOWS ARE THROWN OPEN AND FACES LIT WITH AWE AND WONDER GAZE AT THE OMEN SCRAWLED IN FIRE ON THE NIGHT.
THERE. THE OVER-TURE IS FINISHED.
COME. WE MUST PREPARE FOR THE FIRST ACT...
ME?? B-BUT...
...OH OKAY.
IT IS PRECISELY 12:07 A.M. IT BEGINS TO RAIN...

NOVEMBER THE SIXTH, 1997 IT IS SIX-THIRTY IN THE MORNING...
I WILL HEAR YOUR REPORTS NOW, GENTLEMEN.
MR. HEYER WILL SPEAK FOR THE EYE.
WE HAVE JUST UNDER THREE MINUTES OF USEABLE FOOTAGE, LEADER. THE LARGE MAJORITY OF OUR V-RECORDERS WERE DAMAGED IN THE EXPLOSION.
TO MY LEFT IS AN ENLARGEMENT OF THE SUSPECT'S FACE. I'M AFRAID THE MASK MAKES RETINAL IDENTIFICATION IMPOSSIBLE.
CLOSE-UP IF YOU PLEASE, MR. HEYER..
AH.
THANK YOU MR. HEYER. MR. ETHERIDGE WILL NOW SPEAK FOR THE EARS.
UH... PHONE SURVEILLANCE INDICATES THAT A LARGE PROPORTION OF THE, UH, PEOPLE ARE TALKING ABOUT THE, UH, EXPLOSION, THAT'S INSIDE LONDON.
ALL SUSPECT OR SIGNIFICANT TRANSCRIPTS ARE BEING FORWARDED TO MR. UH, ALMOND AT THE FINGER.
MR. ALMOND IS WITH ME AT PRESENT. I SHALL INFORM HIM. MR. FINCH WILL SPEAK FOR THE NOSE...
WE'VE FOUND THE DEVICE PROBABLY USED TO LAUNCH THE FIREWORKS AND SOME SPENT CASINGS. INDIVIDUALLY WEIGHTED FLARES AT A GUESS.
DESPITE IT'S SOPHISTICATION I SHOULD SAY THAT THE DEVICE WAS ALMOST CERTAINLY HOME-MADE, AND THUS UNTRACEABLE. SORRY, LEADER. NOTHING ELSE YET.
THANK YOU, MR. FINCH. THE THREE OF YOU WILL INFORM ME OF ANY FURTHER DEVELOPMENTS AND AWAIT MY DIRECTIVE. ENGLAND PREVAILS, GENTLEMEN.
LEADER, I.
WELL, WE HAVE HEARD FROM THE REST OF THE HEAD. THAT LEAVES YOU, MR. ALMOND. THREE FINGERMEN WERE KILLED LAST NIGHT BY ONE SOLITARY LUNATIC.
IT IS ALSO HIGHLY PROBABLE THAT THIS SAME PERSON HAD EARLIER PLANTED AN EXPLOSIVE DEVICE OF STARTLING CAPABILITY WITHIN THE HOUSES OF PARLIAMENT.

YOU WILL BE SILENT, MR. ALMOND!
YOUR INCOMPETENCE HAS COST US OUR OLDEST SYMBOL OF AUTHORITY AND A JARRING PROPAGANDA DEFEAT. DO YOU UNDERSTAND WHAT HAPPENED LAST NIGHT?
SOME-ONE DID THE UN-THINKABLE. SOME-ONE HURT US.
...AND YOU ALLOWED THEM TO DO IT. I WANT THIS CREATURE AND HIS ASSOCIATES FOUND, MR. ALMOND. I WANT HIS HEAD.
...OR BY GOD I'LL HAVE YOURS INSTEAD.
YOU WILL CONSULT MR. DASCOMBE AT JORDAN TOWER BEFORE MAKING ANY OFFICIAL PRO-NOUNCEMENTS.
THAT WILL BE ALL, MR. ALMOND. ENGLAND PREVAILS.
ENGLAND PREVAILS, LEADER.
JORDAN TOWER, SEVEN O'CLOCK:
OF COURSE YOU DID, LEWIS! WE ALL GOT UP EARLY THIS MORNING, DIDN'T WE? NOW IF WE CAN JUST RUN THROUGH IT ONCE MORE BEFORE WE PUT IT IN THE CAN, THEN...
PUT YOUR TRUST IN FATE
AH. EXCUSE ME FOR A MOMENT, LEWIS...
DEREK!! WE DON'T SEE YOU DOWN HERE IN THE MOUTH VERY OFTEN...
OOH! 'DOWN IN THE MOUTH'! I COULD HAVE MADE A JOKE OUT OF THAT, COULDN'T I?
YOU HAVE DONE, DASCOMBE. SEVERAL TIMES. WHAT'S FATE PUTTING OUT ON THE PARLIAMENT BOMB-ING?
WE-E-LL, FATE WANTS US TO SAY IT WAS A SCHEDULED DEMO-LITION UNDERTAKEN AT NIGHT TO AVOID TRAFFIC CON-GESTION.
IT'S GOING OUT ON THE EIGHT O'CLOCK BROADCAST... I WAS JUST RUNNING THROUGH IT WITH LEWIS WHEN YOU CAME IN.
LEWIS?
LEWIS PROTHERO. HE DOES THE VOICE. THE VOICE OF FATE.

GOOD MORNING, LONDON. THIS IS THE VOICE OF FATE BROADCASTING ON 275 AND 285 METRES IN THE MEDIUM WAVE...
Chapter Two
THE VOICE
HMM. WHAT ARE YOU SAYING ABOUT THE FIREWORKS?
FATE DOESN'T THINK WE SHOULD MENTION THE FIREWORKS. IF ANYONE ASKS LATER WE'LL SAY IT WAS A FREAK EFFECT OF THE BLAST.
LISTEN TO LEWIS... ISN'T HE MARVELLOUS? IF FATE REALLY HAD A VOICE IT WOULD SOUND JUST LIKE THAT. IF ONLY PEOPLE KNEW WHAT A GOOD JOB HE'S DOING...
DON'T BE STUPID, DASCOMBE. THE WHOLE IDEA IS THAT PEOPLE THINK IT'S FATE TALKING. IT MAKES FATE APPEAR MORE HUMAN. GIVES PEOPLE CONFIDENCE.
HMMM...
HE COLLECTS DOLLS, YOU KNOW. WOULDN'T THINK IT, WOULD YOU? BIG MAN LIKE THAT, COLLECTING DOLLS. HE'S SENSITIVE, YOU SEE. YOU CAN TELL BY HIS VOICE.
YES, A LOT OF YOU MEDIA PEOPLE ARE "SENSITIVE," AREN'T YOU? I DON'T KNOW WHY THE LEADER TOLERATES YOU.
MY DEAR DEREK... THE LEADER IS THE MOST SENSITIVE OF US ALL.
...IN FACT, WHEN YOU'D FINISHED EXPLAINING HOW A LONE LUNATIC COULD KILL THREE FINGERMEN AND BLOW UP PARLIAMENT, I SHOULD IMAGINE HE WAS VERY SENSITIVE.
YOU'RE A DEGENERATE, DASCOMBE.
YOU'RE BITTER, ALMOND.
"BITTER ALMOND"! OH DEAR ME! HA HA HA HA HA HA!

PLEASE YOURSELF.
ALRIGHT, LEWIS... FROM THE TOP.
"BITTER ALMOND"! OH DEAR ME! HA HA HA HA HA!
THE SHADOW GALLERY:
LOOK, I DON'T WANT TO SOUND UNGRATEFUL, I MEAN, AFTER YOU RESCUED ME? BUT I DON'T UNDERSTAND ANY OF THIS. WHO YOU ARE, OR WHAT YOU WANT OR ANYTHING.
I MEAN, I KNOW YOU MUST HAVE HAD A REASON FOR BLINDFOLDING ME WHEN YOU BROUGHT ME HERE, BUT COULDN'T YOU JUST TELL ME WHERE WE ARE? ARE WE STILL IN LONDON?
WE ARE IN THE SHADOW GALLERY. THIS IS MY HOME.
DO YOU LIKE IT? I BUILT IT MYSELF, YOU KNOW.
IT... IT'S UNBELIEVABLE! ALL OF THESE PAINTINGS AND BOOKS... I DIDN'T EVEN KNOW THERE WERE THINGS LIKE THIS.
YOU COULDN'T BE EXPECTED TO KNOW. THEY HAVE ERADICATED CULTURE... TOSSED IT AWAY LIKE A FISTFUL OF DEAD ROSES...
ALL THE BOOKS, ALL THE FILMS... ALL THE MUSIC...
THE MUSIC IS BEAUTIFUL! YOU MUST THINK I'M REALLY STUPID... ALL I'VE EVER HEARD IS THE MILITARY STUFF THEY PLAY ON THE RADIO.
BUT ALL THIS STUFF ON YOUR DUKE-BOX SOUNDS SO... I DUNNO... ALIVE! WHAT'S THIS PLAYING NOW? THE WOMAN'S VOICE DOESN'T EVEN SOUND ENGLISH.
IT'S NOT. AND THE WORD IS "JUKE-BOX" WITH A "J".
THE SONG IS CALLED "DANCING IN THE STREETS." IT'S BEING SUNG BY MARTHA AND THE VANDELLAS. PERHAPS THE TERM 'TAMLA MOTOWN' IS FAMILIAR TO YOU?
OBVIOUSLY NOT. HARDLY SURPRISING, I SUPPOSE. AFTER ALL...

...THEY ERADICATED SOME CULTURES MORE THOROUGHLY THAN THEY DID OTHERS.
NO TAMLA AND NO TROJAN. NO BILLIE HOLIDAY OR BLACK UHURU...
JUST HIS MASTER'S VOICE. EVERY HOUR. ON THE HOUR.
WE'LL HAVE TO SEE WHAT WE CAN DO ABOUT THAT...
SORRY. THIS COMPARTMENT IS FULL.
FULL?? DON'T BE RIDICULOUS, MAN! IT'S EMPTY APART FROM YOU THREE! THERE'S PLENTY OF..
I SAID IT'S FULL, CRAPHEAD.
OH MY GOD. I'M SORRY... I DIDN'T REALISE.
FULL. YES, OF COURSE. FULL.
WELL BLOCKED, TED! CAN'T HAVE THE CARRIAGE FULL OF CIVILIANS. CIVILIANS DON'T APPRECIATE TRAINS. TAKES A MILITARY MAN TO APPRECIATE TRAINS...
LIKE DOLLS. YOUR AVERAGE CITIZEN DOES NOT GIVE A MONKEY'S ABOUT DOLLS. NO APPRECIATION, YOU SEE? DID I TELL YOU I COLLECTED DOLLS, GEORGE?
ER...YES, MR. PROTHERO. I THINK YOU MAY HAVE MENTIONED IT ONCE OR TWICE. VERY INTERESTING.
INTERESTING! THAT'S EXACTLY RIGHT! MIND YOU, YOU'RE A MILITARY MAN. ASK YOUR AVERAGE CITIZEN. HE'D SAY DOLLS WERE FOR POOFTAHS. IGNORANT, YOU SEE.
MYSELF, I'VE ALWAYS BEEN A LADIES' MAN. TALES I COULD TELL YOU ABOUT WHEN I WAS IN ADEN. I REMEMBER ONCE, PORKY APPLEBY AND MYSELF MET THESE TWO NATIVE GELS...

JESUS CHRIST! WHAT THE HELL'S THAT??
WHAT WAS WHAT?
JUST BEFORE WE WENT INTO THE TUNNEL I THOUGHT I SAW SOMETHING UP ON THE BRIDGE.
I DUNNO... IT COULD HAVE BEEN RAGS CAUGHT ON A FENCE OR SOMETHING, I SUPPOSE.
HMMM.
...SO ANYWAY, WE'D BOTH HAD A FEW TINCTURES BY THAT TIME, AND PORKY SAYS TO ONE OF THESE LOCAL BINTS... THE ELDEST GEL, I THINK IT WAS... HE SAYS...
...EXCUSE ME, MR. PROTHERO...
TED... DID YOU JUST HEAR SOMETHING? A BANG ON THE ROOF OF THE TRAIN?
I SAY! WE'RE STOPPING! IS EVERYTHING ALL RIGHT, D'YOU THINK?
I DON'T... AY!! WHAT'S HAPPENED TO THE LIGHTS?
...OH BLOODY HELL...
0730

HMMPH. SHOULDN'T WORRY IF I WERE YOU, LADS. BRITISH RAIL ACTING UP AGAIN. LIGHTS'LL BE BACK ON IN A MINUTE, YOU'LL SEE.
NOW, AS I WAS SAYING, THERE WAS PORKY WITH ONE HAND...
JUST A MINUTE, MR PROTHERO! SHOOTERS OUT, TED. JUST IN CASE.
I'M SORRY, MR PROTHERO... PLEASE GO ON....
AND SO THE ELDEST GEL SAYS "WITH A MONKEY??! SHOULD BLOODY COCOA!!" HA HA HA HA! GOOD ONE, EH?
HMM. THEY DO SEEM TO BE TAKING THEIR TIME, DON'T THEY? PERHAPS YOU SHOULD GO AND HAVE A WORD WITH THE DRIVER, GEORGE.
GEORGE?
... GEORGE?
DON'T TAKE OFFENCE, GEORGE. IT WAS JUST A NAUGHTY YARN. WE'RE ALL MEN OF THE WORLD, EH, GEORGE?
...GEORGE?
OH MY GOD! TED, IT'S GEORGE! HE'S...
...TED?
OH LORD: WHAT'S THE MATTER WITH THE PAIR OF YOU?? FOR CHRIST'SAKE, SOMEBODY SAY SOMETHING!!
HELLO.

NOVEMBER 6TH 1997...
...SO LET'S JUST HEAR IT ONCE MORE IN YOUR OWN WORDS. THE TRAIN ENTERED THE TUNNEL... AND THEN WHAT?
W-WELL, I MEAN, IT'S DIFFICULT TO SAY. IT ALL HAPPENED SO QUICK, DIDN'T IT?
I DIDN'T ACTUALLY HEAR ANYTHING... JUST SORT OF CAUGHT SOMETHING MOVING OUT THE CORNER OF ME EYE. AND BY THEN IT WAS ALL OVER, WANNIT?
COULD YOU GIVE US A DESCRIPTION OF YOUR ATTACKER? HEIGHT, DRESS, ANYTHING LIKE THAT?
WELL, IT WAS JUST SORT OF BLACK, KNOW WHAT I MEAN? JUST THIS BIG, BLACK SHAPE COMIN' AT ME FROM THE SIDE-WINDOW OF THE CAB...
AND IT HAD A FACE, ONLY NOT A PROPER FACE, SEE? AN' IT WAS SMILING.
I SEE. AND THEN WHAT HAPPENED? DID IT HIT YOU, STRIKE YOU IN ANY WAY?
NO. I MEAN, THAT WAS THE FUNNY BIT. IT JUST SORT OF TOUCHED ME, UP HERE ON ME NECK.
I FELT THIS... IT WAS LIKE AN ELECTRIC SHOCK, SORT OF. AN' THEN I JUST PASSED OUT.
...AND CAME TO AN HOUR LATER WHEN THE SECURITY FORCE ARRIVED ON THE SCENE. I SEE.
WELL, I THINK THAT'S ABOUT IT, MR. BISHOP. THE OFFICER WILL TAKE YOUR ADDRESS IN CASE WE NEED TO CONTACT YOU. THANK YOU FOR YOUR TROUBLE.
WELL, MR. FINCH, WHAT DO YOU THINK? IS IT THE SAME BLOKE WHO DID THE PARLIAMENT BOMBING, OR WHAT?
I HOPE SO, DOMINIC, BECAUSE IF IT'S NOT, THEN THERE MUST BE TWO OF 'EM...
...AND THAT'S A POSSIBILITY I'D RATHER NOT CONSIDER WITHOUT A STIFF DRINK TO HAND.

ME NEITHER, MR.FINCH. WHAT EXACTLY ARE WE UP AGAINST HERE? WHO IS THIS CHARACTER?
I MEAN, ALL THIS BUSINESS ABOUT BOARDING MOVING TRAINS IS LIKE SOMETHING OUT OF THE PICTURES. NORMAL PEOPLE CAN'T DO THINGS LIKE THAT.
YOU'RE RIGHT, DOMINIC. OR KNOCK OUT A THIRTEEN STONE TRAIN DRIVER BY TOUCHING HIM LIGHTLY ON THE NECK. NORMAL PEOPLE CAN'T DO THINGS LIKE THAT.
... IN FACT, I DON'T THINK IT'S GOING TOO FAR TO SAY THAT MOST NORMAL PEOPLE HAVE NEVER EVEN CONSIDERED BLOWING UP THE HOUSES OF PARLIAMENT.
SO WHAT WE'RE UP AGAINST IS SOMEONE WHO ISN'T NORMAL PEOPLE... EITHER PHYSICALLY OR MENTALLY. IT'S THE "MENTALLY" BIT THAT BOTHERS ME.
BECAUSE IF I'M GOING TO CRACK THIS CASE... AND I AM... I'M GOING TO HAVE TO GET RIGHT INSIDE HIS HEAD, TO THINK THE WAY HE THINKS. AND THAT SCARES ME.
AHH, HERE WE ARE.
ANYTHING BEEN TOUCHED IN HERE?
NO, SIR, EVERYTHING'S AS WE FOUND IT WHEN WE GOT THE TRAIN OUT OF THE TUNNEL.
Chapter Three
VICTIMS
HMM... I'LL NEED SOME PHOTOGRAPHS OF THIS CHEST WOUND. IT WASN'T A KNIFE OR BULLET THAT DID THIS...
IN FACT, I'VE GOT A NASTY SUSPICION THAT WHOEVER DID THAT DID IT WITH THEIR FINGERS.
WHAT DO YOU MAKE OF THIS, MR.FINCH?
DAMNED IF I KNOW. GET A PHOTOGRAPH OF IT, AND LET ME HAVE SOME PAINT SCRAPINGS FOR ANALYSIS...
PERHAPS THE FORENSIC PEOPLE BACK AT THE NOSE WILL BE ABLE TO TELL US SOMETHING. ALTHOUGH FRANKLY I DOUBT IT.
...OTHER THAN THAT, JUST THE USUAL STUFF. DUST THE CARRIAGE FOR DABS, GET A PATH REPORT ON THE BODIES.
FATE WILL WANT A COPY, REMEMBER...

HELLO. WHAT'S THIS?
A ROSE. A "VIOLET CARSON" ROSE. FUNNY... I THOUGHT THEY'D BEEN EXTINCT SINCE THE WAR...
OUR FRIEND IN THE MASK HAS GOT QUITE A THING ABOUT THE LETTER "V" WOULDN'T YOU SAY?
AND UNLESS WE FIND A BODY IN THE NEXT COUPLE OF HOURS, IT LOOKS LIKE HE'S GOT LEWIS PROTHERO AS WELL.
BLOWING UP THE HOUSES OF PARLIAMENT, KIDNAPPING OUR TOP BROADCASTER...
DO YOU THINK HE'S TRYING TO TELL US SOMETHING?
I DON'T KNOW, SIR. JESUS CHRIST, WHAT HE'D DONE TO THOSE MEN...
I'VE SEEN WORSE, DOMINIC, PHYSICALLY SPEAKING. LIKE I SAY, IT'S THE MENTAL SIDE THAT BOTHERS ME... HIS ATTITUDE TO KILLING.
THINK ABOUT IT. HE KILLED THEM RUTHLESSLY, EFFICIENTLY, AND WITH A MINIMUM OF FUSS. WHATEVER THEIR FAULTS, THOSE WERE TWO HUMAN BEINGS...
...AND HE SLAUGHTERED THEM LIKE CATTLE!
THE SHADOW GALLERY...

ANNIE
VICTOR McLAGLEN
WAIKIKI WEDDING
THE CAT
THE 4 MARX BROTHERS
OH.
I- I'M SORRY. YOU STARTLED ME. I DIDN'T HEAR YOU COME IN...
NOBODY EVER DOES. YOU'VE BEEN CRYING.
YES. DON'T TAKE ANY NOTICE OF ME. I'M A BABY.
I-IT WAS WHEN YOU WENT OUT EARLIER ON AND DIDN'T SAY WHERE YOU WERE GOING... I THOUGHT ... I DIDN'T THINK... THAT IS, I MEAN...
I WAS SCARED YOU WOULDN'T COME BACK.
I KNOW I'M STUPID, BUT MY LIFE'S SUDDENLY BE-COME VERY STRANGE. I DON'T KNOW WHAT'S HAPPENING ANYMORE.

LAST NIGHT... THOSE MEN. THEY WERE GOING TO... THEY SAID THEY'D KILL ME. AND YOU RESCUED ME.
YOU RESCUED ME AND BROUGHT ME TO THIS FANTASTIC PLACE, AND IT'S SO BEAUTIFUL AND IT MAKES ME FEEL SO SAFE AND...AND...
...AND I DON'T EVEN KNOW WHAT YOUR NAME IS.
I DON'T HAVE A NAME. YOU CAN CALL ME "V."
WHAT SHALL I CALL YOU?
MY NAME IS EVEY... EVEY HAMMOND.
I'M NOBODY. NOBODY SPECIAL. NOT LIKE YOU.
EVERYBODY IS SPECIAL. EVERYBODY. EVERYBODY IS A HERO, A LOVER, A FOOL, A VILLAIN. EVERYBODY.
EVERYBODY HAS THEIR STORY TO TELL. EVEN EVEY HAMMOND. I SHOULD VERY MUCH LIKE TO HEAR EVEY HAMMOND'S STORY.
B-BUT THERE'S NOTHING TO TELL. I'M ONLY SIX-TEEN. I HAVEN'T DONE ANYTHING.
SIXTEEN. THEN YOU WERE BORN IN 1981?
Y-YES. IN SEPTEMBER. WE USED TO LIVE ON SHOOTERS HILL IN SOUTH LONDON. IT WAS NICE THERE. I-I'VE GOT A PHOTOGRAPH IF YOU WANT TO SEE...
JUST ME AND MUM AND DAD. I DIDN'T HAVE ANY BROTHERS OR SISTERS... DAD SAID HE COULDN'T AFFORD ANY MORE KIDS...
THIS WAS DURING THE RECESSION OF THE EIGHTIES?

YEAH... I DON'T REMEMBER MUCH ABOUT THAT... I KNOW DAD SAID THINGS DIDN'T GET MUCH BETTER WHEN LABOUR GOT INTO POWER...
HE SAID THAT THE ONLY ELECTION PROMISE THAT THEY KEPT WAS GETTING RID OF THE AMERICAN MISSILES THAT WERE STATIONED OVER HERE.
AND THE WAR, EVEY. DO YOU REMEMBER THE WAR?
"OF COURSE I DO. I WAS ONLY SEVEN BUT I REMEMBER WHEN THE NEWS CAME OVER THE RADIO. DAD KEPT TELLING MUM NOT TO WORRY. HE WAS SCARED TO DEATH... IT WAS ABOUT POLAND AND THE RUSSIANS. WASN'T IT? AND PRESIDENT KENNEDY SAID HE'D USE THE BOMB IF THEY DIDN'T GET OUT. THAT'S WHAT DAD TOLD ME.
"IT WAS HORRIBLE. NOBODY KNEW IF BRITAIN WOULD GET BOMBED OR NOT. I REMEMBER MUM SAYING 'AFRICA'S NOT THERE ANYMORE.' THAT'S ALL SHE SAID.
"I THOUGHT ABOUT ALL THE LIONS AND ELEPHANTS BEING DEAD. IT MADE ME CRY. I WAS ONLY SEVEN.
"BUT BRITAIN DIDN'T GET BOMBED. NOT THAT IT MADE MUCH DIFFERENCE. ALL THE BOMBS AND THINGS HAD DONE SOMETHING TO THE WEATHER. SOMETHING BAD.
"I REMEMBER ONE DAY DAD CALLED MUM AND ME INTO THE BACK BEDROOM. HE SAID HE WANTED TO SHOW US SOMETHING...
"WE COULD SEE RIGHT ACROSS LONDON FROM THE BEDROOM WINDOW. IT WAS NEARLY ALL UNDER WATER. THE THAMES BARRIER HAD BURST.
"THE SKY WAS ALL YELLOW AND BLACK. I'VE NEVER SEEN A SKY LIKE IT. DAD SAID LONDON WAS FINISHED. HE WANTED TO TAKE MUM AND ME TO THE COUNTRY.
"MUM WOULDN'T GO. JUST AS WELL, I SUPPOSE. IT TURNED OUT THAT THE COUNTRYSIDE WAS WORSE THAN THE TOWNS.
"THE WEATHER HAD DESTROYED ALL THE CROPS, SEE? AND THERE WAS NO FOOD COMING FROM EUROPE, BECAUSE EUROPE HAD GONE. LIKE AFRICA.

"I-I DIDN'T LIKE TO THINK ABOUT THE NEXT FOUR YEARS. WE'D GOT TOGETHER WITH SOME NEIGHBOURS IN A PROTECTION COMMITTEE. IT DIDN'T HELP MUCH...
"THERE WAS NO FOOD, AND THE SEWERS WERE FLOODED AND EVERYBODY GOT SICK. MUM DIED IN 1991. DAD WOULDN'T LET ME SEE HER.
"THERE WERE RIOTS, AND PEOPLE WITH GUNS. NOBODY KNEW WHAT WAS GOING ON. EVERYONE WAS WAITING FOR THE GOVERNMENT TO DO SOMETHING...
"BUT THERE WASN'T ANY GOVERNMENT ANYMORE, JUST LOTS OF LITTLE GANGS, ALL TRYING TO TAKE OVER. AND THEN IN 1992, SOMEBODY FINALLY DID...
"IT WAS ALL THE FASCIST GROUPS, THE RIGHT-WINGERS. THEY'D ALL GOT TOGETHER WITH SOME OF THE BIG CORPORATIONS THAT HAD SURVIVED. 'NORSEFIRE' THEY CALLED THEMSELVES.
"I REMEMBER WHEN THEY MARCHED INTO LONDON. THEY HAD A FLAG WITH THEIR SYMBOL ON. EVERYONE WAS CHEERING. I THOUGHT THEY WERE SCARY.
"THEY SOON GOT THINGS UNDER CONTROL, BUT THEN THEY STARTED TAKING PEOPLE AWAY... ALL THE BLACK PEOPLE AND THE PAKISTANIS...
"WHITE PEOPLE, TOO. ALL THE RADICALS AND THE MEN WHO, YOU KNOW, LIKED OTHER MEN. THE HOMOSEXUALS. I DON'T KNOW WHAT THEY DID WITH THEM ALL.
"DAD HAD BEEN IN A SOCIALIST GROUP WHEN HE WAS YOUNGER. THEY CAME FOR HIM ONE SEPTEMBER MORNING IN 1993...
"IT WAS MY BIRTHDAY. I WAS TWELVE. I NEVER SAW HIM AGAIN.
"THEY MADE ME GO AND WORK IN A FACTORY WITH A LOT OF OTHER KIDS. WE WERE PUTTING MATCHES INTO BOXES.
Lucifer
"I LIVED IN A HOSTEL. IT WAS COLD AND DIRTY AND I JUST USED TO CRY ALL THE TIME. I WANTED MY DAD."
...THAT'S HOW IT WAS FOR FOUR YEARS... NOT ENOUGH FOOD, NOT ENOUGH MONEY. SOME OF THE OLDER GIRLS MADE MONEY GOING WITH MEN.
THAT'S WHAT I WAS GOING TO DO, LAST NIGHT. BUT THEY WERE FINGERMEN. THEY WERE GOING... THEY WERE G-GOING TO...
THEY WERE GOING TO RUH... RUH... RUH...

HUSH, CHILD, HUSH. IT'S OVER NOW. YOU'RE SAFE. THE PAST CAN'T HURT YOU ANYMORE. NOT UNLESS YOU LET IT.
THEY MADE YOU INTO A VICTIM, EVEY. THEY MADE YOU INTO A STATISTIC. BUT THAT'S NOT THE REAL YOU. THAT'S NOT WHO YOU ARE INSIDE.
JUST TRUST ME, EVEY, AND WE CAN WIPE IT ALL AWAY. ALL THE PAIN, ALL THE CRUELTY, ALL THE BEREAVEMENT. WE CAN START AGAIN.
THERE, YOU SEE?
ALL GONE.
...AND EVEY HAMMOND SOBS LIKE THE CHILD SHE IS, SOBS BECAUSE AT LONG LAST, HER NIGHTMARE IS OVER...
NOW, LEWIS PROTHERO, ON THE OTHER HAND...
MNNUH
WHERE AM I? WHAT HAPPENED?
...AND WHAT AM I DOING WEARING THIS UNIFORM?
HIS NIGHTMARE IS ONLY JUST BEGINNING!
OH MY GOD.
LARKHILL RESETTLEMENT CAMP

NOVEMBER THE SEVENTH, 1997. THE LEADER AND MR. FINCH.
I THINK HE'S A PSYCHOPATH, LEADER.
I USE THE WORD IN ITS MOST PRECISE SENSE.
I SEE. THEN WE CAN'T ASSUME THAT "CODE-NAME 'V'" WILL BEHAVE LIKE A CONVENTIONAL TERRORIST.
WE CAN'T ASSUME THAT HE WILL EVENTUALLY ISSUE A SET OF DEMANDS OR ASK FOR THE USUAL CONCESSIONS.
I DON'T THINK HE'S OUT FOR CONCESSIONS, LEADER.
I THINK HE'S OUT FOR BLOOD.
THEN HE'S CERTAINLY GETTING IT, ISN'T HE, MR. FINCH? HE'S BLOWN UP THE HOUSES OF PARLIAMENT, DISPATCHED FIVE OF MR. ALMOND'S FINGERMEN..
...AND NOW HE'S ABDUCTED OUR TOP BROADCASTER. IF PROTHERO IS UNABLE TO MAKE HIS "VOICE OF FATE" BROADCASTS AS SCHEDULED, OUR CREDIBILITY WILL SUFFER.
TWO DAYS, MR. FINCH. THAT'S ALL ITS TAKEN HIM.
COULDN'T MR. DASCOMBE ARRANGE A STAND-IN FOR PROTHERO, LEADER?
OH YES. BUT THE PROBLEM IS THAT MR. DASCOMBE IS TOO GOOD AT HIS WORK. THE PEOPLE ACTUALLY BELIEVE THAT THE VOICE OF LEWIS PROTHERO IS THAT OF THE FATE COMPUTER.
BRITAINS BELIEF IN THE INTEGRITY OF FATE IS THE CORNERSTONE OF OUR NEW ORDER. ANY CHANGE IN THE VOICE AND.. IT JUST WON'T BE THE SAME.
I SEE. FROM A PROPAGANDA ANGLE WE'VE BEEN PUT IN A BIT OF A SPOT, HAVEN'T WE?
ALTHOUGH PERSONALLY I DON'T GO MUCH FOR THIS "NEW ORDER" BUSINESS. IT'S JUST MY JOB, TO HELP BRITAIN OUT OF THIS MESS. YOU ALREADY KNOW THAT, LEADER.
INDEED I DO, MR. FINCH. YOU HAVE EXPRESSED SUCH SENTIMENTS BEFORE. THAT YOU ARE STILL ALIVE IS A MARK OF MY RESPECT FOR YOU AND YOUR CRAFT.
LEAVE ME NOW. THERE ARE MANY PROBLEMS TO CONSIDER. I WISH TO SPEAK WITH FATE.
ENGLAND PREVAILS, MR. FINCH.
ENGLAND PREVAILS, LEADER.

THE SHADOW GALLERY. EVEY HAMMOND:
V...
HMM?
OH... UH... NOTHING. I WAS JUST TRYING TO GET USED TO SAYING IT OUT LOUD. V... IT'S A FUNNY THING TO CALL YOURSELF.
I'M A FUNNY PERSON, EVEY. YOU'LL FIND THAT OUT WHEN YOU'VE KNOWN ME LONGER. A VERY FUNNY PERSON INDEED.
YOU'RE A KIND PERSON. LISTENING TO ME TELLING YOU MY SOB STORY, ALL ABOUT THE WAR, AND MUM AND DAD. ALL ABOUT MY STUPID LIFE.
HAL MONTY
MORECAMBE AND WISE
WHAT ARE YOU GOING TO DO, V? THE WORLD IS SO BIG AND HORRIBLE AND THERE'S JUST YOU... AND ME, I SUPPOSE.
YOU AND ME, EVEY. YOU AND ME AGAINST THE WORLD! HA HA HA HA! MELODRAMA, EVEY! ISN'T IT STRANGE HOW LIFE TURNS INTO MELODRAMA?
THAT'S VERY IMPORTANT TO YOU, ISN'T IT? ALL THAT THEATRICAL STUFF.
IT'S EVERYTHING, EVEY. THE PERFECT ENTRANCE, THE GRAND ILLUSION.
IT'S EVERYTHING.
...AND I'M GOING TO BRING THE HOUSE DOWN.
THEY'VE FORGOTTEN THE DRAMA OF IT ALL, YOU SEE. THEY ABANDONED THEIR SCRIPTS WHEN THE WORLD WITHERED IN THE GLARE OF THE NUCLEAR FOOTLIGHTS.
I'M GOING TO REMIND THEM, ABOUT MELODRAMA. ABOUT THE TUPPENNY RUSH AND THE PENNY DREADFUL. YOU SEE, EVEY, ALL THE WORLD'S A STAGE, AND EVERYTHING ELSE...
KING OF SCOTLAND
...IS VAUDEVILLE.
THE SHADOW GALLERY. LEWIS PROTHERO:
HELLO? I SAY, IS THERE ANYBODY THERE?
Chapter Four
VAUDEVILLE

Hanif Kureishi
b. 1954

Hanif Kureishi embodies the complexities of postwar British society. Born in Kent, England, and raised in a middle-class London suburb by a British mother and a father who worked as a journalist in both England and his native Pakistan, Kureishi is part of what is called "Black Britain": the second generation, British-born children of returning colonials from the far-flung British empire in India and Pakistan, in Africa and the Caribbean. His electrifying screenplays, stage plays, novels and short stories have delineated the mélange of cultures, races, and histories that form the multicultural society of today's England.

Throughout his childhood, Kureishi was subjected to the racist taunts and even beatings that had become commonplace as nationalistic politicians such as Enoch Powell stirred up racial enmity among working-class and middle-class Britons. "Paki-bashing" became a sport of working-class white youths, especially as many cities developed large Pakistani communities. The Pakistanis drew together with Asian and Afro-Caribbean immigrants under the self-proclaimed banner of "Black Britain," a cultural solidarity movement that opposed all types of discrimination. Kureishi's writing is hardly demagogic, though, nor is it purely political in the sense of arguing in a systematic way against discrimination. It is instead antic and comic, filled with picaresque elements and absurdist humor drawn from everything from the Beatles to Monty Python and Beyond the Fringe, and develops a special mode of comedy predicated on self-deprecating yet also politically radical subversions.

Kureishi's works generally depict a semiautobiographical figure who, with a combination of naivete and passion, attempts to negotiate the twists and turns of urban existence, racial and class prejudice, sexual ambiguity, and the sheer comedy of manners that is Britain today. Somewhat like V. S. Naipaul—although without his pessimism or misanthropy—Kureishi refuses to make simplistic analyses that would have the British always in the wrong, their former colonial subjects always right, a balance amply illustrated in *Something to Tell You*. Kureishi sees the shades of gray, rather than merely blacks and whites, and makes pointed yet hilarious comedy of the wild and inevitable conflicts of a society now filled with immigrants. His tribute to the creative energies of the problematic society he calls home is symbolized in the title of his 1995 novel, *The Black Album* (1995). Naming his book after the Beatles's *White Album*, the most mysterious and evocative of their recordings, Kureishi pays homage to a Britain he himself helps to name Black.

Something to Tell You

The plane must have touched down around three in the morning. I had to slap and shake Miriam awake. She'd been living in a squat[1] in Brixton and was eager to get away. The area had recently been torn apart by anti-police riots. Miriam had been up for a week throwing bricks and helping out at the Law Centre. The contemporary graffiti advised: "Help the police—beat yourself up."

Inevitably, Miriam had taken something to calm her nerves on the flight, cough syrup I think, one of her favourites, which had poleaxed her. I helped her throw her stuff into her various hippie bags and shoved her out into the Third World. Lucky them.

1. Illegally occupied apartment.

It was still dark but warming up. In the chaos outside the airport, scores of raggedy beggars pressed menacingly at us; the women fell at, and kissed, Miriam's red Dr Martens.

Wanting to escape, we got into the first car that offered a ride. I was nervous, not knowing how we'd find our way around this place, but Miriam closed her eyes again, refusing to take responsibility for anything. I'd have dumped her if it wouldn't have caused more problems than it solved.

We can't have been in Pakistan, the land of our forefathers, for more than an hour when the taxi driver pulled a gun on us. He and his companion, who looked about fourteen and was wrapped in a grim blanket against the night cold, had been friendly until then, saying—as we took off from the airport to Papa's place with Bollywood music rattling the car windows—"Good cassette? Good seat, comfortable, eh? You try some *paan*? You want cushion?"

"Groovy," murmured Miriam, shutting her eyes. "I think I'm already on a cushion."

This was the early Eighties; I had graduated, Lennon had been murdered, and the revolution had come at last: Margaret Thatcher was its figurehead. Miriam and I were in an ancient Morris Minor with beads and bells strung across it. She must have thought we were approaching some sort of head idyll and would soon run into Mia Farrow, Donovan and George Harrison meditating in front of a murmuring Indian.

The driver had taken a sharp left off the road, through some trees and across a lot of dirt, where we came to a standstill. He dragged us out of the car and told us to follow him. We did. He was waving a gun at our faces. It was not Dad's house; it was the end. A sudden, violent death early in the morning for me—on day one in the fatherland. I wondered whether we'd be in the newspapers back home, and if Mum would give them photographs of us.

Not that Miriam and I were alone. I could see people in the vicinity, living in tents and shacks, some of them squatting to watch us, others, skinny children and adults, just standing there. It looked like some kind of permanent pop festival: rotting ripped canvas and busted corrugated metal, fires, dogs, kids running about, the heat and light beginning to come up. No one was going to help us.

We considered the shooter. Oh, did we take it in! Sister and I were shouting, indeed jumping up and down and wildly yelling like crazies, which made the robber confused. He appeared to get the message that we didn't have any money. Then Miriam, who was accustomed to intense situations, had the stunning idea of giving him the corned beef.

She said, "It's not sacred to them, is it?"

"Corned beef? I don't think so."

She became very enthusiastic about it. She seemed to believe they should want corned beef, perhaps she thought they'd had a famine recently. They did indeed want corned beef. The robber grabbed the heavy bag and kept it without looking inside. Then he and the other man drove us back to the road, and then to Papa's place. Even robberies by taxi drivers are eccentric in Karachi.

"Papa won't be getting a brand-new bag then," I said as we hit the main road.[2] Miriam groaned as we swerved past donkey carts, BMWs, camels, a tank with Chinese markings, and crazy coloured buses with people hanging from the roofs like beads from a curtain.

2. Jamal, our narrator, puns on the title of the 1965 James Brown hit, "Papa's Got a Brand New Bag."

Luckily, along with the reggae records Dad had requested, I'd put an extra couple of cans of corned beef in my own bag. Papa wasn't disappointed. Although, apparently, he had told Miriam that corned beef was the thing he missed most about Britain, I can't believe he'd have wanted a suitcase full of it. He was partial to the stuff though, sitting at his typewriter eating it from the can, helped down with vodka obtained from a police friend.

"It could be worse," he'd say. "The only other thing to eat is curried goat brain."

Mother had wanted us to come here. She was sick of worrying about Miriam when she wasn't at home, and arguing with her when she went there to crash. Mother was also, at times, bitterly angry with Father. She had found us hell to cope with, and she had no support. It would benefit all of us to spend time with him, getting to know how he lived and how he really felt about things. Even Miriam agreed.

Long before we got to Pakistan, like a lot of other "ethnics," she'd been getting into the roots thing. She was a Pakistani, a minority in Britain, but there was this other place, where she had a deep connection, which was spiritual, even Sufic. To prepare for the trip, she'd joined a group of whirling dervishes in Notting Hill. When she demonstrated the "whirling" to me, at Heathrow, it was pretty gentle, a tea dance version. Still, we'd see just how spiritual the place was. So far we'd had a gun at our heads.

Soon Papa's servant was making us tea and toast. Papa, not only thin but as fragile as a Giacometti,[3] yet dignified in his white salwar-kamiz[4] and sandals, informed us we would not be staying with him, but with our uncle, his older brother Yasir. To be honest, it was a relief.

"What the fuck is this, a squat?" Miriam said, when we were alone.

It turned out that Father, an aristocrat to those he left behind, was living in a crumbling flat, the walls peeling, the wires exposed, the busted furniture seeming to have been distributed at random, as though a place would be found for it later. Dust blew in through the windows, settling among the ragged piles of newspaper rustling on the floor and the packets of unused white paper, already curling in the heat.

Later that morning, saying he had to write his column, Papa got his servant to drive us to Yasir's. It was a broad one-storey house that looked like a mansion in movies set in Beverly Hills, an empty swimming pool full of leaves in the front, and rats rushing through them.

Miriam was annoyed we weren't staying with Dad, but I went along with the adventure. For a suburban kid with not very much, I like my luxuries, and luxuries there were at Yasir's.

It was a house of doe-eyed beauties. There were at least four. The Raj Quartet[5] I called them. I was still mourning Ajita, of course, as well as assuming we could get back together when she eventually returned to London. I had never given up on her. We would be closer than before; we would marry and have children.

Meanwhile, it occurred to me that this quartet of dark-skinned, long-haired women staring at us from a doorway, Uncle Yasir's daughters, might help me bear my pain.

I was looking at the girls, confronting the anguish of choice, not unlike a cat being offered a box of captive mice, when there was a commotion. Apparently there was a rabid dog on the roof. We rushed out to see it being chased by servants with long sticks. The servants got a few good cracks in, and the dog lay injured in the road

3. Alberto Giacometti (1901–1966), Swiss sculptor, known for his rail-thin human figures.
4. Suit of loose-fitting trousers and tunic.
5. A series of four novels (1965–1975) by Paul Scott about India under British rule.

outside, making god-awful noises. When we went our later, it was dead. "You like our country?" said the house guard.

Miriam was told that she not only had to share a room with two of her cousins, but with a servant, too, a couple of children and our grandmother, who was, apparently, a princess. This old woman spoke little English and washed her hands and clothes continuously; the rest of the time she spent either praying or studying the Koran.

It was a large house, but the women kept to their side of it and they were very close with one another. So Miriam and I were separated, and each day we did different things, as we always had at home. I liked to read the books I'd brought with me, while Miriam would go to the market with the women and then cook with them. In the evenings dad and his friends would come over, or I'd go with him to their houses.

When Papa was writing his column, which he began early in the morning, I'd sit in his flat listening to the heroes of ska and bluebeat, while being shaved by his servant. Papa was working on a piece ostensibly about families called "The Son-in-Law Also Rises." It was giving him difficulty because, having written it straightforwardly, he then had to obscure it, turning it into a kind of poetic code, so the reader would understand it but not the authorities.

Dad's weekly column was on diverse subjects, all obliquely political. Why were there not more flowers bordering the main roads in Karachi? Surely the more colour there was—colour representing democracy—the more lively everything would be? His essay on the fact that people wash too often, and would have more personality if they were dirtier—thus expressing themselves more honestly—was about the water shortages. An essay ostensibly about the subtle beauty of darkness and the velvet folds of the night was about the daily electricity breakdowns. He'd hand them to me for my suggestions, and I even wrote a couple of paragraphs, my first published works.

After this was done, at lunchtime we'd tour the city, visiting Dad's friends, mostly old men who'd lived through the history of Pakistan, ending up at my father's club.

In the evening we'd go to parties where the men wore ties and jackets, and the women jewellery and pretty sandals. There were good manners, heavy drinking, and much competitive talk of favours, status and material possessions: cars, houses, clothes.

Far from being "spiritual," as Miriam understood it, Karachi was the most materialistic place we had been. Deprivation was the spur. However, I might have considered my father's friends to be vulgar and shallow, but it was I who was made to feel shabby, like someone who'd stupidly missed a good opportunity in Britain. I was gently mocked by these provincial bourgeois, with my father watching me carefully to see how I coped. What sort of man, half here and half there, had I turned out to be? I was an oddity again, as I had been at school.

All the same, my father was educating me, telling me about the country, talking all the time about partition, Islam, liberalism, colonialism. I may have been a feisty little British kid with Trot[6] acquaintances and a liking for The Jam,[7] but I began to see how much Dad needed his liberal companions who approved of Reagan and Thatcher. This was anathema to me, but represented "freedom" in this increasingly Islamized land. Dad's friends were, like him, already alienated in this relatively new country, and he believed their condition would get worse as the country became more theocratic. As Dad said, "There are few honest men here. In fact, I may be the only one! No wonder there are those who wish to establish a republic of virtue."

Many of my father's friends tried to impress on me that I, as a member of the "coming up" generation, had to do my best to keep freedom alive in Pakistan. "We are dying

6. Trotskyite.

7. British punk band.

out here, yaar. Please, you must help us." The British had gone, there'd been a vacuum, and now the barbarians were taking over. Look what had happened in Iran: the "spiritual" politics of the revolution had ended in a vicious God-kissed dictatorship with widespread amputations, stonings and executions. If the people there could remove a man as powerful as the Shah, what might happen in other Muslim countries?

I learned that Father was an impressive man: articulate, amusing and much admired for his writing. He'd almost gone to jail; only his "connections" had kept him out. He had been defiant but never stupid. I read his pieces, collected at last, in a book published only in Pakistan. In such a corrupt place he represented some kind of independence, authority and integrity.

If he seemed to have the measure of life, it wasn't long before I had to put to him the question I was most afraid of. Why hadn't he stayed with us? What made him come here? Why had we never been a proper family?

He didn't shirk the question but went at it head on, as if he'd been expecting it for years. Apart from the "difficulties" he had with mother—the usual stuff between a man and a woman, at which I nodded gravely, as though I understood—there had been an insult, he said. He had liked Mum. He still respected her, he said. It was odd to hear him speaking about her as a girlfriend he'd had years ago, but now, clearly, was indifferent to.

I learned, though, that he had had, briefly, at the same time as Mum, another girlfriend, whose parents had invited him to dinner at their house in Surrey. They were eating when the mother said, "Oh, you can eat with a knife and fork? I thought you people normally ate with your fingers."

This was to a man who'd been brought up in a wealthy liberal Indian family in colonial Bombay. Among the many children, Father was the prince of the family, inheritor of the family talent. "Isn't he a magnificent man?" Yasir had said to me. "Your grandfather told me to look after him always."

Dad had been educated in California, where he'd established himself on the college circuit as a champion debater and skilful seducer of women. He believed he had the talent and class to become a minister in the Indian government, ambassador to Paris or New York, a newspaper editor or a university chancellor. Dad told me he couldn't face more of this prejudice, as it was called then. He had "got out," gone home to the country he had never known, to be part of its birth, to experience the adventure of being a "pioneer."

As we drove around Karachi—him tiny behind the wheel of the car—he began to weep, this clean man in his white salwar-kamiz and sandals, with an alcohol smell that I got used to, and came to like. He regretted it, he said, the fact that we as a family weren't together and he couldn't do his duty as a father. Mother wouldn't live in Pakistan and he was unable to live in England.

If he had left us in Britain, it was, he added, as much for our sake as for his. It was obvious we would have more of a chance there. What should have happened, he said, was that his family should never have left India for Pakistan. India was where his heart was, where he'd belonged, where he and Yasir and his sisters and brothers had grown up, in Bombay and Delhi.

He now realized that Bombay, rather than Karachi, was the place where his ideals could have been met, crazy though it might be there. In Pakistan they had made a mess of things. He admitted it could have been predicted by a cursory reading of history. Any state based on a religious idea—on one god—was going to be a dictatorship. "Voltaire could have foretold, boy. You only have to read anywhere there to realize."

He went on, "Liberals like me are marginal here. We are called the 'high and dry' generation. We are, indeed, frequently high, but rarely dry. We wander around the city, looking for one another to talk to. The younger, bright ones all leave. Your cousins will never have a home, but will wander the world forever. Meanwhile, the mullahs will take over. That is why I'm making the library."

Packages of books from Britain and the US arrived at Papa's flat a couple of times a week. He didn't unpack them all, and, when he did, I noticed that some of them were volumes he already had, in new editions. With Yasir's money, Papa was building a library in the house of a wealthy lawyer. Such a darkness had fallen upon the country that the preservation of any kind of critical culture was crucial. A student or woman, as he put it, might want access to the little library, where he knew the books would be protected after his death.

Dad insisted I go to meet his older sister, a poet and university lecturer. She was in bed when we arrived, having had arthritis for the last ten years. "I've been expecting you," she said, pinching my cheek. "This will be difficult, but there's something you need to see."

We got her up and on to her walking frame and accompanied her to the university, which she was determined to show me, though it was closed due to "disturbances." She, Dad and I shuffled and banged our way through the corridors and open rooms, looking at the rows of wooden benches and undecorated, crumbling walls.

She taught English literature, Shakespeare, Austen, the Romantics. However, the place had been attacked frequently by radical Islamists, and no one had returned to classes. The books she taught were considered "*haram*," forbidden. Meanwhile madrassas or "bomb schools" were being established by President Zia.[8] This was where many poor families sent their kids, the only places they would receive education, and food.

When I wondered what it meant for my aunt to teach English literature in such a place, to people who had never been to England, she said, "They've gone, the British. Colonialism restrained radical Islam, and the British at least left us their literature and their language. A language doesn't belong to anyone. Like the air, everyone can use it. But they left a political hole which others fill with stones. The Americans, the CIA, supported the Islamic revival to keep the Communists out of the Middle East. That is what we English teachers call an irony." She went on, "It is the women I fear for, the young women growing up here. No ideology hates women more than this one. These fanatics will undo all the good work done by women in the Sixties and Seventies."

She would return to the university when the time was right, though she doubted that she'd live to see it. "A student said to me, 'We will kill ten thousand people, which will destroy this country's institutions and create a revolution. Then we could attack Afghanistan and go upwards . . . There will be the believers and there will be the dead. The West will defeat Communism but not Islam—because the people believe in Islam.' "

Meanwhile my aunt was content to remain in her room and write poetry. She had published five volumes, paying for the printing costs herself, the Urdu on one page, the English on the other. She adored the Trinidad poet Derek Walcott, who was her light. "His father, I'm sure, was a clerk in the colonial administration, like so many of our educated." He had taught her that she could write from her position—"cross-cultural," she called it—and make sense. Other local poets met at her house,

8. Muhammad Zia-ul-Haq (1924–1988), President of Pakistan, 1978–1988.

to read their work and talk. They wouldn't be the first poets, nor the last, to have to work "underground."

"I envy the birds," she said. "They can sing. No one shuts their mouths or imprisons them. Only they are free here."

Language; poetry; speaking; freedom. The country was wretched but some of the people were magnificent, forced into seriousness. Dad would have known the effect this would have on me.

Our lives had been separate. Dad had never visited our schools or even our house when he was in Britain; there'd been no everyday affection. But as he drove about Karachi he did ask me, What is it you really do? As though he needed to know the secret I'd been keeping from the anxious enquirers at the dinner parties.

I didn't have much of a reply. I said I was going to do a PhD on the later work of Wittgenstein.[9] I'd say this to anyone who enquired about my choice of career, and I did so to Papa. He could show me off or at least shut the questioners up; I had, after all, graduated with honours—whatever they are—in Philosophy.

This was, though, only for the benefit of others and Dad knew it. When, in private, he called me a "bum," which he did from time to time, often appending other words like "useless" or "lazy" or, when he was particularly drunk, "fucking useless lazy stupid," I tried to defend myself. I was not bringing shame on the family. I did want to do some kind of intellectual work and had even considered doing an MA. But really I only considered Philosophy as the basis of intellectual engagement, a critical tool, rather than anything that seemed worth pursing for itself. Who can name a living British philosopher of distinction? Later, psychoanalysis came to interest me more, being closer to the human.

This was all too vague for Papa, and the "bum" taunts didn't stop. He'd say, "Your other cousins, what are they doing? They're training to be doctors, lawyers, engineers. They'll be able to work anywhere in the world. Who the fuck wants a Philosophy PhD? Yasir was like you, doing nothing, sitting in pubs. Then our father, who was in Britain, kicked his arse and he opened factories and hotels. So, you can consider your arse to be kicked!"

How could I put pleasure before duty? What could be more infuriatingly enviable than that? Papa had kicked my arse. Where had he kicked it to? I felt worthless, and glad he hadn't been around in London: one of us might have killed the other.

As I considered the serious side of Papa's attack, I drifted around Yasir's house, wondering what to do with myself. I'd already learned how difficult it was to find solitude in this country. The price of an extended and strong family was that everyone scrutinized and overlooked one another continuously; every word or act was discussed, usually with disapproval.

One day I discovered that my uncle also had a library. Or at least there was a room called "the library," which contained a wall of books, and a long table and several chairs. The room was musty but clean. No one ever used it, like front parlours in the suburbs.

I took in the books, which were hardbacks. Poetry, literature, a lot of left-wing politics, many published by Victor Gollancz. They'd been bought in London by one of my uncles and shipped to Pakistan. The uncle, who lived in Yasir's house but now "roamed around all day," had developed schizophrenia. In his early twenties he'd been a brilliant student, but his mind had deteriorated.

9. Ludwig Wittgenstein (1889–1951), Austrian-British philosopher.

I sat at the library table and opened the first book, the contents crumbling and falling on the floor, as though I had opened a packet of flour upside down. I tried other volumes. In the end my reading schedule was determined by the digestion of the local worms. As it happened, there was one book less fancied by the worms than others. It was the Hogarth edition of *Civilization and Its Discontents*,[1] which I had never read before. It occurred to me, as I went at it, that it was more relevant to the society in which I was presently situated than to Britain. Whatever: I was gripped from the first sentence, which referred to "what is truly valuable in life . . ."

What was truly valuable in life? Who wouldn't have wanted to know that? I could have ripped at those pages with my fingernails in order to get all of the material inside me. Of course, I was maddened by the fact that whole sentences had been devoured by the local wildlife. Indeed, one of the reasons I wanted to return to London was that I wanted to read it properly. In the end, the only way to satisfy my habit—if I didn't want to ask my father for books, which I didn't—was to read the same pages over and over.

Often, my only companion was my schizophrenic uncle, who would sit at the end of the table, babbling, often entertainingly, with a Joycean flow. The meaning, of course, was opaque to me, but I loved him, and wanted to know him. There was no way in. I was as "in" as I was going to get.

While I settled into a daily routine of carefully turning the medieval parchment pages of old books, I noticed a movement at the door. I said nothing but could see Najma, at twenty-one the youngest female cousin, watching me. She waited for me to finish, smiling and then hiding her face whenever I looked at her. I had played with her in London as a kid. We had met at least once a year, and I felt we had a connection.

"Take me to a hotel, please," she said. "This evening."

I was mad with excitement. The bum also rises.

This advent of heterosexuality surprised me a little. I had already been made aware of the broad sensuality of Muslim societies: the women, for instance, who slept in the same room, were forever caressing and working one another's hair and bodies; and the boys always holding hands, dancing and giggling together in someone's bedroom, playing homoerotically. They talked of how lecherous the older men were, particularly teachers of the Koran, and how, where possible, you had to mind your arse in their presence. Of course, many of my favourite writers had gone to Muslim countries to get laid. I recalled Flaubert's[2] letters from Egypt. "Those shaved cunts make a strange effect—the flesh is hard as bronze and my girl had a splendid arse." "At Esna in one day I fired five times and sucked three." As for the boys, "We have considered it our duty to indulge in this form of ejaculation."

I had been introduced to young men of my age, and went out with them a few times, standing around brightly decorated hamburger and kebab stalls, talking about girls. But compared to these boys, after Ajita, I had little hope; they seemed too young, I was alienated, and had no idea where I belonged, if anywhere now. I would have to make a place. Or find someone to talk to.

It took Najma three hours to get ready. I'd never waited so long for a girl before and hope to never again. I was reminded, unfortunately, once more of Ajita, who was inevitably late for classes, giving the excellent excuse that she didn't want the lecturer to see her with bad hair.

1. A meditative work by Sigmund Freud (1930).

2. Gustave Flaubert (1821–1880), innovator in modern French fiction.

Najma turned up, aflame with colour, in a glittering salwar-kamiz with gold embroidery. On her wrists she had silver bangles; on her hands there was some sort of brown writing; her hair resembled a swinging black carpet, and she wore more make-up than I'd seen on anyone aside from a junkie transvestite friend of Miriam's. Najma didn't need the slap; she was young and her skin was like the surface of a good cup of coffee.

I assumed we were going to the hotel to fuck. I didn't realize that the Karachi hotels were the smartest places in town, where all the aspiring courting couples went. The radical Muslims were always threatening to bomb these hotels—and did occasionally—but as there were no bars and few restaurants in the city, there was nowhere else to go apart from private houses.

Sitting there in my ragged black suit—I could scratch my crack through the gash in the behind—drinking nothing stronger than a salted lassi,[3] all I did was worry about the size of the bill and feel as out of place as I did on the street. But in the car on the way home she asked if I'd let her suck me off. It sounded like a good idea, particularly as I doubted whether I'd be able to find my way through the complicated layers of clothes she seemed to be wearing. She pulled over somewhere. As I ran my fingers through Najma's black hair I though it could have been Ajita—in a neighbouring country—who was satisfying me. At the end she said, "I love you, my husband."

Husband? I put this down to the poetic exaggerations of passion. Najma and I had a lot of time together and after our first lovemaking she made it clear she was in love with me. I liked that about her. I fall in love too easily myself. You see a face and the fantasies start, like tapping on the magic lantern.

She liked to deride the West for its "corruption" and "excess." It was a dirty place, and she couldn't wait to move there, to escape the cul-de-sac which was Pakistan, the increasing violence, the power of the mullahs, and the bent politicians. I would be her ticket.

I'd read and she'd lie with her head in my lap, talking. Other women who came to the house were training as doctors and airline pilots, but the Chekhovian women in my family only wanted to get away, to America or Britain—Inglestan it was called—except that they couldn't do it without a sufficiently ambitious husband. The ones left behind, or waiting to leave, watched videos of Bollywood movies, visited friends and aunties, gossiped, went out for kebabs, but otherwise were forced into indolence, though their imaginations remained lush and hot.

I didn't want the sucking to stop. I liked it a lot, along with the spanking and other stuff I hadn't yet got round to. She liked—she was very fond of—the economics, too. Not a Merc, darling, I'd say, when she seemed to think that that was what we'd move around London in. I'd prefer a Jag. I've had Jags, even a Roller, a Bentley for a week, but I sent it back. I've had a lot of trouble with Mercs, they're always breaking down, the big ends go, Jesus.

Then I'd tell her New York wasn't enough for her. We would have to go out to LA, to Hollywood, where the swimming pools were top class and maybe she could become an actress, she had the looks.

"Next week?" she said.

"Maybe," I said, hastening to add that though I might seem a bit short of money at the moment, I'd had it before and soon would again, once I started back at work. It wouldn't take someone as smart as me long to make real money.

3. Yogurt-based drink.

I have to say I didn't begin by wanting to deceive Najma with these spidery nonsense nets. She had taken it for granted that I was already wealthy, and could become even wealthier in the near future, like her male cousins. She'd been to Britain often, but had little idea of what it was really like. Most people, in fact, seemed to think that Miriam and I were rich. If we weren't we must have been stupid, or mentally weak. One time I saw a young servant of Yasir's wearing my shoes, then a pair of my suit trousers. When I remonstrated with him he just grinned.

"But you are rich," he said in strange English.

"Get that stuff off," I said, "I'm going to tell Yasir."

He acted like I'd hit him. "Please, I beg you, no, no," he pleaded. "He sack me."

Off he went in my gear. What could I do? He earned almost nothing. Miriam, being generous and ingenious, found a way to fund him while benefiting us. She got him to bring us joints which we'd smoke on the roof. Not long after, I discovered from Najma that Papa was referring to us as "*les enfants terribles*." His own children!

Not that we weren't looking into him too, eager to get the low-down. I knew little about his romantic life, whether he had anyone or not. It seemed unlikely. He had his routine, his worries and his books.

There was, though, his second wife, Miriam, and I went to her office, where she was the editor of a woman's magazine. She was very cool, small with fine features, polite, curious and intelligent. She had an English upper-class accent with the head-wagging Indian lilt I'd liked since meeting Ajita. I could see Miriam getting a crush on her. But she wasn't for a moment emotionally engaged with us. She didn't talk about Papa or our lives without him. After our visit, Miriam phoned a couple of times but was told she was away.

Things began to go bad. One time I was in the library and Najma was waiting outside as she always did. I went to her, checked for prying eyes, and kissed her shiny lips a little and began to touch her, but she was cold and pushed me away. She was silent for a while, letting me take in her hurt, before beginning to abuse me in Urdu. Her father, in a rage, came in. They talked a lot in Urdu too. I got out of there. It was breaking down.

It turned out that Najma had gone to Miriam and confessed to her. We were in love, we were going to marry, we were off to London, New York, Hollywood, in a Merc, or was it a Jag?

Miriam calmly told her to forget it, Jamal was marrying no one. He's not even a student; he's got the degree but so does every bum and semi-fool in London Town. Forget the Jag, the fucker might be able to drive but he hasn't taken his test, they wouldn't let him on the road in England. If he's intending to marry, she finished off, he hasn't mentioned it to me, and he mentions everything to me, otherwise I slap him.

I was in a rage with Miriam. Why did she do this? She liked the girl, she said. She felt sorry for her being subjected to my lies and stupid stories. But what was she doing herself?

It was taken for granted I'd accompany Papa during the day (I was learning a lot), just as he took it for granted that Miriam would stay at the house with the other women. They would discuss "women's things." But, apparently, she had stopped doing this. Instead, she had taken to driving off in Uncle Yasir's car, often with her head uncovered. When asked where she's been, she'd reply, "Sightseeing." I had some idea of what these sights might be when she told me that her favourite thing in Karachi was to go to the beach and there, under a palm tree, split open a coconut and pour half a bottle of gin into it.

Most of the sightseeing she did was from within the arms of one of our cousin's fiancés, an airline pilot, who had a beach hut. He and our cousin were to be married later that year, but the pilot was taking the opportunity to get to know the further reaches of the family. He and Miriam had also been meeting in rooms in the hotel I'd visited with Najma, where he knew the manager.

They'd been spotted. Gossip was one of the few things that moved urgently in Karachi. He'd taken it for granted that English girls were easy, and when he ran into Miriam he knew he was right. I'd been wondering how she knew so many little things about the country. Of course our cousin went crazy, and threatened to stab Miriam. Miriam was outnumbered. I refused to help her.

Miriam had thought we could live in Pakistan a while, get a job, save a bit, hang out on the beach and deal hash, and so on. But in a little less than a month the whole thing had become impossible. We were too alien; there was no way we could fit in. There were American and British wives living there, but they had gone native, wearing the clothes, doing the accent, trying to learn the language in order to speak to the servants.

Outside, if Miriam wasn't covered, she was jeered and hissed at. They even pinched her. She picked up fruit from stalls and threw it at people. I was terrified she'd get into a fist fight or worse. I kept my head down, but Miriam, being a modern woman of the most extreme kind, fucked them all up. Our grandmother, the Princess, had already gone to her, placed her hand on her forehead and said, "I'm going to recite a small prayer which will drive out the devil and the evil spirits which possess you. Satan, be off! Give us victory over those who disbelieve!" The following morning she had two sheep slaughtered. The meat was distributed among the poor, who were asked to pray for Miriam's quick recovery.

It all blew up at Papa's flat one morning when I heard a commotion in the sitting room. There were raised voices. Then I heard what sounded like a large object being thrown across the floor. I guessed the large object might be Papa. When I ran in, followed by the servant, Miriam was sitting on Papa, rather as she used to sit on me, screaming at him. He was trying to protect his face as well as trying to strike her. She was strong and difficult to pull off. There was something she wanted to tell him.

"He's been abusing me!" she said, as we held her, trying to pin her arms behind her back.

Papa was dusting himself down. Then I saw she had spat at him, that her spittle was on his face. He took his handkerchief and cleaned himself.

She said, "He says I kiss the arse of whitey! He calls me 'a rotten girl' and a dirty slut who can't behave! Yet he left us there in London! He abandoned us! What could be worse than that!"

"Get out," cried Papa in a weak voice. He went into another room and shut the door.

It was the last time we saw him.

Dad must have spoken to Yasir. When we got back to his house we were informed that we were leaving later, around one in the morning. We were not given any choice. The servants were already packing our bags. No one said goodbye or waved. We weren't allowed to say goodbye to the girls.

The funny thing was, we spotted Miriam's lover, the pilot, going through the "crew lane" in the airport. Later, during the flight, he came to collect her. Apparently she "guided the plane." A packed 747 with Miriam at the wheel, sitting on the pilot's knee, with, no doubt, her hand in his fly.

Mother had wanted us to see father "in his own environment." She thought it would be informative. It was. We could no longer idealize him. In most ways he was worse off than us. He couldn't save us, nor we him. He couldn't be the father we had wanted him to be. If I wanted a father, I'd have to find a better one.

By the time we returned to London, Miriam and I weren't speaking. I hated her and didn't want to see her again. I didn't want to be the little brother any more. Usually I'm quite passive, if not evasive; I go along with things, to see what's happening, not wanting to make things worse by tossing my chillies into the stew. But I had said to Miriam, as we left Papa's, that she had ruined the whole trip.

"No wonder Papa thinks you're an idiot and a bitch," I explained. "You can't control yourself for five minutes! These people have their own way of life and you just pissed all over it! There can be few people in this world who are more selfish then you!"

She was so sullen and freaked, traumatized, I supposed, she couldn't even hit me. It occurred to me that she'd either damage herself in some way or go back on the smack.

We rode back into London on the Tube. The little houses and neat gardens sitting there in the cold looked staid, cute, prim. Saying nothing, hating everything, we both had furious eyes. This was our land and it was where we had to live. All we could do now was get on with our lives—or not. At Victoria Station the two us parted without speaking. I went home to Mum and Miriam went to stay with someone who had a council flat in North Kensington.

I knew that whatever happened, I needed to get a job. Luckily, I had a friend from university who was working in the British Library, and he said he could get me something there.

The one person I didn't expect to see again was Najma, but she turned up a year later in Britain and rang Mother, asking for me. For a moment, in my confusion and with Mum's lack of clarity—"an Indian girl phoned"—I thought it was Ajita. I began to cry with relief. She hadn't forgotten me. She was coming back.

Najma had married a Pakistani who came here to study engineering, and the two of them were living in Watford, with twins. I went out to see them a few times.

One kid had a fever, the other was perhaps a little backward. The couple had been racially harassed, knew no one, and the husband was out all day. Najma would cook for me; she knew I loved her food, and we'd sit together, chastely, while she talked of everything she missed "back home." Exiled, she continued to curse the West for its immorality, while blaming it for failing to dispense its wealth to her family with the alacrity her fantasies demanded.

I took the husband out for a drink, and had to listen to him complaining about the excessive price of prostitutes in Britain.

I could only say that Britain might turn out to be more expensive than he thought.

2007

Nick Hornby

b. 1957

Fanaticism is Nick Hornby's meat and potatoes. He came to the attention of the British reading public in 1995 with his memoiristic *Fever Pitch*, about his devotion to the English football club Arsenal; the 2005 American film adaptation substituted comic Jimmy

Fallon for Hornby, and baseball's Boston Red Sox for Arsenal F.C.—but a fanatic's a fanatic. The analysis was then extended in Hornby's first novel *High Fidelity* (1995), which takes its title from an Elvis Costello song; in this case, it's young males' blind devotion to music, rather than sport, to which Hornby turns his attention. It may be the best fictional treatment we have of what it means to be a rock fan, note-perfect in its rendering of what it's like to consume and be consumed by the music, and it brought Hornby a measure of celebrity throughout the English-speaking world.

Hornby was born in Maidenhead, thirty miles west of London. He graduated from Cambridge University and taught English at a community college in Cambridge for a time before turning his attention full-time to writing. Hornby has managed very successfully to combine fiction writing with popular journalism; he has written for *GQ*, *Esquire*, *Vogue*, and the *New Yorker*, among others. Some of his music writing is collected in *Songbook* (2002), a National Book Critics Circle Award finalist; profits from the book, along with those from an anthology of short fiction that Hornby edited, *Speaking with the Angel* (2001) from which *NippleJesus* is taken, go to Treehouse Trust, a charity that works with autistic children. He currently lives in Highbury, Islington, in central London.

Hornby has been called the father of "lad lit," novels about immature and commitment-phobic young men seeking to remain in a state of perpetual adolescence; the actor Hugh Grant seems almost to have been type-cast in the starring role of Chris and Paul Weitz's 2002 film treatment of Hornby's *About a Boy*. As Rob Fleming, the protagonist/narrator of *High Fidelity*, puts it in a rare moment of self-recognition: "I've been thinking with my guts since I was fourteen years old, and frankly speaking, between you and me, I have come to the conclusion that my guts have shit for brains." But as Rob's confession suggests, Hornby has matured beyond his narrators; the protagonist of *NippleJesus* finds himself at a crossroads of sorts, both in terms of his family life, his career, and his own aesthetic and emotional development. By the end of the story, he has gone a long way toward leaving the lad behind.

"Hornby believes that beautiful songs, beautiful books and yes, the beautiful game, are the great redemptive forces," Zadie Smith has written. "He loves good stuff so much that one might call him the European Ambassador of Goodness."

NippleJesus

from Speaking with the Angel

They never told me what it was, and they never told me why they might need someone like me. I probably wouldn't have taken the fucking job if they had, to tell you the truth. And if I'd been clever, I would have asked them on the first day, because looking back on it now, I had a few clues to be going on with: we were all sat around in this staff-room-type place, being given all the dos and don'ts, and it never occurred to me that I was just about the only male under sixty they'd hired. There were a few middle-aged women, and a lot of old gits, semi-retired, ex-Army types, but there was only one bloke of around my age, and he was tiny—little African geezer, Geoffrey, who looked like he'd run a mile if anything went off. But sometimes I forget what I look like, if you know what I mean. I was sitting there listening to what this woman was saying about flash photography and how close people were allowed to get and all that, and I was more like a head than a body, sort of thing, because if you're listening to what someone's saying that's what you are, isn't it? A head. A brain, not a body. But the point of me—the point of me here, in this place, for this job—is that I'm six foot two and fifteen stone.[1] It's not just that, either, but I look . . . well, handy, I suppose. I look like I can take care of myself, what with the tattoos and the shaved head and all that. But sometimes I forget. I don't forget when I'm eyeballing some little shitbag outside a club, some nineteen-year-old in a two-hundred-quid[2] jacket who's trying to impress his bird by giving me some mouth; but when I'm watching something on TV, like a documentary or something, or when I'm putting the kids to bed, or when I'm reading, I don't think, you know, fucking hell I'm big. Anyway, listening to this woman, I forgot, so when she told me I'd be in the Southern Fried Chicken Wing looking after number 49, I never asked her, "Why me? Why do you need a big bloke in the Southern?" I just trotted off, like a berk.[3] I never thought for a moment that I was on some sort of special mission.

I took this job because I promised Lisa I'd give up the night work at the club. It wasn't so much the hours—ten til three Monday to Thursday, ten til five Friday and Saturday, club closed on Sunday. OK, they fucked the weekends up, and I never saw the kids in the morning, but I could pick them up from school, give them their tea, and Lisa didn't have to worry about childcare or anything. She works in a dentist's near Harley Street, decent job, nice boss, good pay, normal hours, and with me being off all day, we could manage. I mean, it wasn't ideal, 'cos I never really saw her—by the time the kids were down and we'd had something to eat, it was time for me to put the monkey suit on and go out. But we both sort of knew it was just a phase, and I'd do something else eventually, although fuck knows what. Never really thought about that. She asks me sometimes what I'd do if I had the choice, and I always tell her I'd be Tiger Woods—millions of dollars a week, afternoons knocking a golf ball about in places like Spain and Florida, gorgeous blonde girlfriends (except I never mention that bit). And she says, no, seriously, and I say, I am being serious, and she says, no, you've got to be realistic. So I say, well what's the point of this game, then? You're asking me what I'd do if I had the choice, and I tell you, and then you tell me I haven't got the fucking choice. So what am I supposed to say? And she says, but you're too old to be a professional golfer—and she's right, I'm thirty-eight now—and you smoke too much. (Like you can't play fucking golf if you smoke.) Choose something else. And I say, OK, then, I'll be fucking Richard Branson.[4] And she says, well you can't just start by being Richard Branson. You have to do something first. And I say, OK, I'll be a bouncer first. And she gives up.

I know she means well, and I know she's trying to get me to think about my life, and about getting older and all that, but the truth is, I'm thirty-eight, I've got no trade and no qualifications, and I'm lucky to get a job headbutting cokeheads outside a club. She's great, Lisa, and if you think about it, even her asking the question shows that she loves me and thinks the world of me, because she really does think I've got choices, and someone else is going to have as much faith in me as she does. She wants me to say, oh, I'd like to run a DIY[5] shop, or I'd like to be an accountant, and the next day she'd come back with a load of leaflets, but I don't want to run a DIY shop, and I don't want to be an accountant. I know what my talent is: my talent is being big, and I'm making the most of it. If anyone asks her what I do, she says I'm a security consultant, but if I'm around when she says it, I laugh and say I'm a bouncer. I don't know what she'd say now. Probably that I'm an art expert. You watch. Give her two weeks and she'll be on at me to write to Antiques Roadshow. I don't know

1. 210 lbs. 1 stone = 14 lbs.
2. Pound sterling (£).
3. Fool.
4. Richard Branson (b. 1950), British entrepreneur, founder of Virgin Records and Virgin Airlines.
5. Do-it-yourself.

what world she lives in sometimes. I think it's something to do with the dentist's. She meets all these people, and they're loaded, and as thick as me, half of them, and she gets confused about what's possible and what's not.

But like I said, it wasn't the hours at the club. There were a couple of nasty moments recently, and I told her about them because they frightened me, so of course she did her nut, and I promised her I'd pack it in. See, the trouble is now, it doesn't matter how handy you are. I mean, half of those kids who went down Casablanca's, I literally could pick them up by the neck with one hand, and when you can do that . . . Put it this way, I didn't need to change my underpants too often. (I do anyway, though, every day, in case you're thinking I'm an unhygienic bastard.) But now everyone's tooled up. No one says, I'm going to have you. They all say, I'm going to cut you, or I'm going to stab you, and I'm going, yeah, yeah, and then they show you what they've got, and you think, fucking hell, this isn't funny anymore. Because how can you look after yourself if someone's got a knife? You can't. Anyway, about a month ago I threw this nasty little piece of work out of the club because he'd pushed it too far with a girl who was in there with her mates. And to be honest I probably slapped him once more than was strictly necessary, because he really got on my fucking nerves. And the next thing I know, he's got this . . . this thing, this . . . I've never seen anything like it before, but it was a sort of spike, about six inches long, sharp as fuck and rusty, and he starts jabbing it at me and telling me that I was dead. I was lucky, because he was scared, and he was holding this thing all wrong so it was pointing down at the ground instead of towards me, so I kicked his hand as hard as I fucking could and he dropped it, and I jumped on him. We called the police and they nicked him, but when they'd gone I knocked off. I'd had enough. I know what people think: they think that if that's the sort of job you choose, you're asking for whatever you get, and you probably want it, too, because you're a big ape who likes hurting people. Well, bollocks. I don't like hurting people. For me, a good night at Casablanca's is one where nothing's happened at all. I mean, OK, I'll probably have to stop a couple of people coming in because they're underage, or bombed out of their brains, but I see my job as allowing people to have a good time without fear of arseholes. Really, I do. I mean, OK, I'm not Mother Teresa or anything, I'm not doing good works or saving the world, but it's not such a shitty job if you look at it like that. But I'm a family man. I can't have people waving rusty spikes at me at two in the morning. I don't want to die outside some poxy club. So I told Lisa about it, and we talked, and I packed it in. I was lucky, because I was only out of work for a fortnight. They wouldn't let me draw the dole[6] because I'd left my previous employment voluntarily. "But this geezer had a rusty spike," I said. "Well, you should have taken it up with your employers," she said. Like they would have offered me a desk job. Or given the kid with a spike a written warning. It didn't matter much, though, 'cos I found this one pretty much straightaway, at an employment bureau. The money's a lot less, but the hours are better. I was well chuffed.[7] How hard can it be, I thought, standing in front of a painting?

So. We had the induction hour, and then we were led through the gallery to our positions. On the way I was trying to work out whether I'd ever been in an art gallery before or not. You'd think I'd remember, but the trouble is, art galleries look exactly like you think they're going to look—a load of corridors with pictures hanging on them and people wandering around. So how would I know if I've been to one before? It feels like I have, but maybe I've just seen one on the telly, or in the films—there's

6. Unemployment insurance.

7. Pleased.

that bit in *Dressed to Kill*, isn't there, where the bloke's trying to pick her up, and they keep seeing each other in different rooms. I can say this for sure, though: I've never had a good time in one. If I have ever been, it was on a school trip, and I was bored out of my skull, like on just about every school trip I was taken. The only one I remember now is when we went to some Roman ruins somewhere, and I nicked a few stones out of this mosaic thing. I stood on the edge and loosened a few with my foot, and while the teacher was talking, I crouched down as if to do up my shoelace and slipped a few in my pocket. And when we got back on the coach, I showed all the other lads what I'd done, and it turned out they'd all done exactly the same, and we were holding half the fucking floor in our hands. And the next thing we knew the bloke in charge of the place was chasing the coach down the street, and we all had to go to the front and put what we'd nicked into a carrier bag. We got in a lot of trouble for that. Anyway, what I reckon is we did go to an art gallery somewhere, and I don't remember because nobody walked off with a painting.

The thing is, this gallery's like the normal sort of gallery for the first few rooms—pictures of fruit and all that, and then it starts to go weird. First we went through a couple of rooms where the pictures aren't pictures of anything, just splodges, and then when we get to our bit, the new exhibition, there aren't many pictures at all. There are bits of animals all over the place, and a tent, and ping-pong balls floating on air currents, and a small house made of concrete, and videos of people reading poetry. It looks more like a school open day than an art gallery. You know, biology here, science there, English over at the back, media studies next to the toilets. . .

"I could have done any of these myself," said this miserable old git called Tommy who'd already moaned once about the length of the coffee breaks. "Yeah, you could now, you old cunt," I said to him. "Now you've seen them. Anyone could now. But you didn't think of it. So you're too late." I was pleased with that. I pinched it off of a teacher at school, apart from the "you old cunt" bit. That's mine. We were reading this poem at school, and some kid said exactly the same thing as Tommy—"I could have done that." Because it was an easy poem. It was short, and we knew all the words, and it didn't rhyme. And the teacher said, "No, you couldn't. You could now, because you could just copy it out. But you didn't think of it." I thought that was smart. Anyway, Tommy hasn't spoken to me since I called him an old cunt, and I'm glad.

I don't give a fuck about whether it's art, or who could do it. The thing is, it isn't boring, our gallery. The other rooms, with the pictures of cows in, they're boring. But our rooms, with the actual cows in, all cut up, they're not. There's got to be a lesson in there somewhere, hasn't there? It wouldn't work for everything, though, I can see that. I mean, it works for cows and tents and small houses, but it wouldn't work for, like, the fucking river. You'd still have to do a painting of that.

Anyway. Our group was getting smaller and smaller, because the woman taking us to our positions was sort of dropping us off, like we were in her bus. And it turned out that I was the last passenger. Like when me and Lisa went on a dodgy package holiday to Spain, years and years ago, before the kids came, and there was a coach to pick us all up at the airport, and every other bastard got dropped off at their hotel before we did, because it turned out that our hotel was two miles from the fucking beach. My painting was sort of the same thing as that. It was off to the side, in a room all of its own, and there was a curtain across the entrance, so it was separate from the others. Outside, there was a sign that said: "WARNING! This room contains an exhibit of a controversial nature. Please do not enter if you feel you might be offended. Over

18s only." The woman didn't say anything about that. She just ignored it—never asked me if *I* might be offended.

"You're in here," she said. "Watch out. We're expecting trouble." And then she went off.

I went behind the curtain, and there on the far wall was this massive picture of Jesus. I'd say it was probably ten feet high, five or six feet wide, something like that. It's kind of like the pictures you've seen before—eyes closed, the old crown of thorns on his head. That was when he was on the cross, wasn't it? It's sort of a closeup, head and shoulders, so you only see a bit of the cross, but what this picture has that the normal ones don't—not to me they don't, anyway—is that you can really tell just how much it must have fucking hurt, being nailed up. Usually, it looks like he's having a kip,[8] but this one, his face is all screwed up in agony. You really wouldn't want to be in his shoes, I'll tell you. So the first thing I thought was, bloody hell, that's a good picture. Because it makes you think, and I don't often think about things like that. I haven't been anywhere near Jesus since Lisa's sister got married, three years ago.

And the second thing I thought—I'd forgotten about the sign and the curtain and all that for a moment—was, who the fuck would get offended by that? Because you can go into any church and see the same sort of thing. Not so realistic, maybe, a bit more PG than R, but, you know, basically the same sort of stuff: moustache and beard, crown of thorns, sad. Because you can't tell how it's done from a distance, see. When you step behind the curtain, you just see the picture, and the face. You have to get quite close up to see anything else. So I couldn't understand it, why there was all the fuss. I just thought: religious people. Nutters. 'Cos they are, most of them, aren't they? I mean, to each his own and everything, but you wouldn't want to marry one, would you?

There's a chair in front of the picture, and I walked towards it to have a sit-down. And as I got closer, I could see that the picture was made up of hundreds—thousands, maybe millions—of little squares, like the mosaics I pinched from the Roman ruins. And when I got really close, I could see that these millions of little squares were actually little pictures, and every single little picture had at least one female breast in it. So . . . you know those pictures that are made up of dots? Well, that's how this Jesus picture was done, except all the dots are nipples. And that's what the picture's called—"NippleJesus." There were big breasts and small breasts, and big nipples and small nipples, and black breasts and white breasts. And some of the pictures had as many as four breasts in them, and I could see then that all of the pictures were stills from porn mags, and he'd cut them all up and stuck them on. Must have taken him years. So now I understood what the sign was about.

I hated the picture then. Two minutes ago I'd liked it, now I hated it. And I hated the bloke who'd done it, too. Wanker.[9] I went to have a look at the name of the artist, and it turned out to be a woman. Martha Marsham. How can you be a woman and do that? I thought. I could have understood some bloke doing it, some bloke with too many dirty magazines and no girlfriend. But a bird? And I hoped that someone did manage to fuck the picture up somehow, and if they did, I said to myself, I wouldn't try to stop them. I might even give them a hand. Because that is offensive, isn't it, a Jesus made out of nipples? That's out of order.

One thing I forgot to say before: this was about six o'clock in the evening, and the exhibition hadn't opened to the public yet. It was opening the next day, but we'd been called in to do the first-night party. I was actually still looking at all the little

8. Nap.

9. Jerk.

pictures when the first people came in, holding wineglasses. I felt a bit of a tosser, like I'd been caught looking at dirty pictures, which is actually what I was doing, if you think about it. Or even if you don't. I stopped looking, quick, and stood by the chair with my hands behind my back, looking straight ahead, like I was on sentry duty, while these two people, a man and a woman, looked at the picture.

"It's rather lovely, isn't it?" said the woman. She was about my age, short hair, quite posh.

"Is it?" The bloke didn't seem too sure, so I decided I liked him more than her, even though he had floppy hair and braces and a suit.

"Don't you think?"

He shrugged, and they left the room. There was none of that stuff, the stuff they take the piss out of in TV comedies, where they stroke their chins and talk bollocks.[1] (There never is, in my experience, which has now lasted two days. Most people don't say anything much. They look and they go. If you ask me they're scared of talking bollocks, which pisses me off, because once I was sat here for a while I wanted the bollocks. Something to laugh at. But there isn't any.) The next couple were younger, early twenties, studenty types, and they were more interested in me than the picture.

"Fucking hell," said the bloke.

"What?"

"Look at him."

And the girl looked at me, and laughed. It was like I was part of the exhibition, and I couldn't hear what they were saying.

"Well," she said. "Can you blame them?"

And then they went, too. By this stage, I was starting to feel a bit sorry for this Martha woman. I mean, you spend fucking who knows how long doing this thing and people come in here, look at me, laugh, and then fuck off again. I might ask her for half her royalties, or whatever it is she gets.

The moment the students left, the curtain swished back, and I heard this woman's voice going "Ta-ra!," and then a whole group of people came in—two younger guys, an older couple, and a young woman.

"Oh, Martha," the older woman said. "It's amazing. That'll get them going." So I looked at the group, and straightaway I guessed it was her mum and dad, her boyfriend, and maybe her brother. Martha is about thirty, and she doesn't really look like I thought she'd look—no dyed hair, no pierced nose, nothing like that. She looks normal, really. She was wearing this long, green, sort of Indian skirt and what looked like a bloke's pinstripe jacket, and she's got long hair, but . . . she's nice-looking. Friendly.

I wondered for a moment whether her mum and dad knew about the nipples and all that, because I liked the picture when I first came into the room. But then I realised that was stupid, and she would have told them something about it before they came, or ages and ages ago. So what kind of parents were these? I know what I would have got if I'd told my dad I was making a picture of Jesus out of women's breasts. He probably would have wanted to see the breasts, but he would have given me a pasting for the Jesus bit. So I looked at Martha's mum and dad and tried to work them out. Her dad was tall, and wearing jeans, and he had long grey hair in a ponytail; her mum was wearing jeans too, but she looked a bit more like somebody's mother than he looked like somebody's father. They all looked like they were artists, though. They looked like they all sat around at home smoking dope and painting. Which was why no one had given her a back-hander for making a Jesus out of porn, probably.

1. Nonsense.

"I want a photo," Martha said. "With all of us in it." And then she looked at me. "Do you mind?"

"No," I said.

"I'm Martha, by the way."

"Dave."

"Hello, Dave." We shook hands, and then she gave me her camera, and I took a picture of them all, standing there grinning and pointing, and I didn't know whether it was right, what with the kind of picture it was. But at that precise moment, I wished that I knew them better, or people like them, because they seemed nice, and happy, and interesting. I wanted a dad with a grey ponytail instead of a miserable old git who was always going on about the fucking Irish and the fucking blacks; it seemed to me that if I had a dad like that, I wouldn't have ended up going into the Army, which was the worst mistake I ever made.

I wanted to ask them questions. I wanted to ask her, Martha, why she'd wanted to do what she'd done, and why it had to be nipples, and why it had to be Jesus, and whether she actually wanted to upset people. And I wanted to ask them whether they were ashamed of her, or proud of her, or what. But I didn't ask anything, and nothing they said made me any the wiser; after the photos they talked about where they were going to eat, and whether someone else that they knew had come to the party, and then that sort of thing. Before they went, Martha came over to me and kissed me on the cheek, and said, "Thank you." And I went, you know, "Oh, that's OK." But I was really pleased that she'd done it. It made me feel special, like I had a proper, important job to do.

Martha smiled, and I was left on my own again.

I told Lisa about the picture when I got home that night, after the party. She couldn't believe it—she said it was disgusting, and how come it was on the wall in a famous gallery. For some reason I found myself sort of defending it, taking Martha's side. I don't know why. Maybe I fancied her a bit, maybe I liked the look of her family—maybe I trusted them, and, like, took my lead from them. Because I knew they were nice people, and if they didn't see anything wrong with "NippleJesus," then maybe there wasn't anything. And anyway, the stuff that Lisa was coming out with . . . it was just plain ignorant. "You should take it outside when no one's looking and smash it to bits," she said.

"After all that work she's put in?" I said.

"That's got nothing to do with it," she said. "I mean, Hitler put in a lot of work, didn't he?"

"What harm is she doing you?" I asked her. "You don't have to go and look at it."

"Well, I don't like knowing it's there," she said. "And I paid for it. Out of my taxes."

Out of her taxes! How much of her taxes went towards "NippleJesus"? She sounded like one of those lunatics you hear on radio phone-ins. I got twopence out of my pocket threw it at her. "There," I said, "there's your tax back. And you're making a profit."

"What you gone all like this for?" she asked.

"Because I think it's good," I said. "Clever."

Lisa didn't think it was clever. She thought it was stupid. And I thought she was stupid, and told her, and by the time we went to bed we weren't speaking to each other.

So yesterday morning, I get on the bus to go to work, and I pick up the paper that someone's left on the seat, and there it is, my painting, all over page seven. "PROTESTORS TARGET SICK PICTURE," it says, and then there's all this stuff about what a disgrace it is, and people from the Church and the Conservative party going on about how it shouldn't be allowed, and someone from the police saying that they might want to interview Martha and maybe press charges of obscenity. And I read it, and I think, I've never been in the news before. Because it is me, sort of. That's my room there, my private space, and I've even started to think of the picture as mine, in a weird sort of way. Probably no one apart from Martha has spent as long looking at it as I have, and that makes me feel protective of it, kind of thing. (Which is just as well, when you think about it, seeing as that's my job.) I don't like these people saying it's sick, because it is and it isn't, and I don't like the police saying they're going to charge Martha with obscenity, and I don't like the idea that they're going to take it out of the exhibition, because it says outside the door that you shouldn't go in if you think you might not like it. So why go in? I want people to see what I saw: something that's beautiful if you look at it in one way, from a distance, and ugly if you look at it in another, close up. (Sometimes I feel that way about Lisa. When she walks into the room when we're just about to go out, and she's got her makeup on and she's done her hair and that, you'd think she could be a model. And sometimes I wake up in the night and I roll over and she's an inch away from me, and she's got bad breath and she's snoring a bit, and you'd think . . . Well, never mind what you'd think, but you wouldn't think she'd make much of a model, anyway. So maybe Martha's picture, it's sort of like that a bit.) But if these people have their way, no one's going to see anything, and that can't be right. Not after all that work. All that cutting up and sticking on.

Did you know you couldn't smoke in an art gallery? Neither did I. Fucking hell.

When I got there, there was already a crowd outside. Some of them were people queuing to see the exhibition, and some of them were protestors—they had placards and they were singing hymns—and there were TV crews, and photographers, and it all looked a bit of a mess. I just pushed through them and knocked on the front door and showed my pass through the glass and one of the guys let me in.

"You're in for a busy day," one of the others said when I went to change into my gear, and I thought, yeah, I'm looking forward to this.

Nothing much happened at first. A steady stream of people came in and looked, and a couple of them sort of clucked, but what's really clever about the picture is that you have to get close up to get offended, because if you stand at the back of the room you can't see anything apart from the face of Christ. So it makes the cluckers look like right plonkers,[2] because they have to go and shove their nose up against the painting to see the nipples, and so you end up thinking they're perverts. You know, first they have to ignore the sign on the door telling them not to go in, and then they have to walk the length of the room, and then they go, "Oh, disgusting." So they're really looking out for it.

After about an hour, I got my first nutter. He looked like a nutter: he had chunks missing from his hair, like he'd been eaten by moths, and he wore these huge specs,

2. Fools.

and he kept blinking, like some demented owl. And he dressed like a nutter too: even though it was a hot day, he was wearing a winter coat covered in badges that said things like "DON'T FOLLOW ME—I'M LOST TOO" and "I'M A SUGAR PUFFS HONEY MONSTER." He stank, and all. So it wasn't like he was hard to spot. He wasn't an *undercover* nutter, if you know what I mean.

He stared at the picture for a couple of minutes, and then he dropped to his knees and started praying. It was all, "Heavenly father who gave his only son Jesus Christ to us so that we might be saved please deliver us blah blah blah," but what was weird was, you couldn't work out whether he was praying because he was looking at Christ, or whether he was praying like they prayed in *The Exorcist*, to get rid of the demons in the room, sort of thing. Anyway, after a little while I got pissed off with it and made up a rule.

"I'm sorry, sir. We don't allow kneeling in the galleries," I said.

"I'm praying for your immortal soul," he said.

"I don't know about that, sir, but we don't allow kneeling. No flash photography, no sandwiches, no kneeling."

He stood up and carried on muttering, so I told him praying was out too.

"Don't you care?" he said.

"About what, sir?"

"Don't you care about where you are going?"

"And where's that?"

"To hell, man! Where serpents will suck on your eyeballs and flames will lick your internal organs for all eternity?"

"Not really, sir." What I meant was, I didn't think I was going to be sent to hell. Not for standing in front of a picture, anyway.

You don't really want to go down that road, the eyeball-sucking road, do you? It's not very . . . *cheerful*, is it? I mean, what must it be like to be this geezer? And what's he doing here? Does he just wander around looking for stuff that's going to make him blink and drop to his knees and mutter away? Does he spend all his life wandering around Soho and King's Cross? Because if he does, then no wonder he's a nutter. If you don't spend any time playing with your kids (and I'll tell you, this is not a bloke with kids), or drinking with your mates (and I'll bet mates are a bit thin on the ground as well), or watching *Frasier* (I like *Frasier*) . . . you're going to end up like him, aren't you?

Just as I was wondering what I was going to do with him, a couple of women came in and he scuttled off, and things went quiet for a while. But then just before my lunch break, just as I was starting to think that it was going to be an aggro-free[3] day after all, a bloke walks in wearing a dog collar. A fucking vicar! He was younger than most vicars, and a bit trendier, too—he had a sort of Hugh Grant floppy haircut, and he was wearing jeans. He came into the room and stopped and stared, and I knew, because I knew all the angles and distances by now, that he couldn't see anything from where he was stood. Or rather, he could see Christ, but he couldn't see the nipples. So when he started to walk down towards the picture, I started to walk towards him, to block him off, and we stood there almost nose-to-nose.

"Why do you want to do that, your honour?" I asked him. "Why don't you just stay where you are?"

"I have to make up my own mind," he said.

3. Aggravation-free.

"You know what's there," I said. "Everyone knows what's there now. Why do you have to go and look at it? Stay where you are. Look. It's beautiful."

"How can anything made out of pornography be beautiful?"

For a moment I wanted to get into a whole different argument. This isn't porn, I wanted to tell him. This is just page 3 stuff.[4] Porn is what we used to watch in the Army, with dogs and lesbians with strap-ons and all that, but you don't want to be talking to a vicar about sex with dogs, do you? I didn't anyway.

He moved to his right to get by me, so I moved to my left, and then we did the same dance the other way round. He was getting annoyed now, and in the end I had to let him through; otherwise I swear it would have all gone off, and I would have been fired for decking him.

"Happy now?" I said after he'd been there a while.

"Why did she do it, do you think?"

"I wouldn't know, your honour. But she's a very nice young lady."

"That makes it even sadder, then."

Not to me it doesn't, I thought. If it had been made by a seedy old git whose hobby was looking up women's skirts, then that's one story, but it's different when you've seen what Martha is like, the kind of person she is. You end up sort of trusting her, and trusting what she does, and why. I did, anyway. I can see that wouldn't work for everyone. It wouldn't make a lot of difference to the nutter, for example.

"I think you've been here long enough now," I said to the vicar. This was completely out of order, of course, but the truth was I was sick of him, and I didn't want him in my room anymore.

"I beg your pardon?"

"We've been told to watch out for people who stay here more then five minutes. You know, perverts and that." That did the trick.

If I'd just read about "NippleJesus" in the paper, or seen it on the news, I'd have thought it was wrong, no question. Sick. Stupid. Waste of taxpayers' money. (You always say that even if you've got no idea if taxpayers pay for it or not, whatever it is, don't you?) And then I'd never have thought about it again, probably. But it's more complicated when you actually stand by it all day. And now I still don't know what I think of it, really, but what's so great about the nutter and the kinky vicar and all the other people who came to have a look that first morning is that they make up your mind for you about whose side you're on. I'm not on theirs, that's for sure, and the longer I have to spend with these wankers the more I hate them. It's so simple, really. The nice ones like the picture, and they get it, and they have a look at how it's done but that's not why they're staring; the horrible ones come in, gaze for hours at the tits, moan to each other (or, if they're really mad, to themselves). . . . You don't need to work out what you think. You just need to have a look at what other people think. And if you don't like the look of them, then think the opposite.

No sooner had the vicar gone than a whole fucking zoo turns up. I recognize a couple of the monkeys in it: there's this woman politician I'm sure I've seen on TV, that fat one who's always banging on about the family and all that, and she's brought a TV crew with her. The interviewer is that bloke who does the local news

4. The British tabloid *The Sun* is famous for its pictures of topless (or nude) women on page 3.

on the BBC. You'd probably recognize him too—smoothy, sharp suits, fake tan. Anyway, you should have heard this woman. She was calling for Martha to be sent to prison, for the people who put on the exhibition to, I don't know, have their licence taken away or something. . . . And the smoothy geezer was just egging her on. "You've been campaigning very hard for a return to family values, and presumably this kind of thing doesn't help your cause . . . " Stuff like that. When they'd finished I wandered over to the interviewer and had a word with him, just to wind him up, sort of thing.

"So," I said, "You getting someone else to say something?"

"How'd you mean?"

"Well you can't have just her, can you?" She was standing about two feet away, having her microphone taken off, so I knew she could hear me. She turned round and looked at me.

"We'll be talking to the artist, too," said the presenter. "She should be here in a second."

"Did you do a closeup of the painting?"

"I would imagine so," he said. All sarcastic, like I was being thick.

"So you're going to show thousands of nipples on the local news? My kids watch that."

"Do they?" he said, like he didn't believe me. Like no one with a skinhead haircut could have kids who watched anything but football. Cheeky bastard. OK, my kids don't watch the news, but that's because they're too young, not because they're too thick. Wanker.

When Martha turned up, I realized I sort of had a crush on her. She looked great—fresh, and friendly, and young, and she was wearing this bright lime-green T-shirt that added to the freshness. The politician was wearing this dark suit, and she had a hard face anyway, and Martha makes her look old and cruel. She said hello to me, and asked me how it was going, and I told her about the nutter and the vicar, and she just smiled.

The interviewer didn't like her, I could tell. He asked her whether she minded offending so many people, and she said she didn't think she had, only one or two. And he asked her what the point of the picture was, and she said that she didn't want to have to explain it, she thought it could explain itself, if she could tell everyone what it meant then she would have just written the meaning down, she wouldn't have gone to all the trouble of sticking all the nipples on the paper. And the interviewer said, well, some people wish you hadn't bothered, and she said, well, it's a free country.

I was disappointed, to be honest. I was hoping she'd talk about how beautiful the picture was—how holy, sort of thing. And I wanted her to explain that if you wanted to see the nipples you really had to get up close, like the vicar had to, and what kind of vicar you were if you wanted to do that. And I wanted to hear why she'd done it, too. I mean, there had to be an idea behind it, didn't there? A meaning, kind of thing. It's not just something you'd wake up in the morning and do, is it? You know, "What am I going to do with all these pairs of breasts I've been cutting out? Oh, I might as well turn them into a picture of Christ on the cross . . . "

Maybe they should have interviewed me. Like I said, maybe I've thought more about this picture than anyone. Because she doesn't know, Martha. She hasn't seen it in action, like I have. And she hasn't spent any time standing in front of it, watching people looking at it. Perhaps she should; then she'd be able to say things about it in interviews.

Just before we closed, the smelly nutter with the badges came back with an egg, and tried to throw it at the picture. I saw it coming a mile off, and I grabbed his arm just as he was raising it, and the egg travelled about two feet and landed splat on the floor. It was so pathetic it made me laugh, and I remembered the kid with the rusty spike outside the club, and why I'd packed that job in; it's hard to be scared by a scrawny weirdo with an egg. I was still angry though, so I didn't let go of him after he'd thrown it—I pinned his arm behind his back with more violence than I needed, and he started yelling. I marched him out, and down the corridor towards the front entrance. I hated the fucker so much that I got carried away a bit—I was twisting his arm and calling him all the names under the sun, and he said he was going to sue me and report me to the police and he wasn't going to pray for my soul and he hoped that all the agonies of damnation were heaped upon me. Pillock.[5]

But he knew what he was doing. As I was shoving the nutter down the corridor, there was a commotion behind me, shouting and crashing and alarms going off and then the sound of running. I let the nutter go and went back to my picture, and a couple of the other security guards were in there staring at the floor. Someone had fucked "NippleJesus" over good and proper. They'd taken it off the wall and stomped all over it and then fucked off. There wasn't hardly anything left of it.

I felt like crying. Really. I'd let Martha down, and I'd been stupid to leave the room, and it was only when I saw the picture smashed up on the floor that I finally realized how much I loved it. But I'll tell you something else, something really weird: seeing Christ on the floor with his face all smashed in like that . . . It was really shocking. What they'd done was much more blasphemous than anything Martha had done. I wonder if they'd thought about that when they were doing it? Whether they'd had any moment of doubt, or fear? Because, I'll tell you, if I was religious, and I thought that there was a hell where serpents suck your eyeballs out and all that, I wouldn't go round stomping all over Jesus' face. Jesus is Jesus, isn't he? No matter what you make him out of. And maybe that's one of the things Martha was trying to get at: Christ is where you find him.

Some people from the gallery turned up, people I'd seen at the party the night before but no one who'd ever bothered to speak to me. And I told them about the nutter and the egg, and how I shouldn't have left my post but I did, and they didn't seem to blame me much. And then a copper came, and I told him the same stuff. He seemed to think it was funny, though. He didn't laugh or anything, but you could tell that it was low down on his list of crimes to solve.

And then Martha came in. I walked towards her because I wanted to hug her, but I worked out just in time that my relationship with her was not the same as her relationship with me, if you see what I mean. I've spent a lot of time over the last couple of days thinking about her, because of my job, but she couldn't have spent much time thinking about me, could she? Anyway. I didn't hug her. I just went over to her and said, you know, I'm sorry and all that, but she didn't seem to hear me. She just stared at the picture on the floor, and said, "Oh my God," which considering the circumstances was about right.

And when she looked up again, her face was all lit up. She was thrilled to bits, excited like a kid. I couldn't believe it.

"This is perfect," she said. "Brilliant."

"How d'you mean?" I said, because I didn't get it.

"Who did this? Did you see?"

5. Idiot.

So I told her about the smelly nutter with the egg, and how I thought he'd done me, wound me up to get me out of the room so his nutter mates could do their stuff, and she loved it. She loved the whole story. "Perfect," she kept saying. "Fantastic." And then: "I can't wait to see the video."

And I was, like, "What video?," and she pointed out the CCTV camera up in the corner of the room.

"That's part of it," she said. "That's part of the exhibition. What I was hoping was that someone would come in and do this on day one, and on day two we could show the film, and . . . I'm going to call it *Intolerance*."

And I thought about the vicar, and the politician, and all the other people who'd come in and stuck their noses up close and then said how disgusted they were and how shocking it was, and I could see that it would be a bit of a laugh for people to see them on the telly. But that was all it was, really, a bit of a laugh.

"So that was the idea?" I said. "Someone would come in and smash it up?"

"Put it this way," she said. "I'd have been stuffed if they hadn't. I'd have been stuck with a portrait of Jesus made out of breasts, and what use is that to anyone? It's Dave, isn't it? Well, Dave. Art is about provocation. Getting a reaction from people. And I've done it. I'm an artist."

I remembered the party, when she thanked me, and I asked her why she'd done that if all she wanted was for someone to smash it up. But she didn't remember thanking me. So I said, you must remember, last night, at the party. When I took your photo, and you came over and kissed me on the cheek and said "Thank you." And she shrugged, and said, "Oh, yeah. I was thanking you for the photo, I think." Like it wasn't a big deal. Which it clearly wasn't, I can see now. I suppose if you're an artist, it doesn't mean anything, kissing someone on the cheek. They do it all the time. "Twenty Marlborough Lights please." Kiss. "Leicester Square please." Mm-mmwa. It doesn't mean, oh thank you for the important and dangerous job you're doing, obviously. Silly cow. I should have just stood there. I shouldn't have gone out with the smelly nutter with the egg. Because, if you think about it . . . the only reason it got smashed up was because I cared about it too much. I could have just stood there, stopped the egg, got rid of the nutter; but he'd got on my nerves, he'd tried to damage my picture—*my picture*—and I wanted to make sure he left the building, maybe give him a couple of digs at the same time. Which is why I wasn't in the room when it got broken. So. She wouldn't understand this, but she needed me for her film as much as she needed them.

When I went home last night, I felt stupid. I felt like I look, if you like: a six-foot-two, fifteen-stone bouncer with a shaved head who doesn't know anything about art. I'd spent two days thinking something was, you know, beautiful, and worth protecting, and all the time it was a piece of shit, stuck on the wall because some bird thought it would be a laugh if someone smashed it to pieces. So everyone's a prat,[6] aren't they? The nutters are prats for doing what they were supposed to do, and I was a prat for trying to stop them . . . The only one who isn't a prat is Martha. She's watching us and having a laugh. Well, fuck her.

Except maybe she isn't as clever as she thought she was. Because the film's showing now, up the corridor, and no one looks at it. It's too long, so most of the time

6. Idiot.

nothing's happening, and you can't see very much anyway—they cocked up the angle of the camera, so you see the painting coming off the wall, but you don't see anyone jump on it. And it's not beautiful. It's just a CCTV film, like you see in a petrol station when you're waiting to get served. And that's what you get instead of the face of Christ in his agony. So who's the prat, eh, Martha?

I've got an onion now. A fucking onion. And some other stuff, beds, and tents and shit, because I'm not in a room by myself anymore; the CCTV film isn't controversial, so they don't need anyone to keep an eye on it. But my chair's by the onion, and it bores me shitless, because there's nothing to think about onions, is there? So I don't. I just sit here and think about what I'd like to do, apart from be Tiger Woods or Richard Branson.

Zadie Smith

b. 1975

Zadie Smith was born in Brent, a northwest borough of London, in 1975. Her first novel, *White Teeth,* was pulished in 2000 and won the Whitbread First Novel Award, *The Guardian* First Book Award, the James Tait Black Memorial Prize for Fiction, and the Commonwealth Writers' First Book Award. Her second novel, *The Autograph Man* (2002), won the *Jewish Quarterly* Wingate Literary Prize. Smith's third novel, *On Beauty* (2005), was shortlisted for the prestigious Man Booker Prize, and won both the Commonwealth Writers' Best Book Award (Eurasia Section) and the Orange Prize for Fiction. Smith has edited an anthology of short entitled *The Book of Other People,* and in November 2009 she publishes a collection of her essays, *Changing My Mind.* Zadie Smith is a Fellow of the Royal Society of Literature.

Martha, Martha

Though the telephone is a perfectly useless indicator of most human qualities, it's pretty percise about age. From her tiny office on the third floor, Pam Roberts looked through a window and correctly identified the Martha Penk she was waiting for, a shrimpish girl pushing twenty-two, lost down there. She had on a red overcoat and cream snow boots, putting her weight on their edges like an ice skater; she seemed to waver between two doorways. Pam opened her mouth to call out "Miss Penk!" but never got to make the curious sound—abruptly the girl turned the corner and headed back down Apple towards the river. Pam went to her own door, opened it, worried her chapped lips with a finger, closed it again. The cold was just too extreme; today the first snows were due, opening performance of a show that would last a dreary, relentless four months. Besides, she had her slippers on. Miss Martha Penk, who appeared to believe that two bedrooms and a garden could be had for a thousand dollars a month, would figure our her second mistake soon enough, come back, discover the bell. The confusion was common; it arose from the higgledy-piggledy arrangement of the ground floor—a busy bookshop and a swing-doored optician obscured the sign that told you of the dentist, the insurers, the accountant and Pam's own dinky realty business at the top of the building; also the antique elevator that would take you to them. Pam tapped her door with a knuckle, warning it she would return, and crossed the room to the filing cabinet. On tiptoes she slid open the top drawer and began flicking through files, her Mozart swelling behind her. She sang along with that section of the *Requiem* that sounds so very like "OH I SEE YOU WILL GO *DOWN*! AND I SEE YOU WILL GO ALSO!," although it could not be this for the words are Latin. As she sang she ground one of her Chinese slippers rhythmically into the carpet and pressed herself into the metal drawer to reach for something at the very back: "OH I SEE YOU WILL GO DOWN, OH! I SEE YOU WILL GO DOWN! ALSO! ALSO!"

Pam found what she wanted, closed the cabinet suddenly with an elbow and sat down in a fat armchair opposite a lithograph of Venice. She put a foot in her hand and said "Phee-yoo! Now, *there* you go," pressing relief into a sore instep. She started picking out every third sheet or so from the listings and laying them on the floor before her in a small pile. At the opening of the "Lacrimosa" she removed her slipper entirely, but then hearing someone gallop up the stairs, replaced it and quickly rose to greet a large, dark, bearded man in a sheepskin overcoat, who stood bent at the knees like a shortstop, trying to recover his breath in the hallway. He took a step towards her, looked up and frowned. He paused where he was, supporting himself with a hand on the door frame. Pam knew exactly why he had come and the two spoke at the same time.

"This temping agency?" he asked, a heavy accent, quickly identified by Pam as Middle-Easterny. A Middle-Easterny scarf, too, and a hat.

"No dear, *no*," said Pam, and let her glasses fall to her chest from their chain, "It's above the *other* Milliner's Books, right? There's two Milliner's Books—you need the one on the corner of Apple and Wallace—this is the wrong Milliner's, this is above the *children's* Milliner's—I don't know why they just don't say that to people—"

The man groaned pleasantly and hit his temple with the hub of his palm.

"I make mistake. Sorry, please."

"No, they just didn't say, they never *do*. It's not *you*, dear, it's them—people always come here by mistake, it's not *you*. It's two minutes from here. Now, you go back down, turn left, then immediately right, you can see it from there. I've got somebody who just did the *exact* same, but *exactly*—only vice versa—she's gone to . . ."

A further thundering on the stairs and three more men, younger, also bearded. They stood bent like their friend, panting, one man crying the involuntary tears of a Massachusetts winter. They stared at Pam who stared frankly back at them, with her hands on her makeshift hips, up there where her black linen trousers began, high under the breasts. A black T-shirt and cardigan finished the thing off. Pam was a recognized doodlenut when it came to clothes, buying the same things over and over, black and loose, like a fat Zen monk. She didn't mind. Her moustache was moist and visible—oh, so let 'em *stare* was how Pam felt about it. Young men did not register with Pam any more.

"My friends," explained the man, and with his friends began the descent, emptying out a demotic mystery language into the stairwell. Miss Penk must have passed them on the bend. A moment later she was in the room apologizing for her lateness.

"Sorry I'm late, I'm sorry," she said, but did not look sorry. Her face, very black, could not blush, and her accent, to Pam's ears very English, could not apologize. She stood in the centre of the room, clumsily divesting herself of the loud red coat. She was short, but more muscular, more solid than she had appeared from three floors up. A cheap-looking grey trouser suit and some fake pearls were conspiring to make her older than she was. The buttons on the jacket looked like rusty spare change.

"No, I saw *you*, you see," began Pam warmly, coming forward to catch what was falling, a scarf, a woolly hat, "There's *two* Milliner's—did you see those men? On the stairs? They did the exact same thing—and I saw you down—"

"The lift's[1] broken, it don't work," said Martha, and now lifted her head and reached out a hand. Pam felt faintly interrupted, but took the hand and gave it a double-handed shake.

"Pam Roberts, we spoke on the phone. It's so good to *meet* you!"

"I'm Martha," she replied and quickly freed herself. She passed a smoothing hand over her own short ironed hair, cut in a flapper's style, a helmet brilliant with some kind of polish. A concrete kiss curl had been plastered on to her left cheek. Pam had never seen anything quite like it in her office before.

"Well. Now, did you come from far? Are you nearby?" Pam asked, a question that had a little business in it.

"Near, yeah" said the girl, firmly. She stood oddly, hands by her sides, feet together, "A hotel, it's called The Charles? It's just like by the river—it's just if you go down by—"

"Oh, I know where it is—it's *very* nice."

"It costs too much, man," said Martha, tutting loudly, removing a pair of childish mittens, "But I came right from London and I didn't have any place arranged—I just arksed the taxi to take me to the nearest hotel—I been there a week, but I can't afford it for much longer, you know?"

Usually Pam would use these minutes in the office to ascertain something about likely wealth, class, all very gently—what kind of house, what kind of taste, what kind of price—but she had been wrong about English accents before, not knowing which were high class, which not. Or whether high class meant money at *all*—if you watched PBS as Pam did you soon found out that in England it could, often did, mean the exact opposite.

"It *is* such a nice place, The Charles. They really do things properly there, don't they? They really make the best of that location, I think. I stayed there once for a realty conference, and I really appreciated the standard of the breakfasts. People talk about pool this, steamroom that, but in actual fact it's the little things, like a *breakfast*. A good hot *breakfast*. But my *God* the price isn't any fun—Martha, we'll have you out of there in no time, I promise, especially if we find something empty—"

"Yes," said Martha, but rather too quick, too desperate, "How long would it be before I could move in somewhere?"

Pam felt herself immediately on surer ground and slipped down a gear into patter, "Well, as I'm saying, dear, it depends on whether the place has people in it at the *moment*—but even then, we can turn it around very *very* quickly. It just needs to happen so that everybody wants to make it work, that's all. Don't worry, we'll find something that works. And if it doesn't work, we'll cut it loose and go on to the next," she said loudly, clapping her hands and glancing at a clock on the wall, "Now, I've got about two hours free—it's really very dry at the moment so there's *plenty* to show." She bent down to scoop the remembered listings from the floor, "I think I understand what you're looking for, Martha, I received your letter, I have it right here—Wait—" Pam reached over to her stereo like a woman with one foot each in

1. Elevator.

two drifting boats; she punched at a couple of buttons to no avail, "Sometimes it gets a little loud. Funny little machine. It's completely wireless! It's like a single unit stereo for single people, very liberating. You can't really adjust it without the remote, though, which is a little frustrating. And I find it gets louder sometimes, do you know? Sort of when you don't expect it?"

"Classical," said Martha, and looked at Pam and the surrounding office with determined reverence, "I want to listen to more classical music. I want to know more about it. It's on my list."

And this she said in such a way that Pam had no doubt that there was such a list, and that renting an apartment *today* was somewhere on it. The girl had a manner that was all itinerary, charmless and determined, and Pam, a Midwesterner by birth, had the shameful idea that she might go far, this Martha Penk, here on the East Coast.

"Oh! Well, I don't know what there is to *know*, really. I mean, I don't know anything at *all*. It's the violins that do it for me, I guess, the way they sound like somebody's crying? The 'Lacrimosa' means crying, I'm pretty sure. Lachrymose—that's from the eye, isn't it? But are you at the university?"

"No!" said Martha but her face at last released a flood of undisguised pleasure, as when a girl is told she could be a model or an actress or do whatever she does amateurishly, professionally, "I wish! Maybe one day. I'm looking for that next level—qualifications, getting forward, raising myself, my consciousness. But that's like a dream, yeah, for me at this stage?"

She looked serious again, began enlisting her hands in her speech, drawing out these "levels" in the air, "It's about stepping a bit further, I mean, for me, I really want to improve myself while I'm here, go up a bit, like listening to different music, like that."

"*Well*," said Pam brightly, and sounded her desk with her hand, "We'll just have to find you the right place where you can do that. Hmm?" But Miss Penk had returned her attention to the CD case, and Pam found herself nodding into the silence, and talking to fill it, "Oh, I just like all kinds of music, really. I am just the *biggest* fan of music. Cuban, classical, hillbilly—or whatever you call that sort of close harmony singing? A lot of jazz . . . don't know a thing about it, though! Oh *my*. Maybe I can't be improved. Too old to be any better than I am," said Pam in a saccharine sing-song, as if it were a proverb.

"Yeah," said Martha, the sort of absent yes that a silly proverb probably deserves. She took the sleeve notes out of the case and opened them up.

"Now," said Pam, struggling a little, "From your letter I understood you were thinking around the thousand mark—but that's really a little *low*—I mean, I'll *show* you those places, Martha, but I can't guarantee you're going to *like* them. I mean, they're not there to be *liked*," Pam said patiently, and gathered up her car keys from her desk, "But we'll find something that works—we just need to get a handle on it. I'd like to show you a big place that's going for two thousand, maybe—maybe lower—it's negotiable with the present owner. In more vibrant times, it's worth at least three. It'll give us some idea anyway. I'm here to make it work for you, so, I'm going to be led by you. . . "

Outside a plane roared low like some prehistoric bird, Pam shuddered; Martha did not move. Pam tried jostling her keys expectantly in her hand; Martha put down the CD case leaving the notes unfolded and walked over to the window. From behind she was an even more neatly made girl than from the front, everything tight and defined, fighting slightly against the banal restraint of polyester.

"We'll take my car, if that's all right," tried Pam, anxious that Martha should not open a window but unwilling to ask her not to. It *was* hot in the room, but it was that time of year: you either fried or you froze. But Martha had already tugged on the sash, in a second her head was out there in the open air. Pam winced. She hated to see people lean all the way out of a window like that.

"Do you get a lot of university people? Students?"

"Oh, *yes*. At the beginning of a semester, certainly. Students around here have some money to spare, if you know what I mean."

Martha took her plastic pearls in her hand and twisted them.

"They must be amazing. Focused people."

"Oh! Well, yes, I suppose. Certainly, they're *bright*. There's just no denying that. But I'm afraid," said Pam in her own, overused, comic whisper, "They can be pretty *obnoxious* as well."

"There aren't any black students," Martha said in a tone somewhere between statement and question. Pam, who was in the middle of forcing her arm though a recalcitrant coat sleeve, stopped in her position like a scarecrow, "Well, of *course* there are students of colour, dear! I see them all the time—I mean, even before the affirmative action and all of that—I mean, there's *always* been the basketball scholarships and the rest—though it's much, much better now of course. They're *completely* here on their own steam *now*. Lots of Chinese young people too, and Indian, many. Many! Oh, there's plenty, *plenty* of people of colour here, you'll see," said Pam and switched off her desk lamp. "But have you been to America before?"

"Only Florida when I was twelve. I didn't like it—it's quite vulgar?" said Martha, and the word was most definitely borrowed in her mouth. Pam, who also occasionally borrowed words, recognized the habit and tried to look kindly upon it.

"Florida and Nigeria are the only places I've been, really, out of England," continued Martha, leaning yet further out, gazing across the square, "And now here."

"Oh, are you Nigerian?" Pam asked, kicked off her slippers and began to replace them with treasured walking boots. When people remarked that Pam had become "so *hard*" recently or suggested that she'd turned into a doodlenut since her divorce, they often meant these boots and nothing more than these boots.

"My parents."

"Penk, it's very unusual, isn't it?" said Pam to Martha's back, "Is that a Nigerian name?"

"No."

Nothing further came. Discovering her remote control behind a coffee cup, Pam stopped the CD and then approached, reaching briskly around Martha to close the window. Clearly, the girl blew hot and cold; in the end Pam just needed her name on a contract, nothing more. Even that was not essential—plenty of people take up your whole afternoon and never call again; Pam called them her one-day stands.

"Look at that sky. It's gonna snow any minute. You know, we should try to get going before it really starts to come down . . ."

With a simple, businesslike nod Pam indicated the coat that Martha had left draped over the photocopier.

About a half-hour later the two of them were completing their tour of Professor Herrin's house, climbing back down the stairs into his open-plan ground-floor lounge. The place was big, but in some disrepair. The carpets felt springy, damp.

Mould was the overarching theme. Martha was stepping over an empty cat-food can, and Pam's voice was taking on the fluidity of a woman who feels she is moving down the home straight of her anecdote, "He's just a very, very impressive man. Not only is he a Professor of Chinese, he holds a law degree—can you imagine—he's on all *kinds* of boards, I'm sure he plays that piano—When the *President of the United States* wants advice on China, the *President*, mind you, he calls up Professor Herrin. It's such a pleasure talking with that man about *Taoism* or, I don't know, *science* or health matters. . . So many men, they just don't achieve anything at *all*—they don't *expect* to—beyond *business* or a little bit of *golf*, maybe. But there's no attention to the spiritual side, not at all. I mean, his wife, well, actually his wife's a little peculiar—but the mind just boggles to think about living with a man like Professor Herrin, I mean, the attempt to satisfy him, *mentally* . . . and it's *such* a beautiful house, a little fusty; but—have you seen this? He carved it, he really did. He's a Zen Buddhist, death for him is just an *idea.* He *made* the bookshelf—and of course that would all stay here—he would just want to know from you how many of his books he'll have to store, I mean how much shelving you would need, and so on. He's already in New York, and he's intending to be there until at *least* next February. He's a sort of an *expert* on relations between the races," whispered Pam, "so he feels it's important to be in New York right now. In its hour of *need,* you know."[2]

"I don't have any books," said Martha, opening the screen door and stepping into a small walled garden, "I'm going to get books, though, prob'ly, I'll—Oh, it's snowing—it must've started when we were in there. It's on the ground, look."

Pam turned to look and already the ebony sheen of Martha's hair was speckled white, like dusting on a chocolate cake.

"This house feels sad, man," said Martha, and lifted one foot off the ground. She reached behind herself and grabbed the ankle, pressing the foot into her buttocks. First one leg, then the other.

"Does it?" asked Pam, as if the idea had never occurred to her, but her passion for gossip was stronger then her instinct for business, "Well, actually his wife is very peculiar, a terrible thing happened to her. Terrible. It's partly why they're moving again—she can't stand to be in one place, she *broods*. Now, aren't you *cold* out there?"

Martha shrugged, crouched, and tried sweeping a half-inch of snow into her hands, began packing it. Pam sat on the piano stool and stretched her legs out in front of her.

"His wife, Professor Herrin's wife—it's such an awful story—she was in *China*, about twenty-five years ago, and this young man stole her bag. Well, *naturally* she reported it—and what do you think? Two months later when she got back to America, she heard he'd been executed, can you imagine? What that would *do* to a person, it's just terrible. It's a terrible weight to bear."

"She shouldn't have said nothing," said Martha, and appeared to think no more about it.

"Well," considered Pam, pushing her glasses up her nose, "I think it's quite a difficult marriage—I think he's quite eager to leave this place, so I imagine he'd be flexible vis-à-vis the rent, Martha. Martha?"

"Yeah? Sorry, what?"

"Now, Martha, let's talk now. What are you thinking—are you at all . . . ?"

2. A reference to New York City in the wake of the September 11, 2001 terrorist attacks.

Martha took her half-packed snowball and threw it limply at the wall.

"I can't afford it. It's too much. Loads too much. Why does it smell weird out here?"

"*Okay*. . . . well, now I wanted to ask about money," said Pam slowly, coming to the opening and hugging herself against the chill, "I mean, are we talking about savings? You're very young. Or will you be working? Just so I have some *idea* of how much space we have to manoeuvre."

Martha stayed where she was in the garden but put both hands out in front of her, awaiting whatever came. The flakes were massive, consistent and quick, as if the snow was not merely falling but being delivered, like manna, because people needed it.

"I've been left some," said Martha quietly, "In a will. My uncle passed. Basically, it's enough for a year. A thousand a month, two bedrooms and a garden, yeah? Maybe a bit more, maybe. I need space for people. To come." She paused. "If they want." Suddenly she seemed agitated, even panicked; she attacked her bottom lip with her teeth and looked up and over into the next garden, "People who might visit, you get me? But this is too too big, I can't afford it. I can't. Don't you have anything I can *afford*?"

It looked for a moment that the girl was about to cry—out of instinct Pam hurried towards her—but by the time she stepped outside Martha had already recovered herself, turning to peer now over the back wall towards the piercing towers and stark white crosses of the university. She seemed calmly framed by them and remote, a figure in a plastic snowstorm.

"Something a bit further out, maybe," offered Pam a minute later as they climbed back into the car.

"If I had all that education," said Martha, fastening her seat belt, "Believe me, I wouldn't live somewhere like *that*."

"Oh no?"

"I'd live somewhere *new*."

"I see," said Pam tersely, starting the car and welcoming the automatic resuscitation of the stereo, Mozart and his death song as background filler. "Well, each to their own, I suppose, Martha, that's what this business is about, of course. Actually, I used to live on this street, at the top end, at this end, in the more modern architecture, and I must say I found it very pleasant for a long time. Though I also enjoy—I have a sort of apartment now, downtown, and that's also very nice, in a different way."

"You used to live in one of these big houses?" Martha asked, with unseemly incredulity, and as she spoke they drove past the very house. For the first time in months Pam resisted the urge to inspect the curtains, the lawn, the little things he'd changed for somebody else.

"Why'd you go?"

"Circumstances. My circumstances changed. I guess you could say that."

"How?"

"My *gosh*, you *are* a nosy parker. I'll guess I'll have to tell you my dress size next."

"I'm just arksing, you don't have to answer."

"You should be a lawyer or something, it's like being cross-*examined*."

"So why'd you go?"

Pam sighed, but in fact she had, some time ago, designed a speech to answer the question, whoever it came from, "Well, I suppose at my age, Martha, and especially in the light of the events of last September, I just think you have to make things work for you, work for you *personally*, because life is really too short, and if they don't work, you just have to go ahead and cut them loose, and that's basically—"

"I'd love to be a lawyer," interrupted Martha, "My friend is a lawyer. She has a house like that. Big-up house. We used to get the bus together to school. Now she's a big lawyer. That's like the best thing you can be."

"You know what?" said Pam, drumming the steering wheel and preparing to lie, "I like what I do. I don't think I'd change it to be a lawyer for all the tea in China. I really don't. I guess that's just me."

Martha pulled down the passenger mirror, licked her finger and began to reshape her kiss curl.

"She's my role model, Kara—she definitely took it to the next level—as a young black woman, you know? She didn't get caught up in a lot of the things you can get caught up in—kids and that. She took it forward. That's where I'm aiming for—if you don't aim high, there's no point, really."

Martha wound down the window that Pam had just closed and Pam felt she might just scream if the girl kept letting the outside in everywhere they went.

"Now, *good* for her! And good for you, too. God knows, when I was your age, all I did was have children, oh *my*. I've *three* girls. But it's such a different world. I wouldn't even want to bring up children in this world now. My *gosh*, it's really snowing. That's a couple of inches since we left the office."

They drove twenty minutes and then parked a street from the one they wanted so Martha would have an opportunity to see a bit of this new neighbourhood by foot. It was cold beyond cold. Everything laid out like a promise, delayed for summer; bleached porches, dead gardens, naked trees, a sky-blue clapboard house, its rose-pink neighbour. Part of the East Coast realtor's skill is to explain what places will look like when the sun finally comes.

"And this just goes the most *incredible* orange when the fall comes. It's like the whole city is on fire. Just life, life, life *everywhere*. Now: the couple we're about to see," said Pam, walking briskly ahead, "They are just darling. Yousef and Amelia. He's Moroccan and *so* handsome and she's American, just American, and they have such a beautiful daughter, Lily."

"Where they going to go, then, if I move in?"

"They're moving to Morocco. It's just what we were saying, they don't really want to bring up children in this country, I'm afraid. And frankly, I can understand that. They're *artists* too, so, they're a little bit flaky. But *very* sophisticated. So witty, and they make you feel comfortable right away, you know? Now, Martha, I've shown so many people this house, but it's a little too small for a family and a little too big for a single person, so it's awkward—but it's *perfect* for you—now, what *is* that—"

There had been a babbling noise the past minute or so, excited foreign voices, and as they turned the corner Martha saw some snow come flying and guessed at children, but the next second revealed the depth of the voices—these were bearded men, with dark, ashen skins—and the argument was over design, a snowman. It was incompetently begun, a tall upturned cone upon which a future head would never sit. And now work had stopped entirely; at the sight of the two women, the men froze and looked at their gloved hands and seemed to find themselves ridiculous.

"But those are the men!" cried Pam when they were not five yards out of hearing range, "From my office. They just came just before you. But isn't that *weird*? They're making a snowman!"

"Is that what they were doing?" asked Martha, and dug into her pocket for a mint she had quietly lifted from the bowl of same in Pam's office.

"Well what *else* were they doing. You know, Martha, they've probably never seen snow. Isn't that amazing—what a thing to see!"

"Grown men playing in the snow," said Martha, but Pam could not be dissuaded from the romance of it, and it was the first anecdote she told as they walked through the door of 28 Linnaean, a canary-yellow first-floor apartment with two porches, front and back, nestled behind a nineteenth-century police station. Yousef was handsome as promised, curly-haired and with eyes many shades lighter brown than his skin; he was frying something with a great deal of chilli in it and offered his elbow for Martha to shake. Amelia was very skinny and freckled, with an angular hip and a toddler perched on it. She had the kindly, detached air of a young mother, the world outside the screen door having grown distant and surreal, brought to her only in tiresome reports from other people. But she good-humouredly let Pam hustle her to a window at the front of the house and followed the direction of her finger.

"Over there, can you see? They're making a *snow*man! Egyptian or Iranian or *something*. They were so *sheepish* about it. They were so embarrassed. I don't think they've ever seen snow before! And I saw these men, an *hour* ago in my *office*. It's the same men. But the *exact* same. Martha doesn't think anything of it, but I think it's darling."

"That *is* sweet," conceded Amelia, and hitched Lily up over her shoulder.

"Amelia—" said Pam, suddenly, taking a step back from her and appraising a small bulge around her middle, "Now, are you pregnant again?"

"NO," called Yousef from the other room, laughing, "She's just a fat girl now! I feed her too much!"

"Four months," said Amelia, shaking her head, "And I'm going to have it in Morocco, God help me. Hey there, Martha. Do you think you'll take this place off our hands? *Please* won't you, please? We're totally desperate!"

"I don't know yet, do I?" said Martha very fiercely and made the odd, contemptuous noise with her teeth again. Lily reached out a doughy pink hand for Martha's face; she flinched from it.

"Oh," said Amelia, reddening, and battling Lily's tiny kicking legs, "I didn't mean to—"

Pam almost blew up right there—she just *could not* understand what kind of a girl this was, where she came from, what kind of conversation was normal for her. She drummed her fingers on the patch of wall behind her—as close an expression of suppressed fury as Pam ever managed.

"Martha, I'm sure Amelia only meant—"

"I was really joking, I didn't—" said Amelia, putting an incautious hand on Martha's shoulder, feeling a taut, inflexible muscle. She soon retracted it, but Martha continued to look and speak to the spot where the hand had been, "I didn't mean that, I mean I meant I think I want to be nearer the university, nearer all of that, yeah? It's very alone up here, if you're alone, isn't it?"

"Well, you know, there's a very convenient bus—" said Amelia, looking over Martha to Pam who was performing a minimal mime with her thumbs to the effect that she did not know the girl well nor could she explain her.

"I'll look around," said Martha, and walked away from them both, down the hall.

"Look everywhere," said Amelia feelingly. She let Lily loose from her struggle, laying her on the floor. "Please, feel absolutely at liberty."

"Oh, she will," said Pam rather tartly, but Amelia did not smile and Pam was mortified to see that she had thought the comment cruel. Without any skill, Pam turned the conversation to the problem of noisy plumbing.

At the other end of the apartment, Martha's walk changed; she was alone. She moved through the two big bedrooms, loose and alert, examining the strange foreign things in them: Arabic writing, meaningless paintings, and all those touches that rich people seem to use to look poor: wood floors, threadbare rugs, no duvets, all blankets, nothing matching. Old leather instead of new, fireplaces instead of central heating, everything wrong. Only the bathroom was impressive; very clean, white tiled. It had a mirror with a movie star's bald light bulbs circling it. Martha locked herself in here, ran both of the taps full blast, and sat on the closed toilet seat. She took a worn-looking, folded photograph from her coat pocket and wept. She was crying even before she had unfolded it, but flattening it out now against her knee made it almost impossible for her to breathe. In the picture a grinning, long-lashed boy, about eighteen months old, with a head like a polished ackee nut, sat on the lap of a handsome black man. Neither the picture nor their mutual beauty was in any way marred by the fact that both of them had sellotaped their noses to their foreheads to give the impression of pigs' snouts. Martha turned over the photograph and read what was written there.

> Martha, Martha, I love U
> And I'm trying 2 tell U true
> For this New Year 2002
> I am going to be there for U
> I know that U have many dreams
> And life is not always how it seems
> But I want U 2 put me 2 the test
> And I will do all the rest
> Together we will get so much higher
> Through my love and our desire
> Don't give up on what we've got
> Cos Ben and Jamal love U a lot!

It took another five minutes to recover herself. She rinsed her face in the sink and flushed the toilet. She came close up to the mirror and gave thanks to God for her secretive skin that told nobody anything; no flush, no puffiness. She could hear a great deal of laughter the other side of the door and wondered what they were saying about her; especially *him*, who was probably the worst, because he'd married like that and those ones that marry white always feel even more superior. She hadn't expected this. She didn't know what she'd expected.

"Martha!" cried Pam as she appeared again in the kitchen-lounge, "I thought you'd been eaten by something. Eaten by a bear."

"Just looking around. It's nice."

Pam sat on a high kitchen stool beaming at Yousef, but he was busy pulling a giggling Lily out from under the sofa by her ankles.

"So you've had a good look around—she's had a good look around, Yousef, so that's something. Now," said Pam, reaching down to the floor to get her bag, "I don't want to hurry anybody. It always helps to get to know each other a little bit, I think. How can we make this work, for everybody?"

"But I don't know if I—I can't—"

"Martha, *dear*," said Pam, returning a pen and pad she was holding back to her bag, "There's no hurry whatsoever, that's not the way this works at all."

"You know what?" replied Martha. With trembling fingers, she undid and then retied the waistband of her coat, "I've got to go."

"Well—" said Pam, completely astonished, and shook her head, "But—if you'll give me—just wait a *minute*, I'll—"

"I'll walk. I want to walk—I need some air."

Pam put down her coffee cup, and smiled awkwardly between Yousef and Amelia on the one hand and Martha on the other, increasing, as only Pam knew how, the awkwardness on both sides.

"I think I want a one bedroom thing," mumbled Martha, her hand already on the doorknob, "One bedroom would be more . . . " she said but could not finish. "I'm sorry," she said, and again Pam could not tell if she meant it. You can't tell anything about a one-day stand. They aren't there to be known. Pam shunted herself off the stool and put her hands out as if for something falling but Martha had already backed on to the porch. She struggled down the snowy steps, felt the same panic that rightly belongs to a fire escape. She could hear the clamour of snowman builders, speaking in tongues, laughing about something.

CREDITS

TEXT CREDITS

Achebe, Chinua. "An Image of Africa" from *Hopes and Impediments: Selected Essays* by Chinua Achebe. Copyright © 1988 by Chinua Achebe. Used by permission of Doubleday, a division of Random House, Inc.

Auden, W. H. "Musee des Beaux Arts" copyright 1940 and renewed 1968 by W. H. Auden, "In Memory of W. B. Yeats" copyright 1940 & Renewed 1968 by W. H. Auden, "Spain 1937" copyright 1940 & renewed 1968 by W. H. Auden, "September 1, 1939" copyright 1940 & renewed 1968 by W. H. Auden, "Lullaby (40 lines)" copyright 1940 & 1968 by W. H. Auden, from *Collected Poems* by W. H. Auden. Used by permission of Random House, Inc. "Law Like Love" copyright 1940 & renewed 1968 by W. H. Auden, "In Memory of Sigmund Freud" copyright 1940 and renewed 1968 by W. H. Auden, "The Hidden Law" copyright 1941 by W. H. Auden from *Collected Poems* by W. H. Auden. Used by permission of Random House, Inc. "Sir, no man's enemy forgiving all" edited by Edward Mendelson, from *Selected Poems*, Expanded Edition by W. H. Auden, edited by Edward Mendelson, copyright © 1979 by Edward Mendelson, William Meredith and Monroe K. Spears, Executors of the Estate of W. H. Auden, 2007 by the Estate of W. H. Auden Introduction and notes copyright © 1979, 2007 by Edward Mendelson. Used by permission of Vintage Books, a division of Random House, Inc.

Beckett, Samuel. "Endgame: A Play in One Act" from *Endgame and Act without Words* by Samuel Beckett. Copyright © 1958 by Grove Press, Inc., © 1986 by Samuel Beckett. Used by permission of Grove/Atlantic, Inc.

Boland, Eavan. "Anorexic" and "Mise Eire" Copyright © 1987 by Eavan Boland, from *An Origin Like Water: Collected Poems 1967–1987* by Eavan Boland. Copyright © 1996 by Eavan Boland. Used by permission of W. W. Norton & Company, Inc. "A Woman Painted on a Leaf" and "The Pomegrante" from *In a Time of Violence* by Eavan Boland. Copyright © 1994 by Eavan Boland. Used by permission of W. W. Norton & Company, Inc.

Bowen, Elizabeth. "The Mysterious Kôr" from *The Collected Stories of Elizabeth Bowen*. Copyright © 1981 by Curtis Brown Ltd., Literary Executors of the Estate of Elizabeth Bowen. Used by permission of Alfred A. Knopf, a division of Random House, Inc.

Chapman, Graham. "Travel Agent" by Graham Chapman et al., from *The Complete Monty Python's Flying Circus: All the Words*, Vol. Two. Copyright © 1989 Python Productions Ltd. Reprinted by permission of Python Productions Ltd.

Conrad, Joseph. From *Congo Diary and Other Uncollected Pieces* by Zdzislaw Najder. Copyright © 1978 by Ralph Lew Wedgewood, executor of the Joseph Conrad estate. © 1978 by Zdzislaw Najder on editing. Used by permission of Doubleday, a division of Random House, Inc.

Crawford, Robert. "The Saltcoats Structuralists" and "Alba Einstein" from *The Scottish Assembly* by Robert Crawford, published by Jonathan Cape. Reprinted by permission of The Random House Group Ltd.

Duffy, Carol Ann. "Elvis's Twin Sister" and "Little Red Cap" from *The World's Wife*. NY: Farrar, Straus & Giroux. "Originally" and "Translating the English, 1989 are taken from *The Other Country* by Carol Ann Duffy published by Anvil Press Poetry in 1990. Reprinted by permission. "The Diet" and "Anon" from *Feminine Gospels* by Carol Anne Duffy. Faber and Faber.

Eliot, T. S. "Burnt Norton" from *Four Quartets* by T. S. Eliot. Copyright 1936 by Harcourt, Inc., and renewed 1964 by T. S. Eliot. Reprinted by permission of the publisher. "The Hollow Men," "Journey of the Magi" from *Collected Poems 1909–1962* by T. S. Eliot. Copyright 1936 by Harcourt, Inc., copyright © 1964, 1963 by T. S. Eliot. Reprinted by permission of the publisher.

Forster, E. M. "The Life to Come" from *The Life to Come and Other Stories* by E. M. Forster. Copyright © 1972 by The Provost and Scholars of King's College, Cambridge. Used by permission of W. W. Norton & Company, Inc.

Gordimer, Nadine. "What Were You Dreaming?" from *Jump and Other Stories* by Nadine Gordimer. Copyright © 1991 by Felix Licensing B. V. Reprinted by permission of Farrar, Straus and Giroux, LLC.

Greene, Graham. "A Chance for Mr. Lever," Copyright 1936, renewed © 1968 by Graham Greene, from *Collected Stories of Graham Greene* by Graham Greene. Used by permission of Viking Penguin, a division of Penguin Group (USA) Inc.

Gunn, Thom. "Lines for a Book," "Elvis Presley," "A Map of the City," "Black Jackets," "From the Wave," "The Hug," "Patchwork" and "The Missing" from *Collected Poems*. NY: Farrar, Straus & Giroux.

Heaney, Seamus. "A Call" and "The Errand" from *The Spirit Level* by Seamus Heaney. Copyright © 1996 by Seamus Heaney. Reprinted by permission of Farrar, Straus and Giroux, LLC. "Act of Union;" "The Gaeltacht;" "In Memoriam Francis Ledwidge;" "Personal Helicon;" "Postscript;" "Punishment;" "Requiem for the Croppies;" "The Skunk;" "The Singer's House;" "Section XII" from "Station Island;" and "The Toome Road" from *Open Ground: Selected Poems 1966–1996* by Seamus Heaney. Copyright © 1998 by Seamus Heaney. Reprinted by permission of Farrar, Straus and Giroux, LLC. "A Call" and "The Errand" from *The Spirit Level* by Seamus Heaney. Copyright © 1996 by Seamus Heaney. Reprinted by permission of Farrar, Straus and Giroux, LLC.

Herbert, W. N. "Cabaret McGonagall" and "Smirr" from *Cabaret McGonagall.* (Bloodaxe Books, 1995). Reprinted by permission of Bloodaxe Books.

Hooley, Teresa. "A War Film" from *Songs of All Seasons.* Jonathan Cape Ltd., 1927. Reprinted by permission of The National Federation of Retirement Pension Association.

Hornby, Nick. "Nipple Jesus" from *Speaking with the Angel,* edited by Nick Hornby, copyright © 2000 by Nick Hornby. Used by permission of Riverhead Books, an imprint of Penguin Group (USA) Inc.

Hughes, Ted. "Wind" and "Relic," from *Selected Poems 1957–1967* by Ted Hughes. Copyright © 1972 by Ted Hughes. Reprinted by permission of HarperCollins Publishers. "Theology" from *Wodwo* by Ted Hughes. Copyright © 1972 by Ted Hughes. Reprinted by permission of Faber and Faber. "Dust As We Are;" "Leaf Mould;" and "Telegraph Wires" from *Wolfwatching* by Ted Hughes. Copyright © 1991 by Ted Hughes. Reprinted by permission of Farrar, Straus and Giroux, LLC.

King, Jon and Andy Gill. "We Live as We Dream, Alone." Written by Jon King and Andy Gill. © 1990 BUG MUSIC, LTD. (PRS) / Administered by BUG. All rights reserved. Used by permission.

Kureishi, Hanif. Chapter 16, pp 137–53 reprinted with the permission of Scribner, a Division of Simon & Schuster, Inc., from *Something to Tell You: A Novel* by Hanif Kureishi. Copyright © 2008 by Hanif Kureishi. All rights reserved.

Larkin, Philip. "Annus Mirabilis," "Aubade," "High Windows," "Homage to a Government," "The Importance of Elsewhere," "Talking in Bed," and "MCMXIV" from *Collected Poems* by Philip Larkin. Copyright 1998, 2003 by the Estate of Philip Larkin. Reprinted by permission of Farrar, Straus, and Giroux, LLC. "Church Going" by Philip Larkin is reprinted from *The Less Deceived* by permission of The Marvell Press, England and Australia.

Lawrence, D. H. "Cypresses" and "Bavarian Gentians" by D. H. Lawrence, "The Piano" by D. H. Lawrence, "Snake" by D. H. Lawrence, "The Song of a Man Who Has Come Through" by D. H. Lawrence, "Tortoise Shout" by D. H. Lawrence, from *The Complete Poems of D. H. Lawrence* by D. H. Lawrence, edited by V. de Sola Pinto & F. W. Roberts, copyright © 1964, 1971 by Angelo Ravagli and C. M. Weekley, Executors of the Estate of Frieda Lawrence Ravagli. Used by permission of Viking Penguin, a division of Penguin Group (USA) Inc. "Surgery for the Novel—or a Bomb" from *Phoenix: The Posthumous Papers of D. H. Lawrence,* ed. By Edward McDonald. Copyright 1936 Frieda Lawrence, renewed © 1964 by the Estate of the late Frieda Lawrence Ravagli. Used by permission of Viking Penguin, a division of Penguin Group (USA) Inc.

Lewis, Gwyneth. "Therapy" and "Mother Tongue" from *Chaotic Angels: Poems in English.* (Bloodaxe Books, 2005). Reprinted by permission of Bloodaxe Books.

Moore, Alan. From *V for Vendetta* © 1989 DC Comics. All Rights Reserved. Used with permission.

Muldoon, Paul. "Aisling;" "Cuba;" "Meeting the British;" and "Sleeve Notes" from *Poems 1968–1998* by Paul Muldoon. Copyright © 2001 by Paul Muldoon. Reprinted by permission of Farrar, Straus and Giroux, LLC.

Naipaul, V. S. "Prologue from a Journal: The Tramp at Piraeus" and "Epilogue from a Journal: The Circus at Luxor" from *In a Free State* by V. S. Naipaul. Copyright © V. S. Naipaul, 1971. Used by permission of Alfred A. Knopf, a division of Random House, Inc.

Ní Dhomhnaill, Nuala. "As for the Quince." Reprinted by permission of the author. "Feeding a Child, "Parthenogenesis," and "Labasheedy (The Silken Bed)" by Nuala Ní Dhomhnaill. Reprinted by permission of New Island Books, Dublin, Ireland. "The Language Issue" from *Pharaoh's Daughter* by Nuala Ní Dhomhnaill, translated by Paul Muldoon, 1993. Reprinted by permission of Wake Forest University Press. "Why I Choose to Write in Irish" from *The New York Times Book Review,* January 8, 1995, p. 3. Copyright © 1995. Reprinted by permission of the author.

Nunez, Sigrid. "On Rereading *Mrs. Dalloway*" from *The Mrs. Dalloway Reader,* ed. By Francine Prose. Copyright © 2003 by Sigrid Nunez. Reprinted by permission of Houghton Mifflin Harcourt Publishing Company.

Orwell, George. "Shooting an Elephant" from *Shooting an Elephant and Other Essay* By George Well. Copyright 1950 by the Estate of Sonia B. Orwell; reprinted by permission of Houghton Mifflin Harcourt Publishing Company.

Rowson, Martin. From *The Waste Land.* Copyright © 1990 Martin Rowson. Reproduced by permission of the author c/o Rogers, Coleridge & White Ltd., 20 Powis mews, London W11 1JN.

Rushdie, Salman. "Chekov and Zulu" and "The Courter" from *East, West: Stories* by Salman Rushdie. Copyright © 1994 by Salman Rushdie. Used by permission of Pantheon Books, a division of Random House, Inc.

Sassoon, Siegfried. "They," "The Rear-Guard," copyright 1918 by E. P. Dutton, Copyright renewed 1946 by Siegfried Sassoon, from *Collected Poems of Siegfried Sassoon* by Siegfried Sassoon, copyright 1918, 1920 by E. P. Dutton. Copyright 1936, 1946, 1947, 1948 by Siegfried Sassoon. Used by permission of Viking Penguin, a division of Penguin Group (USA) Inc.

Shaw, Bernard. *Pygmalion* by Bernard Shaw. Copyright 1913, 1914, 1916, 1930, 1941 George Bernard Shaw. Copyright 1957 The Public Trustee as Executor of the Estate of George Bernard Shaw. Reprinted by permission of The Society of Authors on behalf of the Estate of Bernard Shaw.

Smith, Zadie. "Martha, Martha" as appeared in Granta 81, pp. 325–39 (2003). Reprinted by permission of A P Watt Ltd.

Spender, Stephen. "Airman," copyright 1934 and renewed 1962 by Stephen Spender. "The Pylons," copyright 1934 and renewed 1962 by Stephen Spender. "The Express," copyright 1934 and renewed 1962 by Stephen

Spender. "What I Expected," copyright 1934 and renewed 1962 by Stephen Spender. From *Collected Poems 1928–1985* by Stephen Spender. Used by permission of Ed Victor Ltd.

Stoppard, Tom. *The Invention of Love*, copyright © 1997 by Tom Stoppard. Used by permission of Grove/Atlantic, Inc.

Thomas, Dylan. "The Force That Through the Green Fuse Drives the Flower" by Dylan Thomas, from *The Poems of Dylan Thomas*, copyright 1939 by New Directions Publishing Corp. Reprinted by permission of New Directions Publishing Corp. "Fern Hill" and "Poem in October" by Dylan Thomas, from *The Poems of Dylan Thomas*, Copyright 1945 by The Trustees for the Copyrights of Dylan Thomas, first published in POETRY. Reprinted by permission of New Directions Publishing Corp. "Do Not Go Gentle Into That Good Night" by Dylan Thomas, from *The Poems of Dylan Thomas*, copyright 1952 by Dylan Thomas. Reprinted by permission of New Directions Publishing Corp.

Tuqan, Fadwa. "In the Aging City" trans. by Patricia Alanah Byrne and Naomi Shihab Nye from *Modern Arabic Poetry: An Anthology*, ed. by Salma Khadra Jayyusi. Copyright © 1987 by Columbia University Press. Reprinted with permission of the publisher.

Trotter, Alys Fane. Poem, "The Hospital Visitor" from *Houses and Dreams*. Oxford: B. Blackwell, 1924. Reprinted by permission of Blackwell Publishing Ltd.

Walcott, Derek. "A Far Cry from Africa;" "The Fortunate Traveller;" Sections L, LII, and LIV from "Midsummer;" "Wales;" and "Volcano" from *Collected Poems 1948–1984* by Derek Walcott. Copyright © 1986 by Derek Walcott. Reprinted by permission of Farrar, Straus and Giroux, LLC.

Waugh, Evelyn. "Cruise" from *The Complete Stories of Evelyn Waugh* by Evelyn Waugh. Copyright © by the Estate of Evelyn Waugh; Foreword Copyright © 1998 by Anthony Lane. By permission of Little, Brown & Company. "The Man Who Liked Dickens" from *The Complete Stories of Evelyn Waugh*, pp. 114–29 by Evelyn Waugh. Copyright © 1998 by The Estate of Evelyn Waugh; Foreword Copyright © 1998 by Anthony Lane. By permission of Little, Brown & Company.

Woolf, Virginia. "The Lady in the Looking Glass: A Reflection" from *The Complete Shorter Fiction of Virginia Woolf*, edited by Susan Dick. Copyright © 1985 by Quentin Bell and Angelica Garnett, reprinted by permission of Houghton Mifflin Harcourt Publishing Company. *Mrs. Dalloway* by Virginia Woolf. Copyright 1925 by Houghton Mifflin Harcourt Publishing Company and renewed 1953 by Leonard Woolf. Reprinted by permission of the publisher.

Yeats, W. B. "Byzantium" and "Crazy Jane Talks with the Bishop," reprinted with the permission of Scribner, an imprint of Simon & Schuster Adult Publishing Group, from *The Collected Works of W. B. Yeats, Volume I: The Poems, Revised*, edited by Richard J. Finneran. Copyright 1933 by The Macmillan Company; copyright renewed © 1961 by Bertha Georgie Yeats. "Lapiz Pazuli," "The Circus Animal's Desertion," and "Under Ben Bulben," reprinted with the permission of Scribner, an imprint of Simon & Schuster Adult Publishing Group, from *The Collected Works of W. B. Yeats, Volume I: The Poems, Revised*, edited by Richard J. Finneran. Copyright 1940 by Bertha Georgie Yeats, Michael Butler Yeats, and Anne Yeats. "Sailing to Byzantium," "Leda and the Swan," "Among School Children," "Meditations in Time of Civil War," reprinted with the permission of Scribner, an imprint of Simon & Schuster Adult Publishing Group, from *The Collected Works of W. B. Yeats, Volume I: The Poems, Revised*, edited by Richard J. Finneran. Copyright 1928 by The Macmillan Company; copyright renewed © 1956 by Georgie Yeats.

ILLUSTRATION CREDITS

Page 1918: Copyright Tate Gallery, London/Art Resource, NY Tate Gallery, London, Great Britain; 1919: © Jon Arnold/JAI/CORBIS All Rights Reserved; 1920: © James Leynse/CORBIS All Rights Reserved; 1921 (top): © Gideon Mendel/CORBIS All Rights Reserved; 1921 (middle-top): CORBIS-NY; 1921 (middle-bottom): © Daniel Hambury/xinhua/Xinhua Press/CORBIS All Rights Reserved; 1921 (bottom): © Bettmann/CORBIS All Rights Reserved; 1922 (top): CORBIS-NY; 1922 (middle): © Bettmann/CORBIS All Rights Reserved; 1922 (bottom): © Peter Turnley/CORBIS All Rights Reserved; 1929: David Damrosch; 1933: London's Transport Museum © Transport for London; 1937: David Damrosch; 1939: William Vandivert, Life Magazine, © Time Inc. Getty Images; 1944: Henry Grossman/Getty Images/Time Life Pictures; 1949: Courtesy of the Library of Congress; 2115: Wyndham Lewis, "The Creditors" (design for Timon of Athens). 1912–13. Courtesy Wadsworth Atheneum, Hartford, Connecticut. The Ella Gallup Sumner and Mary Catlain Sumner Collection Fund; 2164: The Yeats Museum, National Gallery of Ireland. NGI 19,412; 2174: Courtesy of the Library of Congress; 2215: Courtesy of the Library of Congress; 2217: "Courtesy of the National Library of Ireland"; 2284: Courtesy of the Library of Congress; 2313–17: David Damrosch; 2331: David Damrosch; 2333: "Princeton University Library." "Sylvia Beach Papers. Manuscript Division. Department of Rare Books and Special Collections. Princeton University Library"; 2349: Getty Images; 2529: UPI/CORBIS-NY; 2577: Getty Images/Time Life Pictures; 2748: © Rune Hellestad/CORBIS All Rights Reserved.

COLOR PLATE CREDITS

Color Plate 21: Courtesy of David Damrosch; Color Plate 22: London Transport Museum; Color Plate 23: Copyright © Tate Gallery, London/Art Resource, New York; Color Plate 24: Tate Gallery, London, Great Britain/Art Resource, New York; Color Plate 25: Imperial War Museum, London, Great Britain/Art Resource, New York;

INDEX